DAV...

EUROPE SINCE NAPOLEON

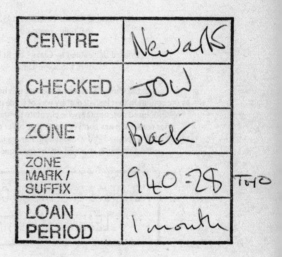

CENTRE	Newark
CHECKED	JOW
ZONE	Black
ZONE MARK / SUFFIX	940·28 TOTO
LOAN PERIOD	1 month

PENGUIN BOOKS

PENGUIN BOOKS

Published by the Penguin Group
Penguin Books Ltd, 27 Wrights Lane, London W8 5TZ, England
Penguin Putnam Inc., 375 Hudson Street, New York, New York 10014, USA
Penguin Books Australia Ltd, Ringwood, Victoria, Australia
Penguin Books Canada Ltd, 10 Alcorn Avenue, Toronto, Ontario, Canada M4V 3B2
Penguin Books (NZ) Ltd, 182–190 Wairau Road, Auckland 10, New Zealand

Penguin Books Ltd, Registered Offices: Harmondsworth, Middlesex, England

First published by Longmans 1957
Revised edition published in Pelican Books 1966
Reprinted in Penguin Books 1990
7 9 10 8

Printed in England by Clays Ltd, St Ives plc
Set in Linotype Times

CONTENTS

CONTENTS

CONTENTS

CONTENTS

CONTENTS

MAPS

MAPS

DIAGRAMS

PREFACE TO THE PELICAN EDITION

SINCE this book first appeared in 1957 the welcome given to it on both sides of the Atlantic has been very encouraging. It attempts to present the history of the last 150 years of European civilization in a new way. The conventional belief that European history must be presented in terms of the separate component nations, and of the coming together of their representatives in wars or conferences, conflicts or compacts, is being more openly doubted. The belief on which this study is based – that tendencies which transcend several nations at once have a rather special historical importance – is gaining ground. If the notion is welcomed that these tendencies, rather than separate governmental policies, are a good and interesting focus for historical study, it is because such an approach can give European studies that greater cohesion and coherence which seem appropriate in our postwar experience.

For this edition the story has been continued to the end of 1963, which means to the brink of the space age. The text and bibliography have been revised in the light of corrections and comments received from helpful readers. I make no apology, even since the collapse of Britain's negotiations to enter the European Economic Community, for having throughout considered the British Isles as a part of European civilization.

DAVID THOMSON

Sidney Sussex College, Cambridge

PREFACE

THIS study of what has been happening in Europe since 1815 has been written on two principles, and it is well that the reader should be aware of them. The first is that a general historical study, if the writing and the reading of it are to be more than the mere drudgery of amassing information, must concern itself with patterns woven by the process of historical change. Certainly, if it is to give any pleasure to the author and any enlightenment to the reader, it must seek to make the process of change intelligible. It must expose the interplay between conditions, events, personalities, and ideas as well as the interconnexions between events themselves. It must set out to show not that certain consequences were in any way predestined or inevitable – for the hazards and unexpected twists of the course of history are part of its very delight – but at least how it was, and as far as possible why it was, that certain consequences did flow from particular temporal conjunctions of material circumstances and human will.

The author offers no apology, therefore, that he has ventured far beyond the tasks of narrative and description, however basic these may be to the work of the historian. There is an art of story-telling and there is an art of description, both of which have their place in the historian's work; but they alone can scarcely be enough. He must apply, also, certain techniques of analysis, explanation, interpretation, in order to elicit from the sequence of happenings, and from our knowledge of their effects upon the fortunes of human beings, some better understanding of how these things came to pass. It is for the reader, not for the writer, of history to infer from these explanations whatever philosophical or ethical or political meanings his conscience and understanding may impose. The better the writer has performed his task of explaining historical events in their own terms of sequence and consequence, the more truthful and valid are such inferences likely to be. The English liberal historian and politician, H. A. L. Fisher, prefaced the famous *History of Europe* which he completed in 1936 with the words: 'Men wiser and more learned than I have discerned in history a plot, a rhythm, a predetermined pattern. These harmonies are concealed from me. I can see only one emergency following upon another as wave follows upon wave, only one great fact with respect to which, since it is unique, there can be no generalizations ....' I, too, detect no plot or predetermined pattern; but I can see certain rhythms of movement and certain patterns of change. They might better be called 'general trends', provided they are not regarded as flowing from eternal causes or proceeding to infinity. It is no part of the historian's duty to be a prophet; but it is his duty to take advantage of his great privilege of hindsight to elucidate what came to pass, even if participants in the events were not always aware of the consequences that would follow from the decisions they took or the course of action they pursued.

This study of modern Europe has been written on a second principle. It is that, just as historical change, in the words of Britain's Poet Laureate, John Masefield, is more than merely 'one damn thing after another', so Europe is something other than just 'one damn country after another'. Of the numerous histories of Europe which fill library shelves, a depressingly large proportion treat their subject as a mere collation of the separate histories of each European nation or state. No historian would think of compiling separate accounts of all forty-eight states and then binding them together with the claim that here is a 'History of the United States'; nor of amassing the local histories of English counties and boroughs and treating the collection as a 'History of England'. Although the states and the nations of Europe have not, perhaps unfortunately, developed within the same common governmental structure as either the states of America or the localities of England, yet they have shared so much in a common historical heritage, they have experienced so much constant interaction, and have so assiduously imitated from one another ideas and institutions of social life, that much of the story of their past can surely be told as one coherent story. Since 1815 the assimilation of modes of life of European nations into one great common pattern has gone far enough for it to be necessary to treat Europe and the United Kingdom integrally if their recent history is to be understood at all. I have, therefore, made no attempt to tell the continuous story of the development of each or any nation for its own sake. I have concentrated upon the 'general trends' discernible in several nations, illustrating these trends from the experience of individual countries. Even so, it has been necessary in doing this to consider all the most important changes in the major states of Europe. In discussing international relations and organizations, as in discussing wars and treaties, the major powers inevitably come in for special and almost continuous attention.

Because it has been written on these two principles, the structure and method of the book have been determined by those unities of time and of place which mattered most in each successive generation. The main Part divisions have been determined by unity of time; so that the generation between 1815 and 1850, the two decades of state-making in central Europe between 1851 and 1871, and the prewar era of 1871–1914 which saw the rapid extension of democracy and socialism, of imperialism and international alliances, are each treated as a unit of time. Since all history is one continuum, and no division by dates has more than a relative validity, the trends of continuity and overlap and interplay have always been emphasized. The eras of two World Wars, as well as the era of French Revolutionary and Napoleonic Wars, deserve special attention because of the combination of internal strains and upheavals with international changes which characterized both. But the great peace settlements have been treated in conjunction with the wars which they ended, as well as with the immediate aftermath of the wars for which they have too often been held responsible. I have emphasized, too, those more long-term forces of change, such as industrialism and urbanization and the impact of new ideas and beliefs, for these have a habit of operating before, during, and after great wars with a disconcerting impetus and persistence which it is beyond the power of statesmen and peacemakers to deflect or modify by more than a very limited degree.

If the main divisions are unities of time, defined with a necessary imprecision in terms of generations or decades, the internal structure of each Part has been devised mainly according to unities of place. The shaping of Europe becomes more intelligible if nations are considered in groups less according to their momentary diplomatic alignments than according to the forces of change which, at a particular time, they were experiencing in common. Geography or economic growth may throw nations into more significant groupings than diplomacy or politics, but over a relatively long time even this grouping or its significance may change. Until about 1850 the peoples of Italy and Germany belonged together more closely with the peoples of eastern Europe, in their phase of political and economic growth; but after 1871 they belonged together more closely with the nations of western Europe, with the United Kingdom and France and Belgium, than with Austria-Hungary, Russia, or Ottoman Turkey. Accordingly the Chapter divisions of Part III, dealing with the generation between 1815 and 1850, are made in terms of the chronological spread of revolutionary movements throughout Europe as a whole; whereas in Part IV, dealing with the era of rapid industrialization in the west and of the making of new states in Italy, Germany, and Austria-Hungary, the main divisions are regional. Then again, in dealing with the longer span of time between 1871 and 1914, the main themes appear to be, on one hand, the internal growth of universal suffrage, of a wealth greater than mankind had ever known, of new organizations of capital and labour, and of socialism; and, on the other, the international rivalries and collisions brought about by the scramble for colonies and for diplomatic alliances. The domestic developments of that period are of such momentous importance for the twentieth century that they have been given somewhat fuller attention than they often receive in a general history of Europe; and although these two themes have been examined separately in Parts V and VI, their interaction has been explained in Chapter 21. Only by some such flexible structure can the broad lines of the complex evolution of modern Europe be made clear. Conventional distinctions between national and international history are artificial, just as differentiation into political, economic, social, cultural, and other aspects of human development is convenient but represents no objective reality. Such distinctions have been treated as of only secondary meaning in this study. Similar methods have been applied to the period since 1914, and it is hoped that the hindsight which has become possible since 1945 has enabled this period of more strictly 'contemporary history' to be interpreted more as a whole and in a more meaningful perspective.

The Parts have deliberately been kept few and large, in order to delineate the general trends and characteristics of the whole period; but they are divided internally into Chapters which have been numbered consecutively throughout the book and which, in turn, have been subdivided. There is, in short, a certain fugue-like quality about the process of historical change, and this has been directly considered in the Epilogue. The structure of the book has been designed to bring out this quality as clearly and as completely as possible.

The history of the United Kingdom has been presented as an integral part of the history of the European continent. Its important initiatives and differences, its special peculiarities, have not, I hope, been neglected; and this might equally be said of every other European nation, since it is as important to indicate contrasts as to stress similarities. It is in the rich diversity and striking contrasts, as well as in the revelation of often concealed undercurrents of general movement, that the alluring interest of modern European history lies.

In a study of this scope and size, about which libraries have already been written, it would be futile to hope for either completeness or perfection. My indebtedness to previous writers on the subject is so great that detailed acknowledgements are impossible. In the Bibliography I have indicated some of the many good books used and consulted, and in which further information or discussion can be found. For the errors of fact or interpretation which must have eluded all efforts to keep them out, I am alone responsible and I shall be grateful if my attention

PREFACE

is drawn to them. The constant need to rethink, and to encourage others to rethink, the recent story of European civilization is perhaps excuse enough for venturing upon an undertaking so large and so ambitious.

This book has been devised chiefly for the use of university students in the United States and in Britain, and rests on close upon thirty years' experience of teaching modern history to such students – mainly in Cambridge, England, but also at Columbia University in New York. My debt to them all, which is very great, may be in part repaid if their successors on either side of the Atlantic find that this account of events which concern us all is of interest, use, and even enjoyment.

I am indebted also to Messrs R. R. Palmer and Joel Colton, authors of *A History of the Modern World*, and to Messrs C. E. Black and E. C. Helmreich, authors of *Twentieth Century Europe*, for maps taken from these books.

To the cartographer Theodore R. Miller, whose maps with simplifications are here included, to the College Department of Alfred A. Knopf, Inc., and to Mr and Mrs Alfred A. Knopf themselves for their many kindnesses, I am most grateful. Mrs Kay Barnes (now Wesley) typed the whole of the work and at every stage in its production gave invaluable help for which I am deeply indebted. To my wife, whose eye for obscurities of expression and inelegancies of style is so acute, I offer apologies for those which have doubtless escaped even her patient scrutiny, as well as gratitude for saving me from all the rest.

DAVID THOMSON

Sidney Sussex College, Cambridge
March 1965

PART ONE

EUROPE IN THE MELTING POT
1789–1814

In the year 1789 two events of world importance happened. The new federal Constitution of the United States of America came into operation; revolution broke out in France. While the New World entered upon an era of integration and expansion within a flexible framework of government, the Old World relapsed into twenty-five years of great disorder and upheaval which shattered its existing political structure.

The sequence of events in Europe during the quarter century after 1789 can be described in four dramatic words: Revolution, War, Dictatorship, Empire. The story can be told, and has often been told, as an epic of heroic grandeur, marching remorselessly toward its predestined end. In this view, violent revolution led naturally to war; revolution and war, in combination, had as their nemesis the dictatorship of a soldier; and military dictatorship led no less naturally and fatalistically to the Caesarist ambitions of Napoleon. These successive upheavals haunted all subsequent development in Europe, for it was by receiving the message of the Revolution, enduring the wars that it caused, experiencing the efficient but exacting rule of Napoleon, and struggling to free themselves from his tyranny, that the nations of Europe took modern shape. This romantic interpretation of the making of modern Europe cannot be accepted. Historians have become suspicious of inevitability, too conscious of complexities and too inquisitive about the mysterious working of historical change, to accept unchallenged this neat standardized account of how nineteenth-century Europe began. The consequences of the French Revolution and the Napoleonic Empire, and of the wars to which both gave rise, were indeed of great importance. But they were variable in importance and by no means the only formative influences on nineteenth-century Europe. Nor was the sequence of events inevitable.

The necessary prologue to an exploration of European history since 1815 is some assessment of how each of these four main phases of change did give place to the next, and of how profound, permanent, and general was their accumulative effect on later generations.

CHAPTER 1

REVOLUTION IN FRANCE

THE REVOLUTIONARY SITUATION

IT is a paradox that no important people or forces in France of 1789 wanted revolution. Revolutions may begin, as wars often begin, not because people positively want them. They happen because people want other things that, in a certain set of circumstances, implicate them in revolution or in war. There had been growing in Europe, throughout most of the eighteenth century, what has been called 'the revolutionary spirit'. This spirit, a spirit of rationalist criticism and of resistance to the established powers of the Roman Catholic Church, the absolutist monarchy, and the privileged nobility, was fostered particularly by the work of a remarkable series of French thinkers and literary men, the *philosophes*. The writings of men like Voltaire, Montesquieu, Diderot, and Rousseau were widely read throughout Europe, and they themselves became European figures of eminence and influence.

But the connexion between their ideas and the outbreak of revolution in 1789 is somewhat remote and indirect. They did not preach revolution, and were usually ready enough to lend support to any absolute monarch who was prepared to patronize them and adopt their teachings. Nor were most of their readers inspired to want, or to work for, revolution; they were mostly themselves aristocrats, lawyers, business people, and local dignitaries, whose lot in the existing order was far from unhappy. The doctrines of the *philosophes* came to be used later on, during the course of the revolution in France, often to justify measures that the *philosophes* themselves would have opposed. Their teachings became more important later; if they had any influence at all on the outbreak and the initial stages of the great revolution, it was only to the extent that they had fostered a critical and irreverent attitude toward all existing institutions. They made men more ready, when the need arose, to question the whole foundation of the old order. What mattered in 1789 – and what made men revolutionary almost in spite of themselves – was the whole 'revolutionary situation'; and in producing that situation the work of the *philosophes* played no very important role.

The essence of the 'revolutionary situation' was that the King, who was the linchpin of the whole established social and political system in

France, was in desperate financial straits. For a decade before, successive ministers had tried to put royal finances on a sounder footing, but all had failed. The costs of government were increasing rapidly, and the cost of wars simply could not be met from the usual sources of royal revenue. It was no new thing for a French king to be hard up; indeed it was the normal situation. But the various means by which he could properly raise taxes had already been so fully and so wastefully exhausted that the country was heavily burdened. By the standards of the time France was a very large, populous, rich, and powerful state. Her foreign trade had increased fivefold since the death of Louis XIV in 1715. She had a bigger middle class of businessmen and small manufacturers and a generally more prosperous peasantry than any other state in Europe. The peasants owned two fifths of the soil and worked almost all of it. But these very facts contributed to the 'revolutionary situation'. It tends to be people with something to lose, and not merely something to gain, who think most eagerly of improving the existing state of society. And that was what people thought of most in 1789. There was an insistent demand for reform of certain abuses, a more efficient and equitable system of taxation and administration, a better system of government. The last thing most people wanted was violent and destructive revolution, which they knew might deprive them of what they had without gaining for them what they wished.

Louis XVI won fresh popularity when he made known his intention of summoning the Estates-General, which was the nearest institution France had to a parliament representative of the whole nation. His action aroused hopes of liberal and constitutional reforms, because it was the traditional role of the monarch to defend the mass of his subjects against abuses and hardships. Just as nobody of importance wanted revolution, so nobody of importance wanted a republic. It was 1792 before a republican movement of any strength appeared, and until then the hopes of reformers centred upon the King and not against him.

Yet the King's well-received action of summoning the Estates-General precipitated revolution. The economic and social structure of France had greatly outgrown her political and governmental system. There was a sharp and bitterly resented contrast between the economically effective parts and the politically effective parts of the nation. Her traditional legal and political structure gave special privileges to the two classes most divorced in outlook and interests from the peasantry and the middle classes – the higher clergy and the nobility. These two segments of the ruling class had much in common, and many of the higher offices in the Church were held by aristocrats. By the time of Louis XVI every bishop was a nobleman, and members of noble families almost monopolized the highest posts of government service and the army. Since they numbered in all only about half a million out of a population of 24 or 25 million, political power was concentrated in very few hands. This was one of the bitterest grievances of the growing and wealthy class of merchants, businessmen, financiers, and lawyers, who collectively also owned a good deal of the land but who were excluded by the chances of birth and social status from most of the more responsible and dignified offices in state and Church. Moreover, because clergy and nobles enjoyed so many exemptions from taxation, the main burden of meeting the expenses of state and Church fell on the middle classes and the more prosperous peasants. The summoning of the Estates-General suddenly gave them an opportunity to make their social and economic weight politically effective. It was a chance they seized with both hands.

By not only arousing hopes of liberal reform but then drawing together many of the people most eager for an overhaul of the social and political system, Louis crystallized the revolutionary situation. He confronted the representatives of the privileged orders, the First and Second Estates of clergy and nobility, with the representatives of the unprivileged orders, the Third Estate of middle class and peasantry. Then by attempting to handle this critical situation through obsolete procedures and creaking, rusty machinery, and with no clear plans or firm sense of direction, the King began a train of events which led in the end to his own downfall. It was only after he had forfeited his original public support by his lack of policy, his wavering and disappointing conduct, and in the end his open betrayal of his own promises, that republicanism grew. Only the king, in eighteenth-century France, could have created a republic.

The King and his ministers were themselves in a dilemma. The situation was inherently revolutionary, because the king and his ministers, with the best will in the world, could not satisfy the demands of the middle classes and peasants for a larger share of political power and a smaller share of taxation without destroying the tangle of ancient rights by which nobles and Church had their own law courts and powers of jurisdiction, monopolized all the most lucrative offices in the state, and enjoyed immunity from the main burdens of taxation. They could not do this without challenging and changing the whole social and political structure of France, the essential character of the old order, in which their own authority was deeply embedded. The French monarchy was a feudal monarchy, based on the centuries-old accumulation of feudal relationships between king, aristocracy, clergy, and all the rest of the population known as the 'Third Estate'. The right of the king to rule existed on the same foundations as the rights and immunities of the privileged orders. To attack any part of this anomalous and fossilized structure was to attack by implication every other part, including royal power itself. Yet the power of the king was regarded as absolute; and it was absolute in so far as there existed no public authority with an acknowledged right to check or deny the power of the king to govern as he chose. It had been checked in the past only by violent resistance on the part of over-mighty nobles or by obstructionist behaviour of the local *parlements*, both reactionary and not reformist forces. The king who claimed to rule by Divine Right and to wield absolute authority was in fact enmeshed in a system that denied him autonomy in jurisdiction, obliged him to rule only through the privileged orders of society, and compelled him to finance his rule by unjust and wasteful fiscal arrangements. His authority came not from God but only from prescription; his power was not absolute, only arbitrary. Only a monarch prepared to be a revolutionary could have escaped from the dilemma.

It was a position of deadlock and stalemate, where reform was inhibited by prudence, and revolution prevented only by apathy. The situation could not have lasted indefinitely, and perhaps the chief cause for surprise is that it had lasted so long. Already other states, notably Great Britain and Prussia, had escaped from similar positions, one by evolving strong parliamentary institutions, the other by concentrating more substantial power in her monarchy. When the Estates-General met, there were many proposals in the air for ways in which France could similarly solve the dilemma. Most attractive and persuasive of these was the argument put forward by the Abbé Sieyès, who was to become one of the most indefatigable constitution-makers of the next twenty years. In his pamphlet, widely read by members of the Estates-General, he asked the crucial question, 'What is the Third Estate?' His answer was that it was nearly everybody, yet it counted for nothing: that it was identical with the nation, yet excluded from the government of the nation. This was exactly what many already believed, but in January 1789 Sieyès put it in a nutshell.

THE CRISIS OF 1789

There was thus, in the France of 1789, an inherent constitutional crisis, if the term may be used of a country that really had no constitution at all in the American or British sense. This theoretically absolute monarchy was in practice powerless to effect the changes that most urgently needed making. When it was obliged to admit its complete bankruptcy as well, a financial crisis was superimposed on the constitutional crisis. But behind these lay an even more serious crisis, which contributed a particularly explosive element to the whole situation. It was the even less appreciated economic crisis in the country caused by prolonged inflation.

Between 1726 and 1780 France had absorbed no less than half the precious metals imported into Europe, and in the course of the eighteenth century her population had increased from roughly 18 to 25 million. With much more metallic currency in circulation, an expansion of credit facilities, an increased demand for goods on the part of her larger population, and a relatively slow expansion in production, prices inevitably rose. As compared with the average general prices of consumers' goods between 1726 and 1741, prices between 1785 and 1789 were 65 per cent higher; and even in the longer period 1771–89 they averaged 45 per cent higher. Average money wages rose only about a third as fast as prices, and the cost of living rose most steeply for those who were living closest to subsistence level. Even nature added to the crisis. The harvests of 1787 and 1788 were bad, partly because of great hailstones in 1788. This brought extreme social distress, which forced many desperate and hungry men into the few large towns. It was this that introduced the element of violence, because it made the Paris mob and led to the peasant riots (or *jacqueries*) of the countryside in 1789.

The political crisis of 1789, which started the course of events that made the revolution, is explicable only in this setting of deep economic and social crisis. When, in preparation for the meeting of the Estates-General in May 1789, the localities were invited to prepare *cahiers* or lists of grievances, it was the long-standing grievances that got listed: the lack of a 'constitution' to restrict ministerial despotism, the need to lighten the burden of indirect taxes and to control taxation by periodic national assemblies, the desirability of ending internal customs barriers and of ensuring freedom of the press. The more immediate discontents of the rural population got eliminated from many of the *cahiers* and were scarcely voiced in the assembly. This neglect only enhanced their importance as a source of violent upheaval and made for a general revolt in the countryside in the summer of 1789.

Although the accumulating crisis could not longer be deferred. it might still have been eased in several different ways. If the King could have found and kept able ministers who had a realistic grasp of the needs of the moment, and if they could have used the Estates-General to put through a clear and comprehensive policy of constitutional and fiscal reforms, it is conceivable that some more durable form of constitutional monarchy might have evolved. But the personalities of all the leading figures militated against this possibility: the character of the King, who was well-meaning but weak-willed; even more the character of the Queen, Marie Antoinette, whose Austrian connexions and notorious frivolity and extravagance made her very unpopular, and who persistently used her influence with the King to kill any projects of reform; the character of the Comte de Mirabeau, the ablest statesman and debater who served the monarchy but also the most personally disreputable and distrusted; the royal entourage, including the King's brothers, whose intransigence and irresponsibility helped to doom the monarchy for the future.

Alternatively, if the privileged orders could have been persuaded to surrender voluntarily their great administrative and juridical privileges and their fiscal immunities, the impasse might have been broken without bloodshed and violence. On 17 June the Third Estate took the title of National Assembly, and was joined by individual clergy and nobles. On 4 August 1789 there took place within it the famous surrender of feudal privileges, when liberal nobles vied with one another in giving up their ancient rights and the clergy competed with them in sacrificing tithes and church rights. But that remarkable burst of generosity was modified in several ways. It is true that such important grievances as aristocratic immunity from taxation, serfdom, forced labour (*corvée*), and the monopolistic and judicial privileges of the nobles were then destroyed, and were destroyed without indemnity. But other important feudal dues were to be commuted and redeemed, and the National Assembly was hoping to salvage the more important feudal property rights by sacrificing the less valuable. Even the genuine sacrifices so made were vitiated by the fact that they came a month too late – after the Paris mob had tasted power in the fall of the Bastille on 14 July, and after the peasants throughout the countryside had begun burning the *châteaux*, destroying feudal archives, and asserting their own freedom from feudal burdens. The Assembly completed its gesture of generosity by conferring on Louis XVI the title of 'Restorer of French Liberty' and then decreed that 'the feudal régime is entirely destroyed'. Frenchmen knew that it was not Louis but the action of the population as a whole which had restored liberty, and that it was the peasants, not the Assembly, who had really overthrown feudalism.

It was part of this new political crisis that the National Assembly was itself out of touch with public opinion, and despite its recent election had slender claim to represent the nation as a whole. The Estates-General was traditionally composed of three assemblies representing the three Estates. The King had decided that the Third Estate should have about 600 deputies out of a total of 1,155, but he had not decided the crucial issue whether voting was to be by head in one single assembly, or by each Estate casting its vote in three separate assemblies. Having decided that the Third Estate should have more representatives than the nobility and clergy together, if he had also decreed that they should be able to use this numerical superiority within one large assembly, he would have ended the political powers of feudalism by his own decision and so kept initiative and leadership. His indecision left it open for the Third Estate to usurp, by its own defiant action, the status of a truly national assembly, and then, after the adhesion of sections of nobility and clergy, to enforce the principle of voting by heads. This happened, after considerable confusion and exacerbation, on June 20, when the representatives of the Third Estate took an oath, in the rain and on the royal tennis court, not to disperse until the constitution of the realm had been firmly established. This act of political usurpation marked the first important stage in the downfall of the absolute monarchy.

The National Assembly also decreed that taxes should continue to be paid only so long as it remained in session, and it took the further logical step of declaring parliamentary privilege. It decreed that the person of each deputy was inviolable. It refused to disperse when the King ordered it to do so. Thus challenged, the King gave way as he had often given way in the past. 'They want to stay?' he asked peevishly, 'then let them stay.' Joined by most of the representatives of the nobility and clergy, the Third Estate henceforth existed as a National Assembly, with the self-imposed task of issuing a Declaration of the Rights of Man and of the Citizen and of protecting the liberty of the nation against the Crown and its ministers. The King, for the first time, found himself on the opposite side from the representatives of the nation. He never succeeded in rejoining them or in reasserting his initiative in reform. Henceforth, if the monarchy was not doomed, at least its existing difficulties were very greatly enhanced. Its political assets were squandered as wastefully as its financial.

Henceforth, too, the constitutional movement became more and more doctrinaire, reflecting the extent to which the lawyers, businessmen, and journalists had imbibed the notions of the *philosophes*. The first consequence was the 'Declaration of the Rights of Man and of the Citizen', which the Assembly, after lengthy debate, adopted on August 26. It had echoes of the American Declaration of Independence, and asserted that 'men are born and remain free and equal in rights', that 'the aim of all political association is to preserve the natural and imprescriptible rights of man', and that 'these rights are liberty, property, security, and resistance to oppression'. The famous declaration, which has remained of considerable importance and as recently as 1946 was

30

'reaffirmed' in the preamble to the Constitution of the Fourth French Republic, was adequately described by its full title.

It was, first, a *Declaration* – a manifesto and a statement of the general principles on which the National Assembly hoped to reform the French system of government. It was, secondly, a Declaration of *Rights* – not a Declaration of Duties. It was an assertion of the new claims and a statement of the political, constitutional, and social rights that its framers held to be essential for making a better régime. It was, thirdly, a Declaration of the *Rights of Man* – a statement intended to have universal application and which certainly had very far-reaching implications. It was drawn up not for France alone, but for the benefit of men everywhere who wanted to be free and to rid themselves of comparable burdens of absolutist monarchy and feudal privilege. This universalism of the original French Revolution was to be of great importance. It was, finally and fully, a Declaration of the Rights of Man and *of the Citizen*, and although the last three words of its title are often omitted they are among its most important. It was careful to specify those civic rights that most concretely expressed the immediate aims of the middle classes which now predominated in the Assembly: equality of all before the law, eligibility of all citizens for all public offices, personal freedom from arbitrary arrest or punishment, freedom of speech and the press, and above all an equitable distribution of the burdens of national taxation and the inviolability of private property. These claims it founded on the two general doctrines that 'the principle of all sovereignty rests essentially in the nation', and that 'law is the expression of the general will'. These doctrines – intended to be universal in application – would clearly, if accepted, destroy the very foundation of the old order of society and disrupt the state everywhere in Europe. This was the inherent challenge of events in France to every one of her neighbours, including Britain. One French historian has called the Declaration 'the death certificate of the old régime'. It certainly remained a charter of liberalism throughout the nineteenth century.

Even so, the Declaration is less abstract and more realistic than it might appear at first. Its omissions, as a manifesto of liberalism, are significant. It made no mention of freedom of economic enterprise or of trade, so dear to its bourgeois makers, because the old order had already in recent years suppressed the guilds and removed controls on the grain trade; it said nothing of rights of assembly and association, nor of education or social security, although many were aware of how important these were, for these matters were less relevant to the immediate tasks of destroying the old régime. Although it tried to be universal, it did not set out to be comprehensive. It deliberately omitted any Declaration

31

of Duties, an omission not remedied until 1795. Its most liberal principles were stated cautiously. Exercise of natural rights is limited by the need to assure enjoyment of the same rights for others. 'Law may rightfully prohibit only those actions that are injurious to society.' Freedom of opinion is limited by the proviso that it must not trouble public order as established by law, and that it must not be abused. Even the sanctity of property is subject to an 'obvious requirement of public necessity'.

The Declaration was not, moreover, a manifesto of democracy. Even the Americans had not yet instituted universal suffrage, and the French contented themselves with stating that 'all citizens have the right to take part, in person or by their representatives', in forming the law and in voting taxes. That they intended neither universal suffrage nor direct democracy became clear before the end of 1789, when a constitution was drawn up by the Assembly. This made a distinction between 'active' and 'passive' citizens and withheld the vote from the latter, defined as those who did not pay taxes equal in value to three days' wages; it set up a purely representative and parliamentary system of government, based less on Rousseau's ideas of popular sovereignty than on Montesquieu's theory of a 'separation of powers'. If the Revolution became the great source of democratic revolutions, that quality was derived from subsequent events, and was not present in either the intentions or the actions of the original revolutionaries.

The most revolutionary doctrine included in the Declaration had also been included in the American Declaration of Independence: the right of resistance to oppression. The Assembly intended, by including it, to justify its own defence of the king and to legitimize the insurrection of 14 July, when the Paris mob had captured the grim old fortress of the Bastille, which symbolized arbitrary power. Paris had then organized, under the liberal noble Lafayette, a new civic or 'National Guard' to protect both public order and the Assembly. In October the principle of resistance had again to be invoked, to overcome the obstacle of the king's right to veto all legislation. In the 'October Days' the ultimate revolutionary sanction of popular violence was decisive. On 5 October some six or seven thousand of the women of Paris marched in the rain to Versailles to clamour for bread and to fetch the King to Paris. After the usual vacillation and muddle, they got their way, and on the afternoon of the following day, in the mud and rain, a strange procession moved into Paris from the palace of the kings. Headed by men of the National Guard with wagons full of wheat and flour, and accompanied by cheering women, the procession included a carriage in which rode the King and his family, with the Marquis de Lafayette, the revolutionary hero of two continents, riding beside it. It also included carriages bearing a hundred deputies chosen to represent the Assembly. The crowd rejoiced that they were bringing to the capital 'the baker, the baker's wife, and the baker's boy'. That night the royal family was housed in the Tuileries, a palace it had deserted for more than a century. Not only had the King, confronted with threats, agreed to ratify the Assembly's decrees; but now, a virtual prisoner of the Paris mob, he could be a constitutional monarch only under obvious compulsion. He had forfeited any hope of appearing to lead the revolution, as well as any material chance of resisting it.

THE ROOTS OF WAR

During the year 1790 two factors, above all others, made still worse the now precarious position of the monarchy. One was the bitter conflict caused by the Civil Constitution of the Clergy and its attempt to make the Church a department of state; the other was the influence of the *émigrés*, the growing tide of exiles who fled from France and incited foreign governments to take up arms against the revolution. The religious schism and the issues of foreign relations combined to effect a transition from revolution to war. This ultimately made the French Revolution an event not only in French but in European history.

Strangely enough, the first negative changes in the position of the Church met with little resistance. On 4 August 1789 the Gallican Church voluntarily gave up its corporate status and its rights to tax and to administer itself; and in February 1790, certain religious orders were abolished with the consent of the higher clergy in the Assembly. Schemes to abolish ecclesiastical tithes and to alienate ecclesiastical land were alike accepted without great resistance. It was the more positive changes of 1790 which aroused fierce opposition. They were not an attempt to separate Church from state, but the contrary – to subordinate the organization of the Church to the dictates of the state, and to fill all ecclesiastical offices by popular election. The French Church was to be separated from the Papacy and its clergy were to become paid officials of the state. These changes were sanctioned by the King and promulgated on 24 August. They aroused enough opposition within the Church for the Assembly to impose on all office-holding clergy an oath that they would uphold the new constitution of the Church. Half of the lower clergy and all but seven of the bishops refused to take this oath, and in March and April 1791, the Pope condemned the Civil Constitution and other political reforms of the Revolution. Henceforth the Church fell into rival and irreconcilable factions. In May relations were broken off between France and the Holy See.

In addition, by the end of 1790 there were already arrayed against the Revolution strong and influential counter-revolutionary forces at Brussels, Coblenz, and Turin. In 1791 an *émigré* army was formed in the Rhineland. The Comte d'Artois established headquarters at Coblenz, and *émigré* agents roamed France persuading other members of *émigré* families to join their relatives in exile and prepare for the 'liberation' of France

The impact of this whole movement upon the position of the monarchy became apparent with the fiasco of the King's flight to Varennes in June 1791. Louis had abandoned his original hopes that he could ride the storm at home, his scruples of conscience about having sanctioned the Civil Constitution of the Clergy had deepened, and the Queen urged that only foreign intervention could now restore his power. Foreign intervention could hardly be expected until the King broke with the Revolution and openly joined the counter-revolution. He was at last, by the spring of 1791, persuaded that he must leave the country. Late on the night of 20 June, disguised as a valet and a governess, Louis and Marie Antoinette escaped from Paris on a planned flight to the stronghold of Montmédy near the Luxembourg frontier. The journey was a whole chapter of miscalculations and accidents. The fugitives were recognized and stopped at Varennes, and were brought back to Paris amid ominously silent crowds. Placed under virtual imprisonment, the royal family could now be regarded as little more than potential traitors to the nation, prepared to join foreign armies and exiles against the cause of the Revolution. There followed a wholesale desertion of royal army officers. The Girondins within the Assembly, a group increasingly favouring war, gained greatly in strength. The enemies of the Revolution could now be depicted as the enemies of France

The Legislative Assembly, in October 1791, under the new constitution, replaced the old National Assembly. In January 1792, it decreed that the Habsburg Emperor of Austria, Leopold II, should be invited to declare whether or not he would renounce every treaty directed against the sovereignty, independence, and safety of the French nation; a fortnight later it ordered the property of the *émigrés* to be sequestrated. This was an ultimatum to both Europe and the *émigrés*. Leopold, himself embarrassed in diplomatic relations with Catherine II of Russia, was ready to be conciliatory. But he died on 1 March. His son Francis II, who succeeded him, was a less intelligent man and more dominated by militarist and absolutist advisers. When he rejected the French ultimatum, the Legislative Assembly on 20 April 1792 declared war 'in rightful defence of a free people against the unjust aggression of a king'.

At once the army of King Frederick William, in accordance with the Prussian alliance with Austria, prepared for active service. Austria and Prussia were joined by Victor Amadeus of Savoy, king of Piedmont. Catherine of Russia, busily engaged in gaining Polish territory, held aloof for the time, as did the British government. The initial conflict was between the revolutionary armies of France and a league of three neighbouring monarchs supported by an army of French exiles.

From the spring of 1792 until the rise of Napoleon the consequences of war and of revolution became inextricably mixed. The immediate causes of the war included the intrigues of the court and the *émigrés*, the war clamour of the Girondins in the Assembly, the aggressive self-confidence of the revolutionaries, the discredit of the King, and the diplomacy of Prussia. But its basic cause lay deeper. It was, in more modern terms, the issue of whether two forms of society based on totally different principles could peacefully coexist. France within her own territories had ended feudalism, destroyed the pretensions of royal absolutism, and founded new institutions on the principles of sovereignty of the people and personal liberty and equality. The old institutions, which had been overthrown in France, remained established in her continental neighbours. The influence of the Revolution was spreading, undermining the position of other rulers and implicitly challenging the survival of serfdom, feudalism, and absolutism everywhere. The revolutionary ideals were too dynamic to be ignored by the established order. The result was the First Coalition of 1793, comprising Austria, Prussia, Britain, the Netherlands, and Spain.

This inexorable conflict became apparent in the rival manifestos issued by each side. In August 1791 the Austrian and Prussian rulers issued the Declaration of Pillnitz, expressing the hope that there would be consultation between the powers about the position of Louis XVI, and hinting at joint armed intervention in the cautiously worded suggestion to employ, in certain conditions, 'efficacious means for enabling the King of France full freedom to set up a monarchical government in conformity with his rights and the welfare of the nation'. This aroused violent resentment in France. Nearly a year later, and after war had begun, the Duke of Brunswick as commander-in-chief of the Austro-Prussian forces issued from Coblenz his famous manifesto, declaring categorically that his armies were intervening in France to suppress anarchy and to restore the king's lawful authority. By threatening that the lives of the deputies and Paris administrators would be held forfeit for whatever harm might befall the royal family, he ensured that the revolutionaries would resist to the death. The Brunswick manifesto of 27 July had its sequel in the revolutionary manifesto of November 1792, in which the French, in the first flush of early victories against Prussia and Austria, offered 'fraternity and assistance' to all peoples wishing, like the French, to assert their liberty. In December the Assembly served notice on Europe that France would enforce revolutionary social principles everywhere. Occupation of any territory by French armies, they declared, would be accompanied by the ending of feudal obligations and the confiscation of clerical and aristocratic property.

The ideological conflict became clear. It was a clash between the old order and the new, now locked in a struggle to the death for the whole of Europe. So, at least, it seemed to men in the winter of 1792. The loudest trumpet call to conservatism had come in 1790 from the Irishman, Edmund Burke, whose violently eloquent *Reflections on the Revolution in France* provided all enemies of the Revolution with a counter-revolutionary philosophy; here was one of the most persuasive expositions of traditionalism ever penned, predicting anarchy and dictatorship as the outcome of such revolution. The revolution in France had become war in Europe: not an old-fashioned, familiar kind of war between monarchs for territory, but a newer ideological war between peoples and kings for the ending of old institutions and the fulfilment of dreams of a new society. In short, war in Europe now meant revolution in Europe.

CHAPTER 2

FRANCE AT WAR

THE JACOBIN TERROR

FROM the spring of 1792 onward, France sustained revolution and war at the same time. The consequences for France were momentous. They were, in brief, the overthrow of the monarchy, the dictatorship of Robespierre, the Reign of Terror, and the rise to power of General Bonaparte. For Europe, too, the consequences were far-reaching.

The first casualty of the war was the French monarchy. The newly elected assembly known as the Convention [1] met on 21 September 1792, the day after the battle of Valmy in which the revolutionary armies led by Generals Dumouriez and Kellermann routed the Prussians. The following day it abolished the monarchy and decreed that the first year of the Republic should date from 22 September.[2] After the further victory of Jemappes on 6 November, as a result of which the French occupied Brussels, the new Republic gained in self-confidence and decided upon the trial of the King. He was executed on 21 January 1793. This act, added to a series of other tensions between France and Britain, led to declaration of war against Britain and Holland at the beginning of February, against Spain in March, and against Hungary in April. This rapid extension of the war to most of Europe outside Scandinavia was soon accompanied by French reverses. A revolt broke out in the western region of the Vendée in March; Dumouriez was defeated at Neerwinden and the French were driven out of Holland in the same month. On 6 April the desertion of Dumouriez to the Austrians created a state of siege and emergency in France.

These events had great repercussions on the course of the revolution in France because they brought to an end the power of the Girondins. As the war party they were discredited by the reverses. Their

1. See p. 39.
2. The romantic and innovating spirit of the time was well expressed in the renaming of the months from September to August with the somewhat absurd names *Vendémiaire, Brumaire, Frimaire; Nivôse, Pluviôse, Ventôse; Germinal, Floréal, Prairial; Messidor, Thermidor, Fructidor.* These have survived among historians because of the French habit of using them to mark the great revolutionary (and counter-revolutionary) incidents. The contemporary English translation of them was an apt comment: Wheezy, Sneezy, Freezy; Slippy, Drippy, Nippy; Showery, Flowery, Bowery; Wheaty, Heaty, Sweety.

failures opened the door to the rule of the more extreme Jacobins: advocates of direct democracy, republicans, and most ardent champions of vigorous national defence against the forces of counter-revolution. In Maximilien Robespierre the Jacobins found a leader of genius and extraordinary fixity of purpose, whose ruthlessness and fanaticism enabled him to dominate the Convention. From July 1793, when he first became a member of its Committee of Public Safety until July 1794, when he died on the guillotine, Robespierre was virtually dictator of France. The revolution, on the defensive, sought salvation in personal tyranny – in the first perhaps, of all the single-party dictatorships of the modern world.

Of all the great French revolutionary personalities, Robespierre remains somehow the most memorable and the most symbolic : more than Mirabeau, who was a better orator and a greater statesman; more than Lafayette, whose statecraft failed to measure up to his inflated reputation; more even than Danton, an infinitely more attractive figure and the generous inspiration of national resistance to invasion and reaction. It is strange that so tumultuous and heroic an event as the French Revolution should remain personified in the slight, bespectacled, and unglamorous figure of this fastidious little provincial attorney. Is it that he in some sense represented the precise mixture of social and ideological impulses which triumphed in the Revolution? Socially, he was the archetype of the provincial lawyer who predominated in the revolutionary assemblies, the feline party intriguer and critic, fluent in the idealistic phrases that so constantly rang through those inexperienced parliamentary bodies. He was the little man of humble origins made great by the upheaval of revolution. In purpose and principle he stood for all that Jacobinism stands for in modern history: a doctrinaire idealism, exalting the principle of the sovereignty of the people, the liberty, equality, and fraternity of all men, the national republic 'one and indivisible'. In his own experience and career he personified the Jacobin revolutionary impulses.

To examine the anatomy of his dictatorship is to reveal the shape of things to come. It set the pattern for further revolutionary activity throughout most of Europe in the century that followed. The cell of revolution remained the club and the secret society, centring on Paris but frequently with provincial branches and committees throughout France. The pattern was, above all, the Jacobin Club of the 'Society of Friends of the Constitution' where, from the Revolution's earliest days, the respectable bourgeoisie of Paris listened intently to Robespierre's sententious moralizings. By its role in exerting pressure upon the elected national assemblies, its capacity to mobilize opinion and discontent in the provinces, its propensity to fall into the hands of the most extremist and ruthless leaders, it eventually triumphed over its many rivals. By the end of 1790 it had 1,100 members, mostly of the middle class, and when the monarchy fell the Jacobin Club had more than a thousand local societies affiliated with it. It remained the only real and effective political organization in France as a whole. It offered the perfect milieu for the full exercise of Robespierre's talents for intrigue, manoeuvre, and persuasion.

The second medium of revolution was the Commune, and here too Paris was the hub. Municipal and local organizations existed for many purposes, mainly administrative and military. In June 1789 the 407 delegates of the several quarters of Paris who had elected deputies to the Estates-General set themselves up at the Hôtel de Ville as an unofficial municipal government. In other towns local risings led to the formation of similar municipal bodies. By December 1789 local communal councils had been set up in all towns and villages. Local revolutionary surveillance committees often came into existence. The National Guard, instituted at the time of the fall of the Bastille and with mainly middle-class recruitment, was also organized in local sections with regional federations. This mass of local bodies tended to fuse together into local insurrectionary organizations, and most significantly in Paris.

In August 1792, with recruits flowing into Paris on their way to the frontiers, and amid fierce discontent in all the working-class quarters of the capital, the populace broke into open revolution against the Legislative Assembly. They stormed the Tuileries, imprisoned the King and royal family, and demanded the election, by universal male suffrage, of a new National Convention. They also set up a revolutionary municipal government or 'Commune' in Paris. Robespierre was elected to it on 11 August and for a fortnight attended its meetings. This body, supported by the extreme Jacobins, remained a rival authority in the capital to the national representative assembly, and exerted constant pressure on it for ever more violent and extreme measures. This was the second great medium of Robespierre's power, to be revived in even more violent form in 1871.[1]

A third was the single-chamber assembly of the National Convention. It was elected on universal male suffrage in the crisis of the fall of 1792 in response to the demands of the Jacobins and the Commune. With the monarchy overthrown, executive power fell into the hands of committees of the Convention. This arrangement lent itself admirably to the machinations of the Jacobins and the special talents of Robespierre. The two most important committees were the Committee of Public Safety,

1. See p. 395.

first created in April 1793, and the Committee of General Security. The former was subject to monthly re-election by the Convention and was entrusted with wide discretionary powers of government. The latter was especially concerned with police functions, and from September 1793 onward its members were chosen by the Committee of Public Safety. Robespierre joined the Committee of Public Safety in July, after the exclusion of Danton, whose heroic efforts to stem the tide of French defeats had plainly failed. The immense powers of both committees were virtually at the disposal of Robespierre and his two closest colleagues, Louis de Saint-Just and Georges Couthon. From August 1792 there had also existed in Paris a special court known as the Revolutionary Tribunal. Set up originally to try political offenders, it became a convenient means by which the government could by-pass the regular courts.

Such was the constitutional basis of Robespierre's 'revolutionary dictatorship', claiming justification in the desperate internal and external condition of France and determined to suppress all resistance by rigorous terrorism. In the frenzy of the time all resistance could be denounced as treason or counter-revolution and punished with the guillotine. This situation also chimed well with the personality of Robespierre, who had a mystical faith in the need for a 'Republic of Virtue'. The word 'Virtue' had echoes of both Machiavelli and Montesquieu, for whom it meant a civic spirit of unselfishness and dutiful self-sacrifice, as well as of Rousseau, who had added to it a more sentimental flavour of personal purity and incorruptibility. Robespierre's dream was of a democracy of loyal citizens and honest men, and he treated it as his personal mission to inaugurate a new democratic religion. In June 1794 he presided over the first festival of the Cult of the Supreme Being, having a month before issued a decree organizing the cult. The second and third articles of that decree were the most significant; they recognized 'that the proper worship of the Supreme Being consists in the practice of human duties', and that 'the most important of these duties are to hate treachery and tyranny, to punish tyrants and traitors, to succour the unfortunate, respect the weak, and defend the oppressed, to do all the good one can to one's neighbour, and to treat no one unjustly'. It was a revolutionary Declaration of the Duties of Man and of the Citizen, a belated but necessary sequel to the Declaration of Rights. It was a sign that the main surge of revolution had run its course; and a month later Robespierre himself fell victim to the guillotine, when his own oppressive tyranny had become at last intolerable. With him died his colleagues Saint-Just and Couthon.

The Jacobin Club, the Commune, and the Committees of the Convention were, in these ways, the three Institutional bases of Robespierre's revolutionary dictatorship. Yet his strange power remains only partially

explained unless there is added to these the atmosphere of restless insecurity and anxiety, the wider elements of revolutionary fervour and
patriotic enthusiasm, the constant blackmailing power of the excited and
ferocious Paris mob, which compelled every political leader to outbid
his colleagues in denouncing treachery and giving proof of his own un-
sullied purpose. The Reign of Terror became possible because of the
overthrow of all familiar established forms of government and the
double menace of counter-revolution at home and invasion from abroad.
That it went so far and lasted so long was due to other causes; above all,
to the power of *enragés* and *sansculottes*, the *bras-nus* and the *canaille* [1] –
in short of proletarian violence and of criminal extremism exploiting the
excitement and savagery of the urban mob. The Terror was directed not
just against recalcitrant nobility and clergy or treacherous *bourgeoisie*,
but even more against the mass of ordinary French men and women
who were unfortunate enough to fall victim to the twists and turns of
party strife. Many were denounced because the chief anxiety was to save
yourself by condemning others. The Terror was not an instrument of
class war, and 70 per cent of its victims belonged to the peasantry and
labouring classes, mostly in rebellion against the state. The Revolutionary Tribunal of Paris condemned to death 2,639 people; revolutionary courts condemned in all about 17,000. The rest of the Terror's 40,000
victims mostly died in summary mass executions in places such as the
Vendée and Lyon where there was open rebellion against the Convention.
Atrocious though it was, by the test of atrocities committed by more
modern dictatorships the Terror was mild and relatively discriminating.

The social incidence of the Terror was matched by the social incidence of the emigration. Over the whole decade 1789–99, the number
of bourgeois, peasant, and working-class refugees outnumbered noble
and clerical *émigrés* by about two to one. It was in 1793, during the
Reign of Terror, that the emigration included mainly the unprivileged,
and became broadly representative of the whole nation. The Revolution
was devouring its own children, and both by execution and exile it was
increasingly alienating large sections of the population. What gave it this
terrifying destructive power was the perpetuation of the war. The ultimate excuse for the Terror was the identification of enemies of the nation
with enemies of the Republic, an equation that the emigration and the
internal rebellions alike helped to strengthen. The revolutionary dictatorship rested on revolutionary war.

Whether it was the Revolution which attacked Europe, or Europe

1. These slang terms meant, respectively, the 'wild men' or republican extremists;
the 'common people' or poor; those 'with bare arms' or the working classes; and
'the rabble' or mob.

which attacked the Revolution, is a question almost impossible and certainly unprofitable to answer. As already suggested, there was an inexorable conflict between the two, and once war had begun, for whatever reason or excuse, the conflict was likely to continue until it burned itself out on the field of battle. The impact of war on the internal reconstruction of France was immense. The converse was equally true. The *levée en masse* or universal conscription for military service, introduced by the Committee of Public Safety in August 1793 on the advice of Lazare Carnot, revolutionized modern warfare. It did not at once mean the mobilization of everyone, which would have simply disorganized the country. At first only bachelors and childless widowers between the ages of 18 and 25 were called up. But the measures established a novel and far-reaching principle: that in time of emergency the state has the right to command the services of all its citizens. It enabled France to put into the field of battle massive formations, organized and equipped by the genius of Carnot, against which the older professional royal armies proved outmoded. The system, perpetuated by the Directory [1] in its Law of Conscription of September 1798, laid a firm foundation for the military dictatorship of Napoleon.

Of necessity imitated by other countries, the system led eventually to the modern citizen-army, and helped to turn war from a battle between armies into a conflict between whole nations. Combined with the doctrines of democracy which prevailed in 1793, it led also to a programme of internal reforms which was full of significance for the future. If persons and services can be conscripted, so can property; and if all must make sacrifices, it is the duty of the state to provide for the needs and welfare of those whose services it commands. The relation between government and governed, between state and society, became an infinitely more reciprocal and intimate relationship than had ever existed under absolutist monarchies. The revolutionary dictatorship undertook to control prices and wages, to organize the distribution of supplies, to regulate currency and trade, to encourage improvements in agriculture, to provide better technical education, to assist the poor, even to abolish slavery in the French colonies. Paternalistic monarchies, too, had done most of these things; but now they were done in the name of democracy, through an assembly of the nation's democratically elected representatives, and in a mood of excited enthusiasm for popular welfare. This connexion between necessities of warfare and the development of welfare was to remain constant throughout subsequent European history.

In August 1793 the main justification for the Terror was that there were five enemy armies on French soil, and Paris had to be organized

1. See p. 44.

like a beleaguered citadel. By the spring of 1794 the tide had turned. The revolt in the Vendée had been broken; the British had been repelled at sea; the Prussian and Austrian forces had been held and then pushed back out of Alsace and forced over the Rhine; in May the Ardennes and western Flanders were reoccupied, and by June all Belgium was again in French occupation. These successes were, in one sense, a measure of how far the Terror had succeeded in its nationally defensible purpose. That the Terror not only continued but greatly intensified during the summer, until the execution of Robespierre, was due mainly to its own impetus – the inability of extremists to drop their habitual demands when there was personal peril in relaxing their grip on power. In June and July the guillotine claimed 1,285 victims. Some pretext for strenuous and harsh government could still be found in the deplorable economic conditions of the country. War on the rich (especially the new rich of profiteers and speculators) for the benefit of the poor could be indefinitely continued, the redistribution of property by confiscation and taxation which Robespierre had proclaimed was certainly not yet completed, and the laws of the Maximum, which attempted to control inflation by setting maximum prices, were undoubtedly widely evaded. But France could not support Terror for such ends alone. It had outlived its usefulness. After the death of Robespierre on 28 July 1794 some 80,000 prisoners were immediately released, and soon all arrests made before his fall were cancelled. Nearly 90 members of the Commune shared Robespierre's fate.

THE DIRECTORY

But if the 'Red Terror' was over, the 'White Terror' of reaction was just beginning. The Convention sat until October 1795, reorganized its committees and readmitted surviving Girondins to positions of power. These last fourteen months of the Convention are known as the Thermidorian reaction (because in the new revolutionary calendar it was on 9th Thermidor that Robespierre was overthrown). It was significantly not a royalist reaction. The forms of revolutionary government went on just as the war went on. But it was a swing back toward moderate Jacobinism, a revulsion against the final excesses of the Terror, a liquidation of party feuds and hatreds. Only in May 1795 was the Revolutionary Tribunal abolished, though its most despotic powers and procedures were taken away from it earlier. The Convention gave up attempts to enforce the laws of the Maximum, and some of the émigrés began to find their way back into France. Abandoning the draft constitutions of both the Girondins and the Jacobins, the Convention now drew up a third, which betrayed not only fear of the executive but also fear of the mob. It began with a declaration of duties as well as of rights. This Constitution came into operation in October 1795, and lasted until November 1799.

The Directory of five, which held executive power under this new Constitution, was ill-fated from birth. The men who successfully became Directors were, except for the patriotic organizing genius of Carnot, disreputable and self-seeking politicians of little ability. The corrupt leaders of a period when the moral standards of social and political life were at exceptionally low ebb, they presided over the final liquidation of the Revolution. The new ruling class which backed the measures of the Directory, as of the latter-day Convention, included businessmen and financial speculators, army contractors and landowning peasants – all those middle-class elements that had profited most from the revolution and the war. These new rich, vulgar in taste and unscrupulous in habits, wanted above all to consolidate and increase their gains. Opposed equally to royalist reaction and to further mob violence, their aims were a constitutional parliamentary system on a narrow social basis, moderate in action and so devised as to prevent personal dictatorship. They succeeded in preventing a repetition of Robespierre's revolutionary dictatorship only at the price of producing Napoleon's military dictatorship. Explanation of how this came about lies in their success in crushing rebellion at home and their failure to produce victory abroad.

At home the Directory more and more openly relied upon the army to defend it against revolt. The Convention had already, in 1795, destroyed the main instruments of revolutionary action when it closed the Jacobin Club, ended the Commune and executed the Communards, reorganized its own committees, and abolished the Revolutionary Tribunal. The Convention had also set the example of relying upon troops to crush insurrection. By the spring of 1795 the severe winter, dislocation of trade, and increase in social distress bred a series of revolts. In April when Parisians rioted and demanded 'bread and the Constitution of 1793', troops under General Pichegru promptly crushed them. In May, when insurgents led by Jacobin rebels occupied the hall of the Convention, regular troops under Murat and Menou drove them out. Barricades hastily erected in the working-class districts were easily demolished. The National Guard, traditional ally of revolutionaries, was reorganized into a truly middle-class body. Again in October, when the Paris mob made one final effort to assert itself against the representatives of the nation, the Convention called to its defence the troops of General Barras. His subordinate was young Napoleon Bonaparte, whose reward for his services was command of the home army. The Directory readily enough followed these examples, and was mainly a mere continuation of the

Thermidorian reaction under the Convention. With an army of more than 800,000 men – the largest ever raised until then by one European power [1] – it felt able to make up for its lack of popularity by frequent use of armed force.

The last episode of the French Revolution was not the fall of Robespierre but the strange and extravagant episode known as the Babeuf Plot of 1796. In October 1795, in resistance to the new Constitution of the Directory devised by the Convention to embody and perpetuate the power of the new rich, a political club was formed called the Society of the Panthéon. It attracted many former Jacobins and held meetings in a crypt by torchlight. It circulated its own paper, the *Tribun*, edited by François-Noël Babeuf, an embittered and fanatical young agitator. While it was hesitating between remaining a political debating society and becoming an active conspiracy, it was attacked by the Directory, which in February 1796 sent General Bonaparte in person to close the meeting place and dissolve the society. The more extremist members, led by Babeuf and Sylvain Maréchal, retaliated by setting up an insurrectionary committee or 'Secret Directory' of six, and preparing revolt. It was to be the final battle for the forgotten revolutionary ideal of equality – the ideal most blatantly derided by the existing conditions of inflation, distress, and corruption.

The Babouvists proposed to revive the Jacobin Constitution of 1793, which had been approved but never implemented, in place of the new Constitution of 1795; to restore the revolutionary movement to its original purity of idealism and sincerity of purpose; and to proclaim a 'Republic of Equals', in which a communistic organization of society would abolish the growing gulf between rich and poor. Revolutionary agents, under the direction of the central committee, were to penetrate units of army, police, and administration. This was the last important attempt to win back the army to the cause of revolution. Preparations for insurrection were remarkably thorough, arms and ammunition were stored, and on the given signal citizens from each district of Paris, to the summons of tocsin and trumpet, were to march behind banners to support the mutineers of the army. Public buildings and bakeries were to be

1. In the eighteenth century it had been Prussia, not France, that had set the example of large standing armies. Although in 1789 the population of Prussia was only one third that of France, she could raise in time of war an army of 250,000. France in 1789 could muster 211,000, or 287,000 if the militia, included at war strength, were added. But the Directory's Law of Conscription of 1798 was the first to introduce the principle that the regular army, as distinct from the militia, should be recruited by systematic national conscription. Though it worked badly and ineffectively, it was later turned to full use by Bonaparte, and through him it affected all Europe.

seized. The Secret Directory would exercise power until completely democratic elections for a new national assembly could be held. But the police had spies within the movement from the start; on the eve of the insurrection its leaders were arrested or dispersed by loyal troops, and the plot came to nothing. The days when a *coup d'état* based on the Paris mob could dictate to France were over for a time, and the strategy of the conspirators already had a somewhat old-fashioned air.

Yet the event became of considerable historical importance because of the mythical and legendary character it acquired. The trial of the plotters, staged in 1797 before a special court and intended to frighten waverers into support of the Directory, lasted for three months and became a platform for expounding the Babouvist ideals. Babeuf made it the occasion for an indictment of the existing régime as well as of the social order, and the Directory rested on so little public loyalty that he hit it just where it was most vulnerable. The execution of Babeuf after his attempted suicide made him the last famous martyr of the White Terror. Through the propagandist work of his colleague, Philippe Buonarroti, the Babeuf Plot became a heroic republican legend among the most active revolutionaries of nineteenth-century Paris. Babeuf won renown by his passionate sincerity. The insurrectionary techniques and inner organization of the Plot were exhaustively studied, imitated, and elaborated. Modern Communism also claims some affinities with the ideals of Babeuf. Perhaps he has acquired greater renown than he deserved, or than the importance of the Plot in 1796 merited. But in revolutions legends are powerful and ghosts can walk.[1]

In foreign affairs, too, the army assumed an ever greater role. By the beginning of 1796 France's only active enemies on land were Austria and Sardinia, and at sea Great Britain. The Convention had made peace with Holland, Spain, and Prussia. By incorporating the former Austrian Netherlands (Belgium) into France in October, it was committed to continuing the war against Austria, which would not accept this loss; while British refusal to make peace, even after the breakup of the First Coalition, kept active the war at sea. Peace had also been made with Portugal, with the German states of Saxony and the two Hesses, with the Italian states of Naples, Parma, and the Papacy. By the beginning of 1796 the Directory was able to concentrate all its efforts on the war against Austria.

On the last day of 1795 Pichegru had signed an armistice with the Austrians on the Rhine front. Using this respite, the Directory planned to send its main armies against Vienna, under the leadership of Moreau and Jourdan, by way of the Black Forest and the Danube. This was to

1. See pp. 144 and 196.

be the decisive frontal attack. To aid it, another army was to create a diversion against Austrian power in Italy. This army was put in the charge of General Bonaparte. By the Battle of Mondovi he defeated the Sardinians and forced them to make an armistice by which they ceded Nice and Savoy to France. Marching on, Bonaparte's army defeated the Austrians at Lodi on 10 May (the very day when the Babeuf Plot was suppressed) and took Milan, where he was greeted as a liberator from Austrian rule. By January 1797 he had succeeded, after a long struggle, in taking the central Austrian stronghold of Mantua, and in routing an Austrian army of some 70,000 at the Battle of Rivoli. Pressing north-eastward to Laibach, he forced the Austrians to make an armistice in April.

Peace was delayed for six months because the main French armies in Austria had made much less decisive progress; but when Bonaparte pressed on even to the Danube, Austria signed the peace of Campo Formio on 17 October 1797. She thereby abandoned Belgium to France and recognized its annexation; recognized the new French creation of a Cisalpine Republic in northern Italy; surrendered the Ionian Islands off Greece; but kept Venice and all her territory in Italy and the Adriatic. Under secret articles the bargain went further. The Austrian Emperor promised to cede to France large districts of the Rhineland, and in return was promised part of Bavaria, the ecclesiastical state of Salzburg, and the exclusion of his rival, Prussia, from any territorial gains. It was a settlement as characteristic of sly Napoleonic diplomacy as the campaign had been of Napoleonic generalship. Only Britain now remained at war with France. (*See* Map 1.)

At home the Directory faced its first political crisis with the elections of 1797, which it was expected would result in an anti-Jacobin majority. Only 13 out of the 216 retiring members of the elected councils were returned: a clear enough protest against the failure of the government to restore French credit and currency or to alleviate the widespread social distress. In September 1797 the Directory forestalled the action of the new hostile and mainly royalist majority. With the help of Bonaparte it expelled the newly elected members from the assemblies. By this *coup d'état* of Fructidor the Directors forfeited their last shreds of legality, and henceforth relied more openly on armed force. Bonaparte's own seizure of power was brought one step nearer. In the further elections of May 1798 nearly all moderates abstained from voting, with the result that the extremists held the field and the Directory resorted to the further *coup d'état* of Floréal, in which it annulled 98 elections. The political system was as bankrupt as the treasury. The elections of May 1799 could not be suppressed with equal impunity, and they brought into the legislative assemblies all the Directory's most active opponents. Of the five Directors, Barras and Sieyès were resolved to resort to the ultimate sanction: open alliance with Bonaparte, the most popular personality in France, with a victorious army at his command.

Bonaparte in 1798 had departed on an expedition to Egypt designed to cut off the British from India and their other eastern possessions. He had captured the island of Malta in June, occupied Alexandria in July, and marched against Syria. Then he suffered reverses. His fleet was destroyed by Nelson at Aboukir Bay in the Battle of the Nile (August 1798). Plague broke out among his troops. By May 1799 he withdrew to Egypt with heavy losses. The campaign produced, too, a second coalition against France, which included Turkey and Russia as well as Britain. Bonaparte sailed from Alexandria in August 1799, evaded the watching British fleet, and reached France in October. Despite his losses and reverses he was the only man in France who enjoyed general confidence, and in the new conditions of emergency it was to him that men turned.

On 9 November (18th Brumaire) in conspiracy with Barras and Sieyès, Napoleon carried out the projected *coup d'état* that brought him to political power. It did not go according to plan. He had hoped that the assemblies, over one of which his own brother, Lucien Bonaparte, presided, could be persuaded to move from Paris to Saint-Cloud, to entrust him with command of the troops in Paris, and then to vote for constitutional revision under his direction. His chief hope was that his undoubted popularity would lead to his being acclaimed almost spontaneously as head of the state. The first two steps in the programme were safely carried out, and at Saint-Cloud he addressed each assembly in turn. But they did not receive him with the acclaim he expected. Instead, on 10 November they rejected his pretensions and affirmed their loyalty to the Constitution. He had to appeal, unwillingly, to armed force. He ordered his troops to chase the assemblies from their hall. A small number of the representatives remained and, in collusion with Sieyès, voted for constitutional revision. They appointed three consuls to carry it out: Sieyès, Bonaparte, and a nonentity, Roger Ducos.

The *coup* succeeded because neither assemblies nor Directory had any popular esteem left, and the population as a whole – even in Paris – accepted the accomplished fact with little resistance. It remained only for that veteran constitution-monger, the Abbé Sieyès, to draft a constitution on his new formula. 'Confidence from below; power from above', and for Bonaparte to adapt it to his own views of the situation, which required his personal autocracy endorsed by popular plebiscite. Executive government was invested in a first consul, with two other consuls subordinate to him; a nominated state council was to initiate legislation; a senate of 60 members was to be nominated by the consuls. When the new arrangement was submitted to plebiscite, it was announced that more than three million votes had been for it, only 1,562 against it. The Revolution had fulfilled the remarkable prophecy of Edmund Burke of nine years before: 'In the weakness of one kind of authority and the fluctuations of all, the officers of an army will remain for some time mutinous and full of faction, until some general who understands the art of conciliating the soldiery . . . shall draw the eyes of all men upon himself. Armies will obey him on his personal account. But the moment in which that event shall happen, the person who really commands the army is your master, the master of your King, the master of your Assembly, the master of your whole Republic.' On Christmas Eve, 1799, only a decade after the Revolution began, that prophecy was completely fulfilled in the formal inauguration of the Consulate.

THE IMPACT ON EUROPE

Meanwhile, the effects of the war upon Europe were little less revolutionary than upon France itself. Until 1914 the French Revolution could properly be regarded as the most important event in the life of modern Europe, comparable in its consequences with the Reformation of the sixteenth century and the religious wars of the seventeenth. It destroyed the landmarks of the old established order in politics, economics, social life and thought, diplomacy, and war. Throughout Europe the impact of revolution and war was enhanced by the previous cult of all things French, which dated from the time of Louis XIV and from the spread of the Enlightenment during the earlier part of the eighteenth century. In Germany particularly, French manners, literature, and thought had become familiar long before 1789. The movement of the Enlightenment (*Aufklärung*) promoted by men such as Gotthold Lessing spread belief in reason and challenged all existing institutions and beliefs. The same was true, if to a lesser extent, in Belgium, northern Italy, and even Great Britain.

This cultural preparation explains the widespread enthusiasm evoked by the early stages of the revolution in France. In Britain and the United States radicals and democrats of all kinds welcomed the signs that the very model of established absolutist monarchy was at last yielding to the need for constitutional reforms. There took place in 1789 a symbolic gesture of the solidarity of the democratic international when Lafayette, the hero of the United States and newly appointed commander of the National Guard, handed to Tom Paine, the republican English hero of America, the key of the Bastille to take to George Washington. In 1792 the National Assembly conferred upon Tom Paine the title of 'French citizen', and he was elected as a deputy of the Convention, where he supported the Girondins. The leading English radical philosopher, Jeremy Bentham, despite his hostility to natural rights and Jacobinism, was also made a citizen of France, and as such he duly recorded his vote for Napoleon in 1799. The dominant classes and parties of revolutionary France, feeling that they were conducting a revolution on behalf of all mankind, welcomed into their ranks men of any other nation whom they regarded as sharing their aspiration. And many generous-minded men of other nations responded to this view of the Revolution – at least until the excesses of the Terror and the aggressions of French armies disillusioned them. The eighteenth century was in culture cosmopolitan, and it fittingly culminated in a cosmopolitan revolution.

It was precisely this universal characteristic of the Revolution – dramatized by the Declaration of the Rights of Man and of the Citizen and by the revolutionary manifestoes [1] – that provoked European rulers into antagonism. It was something that would not let them alone, and which therefore they could not ignore. But this recognition was not immediate. If radicals were over-enthusiastic in their welcome of revolution, rulers were at first equally exaggeratedly apathetic. France was a traditional rival of all her neighbours, and for the French king to find himself enmeshed in difficulties at home was no unwelcome news to them. There was a rough balance of power in the Europe of 1789, a tolerable equilibrium between Bourbon and Habsburg, Austria and Russia, Russia and Turkey. There was, as yet, no concert of Europe, no organization for regular consultation about common European problems, no 'Holy Alliance' to lead a crusade against revolution. All these were consequences of the revolutionary decade between 1789 and 1799, not factors in it. Even at war France found herself opposed only by partial and unstable coalitions, held together mainly by British strategy and subsidies, and then not for long. Normal diplomatic relations were governed by considerations of dynastic security and acquisition of territories. Poland was partitioned during the Revolution itself, when in 1793 and 1795 the rulers of Prussia, Russia, and Austria completed the carving-up that had begun twenty years before. In January 1795, indeed, the monarchs of Russia and Austria made a treaty for the partition or acquisition not only of Poland, but of Turkey, Venice, and Bavaria as well. The sweeping successes of the first revolutionary armies become understandable only if this greedy and separatist characteristic of their opponents is realized.

The disillusionment of democrats with the early promise of the Revo-

1. See p. 34.

lution is not to be explained only by the Terror and the course of the Revolution inside France, though all Europe watched that struggle with the liveliest attention. It is related even more directly to the shift in pretension and behaviour which came about in the revolutionary armies themselves in 1793. The declared war aims of the revolutionary government became more and more selfishly nationalistic in character, less and less distinguishable from the time-honoured aggressive policies of the French kings. Danton's doctrine of the 'natural frontiers' of France included not only the indisputable ones of the Atlantic, the Mediterranean, and the Pyrenees, but also the highly debatable ones of the Rhine and the Alps. This seemed but old Bourbon dynasticism writ large. When the Convention supported these claims to the extent of annexing Nice, Savoy, and Belgium, and attacking Holland, and when it openly defied existing public law and practices in Europe, the claims had to be taken seriously. They were of a kind that neither kings nor peoples could accept with equanimity, for they violated both dynasticism and nationalism.

The rigorous introduction of the novel French laws and institutions into annexed or occupied territories was further proof of French intentions. The task of gallicizing Europe, which the *philosophes* had begun in cultural matters and which Napoleon was later to attempt in imperial administration, was equally vigorously attempted by the revolutionaries. They were aided, indeed, by native supporters, and the destructive side of their work was often welcome enough. It was only when populations found French masters no less exacting than their old régimes that they were fired to ideas of self-government. The idea that 'sovereignty of the people' should lead to national independence was the indirect result of French occupation: its original meaning, of abolishing privilege and universalizing rights, came to merge into this new implication only as a result of conquests. The French revolutionaries spread liberalism by intention but created nationalism by inadvertence.

Under the arrangements made at Campo Formio in 1797 much of the Rhineland and northern Italy were added to the territories directly under French administration. By then the need for the French armies to live on local supplies and to make war profitable, combined with Bonaparte's tendency to exact heavy tribute from the occupied territories, further intensified anti-French feelings. The whole of western Europe between the Pyrenees and the Baltic was infused with a strange mixture of general sympathy for the original ideals of the Revolution and an immediate hostility to the practices of the French. It was the perfect mixture for nourishing the seeds of nationalism. (*See* Map 1.)

In the belligerent states that remained beyond French rule, the results were naturally different. In Austria and Prussia the major effect of the

Legend:

French Republic 1798 · Dependent Republics 1798 · German Church States to be absorbed by other German States

North Sea · Rügen · ENGLAND · Hamburg · Berlin · PRUSSIA · BATAVIAN REP. · OTHER · BELGIUM (ANNEXED 1792) · Pillnitz · SILESIA · Lille · Fleurus · GERMAN · Paris · Varennes · Lunéville · STATES · BADEN · Vienna · Versailles · Danube R. · AUSTRIA · Loire · Basel · Budapest · FRANCE · HELVETIC REP. · SAVOY · PIEDMONT · Campo Formio · Verona · Lyons · CISALPINE REP. · Milan · Venice · Marengo · Genoa · Po R. · Avignon · Nice · LIGURIAN REP. · TUSCANY · Adriatic Sea · OTTOMAN EMPIRE · Marseilles · SPAIN · CORSICA · Rome · ROMAN REPUBLIC · Mediterranean · SARDINIA · Sea · PARTHENOPEAN REP. (1799) · IONIAN IS.

FRENCH REPUBLIC
AND ITS SATELLITES
1798–1799

200 MILES

MAP 1. THE FRENCH REPUBLIC AND ITS SATELLITES, 1798–9

After 1792 the war aims of the revolutionary governments in France became more selfishly nationalistic and less distinguishable from the traditional policies of conquest of the French kings. In expanding eastward to her 'natural frontiers' of the Rhine and the Alps, France annexed Belgium, Germany west of the Rhine, Savoy, and Nice. In the treaty of Campo Formio (1797) these annexations were recognized by Austria, and German princes ousted from the Rhineland were compensated by receiving the territory of erstwhile church-

wars was to impose strain upon their financial resources and domestic administrations. Reverses shook the position of their governments at home and enhanced the hardships and burdens of war. Otherwise the short-term effects were not vastly different from the effects of more familiar kinds of inter-dynastic struggle. Never was there any likelihood of an outbreak of revolution. And court circles, in Vienna and Berlin as much as in the majority of the smaller states of Germany, were in general stiffened in their existing tendencies of conservatism, scared away from any previous thoughts of alliance between monarchy and the Enlightenment. They kept their power over territories which were economically and socially still unfavourable to the reception of revolutionary propaganda. In Russia, Catherine II and her successor Paul did all in their power to seal off the country against the infiltration of French influences and agents; they succeeded sufficiently well to prevent revolutionary ideas from reaching Russia until a whole generation later.

Of all the opponents of France, it was the most persistent, Great Britain, that was most immediately and most profoundly affected by the course of events. By dint of her own turbulent past in the seventeenth century, her relatively advanced constitutional development, her early progress in industrialism, Britain was especially receptive to the revolutionary ideas. Not only did her active radical leaders like Tom Paine, Horne Tooke, Thomas Hardy, and those who formed a coterie around Lord Shelburne, welcome the Revolution as the greatest event since American independence, but the large and influential Whig party, led by Charles James Fox, was at first prepared to defend it in parliament. The moderate Tory government, led by the younger William Pitt, had from 1784 onward sought to introduce many financial and administrative reforms, and it had even considered parliamentary reform. It took time for the opinion of the influential classes of England to set against the Revolution; and only after the King's execution, the Terror, and the outbreak of war did the bulk of the Whig party, headed by the Duke of Portland, take the fateful decision to desert Fox in opposition and to support the war administration of Pitt.

Fox, though himself very far from revolutionary, was impulsive and generous by nature. He refused to believe that in England Jacobinism could ever be dangerous enough to justify repression of free speech and

---

states scattered throughout Germany and Austria. By 1799 six republics dependent on France were set up in the Netherlands, Switzerland, and Italy. Thus enlarged and screened with satellite states, France in November 1799 came to be ruled by the Consulate, with General Bonaparte as First Consul.

association. But others were panicked by the rapid growth of a host of radical societies and clubs, often on the model of the French and in contact with the French. The London Corresponding Society included mainly small tradesmen, artisans, and lower-class elements; and it had affiliated societies in northern cities. The Constitutional Society and the Friends of the People were societies of gentry and tradespeople. They and many others demanded reform of the constitution and varying degrees of democratic freedom. In November 1793 there even met, in Edinburgh, a 'British Convention' demanding universal suffrage and annual elections. But with prolongation of the war such activities came to seem more and more unpatriotic, the government hardened in its repressive policy as it won broader national support, and the outcome was on the one hand a deepening of radical sentiments among the working classes, and on the other a consolidating of Toryism into a policy of resistance to all reform. Parliamentary reform, which had seemed near at hand before 1789, was postponed until 1832. The demands of the war, including payment of subsidies to Britain's continental allies, imposed heavy financial burdens on the country. Pitt borrowed money and thus increased the national debt and the *rentier* class. In 1798 he introduced a novelty which was to have an immense future: the income tax.

As the century reached its close, so did the war in Europe. The First Consul knew that because his power rested on the support of the army, he must ultimately give the army conquest and glory. He also knew that his popularity at home depended upon his giving France a more stable, efficient, and businesslike government than she had hitherto known. To settle and consolidate his position in France, to establish order and security, he needed a truce. He therefore fought Austria to a standstill at the Battle of Marengo in June 1800, and when this was followed up by Moreau's victory at Hohenlinden in December, the result was the treaty of Lunéville in February 1801. It confirmed the terms of the treaty of Campo Formio. In the same year Bonaparte made a concordat with the Vatican and settled the religious issue for the rest of his reign. In 1802 even Britain agreed to make peace and signed the treaty of Amiens. The Second Coalition of 1799, which had included Austria, Russia, Britain, Naples, and Portugal, broke up, as did its predecessor of 1793.[1] The revolutionary wars were over; the Napoleonic wars proper had not yet begun. In the interval Napoleon dazzled France and Europe with the achievements of dictatorship.

1. See p. 35.

CHAPTER 3

DICTATORSHIP IN FRANCE

NAPOLEON BONAPARTE

THE man who was to rule France and much of Europe for the next fifteen years was only thirty years old when he became First Consul – the same age, exactly, as his greatest military opponent, Arthur Wellesley, later Duke of Wellington. A Corsican by birth, Napoleon was French only because the island of Corsica had been annexed to France the year before he was born. He was trained as an artillery officer in French schools, self-consciously a foreigner and sensitively solitary. By 1793 he had been converted to Jacobin ideas, and won some repute for his services in repulsing the British from Toulon. His first great series of victories, in the Italian campaign of 1796–97, was due to his skilled application of new principles of warfare which as a young officer he had studied and elaborated. Scientific improvements had encouraged a new and more offensive type of warfare. Better roads and maps, combined with more mobile artillery more closely co-ordinated with the movements of infantry, were revolutionizing armies and their uses. Instead of using cumbrous equipment suited best to slow movement and siege warfare, it became possible to organize campaigns of swifter movement, more rapid concentration of force, and greater surprise. The infantry, too, drawn less from professionals and mercenaries and more from the whole body of citizens through the *levée en masse*, had greater dash and *élan*. New generalship had to be resourceful and adaptable, mastering a greater mass of details and combining versatility of tactics with precision in their execution. Great military opportunities lay before a soldier of genius who chose to seize them. Bonaparte, with his insatiable ambition and boundless energy, did not hesitate to do so.

It is a constant temptation, in looking back upon the meteoric rise of a great conqueror such as Napoleon, to invest him not only with indomitable will-power, which he undoubtedly had, but also with a degree of foresight and control over events which seems uncanny. The true genius of Napoleon is distorted unless this temptation is resisted. At several crucial moments in his career, when his fortunes hung in the balance, he showed unexpected hesitation and uncertainty of purpose. One such moment was in the *coup d'état* of Brumaire itself, when he was fraught with nervous anxieties and his brother Lucien showed greater presence of mind and more capacity to control events than did Napoleon himself. It might even be argued that so long as his character permitted of this degree of hesitancy, which revealed some humility and also bred prudence, his plans were usually successful; it was when unbroken triumphs had fostered excessive confidence and destroyed all humility that he began to fail. The nervous excitement and anxiety that he was wont to suffer at critical moments serve to remind us that to even the greatest historical figures each momentous decision was a choice between relatively unknown alternatives. Every move was, at the time, a leap in the dark.

Bonaparte was the supreme opportunist, driven by a burning desire for power, which consumed his energies, and guided by a highly intelligent insight into the forces at work in the Europe of his time. He was a masterful opportunist partly because the opportunities before him were so great. The momentum of the revolutionary movement in France had burned itself out, and, as Burke had foreseen, the time was now ripe for a popular soldier with a genius for organization to take over authority. Provided he could discriminate between the durable results of the Revolution which could now be consolidated and its excesses and aberrations which had to be suppressed, he could make for himself a unique position as the heir and legatee of the Revolution.

INTERNAL REORGANIZATION

Between 1800 and 1803 Bonaparte as First Consul was free to devote his energies mainly to the internal reorganization of France. It was in this period, one of the most important in the whole of modern French history, that his most constructively valuable work was done. He brought to the task of reorganization the qualities of swift decision and action, the same precision and concentration upon essentials which had already brought him success in war. The spirit behind the great reforms of the Consulate at home was the transference of the methods of Bonaparte the general to the tasks of Bonaparte the statesman. And, as in war, he was able to enlist in his service a band of men imbued with the same spirit and devoted to the same ends.

Many reforms had been projected during the Revolution but only some of them had been carried out. The division of France for purposes of local administration into a fairly symmetrical pattern of communes and departments had been made in 1790; the administration of the public debt had been unified by Joseph Cambon in 1793; the metric system had been introduced in 1793; the beginnings of more modern technological education had begun in 1794, with Carnot's foundation in Paris of the Polytechnic School (École Polytechnique). But other reforms had been only partially launched or merely projected: the erection of a central administration for assessing and collecting taxes attempted by the Directory in 1797, and the codification of the law which was begun between 1792 and 1796. Now, using the ablest men regardless of their past loyalties, ranging from former servants of the monarchy such as the financial bureaucrat Martin Gaudin to former regicide members of the Committee of Public Safety such as the administrator Jean Bon Saint-André, Bonaparte provided the concentrated drive that got things done. He was the architect, they the technicians. His over-all purpose was a systematic reconstruction of the main legal, financial, and administrative institutions of France, which gives Bonaparte a strong claim to be the last and greatest of the eighteenth-century benevolent despots.

Financial administration and taxation, the cancers of the old régime, were among the first to be overhauled. The Bank of France was founded in 1800, its constitution drafted by a leading Paris banker, Perregaux. The only four existing banks of any importance had been created since 1796. Although at first an independent corporation, the Bank of France was from the outset linked with the management of government loans and tax-collectors' deposits, and in 1803 it was given the monopoly of issuing bank-notes. The system of collecting taxes, which the Revolution had entrusted to autonomous local authorities, was now centralized and made more efficient by Gaudin. Local government itself was at the same time centralized by putting a prefect, appointed by the First Consul, in sole charge of each department. Local elected councils were left with only advisory powers, and even the mayor of each commune was centrally appointed. These measures virtually restored the centralized authority of the old régime with its powerful intendants, since the prefects, who enjoyed immense local power, were all in turn completely under the direction of the central government.

The enormously complex task of codifying French law was completed. In 1789 France knew no common law, but only a medley of local laws and jurisdictions, all overlaid with a tangle of feudal custom, royal edicts, and ecclesiastical Canon Law. Property rights and civic rights had been entirely changed by the upheavals of the Revolution, and to define, stabilize, and codify the new situation had become a vital need. The powerful Council of State, itself a revival in modern form of the old *curia regis* or royal council, was the machine through which Bonaparte remodelled the law. It held 84 sessions to discuss various drafts of the new codes, with Bonaparte himself presiding over 36. It hammered out a synthesis between the liberal, customary, and 'natural law' theories of the Revolution and the Roman law theories which, under the Directory, had been revived in reaction against the Revolution. The synthesis, which was eventually embodied in the 2,287 articles of the Napoleonic Code of 1804, was itself made possible by Bonaparte's readiness to employ men of talent whatever their past. On the Council of State former revolutionaries like Théophile Berlier and Antoine Thibaudeau upheld the claims of customary law, while former royalist jurists like Jean Portalis upheld the claims of Roman law.

The Code gave prominence to the principles of Roman law – a fact that made the Napoleonic Code acceptable to other European countries in later years. This basis affected especially the laws of the family, marriage and divorce, the status of women, paternal authority, and property. The authority of the father over his wife, his children, and the property of the family was strengthened, as against the revolutionary tendency toward equality of persons and equal division of property. Under the new Codes wives were subjected to husbands, divorce was made more difficult, and property up to a quarter of the whole could be bequeathed away from the family. If Bonaparte supported these changes, it was less as a champion of Roman law than as an astute statesman, eager to end the laxity of manners and morals which had existed under the Directory. In other respects equality of civic rights was preserved. The Code confirmed the rights of private property and the land settlement of the Revolution, and reassured all who had acquired the former lands of Church and nobility that their existing rights would be preserved. Bonaparte ensured, above all, that there would be no counter-revolution – and this rallied middle classes and peasants alike behind the Consulate.

An ecclesiastical settlement was no less urgent and important. Bonaparte himself shared the scepticism of the *philosophes* but not their violent anti-clericalism. He had a lively sense of the political importance of religion, which he valued chiefly as a social cement. His only aim was therefore to end the religious strife of the Revolution and find a realistic settlement. He wanted to separate royalism from Catholicism, and to satisfy both the strong Catholic religious feelings of large parts of the population, including peasants and intellectuals, and the anxiety of all who held former Church lands and wished to avoid any ultra-Catholic reaction that might seek to restore the Church's secular power and property. Taking advantage of the accession in 1800 of a new pope, Pius VII, Bonaparte began negotiations for a concordat with the Papacy which would serve these ends.

By July 1801 he completed the bargain. He guaranteed freedom of worship subject only to the preservation of public order, and recognized Roman Catholicism as 'the religion of the majority of Frenchmen'. He undertook to pay the salaries of bishops and clergy, and so won papal recognition for the revolutionary confiscation of Church property. In return, too, the Pope agreed that all existing bishops would resign, and that in the future, bishops nominated by the French government would be instituted by the Pope. In April 1802, Bonaparte embodied the Concordat in a general Law of Public Worship, which applied also to other religious denominations and he added provisions, not agreed to by the Pope, which subjected the clergy to minute state regulation. Here, too, Bonaparte in effect reverted surreptitiously to the pre-revolutionary Gallican Church, closely linked with the state and in a certain defiance of the Vatican. The ecclesiastical settlement proved to be among the less durable of his achievements. It alienated many devout Catholics as well as the more violent anti-clericals. It was, in the nature of things, not a synthesis, as were the legal codes, but a compromise; and like many compromises it left both extremes actively dissatisfied.

Apart from all these institutional reforms of the Consulate, it achieved much that was more silent and constructive. Bonaparte disciplined France and established order. Brigandage was stopped. Life and property were made secure. Public works were begun. The 'career open to talents' and free social and educational opportunity were ensured. The system of education was developed with the opening of *lycées* or secondary schools, where boys were taught to be good citizens and above all to be good soldiers. Scientific research and technological education were encouraged. The Consulate began a healing process in French life, and built a framework of public order and more efficient government within which the energies and genius of the French people could again labour fruitfully. Bonaparte took pride in supporting the sciences and the arts; and as on his famous expedition to Egypt, so also as ruler of France, he liked to surround himself with *savants* and scientific experts. He helped to modernize France, and during the truce of Amiens people from Britain and elsewhere flocked to Paris to behold the impressive new scientific system of government which had at last emerged from the Revolution.

THE RENEWAL OF WAR

But the Consulate was devoted also to extensive preparations for the renewal of war in Europe. Bonaparte, like many Englishmen and Austrians, regarded the Peace of Amiens as bound to be only a truce. He planned to rival British supremacy, and pressed on with the expansion of ports and dockyards. He began extensive shipbuilding and fitted out colonial expeditions to Mauritius and Madagascar, ominously on the route to India. He reorganized the Cisalpine Republic in northern Italy, the Batavian Republic in Holland, and the Helvetic Republic in Switzerland, all previously set up under the Directory, as tributary and satellite states of France (*see* Map 1). In 1803 with the consent of the Tsar of Russia he devised a new imperial constitution for Germany which recast the old map of tiny principalities and greatly reduced their number. In particular Prussia gained most of Westphalia in the heart of Germany, and Habsburg predominance in the Diet was destroyed. In 1802 Bonaparte made himself Consul for life, instead of only for the period of ten years originally fixed in 1799. In 1804 he took the further step of becoming 'Emperor of the French', inducing the Pope to come to Paris in December for the ceremony of coronation and then, at the crucial moment, placing the crown on his own head. It was a realistic gesture: he was a self-made emperor, well suited to the new era of self-made men which the industrial revolution was bestowing upon Europe.

In the decade between 1804 and 1814 Europe beheld in France a system of government which was as much a defiance of the traditional basis of existing governments as had been the revolutionary dictatorship of Robespierre. It surrounded itself with many of the trappings of more traditional monarchies: a court of brilliance and elaborate etiquette, imperial titles and honours, new uniforms and old ceremonials. Napoleon even took care to marry into the most grandiose dynasty of all, the Habsburgs, when in 1810 he married the Archduchess Marie Louise, a niece of Marie Antoinette. But these old-fashioned trimmings of respectability barely hid the realities of an upstart military dictatorship. Unlike the monarchs of Vienna or St Petersburg, Berlin or London, Napoleon could never claim to derive power from descent and from the past. Instead he claimed to derive authority from the present: from popular will. He took care to endorse all his main seizures of power with the subsequent approval of a plebiscite. In reality, as all knew, he derived political authority from military power. He ruled France because he had been a successful and popular general, because the army remained loyal to him, because he devoted all his life, talents, and energies to winning and keeping this military power. It was only if the doctrines of the Revolution and the ideas of democracy were true, that his position could be justified. A child of the Revolution, he combined the substance of old absolutism with the new sanction of popular approval. He was even more of a challenge to other monarchs than was the Revolution itself: a crowned and anointed Jacobin, a usurper legitimized by the will of the sovereign people.

As emperor he continued the constructive work of the Consulate.

By 1808 he produced the scheme for the 'University of France', a form of centralized Ministry of Public Instruction which was to supervise all levels of education. By 1813 he made the system of secondary education in France the best in Europe, though primary education was neglected. Paris was beautified and schemes of public works continued. But now such beneficial schemes were accompanied by an increased stifling of social life and political freedom. The Ministry of Police, suppressed in 1802, was revived in 1804 under the care of Joseph Fouché. A decree of 1810 virtually revived the hated *lettres de cachet* of the old régime, for it set up state prisons and allowed arrest and detention without trial on the authority of the Council of State. The press was heavily censored and by 1810 only four papers appeared in Paris. Correspondence was censored too. An army of spies and secret agents kept Napoleon well informed of any opposition, and he could crush it ruthlessly whenever he chose.

France relapsed more and more into a police state, under an autocracy often heavy-handed and tempered only by the military needs of the Emperor. To meet these he was prepared to perform – and to drive others to perform – prodigies of organization, of labour, of self-sacrifice. Yet he had none of the extravagance, showed none of the wastefulness, of the old régime. His serious and dull court had none of the frivolity of the Bourbon courts. He had a passion for financial solvency, pared down every state expenditure, and constantly urged frugality and thrift upon his whole administration. By inflicting heavy exactions upon other countries, he spared the pockets of French taxpayers, even during his costliest campaigns. Only in 1813 did French taxes have to be sharply raised, and when he abdicated in 1814 the French public debt was only 60 million francs. Never had a great state been run more economically. At the same time he saw to it that industries were encouraged, unemployment relieved, food supplies maintained. He was anxious to make empire, and even war, sound business for France.

The dictatorship of Napoleon in France was a utilitarian, efficient, industrious, hard-headed government. Its oppressiveness must not be exaggerated. It lacked the fanaticism and passions of the rule of Robespierre and the harsh all-pervasive ruthlessness and brutality of twentieth-century dictatorships. Although extreme royalists, fervent Roman Catholics, and more doctrinaire Jacobins were never reconciled to it, Napoleon contrived to rally the support of the great majority of the French people. From about 1808 onward the growing tensions within his Empire, the protracted wars, and the shadow of defeat increasingly tarnished his régime, but the order, efficient government, and prestige that it provided satisfied most Frenchmen. Part of his strength was the absence of any acceptable alternative to his government. At a time when memories of revolutionary excesses were still fresh and fears of royalist reaction still active, Bonapartism seemed preferable to both, even though the price to be paid for it was incessant war.

A further element of strength was the economic advantages that Napoleon's policy brought to French industrialists, farmers, and traders. The Continental System, the attempt to seal the continent of Europe against British trade, was more than a device of economic warfare against Britain. It was a vast system of economic preference and protection in favour of France, and against not Britain alone but the rest of Europe. Italy was almost turned into an economic colony of France, providing raw materials for French industry and a market for French textiles. The economic development of Holland was entirely subordinated to that of France. While the introduction of machinery was encouraged in France, it was discouraged elsewhere. The French cotton and sugar-beet industries prospered behind a heavily protective screen. In economic terms the Empire undoubtedly paid handsomely, at least on the short run.

The Napoleonic Empire was doomed because of its inherent and self-defeating contradictions. Its programme of conquests ensured remorseless British resistance. From May 1803, when war began again, until the abdication of Napoleon in 1814, there was no more truce. After the failure of his invasion plans in 1804–05 and the Battle of Trafalgar in October 1805, when Nelson annihilated the main body of the combined French and Spanish fleets, it was clear that Britain remained superior at sea. Napoleon resorted to the Continental System in an effort to undermine naval power by economic weapons – sapping British trade and undermining her commercial prosperity. To make the system effective he had to extend his territorial conquests and gain control of more and more of the continental coastline. But such further aggressions only intensified British resistance and threw more of Europe into active hostility. It was a vicious circle of conquest and resistance, which British trade could survive so long as the other continents of the world were open to it. The Continental System had to be virtually abandoned in 1813 because it was a failure. The Empire was self-defeating, too, in the inner contradictions between Napoleon's dynastic and nationalist policies. He placed his brothers on the thrones of Holland, Naples, Westphalia, and Spain, creating a new dynastic system in Europe. But the junior branches of the dynasty struck no native roots because it was Napoleon's policy to subordinate their countries so completely to French interests. 'My policy,' he wrote in 1810, 'is France before all.' Old family dynasticism and modern exclusive nationalism do not go together: since the revolutionary ideas as well as the revolutionary example had served to stimulate ideas of national self-determination, he was committed to frustrating the very tendencies to which he owed his own position. Thus it was the Empire that completed the whole process of upheaval and transformation in Europe which had begun in those far-off days of 1789.

CHAPTER 4

NAPOLEONIC EMPIRE

THE EMPIRE AND ITS EFFECTS

THE Empire of Napoleon in Europe was established as a result of the great series of brilliant victories by which, within two years, he smashed the Third Coalition of 1805. In 1805 Pitt constructed a coalition of Great Britain, Austria, and Russia. In the Treaty of Pressburg in January 1806, Austria made peace after being defeated at the battles of Ulm in October and Austerlitz in December 1805. When Prussia joined the coalition, she too was defeated – at the battles of Jena and Auerstädt in October 1806 – and forced to cede large territories to Napoleon. He then routed the Russian armies at Friedland in June 1807, and by a brilliant stroke of diplomacy induced the Tsar Alexander I not only to make peace but to become an ally of France for five years.

The emperors of France and Russia met privately on a raft in the river Niemen, and the outcome was the Treaty of Tilsit in July 1807. Napoleon won Alexander's recognition as Emperor of the West in return for the entrancing vision he depicted of Alexander's own possible future as Emperor of the East. The only obstacle to both was the stubborn resistance of Britain, which barred Napoleon's path in the west as she checked Alexander's expansion towards Turkey, Persia, Afghanistan, and India. In November 1806 Napoleon had issued from conquered and occupied Berlin a decree forbidding the importation of British goods into any part of Europe under his control or allied with him. Russia and Prussia both agreed to enforce this decree, and within a few months they as well as Austria declared war against Britain. Not only was the Third Coalition smashed – it was reversed. The Continental System, an economic boycott of British trade throughout Europe set up by the Berlin Decree, was the basis of the new Empire.

The Treaty of Tilsit and its consequences represent the moment when the Napoleonic Empire reached not its greatest extent but its firmest consolidation (*see* Map 2). Annexed to France were Belgium, Nice, Savoy, Genoa, Dalmatia, and Croatia. As an inner ring of satellite states were Holland (with Louis Bonaparte as king), the Confederation of the Rhine (formed in 1806), the kingdom of Westphalia under Jérôme Bonaparte (formed in 1807 out of Prussia's Rhenish lands), the kingdom of Italy (formed in 1805 with Napoleon as king), the Grand Duchy of Warsaw (formed in 1807 mostly out of Prussia's Polish lands), and Switzerland. Joseph Bonaparte was made king of Naples and Sicily in 1804, and after 1808 king of Spain. The Confederation of the Rhine was extended in 1807, the Duchy of Warsaw in 1809. As allies, France had Bavaria and Württemberg, Denmark and Sweden, Spain, Russia, Prussia, and Austria. Britain was diplomatically isolated; her great war leader Pitt had died in January 1806. There were to be further additions of territory until 1811, when the Grand Empire and its allies covered the whole European mainland, except the Balkans. But by then Napoleon was faced with rebellion and war in Spain and Portugal, renewal of the war against Austria, and the breakdown of his Continental System caused by organized smuggling and the counter-measures of the British naval blockade.

The extent of the Empire at its greatest was made possible by the separatist and expansionist rivalries of the other main powers. Just as the early successes of the French revolutionary armies had been facilitated by the absence of any concert of Europe,[1] so the great victories of Napoleon were won against incorrigibly unstable and unreliable coalitions. He was able to defeat his enemies one by one. Pursuing their separate and often rival purposes, beset by mutual distrusts, the powers were as ready to ally with Napoleon as against him. He was simply more successful than they in doing what they were all doing – seeking to acquire territories, extend influence, enhance prestige. British colonial expansion, Prussian ambitions for leadership in northern Germany and eastern Europe, Habsburg imperial aims in the Danube valley, Russian aspirations in Poland and Turkey, were different from French aims more in degree and in incidence than in kind. But they worked to closer horizons, save perhaps the visionary Alexander I. Prussian and Austrian aims were regional rather than continental in scope. The chief concern of Britain was to preserve some balance of power in Europe; for unification of European resources under a single hostile power would threaten her national security, end her naval superiority, and impede development of her overseas trade. The uniqueness of Napoleon's Empire lay partly in its generalized aim of dominating the whole continent, but even more in the immense energy, ingenuity, ability, and success with which he pursued his objective.

It may be doubted whether, even in 1807, he had any precise and far-reaching design of imperial organization outside the limited regional area of France and her surrounding annexations and satellites in western Europe. Within this area he evolved certain techniques of empire. These

1. See p. 50.

included, besides the enthronement of his brothers and intermarriage with older ruling houses, besides the economic policy implicit in the Continental System, such devices as the introduction of the *Code napoléon* into conquered territories and the establishment of a relatively uniform system of administration and justice. Napoleon was wedded to the idea of government as a rationally and scientifically constructed system, a matter of technique capable of being applied anywhere regardless of historic traditions. What people wanted was public order, equitable administration, efficient organization. This, he believed, he could provide through his legal codes and trained administrators. He did so, for a time, in Belgium, Holland, Italy, and Germany. Beyond these areas he had to deal with established régimes less easily overthrown – as in Russia and Austria – and in these he relied not on imperial organization but merely on diplomacy. Whereas in the West he aimed at some unity, in the East his concern was to exploit disunity. His aim, indeed, was to prevent any general settlement or pacification of Europe. He avoided congresses and general negotiations, and insisted on dealing separately with each power. He contrived to play upon their mutual fears and jealousies in order to keep them from combining. Unification in the West had to be accompanied by constant division and conflict in the East; and his power was never consolidated east of the Elbe and the Adriatic.

The special characteristics of his Empire can best be described by comparing it with the other empires of his day. It was quite unlike that insubstantial medieval relic, the Holy Roman Empire, which Voltaire had derided as being neither Holy nor Roman nor an Empire. In 1804 when Francis II promulgated the Austrian Empire as distinct from the Holy Roman Empire of which he was the Habsburg heir, he tried to substitute a more substantial reality for the shadow of a defunct system; and in 1806 the Holy Roman Empire was formally dissolved by Napoleon, who gathered his 15 client German states into the new Confederation of the Rhine. It resembled more closely the Habsburg Austrian Empire, which was basically a mere conglomeration of territories, with some geographical unity in the Danube valley, but held together only by the common overlordship of the Habsburg dynasty. It was totally different from the British Empire, which was a maritime, overseas, commercial entity, held together by trade and settlement and defended by naval power. The western Empire of Napoleon was the transient product of lightning war and diplomatic *coups*, hastily bound together by dynastic settlement of thrones upon members of his family and by the emergency devices of the Continental System. It did not last long enough even in the west for the more durable mortar of a common code of law, justice, finance, and administration – which he injected into its joints – to set hard and bind it into a real imperial system. Opportunism and expediency haunted it throughout.

Its most destructive achievements were among its most permanent. Napoleon extended and perpetuated the effects of the French Revolution in Europe by destroying feudalism in the Low Countries, in much of Germany, and in Italy. Feudalism as a legal system, involving noble jurisdiction over peasants, was ended; feudalism as an economic system, involving payment of feudal dues by peasants to nobles, was ended, though often in return for compensation and indemnity. The claims of the Church were never allowed to stand in the way of this reorganization. Middle classes and peasants became, like nobles, subjects of the state, all equally liable to pay taxes. The system of levying and collecting taxes was made more equitable and efficient. Old guilds and town oligarchies were abolished; internal tariff barriers were removed. Everywhere greater equality, in the sense of careers open to talents, was inaugurated. A gust of modernization blew through Europe in the wake of Napoleonic conquests. His violent attempts to hammer western Europe into one subservient bloc of annexed or satellite territories succeeded, at least, in shaking it free from accumulated relics of petty feudal power, from antiquated jurisdictions and privileges, from outworn territorial divisions. Most of what he swept away could never be restored. If the French Revolution had thrown Europe into the melting pot, Napoleon stirred it about, making sure that much of the dross was removed and giving it a shape it was never to lose. Europe could never be the same again, however earnest and extensive the attempts at 'restoration' after his fall.

MAP 2. EUROPE, 1810. See following pages.
This map shows the power of Napoleon at its height. To the conquests of the revolutionary armies (see Map 1) he had now added the Netherlands and northern Germany, Piedmont, Genoa, a kingdom in western Italy, and the Illyrian provinces of the Dalmatian coast. By means of dependent régimes he controlled all the rest of Germany and Italy, Spain, and the Grand Duchy of Warsaw. His allies included, at this time, Sweden, Denmark and Norway, Prussia, Austria, and Russia. Britain, Portugal, and the Balkans ruled by the Ottoman Turks, remained beyond his grasp. His invasion of Portugal in 1810 was repelled by Wellington. Anxiety to keep Russia within the orbit of his power led in 1812 to his fateful campaign (see inset), which was to end in the catastrophe of his retreat from Moscow and the crumbling of his Empire.

DESTRUCTION OF THE EMPIRE

The methods by which the Empire was created were one of the main reasons for its defeat. The internal contradictions of the Napoleonic Empire in France have already been suggested; they were matched by its broader European contradictions. It had none of the qualities of permanence of his domestic work as First Consul. It was experience of how territories were consistently snatched from them after military victories, of how dynastic interests were violated by diplomatic manoeuvres, that eventually persuaded the great powers of Europe to combine in a concerted effort to destroy Napoleon. Motivated as they were by separatist interests, it was only the proven necessity for joint action to defend these interests which at last induced the rulers of Europe to make common cause. The most important contribution of Britain to his defeat was to remain intransigently at war until, one by one, her former allies came round to the view that yet a fourth coalition must be formed and kept in being until victory. Meanwhile Britain contained Napoleon's power within Europe, strangling it by her naval supremacy and the power of her blockade. Only the threat posed by Napoleon could have united the governments of Europe in so solid and formidable an alliance: he made the Grand Empire, and he destroyed it.

While defeats, territorial losses, and diplomatic humiliations drove the governments of Europe into alliance, so the disastrous effect of French economic exactions and of the continental blockade aroused among the peoples of Europe a deeper, more national resentment against the rule of Napoleon. It is easy to exaggerate the extent and the depth of the forces of nationalist feeling aroused in Germany and Italy, Spain and Russia, by Napoleon's victories. Such reactions were strongest in Italy and Germany, and, in the romantic cultural environment of the time, hurt national pride readily took semi-political forms. But what most impressed ordinary people was no doubt the glaring contrast between the professed French aims of popular sovereignty and liberation from oppression, and the actuality of the more efficient despotism clamped upon France and Europe by Napoleon. This impression was powerfully backed by bitter experience of high prices, acute shortages, and even occasional starvation, caused by his economic policy of protecting France and fighting Britain by disrupting the whole of Europe's trade. Resistance to him at a popular level in Europe was mainly regional and economic, a matter of guerrilla warfare as in Spain or of bitter economic grievances as in Holland and Italy. It became truly national only later and often only in retrospect, as there grew up the legend of mass popular revolt against the foreign tyrant. But the amalgam of governmental resolve to destroy him by a concerted use of regular, professional state armies, with popular revulsion against his treatment of conquered peoples, was powerful. It proved sufficient to make his Empire but a transient episode in the history of the continent.

Open and active revolt came first in Spain where British naval and military help were most readily forthcoming. It was there that Napoleon suffered his first serious reverses on land. The Spanish people had profound regional and local loyalties, and a certain national pride in their great past. Unlike Germany or Italy, Spain was a single kingdom, though governed by an effete and corrupt monarchy. This monarchy, beset by quarrels between the reigning Bourbon king, Charles IV, and the crown prince Ferdinand, headed a régime so little rooted in popular loyalties that Napoleon expected little resistance. He forced Spain into war against her neighbour Portugal in order to deprive Britain of harbours, and he took the opportunity to billet French troops in Spain. In 1808 Charles IV abdicated in favour of Ferdinand, but Napoleon induced him to repudiate his abdication and surrender all his rights as king of Spain to the Emperor of the French. In May, Joseph Bonaparte was declared king of Spain. The Pyrenees, it seemed, no longer existed. But the Spanish people, by provinces and cities, broke out in open revolt against this purely dynastic handling of their fate, and Britain at once sent them help.

Napoleon found himself fighting a war that cost him half a million men, and he was later to blame 'the Spanish ulcer' for his downfall. The Peninsular War, which dragged on for the rest of his reign, gave Sir John Moore and Arthur Wellesley ideal battlegrounds. Backed by British naval power and by the fierce guerrilla fighters of Spain, they kept large French forces preoccupied and subject to steady losses when Napoleon was sadly in need of them elsewhere in Europe. In 1810 the Spanish parliament (*Cortes*) was summoned in response to popular demands, and it proceeded to draft a new constitution on the pattern of the French revolutionary constitution of 1791. It prescribed a single assembly based on universal manhood suffrage; it rested on the principles of the sovereignty of the people, freedom of the press, and individual liberty. This Constitution of 1812 was to become the ideal of nineteenth-century liberals in many countries besides Spain. It served to accentuate the contrast between the original revolutionary ideals and the autocratic despotism of Napoleon.

The Peninsular War placed Napoleon at every disadvantage. Although when he himself led his troops in Spain he was able to win victories, his generals with smaller forces found their task hopeless. The dispersed nature of the fighting, the guerrilla tactics of the Spaniards, the backing of British naval superiority, all prevented his usual tactics from reaping their usual reward. He could not by concentration of overwhelming force and mastery of strategy inflict decisive defeats on his enemies. The irregular warfare and the difficult terrain compelled a dispersal of forces amid a hostile population. His natural impulse, to throw in superior weight and crush resistance, was inhibited by difficulties he was encountering in other parts of his Empire, which were in turn stirred to fresh energies by news of his reverses in the Iberian peninsula.

These other difficulties were ubiquitous. They arose in France itself, where his chief diplomatic agent, Talleyrand, and his chief of police, Fouché, were making preparations for their own future careers should Napoleon be overthrown. Both these supple and unscrupulous individuals, who had served the pre-revolutionary monarchy and the Revolution with equal impartiality, as they were to serve the restored Bourbons after Napoleon's fall, were men of great abilities whose treachery was to contribute to his downfall. It is a measure of how fragile his Empire was that, at the very first hints of adversity, his highest servants were ready to abandon him. The price of its survival was continuous and unfaltering success – a price that even the genius of Napoleon could not pay. The next difficulty arose in Austria, where moves were afoot by 1809 to resist any further French aggressions. Napoleon declared war on Austria in March and, after temporary reverses, defeated her at the cost of great losses to both sides at the battle of Wagram in July. But the victory had ominous features. While the French armies had deteriorated in quality, being heterogeneous and with less *élan* than the old French armies, the generals of Europe had learned a lot from the previous tactics of Napoleon himself. The balance was evening up. And the Tsar, in spite of his formal alliance with Napoleon and in spite of the lavish protestations of friendship between them at the great celebrations at Erfurt in 1808, had lent him no real support against Austria.

Napoleon's friends were deserting him in Europe as well as in France, just when his needs were becoming greatest. The case of Marshal Bernadotte was symbolic. Bernadotte, like Bonaparte himself, had been a soldier under the Republic, and, although disliking the *coup d'état* of Brumaire, he had served Napoleon faithfully and with outstanding success. After Austerlitz he was given the title of prince. In 1809 the Swedish king, Gustavus IV, was deposed by revolution and succeeded by his childless uncle, Charles XIII. When the Swedish Diet, in default of an heir, elected Prince Bernadotte to succeed Charles XIII, it hoped to stake out for Sweden a more favourable position in Napoleon's empire. The country suffered severely from the Continental System, having lost most of its Baltic and British trade, and was in considerable distress. To have as its ruler a marshal of France seemed a good way to improve its economic conditions. But Bernadotte, who in 1810 became heir apparent to the Swedish throne and held highest place in her government, joined the allies against Napoleon in 1812 and played a large part, as a military commander, in the final campaigns against the Empire.

It was from the direction of Russia that the greatest threat came, and it was in the east that Napoleon's empire suffered its first shattering blow. The French-Russian alliance rested on no common interests, only on temporary convenience. The ambitions of Napoleon and Alexander were ultimately in complete conflict, for both wanted to dominate the Near East and to control Constantinople and the Mediterranean. The famous campaign of 1812, in which Napoleon undertook to invade and defeat Russia, shows to what extent power had corrupted Napoleon's judgement and how far he had lost his former sense of what was possible. To embark on so vast an undertaking in the east while Britain remained unconquered in the west was a mistake that Hitler was to repeat 130 years later.

Yet the very repetition of history suggests that both would-be conquerors of Europe were confronted with an identical dilemma. Even a united Europe depends not upon its own will or that of its ruler, but upon the acquiescence of its two great flanking powers, Britain and Russia. Unless a European ruler comes to terms with one of these peripheral and semi-European powers, he must face this disastrous dilemma. Napoleon faced it, as did Hitler, by accepting naval inferiority in the west and gambling on winning land superiority in the east – a decision natural to a continental land power. Each precipitated an east-west alliance and was then crushed, as in a nutcracker, by a devastating war on two fronts.

The ostensible reason for Napoleon's attack on Russia was the Tsar's refusal to accept the Continental System and cooperate in the blockade of Britain. Napoleon's creation of the Duchy of Warsaw out of most of the former Polish territories taken from Prussia and Austria was regarded as a standing threat to the Tsar's retention of his Polish territories. But these reasons only masked the irreconcilable conflict between rival empires coveting supremacy in the Near East. In 1812–13 Britain and Sweden allied with Russia, and the nucleus of a fourth coalition existed. Prussia and Austria, it was known, would join it as soon as the moment was ripe. At the end of June Napoleon sent his Grand Army of some 450,000 men across the Niemen river, against a

Russian army much less than half its size. His aim was to defeat this army and strike at Moscow, some five hundred miles from the Niemen. But, as in Spain, the improved generalship of his opponents, combined with peculiarly difficult country and extremes of climate, robbed him of success. The Russian commander avoided battle and retreated; when battle was engaged at Borodino, it cost Napoleon heavy and irreplaceable losses; when he reached Moscow, he found it abandoned and soon in flames. Winter approached with no sign of Russian surrender, no decision reached, lengthy communications to maintain, and vast areas to control against the savage attacks of Cossack cavalry. Disease and desertions as well as battle losses depleted his forces. He could not afford to stay on in Moscow. The bitter Russian winter set in as his weary troops continued their retreat from Moscow back to the Niemen, through a countryside of 'scorched earth' and devastation. He lost some 250,000 killed and 100,000 taken prisoner. It was his most dramatic and costly defeat.

Never did Napoleon's resources of energy and will show themselves to greater advantage than in 1813. He squeezed more men and resources from France and his subject territories. He mustered again half a million men. But now Prussia too was stirring restively. With her civil administration and her army overhauled by the great reformers Stein and Hardenberg, Gneisenau and Scharnhorst, with a youthful patriotic movement fermenting among her students and intellectuals, Prussian popular sentiment was more ready to resist than was the government of the cautious Frederick William III. But even he, in January 1813, made alliance with Russia and agreed not to make a separate peace; and this alliance began to attract Austrian support. The Fourth Coalition took shape as the drama reached its climax. The Russians and Prussians drove Napoleon west of the Elbe, back to the borders of his more firmly consolidated empire. Even now he won important victories, at Lützen and at Bautzen, against the Russians and Prussians. Metternich, the Chancellor of Austria since 1810, proposed an armistice that would prepare for a general peace conference. Napoleon signed it in June 1813, but negotiations broke down and Austria declared war. With close on a million men the new alliance heavily outnumbered Napoleon's forces.

Napoleon began with yet another victory, at Dresden. But few now believed in his final victory. Metternich by skilful diplomacy won over most of the states in the Confederation of the Rhine. In October 1813 Napoleon suffered one of his greatest defeats at the battle of Leipzig, in which he lost 50,000 men and had to fall back to the Rhine. While French troops were cleared from the east of the Rhine, Wellesley entered France from the south, from Spain. The ring was closing, and for the first time since 1793 France was herself invaded. But as the war became again a patriotic war for national defence against invasion, and as the invaders behaved cruelly and stupidly, they encountered in France a tide of popular resistance. Napoleon inflicted a couple of costly defeats on the Prussians, the allied commanders acted with little real agreement on strategy, and even now it seemed possible that Napoleon at bay might hold his own. But he was too heavily outnumbered, his resources were too exhausted, the loyalty of his subordinates was too shaky. When Paris capitulated, he signed, on 7 April 1814, his abdication as Emperor of the French. He also renounced his other claims in Europe and retired as sovereign lord of the tiny island of Elba. The brother of Louis XVI returned to the throne of France as Louis XVIII, agreeing to a constitutional charter guaranteeing certain liberties and rights. A general settlement of the problems of Europe was to be undertaken at a congress to be held in Vienna, and it was agreed that France should be given the frontiers she had in 1792, before the revolutionary wars began.

But Louis XVIII had barely begun to establish his rule, the diplomats at Vienna had scarcely involved themselves in the tangle of petty jealousies which were evoked by the prospect of a general settlement, when the thunderbolt struck. After only ten months Napoleon escaped from Elba, and in March 1815 he landed in the south of France. The bulk of the army deserted Louis XVIII, who fled. The masses of Frenchmen joyfully welcomed Napoleon back. One great victory might even yet serve to restore Napoleon to power, for the diplomatic squabbles at Vienna had already helped to disrupt the Fourth Coalition. Such seems to have been his hope. But Europe had in fact outgrown Napoleon. The powers at Vienna declared him an outlaw. They had suffered too much at his hands to turn back now, and it is likely that the campaign that culminated in Waterloo was foredoomed to failure. The 'Hundred Days' that elapsed between Napoleon's return to France and his second abdication in June 1815, have an interest in showing the smouldering survival of Bonapartist enthusiasm among the French peasants and soldiers, in giving yet a further example of the amazing vigour and versatility of the conqueror, and in affording him an opportunity to pose as the misunderstood liberal whose enlightened schemes for a federation of Europe had been frustrated only by Britain. These were all to become of importance later in the century. But at the time the outcome was in little doubt, for Napoleon was denied even the military victory that he needed to grasp power. This is the significance of the battle of Waterloo: it was the end of a very great adventure; not merely of the wild escapade of the 'Hundred Days', but of the whole vast adventure that had begun when King Louis XVI, in the spring of the year 1789, summoned the Estates-General of France. 'What a tragedy,' remarked Talleyrand of Napoleon, 'that he gave his name to adventures instead of to the age.'

The immediate consequences of Napoleon's defeat at Waterloo were simple and important enough: his own permanent exile to the storm-swept Atlantic island of St Helena; the second restoration, on 8 July, of Louis XVIII and his court; the completion of a general settlement of Europe at the Congress of Vienna. A whole chapter was ended, though like the chapters of all good stories it contained the beginnings of later chapters.

THE NAPOLEONIC ERA

The problem remains of how far the inner history of this epic period was itself an inevitable and predetermined process. Was there indeed an inherent fatalism linking Revolution with Empire through the mediations of War and Dictatorship? A great French historian has suggested that although there was no active republicanism in France until 1792, there was, in the improvised arrangements of the constitutional monarchy, a 'republican allure' – an intrinsic bias towards outright republicanism to which the behaviour of the king gave added impetus. So, it might be said, there was in the course of the Revolution a bias towards dictatorship which made itself apparent in the rise of Robespierre and the power of the Directory, and to which the needs of the war gave added impetus. Likewise, in the Consulate, which was born of republican victories in war, there was perhaps a certain bias towards empire, a tendency for a reinvigorated and ebullient nation to seek expansion and prestige in continental conquests. The social and economic revolution in France released dynamic and explosive forces that caused general upheaval in Europe, now taking the form of destroying old political systems, now of launching invasion and war, now of a creative energy devoted to building more efficient social and political organizations. But in shaping the course that events actually took, individuals of genius played a striking part, and to exaggerate the predetermined bias of events is to neglect the role of masterful men. Revolutionary victories without Carnot, Jacobinism without Robespierre, are as difficult to imagine as the Empire without Napoleon. The battle of Trafalgar may only have made obvious what existed: British superiority over France at sea. Yet it was important that it was fought, and events would certainly have been very different had Nelson not been there to win it.

In assessing the place of the whole epic in European or world history, there is likewise need for caution. It is certain that the nineteenth century in Europe would have been a period of profound change and great expansion even if the French Revolution had never happened, or if Napoleon Bonaparte had never been born. American independence had been won before the French Revolution began, and that was full of significance for the future of Europe and of the world. The tide of radical and democratic opinion was strong and forceful in both Britain and America before 1789, and that too would have produced great liberal changes. The industrial revolution, irresistible in its impetus, had begun. The revolutions in science and in culture, which are also the very roots of nineteenth-century changes, were already well advanced before 1789. The French scientist, Antoine Lavoisier, published in 1789 his revolutionary theories which made him the father of modern chemistry; and at the same time the English utilitarian philosopher, Jeremy Bentham, published his *Introduction to the Principles of Morals and Legislation*. The basis of classical economics was laid by Adam Smith as early as 1776. The romantic movement in art and literature preceded the Revolution and did much to shape its character. The period was one of giants in the arts whose work was profoundly affected by events but whose genius would surely have flourished without the upheavals of revolution. In Germany, Ludwig van Beethoven was nineteen, Wolfgang Goethe forty, when revolution began in France. Their importance is quite unaffected by their relation to Napoleon. Beethoven first dedicated his *Eroica* Symphony to Bonaparte, but angrily struck out his name when he heard that he had proclaimed himself Emperor in 1804. Goethe attended the festivities at Erfurt in 1808, where he was decorated and flattered by Napoleon, who was at the height of his prestige, and admired him in return. Beethoven and Goethe outlived Napoleon (who died at last on St Helena in 1821) both in their own lives and in the grandeur of their contributions to human civilization. In the longest perspectives of history, even the most shattering political, military, and diplomatic events of the period seem but limited factors among the many that mould the history of man. The men who shaped Europe's future were not only the leading participants in these heroic events but also men such as Antoine Lavoisier and Adam Smith, James Watt and Jeremy Bentham. When the thud and smoke of gunfire had died away, more permanent forces of human destiny could be seen, shaping nations and states and the fate of individuals.

Perhaps the final significance of the quarter-century of turmoil is that too much history happened in too short a time. The old order would have died anyhow, but it could have died more slowly and peacefully. The explosion of pent-up forces in revolution, the long agony of wars, the dynamism of successive forms of dictatorship, the prodigies of empire, were all so congested in time, and overlapped so closely in their happening, that they mangled and disrupted the processes of historical change. The time was overprolific of energies, overrich in epic incidents, and exercised for later generations a strange spell and fascination. Frenchmen, as if despairing of ever again being original, thought only of a restored monarchy, a Second Republic, a Second Empire. Liberals everywhere in Europe clamoured for the Jacobin Constitution of 1793 or the Spanish Constitution of 1812. The champions of legitimism, Jacobinism, anticlericalism, Bonapartism, went on fighting their battles in Europe for another half-century and more to come – even when these battles came to be old-fashioned and of small relevance to the more urgent problems and more novel needs of the nineteenth century. Legitimism soon became a lost cause, Jacobinism a dogma, anticlericalism a republican scarecrow, Bonapartism a bogey; but men went on fighting for them, or at least arguing about them, as if they could never allow anything that had happened in that magic age to pass away.

Meanwhile the problems created by a fast-growing population, by industrialization and technology, by the growth of democracy and of science itself, went on accumulating only half noticed on the periphery of politics, and fresh revolutionary situations built up. It was a peculiarity of European politics, for the next half century at least, to be out-of-date. Party loyalties and party alignments were often irrelevant or only semi-relevant to contemporary issues, political systems lagged behind vital changes in social structure, and it became fashionable to think of politics as something separate from economics. Yet after 1815 these things did not need to happen. The explanation of why they happened lies in the balance of forces of continuity and change which existed after 1815.

PART TWO

EUROPE IN 1815

WHAT must we think of when we think of 'Europe' in 1815? Of a mere collection of separate and quarrelsome states, so distinct in character and so separate in organization that the continent of Europe was no more than what Metternich called Italy of that time, 'a mere geographical expression'? Or can we think of civilization, a community of peoples with enough in common to justify our regarding Europe as a more organic entity, sharing a culture, an economy, a complex of traditions which made it in a real sense one?

Neither of these images would be accurate. Each would be flat, distorted, at best two-dimensional. To get a more vivid and realistic three-dimensional impression, we must contrive to superimpose one of these images on the other. Just as nineteenth-century diplomats thought of a 'balance of power' in Europe which, by holding a certain equilibrium between the largest states, allowed all states to coexist peacefully, so we may picture the cohesion of Europe as being compatible with its great diversities by a sort of internal balance of forces. In some important respects it was one thing; in other equally important respects it was many things. And from the tensions between these two contrary qualities came much of that inherent impetus to development, change, and greatness, which made Europe the most important and dynamic continent in the world of the nineteenth century.

There existed within Europe a further tension between forces of continuity and forces of change. The former included the institutions of monarchy, Church, landowning aristocracy, and a widespread desire for peace and stability after a quarter-century of revolutionary turmoil and war. The latter included such long-term trends as the rapid growth of population and the spread of industrialism and urban life, as well as the ferment of nationalism and of political ideas disseminated throughout Europe by the French Revolution and the conquests of Napoleon. The conflicts between these opposing forces were to dominate the generation after Waterloo.

CHAPTER 5

THE UNITY AND DISUNITY OF EUROPE IN 1815

INTERNAL COHESION AND DIVERSITY

BENEATH the patchwork design suggested by a political map showing the division of Europe into states (*see* Map 2), there was a vast substratum of historical heritage and continuity. Unlike America or Australasia, Europe is an old continent, in the sense that it has a long and continuous history of some two thousand years. Even when it suffered severe changes and considerable disintegration, as during the barbarian invasions of the fifth century, enough of its past always survived to provide real continuity. The greatest turbulance never destroyed all elements of the old order. Whereas the primitive civilizations of the North American continent contributed virtually nothing to the later development of the United States or Canada, European civilization has been built of layer upon layer of deposits from each phase of its history. Ancient Greece, the Roman Empire, the Frankish kingdoms, the Roman Catholic Church took over in turn this accumulating heritage, absorbing and often greatly transforming it, yet never losing its essentials. From the sixteenth century onwards, even while Europe itself was dividing with increasing sharpness into separate territorial kingdoms and different religious beliefs, much of this common heritage was transported and disseminated to the New World. At no time was it possible to wipe the slate clean and start afresh. It was the discovery that this was impossible in Europe that drove many people to migrate to the New World, where it was hoped this might be done. The double process, of speedy internal change and simultaneous dissemination overseas, not only continued in the years after 1815 but immensely quickened in pace.

Some of this historical heritage therefore came from the remote past, some from the very recent past. In the ancient world much of Europe was included within the Roman Empire. Medieval Europe inherited from Rome systems of law and institutions of government which provided some common elements in Italy, France, and Germany. By the sixteenth century the shadow of medieval political unity was destroyed. But some of the reality remained in the general pattern of dynastic hereditary monarchy, now territorial in basis and without universalist pretensions. And in so far as the Roman Catholic Church was the substantial heir and transmitter of medieval dreams of the unity of Christendom and a universal canon law, it emerged even as late as 1815 as a more militant and powerful force transcending state frontiers. Rome claimed the loyalty of millions of men and women in every European state.[1]

Other living relics from earlier ages were the landed aristocracy, either cherishing their feudal rights of administering justice and exacting dues from their vassals, as in Austria and Russia, or reasserting with all their might claims to a restoration of such rights in countries like France and Germany. The economy of every European country still rested, as it had rested in the Middle Ages, on the labours of peasants in the fields. The peasantry were the mass of the population. Except in parts of north-western Europe, they worked the land using methods and tools that were little different from those used by their medieval ancestors. Much of the political history of the nineteenth century is concerned with the activities of the non-peasant sections of the population; but it must be constantly recalled that these activities were peripheral and at the time even superficial, as compared with the daily productive toil of the millions of peasant families spread throughout the continent. Some, as in western Europe, were now rapidly improving their social and legal status. They were unburdening themselves of feudal services and payments, as well as improving their economic status by new methods of farming. Others, especially in eastern Europe, made little advance of either kind until nearer the end of the century. But whatever their fortunes in these respects they were, as a class, the foundations and fabric of European economy.

Behind the patchwork political map there existed, too, a general monarchical dynastic system which reduced conflicts between states to somewhat simpler categories of rivalries between a few large families. For some three centuries before 1815, the Bourbons of France and the Habsburgs of Austria had disputed possessions in Spain and Italy. Between them these two families, at many points intermarried, provided most of the states of Europe with their ruling monarchs. This 'cousinhood of kings' remained, even in 1815, an important factor in European diplomacy. The era of great dynastic wars, of wars for the Austrian or Spanish succession which had dominated the previous century, was now past. But the political shape of Europe had been moulded by generations of dynastic alliances, marriages, disputes, and wars. In eastern Europe the chief basis of political unity remained the organizations needed to rule from Vienna the sprawling and diversified lands accumulated by the Habsburgs; to rule from St Petersburg

1. See p. 103.

the territories acquired by the Romanovs; and to rule from Constantinople the vast Balkan domains conquered by the Ottoman Turks. Until 1837 such links joined the United Kingdom with Hanover, and so with the intricacies of German politics. Even in 1887, when Queen Victoria celebrated the fiftieth year of her reign, most of the rulers of Europe who attended the Golden Jubilee were related to her, either through her own ancestors or by marriage to members of her own large family.

At a cultural level, too, there was a great common heritage, much of which was very recent and French. For centuries Christianity had set a pattern of worship, of morals, of conceptions of justice and law. Greek philosophy had penetrated much of the thinking of Europe. But during the eighteenth century it was rationalism, as interpreted by the *philosophes* of France like Voltaire, Montesquieu, Rousseau, and the Encyclopedists, which determined a great deal of the intellectual activity of all countries. Just as French, since the days of Louis XIV a century before, had replaced Latin as the normal language of diplomacy and as an international tongue, so the rationalism of French thought, deriving from the mathematician René Descartes, conquered the minds of Europe. Englishmen such as Edward Gibbon, the great historian, and Jeremy Bentham, the great radical, wrote, and spoke in French as readily as in their mother tongue. The greatest 'enlightened despots' of eighteenth century Europe, Frederick the Great of Prussia and Catherine the Great of Russia, adopted French writers and artists with enthusiasm. Members of the aristocracy all over the continent were familiar with the writings and ideas of France. Not since the great days of chivalry, *courtoisie*, and crusades in the high Middle Ages had Europe been so united in its Frenchness. More recently still, during the Napoleonic Empire of 1800–14, French laws, institutions, administrative methods, and systems of weights and measures had been spread throughout western and central Europe. Much of the material and cultural unity of European civilization came from France, the greatest of the continental states.

After the territorial settlement reached by the Congress of Vienna in 1815 (*see* Map 3), the political map of Europe showed in certain areas more simplicity and greater unification than is shown on a modern map. In both the north-west and south-east of Europe the frontiers between states were less chequered than they are now. Norway and Sweden were combined into one kingdom, as were Belgium and the Netherlands. France, Portugal, and Spain had broadly their present boundaries. In the east the Russian frontier included within it Finland and part of Poland. The whole of the Balkan peninsula, except Montenegro which is part of present-day Yugoslavia, was ruled by the Turkish Empire. The Austrian Empire comprised not only Austria, Hungary, and Bohemia but large parts of modern Poland, Italy, Germany, and Yugoslavia. On the other hand, the territories of Italy and Germany were then a mosaic of little states and principalities; and the repeated efforts to unify each of these areas into their more modern shape were to dominate much of the history of Europe during the following fifty years.

EXTERNAL PRESSURES AND CONNEXIONS

The degree of cohesion and unity in Europe can be measured not only in terms of internal conditions, but also in terms of the relations between European states as a whole and other parts of the world. In 1815 no western European power held any of North Africa, except for Spain's control of Tangier on the northern tip of Morocco. The Mediterranean, for practical purposes, was the frontier between Europe and Islam except for the deep encroachment of Turkish power into the Balkans. For centuries the frontiers of Christendom against Islam had been held in the south-west by Spain, after the expulsion of the Moors, and in the south-east by the Habsburgs, against the Turks. These defensive points were now stabilized, and some of the cohesion and general prestige of the Habsburg Empire derived from these frontier, defensive functions that it performed for the benefit of the whole of Christendom. As Metternich put it, Asia began at the *Landstrasse* – the road running out of Vienna towards the east.

Overseas connexions were almost restricted to the western maritime powers, in particular to Great Britain, France, Spain, Portugal, and the Netherlands; and the relative importance of powers within this group had recently been greatly changed. In the course of the eighteenth century Great Britain lost control over her former American colonies but consolidated her ties with Canada by ousting the French; she also confirmed her connexion with India, and established new colonial foot-

---

MAP 3. EUROPE, 1815. See following pages.
The frontiers shown were drawn by the Congress of Vienna in 1814–15. The relatively simple design of north-western and south-eastern Europe was soon to be broken by the separation of Belgium from Holland, by the independence of Serbia and Greece, and the autonomy of Moldavia and Wallachia. The very complex pattern of central Europe was, within the next half century, to be simplified by the unification of Italy and of Germany. The black areas show the new size and importance conferred upon Prussia by the settlement of 1815. For the racial complexity of Austria–Hungary, which was eventually to disrupt that state, see Map 4. In the period 1815–48 the Austrian Empire under Metternich remained, however, the dominant power in central Europe.

EUROPE, 1815

holds in Australia though not yet in New Zealand. Despite the independence of the American colonies, in 1815 Great Britain was already the greatest colonial power in the world, with territories or bases in all continents. Most of this empire was not administered directly by the British government. In northern Canada the Hudson Bay Company, in India the East India Company, were the chief administrative authorities. The most prized and prosperous part of the Empire was the West Indies. The slave trade had been abolished throughout the Empire since 1807. This greatly diminished the importance of the west African territories of the Gold Coast and Gambia, which had been the chief source of slaves. Cape Colony, gained in 1814, was valued chiefly as a stopping place on the long route to India, and Australia as a dumping ground for convicts. At home, interest in the colonies was slight; it was lively only among missionary societies and certain trading interests. The radicals, becoming increasingly influential in English politics after 1815, were opposed to colonial connexions, which they condemned as merely strengthening the aristocratic influence in the constitution. Free traders were not only opposed to efforts to regulate overseas trade, but looked to the emancipation of all colonies as a natural development. The greatest colonial power was paradoxically anti-colonial in spirit.

The rupture of European political connexions with the American continent was completed by the loss of the vast Spanish empire in South America, which began during the Napoleonic Wars and was completed by 1823; by the separation of Brazil from Portugal, completed in 1825; and by the Monroe Doctrine, formulated by President James Monroe in December 1823, and reinforced as regards Latin America by the power of the British navy. The French, who throughout the previous century had rivalled the British in India, Canada, and West Africa, had now lost many colonial territories. Their overseas connexions were limited to a few small areas of India, and to Guadeloupe and parts of the West Indies. In 1815 France was obliged to cede to Britain the island of Mauritius as a naval base on the way to India; in the West Indies, Tobago, and St Lucia, which were of strategic importance; and in the Mediterranean, Malta, which Napoleon had conquered but which Britain had taken from him. Her losses were more naval and strategic than commercial, for she kept her fishing rights in the St Lawrence and off Newfoundland, and her trading stations and trading privileges in India.

Besides settlements in South Africa, the Netherlands had an immensely rich overseas empire in the Dutch East Indies; though only the island of Java was at all fully occupied and developed. With Australasia still mostly unexplored and undeveloped, and colonial territories in Africa limited mostly to mere coastal belts and ports, the colonial world was still fragmentary and undeveloped. In this, as in so many other fields, the expansion of Europe during the nineteenth century was to effect a complete transformation.

REGIONAL DIFFERENCES

Geography has always broken up the continent of Europe into fairly distinct regions: the north-western maritime nations, the almost closed sea of the Baltic, the great northern plain of Germany and Holland, the Mediterranean region south of the Alps, the mountainous peninsulas of the Balkans and Iberia. These in some instances coincide with the historic political divisions, as in Spain and Italy, in the Habsburg dominions of the Danube valley, and in the kingdom of France with its strongly marked natural frontiers of Atlantic and Mediterranean coastlines and the Pyrenees. In others they cut across the political frontiers, as in the great disputed areas of the Rhineland and the eastern marchlands of Poland. Events between 1789 and 1815 deeply accentuated the difference between the countries of the north-western maritime region and all other regions of Europe; for whereas the rest of Europe remained wedded to a traditional agrarian economy, the maritime states were already beginning to enjoy all the economic advantages of more efficient agriculture, more extensive industrial production, and the use of world markets and overseas investments. These advantages they owed, in part, to their favourable geographical position and to the great developments in shipping, banking, and commercial organization by Dutch, British, and French during the previous centuries. The concentration in their hands of overseas connexions gave them rich opportunities to exploit these advantages in the generation of relative peace which the settlement of 1815 ensured.

In a continent where railways and even good roads were unknown, and where the chief means of transport were by river and canal, by horse-drawn vehicles and coastal vessels, such regional differences were pronounced. The bulk of trade was still internal and domestic, and the removal of internal barriers to trade which Britain had enjoyed in the eighteenth century and which France now enjoyed after Napoleon was in itself a great stimulus to trade. Because Italy and Germany were splintered into many little states, they were robbed of this advantage; though the growth of customs unions and the lowering of barriers to trade were to be a feature of German development in the next twenty years. The Austrian empire, because of its predominantly primitive peasant agriculture and its strong provincialisms, fared little better than Germany.

The Continental System imposed on Europe by Napoleon, combined with the blockade imposed on it by Great Britain, had tended to destroy the overseas trade of the continental nations. Most of this trade was monopolized by Britain, whose superior naval power gave her an open door to it. Her foreign export trade trebled between 1789 and 1815, and after 1815 her trade tended to become more and more predominantly a maritime, overseas trade; while France, weaker than before in her transatlantic and far-eastern connexions, tended to develop her trade with continental Europe and with the Near East. Such a change was characteristic of the new twist given to relations between Europe and the rest of the world by the preceding twenty years of war. The Dutch continued to play a considerable part in the shipping and finance of international trade. The modernization of the French financial system and the establishment of the Bank of France in 1800 were soon to make Paris an important rival to London and Amsterdam as a financial centre of western Europe. But in 1815 the Bank of England was the largest centre of deposit in the world, and London became beyond dispute the banking capital of Europe.

The underestimated colonies, and especially the commercial connexion with India, were to help Britain to gain an easy supremacy over all her western neighbours within the next generation. Here was a vast market capable of absorbing the goods that Britain could most cheaply and efficiently produce in the early phases of her industrial revolution – cotton yarns and cloths. It was probably the greatest single impetus to mechanization of production. The goods most demanded by these overseas markets, such as the cotton cloths worn in India, were of the kind most suitable to mass production by relatively simple machinery. Already, in the eighteenth century, these demands of overseas markets had stimulated such inventions as Hargreaves's spinning jenny, Arkwright's water frame, and Crompton's mule. Only with access to a market capable of absorbing cotton products in very large quantities did it pay to use such machines. The 'dark, satanic mills' deplored by the poet William Blake, which grew up so fast in Lancashire in the early nineteenth century, were the result of exporting to these almost insatiable overseas markets. In return, Britain imported food and raw materials to feed and employ her fast-growing population. Once the circuit of manufacture and trade had been established, it spun the wheels of industry faster and faster, leading to ever more specialization of labour. Because Britain turned herself into 'the workshop of the world', she relied increasingly upon imports from abroad to supply her raw materials and her essential foods.

For half a century to come this exchange of manufactures for food and raw materials remained particularly profitable. Agricultural produce stayed cheaper than manufactures, even when manufactured goods became cheap. The rate of exchange was favourable to the industrialist. France, the country most likely to rival Britain, was inhibited by a factor that was otherwise an asset: the ability of her agriculture to feed her people. Not having to buy food, she did not need to sell manufactures. The total amount of her foreign trade was inevitably less than that of Britain, and so she drew less profit from the exchange of manufactures for agricultural products during the period when such an exchange was especially profitable.

For these reasons, the industrial revolution in western Europe brought about a redistribution of wealth, power, and political influence. So long as the two essentials of a nation's prosperity had been fertile soil and a large population, France was inherently stronger than Britain. (Even in 1815, her population was more than half again as large as that of the United Kingdom.) But as soon as prosperity demanded access to large overseas markets and to mineral resources such as coal and iron, the situation was reversed. This fact, more than any political events, underlay the rise of British power and the decline of French in the first half of the century. Germany, which had the relevant assets of coal and iron, was for half a century impeded by her political disunity and by exclusion from overseas markets. So, until at least the 1860s, Britain enjoyed an easy economic supremacy as against her most serious continental rivals. Towards the end of the century the loss of that lead marked a further revolution in the power relationships of all European nations, and began a new era in European history.

RIVAL CONCEPTIONS OF EUROPEAN ORDER

The Empire of Napoleon had given Europe, for a time, one form of order and unity: that imposed from above by conquest. In common resistance to this French domination the governments of Britain and Europe had evolved another form of unity: that of concerted alliance for the single purpose of defeating France. At the Treaty of Chaumont, made between the United Kingdom, Austria, Prussia, and Russia in March 1814, these allies undertook to remain in alliance for twenty years. The immediate purpose of overthrowing Napoleon was in this way widened into the long-term purpose of preventing any similar domination of the continent by a single power. The aim of the allies was to preserve the political division of Europe into dynastic states; but at the same time to find some means of settling disputes between them and of concerting action among the largest powers of the continent. Out of this double purpose arose the territorial settlement of Europe agreed upon at the Congress of Vienna in 1815, and the 'Congress System', which was intended to embody and perpetuate the idea of a 'Concert of Europe'. This settlement was the most thoroughgoing attempt made, until then, to construct new organizations for keeping the peace among the great powers of modern Europe. Not since the Congress of Westphalia, which met in 1648 at the end of the Thirty Years' War, had an assembly so representative of all Europe met to consider issues of general European importance. The settlement as a whole was embodied in four different yet interlocked arrangements: the Treaty of Chaumont, the two Treaties of Paris, the Treaty of Vienna, and the Quadruple Alliance. Taken together these treaties shaped the course of European history for the next half century. A fifth arrangement, the Holy Alliance, expressed yet another conception of European unity and order, to which Britain never acceded.

1. *Treaty of Chaumont, March 1814.* Made as the formal culmination of the military alliance of the United Kingdom, Austria, Russia, and Prussia against France, this treaty bound the signatories first to overthrow Napoleon and then to remain in alliance for twenty years, in order to maintain the territorial and political settlement to be reached as soon as Napoleon should be defeated. They agreed to restore the Bourbon dynasty to France, and proceeded, by the end of March 1814, to occupy Paris. The next month Napoleon abdicated. The peace terms with France were then embodied in the First Treaty of Paris of May 1814.

2. *The Treaties of Paris, May 1814 and November 1815.* By the first Treaty of Paris the boundaries of France were fixed at those of 1792, with some slight additions later. This meant that France had to give up Belgium and the left bank of the Rhine, which she had held for more than twenty years. She also surrendered several colonial possessions. But she was not to be disarmed or occupied or made to pay any indemnity; treatment of her was remarkably generous as compared with either the previous or the subsequent treatment of defeated powers in similar post-war settlements. As a respectable legitimist monarchy, France was able to claim representation at subsequent congresses of the powers, and her brilliant representative Talleyrand proceeded to manipulate the balance of power to his own advantage. Negotiation of a more general settlement in Europe was abruptly interrupted by the escape of Napoleon from the island of Elba to which he had been exiled, and his triumphant return to France. After his final defeat at Waterloo and his

safer imprisonment on St Helena, the allies made more severe terms for France.

The second Treaty of Paris, signed after Waterloo, pushed back the frontiers of France from those of 1792 to those of 1790; this meant that she lost further points of strategic importance on her north-eastern frontier. She narrowly escaped having to cede Alsace and Lorraine. She had to submit to occupation by an allied garrison until 1818, and was made to pay a large indemnity.

3. *Treaty of Vienna, June 1815.* The plenipotentiaries to the general congress of European powers which met at Vienna in the fall of 1814 included Talleyrand, for it was not technically a peace conference. Peace had been made by the first Treaty of Paris, and it was assumed that the issues between France and her victors had been settled. There was no reason why she should not now be admitted to the assembly of European powers as an equal. The Treaty of Vienna was signed in June, before the Battle of Waterloo, and it remained substantially unaltered save for the provisions of the second Treaty of Paris. The settlement reached at Vienna was concerned with the continent as a whole, and was intended to settle all outstanding issues.

It was made, in effect, by the representatives of the five major powers. These were the Tsar Alexander I of Russia who usually acted personally; Metternich the Chancellor of Austria, who had constant help from the secretary, Gentz; Hardenberg, who usually acted for King Frederick William III of Prussia; Lord Castlereagh (and in later stages the Duke of Wellington), who represented the United Kingdom; and Talleyrand, the skilful and wily spokesman of France. Although practically every European state and principality was represented and the congress was in form a general assembly of Europe, all important decisions were made by the Big Five. Throughout the eight months of its duration, the Austrian government sustained in Vienna an elaborate system of spies and secret agents who opened letters, collected backstairs gossip, and surrounded the gathering with a fog of mutual suspicions and distrust.

Among the oddly assorted assemblage of characters, the Tsar was the most enigmatic and aroused the most Utopian hopes of a liberal settlement; Metternich was the most consistently conservative and stubbornly hostile to all liberal hopes; Castlereagh was the most anxious to achieve a moderate and generally agreed settlement, because British interests lay in a peaceful Europe with which trade could be established; Talleyrand was the most insinuating and clear-sighted, having the simple objective of promoting and safeguarding French interests. Over the future of Poland and Saxony, Metternich, Castlereagh, and Talleyrand were driven to make a secret alliance, preparatory to war against Russia and Prussia should these persist in an arrangement which, it was felt, would upset the balance of power.

In retrospect the Big Five might be thought of as grouped differently. Great Britain and Russia were alike in that both were great powers flanking Europe but not in it. Each had growing areas of interest outside Europe, vast hinterlands of space into which they were to move, in the course of the next century, by settlement, trade, and economic expansion. Although the British hinterland was oceanic and Russia's Asiatic, the pull away from Europe was for both so strong that the full and concerted weight of these peripheral powers was not to be felt again in Europe until 1914. They tended for the next century to intervene in Europe only when there was question of the Ottoman Empire – the power which held the key position between three continents, where Anglo-Russian interests clashed. France and Austria were alike in that both were essentially continental European powers, whose orbits of influence touched in Germany and Italy, the two main storm centres of the next half century. Neither had important extra-European interests. It was because of this neat balance of forces, in which Britain and Russia averted their attentions or neutralized one another, and France and Austria served as mutual counterweights, that the fifth power, Prussia, was given a unique opportunity for consolidation and aggrandizement during the ensuing half century. The least among the Big Five in 1815, limited in size, resources, and influence, she held the key to the future in her central concentration of European interests. But in 1815 these groupings were masked and blurred by the more short-term fears and policies of the governments concerned.

In the end, the territorial settlement included drastic safeguards against a resurgence of France (*see* Map 3). The Austrian Netherlands (later to become Belgium) and Luxembourg were combined with Holland to make a buffer state in the north; Prussia was given the Rhineland; Genoa and part of Savoy went to the Kingdom of Sardinia (Piedmont). The territories of Germany were shared out to meet the interests of Prussia and Austria, and a German Confederation, comprising the 39 states to which Germany was now reduced, was set up under the presidency of Austria. In Italy, Austria rewon Lombardy and took Venetia as compensation for the loss of the Austrian Netherlands; the Papal States went back to the Pope; the Bourbons were restored in Naples; and the three little duchies of Parma, Modena, and Tuscany were placed under Austrian princes. In the Baltic, Norway was transferred from Denmark to Sweden, Finland from Sweden to Russia. The Treaty guaranteed the independence and neutrality of Switzerland. Various agreements were made, under British pressure, to abolish the slave trade.

Like any general settlement of the kind, the settlement of Vienna was a network of bargains and negotiated compromises. But so far as any general principles ran through its provisions, they were – in addition to the building of bulwarks against further French aggression – the two principles of legitimism and of balance of power. In the domestic settlement of Europe the source of political authority most generally favoured was that of hereditary dynastic monarchy. As far as possible legitimist monarchs were restored and supported, especially in Spain, France, and Italy. On the other hand, for the purposes of international pacification, it was felt wise to establish some system of a balance of power. For this reason Russian ambitions in eastern Europe were resisted by Britain and Austria, the German settlement included both Prussia and Austria in the new Confederation, Bourbon princes were reinstated as well as Habsburgs, and periodic congresses were planned in which the five major powers would seek to settle any disputes that might arise. The aim was to find and keep a balance among themselves which would prevent any one of them from dominating too large an area of Europe.

It was, on the whole, a reasonable and statesmanlike arrangement, of which the chief defect was that it underestimated the dynamism of nationalism. Territories such as Norway, Finland, and Belgium were used as pawns in the calculations of the treaty makers, regardless of the wishes of their inhabitants. Considerations of strategy, power, and dynastic convenience took priority over national or economic interests. It was a settlement framed by monarchs and aristocratic diplomats of the old order, and it was infused with the spirit of the eighteenth century. As such, it could have only limited applicability and longevity in the faster-moving world of the nineteenth century. But it would be wrong to blame the makers of the settlement for failing to appreciate the power of nationalism or liberalism, which few realized in 1815; nor can they be regarded as having had a free hand to achieve more than they did achieve. They were bound not only by agreements previously reached among themselves, but still more by the need to reach some compromise between the conflicting political interests of the major participants. Vienna had the practical merit of giving Europe nearly half a century of comparative peace, and this was what most Europeans most fervently wanted in 1815.

4. *The Quadruple Alliance, November 1815.* The peacemakers realized that force must be put behind the settlement if it were to be preserved. Accordingly, on the same day as the Second Treaty of Paris (20 November 1815) the four allied powers signed a further treaty perpetuating

the Quadruple Alliance. They pledged themselves to maintain by force, for a period of twenty years, the arrangements reached at Chaumont, Vienna, and Paris. This undertaking created the so-called 'Concert of Europe', because the four powers also agreed to periodic meetings of their representatives 'for the purpose of consulting upon their common interest and for the consideration of the measures most salutary for the maintenance of the peace of Europe'. From the outset, however, Castlereagh made it clear that while Britain would join in keeping the settlement of frontiers and in excluding a Bonaparte from the throne of France, she would not undertake to support Louis XVIII as against any other form of régime in France, nor would she back intervention in the internal affairs of any other state. When the Tsar pressed for an undertaking to intervene in support of Louis XVIII, Castlereagh refused. This difference of principle was to become the main bone of contention between Britain and her partners in the ensuing years, and the cause of her eventual withdrawal from the Congress System. The sharpening differentiation of Britain from the rest of Europe, based on her new economic advantages, led to diplomatic separation.

5. *The Holy Alliance, September 1815.* Britain was equally firm in her refusal to join the Holy Alliance which the Tsar set up in 1815, and which came to be popularly confused with the Quadruple Alliance. By this extraordinary document the rulers of Russia, Prussia, and Austria bound themselves together in a Christian union of charity, peace, and love. They undertook 'to consider themselves all as members of one and the same Christian nation, the three princes looking on themselves as merely delegated by Providence to govern three branches of One Family, namely Austria, Prussia, and Russia, thus confessing that the Christian world, of which they and their people form a part, has in reality no other Sovereign but Him to whom power alone really belongs'. It seems likely that this appeal to the Christian foundations of European civilization was sincere on the part of the Tsar, and that it was prompted by a sense of the great revival of religious faith which, in reaction against the rationalism and scepticism of the Enlightenment, marked these years.[1] It was eventually endorsed by every monarch in Europe except the Prince Regent of England and Pope Pius VII who refused to sign, and the Sultan of Turkey who, as an infidel, could hardly be invited to sign. It was even signed by the President of the Swiss Republic.

If the Tsar Alexander intended it seriously, few of his colleagues did. Metternich dismissed it as 'a high-sounding Nothing', Talleyrand as 'a ludicrous contract', Castlereagh as 'a piece of sublime mysticism and

1. See pp. 103–4.

nonsense'. In his memoirs Metternich asserted that the main motive of Austria and Prussia in signing was 'to please the Tsar', which they could afford to do because of the meaninglessness of the whole scheme. Castlereagh warned the British Prime Minister that 'the Emperor's mind is not completely sound'. The general reception of the scheme by other governments was that it would lead to little but could do no harm; its interpretation by liberal opinion was soon to be that, combined with the more realistic Quadruple Alliance, it represented a sinister and far-reaching attempt to justify universal interference by despotic monarchs in the internal governments of smaller nations. Its historical importance is that it shows how weak was a sense of Christendom, even in this time of religious revival, as compared with the realistic politics of balance of power.

The settlement as a whole reflected that mixture of elements of unity and diversity which has been described above. The principles of legitimism, which were made the basis for the internal government of states, had their counterpart in the Tsar's scheme for a Holy Alliance. The Holy Alliance, appealing to the old notion of the unity of Christendom, presupposed a community of like-minded states, with legitimist, monarchical government within each. It was workable only on the assumption of a fairly uniform pattern of this kind. On the other hand the principle of establishing a balance of power between states, which underlay the territorial terms of the settlement, did not presuppose or imply like-minded monarchies. On the contrary it assumed recurrent rivalries and tensions between states, and was applicable to interstate relations however diverse might be their internal forms of government. The Quadruple Alliance, with its scheme for periodic congresses of the major powers to readjust the balance of power and settle possible disputes among them, was in conformity with these notions of territorial balance. It was compatible with different internal régimes, and left room for divergent political developments. The British attitude was therefore logical, in signing the Quadruple Alliance but not the Holy Alliance; and in repudiating the doctrine of joint intervention in internal affairs which the Tsar, from his point of view, was equally logical in demanding. These two different sets of principle and outlook have, indeed, haunted every attempt at a general European settlement. In 1919 it was assumed that all European states would in future be democratic in structure, and therefore sufficiently like-minded and peace-loving to make the machinery of the League of Nations work effectively.[1] The League was regarded not as a supplement to the balance of power – a

1. See p. 640.

notion then discredited by the prewar system of alliances which had precipitated war in 1914 – but rather as a substitute for it, a sort of permanent and universal congress system, systematically removing all disputes liable to lead to war. Among the chief reasons for its failure was the fact that an increasing number of states ceased to be democratic in structure or peace-loving in purpose. The Congress System of 1815 was more realistic in this respect, that it did not presuppose a greater degree of unity and uniformity in Europe than actually existed. It provided machinery for peaceful change by means of periodic consultations between the greatest power-units in Europe. Its misfortune was that it came to be manipulated by Metternich for the almost exclusively conservative purpose of preventing change, in an age when the forces of change were rapidly gaining in strength as against the forces of order and continuity.

From the outset the post-war years were haunted by economic distress. The year 1815 and 1816 were both years of bad harvests and of economic hardship throughout Britain and Europe. The depression spread to industry and business, thousands of banks and commercial companies failed, taxes remained high, and there was widespread unemployment. These facts in themselves undermined popular confidence in the new order, and soon encouraged demands for radical reforms, which the legitimist governments were too frightened to attempt. There was no interlude of real stability following Waterloo and the Vienna settlement. The nineteenth century was destined from the start to be one of unusual restlessness, mobility, and revolution.

Most of the drama and interest, as well as much of the unity, of European history in the hundred years between 1815 and 1914 derives from the fluctuations of balance between the forces of continuity and the forces of change; or, in their most extreme and dynamic forms, between the forces of reaction and the forces of revolution. To set the stage, then, for the great events of that century, the components of the two sides of this balance must be described.

CHAPTER 6

THE FORCES OF CONTINUITY

THE INSTITUTIONS OF MONARCHY

THE traditional and most generally accepted focus of loyalty for all whose interests and sentiments lay on the side of order and conservatism was a monarch. Even the French revolutionaries of 1789 had no intention, at first, of overthrowing the monarchy, and it was 1792 before they took the daring step of setting up a republic. The only republics in Europe were Switzerland, Venice and Genoa, and they seemed to be exceptions that proved the rule. The experience of the federal republic of the United States was short and offered little example for the peoples of Europe. The traditions of dynastic absolutism, on the other hand, were deep-rooted and well-tested. It is wrong to think of the *ancien régime* as having been totally destroyed by the French Revolution and the conquests of Napoleon. It is unlikely that a form of government which had evolved and prospered so extensively during the previous hundred and fifty years should have been obliterated within twenty-five. Not only did many of the ideas and institutions of the old monarchies survive throughout the upheavals of the period 1789–1815; they enjoyed a new popularity and struck fresh roots in the generation after Waterloo.

The basic idea of monarchy was the idea that hereditary right gave the best title to political power. The tasks and scope of government were still thought of as severely restricted. They were mainly the elementary functions of organizing security for the whole of the kingdom at home and abroad. But these tasks were, in themselves, difficult enough, and seemed best left to the men especially fitted and most expert in them. The twin dangers to public peace and order were, traditionally, the challenge of overmighty subjects and invasion or subjection to foreign powers. Any king who succeeded in repelling these dangers attracted the general loyalty of his subjects. The dangers of disputed succession were best avoided by hereditary succession: ruling families had a natural interest in passing on to their descendants enhanced power and prestige. While conceptions of a 'nation' and even of 'a state' were still only dimly formed and slightly appreciated, the personal allegiance rendered to a monarch seemed the best possible kind of political cement and social cohesion. Monarchy was to most people the most natural form of government in the world.

To the traditions and institutions of monarchy, the rulers of Europe since the late seventeenth century had added the ideas and the practice of absolutism. These rested on the success with which many kings and their ministers had crushed or by-passed the limitations on royal power which had previously been imposed by great feudal factions, local assemblies and corporations, and the Church. The pattern of this new type of absolute monarchy had been set by Louis XIV of France. He inherited a throne that was strong because the squabbling feudal and religious factions in France had exhausted themselves to a point where they could be subdued by royal power. Louis kept the nobles weak by offering them the unattractive choice between impoverishing themselves at the costly court of Versailles, or exiling themselves to their estates in the provinces, far from the fountainhead of pensions and honours. He also subordinated the Church in France to his control, and took from the French Protestant communities, the Huguenots, the rights and liberties they had formerly enjoyed.

The preponderance of French wealth, power, and influence during his reign (1660–1715) tempted eighteenth-century monarchs all over Europe to imitate his methods, to adopt French culture and even the French language, and to claim for themselves comparable absolute powers. Frederick the Great of Prussia, Catherine the Great of Russia, Maria Theresa of Austria, were alike infatuated with the idea of strengthening their power, centralizing government in their own hands as against local and feudal privileges, and so acquiring more absolute authority in the state. Moreover, the very dynastic rivalries and conflicts between these eighteenth-century monarchs drove them to look for ever more efficient methods of government: their increased expenditure on government called for more systematic methods of taxation, and the wars to which their rivalries gave rise demanded better organization and systems of administration. A would-be absolute monarch had to be a more efficient ruler; and he had to seek popular support against nobles and Church, support that he tended to buy with experiments in popular reform and enlightened government. So absolute monarchy became 'enlightened' or 'benevolent despotism', anxious to justify its existence by fostering material progress and adopting more enlightened methods of government.

The French Revolution had not been regarded as a threat to such forms of government so long as it tried only to create a constitutional monarchy, with royal power buttressed by a national assembly representative of the whole kingdom. Many of the reforms achieved in France between 1789 and 1792 were only more thoroughgoing versions of reforms which the enlightened despots had been trying to achieve elsewhere. But when the Revolution had gone on, in disillusion with the king, to attack the Church, establish a republic, and threaten to spread revolution throughout Europe, absolutism was bound to react violently against it.

So strong were the traditions of dynastic monarchy that even Napoleon, feeling himself a usurper, took care to marry into the greatest of the old dynastic families, the Habsburgs. He was not opposed to the institutions of monarchy, but aimed at making himself head of a new and grander dynasty. He made his elder brother Joseph, king of Naples; a younger brother Louis, king of Holland; and his youngest and most frivolous brother Jérôme, king of Westphalia. Even after the upheavals of the Revolution, and perhaps even because of the upheavals of the Revolution, legitimism was still felt to offer the best possible credentials for claiming political authority. It is hardly surprising that when the statesmen of the Vienna Congress in 1815 wanted to re-establish order in Europe, it was to the principle of legitimism, shrewdly suggested to them by Talleyrand, that they instinctively turned. As a result of the settlement at Vienna the ideas and institutions of hereditary, absolute monarchy were given a new lease of life throughout Europe.

The scene was dominated by rulers of the governments that had not been overthrown by either the Revolution or Napoleon, but had weathered the storm: pre-eminently the Tsar Alexander I of Russia, whose mystical sense of the dangers of revolution gave birth to the Holy Alliance; the king of Prussia, Frederick William III, whose power had come near to extinction by Napoleon at the time of the Treaty of Tilsit in 1807, but who had survived as a strategic buffer between France and Russia; the Emperor of Austria, Francis I, who clung to the negative policy, 'Govern and change nothing', and who relied on his energetic chancellor, Prince Metternich, to hold his ramshackle and diversified dominions together. Among this trio the representatives of Great Britain, first Lord Castlereagh and at later congresses George Canning, who ranked as conservatives at home, appeared as liberal rebels. At first the triumph of monarchy, and all that it stood for, seemed complete.

It was later to become the fashion, especially among liberal historians, to ascribe the downfall of Napoleon's ambitions to the rising dynamism of the new national and liberal forces in Europe, and to make much of the resistance to his rule put up by popular movements of revolt in Germany and Russia, and by guerrilla fighters in Spain. These indeed had played their part. But in the end what had defeated Napoleon was an efficient coalition of the great powers of Europe, launching against him the concerted attacks of their professional armies, led by the royalist generals of Russia, Prussia, and Great Britain. In 1815 few had any

doubts that the defeat of Napoleon was a victory for the allied monarchical governments acting in a grand alliance; and that Waterloo had
not been won by popular uprising or guerrilla fighters, but by the hard-
bitten, tough soldiers of the British and Prussian armies.

Under the auspices of the victorious monarchs, the little kings came
out into the sun again. In Germany the Holy Roman Empire had been
abolished in 1806, and no attempt was possible to revive that shadowy
ghost. Nor was it thought possible or desirable to restore all of the 396
tiny principalities, ecclesiastical states, and free cities that Napoleon,
during his occupation, had so thoroughly demolished. From the old
multitude of states there emerged 39, the largest of which were Austria,
Prussia, and Bavaria. These were formed into a loose Germanic confederation (*Bund*). Though decimated in number, they effectively kept
Germany disunited, for they were widely diverse in character. To each
returned its monarch or princeling, reclaiming his absolutist powers and
reviving all the old courtly pomp, extravagance, officialdom, and inefficiency. With each monarch came most of the old aristocracy, more
assertive than ever of its social privileges and political rights. The chief
instrument of co-ordination in the Confederation was the Diet (*Bundestag*), which sat in Frankfurt and was presided over by Austria. Its members represented only the governments of the states, and they were
bound by government instructions. The Diet as a whole had no executive
authority, and was indeed devised to preserve intact the sovereignty of
the princes. In the eyes of Metternich, its chief creator and manipulator,
it was a body for the defence of German sovereigns against French
interference and against liberal forces internally.

To the throne of Spain returned Ferdinand VII, who set to work
to undo the revolutionary changes introduced by the Cortes of Cadiz
since 1812. He annulled the Constitution of 1812 and resumed all the
prerogatives of the absolutist monarchy. He produced a 'confusion of
abuses' which shocked his more astute cousin Louis XVIII of France.
In Italy the restoration took a form similar to that in Germany, with
various arrangements designed to secure the predominant influence of
Austria. While Bourbons returned to France and Spain, Habsburgs or
Habsburg family connexions returned to Italy. In the north, Lombardy
and Venetia, the richest and most strategically important parts of Italy,
were governed directly from Vienna by the Emperor of Austria. The
king of Sardinia was his cousin, as was Francis IV, the duke of Modena.
His brother, Archduke Ferdinand III, became duke of Tuscany; and his
aunt, the queen of Naples. Ferdinand I, king of Naples and Sicily, behaved in as blindly reactionary a manner as did his Bourbon nephew,
the king of Spain. The administration of the Papal States, which geo-

graphically cut the long peninsula of Italy in half, was among the worst in Italy. By 1812 the powers were even obliged to issue a complaint against the abuses, which included at one extreme an uncontrollable brigandage and at the other an oppressive political police. The Kingdom of Piedmont, ruled by Victor Emmanuel I, was destined to assume a role corresponding to that of Prussia in Germany: each evolved an unusually efficient system of administration and devoted considerable attention to its army. These qualities were later to make each of them the leader of a successful campaign for national unification of these sadly disunited countries.

Despite these almost universal restorations of monarchy, the traditions of kingship had been badly shaken. Much of the magic of monarchy had gone, since kings had been bowled over like skittles by French armies, and moved about like chessmen by an autocratic emperor. Many of the kings who climbed back to their thrones in 1814 – and none more so than Louis XVIII of France – suffered from the disadvantage that they had been patently imported in the baggage of the allies. The unceremonious scuttling of Louis during the Hundred Days when the great Napoleon returned, and his second and even more humiliating restoration after Waterloo, emphasized still more sharply how fragile royal authority might be. Legitimism alone seemed an ineffective basis for government, when force of arms loomed large in the foreground. But other elements combined to make the next generation in Europe an age of restored and revived monarchy. What were these other forces?

THE CHURCH

One was the revival of religious faith and the restoration of the power of the Roman Catholic Church. A close alliance between throne and altar was traditional in Europe. The Church, especially in France, had suffered from the attacks of the Revolution as much as had the feudal nobility and the monarchy. The Civil Constitution of the Clergy in 1790 had reduced the Church in France to the position of a department of state, and many higher clergy had joined the aristocratic and royal *émigrés* in exile abroad. Napoleon had, for expediency's sake, come to terms with the Church in his Concordat with the Papacy in 1802. But that bargain had left him in considerable control over the clergy in France, and with the growth of state universities and schools the Church lost most of its former grip over education.

By 1815 the Roman Catholic Church was beginning to reap some of the ultimate advantages of being persecuted, and of the inevitable reaction that set in against the rationalism and freethinking of the eighteenth century, now widely identified with the ideals of the Revolution. The violence and extremism of the Revolution bred a revival of faith and a renewal of clericalist sympathies, most strongly among the royalist and aristocratic classes that now dominated European politics. In 1815 the Roman Church regained a highly privileged position. Where, as in France, it was impossible to restore to it the lands and property that the Revolution had taken away, it was supported by generous grants from the government and resumed its control over education. In other countries it retained its lands and regained influence. Even Protestant powers, such as Britain and Prussia, were prepared to support the revival of papal power in Europe; and they were backed in this by the other great non-Catholic power, Russia. Pope Pius VII enjoyed the personal sympathy that had been aroused by his humiliation at the hands of Napoleon,[1] and in 1814 he made a triumphal return to Rome. The Jesuit Order won official favour at the Vatican, and set about reorganizing its power throughout Europe. The Pope re-established the Index, and even the Inquisition reappeared in Rome and in Spain. It was like a second Counter-Reformation. By a series of concordats the Church recovered much of its freedom of action in Spain, Sardinia, Bavaria, and Naples. The ultramontane policy it followed soon met with some official opposition in the greater powers, and in France and Austria even the monarchical governments were forced to resist its full claims. They especially disliked the spread of the Jesuits. The Jesuits organized societies of Catholic laymen, especially in France, Spain, and Italy, and through the activities of these congregations clericalist influence penetrated into politics, administration, and education. Within a few years France was passing legislation to restrict Jesuit activities, and the Tsar was expelling the Order from Russia. But the recovery of Catholicism after its low ebb at the end of tthe eighteenth century was rapid and remarkable. This decade of militant ultramontanism goes far towards explaining the resurgence of violent anti-clericalism by the middle of the nineteenth century.

In England the Anglican Church still enjoyed a highly privileged position, and its influence at this time was predominantly conservative. Until 1828 Protestant dissenters remained subject to many disabilities. They were excluded by law from all important civil and military offices, as well as from teaching offices in the universities. Even the evangelical wing of the Church, concerned with missionary work at home and abroad and with attacking slavery, remained broadly conservative in politics. Churchmen lent little support to movements for reform, even for such humanitarian causes as reform of the prisons and of the penal code. They belonged to the forces of established order; and an Anglican

2. See p. 60.

cleric, the Whig wit, Sydney Smith, suffered loss of preferment for the more generous views he so pungently and courageously expressed.

These reassertions of clerical powers and the consolidation of Church establishments were accompanied, and indeed made possible, by a broader revival of religious faith. Rationalist ideas of the natural rights of man, secularist doctrines of state power, were tarnished by the excesses of the revolutionary and Napoleonic era. Many of the greatest intellects in Europe, and some of the most biting pens, devoted themselves to affirming the dogmas of Christianity and old religious beliefs. Edmund Burke, whose tremendous literary attack on the ideas of the French Revolution in his *Reflections on the Revolution in France* of 1790 made him the spokesman of conservatism throughout Europe, had stated eloquently the case for traditionalism and reverence for established institutions. In France Joseph de Maistre and the Vicomte de Bonald linked insistence on the supreme need for order with support for the legitimist monarchy and the power of the Papacy. Their brilliant polemics seemed for a time to demolish the ideas and arguments of liberalism, and their influence spread outside France to Italy and Germany. Their ideas were further popularized by Lamennais, who showed the connexions between religious faith and social and political order; though in his later writings he tried to separate the cause of the Church from that of the monarchy, and argued that the excessively close alliance of altar and throne was bringing the Church into unnecessary disrepute. The keynote of their thought was the demand for authority – authority both in state and in church, as the only bulwark against revolution and atheism.

Before 1800 the most influential intellectuals had been on the side of rationalism, democratic ideals, and anti-clericalism. Now, for over a decade, the greatest intellects supported traditionalism, conservatism, and the Church. To all who had been frightened by the experience of revolution, this appeal to history and tradition, to old establishments and creeds, was strong. It seemed to tap the only source of authority rich enough to withstand the disturbing notions of democracy and nationalism on one hand, and the upstart claims of military dictatorship on the other. For at least a decade after Waterloo these forces of conservatism enjoyed more positive prestige and power than at any time since the reign of Louis XIV.

THE LANDOWNERS

To the powerful conservative forces of monarchy and religion must be added a third: the universal conservative tendencies of all whose wealth lay mostly in land. The ultimate foundation, both in theory and practice, of the pre-revolutionary absolutist monarchy had been the feudal system of landownership. In an age that knew only the beginnings of an industrial revolution and little mechanization of production and transport, land was still the most important form of property and carried with it an implicit right to social importance and political power.

The upheavals of the years between 1789 and 1815 in France brought an unprecedented transference of landed property from great landowners and great corporations (particularly the Church) to a number of smaller property owners. It is not known how extensive was this redistribution of land, nor just how much of it was regained by the aristocracy at the restoration. But the larger estates, along with those of the Church, were declared national property and either put up for sale or exchanged for the paper bonds (*assignats*) which were issued on the security of the confiscated Church lands. Many middle-class folk – financiers, lawyers, millers, brewers – made fortunes by speculating in the *assignats*. Sometimes existing tenant farmers took the opportunity to buy their land, and sometimes peasants added to their existing holdings.

When Napoleon came to power he found large stocks of land still not sold or granted away, and from this he endowed a new Napoleonic aristocracy. It was drawn mainly from middle-class people who as soldiers, lawyers, or bureaucrats served his dictatorship. Usually these new landowners simply stepped into the shoes of the old, and leased the land for rent to farmers who cultivated it. The general effect seems to have been considerable acquisitions of land by the middle classes, and some acquisition by the peasants. The peasants enjoyed the further immense gain of being relieved of their old burden of paying feudal dues and tithes. At the restoration there were still unsold national lands, and these were mostly returned to their former aristocratic owners. It was impossible for the king to meet the nobles' demands that their property rights be completely restored, for even to attempt this would have alienated too large a proportion of the population. But by repurchase and regrant, it is thought that by 1820 the old nobility had made good about half its losses – a proportion big enough to give the returned *émigrés* great political power.

The limited diffusion of landed property involved a correspondingly limited extension of political rights. The equation between land and political power remained intact. It was, on the whole, the old aristocracy, the wealthy capitalist bourgeoisie, and the most substantial peasant proprietors who gained from the redistribution of land. The bulk of the land of France was still, therefore, owned by a relatively small class, though it was a differently constituted and somewhat larger class than in 1789. Political power was confirmed to this class by the simple device of fixing the qualification for voting for the new French parliament in terms of the amount of money paid annually in direct taxation. The vote for the Chamber of Deputies went only to citizens who were 30 years of age or more and paid at least 300 francs a year in direct taxation. The electorate was thus only some 90,000 in a population of 30 million. To be a deputy a man had to be over 40 and pay at least 1000 francs a year in direct taxation, and he was indirectly elected. In addition, parliamentary power was shared with an upper chamber, the House of Peers, in which sat the higher aristocracy and clergy. The rights of landed wealth were in these ways deeply entrenched in the new monarchy, and this was a guarantee that its whole policy would be intensely conservative. The king's ministers were drawn mainly from the aristocracy, and his chief ministers were at first the Duc de Richelieu and the Comte Decazes, whose reactionary tendencies were moderated by a political sense of the practical unwisdom of trying to turn the clock back too far. Between 1814 and 1830 the restored monarchy rested on a balance between the powers of the old aristocracy, now much depleted and impoverished, and the power of the new business oligarchy, rapidly growing in power. The *milliard des émigrés*, granted as indemnity in 1825 to those whose lands had been confiscated during the Revolution, more often went into industrial and commercial investment than into land. The aristocracy became more an officeholding than a landowning class. It shared power, in effect, with the wealthy bourgeois who owned a landed estate on which he paid heavy taxes, and the wealthier manufacturer who paid taxes on his membership in a corporation.

The régime represented a balance and a compromise between aristocracy and oligarchy, and the working of the corrupt parliament held little interest for the mass of the nation. The Chamber of Deputies had a permanent majority on the right, and a permanent minority on the left. No party system was possible, and opposition had to content itself with spasmodic attacks and a running fire of verbal criticism of the government, without prospect of assuming ministerial responsibilities. As under the *ancien régime*, government remained exclusively the job of the king and his ministers, and the principle of ministerial responsibility to parliament was neither fully understood nor practically possible.

In Britain, where demands for parliamentary reform had been smothered by the exigencies of the long war against France and by the reaction against the ideas of Jacobinism, similar arrangements existed. There, too, the landed aristocracy of the eighteenth century, reinforced by the ennobled generals, admirals, and administrators of the war years and by the faster-growing class of financiers, merchants, and manufacturers, virtually monopolized state power. The House of Lords, from which most ministers of the Crown were still drawn, preserved its control over legislation. Through individual influence and patronage the aristocracy controlled a large share of the borough representation in the House of Commons. The electorate was determined by an antiquated and complicated system of property qualifications which gave the vote to only some 400,000 men, and effective power to the landed gentry in the countryside and the large landowners and men of wealth in the towns. The regular system of patronage, corruption, and intimidation secured the return of a high proportion of placemen and younger sons of the nobility. The Landed Property Qualification Acts stipulated that members of Parliament for the counties must own a landed estate of at least £600 a year; and for the boroughs, a landed estate of £300 a year.

The larger part played by trade and industry in the life of Britain than in the life of France was reflected in the fact that in Britain the *bourgeoisie* had staked for themselves a larger share in power, alongside the aristocracy. But the principles on which the régime rested were very similar. Parliament existed to represent not persons but property: despite the clamour of radical reformers, the changes made before 1815 had merely admitted certain forms of wealth other than landed property to a very limited share in power. The predominance of the landed and agricultural interests in 1815 is shown well enough by the Corn Law passed in that year; it gave farmers protection by prohibiting the import of corn from abroad until the price at home had reached the high level of 80 shillings a quarter. It is shown, too, by the maintenance of the harsh Game Laws, which made it illegal for anyone who was not a squire or a squire's eldest son to kill game, and for anyone to buy and sell game. In 1816 these old restrictions were added to; a new law provided that the cottager caught with his snares at night, in quest of a hare or a rabbit, could be transported for seven years. Pheasant preserves could be protected by spring guns and man traps, and the practice was upheld by the law courts until 1827.

Great Britain and France were, politically as well as economically, among the most advanced and liberal countries in Europe. In much of Germany, Italy, Spain, and the Austrian empire, the landed aristocracy held on to most of their estates and the political predominance that went with them. Lacking a middle class of merchants and business people as strong as in Great Britain or France, these countries remained more completely a mere perpetuation of the *ancien régime*. Yet even here there were significant changes, most of which derived from the sheer impossibility of undoing some of the things Napoleon had done. In the Rhineland and in Belgium, French rule had meant confiscation of Church lands, abolition of feudal exactions and dues, and considerable redistribution of the land to small owners who cultivated it. The system of landholding in Germany west of the Elbe was already, for historical reasons, very different from that east of the Elbe. Large seignorial domains were almost unknown. Peasants enjoyed rights of life tenancy and hereditary tenancy, subject to payments of quit rent, so that they had effective control over cultivation. Holdings were on the average small. East of the Elbe, where the Germans had been originally a conquering race with a subject population of Slavs, lay an area of mainly large estates, cultivated by servile labour. The Prussian Junkers, like the English squires, were enterprising and progressive in their methods, and tended to expropriate the peasants and build up ever larger estates: unlike the English landowners, they did not let the land out to be cultivated by tenant farmers but organized its use under their own supervision. The emancipation of the peasantry in Prussia from heavy feudal obligations and servitude, decreed by edicts of the monarchy between 1807 and 1816, proceeded slowly. It often resulted in the economic subjection of the peasants and the surrender of large portions of their lan̄d to the Junkers as compensation. For these reasons, Germany remained, throughout the century, divided into two fairly distinct regions, with an even greater concentration of landed wealth in the hands of the conservative Junker class. It was this class that provided the Prussian monarchy with many of its ablest administrators and officers.

In Poland and Russia the power, both economic and political, of the landowning aristocracy remained more intact in 1815. They showed themselves not hostile to emancipation of the serfs who provided the labour on their lands, provided it could be carried out on the model of the Prussian Junkers. But the peasants were bitterly opposed to achieving their personal emancipation from serfdom at the cost of losing land; it was a common saying, 'We are yours, but the land is ours'. Eventually, in 1861, they were to be emancipated by an edict of the Tsar, but both nobles and peasants were left dissatisfied with the process. Until then Poland and Russia remained essentially under the *ancien régime*, with the persistent disadvantage that the aristocracy of these lands had none of the flair for efficient estate management shown by the landowners of Britain and Prussia; while the peasants remained more impervious than the peasants of these countries to the progressive methods of cultivation and husbandry increasingly adopted in the western nations.

THE POPULARITY OF PEACE

To these three main components in the forces of conservatism in 1815 must be added a fourth, latent yet powerful, which operated throughout Europe. Almost every country had known more than two decades of recurrent war. Except in France, warfare did not yet involve a total mobilization of national resources. But great campaigns such as those of the French wars imposed unusual strains on all the combatants. The continental blockade had affected standards of living throughout Europe; and Britain, as Napoleon's most remorseless enemy, had endured heavy burdens and strains. To the fears aroused in all governments by the ideas of Jacobinism must be added the war-weariness and longing for peace and stability induced in all men by the incessant fighting. France herself knew great exhaustion, especially after the disasters of the Russian campaign. As usual, pre-war conditions seemed rosier in retrospect, and all who merely wanted peace and freedom to live their own lives welcomed a substantial reversion to conditions of peace. With such conditions, monarchical rule and even clericalist influence were inseparably connected. This mood of exhaustion and indifference was unlikely to last very long. It was always likely that the errors and excesses of returned émigrés would, in turn, make the exciting ideals of Liberty, Equality, and Fraternity more attractive again. But the interval, at least, belonged to the old order, and the prevailing mood favoured the forces of conservatism.

Only this mood can explain the relative ease with which the western conservative governments could get parliaments to adopt measures of repression which, before 1789, would have evoked violent protest. In 1817 the Tory government of Britain suspended the Habeas Corpus Act, bulwark of individual rights. In 1819 it passed Sidmouth's Six Acts, which were designed to prevent large public meetings, undermine the whole movement for radical reform, and kill or at least control the radical press. Although both measures aroused some vigorous protests in the country, they passed through Parliament without much difficulty. In France the Chamber of 1815, dominated by ultra-royalists in a mood for revenge, passed a series of acts giving the king power to suspend the liberties of the individual and the freedom of the press newly guaranteed in the Charter of his restoration. It authorized savage laws of proscription which sent many of the most eminent Frenchmen of the previous years into exile. In Austria, Metternich organized his famous 'system', designed to keep public order by a network of spies, secret police, and terrorists. It reached a climax of repression in the Carlsbad Decrees of 1819, which applied throughout Germany. In every country governments relied ominously on informers and *agents provocateurs*, on secret police and military repression. In lands like Naples and Sicily the poorest elements in the population could be mobilized against middle-class liberals; elsewhere the fears of propertied classes could be exploited to justify repression of popular disturbances. Such excessive repression, though resisted by shrewd monarchs like Louis XVIII of France and by moderate aristocrats like the Whigs in England, went far enough to ensure a violent resurgence of liberal and radical movements in the 1820s. It meant that the generation after Waterloo, which was in England to become known as an age of reform, would in Europe be an age of revolution.

But though the years between 1815 and 1854 were an era of revolutions, they were not an era of war. Indeed, by comparison with the hundred years after 1854, this period was remarkable for the absence of large-scale fighting in Europe. It was one of the longest interludes of peace known to modern Europe, and no period since has equalled it, either in length or in peacefulness. It was followed by a period equally remarkable for its wars. Between 1854 and 1878 there were no fewer than six important wars in which major powers took part. These were the Crimean War (1854–6), involving Britain, France, Russia, and Turkey; the War of 1859, involving France and Austria; the War waged by Prussia and Austria against Denmark (1864); the Austro-Prussian War of 1866; the Franco-Prussian War of 1870; and the Russo-Turkish War of 1877, which almost turned into a general European conflict.

The contrast between the forty years before 1854 and the twenty-four years after it is so striking that it prompts the suggestion that revolutions had served as a kind of substitute for war; or, more precisely, that one of the reasons for international peace after 1815 was the endemic civil war that produced the great outbreaks of insurrection in 1830 and 1848, as well as a host of intermediate revolts. National cohesion was not yet strong enough to override sectional interests and the conflicts of political principle: human energies were devoted more to seeking an overhaul of internal political and social systems than to pursuing the nationalist causes of war against foreign states. Governments, conscious of revolutionary threats at home, received no encouragement to engage in battle with other states. Peace was popular not only with governments aware of their own fragility, and not only because exhausted peoples welcomed a respite from war, but also because enemies at home seemed more immediate and more menacing than enemies abroad, and civil war absorbed belligerent spirits later to be diverted into the cause of militant nationalism.

CHAPTER 7

THE FORCES OF CHANGE

FOR the combination of reasons just described, the years after Waterloo were marked by the almost universal ascendancy of the forces of continuity, order, and resistance to change. Yet it was from the first certain that Europe had entered upon an era of rapid and fundamental change. The consequences of this change for the political and social systems of the continent were, of course, still indefinable. But even before 1789 there were detectable powerful currents, flowing like rivers that run beneath the surface of apparently calm oceans. They would have transformed life in Europe even had there been no French Revolution, no Napoleonic Empire, and no wars. These events lent such currents a new significance, and may even have in some ways diverted the direction of their flow – but they in no way created the currents.

GROWTH OF POPULATION

The most momentous and far-reaching of all these long-term forces of change was the new rate at which the population of Europe as a whole had begun to increase since about the middle of the eighteenth century. Between 1750 and 1950 the population grew at roughly the following rate:

Year	1750	1800	1850	1900	1950
Population (in millions)	140	180	266	401	540

It increased nearly fourfold in two centuries. The speed of this growth was a completely new phenomenon. During the twelve centuries before 1800, Europe's population had slowly climbed to 180 million; then within one century it more than doubled itself. No social and political order could have remained unaffected by so immense an increase of humanity; and the events of the nineteenth century remain unintelligible unless this greatest revolution of all is kept constantly in mind. It changed the course of world history, for between 1815 and 1914 some 40 million Europeans migrated to the other Continents. The United States, Canada, Austrialia, and many other parts of the globe were populated mainly from the overflow of Europe. In 1815 the whole population of Europe was only 200 million; by 1914 that number of people of European birth or stock existed outside Europe, while the population of Europe itself had risen to 460 million. The smallest of the continents had provided about one third of the human race, and European civilization was spread throughout the earth.

Many different reasons for this growth have been suggested, though their relative importance is impossible to fix. It was certainly due much more to a decrease in death rates than to an increase in birth rates. Populations grew not so much because more people were born as because more survived, and more stayed alive longer. The probable reasons for lower death rates include the improvements in public order and security which came with the stronger monarchies set up throughout most of Europe by the beginning of the eighteenth century; these ended civil and religious wars, destroyed some of the brigandage and violence that had marred human existence in earlier centuries, and did much to relieve famine, plague, and destitution. The reasons certainly include the striking advances in medical science which came in the eighteenth century. These freed western countries from the worst endemic diseases and plagues that had taken a constant and heavy toll of all populations down to the seventeenth century. Infant death rates fell, fewer mothers died in childbirth, and more people lived to a more advanced age. Diseases that had formerly struck cattle and crops began likewise to be conquered, so food supplies improved. Better transport, first by road and canal and later by railway and steamship, made it possible to end localized famine and shortages.

From 1800 onwards there took place an agricultural revolution that vastly increased food production, and so made possible the feeding of this increasing number of mouths. The even more striking increase of population in the United States in the same period raised no problems of food supply, because there was always an abundance of new land to bring under civilization. But in Europe, where all the best land available was already under cultivation, greater supplies of food could be obtained in only two ways: by more intensive cultivation or by importation. Europeans used both methods. By use of winter root crops such as turnips and beetroot, and of green crops such as clover and alfalfa, the old method of three-field rotation in which one third of the land was left fallow each year could be replaced by a four-course rotation. This utilized all the land each year and provided enough cattle food to keep larger stocks of cattle alive through the winter. The increased stock of cattle not only yielded more meat and milk for human consumption, but provided more manure to keep the land fertile. By use of cheaper means of transport during the nineteenth century, the great food reservoirs of the United States, Canada, and latterly Australasia were made available to feed Europe.

The growth of population varied, naturally enough, from one country to another, as did the readiness with which the new methods of farming were adopted. The pace was set in both by the United Kingdom (constituted in 1801 by the union of Ireland with Great Britain). Its population stood at about $18\frac{1}{4}$ million in 1811, and at more than double that figure in 1891. France, which in the previous century ranked as the largest European power, grew more slowly than her neighbours. She had a population of just over 29 million in 1806, and of $38\frac{1}{2}$ million in 1896. Germany, like the United Kingdom, doubled from nearly 25 million in 1815 to nearly 50 million in 1890; and Belgium from $3\frac{1}{4}$ million in 1831 to nearly $7\frac{1}{2}$ million by 1910. It was in these countries that the new methods of more efficient farming were adopted soonest and most readily.

Italy and Spain grew less rapidly, though in the end they too doubled in population between 1815 and the 1920s. The only European country that exceeded the British rate of growth was Russia, which roughly doubled in population during the first half of the nineteenth century, and doubled again during the second half; a fact that helps to explain not only her vast expansion eastward into Asiatic Russia during the century, but also her pressure on south-eastern Europe during most of the period. Part cause and part effect of the slowness of Russia to adopt more intensive agriculture was the possibility of expansion and settlement of new land in the forests and the steppes. This expansion much enhanced both the territories and the power of the Tsars, who were impelled to defend new frontiers against nomadic tribes and so to annex more and more territory.

If nineteenth-century Europe appears in history as unusually restless, explosive, and prone to revolution, this remarkable demographic fact is at least one explanation. Against this tide no social and political order could stand intact. No mere 'restoration' of old institutions and traditions could suffice to meet the needs of the new masses of humanity which so abruptly made their appearance on the old soil of Europe. Only constant inventiveness, reorganization, and experiment in new forms of social life could sustain civilization. In the sphere of economic production and distribution, this inventiveness and reorganization took the form of what is traditionally called the 'industrial revolution'; in the sphere of social life and organization, it took the form of urbanism and, eventually, suburbanism.

INDUSTRIALISM AND URBANISM

It is unnecessary to accept a materialistic or Marxist conception of history in order to hold that changes in how people make a living and in the environment in which they live are among the most important changes in human history. People who earn a wage by working regular weekly hours in a mine, business office, or factory and who live in crowded cities will have different needs, interests, and outlooks from people who till fields, tend flocks, and live in tiny isolated villages. It was the century between 1815 and 1914 which saw the transformation of one national community after another, throughout Europe, from a situation where the last of these conditions predominated to one where the former predominated. The ancient continent, where so much of its long past still survived in Roman law, Greek culture, Christian religion, feudal and monarchical institutions, had not only to provide quite suddenly a home and a livelihood for hundreds of millions more people; it had at the same time to suffer the adjustment of its traditions and its civilization to the new world of machinery and steam, of factories and towns. This immense process had begun in the United Kingdom and western Europe by 1815; it was soon to spread, with increasing impetus, eastward to Germany, Italy, and eventually Russia. It was a more intensive and fundamental process of transformation than had ever been known before. A European born in 1815, who lived to the age of eighty-five, lived through greater changes than had any of his ancestors – though perhaps not through greater changes than his descendants would experience. Not the least important facts about the acceleration of historical development that began around 1800 is that it still continues.

The basis of the industrial revolution was the application of steam power to machinery for purposes first of production and then of transport. Instead of making things by means of tools, set in motion by man's physical strength, it became more and more common to make things by machinery, set in motion by steam. Previously machinery had been worked mainly by animal power or by wind and water power. But animal power is not basically different or markedly greater than human strength, wind was cheap but unreliable, and water was very much limited by natural conditions. What made the use of machinery more generally possible was the invention of the steam engine. It suffered from none of these limitations. For decades stationary steam engines had been used for such purposes as pumping water out of mines. It was only when James Watt, in the later eighteenth century, greatly improved the mechanism of the steam engine and adapted the piston

115

to rotary motion that its immense possibilities became apparent. Before 1789 the firm of Boulton and Watt was busy making steam engines, some of them for export.

The needs of the steam engine created a new demand for iron to make it from and for coal to make the steam. Countries rich in these two commodities were thereafter best equipped to make industrial progress; this gave Britain a great natural advantage over France. At the same time the increasing use of expensive machinery for making cloth or metal goods necessitated the concentration of workers in larger units and factories. Hitherto, although a large proportion of the population was engaged in industry, the use of cheap tools had made possible the domestic system (where workers worked in their own homes) and the system of small workshops (where a few worked together using simple tools or machinery). Shuttles and spinning jennies could be used at home. Even extensive industrial activity, such as prevailed in Britain before 1800, had not brought extensive urbanization because it did not involve large factories and the concentration of workers.

But mechanized industry did involve urbanism, first in textile production, then in the heavy industries of coal, iron, and steel. For working the new machines, unskilled labour was mostly good enough. Not only did skilled workers find themselves lowered in status and in less demand, but women and children could often be employed, at wages lower than those of men, and this revolutionized the whole character of the labour market. In overcrowded homes in drab factory towns lived thousands of families, overworked and underpaid, creating a new social problem of immense proportions. Their employers, engaged in fierce competition with rival firms and uncontrolled by any effective legislation, forced conditions of work and wages down to the lowest possible level. Economic life took on a ruthlessness, a spirit of inhumanity and fatalism, that it had not known before.

It was, in general, this transformation of industrial life – which began in England in the later eighteenth century, continued throughout the wars, and resumed its course with renewed speed after Waterloo – that during the next century was to spread eastward into Europe. Its impact and repercussions varied according to the conditions and character of each country, and according to the precise time and stage at which it operated most fully in each country. When after 1830 steam power was extended from production to transportation, it caused yet further profound changes in economic life and in the balance of advantages between the different European states.[1] While this whole process was going on, each government was confronted, in quick succession, with

1. See p. 289.

a host of novel social problems. A great variety of new kinds of organization appeared, ranging from big capitalist enterprises to trade unions, from railway companies to municipal councils. The law and administration of every state had to accommodate themselves to dealing with such organizations. The restricted, paternal, or aristocratic traditions and institutions of monarchical government were seldom well suited to dealing with problems and conflicts of this kind. In one country after another revolutions were precipitated by the discontent of manufacturers and workers alike with the inadequacy of the existing régimes.

It is important, however, not to exaggerate either the earliness or the speed of these great changes. Even in Britain in 1815, only a relatively small proportion of all the industrial workers were engaged in large factories, and most Englishmen lived in little towns and villages. In France industrial units remained mostly comparatively small in size until the twentieth century, and only in this century have large parts of eastern Europe become industrialized. Big cities became common in Europe only after 1870. The whole process was prolonged, complex, and variable. It gained fresh impetus and new twists of direction from the use of steamships in the later half of the nineteenth century, and from the use of the internal combustion engine and electricity at the end of the century. The demands of wars deeply affected it in the twentieth century. But industrialization had begun in Britain to a significant extent by 1815; and it remained until the present day one of the greatest forces of fundamental change in social life, constantly creating new problems that only strong governments and efficient administrations, enjoying general popular support, could effectively solve. The growth of technology has continued to revolutionize European civilization in all its aspects.

The chief way in which industrialism affected government and politics was in its conferring new wealth and power upon the growing middle class of enterprising traders, manufacturers, and financiers, and in its creation of a new industrial proletariat. Just as the landowners were in general a bulwark of conservatism, so the middle classes were one of the prime movers of change. The 'captains of industry', the self-made millowners of Lancashire, the energetic, thrifty, and hardworking manufacturers of northern England, the Netherlands, and France, were still in 1815 a small minority. They were the new men, the first generation of a new class which would inevitably resent the old aristocratic idleness and contempt for earned incomes. They were increasingly taking their place alongside the older families of business and industry. The established financial groups – such as the Rothschilds, Barings, Laffittes, and Hopes – assumed a new pre-eminence in a world where capital and credit were in immense and profitable demand. Western Europe was fast becoming one commercial, industrial, and financial society as was made evident by the international repercussions of the financial panics of 1816–17, 1819, and 1825–26. Within this economic community, transcending the frontiers of politics, grew both interdependence and common impulses. Restrictions imposed on trade or manufacture by conservative governments in the interests of agriculture were resented and attacked. The new wealth demanded greater political representation and power, the removal of petty restrictions and out-of-date laws, social recognition for the men whose energies and enterprise brought employment to millions. The result was a tide of liberal opinion hostile to the existing order. It was the most potent force of change in mid-nineteenth century Europe.

Meanwhile industrialism also created the new wage-earning classes of the factories, mills, and mines. Their interests coincided, in some respects, with the interests of their employers. Both wanted food to be cheap, trade unimpeded, business to prosper. But confronted with the harsh conditions imposed upon them by the industrialists, with their own weak bargaining power in an overcrowded labour market, and with the bad living conditions of the new industrial towns, these wage-earning classes were soon to look to the state for protection of their interests also. When it became clear that governments would concern themselves with working-class interests only when compelled by political pressure, they, too, demanded votes and rights of free association. Thus the forces of conservatism were faced with a double demand: from the middle classes and from the working classes. Fearing the second more than the first, they often contrived to win middle-class support by timely concessions, so as to resist effectively the more far-reaching and radical demands of the workers. To the tide of liberal opinion was added a tide of democratic and eventually socialist opinion, both alike beating strongly against the entrenched positions of the forces of conservatism.

The total effect was to revolutionize the whole meaning and function of government and politics. Instead of being concerned only with general matters of public order and national security, government had to act at the deepest levels of social and economic life. What modern Europe was groping for was a completely new kind of state, a state in close mutual relationship and constant interplay with the community. The old dynastic conception of ruler and subjects had to be totally replaced by the conception of a state and its citizens. This notion of government and society as mutually interdependent and enmeshed, with a state emanating from the community it governs and the community demanding the constant service of its state, was the most revolutionary notion of modern history. It was utterly incompatible with the old order, and with the sharp dynastic distinctions between ruler and subjects. It was the common basis of all the greatest movements of nineteenth-century Europe: on the one hand nationalism, and on the other, liberalism, democracy, and socialism.

NATIONALISM

A nation may be described as a community of people whose sense of belonging together derives from their belief that they have a common homeland and from experience of common traditions and historical development. In this broad sense nations had certainly existed many centuries before 1815. A lively sense of nationality existed in England of the Tudors in the sixteenth century, and France under her strong central monarchy developed a similar sense of community feeling. But European nationalism in its modern sense, of the desire of such a community to assert its unity and independence vis-à-vis other communities or groups, is mainly a product of the nineteenth century. It was first launched upon its course of triumphant development throughout Europe by the French Revolution and the Napoleonic Empire.

The Jacobin doctrine of the 'sovereignty of the people' was doubleedged. It asserted, on one hand, the claims of the nation as a whole against its monarch, and the right of a people to determine its own form of government and to control the conduct of that government. It implied, on the other hand, the democratic doctrine that government should be the voice of 'the people' and not merely of 'a people'; that is, in conjunction with the revolutionary ideals of Liberty, Equality, Fraternity, it proclaimed the rights of all citizens, regardless of wealth or status, to have an equal voice in the decisions of politics. Whereas the excesses of Jacobin rule during the Reign of Terror (1793–94) discredited the democratic ideas of the Revolution, the conquests of Napoleon in Europe strengthened the ideas and sentiments of nationalism. So by 1815 nationalism was a much livelier force in Europe than was democracy.

The countries where nationalist feelings were most vigorously stirred were Germany and Italy, though Napoleonic imperialism had similar effects in Spain, Poland, Russia, and Belgium. At first nationalism was a spirit of resistance to the exactions and heavy-fisted domination of foreigners, and it was therefore anti-French. New value was attached to local institutions, native customs, traditional culture, and national language. French rationalism and 'enlightenment' were cosmopolitan, universalist, antinationalist in flavour. In reaction against them the new nationalism was romantic, particularist, exclusive in character.

It happened that Germany at the time was enjoying a great cultural renaissance, and could justly claim pre-eminence for her musicians, men of letters, and philosophers. It was the age of Beethoven, Goethe, Schiller, Kant, and Hegel. This enabled Germany in the nineteenth century to oust France from the cultural predominance and intellectual leadership that she had enjoyed in the eighteenth. The philosophers Herder and Fichte taught Germans to cherish and reverence the *Volksgeist*, or peculiar national character, which they presented as the foundation of all good culture and civilization. Prussia, after her defeat by Napoleon at Jena in 1806, which almost extinguished her as a power, drastically reorganized her army under the guidance of Gneisenau and Scharnhorst. Her machinery of government was overhauled by Stein and Hardenberg. After 1815 she emerged as the chief focus of German nationalist hopes, in contrast with Austria, whose ascendancy in the new Confederation was used to keep Germany politically disunited. The chief intellectual support for the regeneration of Prussia and the growth of nationalism in Germany came from the new University of Berlin, in the city that Napoleon had occupied after his victory at Jena. There G. W. F. Hegel was to expound a new philosophy of authority and state power which captivated many German, Italian, and even English thinkers during the nineteenth century.

Much of the reorganization of the Prussian state, which was guided by the dual motive of military recovery and internal efficiency, was but an imitation of French revolutionary reforms. As Hardenberg wrote to the Prussian king in 1807, 'We must do from above what the French have done from below.' He especially envied the success of Carnot's *levée en masse*, the conscription of the whole of French manhood and its inspiration with a sense of national mission. The reformers of Prussia, impressed by French successes, were particularly struck by 'what endless forces not developed and not utilized slumber in the bosom of a nation'. They valued most the creative and irresistible energy that could be generated by a people in arms. They set about building a strong central authority, a truly national army, and a system of national education designed to infuse a common spirit into the whole people, a patriotic reverence for the German heritage and a devotion to the cause of German nationalism.

Meanwhile Napoleon had been unwittingly paving the way for greater unification in Germany by his destruction in 1806 of the Holy Roman Empire; by his assembling Bavaria, Württemberg, Baden, Hesse-Darmstadt, Saxony, and twelve other smaller states into the Confederation of the Rhine; and by his introduction into all western Germany of the *Code napoléon*, to replace the tangle of antiquated laws and judicial procedures. In every aspect German nationalism began as a strange mixture of benefits derived from adopting French methods or institutions, and resentful reactions against French thought, domination, and victories.

At a more popular level German nationalism was further aroused by the Prussian victory at Leipzig in 1813. It was interpreted as the fruit and the justification of all that nationalists had been preaching and reformers doing to regenerate Prussia. It became a patriotic legend. The battle forced Napoleon out of most of Germany, and even freed the left bank of the Rhine. It was in fact an allied victory, and it was made possible in part by Napoleon's disastrous campaign in Russia the year before. But it consoled German national pride, heartened German patriots, and gave a new fillip to ideas of total liberation.

The nationalistic spirit aroused by Napoleon in Italy offers certain contrasts with the effects in Germany. In Italy his régime was longer and more continuous, for it lasted from 1796 until 1814. It was also more acceptable. Italian sentiment was less anti-French than was German or Spanish. Middle classes in the towns welcomed the greater efficiency and the weakening of clericalist influence which came with the demolition of the power of petty princes and of the Pope himself. As in Germany, Napoleon's reduction in the number of states to three encouraged ideas of ultimate unification. Murat, while ruler of Naples, conceived the idea of uniting the whole of Italy in his own hands, and in 1815 he proclaimed the Union of Italy. He was soon defeated and shot, but this dramatic gesture was not forgotten by Italian patriots.

In Germany and Italy, and in Germany more than in Italy, the effect of French rule was to stimulate directly a new and more pervasive spirit of nationalist pride and hope. It was significantly the unification of these two countries which loomed largest in general European affairs between 1850 and 1870. In other countries the effects of French rule were less clear-cut and more indirect.

'The Spanish ulcer destroyed me,' Napoleon later complained. At the Battle of Baylen in July 1808, two French divisions capitulated to Spanish forces, and Spanish guerrilla bands played an important part in French defeats in the Peninsular War. Such achievements were later glorified as expressions of Spanish national spirit. In fact the forces in Spain most actively hostile to Napoleon were the royalist and clerical elements in the country. The insurrectionary Juntas, which organized local resistance, were mostly run by nobles and priests, who were enraged by Napoleon's treatment of the monarchy and by the French efforts to secularize Church property. Popular resistance was led by the lower clergy and the monks, and was not at all typical of nationalist uprisings. Without the military genius of Wellington and the efficiency of the British infantry, the Spanish guerrillas would soon have collapsed before the Grand Army. The strongest stimulus to a real nationalist spirit was the savagery of the fighting in the Peninsular War, immortalized in the pictures of Goya. But Spain had no large or important liberal middle class, which was the characteristic basis for nineteenth-century movements of national unity and independence.

Poland was the centre of aggrieved nationalism in eastern Europe. Between 1772 and 1795 the former Polish state had been obliterated from the map and partitioned among the empires of Russia, Prussia, and Austria. When Napoleon, in 1807, set up the Grand Duchy of Warsaw with a new constitution, it was welcomed by Poles as a step towards restoration and independence. But he kept it subservient to himself, and it soon became clear that he was interested in it only as a pawn in his relations with Russia. When he began his Russian campaign in 1812, he gave the Poles only vague promises of future independence. The victory of the eastern empires in 1814 again obliterated Poland as a state. But the *Code napoléon*, with the ideas of the French Revolution embedded in it, had been introduced into the territory; and even bitter disappointment only added fuel to the burning resolve of Polish patriots to regain national unity and independence. That resolve persisted for another century, until it achieved its aim in another peace settlement in 1919 (*see* Map 14).

The impact on Russian national feeling was even more diffuse and remote. The heroic resistance that led to the burning of Smolensk and Moscow and the epic retreat of the Grand Army through the snows had all the makings of a supreme national legend. The pillaging and devastations of the French troops consolidated the resistance of all classes in Russia as nothing else could have done. The Tsar dared not think of negotiating, so thoroughly roused was the hatred of Napoleon among nobles and peasants alike. The virtual destruction of the Grand Army was the most devastating blow Napoleon ever suffered. Just as Germany made a patriotic legend out of the Battle of Leipzig, so could Russian patriots from the Moscow campaign. But so backward was national feeling in Russia, so divorced from popular life was the régime, that these events had little immediate effect on nationalism.

In all his relations with Europe, Napoleon probably had little coherent policy, beyond a desire to make conquered countries satellites of France and adjuncts to his own dynastic ambitions. He certainly followed no consistent policy of arousing nationalities against their governments, doing so only as expediency dictated. He worked out no principles for organizing his empire, beyond the general introduction of the French legal codes and administrative system. How he organized it in fact varied according to the military needs of the moment and the requirements of his Continental System, and as he was never at peace for long, the pressure of these necessities was constant and decisive. Likewise the results of his conquests varied according to the conditions of each country; and to the existing diversities of European states he added not uniformity, but merely further complexity. During the interlude of the Hundred Days he posed as having liberal and constitutional aims, and it was part of the Bonapartist legend concocted on St Helena that he had had the interests of national independence at heart. His greatest contributions to the growth of nationalism were, in fact, unwitting. They were – as in Germany and Italy – more the outcome of revolt against his empire than the deliberate intention of it. The most important result of this was that the first half of the century saw an alliance, which now seemed natural, between nationalism and liberalism.

LIBERALISM, DEMOCRACY, SOCIALISM

Liberalism, in its continental European sense more clearly than in its English or American sense, was like nationalism in that it rested on the belief that there should be a more organic and complete relationship between government and the community, between state and society, than existed under the dynastic régimes of the eighteenth century. Instead of government and administration existing above and in many respects apart from society – the exclusive affair of kings and their ministers and officials – they should rest on the organized consent of at least the most important sections of the community, and they ought to concern themselves with the interests of the whole community. The ideas that Americans had asserted in 1776 had still not been accepted by European governments: ideas that 'governments are instituted among men' to secure individual rights, and derive 'their just powers from the consent of the governed'. European liberals stood, fundamentally, for these American ideals. The biggest obstacles to a broader basis of government were the powers and privileges of the aristocracy and the Church, and the lack of privileges of the merchant, business, and manufacturing classes. Thus the spearhead of the liberal attack against feudal rights and clericalist power was, in each European country, the underprivileged middle and professional classes. It was these classes, backed in the course of events by the peasants and by the Paris mob, that had been the central driving force of the French Revolution, and the chief gainers from it.

In doctrine, therefore, continental liberalism derived from the rationalist movement of the eighteenth century which had made so corrosive an attack upon inequality and arbitrary power. Its most characteristic method was parliamentary government; it sought in constitutional arrangements and in the rule of law a means of expressing middle-class interests and opinion, a vehicle of social reform, and a safeguard against absolutist government. It was distinct from democracy, or radicalism, in that it favoured ideas of the sovereignty of parliamentary assemblies rather than of the sovereignty of the people; it wanted an extension of the franchise to include all men of property but to exclude men without property; it valued liberty more highly than equality; and it appealed to broadly the same classes as the growing sense of nationalism. To liberals, the French Revolution had condemned itself by its excesses: the Reign of Terror and mob democracy had bred the era of reaction and led to military dictatorship. The most desirable régime was either a constitutional monarchy, guaranteeing certain rights equally to all citizens, or a parliamentary republic, resting on a restricted franchise but upholding the equality of all before the law. Their objections to the settlement of 1815 were less that it violated nationality than that it restored absolutism and threatened to restore aristocratic and clerical privileges.

Democracy resembled liberalism in that it derived its ideals from eighteenth-century rationalism and was equally opposed to the inequalities of the old order. It differed from it in holding to the view that sovereignty lay not in constitutional systems or in representative parliamentary assemblies, but in the 'general will' of the whole people, as Rousseau had taught. It favoured universal male suffrage, the subordination of parliamentary bodies to the will of the electorate as a whole, and even devices of direct democracy such as the plebiscite or the referendum. It was devoted to the ideal of equality of political and civil rights. In its more extreme forms it even demanded greater social and economic equality. Like liberals, democrats demanded equality of all before the law and equality of opportunity for all; but unlike liberals, they wanted to secure these rights even at the cost of greater economic levelling. For this reason, in the first half of the century democracy was treated as a more revolutionary and frightening doctrine than liberalism. The fear of Jacobinism, which haunted the conservative governments of Europe between 1815 and 1848, was partly the fear of the resurgence of French power; it was even more the fear of radical democracy. To resist this menace, liberals were often ready to join with conservatives to crush popular movements and uprisings that favoured democratic ideals. The nearest twentieth-century counterpart to this fear was the universal fear of bolshevism after 1917 : a fear irrational enough to produce strange alliances of otherwise incompatible and hostile forces, yet well enough founded to create a series of violent revolutions and savage repressions. Democracy, even more than liberalism, was a central cause of change and revolution in the century after Waterloo.

Until after 1848 and the rise of Marxism, the word 'socialism' had a somewhat less frightening sound to established authorities than the word 'democracy'. In its early, vaguer, Utopian, and humanitarian stages, socialism was connected in men's minds either with relatively harmless if picturesque cranks, or with the multitude of pietist Christian communities which fled to the United States in order to lead a simple community life, free from the complexities of the old order in Europe and from the strife of industrialism and national war. Until after 1850 or so, socialism and communism (at first hardly distinguishable as political ideas) found their natural home not in Europe but in the United States, where abundance of land and free immigration offered a new mode of life to all who wanted to escape from the restored monarchies of Europe. Such experiments as Robert Owen's New Harmony in Indiana or Étienne Cabet's Icarian Community in Illinois were the dream worlds of early socialism. Based on a system of complete human equality and self-government, they expressed exactly what socialism and communism, before Marx, would have liked to create in Europe. Their migration to the New World was a tacit admission of growing despair that such an order could ever be built in the old world.

Socialist ideas, too, derived from the doctrines of Rousseau and from the ideals of the French Revolution. Just as liberals placed greatest emphasis on the ideal of liberty, and democrats on the ideal of equality, so socialists cherished particularly the ideal of fraternity. Men are by nature good, and without the artificial distortions of social inequality and poverty they would naturally behave to one another as brothers. Cooperation rather than competition would be their instinctive desire. Press the ideals of liberty and equality far enough – even to the point of establishing complete freedom of self-expression and complete equality of opportunity and of wealth – and the reign of fraternity would begin. Often protesting against industrialism as a new cause of poverty and inequality, early socialist movements could never find roots or room in Europe. It was only when socialist theory had been transformed at the hands of state socialists like Louis Blanc and of more scientific economic theorists like Karl Marx that it could accommodate itself to the necessities of life in the increasingly industrialized nations of Europe.

There was enough common ground among liberals, democrats, and socialists for them to join forces on the barricades at great revolutionary moments, such as in 1848 and 1871. Not only were all travelling for at least a certain distance along the same road and finding themselves obstructed by the same forces of conservatism, but all had the common desire to make government, in varying degrees, an organ and agency of society. The socialists, from Louis Blanc to Lenin, found themselves constantly confronted with the problem of how they could cooperate with liberals and democrats, and at what point in the common journey they might suddenly find the liberals and democrats changing front and fighting on the other side of the barricades. Similarly, none of the three could depend upon a reliable alliance with the forces of nationalism. Until 1848 liberals and nationalists seemed to be in natural harmony and alliance. To make a constitutional system work satisfactorily, liberals felt that they needed the natural cohesion in community life which came from nationality. To achieve national unity and independence, patriots felt that they needed the support of all classes which liberalism or democracy could enlist. The fiasco of the liberal-nationalist alliance in 1848 led to a drastic realignment of forces.[1]

Likewise socialism, cosmopolitan and internationalist in its early phases mainly because of its affinities with liberalism and democracy, came by the end of the century to seek closer alliance with authoritarian nationalist governments and undemocratic régimes. The German socialist leader, Ferdinand Lassalle, was prepared to come to terms with Bismarck; socialists in all countries supported their national governments at the outbreak of war in 1914; and bolshevism in Russia created a new combination of nationalism and communism within a single-party dictatorship, under the guise of 'socialism in a single country'. Combinations and permutations of movements of this kind are one of the most significant themes of modern European history, and indeed of world history. They will be one of the recurrent themes of this book.

1. See p. 232.

PART THREE

THE AGE OF REVOLUTIONS
1815–50

THE generation between 1815 and 1849, as already suggested, was a time of endemic civil war. The forces of conservatism triumphed with the restoration of the old order in 1815 and then proceeded to entrench themselves in power in most of the states of Europe. Their strength is measured by the tenacity and the partial success with which they held the forces of change at bay for another whole generation. But their greatest strength lay at the level of political power; and political power alone became less and less sufficient to resist the most powerful forces of change. These were basically the rapid increase in population and the growth of industrialism, but they soon assumed political shape in the movements of nationalism and liberalism. The kind of social and economic order for which the institutions of dynastic monarchy and privileged aristocracy were peculiarly fitted was a more static order, based on landed property and agriculture, on religious faith and political inactivity. The kind of social and economic order which was coming into existence, first in western Europe and later in central and eastern Europe, was based on commercial and industrial wealth, on faith in science and seething popular energy. The old bottles could not indefinitely hold the new wine.

By 1848 it became obvious that the forces of conservatism were fighting a rear-guard action and a losing battle. New forms of government, better adapted to the needs of the new society, were set up. New political and social ideals, springing from the inherent nature of an industrial capitalist economy, fermented first in men's minds and then in movements of political and social revolt. Revolutions happened mainly because the spreading roots of a new system for producing wealth first cracked the hard foundations of the old order. The policies of governments were left behind by the quick advance of the human societies they purported to rule.

CHAPTER 8

THE PHASE OF CONSERVATISM, 1815–30

THE SYSTEM OF METTERNICH

MOST fully characteristic of both the ideals and the arrangements of conservative government was the Austrian Empire of the Habsburgs. It lacked a strong middle class of merchants, businessmen, and manufacturers. A landed aristocracy was the predominant class, and the bulk of the population were peasants. The Austrian provinces themselves, as well as the more peripheral parts of the empire inhabited by Hungarians, Czechs, Slovaks, Croats, Rumanians, and Poles, usually had provincial diets or 'estates' on the medieval model, but these met rarely and irregularly and had no real power. So far as government and administration were carried on at all, it was by local nobles and by the police, army, and bureaucracy controlled from Vienna. Since the central administration was itself only loosely co-ordinated and slackly directed, the hand of government was light in every respect save in its systematic suppression of any forces which might send the whole intricate structure tumbling to the ground.

After 1815 these forces were pre-eminently those of liberalism and nationalism. They were most active in the universities, among a few army officers, in the small commercial middle classes, and above all on the periphery of the territories ultimately controlled by Austria. After the settlement of Vienna these included the Italian areas of Lombardy and Venetia, and most of the German Confederation over which Austria presided. Both the internal condition and the general European situation of Austria destined her government to be the avowed enemy of liberalism and nationalism throughout Europe. In Germany, Italy, and Poland especially, she stood as the major obstruction to movements of change. And these were the three countries where, as shown above, nationalist feeling had been especially stimulated.

The Austrian Chancellor, Prince Metternich, devised his famous 'system' as the master plan for the preservation of Habsburg dominion. His system was no attempt to bring the motley territories of Austria into greater unity. That was accepted as being impossible. It rested, rather, on the exploitation of their disunity, on the time-honoured Habsburg principle of 'divide and rule'. It meant stationing German regiments in Bohemia, and Hungarian troops in Lombardy. It meant

130

keeping the German Confederation (*Bund*) a loose Organization of princes such as Austria could dominate.

When the Diet of the Bund first met at Frankfurt in 1816, it was clear from the outset that here was no fulfilment of German nationalist hopes, but rather the deliberate frustration of them. In September 1819 this body, at Metternich's instigation, ratified the Carlsbad Decrees. These decrees attacked particularly the patriotic student societies (*Burschenschaften*) that had appeared at most German universities after 1815, dissolving them and setting up inspectors for each university. They also enforced a more rigid and general censorship of the press. The following year Metternich persuaded all the German states to limit the subjects that might be discussed in parliamentary assemblies and to recognize the right of the federal authority to intervene in even the more liberal states of the Bund. In the southern states, Bavaria, Württemberg, Baden, Hesse-Darmstadt, and Saxe-Weimar, the rulers had recently set up new constitutions (*see* Map 6). In the most liberal of these the vote was narrowly limited, as in France, to men of wealth, and elected assemblies enjoyed slender control over the governments. But even this degree of liberalism was highly suspect to Metternich.

In 1817, through his agent Prince Wittgenstein, he succeeded in frightening King Frederick William III out of granting a similar constitution to Prussia, and so delayed the moment when Prussia might replace Austria in the leadership of Germany. It is anyhow doubtful whether a more constitutional and less bureaucratic régime could have governed the diverse and sprawling lands incorporated into the Prussian kingdom after 1815. In return for the loss of some Polish territory, Prussia gained at Vienna large slices of Saxony, Westphalia, and the Rhineland provinces. The latter, Catholic in religion and geographically detached from the rest of Prussia, presented very special problems of administration. They were traditionally linked more with the West than with the East, and had enjoyed the benefits of French law and government. In outlook, traditions, and interests they were particularly difficult for Prussia to assimilate, and they resented the new authority exercised over them from Berlin. The kingdom as a whole had more than doubled its population by the addition of $5\frac{1}{2}$ million subjects in the new territories. The Prussian government found its power enhanced, both by the excuses for greater centralization provided by these changes and by its sheer size in relation to other German states. But for some years to come it was kept preoccupied with the tasks of administration and reorganization involved, and throughout the Bund as a whole Austrian influence was left predominant.

Italy had not even the loose federal structure of the German Bund, and there Metternich made his influence felt partly through the Habsburg princes restored to power in 1815, partly through the ubiquitous secret police. It was resented more in Italy than in the German states, because Italy had fared better under Napoleon. She had enjoyed a longer period of national cohesion, and had a more considerable middle class, at least in the northern provinces most directly subjected to Vienna. Habsburg methods proved particularly irritating in Lombardy and Venetia. To install Germans and Slavs in all the most important administrative posts and to refuse any real local autonomy were, in Italian eyes, unforgivable errors. Napoleon had taught the merits of a 'career open to talents'; now Metternich closed all such doors.

His influence in the smaller Italian states is well illustrated by the example of the little duchy of Parma. There ruled Marie Louise, the Habsburg princess who had married Napoleon for her country's good. She had neither hated nor loved him, and her chief emotion when news of Waterloo arrived was one of delight that the messenger admired the beauty of her ankles. Already the Austrian government had taken the precaution of giving her as a lover, a dashing but one-eyed cavalry officer, and through him it now controlled her duchy of Parma. In the south, in Naples and Sicily, ruled the Bourbon Ferdinand I, intent upon keeping his autocratic powers discreetly masked behind a façade of benevolence. Everywhere there was censorship, popular ignorance, illiteracy, and economic squalor. The strength of Metternich's system in Italy lay in the divisions so carefully maintained in the peninsula. They gave great natural safeguards against any concerted nationalist movement of independence. There was no forceful Italian leadership, for the king of Piedmont and Sardinia, the most likely candidate for that role, was even more intent on eliminating French influences than on resisting Austrian.

Yet Metternich's control over Italy was never as complete as over Germany. When he tried to form a confederation of Italian states corresponding, both in form and purpose, to the German Bund, Piedmont and the Pope successfully resisted this attempt to make them more dependent on Austria. They equally held out against his efforts to entice them into making separate treaties with Austria. Victor Emmanuel, the king of Piedmont and Sardinia, even tried to form a league of small states to oppose Austrian power in Italy. It was to include Piedmont, the Papal States, Bavaria, and Naples, but this too came to nothing because Naples and the Papacy refused to join. For these reasons Italy was the Achilles' heel in the system of Metternich, and it was to impose some of the earliest and most severe strains on his ingenuity.

In all his negotiations and arrangements the Austrian chancellor usually included a request that looked innocent but was a crucial part of his system. He proposed postal conventions that would enable foreign correspondence to pass through Austria. In Vienna he set up a special office for opening, decoding, and resealing all correspondence that came through the post. Everything of interest was copied and passed on to the Chancellery. This gave Metternich an astonishing amount of information about all foreign governments, and it was supplemented by constant reports from his army of spies and secret agents, as well as from the police. To know in intimate detail what was going on everywhere became something of an obsession with him. He occasionally shocked foreign ambassadors by careless revelations of how much he knew, and pride in his own omniscience was one of his greatest weaknesses. But it was often well founded.

The lasting tension bequeathed to the empires of Austria, Russia, and Prussia by their partitioning of Poland at the end of the eighteenth century had made it necessary to shelve the eastern question at Vienna in 1815. No agreement among them could have been reached had that explosive issue been handled. Austria held the large Polish province of Galicia. It resembled Italy in being the only other Austrian province to have a strong native nobility. The Polish landed nobility did not owe their position to the Habsburgs, and never forgot that they were Poles. Polish nationalism – the desire to reunite the territories torn apart in the partitions – was stimulated when the Tsar Alexander I in 1815 created a small and sadly truncated 'Kingdom of Poland'. Though this area was entirely within Russian territory, and enjoyed little effective autonomy under tsarist overlordship, it served as a constant reminder of future possibilities. Metternich, inevitably, disapproved strongly of even this much concession to Polish memories and aspirations.

The Polish revolt of 1830 was one of the most serious of that year of revolutions. It was a revolt of the Polish nobles and intellectuals of Galicia which, in 1846, was to give the first warning of the more general European revolutions of 1848. The revolt of 1846 was checked by the characteristic Austrian method: the peasants of the area were incited to rise against their landowners, and the revolt was converted into a *jacquerie* of Polish peasants against Polish landlords, which could then be easily and ruthlessly suppressed. But during the peasant revolt the Austrian authorities had to abolish the hated *Robot*, or labour rent, the last legal tie that held the peasant to the soil. It was generally abolished in 1848. In this way, Habsburg methods of holding the territories in subjection carried within themselves the seeds of their own destruction.

To sustain Habsburg domination by so intricate and subtle a balance between rival nationalties in the Austrian empire was an exacting and strenuous task of statecraft. It called for constant vigilance and remorseless determination. Both of these qualities Metternich had. But it was not only the needs of Austria which made him the master of the conservative forces in Europe. He had a vision that stretched beyond the boundaries of Austria. Metternich was by birth a west German – a Rhinelander – and he understood the interests of stability in Germany as a whole. He also had a philosophy of conservatism, a theory of how balance might best be kept in Europe as a continent. The contention of Metternich was that internal and international affairs were inseparable : that what happens inside one state is of some concern to other states, and entitles other states to take notice of, and even concerted action against, certain internal developments. Alexander stated this same doctrine in its most extreme form. He wanted a standing alliance of rulers to crush revolution anywhere. Metternich resisted this extreme version of his own doctrine, because he was also concerned for the over-all balance of power in Europe. But both wanted governmental action to extend horizontally and not merely vertically. Nationalists and liberals were alike opposed to this doctrine; and asserted instead the contrary doctrine that a government should be in specially close and mutual relationship with the people whom it governed. They wanted governmental action to be completely vertical, in the double sense that a government should rest upon national solidarity and unity, and should also express the wishes and serve the interests of the nation as a whole. They opposed its being horizontal because this violated the ideal of national independence and self-determination, and because it sacrificed a people's wishes and interests to those of foreign governments. Here were two totally contrasted conceptions of European order and policy. Between 1815 and 1848 they were fought out between Metternich and the revolutionaries of Europe, and there could be no compromise.

Viewing the international scene in Europe after Waterloo, Metternich reached the conclusion that the restored monarchs must hang together if they were not to hang separately. There must be some machinery for concerted action. France, the traditional enemy of Habsburg power in Europe, had just been defeated. Safeguards against an early revival of French power had been erected at Vienna. But disputes which he knew French diplomacy would certainly exploit – disputes between Austria and her eastern neighbours, Russia and Turkey; disputes between Austria and her rivals in Germany and Italy, Prussia and Piedmont – would surely arise. So these must be settled as promptly and as smoothly as he could contrive. The means of settling them should be a 'concert of Europe' of the kind that had defeated Napoleon, and which must somehow be kept in existence after the immediate threat of Napoleon had been dispersed. Periodic congresses, at which the governments of the major powers could agree to a settlement of all disputes that might endanger the settlement and the peace of Europe, were the device that he, more than anyone else, invented. Four such congresses, shadows of the great Congress of Vienna, met – at Aix-la-Chapelle in 1818, at Troppau in 1820, at Laibach in 1821, and at Verona in 1822. The 'congress system' reveals both the aims and methods of the forces of conservatism, and the increasing tensions that opened the doors to liberal and nationalist revolts.

CONGRESS DIPLOMACY

Aix-la-Chapelle, 1818. The first of the series, the Congress held at Aix-la-Chapelle in 1818, was concerned primarily with the full reinstatement of France. Since 1815 an ambassadorial conference in Paris, under the Duke of Wellington, had watched over France. It supervised the forces of occupation and arranged for the collection of the indemnity. By 1818 this work was completed and representatives of the major powers met to agree upon their future relations with France. They invited France to join a Quintuple Alliance to preserve the peace, but at the same time secretly renewed the old Quadruple Alliance as a safeguard against her. The Tsar Alexander seized the opportunity to put forward some of his favourite idealistic projects – a scheme for disarmament, the formation of an international army, a general union to protect existing governments against revolution. Lord Castlereagh for Britain and Metternich for Austria opposed these schemes and conspired to block them. They placated Alexander by adopting a general slogan of 'moral solidarity', and secured the substantial gain of readmitting France to a status of diplomatic equality with the other great powers of Europe. The indemnity was paid; the troops of occupation were withdrawn. The only other result of the Congress was to emphasize the continued contrast between the 'balance of power' policies of Metternich and Britain, and the 'Holy Alliance' policies of concerted intervention favoured by Russia. The Tsar's attempt to organize collective help for the Spanish king against the South American colonies met with no support. It was Lord Castlereagh who induced the Congress to refuse such help; and he was eventually joined by Metternich, who preferred subtler intervention to so defiant and sensational a way of supporting absolutism.

Troppau and Laibach, 1820–21. The same divergence of policies was the occasion for the Congress of Troppau in 1820 and its continuation at Laibach the following year, and again it was Spain that provided the bone of contention. A successful military revolution in Madrid forced the king of Spain to revive the very democratic Constitution of 1812. The Tsar Alexander took fright at the news. He circularized the monarchs of Europe calling for a congress to crush this constitution, if need be by armed intervention. This evoked a rejoinder from Lord Castlereagh, in his famous State Paper of May 5 1820, which became the basis for future British foreign policy. He insisted that the Spanish revolution was entirely an internal concern of Spain, and to set up a system for automatic and collective intervention by other states in the internal affairs of any country undergoing revolutionary change was 'impracticable and objectionable'. He appealed to the governments concerned to keep the alliance 'within its common-sense limits'. Metternich, too, was at first opposed to summoning a congress for such purposes, but he agreed to one when revolutions broke out in Portugal, Piedmont, and Naples, each demanding likewise the Constitution of 1812. Britain and France agreed only to send observers to the congress.

At Troppau Alexander persuaded the rulers of Austria and Prussia to join with him in threatening to make war on revolutions in the interests of kings. They jointly announced that they could never agree to recognizing the right of a people to restrict the power of its king. Despite further protests from Britain, Metternich undertook to suppress the constitutions of Piedmont and Naples. In March 1821, the Austrian armies moved into these states and restored the power of their kings. Until September 1822 an Austrian army 12,000 strong remained in Piedmont. Rebels were hunted down in the neighbouring states, and thousands of patriots and liberals escaped abroad.

In Portugal a revolutionary situation had arisen because of the long absence of the royal family in Brazil. From 1809 to 1820 Portugal was in effect governed by the British soldier, Marshal Beresford, whose rule was resented by the upper and middle classes on both nationalist and liberal grounds. Encouraged by the Spanish revolution, the Portuguese army led a revolt in Oporto, which quickly spread to other towns. A provisional government was set up, demanding the return of the monarch from Brazil. A national assembly drafted a new constitution on the Spanish model. The aims of the movement are shown clearly enough by the new constitution. It established a single-chamber parliament, abolished feudalism, and guaranteed freedom of the press and the equality of all citizens. The new liberal government suppressed the Inquisition and some religious orders, and confiscated some of the Church lands. In October 1822, King John VI swore allegiance to the new constitution, which he was soon to abrogate – in 1826 and 1827 even

Britain was obliged to interfere in Portugal to preserve the forms of constitutional government. Meanwhile his eldest son, Dom Pedro, whom he had left as regent of Brazil, proclaimed its independence from Portugal and accepted the title of Emperor. By 1825 Portugal was compelled to recognize the loss of Brazil. Combined with the successful breakaway of the Spanish South American colonies, this severed the direct dynastic and governmental links between Europe and the whole of Latin America, save for the Spanish territories in Cuba and Puerto Rico, and the small British, Dutch, and French possessions in Guiana.

Verona, 1822. The Congress of Verona in 1822 was occasioned by revolution in yet another part of Europe. In March 1821 the Greeks revolted against the Turks. It was a national movement of Christian Greeks against the tyranny of Moslem Turkey. The immediate danger, from the point of view of Metternich, Castlereagh, and all who wanted to keep the peace in Europe, was that the Tsar Alexander would go to war with Turkey in support of the Christian Greeks. To Metternich the interests of monarchy and of the balance of power took precedence over all such religious affinities. He accordingly pressed for one more congress, to meet in the autumn of 1822. But during the summer disturbances in Spain continued and France showed signs of interfering there; and when the Congress met at Verona it had to give even more attention to the affairs of Spain than to those of Greece. By then Castlereagh had committed suicide and was succeeded by George Canning, whose hostility to congresses and projects of armed intervention in other states was even more vehement than Castlereagh's. His firm resistance to intervention prevented any joint action in Spain, although France in 1823 separately invaded Spain, abolished the constitution, and restored King Ferdinand. The danger of Russian intervention in Greece was avoided by Britain's extracting a promise from the Turkish government that it would institute reforms, and for a time the Greek revolt continued without any interference. Verona marked the completion of the breach between Britain and her partners in the Quadruple and Quintuple Alliances. Canning had less knowledge than Castlereagh of European affairs. He was a more impetuous and intransigent man, and felt stronger sympathies with liberal movements abroad. On October 30 1822, when the Duke of Wellington communicated to the Congress Canning's firm refusal to intervene in Spain, it was received as a bombshell. It meant the end of the alliance so far as the western powers were concerned. 'Things are getting back to a wholesome state again,' remarked Canning, 'every nation for itself and God for us all.'

By 1823 the outcome of the Congress system was the disintegration of the diplomatic alliances made in 1814 and the hardening of the positions of both the forces of conservatism and the forces of change. On one hand, the successful suppression of movements of revolt in Italy and Spain left Austria stronger than ever in Europe, and with her triumphed the cause of absolutist monarchies. On the other hand, the old order had been more successfully challenged in Portugal and Greece, and Britain had come out openly as the champion of movements for national independence and constitutional government. These revolts were not, it must be noted, in any sense connected with the growth of population or of industrialism. They were characteristically nationalist revolutions, protests against foreign influences and interference and against the excesses of absolutist and clericalist government. They were strongly tinged with liberalism and constitutionalism, but not always with democracy and never with socialism.

In two major ways the outcome was of great importance for the future of nationalism and liberalism. One was that the independence of the Spanish colonies was confirmed. The successful intervention of France in Spain in 1823, and the ferocious reaction that Ferdinand led after his restoration in Madrid, prompted Canning to look elsewhere for revenge. To forestall any plan to bring the South American colonies back to Spanish rule, and to promote the growing trade between England and these colonies, Canning encouraged President Monroe to throw the weight of the United States on to their side. Monroe's famous Message to Congress of December, 1823, did this; and it was delivered with the knowledge that British naval power would ensure that the policy of proclaiming 'hands off South America' had some sanction behind it. In 1822 the United States had already recognized the new republics of South America, and in 1825 Britain recognized the independence of Argentina, Colombia, and Mexico. By 1830 the present states of Argentina, Bolivia, Chile, Colombia, Ecuador, Mexico, Paraguay, Peru, Uruguay, and Venezuela had been formed by the division of the independent colonies. The five central American states joined in 1823 to form the Confederation of the United Provinces of Central America, which survived until 1838. Canning flamboyantly declared that he had 'called the New World into existence to redress the balance of the Old'.

The other impetus to nationalist and liberal movements came from the successful Greek War of Independence. From 1820 until 1825 the Greek patriots fought alone, and the only help they got from sympathetic powers was the withholding of help from both sides in the struggle. Russia was restrained from helping the Greeks by Austrian and British pressure. Metternich wanted to let the revolt burn itself out 'beyond the pale of civilization'. But in 1825, when the sultan of Turkey received highly successful help from Mehemet Ali, pasha of Egypt, Russia could be held back no longer. Britain joined with her in putting pressure on Turkey to grant the Greeks an armistice and some degree of independence. The reluctance to use force caused further delay until 1827, when France joined them in making a treaty (6 July 1827) to use force if necessary in order to get Turkish agreement. In October, soon after Canning's death, squadrons of the British, French, and Russian fleets destroyed the Turkish and Egyptian navies at the Battle of Navarino. The following year Russia formally declared war on Turkey, and France sent troops to compel Turkish withdrawal from the Morea. Turkey made peace in the Treaty of Adrianople (September 1829). In 1830 Greek independence was ensured, and was guaranteed by Russia, France, and Britain. The new state became a monarchy in 1833 when a Bavarian prince was crowned as Otto I, King of the Hellenes. The long and desperate struggle of the Greeks enlisted immense enthusiasm among liberals everywhere in Europe. It was a heroic and epic struggle, and became a token of nationalist success. Philhellenism was the special form that nationalism took in this age of romanticism; its victory gave inspiration to the revolutionaries of 1830.

In so far as the congress system meant that the great powers of Europe could usefully meet together from time to time to resolve disputes among them and to preserve a certain balance of power in the continent, it met with partial success and helped to keep the peace. At successive congresses such questions as the abolition of slavery, navigation of the Danube, and arbitration of disputes were considered. But in so far as it came to serve the purposes of the Holy Alliance and of at least some partners of the Quadruple Alliance, it was a disturbing force in Europe. The principle of joint intervention, generally accepted in reference to the ex-enemy state of France, became an excuse for a universal meddlesomeness that chimed with the real interests neither of Metternich nor of Britain. Each power in turn was prompted to intervene: Austria in Piedmont and Naples, France in Spain and Greece, Britain in Portugal and Greece, Russia in Greece. Britain, alarmed by the interventions of reactionary monarchs and by the ambiguous aims of Russia in Turkey, found herself committed to the paradoxical policy of 'intervening to prevent intervention'. Even the long and tense achievement of 'holding the ring' during the Greek revolution broke down in the end, and meanwhile brought terrible losses to the Greeks. The protest of the Monroe Doctrine against the practice of intervention for or against existing régimes helped to force upon public attention this fundamental issue of international relationships. Neither the forces of conservatism nor those of nationalism and liberalism derived unmitigated benefits from it. Intervention favoured monarchs in Spain and Naples, liberal rebels in Portugal and Greece; but neither dynastic monarchy nor national independence stood to gain in the long run from accepting the doctrine that external powers might properly intervene in the internal affairs of states. It was discovered by experience that the congress system could mean generalizing, and so magnifying, every dispute; it meant alerting governments everywhere whenever there was an insurrection anywhere. By making peace 'indivisible' it made peace more fragile, for the rival interests of the major powers were implicated in each revolutionary crisis. The 'concert of Europe', viewed by the conservative powers as a dam against revolution, was thought of by Britain rather as a sluice gate, allowing for a measured flow of national and liberal progress. This conflict of purposes was to last for half a century.[1]

THE ROMANTIC REVOLUTIONARIES

The suppression of revolutions, in the 1820s drove the most enthusiastic nationalists and liberals underground or into exile. It inaugurated an age of secret societies and conspiracies, of which the epidemics of revolution in 1830 were the direct consequence. The dispersal of Italian, Spanish, and Greek patriots throughout Europe – mostly to the more tolerant countries of Britain, Switzerland, and the Netherlands – made liberalism more of an international movement. The concerted action of the governments to crush revolution, organized in the system of Metternich and the congresses, produced a similar concerted action of revolutionaries. The cousinhood of kings fostered the brotherhood of rebels; and ferocity of repression gave rise to an equal fanaticism of resistance.

Secret Societies. The ultimate models for most secret societies were the Lodges of eighteenth-century Freemasonry, and from them was derived much of the ritual, ceremonies of initiation, secret signs, and passwords. The more immediate models were the secret societies formed in Italy and Germany to resist the rule of Napoleon: especially the *Tugendbund* (League of Virtue) in Germany and the *Carbonari* (charcoal burners) of Italy, both founded by 1810. But a rich variety of similar organizations appeared throughout Europe: the *Federati* of Piedmont and the *Adelphi* in Lombardy, the Spanish liberal societies after 1815, the Philomathians of Poland modelled on the German students' *Burschenschaften*, the Russian Union of Salvation of 1816 and the republican Society of the South.

These societies were in very much less close touch with one another than Metternich and most governments believed. They nursed very dif-

1. See pp. 176 and 322.

ferent aims and rested on widely varied social bases. Some attracted army officers; others students, professional people, and intellectuals; others the lower clergy or small proprietors. They inevitably included some adventurers and even criminals, and it was seldom difficult to get spies inserted into their ranks. Their most common feature was a spirit of patriotic and nationalist independence, a desire to throw off foreign rule or break the bonds of absolutist monarchy. But within that common characteristic they might be constitutionalist or republican, clericalist or anti-clericalist, aristocratic or plebeian. Even when they kept in communication with one another, and partially concerted action as in 1820 and 1830, they seldom acted with real unanimity. Attracting desperate and usually brave men, compelled to work under conditions of secrecy and mystery – for they risked their lives if they failed – they favoured heroic insurrections and the wildest hopes. It was the perfect breeding ground for idealists and dreamers, no less than for charlatans and ruffians. No project was too fantastic, no vision too unrealistic, to attract their enthusiasm. The revolutionary movements between 1815 and 1848 are incomprehensible until it is recalled that these were the years of the romantic movement in Europe, and they were indeed one facet of that movement.

Romantic Movement. It is true that some of the greatest romantic writers of the early nineteenth century were in temperament religious and conservative. Sir Walter Scott in Britain revived, in his great series of Waverley novels, an interest in the Middle Ages and so in traditionalism, and was an ardent Tory. His novels were widely read in Europe, and the Tsar Nicholas I of Russia read them aloud to his Prussian wife. The Lake poets, William Wordsworth, Robert Southey, and Samuel Taylor Coleridge, had all in their day been enthusiastic in support of the French Revolution; by 1815 they were all supporters of conservatism, traditionalism, and religion. In France, until 1824, the novelist and poet René Chateaubriand supported the restoration of the Bourbons; he represented Louis XVIII at the Congress of Verona, and even served as minister of foreign affairs. His *Génie du Christianisme* of 1802 was a glorification of ultramontane Roman Catholicism. His royalism was tempered by a desire for constitutional monarchy, and under Charles X of France he joined the opposition to the absolutist policies of that monarch. But he remained ultramontane in belief, and never became republican. His influence on French literature was almost supreme in his generation, and it was in general a conservative influence. In Germany, the great romantics Friedrich Novalis and Friedrich Schlegel repeated the spiritual and political pilgrimage of the English Lake poets. Both came to attack the rationalism and 'enlightenment' of the eighteenth century, to defend authoritarian and paternalist government, and to idealize the Middle Ages. The Roman Church had no more devoted apologists. The greatest of all German literary figures, Wolfgang Goethe, was aged sixty-six in 1815, though he lived until 1832. He had admired Napoleon, and lent no support to the liberal or insurrectionist movements.

Despite the extent to which all these romantic writers shared in the conservative and clericalist trends of the times, the romantic movement as a whole corroded the cosmopolitan and non-nationalist outlook on which absolutism had prospered. Even when their works did not directly spread liberal ideas, the romantic writers did promote nationalist sentiments. As the Germany of Goethe, Novalis, and Schlegel replaced France as the focus of cultural and intellectual interests, so emphasis shifted to pride in nationalism and *Volksgeist*, the particular genius of a people, and away from rationalism and cosmopolitanism. The romantic movement, in all its cultural forms, emphasized emotion and sentiment rather than reason and intellect. By turning attention to a misty past, it stirred pride in folk tales and past heroisms. By its very traditionalism, it appealed to sentiments of separatism: it reminded men of all that was special, individual, and personal. By its emphasis on creative and original genius, it made human personality seem more important than society and implicitly condemned restrictions on individual freedom of expression; and in its search for the creative genius of an age or of a people it nourished belief in the supreme value of popular traditions and national development. It made it easy to abandon rationalism for nationalism.

Moreover, the younger generation of romantic artists and writers who took the stage after about 1820 had more affinities with liberalism and democracy than with conservatism. For a time the greatest figures in European romanticism were again French and English rather than German. Victor Hugo, Alphonse de Lamartine, Prosper Merimée, Honoré de Balzac, Percy Bysshe Shelley, John Keats, and Lord Byron began to dominate the scene. This new generation saw romanticism as the literature of emancipation, and were not averse to allying their artistic revolt with political revolution. Byron proclaimed, 'I have simplified my politics into a detestation of all existing governments', and he became an immense personal influence throughout Europe in support of nationalist and liberal causes. Hugo put it simply that 'Romanticism is liberalism in literature'. Even the widespread influence of the German romantic movement in eastern and northern Europe flowed partly through the medium of *De l'Allemagne*, the remarkable study of German nationalism by the Frenchwoman, Madame de Staël. In Russia the poet and dramatist, Alexander Pushkin, wrote his two greatest works, *Boris Godunov* and *Eugen Onegin*, in the 1820s; and in Poland the young liberal Adam Mickiewicz produced his great epic of the Polish nation, *Conrad Wallenrod*, in 1828. Both showed the impact of Byronic themes and spirit. Among the Austrian subjects of the Balkans appeared Czech, Magyar, and Serbian poets to revive popular interest in the folk legends and wistful memories of past glories. In the Scandinavian lands collections were made of legends and folk-songs.

The strongest link between the revolutionaries and the romantic movement was the movement of Philhellenism, formed by all throughout the continent who sympathized with the long Homeric struggle of the Greeks against their Turkish rulers. The Greek war for independence aroused every impulse behind the romantic movement. It recalled the crusades in its heroism and in its struggle between Cross and Crescent. It sufficiently evoked the old sense of the unity of Christendom for both the Pope and Louis XVIII of France to contribute money to the cause. As committees in nearly every country, including the United States, raised funds to help the Greeks, the new generation of romantic writers threw its influence into the struggle. Chateaubriand and Hugo in France, above all Shelley and Byron in England, sponsored the cause. 'We are all Greeks,' exclaimed Shelley, and the young Lord Byron, dying in Greece in 1824, became the symbol of the new spirit. Philhellenism created a new current of European opinion – a great flow of opinion in favour of nationalism and liberalism – running counter to the policies and practices of most existing governments. It won its greatest triumph when it compelled the governments of Britain, France, and Russia to intervene on behalf of the Greeks in 1827.[1]

Mazzini and Buonarroti. Typical of the romantic enthusiasm infused into the new revolutionary movements was the career of Giuseppe Mazzini. He was the son of a doctor and professor of anatomy in Genoa. From very early youth he was brought into the nationalist and democratic movement in Italy. In 1815 when he was only ten years old, Genoa was put under the uncongenial rule of Piedmont, and Genoa as a city bitterly resented this forfeiture of its republican liberties. When the *Carbonari* risings of 1820–21 were crushed, the city was filled with defeated Piedmontese liberals, and their plight left a deep impression on the young Mazzini. As a student in the 1820s he devoured most of the great works of the romantic writers of Italy, France, Britain, and Germany. He claimed later that his favourite books were the Bible and Dante, Shakespeare, and Byron; but he read, too, Goethe and Schiller, Scott and Hugo, Herder and Mickiewicz. His life is one of the best

1. See p. 138.

examples of how close became the affinities between romanticism and revolution. Mazzini and his friends saturated themselves in contemporary romanticism, with a good leavening of the greatest Italian writers of the past – Dante and Machiavelli especially – who embodied traditions of Italian patriotism. Devotion to literature competed, throughout Mazzini's life, with service of politics. In his journalistic writings of this decade, mostly contriving to cheat the censorship by concealing political arguments behind literary essays, he drifted more and more into the work of a liberal agitator. He joined the *Carbonari*, though he was well aware of its defects and its relative ineffectiveness. From these experiences he derived the idea of a new movement of his own, appealing more directly to the younger generation. By 1831 this idea bore fruit in the 'Young Italy' movement.[1] It was men of Mazzini's generation and outlook who were to make the European revolutions of 1848.

It was amid this stirring of nationalist sentiments and in this swiftly changing scene that the secret societies and conspirators went to work. The *Carbonari* spread its activities throughout Europe and gave rise in 1821 to its French counterpart, the *Charbonnerie*. In 1828 there appeared in Brussels a work, written by a veteran French revolutionary, Philippe Buonarroti, that was to become a textbook of revolutionaries. This strange man had shared in the famous plot led by Gracchus Babeuf in 1796.[2] Buonarroti's book now made it the basis of a great republican legend. He had promised his fellow conspirators that he would eventually tell the full story of the plotters and their aims, and this task was fulfilled in his two volumes on *Conspiration pour l'égalité dite de Babeuf*. It gave the revived liberal movement a direct and symbolic link with the great Revolution. Since 1815 Buonarroti, who was by birth an Italian, had turned his attention to the liberation and unification of Italy through republicanism. This preoccupation brought him into touch with the *Carbonari* and with Mazzini's 'Young Italy' movement. He tried to found a Society of *Sublimes-Maîtres-Parfaits*, or trained revolutionary *élite*, and urged the use of Freemasonry as a façade for conspiracy. He lived in Geneva until 1823, when he moved to the Netherlands. He did not return to France until after the July Revolution of 1830. But meanwhile, through the *Carbonari* and through his book, he acquired the respect and attention of the new generation of young revolutionaries of western Europe. This influence grew rapidly in France after 1830.

The combination of internal and international tensions during the 1820s gave nationalist and liberal movements a new leverage for gaining

1. See p. 171.
2. See p. 46.

their ends against conservatism. Whether this new leverage produced piecemeal reforms and concessions, or a more disruptive accumulation of grievances liable to explode in violent revolution, depended chiefly on the policies followed by each state. A parliamentary and constitutional régime like the British fostered a moderate and even liberal toryism, and marked the beginning of an age of reform. A semi-parliamentary and semi-constitutional régime like the French raised more hopes than it could satisfy, and ended in a change of monarch but little change of national policy. A completely unparliamentary and absolutist régime like the Austrian or Russian produced violent revolution, which the forces of conservatism were still powerful enough to crush. There was a sense in which each régime got the kind of liberal revolutionaries it deserved. The differing characters and outcomes of the upheavals of 1830–32 in each country were determined by the nature of the politics pursued by the governments between 1815 and 1830; and it is necessary to examine these before considering the events of 1830.

NEW WINE IN OLD BOTTLES

The Restored Monarchy. The failure of the restored monarchy in France was by no means a foregone conclusion. The restoration rested on a Charter, granted by Louis XVIII in 1814, and in this respect it was fundamentally different from the monarchy of Louis XVI. The existing Legislature drew up a draft constitution that, on 2 May 1814, Louis XVIII accepted in principle. He announced that he was returning to his ancestral throne, but that he would invite members of the Senate and the Legislative Body to help him to draw up a constitution. This was duly done by 4 June. Its first articles guaranteed certain fundamental liberties: equality before the law and equal eligibility for civil and military office; freedom from arbitrary arrest and trial; freedom of conscience, worship, and expression; inviolability of private property, including purchases of the national lands. Political opinions and actions prior to the restoration would not be inquired into. France was given a system of parliamentary government with two chambers and responsibility of ministers. The restored monarchy was in form a constitutional, parliamentary régime, designed to safeguard individual rights.

On the other hand, the forms and ideas of an absolute and hereditary monarchy were also preserved alongside these provisions. Louis claimed that he had really been king since his brother's execution, and referred to 1814 as 'the nineteenth year of our reign'. He insisted in the preamble to the constitution that it was granted 'voluntarily, and by the free exercise of our royal authority'. Whereas royalists could point out that what the king had given he could also take away, constitutionalists could point to the king's oath that he would keep the conditions laid down in it. These ambiguities and inconsistencies of the new régime betray its effort to find a compromise between monarchy and liberalism.

Divine right and constitutional limitations were uneasy bedfellows. Yet they might have reached eventual harmony had Louis been succeeded by a monarch of equal tact and similar determination not to go on his travels again. The Bourbon restoration in France repeated the story of the Stuart restoration in England after 1660. Just as Charles II was succeeded by his more intransigent brother, James II, who forfeited the throne after three years, so Louis XVIII was succeeded in 1824 by his unstatesmanlike brother, Charles X, who forfeited the throne after six years. In each case a combination of ultra-royalist principles and extremist religious policies led to violations of the constitution, unscrupulous political manoeuvres, and eventual revolution. But there was nothing inevitable about this revolution in 1830, as so many liberal historians have assumed. It was the result of policies which could have been different had the factors of royal personality or even of governmental behaviour been other than they were. Republicanism was not strong after 1815, nor was Bonapartism; and many liberals were content enough with a Bourbon monarchy provided it loyally accepted constitutional limitations on absolute power and worked through parliamentary institutions.

A further factor of importance was France's relative inexperience with working parliamentary institutions. In this respect France was very different from Great Britain. British constitutional government was able to develop, even during the period of die-hard conservatism and repression, because behind it lay centuries of practical experience in how representative institutions could impose controls on kings and parliamentary procedures on their ministers. French parliamentary traditions were only a quarter of a century old in 1815, and the record of representative assemblies in France was broken, turbulent, and inconclusive. In Britain a series of subtle conventions, not laid down in any charter, determined the conditions on which governments could secure a reliable parliamentary majority, the circumstances in which they must resign or in which they could expect the monarch to dissolve parliament and appeal to the electorate, the procedures of parliamentary debate, and above all the responsibilities of ministers, individually and collectively, to the House of Commons. Some of these conventions and almost tacit understandings were of fairly recent date; but by 1815 they were accepted without challenge. In France precedents were contradictory and indecisive. The Charter merely stipulated that although the executive power belonged to the king, 'his ministers are responsible'. It provided no clear ways in which the legislature could make them responsible to it. At first there was no party system, and ministers were not questioned in the Chamber. France, like Britain, had a certain number of skilled and experienced parliamentarians, with an instinctive understanding of how to work large assemblies; but they were not the men who found most favour in the Chamber after 1815, nor among those who surrounded the king. Nor was their role in opposition to the ministry at all well defined, whereas it was in 1826 that the English radical M.P., John Cam Hobhouse, first coined amid parliamentary laughter the significant phrase, 'His Majesty's Opposition'.

Apart from these important differences, the governments of France and Britain between 1815 and 1830 rested on similar foundations. In each country the vote was restricted to a small and wealthy section of the population; in each the government of these years was predominantly conservative in policy. Compared with most other monarchies in Europe, they were constitutionalist and parliamentary. In their general policy in Europe they found a good deal in common, for both resisted the attempts of Metternich to manage European affairs from Vienna. The liberal-tory ministries that governed Britain in the 1820s were sensitive to the needs and the demands of the growing business and commercial interests. At the Board of Trade Thomas Huskisson and F. J. Robinson (later Lord Goderich) relaxed the restrictions on shipping and simplified and reduced duties on imports and exports. These measures were typical of the gradual liberalizing of domestic policy in England during these years. The governments of Louis XVIII were equally responsive to business interests. They were honest and prudent in their financial policy, and gave the country solid prosperity while they put the state on a sounder financial footing than it had ever known under the old monarchy. Public loans were raised with such striking success that leading bankers, who had distrusted Bourbon loans and leaned towards the opposition, before long begged the government for a share in the profitable business. In both countries the trend of conservative parliamentary government was towards enlisting the support of the rising *bourgeoisie*. To this extent Louis XVIII and Charles X had a more solid basis for their power than their brother Louis XVI had ever had.

The men who served the restored Bourbons as ministers were partly *grands seigneurs* of the old order, like the Duc de Richelieu, the Vicomte de Martignac, who held power in 1828–29, and the Prince de Polignac, whose ultra-conservative temperament appealed particularly to Charles X. They were partly, too, new men of more humble origin whose fortunes and abilities had brought them to the forefront. Pre-eminent

147.

among these was the Comte de Villèle, who led the government for nearly seven years (1821–28). During the French Revolution he had settled in the French colonies in the Indian Ocean, married the daughter of a rich planter, and made a fortune under the Empire by selling indigo and other colonial exports in France. Another minister who had risen suddenly was the Duc Decazes, favourite of Louis XVIII. He had begun his career as secretary to Napoleon's mother, and entered politics through the bureaucracy. In general the new men served the restored monarchy rather better than did the men of the old aristocracy. They had a more instinctive and businesslike sense of the country's needs, and were more in tune with the interests of the restive *bourgeoisie*. Another category, making a more direct link of continuity with the Napoleonic régime, included those old unfaithfuls, Talleyrand and Fouché, who had served in turn the Revolution and Napoleon, and were resolved not to allow their careers to be interrupted by such minor intrusions as a royalist restoration. Baron Louis who took charge of finance and Baron Pasquier who took the Ministry of Justice were likewise Napoleonic functionaries who had survived the events of 1815.

The restored monarchy enjoyed other continuities with the Empire besides those of personalities. Louis kept intact the legal codes and judicial procedures, the centralized administrative system resting on the prefects and subprefects in each *département*, the whole system of direct and indirect taxation with the machinery for collecting it, including even the protective duties designed to benefit the big landowners and manufacturers. All this gave the restored Bourbons a degree of strength, efficiency, and centralized authority unknown to their royal predecessors. The crucial question was whether this enhanced power of the central government would be used in conformity with the principles of constitutional government, or whether it would come to be used as a weapon against constitutionalism. It was, as Napoleon had designed it to be, the machinery of despotism, and it lost little of its strength by the mere change of personages on the throne. When the first elections of July 1815 gave the extreme royalists a majority of 350 out of 420 in the Chamber of Deputies, and 100 new peers were added to the upper house, the ultra-royalists hoped to use their power to exceed even the king's wishes for a counter-revolution. Hence the paradox that in the early years it was the extreme right that was most insistent that ministers should be subject to the wishes of the Chamber, and that government policy should be shaped in accordance with the wishes of the majority in parliament; it was the moderates who wanted the milder policy of the king to prevail. The ultras, being more royalist than the king, were also more parliamentarian than the constitutionalists – but only so long as they could rely on the 'Incomparable Chamber' (*Chambre introuvable*) of 1815.

Their earliest use of this power was to pass laws setting up special military tribunals, laws against seditious writings, and laws of proscription which sent into exile many of the most eminent men of the Empire. The result was that in September 1816 the king dissolved the Chamber, and the elections gave the moderates a majority. Led by Decazes, Pasquier, Royer-Collard, and Guizot, these moderate royalists followed the policy of 'royalizing the nation, nationalizing the Crown'. Winning the confidence and support of the wealthier *bourgeoisie* by an efficient financial policy aimed at restoring stability and balance to state finances, they made possible the rise of a still more liberal group of moderate parliamentarians, calling themselves 'Independents'. These included bankers like Laffitte and the Delessert brothers, merchants like Ternaux, and businessmen like Casimir-Périer. To the left of them again appeared a republican group, led by the veteran Lafayette, and including such famous names as Voyer d'Argenson, Benjamin Constant, Godefroy Cavaignac, and Hippolyte Carnot. By 1818 these Independents and Republicans combined with unrepentant Bonapartists like General Thiard, a former aide-de-camp of Napoleon, to form a more concerted opposition party. The moderate governments of the Duc de Richelieu, General Dessolle, and Duc Decazes which held power between 1817 and 1821 had therefore to steer a middle course between the pressure of the ultras from the right and the demands of this new opposition on the left. When they failed, because of a resurgence of ultra-royalism in 1821, their place was taken by the more extreme right ministry of Villèle.

Villèle, always the shrewd and realistic man of business, pursued the aims of the extremists with the prudence and studied caution of the moderates. His policy was to restrain the impatient ultras but to win France to their cause by making her drowsy with material prosperity, peace, and good business. Using the machinery of public order even more systematically but also more wisely than did his predecessors, he skilfully kept bourgeois opinion just apprehensive enough of risings and conspiracies to preserve its support. Every actual attempt of the romantic revolutionaries to spread republicanism was exposed and exploited to the full; and even more tenuous plots could always be exaggerated when there were no serious conspiracies to suit his convenience. If real culprits could not be caught and savagely punished, victims could be found to serve the same purpose. This insidious and clever policy was bearing fruit, despite the growing feud between Villèle and Chateaubriand about the latter's desire for a more active and interventionist foreign policy, when Louis XVIII died in August 1824. His hopes of reconciling Crown and nation had by no means been achieved. The accession of Charles X, who as Comte d'Artois had been for fifty years the favourite of the ultras, meant that it would never be fulfilled.

The Chamber of 1824, elected at the end of the previous year in elections that were thoroughly 'managed' by the prefects and other government officials, was so reminiscent of the original *Chambre introuvable* that it was christened the *Chambre retrouvée* (Comparable Chamber). When Charles X succeeded to the throne in September, the ultras felt that they had a free hand. The new king was the king of a party in a sense that his brother had not been. They proceeded to carry out much of their original programme. Control of education was given to the Church by making a bishop minister of education. An indemnity, amounting in practice to some 650,000 francs, was paid to the *émigrés* who had lost their estates. The first of these measures flouted the anti-clericalist sentiments of the *bourgeoisie*, the second attacked their pockets. The money was found by converting 5 per cent annuities into annuities of 3 per cent.

Charles insisted on being crowned at Reims with the elaborate ritual of the *ancien régime*, and this was taken as symbolic of his intention to revive the whole of the pre-revolutionary order. When the Jesuits reappeared and sacrilege was made a crime punishable by death, widespread fears of an extreme clericalist reaction were aroused. The government's attacks on its liberal critics, the prosecutions of publishers and the imprisonment of journalists, solidified liberal opposition. Though opposition was not strong inside parliament, it gained in strength in the country. The extremist policy, moreover, split the ranks of the royalists themselves, for many churchmen feared and opposed the power of the Jesuits. At the elections of 1827 the opposition gained a majority of 60, and in January 1828 Villèle was obliged to resign. The loss of his ability and astuteness was a prelude to the downfall of the king himself.

His successor, the Vicomte de Martignac, adopted a more conciliatory policy. He abolished the censorship of the press and checked the growth of clericalist control over education. This policy eased the tension but was disliked by the king. In 1829 Charles X replaced Martignac by the Prince de Polignac, a former *émigré* and an ultraroyalist of the most extravagant kind. Polignac formed a ministry of the extreme right, which was bound to be in complete conflict with the existing Chamber. The open clash came in March 1830, when the Chamber reminded the king that 'the permanent harmony of the political views of your Government with the wishes of your people is the indispensable condition for the conduct of public affairs'. That was the permanent constitutional issue of the restoration: should ministers be responsible to the king alone, or to parliament? When Charles dissolved the Chamber, he was asserting that they must be responsible to him alone; and when the elections of July returned an opposition that was 53 stronger than before, the king was obliged to fall back on royal prerogatives and attempt a virtual *coup d'état*. In itself an admission that constitutional monarchy had failed in France under a Bourbon king, this was a signal for open battle between king and country. The result, the Revolution of July, is described below.[1]

The Bourbons, it was often said, had 'learned nothing and forgotten nothing'. This is less than just. Louis XVIII had learned that royal power had to be reconciled, partly by kingly prudence and partly by acceptance of parliamentary rules, with the new forces of liberalism and the interests of the wealthier *bourgeoisie*. He had chosen ministers whose abilities and statecraft restored French prestige in Europe while they brought speedy national recovery in economic life and in financial stability. Until the depression of 1825 France's commercial prosperity was great and her credit high. Her population grew by 3 million in the fifteen years between 1815 and 1830. Her material progress, in agriculture, industry, and transport, was solid. By 1829 gas lighting had become general in the city of Paris. The age of railways was just beginning. In the very month of revolution, July 1830, the completion of the conquest of Algiers marked the beginning of a great new colonial empire in Africa. But the Bourbons, and especially Charles X, had not learned that in nineteenth-century conditions material prosperity and progress were no substitute for constitutional liberties and responsible government. The restored monarchy failed because it accommodated itself to nationalism but not to liberalism.

Liberal Toryism in Britain. The comparison with contemporary happenings in Britain is illuminating. There, with parliamentary traditions, conventions, and habits well established and generally accepted, constitutional government worked more smoothly. Tory governments held power under Lord Liverpool until 1827, and then under George Canning, Lord Goderich, and the Duke of Wellington until 1830. Prudent financial policies and the businesslike handling of public affairs encouraged a revival of economic prosperity after the agricultural depression of 1815–16 and the commercial crisis of 1819. In Britain, as in France, more liberal and radical reforms were stubbornly resisted. But conservatism in Britain was more ready than was royalism in France to make timely concessions and to place public welfare above party interests.

It was not that monarchy was particularly popular. Until 1830 the

1. See p. 165.

regency and then the reign of George IV brought it no enhanced prestige, for neither in personal behaviour nor in political shrewdness was he admirable. When he died in 1830 *The Times* commented, 'There never was an individual less regretted by his fellow-creatures than this deceased King. What eye has wept for him? What heart has heaved one sigh of unmercenary sorrow?' His brother William IV, who succeeded him until 1837, was considerably more popular but was held in little respect. As *The Spectator* wrote on his death, 'His late Majesty, though at times a jovial and, for a king, an honest man, was a weak, ignorant, commonplace sort of person. . . . His very popularity was acquired at the price of something like public contempt.' The monarchy, before the accession of Queen Victoria in 1837, was surviving in spite of the monarchs.

Two enactments of these years express precisely the cautious reformism of the new conservatism in Britain. One was abolition of the Combination Laws in 1824, the other the giving of civil equality to Protestant dissenters in 1828 and to Roman Catholics in 1829. The Combination Laws had been passed in 1799 and 1800, at the height of the wartime repression. They had forbidden associations of various kinds, and in particular had made working-class organization illegal and laid trade unions open to the charge of conspiracy. Manufacturers came to believe that this prohibition caused trouble rather than prevented it. Francis Place, the 'Radical tailor of Charing Cross', led a movement for the repeal of these laws. He believed that once workers had the legal freedom to form trade unions and conduct collective bargaining with their employers, they would not need to do so and trade unions would die a natural death. Place and his chief agent in Parliament, the radical Joseph Hume, steered through the Commons a bill putting trade unions on a status of legal equality with employers' associations. As soon as the bill was passed, there was an epidemic of strikes accompanied by violence. In 1825 a second act was therefore passed, severely restricting the use of intimidation and violence but accepting the legality of trade unions for regulating wages and hours of labour. Using this moderate freedom, trade unions during the following decade greatly extended their activities. They were freed from the need to behave like secret societies. New unions were formed, with open constitutions and published books of rules. They could freely bargain about conditions of work.

The repeal of the Test and Corporation Acts in 1828 made it possible for Protestant dissenters to hold legally most of the highest offices in civil government, and commissions in the armed services, which had hitherto been a monopoly of members of the Church of England. Al-

though dissenters had come to enjoy a large measure of practical toleration, it was the denial of religious and legal equality which rankled,
and which had come to seem out of tune with nineteenth-century ideas.
The growing strength and numbers of Methodism reinforced the demand. Nonconformists now numbered some two million out of a population of fifteen million. This victory for the principle of religious
equality paved the way for tackling the more difficult issue of Roman
Catholic emancipation. Roman Catholics in England numbered only
some 60,000. It was in Ireland that the issue was most burning. Since
1801 Ireland had had no parliament of its own, but had the right to elect
members to the United Kingdom parliament in Westminster. The legal
disabilities imposed on Roman Catholics did not prevent them from
voting but kept the great majority of the Irish population from holding
responsible civil or political office. Daniel O'Connell revived an older
'Catholic Association', with wide popular membership and a subscrip-
tion of a penny a month, nicknamed the 'Catholic rent'. Its aim was to
promote the candidature of members of Parliament pledged to support
Catholic emancipation at Westminster; but all such members had to be
Protestants, since Catholics could not sit in parliament.

Because 200,000 Irishmen had a vote and because freedom of association was legally permitted, the Association was able to avoid all the
characteristic weaknesses of the secret conspiracies of contemporary
Europe. Its meeting and proceedings were open, its methods peaceful.
In 1828 O'Connell was elected member of parliament for County Clare,
and the election was accompanied by no disorder or illegality. The government of the Duke of Wellington was confronted with the dilemma
that the Association had so skilfully created. Because O'Connell was
a Roman Catholic he was legally incapable of taking his seat at Westminster. Either the government must remove this legal incapacity, or
find one Irish constituency after another following the example of
County Clare, with the increasing likelihood of deadlock and civil war.
George IV tried to prevent any proposal for Catholic emancipation
from being put before parliament, but when the ministry offered its
resignation, he gave way. While Sir Robert Peel moved the bill in the
Commons, the Duke of Wellington in the Lords pointed out that the
alternative would be civil war. The Tory government forced the bill
through parliament, making Roman Catholics eligible for all but a few
specified offices in the United Kingdom and giving them equality of
civil rights with Protestant dissenters. Like the growth of trade unions,
it was a triumph for the methods of constitutional and law-abiding
popular associations, and an example that others were soon to imitate.

But there are three features of the whole matter which have to be noted. First, it was an important liberal reform granted by a strongly Tory government, contrary to the vested privileges of the Church of England which normally expected the Tory party to safeguard its interests. It was the 'Victor of Waterloo' who 'let the Papists into Parliament'. Conservatism in Europe seldom showed this spirit of compromise and concession. Secondly, this concession was nevertheless made late and only in face of a situation threatening great disorder and violence. It won little respect or good will. The spirit of liberalism still did not prevail strongly enough to win such reforms easily. Thirdly, conservative fears were strong enough as regards Ireland to prompt the government to take away with one hand a lot that they had given with the other. The Emancipation Act was accompanied by disfranchisement of the mass of small Irish freeholders, which reduced the electorate in Ireland to only 26,000 voters, and by suppression of the Catholic Association. Religious equality was given but civil and political liberties were taken away. Good will was lost, and a rankling grievance remained to poison Anglo-Irish relations for another half century.

Radicalism in Britain. The moderate freedom given to popular associations, whether economic such as trade unions or religious such as the Catholic Association, was shared also by political movements of radicalism. From these movements was to come much of the pressure that eventually secured the Reform Act of 1832. Before 1815 the veteran radical, Major John Cartwright, had founded Hampden Clubs, which demanded the reform of parliament and eventually universal suffrage. Their membership was small and scattered, mostly in the larger towns. They extended their activities during the economic crisis of 1815-16. The tactics of the radicals were to create the illusion that every expression of distress and discontent was linked with one common tide of political opinion demanding political reform. In fact even the London radicals, who took the lead, were divided among themselves, and moderate men like Francis Place distrusted and despised more demagogic characters like Cartwright, Henry 'Orator' Hunt, and William Cobbett, who worked to arouse discontent in the country. The methods common to all the English radicals were not so much mass meetings or even popular associations, as devices like simultaneous petitioning, which rested on the ancient right of any subject to petition king and parliament for redress of grievances. Although an Act of 1661 against Tumultuous Petitioning restricted the conditions in which more than 20 signatures could be lawfully solicited for a petition, this did not prevent the simultaneous preparation of a large number of identical petitions. Similarly, although the same Act forbade that the petition be presented to parliament by more than 10 persons, it remained lawful for each of several petitions to be presented by 10 persons. By keeping within the law, it was still possible for radical clubs to arouse public opinion and bring it to bear upon the government. This safety valve was usually lacking in European countries at that time.

Radical leaders like Cartwright and sympathetic Whigs like Sir Francis Burdett became adept at using every lawful means for this end. Union Societies began to be formed – first at Oldham in Lancashire in 1816, and soon in many other towns throughout the industrial and distressed northern counties. Their membership was small; their aim, the political education of the people; their most practical achievements, the organization of petitions. They agitated against the Corn Law of 1815 on the grounds that it made bread dear, and they soon joined forces with the Hampden Clubs. At the same time William Cobbett, in his *Political Register*, mobilized the resources of the press and of his own biting pen in their cause. The virulence of his attacks on the government, however, alienated moderate reforming Whigs. Whigs like Burdett and Lord Brougham were prepared to urge household suffrage but not universal suffrage.

Repressive measures were passed by the government in 1819, after the 'Peterloo massacre', when a crowd of some 60,000 at Manchester was charged by the mounted yeomanry with the result that 11 people were killed and about 400 wounded. Although the severity of the Six Acts and the general measures of repression checked radicalism for a time, 'Peterloo' passed into popular mythology as an outrage on popular freedom and did much to offset the Tory credit for Waterloo. In its treatment of political radicalism, conservatism in England repeated the story of its treatment of trade unions and of the Irish Catholics: it forfeited good will despite its concessions, and showed that its fears of democracy exceeded its repect for constitutional liberties.

Yet the fears of toryism were not without some foundation in experience. In the later eighteenth century large meetings had often led to riots, and with no reliable machinery for keeping public order until after 1829, when Sir Robert Peel first instituted the metropolitan police in London, the government justifiably distrusted any large assembly of ill-educated people. The crust of law and order was very thin. During the French Revolution popular clubs and societies had spread extreme radical and Jacobin ideas, and like all its European contemporaries the British government regarded Jacobinism as a species of plague which would bring disaster unless stern preventive measures were taken. Statesmen were haunted by still fresh memories of the Reign of Terror.

Toryism had, too, a certain philosophy. It regarded social distress and economic depression as evils entirely divorced from politics – as afflictions that any society must from time to time suffer because of bad harvest or disturbance of trade. Political agitation that played upon conditions of social distress and held out hopes of betterment through political reform seemed, therefore, both irresponsible (since it might endanger public order) and hypocritical (since it raised false hopes). The purpose of the Six Acts and of repression in general was to prevent political agitation from penetrating lower socially than the relatively well-educated middle classes. For popular orators to preach radicalism to mass meetings of hungry and ill-educated men in the winter of their distress was little short of revolutionary activity. This attitude was shared by Tories and Whigs alike: the growing mass of the labouring classes were unfit to take any responsible or intelligent part in politics; in time, with prudent government, their lot might improve; but radicalism and democracy bred only dangerous delusions.

In the 1820s radicalism in England became more quiescent. The harshness of repression had scared off many agitators. Improvements in material prosperity softened the economic distress that had nourished popular excitement. A generous though wasteful system of poor relief, administered locally and financed by poor rates, saved the most destitute from starvation. Interest in parliamentary reform declined until 1830, when the revolution in France and the fall of the Bourbon monarchy revived hopes of democratic advance. George IV died on 26 June 1830, and the general elections that followed took place amid the exciting news from Paris.

The London Radical Reform Association and the Birmingham Political Union directed the excitement toward hopes of parliamentary reform in England. Once again conservatives came to feel that some kind of overhaul of the electoral system could not much longer be postponed. When that autumn the Duke of Wellington went out of his way to defend the existing constitution, his government was defeated within a fortnight. The Whig ministry headed by Lord Grey, which succeeded him, was from the outset pledged to a reform bill. Grey held that timely concession to a sustained and widespread popular demand was the right policy, not in the sense that it should be the first step towards broader democracy but rather that it should be a final settlement and reconciliation between the governing aristocracy and the nation. His ministry was solidly aristocratic in its conception, and when rural disturbances and urban strikes broke out the government repressed them with all the old severity. The Whigs were at one with the Tories in resisting democracy and in crushing popular movements; they differed from the Tories only in a more realistic readiness to forestall more violent pressures by the timely granting of moderate reforms, which would 'afford sure ground of resistance to further innovation'.[1]

The Restoration in Europe. In most other countries before 1830 the old bottles proved strong enough to contain the new wine, though at times there was violent fermentation. Victor Emmanuel I of Piedmont was confronted, in March 1821, with the simultaneous revolt of several military units. The revolt was engineered by a small group of aristocratic army officers, demanding war with Austria under a constitutional national government. Half the army remained loyal to the king, but Victor Emmanuel lost his nerve and abdicated in favour of his brother, Charles Felix. His abdication was followed by the resignation of all his ministers, one man with unconscious humour pleading as excuse the death of his grandmother. Prince Charles Albert was declared Regent, and under strong popular pressure fomented by the *Carbonari* he proclaimed the famous constitution of 1812. Charles Felix appealed for Austrian help, which was readily given, and Charles Albert was sent into exile while the Austrians crushed the revolt and installed the more resolutely reactionary Charles Felix on the throne. He held it, with little further resistance, until his death in 1831, when Charles Albert succeeded him.

In Russia the turning point in relations between the monarchy and the nation came in 1825, with the so-called Decembrist Revolt. Tsar Alexander I had extended his liberalism to include grants of self-government and partial independence to the two most sharply defined national groups within his dominions, the Finns and Poles. In 1809, when he became grand duke of Finland, he kept the constitution Finland had previously enjoyed under Swedish rule. This left the Finns with their own laws and law courts, their own army and administrative system, all staffed by Swedes or Finns but not by Russians. Under these arrangements the country suffered little change because of its compulsory transference in 1815, and remained prosperous and generally contented. In the Kingdom of Poland, which comprised little more than a fifth of Russian Poland, he set up a similar constitutional system that guaranteed freedom of speech and of the press, and rights of free association, and included a Diet, or parliament, based on the most liberal franchise in Europe. The army and civil administration were staffed by Poles. But in practice the régime proved less liberal. The army was kept under Russian control and the Tsar, in his capacity as king of Poland, could dominate the proceedings of the Diet. His brother, the Grand Duke Constantine, headed the army; and the Tsar's special 'Commissioner for the Kingdom', Novosiltsev, acquired a degree of personal local power inconsistent with the intentions of the constitution.

1. See p. 172.

In Polish territories the Tsar's hesitant liberalism was closely comparable to the spirit that guided the actions of Louis XVIII in France or of liberal toryism in Britain. In 1819 censorship was set up. The session of the Diet in 1820 was hastily ended when it rejected bills proposed by the government. Clericalist influences and the Jesuits supported Novosiltsev in his repressive policy. From 1821 onward Lubecki, a Polish aristocrat entrusted with public finance, brought sound administrative methods and considerable commercial and financial prosperity to the country. He began the solid industrial development of Poland. As in France and Britain, political conservatism was accompanied by prudent finance and material prosperity. In 1825 the third session of the Diet was again abruptly ended, and that year Alexander died. He had intended that his younger brother, Nicholas, should succeed him, although Constantine was next in the line of succession. The absurd situation arose in which Nicholas, at St Petersburg, proclaimed Constantine Tsar; while Constantine, at Warsaw, proclaimed Nicholas. For nearly three weeks in December 1825 the throne remained vacant. The secret societies seized the chance to stage a revolt of the army at St Petersburg, with the aim of summoning a national assembly. But the plotters had no clear plan or organization, and had made no adequate preparations. They were crushed with great severity. The only consequences of importance were that Nicholas, who now succeeded to the throne, was haunted for the rest of his days by the spectre of revolution, while the 'Decembrist Revolt' entered into the mythology of the secret societies as a romantic legend.

The next thirty years of Russian history, which constituted the reign of Nicholas, were predominantly a time of more complete separation of monarchy from nation. Despite some administrative and legal reforms the tsarist government relied more than ever on the army and police, now fortified by the notorious 'Third Section', or political police. By 1830, when liberal and constitutionalist risings broke out in most of Europe, Russia remained within the grip of the bureaucracy and the police dictatorship of Tsardom. Only in Poland was there a revolt powerful enough to expel Constantine and set up a provisional government; but within a year that was savagely crushed, and Russian Poland reduced to complete subjection.[1]

The policies followed in these years by other restored monarchies were but reflections and repetitions of those already described. The lines in which Lord Byron pilloried Alexander's character and policy might well apply to the policies pursued by conservative monarchies and governments everywhere between 1815 and 1830.

1. See p. 171.

Now half dissolving to a liberal thaw,
But hardened back whene'er the morning's raw;
With no objection to true liberty,
Except that it would make the nations free.

Sensitive to the precariousness of their own position, haunted by memories and fears of revolution, monarchs of the restoration wavered between partial concessions and panicky repression. Where, as in England and to some extent in France, an outlet for opposition was provided through constitutional procedures, the concessions were consolidated. Where, as in Piedmont or Russia, there was no such outlet, there were sporadic revolts led by small groups of army officers, journalists, or students, followed by severe reprisals and bitterness. But everywhere the forces of change remained both dissatisfied and more resolute by 1830.

159

CHAPTER 9

THE LIBERAL REVOLUTIONS
OF 1830-3

ECONOMIC CONDITIONS

IN 1830 Europe stood on the brink of the railway age. Within the succeeding generation the building of railroad networks throughout the continent would revolutionize international relations as well as internal economic systems. The economic progress achieved between 1815 and 1830 was of the more elementary and less revolutionary character consonant with the political characteristics of these years. Agricultural change was slow and unspectacular; improvements in means of transport were limited to improvements in roads and canals, and to the growth of ocean-going shipping, which was still predominantly sail rather than steam; industrial progress was more striking, but almost confined to certain trades (particularly textiles) and greatest in western Europe; commercial policies were still (other than in Britain and France) more concerned with lowering internal customs barriers than with establishing freer trade between states. The sound financial policies followed by the governments of Britain, France, the Netherlands, and Prussia brought these countries a real prosperity interrupted only by years of bad harvest and periodic depressions in trade.

Western Europe. The most characteristic economic achievement of the restored Bourbons in France was the systematic extension of the system of canals. They continued the admirable traditions of their royal predecessors and of Napoleon in attending to roads and canals; this was of special importance to the welfare of a country whose trade was still predominantly internal. (In 1830 the whole foreign trade of France amounted to only about 6 dollars – 30 shillings – per head of the population in a year.) In 1818, as soon as the forces of occupation were withdrawn from French soil, the governments drew up a programme of systematic canal building, financed by special loans. By 1830 it added more than 900 kilometres to the 1,200 kilometres previously in existence. In addition to cheapening transport, this programme of public works stimulated national recovery. It has been suggested that by the 1830s the facilities for transport by road and canal in France were so good and so well managed by the state that they retarded the development of railroads; the relatively poorer conditions of transport in the United Kingdom meant that railroads were welcomed more eagerly. Elsewhere in

Europe roads were good mainly where administrative or military considerations required them to be. In Prussia the length of made-up roads maintained by the state more than doubled – from some 420 (Prussian) miles in 1816 to 902 in 1831 – mostly in the central and western territories. In Russia the main communications were by rivers (many of which had the defect of running shallow in summer and freezing in winter) and by roads (which being only of earth turned to mud in spring and autumn). Although Alexander I set up, in 1809, the Institute of Means of Communication, run by French engineers specially lent by Napoleon, these conditions improved little until the extensive railway construction of the decades 1840–70. Then the new possibilities were seized upon all the more avidly, and by 1900 they had completely changed Russian economic life. The role of improved communications and transport in welding a country more closely together, and so promoting feelings of nationalism, is undoubted although it is difficult to assess.

The extent of industrial change in the economically most developed countries – Britain, France, and the Netherlands – can best be gauged by a few figures of the growth of their major industries. Britain's most booming textile industry, cotton, expanded immensely in these years. Wooden spinning jennies, turned by hand, remained in very common use; but for weaving it was estimated in 1830 that in England and Scotland there were maybe 60,000 power looms to 240,000 hand looms. In France power looms were not introduced until long after they were in general use in Britain, partly because hand labour was cheaper and partly because the capital cost was greater. Yet in Alsace there was a highly localized introduction of power looms during the 1820s, and 2,000 were in use there by 1830. French coal production was sharply reduced by the Vienna settlement, because most of her best working mines were in territory that in 1815 became Dutch and in 1830 Belgian. Her annual output was less than 900,000 tons in 1815, though this rose to nearly 2 million tons by 1830. By 1830 Belgium was producing three times as much coal as France. Britain's coal production doubled from 15 million tons to 30 million tons between 1815 and 1829. So far as there was social distress in these years, it was due much less to the introduction of machinery, which at this time created new occupations almost as fast as it displaced old ones, than to the aftermath of the wars and to years of bad harvest and high food prices. Industrialization, in the more drastic forms it was to take during the next two decades, was little known even in Britain before 1830. Bad housing conditions, low wages, long hours of work, and employment of women and children in conditions of sweated labour existed in countries where little or no machinery had been introduced.

They were normal, not a novelty, and throughout Europe they were as common in agriculture as they were in industry.

By 1830 the main social and political consequences of economic change was a strengthening of the numbers, wealth, and influence of the men who were engaged in manufacturing, business, and trade. It is here that there is a more direct connexion between the early phases of the industrial revolution and the growth of liberalism. The new men who grew rich on Lancashire and Alsatian textiles and on Belgian coal claimed a policy more favourable to their interests, and therefore a form of government more sensitive to their opinions. Resenting Corn Laws, which had been passed to protect the landed and farming interests, because they impeded trade with which they were more directly concerned, first the merchants and later the manufacturers of the United Kingdom pressed for the repeal of such regulations. The gospel preached half a century earlier by Adam Smith in the *Wealth of Nations* lay ready to their hand. In 1820 the London Merchants presented to Parliament a petition embodying its principles. Two of the most important were:

That freedom from restraint is calculated to give the utmost extension to foreign trade, and the best direction to the capital and industry of the country.

That the maxim of buying in the cheapest market and selling in the dearest, which regulates every merchant in his individual dealings, is strictly applicable as the best rule for the trade of the whole nation.

In its report the committee of the House of Commons, set up to consider the matter, agreed with the general principles of the merchants. But despite piecemeal reforms and simplification of duties, no substantial relaxation of protective measures took place until after 1832, when the reform of the electoral system gave greater power to the big towns and to the middle classes.

European Trade. In France, where no large section of the community was directly involved in foreign trade, a policy of protection was continued and even intensified. During the period following 1790 internal tariffs and regional restrictions had been swept away, but this opening of the home market was accompanied by the raising of even higher barriers to foreign trade. After 1815 the Bourbons dared not expose French manufacturers and merchants to the competition of the more highly industrialized production of Britain. In 1816, 1820, 1822, and 1826 tariffs were raised on agricultural produce, to please the landed interests which dominated Parliament, and on coal, iron, and cotton goods to please the industrialists. Industrial and trading interests were strong enough in France to demand this much consideration.

Because British goods were increasingly finding European markets, similar anxieties to protect home industries against British competition governed the commercial policies of most other European states. Prussian policy was of special significance for the future. Prussia's two chief exports were corn and linen, and both were directly affected by British policy. She turned to the task of freeing the German home market from internal obstructions, partly in order to ensure easier sale for these goods. In 1818 the government removed the internal customs boundaries dividing one province of Prussia from the other and set up a uniform tariff against the rest of the world. By 1826 several of the smaller German states enclosed by Prussia's sprawling territories joined the system, and by negotiations with other states a large North German area of internal free trade grew up. Similar unions were next set up between Bavaria and Württemberg in the south, and between Hanover and Saxony in the north. By 1834 the three unions merged into the *Zollverein*, or customs union, comprising 17 states and some 26 million people. The chief German power excluded from this great new free-trade area was Austria, which consistently refused to join and so left to Prussia a new role of economic leadership and domination in German territory.

Russia's chief export to Britain was corn, and the government met with constant outcry from Russian manufacturers and merchants that because Britain, France, and Austria had high tariffs and prohibitions on trade, Russian industries were being discouraged or ruined, while agriculture could find no foreign market. Even when the Tsar favoured, as did Alexander I, a general freeing of trade, the governments were so anxious to collect revenue and prevent money from flowing out of the country that they readily gave way to these pressures. The result was a series of measures in 1816, 1819, 1822, 1825, and 1830 which fluctuated between absolute prohibition of imports of iron and textiles, and very high protective duties on all imports except such raw materials and foodstuffs as were regarded as essential. Least affected by the tariff policies of Britain, France, and Russia was Austria, which enjoyed a large and somewhat freer home market and had an outlet for her exports in the Mediterranean. But Italian trade remained heavily hampered by state frontiers, and by internal customs barriers and tolls.

The conditions of European trade by 1830 were, therefore, in an intermediate phase of development closely comparable with the partial and localized growth of transport and communications, and of mechanization in industry. What had been achieved was a very considerable freeing of the movement of goods within each country, by the removal of internal barriers and tolls. The resulting creation of larger home markets was in itself a change of great importance for the national development of France, Austria, Russia, and above all Prussia in Germany.

But as regards trade between states the general pattern of European policy was still highly protectionist. While enlarged free-trade areas fostered national growth, the hampering of inter-state trade helped to account for periodic trade depressions, which in turn fostered movements of democratic and socialist discontent. The outstanding exception to the general pattern was the United Kingdom. After the union with Ireland in 1801 the United Kingdom had become for a time the largest single area within which trade could be carried on without running into any artificial barriers that increased costs and delays. By 1830 it was losing this unique advantage, which had greatly helped its rapid commercial expansion. It was now, therefore, moving on to seek corresponding freedom for its foreign trade. British merchants and manufacturers, fearing no competition, pressed for the United Kingdom to set the example and the pace in world free trade – a policy that triumphed during the generation after 1830, but found little support from European governments until the 1860s.

Business and Finance. The growing social and political power of merchants and manufacturers was reinforced by the development of business and financial organizations with similar interests and antipathies. While trade between states was still so limited in scope both by the absorptive capacity of home markets and by tariff barriers, the wholesale exporter was extremely rare, and the further east one went the less important he became. But bankers everywhere assumed new importance, and with the growth of large national debts and foreign loans and investments, financial organization became the basis of a class with new wealth and importance. In 1815 the national debt of the United Kingdom stood at more than £800 million, much more burdensome than that of defeated France; nor was this much reduced by 1830. Even so, the Bank of England was well able to organize foreign loans, and continued to do so on a large and profitable scale. The Bank of France, founded in 1800, was likewise in close relations with the government, and enjoyed the exclusive rights of issuing notes until 1817, when banks in Rouen, Nantes, and Bordeaux were also given the privilege. The Netherlands Bank, founded in 1814, had the same monopoly in the Netherlands and Belgium until, in 1822, Belgium gained the right for its new *Société générale,* a joint-stock banking company. In addition to the growth of national banks, great international financial families had built up their organization and wealth by handling the £57 million subsidies and loans that Britain had made to her allies during the French wars. After 1815 men like Nathan Meyer Rothschild and the Baring brothers floated foreign state loans on the London market, and the Hopes did the same in Amsterdam. The Rothschilds had members in all the key centres of London, Paris, Vienna,

Naples, and Frankfurt. They were the leading organizers of the new type of international investment, which brought an increasing interlocking of the nations of Europe, and eventually of the world. Until the railroad boom after 1830 this did not develop much, though it was already beginning. In the 1820s there was a bubble of crazy speculation and overtrading. Loans were floated in aid of a quite fictitious South American republic, and skates and warming pans were being exported to Rio. It is significant of the new international solidarity of bankers that in 1825, when this bubble burst and there was financial crisis, the Bank of France readily lent its rival, the Bank of England, nearly £2 million to save it from difficulties. The financiers played a new role in politics even by 1830, as is shown by Laffitte and Casimir-Périer, the bankers who backed the monarchy of Louis Philippe and became in turn prime minister. But this group was still small in number and somewhat restricted in its influence. In finance, as in industrialization, transport, and trade, Europe was still only on the brink of a new stage of economic expansion.

THE REVOLUTIONARY TIDE

The second half of the year 1830 saw revolutions in France, Belgium, parts of Germany, Italy, and Switzerland, and in Poland. In Portugal and Spain civil war began, which lasted in Spain until 1840. These revolutions were unlike the risings of 1820, which had been essentially nationalist risings led by military groups, in that they were liberal revolts led by broader elements of the wealthy middle classes. They were primarily protests against the rigidities and shortcomings of the conservative policies adopted since 1815; and the limited extent of their purposes and their success derived from the economic conditions already described. What they had in common was a desire to bring governments into closer relationship with society, as society had developed up to that date. When the course of events carried the revolutionary movements beyond that point, they lost impetus and were checked.

The July Revolution in France. In France the liberal opposition to the ultra-conservative government of Charles X was able to take its stand on the Charter of 1814. As a result of the elections of July 1830, the liberal opposition in the Chamber grew from 221 to 274. Polignac's ministry decided on a *coup d'état.* It took the legitimist royalist form of issuing a set of five Ordinances on 25 July. These dissolved the newly elected Chamber before it could meet, reduced the electorate from 100,000 to 25,000, called for new elections on this basis, and forbade any publication not authorized by the government. In spirit, if not entirely in the letter, they destroyed the Charter and the existing constitution. The liberal politicians and journalists, led by men like Adolphe Thiers, François Guizot, and the banker Jacques Laffitte, met to draw up protests, defy the prohibition of free publication, and bring the force of public opinion to bear upon the king. On the day after the fateful Ordinances appeared, crowds formed in the streets of Paris; and on the day after that the republican groups, led by Raspail and Cavaignac, organized bands of students and workers to throw up the barricades. On 28 July these groups captured the Hôtel de Ville (seizure of the city hall being the traditional prelude to Paris revolutions). They raised the tricolour flag, the red, white, and blue of the revolution, and paraded in the boulevards. The royal troops were without guidance or direction because of the inaction of the king and his ministers, and lost control of the city. By 30 July the rebels had complete mastery of the capital, and Charles X abdicated in favour of his grandson, the Duke of Bordeaux, henceforth known to his supporters as 'Henry V'. The downfall of the Bourbons was almost bloodless.

The insurgents were divided as to what to do next. The more democratic republicans, with headquarters at the Hôtel de Ville, wanted to set up a republic under the presidency of the eminent Lafayette, now 74, the 'hero of two worlds' and idol of the National Guard. The liberal politicians and journalists, as the parliamentary majority under the existing constitution, wanted to make the Duke of Orléans king. Orléans, backed not only by the parliamentary majority but also by the astuteness of Thiers, the diplomacy of Talleyrand, and the wealth of Laffitte, was by far the strongest candidate. Descended from a younger brother of Louis XVI, the Orléans family had been the traditional rivals to the Bourbon kings. The Duke's father, 'Equality Philip' (*Philippe Egalité*) had conspired against Louis XVI, and during the Revolution he had adopted republican and revolutionary ideas – though these had not saved him from the guillotine in 1793. The Duke himself had known poverty and exile, but was now a wealthy, thrifty man of 57. He resolved to play the role of citizen king, model of bourgeois virtues and respectful of constitutional liberties. He gained formal power by accepting the office of Lieutenant-General of the kingdom, first from a group of the parliamentarians and then from Charles X himself. He captured republican support by visiting Lafayette at the Hôtel de Ville on 31 July, relying on the fact that that conservatively minded hero preferred monarchy to Jacobinism. When he appeared on the balcony with Lafayette and the two men embraced one another wrapped in an enormous tricolour, the Paris crowd went mad with delight. This kiss won him republican support as well as the support of the National Guard, of which Lafayette was now commander. Charles X fled to England, prudently taking his grandson with him, and a week later Parliament declared the throne to be vacant. Within two days it proclaimed Orléans king as Louis Philippe, 'King of the French by the Grace of God and the will of the nation'. Consolidation of the constitutional monarchy seemed complete, and the revolution, skilfully manufactured in Paris, was accepted with little resistance by the whole of France.

With the form of the régime so quickly settled by the 'Three Glorious Days' (July 27–29) the parliament now proceeded to revise the Charter and impose it upon the new king. The revisions indicate clearly the liberal ideas of the majority. The Chamber of Peers was weakened in its hereditary character by being turned into an upper house of life members only, nominated by the king, and a batch of new peers were created to guarantee the change. The electorate was widened by lowering the age qualification for voters to 25 instead of 30, and the property qualification from 300 francs to 200. Citizens were eligible to become deputies at the age of 30 instead of 40. Censorship was abolished, cases involving the press were referred to trial by jury, and extraordinary tribunals or judicial commissions were prohibited. Roman Catholicism was recognized as the religion of 'the majority of Frenchmen', but the connexion between altar and throne was ended, some religious orders were expelled, and provision was made for state-aided primary schools to be set up in each commune.

The men who imposed these conditions on the king had clear ideas of what they wanted. They did not want universal suffrage or democracy; they did not want a republic, too closely associated in France with Jacobinism and extreme democracy; they did not want to found the new régime on revolution, or even on a plebiscite – hence the manoeuvres, engineered by Laffitte and his friends, to place on the throne a man who combined the necessary credentials of royal descent with a personal readiness to accept the restraints of the Charter and of ministerial responsibility to Parliament. The merit of the new régime, in their eyes, was that it got rid of the absolutist and clericalist proclivities of the Bourbons while guaranteeing property and public order against the encroachments of democracy and republicanism. It held a balance between liberty and order, parliamentarism and authority. It would from the outset have bitter enemies – the clerical and the legitimist royalists, who regarded Louis Philippe and his supporters as traitors; the republicans, who felt cheated; the surviving enthusiasts for Bonapartism. Like every other régime France had had since 1815, it was confronted with a large and disloyal opposition, which regarded it as a fraud and a betrayal. But it would, its supporters hoped, give France a period of peace, prosperity, and settled order in which trade and industry could flourish and men could grow rich in security. This, the king knew, was the commission he had been given. His personal tastes and inclinations coincided happily with these expectations. His chief interests were to stay on the throne and to stay rich.

Alexis de Tocqueville, one of the greatest liberal writers of the century, wrote a description of the new king:

He had most of the qualities and defects which belong more particularly to the subaltern orders of society. He had regular habits and wanted those around him to have them too. He was orderly in his conduct, simple in his habits, his tastes were tempered; he was a born friend of the law, an enemy of all excesses, sober in his ways except in his desires. He was human without being sentimental, greedy and soft. He had no flaming passions, no ruinous weaknesses, no striking vices, and only one kingly virtue: courage. He was extremely polite, but without discrimination or greatness, the politeness of a merchant rather than of a prince. He hardly appreciated literature or art, but he passionately loved industry. His memory was prodigious and capable of retaining the most minute detail. His conversation was prolix, diffuse, original and trivial, anecdotal, full of small facts, of salt and significance.... He was enlightened, subtle, flexible: because he was open only to what was useful, he was full of proud disdain for the truth, and he believed so little in virtue that his sight was darkened.... He was an unbeliever in religion like the eighteenth century, and sceptical in politics like the nineteenth; having no belief in himself, he had none in the belief of others.

He was, in short, everything that a liberal king in 1830 could be expected to be: middle class, respectable, and unspectacular.

Belgian Independence. The July Revolution in Paris had great repercussions in Belgium. The resentment of the Catholic, French, and Flemish sections of the southern Netherlands against their domination by the Dutch since the compulsory union of 1815 had steadily grown in strength. It rested as much on nationalist desires for independence as on liberal opposition to the rule of William I. Within the union Belgians outnumbered the Dutch by two to one, yet they had only equal representation in the States-General. The country was run mainly in the interests of the Dutch minority, and mainly by Dutch officials. By 1828 the two main sections of opposition, the conservative Catholics and the Liberals, united to resist Dutch domination. The fall of the legitimist monarchy in France and the victory of liberalism there overthrew one main pillar of the restoration settlement of 1815. Might not Belgian revolt destroy another?

On 25 August occurred demonstrations at the Opera House in Brussels, and as though by pre-arranged signal there were at once revolts in the provincial towns. The wealthy classes in the towns, fearing street disorders, organized themselves into Committees of Safety and armed Civil Guards to protect property. The king dared not use troops, but sent his two sons, the popular Prince of Orange and Prince Frederick, to Brussels with a few thousand men. The Prince of Orange, finding barricades in the streets, courageously entered the city alone and undertook to support the liberal programme of complete separation of Belgium from Holland 'leaving no point of contact except through the reigning dynasty'. The king agreed to summon the States-General, which on 29 September voted for separation. But meanwhile the insurrection in Brussels, backed by bands of volunteers from other towns, had taken control. Dutch troops, 14,000 strong, were driven away. A provisional government was set up, uniting the old Catholic nobility with the younger middle-class Liberals. On 4 October it proclaimed the complete independence of Belgium, and by 28 October signed an armistice with the Dutch.

Elections for a new National Congress were held on 5 November. Out of a population of some 4 million, 30,000 electors chose 200 deputies. The National Congress met a week later, and on 18 November it unanimously confirmed Belgian independence. It then proceeded to declare members of the Dutch family of Orange-Nassau ineligible to hold any office. By February 1831 it promulgated a new constitution, which was the most liberal in Europe at that time. It declared that 'all powers have their source in the nation', and established a constitutional monarchy with strictly limited royal powers. The king was to be chosen by the representatives of the people, and the organ of popular will was to be parliament, elected on direct and frequent elections by secret ballot, but by an electorate limited by certain property qualifications. The monarch chosen by the congress in June was Prince Leopold of Saxe-Coburg-Gotha, who in July took the oath to maintain the constitution and become King Leopold I.

The new régime was, however, conditioned more by the action of the other European powers than this simple account would suggest. The governments of Austria, Prussia, and Russia wanted to check the Belgian revolution and preserve the position of 1815. The governments of Britain and France wanted to prevent intervention, and took the initiative in summoning a conference of the five powers in London to protect the peace of Europe. It met on 4 November 1830, just as the elections to the Belgian National Congress were taking place. At the same time a gale of liberty blew through Europe. Poland and Italy began to stir, and in England the Tory government of Wellington was replaced by the Whig government of Grey. In December the conference recognized the principle of Belgian independence, and in January it issued a protocol proclaiming that 'Belgium forms a perpetually neutral state'. Under force of circumstances, Belgium won international recognition of her independence and her neutrality.

Accordingly, when in 1831 the Dutch invaded Belgian territory in a last effort to regain it and in ten days defeated the Belgian forces, France sent troops and forced the Dutch to withdraw. The London Conference regulated Dutch-Belgian relations by the Treaty of the Twenty-four Articles, establishing Belgian frontiers, which the Belgians accepted in November. Britain and France blockaded the coast of Holland to force the Dutch to agree, and a French force blockaded the Dutch troops holding out in Antwerp. It was May 1833 before the Dutch and Belgians reached agreement, although it left each in control of territories which the Conference had allocated differently; and it was 1838 before the Dutch accepted the Treaty of 1831 and so recognized Belgian independence. The status of Belgium as independent and neutral was finally determined by agreement of the powers in 1839. Leopold I, who was aged 40 when he accepted the Belgian throne, was to rule the country with skill and good sense for the next 34 years. The youngest son of a petty German prince, he belonged to the class of the ruling dynastic families of Europe. In 1831 he married the eldest daughter of Louis Philippe, and so consolidated his position among the western powers. Under his guidance Belgium was set to follow a course of development closely parallel to that of France, reconciling nationalism with constitutional government, Catholicism with liberalism, in a spirit of bourgeois moderation.

Central Europe. Meanwhile, throughout the lands of central Europe, ripples of revolution were spreading, even to the cantons of Switzerland. The governments of the 22 cantons were mostly in the hands of local aristocracies, and until 1825 they were solidly conservative. Since that year a few had won more liberal and democratic constitutions. Between 1830 and 1833 most of the others gained similar constitutions, under the pressure of small liberal groups who were influenced by the course of events in Greece, France, and Belgium. Students, journalists, and the men of wealth connected with the growth of local industries backed these movements. They regarded the new constitutions as preliminary to an overhaul of the national federation which, since its reorganization in 1815, had little real power. But that further change did not come until 1848.

In the German Confederation, likewise, local revolts occurred. In Brunswick the ruling duke was driven out and his successor compelled to grant a more liberal constitution. In Hanover, Saxony, and Hesse-

Cassel similar concessions were forced from the rulers. In Bavaria, Baden, and Württemberg, where parliamentary systems existed, liberal oppositions gained in strength at elections and the press became more critical of the governments. By 1832 Austria and Prussia felt constrained to get the Diet at Frankfurt to pass the Six Acts, which re-established repressive measures throughout all German states, strengthened the hands of princes against parliamentary assemblies and curbed the more outspoken sections of the press. In 1833 a party of German students and Polish exiles seized the guardhouse in Frankfurt and tried to overawe the Diet. They were defeated, and the Diet set up a special commission to round up such agitators, now beginning to form themselves into a 'Young German' movement. In Germany, by 1835, reaction was again triumphant. In Austria, where Metternich's system for preserving order was at its strongest, the breath of revolution was hardly felt at all.

But in Italy, the home of secret societies, which were now establishing more regular contact with liberals in France and Belgium, revolutions took place on a more concerted plan. At the end of 1830 Francis IV of Modena was driven from his capital by a revolt, and within a few weeks Marie Louise of Parma suffered the same fate. In the papal territories east of the Apennines other revolutions set up a provisional government. It was certain that Austria, backed by Prussia and Russia, would intervene to crush any insurrection so close to her own provinces in northern Italy, and the chief hope of the revolutionaries was that Louis Philippe would send them help. This help was not forthcoming from either the Chamber or the more cautiously liberal ministry of Casimir-Périer. Austria, unimpeded, sent her troops into Italy to restore the rulers to their thrones and support them in the severe repressions that accompanied their return. But Mazzini, who in 1830 was imprisoned for his Carbonarist activities, settled in Marseilles and founded the 'Young Italy' movement, designed to arouse the whole of Italy to greater unity in the cause of national independence. By 1833 the movement had attracted 60,000 supporters, with local committees in all the main Italian cities. The following year he also founded a 'Young Europe' movement to run national committees for similar patriotic agitation in Germany, Poland, and Switzerland. Despite their immediate failures, the revolutions of 1830 thus gave birth not only to the Italian *Risorgimento*, or movement for national regeneration, but also to a wider European movement that was to bear fruit in 1848.[1]

In Poland revolution began at the end of November 1830, led by a secret society and by university students. It was no very formidable force, but Constantine, leader of the army in Poland, panicked and left

1. See p. 204.

the country. The rebels set up a provisional government chiefly of members of the landed aristocracy of Poland, which tried to bargain with the Tsar for reforms. But the rebels split, the Tsar refused to grant reform, and in February 1831 he sent a Russian army into Poland. Again, the only hope was western intervention, but that was no more forthcoming for Poland than for Italy. By the autumn of 1831 the revolution was crushed and the Russians took ferocious revenge. Warsaw, where the more extreme democrats had triumphed and which had been the centre of Polish cultural life, was turned into a military garrison town and its university closed. Poland was subjected to severe suppression and military government for another generation. Many hundreds of her intellectual leaders were driven into exile, and they took refuge mainly in the western countries and America.

In Portugal and Spain constitutional régimes were preserved against counter-revolutions only by British and French intervention. Each country had a pretender to the throne: Dom Miguel, the queen's uncle, in Portugal and Don Carlos, brother of King Ferdinand VII, in Spain. These pretenders were both leaders of the most extreme reactionary and ultra-royalist forces. Dom Miguel seized the throne in 1828 and proceeded to crush all liberal movements. When Pedro, recently deposed emperor of Brazil, came to defend the rights of his daughter, the young Queen Maria, civil war ensued. Then in 1833, when Ferdinand VII died and his daughter became queen, her Liberal ministers drew up a new constitution modelled on the French, Dom Miguel and Don Carlos joined forces against their queens, and civil war began in Spain. The pretenders were driven into exile only when France and Britain intervened on behalf of the liberal monarchs. Their intervention preserved at least the forms of constitutional government in the Iberian peninsula.

Parliamentary Reform in Britain. The British counterpart to the liberal revolutions of these years was the great parliamentary Reform Bill passed in 1832. As already described,[1] the ministry of Lord Grey came to power in the autumn of 1830 pledged to promote a Bill for reform of the electoral system. The first Bill he introduced passed the House of Commons by a majority of only one vote, and Grey demanded fresh elections, which were fought amid great excitement on the main issue of parliamentary reform. This reference of a major constitutional issue to the electorate was itself an implicit concession to liberal ideas. These elections gave the Whigs, led by Grey, a majority in the House of Commons, but the Bill was twice defeated in the House of Lords which had a Tory majority. It was only after Grey had forced the Lords into

1. See p. 156.

passing the Bill, by the threat that the king would create enough new peers to give the Whigs a majority in the Lords, that they gave way; William IV had agreed to so drastic a threat only because there was no other practicable alternative; Grey had already resigned and Wellington, the Tory leader, not having the confidence of the country, had refused to take office. The bill was in this way prefaced by events that vividly coerced both king and Lords into bowing to the wishes of the Commons and of public opinion. This was but a more sensational continuation of that yielding of conservatism in face of immediate threat of violence and civil strife which has already been noted in relation to the grant of freedom of association and of religious equality during the previous decade.

The 'Act to amend the representation of the people in England and Wales,' which eventually passed through Parliament in 1832, was very much less democratic in effect than either its title or the stormy events that preceded its enactment might suggest. The most substantial change it made was to redistribute the strength of the constituencies. The House of Commons consisted, as before, of 658 members elected for boroughs and counties. But whereas 262 boroughs had returned 465 members, 257 now returned only 399; and whereas county members had been 188 they now numbered 253. The universities of Oxford, Cambridge, and Dublin each returned two representatives. These changes, which strengthened the power of the country gentry and the big towns at the expense of the landed proprietors and borough-mongers who had controlled scores of small borough constituencies, gave more weight in politics to the wealthy business and commercial classes of the large northern towns, hitherto greatly under-represented in parliament. Of the small towns, 86 lost the right to return either one or two members to the Commons. These included some, such as the notorious Old Sarum, which had long ceased to be towns at all and whose representatives had been virtually nominated by the 'borough owner'. At the same time 22 new boroughs were allowed to return two members each, and 21 others one member each; and these were the big new towns, mostly in the north, which had grown up around the ports, industries, and mines. These changes were not great enough to destroy the preponderance of the landed interest. There remained nearly 50 boroughs and well over 60 members still directly dependent on the peers and landowners of England and Wales. But the men whose wealth depended on trade and manufacturing were given a share of parliamentary power alongside the old landed interest – a share large enough to enable them to assert their interests, as subsequent legislation was to show.

At the same time the Act protected both landed and industrial interests against the dangers of democracy by a host of other provisions, the chief of which were the changes in the qualification for voting. These remained complex, but all depended on property qualifications. In the boroughs a voter had to be owner or tenant of a property worth at least £10 annual value. This effectively kept out of the electorate all the working classes, confining it to men of some wealth and social standing. The old electorate of less than half a million was increased by about 50 per cent in England and Wales. No provision was made for secret ballot, which meant that the old methods of bribery, influence, and intimidation at elections remained as effective as ever. The detailed arrangements laid down in the Act for the keeping of registers of electors in each constituency gave party organizations a new incentive to spread their efforts into every constituency. With a large body of voters to be canvassed, sharper competition between party organizations, more frequently contested elections, and no effective restraint on bribery and intimidation, electioneering in England became more costly, corrupt, and disorderly than ever before. Yet the electoral system succeeded in returning to the Commons, now enhanced in its prestige and powers in relation to king or Lords, men who broadly represented the main interests and opinions of the country. The radical democrats, whose agitation had done so much to bring about the reform, remained as bitterly disappointed as were the contemporary republicans of France after the July Revolution. It was the Whigs who had won the day; though by effecting this first deliberate overhaul of the parliamentary system they had made it more difficult, in future, to resist further such changes when the mass of opinion in the country demanded them.

One of the first Acts of the reformed parliament of 1833 was to carry out a further liberal revolution, no less momentous in its consequencies and significance than any other revolution of the period. It abolished slavery as an institution throughout the whole of the British Empire. The trade in slaves had been prohibited since 1807, and an Abolition Society, headed by Sir Thomas Fowell Buxton and Zachary Macaulay, had ever since pressed for abolition. In 1833 Lord Stanley, backed by Buxton, steered through parliament a Bill that ended slavery in all British territories and provided for compensation to slave owners, from the pockets of the British taxpayer, to the extent of £20 million. Critics of the emancipating enthusiasts of the liberal Parliament pointed out that their consciences were less tender as regards the sweated labour of women and children in mines and factories nearer home. But with the growing tide of liberalism reaching its height, these abuses, too, were soon to be tackled. The British example in abolishing slavery was followed by most other countries in the next fifty years: by France in

1848, Argentina in 1853, the United States in 1862–5, the Netherlands in 1863–9, Portugal between 1858 and 1878, Brazil in 1871–88.

'NOW HALF DISSOLVING TO A LIBERAL THAW'

The passing of the great Reform Bill in Britain consolidated the new alignment of political forces in Europe. From the revolutions and other changes of 1830–33 Europe emerged divided more sharply than ever into two political regions. In Germany, Italy, and Poland the forces of conservatism triumphed over those of liberalism, and revolutions were crushed by the concerted actions of Austria, Russia, and Prussia. In France, Belgium, Switzerland, Portugal, Spain, and Great Britain liberalism triumphed, backed at times by the power of France and Britain. Europe roughly west of the Rhine was moving towards a pattern of liberal, constitutional, parliamentary government geared to the special interest of a growing commercial and industrial middle class. Europe east of the Rhine preserved all the main lines of its economic and political pattern of 1815. This remained the basic fact in international relations until 1848.

The maintenance and development of constitutional government in the western nations had involved a tightening alliance between the movements of nationalism and the movements of liberalism. The more monarchs isolated themselves from the nation, as did Charles X in France or William I in the Netherlands, the more liberalism stood on the side of the nation. Belgian achievement of national independence was a liberal achievement, enlisting the cause of constitutionalism against the power of the Dutch. In Italy, Mazzini preached liberalism as the necessary path to national unification and independence. Similarly, the triumphs of dynasticism in eastern Europe involved royal denials of both nationalist and liberal aspirations in Germany, Italy, and Poland. Because, as in France, Portugal, and Spain, ultra-royalists in politics were usually also ultramontanes in religion, they were opposed by all who regarded clerical power as an obstacle to both national independence and liberal reforms.

The revolutions that took place all over Europe between 1815 and 1830 made considerable breaches in the political and the territorial settlements of 1815. The overthrow of the legitimist Bourbon monarchy in France and the separation of Belgium from Holland were direct reversals of the treaty arrangements. Norway, which had been allotted to Sweden in 1814, had contrived to assert a greater degree of real independence and self-government than had been contemplated at Vienna. She had accepted her place in a dual monarchy under Crown prince Bernadotte of Sweden, but contrived to keep her Eidsvold constitution of May 1814, which gave her a single-chamber Parliament, able to defy the royal veto by passing a bill in three successive assemblies. This little nation of less than a million fisherfolk and farmers decided to abolish its nobility by an act of parliament. When the king rejected the Bill in 1815, it was passed again in 1818 and in 1821, and became law in spite of Bernadotte. Friction between king and Parliament continued because Bernadotte tried to extend the Swedish system of government to Norway. But by 1830 he was compelled to give up his attempts to change the Eidsvold constitution, and accepted the virtual self-government of Norway. The chief result of the union was a growing nationalist movement in Norway, soon spreading even to the adoption of a full national language, Landsmaal, with a literature of its own. These developments had certainly not been an intention of the settlement of 1815. In other ways, too, the political landscape of Europe had changed: most strikingly with the independence of Greece, and with the development of the *Zollverein* in Germany by 1834. Even where rulers had been reinstated by force, as in the Italian and German states, their temporary overthrow had reminded kings everywhere how fragile was their position, and how dependent they were on the general system of Metternich, already under attack from so many directions.

That system, however, remained at least formally intact and almost invulnerable. The provinces of Austria were kept completely subject to Vienna in government and administration. In Russia, with the resubjection of Poland, and the rule of Nicholas I, reaction reigned triumphant. In Prussia, too, no substantial progress had been made towards more constitutional or liberal government, despite the more liberal economic expedients of the *Zollverein*. By concerted diplomatic action in 1830 and 1831 the three eastern powers had successfully held off any attempts by the western powers to intervene in Italy or Poland. In 1833 they even made a formal treaty of alliance, the Convention of Münchengrätz, which gave to any sovereign threatened with revolution the right to call on them for help to repress it. In the international settlement of the Belgian question, as of the Greek, the old idea of a 'concert of Europe' remained operative. But in nearly every other respect the idea of a general concert had given way to the new reality of rival groups, each acting with concert but in hostility to one another. When France and Britain undertook joint intervention to preserve constitutionalism in Portugal and Spain, Lord Palmerston hailed this action as a new counterpoise to the solidarity of the eastern powers. 'The treaty,' he declared, 'establishes among the constitutional states of the West a Quadruple Alliance which will serve as a counterpoise against the Holy Alliance of the East.' This double 'concert of Europe' was, however, an admission that any hope of a general concert was at an end. It implied, instead, a new 'balance of power', with the rival sides divided by conflict between liberal and nationalist ideologies on one hand, and the preservation of the old order on the other. These conditions allowed more opportunities for the pursuit of separate national interests and for the progress of liberal movements than the restoration settlement, contrived at Vienna, could ever have permitted. The consequences soon became apparent between 1833 and 1848.

CHAPTER 10

THE ECONOMIC REVOLUTION
OF 1830–48

WESTERN ECONOMIC EXPANSION

THE constitutional and political adjustments to new needs, achieved in the western nations by 1833, were followed by a new era of rapid expansion in industrial production and trade. The lead in this expansion was taken by Britain and Belgium, though France and the Scandinavian countries shared in it too. Elsewhere in Europe economic advance was slowed down by the subordination of the enterprising classes of manufacturing and business to the interests of landowners and aristocracies.

Transport and Industry. In Britain these years were pre-eminently the heroic age of railway building. At first railroads were stubbornly resisted by the existing interests of roads and canals. What, it was asked, was to be done to safeguard all those who had advanced money for making and repairing the turnpike roads and the canals? Or the large number of people who made a living as coachmakers, harness makers, horse dealers, innkeepers? The first attempt to get through Parliament a Bill permitting the making of the railroad between Liverpool and Manchester failed because one noble duke protested that it would spoil his fox covers; and it cost £70,000 to secure parliamentary permission in 1826 even before starting the heavy capital outlay needed to buy the land and construct the line. Because British railroad builders were pioneers, they incurred the costs and burdens of all pioneers, and paid the price for technical experiments and mistakes that other countries were able to avoid. The opening of the Liverpool and Manchester Railway in 1830, using the steam locomotive, inaugurated the new era. By 1838, when Russia was building her first railroad, there were 490 miles of railroad in England and Wales, and 50 in Scotland; and their construction had cost more than £13 million. By the end of 1850 there were 6,621 miles in operation. The two boom periods of building came in 1836 and, much more spectacularly, in the years 1844–7. Despite wild speculations and financial disasters in 1847, there was considerable consolidation of lines which had been built piecemeal and often wastefully. The British 'Railway King', George Hudson, devoted his business and administrative skill to bring about extensive amalgamations and improvements in their general running.

The revolution in transport which came with the railroads brought with it vast new demands for coal and iron, and stimulated a counterpart revolution in the heavy industries, especially in mining and metallurgy. Britain's coal output, only some sixteen million tons in 1815, rose to thirty million by 1835 and fifty million by 1848. Her output of iron doubled from one million tons in 1835 to two million in 1848; and by the middle of the century probably half the whole world's production of pig iron took place in Great Britain. Engineering proper, and the industries devoted to making machines, were still small-scale even in 1848, and the main progress in engineering techniques came only after that date. The railroads also encouraged the rise of big contractors, and offered employment to thousands ranging from the gangs of navvies who laid the tracks to the drivers, firemen, and other staff who ran the lines. A great new industry was born in little more than twenty years, and fears of unemployment among those who worked on the systems of roads and canals proved unfounded. There was a general stimulus to the whole economic system, and better facilities for quick and cheaper transport in turn stimulated other industries, such as textiles.

In British economy this was, indeed, almost as much the age of cotton as of coal and iron. It was cotton above all other commodities which was linked with the expansion of British overseas trade. Already in 1830 three quarters of the raw cotton came from the United States, and in 1849 the total import was as high as 346,000 tons, estimated to be worth £15 million. By the middle of the century more than half a million people were engaged in the cotton industry alone, and textiles as a whole employed well over one million. Textile manufacture was the industry most representative of the age of machinery and power. Although mechanization was still slow, cotton set the pace in factory production. The cotton trade boosted shipping. Between 1827 and 1848 the total tonnage of British shipping, both sail and steam, rose from two and a half to four million tons. At the middle of the century 60 per cent of the world's ocean-going tonnage was British; and the tonnage of all shipping entered and cleared from ports in the United Kingdom (excluding coastal trade and trade between Britain and Ireland) rose from six million tons in 1834 to more than fourteen million tons in 1847. This is perhaps the most vivid index of how much the prosperity of the country had come to depend on overseas trade. By 1850 the United Kingdom had triumphantly established itself as not only 'the workshop of the world' but also as the shipper, trader, and to a great extent the banker, of the world.

In continental Europe, Belgium set the pace in railroad-building. Her rich supplies of coal and the spirit of national enterprise released by her newly won independence made possible an industrial revolution comparable in intensity, if not in scale, with Great Britain's. The line from Brussels to Malines, opened in 1835, carried in its first year more than half a million passengers; this was more than were carried by all the British lines in 1835. Belgium was ahead of Britain in having a railway policy and in planning railroad construction as a national concern to serve national needs. Designed to take full advantage of Belgium's geographical and economic position as a land of passage, the lines were planned to link up England, France, Germany, and Holland, and make Belgium the commercial entrepôt of western Europe. The plan, begun in 1834, was completed within ten years. Throughout this period Belgium produced more coal than France, mainly because in 1815 she had inherited mines that had been among France's greatest. Liège and Southern Hainault were the first developed coal-mining areas of the continent, and the Liège district was a well-established metallurgical centre. Belgium sent machinery all over Holland, Germany, and even Russia. Her spirit of national enterprise and traditions of craftsmanship, her urban society and her new network of transport, conspired to give her an economic lead in Europe second only to Britain's.

French economic development was more gradual, though it was real. Under the Orléanist monarchy greater freedom and encouragement were given to industry and trade. The first railway worth the name was opened between Paris and Saint-Germain in 1837, and by 1848 France had some two thousand miles of track: a third as much as Britain, in a country double the size. Local roads were immensely improved as a result of the law of 1836, and this led to a widening of the areas within which farmers could profitably sell their produce – a change of special importance in view of the supremacy of the home market in France. The problems, social and political, caused by industrial towns are prominent in French discussions of these years – more, in fact, than the development of large-scale industry seems to warrant. By 1846 there were hardly more than a million workers employed in large-scale industries. But they were congested into a few big towns and industrial areas – the cotton and textile areas of Alsace, Normandy and the Nord, the metallurgical areas of Lorraine and the basin of the Loire, the silk area around Lyon. This meant the quite abnormal growth of a few towns. In the ten years 1831–41, Saint-Etienne grew from a population of 16,000 to one of 54,000; Roubaix from 8,000 to 34,000. The unregulated employment of women and children for excessive hours and in bad factory conditions exposed the growing class of industrial workers not only to insanitary living conditions and hardship, but also to widespread tuberculosis and epidemics of the cholera, which ravaged both France and Britain in 1831–2, and again in 1847–8. It was found, in 1840, that out of every 10,000 young men drafted for military service in the ten most industrialized departments of France, 9,000 had to be rejected as medically unfit. This severe toll on human well-being was the price paid for such growth, and is an explanation of the rise, in these years, of social revolutionary movements in France.[1]

East of the Rhine, railways came more slowly and piecemeal, and the corresponding advances in manufacturing spread gradually. The first German railway opened in 1835 in Bavaria, and already the economist Friedrich List, just back from America, was pressing the idea of a general German system of railways. At first he succeeded in having a line built in Saxony from Leipzig to Dresden, which began in 1839. In its first year it carried 412,000 people, some lady travellers keeping needles in their mouths to prevent familiarity in the darkness of its single tunnel. List's persuasive propaganda played a part in overcoming the doubts, hesitations, and frank hostility of many of the existing forces in Germany, and the crown prince of Prussia (the future Frederick William IV) became an enthusiastic supporter. By 1840 the line ran from Leipzig to Magdeburg, and companies had been formed to build more lines radiating from Berlin. By 1848 there were 1,500 miles of track on Prussian territory, and meanwhile other German states – following the Belgian planned system rather than the more hesitant Prussian model – had begun to build. As a result, by 1849–50 Germany's total of more than 3,000 miles matched France's 2,000 miles, and compared very favourably with Austria's 1,000 miles. Italy and Russia still had very few and very fragmentary lines. But it was now possible to travel by rail throughout the whole of northern Europe from Paris to Hamburg, Dresden, Berlin, Vienna, Warsaw. Apart from gaps in south-eastern Europe, rail links were by now nearly complete from the Baltic and the North Seas to the Adriatic.

The revolutionary effect of the railway was even greater in some respects on German life than on life in more industrialized countries like Britain and Belgium. With a road system that was so imperfect, and towns still small and semi-rural, the changes brought by both the constructing and the running of the railways were more obvious and more spectacular. Country people were shaken more abruptly out of their traditional outlooks and habits. Germany was set to become the centre of the continental system of transport and distribution in a way inconceivable hitherto. Her natural geographical and political characteristics had operated in the opposite direction: a small coastline discouraged shipping; the flow of many of her rivers to the closed sea of the Baltic, the freezing of her canals in winter, her backward roads, had all made

1. See p. 195.

transport difficult, while her tangle of internal customs and tolls had made it expensive. The new iron tracks opened up the interior lands of Germany as they were opening up the interior of America, exposing them to new forces, bringing a new stimulus to trade, offering new opportunities to men of enterprise in every sphere of business. Just as the *Zollverein* removed the artificial impediments, so the railways removed the natural impediments to German integration and prosperity. They made possible the rapid expansion of the German economy after 1850, and paved the way for the political unification of Germany in 1871. At the same time they gave her an enhanced importance in Europe, as the central power par excellence, and within that new era Prussia held all the advantages as against Austria, for future leadership and domination.

Yet, despite this revolution, economic and social conditions in most of Germany were still backward as compared with the more western countries. Agriculture still employed more than two thirds of the whole population. The middle classes were relatively small, and consisted mainly of small manufacturers, merchants, officials, and professional people, and the more well-to-do peasants. The centres of industry were sparse and scattered. The most important industry was textiles, manufactured mainly by small handicraft plants with little use of powered machinery. Metallurgy was growing with the construction of railways, but although the Krupp works had been founded in 1810, it still employed only 140 workers in 1846. Even by 1850 Germany was producing little more than 200,000 tons of iron. The country in general was poor, and at the middle of the century expansion still remained potential rather than actual.

Trade. The overwhelming preponderance of the United Kingdom in overseas shipping and commerce helped to block the expansion of overseas trade in western Europe. French commerce did not recover until 1825 the volume of foreign trade it had enjoyed in 1789. Even in 1848 most European trade was domestic and continental. But the expansion of means of overseas transport was beginning to open new doors there too. In 1839 the Peninsula and Oriental Line set up a regular steamship service between England and Alexandria. The following year Samuel Cunard founded the Cunard Steamship Line, which twelve years later was running a regular weekly service between Liverpool and New York. Steamers, which had for some years been used for river and coastal transport, came increasingly into use as ocean-going ships; though here, too, they assumed major importance only two decades later.

Overseas trade had become important enough for some major British industries to demand a drastic change in Britain's commercial policy. Controversy centred on two issues: the Corn Laws, resented by the manufacturers and merchants because they hampered free exports, and the Navigation Laws, resented by the same interests because they hampered transport. Between 1846 and 1849 both these protective measures were repealed, though the manner in which their repeal took place shows the tenacity and strength of old ideas and interests in even the most industrialized of European states. In 1836, when the price of corn was high, London radicals formed the first Anti-Corn Law Association; but Lancashire of the cotton mills was the natural home of the free trade movement. Raw cotton had to be imported; cotton goods formed a large proportion of exports. The prosperity of Lancashire depended directly on foreign trade; and the main impediment to foreign trade was the Corn Laws, designed to protect home-grown corn and keep its price high. The cry for cheap food was both simple and popular.

In the 1830s Richard Cobden, himself a cotton manufacturer, became the leading parliamentary spokesman of the movement, and was joined by the Quaker, John Bright. They wanted free trade in general, and 'Cobdenism' developed into a whole philosophy of the benefits of peace, order, and prosperity which could accrue from freedom of international trade. But it was natural first to concentrate their fire on the hated Corn Laws. On this issue the conflict between the conservative agricultural interest and the liberal manufacturing and commercial interests reached its height. An Anti-Corn Law League was founded, with headquarters in Manchester. Its propaganda through pamphlets, press, mass meetings, parliamentary oratory and pressure, set a new model for high-powered, intensive, and simple popular agitation. In 1843 its weekly publication, *The League*, reached a circulation of over 20,000 and in London twenty-four mass meetings were held at Covent Garden theatre. At some moments, as in 1842, the movement became almost revolutionary in character. As its activities spread to the countryside, rick burning and agrarian unrest spread too. In 1845 the harvest was bad, and a devastating disease ruined the potato crop. Since potatoes rather than corn were the staple diet of Ireland, this brought acute famine in Ireland. The League demanded the immediate and complete repeal of the laws which kept out imported food when families were starving.

Confusion prevailed among both the political parties. The Tory, Sir Robert Peel, resigned, but the Whig, Lord John Russell, failed to form a minority government. Peel formed a new cabinet, little different from the old, and tackled an overhaul of the whole fiscal system. His previous budgets of 1842 and 1845 had already almost abolished duties on the import of raw materials. He now completed the process of abolishing the duty on maize, greatly reducing the duties on other grains, including wheat, and permitting free importation of most foodstuffs. It was ten years after the first Anti-Corn Law Association had been formed before the Corn Laws were abolished. It took a hectic decade of incessant clamour to get them repealed; and only famine eventually forced the government's hand even in the reformed Parliament. But the manufacturing and commercial interests, backed by widespread popular support, in the end won total victory.

In 1849 with considerably less agitation the Navigation Laws, which had been designed to protect British shipping in much the same way as the Corn Laws had been intended to protect British farming, were abandoned. The shipping interests by then enjoyed so great a natural superiority in the world that they, like the cotton manufacturers and traders, had nothing to fear from competition. By the middle of the century in Britain, duties remained on imports and exports primarily for reasons of revenue, and not for purposes of protection. The United Kingdom had become an industrial state, in policy as well as in internal development. In 1831 agriculture had directly engaged some 275,000 families in Great Britain. At the middle of the century the number was still roughly the same. It was not that agriculture positively declined in these years, but that in a larger population the proportion that made a living out of industry, trade, and the great new occupations of transport and communication immediately increased. In short, industry and trade virtually absorbed the whole of the four and a half million increase in population between 1830 and 1850.

There was no comparably drastic change in the commercial policy of European countries in these years. Most remained unrepentantly protectionist, largely out of fear of British competition. In Germany the freeing of internal trade continued, with the extension of the *Zollverein* to include the northern and southern states originally excluded. But between 1834 and 1848 there was a tendency for the duties imposed on manufacturers by the whole *Zollverein* to become much heavier, especially on English pig iron and cotton yarn. In France there were interests, enjoying enhanced power after 1830, which favoured a certain freeing of trade. Winegrowers, shippers, consumers of large quantities of iron and steel such as the new railroad companies, and academic economists wanted some relaxation in the severely protectionist measures of the restored monarchy. But in general French farmers and manufacturers joined hands in wanting protection. The economic crisis of 1831, when the price of wheat soared, brought down the tariff against grain imports but only for one year to tide over the crisis. Free transit of goods through France was permitted to boost the carrying trade. The governments tended to be more favourable to the lowering and the simplification of duties than was the general body of manufacturers and farmers, but they were sufficiently subject to their parliamentary pressures to take no step likely to alienate their support. The chamber of 1836, for example, included as deputies 45 industrialists, bankers, or commercial men, and 116 *rentiers* or proprietors. In addition, most deputies represented the wealthier proprietors of rural constituencies. In 1840 Guizot, who served as Louis Philippe's chief minister from then until 1848, wrote to Lord Palmerston:

Another class, that of great manufacturers, metallurgists, and merchants, is favourably disposed toward the government of the king, and has supported and continues to support it on every possible occasion with its energy, its intelligence, its wealth, and its social influence. It is impossible for the government of the king not to be attentive to the interests and desires of the class of the population which has become attached to it. . . .

This was a precise and apt description of the working of the 'bourgeois monarchy', and it could have applied equally well to the governments and policies of Britain and Belgium in these years.

In eastern Europe governments remained broadly protectionist in policy for the traditional reasons. In Russia under the ministry of Count Cancrin, between 1823 and 1844, a series of rearrangements of the tariffs took place in order to help home trade and raise revenue. The general effect was that many duties were lowered, and protection took the place of prohibition. In 1846 began a new phase of freer trade, partly as a result of English negotiations; by 1850 there was a very substantial freeing of both import and export trade, and the former customs barriers between Poland and Russia were broken down.

Economic Crisis. One consequence of the growth of international and overseas trade was that Europe as a whole experienced periods of acute and general economic crisis. The story of the crises of 1818–19 and of 1825 were repeated in the much greater crises of 1838–9 and of 1846–7. The fluctuations of cotton prices in the United States in 1837, and the winding up of the Bank of the United States which involved the loss of £6 million of European capital invested in America, had severe repercussions in Europe. In Britain and Belgium companies failed, banks ran into difficulties, and again as in 1825, the Bank of England was given help through the Barings from the Bank of France. In 1845 and 1846 corn harvests in Britain and Europe were bad; and in 1847, although the English harvest was better, those of France and Germany were again bad. The effect on food supplies and prices was intensified by the failure of potato crops, especially in Ireland. Food had to be imported from further away, from America and southern Russia, and payment for it drained away gold. Speculative dealings in foodstuffs, especially in Britain, caused still further financial difficulties. There were large-scale mercantile failures, bankruptcies, and closures of banks.

These sharp but short-period ups and downs in the cost of living caused great social distress in the semi-industrialized condition of Europe. When added to the consequences of actual famine, the human misery caused by an uncontrolled exploitation of cheap labour, and the growing tide of political discontent, they helped to make the year 1848 a year of remarkable social and political revolution throughout Europe. Just as conservative governments of the years before 1830 had been generally too inhibited by their outlook and interests to handle effectively the movements of liberal discontent, so now the liberal governments after 1830 were too inhibited by their dependence upon mercantile and manufacturing interests to handle effectively the social distress of their peoples. It became evident, in one country after another, that governments had still not been brought into sensitive enough relationship with the needs of the whole of society to serve those needs efficiently. The inevitable result was a swelling demand for still further liberal reforms and for immediate extensions of democratic and even socialist policies. To understand the pent-up forces that brought almost universal revolution in 1848-9, the limited extent of liberal reforms between 1830 and 1848 must be examined, and the movements for more radical social revolution must be described.

LIBERAL REFORMS

The reform of the electoral and parliamentary systems in 1832 helped to make legislative enactment the normal means of administrative and social changes in Great Britain. Just as the abolitionists succeeded in getting the reformed parliament, now more sensitive to currents of organized opinion, to end slavery, and just as the free traders induced Parliament to repeal corn laws and navigation laws, so a host of other zealous improving movements now concentrated upon parliamentary action as the road to reform. These movements of parliamentary pressure were of all political colourings and of none. Leaders of these movements might be individual philanthropists and aristocratic Tory humanitarians, like Lord Shaftesbury, who took up the cause of improving factory conditions, shortening working hours, checking the labour of women and children in mines, and ventilating the hardships suffered by little boy chimney sweeps. They might be evangelicals, interested in Christianizing industrialism. They might be reforming Whig lawyers, like those who put through the municipal reform act of 1835, replacing the old borough corporations, many of which had been exclusive and sometimes corrupt oligarchies, with new municipal councils elected by ratepaying house-holders of three years' standing. They might be humanitarians, who kept up a steady demand for the reform of the penal law and conditions in prisons. But most often they were radicals of diverse hues, ranging from Chartists seeking democratic reorganization of the electorate and parlia-ment, to 'philosophical radicals' like Edwin Chadwick and John Stuart Mill, disciples of Jeremy Bentham, who sought to remodel public ad-ministration and the system of justice in terms of greater efficiency and responsibility to the people. On some issues, such as humanizing the penal code and methods of punishment, these different movements would combine forces; on others they would fall into dispute. But the common framework within which all worked was constitutional govern-ment, and the purpose of most of their activities was to get a Bill through Parliament. They turned Parliament into an instrument of social welfare.

Although radicalism in general remained frustrated and dissatisfied with the extent of parliamentary and electoral reform accomplished in 1832, it began to exert a strong influence on administrative reform. The utilitarian philosophy expounded by Jeremy Bentham and his followers proved to be a particularly corrosive force when it was applied to the antiquated methods of judicial procedure, the confusion of laws on the statute book, and the wasteful and corrupt habits of public administra-tion. Bentham was not himself a Liberal, in that he urged the prior claims of efficiency and social utility, even against the ideals of individual rights and freedoms. But the outcome of his campaign for substituting the test of usefulness for that of mere antiquity when judging the value of legis-lation and procedure was a loosening and undermining of the estab-lished order. Holding the unheroic view that men are guided in their actions by the desire to avoid pain and seek pleasure, he contended that the aim of government should be to use this fact in order to promote 'the greatest happiness of the greatest number'. Because they shun pain, men can be induced to obey the law by inflicting upon them more pain than they derive pleasure or advantage by breaking it; but because pain is in itself bad, the penal law should inflict no more pain than is necessary to deter men from breaking the law. Benthamism thus became the sworn enemy of the excessive punishments commonly inflicted on lawbreakers, either by transportation or capital punishment for petty thefts, or by the brutal conditions of nineteenth-century prisons. It also became the philosophy underlying the important reform of that system of poor relief which had grown up in England during the previous genera-tion.

Poor Relief. The practice of giving outdoor relief to supplement wages and in proportion to the number of dependents had done something to save the poor from destitution during years of economic depression, and had gone far to mitigate the rigours of the early industrial revolution. But it had been wastefully and often corruptly administered, and the methods of raising the money from poor rates levied in each parish and of subsidizing the wage bills of unscrupulous employers had led to widespread abuses. The radical reformers succeeded in getting through Parliament, in 1834, an Act to reform the whole system. It checked payments to supplement wages, reorganized the running of the workhouses, and set up a central Poor Law Commission to supervise the system. Workhouses were to be run by local Boards of Guardians elected by the ratepayers, who would have a natural interest in keeping down the total expenditure on relief. Outdoor relief was to be eliminated by a 'workhouse test', which meant that since conditions inside the workhouse were always to be harsher than those outside, only those in real need of assistance would enter the workhouse. Ratepayers' money would no longer be squandered on the lazy able-bodied or on needlessly subsidizing employers; but the needy poor, unable to do work, would be cared for.

The reorganization did not work out as had been intended by its most enthusiastic supporters. They had meant a distinction to be kept between the aged, the sick, and orphans, who could not work, and the able-bodied who could. The harsh workhouse test was meant to apply only to the latter. In effect, for reasons of economy and because of local insensitivity to human suffering, it was too often applied indiscriminately to all. The hated 'bastilles', as the workhouses came to be called, played a fearsome part in the life of the poor for the next generation. They were apt to be run by bullies and sharpers, such as Charles Dickens satirized in *Oliver Twist*. But the effect in the end was to yield a system of poor relief more efficient in its working and more subject to democratic control than the old. The principle of delegating tasks of national administration to specially created authorities subject to locally representative bodies was imitated for subsequent reforms – most significantly for the protection of public health.

Public Health. The many problems of street paving and lighting, drainage and sanitation, water supply and fire precautions, the prevention of epidemics and an adequate medical service, had hitherto been left to be tackled by local authorities. This meant that usually they had not been tackled at all, or had been tackled badly; and the situation was worst of all in the large and growing industrial towns where these problems were especially acute but where local pride and civic responsibilities were weakest. In 1846 Parliament set up a commission of inquiry into the health of towns. It reported that of fifty large towns the water supply was good in six, indifferent in thirteen, and in thirty-one insufficient or impure. In Newcastle eleven out of twelve houses were without water supply. An Act of 1848 set up a central board of health on the lines of the Poor Law Commissioners, with power to create local boards on the petition of 10 per cent of the inhabitants of a district, and to enforce the setting up of local boards wherever the annual death rate was above 23 per thousand. The long struggle for better organization of town life owed its success to two factors in particular. One was sheer necessity, caused by the recurrence of the dreaded cholera in 1831-3 and in 1847-8, but local boards of health set up in the first epidemic soon lapsed and had to be re-created in the second. The other cause was the persistence of Edwin Chadwick and his disciples, who fought the battle for systematic protection of public health with an enthusiasm, skill, and insistence that in the end wore down all the obstructions of official apathy, vested interests which objected to expenditure of money on such purposes, and parliamentary reluctance to undertake so vast a task.

Social and administrative reforms of this kind in the first half of the century revealed all the faults of the time. They came slowly, belatedly, and only after their complete necessity had been abundantly proved. They encountered apathy and timidity, greedy self-interests and officious bumbledom, local resentment of central authority, and central hesitation in face of tasks that were formidable for a state which still had no expert and impartial civil service at its command. But their accomplishment, despite these obstacles, revealed also the great qualities of British life at that time. They reflected a growing conscience about social ills; a readiness to treat poverty, disease, squalor, and human suffering as remediable; and a willingness to try new ideas and embark on novel experiments in public administration. The social evils they attacked were not new in kind but they were new in scale and social importance. Politics came to be concerned more urgently and more continuously with the welfare of the community as a whole, and with the organized provision, through state legislation and state action, of the minimum conditions of a civilized life. The nation and the state had found one another, and British life was enriched by their meeting.

France and Belgium. In France the July Monarchy brought a move in the same direction. Just as the British Parliament in 1833 passed Althorp's Act regulating conditions for employing young people in textile factories, so in 1841 the French Parliament passed a Factory Act restricting the use of child labour in undertakings employing more than 20 persons. But whereas the merit of the British Act was that it instituted factory inspectors to enforce the law, the French Act did not, and its provisions were consequently largely ineffectual. It was 1848 before an inspectorate was set up, and then the February Revolution of that year prevented the scheme from operating. Just as the English Whigs reformed municipal government, so the French Liberals in 1831 set up general and district councils on which elected members could sit beside others nominated by the government. Although such elected departmental councils remained henceforth a permanent feature of local administration in France, at this time they had little real power.

But they were entrusted with the care of certain social welfare activities. In 1838 they were made responsible for the maintenance of public asylums for the insane. Although the first cholera epidemic of 1832 killed some twenty thousand people, including the Prime Minister Casimir-Périer, little was done to improve public health in the big towns. In 1828 the state undertook a general supervision of the work of local Poor Law authorities, which varied from that of charitable voluntary bodies to local administrative provisions. But the French state was slower than the British to take any direct share in Poor Law administration, and it was a national tradition that such poor relief, where undertaken at all apart from the family, was the duty of private or ecclesiastical charity.

In education, however, the opposite was true. In 1833, when the British Parliament voted the first meagre grant of £20,000 from public funds for the promotion of elementary education, the government of Louis Philippe passed its Education Act, planning to set up state-aided primary schools in every commune. In Britain the parliamentary grant was shared between the National Society (which was Anglican) and the British and Foreign School Society (which was undenominational), and both used it mainly for building schools. In France the purpose of the Act, as defined by Guizot, who presented the Bill, was 'to calm and quench the people's thirst for action, as dangerous for itself as for society, to restore in their minds the inner sense of moral peace without which social peace would never return'. Both measures, in short, were concessions by the middle classes to encourage moral improvement and thereby social peace.

The wealthy *bourgeoisie* of Belgium in these years showed even less concern for social problems, though conditions in mines and factories in Belgium were no better, nor effects of economic depression any less severe, than in Britain or France. Liberal and Catholic parliamentarians, representing the same social class, were in agreement that social questions did not matter politically. Wages were determined by the laws of supply and demand, and the poor had no rights save to appeal to charity. In 1842 the government passed a law requiring each community to support a primary school, but in most cases the former Catholic Church schools were merely adopted by local authorities, with even the same clerical teachers and supervisors in charge.

Germany. The most industrialized part of Germany was the Rhine provinces of Prussia, and as early as 1824 the Prussian minister of education tried, though with little success, to restrict the hours of child workers in factories. The consideration that characteristically induced the Prussian government to take sterner action was the discovery in 1828 that the industrial Rhine regions were unable to contribute their full contingents to the army because of the physical deterioration of the population. Even then there was further delay, until in 1839 a Factory Law was passed prohibiting the employment of children under nine and restricting the working day of children between nine and sixteen to ten hours. The law was not fully enforced, and even when a factory inspectorate on the English model was instituted in 1853, the work of inspectors was limited to a few areas and was stubbornly resisted by employers and local authorities.

In German traditions, especially in the Protestant states, the work of poor relief was left to the communes. But it was of small effect, and it was only in Prussia and only after 1840 that more systematic efforts were made to tackle the problems of poverty through the reformed system of local government authorities. In other respects the Prussian traditions of state paternalism led to readier state action on behalf of social progress. Between 1810 and 1845 the guilds were shorn of their powers in so far as these restricted the development of industry, but they were left in charge of apprenticeship. From the middle of the century onwards they were entrusted with new functions of social insurance. Throughout the period the state system of education continued to develop, and its benefits were made more and more accessible to the people. But elsewhere in Germany the relatively backward economic conditions were reflected in little effort to achieve social reforms. Small firms and handicraft trades persisted, and governments were scarcely conscious of the pressure of more modern industrial problems.

Resistance to Reform. Similarly, elsewhere in Europe no pattern of liberal reform could be detected. In Scandinavia the Danish kings, Frederick VI (1808–39) and Christian VIII (1839–48), preserved their absolutist powers virtually intact; but the Swedish king, Charles XIV (Bernadotte), had by 1840 liberalized his government both in Sweden and in Norway. In 1840 William I of the Netherlands had so used his autocratic powers that he was forced to abdicate in favour of his more popular son, William II; and in 1843 Otto I, king of the Hellenes, was compelled by insurrection to grant a new constitution. But in general the forces of conservatism remained dominant and usually repressive. The doctrines of Metternich were generally accepted, and social peace was preserved more by suppression of disturbing elements than by timely concession to their demands. Years of bad harvest and acute distress were endured with a medieval sufferance and fatalism; poverty was regarded as irremediable, and to be alleviated only by private charity. Only among agitators and extremists was the exciting notion coming to be accepted: that human suffering could be limited by better administration, greater inventiveness and ingenuity, and more strenuous public action, and that governments might be capable of performing for their subjects tasks of emancipation and material improvement far beyond anything so far dreamed of. In the next two generations, as industrialism spread from the West throughout Europe, this startling notion was to captivate opinion in one country after another, until in the twentieth century it proved irresistible everywhere. But in 1848 it was still a revolutionary idea which no existing government received with noticeable enthusiasm.

MOVEMENTS FOR SOCIAL REVOLUTION

The outcome of the revolutions of 1830–33 left reasons enough for active discontent. Governments that had made concessions had without exception been careful to keep in their hands effective ways of turning the edge of real democratic movements. Everywhere the right to vote was defined in terms of property qualifications, and such qualifications were fixed high enough to keep out of political power all save the wealthier middle classes. Everywhere facilities for rigging elections and handicapping parties in opposition to the government remained quite adequate to protect the power of established authority. In Britain the limited franchise, the preservation of boroughs which could be bought or influenced, the lack of secret ballot, kept the Whigs safe from excessive radical pressure. In France the limited franchise and the whole machinery of administrative influence over elections served a similar purpose. The Ministry of the Interior, through its prefects at the head of each *département*, was expected to manage or 'make' elections favourable to official candidates, and it usually succeeded admirably.

In 1831 Casimir-Périer set the tone of the whole régime when he instructed his prefects:

The Government insists . . . that the electoral law be executed with the most rigorous impartiality. At the same time, the Government wishes it to be known that the distance between impartiality and administrative indifference is infinite. The Government is convinced that its continuance in office is vital to the interests of the Nation.

Occasionally prefects would resort to heroic measures to carry out such orders. In 1837 the prefect of Morbihan discovered with consternation that the 'reliable' candidate in the forthcoming elections, M. Hello, was not eligible because he had not resided in the *département* for the necessary six months. Three days before the polls the opposition candidate learned this fact and placarded the information round the town. The electoral registers were stored in the subprefecture. The prefect opportunely burned it down, and by return of post the minister of the interior agreed that elections could not possibly be held without proper registers. By the time the new registers had been compiled M. Hello had resided for the statutory six months and all was well.

Given such blatant manipulations of electoral and parliamentary machinery in even the most constitutional states of Europe, radicals and democrats had abundant grounds for claiming that abuses of this kind could be removed only by universal suffrage and more drastic overhauls of electoral procedures. Given, too, the growth of industrialism and urbanization in western Europe [1] and the recurrence of economic depression and crisis for which the social reforms carried out by governments were quite inadequate, it was natural that radical clamour for political and constitutional reform should link up with movements for more drastic social and economic reform. The Tory–Whig thesis, that political agitation and reform could have no relevance to the alleviation of social distress, became very threadbare in face of the timid experiments actually made to alleviate it and of the growing conviction that poverty might be in fact remediable by new methods of administration and vigorous action. Democratic political reforms were urged as the first and necessary step towards social and economic reforms. Daily evidence of how the middle classes were able to use their enhanced political power to promote and protect their own economic interests robbed them of the pretence that democracy would not bring broader material advantages to the working classes. The shrewdness of the common man taught him that what was sauce for the bourgeois goose was likely to be sauce for the proletarian gander.

Chartism. This radical pursuit of democratic rights in order to improve social conditions was especially clearly illustrated by the Chartist movement of these years in Great Britain. Its roots were partly political and partly economic. It arose out of popular discontent with the Reform Act of 1832, out of the failures of early experiments in trade unionism, and out of movements of mass discontent in Lancashire and Yorkshire caused by economic depression and industrial exploitation. These different movements fused together into one of the most dynamic outbursts

1. See pp. 178–82.

of working-class agitation so far known in England. In 1838 the cabinet-maker William Lovett and the tailor Francis Place drew up the 'People's Charter' as a common political programme. Its famous 'Six Points' called for universal male suffrage, equal electoral districts, removal of the property qualification for Members of Parliament, payment of Members of Parliament, secret ballot, and annual general elections. The first five of these six demands were granted between 1858 and 1918, but the sixth indicates the radical character of the programme. It was intended to make Parliament entirely subject to the will of the people. Against the Whig doctrine of the sovereignty of Parliament, the radicals raised the principle of the sovereignty of the people.

Although Chartism, in this political form, originated among the respectable artisans and radicals of London, it found its mass support, as did the free-trade movement, among the industrial populations of northern England. The Birmingham Union, dating from 1816, and the radicals of Leeds soon joined it and imported into it an element of mass agitation and extremism. Fiery popular orators like the Irishmen Bronterre O'Brien and Feargus O'Connor staged exciting torchlight processions at night, harangued huge meetings of hungry men and women, and conducted violent propaganda through O'Connor's paper, the *Northern Star*. 'The Charter' became the battle cry for a nation-wide movement, rallying to its support currency reformers like Thomas Attwood of Birmingham and European refugees who saw in it a cause for which they had themselves suffered exile.

The climax of the agitation was the calling of a National Convention, to meet in Westminster Palace Yard very near the Houses of Parliament, and the presentation to Parliament of a monster petition for which hundreds of thousands of signatures had been collected. The Convention was deeply split over what it should next do if the petition were rejected. Lovett, Place, and their southern followers were in favour of constitutional methods only, and urged a further campaign of peaceful agitation and popular education. O'Connor and his more extreme revolutionary northern supporters wanted to resort to violence and a general strike. One Polish exile published articles on revolutionary tactics, and pamphlets were sold on how best to build barricades. There was a tang of civil war in the air. In July 1839 the petition with one and a quarter million signatures was rejected by the House of Commons. Riots, strikes, and even insurrections followed, but not revolution. The moderate Chartists resorted to peaceful propaganda, the extremists persisted with their agitation during the 1840s.

In 1842 and again in 1848 further petitions were presented, and each time rejected by Parliament. Latterly only the cranks and fanatics, the rabble, and a few sections of the working classes remained faithful to Chartism. Middle-class sympathizers were diverted to the Anti-Corn Law agitation of these years, the artisans reverted to peaceful agitation, and the working classes began to turn to trade unionism. But, throughout, the fortunes of the movement fluctuated with changes in material conditions. Its periods of greatest activity coincided with periods of economic depression and distress. It declined in times of reviving prosperity. The rise and fall of Chartism were a barometer of industrial and agricultural conditions. It shook the hardening complacency of Victorian England more profoundly than did any other comparable movement, fostered a new social conscience and national consciousness about the ills of industrial Britain, and gave an eventual impetus to further reforms.

The Revolutionary Tradition. In France radical action took less public and more conspiratorial shapes. The secret societies of the restoration period and the revolutionary tradition of mob violence combined to make democratic movements more violent. The first five years of the reign of Louis Philippe were particularly rich in revolts, strikes, and demonstrations, prompted largely by the republicans' sense of having been cheated in 1830. In the silk centre of Lyon wages were unduly low, and there had been experiments in collective bargaining with employers for minimum wage scales. In November 1831 the silk workers broke out into open insurrection. The immediate provocation was that 104 of the 1,400 manufacturers in the area refused to observe the agreements and threatened to close their works. The government, fearing the spread of revolt from a city where the weavers were for a time in control, stepped in and not only crushed the rising but declared collective bargaining illegal.

The incident dispelled working-class hopes that the new régime might protect their interests, and drove them to support the secret republican societies. Such societies abounded, and ranged from fairly open associations like the Society of the Rights of Man, to the traditional type of conspiracy, such as the 'Families' or the 'Seasons'. Even the more moderate societies, like that of the Rights of Man, tended in the propaganda they aimed at the working classes to conjure up the vision of a republic in which economic inequalities would be less. Others, especially those influenced by Philippe Buonarroti or Auguste Blanqui, were more frankly and thoroughly socialistic or communistic in their aims.

Auguste Blanqui deserves special mention as one of the most outstanding of the professional revolutionaries who haunted Paris under the July Monarchy. He inherited the role and many of the ideas of

Buonarroti, who died in 1837.[1] Blanqui was the son of a Napoleonic official and was born in 1805. He had joined the *Charbonnerie* as a student, and for his part in the rising of 1830, which eventually brought Louis Philippe to the throne, he was awarded a medal by the new government. This was the only official recognition, apart from sentences of imprisonment and death, that his activities were ever to receive. He spent nearly half his long life in 15 different prisons, and much of that time was spent in solitary confinement. In April 1834 the government passed a law restricting the rights of association, and in Lyon, which had just endured one of its periodic strikes, protests against the new law resulted in six days of bitter fighting. In the eastern districts of Paris there was, almost simultaneously, a rising planned by the Society of the Rights of Man. Adolphe Thiers who directed its suppression was ever after hated by the republicans for what came to be known as the 'massacre of the Rue Transnonain'.

These events induced Blanqui to set about organizing a new secret society, powerful enough to secure political ends but secret enough to evade police espionage. The result was the Society of Families (*Société des Familles*), modelled on Carbonarist principles and with the immediate purpose of military action. A unit of six members was called a Family; five or six Families, under one Chief, constituted a Section; two or three Sections made up a Quarter. It was so organized that its leaders would remain unknown until the moment for action should come, and orders were issued by a central committee of unknown membership. By 1836 it numbered some 1,200 people, had infiltrated two regiments of the garrison of Paris, and owned dumps of arms and a factory for making gunpowder. To evade the attentions of the police, it then had to be dissolved, but was almost immediately reconstituted as the Society of the Seasons (*Société des Saisons*), with even more picturesque labels. Each group of six was known as a week, commanded by a Sunday; four weeks formed a month, under the orders of July; three months a season, led by Spring; and four seasons a year, directed by a special agent of the central committee. It was led by Blanqui, Martin Bernard, and Armand Barbès. They timed the rising for the spring of 1839.

The Society published clandestine newspapers and organized working-class support in Paris, Lyon, and Carcassonne. Economic distress was bringing unemployment among the town workers and discontent among the peasants, and this swelled the Society's ranks. On Sunday mornings, marching in formation but unobserved because they mingled so skilfully with the Sunday crowds, they were 'reviewed' by Blanqui from some secluded spot. On the fine warm spring morning of 12 May

1. See pp. 46 and 144.

1839, they were at last summoned to action stations. The police, it was hoped, would be preoccupied controlling the crowds at the races at the Champs de Mars. The conspirators' forces concentrated around the gunsmiths' shops and stores in the Paris districts of Saint-Denis and Saint-Martin. The stores were duly raided – the inevitable prelude to rioting – and barricades were thrown up. The Palais de Justice and the Hôtel de Ville were occupied and the Republic was proclaimed while the mob shouted the *Marseillaise*. A few soldiers were killed. Then the National and Municipal Guards were called out, the military garrisons stood to arms, and the insurgents were driven back behind the barricades in the working-class districts. By nightfall they had been completely routed and most of their leaders captured. Blanqui himself was caught after five months of living in cellars, attics, and sewers, and sent to prison for the next eight and a half years – until the Revolution of 1848 set him free again. The conspirators failed utterly, chiefly because they had wrongly relied on the readiness of the mass of Parisians to support them spontaneously once the initial *coup* had been made.

This and the comparable failure of other risings during the 1830s served to discredit the men and methods of the secret societies, and in spite of even more acute social distress at certain times during the 'Hungry Forties', the government was freed from the standing threat of insurrection. But even in prison the social revolutionaries were incessantly active. Between 1815 and 1848 people of all kinds and creeds were liable to find themselves together in prison, and therefore prison life became one of the main breeding grounds for republican propaganda and socialist ideas. Several descriptions have been given, by inmates, of the prison of Sainte-Pélagie where political prisoners were mainly housed. A whole section of it was reserved for 'politicals', whether legitimist royalists or republicans. But there were strict divisions between middle-class and working-class prisoners, though Raspail the republican would at times give the workers lessons on hygiene or the principles of science, and the Vicomte Sosthènes de la Rochefoucauld, imprisoned for writing a legitimist pamphlet, organized weekly concerts at the governor's house to which he invited prisoners of both parties. Though prolonged imprisonment evoked remarkable stoicism, it did not encourage realistic political thinking. The social revolutionary movement in France, deprived for long periods of its most militant leaders, fell out of touch with real working-class life.

What was true, in this respect, of France was no less true for the rest of continental Europe. Republican, nationalist, and revolutionary movements stayed alive, and at moments flared up into local insurrections. But nowhere, until 1848, did they succeed in turning revolt into revolution. In countries where industrialism was less developed, liberal or democratic fervour weaker, and the oppressive power of governments stronger, they had even less hope of success than in France. But though revolutionary action was, in general, paralysed, revolutionary thinking flourished. Most important of all for the future, there grew up in these years new and diverse schools of socialist thought, more closely adapted than the more old-fashioned radical democracy to the novel needs and sentiments of an industrial society. The decade after 1830 was especially the birth-time of socialism.

Early Socialism. As already shown,[1] socialist ideals and doctrines stemmed from Rousseau, from extreme Jacobinism during the French Revolution, and from the general tendency to extend the ideals of liberty, equality, and, above all, fraternity to social and economic life no less than to politics. There was a certain infusion of socialism into Chartism, and Bronterre O'Brien in 1836 produced an abridged English translation of Buonarroti's book on the conspiracy of Babeuf. But in Britain socialism first became of some importance with the activities and writings of Robert Owen. As early as 1800 he had begun the experiment of creating a model factory at New Lanark, and attracted international attention by its apparent proof that workers could be treated well, even generously, without their employer's failing to make a profit. His fellow mill-owners were impressed. If even philanthropy could make profits, then the men of Manchester were interested in philanthropy. His more ambitious experiment of 'New Harmony' in Indiana in 1825, designed as a voluntary and freely self-governing cooperative community, was a failure though not without its value in spreading an ideal. Like many other self-made and spectacularly successful business men, Owen became a dreamer of dreams. His writings became more and more unrealistic and visionary. But the core of his message was clear enough. It was that the condition of men would improve if they would replace competition by cooperation as the mainspring of their economic activities and their social life. If social conditions are bad they can be changed. In so far as they are bad because men are bad and behave inhumanely to their fellow men, then men can undergo a change of heart. The great need is for education, social and moral. By moulding men's minds to the truth of cooperation, society and even human nature can be transformed for the better.

Robert Owen had a decisive influence on the two most successful working-class movements in his day, trade unionism and the cooperative movement – though neither had shed its growing pains before he died in 1858. Impressed by the potentialities of trade unions, as they deve-

1. See p. 124.

loped after gaining legal rights in 1825, Owen set up a Grand National Consolidated Trades Union that was intended to raise unionism to the level of one comprehensive national organization. It was much too ambitious a project, given the state of industry in his day. Under its inspiration or example countless schemes for the complete reorganization of economic life on cooperative lines were put forward. A Grand National Union of Builders was proposed, to take over and run the entire building trade of Britain. By the use of labour exchanges and 'labour notes' as currency, Owen proposed to build a new labour commonwealth. By 1834 the project collapsed. It culminated not, as planned, in one vast general strike but in many local, sporadic, and usually futile strikes. Its death-blow came with the trial and punishment of a handful of Dorsetshire agricultural labourers for taking 'unlawful oaths' as members of a union which was to be part of the Grand National Consolidated Union. These ignorant and unfortunate men, known thenceforth as the 'Tolpuddle Martyrs', were sentenced to transportation, as a savage warning to others.

The pathetic incident turned the enthusiasm of Owen and his followers away from unionism towards cooperative movements. In 1844 twenty-eight Lancashire working men, inspired by Owenism, opened a little store in Toad Lane, Rochdale. The idea of self-help through common ownership and management of a little shop caught on, and by 1851 there were some one hundred and thirty cooperative stores on a similar pattern in the north of England and in Scotland. The idea was to become, by the end of the century, the origin of an organization nation-wide and even, through British emigration overseas, empire-wide. The principle of distributing dividends, according to purchases, among registered members of the society kept it very democratic in shape, and gave it a strong appeal to thrifty housewives.

France was even more fertile than Britain in producing new socialistic theories and movements, though they bore less concrete results in France than in Britain. The two leading French socialist thinkers were Henri, Comte de Saint-Simon, and Charles Fourier. Both, like Owen, belonged to an age when the romantic movement was at its most influential, and their thought had a correspondingly idealistic and emotional flavour.[1] Saint-Simon was by birth an aristocrat, and even claimed descent from Charlemagne. He had renounced his title during the French Revolution of 1789 and then made a fortune through speculating in church lands. His life was spent in the quest for a new source of authority and faith in an industrial age. He preached the gospel of work – 'man must work' – and insisted that property rights must depend on

1. See p. 141.

their social utility, not on any imprescriptible individual rights. He coined the slogan that was to become so popular with later socialism: 'from each according to his capacity, to each according to his work'. But he remained sceptical of democracy, and wanted rule by an intellectual aristocracy. His chief influence came after his death in 1825, when a band of his disciples formed a Saint-Simonian Church, with six departmental churches throughout France and considerable influence in Germany.

Charles Fourier, the slightly younger contemporary of Owen and Saint-Simon, was the son of a well-to-do draper who came to regard commerce as the great enemy. He attacked above all the ills of a commercial civilization which made vice more profitable than virtue and set men in enmity with one another. The great sources of evil are cut-throat competition, deceit, greed, and inhumanity; and the great remedy is association and cooperation to restore harmony to human life. To make work attractive each worker must share in its produce and be guaranteed a sufficient minimum to free him from anxiety. Fourier's ideas were invariably wrapped up in a mass of fantastic speculation and dogmatic theorizing which concealed the grains of shrewdness and common sense which they contained. Thus the dirty and unattractive work of the community would be done, he suggested, by 'little hordes' of children, who at a certain age have been providentially endowed with a love of being dirty. They would be 'passionately attracted' to scavenging, and would be always on foot (or riding on their Shetland ponies) at 3 a.m. even in the depths of winter, repairing roads, killing vermin, attending to animals, and working in the slaughterhouses. But the core of his thought – the argument that cooperation should replace competition – had a wide appeal. Fourierist communities were set up during the 1840s in New Jersey, Wisconsin, and Massachusetts, and he was eagerly read in Russia as well as in France.

The ideas common to these early socialist writers all hinged upon the concept of harmony in social life. Their protest was against the degradation of human labour in the early phases of industrialism, against inhuman capitalist treatment of labour as merely a marketable commodity used to bring profit, against the demoralization of social life by cutthroat competition and the unrestrained devotion to the purpose of making profits regardless of human suffering. Their concern, therefore, was to reassert the moral values of cooperation among men, the dignity and function of work, the need for a harmonious society to regenerate mankind. Their romanticism and their visionary qualities deserved the label that Marxists were later to affix to them, of 'Utopian socialists'. Their very perfectionism doomed them to disillusionment. But they had a profound influence on the seething discontent of the mass of working people in their day, and it was no bad thing that human values should be so prolifically reasserted in these years of ruthless industrial expansion. Their work meant that, when the revolutions of 1848 broke out throughout Europe, there were usually small but active groups of socialist-minded men seeking to use the moment to demand political and social rights for working men. By then, too, more practical-minded thinkers such as Louis Blanc in France and John Stuart Mill in England were proposing more immediate and concrete measures to alleviate working-class conditions.

Blanc in 1839 published his famous book on the *Organization of Labour* (*L'organisation du travail*), which almost at once became a best seller. He argued downrightly that political reform is the only means to achieve social reform, and that socialism must be state socialism. If the state is not used as an instrument it becomes an obstacle. The state must acknowledge and implement the 'right to work', and must in every other way protect the weak and the poor. As the 'supreme regulator of production' the government should, for example, set up 'social workshops' (or *ateliers sociaux*) in the most important branches of industry, and these will treat their workers fairly and be eventually run democratically by the workers themselves. In initial competition with private employers they will attract the best workers and in the end will put unscrupulous employers out of business, defeating them by their own principles of free competition. With Blanc, socialism came nearer to the earth and entered more practicable politics. His ideas were welcomed with widespread enthusiasm by French workers, who knew only too well from experience the hardships of a *laissez-faire* state. That was why Louis Blanc was able to play a prominent role in the revolution of 1848 in France.[1]

Karl Marx. Meanwhile other men, of German origin, were taking a place in the strange medley of extremist socialist and communist groups which worked mostly in exile in Paris, Brussels, London, and Switzerland. A group of German refugees in Paris founded, in the 1830s, a society linked with the working-class movements of Buonarroti and the other disciples of Babeuf. They called it the League of the Just, and it was joined by a young tailor, Wilhelm Weitling. In 1842 he published a communist book called *Guarantees of Harmony and Freedom* and established himself as one of the most important German working-class leaders. In 1846 he attended in Brussels a meeting held 'for the purpose of agreeing, if possible, in a common tactic for the working-class movement'. There he met two very forceful men engaged in devising such a

1. See p. 207.

tactic. These were described by a young Russian traveller, Annenkov, who was present at the meeting. Of one, he wrote:

A type of man all compact of energy, force of character, and unshakable conviction – a type who was highly remarkable in his outward appearance as well. With a thick black mane of hair, his hands all covered with hair and his coat buttoned up askew, he gave one the impression of a man who had the right and the power to command respect, even though his aspect and his behaviour might seem to be rather odd.... He never spoke at all except in judgements that brooked no denial and that were rendered even sharper, and rather disagreeable, by the harsh tone of everything he said. This note expressed his firm conviction of his mission to impress himself on men's minds, to dominate their wills, and to compel them to follow in his train....

The other man he described as tall and erect, 'with English distinction and gravity'. The former was Karl Marx, then aged 28; the latter his devoted friend and collaborator, Friedrich Engels.

Marx joined the League of the Just, now rechristened the Communist League, in the spring of 1847. It was a time of the worst economic depression modern Europe had known, when bad harvests coincided with a business slump after the boom in railroad-building. That autumn Marx and Engels jointly composed a manifesto for the little Communist League, which was destined to replace the Utopian and visionary socialism of Owen and Saint-Simon, Fourier and Blanc, by a new dynamic doctrine of class war and world revolution. The *Communist Manifesto* for the first time delineated not only a complete doctrine of social revolution, but also a strategy of social revolution. It substituted for the old slogan of the League of the Just, that 'All men are brothers', the single purpose of 'the forcible overthrow of the whole existing social order'.

The Manifesto dramatically presents all history as the story of class struggles and depicts modern society in the grip of great revolutionary forces. Technical advances in the methods of producing wealth change the nature and the balance of social classes. Modern industry and commerce give power to the *bourgeoisie*, the industrial, commercial, and financial capitalists who own the means of production and whose ruthless exploitation of the world's resources and of the labour of those who do not own the means of production (the *proletariat* or wage-slaves) shapes contemporary history. This dominant, enterprising class controls the liberal state and uses it for exploiting and repressing more fully those who have only their labour to sell. The proletariat is destined, by the remorseless process of history, to grow in size, misery, and self-consciousness, until it is able to overthrow its oppressors. 'What the bourgeoisie produces, above all, are its own gravediggers. Its fall and the victory of the proletariat are equally inevitable.'

It follows that democracy is a sham, for parliamentary government is only a mask for the class-rule of the capitalists; that the workers should have no national loyalties, since they have common interests with the oppressed wage-slaves of other lands but none at all with their own employers; and that the destined proletarian revolution will be also a world revolution, inevitably triumphant, inaugurating first a proletarian state (the 'dictatorship of the proletariat') and eventually a truly classless society. Marx and Engels end with their famous plea: 'The proletarians have nothing to lose but their chains: they have a world to win. Workers of all countries, unite.'

The *Manifesto* first appeared in London in February 1848, the month of revolution in France. It played no part in precipitating that revolution, and at the time it was little read. But within the next two decades it permeated Europe, twelve editions appearing in Germany alone. It preached a gospel that a century later had become the official political creed of half the human race, and it is beyond doubt one of the most important documents of modern history. Its appearance in 1848 would alone make that year memorable in the history of Europe. But, for the moment, events took charge, and by June the whole face of Europe was changed by a series of eruptions caused primarily by the accumulated economic hardships of the previous two years, and by the stirring of nationalist aspirations for unity. The 'Year of Revolutions' had come, and the 'Age of Revolutions' had reached its climax.

CHAPTER 11

THE NATIONAL REVOLUTIONS
OF 1848–50

THE SEQUENCE OF REVOLUTIONS, 1848

On 12 January 1848, the people of Palermo in Sicily came out into the streets in open rebellion against the misrule of Ferdinand II of Naples. Within a month there were similar riots in nearly all the large Italian cities. On 12 February 1848 the liberal opposition to the conservative government of Guizot in France reduced the government's majority to only 43 in the Chamber of Deputies, and forthwith proclaimed their intention to hold a propaganda banquet on 22 February. When the government in panic banned the banquet, the people of Paris came out into the streets to demonstrate and by nightfall the barricades were thrown up in the working-class streets. These two incidents touched off the two different kinds of popular insurrection which in the course of the year started a series of revolutions all over Europe. Most of the revolutions in Italy, Germany, Austria, and Hungary were on the pattern of Palermo – nationalist and popular insurrections against foreign rule and against the dreary repressive policy of Metternich and his allies. The revolution in Switzerland and the disturbances in Belgium and Britain were on the French pattern – democratic protests against the exclusiveness and inadequacies of middle-class government and a demand for social and democratic reforms. Despite these important differences the risings merged into one great European upheaval, a tide of exasperation and discontent, taking diverse forms and suffering diverse fates in different countries. Its greatest political achievement in Europe was to end the rule of Metternich and secure the overthrow of his 'system', which had prevailed since 1815. Its greatest social and economic consequence was to destroy feudalism in most of eastern Europe.

Italian Initiative. At first the initiative lay with Italy. The hopes of Italian liberals had come to centre upon two men: Charles Albert of Savoy, who in 1831 had succeeded to the throne of Piedmont-Sardinia and was more actively sympathetic than his predecessor had been to nationalist hopes; and Pope Pius IX, who in June 1846 had succeeded Gregory XVI and had shown liberal sympathies by conceding a partial political amnesty and permitting the formation of a Civic Guard in Rome. Either or both, it was thought, might take a lead in ending

Austrian domination of the Italian peninsula. With these more favourable auspices, the secret societies (*Carbonari* and the rest) and the Mazzinian republican movements were active everywhere. The earliest popular risings, in Palermo and Milan, were directly due to them, and without the dynamism provided by these popular movements it is doubtful whether revolution would have begun in Italy in 1848.

Charles Albert, in his reorganization of his composite kingdom of Piedmont, Sardinia, and Savoy, reformed the finances and the army, promoted agriculture, and lowered tariffs. But he ruled as an absolutist monarch, and police and spies were as active in repression in his kingdom as they were anywhere else in Italy. He made the mistake of thinking he could be enlightened in economics and reactionary in politics; and when he permitted meetings of local agricultural societies, he found it impossible to stop their talking politics. It was easy to move from talk of cabbages to talk of kings, and the kingdom of Piedmont became one of the most politically conscious and active parts of Italy. At the same time Pope Pius IX seemed bent on fulfilling liberal expectations; so much so that when, in 1847, papal liberalism began to be imitated in Tuscany, Metternich occupied the papal city of Ferrara. The Pope at once circularized the powers of Europe, there was an outcry in the press, and Charles Albert put his forces at the Pope's disposal for the defence of his states. By December 1847 Metternich was obliged to withdraw the Austrian troops from Ferrara and to admit diplomatic defeat.

These early skirmishes were forewarning of the troubles to come. The weakness of the Italian nationalist forces in general was that because there were three possible national leaders – Charles Albert, the Pope, and Mazzini – there were also three quite different political programmes and movements for national liberation. These were widely canvassed during the later 1840s by influential Italian writers. Massimo d'Azeglio attacked papal rule and urged that since Italy would have to fight Austria to win her independence, all Italian patriots should rally behind the king of Piedmont, as the most independent ruler with resources enough to fight Austria. On the other hand the Abbé Gioberti appealed to moderate conservatives and intellectuals in Lombardy with his plea, in *Il Primato* of 1843, for a federation of all Italian states under the Papacy, with a college of princes as its executive authority. Mazzini opposed both, and was the most influential advocate of republicanism. He urged the expulsion of Austria by a mass popular uprising, the abolition of the temporal power of the Papacy, and the union of all Italy under a democratic republic. It was clear that little compromise and no union was possible between these three fundamentally different programmes. The choice between them was, in the end, decided by the course of events.

Mazzinian enthusiasts not only touched off the revolution by the revolt at Palermo; they won a victory of immense moral importance by compelling Ferdinand II of Naples to grant Sicily the Constitution of 1812 which democrats had always demanded, and with it independence from Naples. By the end of January 1848 Ferdinand had tried to substitute a new constitution for his whole kingdom of Naples and Sicily, on the model of the French constitution of 1830, with two chambers, a free press, and guarantees of individual liberty and rights. But the island of Sicily held out for its complete independence, and its example was infectious. In Piedmont, Tuscany, and Rome similar constitutions were hastily granted by their rulers in a last-minute effort to stave off revolution. The joint pressure of liberal constitutionalists and democratic republicans seemed, by the end of February, to have opened a new era of liberal government in Italy.

Second French Republic. But now the initiative reverted to France and it was to Paris, the traditional prompter for revolutionary performances, that rebels everywhere in Europe began to look. Faced with the popular rising in Paris on 22 February, Louis Philippe decided to dismiss Guizot and his ministry. But the Paris mobs were fast getting out of hand, and the mischance of a volley from a company of regular troops which killed or wounded 52 of the crowd tipped the scale. Barricades were erected everywhere, gunsmiths' shops were looted, and Paris found itself in total revolution. The middle-class National Guard turned against the king. It was supported by moderate socialists like Louis Blanc and by extremist social revolutionaries, the disciples of Blanqui. On 24 February Louis Philippe was forced to abdicate, and in the Chamber of Deputies the poet Lamartine announced a list of liberal parliamentarians to form a new provisional government. They adjourned to the Hôtel de Ville to agree on the allocation of offices. Lamartine himself took Foreign Affairs, the democratic radical Ledru-Rollin Home Affairs, with the aged Dupont de l'Eure as President. But it was one thing to set up a provisional government on paper, quite another to establish its authority in Paris and in the rest of France.

This group of moderate parliamentarians formed a self-constituted provisional government, acclaimed by the mob at the city hall. They were largely the journalistic staff of *Le National,* the liberal opposition paper founded in January 1830, which had helped to undermine the rule of Charles X and had remained the chief opposition journal under the July Monarchy. Now a rival group formed around the contributors and staff of the more radical and socialistic journal *La Réforme,* which included Ledru-Rollin and Louis Blanc. The inclusion of Ledru-Rollin in the government proved insufficient to placate popular feeling in Paris, and after hectic negotiation the government was widened still further to include Louis Blanc and other lesser men, such as Albert, a working man included as a gesture to the mob. By midnight on 24 February enough agreement had been patched up between the two factions to produce the statement: 'The Provisional Government gives its vote for the Republic, subject to ratification by the People who will be consulted forthwith.' This formula reflected the divergent points of view within the new government; for the moderate liberals wanted merely to establish constitutional parliamentary government and were anxious above all to prevent relapse to mob disorder, whereas the radical democrats and socialists demanded universal suffrage and wanted to ensure a republic that would tackle social reforms. All the individual members, save Albert were middle-class and professional men, lawyers, intellectuals, and journalists, and none wanted a new reign of terror. Yet on 25 February only Lamartine's eloquence prevented the republican tricolour from being replaced by the red flag of the extreme left; and throughout its existence the provisional government was under heavy pressure from the force of the mob, roused and directed by extremists of the secret societies and disciples of Blanqui, whom the revolution now released from prison.

Under the double pressure of the radical democrats within and the armed mob without, the government proceeded to arrange hasty measures of social and political reform. It reduced the daily working hours to ten in Paris and eleven in the provinces. It recognized the 'right to work', and in order to deal with unemployment in Paris set up so-called 'National Workshops', whose first task was really poor relief rather than the socialist experiments in cooperation advocated by Louis Blanc. It set up a permanent commission at the Luxembourg Palace under the presidency of Louis Blanc himself to examine labour problems. It removed restrictions on the press and on the liberty of the citizen, and on 5 March decreed that in elections to a National Constituent Assembly, to be held in April, every Frenchman over 21 should be entitled to vote. At one stroke it thus increased the electorate from two hundred thousand to some nine million, most of whom were illiterate and had no experience of political responsibility.

Deferment of the elections until 23 April meant that two months passed between the original revolution in Paris and the polling in the provinces. During that interval the instinctively conservative mass of small rural proprietors had ample time to be alarmed by news of the disorders and the social experiments in the capital. They used their vote – and 84 per cent of the new electorate voted – to inflict a severe defeat on the radicals and socialists. Out of 876 seats these parties won only 100. The majority of the new assembly were either legitimist royalists, former supporters of Louis Philippe, or moderate Liberals and Republicans. To this assembly, when it met in May, the provisional government surrendered its executive power, which was then entrusted to a new Executive Council. It included Lamartine and a few other members of the late government, but it excluded Louis Blanc and Albert.

It was not long before the assembly and its Executive Council were subjected to a further attempt at a *coup* from the extreme left. On 15 May, after three days of demonstrations, the assembly was invaded by a mob, its dissolution proclaimed, and a new emergency government set up at the Hôtel de Ville. Blanqui, Barbès, and the socialist clubs were attempting a second revolution, designed to reassert the revolutionary leadership of the Paris mob against the express wishes of the rest of France. But this time they failed. The National Guard took the side of the assembly against the mob. The new Mobile Guards, formed by the middle classes to protect property, cleared the assembly. Not only were Blanqui and Barbès promptly thrown into prison and their clubs and societies disbanded, but Louis Blanc fled and Albert was arrested. The Hôtel de Ville was reoccupied. By challenging the existence of the Republic, newly endorsed by the overwhelming majority of the largest electorate yet in French history, the social revolutionaries had seriously injured their own cause and made a conservative reaction almost inevitable. The Blanquist traditions of violent *coups* and fighting on the barricades had rashly been turned against the institutions of parliamentary constitutional government; and the forces of republicanism in France began to neutralize one another, leaving the door open to conservative reprisals.

Germany and Austria-Hungary. Meanwhile the example of these events in France stirred revolutionary hopes throughout Europe. In February, three days after the abdication of Louis Philippe, there were big popular demonstrations at Mannheim in the Rhineland, followed by disturbances throughout Germany. German liberalism, as it was understood by the middle and professional classes and the new industrialists, was a national liberalism favouring internal free trade as represented by the *Zollverein* but with little tincture of democratic ideas. Social revolutionaries, active enough in the industrial Rhineland, were elsewhere very small in numbers and unimportant. Germany had neither a liberal parliamentary tradition like the British, nor a violent social revolutionary tradition like the French. The central revolutionary impulse was one of nationalism – for the overthrow of Austrian domination and of the princely sovereignties which served that domination, and for the unification of German territories into one state.

Liberal hopes had been roused in Prussia in 1847 when the Prussian king, Frederick William IV, summoned in Berlin the *Landtag*, representative of the various Prussian territories, to secure authority for a loan to build railways; they were dashed when he dissolved it. This irresolute behaviour was characteristic of that romantic mystic who had come to the throne in 1840. He had relaxed the censorship, and then restored it when journalists criticized him. He had released political prisoners, and then denounced them when they refused to recant. But throughout the states with more liberal forms of government – in Baden, Württemberg, Saxony, and Bavaria – Liberal ministers began to be included in the governments and the Press was granted more freedom. Ludwig I of Bavaria was even obliged to abdicate.

The very particularism of the German states made it impossible for Prussia and Austria to check so many scattered revolts. The hesitations of the Prussian government produced riots in Berlin, and on 17 March the king decided to try to make enough concessions to stem revolt. He declared himself in favour of a federal German *Reich* to replace the existing Confederation, with an elected Parliament, freedom of the Press, one national citizenship, and a national army. As in France less than a month before, a clash between troops and mob provoked civil war in the capital. Barricades were thrown up in the working-class areas, and Berlin imitated Paris. The king formed a liberal government under Ludolf Camphausen, one of the best-known Liberal leaders from the Rhineland, and a constituent assembly was elected which apathetically pursued its labours of constitution-making during the summer until the revolutionary moment had passed. Within Prussia things never got completely out of hand.

It was otherwise in Austria and Hungary. When news of the downfall of Louis Philippe reached Vienna in the first week of March 1848, the opposition to the long rule of Prince Metternich reached its climax. It was drawn from all social classes, and included court factions and liberal aristocrats who had come to detest his rule, middle-class and professional people who resented their long exclusion from political power, and working-class folk whose conditions of life and work had deteriorated during the recent years of depression. On 13 March demonstrations in Vienna forced the resignation of Metternich, and won permission for the middle classes to form a National Guard; two days later the Emperor Ferdinand undertook to summon the Diet, with additional middle-class members, to discuss a new constitution. In Hungary, which the emperor of Austria ruled as king and which had an aristocratic Diet of its own, a great national leader appeared in the person of Louis Kossuth. A lawyer and journalist, with a talent for popular oratory as great as that of O'Connell or Lamartine, he persuaded the country gentry of Hungary to lead the anti-feudal movement so as to preserve the unity of the nation. On 14 March Kossuth harangued the Hungarian Diet meeting at Pressburg. The next day the crowds of peasants, gathered in Buda-Pest for the great annual fair on the Ides of March, took matters into their own hands under the guidance of students and the young radical poet, Alexander Petöfi.

In this way events moved too fast in both countries, between 13 and 15 March, for the government of Vienna to refuse concessions. In both Hungary and Austria moderate governments were set up, making piecemeal concessions to liberal demands but determined not to give way to social revolution. Kossuth's demands for virtual Hungarian home rule were granted by the 'March Laws'. The court and the ruling aristocracy of Vienna played a waiting game, like that of the Prussian government: the main thing was to let the revolutionary moment pass, holding on to enough power to ensure decisive reaction later.

The remarkable simultaneity and initial successes of the revolutionary movements in Prussia, Austria, Hungary, and most of the smaller German states made possible a new phase in the effort to win German unity through one central representative body. A *Vorparlament*, or provisional general assembly, met at Frankfurt at the end of March. It consisted of 500 members drawn from the parliamentary assemblies of the different German states. By its very nature it represented particularism, and achieved no results of any importance save to arrange for the election of an all-German assembly. This new assembly was elected so as to bypass the existing governments of the states, and met at Frankfurt-on-the-Main in the Rhineland, in May 1848. This famous body, which sat for a whole year, represented the aspirations and feelings of all more nationally-minded Germans, but it suffered the initial handicap of having no sort of executive authority or executive organs. It was the voice of the embryonic German nation, echoed through its intellectual and professional classes, but it was a voice crying in a void. The delegates to Frankfurt could discuss, which they did at great length; but since there was no one to whom they could give orders, and nothing could be done except in so far as the separate state governments chose to act, the new-found unity was peculiarly impotent. The Frankfurt Assembly was, in effect, as much bound by particularism as the Diet of the old Confederation or even the *Vorparlament* itself.

The delegates to the Frankfurt Assembly were politically like the reforming Whigs of England or the moderate constitutional Liberals of France and Belgium. They were mostly university professors and businessmen, lawyers and judges, civil servants and clergy. In outlook they were mild, legalistic, and immensely earnest, opposed to violence and to social revolution. They wanted Germany to be federal, liberal, constitutional, and united. One of their leading spokesmen who drew up the first draft of the new German constitution was, characteristically, the eminent historian Friedrich Dahlmann, who in 1837 had been expelled from his professorship at the University of Göttingen for upholding liberal principles. As in Italy, so in Germany, the ranks of nationalists were deeply divided about how these agreed ends were to be achieved. Before long the debates of the assembly revealed two main conflicting programmes of unification; and because it could never reach solid agreement about the choice between these two schemes, the Frankfurt assembly was doomed to frustration.

At bottom it was a dispute about what the notion of 'Germany' amounted to on the map. The existing *Bund* had very hazy borders. East Prussia was not within it, though the bulk of Prussia was. The duchy of Holstein was within it, though it belonged to the Danish king; and Denmark as a whole, including the neighbouring duchy of Schleswig, was not in the *Bund*. It included a large part of the Austrian Empire but not Hungary; and the part of Austria within its boundaries included non-German peoples like the Czechs of Bohemia, while German-speaking communities existed in Hungary and Switzerland, beyond its frontiers. Neither the existing Confederation nor the test of German language offered any clear guide. What principle, then, could be used to define the geographical limits of a new 'Germany'? It was almost inevitable that there should be two answers, one more ambitious and inclusive, and the other more cautious and exclusive; and accordingly the assembly divided into a majority of 'Great Germans' and a minority of 'Little Germans'.

The Great Germans argued that the new federal state should include the Austrian lands except Hungary, even though that would incorporate many different Slav peoples. These they regarded as anyhow destined to be Germanized, and they were impatient at any separatist Slav nationalisms, such as the Polish and Czech, which obstructed their project. Their policy necessitated offering the federal crown to the Habsburgs and accepting Austrian leadership, and their predominance led to the appointment of the liberal Archduke John as Imperial Regent (*Reichs-Verweser*). The Little Germans were willing to leave out the mixed races of Austria in order to unify the rest of Germany more tightly, and wanted to include the whole of Prussia, which meant looking to the Prussian king for leadership. Roman Catholics tended to look to Austria as the leading Catholic power in Germany, Protestants to look to Prussia as the leading Protestant power; so the religious division also affected the alignment of opinions in this crucial issue. The dispute dragged on inconclusively until, again, the revolutionary moment was well past.

By the end of May 1848, the general position in Europe was that the first wave of revolutionary movements had won initial victories, but had spent its main force. In Italy liberal constitutions had been extorted from the kings and princes and when, in March, Austria had tried to suppress the revolts in Milan and Venice, Charles Albert of Piedmont had successfully intervened with armed force to uphold their freedom. But by the end of May the war reached a position of stalemate. No help came from France, where the Second Republic was being installed resting on universal suffrage, but where the large conservative majority in the Constituent Assembly represented provincial resistance to the revolutionary elements in Paris. In Prussia the situation was similar, and in Austria and Hungary Metternich had gone but moderate governments were in the saddle. In Germany as a whole the liberal movement for national unification had become bogged in the disputes of the Frankfurt Assembly. Nor was there sign of new revolutionary successes elsewhere in Europe. In Britain the last great Chartist demonstration failed in April, and Chartism ended in an atmosphere of ridicule when it was found that the petition included not the boasted five or six million names, but only two million, and many of these were plainly bogus since they included the signatures of Queen Victoria and the Duke of Wellington. In Ireland the 'Young Ireland' movement, which had indulged in a great deal of revolutionary and nationalist talk, found no broad popular backing, and as in the rest of the United Kingdom the government was well able to deal with isolated cases of violence and disorder. Spain, which had generated so much revolutionary energy since 1815, registered no more response to the European upheavals than an ill-timed revolt in Madrid at the end of March, which was quickly and easily suppressed by the government, and another at Seville in May which suffered the same fate. In Belgian cities there were sporadic riots throughout March, but they never assumed the character of a revolutionary movement. The dominant middle classes, ruling through an exceptionally liberal constitution, made enough concessions and showed enough solidarity to keep revolution at arm's length. They lowered the property qualification for voters and increased the electorate enough to appease the lower middle classes. They instituted public works and gave more poor relief to rescue unemployed industrial workers from destitution. The elections of June brought a sharp defeat for the Belgian radicals.

Switzerland. In Switzerland alone had liberals and radicals won a victory that was to prove permanent; and they won it partly because the revolutions in Europe prevented intervention by the eastern powers. Since 1845 the seven Catholic cantons (Uri, Schwyz, Unterwalden, Zug, Fribourg, Lucerne, and Valais) had formed themselves, in violation of the Federal Pact of 1815, into a separate political and military league, or *Sonderbund*. In the last two months of 1847 civil war had broken out between the *Sonderbund* and the forces of the Federal Diet, supported by the other, predominantly Protestant, cantons and by liberals and radicals everywhere in the country. It was, like the American War between the States, a war for the preservation of the union, and the overwhelming strength of the federal forces under the skilled generalship of William Henry Dufour of Geneva ended the struggle in twenty-five days. The intervention planned by Austria, Prussia, and France was prevented by the speedy end of the war and by the outbreak of revolutions in Italy and France. A new constitution was created by September 1848, which transformed the Swiss 'League of States' into a real Federal State. It guaranteed republican forms of government in all cantons, equality of all before the law, and liberty of conscience, speech, press, and public meeting. The power of legislation was now invested in a Federal legislature on the pattern of the United States Congress. Within the next few years unified national systems of coinage, postage, and weights and measures were introduced, and internal customs barriers were removed. The material life of the country thrived in consequence, and the new constitution lasted until 1874, when it was replaced by the present system.

Counter-revolution. The summer of 1848 brought a completely new phase in the European revolutionary movement. It was marked in most countries by counter-revolution, led in some by the moderate liberals and conservatives, in others by the more extreme forces of reaction. On 12 June the capture of Vicenza by the Austrian troops under Radetzky began the counter-offensive against Piedmont and the Italian nationalists. It culminated in an Austrian victory at Custozza on 23 July. By 9 August Charles Albert was obliged to make an armistice. This first war of Italian independence ended in defeat, because it was less a concerted effort to attain peninsular unity than a purely anti-Austrian campaign, conceived by Charles Albert as having the limited aim of forming a kingdom of Northern Italy. Only the prompt mediation of Britain and France saved Piedmont from invasion. In France the government decided to close the national workshops in Paris, and precipitated that still mysterious outburst of popular fury known as the 'June Days'.

On 21 June, when the decree abolishing the national workshops was issued, bands of workers swarmed through the streets shouting the *Marseillaise*. Large open-air meetings were held. Two days later barricades sprang up everywhere, and by 24 June a state of siege was declared. It seems to have been a virtually spontaneous popular rising, born of desperation and exasperation, without known leaders or clear organization. Opposed to the insurgents were the formidable forces of the army, the National Guard, and the new Mobile Guards, under the command of the African veteran, General Cavaignac. Pitched battles took place on 24 and 25 June, when guns were trained on the barricades and workers were mercilessly massacred. By the evening of the 25th the fighting was over, but it was followed by summary executions and the judicial punishment of more than eleven thousand prisoners. The ferocity on both sides gave the most vivid support so far to the theories of unlimited class warfare put forward by Marx and Engels. The 'June Days' killed all hopes of a social and democratic republic, and drove the parliamentary government into the arms of reaction. The new constitution of the Second Republic, at last adopted in November, included no mention of the much-discussed 'right to work', and it entrusted all executive power to a president to be directly elected by the people. At the presidential elections the following month, out of seven and a half million votes five and a half million went to Louis Napoleon Bonaparte, nephew of the great Napoleon. Lamartine gained less than 21,000. This marks the swing of opinion in France between the beginning and end of 1848. Out of terror of a social republic, French democracy doomed even the liberal republic; for with a Bonaparte in the saddle a military dictatorship was not far off.

With the turning of the tide in Italy and France during the second

---

MAP 4. THE HABSBURG EMPIRE, 1848

The three main racial and linguistic groups within the patchwork Empire were the Germans, who predominated in the west; the Magyars, who predominated in Hungary; and various Slav peoples who existed in two large blocs – in Bohemia, Moravia, Slovakia, and Galicia, in the north; and in Carniola, Croatia, Dalmatia, and Slavonia in the south. But everywhere there was liable to be intermixture, and in certain areas (e.g., Lombardy and Transylvania) Latin peoples such as Italians and Rumanians dwelt in large numbers. The political structure of the Empire hinged upon the ascendancy of Germans in the West, of Magyars in the east. The nations of contemporary Europe emerged from the disruption of the whole Empire, in the course of which the northern Slavs (Czechs and Slovaks) cohered together, and the Slavs south of the Danube found a nucleus of unity in Serbia (compare Map 15).

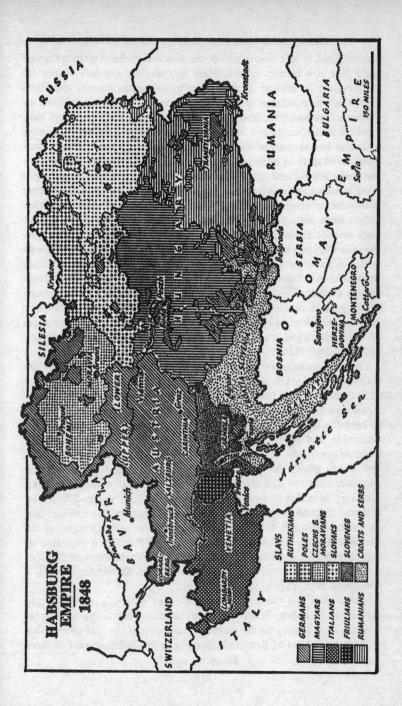

HABSBURG EMPIRE 1848

RUSSIA

BULGARIA

Sofia

RUMANIA

Kronstadt

TRANSYLVANIA

HUNGARY

Lemberg

Krakow

SILESIA

Belgrade

SERBIA

BOHEMIA

BAV.

Danube R.

Munich

Innsbruck

Trent

Vienna

Gratz

AUSTRIA

Carniola

Carinthia

SALZBURG

STYRIA

CROATIA

SLAVONIA

Trieste

Venice

ISTRIA

SWITZERLAND

LOMBARDY

VENETIA

Milan

ITALY

Verona

Padua

Mantua

DALMATIA

Adriatic Sea

BOSNIA

HERZE-GOVINA

Sarajevo

MONTENEGRO

Cattaro

OTTOMAN EMPIRE

150 MILES

SLAVS

RUTHENIANS

POLES

CZECHS & MORAVIANS

SLOVAKS

SLOVENES

CROATS AND SERBS

GERMANS

MAGYARS

ITALIANS

FRIULIANS

RUMANIANS

half of 1848, it was events within the borders of the Austrian Empire itself that now became crucial. Here still was the ultimate bastion of conservatism in Europe. If revolution triumphed in Austria and Hungary, the whole balance of advantages would be permanently tilted in favour of nationalism, liberalism, and democracy. If revolution here were crushed, it could also be crushed eventually in Germany and Italy. The situation, as usual in the Habsburg dominions, was immensely complex (See Map 4). In its simplest terms it was a triangular contest between the three main racial groups of Germans, Magyars, and Slavs, each reluctant to concede to the other the national rights and ambitions which it claimed for itself. But not only was each racial group sharply divided within itself among those championing different views of the future; each provincial area suffered further internal conflicts of interest between landowners great and small, middle and professional classes, and peasants. Faced with this situation, the Habsburg ministers and generals were able to follow cheerfully their policy of playing off one group against the other in order to survive and dominate them all. The novelty of the eastern revolutions of 1848-49 was, however, that this time a permanent residue of change was left; these territories underwent some of the basic legal, social, and political changes effected in western nations before 1815.[1]

The Slav peoples were stimulated to find some common policy by the movement for German unification. The 'Great German' programme of including Austria (though not Hungary) in a more unified German *Reich* was opposed by the Czechs, whose moderate leaders preferred to keep the loose Habsburg structure within which they sought greater autonomy, and by the Slovaks who had no desire to be left separately under Magyar rule. In April 1848 the Czech leader, Frantisek Palacký, declined to attend the Frankfurt Assembly and declared that had the Austrian state not already existed for centuries, it would have been necessary to create it. In May the German radicals resigned from the National Council in Prague, and the cleavage between Slav and German nationalists widened. In June a Slav Congress was held at Prague, as the Slav rejoinder to Frankfurt. Presided over by Palacký, it consisted of three sections: Czechs and Slovaks, Serbs and Croats, Poles and Ruthenians. This threefold division foreshadowed the Slav states of 1919 - Czechoslovakia, Yugoslavia, and Poland.

Like Italian and German nationalists, Slav nationalists were deeply divided as to policy. While extremists dreamed mystically of a great confederation uniting all the scattered fragments of the Slav race (which aroused fresh fears of Russian leadership in the Balkans) most of them

1. See pp. 51 and 57.

were primarily concerned with preventing the mere partition of sub-jected Slav peoples between Germans and Magyars. While the more moderate Czech politicians wanted to remain within a liberalized Aus-trian federation, in which they hoped Slavs would eventually predomi-nate, the Poles wanted to recreate an independent Polish state. The Yugoslavs wanted complete independence from Hungary, while the Slovaks wanted only equal rights. The Imperial Court, which in May had fled from Vienna to Innsbruck to escape popular pressure in the capital, busily encouraged Czech resistance to Germans and Slovak re-sistance to Magyars. It was the old policy of 'divide and rule' which had so often proved its effectiveness. On 12 June the people of Prague imitated the people of Vienna, and broke out in revolution led by students and workers. In five days General Windischgrätz, the Austrian commander, foreshadowed the work of Cavaignac in Paris a week later and of Radetzky in Milan seven weeks later. He crushed the revolution-ary popular movement bloodily and decisively.

The provincial diets, which had revived in most provinces of the Austrian and Hungarian territories during the 1840s, in general proved unable to serve the cause of liberal nationalism. They voiced prevalent discontent with the central government and represented the great land-owners, the smaller landed gentry, and the professional middle classes, whose desire was broadly for greater autonomy and local privilege, rather than for national or racial independence or for social revolution. In Bohemia the Diet stood for the patriotism of the landowners. The Bohemian middle classes, like the French, mostly wanted greater con-stitutional liberties, but they did not want social revolution. The rising in Prague attracted, therefore, no general national enthusiasm.

Kossuth. At first it seemed likely that a similar situation would occur in Hungary. The Pressburg Diet of March, and even the new Assembly which met at the beginning of July, included large majorities that wanted to avoid a complete break with Austria. The Hungarian nation-alist movement could not make common cause with the Slavs. The Croats and Slovaks, under Magyar rule, saw independence from Mag-yars as more important than freedom from German rule; and just as the Austrian government could find an ally in Czech fears of social revolu-tion in its effort to suppress popular revolution in Prague, so it could find an ally in Croat and Slovak fears of Magyar domination to resist the chauvinistic claims of Magyar nationalism. Moreover, Hungarian politics were increasingly governed by the remarkable personality of Louis Kossuth. A petty nobleman by birth, he stood for the lesser nobility or gentry, roughly a third of a million strong, buried in the countryside, as against the great Magyar nobles. He therefore favoured racial and linguistic Magyarism, rather than landownership or territorial rights, as a basis of Hungarian national claims. He became a popular hero, not only within Hungary but throughout Europe, though his radicalism was more completely permeated by intransigent nationalism than was radicalism in the west. His closest counterpart, perhaps, was Mazzini. Under his influence during the 1840s Magyar had replaced Latin as the exclusive language used in Hungary for laws, government business, and public education. Magyar language became, for the gentry, the double protection against German imperial officials and upstart Slav nationalists. This group backed Kossuth's ideal of making Hungary a Magyar national state, although large tracts of it were inhabited by Slav peasants and Magyars were actually a minority of its total population. For these reasons Magyar nationalism was inevitably even more at cross purposes with Slav nationalist movements than with German; and indeed the Great German programme, which would leave Magyars in control of Hungary, suited them admirably. They had a 'Great Hungarian' programme of their own claiming extended authority over Transylvania and Croatia.

The 'March Laws' that Kossuth had piloted through the Diet, and that the events of March in Vienna and Budapest had obliged the Austrian government to accept, provided for Hungarian home rule under nominal kingship of the Habsburgs, with a separate parliament at Buda-Pest elected on a restricted suffrage. The nobility lost their exemption from taxation, and the towns were given representation in Parliament. This new assembly met in July 1848. The same events had forced the Austrian government to create a *Reichstag* for the Austrian half of the Empire, and this also met in Vienna in July. It was the only full imperial Parliament in the history of the Austrian Empire, and represented an attempt to meet simultaneously the Czech fears of 'Great German' nationalism, the German fears of Slav nationalism, the general autocratic and middle-class fears of social revolution, and the Habsburg need for broader backing against Hungarian nationalism. Both the Austrian and the Hungarian Parliaments represented mainly the gentry and the middle classes. As in France and Prussia, the moderates were by July well established in power; and it remained to be discovered how far they could retain that power against radical revolution from below and military reaction from above.

Only eight hours after the Hungarian assembly met on 4 July, Kossuth had to proclaim 'the country in danger', because the subject Slav races were already in revolt in Croatia and Serbia, encouraged by the Austrians. If Slav nationalism should mean Russian intrusion into the Balkans, then Magyar nationalism must prefer an alliance with Vienna and even with Frankfurt. Kossuth appealed for, and was granted, power to raise an army of 200,000 men to enable Hungary to defend herself. But in the end 40,000 of these were sent to support Austria on condition that they should not be used 'against the freedom of the Italian nation'. By the end of August, Radetzky had defeated Charles Albert at Custozza and taken Milan and all Lombardy; and Windischgrätz had crushed Prague. The Austrian government now felt able to settle things with Hungary, and tried to revoke the 'March Laws'.

On 11 September the imperial army from Croatia invaded Hungary, and Kossuth appealed to the Constituent Assembly of Vienna to mediate between Hungary and the Habsburgs. But in that assembly German and Slav sentiment combined against Magyar claims, and gave the government a majority. The deadlock precipitated a second mass rising in Vienna in October, aimed at creating a national Germany and a national Hungary. The democrats of Vienna were now, however, crushed by Windischgrätz as decisively as had been those of Prague; and with both popular movements suppressed, the way was at last clear for general reaction. In November Felix Schwarzenberg was made Austrian Prime Minister, backed by a cabinet composed of a mixture of liberals and radicals. Schwarzenberg was brother-in-law of Windischgrätz and had been adviser of Radetzky in Italy. He was a man of violence whose chief aim was to accumulate power and use it boldly to restore order and central authority in the Austrian Empire. In December the feeble and imbecile Emperor Ferdinand abdicated in favour of his eighteen-year-old nephew, Francis Joseph, whose aims were likewise the preservation of the prestige and military power of the monarchy. By the end of 1848, although Kossuth was yet to gain further temporary successes in 1849, the Habsburgs were back in the saddle and the Magyar nationalist movement was doomed.

Turkey. With so much unrest in the Habsburg territories it was inevitable that their neighbours and traditional enemies, the Ottoman Turks, should experience some repercussions. The Turkist Empire, which had already suffered the loss of Greece,[1] was from 1839 to 1861 ruled by the reforming Sultan Abdul-Medjid. In 1839 he had promulgated a charter that gave equality before the law to all classes of Ottoman subjects and guaranteed their lives and property. Although proclaimed with great solemnity throughout the provinces of the Empire, this enlightened policy encountered enormous local resistance, which was often effective. The provinces most affected by the revolutionary movements were those of Moldavia and Wallachia which, together with Transylvania then under Habsburg rule, came after 1919 to form the bulk of

1. See p. 139.

modern Rumania. By the Treaty of Adrianople of 1829 Russia had occupied these provinces, where she had previously established certain treaty rights, as a guarantee that Turkey would pay the war indemnity. During her occupation Russia had set up in each province assemblies representative of the landowning classes (*Boyars*), and during the 1840s limited economic and social reforms were carried out. Schools were set up and customs barriers between the two provinces were abolished. From 1830 onward there grew up in these two provinces a strong desire for union not only with each other but also with Transylvania on the western slope of the Carpathians, inhabited by Rumans similar in language and race.

Transylvanian resistance to Magyar rule in 1848 stimulated nationalist enthusiasm in Moldavia and Wallachia, where there were riots and local insurrections. In Bucharest, chief town of Wallachia, a provisional government was set up in June on the European pattern. Here, too, it was mainly the work of a nationalist intellectual, the historian Nicholas Balcesco, leader of a secret society. But moderates quickly gained control of it, as in France, and the problem of emancipating the serfs was shelved by appointing an Agrarian Commission which never reached any decision. On the advice of the Tsar, Nicholas I, the Turks sent an army into Wallachia and dissolved the provisional government. By the end of the year the two provinces were again subjected to joint Russo-Turkish occupation, and meanwhile in Transylvania the Habsburg policy of playing off Rumanian forces against Hungarian brought its reward in the collapse of nationalist hopes in that territory too. The story of the Rumanian revolt is a repetition, in miniature, of the European revolutionary movement as a whole. In March 1848 the Society of Rumanian Students in Paris sent a delegation to the French provisional government. It voiced the claim which, in so many other forms, re-echoed throughout the continent that year. 'The Wallachians, the Moldavians and the Transylvanians all declare that they are Rumanians, and that their land, which has so long been witness of their distress, is called Rumania.' It was 1919 before such claims were satisfied for Czechs and Poles, Slovenes, and Rumanians, and during the intervening sixty years many nationalist aspirations fermented and turned sour.

Collapse of Revolution. The year of revolutions ended, then, with the suppression of democratic radical movements in the crucial areas of Italy, France, Austria, Prussia, and Turkey, and with the triumphs of moderate liberals in Belgium and Britain. The ascendancy of these forces, all alike opposed to social revolution, was consolidated in various ways. In Naples, Ferdinand II had already suspended the constitution and reverted to his normal reactionary methods of government. In Frankfurt there was a popular rising against the Assembly in September, and it was crushed by the use of Prussian and Austrian troops. Henceforth the Assembly suffered under the insuperable handicap that it had forfeited popular support and made clear that it existed only by grace of Prussia and Austria. In November Frederick William IV appointed as his chief minister Count Brandenburg, a cavalry officer who had recently restored order at Breslau, and in December he dissolved the Prussian Constituent Assembly, which had failed to devise a new and more liberal constitution for Prussia. The Civic Guard was disbanded, clubs were closed, public meetings banned. The governments of Brandenburg in Prussia, Schwarzenberg in Austria, and Louis Napoleon Bonaparte in France were the paradoxical culmination of the year of revolutions, and an omen of the next phase in Europe's history.

Among the major forces of counter-revolution must be included fate itself, in the form of cholera. The year of revolutions was also the year of plague in Europe. Filling people with fear akin to the modern terror of cancer, this particular epidemic had begun in China in 1844, reached Russia by 1847, and now in the autumn of 1848 began to spread rapidly and devastatingly westward across Europe. It reached Britain in October and went thence to the United States. What had begun in Turkestan ended on the Mississippi. Producing hundreds of deaths each day, it struck especially at the towns, the very centres of revolution. It left behind a heavy death toll and great social dislocation. Among the living it left physical exhaustion and a dispirited apathy that quenched the fires of revolt. All known treatments were almost ineffective, and the physical and psychological condition of survivors made prolonged effort of any kind impossible – least of all the building of barricades and the raising of revolt. The year of revolutions was bounded by calamity, and the embers that had been partly kindled by hunger were partly quenched by disease.

THE SEQUEL OF REVOLUTION, 1849–50

At the beginning of 1849 revolutionary nationalist movements remained active in only two main areas: Italy and Hungary. Elsewhere in Europe power was securely held by moderate liberals or by conservatives, and in places (such as France and Prussia) a current of more severe authoritarian reaction set in. But in Italy and in Hungary the struggle between revolutionary nationalists and moderates continued until the autumn of 1849, and this prolonged sequel to the great 'Year of Revolutions' throws further light on the nature of the revolutionary movement as a whole.

Italy. In Italy the crucial new fact was that, at the beginning of 1849, it was impossible to look for national leadership to either Piedmont or the Papacy. Charles Albert, having been forced to make an armistice with Austria in August after Custozza, had been accused by the more militant Milanese of betraying the national cause; and although democratic government and enthusiasms continued at Turin, his army was in no condition yet to renew the fight. In November, finding republicanism in Rome so strong and disorder so great, Pius IX had fled from the Vatican to Gaeta, in the Kingdom of Naples. With both Piedmont and the Papacy out of the running for leadership of the anti-Austrian movement, initiative lapsed to the republicans, led by Mazzini in Rome and by Daniele Manin in Venice. Mazzini proclaimed that now the war of kings was over; the war of the people must begin. He clung to his ideal of national liberation and unification through a mass democratic rising and the creation of an Italian republic. Since June 1848 he had been joined by the colourful figure of Giuseppe Garibaldi, who had been training his red-shirted Italian Legion in Uruguay and with it defending the republican liberties of Montevideo. Garibaldi had reached Leghorn only in June, too late to take any important part in the war; but he withdrew to the hills to plan guerrilla warfare, in which his red-shirted volunteers excelled. The republicans were resolved to continue the fight even in isolation and against the heaviest odds.

In its new phase the Italian revolutionary movement hinged upon the three pivots of Florence, Rome, and Turin, with the independent island republic of Venice, under Manin, as an isolated outpost of defiance. In Tuscany, the Papal States, and Piedmont strong and vocal radical movements still demanded constituent assemblies elected on universal suffrage, more republican forms of government, and the renewal of the war against Austria. In their chief cities of Florence, Rome, and Turin relatively democratic governments already existed, and the crucial question was how far they could achieve any concerted action for one common policy. In February 1849 a Constituent Assembly met at Rome, elected on universal suffrage and including thirty-seven deputies sent to represent Tuscany, whose Grand Duke Leopold had fled in January to join Pius IX at Gaeta. On 9 February this Assembly voted that 'the form of government is a pure democracy, with the glorious title of the Roman Republic'. But despite Mazzini's efforts Tuscany was not persuaded to unite with Rome as one Republic, mainly because its country districts remained loyal to Leopold. Nor could Gioberti, now premier of Piedmont, be induced to send representatives to the Assembly in Rome. Opinion in Piedmont was, indeed, predominantly faithful to its monarchy and against a republicanism imposed on Italy from Rome. But it favoured ending the truce with Austria, and on 20 March Charles Albert embarked on the ill-conceived compaign that, within six days, resulted in his defeat by Radetzky at Novara. Departing in humiliation to Portugal, he lived for four months in seclusion and died on 28 July.

Novara made possible an Austrian reconquest of Italy. Venice was under blockade. In April the moderate constitutionalists in Florence suppressed the Tuscan assembly and invited Leopold to return. He was duly restored by Austrian armies, though only after bitter fighting in the radical port of Leghorn on 28 July, and he never regained the respect of his people. Restoration of the Pope was a more complex issue, for it affected not only Italy but all the Catholic powers of Europe. At the end of March a conference of representatives of France, Austria, Spain, and Naples met at Gaeta, to consider ways and means. France was particularly concerned to prevent the unconditional reinstatement of the Pope by Austrian arms, and in April forced the issue by sending General Oudinot with 10,000 men to occupy Civitavecchia as the gateway to Rome. The other three states thereupon sent armies too, and at the end of the month the Roman Republic found itself isolated with four foreign armies converging upon it. Under the leadership of Mazzini and Garibaldi the city decided to resist, and went into a state of siege.

When Oudinot first advanced, he was soundly beaten by Garibaldi and retreated to Civitavecchia to demand large French reinforcements. On 3 June, with 30,000 men and full siege equipment, he again advanced. The city held out for a month, in a desperate and heroic defence that became an epic in the story of Italian nationhood. At the beginning of July, Garibaldi left the city with some 5,000 of his men and, pursued by four armies, defied capture in the hills and at last found refuge in Tuscany. Behind French bayonets the cardinals and the Pope returned, and when in August Venice, too, was forced to surrender, the last foothold of republicanism in Italy was destroyed. There Daniele Manin, since the proclamation of the Republic at Venice in March 1848, had assumed a role that was the counterpart to Mazzini's in Rome. The defence of Venice revealed an equal heroism. These final phases bred a new legend of republicanism, strong in the great cities but not in the countryside. It was a legend that inspired fresh efforts a decade later. But it also, paradoxically, meant that the republican solution for Italy's problems could not be discounted. The failure of the Roman Republic to command wider support in Italy revived faith in constitutional monarchy as the only generally acceptable solution. Papal federalism was killed by Pius IX's reversion to absolutism and by his reliance on foreign force. Only Piedmont could now command support, and the last desperate attempt at Novara had restored Piedmont's prestige. It was henceforth plain that only force kept Italy politically disunited; and it was equally plain that only a national army, under the House of Savoy, was likely to expel that intrusive foreign force of disruption.

Hungary. Strangely parallel events had meanwhile been taking place in Hungary. There, too, the nationalist cause found fresh reserves of popular enthusiasm and heroic powers of resistance evoked by Kossuth. But Hungary had to improvise an army, and to crush irregular forces of Serbs and Slovaks within her own territory. She could look for no help from liberal forces in Austria, because early in March 1849, Schwarzenberg overthrew the new constitution and dissolved the ill-fated Austrian *Reichstag*. But Kossuth, faced with anti-Magyar risings of Slovaks in the north, Serbs in the south, Rumanians and Germans in the east, and Croats in the south-west, whipped up Magyar national feeling to a frenzy at the end of 1848. Although Windischgrätz, in the winter of 1848, advanced into Hungary and even occupied Buda-Pest, he was compelled to withdraw again by April 1849. On 14 April the Hungarian Parliament deposed the Habsburgs and elected Kossuth as Governor. He issued a declaration of Hungarian independence, and on 6 June entered Buda-Pest in triumph.

But his rule lasted only a few weeks. As in Italy, popular feeling began to turn against republicanism and revolutionary excesses, and there was no real agreement among leaders of the movement for independence. And, as in Italy, it was the intervention of a foreign army which ended the revolution. Nicholas, Tsar of Russia, believed that monarchs must help one another against revolutionaries. He disliked the successes of the Polish generals who had become so prominent in the Hungarian army. Since March, when Russian troops had been driven back out of Transylvania, a Hungarian division had sat near the Galician frontier to encourage the Poles to rebel against Austria; and he was very sensitive about the effect of Hungarian example on Galicia, since the troubles there only two years before. In May he decided to send military help to the Habsburgs, and a Russian army invaded Hungary. In August the Hungarian army surrendered to the Tsar at Világos. Kossuth buried the Hungarian crown near the frontier and fled to Turkey.

For nearly fifty years he sustained a virulent anti-Habsburg propaganda in Britain and in the United States. The Austrian general, Haynau, who had replaced Windischgrätz, exercised and permitted the most extreme brutalities in his ruthless suppression of the defeated kingdom. Kossuth had a final moral victory over Haynau some years later. Known in England as the 'Hyena' for his cruelties, which Kossuth had publicized, Haynau was mobbed and severely handled by the draymen of Barclay and Perkins breweries when he visited Britain. Lord Palmerston, the British foreign secretary, sympathized with the workmen. He angered Queen Victoria, but added to his popularity in the country, by refusing more than a perfunctory apology for the rough treatment of the General, and proceeded soon after to extend a very friendly welcome to Kossuth.

Reaction. By August 1849, therefore, with the fall of Rome and Venice and the collapse of the Hungarian revolution, the hectic period of revolutions was at an end. There was still sporadic unrest, but no new revolutionary movement took shape. The feeble and dilatory Frankfurt Assembly received its deathblow in April, when at last it decided to offer the Imperial Crown of a united Germany to the king of Prussia. Since Schwarzenberg had made it clear at Frankfurt in December 1848, that he intended to keep Austria-Hungary as one state and to revive the old German *Bund*, the Assembly turned of necessity to Prussia. But Frederick William IV, now more secure in his own autocratic powers in Prussia, refused the offer. Both Austria and Prussia withdrew their representatives from Frankfurt, leaving the Assembly a mere rump of small states which formally approved a new German constitution. In September 1849 Austria and Prussia jointly killed the whole project and took upon themselves the functions of a central German authority. Already in April and May, when revolts occurred in Baden, Bavaria, and Saxony, Prussian troops had promptly been sent into these states to restore order. Determined to prevent further acquisitions of Prussian power, Schwarzenberg took the first opportunity to check this tendency. In 1850 disturbances in Hesse-Cassel prompted him to send in 200,000 Austrian troops. Prussia mobilized in reply, and a few clashes occurred. But Frederick William as usual gave way, and in November, by the pact of Olmütz, Schwarzenberg dictated a settlement of the dispute and left Prussia completely humiliated. He then completed his plan of reinstituting the old *Bund*, intact and as much under Austrian presidency and control as in the great days of Prince Metternich.

By the end of 1850 the clock seemed to have been firmly put back. The turbulent movements for Italian and German unification had been as totally frustrated as had the movements for Slav, Hungarian, and Rumanian independence. Throughout central and eastern Europe the old order had been restored. Naturally enough, even the moderate achievements of more liberal constitutions within Austria and Prussia were among the next casualties. In January 1850 a new Prussian constitution paid lip service but made no substantial concession to liberal ideas. At the end of 1851 the Austrian constitution reverted to a form of complete absolutism. More unexpectedly, even France moved in the same direction. In December 1851 Louis Napoleon secured by a *coup d'état* the extension of his presidency of the Second Republic for another ten years; and one year later he was to give his already autocratic power full Bonapartist form by proclaiming the Second Empire. All these events, too, were the sequel to the year of revolutions. The sense in which they were the true aftermath can be seen if the variegated pattern of revolutionary activity is examined more closely.

THE PATTERN OF REVOLUTIONARY ACTIVITY

Although the revolutions of 1848 and their sequels in 1849 and 1850 are so diversified, they are also of one piece; and their origins and aims, their course and their outcomes, have certain common features. Their special characteristics derive from that balance of unity and disunity in European civilization already described,[1] as well as from the impact of the great economic and political changes of the generation between 1815 and 1848.

Revolutionary situations arise when established authorities find themselves challenged by movements that are superior either in numbers and strength, or in organization and resources, or in both. The reasons why the governments of so many European states found themselves simultaneously challenged by formidable revolutionary movements in 1848 varied considerably from place to place. Disloyalty was created more by a sense of political frustration in France and in Italy than in Germany or Austria: more by an economic revulsion against feudalism in Austria and Hungary than in France or Italy. In eastern Europe industrialism and socialism had little share in causing political disturbances, though the coming of railways had some effect. The extent to which intellectuals, journalists, and students concerted their activities internationally was greatly exaggerated by the frightened governments, just as the rebels frequently exaggerated their own capacity to organize revolutionary mass movements of peasants or working men. It seems likely that the work of secret societies was more important in Italy than in France, and more important in both Italy and France than in Germany or Austria. For a complex of causes modern Europe had reached a critical stage in its political, social, and economic development, which governments little understood and in which they found themselves so impoverished in popular allegiance that they could survive or recover only by the use of extreme violence. Events therefore tended to follow a certain

1. See pp. 81–5.

sequence, and to end in similar results. Yet there is no simple or unitary pattern but rather several interwoven designs.

1. The Pattern of Time and Place. First, and most strikingly, revolutionary movements occurred a generation after the great settlement of Europe in 1815, and in their general character they were all protests against that settlement, all attempts to destroy it. In France the revolution of 1848, much more than the revolution of 1830, was a self-conscious re-enactment of the great Revolution of 1789: a revival of rationalist and democratic idealism, an abandonment of the attempts to reconcile with monarchical government the traditions and aspirations of the revolutionary tradition, a hasty reassertion of French initiative in the art of revolution and of French leadership in Europe. In Italy and Germany the revolutions were even more directly an onslaught on the territorial and dynastic settlement of Vienna and on the hegemony of the Habsburgs which Metternich's 'system' had clamped upon Europe. Simultaneously seeking to overthrow absolutist and conservative government in the several Italian and German states, and to end the dynastic partition of power which kept aspirations for national unification at bay, they involved a natural union of liberalism with patriotism. Through representative institutions and new constitutional arrangements it was hoped to integrate the peoples of Italy and of Germany into self-governing and independent political units. In Hungary the comparable movement was internally involved in the rival struggles for independence of Magyars and Slavs. In Austria and Prussia, on the other hand, movements for liberal self-government and greater constitutional liberties could exist apart from patriotic struggles for national unification and were correspondingly less dynamic. Outside Austria itself, the revolutions shared the common characteristic of being anti-absolutist, anti-conservative, anti-Austrian. Beyond this unanimity about negatives, they were deeply divided as to the most desirable procedures, methods, and aims of liberal nationalism. That was one reason why they failed.

Secondly, the sequence of the revolutions in time and their incidence in place suggest that there were ultimately two separate storm centres from which the hurricane originated, France and Italy; and the greater of these (contrary to contemporary expectation and subsequent belief) was Italy rather than France. The rising in Palermo and in other Italian cities preceded the outbreak of the February Revolution in Paris, and the real initiative lay with Italy. Again in 1849 it was in Italy that republicanism found its second wind and demonstrated its most heroic and epic qualities. But France was still thought of so universally as the prompter of revolutions and Paris remained so pre-eminent as the headquarters of expert revolutionaries, that events there gave stimulus and inspiration to the European movement in general. If Italy set the example, it was France that give the signal for a more general activity; and in Germany, Austria, and Hungary the risings of March came only after the proclamation of the Second Republic in France. Once revolutionary action had become general, the crucial points were not in Paris, where Lamartine and the cautious assembly failed to produce the support that foreign revolutionaries had hoped for, but in Vienna and Buda-Pest, Turin and Rome, Florence and Venice. This relegation of France to a second place in the leadership of European revolutions was symptomatic of her already declining demographic and diplomatic importance, and suggestive of the basically nationalist character of the revolutionary movements themselves. France, like the United Kingdom, was already a united nation and had no irredentist claims; Italy was engaged in her *Risorgimento*. Her patriotic dreams of national unity and independence chimed more with the corresponding aspirations of Germany or Hungary, Poland or Rumania, than with the more conservative and satisfied spirit of France or Britain.

Thirdly, of considerable significance, is the list of countries which escaped revolution and knew nothing more than disturbances while the rest of Europe was ablaze. It includes the United Kingdom and Belgium in the west, Poland and Russia in the east: two of the most industrialized and two of the least industrialized of European states. The revolutions were pre-eminently central European events. They happened in the only slightly industrialized territories of Germany, Switzerland, and Italy, and in the predominantly agrarian and peasant countries of the Balkans. Revolution did not happen in Britain and Belgium because these countries already had flexible constitutional systems of government which could absorb the attacks of radical and democratic movements without being shattered; because their industrial systems were far enough advanced to absorb the rapidly growing population in new forms of employment; and because facilities for emigration eased the pressure on both their internal economies and their internal political systems.

That revolution did not happen in Poland surprised most liberals of the time because, next to Greek independence, the restoration of a free and united Poland was the most cherished cause of the international revolutionaries. But the Poles, unlike the Italians, had no single common enemy. To Polish patriots Prussia, Austria, and Russia were all alike enemies because each held in subjection a part of the body of the Polish nation. Moreover the recent abolition of the *Robot* in the Austrian-held province of Galicia, the area most likely to revolt in the conditions of 1848, had taken the basic impulse from peasant revolt; while the Russian portion, since the crushing of revolt in 1831, was held in a military subjection too tight to permit of serious rising. Only in Prussia were Poles encouraged to hope for more liberal treatment, and this not for long. That revolution did not come within Russia itself is perhaps explained chiefly by the eastward migration of Russians into Asia during the first half of the century, which absorbed the growing population just as westward expansion absorbed that of the United Kingdom. It is likely that movement east acted as a safety valve, offering more food and more freedom than could be found in European Russia where both were restricted and in short supply.

2. *The Economic and Social Pattern.* The connexion between the revolutions of 1848 and the economic expansion of Europe during the previous generation is no less close than their connexion with the political idealism and radicalism inherited from the French Revolution.[1] Basically the revolutionary mood was conditioned by a combination of three things: by the ferment of new ideas and ideals, deriving from the years before 1815 and sustained by the secret societies and the various liberal and democratic revolutionary parties of the continent; by the demographic restlessness caused by the unprecedented growth of population; and by the economic development in transport and industry which were changing the whole outlook of society. The relative importance of these three factors varied greatly from country to country; and if central Europe rather than France is regarded as the major storm centre, then the most important of these factors were the last two rather than the first.

It was in the economically more backward and agrarian lands of Austria and Hungary that the pressure of the growth of population was felt most acutely. During the first half of the nineteenth century the population of Austria probably increased at about the same rate as that of France – that is, by roughly thirty per cent – that of Hungary grew even faster. Not only was agriculture primitive in methods and medieval in organization, but feudal privileges and powers survived throughout most of the Habsburg lands. The Act of Emancipation passed on 7 September 1848 by the Constituent Assembly of Vienna was probably the greatest and most durable achievement of the year of revolutions. It abolished, without compensation, the hereditary rights of landlords in jurisdiction and administration. To the peasant who occupied the land of a noble it gave security of tenure. It abolished the labour service (*Robot*), which had been abolished in Hungary in March and in Galicia in 1847.

Because the landowners had no interest now in keeping large numbers of peasants on the land, the smaller peasants tended to sell their land to the wealthier and move into the towns, so easing class tensions between nobles and peasants in the country while intensifying nationalist

1. See pp. 178–203.

tensions in the towns between the predominantly German townsfolk and the mainly Slav immigrants. Freed from the burden of the *Robot* the larger estates could be run more economically and more productively. With greater security of tenure and more land of their own, the remaining peasant farmers became wealthier, more independent, and more nationalistic. Peasant parties in the future were conservative in social affairs and nationalistic in politics, like the French. The compensation paid for abolition of the *Robot* made the aristocracy more capitalistic, for the landowners tended to invest it in industrial enterprises. The poorer peasants who drifted into the towns provided them with a new labour supply, and the basic conditions that had boosted industrialism in Britain half a century earlier now prevailed in much of eastern Europe. The sudden ending of feudalism brought the beginnings of a real agrarian and industrial revolution to the eastern marchlands of Europe.

The revolutions of 1848 were, in origin and impetus, the work of towns. Throughout the whole of Europe the course of events at first turned upon the actions of town dwellers: it was London and Birmingham, Paris and Brussels, Rome and Berlin, Vienna and Buda-Pest, that set the pace. But again this universal pattern conceals a basic difference. Paris and Brussels were in revolutionary mood because they were industrial cities. Vienna and Rome were revolutionary because they were capital cities, not because they were industrial. It has been pointed out that in 1848 a revolution occurred in eastern Europe wherever there was a town with more than 100,000 inhabitants; and that north of the Alps there were only three such Austrian towns, Vienna, Buda-Pest, and Prague. Vienna, with over 400,000 inhabitants, had almost doubled in size since 1815. The increase came largely from immigration from the countryside, and industrial development was not sufficiently advanced to absorb this rapid increase. Before 1848 the labour supply grew faster than industry, with the result that the towns experienced a declining standard of life and a phase of acute hardship and unemployment. The conditions bred the revolutionary spirit and provided the concentration of numbers and strength which a revolutionary movement needed in order to challenge established authority. Similar conditions existed in Milan, Florence, and Rome, and to a lesser extent in Berlin; they did not exist in Buda-Pest or Prague, which were smaller and were growing more slowly.

Within the towns leadership came from the intellectuals – from university professors and students, journalists and poets; and the events of 1848 in Germany have been called 'the revolution of the intellectuals'. This, again, was a universal characteristic, outside Britain. Poets like Lamartine and Petöfi, journalists like Mazzini and Kossuth, historians like Palacký, Dahlmann, and Balcesco, brought to the movements their peculiarly romantic, academic, and intellectualist flavour. They lent inspiration and infused nationalism. But as leaders of political movements they were weak because they were men of ideas rather than the responsible spokesmen of broad social interests or groups. It is their leadership that gave the revolutions their fragility and brittleness – if also their brilliance and heroism.

In Germany, where the dominance of intellectuals was particularly heavy and prolonged, the endless debates of the Frankfurt Assembly are their chief monument. Lamartine was to a large extent responsible for the lack of French support for revolutionary movements abroad, and his *Manifesto to Europe* in March 1848 was designed to reassure the governments of Europe that the Second Republic would not embark upon war despite all its professions of sympathy for liberalism and nationalism. Where, as in Prague, the revolution remained in the hands of intellectuals and university students and failed to enlist the mass support of either peasants or town proletariat, it suffered early defeat. Where, as in Hungary through the mediation of Kossuth, the revolution was captured by the gentry, it lasted longest and proved the most difficult to crush.

But although the initiative in revolution lay with the intellectuals and the populace of the towns, its ultimate fate lay in the hands of the peasants. Where, as in France and Austria, the conservative interests of landowning peasants made themselves felt, counter-revolutionary forces quickly triumphed. In such lands universal suffrage proved to be a decisively conservative weapon, and liberal expectations were frustrated by the operations of democracy. In Habsburg territories, once feudalism had been destroyed and peasant lands freed, the wealthier peasants lost interest in further revolutionary activity and the poorer peasants lacked any common purpose. Only in Italy and Germany, where there was a more considerable middle class, did the yearning for national integration voiced by the intellectuals linger on in a form capable of resurrection into an effective political movement.

In the more advanced industrial nations, pre-eminently Britain, France, and Belgium, but also to an extent Germany and Italy, socialism had found roots in the industrial working classes. It was henceforth associated on the continent with the desperate attempts at a 'second revolution', expressed in the 'June Days' in Paris and Prague, and the October revolt in Vienna. This association was not altogether justified, though socialists and communists claimed credit for these mass revolts of a desperate town populace. Karl Marx proceeded to analyse in detail the events of these years in *The Class Struggles in France, 1848–1850* and in *The Eighteenth Brumaire of Louis Bonaparte*. He wrote:

The workers were left no choice: they had to starve or let fly. They answered on 22 June with the tremendous insurrection in which the first great battle was fought between the two classes that split modern society. It was a fight for the preservation or annihilation of the *bourgeois* order. The veil that shrouded the republic was torn asunder.

Certainly, as a result of 1848, liberal constitutionalists ceased to fear universal suffrage as a gateway to socialism, though they began to fear it as an introduction to dictatorship; and there appeared a wider gap than hitherto between democracy and socialism.

3. The Political Pattern. The event of these years demonstrated that nationalism, in the sense of the demands of self-conscious peoples for self-determination, was the most potent general force in European politics. It might mean the demand that governments holding parts of a nation separate, as in the states of Germany and Italy, should be destroyed in favour of new comprehensive nation-states. It might mean the demand that comprehensive dynastic states, like the Habsburg Empire in Austria or the Kingdom of Hungary, should be destroyed in favour of smaller, more intensive nation-states. But whether it involved the integration or disintegration of existing states, it had been shown to be an impulse that could evoke a loyalty and a spirit of self-sacrifice vastly more intense than the allegiance normally accorded to existing governments. That it was likely to introduce great complexity and confusion into European affairs was already suggested by the distinction that had appeared in 1848 between the so-called 'historic nations' such as Greece, Poland, Hungary, and (more arguably) Italy and Germany, and the Rumans or various Slav peoples such as the Croats, Serbs, and Slovaks which had been previously submerged by their German, Hungarian, or Turkish conquerors. Of the Slav peoples, indeed, only Russians, Poles and Czechs could plausibly claim any past record of unity or independence; the nationalist claims of others had to rest on ethnography and philology rather than on history. Mutual jealousies and squabbles were inevitable even among nationalists, for German patriots were committed to denying Czech autonomy; Hungarian, to resisting Croatian and Serbian independence. The dreams of fraternal rose-water revolutions cherished by western nationalists like Lamartine and Mazzini were rudely dispelled.

The prevalence of nationalism meant that movements aiming at the creation of new states (as in Italy and Germany) became linked with movements aiming merely at capturing control of existing states (such as liberalism and democracy). It was the contention of men like Mazzini and Kossuth that the states they wanted must be new not only in territorial frontiers and population, but also in structure and institutions. It was also the contention of liberals like Count Camillo Cavour in Piedmont that only in territorially larger and more homogeneous states could the kind of political arrangements that they wanted be successfully established. There was an important difference of purpose between those who saw liberalism or democracy as the essential steps toward national self-determination, and those who saw national unification as the necessary prelude to liberalism and democracy. Until the disillusionments of 1848–50 both could work together, and it seemed as natural for patriots to be liberals or democrats as for liberals and democrats to be patriots. The strength of 'a people' lay in 'the people'.

After 1850 some nationalists came to believe that what liberalism or democracy had failed to give them might be got from more authoritarian sources and by more militaristic means. Cavour, who in 1850 became the Piedmontese minister of agriculture, commerce, and marine, held that only by the economic and military strengthening of Piedmont and by timely alliance with foreign powers could Italy be united. Diplomacy and force must be used to expel Austria and weld together the divided peninsula. This change of mood and outlook, a transition from reliance upon liberal idealism and popular enthusiasm to reliance upon realism and power, was perhaps the most important political result of the failures of 1848. In Germany distrust of liberalism and of parliamentary methods went further and deeper, because the failure of 1848 in Germany had been ever more complete than in Italy; though Prussia needed another decade of reorganization before she could become more clearly the hard core of a new Germany. After 1850 France, too, under the guidance of her Bonapartist ruler, became once again an authoritarian, militaristic state, temporarily abandoning her enthusiasm for republican ideas and parliamentary rights.

Throughout most of Europe the two decades after 1850 were, therefore, another era of conservatism and reaction. As after 1815 the power of the Roman Church revived. The Papacy made new concordats with Spain and Austria. The Church's role in education grew after 1850 in France and England. But in character this new phase differed profoundly from the previous phase of conservatism between 1815 and 1830. Outside Prussia and Russia dynastic monarchy had suffered crippling blows. The system of Metternich seemed old-fashioned – even more old-fashioned than the heroics of Lamartine and the secret societies – and could never return. France was never again to have a monarchy after 1848, and even at the height of his imperial power Napoleon III based his empire on a broader popular and parliamentary foundation than had Louis Philippe. Henceforth greater lip service, at least, had to be paid to the ideas of liberal constitutionalism and the dreams of democracy. Men won and held power to the extent that they represented (or could persuade others that they represented) broad sectional interests or national purposes, and not to the extent that they could claim hereditary right or legitimist authority, or in proportion to their intellectual eminence. In this ultimate sense most governments became increasingly more accountable to the people they governed and came to be regarded as rightly accountable. More than ever before they had to promote solid material interests, and show themselves competent and in command of real power, if they were to survive.

For 1848 had inaugurated the age of the masses. Just as the revolutions originated in the towns, so their characteristic device was the barricades, the instinctive gesture of urban revolt. Radical agitators had prepared the revolutions, and nationalist leaders emerged once they had begun; but the initiative in making revolution came not from such leaders but from the masses themselves. The timing of them was decided by those conditions that affected the masses everywhere: the aftermath of the financial crisis of 1846, the bad harvests of 1846 and 1847, the declining standard of living in the towns. Governments in future had to accept the fact that the masses held the master key of politics, and to lead or mislead mass opinion made vocal by universal suffrage became the first necessity of politicians. Moreover, parliamentary assemblies had gained no credit from the events of 1848–50, whereas it was the armies that had won in the end. When gatherings of enthusiastic middle-class representatives had finished talking, it was the professional armies of Russia, Prussia, and Austria, under their professional generals, which had settled the fate of Europe. Governments would in future rely more on organized military power to achieve their ends. Bismarck's age of 'blood and iron' had begun. For all these reasons the sequel to the era of revolutions was an era of authority and realism, of diplomacy and war; and it was in these conditions that a united Italy and a united Germany were at last to appear.

PART FOUR

THE EMERGENCE OF NEW POWERS, 1851–71

THE outstanding developments of Europe during the two decades between 1851 and 1871 were the industrial and commercial supremacy of the United Kingdom in the world; the temporary resurgence of French power and influence under the rule of Napoleon III; the achievements of political unification in Italy under the leadership of Piedmont and in Germany under the leadership of Prussia; and the remarkable expansion of European power into other continents. For many purposes the period can usefully be divided into two halves, because the years 1861-2 brought a turning point in the internal development of several major countries. In March 1861, the movement for Italian unification culminated in the proclamation of the Kingdom of Italy by the first Italian parliament. Though the city of Rome remained outside the kingdom until 1870, Italy ranked as a major power in Europe after 1861. In November 1860 Napoleon III began to relax his autocratic power and inaugurated the phase of so-called 'Liberal Empire', which brought a revival of parliamentary and electoral activity in France. In February 1861 the Tsar emancipated the serfs, so beginning a new era in the economic evolution of Russia; and he granted concessions in Poland. In September 1862 Bismarck became President of the Prussian Ministry, and began his single-minded policy of unifying Germany under Prussian domination. After three major wars he succeeded triumphantly when, in January 1871, the King of Prussia was crowned as German Emperor. During the second decade of this period European affairs were dominated by the German problem, and they were to remain dominated by it until 1945.

But the two decades, taken together, have a coherence of their own. This coherence comes partly from the common characteristics of the men who now occupied the European diplomatic stage: Lord Palmerston, who was Britain's Prime Minister from 1855 until 1865, except for a brief interlude in 1858-9; Napoleon III, who ruled France throughout; Count Cavour, who led Piedmont from 1852 until 1861; Bismarck, who controlled Prussian policy from 1862 until 1890. All four men had dynamic personalities, pursued forceful policies, and engaged in militant diplomacy and war. Each expressed a vigorous spirit of self-assertive nationalism, and each helped to transform the European scene into an arena of more naked struggle for national

237

prestige and power. For all four, liberalism took second place to nationalism, although Palmerston and Cavour contrived at least in some degree to reconcile the two.

The coherence of the period derives, too, from the prevalence of major wars. As previously suggested,[1] the age of revolutions was succeeded by an era of great wars between major powers, a natural consequence of the militant policies followed by the leading statesmen. Of the five major wars between 1854 and 1870, France, Prussia, and Austria were each engaged in three, Piedmont in two. But except for the first, the Crimean War, none lasted more than a few weeks or months. They were in general wars between regular and professional state armies, and except in Prussia national conscription did not yet make them wars between whole nations. They were wars that were truly 'continuations of policy by other means'. The period is distinct from the generation which preceded it in that governments came to fear other governments more than they feared revolutionary uprisings from within their own countries, and armies fought other armies rather than revolutionaries at home. It is distinct from the generation which followed it in that the French rather than the German Empire was still regarded as the greatest threat to the balance of power in Europe, and relations among the powers were more fluid and governed less by treaty alliances than they were to be after 1871.

A third source of coherence is more concealed than these other two, but none the less real. It was a time of general internal political reorganization in Europe, the impetus for which had been given by the experience of nationalist and liberal revolutions in 1848-9 and by the revival of a more intelligent and subtle conservatism after 1850. These were decades of remarkable fertility and ingenuity in the devising of new kinds of public administration, new forms of federal structure, and new economic and political organizations. Many factors combined to cause this: the rapid growth of population and of large towns, the speed of economic development and of industrialization, the old fear of revolution and the new fear of imminent war, a new expectation of greater efficiency and honesty in public life. To regard the central theme of the period as merely a continued conflict between the forces of conservatism and continuity and the forces of change and revolution would be misleading and superficial; as would be a purely diplomatic picture of the conflicts between the western parliamentary states of the United Kingdom, France, and Belgium on one side, and the central and eastern autocratic monarchies on the other. More important than either of these was the more silent and unobtrusive overhaul of the whole apparatus

1. See p. 111.

of public order, law, administration, and government which was taking place in nearly every country. France, Italy, and Germany were outstanding only in that the militant nationalism of these three great countries filled the headlines with dramatic events and mobilized in its cause the new masses of population, the new economic and military resources of society, and the harsh power of forceful and ruthless leadership. But it is the task of the historian to look behind the headlines, to the less conspicuous and less sensational changes that eventually helped to make modern Europe.

In the longest historical perspective, events of these years in eastern Europe might even be regarded as of more far-reaching significance than those in the west. The invention of the dual monarchy in Austria-Hungary, the emancipation of the Russian serfs, the crumbling of Ottoman Turkish power in Europe and north Africa, the consolidation of expansionist Balkan states in Greece, Serbia, and Rumania, were events no less pregnant with meaning for the future of the world than the attainment of commercial and industrial supremacy by Great Britain, the devising of new systems of government in France, or the making of new states in central Europe. The era of state-making was just beginning, and it was beginning in central and eastern Europe. While Abraham Lincoln was fighting to preserve the Union in America and Britain was devising a new and elastic federal constitution for Canada, while Cavour and Bismarck schemed to unite Italy and Germany, and small Balkan nationalities struggled to attain separate statehood, comparable tendencies were beginning to develop in Russia and Turkey. Finnish and Polish, Lithuanian and Ukrainian nationalisms were stimulated and strengthened; Bulgarian national aspirations were kindled and Slav peoples stirred under Turkish misrule. Nor were the reverberations of the great upheaval restricted to Europe. They were already felt throughout the vast Asiatic hinterland. The opening of Japan to western influences by Commodore Perry in 1854, the establishment of the treaty system in China between 1842 and 1858, and the ending of the East India Company rule in India in 1859 laid foundations for continuing the process of westernization, and so of industrialization and eventual state-making, which was already so evident within eastern Europe. Viewed in this way, the century between 1850 and 1950 was one long story of the extension of western European ideas, influences, and modes of organization in politics, economics, and social life, to the other continents of the world and to the larger part of mankind.

CHAPTER 12

THE BALANCE OF POWER IN EUROPE, 1850-70

THE GREAT POWERS AND THEIR RELATIONSHIP

AFTER the storm, a strange calm. The year 1851 was a year of peace in Europe, and its symbol was the Great Exhibition of the works of industry of all nations held in the Crystal Palace in London. But outside the United Kingdom itself the calm was due less to the prosperity of industrialism than to the temporary exhaustion of revolutionary impulses, to the retrieval of a balance of power in Europe, and to the resumption in modified form of the Holy Alliance against revolution. The main components of this balance were the same five great powers that had made the settlement of 1815: in the West, the United Kingdom and France; in central Europe, Prussia and Austria; in the East, Russia. Because of the economic transformations since 1815 and the events of 1848-50, the relative importance of these five powers had changed and was still changing.

In population France remained larger than any power except Russia, and because of her republican institutions and revolutionary traditions she was still thought of as the most likely threat to European order and peace. The United Kingdom was the only industrial and commercial power of great importance. She produced fifty-seven million tons of coal when France produced only four and a half million and the whole of the German *Bund* only six million; more than two million tons of pig iron when France, her only rival, produced less than half a million tons; and she commanded more than half the whole world's tonnage of ocean-going shipping. But in terms of immediately available military power she lagged behind other states, for the long period of peace and a policy of financial economy had allowed both her army and navy to fall into remarkable decline. For powers that still thought predominantly in terms of land warfare, armies mattered more than navies. The German fleet was even sold by auction in 1853. Russia, the only one of the powers which could claim to have more than a million serving soldiers, was rated next to France as the most likely source of aggression.

The formal basis of Austro-Russian relations remained the agreements of Münchengrätz made by Metternich in 1833,[1] and these also in-

1. See p. 176.

volved Prussia. They bound all three powers to oppose the doctrine of
non-intervention should any independent sovereign appeal for help
against liberalism and revolution. They more specifically bound Austria
and Russia to act together to preserve the *status quo* in Turkey and to
provide mutual help in case of rebellion in Poland. The most sensitive
point was then regarded as Poland, because of the recent Polish revolts
of 1830; and thereafter garrisons were kept by Russia in Warsaw, by
Austria in Cracow, and by Prussia in Posen. The next most sensitive
point was Italy, and Austria kept the bulk of her forces in northern
Italy. In the west, because of fears of France, Prussia kept most of her
forces in the Rhineland fortresses, and British naval bases were all
pointed against France.

Of the five powers in 1851, Prussia was the smallest in population
and, since the 'humiliation of Olmütz' in 1850, the weakest in prestige.
Having then been forced to give up the Erfurt Union which, in March
1850, she had formed with most of the smaller German states, Prussia
was induced to enter the revived *Bund* under Austrian presidency in
November 1850. Within the *Bund* the old clericalist and conservative
tendencies were renewed in all German states, and even Prussia, while
keeping the constitution of 1850, fell into line. For a time, at least, her
inferiority to the Austria of Schwarzenberg was accepted and her weight
thrown into the same side of the European balance as Austria's. In May
1851 the two countries signed an alliance, to last for three years, that
was designed to prevent further revolution in Europe. If it was a revived
Holy Alliance, it had the important difference that it excluded Russia,
because Nicholas I refused to join, and it was more flimsy in that it
involved one-sided advantages for Austria. While it involved Prussia in
guaranteeing Austrian power in Italy, it left her with no corresponding
guarantee for her own territories in the Rhineland. By keeping out of
commitments, the Tsar hoped to enjoy an automatically favourable
balance of power. It seemed that by 1851 a nice system of checks and
balances had been established. In Poland the enforced partition gave
Russia security in Warsaw. Despite Austrian hegemony in Germany, the
Zollverein remained and Prussia had succeeded in preventing the incorporation of the whole of Austria in the *Bond*. In Italy, Austria
backed by Prussian guarantees remained strongly enough entrenched to
check both revolution and French aggression. In western Europe, Prussian power in the Rhineland combined with British naval strength
seemed capable of checking France. These subtle balances left Russia
able to stand out of entanglements while enjoying an automatic protection of her main interests. As a result, she fought the Crimean War
without allies.

Points of Tension. It was on the periphery of the continent that new points of tension appeared; this signified the new problems created by the expansiveness of the powers and the growing importance of maritime strength. The two points of tension were the Baltic provinces of Schleswig and Holstein, under Danish control, and the Straits of the Dardanelles and the Bosporus, controlling access to the Black Sea. These two strategically important areas were to be directly involved in the wars of this period.

International agreements about the Elbe duchies of Schleswig and Holstein dated from the eighteenth century. So long as Britain depended for much of her timber and ship stores on the Baltic, and Russian exports of timber found their outlet chiefly through the Baltic, it was of interest to both that the entrance to that sea should not be controlled by a rival power. In agreement with France they had contrived that the Elbe duchies should remain attached to the Danish crown. Now the situation was changed. Britain, with the development of steam and of overseas connexions, and Russia, with the growth of her southern export trade in wheat, were less concerned with the Baltic. While Britain looked overseas, Russia looked south to the Ukraine and the Straits. The Baltic accordingly was open for expansionist German national claims, on the grounds that Schleswig, though predominantly Danish, had German minorities in its southern part, while the southern duchy of Holstein was entirely German and since 1815 had been included in the German *Bund*.

In March 1848 the Estates of the two duchies broke from Denmark and sought support from the German *Bund*. By May, Prussian troops, acting nominally on behalf of the *Bund*, had expelled the Danes from the duchies; and when they entered Jutland, a part of the Kingdom of Denmark itself, Palmerston intervened and urged an armistice. In August, Prussia and Denmark signed the Armistice of Malmö, which caused both Danish and Prussian troops to be withdrawn from the duchies. They were to be temporarily administered by a joint Prussian-Danish commission – a solution that outraged nationalist feelings in both countries. Peace was concluded in 1850. In May 1852 the Treaty of London, signed by all five great powers as well as by Denmark, Sweden, and Norway, settled the succession to the Danish crown on Christian, Prince of Glücksburg, and included the two Elbe duchies among his dominions. It also gave assurances that the relation of Holstein to the *Bund* was not thereby altered. The aim was declared to be 'the maintenance of the integrity of the Danish Monarchy, as connected with the general interests of the balance of power in Europe'. The treaty was not accepted by the Diet of Frankfurt on behalf of the *Bund*, and was resented by Prussia as a frustration of German nationalism by the concert of powers. Europe was to hear much more of the Elbe duchies as soon as Prussia was able to revive her claims, and it was by exploiting their complex position that the first steps toward German unification were to be taken.[1]

The question of the Straits was likewise formally regulated by previous international agreements. By the Treaty of Adrianople of 1829[2] Turkey had agreed that there should be freedom of trade and navigation in the Black Sea, that the Bosporous and Dardanelles should be open to all Russian merchant ships and to the merchant ships of all other powers with which Turkey was at peace. In 1833 Russia established herself for a time as the chief protector of Turkey, with paramount power in Constantinople, and induced the Turkish government to agree to close the Dardanelles to all foreign warships should Russia be engaged in war. This turned the Straits into a Russian outpost, for it left her fleet with free access to the Mediterranean while excluding her enemies from the Black Sea. But in 1840 Palmerston insisted that the affairs of Turkey were of general European concern, and the Straits Convention was made in July 1841 by the five great powers and Turkey. It closed the Bosporus and Dardanelles to all foreign warships when Turkey was herself at peace.

Regulation of Russo-Turkish relations in these respects did little, however, to solve the basic issues of the Middle East. These sprang from the increasing weakness of Turkish rule in the Balkans and from Russian pressure southward, combined with attempts to make herself the protector and champion of Balkan Slav nationalities against the Turks. Russian occupation of Moldavia and Wallachia, though ended in 1851, left other powers suspicious.[3] The Tsar was apt to speak of Turkey as 'a very sick man' who might suddenly die on the hands of Europe, and to urge the prudence of preliminary agreements about disposal of his property. Britain resisted this view and followed her traditional policy of keeping Turkey whole as a buffer against Russian expansion. In the Holy Land the claims of Turkey, Russia, and France were in conflict over the special question of management of the places of pilgrimage at Jerusalem and the Church of the Nativity at Bethlehem. The Turks were formally in control; the French claimed a traditional right, dating sentimentally from the crusades and diplomatically from a treaty of 1740, to protect Christians against infidels in the East; and Russia now claimed special interests in the position of Orthodox Christians as against Roman Catholic Christians in the Holy Land. Since 1815 both France and Britain had established strong commercial interests in the Levant, and neither welcomed a prospect of further extensions of Russian in-

1. See p. 309.   2. See p. 139.
3. See p. 220.

fluence into the Near East and the Mediterranean. Everything indicated the 'Eastern Question' as a future cause of trouble.

By 1854 the peace of Europe depended upon whether the disruptive tendencies of these tangled and troublesome conflicts in the Baltic and the Black Seas could be removed or contained by the existing forces of European order. Although the 'system' of Metternich had been destroyed in 1848, the desirability of preserving a general 'balance of power' and the methods of preserving it by a 'concert of Europe' were still accepted by the leading states. The revival of conservative forces after 1850 perpetuated many of the pre-revolutionary habits and mechanisms for another decade. The emergence after 1848 of militant nationalism and liberalism was a standing challenge to the working of the old diplomatic system. The insistence that national independence and unity mattered more than stability or concert, that settlement of territorial frontiers by the joint decisions of autocratic governments was a violation of nationalist and liberal principles, that governments and peoples should work in closer mutual relationships, corroded the old system. But for a decade at least these forces were kept at bay.

Balance of Power. The concept of a 'balance of power' kept a special meaning in the 1850s which it lost by 1914. It did not yet mean a balance between rival alliances of hostile states, but rather a balance of territorial possessions. It meant that no state should gain additions of territory in Europe without the agreement of the other states. In consequence, the 'concert of Europe' meant the mechanism by which this agreement was reached and registered. The anxieties of foreign offices during the revolutionary turbulence of 1848 and 1849 had been that these upheavals might offer opportunities for unwarranted and unagreed transfer of territories. In 1849 Palmerston, sympathizing with Hungarian national aspirations yet fearful of Russian intervention, argued in the House of Commons that the survival of Austria was essential to the balance of power in Europe. 'Austria,' he said, 'is a most important element in the balance of European power. Austria stands in the centre of Europe, a barrier against encroachment on the one side, and against invasion on the other. The political independence and liberties of Europe are bound up, in my opinion, with the maintenance and integrity of Austria as a great European Power. . . .'

Between 1815 and 1860 every important change in the territorial settlement reached at Vienna was ratified by the concert of major European powers: the independence of Greece in 1832 and of Belgium in 1839, the affairs of Turkey and the Straits in 1840–1, control over Schleswig and Holstein in 1852, and the disputes involved in the Crimean War in the Treaty of Paris in 1856. On the first of these five occasions,

Great Britain, France, and Russia were concerned; on the other four occasions, all five great powers were involved. After the Congress of Verona in 1822 the concert of Europe worked not through regular congresses but through *ad hoc* international conferences. But it worked nevertheless, and on very similar principles: the greatest of which might be described as 'no annexation without ratification'.

The most important implication of this principle was that a settlement should be reached not merely bilaterally, between belligerents which had just ended a war, but should include participation of other non-belligerent powers recognized as being actively interested in the settlement. On these grounds the great powers had collectively recognized Belgian independence and joined in the Straits Convention; and a non-belligerent power like Prussia was invited (though grudgingly) to take part in the Congress of Paris in 1856. The assumption was preserved that the interests of great powers as such were likely to be concerned in any major changes of power relationships, and that they all had a claim to some voice in treaty settlements.

But the next four wars, which were to be fought between 1859 and 1871, were ended abruptly by the dictates of the victors and the concert of Europe was sharply ignored. By being ignored for such major purposes as the achievement of Italian and German unification and after the defeat of major powers like Austria and France, it was in effect destroyed. The concept of a 'balance of power' lost its old meaning of territorial balance, and began to assume its more modern meaning of a diplomatic balance, a seesaw between rival groups of powers united by treaty alliances. In 1918, when reaction set in against this new system, the notion of a general concert was revived in the greatly extended form of the League of Nations. The Crimean War is, therefore, an important landmark in the development of modern Europe. That a war involving three great powers occurred at all in 1854 was the first failure of the old system to keep the peace; that it ended in a general treaty settlement agreed upon by all five great powers was a twilight triumph for the fading conception of the concert of Europe.

THE CRIMEAN WAR, 1854-6

Although the dispute between France and Russia which precipitated the Crimean War was ostensibly about the Holy Places and the protection of Latin and Orthodox Christians in Turkey, it soon involved the whole tangled skein of the 'Eastern Question'. A test of prestige between France and Russia, it became also a conflict between Russian attempts to control the Turkish government and British fears of Russian expansion; and inevitably this aroused Franco-British anxieties to preserve the balance of power by upholding Turkish integrity. The original dispute was trivial, in itself no justification for breaking the forty years' peace and wrecking the concert of Europe. The two years of protracted manoeuvres which preceded hostilities suggest that the powers did not readily resort to war in 1854.

In February 1852 after two years of French diplomatic pressure and threats of naval action, the Turkish government recognized the full claims of the Latin Christians in the Holy Land to share in administration of the disputed sanctuaries, while denying their claims to exclusive possession. By the end of 1852 Turkish officials were frankly allowing the Latins full control of the Church of the Nativity in Bethlehem. The Tsar decided to adopt open threats of force comparable with those by which France had successfully upheld Latin claims; and in January 1853 he moved Russian troops towards the borders of the Turkish provinces of Moldavia and Wallachia, which he had evacuated only two years before. Backed by this standing threat, in February he sent to Constantinople a special commission under Prince Menshikov, charged with the task of getting as clear a treaty right for Russia to protect the Greek Orthodox Church as France already enjoyed to protect the Roman Catholic Church in Ottoman territories. As re-insurance against the failure of Menshikov, he proposed to the British ambassador, Sir Hamilton Seymour, a plan to partition Turkish territories. Such an arrangement, he hoped, would preserve both the balance of power and the concert of Europe and would be generally accepted. The Tsar still, indeed, accepted the old principle of 'no annexation without ratification'.

The Tsar's hopes of securing Russian aims without general war were frustrated by the course of events, including not least the new factor of violent public outcry in Paris and London against Russian ambitions. When the Sultan of Turkey, on advice from the British ambassador, made concessions about the Holy Places but firmly refused to recognize a general Russian protectorate over Christians in the Balkans, Menshikov left Constantinople and the Russian armies reoccupied Moldavia and Wallachia. Even now the powers headed by Austria tried to prevent war and summoned a conference at Vienna. Their efforts failed and in October 1853 Turkey declared war on Russia. By the end of the month the French and British fleets passed through the Dardanelles as a gesture of deterrence. Near Sinope a Russian fleet attacked and destroyed a Turkish naval squadron. In Britain such behaviour seemed intolerable both to Palmerston and to an excited public opinion susceptible to the popular Press; and in France Napoleon III felt impelled to meet clericalist demands for action and to live up to the militarist traditions of his name. In March, Britain and France declared war on Russia. Before long Russia, under threat of Austrian attack so long as she kept troops on the Danube, withdrew from Moldavia and Wallachia. These provinces were at once garrisoned by Austria, which held them until they were returned to Turkey at the end of the war. With serious outbreaks of cholera in the ill-prepared French and British forces, and with the immediate occasions of the war removed, peace might now have been reached. But both sides felt too heavily committed to withdraw so soon. National prestige was involved, and war continued with a joint attack of Turks, French, and British on the Russian naval base of Sebastopol on the southern tip of the Crimean peninsula.

The conduct of the siege of Sebastopol was remarkable for the inept way in which the allied command threw away their initial advantages. They landed to the north of Sebastopol and after hard fighting forced open the road to the city. Then, instead of driving straight for it, or even establishing a blockade on the north, they embarked on the long and difficult march round to the south of it. This delay enabled the Russians to prepare fortifications that held them at bay for a whole year, until September 1855. The allied fleets, based on Balaclava, contrived to sink the Russian ships in the mouth of the harbour of Sebastopol and so prevented their own entry. Naval strength played a less decisive part in the war than had been planned. The besieging forces, harassed by the Russian winter and by cholera and typhus, as well as by Russian land forces, suffered great losses. The ineptitude of leadership and the sufferings of the men in frozen, disease-ridden camps were made known to shocked populations at home by the dispatches of war correspondents. It was the first general European war in which the telegraph and the popular Press played any important role.

As the campaign dragged on, the diplomatic scene changed. In December 1854 Austria joined in a defensive and offensive alliance with the western powers, but did not take part in hostilities. The next month Piedmont, under its astute leader Count Cavour, joined the allies. In February 1855 Lord Palmerston succeeded Lord Aberdeen as British Prime Minister. In March the Tsar Nicholas I died, and his successor Alexander II was more ready to consider peace. When Austria threatened to enter the war, he decided to give way, and because the strain of war was deeply affecting Russian government the Tsar signed preliminaries of peace in February 1856. The terms of settlement were to be reached at Paris. Prussia, despite her continued neutrality, was invited to attend the Congress, though only after the peace terms had been negotiated, and then under Austrian patronage and against British resistance.

The Settlement of 1856. The settlement was concerned partly with the immediate issues that had led to war, partly with broader definition of rules governing relations between the powers. The independence of Turkey was affirmed, and it was laid down that no power had the right to interfere between the sultan and his Christian subjects. Turkey was admitted to the 'Public Law and System (*Concert*) of Europe,' which meant that for the first time she was brought within the ranks of the great powers and accepted as a component in the balance of power. As encouragement for her government to implement its enlightened professions, the powers recognized 'the high value' of the recent decree by which the Sultan recorded 'his generous intentions towards the Christian population of his Empire'. The Straits Convention of 1841 was 'revised by common consent', so as to declare the Black Sea neutralized, its waters and ports thrown open to merchant ships of all nations, but the Straits closed to foreign warships in peacetime. Turkey and Russia made a separate convention governing the number of light vessels that each might keep in it 'for the service of their coasts', and this convention was not to be annulled or modified without the assent of all the powers. In similar spirit, the free navigation of the Danube was ensured on the principles first laid down in 1815, and the powers declared that this arrangement 'henceforth forms a part of the Public Law of Europe, and take it under their Guarantee'.

The territorial settlement involved concessions from both Turkey and Russia. Russia gave up part of the province of Bessarabia, which was annexed to Moldavia. The principalities of Moldavia and Wallachia were to 'continue to enjoy under the Suzerainty of the Porte, and under the guarantee of the Contracting Powers, the privileges and immunities of which they are in possession'. The Sultan undertook to grant them (modern Rumania) a large measure of independence and self-government, under supervision of a special commission of the powers. Another Danubian principality, Serbia, was to enjoy similar rights under the collective guarantee of the powers. Serbia had gained some local privileges by revolts early in the century, and her rights had been secured by the Treaty of Adrianople of 1829. After 1856 she enjoyed considerable autonomy under her national prince, Milosh Obrenovitch, though Turkish garrisons remained in Belgrade until 1867. She did not become an independent kingdom until 1878. In these respects the settlement marked further steps towards the disintegration of the Ottoman Empire, which the victorious powers had ostensibly fought the war to prevent.

The signatories of the treaty at the same time signed a 'Declaration respecting Maritime Law' which became a landmark in the regulation of naval warfare. Privateering was declared abolished; enemy goods were not to be seized in neutral vessels, or neutral goods in enemy vessels, unless they could be classed as 'contraband of war'; and blockades, to be binding, were to be effective and not merely declarations on paper. These principles marked a concession on the part of the United Kingdom, for she had long resisted them and they would have made improper a general blockade of the kind which she had declared against Napoleon. In this respect, as in others, the Congress of Paris continued the elaboration of a system of international law and agreements on the pattern laid down in 1815. At least two thirds of the deaths in war had been due to disease – to pneumonia, typhus, cholera, and gangrene. The sufferings endured by soldiers on both sides aroused widespread concern, and the improvement of nursing and medical services effected by the work of Florence Nightingale and others was one lasting benefit derived from the war. The same concern led to the International Red Cross, established by the Geneva Convention in 1864.

The chief significance of the settlement lay in its efforts to remove the sources of tension which had produced the first general war in forty years: the relations between the Turkish government and its subjects, and between Turkey and Russia; the question of the Straits and of the Danube; the breakdown in the concert of Europe. None of these ends was finally achieved. Turkish power went on declining and Turkish promises were seldom kept. Russian ambitions in the Balkans and the Black Sea were not destroyed. The concert of Europe had suffered a serious blow, and other wars were soon to come. The outcome of the Crimean War was as indecisive as its outset had been casual. But its consequences for the major participants were great. No belligerent had reason to be proud of its military organization and leadership, and it became clear that armies had to be modernized and overhauled. The charge of the Light Brigade, honoured by Lord Tennyson, was heroic but it was not war. Both Britain and Russia proceeded with this task, and states became conscious of the need for more efficient preparations for war.

Napoleon gained in personal prestige, at home because he could boast of a victorious war, and internationally because the congress was held in Paris. Cavour gained the opportunity he had hoped for, of exalting his country's status by appearing at an international conference alongside the great powers; but his battle for Italian unification and recognition had still to be fought. Austria and Prussia gained as little from the settlement as they had contributed to the war, save that Russian influence in Vienna and Berlin was now greatly reduced. Russia, under her new Tsar Alexander II, suffered the humiliation of defeat and loss of territory, and her administration and economy reeled under the strain of war. Her power in eastern Europe was broken and fear of it abated. Collectively, the belligerents lost about half a million men, which was a total larger than that incurred in any other European war between 1815 and 1914. Of these, the Russians lost over 300,000, the French nearly 100,000, the British 60,000. If small by twentieth-century standards of warfare, these losses were large by nineteenth-century standards. They denoted the new destructiveness of modern warfare.

In long-term perspective the Crimean War was a strange combination of recurrent and of unusual features in European history. In so far as it was a war between Russia and Turkey, it was but one of the long sequence of Russo-Turkish wars, roughly one every generation, stretching from 1768-74, 1787-92, 1806-12, 1828-9 and going on to 1877-8. They were the result of the persistent pressure imposed upon Turkey by Russian desire to extend influence into the Black Sea, the Balkans, and the Mediterranean. In so far as it involved a western invasion of Russia, it was likewise one of a long historic sequence that included: the invasions of Napoleon in 1812, of the Germans in 1916-18, the western allies in 1919-20, and Hitler in 1941-4. On the other hand, it was the first war of recent times in which Britain and France fought on the same side; the first in which women, led by Florence Nightingale, took an important share; the first in which the telegraph and Press exerted any influence on the course of events.

This mixture of familiar and novel features suggests its intermediate position in the history of modern Europe, just as the inconclusiveness of its achievements fixes its significance in diplomatic history. It was fought not so much for Turkey as against Russia. Europe, in the decade after 1848, stood at the parting of the ways. The old concert was dying, the balance of power was beginning to shift, the new era of realism was dawning. In a strange semi-twilight, contemporary Europe – the Europe of large, populous, industrial states, of restless dynamic forces of expansion and explosion, of war fears and acute insecurity – was rapidly coming into existence. Involving as it did the two great peripheral powers – only semi-European in interests and character – of Great Britain and Russia, the Crimean War was token of a profound change in the place of Europe in a wider world. It was a fumbling war, probably unnecessary, largely futile, certainly extravagant, yet rich in unintended consequences. It broke the spell of peace, and it removed the shadow of Russian power from central European affairs. It therefore cleared the way for the remodelling of Germany and Italy by means of war.

THE SHIFTING ECONOMIC BALANCE, 1850-70

These two decades saw a continuation, but in some countries a slowing down, of that remarkable growth of European population which had characterized the first half of the nineteenth century.[1] In 1850 there were roughly sixty-six million more inhabitants in Europe than there had been in 1815, and the United Kingdom and Russia had been growing faster than any other European countries. During the next two decades another thirty million were added, making by 1870 a total of about 295 million. This general rate of increase – roughly 11 per cent – was slower than in the preceding twenty years, and slower than in the subsequent twenty years. The fears of overpopulation which had haunted Britain and France earlier, when the ideas of the economist Thomas Malthus held the field, now disappeared in the surge of mid-Victorian optimism and Napoleonic self-confidence. France even began to fear relative underpopulation. Already in 1851 the French birth rate, like the the Irish, was falling, while that of the Scandinavian countries was reaching its peak; and whereas the population of Germany by 1870 had been increasing at the rate of eight per cent, that of France had increased by roughly seven and a half per cent. The transfer of Alsace and Lorraine with their one and a half million inhabitants from France to Germany in 1871 permanently destroyed the former predominance of France. After the transfer Germany had forty-one million as against France's thirty-six. This sudden change, more than the uneven distribution of population growth between different countries, affected the balance of power in Europe. There was, moreover, a flourishing cotton industry in Alsace and a rich field of iron ore in Lorraine.

The population of the United Kingdom also grew faster than the French by reason of natural increase, despite a more massive emigration and despite the decline in the Irish birth rate. The inhabitants of England and Wales increased by some five million between 1851 and 1871. This was due to all three causes that can increase population: a higher birth rate, a lower death rate, and immigration. In these twenty years the annual birth rate rose from 33·9 per 1,000 to 35·3 per 1,000; the death rate fell from 22·7 per 1,000 to 22·4 per 1,000. Immigrants came mostly from Ireland and Scotland. But, in all, the United Kingdom sent out some 3,700,000 emigrants, mostly to America. It was an age of large families and improving public health, of apparently boundless prospects of prosperity and expansion.

The incidence of urbanization varied even more sharply from one country to another; but nearly everywhere the migration from country to town was greater than the migration overseas. In 1851 half the population of Great Britain, excluding Ireland, was urban. In England from 1861 onwards although the population was growing so fast, there was an absolute decline in the rural population; yet the number engaged in

1. See p. 112.

agriculture remained almost constant, and larger than the number employed in any other industry. In France the towns absorbed nearly the whole of the natural increase in population. In Germany the movement into towns came mainly after 1871, but then it came fast. Whereas only one Frenchman and one German in every three lived in towns in 1871, by 1914 two Germans in every three did so, but only one Frenchman in every two. In Russia, as in eastern Europe, the vast bulk of the population remained entirely rural, though urbanism was spreading. It has been estimated that out of every seven persons added to Europe's population between 1815 and 1871, one went abroad and four or five to the cities. In these ways the whole texture and fabric of social life were changing throughout most of western and central Europe, creating novel or more acute problems of urban housing, sanitation, public order, and organization.

Urbanization usually went hand in hand with industrialism, though the two changes are by no means identical. The growth of industrialism in these decades was even more revolutionary and startling than the growth and redistribution of population. World trade more than doubled in bulk, and Europe had more than its usual share of it. The years 1852-6 were in particular years of boom. The consolidation of conservative governments in Europe, the rapid expansion of railways, the official encouragement given to industry and commerce by, most notably, the governments of Britain, France, and Piedmont, all fostered a new spirit of confidence and enterprise. Fed by the fresh capital resources of gold from California and Australia, better facilities for credit and banking, and more progressive forms of business organization, western industry and trade expanded fast. Prices rose and wages tended to follow. The building of railways proceeded apace, textile industries expanded, engineering and heavy industries grew. The Belgian, French and British railway systems were almost complete by 1870, and had undergone consolidation and modernization. The import and export trade of both France and Britain more than trebled, France's coal production trebled, her iron production more than doubled, as did her import of raw cotton. In Britain by 1871 more than three quarters of a million people were employed in metal, engineering, and ship-building trades, and another half million in mines and quarries. For the countries of western Europe, these decades were a time of very rapid industrial and commercial growth.[1]

Throughout central and eastern Europe, with the exception of a few small areas such as Piedmont, industrial and commercial growth was much less rapid. The rest of Europe was not yet ripe, socially or politically, for this spectacular advance. Industrialism was impeded by less

1. See p. 255.

positive government encouragement, by the sheer competition of British and French advance, by political disunity. The various administrative and political changes effected by 1871 were paving the way for a correspondingly rapid economic development in central and eastern Europe after that date. Meanwhile commercial and financial links were strong enough to make the operations of the trade cycle affect the life of these areas. The great financial crisis which broke in 1857, and which ended the boom of the five previous years, began in the United States, spread to Britain and thence to France, northern Germany, and eventually to Russia. It was a more spectacular repetition of the crisis of 1846-7.[1] It shook the financial structure of central Europe and probably contributed to the renewal of agitation for political unity and consolidation. Political strength and stability seemed all the more desirable amid this new economic instability. There was another severe commercial crisis in 1866 to serve as a reminder of this growing interdependence of European countries in an age of railways, new credit facilities, and international trade and finance.

Despite the new importance of world trade in the economic life of all countries, the changes of the years between 1850 and 1870 are best considered separately for the three broad geographical zones of western, central, and eastern Europe. This threefold division, which has already been described as resting on broad social and political differentiations, was of special relevance in these decades.[2] The United Kingdom and France, with the initial advantages of political unity and rich natural resources, reoriented their internal economies and their commercial interests, and evolved new patterns of internal administration and of business enterprise. Their power was in the ascendant during these years. The lands of central Europe, in particular the states of Italy and Germany, were mainly preoccupied with the attainment of political unification, although in parts they also enjoyed considerable demographic and economic growth. The lands of eastern Europe, particularly of the Habsburg Empire and of Russia, were undergoing a more elementary agrarian transformation, with the ending of serfdom, the extension of railways, and improvements in administration. As yet they knew relatively little industrialization and had taken no clear shape of national separatism.

All three regions can now be seen to have been moving in an ultimately similar direction - toward greater industrial expansion and urbanization, toward national separatism and political reorganization. But in 1870 they were still in notably distinct stages of change. Their distinctive courses of growth as well as their mutual interactions must be more

1. See p. 185.
2. See p. 91.

closely examined. The expulsion of Russian influence from central Europe by the Crimean War and the reorientation of western interests overseas made possible the remaking of Italy and Germany. That change in turn shifted the whole balance of power in Europe; but this shift had already been prepared by the economic development of western and of central Europe before 1870. Cavour and Bismarck achieved momentous results; but they were able to do so only because the tide of economic change was in their favour and because they knew how to ride its currents.

CHAPTER 13

THE REORIENTATION OF WESTERN EUROPE

ECONOMIC AND COLONIAL EXPANSION

DURING the years 1850–70 the proportion of western European trade which was purely internal decreased and the proportion which was external and international vastly increased. This change is commonly described, for the United Kingdom, as her becoming 'the workshop of the world' – a change which was well on the way by the time of the Great Exhibition in 1851, but which was to become of supreme importance, both for Britain and for Europe, by 1871. What had been true for the cotton industry in the first half of the century became more and more true for the heavy industries and for the ship-building and engineering industries in the third quarter of the century. Their prosperity depended on imported raw materials or on exported manufactured goods or on both. In general Britain came to rely for essential foodstuffs – especially grain – upon imports. She paid for these imports by exporting industrial products, by shipping and insurance services, and by interest upon her capital investments abroad. Britain committed herself fully to being an industrial state. In consequence she became a crucial factor in the whole economy of the world.

Her chief competitor until 1871 was her traditional rival, France. The Paris Exposition of 1855 matched the Crystal Palace Exhibition of 1851, and showed that French enterprise was far from backward. But the spirit of cooperation which existed earlier between the Bank of England and the Bank of France in face of a common threat of financial crisis was not absent from other fields of economic life. The Cobden Treaty of 1860, negotiated by Michel Chevalier for France and Richard Cobden for Britain, marked the climax of recognition of common interests between the two major western powers. It involved a temporary reversal of the traditional French protectionist policy, which was no less significant than Britain's adoption of free-trade principles in 1846. It reduced French duties on coal and on most manufactured goods to rates not exceeding thirty per cent. In return Britain lowered duties on French wines and brandy. Within the next decade the value of both British exports to France and French exports to England doubled. This began a movement toward creating a large free-trade area in western Europe. As a direct result of it similar treaties reducing tariffs were made by both countries with Belgium. By further treaties with the German *Zollverein*, Italy, Switzerland, Norway, Spain, the Netherlands, Portugal, and even Austria, France of the 1860s became for a while the focus of a great European movement for the freeing of international trade.

This movement indicates the wider pattern that the economic life of Europe was assuming. It operated in two great zones. One, centring on the United Kingdom, France, and Belgium as the most highly industrialized countries, was now spreading out to comprise the whole of western Europe, including parts of Germany and northern Italy, and even the eastern states of the United States. The other zone comprised the large agricultural areas of southern and eastern Europe, the agrarian regions from which came raw materials and food; it extended eastward to Russia and westward to the western and south United States and South America. It even stretched, through British imperial connexions, to Australia and India.

British Enterprise. The chief initial impetus for this extension of economic life had come from Great Britain. In the 1850s many of the railways in western Europe were built by British contractors, partly with British and partly with local capital. In the following decade western European enterprise completed the railroad networks, expanded home industries, and mechanized manufacture. Meanwhile, after the financial crisis of 1857 and the Indian Mutiny of the same year, British interests moved on to the outer zone of raw-material supplies. The great age of British railway-building in India began, financed almost entirely by British capital; and in Argentina and Brazil the first railways were built in the 1850s. With the new links of railroads and, during the 1860s, of ships – which it had become a great new industry of Britain to build – the two zones became more and more closely interconnected. The opening of the Suez Canal in 1869 was the symbol of the demand for quicker transit between the centre and the periphery of this new economic complex. Though it was built with French capital and by French enterprise, more than half the shipping that passed through it was British. Sometimes British and French cooperation took more deliberate forms, as when these countries went to war against the Chinese Empire and in 1860 exacted from it not privileged concessions or separate spheres of influence, but the opening of new ports to world trade and the reduction of tariffs to five per cent. It seemed natural for the powers engaged in making the Cobden Treaty to try to extend the principles of free trade from European to world trade.

Britain, because of her world-wide colonial connexions, set the pace in forging new economic links between the inner and outer zones. After the middle of the century the colonies were turned from remote outposts and bases, difficult of access, into a more closely knit mesh of economic interests. Along with greater readiness to loosen the political controls and the commercial regulations that had previously been regarded as natural bonds of empire, came a closer actual integration of the economic development of the colonies with that of Great Britain. Their economic status continued much the same, even as their political status changed. They remained primarily sources of raw materials and markets for British manufacturers; this division of labour was even extended as the influx of British capital investment joined the flow of British manufactured goods. This development, in turn, changed the whole focus of British capital investment and narrowed its geographical spread. In the first half of the century capital had flowed out to the whole world but little to the colonies; in the third quarter of the century it concentrated increasingly in the colonies. In 1850 about one third of England's foreign investment was in America, the rest mainly in Europe. In 1854 the total everywhere is estimated to have amounted to about £300 million; by 1860 it totalled £650 million. By 1868 more than £75 million had been sunk in Indian railways alone; and in 1870 well over a quarter of the total of over £750 million was invested in the loans of colonial governments.

At the same time the balance of British imperial interests in general had shifted since 1830. The old colonial empire had centred mainly on the North Atlantic – in Canada and the Caribbean, and in strong commercial and financial connexions with the United States. With the growth and consolidation of British power in India, Ceylon, Burma, Australasia, and the South Pacific, such ports as those of West Africa, Cape Colony, and the chains of intermediate islands formed stepping stones on the route between the North Atlantic region and the Indian and Pacific Oceans, By then, too, the West African trading posts were growing into large colonial territories, the Cape was becoming the springboard for immense expansion northward, and on the western shores of the Indian Ocean lay a corresponding chain of British possessions. In the South Pacific what had been mere footholds in Southern Australia and Northern New Zealand were fast becoming a solid continent under British control.

The old commercial assessment of the value of colonial territories was itself undergoing change. They were valued less for their own commerce and more as guarantees of a world-wide trade, keeping open the supplies and markets of the world to British manufactures; as points of strategic advantage and strength; as offering opportunities for investors, missionaries, and emigrants; as providing national prestige in an era of intensifying nationalist rivalries. Special local commercial advantages in the colonies themselves now seemed of much less importance, and so the old Navigation Acts of 1651 and 1660, which had excluded foreign ships from the carrying trade between Britain and her colonies, were repealed in 1849. Greater freedom of trade and shipping was encouraged, and the establishment of responsible self-government on the lines that Lord Durham had adumbrated for Canada was encouraged elsewhere. The Colonial Laws Validity Act of 1865 gave a general assurance of internal self-government to all the colonial legislatures; new constitutions for New South Wales, Victoria, South Australia, and Tasmania were set up in 1855; and in 1867 the British North America Act opened the door for the federation of all the Canadian provinces except Newfoundland.

The growth of Europe's whole population, combined with the relatively slight improvements in agricultural production, meant that Europe as a whole, and particularly western Europe, was becoming dependent for its corn on sources extending beyond the granaries of eastern Europe. In normal years France could feed herself. The German states, in aggregate, had a surplus of corn for export, as had eastern Europe, including Russia. As of old the surpluses of the whole Vistula basin still went downriver to Danzig in the Baltic; from there much was imported to western Europe, particularly Holland, which had for long had to import grain. Some Russian wheat came from the Black Sea and found its way on to the European market. But after the middle of the century more and more corn came from the American continent and from Russia. Here were the boundless new supplies needed to feed Europe's enlarged population.

France and the Low Countries. France, like Britain, got most of her raw cotton from the United States, and cotton imports made the fortune of Le Havre as a port. During the Second Empire, France's exports tended to exceed her imports, and she was sending capital abroad heavily. But this was for the first time, and most of it went into railways, canals, mines, and government bonds. Internally, there was great concentration in the control of certain industries, most notably in iron. The famous Comité des Forges was founded in 1864, and its interests were extended into Belgium and Germany. Great families like the Péreires and the Foulds controlled large sectors of national industry and business. French colonial possessions were increasing too, though less spectacularly than Britain's. Algeria had been completely taken over by 1857. Though its products were too similar to France's own for it to serve the same purposes as were served by Britain's colonies, it became a good market for French cotton goods. Tahiti and the Ivory Coast had been added, even before 1850, and the Second Empire sent expeditions to Peking in 1859–60 and to Syria in 1861, explorers to West Africa, and new settlements to Dahomey and the Guinea coast. New Caledonia was occupied in

1853, and after the capture of Saigon in Indochina in 1859 three provinces in Cochin-China were annexed and a protectorate was established over Cambodia. In these ways France, like Britain, became indisputably a world colonial power, with national interests straddling both the inner and outer zones of the world economy. She differed from Britain in that her colonies were not used primarily for settlement, being mainly (apart from Algeria) tropical or semitropical in character; and her industrial development, no less than her geographical position, anchored her firmly in Europe.

Until the 1860s Belgium was the only European country to keep pace with Britain in industrial growth. In her resources of coal, iron, and zinc she was particularly fortunate, and she enjoyed, as did Britain, the advantage of the early establishment of iron and engineering industries. By 1870 she, too, had adopted a policy of free trade as regards the import of food and raw materials. By that date her own mineral resources of iron and zinc were becoming exhausted, but she remained a manufacturing and exporting country because she had the technicians and skilled workers, the industrial plant, enterprising management and business organization, and good communications. She exported heavy equipment such as machines, locomotives, and rails, as well as lighter goods such as glass and textiles. In the 1860s she was exporting capital for the construction of railways in Spain, Italy, the Balkans, and even South America. On balance she was, like Britain, a heavy importer of food, particularly wheat and cattle feed. After her separation from the Netherlands, Belgium lacked colonies until she acquired the rich territory of the Congo in the last quarter of the century.

The Netherlands, however, kept its profitable connexions with the Dutch East Indies and ranked as one of the chief colonial powers. The Dutch spread their rule over the three thousand miles of the archipelago of the East Indies, and exploited it by a form of forced labour whereby farmers had to deliver fixed amounts of certain crops as a kind of tax. A freer system was introduced only after 1870, though no moves were made in the direction of greater colonial self-government. Although much less industrialized than Belgium, the Netherlands was strong in particular industries, including its traditional trade of ship-building. Commercially, it was an *entrepôt* for such colonial products as coffee, tea, sugar, and the traditional spices.

Despite important differences of emphasis between them, the western states of the United Kingdom, France, and the Low Countries were all sharing in a broadly similar process of economic change. Together they formed the most intensively industrialized core of the European economy. They were exerting a strong influence upon the growth of central and eastern Europe. But as the chief maritime powers they were looking increasingly outward to the oceans of the world across which sailed their shipping and their emigrants, their raw materials and food-stuffs, their manufactured products and capital investments. They stood balanced between an economic and political pull inward to continental Europe, and a commercial and imperial pull outward to the other con-tinents of the world. Their interests were being reoriented. Trade among the European states remained both large and important. Although French coal production trebled between 1850 and 1870, much of her coking coal for iron smelting came from Britain and from Westphalia in Germany. This was paid for by exporting French silks and wines to Britain and Belgium. For Britain the export of coal became important only after 1850. The five million tons she exported in 1855 were only two and a half per cent of her total exports, and went mostly to France, Germany, Russia, Denmark, and Italy. Of her very much larger exports of cotton goods at that time, one quarter went to Asia, mostly to India. Another very good customer was the United States, which supplied her with most of the raw cotton she needed. But by 1860 the destinations of British cotton goods had shifted. Asiatic and African customers were taking as much as one half of them, and they were to take still more in the course of time. For France and the Low Countries, too, overseas trade was becoming a more and more important sector of their commerce.

Iberia and Scandinavia. The south-western states of Spain and Portu-gal, and the north-western states of Norway, Sweden, and Denmark, shared somewhat less directly and drastically in this burst of industrial-ization and overseas expansion. Whereas the Scandinavian states had no colonial connexions but were expanding their industries, the Iberian states made little industrial progress but had colonies of some impor-tance. Spain held the Canaries, and Cuba and Puerto Rico in the Carib-bean. Portugal held the scattered Atlantic islands of the Azores, Madeira, and Cape Verde; since 1848 she had occupied the area of Angola on the West African coast, and in 1857 she settled a European colony at Mozambique on the East African coast; in India she still held Goa. But both Spain and Portugal, despite the richness of their mineral de-posits of iron, lead, copper, and other metals, developed these industries very slowly. They were handicapped by a shortage of good coal, scarcity of capital, and lack of technical skill and equipment. Both were predom-inantly agricultural and remained backward in techniques. There were large peasant risings in Castile, Aragon, and Andalusia in 1840, 1855, 1857, 1861, and 1865, caused by the breakup of common lands and ex-treme rural poverty. Sweden and Norway, in sharp contrast, underwent an industrial revolution between 1840 and 1860, under the benign rule of

Oscar I, and foreign trade grew almost in proportion. A policy of free trade was adopted in 1857. Norway shared in this prosperity and her trading interests were more widespread and even more important than those of Sweden. Denmark – the Denmark of Hans Christian Andersen – stood economically as well as geographically midway between central Europe and north-western Europe.

The homogeneity of western Europe as a whole derived not only from this common pattern of economic change and maritime expansion, but also, to an increasing extent, from a common direction of political tendencies. Liberal and democratic ideas were fermenting more vigorously because they were less impeded by irredentist nationalism than in central or eastern Europe. Save for Norwegian desire for independence from Sweden, which was blunted by the new prosperity, and the thorny issues of Schleswig and Holstein, which bedevilled Danish-German relations and impeded Danish economic development, western Europe already enjoyed political unification and national independence. On this basis there was growing up a new machinery of government, a closer interrelation between state and society established by new methods of administration and of social organization.

THE NEW MACHINERY OF GOVERNMENT

Poets make bad politicians. That seemed to be one of the general lessons of 1848. The spread of parliamentary institutions throughout most of western Europe brought into prominence the professional politician – the more prosaic but usually astute parliamentarian who mastered the arts of public persuasion, parliamentary debate, ministerial combination, and active opposition. Civilian rather than military, middle-class rather than aristocratic, gaining his ends more by manipulation and management than by force, and more by dint of personal talents than of high birth or great wealth, this relatively new type of political leader predominated in western countries during the second half of the century. In these new circumstances the men who came to power were men like Benjamin Disraeli and William Ewart Gladstone in Great Britain, Eugène Rouher and Émile Ollivier in France, Charles Rogier in Belgium and Johan Rudolf Thorbecke in the Netherlands, Baron Louis de Geer in Sweden. Financial acumen was becoming as important as political sense or parliamentary skill for governing the new industrial societies of western Europe. Between 1852 and 1868 Disraeli and Gladstone alternated as chancellor of the exchequer before they began to alternate as prime minister. A wealthy middle-class electorate interested in liberal, financial, and administrative reforms supported such men in power. It was under their guidance that the economic and colonial expansion already described took place.

Political Reforms. The economic and social changes, combined with the new personnel and the new spirit of politics, made for important developments in the machinery of government and administration. There grew up an uneasy feeling that parliamentary institutions, as they had developed by 1850, were inadequate for the needs of the changing societies of western Europe. In Britain these were decades of widespread popular agitation for improvements in the parliamentary system, which the failure of Chartism had left unrealized. Men like John Bright campaigned for the secret ballot, liberal-minded Whigs like Lord John Russell introduced into parliament bills for further reform of the franchise and further redistribution of seats, and in 1859 the Conservative Disraeli proposed a complicated bill for parliamentary reform which crashed Lord Derby's government. But it was 1867 before a real reform of parliament and electorate was achieved by Disraeli.

His Representation of the People Act nearly doubled the electorate of England and Wales, mainly by giving the vote to all householders of one year's residence in boroughs and all farmers in the counties paying an annual rent for their farms of £12 or more. In effect it admitted to electoral power the whole of the lower middle class and the more well-to-do artisans of the towns. It also redistributed forty-five seats in the House of Commons, transferring them from the smaller boroughs to the counties and to the larger industrial towns. This adjusted the balance between small boroughs and counties, but even so the small boroughs were still over-represented in the House of Commons. For the first time in English history the boroughs contained more voters than the counties: they had always had more representatives. This brought the electorate more into line with the consequences of social and economic change, and with the shifts of population described above.[1] In 1868 it was followed by comparable reforms in Scotland and Ireland.

Although this important measure of parliamentary reform was so long delayed – chiefly because Lord Palmerston, who died in 1865, had thrown all the weight of his authority and influence against it – the decades between 1848 and 1868 were years of incessant agitation for other reforms of all kinds. Reformers had learned well the lessons of Daniel O'Connell's Catholic Association and Richard Cobden's Anti-Corn Law League. Their instinctive and regular recourse was to form popular associations for propaganda, petition, and agitation. The Financial Reform Association of Liverpool kept alive the doctrines of Manchester liberalism by pressing for freer trade; the Administrative Reform Association

1. See p. 250.

and the more radical State Reform Association, both of 1855, demanded an overhaul of the civil service; the radical National Education League and the church National Education Union, divided on issues of secular education, pressed for the expansion and improvement of public education. Radicals had the satisfaction of seeing the methods of popular agitation and persuasion, which they had perfected, adopted by movements of all political shades which wanted some change in existing arrangements. Every Englishman developed a conscience about something, no cause lacked its enthusiasts, and expectations of change by means of parliamentary enactment were boundless.

This striking development, a warning against hasty generalizations about the 'complacency' of mid-Victorian England, produced a peculiar constitutional situation. The organization of political parties was still far from strong. The Reform Act of 1832 had encouraged more elaborate and systematic party organization both in the constituencies and at the centre, but until after the Reform Act of 1867 really large-scale party organization was hardly needed. The old habits of corruption and influence continued little checked by the Corrupt Practices Act of 1854, and electorates remained small enough to be manageable by relatively simple and rudimentary machinery. There was growing up a whole galaxy of 'pressure groups', in the form of popular movements demanding specific reforms, before the political parties were in a condition to transmit these demands into legislation or policy. The result was a growing sense of frustration which reached its climax in 1867, and which helped to make Disraeli's measure much more radical in character than he had intended or than his Conservative colleagues in power expected. Although enthusiastic movements in the country proved so little able to move governments to action before 1867, it was significant that they all focused upon parliament. Once again, as in 1829 and 1839 and 1848, the British constitution with all its defects proved flexible enough and stable enough to attract a general loyalty and to confine the forces of change to peaceful and constitutional procedures. Never was there a threat of revolution, never was the survival of the parliamentary régime itself challenged.

The monarchy, indeed, went through a period of considerable unpopularity in the 1860s, and shared in the general mood of discontent with the existing constitutional system. Queen Victoria's large family was becoming increasingly costly to maintain, and after the death of the Prince Consort in 1861 she withdrew into seclusion for so long that many began to ask whether a monarchy that offered so few colourful occasions in public life was worth so great a cost. A lively republican movement grew up, led by Sir Charles Dilke and Charles Bradlaugh, and much influenced by the course of events in France. But it was abruptly killed in 1871–2, by the astonishing wave of popular sympathy with the Queen when the Prince of Wales nearly died on the tenth anniversary of his father's death, and when an unsuccessful attempt was made to assassinate her. From these events dates the modern British monarchy, cultivating a dignified yet popular esteem by frequent contacts between the monarchy and the people.

New Organizations. The patience of reformers was rewarded as soon as the Reform Acts of 1867 and 1868 opened the door for more direct electoral pressure on political parties. With the electorate doubled, parties had to organize much more thoroughly. In 1867 the National Union of Conservative and Constitutional Associations was created, composed of two delegates from each local association. It was pre-eminently a machine for helping to win elections. Ten years later the Liberal party set up its counterpart, the National Federation of Liberal Associations, with Joseph Chamberlain of Birmingham as its president. The two great political parties, which were to alternate in power for the rest of the century, were fast becoming great election-fighting machines, outbidding one another in appealing for the support of the larger and more democratic electorate. The link that had hitherto been missing, between the pressures of public opinion and the systematic operation of these pressures within parliament on the government of the day, was now forged; and the British parliamentary system entered on its modern phase of development.

Meanwhile Gladstone's first administration of 1868–74 made itself a landmark in nineteenth-century English liberalism because it put into effect so many of the reforms which popular associations of the previous two decades had urged in vain. In 1872 it established secrecy of the ballot for all parliamentary and local elections; after 1870 it abolished patronage in the civil service and enforced recruitment by competitive examination; it carried out similar reforms in the army and greatly improved the conditions of military service; it reorganized the judicial system by the Judicature Act of 1873, remodelling both the legal system and the courts themselves. By these reforms it equipped the state to perform more efficiently the increasing burden of work which the needs and demands of a more democratic electorate would soon impose upon it. By the financial reforms in his budgets between 1853 and 1860 Gladstone had already completed the reorganization of the fiscal system begun by Peel. The auditing of public accounts was modernized by an act of 1866.

The forms and techniques of private business organization were likewise changing. The widespread use of the limited liability company, making possible larger concentrations of joint-stock capital for investment and changing the relations between ownership and management, became possible only after the company legislation of 1855 and 1862, matched in France by laws of 1863 and 1867, and in Germany by the commercial code of 1861. From the 1860s onward joint-stock companies became more and more the normal form of business organization in western Europe, and were regarded as 'democratizing' capital just as a wider franchise was democratizing government. Accountancy became a profession, with the incorporation of societies of accountants and the elaboration of more ingenious and scientific methods of financial accounting.

Labour organization kept in step with the growth of larger units in industry and business. In 1871 British trade unions were given legal protection for their funds and for their methods of collective bargaining, and were protected against the charge of being conspiracies at common law. The first meeting, in Manchester in 1868, of a limited Trades Union Congress, representing some 118,000 trade unionists, marked a new stage in the national organization of British labour. By 1871 it may be said that by diverse forms of new organization, whether of political parties, of the financial, administrative, and judicial machinery of the state, or of capital and labour, Britain had equipped herself for grappling more efficiently with the problems of a modern industrial and democratic state.

Napoleon III. France offers certain striking parallels in these years, despite the superficially very different course of her political development. When Louis Napoleon, in December 1852, made himself emperor of France by a *coup d'état*, he reverted to a system of government closely modelled on that of his famous uncle. His rule was a usurpation of power, for a year earlier he had violently overthrown the republican parliamentary régime which, as its elected president, he had sworn to preserve. He tried to mask and to legitimize this usurpation by three devices: by preserving the shadow of parliamentary government in the form of packed assemblies based on managed elections; by popular plebiscites; and by giving France, in his policy, what he thought would be most popular and most beneficial to the nation. His rule became a strange mixture of authoritarian government with increasing concession to parliamentary power and popular demands. Yet the final result was a development of France's parliamentary institutions which made the Third Republic of 1875 possible. This paradox of French politics in these decades springs initially from the enigmatic character of Napoleon III himself.

This strange man, to whom in 1848 five and a half million Frenchmen had been persuaded to entrust the presidency of the democratic

Second Republic,[1] had already had a colourful and varied career. Son of Napoleon's brother, Louis Bonaparte, king of Holland, he had assumed headship of the Bonapartist family and cause in 1832 when Napoleon's own son (called by courtesy Napoleon II) had died. In 1836 and again in 1840, with a handful of personal followers, he had tried to overthrow Louis Philippe by local risings that failed ridiculously. Imprisoned in 1840 he had escaped in 1846 by simply walking out of the fortress of Ham disguised as a stonemason. In the early months of 1848 the man who in the 1830s had belonged to the *Carbonari* secret societies and who never lost his taste for cloak-and-dagger intrigues could have been seen parading Piccadilly in the role of a special constable, defending the government of Queen Victoria against the dangers of Chartism. Always a dreamer and intriguer rather than a practical statesman, he combined a nostalgic faith in the destinies of his family with a genuine concern for the welfare of the poor and the French people as a whole. From the moment when he was elected president of the Second Republic of 1848 by so overwhelming a majority, it seems certain that he intended to revive the régime, and if possible the glories, of the empire of Napoleon I. Nor was he without considerable abilities and qualities worthy of admiration. He had quickness of mind and imagination, ready sympathies for all in distress, great moral and physical courage. But he lacked a grasp of realities, and his ambitions and sympathies clouded his judgement both of men and of events. He had not the infinity of energy and patience needed to master details and clarify his purposes. His poor physical health increasingly impaired his power of decision, and from middle age onward (he was already forty-four when he became emperor) he suffered from disease and bad health. He had undoubted talents, but he certainly lacked the genius of Napoleon I.

The new constitution which he inaugurated in 1852 rested on principles which, in a preamble, he carefully expounded to the country. He himself, as chief of state, assumed almost monarchical powers: the power to make war and treaties, to choose ministers and nominate to all important offices in the state, to initiate legislation, and to frame the regulations in which the laws were embodied. The Legislative Body, of not more than 260 members elected by universal male suffrage, sat for only three months a year and had little real power. A senate of life members, chosen *ex officio* or nominated by the chief of state, had the duty of examining legislation to make sure it did not conflict with the constitution. Ministers were responsible only to Napoleon, and there was no collective cabinet responsibility. In short, as he explained, 'Since France has only maintained itself in the last fifty years by means of the admini-

1. See p. 214.

strative, military, judicial, religious, and financial organization provided by the Consulate and the Empire, why should we not adopt the political institutions of that period?' Accordingly, he revived the Council of State, the very core of Napoleonic autocracy, 'an assembly of practical men working out projects of law in their special committees, discussing this legislation behind closed doors, without oratorical display'. In such a system, it was clear from the first, parliamentary power was reduced to a minimum, and France was ruled by a centralized despotism tempered only by opportunism and necessity.

Yet within the next eighteen years, because universal suffrage and parliamentary institutions did survive if only in attenuated form, because the ideals and habits of democratic government had become so deeply rooted in France, and because Napoleon found that a series of reverses in foreign policy corroded his personal popularity and prestige and forced him to seek fresh support from parliament, France recovered bit by bit a more genuine system of parliamentary government. Universal male suffrage, instituted in 1848, he never dared to infringe, though he manipulated elections. In 1860 he had to make important concessions to parliament. The Legislative Body was allowed to debate its reply to the speech from the throne, which expounded government policy: a restoration of the right that had been used with great effect by the parliamentary opposition between 1815 and 1848. Ministers began to defend government measures before the Legislative Body and became more accountable to it. The Press, despite continued control and censorship, was allowed to publish fuller reports of parliamentary debates. From 1866 until 1869 further concessions had to be made to the growing clamour of the republican opposition. Control of the Press and of public meetings was relaxed. Ministers could be questioned more closely and opposed more openly in parliament. Despite the resources of electoral management in the hands of the prefects and the powers of police supervision at the disposal of the government, a vigorous and eventually successful republican opposition grew up, led by men of the calibre of Adolphe Thiers, Léon Gambetta, and Jules Ferry. The so-called 'Liberal Empire' which came into existence after 1860 was at least as real a parliamentary régime as was the constitutional monarchy before 1848.

The decline of autocracy in France can be measured by election results. In the elections of 1857 only seven candidates hostile to the government of Napoleon were returned; in those of 1863 thirty-five were returned; and in those of 1869 ninety-three. The big cities of Paris and Marseilles, Lyon and Bordeaux, especially opposed the Empire. This impressive development was due above all to the growing strength and effectiveness of the republican Press. Under stringent Press controls set up in 1852, the political Press had been almost stifled. But, as under Charles X, there was an immediate increase in the number and the circulation of literary, philosophical, and apparently innocuous publications in which critics could make their political arguments obliquely but, to the initiated, very effectively. The amnesty granted to political prisoners and exiles in 1859 brought a rebirth of republican activity, especially in journalism. The strongest surviving moderate republican paper, *Le Siècle*, by 1866 reached the large circulation of 44,000. In 1868, when Press controls were relaxed, 140 new journals appeared in Paris within a year. *Le Rappel* contained the biting attacks of the literary giant Victor Hugo; and the mordant wit of the journalist Henri Rochefort won for *La Lanterne* a circulation of no less than 120,000. 'The Empire,' ran its famous opening sentence, 'contains thirty-six million subjects, not counting the subjects of discontent.'

The Empire, discredited by its succession of reverses abroad [1] and in the failing grip of its sick emperor, could not have long survived such opposition even without the military defeat of 1870 to serve as its Waterloo. Ranged against it, too, were legitimist royalists like Antoine Berryer who wanted to go back behind 1830, moderate constitutional liberals like Thiers who wanted to go back behind 1848, the growing forces of socialism and of revolutionary communism represented by Blanqui and the supporters of the recently formed First International. But the toughest opposition came from two main groups, the liberals led by Thiers and the republicans led by Gambetta.

Before 1863 the parliamentary opposition was still no more than the five republican deputies for Paris and two others elected at Lyon and Bordeaux. But a liberal and republican opposition in the country was forming fast. It attracted brilliant lawyers like the 'three Jules' (Jules Favre, Jules Simon, and Jules Ferry); and government prosecutions of journalists and agitators gave excellent opportunities for republican lawyers, as counsel for the defence, to expound republican principles within the immunity of courtrooms. The young Gambetta first revealed his formidable forensic and oratorical talents in helping to defend a group of republican journalists in a famous Press trial of 1868. The opposition attracted eminent literary men like Victor Hugo, whose work *Punishment* (*Les Châtiments*), written in exile, constituted a devastating attack on the Second Empire. When, in the elections of 1863, the Liberal Union (Union libérale) won two million votes and thirty-five seats, half of the thirty-five were republican. In 1864 Adolphe Thiers made his famous demand for the 'five fundamental freedoms', which he defined as 'security of the citizen against personal violence and arbitrary power;

1. See p. 314.

liberty but not impunity of the Press, that is to say liberty to exchange those ideas from which public opinion is born; freedom of elections; freedom of national representation; public opinion, stated by the majority, directing the conduct of government'. This remained the essence of left-centre liberal programmes for many years to come.

By 1868-9 the activities of the opposition became more open and militant. In the Paris *salon* of Juliette Adam, the banker's wife, republican leaders could discuss politics freely over dinner parties, and Gambetta found a new milieu of influence. By 1869 when he stood for the working-class Paris district of Belleville, he was able to expound what came to be known as the 'Belleville Manifesto', a programme of radical republican reforms. It was the outcome of the years of courageous republican opposition, and its essentials had already in 1868 been set out in Jules Simon's *Politique radicale*. It went much further than Thiers's 'five fundamental freedoms', and included universal suffrage, for local as well as parliamentary elections; separation of church and state; free, compulsory, and secular primary education for all; the suppression of a standing army; and the election of all public functionaries. As yet this radicalism represented only the advanced ideas of the working classes and lower middle classes of the big towns, and Gambetta was triumphantly elected not only in Belleville but also in Marseilles. It was well in advance of what even most republicans wanted. But it foreshadowed the programme of basic democratic reforms on which the great Radical party of the Third Republic was to build. In the new republic soon to be created Gambetta became the key man in the Republican Union, prototype of more modern party organization in France. The paradoxical achievement of the Liberal Empire was to accustom France to the existence and the consequences of an energetic constitutional opposition party, and to nurture a new movement of secular radicalism.

Bonapartist Benefits. The Second Empire achieved much else, more deliberately, in the sphere of social and administrative reorganization. Its most impressive achievement in the eyes of foreign visitors was undoubtedly the transformation of Paris. By a decree of 1860 the area of Paris was extended to include all the outskirts and villages between the customs barriers and the fortifications; this increased its administrative area from twelve to twenty administrative units. Whereas in 1851 Paris had just over one million inhabitants, in 1870 it had more than 1,800,000. The rapid growth of industry combined with the replanning of the city by Baron Haussmann, under the strongest encouragement of Napoleon III himself, changed the whole character of the capital. It changed it socially, for the pulling down of houses in the old labyrinths of the centre to make way for Haussmann's broad new boulevards, squares, and parks forced many workers to the outskirts, where new factories grew up to utilize their labour; omnibus and local railway services made a larger city possible. It changed Paris administratively, for a much more highly organized system of local government and police had to be devised to rule so large a city. The broad straight boulevards had political significance, for they made the raising of barricades in working-class districts less practicable, and the charges of cavalry, police, and troops more effective. It changed Paris architecturally, for the Emperor's programme of spectacular public works included the building of the new Opera house and extensions to the Louvre, new squares and churches; the encouragement of big new stores like the Bon Marché, the Printemps, and the Samaritaine, and of joint-stock banks like the Société Générale and the Crédit Lyonnais.

With the new network of railways and steamship services Paris became more than ever the economic, social, and cultural centre of France. Napoleon did all in his power to make it also the capital of Europe. Great exhibitions or world fairs were held in 1855 and 1867, and it was regarded as a diplomatic triumph to have the conference of powers which ended the Crimean War held in Paris. International showmanship, both commercial and political, was a constant feature of the Second Empire. It was an era of organization and depended on capital accumulation and investment, which Napoleon encouraged. Much of the real estate development on the outskirts, which led to the present-day distinction between the central business and middle-class area and the outer 'red belt' of working-class and industrial areas, was made possible by bankers like the Péreire brothers, Émile and Isaac, or the Paulin Talabot family. Inspired by the ideas of Saint-Simon, these new financial organizers hoped for a transformation of society through industrial progress and improved methods of social and economic organization. Down their bright new boulevards the inhabitants of the scientific, gas-lit Empire danced their way to the tinkling tunes of Offenbach – their way to the national disaster of Sedan and to the horrors of the Paris Commune of 1871.

It was a time when the more modern pattern of industrial society was taking shape. The year 1864, which saw the foundation of the industrial combine of the Comité des Forges, saw also the repeal of the clause in the French Penal Code which made concerted industrial action a crime. Trade unions, which since 1791 had laboured under the stigma of illegality, were now tolerated, and prosecutions slackened. Just as industrial workers found their own separate dwelling places in the expanding outskirts of Paris, so they found their own separate economic and political organizations in the trade unions. In 1864, too, the First International was formed. Before this Napoleon III had permitted and even encouraged mutual insurance groups – had he not, in 1844, written a pamphlet on the conquest of poverty? In 1862 he sent a delegation of workers, at public expense, to see the British Exhibition. They returned impressed with the new opportunities of collective bargaining which the British trade unions were discovering. After the legalization of labour unions in 1864 two main types evolved: the local association or trades council (*chambre syndicale*) and the more militant unit for collective bargaining (*société de résistance*). Even so, labour organization did not become large in scale until near the end of the century, and it was 1884 before it won full legal rights. Meanwhile Napoleon, by a decree of 1853, implemented an idea which he had put forward in his pamphlet *The Ending of Poverty* (*L'extinction du paupérisme*). It revived and extended the Napoleonic idea of conciliation boards (*Conseils de prud'-hommes*), composed half of representatives of employers, half of representatives of workers, with their chairmen, vice-chairmen, and secretaries nominated by the government. Designed to settle labour disputes and so prevent strikes, they were intended by Napoleon as an agency of public order and discipline. They were often means of improving working conditions and wages, and could sometimes become a focus for labour organization and agitation.

In general, the French people gained from having a paternalist government during these years of rapid industrial growth. They escaped something of the hardships caused in Britain by a more rapid industrial growth in a period when doctrines of minimum state interference held the field. Napoleon himself has been called 'Saint-Simon on horseback', and there is no reason to doubt either the sincerity of his desire to improve material conditions or the reality of the benefits his rule conferred. Politically, his policy vacillated as he sought to appease now the Catholics, now the liberals, now the socialists, and always the demands of the populace as a whole. 'Today,' he had written before coming to power, 'the rule of classes is over, and you can govern only with the masses.' His efforts to govern with the masses led to a series of disasters in foreign policy, for he believed (not entirely without justification) that the masses wanted glory and were intensely nationalistic. But these failures should not obscure the more positive material gains that France derived from his rule. 'Half-pint Napoleon' (*Napoléon le petit*) Victor Hugo had scornfully dubbed him. The Second Empire, judged in terms of military glory or original achievement, was indeed only a pale shadow of the First. But it has considerable importance for the material development of France and for the shaping of modern Europe.[1]

1. See p. 301.

Belgian Liberalism. Throughout most of these years Belgium was governed by the liberal party of Charles Rogier and H. J. W. Frère-Orban, with the Catholic party in opposition. After a three-year Catholic government between 1854 and 1857, Rogier assumed power and kept it until 1870. It was 1879 before the Socialist party was formed. As in other countries the Liberals tended to fall into two wings: the more doctrinaire liberals demanding constitutional freedoms and believing in an economic policy of *laissez faire*, and the more radical liberals concerned with extension of the franchise and improvement of social conditions. As in France, this division became especially important from 1863 onward; and, as in France, trade-union organization was prohibited under the penal code. Only in 1867 did it become legal to organize workers, though labour organizations remained severely hampered in all their activities except as friendly societies and mutual-aid associations. Belgian workers were, in effect, kept disarmed and disorganized before increasingly powerful employers' organizations until 1921. Only then were labour unions granted full legal protection and rights.

Belgian politics of these years were dominated by two other major issues: the struggles between clericals and anticlericals, especially for control over the developing system of national education; and the growth of the strongly nationalistic Flemish movement, hostile to the domination of French institutions and culture. The problem of relations between church and state was the chief bone of contention between the Liberal and Catholic parties, and Rogier's ministry of 1857 had as its central aim 'the protection of liberty against the attacks of the Church'. By a series of laws it diminished the power of the clergy in primary and secondary schools, while tolerating the existence of church schools and seminaries. The Flemish movement, which began under Dutch rule before 1830 but became particularly vigorous after 1850, demanded the use of the Flemish language in the schools and colleges of Flanders and in the university of Ghent, in the courts whenever a Flemish defendant requested it, and in separate Flemish-speaking regiments of the army. The movement, though cultural and linguistic in origins, seemed to the Liberals to threaten the territorial unity and cohesion of the state as much as the power of the Roman Catholic Church. Its claims were therefore resisted until after 1870.

The Parliamentary Pattern. In the development of parliamentary government in Britain, France, and Belgium between 1850 and 1870 a certain common pattern can be discerned, underlying the more obvious differences. In all three the institutions of parliamentary government were undoubtedly more deeply rooted, more resilient, and more fully developed by 1870 than they had been in 1850, or than they were elsewhere in 1870. Elected assemblies asserted their power to control ministers responsible for executive government and administration; political parties evolved more efficient and thorough organizations both in the constituencies and within the parliamentary assemblies; the proper functioning of parliamentary oppositions was better understood; the conducting of elections was freer from abuses of corruption, influence, and intimidation. The rights of public association, public meeting, freedom of the Press and of speech, were asserted and given stronger protection. Economic expansion was producing not only new types of industrial and commercial organization, but also new forms of labour organization, which claimed and won legal recognition by the state. Powerful groups other than the state – whether churches, capitalist corporations, trade unions, or cultural movements – were claiming rights even against the state, and certainly through legal recognition by the state.

But in all three countries national cohesion and unity remained strong, looking to a strong central political power for improvements in social life and for protection or support against foreign interference. Nothing cemented Belgian national unity more firmly, and nothing caused more acute friction between the three countries in these years, than the recurrent fear that Napoleon III nursed designs against Belgian independence. In 1852 he exerted pressure on the Belgian government to restrain the virulent Press campaign of the French refugees who had fled to Belgium after the *coup d'état* of 1851. His proposals for a customs union were resisted as a device for subordinating Belgian economy to French. His schemes for gaining 'compensation' for Prussian gains at the expense of Belgium and Luxembourg were a direct threat to her territorial and political independence. On each occasion British support for Belgium was decisive in restraining Napoleon's ambitions. In 1870 Britain obtained the signatures of both France and Prussia, then engaged in the Franco-Prussian war, to a treaty that renewed their engagements of 1839 guaranteeing Belgian neutrality and independence.[1]

The northern European states shared, to a large extent, in this common pattern of evolving parliamentary constitutional government. The Netherlands adhered to a parliamentary system after 1849. Its strong Liberal party, led and largely created by Thorbecke, alternated in office throughout these years with the rival Conservative party. Thorbecke's reforms characteristically included an overhaul of the electoral laws and the administration, a simplification of the fiscal and commercial regulations, and the conversion of Haarlem lake into good pasture land. Beset by quarrels between Roman Catholics and Protestants, the governments of the time also had to grapple with problems of ecclesiastical control

1. See p. 170.

over education and of religious instruction in schools. In 1866 Sweden instituted a bicameral parliamentary system. Universal suffrage without property restrictions did not come, however, for another fifty years, as a result of reforms between 1906 and 1920. In south-western Europe less solidly based constitutional systems fared less well, and these were years of acute instability. In part the alternations of reaction and revolution in Spain and Portugal were due to the instability of the monarchies themselves. Queen Isabella of Spain was eventually deposed in 1868, after successive experiences of her wayward and irresponsible character; and in Portugal a series of royal deaths involved short reigns. But instability came mainly from the backward social development of these countries, which meant that no strong Liberal parties could take shape. They lacked not only traditions of constitutional government and the habits engendered by them, but also the economic and social foundations on which the parliamentary parties of other western countries were developing. The Iberian peninsula proved unripe for the consolidation of a form of government which was, for the most part, a foreign importation with only shallow roots.

The inferences suggested by the changes in political and social organization in western Europe during these decades are that liberal constitutionalism and parliamentary institutions matched closely the needs of an expanding industrial, urban, commercial society. The countries most advanced in industrialization and urbanization – Britain, France, Belgium, the Netherlands – provided the most suitable soil for the flourishing of parliamentary government. Constitutional government in all its diverse forms calls for certain minimum conditions if it is to survive and thrive: a certain abatement of violence, a willingness to tolerate disagreement even about profoundly important matters, a readiness to come to working terms with rivals and opponents. These qualities of mind and outlook are fostered by a commercial society, and are inherent in the habits of business men and manufacturers. Where they had not been widely accepted as desirable qualities and were not commonly found, as in Spain or Portugal of these years, the indispensable conditions for parliamentary government did not exist. These qualities were encouraged in western Europe not only by industrialism and trade, but also by the ever-growing respect won for science and technology. The 'scientific spirit' had traditionally fought against bigotry and fanaticism, intolerance and repression. A society coming to be more and more dedicated to a belief in scientific truth was also a society anxious to end religious strife and political instability by devising a more peaceful, efficient, and non-violent machinery of government. The subsequent history of Europe owes much to the triumphs of science, both as a system of knowledge, a

274

way of thought, and a source of applied technology; and these were years of such triumphs.

THE GROWTH OF SCIENCE AND TECHNOLOGY

By 1850 the explorations of scientists had reached a point where truths discovered in different fields of research began to fit together. Knowledge that had so far appeared fragmentary and disjointed began to reveal interconnexions and so to assume a quite new significance. The most momentous 'discoveries' of pure science have, indeed, been a sudden revelation of hitherto unappreciated relationships: a perception of coherence and a glimpse of new synthesis. Newton related movement to mass and discerned, behind the complex working of the universe, general principles governing the motion of all material bodies; Lavoisier detected an elemental chemical pattern within the structure of nature; Lamarck used the vast accumulation of botanical and zoological information to support the hypothesis that throughout a very long period of time a slow process of evolution had changed one form of creature into another in an ascending series, so that all living organisms have some evolutionary interconnexion. These discoveries of general 'laws' hidden behind a hitherto puzzling diversity of observed facts, even though these laws may later be considerably modified and revised, are what constitute the great landmarks in the history of science. The momentous insight may be prepared by the labours of countless others, often obscure; and without the compilation of data which is reliable because it is experimentally verifiable, such insights would be unlikely to occur. But the insight itself, once propounded and found acceptable to a consensus of expert opinion, assumes an importance that stretches far beyond the confines of the particular field of study in which it originated. It begins to influence all thought, to challenge religious belief, and pose fresh philosophical problems. It constitutes a 'revolution' in thought because it affects the whole of human life.

The century between 1750 and 1850 had been one of intensive researches into every field of scientific exploration: mathematical, chemical, physical, biological, and technological. France had taken a pre-eminent place in this work. Her great mathematicians, physicists, chemists, and biologists had contributed more than those of any other country to extending the frontiers of scientific knowledge. Their characteristic faith was expressed by the great chemist Antoine Lavoisier in 1793, when he submitted a memorandum on national education to the Convention. All branches of science and technology, he argued, are linked together, all scientists serve a common cause and have a common interest. They

275

are an army that must advance on an even front and move in coordinated fashion. All forms of knowledge are threads on one great tapestry, and we are assured of one ultimate pattern and design because there is a unity behind all knowledge.

By the middle of the nineteenth century the tapestry seemed to be nearing completion, although now, a century later, we know that its completion is still very far off. By 1850 the rapid progress of knowledge fostered a mood of boundless optimism, an ebullient hope, which may have closer connexions with the roots of the romantic movement of these years than historians have yet discovered. Stimulated by this optimistic mood, scientists became bolder – even rasher – in venturing upon generalizations and in suggesting relationships between hitherto isolated facts. The Newtonian theory of motion and weight in physics and Lavoisier's theory of elements in chemistry were brought together by the study of atomic weights, thermodynamics, and the kinetic theory of gases. An international convention of chemists at Karlsruhe in 1860 standardized the system of atomic weights which, by 1871, became systematized into the periodic table by Dimitri Mendeléyev. This whole development made possible a clearer understanding of molecular structure and changed the whole concept of matter. At the same time, with the work in Britain of Michael Faraday and James Clerk-Maxwell in the fields of electromagnetism and thermodynamics, the concept of energy was being similarly transformed. The basic concept of energy, which could take various forms of heat, light, sound, or motive power and which could be interchangeably chemical power or electrical power, brought the sciences together into a quite new synthesis. It served as a common denominator for the study of physics, mechanics, and chemistry. The law of the conservation of energy – the notion of a natural store of force which merely takes a diversity of forms but itself remains constant – was a concept particularly susceptible of popularization, and one from which the most far-reaching philosophical inferences could be drawn. By 1870, too, the kinetic theory of gases evolved by Stanislao Cannizzaro, Clerk-Maxwell, and Marcelin Berthelot was linking up the theories of thermodynamics with those of molecular structure and atomic weights. The measurements of heat transformations in chemical reactions suggested affinities between energy and matter. Everything was falling into place so fast that the secrets of nature appeared infinitely discoverable (*see* Diagram 1).

Philosophical Synthesis. The urge to relate different fields of knowledge was no doubt strengthened by the metaphysical philosophy of G. W. F. Hegel, which at this time was gaining impressive ascendancy in Germany. When Hegel died in 1831, his disciples had seriously doubted whether there was anything left to be said – he had so systematically and exhaustively encompassed the whole of thought. The element in his philosophy which was most easily transferable to other studies was the notion that all change and all progress come about by a process of 'dialectic' akin to intellectual conversation. An idea is stated (a 'thesis'). It is then attacked or denied (the 'antithesis'). Then a more complete and rounded truth emerges from the conflict between the two (the 'synthesis'). This result includes something from both its predecessors, and it could not have come into being without them. It marks an advance towards a more perfect understanding and a more complete knowledge of reality. And it, in turn, being a positive 'thesis', then becomes the first stage in a new dialectical argument, to be carried forward by a further negation and synthesis into a still more complete truth; and so on, ad infinitum. Thus history, in Hegel's view, was the progressive realization of a great ultimate truth or idea, and every aspect of human activity had its place in this all-comprehensive system. Hegelianism was a dynamic, evolutionary philosophy of life, in tune with the more dynamic, evolutionary qualities of scientific thought and of life itself in nineteenth-century Europe. It was from him that Karl Marx took the idea of a dialectical process underlying history, though Marx insisted that this process occurred at the level of economic and social conditions, and not, as Hegel taught, at the level of metaphysical Ideas. Similarly, the great authority of this new metaphysical philosophy lent support to all who wanted to bring together the scattered truths of different branches of scientific knowledge and discovery, and synthesize them into provocative new generalizations.

The New Biology. Darwinism had great effects on nineteenth-century thought because it was yet another wonderful new synthesis. It was connected, by dimly perceived links, with the other revelations of physical nature. Organic chemistry, and even more bacteriology, were already forging some links between the mathematical and physical sciences and the biological sciences. It was suggested that life is a process of chemical change. Louis Pasteur and Joseph Lister, from 1854 onward, studied micro-organisms and devised the modern germ theory. Charles Darwin brought together these and other ideas to propound a new theory of life itself. Darwinism was the supreme achievement of contemporary trends towards synthesis, and the publication of *The Origin of Species* made the year 1859 a turning point in modern science and philosophy.

It was characteristically rooted in the material and technological progress of the time. The geological knowledge from which Darwin began had been greatly enhanced by the collection of fossils which came from excavations in building canals, railroads, and ports; the knowledge of selective breeding of plants and animals came from practical agriculture as much as from the experimental laboratory. The component ideas were familiar but so far disjointed. Conceptions of evolution, and even of the role of evolution in differentiating species, had been much discussed during the previous half century as a result of the work of Lamarck. The idea of the unity of life – of a fundamental relationship between all living things – had been defended as the basis of biology by Geoffroy Saint-Hilaire in France. The idea of environment as a totality of surrounding conditions determining life and human society was familiar to historians such as Hippolyte Taine and H. T. Buckle even before Darwin wrote. The notion of competition as a principle of social life and economic activity, of progress coming through a struggle for survival, underlay the economic theories of Adam Smith, Thomas Malthus, David Ricardo, and all the *laissez faire* arguments of the early nineteenth century. When Darwin brought together these scattered ideas and integrated them into his daring thesis – that it is by constant adaptation to environment through a process of natural selection and struggle for survival that all species of living things have become differentiated – it was as if the whole Ark-load of animals had suddenly landed in the Garden of Eden, converting it into a jungle 'red in tooth and claw'.

Darwinism apparently denied the act of Divine creation, and with it the whole familiar concept of great catastrophic occasions – the Fall, the Flood, Divine revelation. It replaced them by a notion of gradual secular transformation and adaptation through millions of years. Darwin was regarded as a blasphemer attacking the very foundations of Christianity. In the hectic debates that ensued, a British Prime Minister, Disraeli, could solemnly announce that if it were a choice between apes and angels, he was on the side of the angels. The whole development of science was brought to a focal point, at which it challenged all existing creeds and philosophies, all accepted notions of the origin, nature, and destiny of mankind.

The challenge of science to philosophy had been there for some time. Until 1848 general theories and philosophical doctrines – of the natural goodness of man, of natural rights and duties, of the universality of reason, of utopian socialism, of Hegelianism and Kantianism – were regarded as of the utmost general importance. Battles about general theories had marked the age of revolutions, of romanticism, even of reaction. But part of the consequence of disillusionment in 1848 was the discrediting of all abstract theories, and a new disbelief in their importance for human life or their efficacy as roads to social change.

This decline in esteem for philosophy left a vacuum that was now filled to overflowing by belief in science. Scientific experiment, method, and theory won credit partly by the striking new syntheses of science which produced general concepts more comprehensible to the ordinary man, more obviously of great human significance, and undeniably of momentous importance for all branches of learning and culture. It was an age of efficient popularization, by lecture, pamphlet, journal, and book, with a large and eager public in most European countries. The impact of scientific ideas was therefore quick and widespread. Because they were mostly products of real interchange and cooperation between the eminent scientists of all countries, scientific knowledge and thought could properly be regarded as an emanation of the whole of European culture. All races, nations, and states had contributed something of value to the general advance, and France lost something of the primacy and leadership which she had maintained during the first half of the century. Data collected in one country or in one branch of study had been taken up by scientists of other countries and other fields, added to and modified, and eventually brought together into a generally acceptable hypothesis; this, in turn, illuminated other sectors of human knowledge. It was all one vast process of integration and vitalization, exciting and wonderful. Tennyson, as usual, expressed perfectly the mood of 1850 when he wrote, in *In Memoriam*,

> Of those that, eye to eye, shall look
> On knowledge; under whose command
> Is Earth and Earth's, and in their hand
> Is Nature like an open book.

The mood of boundless confidence and optimism did not long outlive the phase of scientific progress which had generated it. By 1870 doubts, questions, unanswerable difficulties, were already being raised.[1] Scientific study began to move again along more specialized and separate channels, knowledge became again fragmentary and uncoordinated, and the mood of supreme confidence has never since been regained. The reception of Darwinism in itself marked the beginning of this new phase. Darwin had first formulated his theory as early as 1842, but delayed publishing it for seventeen years. It was not fully expounded until *The Descent of Man* appeared in 1871. But the first popularizers of it, notably T. H. Huxley, met an immediate gust of religious hostility and moral objection. The theory, indeed, seemed to minimize the importance of individual behaviour and moral values. It depicted human progress as the result of an impersonal process, the blind product of the struggle of species for survival by very long-term adaptations to environment. It was

1. See p. 423.

DIAGRAM 1. THE CULT OF SYNTHESIS, 1800-1870

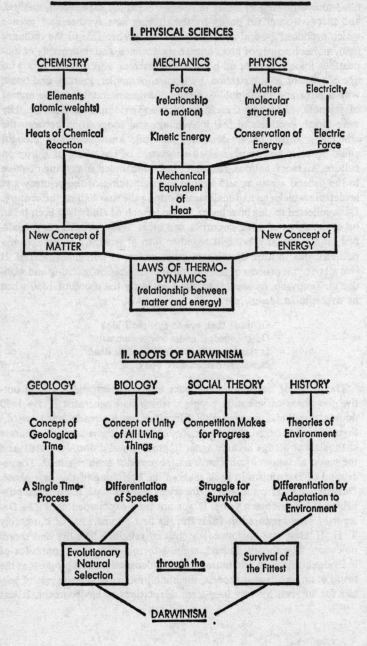

I. PHYSICAL SCIENCES

CHEMISTRY | MECHANICS | PHYSICS

Elements (atomic weights)

Force (relationship to motion)

Matter (molecular structure) | Electricity

Heats of Chemical Reaction

Kinetic Energy

Conservation of Energy | Electric Force

Mechanical Equivalent of Heat

New Concept of MATTER

New Concept of ENERGY

LAWS OF THERMO-DYNAMICS (relationship between matter and energy)

II. ROOTS OF DARWINISM

GEOLOGY | BIOLOGY | SOCIAL THEORY | HISTORY

Concept of Geological Time

Concept of Unity of All Living Things

Competition Makes for Progress

Theories of Environment

A Single Time-Process

Differentiation of Species

Struggle for Survival

Differentiation by Adaptation to Environment

Evolutionary Natural Selection

through the

Survival of the Fittest

DARWINISM

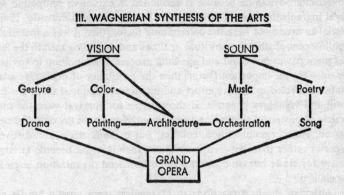

III. WAGNERIAN SYNTHESIS OF THE ARTS

VISION   SOUND

Gesture   Color   Music   Poetry

Drama   Painting — Architecture — Orchestration   Song

GRAND OPERA

IV. SOCIAL AND POLITICAL THEORY: *RIVAL SYNTHESES*

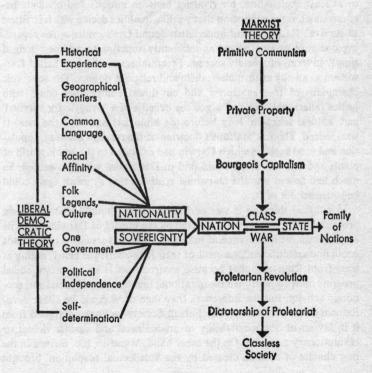

LIBERAL DEMOCRATIC THEORY

Historical Experience
Geographical Frontiers
Common Language
Racial Affinity
Folk Legends, Culture
One Government
Political Independence
Self-determination

NATIONALITY
SOVEREIGNTY

MARXIST THEORY

Primitive Communism

↓

Private Property

↓

Bourgeois Capitalism

↓

NATION — CLASS — STATE — Family of Nations
WAR

↓

Proletarian Revolution

↓

Dictatorship of Proletariat

↓

Classless Society

intellectual dynamite because it contained in explosive compound several ingredients, each of which could be interpreted differently. If material environment were the determining factor, then it was a materialist philosophy, challenging spiritual qualities and degrading men to the level of mere pawns in a blind and age-long process. If adaptation to environment were the important factor, then the possibility of deliberate adaptations effected by human effort and intelligence restored scope for free will and voluntary progress. If the struggle for survival were the main cause of successful adaptation, then again the emphasis lay on selfishness, greed, violence, competition, conflict; but if the struggle were between species rather than between individuals, then it could become an argument for closer human cooperation, better social organization, even for socialism.

Although the first reactions to Darwinism were mostly hostile and bigoted, the long-range reactions were very diverse and eclectic. Many different schools of thought could find in it fresh support for their old beliefs. Nationalists and believers in *Realpolitik* could find justification, or at least explanation, for rivalries between nations and conflicts between states in the suggestion that warlike qualities decide which is 'fittest to survive'. Racialists and imperialists found fresh evidence for regarding one race or one power as inherently superior to another, judged simply in terms of worldly success. Freethinkers of all kinds hailed Darwinism as an ally against clericalism and religious dogma. The economic champions of free enterprise and cut-throat competition could with justice reflect that they had urged the benefits of a 'struggle for survival' and 'natural selection' long before the biologists had used the idea. It was, indeed, Thomas Malthus's doctrine of the relation between population and food supplies which Darwin had extended to the whole world of plants and animals. Each could find in Darwinism what he wanted. So much had flowed into the Darwinist synthesis that as much again could be squeezed out of it.

In political thinking it was perhaps socialist thought that was most profoundly and permanently affected by the impact of Darwinism. In its emphasis on the importance of material conditions socialists of all kinds could find scientific endorsement of their long-cherished belief, dating at least from Rousseau, that because environment is so important social progress must come from a more rational organization of social and economic activity. But the inferences they then drew could be either revolutionary or evolutionary. The Fabian Society in England argued from it in favour of 'the inevitability of gradualness' and against violent or revolutionary measures. On the other hand, Marxism, too, thrived in the new climate of opinion created by the 'intellectual revolution' brought about by Darwinism. The theories of Marx and Engels claimed to be based on economic data patiently observed, collected, and verified; the hypotheses they used to explain these data – the theory that changes in social and political life are explicable only by underlying changes in the means of production and that the clue to all history is the struggle between economic classes – claimed to have the same validity as scientific hypotheses. As Benthamism in its day purported to be doing for social science what Newtonism had done for physical science;[1] so now Marxism claimed to be doing for the social sciences of economics, politics, history, and sociology, what Darwinism had done for biology.

Marx was purporting to replace the older romantic or 'utopian' socialism of Robert Owen, Saint-Simon, and Fourier with a new 'scientific' theory of socialism, claiming validity and credence by reason of its strictly scientific foundations. Like Darwinism, it dealt not with matters of human motive or intention, but with the inevitable long-term trend of human life; it also placed emphasis on the importance of material environment as a conditioning or even determining factor; it also spoke in terms of struggle and conflict. Marx was so conscious of the affinities of his own theories with Darwinism that he wanted to dedicate to Darwin his greatest work, *Das Kapital*, of which the first volume appeared in 1867, but Darwin cautiously declined the honour. When Engels made a funeral oration over Marx's grave in 1883, he claimed that 'Just as Darwin discovered the law of evolution in organic nature, so Marx discovered the law of evolution in human history'.

If the comparison was by no means as simple as that, there is still a sense in which Marxism and even Benthamism belong to the same world of thought and the same mode of belief as mid nineteenth-century thermodynamics and Darwinism. A science of society resting on a dynamics of competition and conflict, whether between individuals or classes, had affinities with a science of nature resting on a dynamics of energy and a struggle for survival. Social and natural sciences alike were marked by an amalgam of abstractions and materialist bias – the abstractions of 'economic man' in the classical economists such as Adam Smith, Malthus, and Mill; of 'economic class' in Marx; of 'solid atoms' measurable by weight in the physicists; of 'species' and 'environment' in Darwin. And the basic notion in all was that of a self-regulating mechanism working according to 'inevitable' laws, whether of supply and demand, of the iron law of wages and the inevitable impoverishment of the wage-earning proletariat, of the 'conservation of energy', or the 'survival of the fittest'. The thought of the whole period has about it a certain homogeneity that made it easy to believe all these things at once.

1. See p. 187.

We act in tune with the mood of these decades between 1850 and 1870 if we discover such an ultimate synthesis of all the most revolutionary and far-reaching ideas to which they gave birth.

The Arts. The quest for a synthesis, which is so apparent in scientific thought, can also be found in the artistic developments of these decades. The most striking example of this is the work of the German musician, Richard Wagner. Wagner contended that all the arts of music, drama, poetry, painting, and architecture should be made to fertilize one another by being brought into a single synthesis, a totality of all artistic endeavour (*Gesamtkunstwerk*). He saw in grand opera the best medium for attaining this result, because it combined the three chief forms of artistic expression – gesture, poetry, and sound. His great project of *The Ring*, a whole quartet of operas based on the Nordic myths of the Nibelungen Saga and planned to occupy four whole evenings in its performance, was completed between 1850 and 1870. After 1861 he enjoyed the support and patronage of King Ludwig II of Bavaria, and in 1872 the great theatre at Bayreuth was begun, though it was not completed until four years later. It was designed to fulfil Wagner's theories. The vision of the whole audience was left unobstructed, the orchestra was sunk from sight between stage and auditorium, and the stage was planned to accommodate elaborate scenery, lighting, and machinery.

In spirit and choice of subject his work had a powerful appeal to surging German nationalism. The works of his great contemporary, Giuseppe Verdi, likewise reflected the spirit of Italian nationalism. His later operas such as *Otello* and *Falstaff* won popularity quicker in Germany than it Italy itself, partly because he was there hailed as a successor to Wagner. In France, his near-contemporary, Hector Berlioz, demonstrated the new artistic opportunities of massive orchestration. When the king of Prussia asked him if it were true that he wrote for five hundred musicians, Berlioz replied, 'Your Majesty has been misinformed: I sometimes write for four hundred and fifty.' In the most influential musical developments of these years there was a characteristic grandiosity – a bias to bigness, power, and comprehensiveness – that matched the trends of the time in economics, politics, and science. Verdi and Wagner became national artists expressing the sentiments of whole peoples, and this is often regarded as the most significant social feature of their work. But of even deeper significance was their passion for synthesis and integration. Orchestration and opera were the artistic parallels to scientific synthesis and political unification.

The intellectual mood and the aesthetic tastes encouraged by science and *Realpolitik* produced an equally characteristic literature and art. From the middle of the century onwards 'realism' in the novel and in painting expressed a new reverence for facts observed and for feelings experienced, and an urge comparable to that of the scientist to make man's physical environment more intelligible. Before 1850 Charles Dickens in Britain, Honoré de Balzac in France, had pointed the way by depicting in vivid detail the social life and problems of their times and countries. With Gustave Flaubert's *Madame Bovary* in 1856, Leo Tolstoy's *War and Peace* in 1866, and in the theatre, Alexander Dumas's *La Dame aux Camélias* in 1852, the new approach was consolidated. In painting the work of the Frenchmen Gustave Courbet, Edouard Manet, and Claude Monet challenged the established romantic tastes of the Paris Salon and founded a new school of naturalism and realism. To see and depict life as it was – even the life of the ordinary people – and to find beauty and meaning in man's immediate surroundings and thereby make them more meaningful and comprehensible: that was their avowed purpose and, to a large extent, their achievement.

Even the specialized art of studying and writing history was powerfully influenced by the same tendencies. The massive collections and publications of historical sources and documents available by 1850 made possible, and indeed essential, a development of research techniques. More rigorous tests of evidence, verification of facts, criticism of accepted generalizations, became the tools of the professional historian. The techniques of the research monograph, with its elaborate apparatus of references and sources, became standardized. In Germany, Leopold von Ranke; in France, Fustel de Coulanges; in Britain, William Stubbs, laid foundations for a more 'scientific' writing of history. If, as in realism in literature and painting, this often resulted in dullness or downright ugliness, it was nevertheless a valuable reaction against romantic history and the uncritical acceptance of age-old superstitions. The basic task of the historian is after all, like that of the scientist, to verify facts, sift evidence, test hypotheses, and find a synthesis that comprises and illuminates all the available knowledge within his province.

In countless ways the arts were affected by social changes and even by political movements. The use of large orchestras became both physically and financially possible because music became more of a democratic enjoyment, involving public performances in large halls. What made the realistic novel popular and effective was the growth of a large reading public; and this depended upon the growth of public education as well as the growth of population, on the reading habits encouraged by a popular Press made cheap by the rotary press and commercial advertising. The national spirit, evident in men as widely different as Henrik Ibsen the Norwegian dramatist; Anton Dvořák the Slav musician; Nicholas Rimsky-Korsakov the Russian composer, reflected the political currents of these years. Art of all forms struck deep social roots in this age of all-pervading synthesis.

The unity of European culture was never shown more clearly than when its universal tendency was toward national differentiation. Even when literature, art, and music were finding their most creative impulses in the separatist forces of nationalism, the peoples of Europe shared sufficiently in one heritage to find common enjoyment in their cultural diversities. The interchange of culture was even facilitated and protected in these years by such arrangements as a series of copyright laws and treaties, beginning with the Anglo-French copyright convention of 1851 and ending with the new German copyright law of 1871. The most eminent men in art and literature, like the most eminent scientists, were of international repute. Wagner and Berlioz, Turgenev and Tolstoy, roamed the continent and found themselves, whether in London, Paris, Vienna, or St Petersburg, members of a European intelligentsia that included public men of all countries. The internationalism of the sciences was matched by the Europeanism of the arts.

Technology. While the world of thought and art was being transformed by new scientific ideas and methods, the material civilization of the western world was being no less strikingly changed by the practical effects of applied science and technology. The steam engine owed little in its origins to the pure scientists; it was a product of the artisan and the mechanic, the practical inventor and adapter. Much of the technical progress of the time likewise had little connexion with the new science. But the railway age, which had come to Europe by 1850, involved a host of technical advances which had great repercussions in other fields: in the perfection of iron smelting and the refinement and applications of steel, in tunnelling and bridge-building, in signalling, in organization both financial and administrative. The Bessemer process of making steel was developed in the 1850s and introduced into the United States after 1867. Only thereafter did the use of the microscope, which had contributed so much to the advances of microbiology, begin to reveal the structure of iron and steel, and open a new age of alloys in metallurgy. The invention of the electric telegraph belonged to the first half of the century, but in the second it led to a European network of speedy communications and in 1866 to the successful laying of a trans-Atlantic cable. The use of the dynamo to generate electricity sprang from the researches of the physicists into the connexions between magnetism and electricity. It began to come into industrial use by 1870, though its greatest utilization still lay further ahead. For building, although the traditional materials of stone, brick, and wood remained most common, increasing use was made of iron and steel and concrete.

The rapid advance of the biological sciences had speedy medical results: in improving sanitation, preventing disease, in aseptic and antiseptic surgery, and in anaesthesia. Food supplies were increased by the growth of more scientific agriculture. In Britain the Royal Agricultural Society had existed since 1838; the Rothamsted Experimental Station for agricultural research was set up in 1842. Bold investment, by both landlord and tenant, in drainage and deep ploughing and in new machinery, introduced the period of 'high farming' which followed the free entry of foreign corn to the home market after 1846. Chemical science produced artificial fertilizers and oil cake for feeding. Steam-driven agricultural machinery was widely used in the 1860s. These improvements were characteristic of western European agriculture in general, and resulted in a much higher output of food.

Confidence that the advances of science would, through technical application, be perpetually and indefinitely useful to man, seemed amply borne out by the progress made during these two decades. Never before had so much knowledge, ingenuity, and skill been used so extensively and so profitably to promote the health, wealth, and welfare of mankind. Even many of the humbler amenities of life now taken for granted date from these years; for example, phosphorus matches and cheap soap, sewing machines and more comfortable furniture.

Yet technological knowledge is ultimately, in human affairs, neutral and equally capable of serving good or evil. Metallurgical skill that produces locomotives and dynamos can also make guns and shells: ploughshares can be beaten into swords. The dramatic triumphs of the new Prussian war machine in 1864 against Denmark, in 1866 against Austria-Hungary, and in 1870 against France, brought home to the whole of Europe how much the very nature of warfare, too, was being transformed by science. Not only did railways make the transport of troops and munitions faster and easier, but long-range field artillery capable of greater range, accuracy, and rate of fire was one of the decisive factors in Prussian victories. The French command in 1870 was defeated largely because it completely miscalculated how long a small body of men, armed with the breech-loading rifle, could hold out against superior numbers, while the telegraph could summon reinforcements brought speedily to the scene by train. The Franco-Prussian War was symbolic of the ambiguous outcome of scientific discovery: a Frankenstein monster, perpetually liable to astonish its creator by its unexpected behaviour and liable always to get out of human control.

Allied with the vastly greater economic and financial resources of western Europe and with new forms of political and social organization, scientific and technical skills constituted a source of power at man's disposal which he has yet to learn to use exclusively for good, under the penalty of being himself destroyed by irresponsible use of it for evil. In so far as the intellectual climate induced by science favoured materialism and realism, it also favoured Marxism and *Realpolitik*. Karl Marx and Otto von Bismarck are the most characteristic products of the new age in Europe, which came into being in 1871. The resources of power made available by technology were put at the disposal of men and societies which infatuation with science had helped to make realistic and materialistic in outlook. It was a fateful conjunction.

CHAPTER 14

THE REMAKING OF CENTRAL EUROPE

ECONOMIC GROWTH AND TERRITORIAL INTEGRATION

By 1850 economic changes had already had great effects throughout the lands of Italy and Germany. As already shown [1] the railway age made it possible for the first time to travel quickly from any part of Europe to almost any other. This opened the way for a rapid expansion of the economy of any state which was ready to take advantages of the new opportunities. Of all the central European states, two were most advantageously placed to do this. One was the constitutional monarchy of Piedmont and Savoy, with its favourable strategic position in northern Italy, its enlightened government anxious to 'westernize' the country, and its prestige as a proven leader of Italian hopes for eventual liberation and unification. The other was the kingdom of Prussia, already in many ways precocious in internal administrative and military organization. With widespread German territories and interests, it was a natural focus for all hopes of German unification without Austria. How did these two countries develop economically between 1850 and 1870, and how did this development affect the destinies of Italy and Germany as a whole?

Cavour. Until his death in 1861 the most important man in Italian politics was Count Camillo di Cavour. Like his contemporary parliamentary leaders in western Europe, he was a convinced liberal both in devotion to constitutional liberties and procedures, and in his desire to develop along more modern lines the agriculture, industry, and finances of his country. He had himself made a fortune out of applying modern scientific methods and mechanization to the farming of his family estates before 1850. As a young man he had travelled widely in England, France, and Switzerland; he was a keen student of advanced western methods in agriculture, industry, and parliamentary government. All the new forms of organization described above [2] fascinated him; and it became the mission of his life to 'westernize' Piedmont and eventually the whole of Italy. He knew that railways, mills, factories, banks, business enterprise, as he had seen them working in Britain and France, were the only road to economic prosperity in Italy. In October 1850 he accepted ministerial office in Piedmont as Minister of Agricul-

1. See p. 181.
2. See pp. 261-75.

ture, Commerce, and Marine. He made a series of commercial treaties with Belgium, France, and England which linked Piedmont to the growing free-trade area of western Europe. As Minister of Finance, which he also became, he raised capital by an internal loan for immediate needs and an external loan from England. With part of it he built more railways. In November 1852, he formed his own Ministry. Its first task was to improve Piedmont's roads, railroads, docks, and ports; expand her commerce; and strengthen her finances. As a young engineer in the army he had imbibed the outlook and aptitudes of the technician, approaching problems of politics with a systematic, well-informed, logical mind, prepared to analyse them patiently and carefully in search of a solution. By 1854, when the outbreak of the Crimean War forced him to turn his attention mainly to foreign relations, he had gone far toward running Piedmont on sounder businesslike lines and assimilating her economic life to that of the West. He passed legislation, on the British and French model, modernizing the structure of business corporations, banks and credit institutions, cooperative societies, the civil administration, and the army. But the rest of Italy, under Austrian or Papal or Bourbon rule, still offered striking contrasts of economic backwardness.

After the end of the Crimean War in 1856 Cavour resumed, for another three years, an even more intensive programme of economic development. Now that war between the great powers had come to Europe after nearly forty years of peace, he had to accumulate military as well as economic strength. The railways of greatest strategic importance were extended. The Mont Cenis tunnel was planned to pierce the Alps and link up Piedmontese territory with French. Genoa was changed from a naval base into a great commercial port with new docks and loading facilities. By rail and steamship Piedmont came to be linked more closely to the West. By the time Cavour died in 1861 he had created, by a series of diplomatic alliances and wars, which shall be described below,[1] a kingdom of Italy with Piedmont as its core but still excluding Venetia and Rome. This political and diplomatic achievement is his most memorable. But it took place against a background of economic development which had an essential place in the whole scheme, and which in itself would have earned for him a high position in the story of Italy. Unlike the constitutional and liberal experiments in Spain or Portugal, that of Piedmont could henceforth rest on the firm and indispensable basis of economic and social modernization.

United Italy. But even after the Kingdom of Italy was created in 1861, Piedmont remained very different from the rest of the country.

1. See pp. 300–307.

In material wealth and development it forged far ahead of Lombardy, Tuscany, the Papal States, or Naples. Whereas Piedmont had some 850 kilometres of railroads connecting the main towns of Genoa, Turin, Alessandria, and Milan, Lombardy had only 200, Tuscany 300, and Naples hardly any. Standards of living and literacy varied greatly. Traditions of separatism and local peculiarities, even of language, remained very strong. The contrast between north and south, accentuated in the 1860s by the exclusion of Rome from the kingdom and for many decades to come by the mere geographical shape of the peninsula, was a contrast between two vastly different ways of life. By 1870, when geographical assimilation was completed by the inclusion of Rome, the short-term effects of political integration had been to cause dislocation and confusion in economic and social life.

The necessary solvents of separatism – a common legal code, a new administrative and educational system, greater economic development – were all long-term remedies. Italy needed two or three generations in which to grow together, before political unification could be reinforced by a more substantial assimilation of economic life and social habits. Meanwhile a disruptive mood of disillusionment set in. Unity had been expected to lighten the burdens of taxation, but in fact it increased them. Political unification was itself expensive because it involved wars. Schemes for administrative and educational reform and capital development made slow progress because the kingdom was chronically short of money. The country had not yet developed the industries needed to sustain the costly equipment of a 'great power' in military and naval establishments. Because Italy was poor in natural supplies of coal and iron, her industrial growth was slow. It was fatally easy for her to overstrain her resources.

These economic difficulties had important effects on the working of the new constitution. The Piedmontese parliamentary constitution, which was adapted to the needs of the new kingdom after 1861, was modelled partly on the French Constitution of 1830 and partly on the English constitution as it existed after 1832. The electorate, determined by property qualifications, was only some 150,000 out of a population of more than twenty million. Widespread illiteracy, strong local patriotism and factions, a weak party system, all threw grit into the works of parliamentary government. Parliamentary groups took shape on a local rather than an ideological basis, and many of them were jealously anti-Piedmontese in sentiment. Governments were unstable and weak. Politics were too often corrupt.

In the 1860s war had to be waged in the south, between the national forces (mostly Piedmontese) and so-called 'brigands', en-

THE REMAKING OF CENTRAL EUROPE

couraged by the former king of Naples, Francis II, from his exile in
the Papal States. It was a civil war, fought with savagery on both sides
and devastating in its effects. For some fifty years to come the south was
reduced to a sullen acquiescence in unification. It was inspired with
little positive enthusiasm for partnership in the new kingdom. Turin,
too far north to be thought of as a real national capital, served only to
isolate parliament from the rest of the country, to the great disadvantage
of both. The double move of the capital, from Turin to Florence in 1865
and to Rome in 1871, dislocated the administrative system. For all these
reasons the new Italy took a very long time to settle down.

If the effects of a decade of strain could have been mainly confined
to the years 1861–71, all might have been well. Venetia was added to the
kingdom in 1866, Rome in 1870. This piecemeal accretion of territories
might even have had some advantage in easing their gradual assimilation
had it been achieved peacefully. But since each acquisition involved war,
and Italy had to be perpetually on the alert and in a state of preparation for war, they were won at excessive cost. Lavish expenditure on
a large conscript army, a new navy of ironclads, great arsenals and naval
bases, in strenuous efforts to live up to her new status as a 'great
power', had to take place before the country was able to afford such
extravagances. Heavy taxation and lavish loans mounted up into a
ruinous national debt that carried forward great financial difficulties
into the years after 1871. Immense annual budget deficits became a
habit. In 1866 more than 2,300 monasteries and convents were suppressed
and their property confiscated, but like all such historical 'windfalls'
this did little to restore national solvency. That even geographical and
political unification took a whole decade, and involved the country in
four wars and in recurrent civil war, meant that the cost of formal unity
was itself almost ruinous.

The diplomatic and international aspirations of Italy went on over-
reaching her material resources, putting severe strains upon both her
economy and her parliamentary system. The prolonged period of uncertainty and excitement made virtually impossible the growth of settled parliamentary government. Despite the welcome given to the new
Italy by liberal opinion throughout Europe, the methods by which it
came into being left fresh sources of bitterness, grievance, and disturbance in central Europe. When the *Risorgimento* reached its culmination
in November 1871 with the opening of the new Italian parliament in
Rome it was a full half century old. It had attracted heroic self-sacrifice
and boundless enthusiasm. It had triumphed partly because of amazing
pertinacity and dauntless courage. But it had also triumphed because of
war and deceit, by a policy modelled on Machiavelli's combination of

force and fraud. Its triumph was bitter-sweet, and its nemesis fifty years later was to be the inflated bombast of fascism.

Unification in Germany. The process of German unification was equally protracted, equally identified with Machiavellian diplomacy and war, equally centred on the leadership of one state, Prussia. But there was one highly significant difference – the economic resources, industrial development, and financial strength of Prussia and of other German territories were much more adequate to sustain the equipment of a great European power. Germany could underpin political unification with a solid foundation of economic expansion. In 1850, whereas Italy had only 400 kilometres of railroad open to traffic, Germany as a whole had 6,000 – a length that Italy attained only by 1870; and Prussian territories already had about the same lengths as in France. This enabled Germany, even by 1860, to exploit her great mineral resources of coal and lignite to a point where her annual output exceeded that of France or Belgium; and between 1860 and 1870 her output of iron increased even more rapidly. The development of both the railroads and the heavy industries was carried out mainly by private capital in Prussia, mainly by state help in other German states. But the Prussian government fully appreciated their military uses. It encouraged the building of strategic railroads by guarantees of interest and similar methods. Military strategy, guided by Moltke, was devised to take full advantage of the new speed with which troops and supplies could be moved. The manufacture of heavy artillery, which this industrial revolution was making possible, transformed field warfare. The needs of the army were never neglected in the policy of the Prussian state.

Prussia was not, like Piedmont, handicapped by shortage of capital; nor was Germany during her years of semi-unification between 1866 and 1871. The Prussian Bank, a joint-stock organization with privately held capital but under state control and direction, had existed since 1847. After the unification of Germany it was to become the Imperial Bank of Germany. Meanwhile other large joint-stock banks, with power to issue notes, had been set up in Cologne, Magdeburg, Danzig, Königsberg, and Posen in Prussian territories; and most other German states developed banks with the authority not only to issue notes but also to promote companies and business enterprises. By 1871 there were thirty-three German banks with the right to issue notes; twenty-five had come into existence after 1850. This rapid and lively growth of a banking system, loosely jointed though it was, played a vital part in mobilizing capital for investment in business and industry; and after 1871 the domination of the Reichsbank welded German banks into a formidable financial power. The growth of population, its drift into the towns, and the decline of rural industries, all provided the mobile sources of labour needed for industrial expansion. The whole fabric of German economic life was better suited than the Italian to absorbing without dislocation the shocks and jars of an industrial revolution and the changes made necessary by political unification.

Even so, there remained considerable disparity between the pace of economic development in Prussia and that in other parts of Germany, though it was less sharp and coincided less with geographical divisions than was the contrast between northern and southern Italy. German states varied considerably in the speed with which, after 1850, they revised the old relationships between peasant and landlord. By 1870 Prussia had largely completed the process of freeing peasants from legal obligations to the landlord in return for their tenure of land, although the manor remained as an administrative unit until near the end of the century. Bavarian peasants were not fully emancipated until a genera·tion later. But though moving at different paces it was broadly true that all were moving in the same direction.

The Zollverein had knitted German trade more closely together. During the 1860s various all-German associations were formed to push this trend of economic unification still further. After 1858 a congress of German economists agitated for free trade, a unified system of coinage, cooperative organizations. In 1861 this body organized a national chamber of commerce (Deutscher Handelstag). Jurists followed suit, working for a unified legal system for all German states. At a political level, the Deutscher Nationalverein of 1859 sought to unite liberals and democrats of all states into a national movement behind Prussian leadership. It was supported, like the older liberal-democratic movement of 1848, by middle-class and professional men, government officials and intellectuals. But it was also supported by the important financiers and industrialists – men like Werner Siemens, who since 1847 had been busy constructing telegraph systems and in 1866 invented the electric dynamo; men like Heinrich Hermann Meier, who in 1857 had founded the North German Lloyd shipping company of Bremen. The growing class of entrepreneurs gave to this new drive for national unification a social backing that previous movements had lacked.

Without the rapid economic development of these decades German nationalism would have been a much weaker force. It would, no doubt have triumphed in any case, since political unification was the work of King William and his great minister Bismarck, and the result of a series of diplomatic and military victories won by the genius of Bismarck and the might of the Prussian army. But as a movement it would have drawn less support, in a critical period, from the most progressive sections of public opinion throughout Germany.

Like Italian unification, German unity was brought about by a sequence of diplomatic manoeuvres and wars: by a skilful exploitation of the disposition of forces in Europe which enabled the Prussian army to fight three successive wars against isolated enemies -- Denmark in 1864, Austria in 1866, France in 1870. Each victory was speedy and decisive; each was accompanied by a further step toward geographical unity and the political ascendancy of Prussia. Just as King Victor Emmanuel II of Piedmont became king of Italy in 1861, King William I of Prussia was declared German Emperor in 1871. The political reshaping of central Europe was pre-eminently the work of two states, Piedmont and Prussia, and of two men, Cavour and Bismarck. But the historical significance of these achievements is distorted if they are considered only as political, diplomatic, and military events - the successful results of deliberate man-made policies implemented by two statesmen of undoubted political genius. They were also a consequence of the changing structure of economic and social life in central Europe. They drew strength from the natural desires of the growing class of liberal-minded entrepreneurs which, like its counterparts in Britain, France, and Belgium in earlier decades, wanted to throw off the legal and administrative arrangements of an old-fashioned order, open up new supplies of free labour and larger free-trade markets, and claim political power through more liberal and democratic parliamentary institutions.

Cavour and Bismarck were above all exponents of *Realpolitik* - the view that government and state policy are matters divorced from moral considerations, to be dictated only by the necessities of power and judged only by success. 'Reasons of state' in their eyes justified any means, provided only that these means yielded the results intended. In later years European and British liberals were to oppose this conception of politics and, like Gladstone, condemn the calculated use of violence to achieve national ends. But the special characteristic of the years between 1850 and 1870 was a close alliance between liberalism and militarism. In 1848 liberalism was already in close alliance with nationalism.[1] The failures of that alliance in 1848-9 bred disillusionment and brought to most of Europe a period of conservatism. At the same time the development of science and technology fostered a mood of realism and even materialism.

Liberal movements in Europe changed in tune with these shifts of mood. Benefits both economic and constitutional which, in 1848, liberals had looked for only from more democratic republics and representative

1. See p. 232.

parliamentary systems, they were now more willing to receive from the hands of kings and their ministers, from diplomatic *coups* and victorious generals. Armies were no longer regarded as the enemy of liberals and nationalists, used chiefly to crush revolutions, but as the agencies of national unification at the expense of foreign powers. Until 1871 support for Prussian leadership in Germany and for Bismarck's policy of 'blood and iron' came from liberals and progressives, from people who favoured parliamentary government, constitutional liberties, freedom of conscience and thought, broader educational opportunities, and scientific and industrial progress.

This new alignment was of far-reaching importance. The chief opposition to the national unification of Germany, as of Italy, came from people who favoured more authoritarian or absolutist government, conservatism, clericalism, traditionalism, and aristocracy. The southern German states held out longest against absorption into a Prussian-dominated Reich partly because of their particularist and conservative traditions, partly because of their Catholicism. What changed European liberalism from the romantic, idealistic, democratic movement of 1848 into the realistic, unscrupulous, opportunist movement of these two decades was more than simple disillusionment after the revolutionary failures of 1848–9. It was the growth, in central Europe, of enterprising businessmen; it was the demonstration given to these men, in the financial crises of 1857 and 1866, that industrialism brought economic loss and insecurity of a kind which only bigger, stronger states could help to overcome;[1] it was the living example of the rapid material progress made by Britain and France and Belgium, countries that enjoyed a degree of political unity hitherto unknown in central Europe. The renewed desire of liberals for substantial national solidarity was not unconnected with the anxiety of bankers and businessmen to enjoy the same political advantages and rights as their rivals in western Europe.

If cautious constitutionalists like Cavour and authoritarian conservatives like Bismarck welcomed this alliance of liberal movements, it was likewise because, in the preceding age of revolutions, liberals had shown themselves resolute opponents of radical revolts and popular risings; because they needed the active support of the new business classes in order to overcome the forces of reactionary separatism; because eventual domination of the new kingdoms by states such as Piedmont and Prussia would be sufficient guarantee against any revolutionary excesses. They had learned from Napoleon III the lesson of how readily republican and democratic enthusiasm could be diverted into support for an authoritarian and militaristic régime by skilful timing of demagogic

1. See p. 252.

gestures and popular plebiscites; and until 1870 there was no comparable evidence of how disastrously, in later nineteenth-century conditions, such adventures could end.

Between 1850 and 1870 a statecraft of cunning realism was the fashion, and it apparently brought very rich rewards. Nothing is more characteristic of Italian unification than the series of plebiscites by which successive territories were transferred after diplomatic agreement or conquest: Savoy and Nice to France in 1860; Tuscany, the Marches and Umbria, Naples and Sicily, to Italy in 1860; Rome to Italy in 1870. Bismarck, equally characteristically, dispensed with the formalities of plebiscites but utilized the device of the North German Confederation of 1867 to consolidate Prussian hegemony in the north, after he had expelled Austria by his victory of 1866. Federalism, like plebiscites, could become a device of autocrats for preserving their power. What neither Italy nor Germany could acquire was a satisfactory parliamentary system within which parties cooperated effectively to produce stable government. Government had to be conducted in spite of, and not through, parliamentary institutions and procedures. In the end, national unity was won at the expense of liberalism.

Dualism in Austria-Hungary. The place of economic changes in the reshaping of central Europe can be further defined by asking: Why was there no comparable movement for national unification in Austria-Hungary? Where is the missing 'third man', to place alongside Cavour and Bismarck? By 1852 the Austrian Empire, guided by Schwarzenberg, had apparently gained strong ascendancy over Prussia as a power in Germany.[1] In the same month as Louis Napoleon's *coup d'état* in France (December 1851) the Emperor Francis Joseph had declared the liberal constitution of 1849 null and void, and replaced it with a series of regulations. These preserved the centralized authority and completed the destruction of local and provincial privileges, but they excluded provision for representative parliamentary institutions to control the central power. Henceforth the Habsburg government had an administrative machine as highly centralized as the French and a central government as autocratic as the Prussian. This remarkable organization, working through a host of local officials, administered the diverse lands of the Habsburgs, which comprised so many different races, nationalities, and languages. It sought to create a sense of common citizenship, akin to that of the United States, but without permitting any important local self-government or any regional and provincial loyalties. By 1859 this system had indeed produced some unity of sentiment throughout south-eastern Europe but it was a sentiment of common resistance to the cen-

1. See p. 241.

tral bureaucracy. The result was that in 1860, when the Council of State (Reichsrat) was enlarged to become more representative (though still not elected), two parties came into existence within it.

One, representing the Hungarian, Bohemian, and southern Slav interests, stood for a federalist programme that would restore greater freedom to these lands and by decentralization give to the landowning aristocracy its old role as intermediary between locality and centre. The other, representing Germanic interests, wanted to preserve a strong bureaucratic authority though it was willing to decentralize some power to new organs of local government. Neither party favoured liberalism or representative government; one thought in historic terms of 'estates of the realm' and the other in terms of autocracy. As a result of financial difficulties – the traditional dilemma of all autocracies since 1789 – the government drifted into a semi-parliamentary system without real social bases. In October, 1860, the Emperor Francis Joseph agreed to exercise his power of legislation only with the 'cooperation' of lawfully assembled diets in the Crown lands and of the central Reichsrat, which would consist of delegates from these diets. The new Reichsrat would control most matters of economic policy – coinage, credit, trade, communications, taxation, and the budget. The local diets would control all other matters. The arrangement satisfied neither party and still less the Hungarian gentry, the liberal middle classes of Vienna, or the Slav nationalists. It was especially strongly resisted by the Hungarian nationalists and liberals, led by Ferencz Deák. They constituted the only element in Austrian development at all comparable with the contemporary nationalist movements in the rest of central Europe; but they spoke for the gentry or squirearchy of the Hungarian countryside rather than for any truly industrial or commercial middle class. In 1850 the whole Habsburg territory had only half the mileage of railways that France had; and although the great Viennese development company, the *Kreditanstalt*, was founded in 1856, the country knew only localized industrial development in this period.

Under the pressure of separate nationalist demands from all the diverse component parts of the empire, both the Reichsrat and the Hungarian diet moved part way toward federal solutions of their political difficulties. Anton von Schmerling, the Viennese liberal who became Habsburg minister in 1860, induced the Transylvanians to send delegations to the Reichsrat. He persuaded neither the Hungarian diet as a whole nor the Croatian diet to follow suit. The Hungarian diet, pursuing a similarly divisive policy, won over the Croatians but neither the Serbs nor the Slovaks. The weakness of Hungarian nationalism was, throughout, that the Magyars were little more than a third of the population of Hungary; and that they were not prepared to concede to the other minorities of Serbs, Slovaks, and Rumanians within their own territories the nationalist claims that they themselves made against the Germans of Austria. This had bedevilled the Hungarian nationalist movement in the time of Kossuth.[1] It haunted it still. In 1867 the conflict between Magyar and German claims was conciliated by the institution of the Dual Monarchy. A complex bargain was struck, by which the Emperor Francis Joseph became simultaneously Emperor of Austria and King of Hungary. His territories were divided by the river Leitha, a minor tributary of the Danube, and there was legally complete equality between both sections. One, dominated by Germans, was ruled from Vienna; the other, dominated by Magyars, was ruled from Pesth. The two governments and systems of administration were separate and distinct as regards all domestic affairs. The Common Monarchy, acting for both the others as regards foreign policy, war, defence, and common finance, was in effect a third government. Within each kingdom the nationalist aspirations aroused among Czechs, Poles, and Slovaks, Croats, Serbs, and Rumanians, were sacrificed to the interest of preserving German and Magyar domination. Deák agreed to the bargain, and in 1868 the Hungarian diet passed a law designed to make nationality a purely individual and personal right, respected by the state in all matters that did not endanger state unity, but not a communal political right involving territorial independence. In the Austrian kingdom liberals hoped that the new parliamentary constitution, with guarantees of civil liberties, would similarly reconcile subject peoples to German domination.

This elaborate compromise clearly rested on an ingenious effort to evade the principles of national unification and independence which were coming to prevail in Italy and Germany. It was a synthetic substitute for nationalism, not an implementation of it. It consecrated political division and national disunity. From an imperial Habsburg point of view it was a masterpiece of conciliatory statecraft, devised to perpetuate the Austro-Hungarian Empire as a power unit in European politics, to postpone indefinitely the separatist hopes of subject peoples for independence, and to consolidate the joint predominance of Germans and Magyars over the dual kingdom. It represented the principle not of unification but of partition: partition of territory between German and Magyar, of political functions between the three governments, of nationality between its personal and its political aspects. It accepted and reaffirmed the view that the Austrian Empire was incapable of national unification in the sense that Italy and Germany were being unified. It

1. See p. 224.

may be condemned as leaving to the twentieth century a tangle of un-resolved problems, as merely papering over the cracks. Yet it lasted for half a century – a long spell on the time scale of modern historical change – and it gave Austria-Hungary a period of relative stability at a time when the rest of central and eastern Europe seethed with unrest. It was, moreover, realistic in that it accepted the undeniable fact that the economic and social development of this area could not yet support a homogeneous nation state. Ferencz Deák and Count Beust, who made the agreement on behalf of the Emperor establishing the Dual Monarchy, showed a spirit of realism worthy of Cavour or Bismarck. But their services were rendered to an ancient dynastic state and not to the cause of integral nationalism. The most highly developed, intransi-gent, and indigestible nationalistic movement, the Magyar, was taken into partnership; and together Germans and Magyars cooperated to hold in check for another generation the eruption of other nationalisms.

Unlike Austria-Hungary, the states of Italy and Germany could be built on homogeneity of language, on strong nationalistic cultural move-ments dating from the years of French revolutionary enthusiasm and Napoleonic government, and on the substantial beginnings of a real industrial and commercial revolution. These are perhaps the main foun-dations for the success of their movements toward national unification. But their political integration had to be engineered, with subtlety and skill, by purposeful men who were prepared to use every lever of diplo-matic intrigue and every instrument of force needed to attain their goals. It was an age of mechanized manufacture, and the nation-state, too, had to be manufactured in Italy and Germany. That process took over a decade, and inflicted upon Europe a series of major wars. It would be as misleading to regard the triumphs of nationalism in central Europe as the inevitable consequences of trends of European history, as it would be to see in them the isolated and individual achievements of two men of dominating genius. What mattered was the interplay of trends and policies, of inherent developments and deliberate design. States are the creation not of nature but of men; and Cavour and Bis-marck created not nations but states. It was these states which then, in turn, created the modern nations of Italy and Germany. They did so because they were designed to do so. The state constructed by Beust and Deák was designed to do the opposite. It also succeeded.

POLITICAL UNIFICATION IN ITALY AND GERMANY

Because the movements to create a united Italian kingdom and a united German empire occurred simultaneously, and made progress by manipulating the diplomatic situation in Europe between 1850 and 1870, their histories touch and overlap at many points. They sometimes wittingly, sometimes unintentionally, helped one another. Their leaders had to deal with a common enemy, Austria-Hungary; a common factor of power, France under the Second Empire of Napoleon III; a single religious force, the Roman Catholic Church. For these reasons their progress becomes intelligible only if the two stories are told interwoven and not separately. Together they form one great event, the total upheaval and political reshaping of central Europe north and south of the Alps. With their joint success in 1871 and its repercussions in France and Austria, the whole balance of power in Europe was fundamentally altered. A gulf was fixed between the continent of the previous eighty years and contemporary Europe of the subsequent eighty years.

Pact of Plombières, 1858. The first chapter of the story centres on the year 1858. In July of that year Napoleon III held an interview with Cavour at Plombières-les-Bains, and they sealed a bargain that came to be known as the Pact of Plombières. It involved three undertakings. First, the daughter of King Victor Emmanuel of Piedmont, the fifteen-year-old Princess Clotilde, would marry Jérôme, cousin of Napoleon III, in order to link together the two states by the old-fashioned dynastic bonds of marriage. Second, France and Piedmont would go to war against Austria. Third, in the settlement that would follow, Piedmont would gain Lombardy and Venetia, to be taken from Austria, and would form a new kingdom of Upper Italy linked with the duchies of Parma and Modena and the Papal Legations. In return, Piedmont would cede Nice and Savoy to France. It was one of the more cynical bargains of nineteenth-century history, and it took some time for the plotters to discover a suitable excuse for declaring war against Austria.

What prompted Cavour and Napoleon to make this remarkable agreement? Cavour had become convinced that the old slogan 'Italy will go it alone' (*Italia farà da sè*) was wrong. The immediate obstacle to northern Italian unity was Austria, which held the vital territories of Lombardy and Venetia. Austria had repeatedly made it clear – especially at the Congress of Paris in 1856 – that she could be made to give up these territories only by force. Piedmont alone could never hope to defeat Austria – Custozza and Novara had demonstrated that. So she needed an ally. Italian unification could make progress only with foreign help. There is little doubt that Cavour would have preferred British help; for Britain was, in general, sympathetic to the cause of liberal nationalism in Italy, and had no immediate demands to make of Italy in return. But British governments had repeatedly made it clear, too, that they would not help by military support. It was an axiom of Palmerston's foreign policy that the survival of the Austrian Empire was necessary for the maintenance, as between France and Russia, of the balance of power in Europe.[1] When in 1857 the archduke Maximilian became viceroy of Lombardy, his policy of leniency and conciliation was warmly approved by British diplomats at Vienna and Turin. Clearly, the most that Cavour could expect from Britain would be benevolent neutrality and an anxiety to avoid involvement in general war. He had engaged in the Crimean War as an ally of Britain and France, and had thereby won a place for his government at the council tables of Paris when the treaty was signed in 1856. His most likely ally was Napoleon III, who made much of his sympathies for the cause of Italian unification and showed a restless readiness to embark on foreign adventures in order to gain fresh prestige for his régime. Cavour, then, nursed hopes of help from France.

That it was forthcoming in 1858 was due to the internal politics of the Second Empire. In the Crimean War, Napoleon had tasted the fruits of popularity and prestige which could be derived from successful war. His natural liking for intrigue, and possibly a genuine ex-*Carbonaro* sympathy with Italian nationalist aspirations, turned his attentions toward Piedmont. A north Italian kingdom owing its very existence to French help would be a welcome and useful element on the diplomatic chessboard of Europe. To gain for France the territories of Nice and Savoy would awaken pleasing echoes of Napoleonic gains and reverse an unpopular provision of the Vienna settlement of 1815. Napoleon I had, even if unwittingly, done service to the cause of Italian unity;[2] it would fit well into the pattern of Bonapartist traditions, as evolved in the legends of St Helena and the earlier writings of Louis Napoleon himself, that the Second Empire should complete the work begun by the First. When the elections of 1857 in France returned only a weak opposition, Napoleon's confidence at home was renewed. He felt free to embark on fresh adventures abroad.

Early in 1858 French-Piedmontese relations suddenly deteriorated when Italian conspirators, led by Orsini, threw bombs at Napoleon and the Empress on their way to the opera. They were unhurt but many others were killed or wounded. The plotters had been supporters of Mazzini, though no support for the plot could be traced to Mazzini himself. Orsini, from prison, wrote to Napoleon urging France to free Italy. The government at Turin took immediate repressive action against the Mazzinians and passed a more severe Press law. Victor Emmanuel sent General Della Rocca to congratulate Napoleon on his escape, but

1. See p. 244.
2. See pp. 121 and 132.

the French minister's protests were so hostile that they evoked spirited replies from both Victor Emmanuel and Cavour. These replies, most unexpectedly, aroused the admiration of Napoleon and appear to have confirmed him in his resolve to encourage Italian unity. 'Now that is what I call courage,' he exclaimed, and he proceeded to publish Orsini's last letter appealing to him to support Italian freedom. Henceforth the scheme matured in negotiations between Napoleon and Cavour, conducted in the deepest secrecy and mystery, yet inevitably leading to rumour and shrewd guesswork in the chancelleries of Europe.

The first step in fulfilling the Pact of Plombières was the simplest to achieve; and in mid September 1858 little Clotilde agreed to meet Jérôme and promised 'if he is not actually repulsive to me I have decided to marry him'. He was not, and she did. The marriage advertised how close was to be the alliance between Piedmont and France. In January 1859 the Pact, hitherto only verbal, was embodied in a formal treaty between the two governments. Two months later Russia was won over by a treaty whereby Napoleon agreed to support revision of the Treaty of Paris of 1856 in return for Russian approval of changes in the settlement of 1815 in so far as it affected Italy. This cleared the field, and insured against Russian intervention. British intervention was taken to be unlikely because, although British distrust of Napoleon was becoming acute, popular sympathies lay with Italy. Prussia was expected to follow Britain in seeking mediation but to be not averse to seeing Austria humiliated; and events fully bore out this expectation.

Piedmont and Austria began to mobilize as the international tension of a war scare intensified. Cavour's diplomacy was geared to the simple aim of forcing Austria to issue an ultimatum at the right moment, so putting herself in the wrong with the other European powers. Mobilization in Piedmont, where it involved the calling up of reserves, created severe dislocation of civil life and inflated the diplomatic crisis. It was more than a precautionary measure, and by committing the government to a policy from which it could not retreat, came near to being a declaration of war. Napoleon, under severe political and diplomatic pressure, showed signs of backing down. By 18 April it even seemed that the concert of Europe was reviving enough to prevent an outbreak of war; and it might well have done so, for the next day Cavour agreed to demobilize. But the Emperor Francis Joseph at that very moment sent the long-awaited ultimatum and refused to demobilize. Cavour's policy of 'defensive provocation' unexpectedly triumphed, and war began with Austria as the technical aggressor. The treaty with France therefore held good.

Villafranca, 1859. After six weeks of fighting the Piedmontese and French forces won two pitched battles, at Magenta and Solferino, and drove the Austrians out of Lombardy. These were decisive victories and betokened the eventual defeat of Austria – unless other powers came to her aid. At this point the enigmatic Napoleon effected one of those incalculable about-turns of policy which were to end in his downfall. Prussia had begun to mobilize; and although Austria had no assurance that Prussia would help her against Piedmont, Napoleon became anxious. Both the French and Austrian governments, therefore, were inclined to make a quick peace. On 11 July Francis Joseph and Napoleon met and agreed to make peace on condition that only Lombardy be given up and that an Italian Confederation be formed under the presidency of the Pope. The rulers of Parma, Modena, and Tuscany, recently expelled by their subjects, would be reinstated. This treaty of Villafranca of 1859 came as a bolt out of the blue to Cavour, who regarded as total defeat any such arrangement that left Austria (as the government of Venetia) a member of an Italian confederation. He promptly resigned. Throughout France, Italy, and many other parts of Europe, Napoleon's betrayal of the nationalist cause in Italy stirred liberal sentiment as nothing else could have done. He had made a mistake that was inexcusable in a former *Carbonaro*: he underrated the passions of liberal nationalism.

In the Italy of 1859 it was impossible to play with the forces of nationalism, inflame them to a fever pitch of expectations, and then dash all hopes by so tortuous a policy. During the fighting the many nationalist groups of central Italy had sprung into action, expelling petty rulers and preparing for liberation. They could not now afford to stop, to allow 1859 to become a mere repetition of 1849; Villafranca made them desperate. In August constituent assemblies met in Parma, Modena, Tuscany, and the Romagna, and formed a military alliance with a common army. They wanted Victor Emmanuel as their king. By December the tergiversations of Napoleon led him to go back even on the terms of Villafranca, and he again began to support the Italian liberal nationalists. In January 1860 Cavour resumed office in Turin, bent upon utilizing this new turn of events to annex central Italy. The following month Napoleon agreed to new terms of the old bargain. Piedmont could have Parma and Modena, as well as Lombardy; but if it took Tuscany then France must get Nice and Savoy. Cavour agreed, regarding Tuscany as essential to the shaping of a solid north Italian kingdom. In March the central Italian states voted almost unanimously, by plebiscite, for union with Piedmont. Europe was presented with the accomplished fact of a new Italian kingdom which included all Italy except Venetia in the north, the Marches and Umbria and the Papal States in the centre, and the Kingdom of Naples and Sicily in the south. These exceptions were

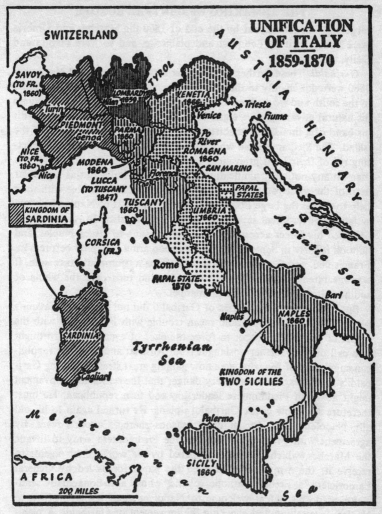

MAP 5. UNIFICATION OF ITALY, 1859–70
The core of Italian unification was the Kingdom of Piedmont and Sardinia. It gained Lombardy from the Austrian Empire at the Treaty of Villafranca in 1859. The following year Parma, Modena, and Tuscany were joined to it; Garibaldi conquered Sicily and Naples; and Cavour annexed to Piedmont all the remaining central states except Rome. When the first Italian parliament met at Turin in 1861, only Venetia and the Papal city of Rome remained unincorporated. These were added in 1866 and 1870, as a result of Bismarck's defeats of Austria and France. By 1871 Italy's political unification was complete.

large and important; but by the end of 1860 the Marches and Umbria were added to it by conquest and plebiscite, and so were Naples and Sicily. (See Map 5.)

Garibaldi. These further acquisitions between March and November 1860 were due mainly to the efforts of the veteran Garibaldi. He started in the south and worked northward – concentrating first on Sicily, where his natural advantages were greatest. In May he landed at Marsala with his band of a thousand red-shirts and proclaimed himself dictator of the island. The Sicilian people who rallied to him were more intent on getting rid of their local grievances and on shaking off the rule of Naples than on any notion of unification with northern Italy. But as a popular hero of the most romantic and glamorous kind, he was able with their help to defeat the large Bourbon army of Francis II of Naples, heir to a system of government sapped by decades of brutality. In August, Garibaldi led his forces across the straits of Messina to attack Naples, and he took it early in September. The Bourbon army collapsed before him, Francis fled, and Garibaldi's progress became a triumphal procession. It was his intention to march on to Rome and turn over the whole of southern Italy to King Victor Emmanuel.

But these dramatic victories of Garibaldi did not at all suit Cavour's plans. To attack Rome would mean trouble with France and with the whole of Catholic Europe; to force the pace of events too hard might also call down a further onslaught from Austria; and since the republican supporters of Mazzini were now gaining great strength among Garibaldi's followers, there was every danger that the nationalist movement might abandon Piedmontese leadership and turn republican. He must therefore somehow check Garibaldi's plans. He turned again to his old ally Napoleon, who for different reasons shared Cavour's fears. By agreement with France, Cavour sent the Piedmontese army to invade the Marches, which had been prepared by the work of his agents to receive it; the army then destroyed the papal forces led by General Lamoricière, a French Catholic royalist whose anti-Bonapartist sentiments made his defeat welcome to Napoleon; and it marched on to Naples, forestalling and checking the movement of Garibaldi. A plebiscite was held in Umbria and the Marches in October, and they were duly annexed to the Piedmontese monarchy in November. In the same month Victor Emmanuel and Cavour rode into Naples, similarly annexed after a popular plebiscite. Meanwhile Garibaldi, refusing all rewards, set sail humbly for his island home on Caprera. His intervention had been decisive, though it had served Cavour's cause more than his own. In January 1861 the first all-Italian parliament met in Turin, with only Venetia and the city of Rome itself still unconquered for

Italian unification. On 6 June Cavour died, dying (like Abraham Lincoln four years later) at the very moment when his survival seemed essential if his work were to be completed and true national unity preserved.

Prussia versus *Austria*. Meanwhile, north of the Alps, comparable movements for unification were gathering strength in Germany. In the month when the Italian parliament met and accepted Victor Emmanuel as king of all Italy, a new king, William I, came to the throne of Prussia. Since Frederick William became incapable of ruling in 1857, his brother William had acted as regent. Though deeply conservative and regarding kingship as a pious divine duty, he also believed in the national mission of Prussia to unify Germany. Nationalists and even liberals welcomed his accession. The situation that confronted him in Prussia and in the German *Bund* had been greatly transformed by the activities of Napoleon and Cavour, and especially by their war of 1859 against Austria and their erection of a new Italian kingdom. The significant decision in Prussian policy had been her refusal to come to Austria's aid in the war of 1859, despite their mutual obligations as members of the German *Bund*. Her motives had been to assert Prussia's role as an independent great power, to play a diplomatic hand as free as Britain's or Russia's, to stay in reserve as a possible mediator of the dispute.

With this aim in mind she resisted, within the Diet of the *Bund* at Frankfurt (*Bundestag*), the scheme sponsored by Bavaria and Austria to appoint a confederate commander in chief to hold office for five years, and alternating between Prussia and Austria. Prussia proposed, instead, a dual system in time of peace, which would place two northern confederate army corps under Prussian control and two southern army corps under Austrian control. In this way the Prussian government backed not the unification but the partition of Germany, for its scheme would have left southern Germany under Austrian political influence as well as under her military supervision. It was, indeed, a scheme for northern German unification parallel with Cavour's initial plans for a kingdom of Northern Italy headed by Piedmont. Both movements began with schemes for partial, not total, unification.

This conflict of view about the organization of the German army was of little importance for its military consequences (the military strength of the smaller states was slender anyhow compared with that of either Prussia or Austria); but it was of great significance for its political implications. It raised the whole issue of Prussia's place in Germany. The defeats of the Austrian troops at Magenta and Solferino in 1859 brought Prussia a relative gain in prestige. Her own decision to mobilize during the war had, moreover, proved a powerful factor in Napoleon's calculations when he made the peace of Villafranca; though otherwise Prussia had no say in the creation of the new Italy of 1861. In July 1861, Otto von Bismarck prepared his famous Baden memorandum on the defence and organization of Germany. He argued that because stability in central and eastern Europe had been destroyed by the breakdown of the Holy Alliance, Prussia now had special responsibilities for the defence of Germany as a whole. These could be exercised only through a body representative of all Germany, in which Prussia would have hegemony. Austria must be excluded, and Germany divided at the river Inn. When the dispute about army reform reached a deadlock soon after William came to the throne in 1861, it was to Bismarck that he turned. The elections of 1862 gave the Liberal opposition a large majority in the lower house of the Prussian parliament. In order to press their opposite view of army reform, they refused to pass the budget. In September, William called in Bismarck as chief minister and foreign minister, with the special task of defying the Liberals and the lower house. At his first meeting with the budget committee Bismarck issued his most famous warning: 'the great questions of the day will not be decided by speeches and the resolutions of majorities – that was the blunder of 1848 and 1849 – but by blood and iron.' He had ample opportunity to make this prophecy come true, for he was to control Prussian policy without interruption for the next twenty-seven years.

Bismarck. This man, who ranks among the greatest heroes of German history and among the most important statesmen of the modern world, assumed power at the age of forty-seven with slender experience of political affairs, but a decade's experience of German and European diplomacy. He had been born in the fateful year 1815, in the Protestant *Junker* estate of Schönhausen in Brandenburg, just east of the Elbe. A massive man of stiff military bearing, he had a quick, sensitive mind, great personal charm, acute intelligence, and indomitable will power. He was by nature passionate and volcanic, a man of action. Though born into a family of landowning gentry and apt to make the most of his *Junker* affinities, Bismarck was in fact brought up in Berlin in contact with the Hohenzollern court. He had a short career in the civil service, then eight years of work as a somewhat unsuccessful rural landowner, and at the age of thirty seemed to be a failure. He was saved from frustration only by happy marriage and family life; and in 1847 he became a member of the Prussian Diet in Berlin. There he opposed every liberal proposal and made a name for himself as a determined reactionary. Inevitably he deplored the events of 1848, welcomed the end of the Frankfurt Assembly, the defeat of the Erfurt Union of 1850, and the restoration of the old Bund. His concern, first and foremost, was with the national interests of the Prussian state. As Prussian representative to the German Bundestag at Frankfurt he learned the arts of diplomacy which he was later to use with such devastating effect. By the time he took over the government of Prussia in 1862 he was convinced that Prussian foreign policy must have two guiding principles: alliance with France and Russia, and a decisive showdown with Austria. These ideas governed his initial policy.

His first duty was to defeat the Liberal majority in the Prussian parliament. This involved him in a four-year battle that revealed his qualities of ruthless persistence and strength of purpose. When parliament refused to vote the proposed taxes, the government collected them anyhow. The struggle showed how shallow were the roots of constitutionalism in Prussia, for a docile population paid taxes to the officials of the state bureaucracy despite their illegal basis. Lack of parliamentary consent meant nothing against royal authority. The taxes were used to enlarge, re-equip, and reorganize the army. There was a case for a larger military establishment, if Prussia was to live up to her status as a 'great power' and to live down the diplomatic humiliations of recent years – the same case as there was for the new kingdom of Italy to spend lavishly on armaments. Since 1815 the population of Prussia had grown from eleven million to eighteen, but the army had not been correspondingly enlarged. It was ominous, for the future of parliamentary liberalism in Prussia, that this was now done only by violating the constitution. Bismarck had no hesitation in violating it, for he despised liberalism and parliamentary assemblies, and believed in order, service, and duty. He was satisfied that by 1866 Prussia would be strong enough to challenge Austria. Meanwhile he set the diplomatic stage for that challenge, as well as trying out his new army, by his skilful manipulation of the dispute between Germany and Denmark about the old question of control over the two duchies of Schleswig and Holstein.

The issue had arisen in 1848 and been settled for the time being by the Treaty of London in 1852. The two duchies had then been included among the dominions of the Danish king, though Holstein was left as a member of the German Bund.[1] (See Map 6.) What revived the dispute in 1863 was a disputed succession to the Danish throne and the desire of the Danes to incorporate Schleswig, which had a large Danish population. The old king died in November 1863 and in accordance with the agreement of 1852 he was succeeded by Prince Christian of Glücksburg. The new king, following the policy of his predecessor, tried to change the administration of the duchies and virtually to annex Schleswig. This immediately met with a nationalistic outcry from the Bundestag of Frankfurt on behalf of Germany. Why, they asked, should the

1. See p. 242.

THE **GERMAN QUESTION**, 1815-1871

North Sea

Baltic Sea

SCHLESWIG

HOLSTEIN

Hamburg

MECKLEN-BURG

EAST PRUSSIA

P R U S S I A

POSEN

Berlin

Vistula R.

WESER

THURINGIA

NASSAU

Frankfurt

(1o Bar.)

BOHEMIA

Cracow

MORAVIA

WÜR-EMBERG

BAVARIA

AUSTRIAN

Vienna

AUSTRIA

EMPIRE

Budapest

TYROL

German
Confederation,
1815-1866
Prussia, 1815-1866
Annexed to
Prussia, 1866
Joined with Prussia in
North German Confederation, 1867
South German States joined in
German Empire, 1871
Alsace-Lorraine, ceded by France
to German Empire, 1871
Austrian dominions excluded
from German Confederation, 1866

Adriatic Sea

**BISMARCK'S
GERMAN EMPIRE
1871**

100 MILES

MAP 6.   THE GERMAN QUESTION, 1815–71

The Confederation (Bund) of 1815 set up only a loose framework within which Austria predominated. But the enhancement of the power of Prussia marked her out as Austria's chief rival. Attempts at unification in 1848–9 came to nothing (see Chapter 11), and until 1866 Germany was divided into thirty-eight states of which only the largest are shown. In 1866 Bismarck began three stages of unification. First, he conquered for Prussia the areas of Schleswig, Holstein, and Hanover, and in 1867 took Mecklenberg, Saxony, Darmstadt, etc., into the Prussian-dominated North German Confederation. Secondly, in 1870–1 he absorbed Bavaria, Baden, Württemberg, and other southern states, and seized Alsace and Lorraine from France. Finally, in 1871 he excluded Austria from the German Reich and established the German frontiers as they were to remain until 1918.

German minority in southern Schleswig be annexed to a foreign power, and permanently lost to the German fatherland? A rival to the Danish throne, Frederick of Augustenburg, who like the Bundestag had never accepted the Treaty of London, lent himself to German intervention. The Bundestag decided to back him and go to war.

Bismarck wanted such a war, but he wanted it to be waged by Prussia and Austria in alliance, not by the whole German Bund. He saw that for Prussia to make a successful war against Denmark in 1864 would serve some of the same purposes as Cavour's timely entry into the Crimean War: it would indicate future leadership, and would raise Prussia's prestige. To act jointly with Austria was both inevitable and desirable; inevitable, because Austria would never agree to let Prussia act alone, and he was not yet ready to defy her; desirable, because any Prussian-Austrian settlement of so thorny a problem would leave ample room for picking a quarrel with Austria later whenever he chose. Bismarck hastily made an alliance with Austria in February 1864, sent a joint Prussian-Austrian army against Denmark, and claimed that it was acting as the agent of the Bund. Denmark was quickly defeated, and in October, 1864, the three powers signed the Treaty of Vienna. The Danish king 'renounced all his rights over the Duchies of Schleswig and Holstein in favour of their Majesties the King of Prussia and the Emperor of Austria'. The claims both of the Bund and of Frederick were completely ignored. Henceforth Prussia, unlike Piedmont, could 'go it alone'.

What were the attitudes of the other three great powers to this open defiance of the principles of a balance of power and the 'concert of Europe' which had, as recently as 1856, been at least partially reasserted?[1] They were directly concerned, because the Treaty of London in 1852 had been signed by all five great powers, as well as by Denmark and Sweden; and they were materially affected because Prussian and Austrian action had forced a small state to surrender territories that were generally regarded as a likely source of international dispute. But each of the three, for different reasons, was inhibited from taking any action. In Britain, Lord Palmerston blustered, but found Queen Victoria, a majority of his cabinet, and the opposition, all against any specific action. Napoleon III had himself, only five years before, connived at a similar defiance of the concert of Europe when he joined with Piedmont to attack Austria; he was by 1864 on bad terms with Britain and faced with growing opposition at home; and since 1861 he had become more and more deeply embroiled in the difficult entanglement of the Mexican expedition, which committed French troops to trying to keep Maximilian, brother of the Austrian emperor Francis Joseph, on the throne

1. See p. 245.

of Mexico. He was at that moment in neither the mood nor the position to exert pressure on Austria and Prussia. Russia exercised no restraining influence because Bismarck had taken the precaution of ensuring her friendly neutrality. Only the year before he had assured Alexander II or support against the Polish insurrection, which had threatened to attract British and French sympathies against Russia. Alexander, grateful for Bismarck's backing against the Poles, was now willing enough to reciprocate as regards the Danes. The new kingdom of Italy, though ranking as a 'great power', had neither the prestige nor the inclination to engage herself against Prussia and Austria together. Bismarck had timed his actions with great insight and skill.

The two duchies were jointly occupied by Prussia and Austria. By the Convention of Gastein in August 1865, Prussia took Schleswig to administer, Austria took Holstein to administer, but the future fate of the duchies remained a joint responsibility. This degree of partition left the partnership most uneasy, and Bismarck knew that his only problem was to time and stage the next war, the German civil war against Austria, as well as he had staged his first. He made overtures of friendship to both Italy and France. In return for Italian promises of help against Austria he promised that Prussia would not make peace until Italy had secured Venetia. In October 1865 he visited Napoleon at Biarritz and contrived to charm him into friendship. British inertia and Russia friendship would, Bismarck assumed, keep them out of action again, as in 1864. Difficulties at home, from an increasingly active liberal opposition, he removed for the time being by proroguing and dismissing parliament. There is no doubt that Bismarck, backed by Moltke and Roon in charge of the Prussian army, wanted and planned for war against Austria as the next step in Prussian domination of Germany. Bismarck might have preferred to gain his ends without war, but he came to regard war as indispensable. Despite the complexities of the Schleswig-Holstein question, it was only a pretext for the war; despite the strenuous diplomatic manoeuvres throughout Europe in 1865 and 1866, and the series of proposals to preserve peace, neither had any chance of preventing Prussia from attacking Austria whenever she chose. In June 1866 Napoleon agreed with Austria that he would keep France neutral and if possible Italy too; and in return Austria promised to hand Venetia over to Italy after the war, whatever its outcome. Napoleon hoped, in his cloudy way, that the two belligerents might be so equally matched that the struggle would be long and France might step in as the decisive force, exacting whatever gains she could from both. But just as he had underrated the passions of Italian nationalism at Villafranca, so he now underrated the power of Prussian militarism.

In June 1866 Prussia forced the issue by proposing that the Bundestag at Frankfurt should be dissolved and the German Bund abolished; she proposed the election of a special German assembly to draft a new constitution excluding Austria and all Austrian lands. Austria retaliated by accusing Prussia of breaking both the Treaty of Vienna and the Convention of Gastein, and demanding mobilization of the federal German forces against her. Austria was supported by nine out of the fifteen states, including Hanover, Saxony, Baden, and Bavaria. Prussia was therefore faced with scattered west German armies, which she could prevent from combining, and with the main Austrian army in Bohemia. War began on 14 June. After only three weeks it resulted in the defeat of Austria and her German allies. On 3 July the decisive battle was fought at Sadowa (or Königgrätz), where the main Austrian army was beaten. In Lombardy strong Austrian forces, pinned south of the Alps by the alliance of Italy with Prussia, defeated the Italians on the old battlefield of Custozza. The Italian fleet was also defeated at the battle of Lissa. These reverses of his Italian allies were especially embarrassing to Bismarck. As in 1864 his great anxiety, as soon as he had attained his aims, was to bring the war to a speedy end. He had to prevent it from spreading, and forestall any danger that a concert of powers might intervene to demand a share in the settlement. Even generous terms for Austria were preferable to that.

In August, Bismarck forced the Prussian king to conclude the Treaty of Prague with Austria. He had all he wanted: the power to expel Austria from German affairs. The treaty arranged for a new federal constitution to be set up for Germany north of the Main, alongside an association of southern German states 'with an independent international existence'. Prussia got Schleswig and Holstein, subject to northern Schleswig's being returned to Denmark if so decided by plebiscite. Bismarck saw to it that this proviso never applied because no plebiscite was held, and Prussia kept the territories until 1919. Austria undertook to claim no further share in the organization of Germany. She was obliged to hand Venetia over to Napoleon, as she had previously promised France; and Napoleon, preening himself on at least this opportunity to appear as a mediator, duly handed it on to Italy. He won no gratitude from Italy, only indignation. At least Italy had done some fighting for it – if not very successfully – and it was Prussia which had promised it to her.

The war had achieved no less and – equally important for Bismarck – no more than he had intended. The excellent organization of the Prussian army, the new needle gun with which it was equipped, the clockwork precision of the campaign, had combined to serve perfectly his diplomatic and political aims. The Austro-Prussian War was a landmark in the history of several states. It was a sharp blow to French power and to Napoleon's prestige, and brought nearer the fall of the Second Empire. It completed the north Italian kingdom and brought Italian unification one step closer. It helped to bring about the Dual Monarchy of Austria-Hungary in 1867. None of these consequences embarrassed Bismarck. The pieces on the European chessboard remained as he wanted them.

Franco-Prussian War, 1870. Meanwhile Bismarck had been busy, even before the Treaty of Prague was signed, staging the next series of diplomatic manoeuvres which would complete the political unification of Germany under Prussia. He signed treaties with Bavaria and other southern states that opened them to Prussian influence. Napoleon III, searching as ever for the basis of a bargain which would bring him prestige, proposed that he might accept Prussian gains if in return he could advance French territories to the Rhine in the direction of Mainz. Bismarck did not at once reject these proposals. He induced the French ambassador, Benedetti, to state the proposals formally, got the Prussian king to reject them in righteous horror, and then published them to the world. Napoleon pursued similar suggestions for the French annexation of Belgium with Prussian connivance. Bismarck made certain that these, too, were put into writing and then kept them by him until 1870, publishing them at a moment when they served to scare Britain and Belgium into anti-French policies.

These unscrupulous tactics succeeded because French opinion regarded Sadowa as a French defeat, and because Napoleon was seeking feverishly for some form of 'compensation' for the great gains made by Prussia, and for the final collapse of his ill-fated expedition to Mexico. In the older conceptions of a balance of power such compensation was reasonable and conventional. In the new world of *Realpolitik* there were no grounds for expecting compensation except at the point of the bayonet. Napoleon, now an ill and failing man, was already old-fashioned and out-of-date in his grasp of the European scene. Bismarck was effecting a revolution in the whole balance of power – that Napoleon understood. But in thinking that the balance could be redressed by diplomatic bargaining instead of by superior force, he was profoundly mistaken.

Bismarck had no such delusions, and proceeded to digest his latest territorial gains in preparation for defiance of France and the final incorporation of the southern German states. By July 1867 the projected North German Confederation was equipped with its constitution. Hanover, Nassau, Frankfurt, and the Electorate of Hesse, having been defeated in battle, were annexed to Prussia. The other north German states

– Brunswick, Anhalt, Oldenburg, and the rest – were included in a federal structure that was designed to make the subsequent inclusion of the southern states easy, yet to ensure the actual domination of Prussia throughout the whole of Germany. The result was a curious hybrid constitution, of importance because it was later adapted to the needs of the German Empire in 1871.

The hereditary head of the new Confederation was the King of Prussia. His chief minister was the Chancellor, through whom he appointed and controlled all other ministers and officials. The Chancellor was appointed by the King, but all other ministers were subordinate to the Chancellor. The federal council representing the different states (Bundesrat) represented not their peoples but their governments; and representation was weighted according to a schedule laid down in the constitution. Whereas no other state had more than four votes, Prussia had seventeen. This gave her automatic predominance in the Bundesrat. As might be expected, the Bundesrat was accorded more decisive powers than was the other federal assembly, the Diet of the Confederation (Reichstag), which was 'elected by universal and direct election with secret voting', as in 1849. As Chancellor of the Confederation, Bismarck now virtually governed the whole of Germany north of the river Main. He exercised very direct influence over the affairs of most of the southern states as well. He was in an immensely stronger position to grapple with the obstacle that he regarded as still his most formidable – France. Inside Prussia new elections brought large conservative gains and liberal losses. Bismarck was emerging as the national hero of Germany – the invincible champion whom it was more than ever unpopular to oppose even within Prussia. Nationalism gained, but the cause of liberalism and of parliamentary institutions had suffered loss.

From 1866 onwards relations between France and Germany remained tense. Napoleon, and behind him an aggrieved national opinion, nursed bitter jealousies of Prussia's gains, mingled with fears of further upheavals in the European balance of power. The 'concert of Europe' had become so threadbare and discredited a conception that no pacification or settlement seemed possible. There existed no international organization for promoting a peaceful settlement of disputes and, as always in such conditions, there began feverish competition in preparedness for war. Across the Rhine, German opinion, too, alerted by Bismarck's clever use of Napoleon's indiscretions, was coming to look upon France as a sworn enemy and an obstacle to further national unification. For a time in 1870 things seemed to have quietened down. The international situation had remained long enough unchanged, after the torrent of changes between 1859 and 1866, for it to seem almost stabilized. The violent dispute between France and Germany about the succession to the Spanish throne, which suddenly blew up in July 1870, came all the more as a rude shock to the chancelleries of Europe – always except to that of Prussia, which was quick to take full advantage of it. It seems certain, indeed, that Bismarck engineered the dispute by supporting the Hohenzollern candidate for the Spanish crown.

Again, the technical details of the dispute mattered little, because it became hardly more than a pretext for war. As already shown,[1] the instability of Spanish politics was closely connected with the character of the Spanish queen, Isabella. She fled into exile in September 1869, and by the summer of 1870 the question of her successor was still unsettled. Prince Leopold of Hohenzollern-Sigmaringen was among those considered. He was related to the king of Prussia, who was head of the Hohenzollern family. Because it was expected that Leopold's accession in Spain would bring still further gains both in prestige and in material benefit to Prussia, it was welcomed in Prussia and equally warmly opposed in France. France feared encirclement, should Hohenzollerns rule on both the Rhine and the Pyrenees.

On 6 July the French Foreign Minister announced that unless the Hohenzollern candidate were withdrawn, France would treat the matter as a cause for war. On 9 July Benedetti, the French ambassador to Prussia, had four interviews about it with the King. On 12 July Prince Leopold, under diplomatic pressure and not reluctant to back down from so insecure a career as that of a Spanish monarch, withdrew his candidature. In France this was greeted with exultation, as a great diplomatic victory over Prussia and as 'revenge for Sadowa'. The French government decided immediately to press their advantage and to demand from Prussia guarantees that the candidature would not be renewed. Benedetti was instructed to seek such assurances personally from the king of Prussia. He again sought out William at Ems on 13 July and presented this demand. The King received him courteously but firmly refused to give any such guarantee. Later in the day, after receiving official news of Leopold's withdrawal, William sent one of his aides to Benedetti to say that he now regarded the affair as closed and that he could not see him again about it. He had a telegram sent to Bismarck in Berlin, telling him what had taken place. There seemed no occasion here for war; and but for Bismarck it would not have led to war.

Bismarck wanted war. He believed that the time was ripe. As before, he wanted the enemy to appear to be the aggressor. He bitterly deplored the King's mild behaviour and on 13 July he was about to resign. He regarded the events of 12 and 13 July as the French did – as a humiliating

1. See p. 274.

surrender before French demands. He was at dinner with Moltke and Roon on 13 July when the telegram arrived from the King at Ems, informing him of the events. He had permission to inform the press and the Prussian embassies abroad if he wished. He saw that if he only slightly edited the telegram he could present the news to the world in a totally different light. He drew up a condensed version which made it appear that the King's refusal to see Benedetti again was due not to his having meanwhile heard news of Leopold's withdrawal, but to the very nature of Benedetti's original demands. It thus appeared that the King had been far from amenable and had curtly rebuffed, from the start, these formal demands of the French government. Both German and French public opinion were so sensitive and so excitable that when this news came out in the Press of both countries it caused hysterical reactions. Never before had the power of the Press played so dramatic a part in international diplomacy. France felt insulted and clamoured for war to avenge her honour; German opinion rejoiced at the King's sturdy defiance of unwarranted claims. On 19 July France declared war on Prussia. Once again Bismarck got what he wanted when he wanted it. He put the match to the powder barrel. That the powder barrel existed was as much the responsibility of France as of Prussia. Neither was anxious to keep the peace. But as soon as war became probable Bismarck claimed it as his own and used it for his own ends.

The war followed the now familiar pattern. The German army, commanded as one unit by Moltke, organized with scientific precision, and equipped with superior artillery and supplies, at once moved smoothly into action. The cumbersome French war machine, lacking clear leadership and surprisingly ill-equipped for action, creaked and split before the concentrated power of the German attack. Marshal Macmahon commanded in Alsace, Marshal Bazaine in Lorraine, with no considered strategy to coordinate their actions. Napoleon III, courageously fighting his own physical weakness, was in no condition to unify the command. On 6 August Macmahon was beaten and withdrew his forces, and Bazaine's army of some 200,000 was encircled at Metz. Macmahon, who should have been falling back to defend Paris, was sent to relieve Bazaine. He got as far as Sedan on 30 August. On 2 September his whole army and Napoleon III himself were forced to surrender. In Paris a republic was proclaimed and a provisional government took over power, calling itself the Government of National Defence.[1] Paris went into a state of siege, and the German army settled down to blockade it. The siege lasted until the end of January 1871, but meanwhile, at the end of October, Bazaine with his army of 173,000 also capitulated.

1. See p. 321.

The war proved longer and tougher than Bismarck had bargained for. Gambetta, escaping from Paris in a balloon, organized provincial resistance from Tours with the object of relieving Paris. He and his colleagues performed prodigies of improvisation, but they had little chance of success. On 28 January an armistice was signed with Bismarck. The war had been kept as a duel, and involved no third power. It was the nemesis of Napoleon's restless policy that France found herself friendless in Europe; it was the triumph of Bismarck's policy that by judicious timing he contrived to isolate the conflict and prevent its becoming a wider European war.

Bismarck refused to make peace until elections had been held for a new national assembly in France. The Assembly which met at Bordeaux in February 1871 accepted in May the severe terms of the Treaty of Frankfurt. France lost Alsace and Lorraine, which Germany annexed. She undertook to pay an indemnity of five billion francs (200 million pounds sterling) and German troops remained in occupation of the northern provinces until it was paid. The peace treaty was signed on 10 May 1871. But meanwhile Bismarck used the defeat of France to complete the unification of Germany. The southern states of Bavaria, Baden, and Württemberg were induced by the surge of nationalist enthusiasm to join the German Confederation. Germany remained partitioned at the Inn – for Austrian territories were excluded – but no longer at the Main. On 18 January in the Hall of Mirrors in the palace of Versailles, the King of Prussia was proclaimed German Emperor.

German Unification. There has been considerable disagreement among historians about whether the long sequence of events which culminated in the new German Reich of 1871 can be regarded as one coherent plan, conceived in the mastermind of Bismarck when he came to power in 1862 and then carried out, with uncanny insight and dominating will power, according to a precise timetable. Both the enthusiastic hero worshippers of Bismarck and his liberal critics have tended to argue that this was so. There is one remarkable piece of evidence which supports this view. According to Disraeli, who met Bismarck at a dinner in London in 1862, shortly before he came to power, Bismarck told him about his whole scheme in the course of half an hour's conversation. Later in the evening Disraeli remarked to Saburov of the Russian embassy in London, 'What an extraordinary man Bismarck is! He meets me for the first time and he tells me all he is going to do. He will attack Denmark in order to get possession of Schleswig-Holstein; he will put Austria out of the German Confederation; and then he will attack France – an extraordinary man!' If this tale is true, and both Saburov and the official biographers of Disraeli vouched for it, there would seem to be no doubt that at least the broad design was in Bismarck's mind when he took office.

But it is so rare in history for even the greatest of statesman to plan successfully ten years ahead and then to impose their plans on the world, that Bismarck's more recent biographers have cast doubts on whether he can be credited with so much uncanny and prophetic insight. Bismarck, it is argued, was not like Metternich or Alexander I, a system maker. He was a brilliant opportunist, whose course of action always remained undecided and flexible until the last moment and whose policy looks more clear-cut and coherent in retrospect than it was at the time. He was first and always a Prussian nationalist who believed that Prussian interests demanded that she should dominate the whole of northern Germany and exclude Austria from German affairs. His policy towards Denmark, Austria, and even France was guided therefore only by the one ultimate test of the interests of the Prussian state. All else was a matter of detail and method, determined by the circumstances of the moment as he, with his profoundly realistic insight into the nature of European politics, understood them. The unification of Germany was incidental, a by-product of his never-ending pursuit of Prussian interests.

His original plan for unification had reached only to the Main; it was extended to the Inn, and so brought in the southern German states, chiefly as a necessity of the war against France. 'Far from using the war to promote unification,' writes A. J. P. Taylor, 'he sought unification in order to continue the war.' He distrusted Bavaria, Baden, and Württemberg as Catholic states, liable to weaken rather than strengthen the predominance of Protestant Prussia in Germany. But he brought them in when it became a military and diplomatic necessity to shorten the war against France and preclude intervention by other powers. The southern states could make a separate peace so long as they remained independent states; once included in the empire they would have to stay in the war. Likewise he at first had no desire to annex Alsace and Lorraine, because the provinces included so many Frenchmen who he foresaw would be an embarrassing national minority in the new Reich. He agreed to annexation only under pressure from the generals who demanded the territories on strategic grounds. This deviation from his original policy was to prove fatal. It made France the irreconcilable enemy of the German empire, plotting revenge and eventually defeating Bismarck's aim of keeping France friendless and isolated in Europe.

In the same way the achievements of Cavour in Italy have been subject to reinterpretation by later historians. He too, they claim, was the brilliant and ingenious opportunist rather than the framer of long-term plans for a speculative future. Neither he nor Bismarck, it is argued, dealt in futures; both were always engrossed with the present. They were supreme practitioners of *Realpolitik*, and their eventual successes are to be explained more by this profound and imaginative grasp of the immediate realities of international politics than by any alleged control over the long-term course of events. They were masterly statesmen, not masterful supermen.

Although these two views of Cavour and Bismarck as opportunists and as planners seem to be so diametrically opposed, they are not entirely irreconcilable. Both men, it can be agreed, cherished certain aims, and both had minimum programmes, which they devoted all their energies to completing. A united kingdom of northern Italy, a Prussian-controlled north German federation, seemed practicable programmes of policy in the 1850s. Both were within the grasp of practical politics if only Austria could be forced back behind the Alps and the Main, and if other great powers – particularly Russia, France, and Britain – could be kept from intervening on Austria's side. Once the sequence of diplomatic movements and military events necessary to achieve these ends had been started, events themselves began to take control. The statesmen of Italy and Germany adjusted their policies to take account of each new situation that arose, and to exploit for their own ends each new set of circumstances as it was revealed. Because the old machinery of a concert of Europe had been demolished, and because the western powers of Britain and France, for different reasons, took no decisive steps to restore it, central Europe was reshaped by the interplay of ruthless and well-devised policy with the course of events. It is the way history often works.

THE SETTLEMENT OF 1871

The year of explosion, of extreme violence, loosened several other pieces in the kaleidoscope of European affairs and allowed them to drop into a new pattern. First, the government of Italy took the opportunity of the withdrawal of French troops from Rome in August 1870 to seize the city a month later. The government first circularized the European powers, describing how it proposed to ensure the freedom and spiritual independence of the Papacy when its temporal power would pass to the Italian state. Austria and Germany, even France and Spain, now accepted the incorporation of Rome as unavoidable. But the Pope himself still rejected the whole idea. He compelled Italy to use force to seize Rome. He then capitulated, and a plebiscite held in the papal state went overwhelmingly in favour of union with Italy. So Italian unification, too, was accomplished in 1870 without foreign intervention.

Secondly, Alexander of Russia took the opportunity to announce in October 1870 that he would no longer feel bound by the naval clauses of the Treaty of Paris of 1856.[1] He claimed the right, denied by that treaty, to build military or naval establishments on the shores of the Black Sea. France was powerless to protest. Gladstone's government in Britain, in concert with Prussia, summoned a conference in London to denounce the unilateral change in a multilateral agreement. But nothing was done to make Russia retract her repudiation of the treaty. Again the 'concert of Europe' suffered a severe rebuff, and a fresh cause of future Anglo-Russian distrust was created.

Thirdly, in France the republican opposition to the Second Empire seized its chance, and on 4 September 1870 a republic was proclaimed in Paris. Although the newly elected National Assembly of 1871 included a majority of monarchists, opinion in the country soon swung round to republican sympathies. By 1875 the parliamentary Third Republic received formal definition in new constitutional laws; but not before there had occurred the violent outburst of the Paris Commune. This insurrection of the capital lasted from mid March until the end of May 1871 and was accompanied by more short-lived risings in other big cities – Lyon, Marseilles, Saint-Etienne, Toulouse, Narbonne, and Limoges. The Commune was many things: a protest of civic pride against the humiliation of defeat; an extreme republican protest against the predominantly monarchist assembly; a social rising prompted by the sufferings of siege and hunger; a socialistic revolt of the urban workers.[2] But in the circumstances of 1871 it was, above all, a demand for drastic decentralization of government – an attempt to displace the centralized nation-state by a federal conglomeration of small self-governing local units, groups, and associations. By crushing this movement so decisively in 1871 Adolphe Thiers, head of the executive power in France, assumed a place in history alongside Cavour, Bismarck, and Abraham Lincoln as one of the great champions of national unity and the nation-state. He ensured that France of the Third Republic would be a middle-class parliamentary state capable of pursuing a unified national policy in world affairs.

Whatever may have been the personal responsibilities of the Piedmontese and Prussian leaders for the events of the period 1850–70, the undoubted effect of their behaviour was that war between states had been used as a deliberate method of political reconstruction. To a degree unknown since 1815, politics were now the politics of intimidation and organized violence. The governments of great powers were dedicated to

1. See p. 248.
2. See p. 395.

war as an effective instrument of national policy; and to diplomacy as a means not of keeping the peace and maintaining the public laws of Europe, but of preparing and timing hostilities so as to yield the maximum advantages. Two great powers only – Britain and Russia – had held aloof from these wars, and had enjoyed years of peace while central Europe rocked with the roll of gunfire. Even the United States, in the same decade, had been torn by war between the northern and southern states. Nor were the defeated powers of Europe left any less bellicose in spirit. The republicans who came to power in France were for long committed to ideas of a war of revenge; the Danes never accepted as permanent the loss of Schleswig to Germany; the Dual Monarchy of Austria-Hungary soon replaced ideas of revenge against Prussia by a tightening alliance with the new German Reich, dictated by fear of Russia and hope of gains at the expense of Turkey. The legacy of the great wars of the 1860s was recurrent international tensions and new systems of alliances in the 1870s and after.

The New Balance. With uneasy relations prevailing between the six great powers of Europe, the whole nature of the balance of power underwent a transformation. It became a fluid conception, a system of diplomacy conceived as a self-adjusting mechanism whereby an equilibrium was constantly re-established by fresh governmental manoeuvres and agreements, some secret, some public. A generation of armed watchfulness and anxious rearmament was the sequel of 1871. The ethical standards of the behaviour of states towards one another – never high in modern history – had sharply deteriorated as a result of the cynical diplomacy of Cavour and Bismarck and Napoleon III. The notion of a public law of Europe, which it was in the common interest of all states to preserve, seemed to have been abandoned along with the idea of a general 'concert of Europe'. The delirium of nationalistic fever which accompanied the outbreak of the Franco–Prussian War in 1870 betokened a new era of popular hysteria in international relations.[1]

Despite these facts, the events that culminated in 1871 can properly be regarded as one of those great periodic settlements of Europe which habitually follow great wars. The map of the continent between 1871 and 1918 was simpler than it had been before or has been since (see Map 7). The total number of states in Europe was greatly reduced. Like the settlement of 1815, that of 1871 inaugurated a period of forty-three years during which there was no war between the major powers. In some respects the new map of Europe and the new pattern of international relations were more radical transformations than those that occurred in 1815. The settlement of 1871 resembled those of 1815 and of

1. See p. 372.

322

1919 in that it represented a consolidation of the outcome of great wars between major powers. It differed from them, and more closely resembled the European settlement of 1945–50, in that it was framed not by general agreement of the victorious powers registered in a large international conference, but rather by a sequence of separate victories and *coups*. It received no more than the tacit and often reluctant acquiescence of the great powers which were not directly involved. Because it was not shaped or supported by an organized concert of the powers, it left behind it no concept or institution of a 'concert of Europe'.

The settlement of 1871 was, in origin and nature, a new arrangement of European frontiers and relationships dictated by events and imposed by German military power. It had happened – it had fallen into shape undesignedly but with dramatic rapidity. It therefore took some time for the governments of Europe to appreciate its essential features and its diplomatic consequences. That two large national states now existed in central Europe instead of the previous multitude of small non-national states was quickly understood and accepted. Their creation was accepted as irreversible, their survival as inevitable. But the precise position of their frontiers was not regarded as fixed. Just as there were Danish and French minorities within the frontiers of the German Reich, so there remained German and Italian minorities outside the borders of the new states. To this extent, at least, the settlement lacked completeness and finality.

The territorial and political settlement rested, no less clearly than that of 1919, on certain underlying principles. Though not deliberately contrived in all its details, it had certain inevitable modes of operation. It rested, primarily, on the principle of nationality: on the belief – which had conquered Europe since 1848 – that people who felt drawn together by bonds of a common national sentiment should proceed to set up a common state and assert their collective independence of other states.

MAP 7. EUROPE, 1871. See following pages.
After the unification of Italy and Germany (see Maps 5 and 6) the political map of Europe was simpler than at any previous time in history. Six big states, more evenly matched in power, now dominated the scene. Outside the eastern marchlands and the Balkans, frontiers were less in dispute than at any time since 1815; but the Ottoman Empire remained 'the sick man of Europe'. Relations between the other powers were increasingly complicated by this 'Eastern Question', and the settlement of it attempted in 1878 (see inset) proved undurable. Because of these issues, and of colonial and other rivalries, the powers formed into two rival alliances which in 1914 were pulled into the First World War (see Part VI and Map 8).

EUROPE
1871

BALKANS
1878

The incorporation of nearly all Italian-speaking people within the new
united Italian kingdom, and of areas such as Schleswig and Holstein,
Alsace and Lorraine, into the new German Reich, were violent assertions of this principle. But these very assertions denied comparable
rights to the French inhabitants of Alsace and Lorraine and to the Danish
inhabitants of Schleswig. It followed that rights of national self-determination belonged only to those nations powerful enough to assert them:
they were implicitly denied to all who lacked superior power. The
tendency to make Europe a continent of nation-states instead of a
mixture of large and small non-national states involved from the outset
this inner contradiction. The settlement of 1871 violated the principles
on which it rested.

The paradox was vividly seen in the settlement of Austria-Hungary
under the Dual Monarchy. Independence for Germans and Magyars
was attained only by the subjection of Czechs and Slovaks, Croats and
Poles. If states were no longer to be frameworks of authority and power
within which peoples of different language, race, religion, and nationality could find a common citizenship, but the political forms of exclusive
nationality, then the Austro-Hungarian Empire was doomed to eventual
disruption in favour of a multitude of small Balkan states. Others would
follow the example of Serbia, and a cluster of mainly Slav states would
take the place of Habsburg power. A similar fate might be expected
to befall Ottoman Turkey and Romanov Russia. The settlement, so far
as eastern Europe was concerned, could be at best only an interim
arrangement. And with continuing jealousy and tension between the
great powers of the continent, Habsburg or Turkish disintegration would
almost certainly bring further major wars. That is the long-term explanation of why the assassination of an Austrian archduke in the little Bosnian town of Sarajevo could, in 1914, precipitate a world war that
embroiled all the great powers of Europe.

The ingenious arrangement of the Dual Monarchy proved able,
though with increasing difficulty and strain, to postpone disintegration
for over forty years to come. The crumbling of Turkish power was to
cause most of the great disputes until 1914. Meanwhile the crucial fact
in Europe was the supremacy of the German Reich. By reason of its
great and growing economic resources, its military might, its large population, its considerable strategic advantages in the new Europe of railways and heavy industries, Germany was the new colossus in Europe.
Stretching in a continuous mass from the Vosges to the Vistula, and
from the Baltic to the Danube, it pressed upon all its neighbours with
relentless economic and political force. It included forty-one million
people when France included only thirty-six, Austria-Hungary thirty-six,

the United Kingdom thirty-one and a half, and Italy twenty-seven million. The disparity increased during the next generation. Of the great powers of Europe only Russia, with some eighty-seven million, had a larger population than the new German empire of 1871. For military purposes these great manpower resources were fully tapped by the new Reich. The Prussian army laws were extended to the whole country, and the military forces were unified under the immediate control of Prussia. Only Bavaria, Saxony, and Württemberg kept independent military contingents, but the king of Prussia, as Emperor of Germany, was in complete control of the whole army; just as his Chancellor had complete authority in matters of foreign policy.

Bismarck remained Chancellor for the next twenty years, and applied his genius to keeping the diplomatic scene favourable to the security and hegemony of Germany in Europe. He preserved and manipulated the settlement of 1871 in German interests, just as Metternich had used the settlement of 1815 in Austrian interests. German economic life made rapid progress under the stimulus of political unification, the indemnity received from France, the absorption of the developed industrial areas of Alsace and Lorraine, and the acceleration of industrial progress already begun before 1870. The western powers of Britain and France and the Low Countries, despite their leadership in industry, trade, and finance, found the Reich a formidable competitor in world markets. The eastern powers of Austria-Hungary, Russia, and Turkey, because of their relative economic backwardness, offered rich openings for economic penetration by the fast-growing German commercial and financial enterprises. A great new dynamic generator of wealth and power had been built into the heartland of Europe; it soon made its impact felt throughout the whole continent.

The Roman Church. The settlement of 1870–1 brought with it an important change in the position of the Roman Catholic Church. In relation to the new nation-states of Italy and Germany the Vatican naturally found itself hostile and on the defensive. The destruction of the temporal power of the Papacy and the loss of the papal territories to Italy remained an inconsolable grievance, and it was not until the Lateran Treaty of 1929 that the Papacy finally recognized the Italian state. Until then each pope regarded himself as a prisoner in the grounds of the Vatican. The domination of the Protestant power of Prussia over the southern, Catholic states of Germany was equally resented, and Bismarckian treatment of Roman Catholics led to a struggle between state and church in Germany throughout the 1870s. In France the simultaneous triumphs of the anticlerical republican parties led to similar difficulties there. Everywhere the spread of a secular spirit, of science and materialism, of state power and capitalist organization, of anti-clerical radicalism and of irreligious revolutionary communism, challenged the dogmas, influence, and claims of the Roman Church.

It so happened that in 1870, when the European crisis was at its height, a Vatican council including representatives from the whole of Christendom had been summoned in order to proclaim the dogma of papal infallibility. This was the climax of a series of papal measures intended to counteract the irreligious tendencies of the times. In 1854 the Immaculate Conception of the Virgin Mary had been announced as dogmatic truth, to doubt which was heresy. In 1864 Pope Pius IX, cured of any earlier proclivities towards liberalism by his experiences of 1848 and 1849, issued a *Syllabus of Errors*. It denounced as errors most of the widely current ideas of these decades – liberalism, rationalism, science, progress, and so-called 'modern civilization'. The oecumenical council of 1870, in accepting and proclaiming the dogma of papal infallibility, completed the triumphs of ultramontanism over Gallican and other national tendencies within the Church itself. It laid down that when speaking *ex cathedra* on matters of faith and morals, the pope speaks with final and supernatural authority. To question or reject such decisions is heresy. The Roman Church thus emerged from the events of these two decades intransigently opposed to their secular trends and achievements: hostile to science and the nation-state, to the devotion of human energies to material progress and social reform. Yet, by reason of its new freedom from local, temporal interests in Rome and its own re-equipment of dogma, it was better fitted to appeal to the spiritual loyalty of its adherents in all nations. To the new tensions and fears between large nation-states were added more frequent conflicts between church and state, as well as between the teaching of religion and the trends of science.

In important respects, the settlement of 1871 was a fulfilment of the aims of 1848 by means quite different from the methods of 1848. The liberal and democratic nationalists of 1848 had wanted to make Italy and Germany unified and independent. They believed that true national unity could come only by popular mass action and through parliamentary or republican institutions. Unity had come to Italy and Germany not by revolution but by war, not through surging republican enthusiasm but through monarchical diplomacy and from above. The new kingdoms were parliamentary in form more than in spirit. Nationalism had triumphed at the expense of liberalism; and when, in the generation after 1871, nationalism was wedded to democracy, it never recaptured fully the liberal idealism of 1848. Many liberals in both countries accepted and even welcomed the gifts of national independence from the hands of kings. Some of them were later to join more intransigent liberals and radicals in opposition to the authoritarian tendencies of nationalistic governments. But, at profound variance with the forces of Roman Catholicism, and with proletarian movements now infused with Marxism, liberalism in central Europe suffered lasting loss from the events of 1871. The defeat of its methods in 1871 was to prove as serious as the defeat of its aims in 1848. The political climate in central Europe remained as different from that of western Europe after 1871 as it had been before.

CHAPTER 15

EMANCIPATION IN EASTERN EUROPE

THE decades between 1850 and 1870 were formative years in the two largest dynastic empires of eastern Europe, Russia and the Ottoman Turkish Empire. Neither yet felt the full throb of the industrial revolution, though to both the railways had come, and more trade with western countries did something to stimulate new social and political forces. Neither, in these years, lost much of its former territory or gained any new lands; for a time after the Crimean War, neither played a prominent part in general European affairs. But there took place profound internal changes in their social life, combined with surprisingly little corresponding change in their political or administrative systems. They differed from the western nations in that the greatest social changes were effected not by economic processes but by legislative action; and from the central European nations in that no overhaul of their governmental systems accompanied such changes. Politics were, in consequence, harshly out of tune with social life. This created, as always, a revolutionary situation.

THE END OF SERFDOM IN RUSSIA

Four years before slavery was abolished in the United States, serfdom was abolished in Russia. It was ended, characteristically, by a decree of the Tsar Alexander II in 1861. This momentous event was a landmark in the modern history of Russia, not so much because it betokened the acceptance of western ideals of individual freedom and rights, but rather because it inaugurated a social and economic revolution, and opened the door to a more massive material westernization of Russian life. Many different circumstances contributed to the abolition. The defeat of Russia by Britain and France in the Crimean War served as a warning that some change was needed. Operating from a great distance and using only part of their resources, these advanced western powers had mounted a highly localized offensive which the Russian Empire had failed to repel, despite its vast size and its obvious strategic advantages.

Alexander II. Alexander II had become Tsar during the war, in 1855, and he decided to enlist as far as possible the help of the liberal intelligentsia of Russia in reorganizing his régime. This class, composed partly of university students and graduates and literary men, found itself sharply cut off both from the majority of the ruling bureaucracy of tsarist absolutism and from the mass of ordinary people who remained sunk in poverty and ignorance. Their spiritual home was western Europe; their closest affinities lay with the most extreme and perfectionist ideas evolving from the cultural development of western and central Europe. They were strange candidates for a political alliance with the tsardom. But Alexander had no other class to turn to – the landowning aristocracy and gentry were mostly indifferent to reforms, the Orthodox Church was too conservative a body to promote drastic change, the official classes were satisfied with their power, and the mass of peasants were too apathetic and depressed to afford any leverage of self-help. So there had to be a sudden, doctrinaire enactment from above.

Alexander wooed the intellectuals by permitting them to travel more freely abroad, by easing the control of universities and of the Press. His father, Nicholas I, had already done something to alleviate the burden of serfdom. Greater freedom of discussion now generated a flow of public opinion which was entirely in favour of emancipating the serfs. The problem was how to do it without ruining the gentry and dislocating the whole economy of the country. As a system of labour relations serfdom was generally recognized, even by the more conservative elements, to be unprofitable and bad. The big landowners of the south, engaged partly in export trade, were finding wage labour more efficient. Serfdom robbed workers of self-respect, initiative, and incentive. It embittered all social life. Local peasant revolts, already endemic, were becoming more frequent. Nor was it only a matter of agricultural labour, though agriculture was by far the largest occupation of the Russian people. Serfs could be used by their owners to work in mines or factories or mills, they could be hired out for that purpose, and they could even be mortgaged as security for debts or loans. Some two thirds of the serfs not owned by the Tsar or the state were, indeed, so mortgaged by 1855. They could be bought and sold, and instead of being bound to the soil as previously in central Europe, they were virtually in bondage to their owners. Humane and paternalist treatment, sometimes to be found, in no way offset the obvious social and moral evil of a system which kept more than forty million people in bondage to landowners or state.

The imperial decree of emancipation gave the Russian peasants legal freedom without economic freedom. They became subjects of the government, and were no longer under compulsion to pay dues to their former owners either in forced labour or in money. But they had to pay redemption money for such services and dues, and for the land which they now received. In all, about half the cultivated land of Russia was henceforth held by the peasants in their own right, though conditions naturally varied greatly from one area to another. They held it, however, not as private property as did the French peasants, but as shares in the collective property of the village or *mir*. The control and restrictiveness of the *mir* largely replaced the old authority of the gentry. It was the *mir* which paid the redemption money collectively – as it already paid taxes – collected it under sanction of forced labour and other exactions, and as before supervised the allocation and cultivation of the land by the members of the village community. Emancipation meant the abolition of personal servitude but the affirmation of communal responsibilities. The committees of nobles or gentry which were set up everywhere to carry out the reform were above all anxious to avoid the evil of the landless labourer which, in the west, had produced the new urban proletariats. The peasant was to be given a stake in the soil, and, unlike the Prussian peasant after emancipation, he was not left free to take up trade or migrate into the towns. To do so he needed permission from his *mir*. Permission was even more reluctantly given now that it meant unloading on the rest of the village the responsibility for paying the redemption. Only when the *mir* ceased to be collectively responsible for village dues and taxes did freedom of movement become greater; and that was not until after 1905.

If emancipation was a mixed blessing for the peasants, it was usually a welcome arrangement for the landowners. The Russian nobility secured nearly half the arable land, were quit of responsibilities for the serfs, and received the redemption money in place of the human property which they had anyhow largely mortgaged. The aristocracy were strengthened, not weakened, by the change. Opposition to the further liberalizing moves of Alexander came not from aristocracy and gentry, but from the intellectuals whom he had hoped to win over. Since the lords now had no jurisdiction over their serfs, new courts replaced the old. By edicts of 1864 the Tsar overhauled the whole judicial system, with the aim of establishing the 'rule of law' on the English model. Trials were now held in public, a jury system was introduced, litigants could choose their own lawyers to represent them in court, and judges were given a better professional training and fixed stipends. At the same time local elected councils (*Zemstvos*) were instituted for districts and provinces, to attend to public health and welfare, road maintenance and education. But no provision was made for a nationally representative body or parliament. The central authority remained detached, autocratic, irresponsible.

Economic Conditions. Nor did emancipation lead to any marked improvements in the methods or output of Russian agriculture. The government excluded priests and former landowners from the *mir*, and this left the supervising authority exceptionally ignorant and unenterprising.

For the next forty years the land was still mostly cultivated in strips, and the time-honoured methods were used to grow the traditional crops. No fresh wind of scientific agriculture or progressive methods blew through the farmlands of Russia. Each male child had a right to land, and the land of the *mir* had to be divided periodically to provide for the new generation. A growing population meant, for the most part, a decline in the size or number of strips which each peasant held. As a man's holding shrank, he had no incentive to improve land that he might lose at the next redistribution. He ceased to be able to live on his holding, unless he could get more land from some other source. Some bought land from the nobles. A few moved on to the eastern frontier, much as the American frontiersman moved west. Because productivity did not keep pace with population, famines and periods of great distress became more and more frequent. Personal and family misfortunes ruined some peasants and offered a chance of gain to others. Great inequalities arose in a closed community which presupposed a broad equality. Redemption had the effect of much heavier taxation, for eighty per cent of the money was advanced by the state and repaid by the peasant to the state in instalments over many years. These repayments were collected along with the regular state taxes. This additional burden proved unbearable, and by 1905 outstanding arrears had to be cancelled in an effort to stave off revolution.

In all these ways the liberal and far-reaching measure of emancipation did little to improve either the economic lot of the mass of the peasants or the economic prosperity of the country as a whole. Nor did it make for a more stable and acceptable political system. The yearning to get distress and grievances remedied was only whetted, not satisfied, by emancipation. Discontent remained sufficiently intense and widespread to make reformist opinion (which was mostly that of the intellectuals) more than ever responsive to the extreme Marxist and anarchist opinions that were infiltrating from the West.[1] The Tsar won neither gratitude nor strength from his reforms. He was nearly assassinated in 1866, in 1873, and again in 1880, before he was finally killed by a bomb in 1881.

The forces of change fermenting in Russian life by 1871 were the consequence of these reforms rather than a result of any marked industrial development. The Crimean War led to a rapid growth of railroads. A special body called the General Company of Russian Railways promoted them, and by 1870 there were more than 10,600 kilometres of track. Combined with the emancipation of the serfs, even this moderate amount of railroad construction was enough to carry Russia forward,

1. See p. 402.

for the first time, into a money economy. Until the middle of the century most of the country had been economically self-sufficing, and the basis of nearly all transactions was services or payments in kind. Barter in purely local markets was the basis of most internal trade. The growth of a foreign trade in wheat, now increased by the new railroads, the demand for money to hire labourers or to pay redemption payments and taxes, the influx of foreign capital from the West, all conspired to develop a money economy. As had happened centuries before in western Europe, social relations that had rested on status and custom were replaced by relations based on contract and law. But this deep transformation could come about only very slowly and with difficulty. Money remained in short supply for a long time, and the protectionist commercial policy of the Tsars was directed, for the rest of the century, to importing bullion and keeping it in the country. Labour only slowly became mobile because of the restrictiveness of the *mir*. Industry remained subservient to the land, and factory workers often went back to agricultural labour in the summer.

By western or German standards industrial progress was slow, industrial organization primitive, until at least the end of the century. In mining, transport, and the building industries, a favourite method of organization was the *artel*, or cooperative labour group. Each member performed his agreed share of the work in return for an agreed share of the earnings, and a leader conducted the bargaining for the whole group. Travelling *artels* of carpenters or masons, numbering anything from twenty to 200, moved from their villages to the towns each year, completing the work contracted for and then returning to the villages for the winter. Spinning and weaving, metalwork and woodwork, were often organized along similar lines in the villages themselves, the peasants working either in their own homes or in cooperative workshops. These peculiarly Russian modes of production had many admirable features. They served to strengthen the bargaining power of the otherwise helpless workers, ensured a good level of craftsmanship and industriousness, and prevented widespread unemployment. But they linked industry very closely to an agriculture that was primitive and to a domestic system that resisted mechanization. The general retarding of the economic development of Russia in these years was to have far-reaching consequences in the twentieth century.

Only in the twentieth century, too, did the greatest safety valve for a growing population begin to operate – emigration. The periodic redistribution of lands in the *mir* favoured large families. For that and other reasons the peasant population was growing rapidly. To the east – in Siberia and Transcaucasia – Russia had vast underpopulated territories.

Yet the government policy until after 1865 did not encourage migration, which it regarded as depleting the supply of labour nearer home and as undermining the bargaining position of the landowners and contractors in their agreements about wages. Nor did the *mir* itself relish any diminution of the number among which the collective tax burden could be divided. The same considerations that restricted the mobility of labour even more strongly resisted permanent migration. As a result movement to the frontiers was small in scale during these years. Underdeveloped areas remained underdeveloped for lack of labour. In the decade after emancipation less than a thousand a year went as free emigrants into Siberia, most of them illegally. The colonization of Transcaucasia was strictly regulated after 1866 by a homestead policy – the government offering for rent homesteads of 135 acres. The railroads did not cross Siberia until 1905, and the marvellous expansion into Russia's Asian hinterland was reserved for the years after that. Most of the colonization was punitive. Between 1853 and 1874 nearly a quarter of a million people were deported to Siberia.

NATIONALIST AND REVOLUTIONARY MOVEMENTS

The well-meant reforms accomplished by Alexander II had little connexion with any sentiment or movement of nationalism. They were autocratic reforms carried out by authoritarian methods. The real nationalist movement of Russia was a revolutionary movement, rooted not in the people as a whole but in the intelligentsia and in that great cultural movement of mid nineteenth-century Russia which found inspiration in the West and had its roots as much in exiles as inside Russia itself. The so-called intelligentsia included some of the nobles themselves, parts of the urban population engaged in trade and the professions, and the majority of university students and graduates, as well as the literary men. It overlapped the bureaucracy, the traders and business men, and the landed nobility; yet it was distinct from them, a thin crust of educated people with a European outlook, intensely self-conscious and profoundly uneasy about the desperate condition of their country in the modern world. The trend towards replacing the old classical education by a more scientific and technical education only made the younger generation more impatient with the political régime and the economic backwardness of their country. This important class of intellectuals was partly the cause and partly the outcome of the remarkable cultural efflorescence of nineteenth-century Russia.

In music and literature Russia quite suddenly enriched the whole culture of Europe. The symphonies of Borodin and Tchaikovsky, the suites and programme music of Rimsky-Korsakov, the songs of Musorg-ski, belong to these years; and all leaned heavily upon legends and folk tales of Russia for their themes. The great novelists Turgenev, Dostoev-ski, and Tolstoi were all concerned with social evils particularly endemic in Russian life; conditions of the poor, the psychological dilemmas aris-ing in conditions of deep distress and violence, the reform of government, were themes especially fascinating to them. Though dealing, like all great art, with eternal human emotions and problems, the works of the Russian composers and novelists of the time expressed a stirring of national con-science, a profound concern for the welfare of the people. They were eagerly received by the whole intelligentsia and helped to give it unity and self-consciousness. They were not repudiated even by officialdom. Conser-vatoires of music were founded in the 1860s in St Petersburg and Mos-cow. Tchaikovsky travelled widely throughout Europe, Britain, and America, and his own fame attracted world interest in Russian culture.

The spiritual stirring of Russia was displayed before the world which, if it found Russian novels and music hauntingly pathetic and exotic, or often gloomy to the point of morbidity, could still recognize them as a great new offshoot of European culture, linked to the West by a thousand subtle ties of form and taste. It differed from more militant nationalistic culture, such as the German, in that these great sons and lovers of Russia yearned not for national unity and independence (which they already had), but for greater human happiness and peace of mind, and a less oppressive social order. Nationalism in Russia was revolution-ary because it was in rebellion against fate and the elements, against his-tory and the harshness of life itself. Patriotic memories of triumph against invasion in 1812 were awakened by Tolstoi's *War and Peace* as much as by Tchaikovsky's famous overture, but that was not a theme that was predominant. Rather it is a culture of struggles of the human heart and problems of the soul, tortured and profoundly moving, echo-ing the cry of a whole people in distress: a culture of revolt even more than of nationality.

Nearly all these great composers and writers came from the classes of nobility and officials. They spoke for the people rather than from them. During the 1860s there grew up a more specifically radical revo-lutionary movement, expressing itself less in literature than in journal-ism, and voicing more crudely, fantastically, and savagely the discontent of the masses of peasants. The socialist journalist N. G. Chernyshevski and the romantic revolutionary Aleksandr Herzen were concerned less with liberals and constitutional reforms, and more with drastic economic change. Both welcomed the emancipation of the serfs in 1861; both were bitterly disillusioned by its results. In periodicals and often illegal pamphlets such writers directly attacked the policies of the Tsar and stirred desperate men to revolution. In a mass of minor literature, revolutionary radicalism was propagated by men who perforce spent much of their lives in prison, in Siberia, or in exile. It was at this level that Marxism and anarchism soaked into the Russian revolutionary movement, producing frequent acts of terrorism and equally frequent reprisals and repressions.

Separatist Nationalities. Russian nationalism was of less immediate concern to the Tsar and his officials than was separatist nationalism in the western fringe of his possessions, especially in Poland. The Poles, as already seen,[1] were perennially the most troublesome nationalist minority of European Russia. Their cause aroused the sympathies of the western world almost as sensitively as did that of the Greeks. The ruler who was prepared to emancipate more than forty million serfs might be expected to have some sympathy for the aspirations of his Polish subjects. Within a week of his decree which emancipated the serfs, Alexander was presented through his viceroy in Poland with a request from the Agricultural Society of Poland to redress grievances. This society, which had existed since the time of the Crimean War ostensibly to promote more scientific farming, had come to be a political organ of the old nobility of Poland, wedded to national independence and to recovery of such former Polish territories as Lithuania. Alexander responded by setting up special bodies to deal with Polish problems and grievances, and entrusting powers of local self-government to provincial councils. It was a timely and well-received gesture.

But the liberal nobles of the Agricultural Society were only one of three nationalistic and revolutionary elements in Poland. There was the Roman Catholic Church, which had retained much of its influence and was permanently opposed to the domination of Russia. There was also the party of impoverished country gentry and the professional classes, closely resembling the supporters of Kossuth in Hungary; it was equally anti-Russian, and had formed a secret committee to run radical propaganda and plan resistance. The Agricultural Society spoke for neither of these powerful movements. The country seethed with revolutionary discontent and when, in January 1863, an attempt was made to draft the young patriotic revolutionaries of the towns into the army, open revolt broke out. The tactics of the Russian government were those of Austria-Hungary in the comparable Polish revolt of 1846: to appeal for support of the peasants by backing their claims against the Polish nobles. The peasants were much more interested in getting land than in winning national independence. They had gained proportionately

1. See pp. 122 and 157.

much less land than was granted to the Russia peasants after 1861. The liberal administration and educational reforms so far carried out had done little or nothing to improve their condition. They were ready enough to fix responsibility and blame on their own landlords. Accordingly, the nationalist revolt organized by the secret revolutionary committee, which spread throughout the country and lasted for most of the year 1863, received only lukewarm support from the peasants in most parts of Poland. By autumn the revolt was almost crushed. The neighbouring Ukrainians gave it little support; the Lithuanians did support it and were brutally suppressed.

The chief embarrassment which the revolt brought to the Tsar was the interest which it inevitably aroused in Europe. On the grounds that Polish autonomy had been granted in 1814 and 1815 by treaties of which they were also signatories, the French and British governments, with half-hearted Austrian support, made representations to the Tsar. Napoleon III asked him to restore Polish self-government, but was rebuffed. Britain asked him to restore the situation of 1815 and grant an amnesty; she received only partial reassurances. Further notes by all three powers proved equally ineffective, because none was prepared to go to war and only force could have deterred the Russian government from suppressing the revolt. The Russian policy had formal Prussian backing, for in February 1863 Bismarck signed a convention with the Russian government providing for similar repression in the Polish provinces of Prussia should the revolt spread to them. Prussia, with a clear common interest with Russia in crushing any moves for Polish independence and reunification, gave the Tsar all the support he needed in order to defy the western powers. His victory was thus not only a military victory against the Poles, but also a diplomatic victory against the western powers. This helped to restore Russian prestige, which had been internationally weakened by the Crimean War. Austria and Russia were now more deeply alienated. Prussia and Russia had moved towards that mutual agreement and friendship which was to be so useful to Prussia in 1866 and 1870, and which Bismarck was to cultivate further after 1871.[1]

The Polish peasants gained substantially from the revolt, which they had done so little to support. The Tsar rewarded them by a more liberal interpretation of the emancipation decrees. They got more land and paid lower redemption payments than the peasants in Russia. A reform of local government also gave greater powers to the rural communes. But national independence was postponed still further. Even the name of the territory was changed from 'Kingdom of Poland' to 'Vistula provinces'. Educational policy was designed to root out the Polish religion and

1. See pp. 312 and 460.

language. In 1869 the university of Warsaw was suppressed and a purely Russian university put in its place. Catholic Church schools and private Polish schools were obstructed or forbidden, and for most official purposes the Russian language was used instead of Polish. An important result was that Polish nationalism lost much of its old romantic flavour and turned to a more realistic policy, designed to make the best of a bad situation. In the 1870s a modern Polish industry grew up, taking advantage of the large domestic market of Russia. Textile industries developed along more modern western lines, and technical education began to produce a new generation of intelligent Polish engineers and managers. In the south-west, coal and iron industries developed. Economic westernization happened sooner and faster in Poland than in the rest of Russia – a strange result of the pitiful failure of the revolt.

The Russian Empire was fringed in the west by other active nationalist movements, especially the Finnish, Lithuanian, and Ukrainian. In 1861 the Tsar experimented with greater autonomy for Finland as well as for Poland. Finland had been annexed by Alexander I in 1809, and kept in 1815 as an autonomous grand duchy. Officially, it was united with Russia only in the person of the monarch. Less prone to violent rebellion and always more realistic in their nationalism, the Finns could continue to be treated as a separate but relatively loyal part of the empire. Lithuanians, as already shown, supported the Polish revolt of 1863 and were in consequence crushed. Having formed part of Poland for four centuries, they were mostly Roman Catholics and had close affinities with Polish nationalist aspirations. A real cultural and nationalist movement, distinctly Lithuanian, come only in the 1880s.

The Ukraine covered the important southern area of Russia stretching from the Austrian and Rumanian frontiers to the Don and the Kuban steppe in the east. Its inhabitants were regarded as 'Little Russians', speaking a language closely akin to Russian, and in religion mostly Orthodox, though the Uniate Church was strong in the western Ukraine and came to serve as a focus of Ukrainian nationalist feeling. Ukrainian peoples straddled the Russian frontiers, for they were to be found in Eastern Galicia and Bukovina in Austria, and in the north-eastern corner of Hungary known as Carpathian Ruthenia. They had become more nationally conscious by 1850 because of a strong literary movement during the first half of the century. By 1847 it assumed political form with the foundation of the secret society of Saints Cyril and Methodius, led by poets and historians, on the pattern of contemporary romantic nationalism.[1] Although this society was suppressed, the period 1850–70 brought greater official tolerance of nationalist activities, and

1. See p. 144.

the heroic land of the Cossacks remained a distinctive though not actively separatist part of the Tsar's dominions.

Finnish, Lithuanian, and Ukrainian separatism was to have importance later in the century.[1] But by 1870 these provinces, like the Polish provinces, seemed for a time reconciled to continued Russian rule. By 1871 the nationalist movements of the eastern marchlands were left unsatisfied but temporarily quiescent. The Russian Empire was to survive intact for another generation. Only in Poland had economic progress begun to lay fresh foundations for a stronger movement of nationalism; and Polish nationalism, like Ukrainian, encountered the resistance not of Russia alone, but of Austria and even Prussia as well. It could bring about no effective change until such time as the whole of eastern Europe might be thrown into the melting pot, and the grip of the three great powers simultaneously weakened. That unlikely event did happen in 1918, with drastic results.

THE FAILURE OF REFORM IN TURKEY

In 1815 the Ottoman Empire had extended across the whole northern coast of Africa as far as Morocco, and into the Balkans as far as the rivers Danube and Pruth. It straddled the mouths and the lower reaches of the Danube, and ended only at the southern ranges of the Carpathians. Even so, it had been progressively pushed back since its maximum extent at the end of the seventeenth century (see Map 8). During the eighteenth century, Austria, Hungary, and Russia had taken the lead in recovering large areas of Hungary and the northern shores of the Black Sea (including the Crimea). The Empire survived the Napoleonic wars only because of the deadlock in the balance of power in eastern Europe between Russians, British, and French. In 1830 the process of dissolution began again with the French conquest of Algeria and the independence of Greece. At the same time the whole structure of Ottoman rule was shaken and loosened by the recognition of Serbia, Moldavia, and Wallachia as autonomous principalities within the empire, and by the emergence of Egypt under Mehemet Ali as another autonomous region. In the Crimean War, Russia pressed still harder upon its northern frontiers, and only the aid of the western powers kept Russia at bay. It was symptomatic of the new era of 'realism' in international affairs that Catholic and Protestant Christians then allied with Moslem Turks against Greek Orthodox Christians – evidence enough that Turkey had become a focus for policies guided in no way by religious considerations but only by anxieties about the balance of power in the Near

1. See p. 479.

East. Even so, an empire that still had a firm base in Asiatic Turkey and whose territories still extended from the Persian Gulf to Tripoli would be an unconscionable time in dying.

The Ottoman Turkish Empire between 1850 and 1870 resembled Russia in four respects. It was impelled to attempt reform and renovation as a result of the Crimean War. It was confronted with a series of disruptive nationalist movements in its western territories. Its difficulties attracted considerable interest on the part of the other great powers of Europe. And like Russia it was not so much a European state as that characteristically Asian phenomenon – a vast sprawling dynastic empire comprising a great mixture of races, languages, and religions held together only by subservience to an arbitrary and harsh central authority. But it differed from Russia in the important fact that the ruling class was Turkish and therefore Moslem, whereas many of the subject peoples were either Jews or Christians. Religious and racial divisions did not coincide: some Slavs had adopted Islam; some Arabs, Christianity. But to western European eyes the general picture was one of an infidel race misruling, and from time to time massacring, Christian peoples; and though this picture was not quite accurate, it was at least true enough at certain periods.

What was abundantly clear was that Turkish power, which had been disintegrating for 150 years past, was likely soon to crumble further before the renewed pressure of Russia and Austria; and when it did, the whole balance of power in the Near and Middle East would be drastically changed. The western powers of France and Great Britain hesitated between an impulse to buttress Turkish power as a barrier against Russian and Austrian expansion, and exasperation with the corrupt and brutal methods by which the Turks misgoverned their Christian subjects. This ambivalent attitude to what was generally known as the 'Eastern Question' became of great international importance in the decade after 1870.

During the third quarter of the nineteenth century, however, the 'Eastern Question' remained a cloud gathering for the future, rather than a storm immediately about to break. The great powers were preoccupied with the dramatic changes in central Europe, and Russia was undergoing the social upheaval of abolishing serfdom. From 1856 onward it seemed that even the Turkish government was bringing itself more up-to-date and was accepting reforms. In that year the Ottoman government issued a reform edict known as the Hatt-i Humayun. The religious groups under separate religious leaders – patriarchs, rabbis, bishops, and the rest – had been the units of government and administration, each separately responsible to the sultan. Now a universal Turkish national citizenship was created for all persons within the sultan's territories. The civil authority of the religious leaders, which had been very great, was abolished. Equality before the law and equal eligibility for public office were guaranteed. Christians and Moslems alike could join the army, hitherto restricted to Moslems. The system of taxation was reformed, and, as in Russia, judicial reforms were undertaken abolishing the use of torture and improving conditions in prisons. The universal corruption and extortions of public officials were to stop. For the next twenty years some effort was made to implement these far-reaching reforms – but with increasing failure and disappointment. The degeneration of the Ottoman administration had gone too far, its corruption was too deep-seated, to permit of easy renovation. The powerful class of legal-religious rulers resented and resisted the changes. The official religion of Islam inhibited equal treatment for non-Moslem citizens. In the provinces the beys and pashas ignored the reforms, and the power of the sultan in Constantinople was neither resolute enough nor efficient enough to enforce his will.

In 1861 the sultan Abdul Mejid drank himself to death and was succeeded by Abdul Aziz, who reigned until 1876. He tried to implement the reforms and to open Turkey to western influences. He allowed freer newspapers and some propagation of western ideas. The first sultan to visit Europe, he travelled to Vienna, London, and Paris. With the help of foreign loans, railroads were built to join the Danube and the Black Sea. A literary nationalist revival began. The admission of Turkey to a status in the public law of Europe in 1856 began to mean something.[1] One part of the Empire in particular, Egypt, made solid material advance in westernization. Railroads were built, mainly with French and British capital and technicians. While the War between the States in America prevented the southern states from exporting as much raw cotton as usual, between 1861 and 1865 Egypt's exports of cotton multiplied fourfold. The khedives modernized their legal and administrative systems and encouraged the building of the Suez Canal. The completion of the Canal in 1869 made the Middle East once again a focal point of world trade and of European rivalries.

In these ways, despite the effeteness of the sultan's power and the internal resistance to all reforms, fresh forces were at work within the Empire. By 1870 it was an open question how far they could transform the Turkish lands, and what results such transformation might bring. But one result most unlikely to be achieved was a thoroughly renovated and consolidated Ottoman Empire. No European government wanted such a result. Russia still dreamed of a warm-water port and worried

1. See p. 248.

about her security in the Straits; Austria cast covetous eyes on Salonika and the Aegean; Prussia cared little about the fate of Turkey; France was anxious to retain her position in Syria and Palestine; Britain and other western powers sympathized with the aspirations of Greeks and Serbs for national freedom. The Balkan peoples themselves instinctively resisted any improvement of the Turkish system which might prolong their servitude. Nobody had an interest in the sick man of Europe becoming any healthier or stronger.

Balkan Nationalism. As in Austria-Hungary and Russia, much the most disturbing element in the whole situation was the separatist aspirations of the smaller states and nationalities. Although Turkey was almost untouched by the wave of revolutions in 1848, its territories had been falling away on the western edges wherever nationalism was strongest. In the 1820s it had been the Greeks who had successfully asserted independence.[1] In the 1830s Serbia followed suit, and so had the Rumanians of Moldavia and Wallachia.[2] These three Christians peoples, Greeks, Serbs, and Rumanians, won further gains during the troubled years between 1850 and 1870; and these gains all undermined Ottoman power in the Balkans. Each developed aims of national unification, miniature versions of the contemporary movements in Italy and Germany. Substantial minorities of each were still under direct Turkish rule in 1870, and the centripetal attraction of neighbouring states or provinces with some degree of self-government and independence continued to be a violently centrifugal force within Ottoman territories.[3]

The Greek kingdom which in 1830 was guaranteed by the powers included only about half the Greek-speaking peoples. It was confined within narrow boundaries chiefly because the western powers had not wanted to weaken Turkey too much. Its economic resources were too meagre; its system of law and order too fragile, to ensure prosperity and security. King Otto, established in 1833, was in 1843 forced by popular uprisings to grant a constitution. In 1862 he had to abdicate, and the following year a son of the King of Denmark was installed as George I. At the same time Britain gave to Greece the Ionian Islands, off its western coasts, whose 'protection' the British had found costly and troublesome. But this only whetted the ardent Greek desire to gain, at Turkey's expense, the Aegean Islands off the east coast and the northern half of the peninsula including Macedonia. Although philhellenic enthusiasm in Europe had waned considerably with further experience of the misery, disorder, and aggressive fanaticism of independent

1. See p. 139. 2. See p. 220.
3. See p. 462.

Greece, it remained strong enough to enlist western sympathies in the cause of further Greek gains. Torn by political factions and obsessed, with hatred against the Turks, the Greeks by 1871 were clearly one of the most likely sources of war in the Balkans.

In 1829 Serbia had also become a semi-independent principality after a generation of struggles for freedom, and by mid century she was raising the issue of southern Slav unification. Her rights were reaffirmed by the powers in 1856. To her south-west lay the tough mountain people of Montenegro, relentless fighters against the Turks; to the west the provinces of Bosnia and Herzegovina were inhabited by Slavs under Turkish rule; on the north were Slavs under Austrian and Hungarian rule; on the east and south lived Slav minorities in territories held by Turkey. The internal politics of Serbia, as of Greece, were an explosive mixture of ferocious domestic feuds and excitable nationalist claims. Prince Alexander of the 'Black George' dynasty ruled from 1842 until 1858, when he was deposed by popular uprising. He was replaced by Milosh, of the rival Obrenovich dynasty, who had ruled from 1817–39. He reigned only until 1860, when his son Michael succeeded to his turbulent inheritance. With the aid of the western powers he contrived, in 1867, to have the last of the Turkish garrisons withdrawn from Serbia. He was assassinated the following year. Michael was succeeded by his cousin, Milan I, who proclaimed a new constitution but kept wide powers for the monarchy. Lacking any seaport, Serbia was primitive in her economy. It depended upon the Danube, which formed her northern frontier, and so she was virtually dependent upon Austria. This did not prevent – it even reinforced – Serbian resolve to fight for western territories that would give her an outlet to the Adriatic.

North of the Danube was appearing a third distinct Balkan state in the form of Rumania. After 1815 Turkish suzerainty over the principalities of Moldavia and Wallachia had become little more than nominal, though rival Austrian and Russian intentions made eventual independence for these provinces problematical. As already seen, they were temporarily occupied by Russia in 1829, reoccupied in 1848, evacuated in 1851, reoccupied in 1853, and evacuated again, under Austrian pressure, in 1854.[1] As a result of the Crimean War they were augmented by the addition of part of Bessarabia surrendered by Russia, and were guaranteed in their rights by the powers, though remaining under Turkish suzerainty. In 1859 they were united under a single government, and until 1866 the consolidated kingdom was ruled by Prince Alexander Cuza, one of the abler Rumanian nobles. He carried out the reforms characteristic of these years, abolishing serfdom, dissolving monasteries,

1. See p. 243.

and promoting education. But the Rumanians deposed him in 1866, and offered the crown to Prince Carol, who was connected by birth with the Hohenzollerns of Prussia and even with the family of Napoleon. His accession was opposed by Austria and Russia but supported by Bismarck, and in the European situation of 1866 Bismarck got his way. Unlike her Balkan neighbours, Rumania was a rich agricultural country and had the capacity to develop more quickly. In 1870 she still suffered from the prevalent deficiencies of Balkan kingdoms. She had no railways, few good roads, an oppressed and poverty-stricken peasantry, and chaotic finances. But with less strident nationalist grievances and claims, and with an able administrator at her head, Rumania was well equipped to consolidate her independence in the near future.

The two great decades of 'state-making' between 1850 and 1870 therefore saw the creation or consolidation of three new Balkan states, destined to remain continuously thereafter on the map of Europe and to extend their frontiers as well as accomplishing more complete independence, by the end of the century. There remained within Turkish territories two other peoples still in a more primitive phase of struggling to attain statehood. On the mountainous eastern coast of the Adriatic was the province of Albania, home of the ancient Illyrians. Its inhabitants were still in a semi-tribal stage of development, in religion partly Moslem and partly Christian, but in civilization the most backward people of Europe. Turkish rule was weak in Albania, less because of nationalist resistance than because of the sheer impossibility of imposing any rule whatever on the tough and barbaric mountain tribes. To collect taxes was to cause ferocious rebellion, and wise Turkish administrators were usually content to leave the province alone. In the eastern Balkans, bordering the western shores of the Black Sea, lived a half-forgotten people, the Bulgars, speaking a Slav tongue but of Finnish-Tartar stock. During the first half of the nineteenth century Bulgar nationalism had revived, and it was encouraged by Russia as a weapon against Turkey. There began a demand for Bulgar education and use of the native language in churches. In 1860 the Bulgarian Christians declared that they would no longer acknowledge the ecclesiastical authority of the patriarch of Constantinople. In 1870 the sultan of Turkey, under Russian pressure, set up an exarch in Bulgaria as head of the Bulgar church. This recognition of Bulgarians as a separate religious nation was their first step towards national independence. Although in 1870 they were still completely under Turkish rule, this strange people was soon to make a dramatic re-entry on the stage of European history and became a focus of great-power diplomacy.[1]

1. See p. 467.

EMANCIPATION IN EASTERN EUROPE

A shrewd observer in 1871 might well have perceived that the whole Eastern Question was ready to burst into flames. The failure of reforms in Turkey, the fraying of Turkish rule throughout the Balkan peninsula, the emergence of three restless new states and of other nationalist movements, the stirring of new economic and political forces in a region of Europe still little affected by the mighty transformations of the nineteenth centry, all betokened a fast-approaching upheaval. But events in western and central Europe served to distract the attention of the great powers from such impending changes in the east. Austria and Russia continued to offset one another in expansionist plans. France and Italy were occupied with their own reconstruction and the consolidation of new régimes. Britain, still obsessed with fears of Russia, cherished the hope that the integrity of Turkey might somehow be preserved. And Bismarck, the most perceptive statesman of Europe, was so engaged in completing the work of unifying the new German Reich that he was prepared to discount the Eastern Question as of negligible importance. The Balkans he declared to be 'not worth the bones of a single Pomeranian grenadier', and he affected 'never to trouble to open the mailbag from Constantinople'. Yet from this time onward the Eastern Question was to demand more and more attention from the statesmen of Europe. It resulted in frequent crises, wars, and revolutions during the remainder of the nineteenth century. It contributed to the causing of two world wars in the twentieth century, one precipitated by events in Serbia and the other by events in Czechoslovakia and Poland. By the 1950s the partition, tension, and balance between the worlds to the West and to the East of Berlin seemed to impose a new pattern upon European and world relationships. The origins of this situation could be traced back to that shift in the orbits of power which had taken place by 1870.

PART FIVE

DEMOCRACY AND SOCIALISM
1871–1914

In their two most significant features the forty years after the settlement of 1871 resemble the generation after 1815. They are a period of internal tensions between forces seeking to consolidate and perpetuate the political and social order that had been established by 1871, and rival forces seeking to transform society by new forms of organization and reform. They are also years of peace following an era of great wars, though years marked by frequent tensions and minor conflicts between the great European powers. Since history never repeats itself, the actual forces and the nature of the issues about which they were in conflict were different from those that shaped Europe after 1815. But in a broad and general way the nations of Europe passed through another phase of postwar settlement and reconstruction, both internal and international; and the phase ended, as the first phase between 1815 and 1854 had ended, in ordeal by battle in 1914.

Whereas the forces of continuity and establishment after 1815 had been mostly conservative institutions, classes, and creeds, their counterparts after 1871 were mostly liberal-conservative institutions, classes, and creeds, attempting to find stability through wider electorates, parliamentary representative institutions, and strong central authority.[1] Whereas the forces of change and revolution after 1815 had been mostly liberal and socialist movements demanding constitutional rights and social reforms, their counterparts after 1871 were socialist, anarchist, and communist movements demanding more complete democracy and economic reorganization. In the earlier generation the forces of change had combined with insurgent nationalism in central and eastern Europe; in the later, they combined with insurgent nationalism in eastern Europe and in Asia.

Whereas international order after 1815 had rested formally on the 'concert of Europe' and more basically upon the continental hegemony of Austria maintained through the 'system' of Metternich,[2] it rested after 1871 ostensibly upon a 'balance of power' between the major European states and more basically upon the continental hegemony of Germany. The system of alliances which Bismarck constructed after

1. See pp. 99–111.
2. See pp. 130–40.

1871 to provide security for Germany provoked a counter-system of alliances hinging upon France; and so long as balance between them prevailed and they served to restrain wanton aggression by either side, they underpinned the settlement of 1871. When, after 1890, they bred mutual fear of aggression and a competition in armaments, they resulted in a series of acute international crises which culminated in war. These crises were closely connected on one hand with the tensions of the Eastern Question, and on the other with the hectic rivalry of the maritime powers for overseas colonies. While dynastic imperialisms of the old kind crumbled in eastern Europe, colonial imperialisms of the new kind clashed in Asia and Africa.

This whole conjunction of conflicts governed the course of European history between 1871 and 1914; their total outcome gave shape and pattern to European affairs in the twentieth century. Part V is devoted to examining the internal developments of European states before 1914, Part VI to the international developments of the same years. What matters most throughout is the interplay between the two, and the intricate reshaping of international relations by domestic changes, of domestic affairs by international relations. This interplay is indicated throughout both parts, and is summarized as 'the system of alliances'.[1]

1. See p. 524.

CHAPTER 16

THE PATTERN OF PARLIAMENTARY DEMOCRACY

THE NEW ELECTORATES

IN almost the whole of western and central Europe, parliamentary institutions developed between 1871 and 1914. They varied widely in form and in effectiveness, in their electoral basis and in the extent of their control over governments. Because most states were still kingdoms (Switzerland, France, and after 1910 Portugal, being the only republics in Europe) these parliamentary institutions were usually, as in the United Kingdom, the bridge between a strong centralized governmental authority and demands of peoples for more direct representation and more general participation in the shaping of national policies. They were at least a provisional solution to the old problem, which had agitated European civilization since 1815, of how to establish a closer mutual relationship between state and society, between government and governed.[1]

Wider Franchise. France was ahead of all other countries in having effective universal male suffrage from 1871 onwards. The electoral laws of 1848, which were revived in 1871 and again in 1875, gave the vote to some ten million Frenchmen. The electorate of the United Kingdom after the reform acts of 1867–8 numbered only between two and a half and three million. But in 1884 Gladstone passed a further act which extended the electorate to about five million, or roughly one sixth of the population. This made the rural electorate as democratic as the urban, and was the first clear recognition of the radical principle that the individual, regardless of property qualification, was entitled to a vote. It applied to Ireland as well as to England and Wales. It was followed by a redistribution of seats which established single-member constituencies for all save the universities and the larger towns – with more than 50,000 inhabitants. In 1883 a Corrupt Practices Act effectively attacked the rowdiness and abuses that had prevailed during elections. Together with the secret ballot, which had been instituted in 1872, these reforms launched Britain on the broad road towards political democracy. In neither Britain nor France were women given the parliamentary vote before 1914, and in Britain nearly a quarter of even the adult male population remained voteless until 1918. But because the general principles

1. See pp. 123 and 233.

of universal personal suffrage had now won the day, it was to be only a matter of time before they permeated the electoral systems of both countries.

Other western states, having instituted parliamentary systems in the years before 1870, developed along comparable lines.[1] Switzerland had universal male suffrage after 1874. In Belgium until 1893 property qualifications restricted the electorate to less than five per cent of the population, but a reform of that year established universal male suffrage with the addition of plural voting for men with special property or educational qualifications. In the Netherlands, reforms of 1887 and 1896 extended the electorate from two per cent to fourteen per cent of the population, but universal suffrage came only in 1917. Spain introduced universal male suffrage in 1890, Norway in 1898. Finland and Norway pioneered female suffrage in 1907. But in Portugal and Sweden the electorates remained comparatively restricted until after 1900. The two great new states of Germany and Italy differed widely in these respects. Bismarck had permitted the Reichstag to be elected by universal male suffrage, but the decisive power wielded by the upper house (Bundesrat), and still more by the Emperor and his Chancellor, ensured that government could be conducted without undue dependence on a democratically elected assembly. Of the German states, Baden adopted universal male suffrage in 1904, Bavaria and Württemberg two years later. In Italy, on the other hand, the constitutional monarchy retained its mid nineteenth-century restrictiveness, and even the electoral reform of 1882 widened the electorate to only about two million, or seven per cent of the population. Most Italian men gained the vote, at last, in 1912. Whereas the age for voting rights was twenty-one in the United Kingdom and France, in most other countries it was more. In the German Reich it was as high as twenty-five; and in Italy, even in 1914, it was thirty.

In the states of eastern Europe the same tendencies were at work, though often more weakly and slowly, as befitted the stage of social development in those lands. Austria adopted universal manhood suffrage in 1907, after adding in 1896 a fifth class representing the mass of the population to her former four-class system based on property. Hungary preserved until 1918 a complex system of franchise restrictions resting on qualifications of age, taxation, property, official status, and national privileges, which admitted only five per cent of her population to the electorate. Rumanian politics were very narrowly restricted. In the Ottoman and Russian Empires there was no suffrage at all, until after the revolutions of 1908 in Turkey, of 1905 in Russia.

Behind the whole chequered story, in spite of all the many diver-

1. See p. 260.

gences and restrictions, there can be discerned a great tide of movement. Democracy was advancing everywhere in Europe, and by 1914 it was lapping the frontiers of Asia. The symbol was the right of the individual citizen to vote – a right increasingly buttressed from the 1880s onwards by secrecy of the ballot. The vote was often endowed, by enthusiastic radicals and frightened conservatives alike, with a magic power. Too many radicals expected universal suffrage to bring the millennium – to sweep away before it the last relics of feudalism, of aristocratic and plutocratic privilege, of popular squalor and ignorance. Too many conservatives and moderate liberals took the radicals at their word, and feared that democracy would demolish monarchy, church, religion, public order, and all that they cherished. Therefore the struggles for extensions of the franchise and secrecy of the ballot were often long and bitter, raising exaggerated hopes on one side, excessive fears on the other.

It was seldom that mere extensions of the vote produced any results as dramatic as this. Constitutional liberals knew many ways, effective enough, to check the operations of full democracy: devices such as separate estates, second chambers, plural voting, party agreements. Elected representatives were usually moderate men, for the most part lawyers and technicians, businessmen and bankers, and a whole class of professional politicians whose skill lay in finding modes of compromise and the practical devices of parliamentary moderation. Napoleon III, Disraeli, and Bismarck had been shrewder than many of their contemporaries or successors in sensing that the vote of the masses was as likely to favour strong government and nationalist policies as it was to support revolutionary or destructive forces. In France, Gambetta converted the peasants to republicanism, but it was to a moderate and somewhat conservative republicanism, respectful of private property and intolerant of the revolutionary excesses of the big towns. The crushing of the Paris Commune in 1871, by the forces of the moderate constitutional government and of the French provinces, was symbolic of the new order in Europe. So was Bismarck's successful manipulation of the popularly elected German Reichstag after 1871, and Crispi's domination of the unruly and weak Italian parliaments.

Growth of Population. The new electorates of Europe were large, not only because of extension of the franchise, but also because of the growth of populations. The immense increase of population in earlier decades [1] was now producing the most momentous of all modern European phenomena – 'the age of the masses'. This, even more than the spread of democratic ideas, compelled every state to overhaul its

1. See p. 251.

machinery of government and administration. The accumulated consequences of this fact were to make the twentieth century unique in its problems and its opportunities. Between 1870 and 1914 Europe as a whole maintained the dizzy speed of its growth, and grew at an average rate of more than one per cent each year. The 293 million in 1870 became 490 million by 1914. The last three decades of the nineteenth century, which saw the increase of Europe's inhabitants by nearly one third, saw also the emigration of twenty-five million more to North America, South America, and Australasia. The earlier rate of increase tended to slow down in the western nations but to accelerate in the central and eastern nations. Between 1871 and 1914 the population of the United Kingdom increased by nearly half, that of Germany by more than half, that of Russia by nearly three quarters. Italy grew more slowly than Germany, from twenty-seven to thirty-five million; but France grew more slowly still, from thirty-seven to only forty million. Many Italians emigrated, whereas in France immigration constantly exceeded emigration. The significance of these differences for the balance of power between the largest states of Europe will more appropriately be considered later.[1] Its significance for internal politics was that every European government now had to administer and serve the interests of larger and denser agglomerations of people than ever before in the history of mankind. When the First World War began, the United Kingdom was still, as she had been since 1815, the most highly urbanized country in Europe, whereas France clung stubbornly to her rural character. But after her political unification Germany swung over sharply from a population almost as rural as the French to a position in which three out of every five Germans lived in towns. This 'flight to the towns' had begun before 1871,[2] but it now took place in Germany at a speed unrivalled by any other nation.

These changes in greater or lesser degree affected all European countries. In terms of politics and administration they meant that all governments were confronted with problems that British governments had been obliged to tackle earlier in the century. These were problems of how to govern densely populated industrial towns; how to ensure adequate provision for public health and sanitation, public order, and police; how to protect industrial workers against bad conditions of working and living. Perplexing social problems were forced upon every government by the course of events; and the parallel growth of democratic ideas and of wider electorates ensured for these problems a high priority of attention.

1. See p. 532.
2. See p. 252.

354

The decrease in death rates, which so largely accounted for the general growth of population in these years, was still further promoted by these improved provisions for public health and sanitation which the growth of large cities made necessary. The researches of Louis Pasteur into the role of microbes in causing disease and of Joseph Lister into chemical methods of destroying these microbes resulted in better hospitalization and better public sanitation. The German physician and scientist, Rudolf Virchow, pioneered the new sanitation in Berlin; while the Benthamite radical Edwin Chadwick, the Tory radical Benjamin Disraeli, and their like in other countries persuaded governments and local authorities that pure water supply, the scientific disposal of sewage, the regular collection of refuse, were essential services in modern towns. Meanwhile a host of research institutes concerned with the study of bacteriology evolved the wonderful science of preventive medicine. The determination of which germs caused the most frequent epidemic diseases and the discovery of how to guard against them by inoculation, quarantine, and appropriate medical care and treatment combined to revolutionize modern medicine.

By 1914 European civilization had discovered how to protect itself against such venerable scourges as cholera, bubonic plague, typhoid, malaria, smallpox, and most of the more deadly destroyers of mankind. As a result, the expectation of life of babies born in England and Wales was over ten years more in 1914 than it had been in 1871. The elaborate organization, and frequently the powers of legal compulsion, which such preventive techniques required could come only from national governments. Nearly every state in Europe, by 1914, had a code of legislation governing the building of houses and the making of streets; ensuring minimum standards of sanitation, safety, and conditions of labour in factories, mines, and mills; regulating the entry of ships into ports; and enforcing standards of purity and cleanliness in food and drink. In Britain the first landmarks were Disraeli's Public Health Act of 1875 and a series of housing acts from 1875 onward. With the rapid growth of large towns and of mechanized industry, a larger proportion of every electorate was an industrial, wage-earning class dwelling in or near large towns and making its living in conditions that demanded greater social discipline, a higher degree of organization, and more sustained administrative activity on the part of governments. Every state, in this minimum sense, was becoming a welfare state even before 1914.

Social Reforms. Accordingly, the politics and policies of all European states came, in these years, to be greatly concerned with social problems. This pressure of demand for a more active state came into conflict, especially in western countries, with the recently dominant tendencies towards free trade, *laissez faire*, and a divorce of politics from economic and social affairs. The more doctrinaire liberals, wedded to notions of free trade and free enterprise, found themselves being pushed from the left – partly by more radical-minded liberals and partly by the growing parliamentary socialist movements and labour organizations. In the novel circumstances of large popular electorates for whose votes rival political parties had to compete, there was a strong temptation for politicians to outbid one another. For this reason many of the social welfare measures passed in these years were the work of conservative parties, or of liberal parties obliged to yield to the pressure of their more radical supporters. Larger towns and larger electorates conspired to change the whole purport of state activity, as well as to make it more democratic.

A host of important consequences followed. Parliaments became busier passing legislation that imposed upon governments new kinds of work and organization; local authorities and officials blossomed into fresh life; and new sources of taxation had to be tapped to finance such activities. By illustrating each of these three tendencies, it is possible to assess the new significance of parliamentary democracy in Europe.

First, legislation extended the activities of governments into new fields. Britain, by 1871, already had extensive regulations governing the conditions and hours of work in factories, mines, and mills. Conservative governments passed laws in 1878, 1891, and 1901, which consolidated previous controls. But it was the Liberal governments after 1905, led by Sir Henry Campbell-Bannerman and H. H. Asquith, and under pressure from organized labour, which undertook more general legislation about social problems. In 1909 a Trade Boards Act attacked 'sweating' in certain trades. It was effective enough to be soon extended to others. Conditions of shop assistants were improved by a Shops Act of 1911, which introduced the principle of a legal weekly half holiday, and a Coal Mines Act consolidated the laws applicable to work in mines. In the same year the National Insurance Act introduced a vast contributory scheme insuring the whole working population against sickness, providing for free medical attention, and insuring some categories of workers against unemployment. Modelled on the German laws of 1883–9, with which Bismarck had contrived to steal the thunder of the socialists by paternalist action on behalf of the workers, it anglicized the scheme to the extent of bringing in friendly societies and trade unions as 'approved societies' to help administer the money benefits for their members. As in education and poor relief, such cooperation between the state and voluntary bodies was characteristic of the British approach to these new social problems. Two years before, a start had been made in providing non-contributory old age pensions, on a very limited basis and as an addition to the many private schemes for superannuation.

Many of the other social welfare schemes introduced into Great Britain in these years were imitated from European examples. The Housing and Town Planning Act of 1909 was in part also prompted by German example, though it proved more of an obstruction than a help to effective town planning. In the 1890s Infants' Welfare Centres began, with schemes for supplying clean milk free to poor mothers (an idea that had originated in France) and 'schools for mothers' (imitated from Ghent). The successive moves to build up a national system of primary and secondary education, culminating in the Education Act of 1902, were largely an effort to catch up on the more advanced educational systems established earlier in France and Germany. The adherence of English liberalism to doctrines of free trade and *laissez faire* was not unconnected with its relative slowness in meeting the pressing social problems of the last years of the century.

In France the traditions of paternalist legislation declined with the fall of the Second Empire, and the prolonged struggle of the republican parties to secure the Republic against its monarchist and Bonapartist threats delayed any serious tackling of social problems. Nor, with her slow industrialization and urbanization, and the prevalence of small towns and villages, small firms and farms, was France faced with social problems of the same scale or urgency as those in Britain and Germany. Characteristically, the most effective French labour regulations derived not from politics at all but from the activities of the bureaucracy, where the traditions of Bonapartist paternalism remained strongest. In the 1890s it set up workers' delegations for the mines, and got laws passed regulating hygiene, limiting women's work to ten hours a day, and providing in part for pensions and accident insurance. In 1900 the maximum working day was limited to ten hours, and in 1906 a six-day week was enforced. When Georges Clemenceau formed his ministry of 1906, with a seventeen-point programme which included various proposals for workers' welfare, it came to practically nothing. But labour legislation was codified between 1910 and 1912, old age pensions were instituted, and enough had been done by 1914 to give French industrial workers as a class some protection and relief from a state which in so many other respects remained more responsive to the interests of small capitalists and landed proprietors.

By 1914 every European country outside Russia and the Balkans had relatively well-developed codes of factory and labour legislation, comparable with the British and French. Austria set up a system of national factory inspection in 1883, and in 1907 issued an elaborate industrial code consolidating regulations that prohibited employment of children under twelve, prescribed an eleven-hour day in industry, and provided for good sanitation and protection against injury. Separate Swiss cantons, led by Zürich, followed the same course, and by 1877 a comprehensive federal statute was passed, applying to all cantons. In the same decade the Netherlands and Belgium introduced comparable laws. Italy and Spain lagged far behind other countries, but between 1886 and 1904 they too made some progress in labour legislation, the Italian being closely modelled on the German.

Just as Germany provided the most spectacular example, in these years, of massive and speedy industrial expansion, so she also set the pace in systematic social legislation. The emphasis in the German system lay neither on factory legislation, which Bismarck distrusted as external interference in employers' affairs, nor on unemployment insurance, which he treated as of minor importance. It aimed at a comprehensive national provision for security against the three commonest vicissitudes of urban life – sickness, accident, and incapacity in old age. Acts tackling successively these three problems were passed in 1883, 1884, and 1889. In 1911 the whole law of social insurance was codified and extended to various classes of non-industrial workers, such as agricultural labourers and domestic servants. Before these laws were passed, a multitude of local provisions had been made voluntarily by benefit societies, guilds, burial clubs, and parishes. The Reich system utilized these older forms but gradually absorbed and replaced them by new local and factory associations which administered the insurance schemes. By 1913 some fourteen and a half million persons were insured in this way. To the sickness and pension funds, both workers and employers contributed and both were represented on their management. In the course of time such benefits as free medical attendance and hospital care were extended, and by 1914 codes of factory legislation and of child labour were at last added. Although the prewar Reich did not set up unemployment insurance, it set up labour exchanges, and some municipalities had local schemes of insurance and relief for unemployed workers. Germans were pioneers in the thoroughness and extent of their welfare system. When war began, German workers were better protected against the hazards of an industrial society than those of any other country. This was a not unimportant element in her national solidarity and strength.

Germany's neighbours, impressed by these further developments, were quick to imitate them in whole or in part. Belgium and Denmark, as well as the United Kingdom, imitated all three forms of insurance.

Austria adopted accident and sickness insurance in 1887-8, Italy and Switzerland in the 1890s. In these same years Britain, France, Norway, Spain, and the Netherlands introduced legislation that obliged employers to compensate their workers for accidents that occurred during work. Everywhere the state shouldered new kinds of responsibility for the safety and well-being of its citizens, and the principle of contributory insurance helped to reconcile *laissez-faire* individualism with this spectacular growth of state activity.

Local Government and Taxation. Secondly, this expansion of social security systems, combined with the urbanization of much of European society, called for a general overhaul of local government and administration. In the United Kingdom a whole new phase in the history of her local government began in the 1870s, led by the big northern industrial towns such as Birmingham and Liverpool. The radical Joseph Chamberlain was mayor of Birmingham between 1873 and 1875. He ran the gas and water supplies as municipal undertakings. He initiated the first successful local programme of slum clearance, public parks, and recreation grounds. In 1880 Liverpool succeeded in its appeal for a loan from private investors for municipal enterprise, instead of borrowing from the central government, and it followed Birmingham's example of slum clearance. A Municipal Corporations Act of 1882 swept away the last legal restrictions on services that municipal corporations could provide. During the next decade municipal enterprise, or 'gas and water socialism', became the most impressive feature of local government. Local Government Acts of 1888 and 1894 democratized all local authorities by creating county councils elected as were the borough councils. To them were transferred nearly all the administrative duties hitherto carried out by un-elected justices of the peace, and by a host of sanitary and education boards which had been set up piecemeal during the previous half century, often with overlapping and confused areas and duties. To meet the objections of the large towns to having any of their services run by county councils, a special new category of county boroughs was created, having all the powers of county councils and so being immune from county interference. Some sixty big towns gained this status. Outside them, the county system was subdivided into urban and rural districts, whose councils were also elected but whose duties were more limited. London, always a special problem because of its vast size, was entrusted to a special London County Council. There the recently formed Fabian Society, led by Sidney Webb, found a rich field for practising its socialist principles. By the end of the century nearly every large town took pride in its municipally owned parks, water supply, gas works, tramway lines, schools, hospitals, museums, art galleries, public baths, and similar amenities of all kinds. In this work individualistic radicals with no enthusiasm for socialism could join with democratic socialists in caring for the welfare of all citizens.

By 1914 most large cities on the continent trod the same path, endowing Europe with a great new equipment of municipal public utility services, markets, laundries, slaughterhouses, hospitals, and labour exchanges. Several countries found it equally necessary to endow local authorities with wider powers in order to enable them to carry out these labours. In 1884 the powers of French municipal councils and mayors were redefined, and the communes were given general authority to provide for all matters 'of communal interest'. Under energetic mayors this led them into wide fields of activity, A few years later Italian provincial and communal administrations were given greater regional freedom from central interference in matters of local government, and municipal services flourished. In lands such as Belgium or Sweden, where provincial and communal independence had preceded the national state itself, local government was inevitably strong and active, and Swedish municipal authorities were democratized in 1909. Germany surpassed most other countries in the massiveness of its municipal activities; and in Vienna the energetic Christian Socialist mayor, Karl Lueger, municipalized most civic utilities and strove to persuade a reluctant city council to tackle the formidable housing problem. All over Europe, while cabinets and chancelleries talked increasingly of guns and warships, local councils and mayors were busy planning schools and hospitals. Without this basic reorganization of civic life which took place everywhere in the generation before 1914, it is unlikely that the structure of civilized life in Europe would have withstood so well the strains and burdens of four years of war.

Thirdly, all the increased activity of central and local governments cost money, and rulers everywhere were driven to find new ways of assessing, collecting, and allocating national revenue. Until after 1871 direct income tax had been an institution virtually peculiar to Great Britain. In the climate of opinion favourable to freer trade (and in the eyes of electorates of consumers) indirect taxes became unpopular. Progressive direct taxation, scientifically assessed and collected in proportion to wealth, came increasingly into favour. Even so, it roused fears of excessive official inquisition into private finances and of unrestrainable public expenditure, and was everywhere greeted with great suspicion. Economic expansion was greatly increasing the national income of every country; but governments had to discover acceptable and preferably painless ways in which to divert a large enough proportion of this wealth into national treasuries.

In Britain the greatest constitutional crisis of the period, involving a long conflict between the House of Commons and the House of Lords, arose over this very issue. In his budget of 1909 the Liberal chancellor of the exchequer, David Lloyd George, included the whole gamut of new fiscal devices which had been evolving for some years: heavy duties on tobacco and liquor; heavier death duties on personal estates, which had first been introduced by Sir William Harcourt in 1894; graded and heavier income tax; an additional 'supertax' on incomes above a fairly high level; a duty of twenty per cent on the unearned increment of land values, to be paid whenever land changed hands; and a charge on the capital value of undeveloped land and minerals. The Conservative majority in the House of Lords broke convention by rejecting this budget until it could be referred to the electorate for approval, and so initiated a two-year battle, which was ended only by the surrender of the Lords and the passing of the Parliament Act of 1911. This important Act permanently removed the Lords' control over money bills and reduced their power over other bills to a mere capacity to delay them for two years. The merit of death duties, income tax, and supertax in the eyes of radicals and socialists – and their infamy in the eyes of conservatives and more moderate liberals – was that once accepted in principle they were capable of yielding an ever greater return by a simple tightening of the screw. The screw was, in fact, repeatedly tightened throughout the following half century.

During the 1890s, *pari passu* with the growth of governmental expenditures on social services and on armaments, Germany and her component states, as well as Italy, Austria, Norway, and Spain, all introduced or steepened systems of income tax. France repeatedly shied away from it, though in 1901 she resorted to progressive death duties; it was 1917 before she at last introduced a not very satisfactory system of income tax. With the drift back to protectionism in commercial policy in the last quarter of the century, indirect taxes generally yielded a higher share of revenue than before. Every state had clung to considerable sources of indirect taxation, and as late as 1900 the bulk of the revenue of most governments came from these sources. Progressive taxation, weighing heavier on the more wealthy, was accepted by liberals as in accord with the principle of equality of sacrifice. To radicals and socialists it was welcome as in itself an instrument for achieving greater equality by systematically redistributing wealth. The modern state was to assume more and more the role of Robin Hood, robbing the rich to feed the poor.

Russia and Turkey. The most striking feature of all these great changes in the size and extent of electorates, in the character and scope of central and local government activity, and in the structure of state finance, was their virtual universality in Europe. Even the two eastern Empires of Russia and Ottoman Turkey, though the forces operating in them were in many ways so different from those in western and central Europe, were not unaffected by these tendencies. District and provincial assemblies (*zemstvo* institutions) had been introduced in Russia from 1865 onwards. Though the noble, landowning, and official classes tended to dominate them, they did considerable work in improving public health, famine relief, road building, and even education. Municipal councils had also been set up in 1870, and in the revolutionary crisis of 1905 these were strong and independent enough to join with the *zemstvo* representatives in demanding full civil liberties and a legislative assembly elected by universal suffrage.[1] In spite of many changes in the fiscal system, the bulk of the Russian government's revenue before 1914 was drawn from the peasants and the town workers. The land tax bore twice as heavily on peasant-owned land as on estates of the nobles. A light inheritance tax was instituted in 1882 but reduced in 1895. Indirect taxation remained extremely heavy. Important duties such as that on sugar worked in the opposite direction to income tax – the tax on sugar was collected mainly from the poor consumers and handed on as subsidies to the exporting sugar producers of the southwest provinces. As in pre-revolutionary France, a complex, unjust, and unscientific fiscal system was important in creating the revolutionary situation of 1917 in Russia. The tsardom financed its colossal war expenditure in 1914 partly from its large gold reserves and partly from extensive foreign loans. It was bankrupt before 1917.

Turkey, after the abortive attempts at constitutionalism and reform between 1861 and 1876,[2] fell for a whole generation under the oriental despotism of Sultan Abdul Hamid II, known as 'Abdul the Damned'. Though a man of considerable ability and shrewdness, he had a deep antipathy to everything Christian, western, and European, especially after his reverses in the Russo-Turkish War of 1877 and the further losses exacted from him by the western powers at the Congress of Berlin in 1878.[3] He therefore devoted his talents to ensuring his own undisputed rule and to excluding, as far as he could, disturbing western influences from his dominions. He lived on a huge national debt, but saw to it that the interest on it due to European investors was promptly paid, even when his own administrators went unpaid. As in Russia, a generation of misrule culminated in revolution. In 1908 the 'Young

1. See p. 405. 2. See p. 341.
3. See p. 464.

Turks', westernized Ottoman patriots, brought about a revolution demanding the revival of the abortive constitution of 1876 which, having bestowed upon Turkey a complete parliamentary system by a stroke of the sultan's pen, had been by the same means entirely overthrown. Abdul blandly granted it – and again tried to abolish it the following year. But this time the Young Turks counter-attacked and deposed Abdul in favour of his more amiable younger brother, Mohammed V. Members of the new Turkish government, though almost as brutally intolerant as their predecessors, unable to carry out much of their programme, and beset by revolts and wars that disrupted the already fragile Empire, did something to modernize the state and open it to western influences.[1]

The revolutionary situations that built up in Russia by 1905 and in Turkey by 1908 were in part due to failures in war; to Turkish losses in 1877–8 and to Russian defeat in the Russo-Japanese War of 1904–5. But these wars only brought to a head inherent tensions which had been apparent in each country during the previous generation. And these tensions were closely related to the absence of that close interplay between state and society which other European states had ensured through widened electorates, parliamentary representative institutions, and all the developments of beneficial governmental activities already described. That the lack of such developments in the two great eastern empires culminated in revolutions is some indication of why revolutionary movements made so little real headway in western and central Europe during these years. It was not for lack of such movements. They existed in abundance and are described below.[2] But it took the prolonged upheaval of the First World War to give them their opportunity; and while the twentieth century was to perpetuate that close relationship between war and revolution which had existed in Europe since 1815,[3] the generation between 1871 and 1900 was for most of the continent a period of internal consolidation and reorganization rather than revolutionary upheaval. From 1900 onwards the air became charged with more menacing revolutionary currents. Wherever parliamentary institutions, however imperfect, and wider electorates, however defective, were firmly established, they had a moderating and civilizing effect, taming revolutionary fervour as much as they tempered arbitrary government, and promoting works of human welfare which made the life of men richer and happier. It became apparent that the age of the urban masses was susceptible, also, to more irrational, sinister, and

1. See p. 471.   2. See p. 402.
3. See p. 111.

363

violently destructive forces. These forces were to have an important future, of which there were a few portents in the decade before 1914.[1]

PUBLIC OPINION AND POLITICS

Every European government after 1871 regarded it as one of its first duties to provide, or to see that others provided, a system of public education which had two main purposes. It would destroy mass illiteracy by compulsory primary education; and it would produce by higher education an adequate number of more specially educated citizens to meet growing national needs for engineers and doctors, technicians, and administrators. Even before 1871 several states – most notably France and Prussia – had gone far towards creating a complete national system, comprising within one structure all stages of education from the primary schools to the secondary and technical high schools and the universities. By 1914 every western state had some such system in fairly full operation. It was an objective upon which different parties could agree, however violently they might differ about how it should be attained or about how far the state should permit the church to have any hand in the work. The attack on illiteracy was implied in the widening of the electorate. 'We must educate our masters' was an idea in the minds of even very conservative statesmen; and in turn the demand for more equal educational opportunities derived fresh impetus from the existence of wider electorates.

Thus in Britain each extension of the franchise was accompanied by a new educational advance which opened fresh doors of opportunity to children of ability regardless of their parents' wealth. Three years after the Reform Act of 1867 Gladstone passed the Education Act of 1870, which for the first time ordained that a primary school should be within the reach of every English child; and in 1880 attendance became compulsory. In 1871 religious tests that had made Oxford and Cambridge an Anglican monopoly were abolished. In 1902 secondary education was greatly extended and better financed, and so became available to many more pupils. But it was not until 1918, when the electorate was more drastically widened, that Britain instituted a coherent and comprehensive national system of free and compulsory public education.

In general the 1870s were a decade of expanding public education throughout Europe; the 1880s saw such expansion consolidated, as public education was made more universally free and compulsory. Prussia nationalized her existing system in 1872 and made education free in

1. See pp. 372 and 529.

1888. Switzerland made attendance compulsory in her new constitution of 1874; Italy, in 1877; the Netherlands, in 1878; Belgium, in 1879. In most countries, however, until the twentieth century, compulsion applied only to children below nine or ten years old. Shortage of buildings and of teachers made the advance of education everywhere a slow and gradual process. Governments were reluctant to spend the necessarily very large sums of money required for so vast an undertaking. But, considering the novelty, scale, and the cost of the whole department, the chief cause for comment is not the slowness and the mistakes that were undeniable, but the persistence and universality of the great adventure. The Prussian government was spending in 1901 more than thirty times as much on primary education as it had spent thirty years before. In 1914 education authorities in England and Wales were spending nearly twice as much on elementary education as they had spent in 1900, although this was also a period of extremely heavy expenditure on armaments; and there were more than six million children attending grant-aided elementary schools, staffed by 120,000 teachers.

In France the greatest changes came in the 1880s, with the controversial educational laws passed by the anticlerical republican Jules Ferry. Since Napoleon I, France had conceived of a single integrated system ranging from the village school to the *lycée* and the universities, all ultimately controlled by the Ministry of Public Instruction. But each régime had hitherto neglected the primary base of the pyramid, and each had become embroiled in bitter wrangles with the Roman Catholic Church about the relationships that should exist between religious and secular education. The outcome of Ferry's tenures of the Ministry of Public Instruction between 1879 and 1885 was a real network of free, compulsory, primary, secular schools. Many 'free schools' run by the churches survived, though under state inspection and limited supervision, and the number of children attending them was steadily declining by 1914.

Church and State. Prolonged and bitter controversy between church and state about education was a feature of nearly every European country in these years. Even in the United Kingdom, where traditions of religious toleration were strong and anticlericalism was weak, religious controversies greatly impeded the growth of an educational system. In France, Belgium, Germany, Italy, Austria-Hungary, this issue dominated the whole story. It resulted everywhere in the eventual toleration of church schools under varying degrees of restraint, but also in the establishment of a strong anticlericalist and even antireligious bias in the education provided in state schools, as well as in the training of teachers to be employed in them.

In France the feud between church and republic, which raged especially around the issue of education, led eventually to the separation of church and state in 1905 and to a deep rift in French national opinion. In Germany the conflict with the Roman Catholic Church was accentuated by unification itself. The North German Federation had been predominantly Protestant. The addition of the south German states in 1871 made the Roman Catholics a very formidable minority in the new Reich. Their political power was concentrated in the Centre Party in the Reichstag. Bismarck's famous struggle with the Roman Church and the Centre Party, known somewhat grandiloquently as the Kulturkampf, lasted until 1878. He passed the 'May Laws' of 1873–5, which required state approval for the training and even the licensing of priests; suspended and imprisoned priests and bishops; and stiffened secular control over the system of public education. But the conflict in Germany was less sharp than elsewhere. In Belgium, as in France, it provoked a long struggle between clericals and anticlericals, begun during the liberal government of Frère-Orban in 1878 and known as the 'war of the schools'. In Italy between 1887 and 1896 the ministries of the liberal anticlericalist, Francesco Crispi, had many reasons for their turbulence; but one at least was his policy of making religious teaching optional instead of compulsory in the primary schools and of attacking the role of religious orders in education. In Austria-Hungary battles between liberals and clericalists for control of education became inevitably tangled up with rivalries between the various nationalities, each anxious to secure its own schools or to make special provision for the teaching of its own language and culture. In Spain, though most schools belonged to the civil authorities, most schoolmasters were devout Roman Catholics, and since the Concordat of 1851 it was compulsory for them to teach the Catholic religion and catechism. Even so, the Church tried to force the state schools to close down for lack of funds, and preached a ferocious antiliberalism. In Scandinavia, where Lutheranism prevailed, there was little friction between church and state.

All Europe, during this period, was going to school. From the age of five or six the rising generation was increasingly compelled to attend classes regularly, to become at least literate, to learn what governments considered it desirable that every citizen should know. Schoolteachers became a more numerous and more influential element in the life of the community. Usually given a special form of training by the state, and often obliged to teach from a syllabus laid down by a department of the central government, the schoolteachers (many of whom were women) tended to become apostles of the doctrines of secularism or nationalism, the advance guard of anticlericalism. Typical of the outlook and doctrines which state-trained teachers were required to impart to their pupils were those prescribed by Jules Ferry, in a circular letter to primary teachers in which he explained the purport of the law of 1882. Emphasizing the role of the teacher as 'a natural aid to moral and social progress', he urged them 'to prepare a generation of good citizens for our country'. Octave Gréard, his right-hand man, whom he described as 'the first schoolmaster of France', told them that 'in history we must emphasize only the essential features of the development of French nationality, seeking this less in a succession of deeds in war than in the methodical development of institutions and in the progress of social ideas'. The civic virtues of loyalty, discipline, devotion to duty, patriotism, were usually taught in a manner which exalted nationalism and undermined religious faith. Only too often the missionary zeal of the teachers brought internal strife to the villages and small towns of Europe, and their lot became unenviable. By 1894 Georges Clemenceau passed this judgement on the excessive narrowness and the unimaginative outlook which infused French primary education:

In futile efforts the pitiful ambassador of the Republic to the inhabitants of the rural districts consumes his time and his strength. The parents are inaccessible to him; the country squires are his enemies. With the priest there is latent hostility; with the Catholic schools there is open war.... They steal his pupils. They crush him in a hundred ways, sometimes with the connivance of the mayor, usually with the cooperation of the big influences in the commune.

Because this remarkable expansion of popular education took place at a time when the new doctrines of science, realism, positivism, secularism, nationalism, were at flood tide, it caused violent controversy. Its collision with the established creeds and institutions of Christian churches, hitherto the chief sources of education, left deep scars on the body of European opinion. The rising generation was divided into those whose education had been provided by the church in militant mood, and those whose education had been strongly anticlericalist and militantly nationalist. To either side indoctrination seemed more important than the spirit of free inquiry and reflective thought. By the twentieth century some of this acerbity had gone; the Roman Catholic Church under Pope Leo XIII, from 1878 onwards, gradually came to terms with the new states of Europe and the feud between clericals and anticlericals partly burned itself out. But outside the United Kingdom and Scandinavia it was always liable to revive whenever questions and subsidies to church schools or official inspection of all schools raised their heads. To a degree quite unknown in the United Kingdom or the United States of America, European education has been haunted by schism.

The social effects of the great attack on illiteracy were immense. One of the less frequently noticed is the incidental training in social discipline. The bringing together of large numbers of children of the same age into a common classroom under the charge of a trained teacher did much more than destroy illiteracy. For the first time it accustomed the urban masses to a highly integrated community life and a standardized form of group discipline. When the children left the discipline of the classroom, at some age between ten and fourteen, an increasing proportion of them passed on to the no less standardized discipline of the workshop and the factory, the business office and the shop. The foreman, manager, or employer took the place of the schoolteacher. It was often a harsher and less benevolent discipline; but how much did it owe its effectiveness to the preliminary training and conditioning achieved in the classroom? When, as in many European countries after 1871, these strong conditioning circumstances were also reinforced by the equally inescapable and still more rigorous disciplines of military training and national service, the moulding forces of the new generation are seen to be quite revolutionary in their effects.

The unit of the family or the village or the church ceased to be supreme among the communities that normally shaped the early life and experience of children. Living in larger, more impersonal, and more highly organized communities was an art that had to be learned. Without it an ordered and civilized life in the big modern communities of cities and nations would have been impossible. Yet the learning of it imposed great burdens of adaptation and conformity, and often brought new senses of frustration, psychological disturbances, and distortions, which might find alternative outlets either in antisocial urges or in a too easy surrender to the instincts of the herd. The millions who in youth and adolescence had known schoolroom, barracks, and factory were bound to be different in outlook and behaviour from their predecessors who had known none of these things. The young people who grew up, worked, and voted in the generation before 1914 were the first generation that had so universally known these experiences. They marked a turning point in the social history of modern Europe.

By 1914 popular education, both in its intended and in its unintended effects, was no doubt the greatest single force moulding and conditioning public opinion in general. From the classroom came many of those basic assumptions and implicit forms of behaviour which unconsciously determined much of what people thought and did. But other great new engines for shaping opinion were coming into operation. One was popular associations of all kinds, and not least political parties; another was the popular Press, enjoying a mass circulation and influence. These two media, more than any other, formed the link between public opinion and politics in the age of wider electorates and parliamentary governments.

Popular Associations and the Press. The rights of free association and public meeting had traditionally been regarded as inherent rights of democracy. They were, for example, stipulated in the Belgian Constitution of 1831. Yet it was only in some European states, and there belatedly, that full freedom for citizens to associate and meet together for private or public purposes was granted before 1914. By 1871 the United Kingdom had come to accept freedom of association, meeting, and speech as normal. The mid nineteenth century was a golden age of large popular associations for promoting every sort of cause.[1] But it was only by 1876 that trade unions won full legal recognition and protection, and their rights were not fully determined until the Trades Disputes Acts of 1906 and 1913. In France the famous Le Chapelier Law of 1791 and the Napoleonic Penal Code forbade all forms of economic association of workers, but this had been partially relaxed in 1864, and in 1884 freedom of association was finally granted. In general, freedom of association was securely recognized and practised in all the Scandinavian and western states before the end of the century; but in central Europe – especially in Germany, Italy, and Austria-Hungary – it was subject to severe curtailment in certain circumstances, despite formal recognition of civil liberties in laws and constitutions.

In all three countries trade unions grew and flourished in spite of periodic setbacks. Other forms of association were less secure. In 1878 when Bismarck, as German Chancellor, was engaged in battle with the socialist parties, he passed a law that gave him power to suppress all independent labour organizations, all socialist political and economic associations, and all their publications. They were forbidden to hold meetings. The law was renewed until 1890, and in the intervening years over 150 periodicals were suppressed by the police, and over 1,500 persons arrested. In 1894 the Italian Premier, Crispi, launched a similar attack against the socialists, dissolving their associations, suppressing their newspapers, and arresting many people. He met with somewhat less success than Bismarck for whereas the German socialists lost nearly a third of their former votes in the elections of 1881, the Italian socialists gained considerably in the elections of 1895. In both countries the repressive measures ultimately failed to achieve their ends, and socialist movements gained in strength.[2] In Austria the constitutional laws of 1867 had authorized the Emperor to issue 'emergency regulations' in

1. See p. 193.
2. See p. 397.

case of need. From 1900 until 1907 Austrian politics fell into such a deadlock that the prime ministers virtually ruled by emergency powers, and constitutional government became a farce. In Russia freedom of association and speech were as short-lived as the brief constitutional interlude of 1905–6; in Turkey they never really existed. Clearly, as one moved further east in Europe, constitutional government and its attendant rights and civil liberties had struck shallower roots. They were still liable to wither and die, unless revolution should plant new seeds.

Freedom of speech and of the Press, closely linked in purport with freedom of association and public meeting, was an equally vital element in the forming of public opinion in politics. Again these rights, so widely canvassed before 1848, had often been embodied in the new written constitutions of Europe: in the Belgian of 1831, the Dutch of 1848, the Austrian of 1867, the Swiss of 1874, the Spanish of 1876. In Britain the last tax on newspapers, condemned as a 'tax on knowledge',. was removed in 1861; and the last restriction, in 1869. Germany in 1874, France in 1881, enacted special laws guaranteeing the Press against governmental interference. Although the political Press was still, in central and eastern Europe, liable to suffer occasional oppression in special circumstances, as under Bismarck's antisocialist law of 1878, there was in general enough freedom of expression for the Press to develop in vigour, scale, circulation, and influence. With the more modern techniques for collecting news, printing papers, and speedily distributing them, new opportunities for popular journalism appeared; and the growth of a much larger literate public, more directly interested in politics, ensured that these opportunities would be seized, whether for profit making and advertising, or for purposes of political propaganda and persuasion. It has been estimated that the number of newspapers published in Europe doubled during the last two decades of the century; and this increase was mainly due to the growth of a new kind of Press. It was less literary and less sophisticated than the old, but more popular in its mass appeal, more sensational and irresponsible, cheaper and more dependent for its finances upon commercial advertising than upon the subscriptions of its readers.

During the 1870s and 1880s there existed a good, vigorous middle-class Press, represented by the British *Daily Telegraph* and *Daily News* (dating from 1846), the French *Le Matin*, the German *Neueste Nachrichten*, and the Italian *Messaggiero*. It was quickly followed in the 1890s and after by a still more popular and proletarian Press, often modelled on the spectacularly successful Hearst Press in the United States and inaugurated by such journals as Lord Northchiffe's *Daily Mail*, the Parisian *Petit Journal*, and the Berlin *Lokal-Anzeiger*. By

1900 each major country had some such papers, exceeding the million mark in daily circulation and fostering a new type of bright popular journalism. They were skilfully calculated to attract the maximum number of readers and therefore the largest advertisement revenue. Highly competitive and commercial in character, they appealed directly to the new literate and semi-literate public. Lord Salisbury might jibe at Northcliffe's *Daily Mail* of 1896 as 'written by office-boys for office-boys'; but this pioneer of the modern Press magnates in Britain had gauged nicely the mentality and prejudices of the public which now mattered most in Britain. He gave it what it wanted – bright accounts of world news, blended with occasional campaigns against some abuse or some alarming foreign government, now arousing hate and then a scare, but always exploiting the excitement of the moment. It paid very handsomely, and others soon imitated it.

Inevitably, political parties and movements came to rely on the Press to keep in contact with their adherents and to rally fresh support to their cause. Every country acquired a political Press as well as a commercial Press, and sometimes the two could be combined in one organ. In Germany the Conservatives had their *Kreuzzeitung*, the Catholic Centre Party its *Germania* (established in 1871), the National Liberals their *National Liberale Korrespondenz*, the Social Democrats their *Vorwärts* and *Leipsiger Volkszeitung*, and each party acquired other local or provincial organs. The German political Press remained basically serious and 'educational' in character, putting heavy emphasis on political issues, editorial opinion, and literary or philosophical articles. It did much to nationalize opinion by focusing it upon issues of importance to the whole Reich, rather than upon those peculiar to the component states. France, too, had strong traditions of political journalism. Of the forty-six general newspapers that appeared in Paris daily in 1914, all save a small handful could be classed as markedly political in bias; but the exceptions were mainly those with the largest circulations which, to maintain sales, carefully avoided alienating any specific category of readers. The demands of party polemics and of mass circulations frequently conflicted in this way, and it is seldom that large circulations have been built on a mainly political appeal. Crime and sport, sex and sensationalism, were the more favourite themes of the largest dailies, before 1914 as since. None the less, party organs were valued and valuable aids in the building of new political and social movements, most obviously the new socialist parties that appeared in most countries by the end of the century. In France *L'Humanité* edited by the socialist leader Jean Jaurès, in Germany the Social Democrats' *Vorwärts*, in Britain the *Daily Herald* of George Lansbury, in Italy *Avanti!*, have a central importance in the history of European socialism.[1]

Public Excitement. Even by 1900 all these tendencies – popular education and literacy, popular associations of publicity and propaganda, and a popular Press – had gone far enough to produce dramatic and often incalculable results in politics, both national and international. As early as 1870 Bismarck's publishing of the Ems telegram, which the following morning set on fire extreme nationalist opinion in both Paris and Berlin and helped to precipitate the Franco-Prussian War, was token enough of the new inflammability and violence of public opinion.[2] The years between 1871 and 1914 were to yield a large number of further examples of the impact of public opinion on politics, of which three may be taken as representative.

One is the prevalence of sensational scandals and affairs in France under the Third Republic. It is improbable that as much corruption, gerrymandering, and political blackmail existed under the parliamentary republic as had existed under its predecessors, the notoriously corrupt monarchy of Louis Philippe before 1848 or the resolutely unjust régime of Napoleon III. The difference after 1875 was partly that the enemies of the republic delighted in uncovering every disreputable fact about it, and partly that social consciences were now more tender and alert. It was easier to excite indignation when so many had cherished high hopes of a democratic and republican régime. In 1887 Daniel Wilson, the son-in-law of the venerable republican leader, Jules Grévy, who had been president of the Republic since 1879, was discovered to have carried on a prosperous traffic in honours and decorations from the very precincts of the president's palace. There ensued a long political crisis, which involved the resignation of both the ministry and the president. In another example the monarchists and Bonapartists hostile to the Republic sponsored the cause of General Boulanger, who had already been active as a popular champion of the demand for 'revenge' against Germany. In 1889 he attempted a *coup d'état*, and the Republic was saved chiefly because his nerve failed him at the last moment. The government took swift action against the chauvinistic League of Patriots and other violent movements that had backed him. Popular excitement, which he had been exploiting, was given timely diversion by national celebrations of the centenary of 1789. Only three years later an even wider scandal concerning the finances of the Panama Canal again rocked the government and the Republic, and led to the trial of six ministers, only one of whom was convicted.

1. See p. 398.
2. See p. 317.

In 1896 came the greatest of the affairs, which split French opinion and had far-reaching effects on the Republic. It was alleged that the chief document on the evidence of which Captain Dreyfus, a Jewish army officer, had been convicted and punished by a military tribunal, had in fact been forged; and that its forger had been protected by the reactionary military authorities, who had seized upon the excuse to expel Jews and Protestants from the armed forces. The great novelist, Emile Zola, published an article 'I Accuse' ('*J'accuse*') in which he deliberately invited legal penalties in order to set out the charges against the army. A whole succession of charges and countercharges meanwhile aroused public excitement to fever pitch, and Zola's trial, in which he was defended by Clemenceau, became a heated political debate. The personal issue of the guilt or innocence of Dreyfus was lost sight of, and the issue became one of general principle. It was a clear issue between the military claim, that the honour and prestige of the army mattered more than injustice to any individual, and the Republican civilian claim, that individual justice must triumph over all else. Both sides exaggerated and inflated the issue until no settlement seemed possible. The Church became implicated on the side of the army, partly because of the unwise behaviour of some of its members and partly because the Republicans were ready to see the hand of clericalism in everything. The affair ended with somewhat half-hearted attempts at a *coup d'état* by extremists of the right, and eventual pardon and reinstatement of Dreyfus. But the depths of bitterness engendered by it, and the violence with which each side fought it for several years, made it seem natural even in 1940 for the overthrow of the Third Republic by Marshal Pétain to be described by Frenchmen as 'the revenge of the anti-Dreyfusards'.

A second example of the impact of public opinion on politics can be drawn from the United Kingdom, where at least parliamentary institutions and traditions of political compromise were by now firmly established. Gladstone touched the chords of the new mass opinion when, in the winter of 1879, at the age of seventy, he stumped the country denouncing Disraeli's policy of imperialism. This Midlothian campaign scandalized Queen Victoria. It had not hitherto been etiquette for a leading statesman to behave in this way. Just before the elections of 1880 he launched a second Midlothian campaign, which his biographer John Morley described as an 'oratorical crusade', but which Disraeli (who did not imitate him) called 'a pilgrimage of passion'. In any case the Liberals won a majority of 137 seats in the elections, so these methods clearly paid. However much the Queen might frown, there was irresistible logic about Gladstone's decision. Now that the franchise had been widened (and Disraeli had widened it), national leaders must expect to have to make some such direct contact with the electorate. Lloyd George was to perpetuate this new kind of electioneering. But the frenzy to which opinion in the whole country could be raised did not become evident until, at the end of the century, Britain became involved in the Boer War against the small Dutch farmers' republics of South Africa. Coming as the climax of a period of colonial expansion, and amid darkening clouds of international tension, it was the first important war in which Britain had engaged since the Crimean War nearly half a century before. The irresponsible swagger with which it was undertaken, and the unexpected reverses that the British forces met with, induced remarkable outbursts of popular anger and rejoicing. Already the crisis of the Russo-Turkish War in 1878 had given the English political vocabulary one word that was to survive because it so aptly fitted the mood. The old conjuror's gibberish word Jingo had become incongruously popular through the music-hall song:

> We don't want to fight, but, by jingo, if we do
> We've got the ships, we've got the men, we've got the money too.

Now the Boer War contributed another, 'mafficking'. It originated in the scenes of popular hysteria with which Londoners, in 1900, greeted the news that the long siege of Mafeking by the Boers had been at last relieved. Jingoism and mafficking were symptomatic of the irrational forces at work in the new age, stirred by the crudest forces of sensationalism and mob emotion. The Boer War, for a time, split the British nation almost as deeply as the Dreyfus Case was, at the same moment, splitting the French; and both coincided with the Spanish-American War, which revealed not dissimilar impulses across the Atlantic.

A third example can best be drawn from the field of international relations. In 1890 the Emperor William II, who two years before had come to the throne of the Reich, dismissed the veteran Bismarck and opened a new era in German policy. Instead of being guided by the shrewd calculations of the realistic Bismarck, Germany was now governed by the theatrical gestures and utterances of her neurotic Emperor and the emotionally unstable ministers whom he chose to advise him. His nervous and inept way of handling German foreign relations made him, even among his own advisers, a byword for clumsiness. The long series of international incidents and crises in which the Kaiser played a central role will be described later.[1] There is little evidence that his behaviour made him at all unpopular at home, and it seems probable that it was accepted as an instinctive reflection of the uncertainties of German national sentiment and the surges of her expansionist aspira-

1. See p. 533.

tions. He was among the first of the great national leaders to exploit the new relationship that was growing up between diplomacy as it had long been conducted by the ruling *élites* of Europe – the frock-coated, top-hatted circles of 'influential people' (*massgebende Kreisen*) – and the new disturbing force, which these men could no longer ignore, of the prejudices, passions, and attitudes of the mass electorate.

Hitherto, although domestic affairs had been directly subject to electoral pressures, diplomatic and military affairs had remained the almost unchallenged province of the *élites* of birth and skill. The Kaiser, by his very vulgarity and emotional instability, was especially sensitive to these pressures. The link between the two was not so much 'public opinion', which suggests something more coherent, rational, and articulated than what actually existed; it was rather 'publicity', the day-by-day reporting of news and views to a gigantic public that was inevitably largely ignorant of the complexities of international relations. This process, which was coming about through the interaction of mass literacy, universal suffrage, and the popular cheap daily Press, was revolutionizing the old diplomacy. The financial burdens of taxation and the personal burdens of military service compelled governments constantly to rally general public support behind their policies, abroad as well as at home. There was an irresistible temptation to short-circuit the process of rational persuasion by appealing to the strongest, because the crudest, of the mass emotions; hatred, anger, and fear. The intensifying competition in armaments which dominated the decade before 1914 was based on this, and so was much of the Kaiser's diplomacy. Long before President Woodrow Wilson demanded 'open covenants openly arrived at', the traditions of secret diplomacy were already giving way to the newer practices of diplomacy by publicity and demagogy. Even before the Kaiser began rattling his sabre, relations among European states were subject to the violent vibrations of national passion and the incantations of imperialism. The murders at Sarajevo, which touched off the great war in 1914, occurred appropriately enough on the day whose patron saint was St Vitus.

CHAPTER 17

SOCIALISM VERSUS NATIONALISM

ECONOMIC AND SOCIAL ORGANIZATIONS

JUST as the growth of Europe's populations and towns brought about a revolution in the electoral basis, structure, and functions of central and local governments, so economic expansion brought about a revolution in the nature and structure of economic organizations. Tendencies that had been apparent before 1871 in Great Britain, Belgium, and France, now became even more dramatically apparent in Germany, Austria-Hungary, and Russia. The whole of Europe was being pulled irresistibly into the pattern of economic development which western nations had been the first to evolve.[1]

German Expansion. Germany outpaced all other nations in the production of wealth, and it was not that western nations stood still. If the output of France's blast furnaces increased sixfold between 1870 and 1904, that of Germany's grew tenfold. By exploiting the rich mineral resources of the Ruhr, the Saar, and Alsace-Lorraine, as well as the newly unified labour power of the Reich, Germany by 1914 had become the greatest industrial nation in Europe. The ratio of industrial potential between Germany and her two western neighbours at that date has been estimated as Germany three: Britain two: France one. This rapid ascendancy of Germany in the economic life of Europe was the most significant feature of the prewar generation. Moreover, whereas France manufactured for home rather than world markets, and her industrial structure of small firms slowed down standardization and total output, Germany manufactured increasingly for export. This made her the chief European rival to Great Britain as the 'workshop of the world', as well as in banking, insurance, and shipping. This rivalry added greatly to the international fears and tensions that sprang from other considerations of national security, naval power, and colonial possessions. The rule of the Iron Chancellor inaugurated an age of iron and steel – commodities which the Reich as he forged it was especially well equipped to produce.

Like Britain half a century earlier, Germany became a food-importing country, despite more scientific and more mechanized agriculture which greatly increased the productivity of her farms. By 1914 about a fifth

1. See p. 178.

of her food was being imported, mainly from the Netherlands, Denmark, and the Danube valley. Already in 1879 Bismarck changed German commercial policy to one of protection, and imposed tariffs in response to pressure from agricultural and industrial interests alike. France, traditionally protectionist, imposed new tariffs throughout the 1880s. During the same decade even the United Kingdom wavered in her free-trade policy. These departures from free-trade policies by the leading industrial nations started a general European movement toward protection. Within the territories of the Reich a rapid expansion of all means of transport and communication – of road, railroads, waterways, mail, and telegraph service – welded the country into one great economic unit. The 11,000 kilometres of railways in 1860 became 19,500 by 1870, 43,000 by 1890, and 61,000 by 1910 (see Diagram 2). Between 1879 and 1884 most of Prussia's roads were brought under state control. Germany's coal output multiplied nearly sevenfold between 1871 and 1913, and her output of lignite, tenfold. The marriage of coal and iron gave her the greatest iron and steel industry in Europe. The firms of Krupp, Thyssen, Stumm-Halberg, and Donnersmark developed huge steel empires. British coal production kept ahead of German, but in the output of pig iron, which is a convenient index of the growth of the iron and steel industries, Germany overtook the United Kingdom before 1900. (See Diagrams 3 and 4.) After 1878 English discovery of the Thomas-Gilcrist process for smelting ore made the phosphoric iron ores of Lorraine available for German steel manufacturing, and was partly responsible for its rapid expansion. The heavy industries of the Ruhr, the Saar, Lorraine, and Silesia became the very foundation of German prosperity and power in Europe.

German electrical and chemical industries expanded no less impressively. Werner von Siemens, who invented the electric dynamo, built up the firm of Siemens and Halske, which specialized in heavy current and in 1903 merged into the Siemens–Schuckert Werke combine. Emil Rathenau created the German Edison Company of 1883, which later became the famous AEG (*Allgemeine Elektrizitäts Gesellschaft*). Between them these two gigantic concerns literally electrified Germany, and by 1906 this new industry was employing more than 100,000 people. In 1913 electrical equipment and electrical goods of all kinds were among Germany's most valuable exports. Her chemical industries prospered partly because her excellent scientific education could be married to rich mineral resources. With the production of a wide variety of industrial and agricultural chemicals, ranging from sulphuric acid and ammonia to pyrites and potassium salts, there grew up important national industries in dyes and fertilizers as well as in explosives and

377

DIAGRAM 2. BUILDING RAILROADS, 1870-1910

approximately in thousands of kilometers

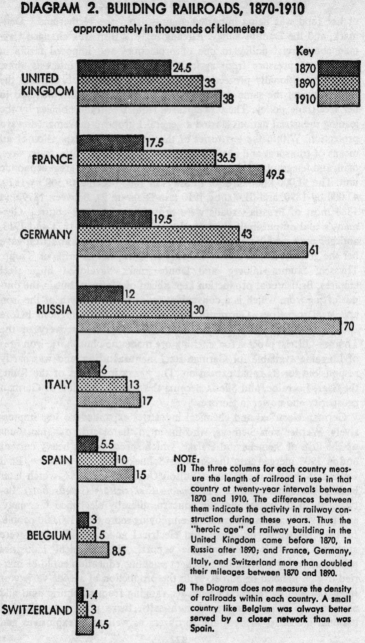

Key
1870
1890
1910

UNITED KINGDOM
24.5
33
38

FRANCE
17.5
36.5
49.5

GERMANY
19.5
43
61

RUSSIA
12
30
70

ITALY
6
13
17

SPAIN
5.5
10
15

BELGIUM
3
5
8.5

SWITZERLAND
1.4
3
4.5

NOTE:

(1) The three columns for each country measure the length of railroad in use in that country at twenty-year intervals between 1870 and 1910. The differences between them indicate the activity in railway construction during these years. Thus the "heroic age" of railway building in the United Kingdom came before 1870, in Russia after 1890; and France, Germany, Italy, and Switzerland more than doubled their mileages between 1870 and 1890.

(2) The Diagram does not measure the density of railroads within each country. A small country like Belgium was always better served by a closer network than was Spain.

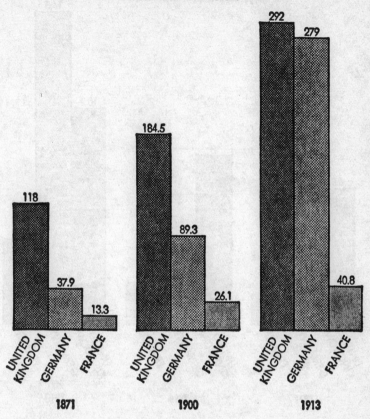

DIAGRAM 3. OUTPUT OF COAL AND LIGNITE, 1871-1913
In millions of metric tons

	1871	1900	1913
UNITED KINGDOM	118	184.5	292
GERMANY	37.9	89.3	279
FRANCE	13.3	26.1	40.8

armaments. The number of people employed in the chemical industries nearly quadrupled between 1885 and 1913, the years of most rapid expansion. The combination of these two especially modern electrical and chemical industries modernized Germany's whole industrial equipment, and gave her immense advantages over other nations.

It was inevitable in these circumstances that German trade should expand, and should come to rival that of the United Kingdom in European markets. The completion of the railway network in Europe brought Germany immense advantages. It even converted her geographical position, previously a handicap, into a positive asset. It no longer mattered

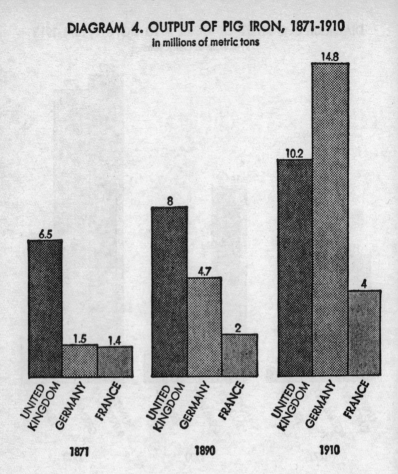

DIAGRAM 4. OUTPUT OF PIG IRON, 1871-1910
in millions of metric tons

6.5 · 1.5 · 1.4

UNITED KINGDOM · GERMANY · FRANCE

1871

8 · 4.7 · 2

UNITED KINGDOM · GERMANY · FRANCE

1890

10.2 · 14.8 · 4

UNITED KINGDOM · GERMANY · FRANCE

1910

that several of her rivers ran northwards into the Baltic, nor that her seacoast was short, nor that mountains hemmed her in on the south. As the great central land power in Europe she became the focus of the whole European network of railroads, with access by rail to Russia and Turkey, by tunnel to Italy, the Balkans, and the Mediterranean ports, by steamship to the Atlantic and Pacific. From 1880 onwards the Reich also promoted the reconstruction of its already good internal canal system, and widened and extended waterways to take steamer traffic. The Kiel Canal was built more for strategic than for economic reasons. From 1886 onwards the great *Hamburg–Amerika* line was expanded by Albert Ballin, until its twenty-two ocean steamers with a gross tonnage

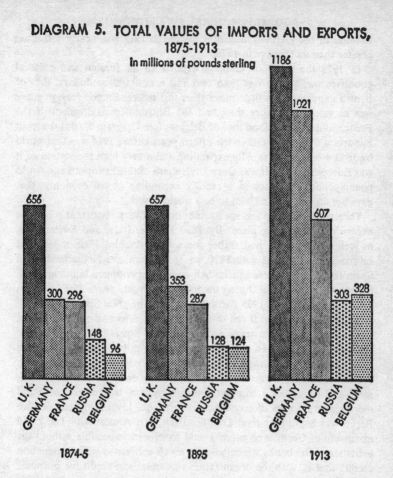

DIAGRAM 5. TOTAL VALUES OF IMPORTS AND EXPORTS, 1875-1913

In millions of pounds sterling

1874-5

- U.K. 656
- GERMANY 300
- FRANCE 296
- RUSSIA 148
- BELGIUM 96

1895

- U.K. 657
- GERMANY 353
- FRANCE 287
- RUSSIA 128
- BELGIUM 124

1913

- U.K. 1186
- GERMANY 1021
- FRANCE 607
- RUSSIA 303
- BELGIUM 328

of little more than 60,500 tons had by 1913 become the HAPAG fleet of 172 steamers, with a gross tonnage of over a million tons. Ballin expanded the lines to the United States, Latin America, and the Far East. He became a close personal adviser of William II. In 1888 its chief rival, the North German Lloyd company (*Nord–Deutscher Lloyd*) of Bremen, began regular sailings to Australia. The ports and harbours of Hamburg and Bremen had to be repeatedly extended, and even between 1900 and 1914 their tonnage of shipping was doubled. When war began, the German merchant fleet was the second largest in the world, exceeded only by Great Britain's. Its steam fleet had come to exceed that of France during the 1880s, and by 1910 was three times as great; and the total tonnage of the German merchant marine in 1913 was nearly 490 times greater than its tonnage in 1870.

In 1913 the value of German exports to all foreign and colonial countries was a little less than two and a half billion dollars; that of British exports was a little more than this figure. French foreign trade was in value little more than half the British; Russian, only half the French and even less than that of Belgium (see Diagram 5). But the most important overriding fact in the fifteen years before 1914 was that world trade as a whole was rapidly expanding and a very high proportion of it was European trade. It was Germany's share of this European and world phenomenon, her place in a rapidly expanding global economy, that gave her an irrefutable claim to be a world power.

Throughout Europe less spectacular but still very important economic expansion was taking place. By 1890 France, Italy, and Switzerland, as well as Germany, had rather more than doubled their mileage of railroads as compared with 1870, while Belgium, the Netherlands, and Spain had nearly doubled theirs. All countries continued building track, though at a slower rate, during the following twenty years. (See Diagram 2.) Between 1891 and 1905 Russia completed the great Siberian railway, as a state undertaking. It ran over some 3,800 miles and opened up vast new Asiatic regions to trade and settlement. Russian railroad mileage nearly doubled between 1889 and 1902. Other railways penetrated right through Asia, and Eurasia became in a quite new sense one continent.

Behind this economic expansion, and the growth of industries, shipping, and trade, lay a complex financial system, linked with new and more gigantic forms of economic organization. In banking and finance Berlin was coming to rival London, Paris, and Amsterdam. The rapid expansion of German economy would have been impossible without the activities of the banks which were so much concerned with 'production credit', that is, with the organization of capital and credit for purposes of business enterprise and expansion. Most of these banks had been formed before 1871,[1] but they were reorganized and expanded after unification. They helped to provide capital and credit, not only for the development of domestic industries and trade, but also for financing scores of enterprises abroad: in Austria and Russia, Africa and the Near East, even in the United States and Latin America. The Deutsche Bank, founded in 1870 and developed by Georg von Siemens, cousin of Werner, was especially active in these foreign enterprises. It took part in the construction of the famous Berlin–Baghdad Railway, which caused such far-reaching international repercussions in the decade before 1914.[2]

1. See p. 293.
2. See p. 518.

Combines and Trusts. In every advanced industrial country there took place a variety of changes which tended in one direction – toward ever larger units of production, distribution, and financial organization. It might be what is known as 'concentration of industry', the growth of larger units of production, bigger factories each producing more than any had produced before. This might be accompanied by the elimination or amalgamation of a previously larger number of small factories. Or it might be the vertical combination of firms at different stages of an industry, as became common in the metal trades – large steel businesses managed the whole making of steel from the mining of the iron ore to the manufacture of rails and steamships. Or it might be horizontal combinations, known as cartels, designed to restrict competition by association among rival producers in order to control output and prices; and the associated firms did not necessarily belong to the same country. European countries before 1914 offered examples of all these types of concentration, combination, and cartel, and of various shades of association which included more than one such type. The Dynamite Trust formed in 1886 by the Swedish inventor of dynamite, Alfred Nobel, having collected a large fortune from international trade in explosives, devoted much of it to the causes of philanthropy and peace. The United States produced its Carnegies and Rockefellers and Fords in these years; Europe had its counterparts.

The new industries, such as the iron and steel, electrical, and chemical industries of the Reich, showed these elephantine tendencies to a marked degree. In Europe, Germany was the extreme example of high-powered integration and concentration into leviathan firms and cartels. But similar things happened in the United Kingdom, Belgium, and even France, despite the French affection for small units of production. French sugar factories, numbering 483, produced an average of 840 tons each in 1883–4. By 1900, there were 334 factories producing an average of 3,000 tons each. By 1912, there were 213 factories averaging more than 4,000 tons each. Even so, as late as 1896 the average number of employees in each industrial unit of France was 5·5. The workshop, not the factory, was still the typical unit of French industry. In Britain the most conspicuous example of concentration in industry before 1914 was the powerful combination of J. and P. Coats which made sewing thread. By 1890 it controlled a third of the thread trade in the United Kingdom; it was then reorganized as a limited liability company and acquired almost a monopoly. Britain's largest combinations, Unilever and Imperial Chemical Industries, developed after 1914, and her banking business became concentrated in the 'Big Five'.[1]

1. See p. 577.

In western Europe it was, naturally enough, the heavy industries that set the pace in amalgamation and unification. The French metal industries had their great trust, the *Comité des Forges*. It dated from 1864, and by 1914 it had come to include nearly every iron and steel firm in the country. Its controlling power was virtually in the hands of half-a-dozen large firms, especially Schneiders of Le Creusot and Wendel of Lorraine. Germany evolved, among others, her two greatest cartels, the Rhenish-Westphalian Coal Syndicate and the Steelworks Union. The former was set up in 1893 and dominated the Ruhr coal area; the latter in 1904, and included all German steelworks except those engaged in making the very finest products. Similar syndicates grew up in Russia after 1900, especially in the heavy industries. Thus Prodamet, formed in 1902, came to include eighty per cent of the entire production of Russian metallurgical works.

The appearance of these vast new economic organizations inevitably had repercussions on politics, and in this way too the interconnexions between politics and economics were reinforced between 1871 and 1914. Concentration of industry meant new concentrations of power. No government, least of all a government concerned directly and increasingly with conditions of labour, social security, and national strength, could ignore combinations as powerful as these. Nor were such enterprises, often engaged in far-ranging international transactions, inhibited from seeking to influence governmental policies. The sinister influence of armaments manufacturers in promoting international rivalries in order to bring them richer profits may often have been exaggerated; but at least the great coal and steel and chemical magnates formed or backed by all kinds of associations which urged courses of action considered desirable in the interests of their business. The Union of Economic Interests (founded in France in 1911) was a powerful association of businessmen within which the *Comité des Forges* had great influence. It exerted a steady pressure in postwar France against governmental controls, state monopolies, and graduated taxation. The creation of the German Navy League in 1898 was prompted by a combination of conservative nationalists, Rhenish steel interests, and northern shipping interests. It had been described as marking 'the entrance of the heavy industries, the mercantile interests, and the financiers into the ranks of the naval enthusiasts'. With the help of newspapers owned by the same steel and shipping interests, it ran a tremendous campaign in favour of naval armaments in rivalry to Great Britain. It was an unexpected consequence of democratic principles, of freedom of association and speech, that such powerful economic groups could most readily avail themselves of the instruments of modern publicity and propaganda; there is little cause for surprise and no reason to doubt that they used these instruments to advance their special interests.

Just as the private consumer was at the mercy of cartels and price-fixing agreements of big business, so the ordinary citizen was subjected to high-pressure propaganda emanating from big business. Growing evidence of this stimulated, by reaction, a host of different social and economic organizations. Two of the most important were cooperative movements and trade unions.

Cooperative Movements and Trade Unions. Cooperative associations, both of producers and of consumers, arose in many countries. France, the home of the producers' cooperative since the 1830s, saw a fresh flowering of the movement in the 1880s. Between 1880 and 1914 the number of such associations rose from 100 to 450. After 1894 their activities were coordinated by a 'consultative chamber'. Britain, on the other hand, was the traditional home of consumers' cooperatives, and the movement that had begun at Rochdale in 1844 likewise bore rich fruit towards the end of the century. The English Cooperative Wholesale Society was formed in 1863; the Scottish, five years later. Both were federations of consumers' societies, designed to cut out the middleman. In the 1870s they extended their activities into production, and even into landowning, insurance, and banking. Strong cooperative movements developed in Germany only at the end of the century – with the formation in 1899 of the Hamburg Society *Produktion* (which propounded an ambitious and aggressive programme of social reconstruction), with the new Wholesale Society of 1893, and with an expansion of mutual credit associations among the agricultural population. In all three countries schemes of profit sharing and copartnership, designed to give workers a direct interest in the business, were introduced by certain firms; most notably in some banks and insurance companies in France, several gas companies in Great Britain, and in a few farming estates in Germany. But this movement, advancing in the 1890s, was sharply declining by 1914.

Other nations adopted cooperative organizations in fields especially appropriate to their economies. In Denmark, Italy, the Low Countries, Finland, and Ireland, they spread most quickly to agriculture and dairies. Danish developments were the most far-reaching, with 1,000 cooperative dairies by 1892; and the bulk of Danish eggs, fruit, and bacon, as well as milk and butter, were produced and marketed by cooperative methods. Italy had more than 400 cooperative dairies by 1900, and masons and less skilled labourers formed a great national association on cooperative lines. In Ghent in 1873 workmen combined to lower the price of bread by setting up a cooperative bakery. By 1880 this example led to the formation of *Vooruit*, which eventually gave rise in every large Belgian town to a great cooperative organization running shops, cafés, libraries, and sometimes a bakery and brewery. The *Maison du Peuple*, which began in Brussels in 1881, followed similar lines, and came to serve as the headquarters of the Second International.[1] In Sweden the movement was small and localized until 1899, when the Wholesale Society (*Kooperativa Forbundet*) was formed; it then sailed on to broader waters, but moved slowly until after 1914. The place of cooperative *artels* in Russian industries has already been mentioned.[2]

Besides specifically economic organizations, a host of social and cultural associations grew up in these years. Here and there, as in Belgium and Germany, these became linked closely with political parties but their greatest functions were not political. These years saw a rich proliferation of voluntary associations of all kinds, ranging from the Workers' Educational Association formed in Britain in 1903 to a host of women's leagues and youth clubs, from the restless German youth movement (*Wandervogel*) to the French Catholic 'Popular Institutes' of around 1900, from chambers of commerce to trades councils. From all these the more literate populations gained experience in organization and management. They were the producers of a new sense of community, a new urge to find intellectual and material improvement through self-help and greater security through national solidarity – an urge born of urbanism, education, nationalism, democracy.

Most important of all, the same reaction against the pressures of big business brought a general renaissance of trade unionism. Labour organization already had long traditions and a rich history in western Europe by 1871.[3] Economic expansion after 1871 brought it fresh opportunities and incentives, and its rapid growth before 1914 forms a pattern common to all areas of Europe which had become industrialized. Combination of workers into larger units became easier with the rise or larger factories and firms. It became more desirable if workers were to hope for any success in bargaining collectively with the powerful new captains of industry. Democratic ideas favoured legislation granting freedom of association and legal protection for union funds, officials, and bargaining activities. Accordingly, these years mark a whole new phase in trade-union history. Trade unions were given legal recognition in Britain by 1871, in France by 1884, in Austria by 1870, in Ger-

1. See p. 418.   2. See p. 334.
3. See p. 152.

many after the lapse of Bismarck's antisocialist laws in 1890, in Spain in 1881.

Until the 1880s labour unions included mainly the more skilled workmen in particular trades, such as building, engineering, mining, textiles, and printing, all of which were expanding. They were predominantly craft unions, constantly preoccupied with mutual insurance and self-help against the hazards of accident, sickness, and death, and only sporadically engaged in strikes to reinforce their demands for better working conditions, shorter hours, and higher pay. They tended to ally with the more radical liberal movements, with John Bright in Britain, the radical republican journalist Barberet in France, the progressive liberals Hirsch and Duncker in Germany. When the first French Labour Congress met in Paris in 1876, it was attended by 255 delegates from Paris and 105 from the provincial towns, representing the trade unions, cooperative societies, and mutual aid societies; when the third Congress met in Marseilles three years later, it fell more under the influence of Jules Guesde who preached a Marxist programme. The mildly reformist Hirsch-Duncker unions in Germany were strongest among the skilled workers in engineering and in the metal industries, but they declined during the 1890s. In the United Kingdom their counterparts were the Amalgamated Society of Engineers, dating from 1850, and its imitators in other skilled trades. The British unions grew bigger sooner, and whereas by 1886 their membership totalled one and a quarter million, that of German unions totalled only 300,000 and of French only 50,000. But in all western industrial countries, by that date, they had not only won legal status but had also become strong enough to exact greatly improved conditions of labour from employers and state alike.

The 'new unionism' that came into existence with dramatic suddenness after 1886 coincided with a period of comparative economic prosperity which lasted until 1892, and which followed years of economic depression between 1882 and 1886. It was heralded by a series of long and bitter strikes, involving the less skilled workers – the strike of Belgian miners and glass workers in 1886, of the London match girls in 1888 and of the London dock workers in 1889, of the Ruhr coal workers in 1889, of the French forest woodmen in 1891 and 1892. These great strikes revealed the stirring of new levels of the working classes, hitherto unorganized or almost unorganized. The enlistment of masses of less skilled workers into the ranks of trade unionism transformed its whole character. Three main changes can be seen. First, there was a great multiplication of different types of labour organization, as unionism became fashionable; and as a result, it came to be more closely linked with political and social creeds, often competing with one another for union allegiance. Secondly, in each country there were movements for creating more national and unified labour organizations, on the self-evident principle that solidarity gives strength. Thirdly, efforts were made to link up labour organizations internationally. Unionism, like so many other things in these years, became a phenomenon of the masses and therefore different in structure and significance from all that had gone before.

The proliferation of several different kinds of labour organization in some ways enriched social life; but in other ways it weakened, because it divided, trade unionism as a movement. In France from 1887 onwards there grew up locally *bourses du travail* – a peculiarly French institution that was a mixture of labour exchange, trades council, and workers' club. These groups catered for a wide variety of local needs. In 1892 Fernand Pelloutier formed them into a national federation, which ten years later combined for many purposes with the new federation of trade unions. In France and Germany, as in other countries, the Roman Catholic Church, encouraged by the encyclicals of Leo XIII, formed separate labour unions of Catholic workers, designed to give them the advantages of trade unionism free from association with anticlerical socialists, syndicalists, and communists. In most countries, too, the closer relations between labour organization and political movements resulted in distinct socialist and communist trade unions, often quarrelling with each other as well as with the older liberal and the newer Catholic unions.[1] This diversification of types brought wider ambits of workers into unionism and catered more specifically for their needs and sentiments; but it also splintered labour organization as a whole and made desirable – though also more difficult – the second development of the period, national federation.

Movements for unification and federation came to a head at the end of the century. The French unions in 1895 formed a national federation, the *Confédération Générale du Travail* (C.G.T.), the name it kept when seven years later it combined with the federation of *bourses*. It was from the start wedded to a policy of industrial action through collective bargaining backed by strikes. The first article of its constitution was that 'elements constituting the C.G.T. will remain independent of all political schools'. It deliberately divorced itself from politics and parliamentary activities. The British Trades Union Congress, formed originally in 1868, had proved able to hold together the old and the new types of union, and by 1900 represented some half a million members. In that year it joined with the socialist societies to set up a

1. See p. 406.

Labour Representation Committee to return workers' representatives to parliament. It put up fifteen in the general election held within a few months of its formation. Only two were successful, but one of them was the Scottish miner, Keir Hardie. British unionism thus followed a course of action quite opposite to the French, and by 1906 gave birth to the modern Labour party. Italian socialist unions formed, in 1906, a General Italian Federation of Labour, but Catholic and syndicalist unions remained distinct. In Germany, as in France and Italy, trade unionism was sharply divided into distinct segments. There were three main kinds: the original liberal Hirsch-Duncker unions; the so-called 'free' trade unions, which were socialist in inspiration; and the Christian unions of the religious groups. By 1913 the socialist unions had by far the largest membership (more than two and a half million, as compared with 107,000 in the Hirsch-Duncker unions, and some 343,000 in the Christian unions). In contrast to both the French and the British, German unionism was highly concentrated. The four million British trade unionists of 1913 were enrolled in over 1,000 unions; the three million German in only 400 unions. The high degree of concentration in German industry was matched by the same phenomenon in labour organization. The small scale and relative weakness of trade unions in France likewise reflected the highly diversified and unconcentrated character of the French economy. The one million French trade unionists of 1913 were enrolled in more than 5,000 local unions.

Finally, trade unionism evolved international affiliations. In this it shared in a broader trend. All such working-class movements tended to project themselves across state frontiers. In 1895 the cooperative movement formed the International Cooperative Alliance, but this organization came to represent the outlook and interests much more of the consumers' cooperatives than of the producers'. From 1889 onwards individual trades established international links; such as the leather workers' international federation of 1889, and its counterparts for the miners, metal, textile, and transport workers. In 1901, after a few abortive attempts, the national federations of Britain, Germany, and the Scandinavian countries set on foot concerted efforts that led by 1913 to the International Federation of Trade-Unions (IFTU). It represented the bulk of organized labour in nearly every European country, though by no means all labour was yet organized.

The history of labour organization in other countries is but a repetition, with variations, of one or other of the patterns of development noted in Britain, France and Germany. Belgian unions, like so many other Belgian institutions, broadly followed the French pattern; in

Austria, Italy, Spain, and the Scandinavian countries, Marxist disciples tended to get control over important sections of the unions; Catholic unionist movements were launched in Belgium, Austria, and Italy. In Russia every attempt by workers to form associations of their own was looked upon by the government with the liveliest distrust, and before 1905 was punished as a crime. In 1906, in response to the revolutionary events of 1905, both workers and employers were given the legal right to form unions, confined to economic purposes. But the legal right to strike was not granted, and the revival of repressive policies after 1906 forced labour unions to perpetuate their old secret and conspiratorial habits. Strikes did occur frequently. In 1913 there were more than 2,400 strikes, mostly very short in duration but mainly in the textile and metal-working industries of the St Petersburg district.

Capital versus *Labour*. There was, in all these ways, a clearly defined pattern of European economic growth between 1871 and 1914. It varied in intensity and time from country to country, and in its details it was infinitely diversified. But everywhere the overriding fact was the emergence of ever larger and more powerful units, chief of which were the big combines of capitalist production and finance on one hand, the massive organizations of labour on the other. In the decade before 1914 these two groups were increasingly coming into conflict about conditions of labour, and engaging in the open warfare of giant or epidemic strikes.[1] The background to this intensifying industrial unrest was the alternation of periods of depression with periods of prosperity. There were spells of general depression and slump between 1873 and 1879, 1882 and 1886, 1892 and 1896, 1900 and 1901, 1907 and 1908, 1912 and 1913. These were separated by spells of economic revival and relative prosperity.

The cyclical business recessions, which seemed now to be a regular characteristic of the European economy and beyond the control of governments, aggravated the conflicts between employers and workers, and help to explain the social tensions of these years. It was significant that the countries that most completely coincided in their susceptibility to business recessions were those predominantly industrial and predominantly engaged in world trade; that is, Britain, France, Germany, the Netherlands, and Sweden. The international solidarity that trusts and trade unions were seeking to achieve by means of economic and political organization seemed to be there already and very effective at a deeper level of their economic activity. The business of one country was peculiarly sensitive to changes in another. European nations were sharing as partners in a single vast economic expansion that

1. See p. 409.

masked, impeded, and at times disrupted by their behaviour at a diplomatic and political level. World trade, world markets, world investment, had raised European society to a new plane of development.

The central problem in understanding the history of European peoples before 1914 is to penetrate behind all these new types of organization of the state, of capital, and of labour, to the transformation that they were effecting in the daily lives and habits of thought of men and women and children. There was a rising social pressure on each individual and on every national state. Any change so far reaching as changes in where most people lived, how they were brought up and made a living, what social and group loyalties they avowed, was bound to revolutionize human behaviour and outlook. The greatest of all reorganizations in these decades was the unplanned, uncomfortable, yet quite relentless transformation of the very texture of social life itself. The new medicine and sanitation, the new education and Press, the new towns and factories, the new subjection to the capricious forces of cyclical boom and slump, the more frenzied rivalries of nation-states, were elements in this over-all transformation. The twentieth century would have been a turbulent, dynamic, violent era even if there had been no world wars to intensify these qualities. That was apparent enough in the ferment of socialist, syndicalist, and even anarchist ideas and movements which occurred among all classes of European workers before the century began. By examining these movements more closely, it is possible to get deeper insight into how the fabric of European life was being transformed; for work is not merely a factor in production – it is one of the main sources of individual experience and it shapes the quality of life of every human being.

ORGANIZED LABOUR AND SOCIAL DEMOCRACY

Trade unions in many countries (most notably France) strove to keep free from political affiliations and to confine their energies to improving the material lot of their members by direct industrial action. But only occasionally did they succeed in staying neutral. In Belgium, where after 1898 the law required incorporated unions to be nonpolitical, they were not. The rise of unions coincided, throughout Europe, with the rise of socialist, communist, syndicalist, and even anarchist political movements; and inevitably the leaders of such movements took an active interest in labour organizations that might bring support and power to their political activities. Socialism, and even more communism, had been virtually submerged as operative forces in European politics during most of the twenty years of state-making prior to 1871. Because socialists were more violently opposed to dynasticism and clericalism than to nationalism and liberalism, they had in general welcomed the creation of a unified Italy and a unified Germany; though individuals such as August Bebel and Wilhelm Liebknecht in Germany had opposed the wars of 1866 and 1870. Socialism had been born in the heyday of romantic liberalism, and shared its enthusiasm for national liberation and self-determination. It likewise perpetuated the internationalist and humanitarian traditions of the democratic and radical movements. It was, accordingly, natural enough for socialist organizations in several western countries to lend support to the First International of Working Men's Associations, which Karl Marx helped to set up in 1866. But within six years this organization was torn apart by dissensions between Marxists and anarchists, and it was disbanded in 1876 without having achieved anything of importance.

The Socialist Dilemma. The choice before trade unions, of remaining purely economic in activity or of becoming political, was paralleled by the equally vital choice which confronted socialists. It was the avowed purpose of all socialist movements to use the state to overhaul and reconstruct the social order so as to further working-class interests. (In this they all differed from the anarchists, whose purpose was to abolish the state.) The choice before them was then one of basic strategy and method. Should they try to get political power by working within the framework of parliamentary democracy and the new electorates, exerting pressure on liberal and conservative government to get concessions in the form of social welfare legislation and state regulation of working conditions? Or should they stand apart from the inevitable compromises and half measures of parliamentary politics, preserving intact their revolutionary impulse and striving to hasten (if need be by violence) the day when the parliamentary state of capitalism would break down and open the door to a socialist revolution? It was on this issue that socialists usually parted company from communists, and chose the reformist rather than the revolutionary path.

In every important European country this issue split socialist parties; and it was indeed a crucial question. To accept the road of parliamentary action involved accepting the democratic processes of discussion and majority decision, and it meant treating the existing state as potentially a source of good. It meant accepting, from the hands of opportunist or of well-intentioned conservative and liberal governments, concessions which the extremists called sops, and which by reconciling workers to existing conditions perpetually weakened the urge of electorates for more drastic measures. The moment of final decision came when there arose an opportunity for socialist leaders to accept a share in government alongside the capitalist parties. Was this merely offering leaders as hostages to the manoeuvres of their political opponents and implicating socialists in repressive policies? The charge of betrayal was regularly hurled against any socialist leader, such as Alexandre Millerand or Aristide Briand in France, who accepted membership in a coalition government. Yet the original decision to work within the existing political and social order in the hope of reforming it from inside could scarcely lead, logically, to refusing all share in power and responsibility when it was offered. If the chief aim was to exact concessions from employers and the state by political action, might not larger concessions be got from inside a government than from mere opposition?

It might be expected that parliamentary socialists would find organized labour a more ready ally than would revolutionary Marxist parties; for both socialists and trade unionists had elected to bargain with capitalists rather than try to abolish them, and therefore both had a natural interest in keeping employers prosperous in order to produce a better bargain. Periods of prosperity and economic expansion, such as the 1850s and the interludes of the later 1880s and 1890s, favoured unionism. Employers needed workers most when business was brisk, and they could more comfortably make concessions when their own profits were high. These were also periods, as already noted, when socialist parties prospered most. On the other hand revolutionary Marxists gained ground in the intervals of economic recession and slump, when unemployment increased and employers hardened in their ability to bargain; and the Marxist analysis of the class war carried more conviction in times of greater tension between capital and labour. For this reason unionism as a whole tended to waver and split between support for the moderate socialists and seduction away to the more violent revolutionary Marxists and anarchists, according to the fluctuations of the business cycle. So long as real wages rose, moderation prevailed. But when real wages rose less quickly – as in Great Britain, France, and Germany between 1880 and 1900, when they rose only some twenty or twenty-five per cent – workers demanded a larger share of the wealth which the new machines could produce.

Moreover, socialist thinkers of all kinds, whether backing parliamentary programmes or revolutionary action, had something in common. They were all less interested than was the ordinary worker and trade unionist in short-term gains such as immediate increases in pay or shortening of hours. They thought more in terms of society as a whole;

they dreamed of long-term reconstruction of the whole social and economic system. They were intellectuals, attracted to general programmes and projects rather than to detailed benefits for particular trades. They liked to think and speak of the working class or of society as a whole rather than to serve the immediate needs of separate groups of workers. The socialist parties were seldom the work of the masses in the sense that trade unionism or the cooperative movement was born of working-class initiative and needs. They were rather the work of intellectuals, political agitators, and a few enterprising individual workers. Such men valued, more highly than did the ordinary worker, the niceties of doctrine and the subtleties of political strategy. It was partly in revulsion again the perpetual ideological debates and the incorrigible quarrelsomeness of socialist parties that the solid ranks of trade unionism and cooperatives tried to hold aloof from politics. Yet the countless small groups of intellectuals, journalists, and propagandists concerned with socialist parties contributed a lot to the political reshaping of Europe before 1914.

The Paris Commune, 1871. In western Europe of the 1870s socialist movements struggled against a heavy tide of resistance and resentment. The dominating fact in men's minds, breeding on the one hand violent fear and on the other hopelessness and apathy, was that strange paroxysm of violence – the insurrection of the Paris Commune in 1871. This event played so important a part, both in the actual history and in the mythology of socialism, that the facts of the matter are of great importance. On 18 March 1871, after the national humiliation at Sedan, after Paris had endured a four months' siege by the armies of Bismarck, after Gambetta's republican Government of National Defence had failed, heroically but decisively, to keep France at war, and after German troops had marched in triumph down the Champs-Elysées in Paris, the city broke into revolt. Its purpose was to defy the efforts of the newly elected National Assembly, and of its provisional government headed by Adolphe Thiers, to make peace with the Germans and build a conservative régime in place of the defunct Second Empire of Napoleon III.[1] It recalled, in its fury, the 'June Days' of 1848, which had left among the workers of Paris a deep class hatred of the *bourgeoisie* and a distrust of all politicians. Power quickly fell into the hands of the medley of extremists which traditionally congregated in Paris, the international home of full-time professional revolutionaries. One reason was that, after the long siege, the population of Paris no longer included many of its more wealthy citizens, but did include some forty thousand evacuees and refugees from the German-occupied industrial provinces of the

1. See p. 317.

north. Another was that the population as a whole was outraged, in its patriotic and civic pride, by the humiliation of defeat and irritated by the decision of the new assembly to meet at Versailles rather than in Paris.

The lead in the revolt, with its echoes of 1793 and 1848, was taken by the few thousand followers of the veteran revolutionary, Auguste Blanqui, idol of the Paris underworld of conspirators. Allied with them were the doctrinaire Jacobins, led by Charles Delescluze and Félix Pyat, experienced in clandestine resistance during the Second Empire and resolved to restore the revolutionary tradition of France to its original purity and idealism. They were also joined by various socialist groups, disciples of Saint-Simon, Fourier, Louis Blanc, and above all Pierre-Joseph Proudhon, whose anarchistic theory of society gave prominence to the role of the small, autonomous unit, the commune. The slogan of 'the Commune' meant something different to each group, but it served well enough as an omnibus rallying cry. The revolutionary government which appeared was a hasty compromise between these main groups, and included also one or two Marxists, notably Edouard Vaillant, who became minister of the interior in the Commune, and Leo Franckel, who kept in touch with Marx himself. But it was neither a mainly communist and Marxist movement, nor even closely connected with the recently formed First International. It was a peculiarly French and Parisian revolt, the apotheosis of the long French revolutionary tradition and an outburst of local pride and distress, fiercely patriotic and anti-German. After two months the national forces of Thiers overthrew and restored Paris to France. The fighting in Paris was conducted on both sides with an atrocious ferocity unwonted even in that city of immemorial barricades. The men of the Commune burned some of the finest public buildings, shot the Archbishop of Paris, and many other hostages, and ruled by methods of terror. The national troops took savage reprisals, shooting prisoners mercilessly and eventually deporting some seven thousand five hundred. Paris relapsed into sullen acquiescence in the new Third Republic which the conservative assembly proceeded to construct.

These startling events, which brought an oriental barbarism into the most civilized and cosmopolitan capital of Europe, had decisive consequences for nascent socialism. Marx wrote his pamphlet on *The Civil War in France*, which hailed the Commune as the dawn of a new era of direct proletarian revolutionary action and a triumph for his own followers and for the International. Frightened property-owning classes everywhere in Europe took him at his word, and saw in the Commune the beginning of a fresh revolutionary menace. Even a confusion of words contributed to this widespread misinterpretation of the Commune. *Communards* (supporters of the Commune) were assumed to be *communists*. *Capitulards* (as the rebels called Thiers and his ministers who 'capitulated' and made peace with Germany) were confused with *capitalists*. The Marxist analysis of the event as a landmark in the class war was made to fit only by a distortion of both facts and words. It can be regarded more accurately as the last dying flicker of an old tradition, the tradition of the barricades of 1789 and 1848, rather than as the beginning of a new. Never again was Paris to impose her will upon the rest of France, as she had done before 1871. The aftermath of the Commune and of its repression was the exile or imprisonment of all the more revolutionary elements in France; and the new parliamentary republic was erected during their elimination from the scene. It was only after 1879, when the republican parties gained full control of the Republic, that amnesties were granted and more active socialist movements could again operate freely in France.

Social Democracy. This temporary expulsion of socialist and communist movements from France enriched her neighbours with socialist agitators and contributed to the growth of socialism elsewhere. The failure of the Paris Commune launched Marxism upon a new phase; the development first in Germany, and soon in nearly every other country, of 'social democratic' parties. The establishment of the German Empire, with its Reichstag elected on wide popular franchise, transformed the conditions of political action in Germany. It made the division of German socialism into rival parties an obvious barrier to electoral success. The party which Ferdinand Lassalle had formed in northern Germany in 1863 (the General German Workingmen's Association) rested on Lassalle's un-Marxist doctrine that universal suffrage and proletarian interests were not incompatible. It was designed from the first to be a political and electoral movement aimed at gaining parliamentary power. The party which Wilhelm Liebknecht and August Bebel formed in southern Germany adopted, as early as 1869, its Eisenach programme, which was distinctly Marxist.

In 1875 these two parties combined to form the German Social Democratic party based on a new programme. This so-called Gotha Programme accepted Marx's doctrines of the class struggle and his materialist interpretation of history, but it abandoned his view of the state in favour of Lassalle's, and regarded revolutionary Marxism as rendered out-of-date by the existence of universal suffrage. The new party set out to capture the state by parliamentary methods, not to overthrow it in favour of a proletarian state. It was attacked by Marx (in his *Critique of the Gotha Programme*), but his attack was not published until many years later. The issue was anyhow smothered until 1890 by Bismarck's antisocialist laws, which closed the socialist ranks and forced them back into underground activities; but meanwhile social democratic movements on the Gotha model grew up in other countries, and after 1890 the German Social Democratic party resumed its original aims more explicitly. It soon became the largest of all the parliamentary socialist parties in Europe.

'Social democracy' became the general pattern of the new socialism in Europe during the 1880s. It was everywhere characterized by that tension between orthodox Marxists and more moderate political socialists which had appeared in Germany. In Great Britain, where Marx and Engels spent most of their time, no specifically Marxist party existed until that wealthy and eccentric old Etonian, Henry Hyndman, set up his Democratic Federation in 1881. In 1883 the poet, William Morris, combined with him to remodel it into the Social Democratic Federation. In France the first Marxist party was formed in 1880 by Jules Guesde. In both countries the existence of a wide franchise encouraged the simultaneous growth of less doctrinaire socialism – with the result that Hyndman's Social Democratic Federation was soon superseded as a political movement by Keir Hardie's Independent Labour Party of 1893, and rivalled by the Fabian Society of 1884; and in France, Guesde's party had several rivals in the Blanquists, Proudhonists, and others.

But wherever extension of the franchise came late, as in Italy or the Low Countries, Marxist parties enjoyed a more undisputed leadership of socialist movements. A narrow franchise, such as existed in Italy until 1913 and in the Low Countries until 1918, discouraged and impeded socialism from building mainly electoral parties committed to programmes of immediate social reform. Its leaders could talk the language of Marxism more plausibly and with less inconsistency than could socialist leaders in Britain, Germany, or France. Thus the Italian socialist party founded by Turati in 1892 was equipped with a Marxist ideology by the young Roman professor, Antonio Labriola. But the economic backwardness of Italy kept it relatively unimportant. The Belgium social democratic party (the Parti Ouvrier Belge) dated from 1885, the Austrian and the Swiss from 1888. Belgian socialism was moderated, despite the narrow franchise, by the growth of other large working-class organizations such as the cooperative groups; it became in spirit realistic and opportunistic. Even a Czech social democratic party was formed in 1887.

In every country the first problem facing political socialism was its own unification, for whether the aim was electoral gains or revolutionary action, unity was important. By the beginning of the twentieth century unity was substantially achieved in Britain and France. In 1900 the Social Democratic Federation, the Fabian Society, and the Independent Labour party combined with the swelling trade-union movement to found the future Labour party. In this new amalgam the Marxist ingredients were swamped. The Social Democratic Federation, never large, was much weakened by the secession in 1884 of its most influential member William Morris. Both the Fabians and the Independent Labour party took from Marxism only those notions that attracted them, irreverently discarding all those that did not. On this basis a broad, solid, socialist movement was built, little divided by doctrinal feuds and backed by massive trade-union funds and support.

In France, partly because trade unionism abstained from politics during the formative years, socialist parties remained chronically weak and splintered until 1905. From the followers of Guesde split the followers of Paul Brousse, known as 'possibilists' because they rejected the all-or-nothing absolutist doctrines of Marx. Alongside these movements grew up an influential group of middle-class intellectuals and individual parliamentarians, calling themselves Independents. They included many who were to become the most eminent leaders of parliamentary socialism – Jean Jaurès, Alexandre Millerand, René Viviani, Such semi-detached socialists of bourgeois origins were liable to be distrusted by the workers. Under the pressures of the Dreyfus Affair the socialists combined in 1905 into a unified parliamentary party headed by Jaurès; but the main trade-union body, the C.G.T., still held aloof, and after the untimely assassination of Jaurès in 1914 the party's short-lived unity broke up. Yet by 1914 there were as many as seventy-six socialist deputies in the Chamber.

The corresponding architect of social democratic unity in Germany was August Bebel. On the basis of the Gotha Programme he led the Social Democrats to a succession of electoral gains until, in the Reichstag of 1912, they were the largest single party with 110 representatives. By 1914 its membership in the country was over one million, and it had 110 daily newspapers with a total circulation of nearly one and a half million copies. Bebel, who ruled it with an iron hand and imposed on it its characteristic discipline, led it for close on fifty years – until his death in 1913 – and made it the most impressive of all continental socialist parties. He combined in his personality and career all the qualities most desirable for a socialist leader. Having been trained as a carpenter and worked with his hands, he had an instinctive sympathy for the ordinary workers and their families. Having been imprisoned on charges of treason, he had a certain halo of martyrdom. As a resourceful organizer he was able to build up the party systematically, and as a persuasive orator he was well qualified to lead it in the Reichstag. He had the power of intellect to cross swords with Bismarck in Germany and with Jaurès in the congresses of the Second International. More than any other socialist leader outside Great Britain, he contrived to base his party on the broad mass of the industrial workers. Its roots were deepest in the big industrial centres – the Rhineland, Berlin, Hamburg, Saxony, and Silesia. Yet even this unusually monolithic party suffered the same kind of schism that developed elsewhere in Europe.

Its doctrinal unity was achieved only by preaching a much more orthodox Marxism than was matched by its parliamentary behaviour; and inevitably there developed within it in the 1890s a more moderate or so-called 'revisionist' wing, led by Eduard Bernstein. Bernstein argued, with considerable truth and effect, that the trend of events was not bearing out the Marxist analysis and predictions. The number of people who owned property was not decreasing as Marx had predicted, it was increasing. The workers were not getting remorselessly poorer and more repressed, they were coming to be better off and freer. There was no sign that the capitalist system would soon reach a point of collapse: in Germany, more conspicuously than anywhere else, it was getting ever stronger and more successful. Socialism should therefore, he argued, regard itself as a movement toward a cooperative system of production, a gradualist and reformist movement transforming society through the achievements of democracy and the constant improvement of working-class life. It must give up talk or hope of cataclysm, and, like the Fabians in England, observe 'the inevitability of gradualness'. He wanted to end the internal contradictions of Gotha and make the 're-vision' of Marxism explicit.

Here, in short, was a socialist programme and theory that fitted closely the inherent aims and methods of organized labour, as well as the established procedures of parliamentary democracy. It compelled the party to modify its ideas. Bernstein was supported in his revisionism by a large number of able young writers who ran their own Press and journals. They drew attention to the usual Marxist neglect of the peasants, and put forward programmes of agrarian reform. They pointed to recent achievements of parliamentary and democratic social legislation in the United Kingdom and the United States, which contrasted with the negative legislative achievements of the German Social Democrats, for all their strength. They even attacked the doctrinal antinationalism and anti-imperialism of the Social Democrats. In the great storm that blew up in the Reichstag in 1907 over their opposition to military expenditure, the revisionist Gustav Noske declared that 'the Prussian Minister of War should know that we have always demanded an armed nation'. Here was foreshadowed the final issue which was to dominate the fate of socialist parties everywhere. Should they support their nation and nation-state in war? Or should they adhere to the strict Marxist teaching that modern wars are imperialistic, destined to injure the interests of the workers who know no country and who in revolution have nothing to lose but their chains?

Within the German Social Democratic party this fundamental issue was smothered until 1914 by the ritual of proclaiming on all official occasions a resolutely revolutionary purpose, while following in normal practice an equally determined reformist and revisionist policy. This meant preserving the formal unity of the party at the expense of alienating all liberal and many middle-class elements in Germany, and of perpetuating an unresolved internal contradiction between principle and practice. These remained two of the greatest weaknesses of German socialism until 1914. They condemned it to the same fate as German liberalism in 1848 :[1] an ineffective combination of absolutist and challenging pronouncements with feeble action. The party reflected, also, the most striking characteristics of German nationalism: subordination of spontaneity and freedom to discipline and corporate efficiency. Its representatives in the Reichstag showed immense loyalty and devotion, and normally voted as one solid block in opposition. Yet the great measures of social insurance were passed by Bismarck, while his anti-socialist laws made cooperation of the party impossible; the Reichstag's lack of control over the government made the party's strength largely illusory in politics; and by 1914 it had a remarkably barren record of legislative achievement. If within the party the legacy of Lassalle triumphed over that of Marx, in Germany it was rather Bismarck who triumphed over Lassalle. In 1881, when he promoted his social insurance schemes, Bismarck said, 'Whoever has a pension for his old age is far more content and far easier to handle than one who has no such prospect.' He was proved right.

The whole complex of political issues which divided Broussists from Guesdists in France and followers of Bernstein from followers of Bebel in Germany beset the socialist movements of nearly every other country. The pattern prevailed in Italy and Austria-Hungary, in Scandinavia and in the Low Countries, though with local variations. Nowhere else did socialist parties attain the size and discipline of the German. The main Italian socialist party, dating from 1892, was returning thirty-two deputies by 1900. Even more than the French it was haunted by internal

1. See p. 210.

dissensions, both over reformism and nationalism, and over syndicalist and anarchist splits of its own. During the war with Turkey in 1911–12, in which Italy claimed colonial territories in Tripolitania and Cyrenaica, the reformist socialist leaders Bonomi and Bissolati supported the war on nationalist grounds and were duly excommunicated from the party.

The Austrian Social Democratic party owed its existence chiefly to Dr Victor Adler, the son of a well-to-do businessman whose ideas were much influenced by Lassalle. By 1888 he succeeded in unifying and consolidating the party to an extent that brought it success in its first task of agitating for wider suffrage. That the vote was in 1907 extended to all men over twenty-four years old in the Austrian half of the Empire was in part due to socialist agitation. But the consequent addition of social issues to the multitude of nationalist issues which already divided the Austrian parliament merely made it easier for the ruling bureaucracy to dispatch current business without much deference to parliament. Austria was not made much more democratic. (The introduction of universal male suffrage in Italy six years later likewise did little to change the power of officialdom in that country.) The Austrian Social Democratic party was itself haunted by the bugbear of all Austrian politics, nationalist divisions. By 1911 it had split into three groups, German, Polish, Czech. Despite their common recognition of Adler as leader, and their collectively large membership of eighty-two in the Austrian parliament, these divisions hamstrung the party as a political power. As Adler remarked in 1900, 'We in Austria have a little International of our own.'

The socialist parties of Scandinavia and the Low Countries broadly followed the British pattern, both in their affection for moderate parliamentary reformist programmes and in the closeness of their relations with trade unions. The Danish Social Democratic party, founded in 1878, was from the first closely associated with the trade unions. It grew steadily in strength by adapting its programme to the needs of agricultural cooperatives and by shunning Marxist doctrines. By 1913 it mustered 107,000 votes and sent thirty-two representatives to the Danish lower house (*Folketing*). This victory led to the formation of a joint government of Radicals and Social Democrats. Sweden's Social Democratic party of 1889 was likewise backed by the trade unions. They cooperated, as in Britain, in getting legislation passed to provide for old-age pensions and sickness insurance. Norway's socialist movement dated from 1887, but made little headway until after the separation of Norway from Sweden in 1905. By 1912 it won nearly 125,000 votes and twenty-three seats in the *Storting*. The Low Countries developed somewhat more along the German and French pattern than the British or Scandinavian.

The main Belgian socialist party led by Émile Vandervelde originated in 1885, the Dutch in 1894. Although the Dutch was more stricken by the familiar feud between reformists and revolutionary Marxists, a special feature of the progress of both was their development of a vast cooperative organization.[1]

The Birth of Bolshevism. The Socialist party of most momentous importance for the future, though few would have predicted that at the time, was the Russian. The rapid industrialization of western Russia in the twenty years before 1914 opened the door to a more western type of socialist movement, distinct from the former anarchist and terrorist organizations to which tsarist repression had given birth. George Plekhanov – in exile in Switzerland – founded the first Russian Marxist party in 1883. It had little influence until, in 1898, attempts were made to found a Marxist Social Democratic Labour party inside Russia. In 1902 was founded a rival Socialist Revolutionary party which appealed more directly to the peasants than to the industrial workers. The absence of constitutional liberties compelled both to work either through secret organizations inside Russia or in exile. Both were simply more up-to-date offshoots of the whole violent tide of Russian revolutionary movements which had come into being during the generation since the emancipation of the serfs.[2] Their common basis was a frenzied hatred of the Tsar and his government, and of the whole social system which they represented. In this broad tide of discontent the intelligentsia took a leading part, many of them belonging to the aristocratic and official class, since these alone were well educated. 'A father,' it has been said, 'would sit in his office as Chief of Police or Governor while his daughter stood at a street corner throwing bombs.' Young students of noble birth set out to destroy all that their parents respected. This revolutionary movement, though professing the French revolutionary ideals and preaching constitutionalism and democracy as an ideal, was compelled by circumstance to adopt every device of conspiracy and terrorism. There could be no question of working through trade unions, for these were not permitted to exist; nor of choosing between reformist and revolutionary strategies, for there was no nationally representative body. So violence, secret plotting, and bomb-throwing it had to be.

The Russian Social Democratic Labour party of 1898 was in one sense a break with this peculiarly Russian tradition. It was the Socialist Revolutionary party of 1902 which perpetuated the old tradition, and concentrated on propaganda among the peasants. It was the Social

1. See p. 386.
2. See p. 330.

Democratic party, modelled at first upon the Social Democrats of Germany, which introduced the more systematic doctrines of Marxism and propagated them among the industrial workers. But at an early stage it was confronted, in especially crucial form, with the choice that lay before all such European parties. Could it, like the German Social Democrats, concentrate upon the special class interests of the workers, their wages, housing, and conditions of work, and so seek to win a place for itself within the existing political system as the articulate voice of the working classes? Or should it concentrate upon the overthrow of the political system and the capture of the state? If it chose the latter course, it was faced in Russia with a life and death struggle, for in the absence of political democracy there was no prospect of changing the régime save by violent revolutionary activity. If it chose the former course, it might even win for itself some kind of semi-legal existence under the tsardom, but only at the expense of losing its revolutionary impulse and of granting to the rank and file of the workers a controlling voice in the conduct of the party. Until its congress held in 1903 the trend of the party was in this last direction, following in the footsteps of the German Social Democrats. But in 1903 its course was abruptly altered mainly by the actions of one man: Vladimir Ulyanov, known in history as Lenin.

Lenin was then thirty-three, son of a minor official of the régime – a district inspector of schools in the district around Moscow. His elder brother had in 1887 been hanged for his share in a plot to assassinate the Tsar Alexander III. Since then, steeping himself in Marxist and other revolutionary literature, and excluded from posts to which his intellectual brilliance entitled him but from which his revolutionary ideas and activities barred him, he had been imprisoned and exiled to Siberia. Returning from Siberia in 1900, he went into exile and threw himself into work for the recently formed Russian Social Democratic party. He edited *Iskra*, the party paper, which was smuggled into Russia from Germany and Switzerland. He was convinced that the old terrorist tradition, in the cause of which his brother had died, was spent: that the future lay only with a highly organized movement and a disciplined revolutionary party.

The party was led and dominated by George Plekhanov, who applied Marxist theories to the new Russian phenomenon of a large industrial proletariat, gathered together in the western towns, factories, and mines. Lenin worked in collaboration with him. The parting of the ways came in 1903, when the party held its second congress to decide its formal constitution and structure. It began, as one writer put it, 'in Brussels in a rat-infested flour mill surrounded by Russian and Belgian detectives; and continued, after two of the delegates had been arrested, in the August heat of the Tottenham Court Road in London'. Lenin and Plekhanov wanted membership in the party restricted to those who 'personally participate in one of the organizations of the party'. A rival group, led by Martov and supported by Leon Trotsky, wanted membership to include all those who 'work under the control and guidance of one of the party organizations'. The first definition would restrict the making of crucial decisions to the narrow circle of militant members and active organizers; the second would produce an open party, guided by the collective voting power of all its enrolled supporters and sympathizers. The first would, Lenin believed, keep intact the party's revolutionary impetus, which was especially necessary for reasons of security and of drive. The second would yield a party comparable to the German Social Democrats, a mass organization broadly based on the Russian working classes. But how could any such party function in tsarist Russia? In the end Lenin's group won by a majority of two votes, and so came to be known as the 'majority-men', or *Bolsheviki*. Martov's group were dubbed the 'minority-men', (*Mensheviki*). Paradoxically, the Leninist 'majority-men' were thus those who stood for controlling the party by means of a small minority of the *élite*, the fanatical and hard-bitten experts who would be ruthless in their revolutionary policy and unswayed by any consideration of the wishes or immediate interests of the majority of members. So was born modern Bolshevism, and the nucleus of the modern totalitarian single-party states of which Russia after 1917 was the model. The whole aim of this party was to capture complete political power for itself by the total overthrow of the existing régime. No compromise or half measures would now be possible: it was war to the death against tsardom. The two groups continued to work together until 1912, when they eventually split. The differences between them had a more desperate significance in the Russian environment than anywhere else in Europe.

Meanwhile the eruption of discontent which Lenin could detect in 1903 was boiling up in Russia. Leon Trotsky had brought further news of it in October 1902 when he had arrived at Lenin's lodgings in London. Even while the congress met, a gigantic general strike had been taking place in southern Russia. The underground revolutionaries in villages and factories were bringing things to a head faster than the exiled leaders of the party could catch up on them. The crisis was precipitated by the strain of the Russo-Japanese War in 1904, and by the brutal massacre of January 1905. This occurred when a crowd of people, led by an Orthodox priest Father Gapon, came to petition the Tsar to call a constituent assembly based on universal suffrage, transfer the land to the people, and decree an eight-hour day. They were shot down on the Tsar's orders. This atrocity provoked the most widespread and comprehensive industrial strikes that Europe had ever known. Lenin, Trotsky, and most of the Bolshevik leaders were caught unawares, and few of them reached Russia in time to take control of the revolution.

By June 1905 there was a mutiny on the battleship *Potemkin*, a general strike in the Black Sea port of Odessa, and committees (*soviets*) of workers were set up in St Petersburg factories. By October, when further waves of strikes began, Trotsky and the local Mensheviks organized in the capital a Soviet of Workers' Delegates, in which both wings of the Social Democratic party took part alongside the Socialist Revolutionaries. Lenin did not arrive until late in November, and the Bolsheviks took no decisive action until he came. It was too late. The Soviet had lasted only fifty days when its members were arrested. It was crushed by the savage reprisals of the government, as were the peasants who had risen against their landlords, the sailors and soldiers who had mutinied, and the workers who had held out behind barricades. It was the bloodiest civil war since the Paris Commune. By the time the Tsar was compelled to summon the first national assembly (*Duma*) in April 1906, it is estimated that his government had killed some fifteen thousand people and arrested seventy thousand. The Bolshevik leaders escaped mostly to Finland and thence into exile, to debate tirelessly the lessons of 1905 and to plan for the next magic moment. Nicholas II dissolved the Duma after it had sat for only two months. Although three more Dumas were elected before 1914, they wielded little power. Russian government relapsed to its familiar routine of despotism, backed in 1906 by a loan of 2,250 million francs from French bankers, which the Russian Prime Minister proudly and accurately described as 'the largest loan made in the history of mankind'.

Minimum and Maximum Socialism. This panorama of the proliferation of socialist parties before 1914 suggests two general conclusions that have great importance for the later history of Europe. One is that within socialism there was a recurrent and inescapable cleavage: between those parties which, from an early stage in their growth, came to terms with the institutions of parliamentary democracy, with trade unionism and the cooperative movements; and those which held to more absolutist revolutionary doctrines, whether of Marxism or anarchism, and so dedicated themselves to the task of fighting and overthrowing all other political parties and institutions. The best examples of the former are the British and Scandinavian Labour parties and the parliamentary socialist groups of France and Italy; of the latter, the supreme example is the Russian Social Democratic party after 1903. It had not yet become customary to distinguish between them by labelling the former Socialists, the latter Communists. That convention arose only after 1918. But here was the origin of the mid twentieth-century cleavage between western parliamentary socialism and eastern revolutionary communism. All the essentials of that conflict were already present in 1914, save that neither socialism nor communism had by then won power in any country.

The second conclusion is that parliamentary socialism, like other working-class movements and organizations, grew and flourished most where the traditions and institutions of liberal democracy had already become most fully established. It was in the United Kingdom, Scandinavia, and France that reformist socialism took shape most quickly and won its earliest triumphs. Wherever universal suffrage remained for a long time impeded, as in Italy and Austria-Hungary, or wherever its operation was severely limited by strong central authority, as in Germany, socialists went on using the language and preaching the ideas of revolutionary doctrinaire Marxism even when their practice and their achievements were more moderate. Where parliamentary institutions and universal suffrage were unknown, as in Russia, reformist socialism could strike no roots and was replaced by extreme revolutionary communism. The pattern of socialism is, so to speak, a pattern superimposed on the territorial distribution of liberalism and democracy, and matches the extent of the new electorates.

These conclusions are clinched by a comparison of the minimum and maximum programmes of policy which the different parties drew up and endorsed at various times. In western countries the parliamentary socialist parties, committed to seeking votes in order to gain political representation, normally drew up minimum programmes of those reforms best calculated to win broad electoral support. Inevitably these were mostly concerned with widening of the franchise, social welfare legislation, an eight-hour day, and improvement of conditions of work. Such was the minimum programme which the Italian Socialist party drew up in 1895. Their more abstract ideological aims were relegated to ultimate or maximum programmes, which appealed more to the intellectuals and preserved something of the party's doctrinal character. Thus, when the main French socialist groups combined in 1905, they drew up a common programme which included a statement of ultimate collectivism, of the group's resolve to socialize the means of production and of exchange, and a protestation that it was 'not a party of reform but a party of class struggle and revolution': but it also included an assurance that 'in parliament, the socialist group must dedicate itself to the defence and extension of political liberties and the rights of workers, to the promotion and realization of reforms which will ameliorate the conditions of life and of the class struggle of the working classes'. The difference of emphasis between French and German socialism emerges if this statement is compared with the German Social Democrats' Erfurt Programme, which they adopted in 1891. It was a more thoroughgoing Marxist statement than its predecessor, the Gotha Programme of 1875. It propounded orthodox Marxist philosophy as its very foundation, and gave this theoretical basis more prominence. But it added, as its immediate and practical aims, demands closely similar to those of Gotha, or of the Italian and French minimum programmes: including universal direct suffrage for men and women over twenty, freedom of expression and meeting, secular education, an eight-hour day, social welfare legislation, and progressive income tax.

The more fundamental difference between all western socialism and Russian communism becomes clear if these programmes are compared with the Russian Social Democratic programme adopted in 1903. It too, in accordance with precedent, was divided into maximum and minimum aims. But it was not exposed to the Italian or French or German danger of exalting the minimum at the expense of the maximum, in order to gain electoral votes. In western countries since 1871 (and even since 1848) the whole notion of a minimum programme depended on its being attainable within the existing framework of capitalist society without revolution; the whole point of the maximum programme was to keep before men's eyes the doctrines and the ultimate ends of socialism, but to relegate them to a distinct category of aims unattainable without revolution. In Russia both minimum and maximum programmes were of necessity revolutionary. The minimum political demands of 1903 began with the revolutionary overthrow of the tsarist régime and its replacement by a democratic republic. The minimum economic demands were those normally included in the minimum demands of western socialists : an eight-hour day and six-day week; effective factory inspection; state insurance against sickness and old age; the confiscation of church lands. But these too, in Russia before 1914, were revolutionary demands, and there was no essential difference between this minimum programme and the maximum programme of the proletarian socialist revolution. Indeed the most important decision taken in 1903, as already shown, was not about programmes at all, but about the actual organization of the party as a militant force, tempered for the struggle against the whole existing order. The point was appreciated from the outset in the manifesto which the new-born Russian Social Democratic Workers' party issued in 1898 : 'The further to the east one goes in Europe, the weaker in politics, the more cowardly and the meaner becomes the bourgeoisie, the greater are the cultural and political tasks that fall to the lot of proletariat.'

These differences of programmes and of organization involve a still wider contrast. It was not merely an issue of whether socialism should be economic or political in its scope, whether it should concentrate on capturing or on destroying existing states. To enter into competition with other parliamentary parties for winning votes, and to win from government concessions of value to the working classes, enmeshed every social democratic party, however vocal its protestations of ultimate proletarian purposes, in more nationalistic ways of thinking and behaving. In universal suffrage what counts is the vote of the individual elector, whatever his class; and in restricted electorates majorities lie with the non-proletarian electors. The leaders of a parliamentary socialist party instinctively think in terms not of classes but of individual voters and of majorities. They find themselves thinking in general, national terms, rather than in narrow terms of class war. Their working-class supporters, benefiting increasingly from legislation in their interests passed and enforced by the national state, likewise think more and more in national and non-revolutionary terms, since they become aware that they have more to lose than their chains. The growth of social democracy and of parliamentary labour parties brought about a nationalizing of socialism. This changing outlook was at variance with the older traditions of universal humanitarian socialism which were inherently internationalist in outlook, just as it was in conflict with the resolutely internationalist tenets of orthodox Marxism. This, above all, is the historical reason why it was Russia that was destined to make the first successful communist revolution. The conflicts between socialist movements that had been domesticated or 'nationalized', and revolutionary movements that still thought exclusively in terms of class war and proletarian action, were fought out before 1914. They repeatedly arose in the many congresses of the First and Second Internationals, until in 1914 the supreme issue seemed to be socialism versus nationalism.

LOYALTIES IN CONFLICT

By the 1890s industrialized Europe had in many respects become one unit, comprising the five major powers of the United Kingdom, Germany, France, Italy, and most of Austria-Hungary, along with the smaller states of Switzerland, the Low Countries, and Scandinavia. Within this *bloc* the fabric of social and economic life was woven on a broadly common pattern : a pattern traced by railway tracks and shipping lines, commercial connexions and urban densities, industrial concentrations and labour unions; a pattern coloured everywhere by the rich reds of violent conflict about religion, wealth, politics, and nationality. To the south and the east of this *bloc* stood areas still only partially affected by this pattern, still no integral part of this new economic fabric: such lands as Portugal and Spain, most of the Balkan peninsula, and all save the western fringe of Russia. The process of interweaving was by no means complete, and the peripheral countries already showed signs of being deeply affected. (See Diagram 6.)

Labour and the State. The great strikes that took place in Russia before 1905 were one such sign. They were part of a much more widespread feature of European life in these years. In Russia they were, it is true, exceptionally violent and persistent, and those of 1905 were closely related to the dislocating effects of the Russo-Japanese War of 1904–5. But they were preceded and followed by a whole epidemic of European strikes of which they can properly be regarded as a part. In France, Belgium, the Netherlands, Italy, and Sweden, there took place a long sequence of general strikes, wider in purpose than the immediate improvement of local working conditions, and aimed against governments as much as against employers. In the United Kingdom and Germany these were also years of large and important strikes which, though more limited in aim, caused alarm because of the contemporary fashion for general strikes elsewhere. As early as 1893 there had been a general strike in Belgium. Another occurred in 1902, accompanied by strikes in Sweden and Spain, and followed by general strikes in the Netherlands in 1903, Italy in 1904, France and Sweden again in 1909. A general strike of the metal workers of Barcelona in 1902 provoked widespread disturbances in Spain and in 1905 led to another in Cordova.

The first decade of the century was hag-ridden by such clashes between organized labour and the state. They were so relatively simultaneous in so many countries that it is tempting to look for a common cause; yet closer scrutiny shows that they differed widely in purposes, character, and success. They were rather multiple facets of a whole surge of industrial and social unrest which was increasingly guided into political channels, leading to the belief that the limits of social justice to be got within the existing framework of society had been reached. This general unrest was itself only part of a much wider crisis of human loyalties.

Both the Belgian strike of 1893 and the Swedish of 1902 were political in purpose, and were directed to forcing the governments to introduce universal suffrage. Each was partly successful. The Dutch general strike of 1903 was aimed against projected legislation that would have made strikes in the public services illegal; it failed completely. The Italian strikes of 1904, though widespread, were quite spontaneous protests against the killing of workers by government troops. They had no other clear objective, and their results were naturally negative. The Spanish strikes were protests against extremely low pay and harsh working conditions, and they failed – that in Andalusia in 1905 being ended by a terrible drought and famine. The Swedish general strike of 1909 was purely about wages, and was the trade unions' reprisal to a general lockout proclaimed by the employers in order to break the unions' resistance to wage reductions. It failed decisively. So did the French general strike of the same year.

In all countries particular strikes, usually about wage claims, were as liable to succeed and to cause severe dislocation as these so-called 'general strikes'. Thus the repeated strikes of miners in Britain, and of postal workers in France in 1908 or of railwaymen in 1910, produced more specific if meagre results. The lead, moreover, was usually taken by socialist trade unions, rather than by the avowedly syndicalist or communist unions; though these were the years when syndicalism, as an economic and political theory, was being most systematically expounded by men like George Sorel in France and his friend Vilfredo Pareto in Italy. It was percolating into Spain where it blended with anarchist movements launched by the Russian aristocrat, Michael Bakunin. Syndicalists, anarchists, and Marxists, were wont to take credit for the strikes which the frightened governments and ruling classes were ready enough to accord to them.

Both syndicalist and anarchist theories, as they were expounded in these years, had closer affinities with Marxism than the bitter quarrels between their advocates and the Marxists might lead one to suppose. All accepted the doctrines of class war and of the proletarian revolution; all believed that it was essential to overthrow existing society and the state. They differed mainly in emphasis and in priorities. Syndicalists argued that the chief weapon of the workers in the class war must be the general strike, and that the medium of proletarian action must be not political parties but the workers' own organizations, the labour unions. It was the task of union leaders to train their followers for the battles of the class war, and strikes were the best training ground. The state would be replaced, after revolution, by federal organizations of the workers, grouped in their functional unions.

Anarchism, as taught by Bakunin, was readier to resort to a wider repertoire of revolutionary deeds, and to seek salvation not in any interim 'dictatorship of the proletariat' but in the total destruction of all state organizations and the breaking down of national communities into local groups, voluntary associations, and municipalities. (In this way his ideas linked up with those of Proudhon, which had played a leading part in the Paris Commune of 1871.) He differed from the syndicalists in refusing to accord labour unions the key position; from Marx, in refusing to think of 'the masses' and of provisional dictatorships; from the social democrats, in his disbelief in the usefulness of parliamentary methods. He looked for salvation not to the industrial proletariat, but to the poor peasantry and town workers in such countries as Russia, Italy, and Spain. For this reason he is the creator of the peasant anarchism of southern and eastern Europe. In Spain and Italy anarchism and syndicalism could, for practical purposes, combine into a movement of anarcho-syndicalism, just as in the rest of Europe socialism and communism could combine into social democracy; but it was never a firm alliance, and beyond initial acts of violence or destruction it produced no concerted programme of action.

It is not to such theories that the general wave of European unrest in the early twentieth century can mainly be traced. Although syndicalist ideas and labour unions calling themselves syndicalist grew up in all the Latin countries of Europe (wherever trade unionism and socialism had made slowest headway), these were too restricted in appeal to explain the wider movement. The syndicalist movement has been well described by W. Milne-Bailey as 'merely that branch of a world-wide unrest that was equipped with a particular philosophy'; and outside the Latin countries and Russia it appealed not to workers so much as to isolated intellectuals who had small influence as compared with social democratic leaders. The tide of industrial unrest, which extended to the United States and Australia as well as Russia, was really the climax of that whole era of expansion of population, towns, industries, nations, and social organizations of all kinds which has already been described. Everywhere men and women were now organized into larger and more powerful units; territorially, politically, socially, industrially. Giant trusts and corporations stood face to face with growing labour organizations inside more powerfully organized states. Friction between them all was more likely; and wherever it occurred it could be more disruptive. The state by its very existence (and its wider electoral basis) was committed to serve interests more general than those of any one type of organization within it. But governments found it more and more difficult to hold the ring, to pacify the contestants, and to reconcile rival claims for shares in the national income. The tendency, most marked in western Europe, for real wages to slacken still further in their increase after about 1909, may explain some of the unrest before 1914.[1]

But behind such specific reasons lay the larger issues of rival claims to popular allegiance. It is not surprising that so far-reaching a transformation of old ways of life should result in a host of new human predicaments, a great crisis of conscience which brought turmoil. A generation of collective bargaining between employers and workers, marred by occasional strikes and lockouts, and accompanied by a generation of Marxist or semi-Marxist argument which taught that class war was endemic in the new industrialism, contributed to popular awareness of rival claims on loyalty. A generation of bitter feuds between church and state, of feuds about control over primary schools which affected every village and every family, contributed also to the universal spirit of sectarianism. A mood of disappointment with universal suffrage, civic liberties, and parliamentary government added still further to the contemporary confusion. Even where these had been early and fully achieved, they had failed to fulfil many of the great expectations which enthusiastic radicals and liberals had cherished. A generation of intensifying nationalist rivalries throughout Europe, by this time involving extensive rearmament, anxious diplomatic alliances, and periodic international scares and crises fully reported by a popular Press, served to exalt the claims of national allegiance above all others. The supreme question confronting most Europeans before 1914, though it was seldom appreciated in its full complexity, was nothing less than the basic question of human loyalties and allegiance. To what community did one most completely belong – to the old-established communities of church and homeland, or to the newer organizations of nation-state and industrial unit? It was a dilemma constantly present and inescapable, because it involved such everyday intimate things as a man's wages and work, how his children should be educated and what they should be taught to believe, whether he should give military service to the state or militant service to movements that claimed to transcend frontiers and lead on to humanity. If old faiths had gone, what new faiths should replace them? Was patriotism enough?

It is a revealing comment on the so-called 'century of nationalism' that not only did many millions of Europeans choose to leave their national homelands and seek their future overseas (*see* Map 10), but also so much migration took place between one European state and another during the last three decades of the century. Higher standards of living and richer opportunities in the modern industrialized states at-

1. See p. 395.

tracted immigration from the more economically backward countries. Never had the metropolis of each nation been so cosmopolitan. Into Britain flowed Irish, Jews, Poles, Germans, and Italians; into Germany came some 200,000 Poles; and into France poured many thousands of labourers from Belgium, Italy, and Spain. Among the wage-earning classes, at least, it seemed that the ties of national sentiment were weaker than the call of material prosperity. The nostalgic and sentimental patriotism that pervaded late nineteenth-century popular songs and legends, with their repeated protestations of devotion to the homeland and love of mother country, came mostly from individuals and families whose exile was voluntary and whose choice of habitation had been made for reasons of material advancement, despite the ties of nationality. Many such emigrants, indeed, eventually returned; those who did not kept a wistful affection for their own nationality and even contacts with their families and friends at home. But most did not return, and found little reason to regret their abandonment of the old world for the new, or of the less advanced for the more prosperous. The next generation was assimilated into the nationality of its adoption. Industrial unrest was but one manifestation of this wider conflict of allegiances. It is significant that syndicalism and anarchism, preaching allegiance to the smaller units of labour fraternity and locality, took root only in those parts of Europe least fully industrialized and urbanized, most consciously regional rather than national: they appealed slightly in France and Italy, more deeply in Spain, the Balkans, and Russia. For that reason they belonged to a dying social order, not, as they claimed, to a glowing future.

Anarchism and syndicalism were the most absolutist protests against the existing economic and political order in Europe. For this reason even movements of discontent which had no natural connexion whatever with the aims of these movements tended to borrow their methods and ideas, and even to link up with them wherever possible. The most surprising examples of this occurred in the United Kingdom, where it might have been expected that parliamentary traditions were strong enough to resist such reversions to force. There two special conflicts arose contemporaneously with the epidemic of strikes in Europe. One was the suffragette campaign, demanding votes for women as the next great step in feminine emancipation. The other was the perennial demand for Irish Home Rule, a more familiar cause of disruption in British political life. The Labour party lent support to their aims, if not to their methods. Although neither was in doctrine anarchist, each adopted methods of destruction and dislocation; although neither was syndicalist in character, each turned momentarily to seek alliance with organized labour. Like called unto like, and there is no more striking testimony to the new climate of the twentieth century than the hysteria and violence that these two political issues generated even around the Mother of Parliaments.

Women's Suffrage. The movement for women's suffrage took organized form in the fateful year 1903, and it began where so much that was revolutionary in Victorian England had begun, in Manchester. A little group of women, meeting in the house of Mrs Emmeline Pankhurst, widow of a socialist barrister, formed the Women's Social and Political Union. Until 1910 this little movement, along with other kindred groups, lobbied members of parliament, staged processions, and in general agitated as nineteenth-century radicals had always agitated when they demanded the extension of civil liberties and political rights. Gradually, meeting with ridicule or at best negative response, they became more militant. They found ingenious ways of heckling political meetings, disturbing debates in parliament, and of making cabinet ministers' lives more uncomfortable. Then, in November 1910, when the Liberal government of Herbert Asquith was in the midst of its battle with the House of Lords,[1] there occurred a scene that heralded the new phase of violence. The Women's Union staged an invasion of the Houses of Parliament, and found themselves blocked in Parliament Square by great numbers of police who had orders to keep them away. Pushing, jostling, and rough treatment went on for nearly six hours, intensifying in violence until the crowd dispersed. A few days later the women invaded Downing Street, where Asquith had to be rescued by the police when he attempted to leave his house. Thereafter relative quietness came, until November 1912.

Then, convinced that Asquith was resorting to endless evasions, the women sprang into action again. They began a campaign of breaking windows, courting arrest and imprisonment, defying the law. They fell more completely under the guidance of Christabel Pankhurst, daughter of Emmeline and an altogether more ruthless and violent personality. For the next two years the 'argument of the broken pane' was backed up by outbreaks of arson in churches and country houses. Paintings in picture galleries were slashed, telegraph wires cut, sports pavilions wrecked. Suffragettes sent to prison went on hunger strike, and the authorities resorted to the cruelty of forcible feeding. On Derby Day, June 1913, Emily Davison threw herself in front of the King's race horse and was killed. The movement had its martyr, its human sacrifice. Hunger strikes might yield more. To forestall this danger, the government passed a law of very dubious constitutionality – the so-called

1. See p. 361.

'Cat-and-Mouse' Bill, which provided that hunger strikers might be discharged when their health became affected but rearrested as soon as they were well again, so prolonging the term of their sentence indefinitely. Labour leaders such as Keir Hardie and George Lansbury took up the women's cause and opposed the bill, but in vain. The Liberal government seemed nearing the end of its resources, but would not accept Keir Hardie's simple proposal that the only answer was to give in. George Bernard Shaw, a leading Fabian, suggested that the Home Secretary, then busy suppressing suffragist papers, 'apparently believes himself to be the Tsar of Russia, a very common form of delusion'. Down in London's dockland Mrs Pankhurst's other daughter, Sylvia, was rousing working-class folk to the cause, and making links with trade unionism. It was all very frightening for the harassed Liberal ministers, betrayed into a most illiberal-looking policy. They were saved from their misfortune by the war in 1914. By then, indeed, the suffragette movement was showing signs of internal division, and public opinion was tiring of the endless violence of its methods. The cause for which the Edwardian women suffered so much was won in 1918, after the greater violence of war had given time for passions to cool. But it was a very revealing episode in prewar Britain.

Irish Home Rule. Nor were strikers and suffragettes the only thorns in the side of Asquith and his colleagues. There were also the Irish – the eternal Irish. In the days of Gladstone the Liberal party had been rent by his efforts to grant Irishmen home rule – the national independence and separation from England that the more ardent Irish partiots had demanded since the days of Daniel O'Connell.[1] In 1870 Isaac Butt had founded an Irish party and coined the slogan of 'Home Rule'. It was intended to be a more positive version of the old demand for 'Repeal' of the Act of Union of 1800, which had made Ireland a part of the United Kingdom and given it representation in the parliament at Westminster. From 1874 onwards, with nearly sixty Irish members in the House of Commons, Butt had repeatedly pleaded the cause of Irish independence and had equally repeatedly been ignored or rebuffed. In 1878 the conciliatory Butt was replaced by Charles Stewart Parnell, spokesman of those who preferred more drastic tactics. Parnell and his colleagues proved as ingenious in devising methods of obstructing business in the House of Commons as the Edwardian women were later to prove in harassing the government of their day. By 1886 Gladstone was persuaded that Home Rule must be granted, but failed to carry the whole Liberal party with him. In 1890, when Home Rule seemed almost assured, Parnell was suddenly discredited by his role in a

1. See p. 153.

divorce case; and Gladstone's Home Rule Bill of 1892, though passing the Commons by a narrow majority, was rejected by the House of Lords.

In 1900 the 'Irish Question' entered a new phase when the Irish party was reconstituted under John Redmond; and its fresh campaign coincided with the onslaught of the strikers and the suffragettes upon the parliamentary system in the new century. With a solid group of now eighty members, the Irish party could with luck control the balance between Liberals and Conservatives in parliament; so no government could afford to ignore it. But while the Liberals were still divided about the issue, the Conservatives were anxious to preserve the Protestant ascendancy in Ulster (the northern counties). They were strongly opposed to any home-rule measure that would subordinate Protestant Ulster to the Catholic south. It was a disruptive issue for both parties, and both manoeuvred with care.

The passing of the Parliament Act in 1911 altered the whole situation. The Conservatives had hitherto been able to rely safely on their permanent majority in the House of Lords to block any attempt, as it had blocked Gladstone's in 1892, to grant home rule to Ireland. Now that the power of the Lords was reduced by the Act to a mere power of delay and not of veto, it seemed certain that the Liberals would pass Home Rule. Asquith had almost promised it when he bargained for Irish support in passing the Parliament Act. The Conservatives, led from 1911 onwards by Andrew Bonar Law, a Scotch-Canadian Presbyterian, were bent on taking revenge for their loss of power in the Lords by mobilizing the resistance of Ulster to any conceivable scheme of Home Rule. The outcome was a sort of Conservative rebellion, a strike of the wealthy classes and the peers against the constitutional government of England. The intricacies of the story are of little importance. What mattered was the outcome, which was that Ulster found its fanatical and violent champion in Sir Edward Carson, a great advocate and a Protestant southern Irishman; that Bonar Law and Carson most recklessly incited Ulstermen to revolt should the Home Rule bill not provide independence for Ulster; and for the next three years there seemed to be no limit to the excesses that responsible political leaders of either party were prepared to perpetrate. So frenzied was the party conflict that by 1914, on the eve of the outbreak of the world war, Conservatives were drilling and arming Ulster volunteers against the day when Ireland would get Home Rule, and were encouraging British army officers to mutiny and desert rather than coerce Ulster; while the Liberals were preparing to coerce Ulster in the name of national freedom, and even to connive at the desertion of their own army officers rather than risk organized mutiny. It was a crisis not only of Irish history, but of English parliamentary government.

The Irish, moreover, like sections of the suffragettes, showed signs of linking up with syndicalists and so importing more violence into the matter. With Ireland heading for civil war – for the Nationalist Volunteers, like the Ulstermen, were drilling and arming – there grew up in Dublin a new syndicalist movement led by James Larkin and James Connolly. It preached the contemporary European creeds of riot, the general strike, guild socialism, syndicalist revolution. Larkin's Irish Transport Workers' Union fought a great transport strike in Dublin in 1913, and it led to a crop of sympathetic strikes and riots. Linked through Connolly with the Irish Volunteers, this desperate syndicalist movement of the workers seemed for a time yet another element in the forthcoming Irish civil war. The violent nationalist group of *Sinn Fein* was gaining in appeal. But here, as elsewhere in Europe, the bigger crisis of 1914 swamped all lesser quarrels. In the summer of 1914 it seemed certain that a general strike would soon occur in Britain. If it had, both Irish syndicalist revolt and Irish civil war would doubtless have merged into it. Sarajevo happened just in time to save the parliamentary system in Britain.

Terrorism. The backcloth of events in Europe, in these same years, was no less lurid. Besides the epidemics of great strikes and industrial unrest and the darkening clouds of war, there had been a remarkable list of assassinations. To be the head of a state or of a government had become a most perilous occupation. When the Austrian archduke Franz Ferdinand was murdered at Sarajevo in 1914, it was striking how many other leading personages had within living memory suffered the same fate. Three Presidents of the United States, an Emperor of Russia (Alexander II in 1881), a President of the French Republic (Sadi Carnot in 1894), an Empress of Austria (Elizabeth in 1898), a King of Italy (Humbert in 1900), a King and Queen of Serbia (Alexander and Draga in 1903), a King of Portugal (Carlos in 1908), quite a few Russian archdukes and several minor princes, had all been assassinated. It was not that assassinations were new, though there were many would-be assassins that did not succeed. Orsini had thrown his bomb at Napoleon III in 1858 and even in peaceful England an attempt had been made on the life of Queen Victoria in 1872. Bismarck's antisocialist laws of 1878 had been passed after two attempts to assassinate the German Emperor. These were episodes in an already well-established nineteenth-century tradition which was born of the age of secret societies and the violent revolutionary tradition, and they had many earlier historical precedents. But the speed with which crowned heads fell in the generation before

1914 was such as to betoken a new era of violence. Men were not slow to trace the cause to the activities of anarchists, communists, and socialists in the Second International, which held frequent meetings from 1889 until 1914. This was to exaggerate the importance and the nature of this body, whose aims were organizational and not isolated acts of terrorism. But the story of the International throws further light on the connexions and conflicts between the different varieties of revolutionary and social democratic movements; and they provided the setting where, more clearly than anywhere else, the issues of socialism versus nationalism were debated to the full.

First and Second Internationals. The First International Association of Workingmen, which had originated in 1864 and to which Marx had given shape and doctrine by 1866, was throughout its existence rent between Marxism and anarchism. Rejecting the constitution first prepared for it by the veteran Mazzini, on the grounds that it was better suited to secret political conspiracy than to the more open encouragement of working-class strength and solidarity, it had accepted Marx's arguments that what was now needed was systematic cooperation internationally between all working-class societies in order to promote emancipation on a broad front. When the new constitution was adopted at its first full congress at Geneva in 1866, socialist doctrines were set out in very general terms. Its immediate concern was with the earliest possible reduction of the working day to eight hours, and better facilities for general and technical education. From this aim few labour organizations or socialist societies could dissent. The next year doctrine was formulated more precisely: means of transport and communication should be socialized. In 1868 came more precision: land, mines, and forests must also become the property of the state, and the principle of 'to labour the full product of labour' must be established. By now the movement included representatives from Britain, France, Germany, Belgium, Switzerland, Italy, and Spain. The International was gaining momentum, despite the wars of these years, and labour unions gave help to one another in times of struggle. It spread to Hungary and Poland. The police estimated its members and supporters at about five million. But in 1869 Bakunin and other anarchists joined it, and thenceforward it was beset with deep internal dissension. They were expelled in 1872 and it was finally disbanded in 1876. It corresponded, in the ambitiousness of its aims by comparison with the meagreness of its powers, with Robert Owen's Grand National Consolidated Trades Union of 1834 in Britain: each overreached what the stage of national industrial development made possible, and each failed because it was unrealistic.

The Second International throve on the lessons that had been so bitterly learned. It came into being in 1889, in the large assembly of socialist societies which gathered in Paris to celebrate the centenary of the French Revolution. It originated in a merger of two separate conferences, one of the Marxian revolutionary parties, the other of the reformist or 'possibilist' parties and trade unionists. It was therefore a reflection of the very divisions which had already rent so many national socialist parties, and was at the same time an attempt to overcome that division. The anarchists it excluded from the first, remembering the fate of the First International – though its early sessions were made almost intolerable by the interruptions and heckling of anarchist groups protesting against their exclusion. The agile and ingenious Italian anarchist, Dr Saverio Merlino, contrived to attend its first meetings and preach his own gospel.

The International held a long succession of congresses – at Brussels in 1891, Zürich in 1893, London in 1896, Paris in 1900, Amsterdam in 1904, Stuttgart in 1907, Copenhagen in 1910, and Basle in 1912; the congress that was to have met in Vienna in August 1914 was abandoned because of the outbreak of war. From 1900 onward it had as a permanent office the International Socialist Bureau, housed in the Maison du Peuple in Brussels and run by Camille Huysmans. It grew considerably in comprehensiveness, and in 1910 the congress was attended by 896 delegates representing twenty-three nationalities. With the growth of socialist movements everywhere in these years, it also gained in solidity. At its best the Second International served to break down the isolation in which socialist leaders had lived and worked; it made working men in at least a score of countries more conscious of the political and social problems which confronted them all in common; and it achieved moments of important solidarity between people of different and often politically opposed nationalities. Much of what it attempted was haunted by frustration and failure. The nearest it ever came to embodying a real international working-class solidarity in face of oppression was the support it gave to the Russian revolutionaries in 1905; though even that proved ineffectual.

The two greatest controversies with which it had to deal, and which reveal most clearly the dilemmas before it, were about whether socialists should accept ministerial office along with members of non-socialist parties, and about the correct action for socialists in time of war. These issues were the touchstones of choice between socialism and nationalism. The first arose at the congress of Amsterdam in 1904, occasioned by Alexandre Millerand's acceptance of office in the government of republican defence of 1899 in France toward the end of the Dreyfus Affair.

French socialists were particularly shocked that his colleague as Minister of War in the same government should be General Gallifet, a man particularly hated by the workers because he had so savagely suppressed the Commune of 1871. Internationally, this situation aroused especial fury among the German social democrats, who blamed the disunity of French socialists for permitting this great betrayal. The issue divided both the French socialists and the International. Debates on the issue between Guesde and Jaurès became so frequent in the next few years that Briand remarked that the party now met in 'annual scissions'. At Amsterdam in 1904 Jaurès debated with Bebel, and the issue before the International became one between French and German conceptions of socialism.

Jaurès attacked the German social democrats for wanting to impose their doctrines and tactics on all other countries, and asserted that the great obstacle to progress was not the behaviour of the French socialists but the 'political powerlessness of German Social Democracy'. This mighty disciplined party suffered, indeed, from the handicap that its strength in the Reichstag was of little consequence so long as the Reichstag itself had so little control over the German government. Jaurès touched a sore spot, too, when he pointed out that the party had 'no revolutionary tradition but only one of receiving benefits – universal suffrage, for instance – from above'. Jaurès was defeated on the motion condemning socialist participation in government, but the voting revealed a deep split in the congress. The men who supported Jaurès or who abstained were those from countries where liberal parliamentary institutions were most fully established – Britain, France, Belgium, Scandinavia, Switzerland. Those who supported Bebel, apart from the Italians, came from countries where they were anyhow unlikely ever to be offered a share in political power. They even included the lone delegate from Japan, Katayama. Nothing showed more clearly the diversity of circumstances with which social democrats had to deal in different countries, or the impossibility of their concerting any single agreed policy and tactic. An amendment moved by the Austrian Adler and the Belgian Vandervelde, allowing for such local variations, was rejected, though only by twenty-one votes to nineteen. On this matter international socialism appeared to be almost equally divided.

The second great controversy arose the following year. It was events in Russia that forced this issue upon the International. It was to dominate all subsequent congresses. What should be the action of socialists in the event of war? Bebel, Jaurès, and most other western social democrats believed that the workers' interest lay in ending the war as quickly as possible by opposing war credits, by a general strike, and by sabotage of the war effort. Lenin and the German Marxist Rosa Luxemburg argued that a European war would so weaken the machinery of the capitalist state that socialist revolution would become possible. Insurrection, they maintained, must aim not merely at ending a war but at the 'overthrow of class rule' and the proletarian seizure of power. The Stuttgart congress of 1907 attempted to reconcile these contrary views by a famous resolution which, in the fashion of German social democracy, contained something for everyone, while committing nobody to anything. It included the now traditional condemnations of militarism and imperialism, and the call for a national militia in place of standing armies. It recited alleged instances of successful socialist action to prevent or end wars; and concluded with the omnibus statement of the role of socialists in wartime:

Should war break out in spite of all this, it is their duty to intercede for its speedy end, and to strive with all their power to make use of the violent economic and political crisis brought about by the war to rouse the people, and thereby to hasten the abolition of capitalist class rule.

The allegedly successful interventions for which the Stuttgart congress claimed credit amounted to very much less than they sounded. After Franco-British tension about Egypt and the Sudan in 1898, English and French trade unionists had indeed got together to reinforce Franco-British understanding – but only after the crisis of Fashoda had been overcome by diplomatic action. During the comparable Moroccan crisis between France and Germany in 1905, the parliamentary interventions of the French and German socialists did little to resolve the crisis.[1] The socialist trade unions in Sweden had demonstrated against war on Norway, but they voiced only a part of a much wider desire to avoid war and it was a government-sponsored plebiscite which peacefully and constitutionally separated the two countries in 1905. Just as the German Social Democrats had little legislative achievement to show, so the Second International, constantly dominated by the Germans, had pitifully little positive achievement to show by 1914.

The arguments and resolution of Stuttgart did little to settle the overriding issue of socialism versus nationalism, or to frame any coherent principles upon which such diverse parties in so many different states could be relied upon to take action in an emergency. Perhaps in even trying to do this, it was at fault; for, as already seen, the spirit and character of socialism, as of labour organization in general, varied immensely according to the economic and political environment in

1. See p. 520.

which it grew up. The International of social democratic movements could be no more coherent in its principles and policies than the coherence of its component national parties permitted; and though they debated at home the issue of war and peace even more constantly than in the congresses of the International, they reached no greater clarity of programme.

Militarism and Pacifism. The issue raised its head whenever national parliaments considered expenditure on naval and military establishments, and this happened very frequently in these years. In the same year as the congress of Stuttgart the question arose in the German Reichstag, and the 'revisionists' gave full support for German military expenditure on the grounds that it was the duty of all citizens, socialists included, to see to it that 'the German people is not pressed to the wall by any other nation'. Both the Gotha Programme of 1875 and the Erfurt Programme of 1891 had specified among their aims 'a people's army in place of standing armies', and 'training in universal military duty'. These were the most common socialist solutions to the problem of national armaments – a militia or 'people's army' in the French traditions of 1793.

It was the solution which Jean Jaurès put forward in France in his study of *The New Army* (*L'armée nouvelle*) of 1910. His purpose was to refute the extreme antimilitarists and pacifists, like Gustave Hervé, who preached unilateral disarmament, and thereby to counteract the nationalists' charge that socialists lacked patriotism; but at the same time to reject the conservative preference for a standing professional army. The Caesarist traditions of Napoleon, recently strengthened by experience of that equally 'good republican' General Boulanger and still more by the crisis of the Dreyfus case, made army reform a foremost issue for French socialism. The army seemed to be a 'state within the state'. How could the Republic be internationally secure without jeopardizing its own domestic survival? Jaurès argued for a citizen army, the 'nation in arms' at the service of democracy and peace. He urged 'a strong democratic militia, reducing barracks to the functions of a training school', and the abolition of all the old invidious dispensations from service. He favoured the Swiss principle of 'the gun behind the kitchen door'. What the republicans as a whole demanded was that length of service should be shortened but equalized; and after three successive overhauls of the system, in 1889, 1905, and 1913, this was accomplished. After 1889 no one was conscripted for more than three years, and after 1905 every young man, regardless of family origin or future career, served for the same period. The conditions of military life were made more democratic, and the army was treated more as a school of citizenship. Jaurès managed to unite socialists in this conception, save for the extreme pacifists and Marxists. But in 1910, the very year his famous book appeared, that former socialist Aristide Briand, who had once advocated the general strike, when in power broke a railway strike by means of the service laws. He called the strikers to the colours and then assigned them, as soldiers, to their former duties. Since mutiny, unlike striking, could be punished with death, it became clear enough that army laws could not so easily be reconciled with socialist activities.

The debate about military and naval establishments could be conducted at, so to speak, several different levels. At a constitutional and political level, most liberals and radicals were in agreement with the socialists that military power must be so controlled as to offer no threat to civilian government. At a more technical level, it was a debate about the most efficient way to run an army – whether as a professional and highly trained fighting force, or as a peacetime framework for training the 'people in arms', whose patriotic spirit would in an emergency bring irresistible *élan* into a war of national defence. The main argument of the socialists was that since no war of conquest can be justified, it is essential to prepare only for a war of defence; to which the nationalists retorted that the lessons of Prussian victories in the 1860s were that a professional army is superior to amateur militias, however enthusiastic. At an economic level, a recurrent difficulty was that military and naval expenditures competed for national resources with the social services and endangered existing standards of living. It was the characteristic twentieth-century dilemma of guns or butter.

Whereas the debate in France was conducted at the first and second of these levels, the debate in Germany was conducted mainly on the first, and mainly about naval rather than military expansion. The first bill expanding the navy was passed by the Reichstag in 1898. It was opposed by the Social Democrats, and many liberals feared that the fixing of the naval budget for seven years ahead would rob the Reichstag of control over expenditure. Anxieties accumulated with each successive approval of naval expansion – in 1899, 1906, 1907, 1908. But each law passed with large majorities, and socialists proved helpless against the tide of nationalist propaganda and sentiment.

In Britain, where compulsory national service did not exist, the debate took place mostly at the third level, that of finance and encroachment on national standards of living. Further naval expenditures in 1909 were resisted even within the Liberal government by Lloyd George and Churchill, who were anxious to develop social reforms – the joint burden led to the famous budget of that year which tapped new sources of taxation.[1] Labour party speakers constantly took this view, and were especially opposed to British alliance with tsarist Russia. In January 1912 the Labour party passed a resolution at its annual conference: 'This conference, believing the anti-German policy pursued in the name of the British Government by Sir Edward Grey to be a cause of increasing armaments, international ill will, and the betrayal of oppressed nationalities, protests in the strongest terms against it.' But the party was still too small to matter. Such were the general sentiments of socialists almost everywhere in Europe: all deploring the race in armaments and the scramble for colonies, most seeking to arouse anti-war sentiments, the most extreme urging a general strike in the event of war. But differences of opinion fell along national as much as ideological lines of division.

It is easy and tempting, in retrospect, to laugh at the high-minded, loquacious, yet strangely ineffectual social democrats of the Second International, at their interminable and somewhat circular debates about how to prevent war, at their bitter sectarianism. Yet their purpose was worthy enough, their hopes noble and humane. They represented the basic pacifist sentiment of the European workers in an age of violence – the great majority of whom refused to differentiate, as Lenin wanted them to, between useful and harmful wars. They wanted no war at all, and their spokesmen at the congresses of the International reflected their desires when they rejected what Lenin or Rosa Luxemburg wanted, an international strategy of revolution devised to turn a 'useful' war into a successful revolution. After 1890 Engels had argued that international socialism must pin its hopes on the continued growth of the German Social Democratic party. The Hohenzollern power in Germany would not survive a world war, and the Social Democrats would inevitably come into power. Since the Russian Tsar was the chief enemy of workers everywhere, German workers would then wage a 'useful' war of liberation against Russia, in the manner of France in 1793. What cut across his calculations was the alliance completed between France and Russia by 1894. To ask French workers to support imperial Germany against Russia was to ask them to accept the government of Wilhelm II as an ally. contrary to all their deep-rooted patriotic and anti-German sentiments. Here was the conflict of socialism versus nationalism in its most acute and concrete form, and the International evaded it simply by condemning all wars between capitalist governments.

It should not have come as a surprise in 1914 that socialist parties in every country voted almost unanimously for war credits and backed their national governments in war. The choice had already been made

1. See p. 361.

by their very refusal to concert a grand strategy of international revolution, by reference to which tactics appropriate for the socialists of each country could have been devised. At no time before 1914 was it possible to enlist support from the mass of French or British workers for the German imperial government in a war against Russia – however neatly that might have solved the dilemma of the German workers. In no country – not even in Germany – were social democrats anyhow numerous enough or in a position strong enough to determine the choice of peace or war.

The Socializing of Nationalism. The surge of social unrest and violence before 1914 was explicable in terms of the incompleteness of industrialization and of democracy. Wherever industrialization had slowed down, as in France or Spain, and wherever electorates were still restricted, as in Italy or Sweden, urban workers felt in some degree excluded from the national community. A sense of isolation and of underprivilege, of being treated as an internal alien group like a national minority, was perhaps as much a source of the workers' unrest as it was of the unrest of the militant suffragettes. Millions of Europeans were moving towards a reorientation of community life. Just as Norwegians felt that they did not belong together with Sweden, or Irish home-rulers felt that they did not belong together with Great Britain whereas Ulstermen felt that they did, so the most class-conscious elements of the new proletarian masses no longer felt a community of interest or of aspiration with the property-owning classes of their states. The masses everywhere sought escape from anonymity – from the harsh impersonal rule of remote management in industry, from the grey uniformity of industrial life, from being, in short, inarticulate masses. The aim of the social revolutionaries, as of Norwegian and Irish patriots or militant suffragettes, was to intensify this decline in national loyalties and to make a counter-appeal of sectional unity.

Wherever, as in the advanced industrial countries of Great Britain and Germany, this feeling was diminished and offset by a wide franchise, social legislation, and freedom of labour organization, the unrest was less explosive. There, strikes were concerned with remedying particular grievances, and agitation had definable and attainable goals. Industrialization was continuing everywhere, democracy and parliamentary institutions were spreading, labour organizations and socialist movements were growing, right up to the brink of war in 1914. Most workers could look forward with reasonable expectation to further alleviations before long, if only peace could be kept. Above all, the existing achievements of socialism and of social security were forging new links of solidarity and loyalty between workers and nation. Men become more conservative when they have something to conserve. The old attachments to locality and country, to national life and traditions, were being intensified by popular education and publicity. It was only where no such ameliorations existed, where the electoral basis of the state remained narrow and the provisions of social security practically non-existent, as in Spain or Russia, that unrest was necessarily political and revolutionary.

Those nation-states of western and central Europe which had undertaken to serve the interests and welfare of all classes in society, and which had admitted organized labour to some share of responsibility and power, were rewarded by a socialism that was in spirit cooperative and unrevolutionary. Wherever the nation-state had been most completely socialized, there also was socialism most completely nationalized. The counterpart to the growth of wider electorates and of social security provision was the growth of social democracy rather than revolutionary Marxism.

This important fact does much to explain the stability and resilience of the western states, even when subjected to the strain of war. In the whole industrialized area of western and central Europe, excluding the Iberian and Balkan peninsulas, the only states to suffer revolution as the immediate result of the First World War were the two defeated Empires of Germany and Austria-Hungary. Outside this area, in Poland, Russia, and the Ottoman Empire, revolution was the rule rather than the exception. And even the two exceptions in central Europe deserve attention. The dual monarchy of Austria-Hungary was disrupted not by Marxist revolution but by the old-fashioned nationalist insurgence of Balkan peoples. The revolution in Germany in 1918 proved to be a much more superficial change of political system that it at first appeared. If the German Reich had been more advanced in its provision of social security than republican France, it had also been a less genuine parliamentary democracy. The turning point had come as early as 1879, when the Third French Republic, designed to be conservative, fell completely into the hands of moderate republicans who controlled its presidency, ministry, and parliamentary majorities. At that same time the Bismarckian Reich broke with the National Liberals, who were inopportunely demanding freedom of speech, Press, and trade, as well as the implementing of parliamentary control over government, and sought support from the conservative Prussian landowners and large industrialists. The French parliament remained, thereafter, a more effective organ of representative democratic government than the Reichstag. Germany lacked this source of moral strength which France, for all her other weaknesses, enjoyed.

Thus, as has been remarked, 'from St Petersburg to Paris the political spectrum of Europe shaded from autocracy to parliamentarianism, preserving the gradations that had distinguished it since the Congress of Vienna'. The point had not gone unnoted by the precursors of the Bolsheviks.[1] It may not be too fanciful to see in so persistant a pattern the basis of divisions in Europe after the Second World War. In eastern Europe the penalties of having repudiated liberal democracy in 1848, and social democracy before 1914, were belated experiments in fragile democratic systems after 1919 and the imposition of new-style 'people's democracies' after 1945.[2] Deviant paths, once followed in history, seldom end at the same destination.

1. See pp. 115 and 408.
2. See pp. 589–600 and 833–6.

CHAPTER 18

THE TEXTURE OF EUROPEAN CULTURE

SCIENCE AND MATERIAL PROGRESS

AFTER the First World War it became common to despise or to ridicule the boundless faith in progress which had prevailed during the nineteenth century. Before 1914, it was suggested, people had taken for granted that material betterment – the mere capacity to produce more and more wealth with less and less labour through the use of machines – was in itself progress. It had been forgotten that man cannot live by bread alone, that knowledge is not the same as wisdom, that the enhanced resources put at man's disposal by science, technology, and superior methods of organization might be used for destruction or tyranny instead of for creation and emancipation. It in no way followed that when a people became more healthy and wealthy, it also became more wise. Spiritually and morally, indeed, to devote so much energy and enterprise to material ends might be not progress but retrogression – the first step in a reversion from civilization to barbarism.

It was natural enough, after the collapse of prewar prosperity and optimism, after experience of the devastations of the first world war, that there should be reaction, and even revulsion, against the whole trend of developments which had led to this catastrophe. But equally, it was neither foolish nor wicked of nineteenth-century men to believe that what had happened in that century had resulted in positive and creative progress. Many of the age-old miseries of mankind had been abolished or were in rapid retreat: slavery had been ended in all save the remotest and most primitive parts of the earth; famine, plague, and disease were being speedily diminished by greater abundance of food, better transport, wonderful drugs, and more skilful medical services; the agonies caused by childbirth and early death were being soothed away by science; decades had been added to the average length of human life; squalor and exploitation were receding before slum clearance and sanitation, factory regulation and social controls; ignorance and illiteracy were in retreat before advancing armies of teachers. The numbers of mankind grew so fast, and within a single lifetime families became so clearly healthier and better fed, cleaner and better housed, more literate and better informed, more mobile and better governed, that none could doubt the truth of vast individual and social betterment.

This material progress was especially obvious in the industrialized western countries, where between 1870 and 1900 real wages – or what incomes would buy even allowing for losses due to periods of unemployment – rose by about half. It was not an absolute fall in the value of real wages after 1900 which provoked industrial unrest, but merely a slowing down of what had come to be regarded as their normal rate of increase – that, and the unevenness of wage levels, which prompted less skilled or less fortunate types of workers to press for a more equitable share in the profits of mechanization. The most liberal minded admitted that many evils remained still to be fought: including the newer evils of drab squalor in mining towns and industrial cities, the ravages of the countryside, the menace of unemployment, the terror of economic crisis, and above all the frightfulness of more scientific warfare. But few doubted that these, too, could safely be added to the list of remediable evils, that the ingenuity of men of good will could in due time overcome all these and other ills. The most observant noted that two new perils loomed ahead: the dangers of mass hysteria and sensationalism in the more gregarious and less religious communities of modern Europe, and the new fact that in a world deficient in international organization national prosperity depended on what happened everywhere else. But even these perils good sense and good will could reasonably be expected to remove, and a new age of prosperity, peace, and plenty seemed at last to be within reach of mankind. Such was the mood of nineteenth-century Europe, so abruptly dispelled in 1914.

'*Miracles of Science.*' If pride is ever justified, the men of nineteenth-century Europe were justified in taking pride in their achievements. If asked what had made so much progress possible, they would have answered, almost with one voice, that it was above all science. It was feats of mechanical engineering that attracted their highest admiration: the quadrupling of the world's railway mileage between 1870 and 1900, involving such masterpieces as the Forth Bridge in Scotland and the Trans-Siberian and Canadian Pacific railways; the erection of the first skyscrapers in New York and Chicago, and of the Eiffel Tower in Paris; the digging of the Suez and Kiel and Panama canals; the great new oceanic liners and the exciting consequences of the invention of the internal combustion engine, which made possible both automobiles and aeroplanes. There were signs of the impending conquest of the air, as well as of land and sea, when in 1895 the Irish-Italian inventor, Guglielmo Marconi, first used radio waves to transmit messages by wireless telegraphy, and when in 1909 the Frenchman Blériot successfully flew the English Channel in one of the new flying machines which

Americans had invented. Next in esteem ranked exploration of the earth's surface, now made more possible by modern resources of transport and medicine. While some Europeans, like David Livingstone and Henry Stanley from Britain, Fernand Foureau and Savorgnan de Brazza from France, Gerhard Rohlfs and Hermann von Wissmann from Germany, the Hungarian Samuel Teleki, and the American Donaldson Smith, penetrated into the interior of the unknown African continent; others, like the Norwegians Fridtjof Nansen and Roald Amundsen, and the Englishmen Robert Scott and Ernest Shackleton, explored the poles of the earth. The exploits and courage of these men were material for a new saga of heroism, to be told to children as inspiring examples of what brave men might achieve. Even a new universe began to come within view when the German astronomer, Johann Gottfried Galle, discovered the new planet Neptune – a discovery that in the opinion of one historian of science, Sir William Dampier, probably 'had a far greater effect in establishing the credibility of scientific method in the civilized world at large than the far more important co-ordination of observation and hypothesis in the preceding fifty years'.

Meanwhile the theoretical and experimental scientists were advancing new hypotheses that opened fresh vistas of progress in man's knowledge of his physical environment. That versatile Scot, James Clerk-Maxwell, who in 1871 became the first professor of experimental physics at the University of Cambridge, put forward an electromagnetic theory of light. Since the velocities of electromagnetic waves and of light waves were shown to be the same, he inferred that light waves were probably electromagnetic in character. He died in 1879, but his theories were further investigated by scientists in many countries, and by 1886 the German Heinrich Hertz measured the actual velocity of electromagnetic waves. This work linked up with a rapid development in the study of radioactivity, of which the enormous importance was fully realized only after 1914. In 1895 the German Wilhelm Konrad Röntgen discovered X rays; the next year the Frenchman Antoine Henri Becquerel showed that uranium gave off rays similar to those discovered by Röntgen; and two years later Pierre and Marie Curie (one French, the other Polish) isolated radium. These discoveries carried much further that inquiry into the secret relationship between energy and matter which had begun before 1870.[1] They brought closer together the physical and biological sciences; and led on the one hand to telecommunications and radio, on the other, to radiotherapy and new methods of attacking disease.

In the experiments of J. J. Thomson and Ernest Rutherford, each in

1. See p. 276.

turn a successor to Clerk-Maxwell in his Cambridge professorship, these theories led to a completely new theory of atomic structure. By 1897 German physicists had discovered that when a high voltage of electricity was applied across two metal plates sealed within an evacuated tube, rays were given off from the negative plate, called the cathode. Thomson proved that these cathode rays consisted of very small particles (ions), travelling at very high speed and carrying a negative charge of electricity. He called them at first 'corpuscles', but they are now known as electrons. The electron was held to be present in all matter, and the conductivity of gases was shown to be due to the splitting up of atoms by the removal of one or more electrons, leaving the atom positively charged. Electrons were found to be one of the simple fundamental units out of which all the different kinds of atoms are built; and though all carry the same electrical charge, they are not identical in mass. The American scientist, Robert Millikan, proved finally that electricity, too, is atomic in nature; and the connexion of energy with matter was established. The chemical properties of matter depend entirely on how electrons are arranged within it. The flow of electricity through a wire means that there is a flow of electrons through the wire; the picture on a television screen is painted by an electron beam. The electron is everywhere, and it is the chief link between what is called matter and what is called energy.

By 1903 Ernest Rutherford and Frederick Soddy evolved a theory to coordinate and explain all the phenomena of radioactivity which had been observed. They suggested that such activity was released by changes within single radioactive atoms as a result of their internal explosive disintegration. Rutherford's book on *Radioactivity* first appeared in 1904, and two years later in *Radioactive Transformations* he added his theory of the transmutation of elements. Though many chemists resisted the view that chemical atoms, hitherto thought immutable, were actually undergoing transmutation, Rutherford was proved to be right. He went on to suggest that the atom was itself like a miniature solar system, with a positively charged nucleus as the sun, surrounded by negatively charged electrons revolving about it like planets, and that even the nucleus might also have a complex structure. Thus apparently solid matter must be thought of as mainly empty space, and both energy and matter were reducible to common units. All this work was abruptly interrupted by war in 1914, when scientists were diverted to research of immediate military usefulness. But the basis had been firmly laid for revolutionary developments in physics in the interwar years, involving the discovery that the neutron, or uncharged particle, is part of the structure of the nucleus of the atom. With this discovery came man's ability to 'split the atom' and so release at will energy hitherto securely locked up inside it.

The New Mathematics. The precision required of modern engineering, and still more the highly complex calculations required in atomic physics, were made possible only by great parallel developments in mathematics. The new mathematics challenged both Euclidean geometry and Newtonian mechanics. In 1900 Max Planck produced the quantum theory. In 1905 an unknown clerk of twenty-six in the patent office of Bern, Switzerland, published an article that was to shake the world. Young Albert Einstein began to propound the theory that came to be known as relativity. In 1908 Minkowski depicted a four-dimensional world, with three coordinates for space and one for time. The effect of these advances in mathematics was to question the old distinctions between space and time, as well as between energy and matter, and to bring into a new relationship astronomy, nuclear physics, and philosophy. Since Einstein's genius, like Darwin's, was above all one of synthesis – the capacity to reveal underlying unities behind apparently disparate observations – he properly ranks as the supreme scientific genius of the early twentieth century. One great flaw in Newtonian mathematics was an unreconciled discrepancy between calculation and observation of the working of gravity in the case of the planet Mercury. Einstein claimed that his modification of Newton's theory would remove this discrepancy. It was found to do so. His other astronomical predictions, such as that light rays from distant stars are bent by passing the sun by double the amount Newton calculated, were tested and proved correct in 1919, when a total eclipse of the sun was visible both in West Africa and in Brazil. The discovery that matter is energy, energy matter, and that space and time are interdependent, constitutes a revolution in human thought closely parallel with Darwinism. Atomic physics and the mathematical theory of relativity destroyed some of the basic conceptions on which science had been built since Galileo and Newton. The idea of a substance as something extended in space and persistent in time becomes meaningless if neither space nor time is absolute. A substance had now to be considered as a series of events, connected together in one continuum, taking place in space time. In matter and in energy, as in organic evolution and the solar system, there occurs a process of everlasting change; and the only thing eternal is change itself. The new scientific synthesis of knowledge was shattering to the old, in all its aspects. But to all save the expert the full implications and consequences have remained largely unappreciated and obscure – whereas the Darwinian hypothesis had immediate repercussions on all human thought.

Biology and Psychology. In the generation before 1914 Darwinism was still the most far-reaching and controversial of all the theories put forward by science. When Darwin published his study of *The Descent of Man,* in 1871, he summed up the firm conclusions to which his work had led. After marshalling the evidence that man is related to all animal life, he wrote:

The great principle of evolution stands up clear and firm, when these groups of facts are considered in connexion with others, such as the mutual affinities of the members of the same group, their geographical distribution in past and present times, and their geological succession. It is incredible that all these facts should speak falsely. He who is not content to look, like a savage, at the phenomena of nature as disconnected, cannot any longer believe that man is the work of a separate act of creation. . . .

Here was the ultimate clash between the new biology and theology. Accepting geological time, Darwinism supposed an endless sequence of minute changes, one vast continuum in time and space, effected not as previous biologists had thought by the inheritance of characteristics which had been acquired by deliberate efforts, but by the impersonal process of natural selection. Giraffes acquired long necks not by stretching, but because over centuries of evolution long necks paid in terms of survival. As T. H. Huxley, the chief popularizer of Darwinism, put it, 'new species may result from the selective action of external conditions upon the variations from the specific type which individuals present'. This selective action comes from the struggle for survival, the very will to live, and it selects by favouring those individuals who happen to possess variations of immediate use to them in their surroundings. These individuals tend to survive and to breed. The same process, repeated countless times for each succeeding generation, results in accumulated minute variations that account for the differentiation of species. The contribution of geologists to the theory was their proof that the earth had existed for billions of years during which this process could have occurred.

Just as the Copernican system of astronomy had deposed the earth from its central place in the universe, so Darwinism seemed at first to dethrone man from his central place in the history of the earth.[1] But from 1870 onwards some reconciliation began to be achieved between Darwinism and its theological critics. Liberal theologians saw the need to adapt themselves to their new environment. Archaeology, anthropology, ancient history, and biblical textual criticism, all contributed to a drastic revision of theological thought which brought it more into harmony with the ideas implied by acceptance of Darwinism. The com-

1. See p. 277.

parative study of religions even suggested a certain relativity in the validity of religious beliefs and rites. Sir J. G. Frazer's eleven volumes of comparisons between religions and myths (*The Golden Bough*) profoundly influenced European thought. While these trends toward readjustment and reconciliation were having effect, a new revolution in thought came from yet another direction – from the detailed study of the nature of man himself, from psychology.

The study of psychology was at first closely related to advances in biology and physiology. In the 1860s Gregor Mendel explored how heredity worked, but his researches were strangely overlooked for a generation. Francis Galton investigated the place of heredity in the mental development of human beings, and by 1872 the German physician, Wilhelm Wundt, showed the interdependence of mind and body, in his *Principles of Physiological Psychology*. During the 1890s psychological research continued on the assumption that understanding of human behaviour could be deduced from experiments on animals: the most famous exponent being the Russian Ivan Pavlov, whose experiments on dogs and their reactions to external physical stimuli led to the theory of 'conditioned reflexes' and to a doctrine that came to be known as behaviourism. Mind, like body, seemed to be governed by mechanical laws, and to consist of matter not fundamentally different from body. It was only when the psychologists put emphasis less exclusively on the physiological side, and more on the unconscious urges and repressions within the mind itself, that revolutionary advances took place. This was achieved around the end of the century by the Austrian Sigmund Freud and his associates, Carl G. Jung and Alfred Adler. The attempt to identify psychology with physiology broke down, and it became apparent that psychology was a science distinct from both physiology and physics, and partly independent of them. Introspection – the less precise yet quite scientific investigation of human mind and will and their inner working – is valid as a source of verifiable data; so that while some psychological laws involve physiology, others do not. Freud's techniques of psycho-analysis opened new doors into the mind. The study of the subconscious made men aware of the power of the emotional, the non-rational, and the instinctive impulses that prompt human behaviour.

The ideas put forward by the psychologists had, like Darwinism, immediate consequences for philosophy and general ideas. This was partly because they were startling ideas about the inner nature of man himself and had obvious and instant implications, and partly because they seemed more comprehensible to the ordinary person than the abstruse mathematical calculations of an Einstein. The researches into the mind of the criminal conducted by the Italian Cesare Lombroso, into the testing of intelligence by the Frenchman, Alfred Binet, into abnormal psychology by Freud, into the meaning of dreams by Freud and of family relationships by Jung, attracted a wide interest. Crude popularizations and perversions by charlatans caused considerable confusion in general understanding of what psychology could achieve. Psychological jargon about complexes and frustrations, inhibitions and repressions, entered wildly into the language of ordinary speech and writing. Novelists found new material for their work in pseudoscientific analysis of character. But when, after the war, much of the turmoil settled, it was apparent that considerably greater understanding of the mind of man had been achieved, if without the precision or finality that the physical sciences could claim.

Lack of Synthesis. Between 1850 and 1870 [1] the advances of scientific thought and of social thought had all tended towards an ever more complete and confident synthesis. Benthamism and Marxism, mid nineteenth-century thermodynamics and Darwinism, had belonged to the same world of thought. It was a world of self-regulating mechanism working according to 'inevitable' laws, whether of supply and demand, of the iron law of wages and the inevitable class struggle, of the conservation of energy or the survival of the fittest. This homogeneity in the world of thought was now disoriented by the rapid advances of science, and it was only in part replaced by a new and quite different homogeneity. In this new world of 1914 notions of self-regulating mechanism seemed too crude to fit into the image of a universe subject to constant change, and of matter which was but diverse combinations of different forms of energy, and of man who was a creature of subtle psychological impulses. If all is one vast continuum and 'things' can be described only in their ever-changing relationship to other phenomena, any notion of simple and inevitable laws seems inappropriate. Thus, although the new trends in scientific thought had a homogeneity of their own which was as great as that of the old, they were all at considerable variance with the sort of synthesis which in 1870 had so confidently been expected.

Moreover, by 1914, the main impression was one of disorientation and dislocation. The new branches of knowledge grew so fast and so unevenly that they lost contact with one another. The growing complexity of scientific study demanded narrow specialization and concentrated devotion. It remained true, perhaps, as Lavoisier had suggested a century before, that all threads of knowledge might be at last woven into one great tapestry of beauty and significance for mankind. But at

1. See p. 276.

this stage of advance men saw only raw ends and tattered edges. The most conspicuous feature of science was no longer synthesis but analysis, not unity but fragmentation. Scientists and mathematicians came to be looked upon not as the great teachers of mankind but as the wonder-workers of the modern world, priests of a mysterious and esoteric cult, practising within their laboratories and publications secret and unknow-able rites beyond the comprehension of all save the most expert and de-vout. The sectarianism of anticlerical liberals and socialists was matched by the sectarianism of scientists. There are many reasons for this; and not the least was that science so consistently produced results which were of obvious material benefit that most men were content to enjoy these boons without inquiring too much how they came to be provided. When the German chemists discovered how to fix nitrogen from the air and so produce in abundance fertilizers that Germany had hitherto had to import from overseas, or when they learned how to extract from coal a rich range of commodities – from drugs to explosives, and from textiles to the dyes with which they were coloured – it was enough to be thankful that these discoveries made the nation more independent of foreign imports, more ready to endure a war. But another reason for the continued fragmentation of knowledge was that philosophy and theology, the traditional instructors of mankind in the meaning of life, failed to serve as adequate interpreters of this new store of know-ledge.

Philosophy spoke with many voices. On one hand there was a power-ful revival of Hegelian idealism, especially in Germany, Italy, and Britain. The philosophers Rudolf Eucken in Germany, Benedetto Croce and Giovanni Gentile in Italy, and the active school of Oxford idealists – stemming from T. H. Green and including Bernard Bosanquet, F. H. Bradley, Lord Haldane, and many other highly influential thinkers – denoted a reaction of philosophy away from the materialistic tenden-cies of utilitarian liberalism, socialism, and science itself. On the other hand, philosophers of realism and of power had a profound appeal in this age of dynamic growth. Characteristically enough, they were most vocal in Germany; and although Arthur Schopenhauer had died in 1860, it was only later in the century that he acquired fame. He taught that the only ultimate reality in the universe is blind, struggling will. His greatest disciple, Friedrich Nietzsche, combined with similar emphasis on masterful will an evolutionary doctrine of eternal struggle to domin-ate both environment and rival wills. He produced thereby his famous doctrine of the superman. The will to power was the driving force of history, and both goodness and truth were merely that which was be-lieved to be useful for survival and for domination. Here was an ethic that chimed well with the current rivalry between states for wealth and territory, and also with the impending notions of relativity. In Britain, Thomas Carlyle preached a milder version of comparable ideas, and the vogue for his writings increased after his death in 1881. His profound respect for German literature and philosophy and his many writings about them earned him the award of the Order of Merit from the Prussian government. At the beginning of the twentieth century the hegemony of Germany in European affairs included the intellectual supremacy of her philosophy and her universities. In the racial theories of the renegade Englishman, Houston Stewart Chamberlain, the philosophies of evolutionary struggle and the will to power were combined into a doctrine of the master race, which was later to be adopted by Adolf Hitler and the National Socialists. Chamberlain became a German citizen and married Richard Wagner's daughter. Kaiser Wilhelm II subscribed to a fund for distributing to public libraries free copies of his work on *The Foundations of the Nineteenth Century* (1899). It became the gospel of Pan-Germanism.[1]

The trend of thought embodied in Nietzsche and Chamberlain was an anti-intellectualist revival of paganism, a frontal attack on the teachings of Christianity. In it the materialistic undertones of nineteenth-century thought ceased to be undertones and came to predominate. While these ideas favouring the principles of strong leadership, state power, and racial imperialism attacked Christian theology and ethics from one side, the swelling tide of Marxist materialism attacked them from another. Not only did Marxism penetrate socialist thought through the new social democratic parties,[2] but the variant of it known as syndicalism became important in the early twentieth century.

The French engineer, Georges Sorel, combined Marx's theories of dialectical materialism and class struggle with Nietzsche's ideas of power and will, to make a unique theory of violence as the medium of change. His *Reflections on Violence* appeared in book form in 1908, and provided a whole philosophy to justify labour unions as the natural medium for proletarian revolution and the general strike as the supreme weapon of class war. He incorporated also into his theories two further ideas that were to have an important future. Adapting Nietzsche's views of truth as relative, he argued that men are moved by myths, by non-rational beliefs that prompt action regardless of whether they are true or false. And adapting Nietzsche's ideas of the superman and an *élite*, he urged the necessity for political leadership by 'audacious minorities', eliciting the energies of the mass of the proletariat by their own will

1. See p. 517.
2. See p. 397.

to power and by use of appropriate 'myths', which it is necessary for men to believe in order to succeed. Through Sorel, who has been correctly described as a 'prismatic thinker', the various philosophical ideas hostile to liberal democracy and rationalism were focused for frontal attack. Although they bore little fruit before 1914, they became, after the Bolshevik revolution of 1917 and the Italian Fascist revolution of 1922, a capacious reservoir of ideas which could be brought to bear against parliamentary democracies by the single-party dictatorships of the interwar years. Sorel had great posthumous significance as an apostle of irrationalism and violence in politics. His Italian friend and fellow engineer, Vilfredo Pareto, reinforced these ideas from his more systematic study of sociology.

In these ways the liberal, utilitarian, and democratic socialist philosophies of the mid-century were being attacked from both sides at once: by a reaction to Hegelianism, and by a more ruthless materialism. At the same time they were being more subtly questioned by the widely influential philosophies of an American, William James, and of a Frenchman, Henri Bergson. James remained, in political opinions, a staunch defender of individualist liberalism and democracy. But his philosophy of pragmatism, with its insistence that experience exceeds logic and transcends reason, reinforced other trends towards accepting as true whatever proved most efficient and successful. Bergson constructed a philosophy based on the fact of evolution, and emphasized the realities that might be grasped by intuition if not by intellect and reason. Philosophy must use the data of science, but it must correct and supplement this knowledge by the use of intuition and insight, in the fashion of the great artists who see more than is seen by simple observation and reason alone. He wrote much about the life force, the advancing current of creative vitality, of which the supreme task is to dominate matter. His metaphysics in many respects recalls Hegelianism, save that for rational intelligence as the unfolding reality in history Bergson substitutes the free creative activity of mind which is broader and deeper than reason. The affinities between Bergson's teaching and the contemporary advances in biology and psychology, as well as in physics, made it the most complete synthesis hitherto attempted between old philosophy and new science. Hence came its widespread influence, both before and after 1914. That his ideas greatly influenced both Georges Sorel and Benito Mussolini is warning enough against regarding such a synthesis as being necessarily a reinforcement of liberalism and democracy; but it had close relevance to the contemporary trends of introspection, 'impressionism' and 'expressionism' in literature and painting.[1]

1. See p. 449.

Religious Conflicts. Theology, like philosophy, moved part way toward making terms with the new currents of thought, but it proved even less successful in achieving a synthesis. Darwinism was a major blow to both fundamentalism and ecclesiastical dogma. As already seen, its rise at first coincided with a strong tendency within the Roman Catholic Church to assert more forcefully the dogmatic basis of Catholic faith.[1] In so far as churches in Europe appeared by 1870 to be on the side of conservatism and established order, and part of an alliance against secular progress, scientific discovery, liberalism, socialism, and even nationalism, they lost most of their appeal to the rising classes of intellectuals and industrial workers. The shift of balance between countryside and towns removed millions of Europeans from the traditional religious bonds of the parish and collected them in larger and more inchoate agglomerations, usually deficient in ecclesiastical organization and spiritual influences. The growing reliance upon the state or local government for provisions of social protection, poor relief, security, education, and welfare meant that men learned to look to the secular state for things that had once been provided mainly by the church. While these tendencies bred apathy towards religion, the contemporary feuds between church and state about control of education fostered in many a more militant hatred for clericalism, dogma, ritual, and the faith which was dubbed superstition. Secular changes, whether the making of new nation-states, the spread of democracy, or the destruction of illiteracy, took place outside or even in spite of the churches. They seemed to be tied to the old order and in blind hostility to the future. This situation existed, though in different degrees of explosiveness, in almost every European country by the 1890s.

But during the twenty years before 1914 it changed with remarkable speed. Toward the ideas and movements of Marxism, syndicalism, and anarchism, Christianity everywhere remained inherently hostile. But increasingly the churches came to terms with the swelling demand for greater social justice, and they came to see that this was in no irrevocable conflict with the essential teachings of Christianity. In England the persuasive school of writers which had appeared by 1850, led by men like Charles Kingsley and Frederick Denison Maurice, had founded a form of Christian Socialism which abandoned doctrines of hell-fire, eternal damnation, and extreme Sabbatarianism, and sought expression for the spirit of Christian charity in work for social welfare. The tide of opinion which they started gained in force during the second half of the century, and the Christian Social Union was set up in 1889 to link the work of the churches with social reform. Fundamentalism took new shapes,

1. See p. 327.

expressing solicitude for material health and social justice. The Christian Science movement, which had originated in America in the 1870s and the Salvation Army, founded in England by William Booth in 1880, were significant signs of the times.

Throughout Europe the accession of Leo XIII to the Papacy in 1878 marked a new era of social Catholicism. The new Pope – though sixty-eight when elected, he lived on to the age of ninety-three – was himself a great humanist, scholar, and artist, more sensitive and sympathetic than his predecessor to the trends of the modern world. In 1883 he opened the archives and library of the Vatican to historical researchers, encouraged the study of church history and of Thomist theology, and staffed the astronomical observatory of the Vatican with eminent mathematicians and physicists. These visible efforts to reconcile religion with science had their counterpart in his famous encyclicals, which restated Catholic social doctrines in terms relevant to modern society: the encyclicals *Immortale Dei* (1885), *Libertas* (1888), and *Rerum Novarum* (1891). He upheld private property as a natural right, but criticized capitalism for the poverty and social injustice it produced; he condemned materialistic socialism of the Marxist kind, but welcomed whatever in socialism was Christian in principle. He encouraged the formation of specifically Catholic trade unions and socialist parties, and by the end of the century Catholics in most European lands had acted upon his advice. He tried to end the quarrels between the Church and the new liberal states of Europe, by urging French Catholics to accept the Third Republic and engage in its political life, and by reaching a *modus vivendi* with the Italian kingdom. The fierce struggles about lay control of popular education during the 1880s prevented this expected reconciliation, but the outcome of the struggle was not always to the disadvantage of the Church. The separation of church and state carried out in France in 1905 freed the Church in France from state control, while putting it more under the direct control of the Papacy. Leo XIII's successor in 1903, Pius X, undertook to stamp out 'modernism' in the Church and in 1907 defined it as a heresy. Thereafter Roman Catholicism remained in considerable hostility to modern science, refusing to modify its basic doctrines so as to reconcile them with scientific beliefs and standing firm on its traditional dogmas and creeds. But the spread of social Catholicism in various forms continued, and forty years later was to bear rich fruit in the Catholic Democratic parties of Germany, Italy, and France.[1]

In world Jewry contrary impulses appeared, both of them hostile to the peaceful coexistence and assimilation of Jews within the new nation-

1. See p. 826.

states. The spread of liberal democratic principles and institutions should have made assimilation easier. The principles of toleration and equal citizenship, and the ending of old disabilities and restrictions, tended to turn Jews into ordinary citizens, and so to loosen their special ties to an exclusive religious and racial community. In politics, business, and the professions individual Jews assumed great eminence. Disraeli and Durkheim, Freud and Einstein were all Jews by birth. But these very tendencies evoked separatist forces by reaction – a nationalist movement among Jews themselves, and a racialist movement among Gentiles who resented the prominence and success of Jews in economic and public life. In 1897 the first Zionist congress met in Basle, representing a special Jewish nationalist movement and demanding that Palestine be made an independent state and a Jewish national home. On the other hand the spread of racialist ideas fostered anti-Semitic forces which at the end of the century swept through many European countries. There were anti-Jewish laws and massacres (pogroms) in Poland and Russia; strong anti-Semitic forces led by Adolf Stöcker in Germany; and the Dreyfus Affair in France, inflamed by the violently anti-Semitic writings of Édouard Drumont and by chauvinistic movements like Paul Déroulède's *League of Patriots*. Anti-Semitism transcended political parties, but it became a favourite theme of ultranationalist propaganda that Jewry represented an alien international conspiracy, operating inside each state to the detriment of national integrity and security. The Zionist and the anti-Semitic movements fed on one another, and the inflaming of all nationalist feelings by 1914 boded ill for the future of the Jews in Europe.

At the same time Judaism itself was divided by the issue of science and 'modernism'. While modernism triumphed in most of central and western Europe as well as in America, a more severe orthodoxy prevailed in eastern Jewry. Like the Orthodox Church and Islam, eastern Jewry remained least affected by the modernist upheavals that troubled the religious communions of Europe. But it was especially subjected to discriminatory legislation in Rumania, Poland, and Russia. In 1891 some three hundred thousand Jews left the tsarist Empire, many to seek new homes in the United States.

Viewed as a whole, the tendencies of European thought by 1914 revealed the most astonishing contrasts and conflicts. In one sense, a keynote of the new trends was precision and refinement. The precision of modern science made possible not only the construction of new giants in liners, skyscrapers, and bridges, but also the investigation of the most minute objects in the universe – micro-organisms and electrons. Comparable applications of exact tests yielded great advances in archaeology, and anthropology, in geology and chemistry. Mathematical precision not only made it possible to measure the speed of movement of celestial bodies and the speed of electrons, but showed that there were mathematical relationships between astro-physics and atomic physics. With closer understanding of the minutest objects came greater attention to the more imponderable and intangible forces – to the meaning of time and the importance of the subconscious impulses in the human mind. In another sense, the keynote of the period was just the opposite. There was a crudity of conflict between religious faith and materialism, between nations competing in wealth and armed might, between races and empires vaunting their superiority; a gross violence of mass hysteria and prejudice, a savage attack on the old human values of personal freedom and rationality, even upon the human intellect itself; a profound disorientation of established beliefs and habits of mind which led to mental and moral bewilderment. A crisis of culture and intellect no less than a crisis in international relations preceded the war of 1914. A moral world, within which men can agree because they share similar assumptions and values and goals and speak the same language, would have had to be remade after 1914, even if the material world also had not had to be remade because of the dislocations of war. Many of the essential elements in the spiritual crisis of the interwar years already existed before war even began.[1]

SOCIAL THOUGHT AND CULTURE

Some of the ways in which the changing concepts of science affected social thought have already been suggested. Through their impact on philosophy and religion, scientific ideas indirectly affected what men thought about social and political life. Study of anthropology and psychology tended to emphasize racial, environmental, and non-rational factors that govern the behaviour of men in society. A series of writers, who may properly be called 'social Darwinists', eagerly applied or transferred Darwinian ideas to the study of society and politics. In Britain the banker-journalist Walter Bagehot wrote during the 1870s a provocative study of *Physics and Politics: Thoughts on the Application of the Principles of Natural Selection and Inheritance to Political Society*. He argued that in order to survive a primitive tribe must hold itself firmly together, and this it does most successfully by forming a 'cake of custom'. The habits of discipline and conformity and the 'legal fibre' which it acquires are essential to its survival. Progress comes from conflict between compact and coherent groups, a conflict in which, Bagehot

1. See p. 460.

argued, the group that is superior in customs triumphs. Thus good customs tend to drive out bad, for it is those groups which have a higher morality and religion which survive. But in later stages of evolution the 'cake of custom' makes for too much stability and becomes an enemy of progress. Then it has to be broken, to make way for the freer operation of intelligence through discussion, and for individual initiative and freedom. In an ingenious way this subtle and ironic writer contrived to combine Darwinism with liberalism. But it was questionable whether so simple a transference of ideas from biology to politics was justifiable.

Sociology. It was natural that in Britain, which gave birth to Darwin, many other political thinkers should likewise absorb the notions of evolutionary biology. Pre-eminent among them was Herbert Spencer, who was ever sensitive to the latest teachings of science as he understood them. He became one of the most popular and important of European political thinkers in the latter part of the century. He held that the laws of evolution apply as much to man himself as to all animal creatures, and as much to man's mental, moral, and social charcteristics as to his body. Human conscience, for example, is a product both of the past evolution of man in society and of the individual's personal experience during his lifetime. But Spencer, whose biological interests and ideas remained in many ways Lamarckian, favoured the un-Darwinian view that purposive adaptations to environment were important. His methods, like his ideas, were less scientific than he liked to think; and his imprecise use of terms, his excessive liking for mere analogies such as 'social organism', have robbed his theories of more permanent value. More lasting in significance were the ideas of the Austrian, Ludwig Gumplowicz, whose influence on American social thinkers was very great. He argued that the state and all other political institutions originate in conflict between groups and in the conquest of one group by another. The state originates in force. In this view his approach was akin to Marxism, though the inferences he drew from it were far from being Marxist. He emphasized the power of social environment to condition the individual's thought and beliefs, but he regarded the ruling classes as likely to be superior to other classes within the state. Nor is the state evil, as it is for Marx. It is the prerequisite of material progress. The theories of Bagehot, Spencer, and Gumplowicz show how scientific theories could be used to serve quite contrary political and social doctrines.

Similarly, it was possible for anarchist theorists no less than conservatives to find support in ideas of evolution. The Russian prince, Pëtr Kropotkin, published articles between 1890 and 1896 which were later collected in 1902 in his *Mutual Aid.* As a student of biology he

443

dared to challenge the basic postulate of the Darwinists (though not always, as he points out, of Darwin himself), that a bitter struggle for existence was the main driving force of evolutionary change. Having travelled in his youth in eastern Siberia and northern Manchuria, where the conditions of environment were exceptionally rigorous, he noted that very severe struggle for survival brought not progress and improvement but impoverishment in vigour and health; that cooperation and mutual support between members of the same species was liable to be more important for the survival of that species than struggle against other species; and that struggle between members of the same species was in fact very rare. These observations led him to contend that habits of mutual aid and group cooperation played a greater part than struggle in evolutionary survival. He applied this idea to the human species and argued in diametrical opposition to the champions of state power and racial rivalries, who saw only ruthless competition and conflict as the source of progress. His inferences from the actual theories of Darwin were as legitimate as those of his opponents; and politically the champions of socialism, cooperation, labour unions, and even anarchism welcomed his persuasive arguments. It was equally legitimate for the English Fabians to infer the 'inevitability of gradualness', and so devise a gradualist and evolutionary school of democratic socialism in opposition to revolutionary Marxism. *Fabian Essays*, to which Sidney Webb and George Bernard Shaw contributed, first appeared in 1889 as the manifesto of English 'gas and water socialism'.[1]

In an age when the behaviour of man in society and new kinds of community life were presenting obvious problems, it was inevitable that a science of social psychology should be developed, linking up with the infant studies of psychology and sociology. In France a group of brilliant pioneers explored the basis of individual behaviour. They included Gabriel Tarde, who emphasized the power of imitation and habit; Gustave Le Bon, who expounded the reasons for the irrational behaviour of crowds in a panic or a mob; and Émile Durkheim, who evolved a theory of 'collective consciousness' and argued that the small local or functional group served the most valuable purposes in society. All were working and writing before 1914. At the same time, in Britain and the United States, the Fabian socialist, Graham Wallas, studied *Human Nature in Politics* (1908) and contended that the art of politics lay largely in the creation of opinion by non-rational inferences and emotional suggestions; and the social psychologist, William McDougall, taught that the basic primary emotions of man were largely derived from animal nature and were relatively few but enormously potent in their

1. See p. 359.

effects on human behaviour. In Britain, too, Herbert Spencer, infatuated with the faith in positivism that he had imbibed from the Frenchman Auguste Comte, tried to synthesize the whole study of society in his three volumes of *Principles of Sociology* (1877–96). But such pretentious studies were of less significance than the more truly scientific approach of men like the Frenchman, Frédéric Le Play, who patiently studied family life in Europe, or the factual surveys of urban life carried out by such men as Charles Booth in London. Booth startled late Victorian England by revealing that one third of Londoners were living below the 'poverty line' of barest subsistence.

Sociology, like social psychology, had a long way to go in the collection of accurate data and statistics before it could validly expose any 'laws of society' such as Spencer claimed to formulate. What was significant was that more close attention and more detailed study were now devoted to the conduct of men in society; and that this led to the almost unanimous discovery that man was prompted much less by rational impulses than nineteenth-century radicals or liberals had commonly assumed. In this way, too, man appeared to be very much less the controller of his destiny and the 'captain of his soul' than had been previously believed. This more passive creature, moulded biologically by natural selection, dominated by the mysterious promptings of his unconscious, and stimulated into action by his social and material environment, seemed a puny, helpless creature, buffeted by an impersonal universe of unending change. To offset this dispiriting picture were the undoubted facts that man had the intelligence, initiative, enterprise, and skill to discover all these new truths and the lurking hope that by conquering nature in all her forms and by discovering her laws he might use them to control his own fate. The climax of a century of unparalleled scientific advance was the paradox that while greater understanding brought ample grounds for humility of spirit and a sense of helplessness, it brought also reasons for pride and hope. If the nineteenth century ended in 1914, it ended here, as in other respects, with a very large mark of interrogation. The famous statue of *The Thinker*, by the French sculptor Auguste Rodin, is a fitting symbol of the age.

The Study of History and Economics. Of all social studies, the two that developed most fruitfully in these years by absorbing the spirit rather than the jargon and analogies of modern science were history and economics. If Darwin was right, if Marx was even partly right, then it was important to study man's past. Historicism was the natural outcome of the new ideas. The cult of 'scientific historiography', which had begun with von Ranke and his counterparts in other countries,[1] bore

1. See p. 285.

fruit by the end of the century in attempts to synthesize the mass of detailed research and specialized monographs, and to make their conclusions available to all. This led to an approach to history which was embodied, if not embalmed, in such cooperative or 'synthetic' histories as the great series of Medieval and Modern Histories, and the *History of English Literature*, published by the Cambridge University Press. Teams of scholars contributed chapters on their own special fields of study. Mandell Creighton, Bishop of Oxford, stated the theory on which the series was compiled in his introduction to the first volume of the *Cambridge Modern History* when it appeared in 1902. He argued that 'Every period and every subject has features of its own which strike the mind of the student who has made that period or subject the field of his investigations. ... Round some definite nucleus, carefully selected, these impressions can be gathered together; and the age can be presented as speaking for itself.' This method, it was believed, would eliminate personal bias or preconceived notions, and 'allow the subject-matter to supply its own unifying principle'. The snare of the argument came in selecting 'the nucleus', which in fact was provided in the scheme for the whole work devised by the liberal Catholic, Lord Acton, in many ways a disciple of the Göttingen school of historians adorned by von Ranke. Acton thought in predominantly political terms and according to very definite moral opinions about the nature of history. The expectation that the result would be objectively scientific was an illusion, though as a work of reference and a source of factual knowledge it was to remain in wide use for some fifty years. Even biography became syndicated in the vast *Dictionary of National Biography* edited by Leslie Stephen. In opposition to such a trend, and as an advocate of the humanistic value of history as a form of literature, George Macaulay Trevelyan attracted a wider public and more general support. In 1913, asserting that Clio was still a Muse, he noted that 'History as literature has a function of its own, and we suffer today from its atrophy'.

Throughout Europe, in contrast with the cult of detached objectivity in the writing of history, historians became caught up in the ecclesiastical, national, and political controversies of the time. The study of ecclesiastical history was greatly stimulated by the growth of ultramontanism under Pius IX,[1] and in Germany Ignaz von Döllinger led the liberal Catholic attack against papal claims. In each country national histories abounded, and if they showed traces of a scientific insistence on accuracy and verification of facts, they were also as a rule cast in the mould of national outlook and nationalistic assumptions. In France, Jean Jaurès, continuing the political traditions of Lamartine, Thiers, and

1. See p. 320.

Guizot, produced the beginnings of his avowedly socialist history (*Histoire socialiste*) of the French Revolution. It was acclaimed by no less an authority than the great historian Aulard as 'a work of scientific inspiration and of scientific execution'. If the historical work written in these years seldom shed completely the flavour of contemporary controversies, at its best it attained a standard of erudition, documentation, and scholarly judgement that was a triumph for the new methods of exact and precise scholarship. The stimulus to reassessment and investigation of the ancient world which came from the advance in archaeology, epigraphy, and kindred studies, and of the medieval world from access to documents and improved techniques of paleography, came in modern history from a more systematic collation of sources and a more discriminating verification of alleged facts. It came also from an increasing concern with social movements, economic processes, and changes in the actual functioning of political institutions. In Britain, Sidney and Beatrice Webb examined the history of cooperative movements, trade unions, local government, and poor relief; William Cunningham founded a systematic approach to economic history; Thorold Rogers used statistical methods to reveal changes in prices and wages; John and Barbara Hammond began their famous series of studies of working-class life in the earlier nineteenth century; Frederick William Maitland brought a lawyer's mind and a humanist's sympathies to the historical study of governmental institutions. Britain enjoyed a veritable renaissance of historical scholarship, less thunderous but perhaps more lasting than the German.

In every country an awakened interest in history, and a stimulus to its presentation in more popular and assimilable form, sprang from the growth of popular education, which called for more good textbooks; from the spread of literacy, which prompted the publication of cheap series of short studies by reputable historians; and from a general concern with social and economic problems which could be explained only in historical terms. The legal and institutional emphasis of older histories began to be thought inadequate; the untilled fields of economic and social history demanded fresh techniques. When the historical approach to all things was becoming more and more prevalent, these shifts in emphasis had a far-reaching effect. The proliferation of such studies as sociology and economics demanded a foundation of historical knowledge which only professional historians could provide. In Germany Max Weber and Werner Sombart studied sociologically the development of modern capitalism. In Switzerland Jakob Burckhardt wrote his classical study of *The Civilization of the Renaissance in Italy* in 1869, and revealed a new scope for historiography. In Italy Guglielmo Ferrero studied ancient and recent history in an anti-Carlylean spirit. In France a galaxy of historians headed by Ernest Lavisse, Alfred Rambaud, Gabriel Hanotaux, and Alphonse Aulard rewrote French history with special concentration on the history of the French Revolution. Everywhere archivists were busy collecting and classifying, and the professional historian suffered not from a scarcity but from an embarrassing bulk and variety of materials for the widened scope of his studies. Fuller understanding of the past became a continuing concern of European scholarship.

Economics, which Thomas Carlyle had christened 'the dismal science', became if not more cheerful at least more scientific. Enjoying like the historians a vastly greater bulk of more reliable sources and improved techniques for handling them, the economists in many countries raised the study to a new level of significance and of usefulness. Just as Marx in writing *Das Kapital* (of which the first volume appeared in 1867, the remaining volumes by 1895) was able to draw upon the mass of official reports, surveys, and statistics compiled in mid-Victorian England, so his successors were able to use an ever-increasing bulk of statistical material. The evolution of large-scale business organization and of great schemes of insurance developed fresh techniques of accountancy and of statistical method.

Economists as a professional class began to secure greater influence and prestige, and nowhere more than in Germany. In the 1870s the 'Socialists of the Chair' (*Kathedersozialisten*) led a revolt against *laissez-faire* economics and a demand for state intervention in social problems. They included conservative economists like Adolf Wagner; liberals like Lujo Brentano, who studied British trade unionism, and Adolf Held, who studied English social history. In 1872 more than a hundred and fifty economists met at Eisenach to discuss 'the social question', and the following year they formed the most important organization of social scientists in Germany, the Association for Social Policy (*Verein für Sozialpolitik*), which survived until 1934. Its original purpose was to press for social legislation, but when this had been largely fulfilled by Bismarck, it continued as a learned society promoting the scientific study of economics and social problems.

In France economists were mainly divided on the similar issue of state intervention in economic life, especially as regards protectionism, and there too they formed professional organizations. Paul Louis Cauwès, whose *Course of Political Economy* (*Cours d'Économie Politique*) first appeared in 1878, became the leading exponent of state action and furnished the chief economic arguments for the protectionists who passed the Méline tariffs of 1892. He founded the Société d'Économie

Nationale and wrote for the *Revue d'Economie Politique*. But the tradition of liberal economics died hard in France, as in Britain, and Cauwès was opposed by Frédéric Passy of the rival Société d'Économie Politique, by Gustave de Molinari, and by the politically influential Léon Say. In critical opposition to both these doctrinaire groups there emerged a third which was more opportunistic and detached, led by Charles Gide whose important *Cours d'Economie Politique* appeared in 1909. There were comparable tendencies in Britain, symbolized by the ascendancy of the teaching of Alfred Marshall, whose standard work on the *Principles of Economics* appeared in 1890, and by Sidney Webb's foundation in 1895 of the London School of Economics and Political Science. In Germany, France, and Britain the modern science of economics was evolving.

Learning and Literature. All learning, indeed, was becoming increasingly institutionalized. A development of these years which was of incalculable importance for all learning, whether scientific or humanistic, was the transformation of old universities and the founding of many new ones. In Britain it was a time comparable with the Renaissance in its prolific extension of new facilities for higher learning and education. In the England of 1871 there existed only the ancient universities of Oxford and Cambridge, and the universities of Durham (since 1832), London (since 1836), and Manchester (since 1851). By 1914 there had been added five more civic universities at Birmingham (1900), Liverpool (1903), Leeds (1904), Sheffield (1905), and Bristol (1909), as well as the University of Wales (1893) and half a dozen university colleges. In addition the older universities had been thrown open to others than Anglicans in 1871 and reorganized in the subsequent decades, and special colleges for women had been established in Oxford, Cambridge, and London. In the Netherlands, Amsterdam acquired a new state university in 1877 and a new Calvinist university in 1905. Portugal founded two new universities in 1911, at Lisbon and Oporto. Although France and Germany had developed their university systems before 1870, these years saw great extensions of other institutions of higher learning such as technical high schools, scientific institutes, and academies of the arts. Learning was being institutionalized and subsidized more extensively than ever before, and it was made available to many more people.

The most striking feature of the literature of the period was its preoccupation with social and national problems in all their complexity, with social criticism and the impact of new ideas on human problems. There was little new in the concern of nineteenth-century novelists and poets with social and national problems. As already seen, there were close affinities between the romantic movement and the nationalist and social-revolutionary movements in the first half of the century. With Balzac and Hugo, Dickens and Tolstoi, social criticism as a function of the novelist had become an honourable and well-established tradition. But the concern of literature with the predicaments of man in society was now greatly deepened, became more widespread throughout the countries of Europe, and spread from the novel to the drama.

The great mid century tradition of Russian literature was continued by Leo Tolstoi and Feodor Dostoevski; in France, Balzac and Flaubert were succeeded in their naturalism and social criticism by Émile Zola and Anatole France; in Britain, Dickens and Thackeray were followed by Thomas Hardy and George Meredith, whose *Diana of the Crossways* (1885) first won him a wide public. The dramatist who towered above all others in Europe was the Norwegian, Henrik Ibsen. His attacks on bourgeois hypocrisy and cramping social conventions began with *Pillars of Society* in 1877 and continued to *When We Dead Awaken* in 1899. Throughout these decades his great plays focused public attention on the social evils of industrial strikes and insanity, on prostitution and the subjection of women, and on psychological problems as they affected human relations. These years preceding the national independence of Norway saw a remarkable flowering of Norwegian culture. Ibsen's contemporaries included the novelist and dramatist Björnstjerne Björnson and the musician Edvard Grieg, who composed the music for Ibsen's *Peer Gynt* as an opera. Ibsen had a profound influence on the Irish dramatist and social critic, George Bernard Shaw, whose plays had by 1914 won a reputation that was to make him Ibsen's successor as the pre-eminent European dramatist. This was the great age of the Irish Literary Theatre, Dublin, where even before Shaw such dramatists as W. B. Yeats, George Moore, and Douglas Hyde began a veritable renaissance of Celtic culture. It was the Irish counterpart to the reawakening of nationally conscious culture in Scandinavia and the Balkans. The poems of Yeats and later the plays of J. M. Synge continued the movement, resting like musical revivals of other countries on ancient legends and folk songs, mystical and sadly nostalgic in tone and often intensely and delicately beautiful.

Next to social criticism the writers of the time were preoccupied with various futuristic aspects of the new science. Often the two were combined, as in the spate of scientific utopias depicted by so many of the novelists. Samuel Butler, influenced by Darwinism and psychology, produced *Erewhon* in 1872. It was in effect a satire on contemporary thought. There followed in quick succession from America, Edward Bellamy's *Looking Backward* (1887) and Laurence Gronlund's *Co-operative Commonwealth* (1884); and from Britain, William Morris's

News from Nowhere (1891) and H. G. Wells's *War of the Worlds* (1898) – all socialistic in tendency, and all concerned with the imaginary consequences of scientific progress. The Austrian, Theodor Hertzka, in 1890 produced another such novel which enjoyed popularity and influence on the continent, *Freiland, ein Soziales Zukunstbild.* It described the founding of a socialist colony in equatorial Africa. Other novels were concerned with science fiction for its own sake, devoid of social criticism, in the tradition begun in the 1870s by the Frenchman, Jules Verne, whose fanciful *Twenty Thousand Leagues under the Sea* won immense popularity. In Britain the chief exponent of this genre before 1914 was H. G. Wells, and the first of a long series, *The Time Machine,* came out in 1895. At a still more popular level of fiction the detective story began to replace to a great extent the older ghost or mystery story. Depending for its appeal on logical deduction and modern scientific police methods, the vogue for detective fiction was firmly established for at least half a century to come by Arthur Conan Doyle's famous stories of Sherlock Holmes, which first began to appear in the 1880s.

Most of the realistic literature of the time which was not sociological was psychological. Émile Zola traced through a score of novels the case history of a degenerating French family; Björnson described the psychological effects of heredity and environment; Thomas Hardy showed the fateful working out of psychological conflicts in the English countryside; Samuel Butler joined the same trend in *The Way of All Flesh* (1903). Ibsen and Chekhov put similar psychological dramas on to the stage. But these sometimes over-sophisticated or morose works appealed less widely than the contemporary versions of traditional adventure stories. Old romance gained a new realism in Robert Louis Stevenson, Bret Harte, Pierre Loti, and Rudyard Kipling – all marking the contacts of European civilization with remote and exotic parts of the earth. It may have been the new blending of familiar types of romantic adventure with topical and tropical circumstances of setting that helped to bring such writers a very large public. In receiving so warmly writers of this high calibre popular taste before 1914 showed that it by no means lacked discrimination. The masses were less introspective, less prone to *fin-de-siècle* cynicism or pessimism, than some of the artistic creations of the intelligentsia might lead one to suppose. They still showed robust enjoyment of a good yarn, which writers of high quality were providing in unusual abundance.

Music and Painting. Germany, so prolific in scientific discovery and in learning, contributed disappointingly little to European literature and arts. None of her dramatists, poets, or novelists of these years attained

European stature, with the two exceptions of Gerhart Hauptmann whose play *Die Weber* (1892) handled mass psychology in a way that attracted wider attention, and Thomas Mann, whose great novel *Buddenbrooks* appeared in 1901. German writers received from Russia and Scandinavia the impulse towards naturalism and social criticism, but they wrote mostly for home consumption, and most of them lacked literary greatness. It was in music – where cultural tradition in Germany was strongest – that she most held her own. Richard Wagner lived until 1883, and enjoyed immense European importance. Like Nietzsche in philosophy, he represented a peculiarly Germanic revolt against western traditions. In Franz Liszt and Johannes Brahms the creative genius of German music showed itself at its best, and in these years Richard Strauss began his long musical career. German culture centred as much on Austria as on the Reich. Brahms spent most of his musical life in Vienna; Liszt was born in Hungary of an Austrian mother and a Hungarian father.

In music as in literature France was prolific in genius. With Massenet and Saint-Saëns, César Franck, Gabriel Fauré, and Claude Debussy, appeared an unrivalled galaxy of younger composers in all the main musical forms. Italy sustained something of her great operatic tradition with the work of Pietro Mascagni, whose *Cavalleria Rusticana* was first performed in 1890; Ruggiero Leoncavallo, whose *Pagliacci* won equal popularity immediately after; and above all Giacomo Puccini, whose operatic heroines Manon, Mimi, Tosca, and Madame Butterfly acquired European fame. Russia, too, continued traditions of past greatness through the works of Tchaikovsky, Rimski-Korsakov, Rachmaninoff, Scriabin, and Glazounov. No less striking a feature than the perpetuation of German, French, Italian, and Russian traditions was an unusually wide diffusion of musical genius among all the nations of Europe.

Everywhere composers found inspiration, as did the Irish dramatists and poets, in the folklore and songs of their native lands. They seemed to draw creative vitality from a new national consciousness. In Britain there were Frederick Delius, Edward Elgar, Gustav Holst, and Ralph Vaughan Williams; in Finland, Jean Sibelius; in Poland, Jan Paderewski; in Bohemia, Bedřich Smetana and Anton Dvořák; in Hungary, Béla Bartók; in Norway, Grieg; in Spain, Manuel de Falla and Enrique Granados. It was the happiest outcome of the intensification of national consciousness in Europe before 1914. The musical counterpart to the great efflorescence of popular fiction of high quality was the international fame acquired by the light music and operettas of the Frenchman, Jacques Offenbach, and the Austrian, Johann Strauss; and the enduring (though less international) appeal of the comic operas of W. S. Gilbert and Arthur Sullivan, which established themselves as a permanent part of English life from 1875 onward. Music, like literature, had a broad and democratic basis, and this is no less meaningful for the historian of European culture than the rapidly changing styles and fashions in the more esoteric forms of these arts.

In all these ways the texture of European culture between 1870 and 1914 was woven on a pattern closely representative of current trends in political, social, and intellectual life. Novelists, dramatists, and musicians wrote for a receptive public both national and European. Their themes were within the comprehension of a wide public; their purposes were didactic or critical; their modes of expression were suited to a cultivated public taste. Literature concerned itself with social criticism and with scientific ideas. Both literature and music were rooted in established national traditions and were in tune with national consciousness. The broad tendency was towards the engagement of artists, as of men of learning, in the spiritual and human conflicts of the age. But at the same time there set in a strong reaction against all such 'engagement'. Many artists became more introspective, more insistent that art should be separated from political and social interests, even from moral considerations. Pure aestheticism, or the doctrine of 'art for art's sake', became a cult. This reaction can be discerned in poetry and music, but it manifested itself most clearly in painting, an art in which France led Europe. A brilliant school of 'impressionists' succeeded now to the strong romantic movement in painting established before 1870 by such artists as Eugène Delacroix, to the realism of Gustave Courbet and Honoré Daumier, and to the landscape painting of Camille Corot. It was led by Edouard Manet, Claude Monet, and Auguste Renoir. A painting, they claimed, should be the spontaneous record of the artist's visual impressions. They abandoned the classical emphasis on studied form, and even the romantic emphasis on composition, in favour of the fortuitous compositions and forms of the photographic camera. Being concerned above all with registering an immediate impression of transient beauty, they depicted refractions and reflections of light and shade, the play of light which produces delicate tints of colour. When the impressionists held their first exhibition in Paris in 1874, they were regarded as rebels, even charlatans, by the orthodox critics.

Paul Cézanne, though strongly influenced by the impressionists, refused to disregard deliberate composition and architectural form. Others again moved on beyond impressionism into the 'expressionist' movement of the Dutchman, Vincent Van Gogh, emphasizing still more absolutely that a picture should reveal the artist's emotions at the moment of painting it. Objective reality was entirely subordinated to the personal emotions and taste of the painter himself. The logic of such an aesthetic theory was that artists must paint regardless of any public, and only to satisfy themselves or at most to please their fellow artists, who alone might be expected to share their sensitivity. Art would be as entirely divorced from society as it would be divorced from intellectual composition and architectural form. It was an aristocratic, not a democratic, conception. Artistic creation would be the concern of coteries and handfuls of disciples, not a public concern at all; it would share in the sectarianism of the scientists already noted. In the 1880s came the inevitable counter-reaction with the carefully studied composition and lines of Georges Seurat, a style that was to displace impressionism almost completely. But amid the fashion for extremism, this, too, led in the early twentieth century to the cubism of the Spaniard, Pablo Picasso, and the Frenchman, Georges Braque, and to an extremely geometrical style.

Nowhere were the vigour and vitality of France's cultural genius shown to better effect than in the originality and experimentalism of her painters, and in the ascendancy she established over European painting in these decades. Though Van Gogh was Dutch, and Picasso Spanish, both found their cultural homes in France. German painting was mostly content to reflect the contemporary shifts of style in French art, moving from the realism of Adolf Menzel through the impressionism of Max Liebermann to the expressionism of Emil Nolde. At no point did it assert a real initiative or rival the supremacy of the French. In poetry the revival of symbolism with Paul Verlaine and Stéphane Mallarmé manifested the same revolt against conventionality and form, the same quest for greater freedom and individuality of expression. In drama Maurice Maeterlinck reflected a similar trend. Here, by 1914, were the counterparts in art and literature to the trends already described in politics, science, philosophy, and social thought: the disorientation of traditional standards and values, the contrasts between an extreme collectivism and an equally extreme individualism.

It was fitting that a Frenchman, Maurice Barrès, should symbolize the final dilemma of European culture in 1914, just as the French sculptor Rodin symbolized its ultimate mark of interrogation. Barrès wrote two great series of novels. The first, between 1888 and 1891, was christened *The Cult of Self* (*Le Culte du Moi*); the second, between 1897 and 1909, was called *The Novel of National Energy* (*Le Roman de l'Energie Nationale*). In psychological analysis and in style he was a pure individualist; in tendency he was a devotee of extreme nationalism. Individual egotism led to national egotism. If personal experience was to be the sole inspiration of thought and action, that experience led remorselessly to acute awareness of roots in time and place, in race and nation. That so many men had to make this spiritual pilgrimage and arrived at the same destination was the most distinctive feature of European culture in 1914.

PART SIX

IMPERIAL RIVALRIES
AND INTERNATIONAL ALLIANCES
1871–1914

THE settlement of 1871, which redrew the map of central Europe, left, apparently intact, the three sprawling dynastic Empires of eastern Europe – Austria-Hungary, Russia, and Turkey. It was in one sense completed by events a few years later. The Russo-Turkish War of 1877 was in essentials a resumption of the Crimean War and but the fifth in the series of such wars since 1768.[1] It was concluded, like the Crimean War, by a general congress of the major European powers, held at Berlin in 1878. The ensuing settlement involved a further demolition of the Ottoman Empire and a new assertion of the immediate interests and ambitions of Germany and Great Britain in the tangled 'Eastern Question'. It also brought Russia back into European diplomacy as an integral factor in the international balance of power. Henceforth diplomacy involved all the six great powers in delicate systems of alliances which, manipulated at first by Bismarck to ensure German security against France, ended by embroiling all the powers in war. The grand designs of big-power diplomacy were complicated by two other elements in the situation: the restless nationalist aspirations of the peoples of the Balkans and the eastern marchlands, and the overseas rivalries of the great powers themselves for possession of colonial lands. Behind these political and diplomatic entanglements lay the economic realities of a shifting relative strength in industrial production, trade, investment, and population.[2] It was all these developments, in combination and interaction, which created the crisis of 1914.

The key to the understanding of international affairs between 1871 and 1914 is the way in which local conflicts, in eastern Europe or overseas, brought about a long sequence of subtle shifts in the attitudes and priorities of policy among the great powers of Europe. The stage for this drama was set by the 'League of the Three Emperors' (*Dreikaiserbund*) of 1873. Until 1875 the prime danger to the peace of Europe seemed to be a recurrence of war between France and Germany. Recovering fast under the adroit leadership of Thiers, France tried to break through the diplomatic isolation that had brought about her ruin in 1870. Bismarck, accordingly, worked to preserve that isolation. Since

1. See p. 250.
2. See p. 376.

Britain needed little encouragement to keep out of formal alliances, he was free to concentrate on remaking the old triple alignment of the 'three Northern courts' of Germany, Austria-Hungary, and Russia, which had first appeared in 1815 as the 'Holy Alliance';[1] it had been weakened by the events of 1848–9,[2] but Bismarck saw that it could now profitably be resumed. The others were willing. After 1870 the Habsburg Emperor Francis Joseph gave up all hope of regaining Austrian hegemony in Germany, or of making an alliance with republican France. Austrian foreign policy was in the hands of the self-confident Magyar aristocrat, Count Andrássy, who wanted alliance with Bismarck against Russia. Alexander II of Russia was anxious for a general demonstration of conservative solidarity of the dynastic Empires and, being frightened of German-Austrian combination against him, he, too, was ready to enter into some alignment with Germany. Given Austro-Russian rivalries and tension in the Balkans, Bismarck saw that what could best bring both governments into line with Germany was a 'League of the Three Emperors'. This he achieved in 1873. It was a fragile alliance, ostensibly devoted to upholding conservative principles and to keeping the peace in Europe, but in reality a useful device for keeping France in diplomatic isolation in the West and attempting to ease Austro-Russian rivalries in the East. It was incapable of surviving a sharp challenge on either front, but it served well enough for its temporary purpose.

In 1875 it received its first challenge in the scare of another war between France and Germany. France would have liked most alliance with both Britain and Russia. This aim seemed checkmated because to Disraeli, whose conservative ministry succeeded Gladstone's in 1874, Russia was the greatest menace to British security in the East. Since the Suez Canal had been opened in 1869, Britain was more than ever anxious to keep open the near-eastern route to India and the Far East. From Canning and Palmerston had descended the policy of checking Russian pressure on Turkey and the Balkans. Russia's repudiation in 1870 of the Black Sea clauses of the Treaty of Paris[3] had reawakened such anxieties in Britain. There was therefore no immediate hope of allying with Britain and Russia at the same time, and France had to choose; but, given British detachment and the *Dreikaiserbund*, had she any choice at all? By 1875 she still found herself isolated in Europe. The purpose of her conservative Foreign Minister, Decazes, was to bait Bismarck into indiscretions that might turn Europe, and especially Britain, against him. During 1875 several minor incidents accumulated

1. See p. 96   2. See p. 241.
3. See pp. 248 and 321.

into a diplomatic crisis. When Bismarck sent a special envoy to St Petersburg in February, the French feared it meant preparation for an attack. When, next month, he forbade the export of horses from Germany, it was interpreted as real evidence of war preparations. In April the German Press published articles on the theme 'Is war in sight?' and the French could claim more plausibly that Bismarck was planning war. When his envoy indiscreetly defended the doctrine of preventive war, both the British and Russians took fright and warned Bismarck against the idea. He protested that it was all a false alarm, and the crisis blew over. But it had revealed, in silhouette, a possible alignment of France, Britain, and Russia against him: a Bismarckian nightmare that was to take solid shape in the end, but a whole generation later. Meanwhile, international relations were dominated by the Eastern Question and by colonial rivalries.

CHAPTER 19

THE EASTERN QUESTION

FERMENT IN THE BALKANS

ONLY two months after the alarm of May 1875 a further crisis appeared in the East, which confronted all the powers with a new phase of the century-old 'Eastern Question'. The main features of that complex problem have already been outlined.[1] The new phase began, as usual, with a rising of the Empire's subject peoples, and they were encouraged, as usual, by the rival powers of Austria and Russia. Habsburg interest in the Balkans, never absent, had been sharpened by desire to recover in south-eastern Europe prestige that had been lost in Italy and Germany, Russian interest, likewise continuous, was intensified by evidences of Austrian interest. Accordingly, risings against Turkey in Herzegovina on the Adriatic coast in July 1875, in Macedonia in September, and in Bosnia, to the north of Herzegovina, by the end of the year, all invited the attention of both Austria and Russia. By the middle of the following year full-scale revolts raged in these provinces and throughout the Bulgarian areas south of the Danube; and the Turks were engaged in suppressing them by the familiar methods of massacre and atrocity. While in Britain Gladstone denounced the pro-Turkish policy of Disraeli, a mob in Constantinople deposed the sultan Abdul-Aziz and replaced him by Murad V. When the Turkish government suspended payment of interest on its large foreign debts, it attracted the hostile attention of investors in France and Britain. The two small principalities of Serbia and Montenegro went to war against the Sultan, still nominally their suzerain, in support of the rebels in the neighbouring territories of Bosnia and Herzegovina. It became evident that the 'Eastern Question' was once again erupting in a way likely to embroil the whole of the Balkans. In August, 1876, Murad was in turn deposed by another palace revolution and succeeded by his crafty and unscrupulous brother, Abdul-Hamid II.

The powers of Europe reacted, at first, in characteristic manner. Russia planned to bring about the complete dissolution of the Ottoman Empire, and so open her own path to the Balkans (see Map 8). Bismarck's anxiety was to prevent any open breach between his two partners, and so he was willing to serve as an 'honest broker' in settling the

1. See pp. 137, 243 and 340.

Eastern Question. If the Turkish Empire, as he believed, was doomed to dissolve, then he wanted it dissolved by joint agreement of the powers. Austria wavered between anxious fears of Russian aims in the Balkans, which prompted her to back Turkey, and willingness to accept a limited and negotiated partition from which she herself could gain territories. France still nursed hopes of revenge against Germany, which were moderated only by fears that Bismarck might decide upon a preventive war to check French recovery. Although her investments in Turkey accounted for anxieties about Turkish collapse, she was averse to any direct engagement in the Eastern Question. The British government led by Disraeli gave first priority to preventing Russian expansion into the Balkans, but it was inclined to hesitate between regarding a bolstered Turkish Empire or strong national states as the best choice of buttress. Disraeli (who had recently bought for Britain from the Khedive of Egypt a large portion of the stock in the Suez Canal) favoured support for Turkey. By either means, the route to India was to be kept open; but if rearrangements of Turkey were to be made by international agreement, Disraeli was resolved to be present at the negotiations.

Crisis in Turkey. After the installation of Abdul-Hamid II in August 1876 the course of events passed through three crises, each in turn involving larger issues for the powers. The first came in September when the army of the new Sultan, under its unusually efficient general, Osman Pasha, inflicted upon the Serbians a reverse so severe that Serbia sought the intervention of the powers. Faced with demands from Russia, the Sultan agreed that terms of peace should be settled by an international conference to meet in Constantinople in December. There Germany mediated between Austria and Russia, and various proposals for redrawing the Balkan map were agreed upon. The Sultan, in time-honoured fashion, catered for the susceptibilities of the West by proclaiming a new liberal constitution, and then rejected these proposals of the powers. But Russia, intent on pursuing her policy of dismemberment, struck a bargain with Austria. In return for undertaking to respect the independence of Serbia and Montenegro, and offering Austria a free hand in Bosnia and Herzegovina, she gained Austrian promises that she could have a free hand in Rumania and Bulgaria. A month after Serbia had made peace with the Ottoman Empire, Russia declared war on it and precipitated a fresh crisis.

The Russo–Turkish War of April 1877 quickly brought in other Balkan states. Rumania joined Russia in May, Serbia reverted to war against Turkey in December, and Bulgarian irregulars supported Russia. Montenegro remained at war with Turkey, as she had been since June 1876. By the beginning of 1878 Russian forces had taken Sofia and were advancing on Constantinople. The Turks asked for an armistice, and made peace in the Treaty of San Stefano in March. They undertook to recognize the independence of Rumania, Serbia, Montenegro, and a greatly enlarged Bulgaria; to cede to Rumania the area of Dobruja south of the delta of the Danube, and to Russia a few towns in the Caucasus; to destroy the Danube fortifications and pay a war indemnity; and to carry out reform of the administration in Bosnia and other areas. The treaty aroused all the inevitable jealousies and disappointments. Rumania, Serbia, and Greece resented the rise of Bulgaria. Austria and Britain feared that Russia would dominate the new Slav state of Bulgaria in the heart of the Balkans. They pressed Russia to submit the settlement to a congress of the powers, and again it was Bismarck, ruler of the most disinterested power but with an overriding interest in reconciling his two partners of the *Dreikaiserbund*, who was the obvious choice as 'honest broker'. Accordingly, the congress met in Berlin in June 1878 attended by Russia, Turkey, Austria, Britain, France, Italy, and Germany.

The Congress of Berlin, 1878. The Congress of Berlin, third episode in this phase of the Eastern Question, was significant more for its effects on the alignments of the great powers than for its efforts to 'settle' the fate of Turkey. Rumania, enhanced by addition of part of the Dobruja, and Serbia and Montenegro, less handsomely augmented, were all reaffirmed in their independence as sovereign states. Russia was allowed to take, as she had stipulated at San Stefano, the few Turkish towns and to reclaim from Rumania Bessarabia, which she had forfeited in 1856. But the projected state of Bulgaria was cut back in size, by exclusion of Rumelia and Macedonia. Bulgaria, thus reduced, was declared to be 'an autonomous and tributary Principality under the Suzerainty of His Imperial Majesty the Sultan', and was to have 'a Christian Government and a national militia'. Rumelia and Macedonia were restored to more

---

MAP 8. DISSOLUTION OF THE OTTOMAN EMPIRE, 1699–1914
The decline of the Ottoman Turkish Empire dated from 1699, when it lost Hungary to Austria. By 1815 Russia had also annexed the areas around the Crimea. By 1830 its Balkan territories (Serbia, Moldavia, Wallachia, Greece) were winning national independence, and France had begun the partition of its loosely held North African possessions by conquering Algeria (see inset). By 1914 the whole of the Balkans had broken away and the whole of North Africa had fallen under the colonial control of the European powers, leaving the Empire cut back to the black-shaded area. By 1923, when a Turkish Republic was set up, the Arabian states had also been lost (see also Maps 16 and 17).

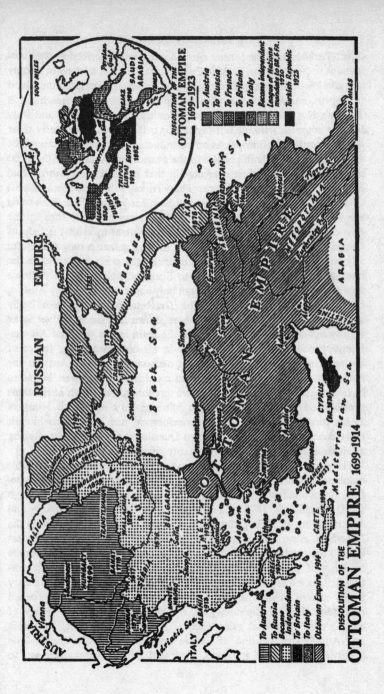

DISSOLUTION OF THE OTTOMAN EMPIRE, 1699–1914

direct Turkish rule, the former being confusingly described as 'an autonomous province of the Turkish Empire'. Austria was allowed to occupy
and administer Bosnia and Herzegovina. Britain appropriated the island
of Cyprus, and France was placated by being promised a free hand in
Turkey's North African territory of Tunisia. Only Germany and Italy
left the congress without territorial gains. It became abundantly clear
that the 'concert of Europe', as now conducted, sacrificed the nationalist
aspirations of all Balkan peoples to the avarice and rivalries of the great
powers. It was more than ever certain that the Balkan volcano would
erupt again in the near future. That Turkey's 'friends' should thus
despoil her of territory so much more than her 'enemies' was a warning
she was to remember; and as soon as the Sultan had duly torn up the
new constitution, he set about reorganizing his army with the help of
German military experts. If Germany thereby gained a new and useful
ally for the future, the immediate effect of the crisis was to leave the
international scene less favourable to Bismarck's plans. His ally Russia
now nursed a profound grievance, not only against his other ally Austria,
but against Germany herself. The *Dreikaiserbund* had been badly
strained at Berlin, and France had been shown that she might yet make
an ally out of Russia. For Bismarck the main lesson was that Austria-
Hungary now held the key position in his diplomacy. The forces of
insurgent nationalism in the Balkans necessarily involved Austria; she
could not countenance the progress of movements which were bound to
have disruptive effects within her own territories, and which at the same
time opened the Balkans to Russian influence. To keep Austria-Hungary
as his foremost ally, Bismarck henceforward had to concern himself
more continuously with the Eastern Question – and any overt backing
of either of his partners must inevitably alienate the other.

The settlement reached at the Congress of Berlin had the remarkable
outcome that it left each power dissatisfied and more anxious than before. It was a defeat for Russian prestige. Britain had sent a fleet through
the Dardanelles in 1878 as a reminder of her interests in Turkey, and
the crumbling of Turkey now left Russia face-to-face with Britain in the
Near-East. Austria-Hungary, too, had patently failed if her real interest
lay in keeping the Ottoman Empire strong; as also had Disraeli, despite
his boast of 'peace with honour' and the acquisition of Cyprus. In general Britain, however, had asserted and reinforced her naval supremacy
in the eastern Mediterranean and the Straits, and France had opened
new doors for her diplomacy of recovery and her future policy of
colonialism. Territorial gains, such as Russia's recovery of Bessarabia
and Austria's occupation of Bosnia and Herzegovina, were of little
profit if the legacy of inflamed, frustrated Balkan nationalism was to

continue to embroil all the powers in future crises and wars. International tension was increased, not eased, by the events of these years. The new balance of power, now clearly centred on Germany, was destined to preserve the peace for another whole generation. But it was doomed to be a most uneasy and unstable peace, subject to recurrent crises and threats of war. The next general European congress met forty years later not in Berlin but in Paris – and at it were to be no representatives of the *Dreikaiserbund*.

Bulgaria. The new storm centre of the Eastern Question had been indicated clearly enough in 1878: it was Bulgaria. There hardy peasants had seen their new enlarged state truncated as soon as it had been set up. They looked favourably upon their Russian protectors only until it was clear that Alexander intended to fill all public offices with Russians and to impose on Bulgaria a constitution designed to produce a deadlock that Russia could exploit. In 1879 they elected as king Alexander of Battenberg, a nephew of the Tsarina and a gallant, well-meaning young man who, if he did not speak Bulgar, was sufficiently German by birth and training to be hostile to Russia. In 1881 he first gained personal power by suspending the constitution and so freeing himself from the hostility of the Bulgarian parliament (*Sobranje*), with its nationalist and anti-Russian majority. Two years later, when he resolved to resist further Russian domination, he restored the constitution and played off nationalists and parliament against the Russians. These symptoms of independence won British support, and British policy began to see in a strong Bulgaria a more reliable barrier to Russia than a disintegrating Ottoman Empire. This marked an important turn in international affairs. It made possible a synthesis of the policies of both political parties in Britain, for it meant supporting Balkan nationalism (which the Liberals favoured) in order to withstand Russian pressure (which the Conservatives had always advocated).

This shift of policy proved important in 1885. Eastern Rumelia, the south-eastern strip of Bulgaria which had been taken away in 1878 and declared 'an autonomous province of the Turkish Empire', demanded reunion with Bulgaria under Prince Alexander. The union was achieved by a *coup* in the Rumelian capital, which was approved of by Alexander and the Sobranje. This defiance of both Turkey and Russia would have precipitated another war had not Britain restrained Turkey from protesting against her loss of suzerainty over Rumelia. Alexander III (who had succeeded to the tsardom in 1881) hesitated to coerce Bulgaria, which Russia had presented to Europe as her protégé. The crisis was caused once again by the mutual jealousies of the Balkan nations themselves. Serbia, always jealous of Bulgaria's rise and guided by her irresponsible King Milan, suddenly declared war on Bulgaria in November 1885. Despite the Serbians' advantages of experience, training, and tactical surprise, they were hurled back in defeat after a desperate three-day battle. Austria, as protector of Serbia, intervened to force an armistice on Bulgaria, and in 1886 peace was signed.

Bulgaria now held Eastern Rumelia, and had asserted her power in the Balkans. Yet later that year Alexander was forced to abdicate, and six months afterward another German prince, Ferdinand of Saxe-Coburg, replaced him on the Bulgarian throne. This prince was a descendant of Louis Philippe of France and was related to Queen Victoria of England. He was therefore regarded by Russia as virtually a candidate of the western powers, but again the Tsar had to accept virtual defeat and restrain himself from intervening. What stabilized Ferdinand on his new throne was partly his own astuteness and patience, partly the backing of the most influential man in the country, Stambulov, who held sway for the next eight years. The son of an innkeeper and an ardent patriot, Stambulov carried out enlightened reforms and public works by strong-arm ruthless methods. He improved agriculture and encouraged industry, built roads and railways and schools, and gave Bulgaria more efficient administration than she had known before. But he silenced opponents by imprisonment and terror, and eventually overplayed his hand. In 1894 Ferdinand made him resign and two years later signed a pact with Russia. Thereafter Bulgaria remained on terms of friendly independence with Russia, and consolidated both her economic progress and her means of national defence.

Internationally, the Bulgarian crisis of the 1880s contributed to the further shifting of power relationships in Europe. In December 1887 Britain, Austria-Hungary, and Italy made an agreement about the Near East. They agreed to keep the peace and the *status quo*, ensuring freedom of the Straits, Turkish authority in Asia Minor, and her nominal suzerainty over Bulgaria. The pact was directed entirely against Russian expansion towards Constantinople, and marked the hardening of British policy towards Russia. But after swallowing her reverses over Bulgaria, Russia lost some of her former interest in the Balkans. Though still anxious for security in the Black Sea, she came to pursue other interests in central Asia and the Far East. The prizes offered there were bigger and easier to come by than in the Balkans where Russia had little investment or trade. With a government in Bulgaria after 1894 that was friendly to Russia, she pinned new hopes in the Trans-Siberian railway – then being built with French loans – and the control that it might bring her over China. This easing of Russian pressure in the Near East gave Austria-Hungary some reassurance. So long as King Milan ruled Serbia,

Austria-Hungary had a reliable and economically dependent satellite of her own in the Balkans. In 1889 Milan abdicated, his popularity undermined by his defeat at Bulgarian hands in 1885. His son and successor, Alexander, in 1894 overthrew the liberal constitution which Milan had introduced the year before his abdication, and revived the old autocratic system of 1869. His high-handed rule lasted another nine years, then in 1903 Alexander and his unpopular queen were assassinated. The rebels called to the throne Prince Peter Karageorgevic, the elderly representative of the royal family which had been exiled since 1858. He ruled Serbia as a constitutional monarch, won recognition from both Austria and Russia, and established the little state among the group of tough, aggressive Balkan kingdoms which were to engage in such violent battles after 1912.

Germany, too, was content enough with the situation that resulted from the Bulgarian crisis. In June 1887 Bismarck made a 'Reinsurance Treaty' with Russia, whereby each promised to remain neutral in any war in which the other became involved, with two exceptions. Russia need not stay neutral if Germany attacked France; Germany need not stay neutral if Russia attacked Austria-Hungary. Bismarck also renewed promises of diplomatic support for Russia in Bulgaria and at the Straits. Since 1879 he had been in defensive alliance with Austria-Hungary, and in 1888 he published the text of this treaty in order to show that it was purely defensive. Austria, Hungary, and the German generals were by then pressing upon him the desirability of a preventive war against Russia. As anxious as ever to preserve peace by manipulation of the balance of power, he firmly refused. 'I shall not give my consent,' he declared, 'for a prophylactic war against Russia.' But that Germany would, in the last resort, stand by Austria left Russia more anxious to find another ally, which could only be France. The new German Emperor, William II, who succeeded to the throne in 1888, favoured close alliance with Austria-Hungary and Britain, and outright hostility towards Russia. His profound disagreements with the policies of the old Chancellor led to the resignation of Bismarck in 1890. Henceforth every thread in the tangled skein of diplomacy which Bismarck had woven felt the violent tugs and stresses imposed on it by the new Emperor and his imperialistic advisers. Germany, like Russia, became more fully engaged in overseas and colonial ambitions. But Russia made her alliance with France in 1893.[1]

Armenians and Greeks. During the 1890s two further crises arose out of the intractable 'Eastern Question', both concerning Turkish rule over her subject peoples. In 1894 Constantinople was confronted with

1. See p. 527.

another revolt, this time among the two million Christian Armenians who lived in the mountainous regions to the north of the city and around the south-eastern coasts of the Black Sea. In the settlement of Berlin the powers had exacted a promise that these people, partly peasants and partly well-to-do men of business and trade, would be better treated and given 'security against the Circassians and Kurds' who were wont to oppress them. From 1890 onwards the Armenians, convinced not unreasonably that such reforms would never be carried out unless they invoked support from foreign powers, agitated in western states for the grant of national independence. Abdul-Hamid II, reassured by German support and resolved to tolerate no further rising of Balkan nationalities, launched his fanatical Moslem Kurds and other Turkish troops against the Armenians in a series of massacres and atrocities which horrified the powers. Despite loud protests in France and England, the refusal of Russia, Austria-Hungary, and Germany to take any action left the Sultan to complete his work with impunity. This defiance of the West by the allegedly 'sick man of Europe' was taken as evidence of his reliance upon German support. When the German Emperor visited Constantinople a few years later, he successfully negotiated the Berlin–Baghdad railway project, and Germany gained valuable openings for economic expansion into the Ottoman Empire.

If the newest of the Balkan nationalist movements thus failed tragically, the oldest was prompted to stake its fortunes on open war against Constantinople, and it was to prove more successful. Greece nursed grievances against the Berlin settlement because it had not granted her larger portions of Thessaly and Epirus, to the north. By negotiation with Turkey she gained Thessaly in 1881. In 1896 the island of Crete, which although close to the southern tip of Greece had been left under Turkish rule, broke into open revolt. It had suffered the miseries of a prolonged civil war between Christian majority and Moslem minority, which had been encouraged by the wily Turk. In 1897 the King of Greece yielded to great nationalist clamour and sent a small force to Crete. This gesture was followed by skirmishes on the Greek-Turkish frontier, which forced the Sultan to declare war. The unprepared and ill-equipped Greeks were driven back in a series of decisive defeats and within a month they had to ask for an armistice. The great powers intervened to force Turkey to grant one. Although Greece had to pay a heavy war indemnity and cede a few strategic villages to Turkey, international pressure saved her from further losses. If Greece did not gain Crete, Turkey virtually lost it. Britain, France, Italy, and Russia joined in making the Sultan grant autonomy to the island and withdraw Turkish troops from it. Again, the power which won a war lost the peace; and

Prince George of Greece was appointed governor by the four protecting powers, even if he acted nominally 'under the suzerainty of the Sultan'.

By 1908 it was obvious enough that the Ottoman Empire had crumbled irretrievably. From its Balkan territories had now been carved no fewer than five independent national states – Serbia, Montenegro, Greece, Rumania, and Bulgaria; and former parts of its possessions, such as Bosnia and Herzegovina, the Dobruja and Crete, were administered by foreign powers. Every stage in its disintegration had reverberated throughout Europe, enlisting powerful liberal sympathies for oppressed nationalities and embroiling the great powers in dangerous diplomatic crises. Every chancellery in Europe was heartily sick of the sick man of Europe. But he was an unconscionable time in dying, and he still held the vitally strategic area around Constantinople and the Straits of the Bosporus and Dardanelles, as well as the central Balkan area of Macedonia. The tale, plainly, was not yet finished. In North Africa, too, the European powers had been engaged in stripping the Sultan of his Mediterranean territories of Algeria, Tunisia, and Egypt.[1] This was the general situation when, in 1908, there took place the 'Young Turk' revolution which overthrew Abdul-Hamid II and in its aftermath tempted Turkey's neighbours into still more looting raids.

The Young Turks. This revolution, as already suggested,[2] was analogous to the revolutionary movement of Russia in 1904–5. The Young Turks were Ottoman patriots, ardent supporters of the process of westernization which Abdul-Hamid II had tried to exclude from his dominions. Events in Russia after 1904 had repercussions in Turkey. They added to the preoccupations of Russia and still further freed the Balkans from Russian pressure; and at the same time many of the younger generation of Turkish noble families were inspired by ideas similar to those held by the liberal intelligentsia of Russia. They had come to realize that successful action against the Sultan lay not in isolated acts of terrorism but in the winning over of part of his armed forces to their cause. Their aim was to revive the abortive liberal constitution of 1876, which the Sultan had unceremoniously discarded as soon as the moment of danger was past. Their 'Committee of Union and Progress' carried out intensive propaganda against the 'Red Sultan', and by July 1908 won over the ill-paid and discontented Third Army Corps stationed at Salonica. Aided by the Second Army Corps, they proclaimed the constitution revived and marched on Constantinople. Abdul-Hamid, faced with so formidable a military revolt, overnight converted himself

1. See p. 466.
2. See p. 362.

into a full-dress constitutional monarch. He ordered the calling of a national parliament on universal male suffrage and stopped all censorship of the Press. The abruptness and completeness of his volte-face took everyone by surprise, and amid universal rejoicing the Young Turks seized all offices, and elections were held. It seemed, for a time, that Balkan nationalism had come full circle, and to the nationalist zeal of subject peoples had suddenly been added the paradox of an Ottoman nationalism ready to embrace Greeks, Rumanians, Bulgars, and Serbs as brothers.

Power lay now in the hands of the managing committee of the Young Turks, led by Enver Bey. The new assembly lacked any political experience and was used as a rubber stamp for Young Turk measures. Abdul bided his time, mobilizing against the new régime all the forces of conservatism and all who were disappointed with the amateurishness and selfishness of the new rulers. By April 1909 he was strong enough to head a counter-revolution, which retook Constantinople and overthrew the government. But at Salonica the Committee of Union and Progress rallied the army once more, and retook the capital after five hours of ferocious fighting. This time they made the parliament depose Abdul-Hamid in favour of his younger brother, Mohammed V, and the dreaded 'Red Sultan' retired with most of his harem to a comfortable villa in Salonica. Mohammed was the ideal figurehead for Young Turkish rule, reconciling the formalities of legitimist succession with a passive acquiescence in whatever his ministers required. The extent to which the Young Turks were to disappoint liberal and nationalist hopes, and to prove no less brutal and tyrannical toward subject nationalities than their predecessor, soon became apparent. But more important for international relations were the immediate consequences of their weakness.

The first was that Austria annexed Bosnia and Herzegovina, which she had hitherto administered under the terms of the Treaty of Berlin. This naturally inflamed Serbian nationalist sentiment against her, since these provinces included a million Serbs, and turned Serbia from a semi-client state into a relentless enemy. Ferdinand of Bulgaria at the same time threw off the suzerainty of the Sultan and proclaimed his kingdom completely independent. Both actions were breaches of the Treaty of Berlin and might be expected to evoke strong reactions from the powers which had taken part in that settlement. But they were not the first, and only Russia showed a lively interest in trying to summon another conference of the powers where she probably hoped to get agreement to the free passage of Russian warships through the Straits as compensation for Austria's gains. Britain and France were lukewarm; Austria-Hungary, backed by Germany, was opposed to any such conference.

None was held. Instead, Turkey was compensated in money for her losses – by Austria-Hungary on her own behalf and by Russia on behalf of Bulgaria, with whom Russia made secret pacts in 1902 and again in 1909. From the whole crisis Bulgaria emerged more closely tied to Russia, Serbia more violently hostile to Austria and therefore by reaction more likely to look to Russia for future support. Once again the acquisition of territory proved a less substantial gain than the winning of reliable allies, and Austria-Hungary was considerably weakened by the new alignments. The pressure that Germany put upon Russia to recognize Austria's annexation of Bosnia and Herzegovina, a pressure amounting to virtual threat of war, left Bismarck's League of Three Emperors in ruins. Austria-Hungary and Germany were now bound more closely together, but Russia was finally thrown into the rival camp of France.

The second international consequence of the Young Turk revolution was that in 1911 Italy seized Libya. Within Italy had grown up a nationalist and colonial party, resolved to assert Italy's claim alongside that of France for colonial possessions in North Africa. In the 1880s France had taken Tunisia; Tripolitania was the corresponding strip of coastline south of Italy, and France had long before conceded Italy's claim to it. The Italians occupied the Turkish island of Rhodes and the Dodecanese archipelago, and bombarded the forts on the Dardenelles. In Libya the Turkish troops withdrew to oases in the interior and refused to make peace. Italy found it expensive to keep both her army and fleet mobilized, and was unprepared for so stubborn a resistance. The war dragged on and might have turned against her had not the outbreak of another war in the Balkans compelled the Turks to cede Tripoli and make peace. Italy acquired little glory from the war, but yet another part of the Ottoman Empire had fallen away.

The Balkan Wars, 1912–13. The Balkan War of 1912 was a third consequence of the Turkish revolution. Nothing but experience of Young Turkish rule could have caused Greeks, Serbs, Montenegrins, and Bulgars to unite into the common front of the Balkan League. The war was the crescendo of Balkan nationalism, forced into a common cause by Turkish intransigence and focused by the complex problems of Macedonia. Even the congress of Berlin had not tried to tackle the Macedonian question. This hill country lying between Greece, Albania, Serbia, and Bulgaria, with its port of Salonica on the Aegean Sea, contained national minorities of all its neighbours. Mutual hatreds, combined with Turkish oppression and tactics of 'divide and rule', kept the land a prey to every form of banditry and misery. As soon as the more zealously nationalist government of Turkey tried to introduce into the territory such typically western institutions as a common law, a national language, and compulsory military service, it inevitably aroused fierce resentment: resentment among Greeks who cherished their separate law courts, among Arabs and Slavs of all kinds for whom distinctive language was the symbol of nationality, and among every minority which feared that its enlisted troops would be used against national liberties. It was impossible for Turkey to become a nation without surrendering its power over other nationalities, and this the Young Turks refused to do. In this sense, Balkan wars were inevitable, and Macedonia was the predestined bone of contention.

On 8 October 1912 Montenegro declared war on Turkey, and within a week Bulgaria, Greece, and Siberia did the same. By the end of the month they had defeated every Turkish army in Europe, and now the Turks held only Adrianople, Scutari, and Janina. This rapid collapse took all the powers by surprise, and the clear victory of Balkan nationalism was a disaster for Austria-Hungary. The disintegration of one old dynastic Empire now brought comparable tensions in a neighbour wherein lived restless national minorities of some of these victorious Balkan states. But Austria-Hungary was in no position to prevent the collapse. Likewise Russia, dragged back against her inclinations to concern about the Balkans, was averse to taking any preventive action. The victory of the Balkan League produced a strange volte-face on the part of each power. Austria-Hungary assumed the unfamiliar role of sponsor of subject peoples by championing the cause of Albanian independence in order to check Serbian encroachment on the Adriatic. Russia took a firm stand against her former satellite, Bulgaria, to prevent it from seizing Constantinople.

The Eastern Question had lost none of its old capacity for producing the strangest somersaults in the policies of the powers. It now had the most surprising effect of bringing Russia and Austria-Hungary closer together, each to resist a Balkan state's advances; and of making Germany seek cooperation with France and Britain in order to keep Russia out of Constantinople. But France, now led by the vigorously anti-German Raymond Poincaré, refused to jeopardize the Franco-Russian alliance; and Britain was prepared to resist only in a general conference of the powers. The crisis was prevented from running its full course by the failure of the Bulgarians to take Adrianople or to press on to Constantinople; and in December the Balkan League had to make an armistice with Turkey. A conference of ambassadors of the powers met in London under the chairmanship of the British foreign secretary, Sir Edward Grey. It could not undo the results of the war, but it could register them and carry out the Austrian demand, to which Russia agreed, that Albania should also become an independent state. Thus the conference carried still further the triumphs of Balkan nationalism: a reversal of the process at Berlin in 1878. In April 1913 the powers even acted in concert to impose their joint decisions – if only against the smallest but the most aggressive of all Balkan states, Montenegro. The powers had allocated Scutari to Albania but it was seized by Montenegro. A western naval demonstration forced her to withdraw. In May 1913 the Treaty of London ended the war and established Albania, though that country's internal condition remained far from settled for decades to come.

The Balkan League immediately broke up, because Serbia had occupied and kept most of Macedonia although the Serbs and Bulgarians captured Adrianople; and the Greeks had similarly taken Salonica and claimed larger stretches of the Aegean coast. Bulgaria, at the end of June 1913, simultaneously attacked Serbia and Greece, her former allies. This second Balkan War – on the more familiar historical pattern of a conflict between Balkan states – gave the Turks under Enver Bey an opportunity to recover Adrianople and brought in Rumania against Bulgaria in the hope of taking the remainder of the Dobruja which had not been transferred to her in 1878. Against such odds the Bulgarians were helpless and in the Treaty of Bucharest, which they signed with Greece, Serbia, and Rumania in August, they paid a price to everyone. Greece kept southern Macedonia; Serbia, northern Macedonia; and Rumania, the southern Dobruja. Turkey kept Adrianople, which in the Treaty of London had been given to Bulgaria. In this way all four states defied the great powers and ignored the Treaty of London. The powers were hamstrung by their own mutual fears, for they knew that a wider war would mean Germany and Austria-Hungary ranged on one side, at least France and Russia on the other. That they had come so near the brink of war over the Balkan disputes of 1912–13 made them more than ever conscious of the dangers to which the system of alliances now exposed them.[1] But the hour for repentance was very late.

The Balkan wars left the international scene more enigmatic than before. No belligerent believed that the decisions about territory would last. Serbia and Montenegro now regarded war against Austria-Hungary, to liberate the Serbs in Bosnia, as inevitable. Bulgaria nursed plans for revenge against her rapacious neighbours, and looked to Turkey and Austria-Hungary as possible allies. Russia, her interest in the Balkans renewed by the evident collapse of Turkey, tended now to side with Serbia and Rumania against Bulgaria. Each state, its appetite whetted by gains or its spirit embittered by losses, remained more warlike than ever. The defiance of the great powers and the contempt for treaties alike

1. See p. 540.

deprived them of any expectations of gain or security by any means other than war. For the first time in a generation the never easy relations of the Balkan nations had relapsed into full-scale wars, and these wars had still produced no definitive or accepted settlement. Any resumption of war in this region was more likely to involve even bigger stakes, for neither Austria-Hungary nor Russia could contemplate, without their participation, the final eclipse of Turkey in Europe.

INSURGENT NATIONALISM IN EASTERN EUROPE

For internal reasons both Russia and Austria-Hungary in these decades were sensitive to whatever happened in the Balkans. This was not merely because both governments pursued foreign policies that intersected in the Balkans, and were concerned with the balance of power in the Adriatic, Aegean, and Black Seas. It was also because the very fabric of these Empires rested upon a denial of the forces of nationalism and political independence which were fermenting so violently in the Balkan peninsula. Whether, at any moment, Austria backed or opposed Serbia, whether Russia backed or opposed Bulgaria, depended upon fine calculations of policy which took into account both the international scene and the internal condition of insurgent nationalities. It would be wrong to think of the rivalries of Austria-Hungary and Russia in this region as a battle only for spheres of influence or only for points of strategic defence. They involved both these considerations, but they also involved a domestic necessity to hold together somehow their own polyglot and multi-national territories.

The importance of insurgent nationalities along the western fringes of the tsarist Empire has already been indicated.[1] Poles and Ukrainians, Lithuanians and Finns, continued to exert a strong centrifugal pull on the Empire after 1870; and the more the régime looked eastward for its expansion, the more these peoples felt that they belonged to the West. Russian policy towards her western nationalities was accordingly one of more intense 'Russification', especially under Tsar Alexander III between 1881 and 1894. This policy, begun in Poland after the revolt of 1863, was extended in the 1880s to all the nationalities of the eastern marchlands. It had the effect of turning the most extreme patriots of these national groups towards the Russian Social Revolutionaries, who were thus soon able to establish close links with Activists in Finland, the Social Democratic League in Latvia, Polish Socialists, Armenian Dashnyaks, and Georgian Socialist-Federalists. All these local movements represented radical nationalism. They wanted socialization of

1. See p. 337.

the land, to be administered by local elected authorities which would grant land to peasant families on a basis of 'labour ownership'. They also wanted a high degree of local national autonomy, amounting sometimes to complete independence. The clash between the Russian government's policy of assimilation or Russification and the more militant movements for national autonomy was the central theme in the history of these years. It reached its climax in the revolutionary years 1905–6, and then subsided into a sullen and sultry deadlock until 1914.

Poland. In Poland of the 1870s Russia combined a progressive social policy with a repressive educational policy. The purpose of the first was to split the Polish national ranks by alienating the landowners from the peasants who gained land at low redemption rates; of the second, to crush the teaching of the Polish language and culture. While local government was reformed so as to give greater power to the rural commune and placate the peasants, private Polish schools were forbidden, Russian schools were supported by the state, and religious education by the Catholic Church was impeded. What saved this ambiguous policy from ending in further revolt was the growth of industry and trade within the Polish territories, and with it greater general prosperity. Textiles from Polish mills found their way on to Asiatic markets in Turkey, China, and Persia, even in competition with Russian textiles, and this expansion was encouraged by the Russian government. It hoped to get the support of the prosperous Polish industrial classes against the nationalistic Polish nobility. The policy of killing Polish nationalism by prosperity paid dividends at the turn of the century, when Russia concentrated on expansion in the Far East. This expansion offered fresh opportunities of employment for skilled Polish engineers and managers. At the same time an agricultural depression set in, affecting Poland along with most of the rest of Europe since it was caused chiefly by the competition of grain imports from the New World. Landed estates went bankrupt, and more of the land was bought by the peasants. Landlords were impoverished. Their families found alternative careers blocked by Russians entrenched in the bureaucracy and by Jewish predominance in business and the professions. These changes stimulated a fresh wave of nationalism among the nobility and middle classes, and it was a less romantic and more realistic nationalism than the old. Only in an independent Polish state could the younger Poles of good education, eager for better careers, hope to find opportunities. Russian policy was now reversed, therefore, and tended to favour the landlords against the growing middle class. Constitutional changes such as the introduction of *zemstvo* institutions in 1911 and city councils in 1913 were carried out so as to weight the rural Polish and the Russian elements against the urban Polish and Jewish elements. As a result, by 1914 Polish nationalist sentiment had strongly revived and widened, and any weakening of tsarist rule would clearly lead to more clamorous demands for the resurrection of an independent Polish state.

This inevitably had repercussions in the Polish territories of Austria, especially Galicia. which enjoyed a much greater degree of autonomy than the Vistula provinces of Russia. In Galicia the administration was almost entirely staffed by Poles, who also controlled the schools, together with the two universities of Lvov and Cracow and the engineering college of Lvov. A separate Diet met at Lvov, elected on a restricted franchise. It was responsible for education, public health, agriculture, and forestry. The viceroy, head of the executive, was always a Pole. Galicia was represented in the Reichstag, the imperial parliament at Vienna, and its representatives were popularly elected on a limited franchise. A special minister for Galicia served as a link between the viceroy and the government in Vienna. In 1907 universal male suffrage was introduced in Galicia, as in other parts of Austria.

The position of the Poles in the German Reich was less auspicious for future national unity. They were a Catholic minority in Protestant Prussia. Just as Russia was Russifying, so in her eastern marchlands Prussia was Germanizing, and her aim was to colonize the province of Poznań with Germans. Bismarck's quarrel with the Roman Catholic Church in the 1870s (the *Kulturkampf*) had led him into conflict with the Polish archbishop Ledochowski of Poznań, who was imprisoned in 1874. When Bismarck went on to attack the use of Polish language in schools, law courts, and the administration, and when he set aside funds, in 1886, to settle German families on the land, he aroused strong nationalist resistance. The Polish population was increasing faster than the German. It rose from sixty-seven per cent of the whole population of the province in 1867 to seventy-one per cent by 1910. Bismarck's successor, Caprivi, at first followed a gentler policy towards the Poles, but this so greatly exacerbated relations between Germany and Russia that from about 1894 onward it was reversed. In 1889 the process of Germanization was reinforced by the foundation of the *Deutsche Ostmarkenverein*, and until 1914 there continued a vigorous policy of colonization. Even so Germany's Poles, like Austria's, enjoyed most of the normal civil liberties, in sharp contrast with the discriminatory legislation and oppressiveness to which Russia's Poles were subjected. By 1918 the simultaneous collapse of all three Empires was to leave a temporary vacuum in which the three parts of Poland were able to unite into one united Polish state.[1]

1. See p. 626.

Ukrainians and Lithuanians. Ukrainians presented the Austrian and Russian Empires with similar problems. They enjoyed freedom only in Galicia, where, during the 1870s, the nationalist movement took the familiar form of literary societies and cultural propaganda. The leading Ukrainian intellectual, Drahomaniv, was a former professor of the university of Kiev who settled in Lvov. He urged not complete separation from Russia, but the reorganization of Russia on a federal pattern which would give Ukrainians wide cultural autonomy. In 1899 a separatist party was formed by Hrushevski, holder of the new professorship in Ukrainian history founded at Lvov in 1894. This National Democratic party was violently anti-Russian and demanded complete independence; it came to absorb the Radical party, formed a decade before by the disciples of Drahomaniv. A Ukrainian Social Democratic party was also formed in Galicia in 1899, and two years later the Revolutionary Ukrainian party was founded in Russia; both were socially revolutionary and politically nationalistic. In Russia the nationalist movement had to be, like all revolutionary movements, illegal and subterranean. Austrian policy was to play off Polish and Ukrainian forces against one another, and to hold both in reserve as possible threats of Russia. Germany, having no Ukrainian minority, was neutral towards Ukrainians but firmly anti-Polish. In 1905, although there were strikes and risings in the Ukraine as in the rest of western Russia, it was only the peasant revolts that had markedly nationalistic flavour. The Ukrainian parties, like the Polish, sent representatives to the first Duma, but made no concrete gains. In 1908 their place was largely taken by the Society of Ukrainian Progressives, a secret organization with socialist and autonomist aims that appealed strongly to the workers. Rural cooperative movements gained in strength, although cultural movements suffered decline and repression. Ukrainian nationalism spread among the peasants until 1914, partly because of agrarian discontent and partly because most of the big landowners were Russians or Poles. It looked mainly to Germany for help, and opposed alike Russian and Polish 'Slav' movements that sought to absorb or crush it. With its emphasis on distinctive language and culture, its complex internal divisions, its 'Young Ruthenian' party of the 1880s, its romantic flavour, it recalled the insurgent nationalism of half a century before.

To the north of Poland, in the Baltic provinces, similar separatist movements were stirring. Lithuanian nationalism, like Ukrainian, encountered hostility from Polish nationalism. Lithuanians, having formed part of Poland for nearly four hundred years were predominantly Catholic. Their Democratic party, formed in 1902, aimed at autonomy within the Russian Empire as a step towards eventual independence. Their

Christian Democratic League, founded three years later, had a similar programme of civil rights and local autonomy but was opposed both to the secularization of education urged by the Democrats and to the anti-Catholic Russification of St Petersburg. A Lithuanian National Congress met in autumn 1905 at Vilna, mostly supporting the Democrats. Socialism in the country faithfully reproduced the usual internal divisions common to socialist movements everywhere. Their neighbours in the great Baltic areas between the Prussian frontier and the Gulf of Finland included the Latvians and Estonians – both mainly Lutheran in religion but differing in language. Each of these peoples also developed a livelier cultural consciousness in the years after 1870. Encouraged by the Lutheran pastors and led by the educated classes, both groups pressed for improved education and linguistic development. A Latvian Social Democratic party was active after 1904, and in 1905–6 took the lead in the revolutionary civil war which accompanied the revolution of Russia. The province suffered correspondingly savage repression in 1906. The 'All-Estonian Congress' which met at Reval in 1905 represented a more conservatively democratic movement, strong among the urban middle classes, which prevented agrarian revolution in Estonia. But in both areas distinctive nationalistic forces were clearly at work, hostile to both Germanic and Russian elements in the Baltic.

Finns, Armenians, Jews. Finland, the other Baltic province of Russia, had long been a model of peaceful coexistence. During the reign of Alexander II the special privileges and rights of the Grand Duchy were respected. So long as Finnish sentiment regarded the Russians as allies against the Swedes who constituted most of the governing class in Finland, this happy situation persisted. Although the Swedes were only some twelve per cent of the population, and included people of all classes, their predominance in the administration, business, and higher education made them a buffer between Russian power and Finnish national resentment. It was the policy of Russification towards the end of the century which here, too, united the three million inhabitants, both Finns and Swedes, against the Russian bureaucracy. During the 1890s isolated moves towards the assimilation of Finland into Russia and the preferential treatment of Russians aroused strong opposition. A climax was reached in 1898 when a new military law exacted longer military service from Finns and drafted them into Russian units or placed Russian officers in command of Finnish units. Against mass petitions and vigorous protests, the law was introduced by imperial decree and the Diet was reduced in powers to a mere provincial assembly. The Finns retaliated by passive resistance. They refused to implement the law. The whole constitution was suspended in 1903, and the next year the Russian Governor General Bobrikov was assassinated by a young patriot. Finland was governed as a police state until the year of revolutions induced the Tsar to repeal the conscription law, and in 1906 to reinstitute the Diet on an even more completely democratic basis. Even female suffrage was introduced. The Social Democratic party (founded in 1903) won a majority in the new assembly, and though governments were formed by coalitions of their more moderate rivals, the Socialists succeeded in pressing for reforms in land rents and industrial working conditions. Finnish independence was short-lived, for in 1910 the Duma again reduced the powers of the Finnish Diet to those of a provincial assembly, and it was then dissolved to make way for extensive Russification. By 1914 Finland, too, was ready for nationalist rebellion. The strength of Finnish nationalism, as of Polish, was the rapid economic development which it shared with most of western Russia. Industry grew on cheap raw materials, especially timber, and on water power; and the number of industrial workers rose from 38,000 in 1885 to 113,500 in 1906. The value of Finland's industrial output grew nearly fourfold between these dates. When Russia sought to protect her own industries against Finnish competition by higher tariffs, she still further weakened links and loyalties between the two countries, and drove Finnish exports to find outlets in other European countries.

Of the other national groups taking clearer and more self-conscious shape in the eastern marchlands during these decades, only two call for mention. The Armenians of Russia, as of Turkey and Persia, began to claim distinctive cohesion.[1] Their chief bond was religion. The centre of the special Armenian religion was the city of Echmiadzin, where the head of the Church, the Catholics, resided. It had been within Russian territory since 1828. During the 1870s the hierarchy of the church was reorganized into a democratic system in which priests were elected by parishioners, and higher clergy by the priests. Under Alexander II the Armenians in Russia founded their own schools and Press, and cultivated the teaching of their own language. Russia permitted them to do so because her policy was to attempt to attract Turkish minorities by tolerant treatment of their neighbouring compatriots. But again the subsequent shift of policy towards Russification and the new militancy of the Orthodox Church combined to bring misfortunes upon the Armenians in the last decades of the century. Instead of treating them as possible allies against Turkey, St Petersburg began to see Turkey as a dynastic monarchy threatened, like Russia, by disruptive nationalism and revolutionary activity. The Russians closed Armenian schools, appropriated church funds, and countered revolts and assassinations by savage re-

1. See p. 470.

prisals outdone only by the Turks. From 1905 onwards the local Russian administration followed a more tolerant policy, even restoring the independenece of the Armenian church, but the impetus to independence once begun could not be checked. After 1890 a particularly violent Armenian Revolutionary Federation (*Dashnyaks*) was at work on both sides of the Russo-Turkish frontiers. Its aim was by crimes and assassinations to invite Turkish reprisals and massacres, and so to create an international scandal that would attract the intervention of the other powers. It split in 1905 between terrorists and moderates, but the latter looked to Russia as a counterpoise to Turkey and as a possible liberator of Turkey's Armenian subjects.

The other national minority, concentrated in no one area but distributed unevenly throughout the whole belt of the marchlands, was the Jews. There were some five million Jews within the Russian Empire at the end of the century, mostly in the Polish provinces and Bessarabia, and in the towns of the eastern marchlands. Until the 1860s the government severely restricted their movement and employment, confining them to the borderlands and excluding them from all professions other than trade. By the 1870s they moved about more freely and spread rapidly. This led in the next decade to anti-Semitic measures and even pogroms under Alexander III. Severe legal restrictions were reimposed in 1882, and irksome discrimination forced large numbers to migrate. With the rise of Zionism at the end of the century and violent outbreaks of Jewish persecutions in Bessarabia, the cause of Jewish nationalism emerged as yet another element in the kaleidoscope of eastern separatisms.

Russia was a multi-national Empire, in which the 'Great Russians' speaking the Russian language were outnumbered by a multitude of smaller nationalities. It was especially sensitive to all such separatist national movements. Yet its fluctuating policy in these years universally resulted in a strengthening of the very tendencies to disruption which were most likely to bring about its decline. Nationalities had been given enough freedom, intermittently, to arouse their hopes, but subjected to enough petty and savage repression, in the intervals, to strengthen their will for independence. Russia before 1914 was showing every indication of succeeding Turkey as the 'sick man of Europe', and in the First World War the diverse peoples of the eastern marchlands were to play a considerable part in weakening Russian war effort and ensuring her defeat. Despite their diversity and their frequently mutual hostility, the most striking feature of their rise was their reduplication of the spectrum of political parties and attitudes then visible in the whole of Europe.[1]

1. See p. 400.

Like nearly every other European nation they divided into liberals and radical democrats, into moderate and revolutionary socialist movements. They too had their social democratic parties and their extreme revolutionary Marxists, their internal conflicts between nationalism and socialism. The pattern of western European history was reappearing in facsimile between the White Sea and the Black Sea; and it was likely even before world war began that when the people of this great area should attain national freedom and self-governing institutions, which their knowledge of the West had taught them to want, they would imitate in the closest possible detail the European pattern of life. The pull of the West was already dooming to extinction the Russian Empire of the Tsars, just as it was condemning to death the Ottoman Empire of the Sultans.

Austria-Hungary. The example of events in Turkey and Russia was bound to have no less explosive effects on the more westerly nations still confined within the borders of the Dual Monarchy of Austria-Hungary. The Habsburgs, like the Romanovs, ruled a multi-national Empire which had already, in 1848, shown its sensitivity to the ideals of nationalism, liberalism, and even socialism. The institution of the Dual Monarchy in 1867 won for the dynasty a temporary reprieve; but, as already suggested,[1] this had been little more than a bargain between Germans and Magyars to keep in each half of the Empire their separate predominance over Slovaks, Czechs, Serbs, Croats. The successive triumphs of the Balkan nations in the fight to liberate themselves from Turkish rule [2] had very far-ranging effects across the Austro-Hungarian borders; and the tensions between Austria-Hungary and Russia gave constant opportunities for the national minorities to exploit the difficulties of their rulers, whether German or Magyar. Here again the central theme of the period is the recurrent interplay between internal and international events.

The Poles were the focal point of this interplay, and as already shown it was the Polish province of Galicia which became the hub of Polish nationalist hopes. In 1910 its inhabitants included four and three-quarter million Poles and some three million Little Russians (or Ukrainians), mainly in the east; but most of the landowners and officials were Polish. Eastern Silesia also included a large Polish minority which was mainly industrial working class and was increasing fast by natural multiplication and by immigration from Prussian Silesia. Polish minorities in other areas brought the total of Poles in the Austrian half of the monarchy to nearly five million, or seventeen per cent of the total population. There were no significant numbers in the Hungarian half. Policies of

1. See p. 326.
2. See p. 473.

Germanization and Russification in the other segments of Poland drove many exiles into Galicia, among them Josef Pilsudski who was to become the regenerator of the Polish state in 1918, and who meanwhile trained Polish riflemen in Austria. The growing hostility between Germany and Austria-Hungary on one side, and Russia on the other, gave men like Pilsudski their opportunity.

To the south the most active minorities were the Serbians of Bosnia and Herzegovina, and Serbo-Croats of Dalmatia, the Slav populations of Styria and Carinthia, Istria and Carniola. All these areas had either Slovene majorities or large and compact Slovene or Croat minorities. Upon them the policies of Serbia and the Pan-Slav propaganda of Russia had effect. To the north were 'the lands of the Bohemian Crown', including Bohemia, Moravia, and Silesia. In two of these provinces Czechs greatly predominated – three and a half million in Bohemia, one and a half million in Moravia. In Silesia, though Germans outnumbered either the Czechs or Poles separately, they did not outnumber both together. There were three quarters of a million Italians, mainly in the South Tyrol. In all, therefore, Germans were struggling to maintain power despite their relative inferiority in numbers; and a resurgence of Czech nationalism in the north matched that of Serbian nationalism in the south and of Polish in the east. Having failed to win Bohemian autonomy, the Czechs turned to systematic obstruction in the Reichsrat. The ten million Germans of Austria constituted little more than one third of the whole population, and could hold their position only with the help of the five million Poles. The exclusively German provinces of Vorarlberg, Salzburg, and Upper and Lower Austria appeared as the Germanic heart of an Empire surrounded on all sides by provinces predominantly non-German and becoming increasingly anti-German.

The kingdom of Hungary, under Magyar rule, duplicated this image. The 'lands of the Crown of St Stephen' comprised Hungary, Croatia-Slavonia south of the Danube, and to the east Transylvania bordered by the Carpathians. Transylvania's Rumanian majority was swamped by incorporation of the territory into Hungary after 1867, but there were nearly three million Rumanians under Magyar rule in 1910, half of them in Transylvania. Nearly ten million Magyars constituted barely half the whole population of the kingdom, and they were grouped in the centre, with fringes containing two million Slovaks in the north, two million Germans in the west and in the towns, some six hundred and fifty thousand Serbs and Croats in the south, and Rumanians with nearly half a million Little Russians in the east.

The Magyars in Hungary enjoyed a more complete control over the subject nationalities than did the Germans in the Austrian provinces. In

1867 they had held the dynasty to ransom because a revolt would then have split the Empire asunder, and they had seized every opportunity to entrench themselves in independent authority. Being both politically astute and masterful, the Magyars saw salvation only in thorough Magyarization. The government tried to eliminate German and Latin languages as well as Slav, and non-Magyar publications suffered constant police persecution. It offered every inducement to assimilation and absorption. Budapest, like Vienna, made no concession to the representation of national minorities in parliament. The franchise was kept narrowly restricted, and so designed as to ensure power for the Magyar landowners. Every kind of corruption and trickery was used to carry elections. The non-Magyar nationalities, who collectively outnumbered the Magyars, never gained more than seventy per cent out of the 453 deputies in parliament. The most indigestible part of the kingdom was Croatia-Slavonia, which in 1868 had contrived to get an unusual measure of local autonomy and even a local legislature of its own. Although it suffered a process of Magyarization as ruthless and ingenious as that in any other part, Croatia-Slavonia, with the magnetic attraction of an independent Serbia so near, never succumbed to the process. It evolved, instead, a more stubborn desire for independence. The Magyars were in consequence even more bitter in their hostility toward Serbia than were the German rulers of Austria.

As the cohesive appeal of dynastic monarchy declined and gave way to the desire for national solidarity and independence, it was inevitable that this great patchwork of the Dual Monarchy should suffer strain at every seam. That it withstood so long the disruptive forces that tore apart the Ottoman Empire and exerted such ominous strains on the Russian, was one of the miracles of the age. It was in part due to widespread personal affection for Francis Joseph himself, who ruled from 1848 to 1916 with the single desire to hold his domains together. In 1876 the Austrian minister, Andrássy, showed that he appreciated the constant danger. 'If it were not for Turkey,' he said, 'all these [nationalistic] aspirations would fall on our heads. . . . If a new state should be formed there, we would be ruined, and it would be we who would assume the role of "the sick man".' Francis Joseph entered the League of the Three Emperors in order to uphold the conservative forces in eastern Europe, just as he tried to impose reforms on Turkey in order to keep Russia inactive, and remained neutral in the Russo-Turkish War of 1877. The settlement at Berlin in 1878 gave Austria-Hungary, as it gave Turkey, a new lease of life – guaranteed not by their own strength but by the backing of Britain and Germany against Russia. It was the international balance of forces which provided the conditions needed for Habsburg survival. The only specific promise in the Austro-German treaty of alliance of 1879 assured Austria-Hungary of German support in case of a direct attack by Russia; this was the price Bismarck paid to keep Austria from looking for help, as in 1856, to France and Britain. But the alliance did not promise German support for Austrian ambitions in the Balkans, and so it bound Austria-Hungary to a conservative policy of preserving the Ottoman Empire. It was a compact to keep the peace, so long as Russia kept it. But the two halves of the Empire could follow somewhat different policies. Hungary looked not to Vienna, but to Berlin, for Germanic support of Magyar supremacy over subject nationalities. With Count Taaffe as minister between 1879 and 1893, the government of Vienna gave concessions to the Poles and tried to placate the separatist nationalities; with Count Koloman Tisza as minister from 1875 to 1890, the government of Budapest imposed Magyar rule on all its subject nationalities, and pursued a policy of Magyarization.

In each half of the Empire, however, the main key to its survival was the same. It was the erection of a centralized administrative system, a new form of machinery of state, within which the diverse elements could be contained. Disruption could be checked, in the last resort, only by centralization. In the Austrian provinces between 1879 and 1897 this centripetal force was provided by giving the nationalities representation in the Reichsrat and by creating a vast bureaucratic machine that ran on a system of spoils, bribes, and manipulation. Both the electoral system and the method of representing separately the four classes of land-owners, chambers of commerce, cities, and peasants gave ample scope for keeping power in the hands of the landowners and the officials. Czechs and Poles were given cultural autonomy as a substitute for political autonomy, not as a road to independence. Germans in Bohemia and Slovenes in Istria looked upon Habsburg rule as a protection against the oppression by Czechs or Italians which greater provincial autonomy would undoubtedly bring. The equipoise upon which the power of the Emperor Francis Joseph rested derived support from every minority that feared local domination by a bigger minority. The large official class by which the country was administered depended upon Habsburg authority for its employment, and upon continued disunity for its perquisites.

In the Hungarian half the survival of the monarchy was ultimately due to a similar situation. There it was brought about by the rapid decline of the independent landowning gentry who, in 1848–9 under Kossuth, had been numerous enough to determine the course of the revolution.[1] Their economic decline was due in part to the abolition of the

1. See p. 217.

Robot in 1848,[1] in part to the coming of the railways and with them competition from imported American wheat. The land became concentrated in the hands of a small number of bigger and more capitalistic landowning magnates, while the landless gentry found employment in the great new state bureaucracy. They ran the state railways and post offices, the educational and health services. They ran the state not, as before, from the countryside, but from the offices of officialdom. By the twentieth century a quarter of a million of them were so engaged. They provided the administrative machinery as well as the political support for the centralized state, and had every interest in carrying out the policy of Magyarization. By a strange alchemy the very forces of disunity, even the old gentry who were the traditional opponents of the centralized state, were thus converted into the mainstay of Habsburg survival. Prevented by its origins and composition from finding any foundations in the solidities of national unity, the Empire ingeniously became a fabric held up by a scaffolding of officialdom and by a precarious equipoise of national animosities both within and without. Being of a kind with the dynastic empires of Turkey and Russia, the Habsburg Empire reached a crisis, too, in the years 1905–6. It was caused, inevitably, by the Magyars.

In 1903 the Magyar magnates challenged the Dual Monarchy by refusing to provide contingents for the common army, as agreed in 1867, unless Magyar became the language of command in their contingents. Stephen Tisza, son of Koloman, undertook to meet the challenge on behalf of the Emperor and the gentry; in January, 1905, he fought a really free election in Hungary, abandoning the normal methods of corruption and influence which his father had used. When he was heavily defeated, the Emperor used the army and the bureaucracy to overthrow the constitution. In 1906 the Hungarian parliament was turned out by troops, and the country was thereafter governed by purely bureaucratic means, with the aid of the Croats. The two most menacing weapons in the Emperor's hand were, paradoxically, the threat (made in 1905) to establish universal suffrage and the threat to encourage Croatian independence. One would have ended the rule of the Magyar magnates; the other would have removed large territories from their rule. Rather than contemplate either prospect, they rallied to the Crown. Besides, Hungarian corn needed Austrian markets, and economic interests cut across the most self-assertive sentiments of nationalism. In April, 1906, the old partnership was resumed. Hungary went on contributing her contingents to the common army, and in return the magnates were allowed to keep their supremacy over the subject nationalities.

1. See p. 228.

By the end of the century the three peoples of Austria-Hungary most clearly ready for the assertion of complete national independence were the Poles, the Czechs, and the Serbo-Croats. Already the outline had appeared of a Southern Slav union – the merger of all the Slav peoples south of the Danube into one large entity, with its nucleus in Serbia just as Italy had found unification around the nucleus of Piedmont. The blurred shadow of a future Poland, Czechoslovakia, and Yugoslavia were detectable in the political situation of eastern Europe before 1914. Along with them Greece, Rumania, Bulgaria, and Albania had already appeared on the political map of the Balkans. The Balkan Wars of 1912 and 1913 [1] showed that these states were likely to remain quarrelsome and separated by profound mistrusts and jealousies. Lesser known and, to western ears, strange submerged nationalities of Lithuanians and Ukrainians, Little Russians and Ruthenians, were astir everywhere along the great eastern marchlands. Dynastic Empires, clearly, were falling rapidly out of repute and into difficulties. Their decline would certainly have great reverberations in all the chancelleries of western and central Europe. But meanwhile these chancelleries were also beset with their own disputes and difficulties outside Europe altogether. For the consolidated nation-states of Europe had entered upon a new phase in their own development, involving themselves in acute rivalries both economic and political in Africa, the Far East, and even the southern Pacific. The conflicts of colonial imperialism were added to those of dynastic imperialism.

1. See p. 473.

CHAPTER 20

COLONIAL EXPANSION
AND RIVALRY

THE URGE TO IMPERIALISM

BY 1815 the world had known some four hundred years of continuous European imperialism, in the sense of the outward expansion of European power over other countries. Spanish, Portuguese, Dutch, French, British colonial Empires had followed one another throughout these four centuries, and always these extensions of control over non-European territories had involved, in varying proportions, trading, missionizing, adventure, settlement, loot, national pride, conquests, and wars between rival powers. The very list of countries mentioned above emphasizes the lead taken in this expansion by the western, maritime peoples. But it is not necessary to cross sea, rather than land, to become an imperial power. The creation of the great dynastic empires of the Habsburgs and the Ottoman Turks, the traditional drive eastwards (*Drang nach Osten*) of the Germans in quest of lands for settlement and trade, the continental conquests of Napoleon, the rapid advance of Russia into southern and central Asia during the nineteenth century, even the expansion westward of the United States during the same period, are all examples of the same process carried out, it so happened, within continental land areas rather than across oceans. In 1870 there was, therefore, nothing whatever new about the extension of European control and power over other parts of the earth. Yet the very word 'imperialism' was, it seems, a mid nineteenth-century invention, and the generation after 1870 has come to be known, in some specially significant and discreditable sense, as 'the age of imperialism'. In what sense can these decades between 1870 and 1914 be so described?

A famous British economist, J. A. Hobson – and following him, Lenin – attributed the colonial expansions of these years to special new economic forces at work in the most industrialized nations of western and central Europe. This economic explanation of the urge to imperialism is usually taken to mean that the basic motives were also the basest motives and that, whatever political, religious, or more idealistic excuses might be made, the real impulse was always one of capitalistic greed for cheap raw materials, advantageous markets, good investments, and fresh fields of exploitation. The argument has commonly been used, therefore, to denounce the events, and to attack the men, parties, and

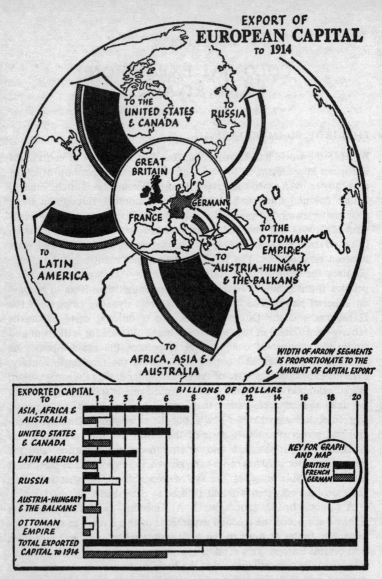

TO THE
UNITED STATES
& CANADA

TO RUSSIA

GREAT
BRITAIN

GERMANY

FRANCE

TO THE
OTTOMAN
EMPIRE

TO
AUSTRIA-HUNGARY
& THE BALKANS

TO
LATIN
AMERICA

TO
AFRICA, ASIA &
AUSTRALIA

WIDTH OF ARROW SEGMENTS
IS PROPORTIONATE TO THE
AMOUNT OF CAPITAL EXPORT

EXPORTED CAPITAL TO	BILLIONS OF DOLLARS
	1 2 3 4 6 8 10 12 14 16 18 20
ASIA, AFRICA & AUSTRALIA	
UNITED STATES & CANADA	
LATIN AMERICA	
RUSSIA	
AUSTRIA-HUNGARY & THE BALKANS	
OTTOMAN EMPIRE	
TOTAL EXPORTED CAPITAL TO 1914	

KEY FOR GRAPH
AND MAP
BRITISH
FRENCH
GERMAN

MAP 9. EXPORT OF EUROPEAN CAPITAL TO 1914

By 1914 the major European powers had become heavy investors in the under-developed countries overseas. British capital flowed mainly overseas to the Americas and Africa, French mainly to eastern Europe and Russia, German mainly to south-eastern Europe, Turkey, and the Far East, though also to the nations that took part in them. The argument, in brief, is that what Hobson called 'the economic taproot of imperialism' was 'excessive capital in search of investment', and that this excessive capital came from oversaving made possible by the unequal distribution of wealth. The remedy, he maintained, was internal social reform and a more equal distribution of wealth. 'If the consuming public in this country raised its standard of consumption to keep pace with every rise of productive powers, there could be no excess of goods or capital clamorous to use imperialism in order to find markets.' It is undeniable that the search for lucrative yet secure overseas investment played a very great part in the European urge to acquire colonies at the end of the nineteenth century.

Lenin elaborated the argument, in his pamphlet on *Imperialism the Highest Stage of Capitalism* (1916), to emphasize the current importance of finance capital rather than industrial, and the priority of the desire to find new outlets for investment rather than new markets. His thesis was that imperialism was 'a direct continuation of the fundamental properties of capitalism in general', and that 'the war of 1914 was on both sides imperialist'. He used this thesis to explain the fact, which Marx and Engels had declared to be normally impossible in a capitalist society, that there was a conspicuous general improvement in the economic condition of workers in the more advanced countries. In the backward colonial peoples, argued Lenin, capitalism had found a new proletariat to exploit; and from the enhanced profits of such imperialism it was able to bribe at least the 'aristocracy of labour' at home into renouncing its revolutionary fervour and collaborating with the *bourgeoisie*. But such improvement could only be temporary, and since imperialist rivalries must lead to war, all workers alike must eventually suffer from it. This argument ignored the awkward facts that much of the foreign investment of the European powers was not in colonial territories at all but in countries such as South America and Russia, and that the standard of living of the working classes was high in countries like Denmark and Sweden which had no colonies, but low in France and Belgium which

---

Americas. Together they held 30,000 million dollars in loan and investments abroad. In addition the Dutch invested heavily in the Netherlands East Indies, and smaller countries such as Belgium, Scandinavia, and Switzerland took part. The flow led to a great development of hitherto backward lands. It raised the general standard of living in Europe because the interest on such investments enabled Europeans to import more goods than they exported. Imperialism, according to some economists, was explicable in terms of this 'glut of capital' seeking safe investment. Most of it was lost or spent in the First World War.

had large colonial territories. Nor, of course, could it be a general explanation of imperialism, which had existed centuries before there was a 'glut of capital' and before finance capital was as plentiful or as well organized as it was in the later nineteenth century. But it was a convenient and persuasive enough case, at the time, for explaining the First World War in exclusively economic terms, and for presenting it as the result of capitalist activities and the maldistribution of wealth. (See Map 9.)

The New Imperialism. What made it seem particularly necessary to find some special reason for modern imperialism was both the dramatic suddenness of its reappearance and its pre-eminence in the policies of the powers during the last quarter of the century. Until after 1870 national policies, and even more national public opinion, in most European countries have been hostile to colonies. By the 1820s several countries, after having long colonial connexions, had lost these connexions without suffering any apparent economic deprivation. By 1815 France had lost most of her colonial possessions in America and in the East, and Spain had lost her vast South American territories. Before that the thirteen colonies in America had broken away from Britain, and by 1822 Portugal lost Brazil. Advanced opinion everywhere welcomed these events. Adam Smith had argued that the burdens of colonialism outweighed its alleged benefits; radicalism favoured *laissez faire*; Bentham urged France to 'Emancipate your Colonies'; Cobdenism preached free trade and the abolition of all commercial privileges; and in 1861 France opened to all nations the trade of her colonies. Gladstone expected the whole British Empire to dissolve in the end, and in 1852 Disraeli, who agreed with Gladstone in little else, made his famous declaration that 'These wretched colonies will all be independent in a few years and are millstones around our necks.' As late as 1868 Bismarck, who until a decade later was opposed to colonial aspirations for Germany, held that 'All the advantages claimed for the mother country are for the most part illusory', adding that 'England is abandoning her colonial policy: she finds it too costly'. But he was wrong, and only four years later Disraeli announced his conversion to a policy of imperial consolidation and expansion. The tide of opinion turned abruptly. The chorus of anti-colonialism before 1870 was so strange a prelude to an era of especially hectic colonial scramble that some extraordinary explanation seems to be called for.

It is improbable that this explanation can be entirely, or even 'basically', economic. However important the economic forces were, they cannot explain why France, one of the least fully industrialized of the north-western European nations, was the one which had already set the

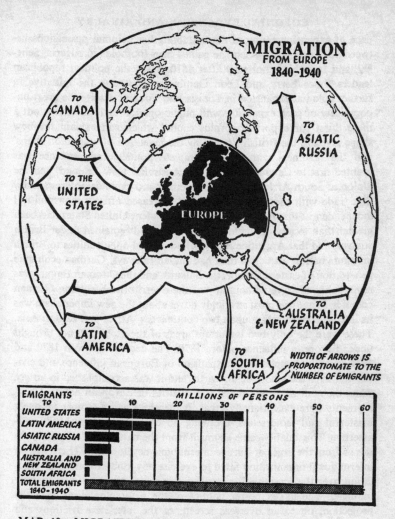

MAP. 10. MIGRATION FROM EUROPE, 1840–1940

The Expansion of Europe after 1815 involved the export of people as well as of capital and goods. In the century before the Second World War more than sixty million people left Europe, distributed as shown in the chart. The greatest reception areas, taking some eighty-five per cent of the total, were North and South America. At the same time seven million Russians moved eastward into Asiatic Russia. This rise of European settlements outside Europe helped to build up a new world economic system focused upon Europe; and explains why one aftermath of war in 1929 was an economic depression that was world-wide in its effects. See also Map 9 and Diagram 5.

493

pace of expansion by more than doubling her colonial possessions between 1815 and 1870, when she gained firm footholds in Algeria, Senegal, and Indochina; nor why after 1870 it was the political republican leaders, Jules Ferry and Léon Gambetta, who took the initiative in further colonial expansion in Tunisia and Tonkin, despite the great unpopularity of such expansion with public opinion in France. It is not a mere thirst for exporting surplus capital which can explain the new shape given to the British Empire by the invention of 'dominion status' and the readiness with which complete political independence was granted first to Canada, and later to Australia, New Zealand, and the Union of South Africa. British commercial and capitalist interests knew that trade with the United States had increased after it won political independence; that migration to the independent United States had been greater than to any of the territories which had remained under British control; and that Argentine railways had offered opportunities to British investors no less attractive than had Indian railways. German economic penetration of eastern Europe, the Balkans, and the Ottoman Empire was remarkably effective without any of these territories becoming German colonies. What was most strikingly novel about the new imperialism was its intense concentration upon two continents – Africa and eastern Asia. These were the only two important areas of the globe still not brought under European influence before 1870. The decades between 1870 and 1914 speedily completed the expansion of European influence and civilization over the whole of the earth, and it was accomplished in an era when the realism, ruthlessness, and rivalries of European national governments were exceptionally great. It therefore had a temper uniquely masterful and remorseless, brooking no obstacles and pushfully self-assertive. This quality came as much from the nature of European politics as from the urges of European economic development. There was no international organization fitted to exercise any kind of control or regulation over the scramble for territories in which the great powers now indulged. The naked power politics of the new colonialism were the projection, on to an overseas screen, of the inter-state frictions and rivalries of Europe. It was this combination of novel economic conditions with anarchic political relations which explained the nature of the new imperialism.

Among the economic forces behind it, the urge to find new outlets for the 'glut of capital' and fresh markets for industrial output were in general more important than either the quest for raw materials or the factor of overpopulation. The special attractions of Africa and Asia were, indeed, that they offered many of the raw materials needed by the multiplying factories of Europe: including cotton, silk, rubber, vegetable oils, and the rarer minerals. The products of the tropics were especially welcome to Europe. But many of these raw materials could be, and were, got by trading without political control. The pressure of population in Europe was becoming great by the early twentieth century, but it still found free outlet in migration to the traditional areas of reception in the United States and Australasia. Neither Africa nor eastern Asia offered climatic or economic conditions inviting enough to attract large-scale white settlements, and the pressure of population within Japan, China, and India was now itself so great as to exert a steady demand for fresh outlets. It was against Asiatic immigrants, not European, that the main barriers began to be raised. Chinese were excluded from the United States after 1882, from Hawaii after 1898, from the Philippines after 1902. The United States excluded Japanese labourers in 1907, and by the Immigration Act of 1917 barred the entry of other non-Europeans, especially Indians and inhabitants of the East Indies. Canada took similar action against the Chinese after 1885; and against the Japanese after 1908. New Zealand restricted Chinese, and in 1901 Australia passed a federal Immigration Restriction Act with the same purpose. The Union of South Africa barred Chinese in 1913, and some South American states followed suit. The main impediments to European migration came only after 1918, and the nineteenth-century flow out of Europe actually reached its peak in 1914. (See Map 10.)

The quest for markets in which to sell manufactured goods was more important. But here, again, the political factor was no less important than the purely economic. Until 1870 British manufacturers of textiles, machinery, and hardware had found good markets in other European lands. After 1870 Germany, France, Belgium, and other nations were able to satisfy their own home markets, which they began to protect against imports from Britain by tariff barriers. They even began to produce a surplus for which they sought markets abroad. With increasing saturation of European markets, all tended to look for more open markets overseas, and in the competitive, protectionist mood of European politics they found governments responsive enough to national needs to undertake the political conquest of undeveloped territories. For this purpose, Africa and Asia served admirably. It was in these economic and political circumstances that the urge to exploit backward territories by the investment of surplus capital could make so much headway. It began especially after 1880, and gained rapidly in momentum until 1914. (Of the annual investment of British capital between 1909 and 1913, thirty-six per cent went into British overseas territories.) By then the main industrial countries had equipped themselves with an abundance of manufacturing plant, and the openings for capital investment at home were more meagre. The vast undeveloped areas of Africa and Asia offered the most inviting opportunities, provided that they could be made safe enough for investment, and there seemed no better guarantee of security than the appropriation of these lands. Again governments were responsive, for reasons that where not exclusively economic. The ports of Africa and the Far East were valuable as naval bases and ports of call, no less than as in-roads for trade and investment. Given the tangle of international fears and distrusts in Europe during these years, and the ever-present menace of war, no possible strategic or prestige-giving advantage could be forfeited. Once the scramble for partitioning Africa had begun, the powers were confronted with the choice of grabbing such advantages for themselves or seeing them snatched by potential enemies. The 'international anarchy' contributed an impetus of its own to the general race for colonies. To say, as it was often said after 1918, that imperialism had led to war, was only half the story; it was also true that the menace of war had led to imperialism.

It was normally the coexistence of economic interests with political aims which made a country imperialistic; and in some, such as Italy or Russia, political considerations predominated. With nations as with men, it is what they aspire to become and to have, not only what they already are or have, that governs their behaviour. There was no irresistible compulsion or determinism, and no country acquired colonies unless at least a very active and influential group of its political leaders wanted to acquire them. Britain had long had all the economic urges of surplus population, exports, and capital, but they did not drive her to scramble for colonies during the 1860s as much as during the 1870s and after. Neither Italy nor Russia had a surplus of manufactures or capital to export, yet both joined in the scramble; Norway, although she had a large merchant fleet which was second only to that of Britain and Germany, did not. Germany, whose industrial development greatly outpaced that of France, was very much slower than France to embark on colonialism. The Dutch were active in colonialism long before the more industrialized Belgians. What determined whether or not a country became imperialistic was more the activity of small groups of people, often intellectuals, economists, or patriotic publicists and politicians anxious to ensure national security and self-sufficiency, than the economic conditions of the country itself. And, as the examples of the British, French, Dutch, and Portuguese show, nations that had traditions of colonialism were more prompt to seek colonies than were nations, such as Germany and Italy, that had no such traditions.

Besides the direct political motives of imperialism – the desire to strengthen national security by strategic naval bases such as Cyprus and the Cape, or to secure additional sources of manpower as the French sought in Africa, or to enhance national prestige as the Italians did in Libya – there was a medley of other considerations which, in varying proportions, entered into the desire for colonies. One was the activities of explorers and adventurers, men like the Frenchmen, Du Chaillu and De Brazza, in equatorial Africa; or the Welshman, Henry Morton Stanley, in the Congo basin; or the German Karl Peters in east Africa. Prompted by a genuine devotion to scientific discovery, or a taste for adventure, or a buccaneering love of money and power – as was Cecil Rhodes in South Africa – men of initiative and energetic enterprise played an important personal part in the whole story.

Christian missionaries played their part too in the spread of colonialism. The most famous was the Scot, David Livingstone. A medical missionary originally sent to Africa by the London Missionary Society, he later returned under government auspices as an explorer 'to open a path for commerce and Christianity'. When he had disappeared for some years in quest of the source of the Nile, Stanley was sent to find him, and duly met him in 1872 on the shores of Lake Tanganyika. When Livingstone died in Africa in 1873, his body was taken to London under naval escort, to be buried in Westminster Abbey as a great national hero. But Livingstone was only one among many, and France, even more than Britain, sent organized missions into Africa to convert the heathen to Christianity. The Catholic missions of France under the Third Republic were exceptionally active, and provided two thirds (some forty thousand) of all Catholic missionaries. They were spread all over the world, including the Near and Far East; and in 1869 Cardinal Lavigerie, installed only the year before in the see of Algiers, founded the Society of African Missionaries, soon to be known because of their Arab dress as the 'White Fathers'. By 1875 they spread from Algeria into Tunisia, and set up a religious protectorate that preceded the political protectorate. Gambetta said of Lavigerie, 'His presence in Tunisia is worth an army for France.' Other French missions penetrated into all parts of Africa, setting up schools and medical services, often in the footsteps of the explorers and adventurers. Belgian missionaries were active in the Congo as early as 1878.

Yet another element in the growth of imperialism was the administrator and soldier – the man with a mission, who was not a missionary but who welcomed an opportunity to bring order and efficient administration out of muddle. Such men became the great colonial proconsuls – Lord Cromer in Egypt, Lord Lugard in Nigeria, Lord Milner at the Cape, Marshal Lyautey in Morocco, Karl Peters in German East Africa.

Without such men the extent and the consolidation of European control over Africa would have been impossible. The sources and the nature of the urge to imperialism were multiple, and varied considerably from one country to another. It was not just that trade followed the flag, but that the flag accompanied the botanist and buccaneer, the Bible and the bureaucrat, along with the banker and the businessman. The unexplored and unexploited parts of the earth offered a host of possible advantages which, in the competitive world of the later century, few could resist seizing; they were seized, amid the enthusiastic approval of the newly literate nationalist-minded masses in Britain and Germany, or amid the sullen resentments of the French and Belgians.

In 1875 less than one tenth of Africa had been turned into European colonies; by 1895, only one tenth remained unappropriated. (See Map 11.) In the generation between 1871 and 1900 Britain added four and a quarter million square miles and sixty-six million people to her Empire; France added three and a half million square miles and twenty-six million people; Russia in Asia added half a million square miles and six and a half million people. In the same decades Germany, Belgium, and Italy each acquired a new colonial empire: Germany, of one million square miles and thirteen million people; Belgium (or, until 1908, Leopold II, King of the Belgians), of 900,000 square miles and eight and a half million inhabitants; and Italy, a relatively meagre acquisition of 185,000 square miles and 750,000 people. The old colonial Empires of Portugal and the Netherlands survived intact and assumed increasing importance. It was a historical novelty that most of the world should now belong to a handful of great European powers.

These immense acquisitions had no close correlation with the ascendancy of one political party. In Belgium they were originally an almost personal achievement of the king; in Britain and Germany they were

---

MAP 11.   AFRICA, 1914

By 1900, and mainly since 1870, the great powers of Europe had divided up most of the African continent. The only independent states left were Liberia, Ethiopia, and the two Boer Republics of the Orange Free State and the Transvaal. Their separate holdings were so distributed that Britain, France, and Germany each aimed at linking up their holdings: the British by a Cape-to-Cairo line running south-north, the French by linking their large western territories with French Somaliland on the east, the Germans by a triangular thrust across the Congo and Angola (see inset). These thrusts led to colonial collisions at Fashoda and to the Boer War (see pp. 514–15), and to international agreements to preserve Belgian power in the Congo and Portuguese in Angola. By 1904 most African colonial disputes had been provisionally settled.

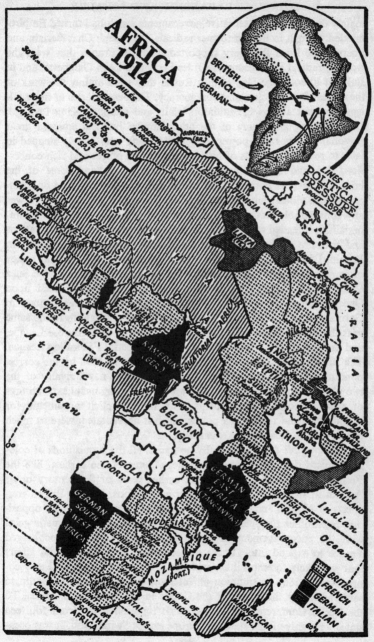

AFRICA
1914

1000 MILES

MADEIRA Is.
(PORT.)

CANARY Is.
(SP.)

RIO DE ORO
(SP.)

Tangier

FRENCH
MOROCCO

GIBRALTAR
(BR.)

30°N

30°N
TROPIC OF
CANCER

BRITISH
FRENCH
GERMAN

LINES OF
POLITICAL
PRESSURE
ABOUT 1898

Dakar
GAMBIA
(BR.)
PORT.
GUINEA

SIERRA
LEONE
(BR.)

LIBERIA

EQUATOR

IVORY
COAST
(FR.)

GOLD COAST
(BR.)

TOGO
(GER.)

RIO MUNI
(SP.)

Libreville

FRENCH

FRENCH
WEST AFRICA

S A H A R A

ALGERIA

TUNISIA

MALTA
(BR.)

LIBYA
(IT.)

EQUATORIAL AFRICA

NIGERIA

KAMERUN
(GER.)

Congo R.

BELGIAN
CONGO

Alexandria
Cairo

EGYPT

Nile

ANGLO-
EGYPTIAN
SUDAN

SUEZ
CANAL

A R A B I A

ERITREA
(IT.)

FRENCH
SOMALILAND

Addis
Ababa

ETHIOPIA

BRITISH
SOMALILAND

Atlantic

Ocean

0°

ANGOLA
(PORT.)

Lake
Tanganyika

Lake
Nyasa

GERMAN
EAST
AFRICA
(TANGANYIKA)

ZANZIBAR (BR.)

BRITISH EAST
AFRICA

ITALIAN
SOMALILAND

Indian

WALFISCH
BAY
(BR.)

GERMAN
SOUTH
WEST
AFRICA

BECHUANA-
LAND

RHODESIA

Zambesi R.

MOZAMBIQUE
(PORT.)

Ocean

Cape Town
Cape of
Good Hope

UNION OF
SOUTH
AFRICA

TRANS-
VAAL

NATAL

CAPE COLONY

TROPIC OF
CAPRICORN

30°S

MADAGASCAR
(FR.)

60°

BRITISH
FRENCH
GERMAN
ITALIAN

499

mainly the work of conservative governments which had turned Empire-minded, though in Britain former radicals like Joseph Chamberlain and liberals like Lord Rosebery supported them; in France they were the work of radical republicans like Jules Ferry and Léon Gambetta, and in Italy, of liberals like Depretis; in Russia they were mainly the work of the official military class and bureaucracy. The beneficiaries of imperialism were not always the initiators of it; and although King Leopold, Cecil Rhodes, and many of the other Empire builders amassed great personal fortunes and power, so too did many who merely stepped in later to reap the rewards of high administrative offices and rich concessions for trading and investment. On the other hand some of the initiators, such as Ferry in France and Crispi in Italy, earned only disrepute and violent hatreds for their achievements. Wherever there was any considerable section of public opinion generally in support of imperialism, it tended to be canalized into active propagandist associations and pressure groups, often distinct from any one political party. In Britain, Disraeli committed the Conservative party to a general policy of imperialism in 1872, backed by the purchase of shares in the Suez Canal in 1875 and by the conferring of the title 'Empress of India' upon Queen Victoria in 1877. In 1882 a Colonial Society was formed in Germany, and in 1883, a Society for German Colonization. In the same year the British conservative imperialists founded the Primrose League, and the liberals soon followed suit with the Imperial Federation League. The British Navy League of 1894 was followed in 1898 by the corresponding German *Flottenverein* – incidents in the naval rivalry of the two powers. Each championed the rapidly increasing naval expenditures of their respective governments. The more explicit arguments for colonialism, and for the sea power which it necessitated, were as much expressions as causes of the expansion.

The Scramble for Colonies. By no means all the acquisitions of colonies caused disputes among the powers. Some of the earliest, like the French conquest of Algeria in the earlier years of the century or of Annam in 1874, and even some later acquisitions, like the British conquests of Nigeria and Ashanti in the 1890s, aroused little or no opposition from other European powers. Occasionally one power made gains with the encouragement or assent of others: Bismarck encouraged France to expand into Tunisia as a diversion from continental affairs that was likely to embroil her with Italy; Bismarck and Jules Ferry co-operated in 1884 to summon an international conference at Berlin to settle amicably the future of the Congo in central tropical Africa. To the Berlin Conference of 1884–5 came representatives from fourteen states – roughly all the states of Europe except Switzerland. It was occasioned mainly by the activities of the International African Association, which had been formed in 1876 by King Leopold II of Belgium. This Association had sent H. M. Stanley on explorations into the Congo between 1879 and 1884, where he made treaties with the native chiefs and established Leopold's influence over vast areas of the interior. By the beginning of 1884 Britain and Portugal, apprehensive of this development, set up a joint commission to control navigation of the whole river. The colony of Angola south of the Congo mouth had been held by Portugal since the fifteenth century, and now Britain recognized Portugal's claim to control the whole mouth of the river. It looked like an alliance of the older colonial powers to strangle the expansion of the new; for France was increasingly interested in the tropical belt north of the Congo River, and Germany in the Cameroons still further north. Leopold therefore looked to France and Germany for help, and the result was the Berlin Conference.

It was concerned with defining 'spheres of influence', the significant new term first used in the ensuing Treaty of Berlin of 1885. It was agreed that in future any power that effectively occupied African territory and duly notified the other powers could thereby establish possession of it. This gave the signal for the rapid partition of Africa among all the colonial powers, and inaugurated the new era of colonialism. In the treaty it was agreed that Leopold's African Association would have full rights over most of the Congo basin, including its outlet to the Atlantic, under international guarantee of neutrality and free trade. Slavery was to be made illegal. Both the Niger and the Congo were to be opened on equal terms to the trade of all nations. The treaty was, in short, a compact among the powers to pursue the further partition of Africa as amicably as possible; and an attempt to separate colonial competition from European rivalries.

For a decade after the Berlin Conference, imperialistic conservative governments ruled in Britain and Germany and anticolonialist protests subsided in France and Italy. Their policies of mercantilism and protection, the popular mood of assertive nationalism in all four countries, favoured colonialism. Expansion into Africa was unbridled. In 1885 the African Association converted itself into the Congo Free State, with Leopold as its absolute sovereign. The success prompted other powers to set up chartered companies to develop other African areas. Such companies, granted by their governments monopoly rights in the exploitation of various territories, became the general media of colonial commerce and appropriation in the subsequent decade. The German and British East African Companies were set up by 1888, the South Africa Chartered Company of Cecil Rhodes to develop the valley of the Zambesi in 1889, the Italian Benadir Company to develop Italian Somaliland in 1892, the Royal Niger Company in 1896. By these and every other means each power established protectorates or outright possessions, and made their resources available for home markets. Germany enlarged and consolidated her four protectorates of Togoland and the Cameroons, German South-west Africa and German East Africa. France took Dahomey, and by pressing inland from Algeria, Senegal, Guinea, and the Ivory Coast, she linked up her west African territories into one vast bloc of French West Africa. She drove inland along the north bank of the Congo to consolidate French Equatorial Africa. On the east coast she established her claim to part of Somaliland and by 1896 conquered the island of Madagascar.

Great Britain was already firmly based on the Cape, and began to push northward. She appropriated Bechuanaland in 1885, Rhodesia in 1889, Nyasaland in 1893, so driving a broad wedge between German South-west Africa and German East Africa and approaching the southern borders of the Congo Free State. This expansion, largely the work of Cecil Rhodes, involved her in constant conflicts with the Dutch Boer farmers, who set up, in the Orange Free State and the Transvaal, two republics of their own. The Boer War of 1899 was the direct result.[1] From the Indian Ocean she also pressed westwards inland, founding British East Africa by 1888 and taking Uganda by 1894. In West Africa, Nigeria was acquired by the activities of the Royal Niger Company between 1886 and 1899. Italy, indignant at the French occupation of Tunisia, had laid the basis of an Italian East African Empire in Eritrea by 1885, and added Asmara in 1889. In the same year she appropriated the large southern coastal strip of Somaliland and claimed a protectorate over the African kingdom of Abyssinia. But in 1896 her expeditionary forces were routed by its native forces at Adowa, and she was obliged to recognize Abyssinian independence. By 1898 the map of the African continent resembled a patchwork quilt of European acquisitions, and south of the Sahara the only independent states were Liberia and Abyssinia, and the two small Dutch Boer republics. The North African coastline, especially the provinces of Morocco in the west and Libya and Egypt in the east, remained a troublesome source of great power rivalries, and as such will be considered later.[2]

The Far East. In the south Pacific and the Far East the same story of separate thrusting, mutual rivalries, and at times joint agreement was repeated (see Map 12). The coming of steamships made islands figure largely in the story. In 1885 New Guinea, where Dutch power was al-

---

1. See p. 514.
2. See p. 519.

ready well established, was partitioned between Dutch, British and Germans. Germany occupied several neighbouring islands (which she christened the Bismarck Archipelago) and the Marshall Islands. By the end of the century she shared the Samoan Islands with the United States and purchased the Caroline and Marianne Islands from Spain, when Spain sold out her Empire after the Spanish-American War of 1898. In 1888 Britain set up a protectorate over North Borneo where a chartered British North Borneo Company had been active since 1881, and where in Sarawak Rajah Brooke had established a remarkable personal power as an independent sovereign. By the end of the century she also took the South Solomon, Tonga, and Gilbert Islands. France occupied the Marquesas, the Society Islands, and other small groups adjoining Tahiti which she had held since 1842. The United States, after her war with Spain, not only annexed Puerto Rico and set up a protectorate over Cuba in the Caribbean, but also took the Philippines and the Hawaiian Islands. The twentieth century began, therefore, with the whole southern Pacific partitioned among the old colonial powers, such as the Dutch who held the East Indies and the British who held the key areas of Malaya and North Borneo, and the new colonial powers of Germany and the United States. Any future war between these powers was bound to be projected on to a world scale, and to affect even remote Pacific islets on the other side of the globe.

In the north Pacific the scramble centred upon China, where it had become a common practice for European powers in search of trade to extract from the crumbling Manchu dynasty concessions of port facilities and territories. The general aim was not to annex land but to establish focal points of influence and centres of trade, commercial

---

MAP 12. IMPERIALISM IN ASIA, 1840–1914. See following pages.
Rivalries of the European powers in the Far East also involved the United States, Russia, and Japan. Until 1900 gains were chiefly made in the southern Pacific. While the British thrust northward into Burma and North Borneo, and the Dutch consolidated their Empire in the East Indies, new Empires were built up by the French in Indochina, the Germans in New Guinea and the Pacific islands, the Americans in the Philippines, and the Japanese in Formosa. Thereafter tensions centred upon the north Pacific and China, where Russians and Japanese competed for control of Manchuria and Korea, and all sought concessions and rights at the expense of China (see inset). These tensions produced the Sino–Japanese War of 1895 and the Russo–Japanese War of 1904–5, as well as the Boxer rebellion of 1899 and the Chinese nationalist revolution of 1911.

IMPERIALISM IN ASIA, 1840-19

ALASKA PUR-
CHASED BY
UNITED STATES
FROM RUSSIA
1867

ALEUTIAN IS.
(USA, 1867)

*Bering
Sea*

KAMCHATKA

*Sea of
Okhotsk*

EMPIRE

S I B E R I A

Lena R.

Yakutsk

SAKHALIN

KURILE
ISLANDS
(JAP, 1875)

North

KARAFUTO
(JAP, 1905)

Khabarovsk

Pacific

AMUR
PROVINCE
1858

MARITIME
PROVINCE
(RUSS, 1868)

Amur R.

Ocean

Lake
Baikal

Chita

MANCHURIA

Harbin

Vladivostok
1860

*Sea of
Japan*

Tokyo

Urga

TER
GOLIA
1912,
SPHERE

INNER MONGOLIA

Mukden

JEHOL

KOREA
(JAP, 1905,
1910)

**JAPANESE
EMPIRE**

Peking

Tientsin

Port Arthur
(JAP,
1905)

Kiao-chou
(GER, 1898)

East China

CHINA

Huang Ho

Nanking

Shanghai
(BR., 1842)

Ningpo
1842

Sea

Chungking

Hankow

Yangtze

Foochow
1842

Amoy

RYUKYU ISLANDS

MARIANAS IS.
(GER, 1899)

YUNNAN

KWANGSI
(FR. SPHERE)

Canton
(BR, 1841)

FORMOSA
(JAP, 1895)

South

GUAM
(USA, 1898)

Hong Kong (BR., 1842)

PESCADORES (JAP, 1895)

Hanoi

Macao (PORT, 1557)

Kwang-chow
(LEASE TO FR. 1896)

HAINAN

PHILIPPINE IS.
(USA, 1898, 1899)

Pacific

YAP

CAROLINE IS
(GER, 1899)

SIAM

Bangkok

FRENCH
INDO-CHINA
1884, 1907

South

Manila

PALAU IS.

Saigon

China

Sea

BR.
N. BORNEO
1888

KAISER
WILHELMSLAND
(GER, 1884)

Ocean

MALAY STATES
(BR, 1800, 1824)

SARAWAK
1888

BORNEO

CELEBES

I N D

NEW
GUINEA

Singapore
(BR., 1819)

SUMATRA

D U T C H

Batavia

E A S T

(PORT,
1859)

TIMOR

AUSTRALIA

Darwin

footholds on the eastern Asiatic coast which could give access into the underdeveloped interior of China. The country was distracted by great disorder, of which the latest symptom had been the Tai-ping rebellion of 1850, resulting after prolonged civil war in the emergence of local war lords. By the 1870s Britain and France had secured, by wars or bargaining, treaties that gave their diplomats and traders considerable opportunities and security for trade with China. In 1842 Hong Kong had been ceded to the British; and more than a dozen cities, such as Canton and Shanghai, were opened to all Europeans as 'treaty ports' where they could settle immune to Chinese law. When they travelled inland, they remained subject only to their own governments, not to the Chinese. To protect Europeans, British or American gunboats policed the Yangtse river in the south, and staffs of European officials were introduced to collect customs duties. The Chinese agreed to impose no import duty higher than five per cent, and the magnet of this vast new free-trade market attracted merchants of all western exporting countries. While the western powers were penetrating China from the eastern shores, large parts of the Empire were annexed to the north and south. Russia pressed down the Amur river and by 1860 established Vladivostok as the gateway of her eastern maritime provinces and the future eastern terminus of her Trans-Siberian railroad. During the 1880s France annexed the rest of Indochina, and Britain annexed the remainder of Burma. China was the Turkey of the Far East, and Manchus, like Ottomans, seemed destined to preside over the dissolution of their own Empire.

A new imperial power, however, appeared to complicate the scene. Japan had first been opened to western influences by the American, Commodore Perry, in 1854. In 1867 she underwent an internal revolution that brought dramatically sudden westernization. The introduction within one generation (the reign of the Emperor Mutsuhito between 1868 and 1912) of industrialism, railroads, schools, a new legal system, modern science and technology, and all the apparatus of western civilization, effected a tremendous transformation. Her population grew with great speed, as did her foreign trade and her naval power. By the 1890s Japan was ready to engage in an imperial expansion of her own. The obvious field for such expansion was the coastline nearest to the islands of Japan, the peninsula of Korea and the large province of Manchuria which lay behind it. In 1876 she helped to detach Korea from its tenuous links with the Chinese Empire by recognizing its independence, and in 1894 she went to war with China over disputes in Korea. Being equipped with much more modern organization and weapons than were the Chinese, Japan won the war. In 1895 she imposed on China a treaty that ceded to Japan not only Korea but also the island of Formosa and the

Liaotung peninsula, the southern tip of Manchuria. Japan's sudden appearance as a formidable rival to the European imperialist powers – blocking Russia's eastern expansion and rivalling the colonialism of France and Britain – led to a joint protest by Russia, France, and Germany which forced Tokyo to restore the Liaotung peninsula to China. Her demand for it had indicated only too clearly that Japan's intention was to dominate Manchuria, for which it was the main outlet to the sea. Japan gave way, with much resentment.

China's reaction to her defeat in the war with Japan was to plan her own westernization, but this only placed her, for a time, still more at the mercy of the western powers. The Russians made her lease to them the Liaotung peninsula, in which to build railroads linking Port Arthur at its tip with Manchurian and eventually Trans-Siberian railroads. Germany took a lease of Kiachow and concessions in the Shantung peninsula, to the south of the Liaotung peninsula. Britain took the port of Weihaiwei and consolidated her 'sphere of influence' in the Yangtse, though she backed the demand of the United States for a policy of 'the Open Door'. This meant keeping open Chinese trade on equal terms to all countries, and was in part directed against further annexations by Russia or Japan, whose military power on the spot naturally exceeded that of the western states. The first rumblings of a Chinese nationalist revolt against these foreign intrusions came the following year, in 1899, with the so-called Boxer Rebellion. A secret society called the Order of Literary Patriotic Harmonious Fists planned attacks on the foreign legations and officials, killing some three hundred people. The European powers, Japan, and the United States combined to suppress the rebellion, exacting a large indemnity as compensation and imposing still more stringent controls over the Chinese government. In the southern provinces appeared a strong Chinese nationalist movement led by Dr Sun Yat-sen. By 1911 it overthrew the Manchu dynasty and began the prolonged revolutionary process that reached its climax in the Communist revolution of 1949.[1]

These events, which may be summed up as the successful imperial penetration of a crumbling Chinese Empire and the consequent stimulation of Chinese nationalist feeling and of more intense rivalries among the imperial powers themselves, led by 1904 to war between Japan and Russia. The bone of contention, inevitably, was the whole area of Manchuria and Korea. With the Japanese in possession of Korea and Formosa, the Russians in control of Vladivostok and the Liaotung peninsula and enjoying concessions to build a railway across Manchuria, there was for a time an equal balance of power. If Russia controlled much of the

1. See p. 844.

mainland and the hinterland, Japan controlled the Sea of Japan and Korea. In 1902 Great Britain and Japan made a treaty of alliance, taken in Europe as a significant sign of the end of Britain's policy of isolation. In 1904 the Japanese, without declaring war, suddenly attacked by sea the Russian base at Port Arthur, and both countries concentrated armies in Manchuria. The Trans-Siberian railway was not completed, which put Russia at the great disadvantage of having to rely on the remote operations of naval power. When she sent her Baltic fleet to the Far East, it was intercepted and destroyed by the new Japanese navy in the Tsushima Strait between Japan and Korea. In Manchuria the two armies clashed in the great battle of Mukden, and there, too, Russia was defeated. President Theodore Roosevelt of the United States intervened to persuade both governments to make peace.

By the Treaty of Portsmouth of 1905 Japan regained the Liaotung peninsula with Port Arthur, and also the southern half of the northern island of Sakhalin; a protectorate over Korea, which remained independent of China; and concessions in Manchuria, which remained technically Chinese. Just as Abyssinia had routed Italy, so Japan had routed Russia; it was clear that coloured peoples might now learn to hold their own against white peoples. Russian expansion, checked in the Far East, was diverted back again to the Balkans,[1] while the internal effects of her defeat precipitated the revolution of 1905. At the same time the moral that rapid westernization had brought Japan victory was learned elsewhere, and encouraged the nationalist revolutions of Persia in 1905, Turkey in 1908, China in 1911. Before 1914 the consequence of imperialism in Asia was already that stimulation of nationalism in the undeveloped countries of Asia which has remained the dominating feature of their subsequent history. All that the war did was to weaken Russia still further, give Japan her unique opportunity to become a great world power in the Pacific, and so to hasten and clarify the tendencies that were already apparent before 1914.

COLONIAL COLLISIONS

The simultaneous expansion of European powers overseas, especially during the twenty years after the Berlin Conference of 1884–5,[2] brought them into frequent collisions at remote points all over Africa and the Far East. The history of international relations in these years is studded with such collisions, and accumulatively this kind of friction – the irritations of rival colonial claims and frontier disputes – no doubt added to

1. See p. 518.
2. See p. 501.

tensions between the powers in Europe. But there is no evidence that colonial issues were in any instance decisive in determining the final alignment of powers in the two great rival systems of alliances.[1] In some respects the relations of powers in the colonial field cut across their relations within the continent of Europe and positively helped to delay the hardening of the rival alliances. It was, significantly enough, only after 1904, when almost all the colonial issues had been substantially settled but when the Eastern Question came to predominate, that the alliances took final shape. Only then began that slithering of the powers down the inclined plane towards 1914, which looks, in retrospect, so fatalistic. In Africa and the Pacific there was usually enough elbow-room for compromise, and until after 1904 even disputes about the Near East could be settled by promising or taking 'compensations' at the expense of the Ottoman Empire in the Balkans or in North Africa. It was when the world's resources of such cheap 'compensations' were exhausted, in the decade after 1904, that European tensions reached breaking point. The beginning of the twentieth century brought not only the 'end of the frontier' in American history; it brought a limit to the expansion of the world's colonial frontiers in general and forced the powers back upon their more dangerous rivalries in Europe where no freedom of manoeuvre remained. Thereafter it was Morocco – the one remaining semi-detached territory in Africa – which remained the only source of important colonial disputes.

It was intense French concentration on revenge for defeat in 1871, on the recovery of Alsace and Lorraine, and on the security of her north-eastern frontier which had led to the war scare of 1875. It was the diversion of French energies and enterprise to colonial expansion in Africa and Indochina which helped, as Bismarck had shrewdly hoped, to ease Franco-German relations. The old rankling anxieties never completely disappeared. They revived from time to time, and in the 1880s General Boulanger could become popular by exploiting the deep-rooted fears and nationalist animosities of the French people.[2] But thereafter Franco-German relations undoubtedly eased until after 1900, when the aggressive gestures of Kaiser Wilhelm II and his advisers resuscitated old fears in France and bred new distrust in Britain – though the Anglo-German naval rivalry began to be a more decisive force in international relations than even Franco-German animosities. Likewise, by making common cause in the Far East against China in the Boxer rising in 1900 and against Japan in 1905, the western powers found a new community of interests and fresh ground for cooperation – just as in 1884–5 they

1. See Chapter 21.
2. See p. 372.

had cooperated in settling the future of the Congo basin. Indeed the satisfactory settlement of colonial disputes became a normal prerequisite for making the alliances; and had colonial rivalries been decisive in shaping alliances, they would have tended to drive Britain more toward Germany than toward France and Russia.

The Anglo-French *entente* of 1904 was made on the basis of resolving mutual conflicts in Egypt and Morocco, the Anglo-Russian *entente* of 1907 on the basis of settling their separate spheres of influence in Persia. Italy, the one power that allowed colonial ambitions to govern its diplomacy, ended by making agreements with all the powers in turn and remained the most unpredictable and unreliable ally of either side. Diplomatically, colonial collisions were always disturbing, but they were certainly not decisive in making the situation that precipitated war between the rival alliances in 1914. There is strong evidence that all the most important colonial disputes had been settled before 1914. The crucial rivalry in naval power between Britain and Germany was by no means exclusively related to the possession of colonies. It affected the national security of the British Isles themselves, and Germany's bid to add great naval power to her existing military superiority in Europe alarmed France almost as much as it spurred Britain into activity.

The main tensions between powers induced by colonial collisions may be listed as the six disputes: between Britain and France about Egypt; between Britain and Germany over South Africa; between Britain and Russia about Persia; between Germany and Russia about the Balkans; between Russia and Japan about China; and between Germany and France about Morocco, involving three crises. It is only by examining briefly the nature of each of these disputes – all of which occurred between 1895 and 1911 – that it becomes possible to assess more precisely the significance of imperialism as a source of world war. In addition to these disputes, which were settled only after causing considerable heat and excitement and in one instance the Russo-Japanese War, there were many others which were arranged more amicably. The opening up of the great Congo basin, which had all the makings of a major quarrel between the competing powers of Belgium, France, Britain, Germany, and Portugal, was satisfactorily settled by the Berlin Conference of 1884–5. Despite the internal barbarities which aroused much hostile comment abroad, Belgian control over the area was eventually established in 1908 and paved the way for the peaceful and mainly beneficial development of the territory ever since. Britain's dispute with the United States over Venezuela in 1895 seemed, absurdly enough, capable of provoking war between them; but it was permanently settled by the eventual wisdom of both governments in appealing to arbitration.

Egypt and the Sudan. Frictions between Britain and France about Egypt and the Sudan, which caused the first dispute, reached their climax in 1898 in the famous incident of Fashoda. They dated back to the years between 1850 and 1870, when French and British business interests and engineers built the Suez Canal and Egyptian railroads, and when Egyptian cotton assumed a new importance in world markets (especially in British markets) during the American Civil War. More than any other part of the Ottoman Empire, Egypt in 1870 had become westernized in its economy and tastes. To celebrate the official opening of the Suez Canal in 1869, Verdi's opera *Aïda* had been first performed in the new opera house built in Cairo by the highly westernized Khedive, Ismail. But the lavish foreign loans needed to keep up this process of westernization put the Khedive more and more at the mercy of French and British banking interests. In 1879 they forced Ismail to abdicate and replaced him by Tewfik, who offered them better opportunities for investment. Britain and France set up a system of financial 'dual control'. Led by Arabi Pasha and the Egyptian army, there grew up a characteristic oriental movement of militant nationalism, opposed both to the foreign intruders and to the government that permitted such intrusions. Riots in Alexandria in 1882 led to British bombardment of the town and to the disembarkation of British troops at Suez and Alexandria. Egypt under Tewfik became, by French default, virtually a British protectorate, holding at bay both the native nationalists and the claims of Turkey. Between 1883 and 1907 Sir Evelyn Baring (Lord Cromer) was established as British consul general, and under his able guidance the country was modernized and efficiently administered. The interest due on loans from British and French investors alike could be paid regularly because the country's economy was expertly developed and the system of taxation was overhauled. British engineers built the Aswân dam in 1902. The French came to resent being ousted so much from Egypt, but consoled themselves by extending their control over other parts of North Africa and the Near East. By the 1890s, with the exploration of the interor of Africa, fresh fields for Anglo-French competition appeared in the Sudan. Nominally governed by Egypt, it was in effect governed by nobody.

Egyptian forces had had to be withdrawn from the Sudan in 1885, after General Gordon had been killed at Khartoum. But Britain, firmly established on the lower Nile, made it clear that she would look upon any advance of the French into the upper Nile valley as a hostile act. In 1895 Sir Edward Grey stated in the House of Commons that the advance of a French expedition from the other side of Africa towards the Nile 'would be an unfriendly act, and would be so viewed by

England'. In March the following year Britain decided to reconquer the Sudan and assembled a strong Anglo-Egyptian force in Egypt under Sir Herbert Kitchener. From Uganda in the south the railroad was pushed northwards, and some began to dream of one continuous Cape-to-Cairo territory all under British control. Frenchmen, meanwhile, had dreamed a dream that cut right across this project – the completion of one continuous belt of French territory stretching from Dakar to the Gulf of Aden, from the basin of the Congo and French West Africa right across the upper reaches of the Nile and joining on to Abyssinia and French Somaliland in the east. The missing link was the gap between the southernmost limits of effective Egyptian power in the Sudan and the northern-most bounds of British power in Uganda. The strategic point in this gap was Fashoda, whose fortress had fallen into bad repair but which gave control of the waters of the Nile, upon which the whole of Egypt depended for its existence.

Towards this nodal point there began in 1896 a great race. The French leader was Captain Jean-Baptiste Marchand, an explorer and soldier still in his thirties, and a passionate opponent of English colonialism. His march across darkest Africa, taking with him in pieces the steamer *Faidherbe* which he could reassemble when he reached the Nile, was itself an epic adventure. Its boiler was rolled on logs for hundreds of miles through the tropical forest. After more than a year Marchand reached Fashoda, on 16 July 1898. He restored the fort, made a treaty with the local chief, who put his territory under French rule, and hoisted the French flag over the fort. A fortnight later two messengers arrived from Kitchener, announcing that British forces had destroyed the Sudanese dervishes at the battle of Omdurman and that Kitchener himself would soon arrive at Fashoda. A few hours later Kitchener arrived with five gunboats and some two thousand men, a force very much greater than Marchand's little band of Senegalese riflemen. The French had won the race in time, but Kitchener was there with superior strength, firmly based on the Nile and on British sea power in the Mediterranean. Marchand's garrison was only an isolated outpost. But it held on bravely, and its leader remembered the bold words of his Foreign Minister when he undertook the expedition: 'You are going to fire a pistol shot on the Nile; we accept all its consequences.'

The deadlock at Fashoda brought Britain and France to the brink of war. When the news reached London and Paris, public opinion reacted wildly and irresponsibly. British opinion was still smarting from the failure of the Jameson Raid in South Africa[1] and the irritation of unpopularity in Europe; French opinion was being inflamed by the

1. See p. 515.

Dreyfus case. Fortunately the two men at Fashoda behaved with soldierly dignity and gallantry.

'I must hoist the Egyptian flag here,' said Kitchener.

'Why, I myself will help you to hoist it – over the village,' replied Marchand.

'Over the fort.'

'No, that I shall resist.'

'Do you know, Major, that this affair may set France and England at war?'

'I bowed,' records Marchand, 'without replying.'

They agreed that Kitchener should hoist the Egyptian flag over an outlying part of the fort, but the French flag remained flying over the fort itself. With this sensible compromise, and with no bloodshed, the soldiers passed the dilemma back to their governments.

Fortunately, too, the Foreign Ministers of the two countries were more reasonable than opinion in Press and country. The new French Minister, Théophile Delcassé, saw the matter in broad perspective. He knew that Lord Salisbury's cabinet would be quite unyielding on the Sudan; that Marchand could easily be overwhelmed and that French naval power in the Mediterranean was no match for British. France's larger diplomacy, of seeking Russian and British support against Germany, forbade an open breach with Britain, from which Germany would be only too eager to profit. Nor would Russia support France on such an issue. British reactions were violent, and both Joseph Chamberlain and Michael Hicks-Beach used strong language, which made compromise difficult. But Salisbury had no desire for war, and was ready to wait to reach diplomatic agreement. At last, in March 1899, agreement was reached. Marchand was withdrawn.

The watershed of the Nile and the Congo was made the dividing line between British and French spheres of influence. Though France was totally excluded from the Nile valley, she secured all her gains west of the watershed. She consolidated the whole hinterland of French West Africa, for Britain agreed not to seek territory or influence westward. Amid the general sense of humiliation and bitterness in France, Delcassé withstood the attacks of the violent nationalists. French interests lay first in security in Europe against Germany; he counted as slight the loss of Fashoda so long as these could be guaranteed by a closer understanding with Britain. When the fury died down on both sides, the two countries paradoxically found themselves nearer to a general understanding. Britain, where many began to feel ashamed of intransigence, reflected on the dangers of being at variance with both Germany and France at the same time; France realized that alliance with Russia alone was not enough. Italy, whose defeat at Adowa by the Abyssinians in March 1896 had first left open the upper Nile to a French advance, remained an unjoyful third party, having gained neither territory nor allies. So did colonial events react in diverse ways on the system of international alliances. With Kitchener had been a young soldier called Winston Churchill; with Marchand, another called Charles Mangin. They were to fight as allies in 1914.

South Africa. The second dispute occurred when relations between Great Britain and Germany were complicated by similar developments in South Africa. South of the equator the relative positions of German and British colonial possessions corresponded to those of French and British north of the equator; that is, British expansion northward from the Cape to Uganda was intersected by the transverse pressure of Germany between German South-west Africa and German East Africa. Here the gap between the two German colonies was filled by the Portuguese possession of Angola and by the Congo Free State. As already shown, the status of the Congo Free State had been determined by the Berlin Conference of 1884–5. In 1898 Germany held secret discussions with Britain about the possibility of partitioning the Portuguese colonies. They led to nothing, because Britain preferred Portugal to Germany as the governing power in these intermediate regions. Fresh dynamism in pressing the Cape-to-Cairo scheme had come from Cecil Rhodes, who in 1890 had become Prime Minister of Cape Colony. His drive into the territories which came to bear his name (Rhodesia) bypassed the two little Afrikaner republics of the Orange Free State and the Transvaal. After British annexation of the Cape in 1814 the simple, obstinate Dutch farmers had increasingly experienced pressure, and had tended to retreat before it. They even began their 'great trek' in 1836 to escape from British rule. Descendants of the original Dutch settlers at the Cape in the seventeenth century, they clung, as did the French settlers of Canada, to their old ways of life and were opposed to the great new mining promoters who flocked into the territory after the discovery of gold and diamonds in the 1870s. Paul Kruger, President of the Transvaal, which had asserted its independence in 1881 at the battle of Majuba Hill, symbolized their attitude of truculent obstruction and old-fashioned resentment towards new trends. When the discovery of gold in the Transvaal attracted a new batch of fortune hunters, Kruger treated them as 'outlanders' and refused them full citizenship. Their status became the formal cause of war between British and Boers in 1899, but the substantial cause was the clash of two opposed ways of life. Meanwhile, in 1895, a band of irregular troops led by Dr Jameson carried out a raid into the Transvaal from the Cape, encouraged by Cecil Rhodes who hoped to precipitate revolt. The raid was a complete failure, and brought upon Britain great criticism in Europe.

Feelings were particularly bitter in Gemany. On the birthday of Kaiser Wilhelm II, in January 1895, Kruger had been entertained by the German Club at Pretoria. In proposing a toast to the Kaiser, he had spoken of Germany as a 'grown-up power that would stop England from kicking the child republic'. Clumsy British protests in Berlin, and even clumsier German counter-protests, set the stage for news of the Jameson Raid and its failure. The Kaiser at once sent Kruger a telegram, congratulating him on successfully repulsing the invaders 'without appealing for the help of friendly powers'. This served only to divert British anger in full blast upon Germany, and made Kruger appear not as an injured innocent but as a plotter with Germany against British power in South Africa. In Germany the naval enthusiasts seized the chance to point their favourite moral: that only greater naval power could equip Germany to withstand such a policy. On both sides relations deteriorated. Friedrich von Holstein, in the German foreign office, seized the occasion of Britain's isolation in Europe to propose cooperation of all the other powers against her. The Dual Alliance of France and Russia might find common ground with the Triple Alliance (Germany, Austria-Hungary, and Italy) in concerting their colonial aims and forming a united front against the arch-imperialist power. But German policy, as others soon suspected, was aimed not at the final estrangement of Britain but only at forcing her into cooperation with the Triple Alliance by demonstrating the perils of isolation. The German proposal discreetly omitted to mention Egypt, which alone might have interested France; in the Transvaal France had no interest whatever. When Britain became involved in the Boer War (1899–1902), it was only Russia who proposed intervention, and Germany who refused to interfere. Although it took three years of fighting to subdue the two Boer republics, they were at last incorporated into the Union of South Africa in 1910 without having become the occasion of a European war. As over Fashoda, European states were apt to draw back from war among themselves about colonial disputes, however much they might snarl and hint at hostilities.

Persia. The third main imperial dispute in which Britain became involved in these years was with Russia about Persia. Russian imperial expansion in Turkestan, east of the Caspian Sea, brought her into contact with Afghanistan and Persia, just as her earlier spread southward, to the west of the Caspian, had led to encroachment upon Persia. The policy of Britain, fearful as ever of Russian designs upon India, was to support Afghans and Persians as buffers against such pressure. In 1885 they settled by arbitration details of the Russo-Afghan frontier in the Pendjeh area. By 1894 they reached an agreement about frontiers between the Russian and Indian Empires in the Pamir mountains on the roof of the world. The biggest remaining problem was Persia. In 1890 the Persian government was given a loan by Britain, who took as security for it the control of customs in the ports of the Persian Gulf. Ten years later it received a comparable loan from Russia, who took as security all other Persian customs. Persia under the Shah was falling into the same position as Turkey under the Sultan – a decrepit and bankrupt eastern state, crumbling before the economic and political pressures of the great powers and losing all control over its own fate.

There was the usual consequence in 1905 – a nationalist revolution that led to the calling of a nationally representative parliament. It was aimed against both the old régime of the Shah and the foreigners to which it had become subservient. Here again it proved possible to compromise. In August 1907 Britain and Russian signed a convention defining their spheres of influence, and erecting neutral zones between them. The northern part of Persia, adjoining the Caspian Sea and the Caucasus, became a Russian sphere of influence, the south-eastern, adjacent to Afghanistan and India, a British sphere of influence. The centre, including the Persian Gulf, was to be a neutral zone. At the same time Russia renounced direct contact with Afghanistan, and Tibet was made a neutral buffer state. The settlement did not, indeed, prove final. Russian ambitions revived, strengthened by the inclusion of the Persian capital of Teheran in their zone. In 1909, when a liberal revolution overthrew the Shah, who was Russia's protégé, it attracted British sympathy. When oil became important, the British found themselves in the more advantageous position to exploit it, and the Anglo-Persian Oil company did so. For these reasons, Anglo-Russian relations remained strained until eased by alliance in war when, in 1915, Russia agreed to British control over the original neutral zone. This was a colonial dispute resolved by the need for alliance in war, not a source of friction causing war—just as the Anglo-Russian convention of 1907 formed part of that general settlement of disputes which had created the Triple Entente of France, Russia, and Britain.

Crucial factors in the forging of this Entente were the proven difficulties of reconciling the three other major colonial conflicts of these years: between Russia and Germany about the Balkans, between Russia and Japan about China, and between Germany and France about Morocco. It was clear that disputes of the kind already described, even when involving issues of national prestige and long-term national security, such as Fashoda and the Boer War and Persia, were capable of being handled so as to preclude war between the major powers. In each of the remaining three disputes, one side felt its national security too intimately involved to yield to the other: Germany could not forgo her eastern expansion into an area of vital economic interests; France could not accept German intrusion into North African and Mediterranean affairs; Russia could not accept permanent exclusion from China by Japanese power. Of all colonial issues, here were three more liable to endanger European peace, more likely to cause war because they were so closely related to the intrinsic policies and interests of the powers. Compared with these, Anglo-French manoeuvres about the Sudan or Anglo-Russian wrangles about Persia seemed remote and peripheral.

Pan-Germans and Pan-Slavs. The fourth major colonial dispute was between Germany and Russia. The ultimate collision of their interests in eastern Europe became evident with the growth of Pan-Slavism and of Pan-Germanism. The incompatibility of German expansion eastward with Russian expansion westward underlay the failure of the Three Emperors' League, Germany's increasing reliance upon Austria-Hungary, and the making of the alliance between France and Russia. In the 1870s Pan-Slavism was propagated by many writers, including the great novelist Fëodor Dostoevski and the publicist N. I. Danilevsky, whose *Russia and Europe* appeared in 1871. It forecast a long war between Russia and Europe, culminating in a union of all Slav peoples and the extension of Slavdom over central Europe and large parts of the Turkish Empire. Romantic in flavour as was the original Prague congress of 1848,[1] Pan-Slavism became in this period a tool of more realistic politics – favoured by the Slavs of the Balkans only as a possible bludgeon against Turkey, by the Russian government only as a mask for Russian imperialism. It played little part in arousing the Balkan revolts of these years[2] which sprang from indigenous nationalisms; yet it exacerbated relations between the great powers, particularly between Russia and Germany, because it stood for an indefinitely ambitious programme of expansion.

Its counterpart, Pan-Germanism, was a more direct emanation from German nationalism, appealing strongly to the fast-growing German middle class. The Pan-German League (*Alldeutscher Verband*) of 1891 was supported mainly by business men, bureaucrats, and intellectuals, and its first president was Karl Peters. Its programme, as it developed during the 1890s, was twofold: the union of all Germans in the world into one great German state, with an enlarged central Germany at its heart; and the claim of this state to rule the world. Its advocates usually

1. See p. 216.
2. See pp. 462–76.

included within it the Netherlands, Belgium, Luxembourg, Austria, Hungary, Poland, Rumania, Serbia, and parts of Switzerland. The Pan-German League helped to co-ordinate the activities of other nationalist societies such as the Navy League, the Army League, and the Colonial Society. It developed powerful connexions and support overseas and in governmental, industrial, and journalistic circles within Germany. In policy it was strongly tinged with anti-Semitism and with anti-Slavism and, alike in its racial streaks and in the boundlessness of its objectives, it was a precursor of postwar National Socialism. The Pan-German programme came close to fulfilment under Hitler after 1940; the Pan-Slav, under Stalin after 1945.[1]

Symbolic of the clash between Pan-Slavism and Pan-Germanism was the project of the Berlin-Baghdad railroad, initiated by the *Deutsche Bank*. For Germany to drive a trade route right through the Balkans to the Persian Gulf required the cooperation of Austria and friendship with Turkey, and it involved head-on collision with Russian ambitions. The ostentatious wooing of Turkey by the Kaiser, who visited Constantinople in 1889, was accompanied by overt German interest in railroad concessions. Ten years later the concession was granted, but only after negotiations, for it had evoked characteristic reactions from the powers. Britain at first welcomed it: men like Cecil Rhodes, who had comparable ambitions of his own for a Cape-to-Cairo railroad, saw it as a useful diversion of German interests away from Africa. France welcomed it as making Germany equally interested in maintaining Turkish independence against Russia, and offered to put up some of the capital. The Russians were afraid of it, and since they could not forbid it, they tried to make an arrangement about it. They proposed that Germany, in return for their consent to it, should promise them control of the Straits. The Germans, having no need to buy Russian consent, refused; but in 1900 Russia made an agreement with Turkey which required Russian consent for the building of railroads in the Black Sea areas of Asia Minor. In fact the railroad took so long to build that it was still only a fragment in 1914; and then France and Britain both reached agreement with Germany about it. The chief importance of the whole scheme had been its contribution to the accumulating frictions between Germany and Russia, and so to the widening of the gulf between the two systems of alliances in Europe.

The Russo-Japanese War. The fifth major colonial dispute, that between Russia and Japan in the Far East, showed how wide the bonds, and therefore the repercussions, of the system of alliances had become. In 1902 Britain signalled her abandonment of the policy of isolation

1. See pp. 795 and 835.

and of 'keeping a free hand', by concluding an alliance with Japan. Each power agreed that it would keep in the Far East 'a naval force superior in strength to that of any third power'. If either were attacked by more than one power, the other promised to come to its assistance. This agreement not only served warning on Germany, who now held colonial possessions in the Pacific, that she would be outweighed in that half of the world; by ruling out the danger of an alliance between Japan and Russia which would have put the British Far Eastern squadron in grave danger, it also enabled Britain to keep the bulk of her growing fleet nearer home. In February 1904 Japan took advantage of her new strength to attack the Russian naval base of Port Arthur, bottling up the Russian Far Eastern fleet. The Russo-Japanese War which ensued,[1] and which ended in Russian defeat, was primarily a colonial war – the only colonial war of these decades fought between two major powers. As a result of it the Japanese gained virtual possession of Korea (which they annexed five years later), annexed the southern half of the island of Sakhalin, and took over the Russian lease of the Liaotung peninsula, which gave them entry to Manchuria. The effects of the war on Europe were great. Although France was the ally of Russia, and Britain the ally of Japan, both countries kept out, while noting how much advantage Germany could gain if either should become involved. It encouraged the conclusion of the *entente* between France and Britain in 1904. The startling disclosure of Russia's governmental weakness, which led to revolution in 1905, and of the military and naval weakness brought about by the destruction of her Baltic fleet dissipated Germany's traditional nightmare of a two-front war, while it left France feeling more exposed by the enfeeblement of her one certain ally. These events in the Far East violently oscillated the balance of power in Europe, intensifying both German intransigence and French determination to find another ally.

Morocco. The sixth main imperial dispute was between Germany and France about Morocco, which was a recurrent bone of contention between them in the twenty years before 1914. By 1895 it was the one remaining part of the Ottoman territory in North Africa which remained at least semi-independent of European control. But in its mode of government it seemed peculiarly ill-fitted for such a status. Muley Hassan, one of the strongest sultans Morocco had known, died in 1894. He was succeeded by a boy of fourteen. Arthur Nicolson, the British consul-general in Morocco, described the land as a 'loose agglomeration of turbulent tribes, corrupt governors, and general poverty and distress'. Half the territory was normally in open revolt. Yet because of its strategic

1. See p. 507.

position at the mouth of the Mediterranean, and because of the strained relations between the great powers of Europe, this unhappy land was to prove a source of international dispute on three occasions between 1905 and 1911. It provides vivid illustration of how relatively minor colonial issues could set the powers snarling at one another in the decade before war began. But it also shows how such issues were resolutely resolved and kept subordinate to considerations that most of the powers regarded as their more vital national interests.

The first Moroccan crisis occurred in 1905. France claimed special interests in Morocco because its southern frontier with Algeria had never been precisely defined and certain oases, essential to communications between Algeria and French Equatorial Africa, were disputed between France and the Sultan. Britain had trading interests in Morocco, as well as possessing Gibraltar on the other side of the straits. Germany, anxious to detach France from the *entente* of 1904 with Britain, decided to exploit the Moroccan question for this purpose. At the end of March 1905 the Kaiser landed at Tangier in Morocco and indicated that his visit was intended to be formal recognition of the Sultan's independence. Since Germany had no traditional or direct interest in Morocco, and since Britain and France had so recently reached agreement about its status, this was a deliberately provocative act. It was also foolish, for it encouraged the Sultan to expect from Germany support that could not be given without incurring the risk of a European war; it rallied French opinion behind Delcassé's policy; and far from dislocating the *entente,* it fostered in Britain a new conception of it as something that had to be strenuously defended against German threats. It was the beginning of a long series of diplomatic blunders on the part of the Kaiser and, even more, of his chancellor, Prince von Bülow – blunders in the double sense that they had results the very opposite to what Germany intended, and that they greatly increased the accumulating fears and distrusts which precipitated war. Bülow made it clear to the French Prime Minister, Maurice Rouvier, that 'so long as M. Delcassé remains in office there is no possibility of an improvement in Franco-German relations'. Delcassé, architect of the *entente,* had been France's Foreign Minister for seven years; in June 1905, he was forced to resign. Nationalist opinion in France naturally stormed at this humiliation, and the apparent pretension of Germany to dictate who might be France's Foreign Minister rallied British sympathy to the French side.

France yielded to Bülow's demands for an international conference to settle Moroccan affairs, which duly met at Algeciras in January 1906. Diplomatic representatives of the great powers, including the United States, Spain, the Low Countries, Portugal, and Sweden, were all there.

Contrary to her expectations, Germany found that only Austria supported her in the conference, whereas Britain, Russia, Italy, and Spain backed France. The mendacity and mystifications of German diplomacy during the conference did her irreparable harm. In the outcome, she gained nothing from the settlement save a share for the *Deutsche Bank* in Morocco's new State Bank. The crucial issues were who should control the police forces and the finances in Morocco. It was decided that the Sultan's Moroccan police should be under joint French and Spanish control under a Swiss inspector general, and that Moroccan finances should be run by a state bank which would be international. In effect this left France in predominant control of the administration of Morocco (despite the formal declaration of its independence), and also in partial control of its finances. It was Germany, not France, which left the meetings at Algeciras feeling humiliated. Whereas the defection of Italy revealed the basic weakness of the Triple Alliance, the *entente* between Britain and France passed, as André Tardieu put it, 'from a static to a dynamic state'. While the conference was meeting, military experts of France and Britain discussed secret plans for landing a hundred thousand British troops in France if war should come.

The second Moroccan crisis arose in 1908, when the French invaded the German consulate at Casablanca in order to arrest three German deserters from their foreign legion. The 'Casablanca incident' coincided with the much more important crisis caused by Austria's annexation of Bosnia and Herzegovina,[1] and Berlin seized upon it as a diversion. It was settled by submission to arbitration at the Hague.[2] In 1909 France and Germany signed a declaration in which Germany recognized France's political predominance in Morocco, and France in return undertook not to injure Germany's economic interests.

The climax of Moroccan crises, the third, occurred two years later, when French troops occupied Fez, the most important town in Morocco, in the cause of maintaining order and protecting the Sultan against rebels, Germany demanded compensation, and indulged in the dramatic gesture of sending the German warship *Panther* to the Moroccan port of Agadir. If the French had been within their rights in marching on Fez, they had thereby aroused sleeping dogs all over Europe, in Madrid and London as well as in Berlin. The *Panther's* arrival in Agadir set these dogs barking, for it looked as if Germany was again brandishing the big stick. Britain's bark took the form of Lloyd George's speech at the Mansion House in London, wherein he declared:

1. See p. 473.
2. See p. 538.

I would make great sacrifices to preserve peace.... But if a situation were to be forced upon us in which peace could only be preserved by the surrender of the great and beneficent position Britain has won by centuries of heroism and achievement, by allowing Britain to be treated, where her interests were vitally affected, as if she were of no account in the Cabinet of nations, then I say emphatically that peace at that price would be a humiliation intolerable for a great country like ours to endure.

Coming from the man who had opposed the Boer War and who was allegedly leader of the pro-German pacifists in the British government, these words had a startling effect. The British fleet prepared for action, and compromise between France and Germany became even more improbable. In November Germany agreed, however, to a French protectorate over Morocco, in return for two strips of territory (100,000 square miles) in the French Congo, and the *Panther* was withdrawn. In all three countries public opinion remained angry, and the German Navy League used the crisis, as usual, to demand more dreadnoughts. The main effect of the crisis of Agadir was to accentuate Anglo-German rivalry and distrust, and to inflame public opinion in the cause of national prestige. This crisis and the Casablanca incident were more ominous forbodings of war than any of the previous crises. Prince von Bülow himself summed it up from the German point of view:

Like a damp squib, it startled, then amused the world, and ended by making us look ridiculous. After the leap of the *Panther* on Agadir there was a fanfare which, on Lloyd George's speech, died down in the most inglorious chamade.

The mere narration of these six main colonial collisions serves to emphasize to what extent political and strategic, rather than economic or financial considerations, governed the behaviour of the great powers in the colonial field. Even where strong economic considerations existed, as with French trading concerns in Morocco or British oil interests in Persia, such considerations were kept entirely subordinate to political and strategic necessities or merely to issues of national prestige and dignity. When strong French financial interests, led by the minister of finance Rouvier, wanted to take part along with Germany in making the Berlin–Baghdad railway, they were prevented by the government under the influence of Delcassé, who was anxious not to annoy Russia. Apprehensions about national security and the quest for reliable alliances so engaged the attention of the governments of most of the powers that their decisions, whether to pursue active imperialist policies or to moderate their policies of expansion and settle colonial conflicts with other powers, were determined first by political calculations and only secondarily by economic. For this reason economic pressure groups tended to operate directly on public opinion, inflaming jingo sentiments for sectional advantage or urging policies that masked economic motives behind nationalistic slogans. Only rarely were the actions of governments directly guided by purely economic motives. International relations were conducted mainly by diplomats of the old school, and even many of the politicians were men who had been trained more in diplomacy than in statesmanship. Their dispatches show very little interest in economic conditions or social forces, and no understanding of the hopes of ordinary folk for a more just social order, but only a profound absorption in the skilled game of power politics. Enshrouded in suspicions, alert to every sign of subtle shifts in the balance of power, they tirelessly and purposefully pursued the interests of their countries as they understood them; and they understood them almost exclusively in terms of alliances and counteralliances, manoeuvres and bargains, always with the single purpose of enhancing national security and power.

For this reason the final understanding of the long sequences of interrelated events which led – in retrospect so remorselessly – to the outbreak of world war in 1914 must be sought neither in the Eastern Question alone, nor in imperialism alone, but in that delicate network of alliances and understandings between the major powers which it was the special craftsmanship of the diplomats to weave and to handle. Here was the snare in which all became eventually enmeshed, set usually in secret and at times wrenched violently by clumsiness of statecraft, yet potent enough, in the absence of any firmer and larger organization of world affairs, to drag all alike over the brink of disaster in 1914.

CHAPTER 21

THE SYSTEM OF ALLIANCES

TRIPLE ALLIANCE AND TRIPLE *ENTENTE*

DESPITE occasional and momentary rapprochements between them, the enduring hostility between France and Germany was one of the most constant factors in international diplomacy between 1871 and 1914. It was on the assumption that this enmity would always, in the end, supervene over all other considerations that the system of great alliances was built. On the side of Germany, Bismarck's main purpose was to preserve the settlement of 1871 [1] and to ensure, for Germany at least, a generation of peace in which to consolidate her new-found national unity. On the side of France, once the most violent passions demanding revenge and the most violent fears of a preventive war had subsided, the main purpose was to find allies that would save her from the friendless isolation which had brought about her downfall in 1871. In this sense, the basic desire of the two most constant enemies in Europe was defensive rather than offensive. Not even the desire to recover Alsace and Lorraine – strong though that desire remained in the hearts of Lorrainers like Maurice Barrès and Raymond Poincaré – was greater than the anxiety to find some counterweight to the new supremacy of Germany in Europe. Germany had usurped France's traditional role as the superpower of western and central Europe, and had destroyed all balance. For the first time in centuries France herself was no longer a threat to the balance of power, but rather, like Britain before her, the mainspring of a policy which sought to recreate a balance of power in Europe.

France found Britain for long unresponsive to taking any share in this task. Britain saw in the existence of five major continental powers, where previously there had been only four, the elements of an almost automatic balance of power. She was so accustomed to regarding France or Russia, rather than Austria-Hungary or Prussia, as the most likely menace to an equable balance in Europe, that she was slow to appreciate the full implications of German ascendancy, both diplomatic and economic. Even in 1904 the disposition of her east-coast naval bases still reflected the belief that France would be the main enemy. Her conception of the 'balance of power' itself had always been different from

1. See p. 320.

the French or Italian. As befitted a nation of shopkeepers who had prospered on becoming the bankers of the world, she thought of it as like a balance at the bank – a reserve of security to be drawn upon for normal purposes, and to be reinforced by her own efforts only when the credit balance looked like disappearing. Her ideal arrangement of Europe was one which, like her own constitution, rested on a system of checks and balances operating smoothly and automatically so as to preserve the liberties and independence of all nations, yet calling for no engagement or commitment on her own part until one power should become so dangerously overgrown as to threaten this stability. Then, but only then, and as an emergency expedient, would she throw her own weight into the balance against it. This was what she had done against Louis XIV, against Napoleon, against Russia in the Crimean War. Meanwhile, it was essential for her, if she was to fulfil this ultimate role successfully, to keep a free hand and avoid firm precommitments to either side. She had interests and concerns enough elsewhere in the world. These she safeguarded by her naval supremacy, which was still, in the 1870s, completely unchallenged. Her traditions, her interests, and – as her leading statesmen mostly conceived it – her duty to Europe, all coincided most happily to justify the policy of 'splendid isolation'.

Bismarckian Diplomacy. Confronted with British isolationism, Bismarck set to work to make Austria-Hungary his major ally. To this he was driven by the precariousness of the Three Emperors' League of 1873, the collapse of which has already been considered.[1] The Dual Alliance of the two Germanic powers, concluded in 1879 but kept secret for some years, became the foundation of the Triple Alliance. The outcome of the Congress of Berlin in 1878 had indicated Austria, not Russia, as Bismarck's major ally, while it had left Russia as a possible ally of France.[2] The Treaty of Vienna in 1879 assured Austria-Hungary of Germany's support in the event of a direct attack on her by Russia; and although the promise was for 'reciprocal protection', this was its most substantial effect. It stipulated that if 'one of the two Empires shall be attacked on the part of Russia, the High Contracting Parties are bound to assist each other with the whole of the military power of their Empire, and consequently only to conclude peace conjointly and by agreement'. If either were to be attacked by any power other than Russia, the other signatory was pledged at least to a benevolent neutrality. This meant that Germany would back no aggressive Austrian policy in the Balkans, while Austria would back no aggressive German policy toward France. It was, therefore, a defensive alliance. It left Bismarck with the

1. See p. 469.
2. See p. 466.

problem of trying to prevent Russia from drifting into alliance with France. The new Tsar, Alexander III, was amenable, and in 1881 Bismarck revived the *Driekaiserbund* with this end in view. But again it foundered on the rocks of Austro-Russian rivalry in the Balkans; hence his Reinsurance Treaty of 1887, wherein Russia undertook not to support France should she make war on Germany, and gained in return a German promise to back Russian interests in the Balkans.

Meanwhile the Triple Alliance was completed in 1882, when Germany and Austria made a further treaty with Italy. Stimulated by her annoyance at the French seizure of Tunis the year before, Italy was induced to make this agreement with her traditional nationalist enemy, Habsburg Austria, and with Germany for whom she bore no affection. Its terms were that both other powers would support Italy if she were attacked without provocation by France. Italy in return was pledged to support either of her allies only if it were attacked by two or more great powers, but would aid Germany if she were attacked by France alone. At Italy's special request, both her allies agreed that in no case would the treaty operate against Great Britain. These stipulations show how carefully the treaty was geared to the peculiar needs of Germany and Italy. Each of them gained further security against attack by France. Italy, however, was not obliged to back Austria except in conjunction with Germany and against at least two other major powers – that is, in the event of a general European war; and even then, if Britain were involved, she had reserved the right to contract out of this obligation. Austria-Hungary gained little from the bargain, save uncertain Italian backing in a general war and the promise of German backing against attack by two other powers, not merely against Russia. She did not secure Italian aid against an attack by Russia alone. In 1883 Rumania adhered to the Triple Alliance, and gradually Turkey also, despite her war with Italy in 1911, was drawn into its ambit. It must be remembered that, in those days of secret diplomacy, Italy did not know of the existence of the Dual Alliance when she signed the Triple Alliance treaty in 1882; and although France in 1883 knew of the existence of the Triple Alliance, its precise terms were not divulged before 1918. This lack of precise knowledge intensified fears and stimulated other powers in their incessant search for allies.

French Diplomacy. The triple *Entente* had its corresponding foundation in the Franco-Russian *entente* of 1893. After Bismarck ceased to be German Chancellor in 1890, his successors abandoned the careful delicacy of his diplomacy. They allowed the Reinsurance Treaty to lapse. Faced with the obvious hardening of the German-Austrian alliance, Russia became more responsive to French overtures, the more so as she urgently needed French loans. At the end of 1893 Russia and France signed a military convention in which Russia undertook, if France were attacked by Germany or by Germany and Italy together, to go to war with Germany; and in return France pledged support for Russia if she were attacked by Germany, or by Austria and Germany together. Again, although the existence of the agreement was admitted two years later, its exact terms were not disclosed until 1918. At the expense of throwing in her lot with Russia to the extent of committing herself to take part in any further Russo-German war, France had by 1893 defeated the central purpose of Bismarck's diplomacy since 1871. Provided that Russian promises could be trusted, France would not again find herself fighting Germany alone.

It is a measure of the strength of British isolationist traditions that eleven more years elapsed before France could secure any assurance from Great Britain. Distrust of Russia reinforced British inclinations to keep a free hand in Europe, and for a time there was even a possibility that she might commit herself to the Triple Alliance, or at least to Germany rather than to France. Britain's alliance with Japan in 1902 was directed mainly against their common enemy, Russia, and might be expected to render still more improbable any *rapprochement* with Russia's ally, France.[1] Only the mounting menace of German naval power and blundering German diplomacy could have overcome this tendency to aloofness. By 1902 they had successfully done so, for Britain nursed bitter memories of the Kaiser's telegram to Kruger; and Joseph Chamberlain, leading advocate of an alliance with Germany, had had rebuffs enough to turn his thoughts towards France. At the beginning of 1902 the German ambassador in London reported that he had learned, in the strictest confidence, of negotiations between Chamberlain and the French ambassador, Paul Cambon, for a general settlement of colonial disputes. In 1903 King Edward VII visited Paris, where he was welcomed with great popular enthusiasm, and the French President paid a return visit to London. Negotiations took nearly a year, but in April 1904 the agreement was signed. It marked the beginning of the *entente cordiale* which was to survive for more than fifty years.

The famous agreement was viewed by the British Foreign Secretary, Lord Lansdowne, as a purely colonial settlement – extensive and important, but exclusively colonial. So, in substance, it was. Its main provision gave France a free hand in Morocco in return for the cession to Britain of her rights and historic position in Egypt. It was in a sense a mutual recognition of spheres of interest and influence in North Africa. It also removed points of friction in other parts of the world – in Siam,

1. See p. 507.

Madagascar, the New Hebrides, Newfoundland, west and central Africa. For European affairs the most significant article was the last, in which the two governments agreed 'to afford to one another their diplomatic support in order to obtain the execution of the clauses of the present Declaration'. This made Morocco the focus of European disputes during the next decade [1] and the occasion of several German discomfitures. Four articles of the agreement only were kept secret, but these were of little importance and added nothing to the extent of formal commitments. France and the United Kingdom were not in military alliance, and the agreement was not aimed specifically at Germany. But the lasting removal of Anglo-French frictions and the reconciliation of the two western powers betokened, as the French Foreign Minister Delcassé foresaw, a new era in European politics. The completion of the Triple *Entente* three years later, by the corresponding compromise about Anglo-Russian disputes in Persia, marked the hardening of Europe into two rival camps. Again, this was no military alliance. British susceptibilities were fully respected by avoiding any commitment to Russia which was inconsistent with her pledges to Japan. But since France was Russia's ally, and Britain and France in the course of the following years entered into undertakings about the disposal of their fleets in time of war, the judgement of most European statesmen, that Britain had at last given her long-coveted casting vote for the *Entente* powers, was not far from the truth. Morally, and in certain circumstances diplomatically, Britain would now back France in any future clash with Germany.

The Alignment of Powers. By 1907, then, seven years before war began, the greater European powers had grouped themselves into two *blocs*: a predominantly military but defensive alliance between Germany, Austria-Hungary, Italy, and Rumania; and a predominantly diplomatic alliance between France, Russia, and Great Britain. Neither, it must be emphasized, was constructed as a preparation for war. Both were attempts to prevent war by appearing so strongly embattled with allies that the other would not dare to launch an attack. Just as Bismarck's original system of alliances had been devised to keep the peace, so, too, the system of rival alliances which grew up after his retirement was intended to keep the peace in Europe. Just as Bismarck's nightmare had been the possibility of a war on two fronts and encirclement, so France's nightmare had been diplomatic isolation and solitary defeat. Now, as France's nightmare had been dispersed, Germany's recurred. From the viewpoint of an easing of those general fears and distrusts in Europe which underlay the competition in armaments and the restless

1. See p. 519.

quest for alliances, the position was no better. It was even worse. German economic and naval might were now growing so fast that her neighbours were justifiably more apprehensive; while her diplomacy was conducted with such reckless neglect for others' fears that hopes of possible reconciliation receded still further. The road to war was paved with good conventions – and bad manners.

So feverish was the state of public opinion in most countries, so busy in their intricate arts were the professional diplomats, that it was scarcely noted how abnormal was the new alignment of powers, or how great had been the diplomatic revolution that made it possible. For centuries Britain and France had been rivals, both in Europe and overseas; now they based concerted action in Europe on an agreed settlement of disputes overseas. Throughout the nineteenth century the shadow of the Russian bear had lain across the lines between Britain and India; now the British had come to amicable terms with Russia about all the frontiers between their two Empires. So complete a reversal of traditional animosities meant a radical change of outlook and a new balance of power in the world. So, too, the arch-enemy of both German and Italian nationalists for a century or more had been Austria of the Habsburgs, and both had fought wars with her within living memory. Yet now they found themselves her allies, pledged to help defend her against even their old friends and sympathizers such as the British and the French. The system of rival alliances marked the liquidation of nineteenth-century relationships, the abandonment of traditional foreign policies, the adoption by others of the new, mobile, dynamic diplomacy invented by Cavour and Bismarck.

The complexities of this new international order are suggested not only by the intricate provisions of the separate treaties of alliance, but also by the further minor alliances – the flying buttresses, as it were, of the new diplomatic fabric. Italy was especially active in the making of such agreements, and in the end made some agreement with every major power. In the Mediterranean Pact of 1887 with Britain, later extended to Austria, she was in effect promising the same sort of help in Tripoli as she might give Britain in Egypt, and in both cases the agreement was aimed against France. Lord Salisbury's promise of broader support was, however, couched in characteristically vague terms – 'in general and to the extent that circumstances shall permit'. Italy exchanged notes with Spain to preserve the *status quo* in Morocco. Together with Britain and Austria-Hungary she agreed to maintain peace and the *status quo* in the Near East, the Straits, and Bulgaria. When the Triple Alliance was renewed in 1887, it was accompanied by new separate treaties with Austria-Hungary and Germany. Germany promised, in effect, to help Italy to get Tripoli if France got Morocco. In 1900 Italy also made the Racconigi agreement with Russia, aimed against Austria. Russia undertook to look favourably upon Italian claims to Tripoli, Italy to favour Russian claims for the opening of the Straits to Russian ships of war. Each promised not to make agreements with a third power about the Balkans without the participation of the other. These promises not only ran counter to Italian obligations under the Triple Alliance, but were followed only a few days later by an agreement with Austria stipulating that neither state would make agreements with a third party without the knowledge of the other. The climax of duplicity was reached in 1902, in a secret agreement with France that each should remain neutral towards the other not only in the case of a war of aggression but also if the other 'as a result of direct provocation, should find itself compelled in defence of its honour or security to take the initiative of a declaration of war'. Italy's twofold determination, to get Tripoli and to have her bread buttered on both sides, led her into an astonishing tangle of conflicting promises until almost any action must involve the breach of some of them. Her secret and inconsistent promises reduced the system of alliances almost to a farce; and she was notably the one power whose European policy was so largely dominated by colonial aims. The others, guided by more constant considerations of national security or national interests in Europe, remained somewhat more predictable and reliable.

Italy's flirtations with both sides, and her eventual desertion of Triple Alliance for Triple *Entente* in 1915, raise the important question of why the promises made in the system of alliances proved so binding. In an age of secret diplomacy and cynical political realism, it might be expected that paper-promises would be felt to be so fragile as to be almost worthless. Germany's dismissal of her treaty-undertaking to respect Belgian neutrality as a mere 'scrap of paper' when it ran counter to German military plans in 1914 suggests that such an attitude was not unknown. Yet the very alarm and denunciation which German action aroused on that occasion suggests, too, that it was rare. The deceitfulness involved in secret diplomacy, except when carried to Italian extremes, was expected to stop short at open breach of promise. Moreover, the greatest sanction behind treaty obligations was fear. The alliances themselves were cohesions of fear. Governments made them because they were afraid, because they came to dread diplomatic isolation, because if allies were in the market, it was always desirable to forestall a rival in buying them. There was always a seller's market for treaties of alliance, which was why Italy could sell to everybody. But since a price always had to be paid, each power found itself committed to backing an ally over disputes in which that power itself had no direct interest; peace became, in a phrase that was to become more prevalent but less applicable between the two wars, 'indivisible'. An outbreak of hostilities anywhere must, if the bonds of the alliances held, lead to a general war. The best hope for peace was that the powers, like bands of mountain climbers tied together with ropes, might contrive to restrain and haul back to safety any member of the party about to stumble over the edge of war. In the great Bosnian crisis of 1908 and in the Balkan Wars of 1912 and 1913 [1] the system of alliances worked in this helpful manner. Allies served as powerful friction-brakes on the headstrong. But with the piling tensions of the international drama, it became ever more possible that the pulls would work the other way: that momentum of the more reckless and clumsy members might drag the cautious and reluctant over the edge with them into the abyss. That happened in 1914.

The philosophy behind the alliances, although their completion marked the total defeat of his purpose, was that of Bismarck. It rested on the assumption, truer in 1871 than it was in 1914, that there were five recognizably 'great powers' in Europe: Austria-Hungary, Germany, Russia, France, and Great Britain. Italy counted by courtesy as a sixth, Ottoman Turkey as a very weak seventh. But in realistic terms there were only five. 'You forget,' said Bismarck to the Russian ambassador Saburov, 'the importance of being a party of three on the European chess-board. ... Nobody wishes to be in a minority. All politics reduce themselves to this formula: try to be *à trois* in a world governed by five powers.' The *Dreikaiserbund,* had it been workable and durable, would have achieved this end for Germany. The Triple Alliance, which omitted Russia and in Italy included only the sixth power, could never serve this purpose. Even buttressed with Rumania and Turkey, it could not serve. The Triple *Entente,* though less formal, less binding, less military in purpose than the Triple Alliance, conformed more completely to Bismarck's principle. All three were undeniably great powers. What frustrated Bismarck's plan was that France – not Germany alone – adopted it. A world in which both these sworn enemies could contrive to be *à trois* was a fantastic, unarithmetical world, where the weights in the scales of power were so evenly balanced that only a long and exhausting tussle between the two sides could establish the superiority of one. Save that his decision to annex Alsace and Lorraine in 1871 saddled Germany with the lasting liability of French enmity, Bismarck was not to blame for the First World War. His conception of alliances was intended for German use only – applied universally it must, like the principle that might is right, end in absurdity. Even his conception of warfare was

1. See p. 473.

the opposite to that of 1914. His use of war was restricted to limited, finite wars for specific ends – instruments of precision for attaining definite objectives by decisive victory over isolated victims. The phennomenon of a general European war for indefinite objectives, even for determining the balance of power, would have been anathema to him. Yet this, in the course of events, is what his policy of alliances and his series of specific wars led to by 1914. The most important thing about the First World War is that it was the unsought, unintended end product of a long sequence of events which began in 1871. No man, no nation, worked for this result, which was the total outcome of the interplay of diverse policies and strategies usually aimed primarily at providing national security, stability, even peace. The first impression is one of fatality and fatalism – a drift of doom. But the historian, peering through the curtain which conceals the significance of events as recent as those within living memory, can detect at least a few features of the true image.

Germany and Britain. By 1900 two facts were certain: Germany was the greatest power in Europe, the British Empire was the greatest power in the world. With a rapidly expanding population of fifty-six million in the heart of Europe, a dynamic economy fast overtaking even that of Britain in industrialization, the strongest and best-equipped army on the continent, a firm alliance with Austria-Hungary, Germany was in 1900 the greatest power in Europe.[1] Yet in the world at large – in that oceanic world which, throughout the previous century, had been dominated by British sea power – the British Empire loomed still mightier. It covered a quarter of the surface of the earth and included a quarter of mankind. Given the isolationism of the United States, and the effective extension of the Monroe Doctrine over central and south America by the growth of Pan-American organizations, British sea power controlled the high seas. Half the world's tonnage of merchant shipping was hers, and the lion's share of the world trade. But unlike Germany's, Britain's populations and resources were not concentrated and compact. Most of her population lived in the widely separated areas of India and the British Isles; the rest were scattered over Africa, Canada, Australasia, and many small islands and outposts. Even by 1914 there were only some twenty-three thousand German settlers in German colonies – fewer than the number of Germans in France. In comparison with Germany's position of concentrated power in central Europe, the British Empire was peripheral and diffused.

This situation at the opening of the twentieth century meant that there was no balance of power anywhere: only an unbalance in Germany's

1. See pp. 376-85.

favour in Europe, an unbalance in Britain's favour in the oceanic world. Between 1900 and 1914, with the expansion of German sea power and world trade on one hand, and the adhesion of Britain to the continental system of rival alliances on the other, there took place a gigantic contest about whether or not Germany's localized superiority could be widened by adding to it enough naval power to destroy British supremacy on the high seas. To do this Germany did not need to build a fleet larger than Britain's. The view of Admiral von Tirpitz was that German aims would be fulfilled by building a fleet which, in time of war, could sink enough British ships to reduce British naval strength below the two-power standard, and so expose it to defeat by any other two naval powers. His policy, like Bismarck's diplomacy, relied for success on Germany's being *à trois* in a world of five great powers. It was equally inappropriate once the Triple *Entente* had been forged. Yet Germany chose that moment to embark upon unlimited competition in naval construction. It was widely inferred, therefore, that Germany's real aim was unilateral world domination, through an extension of Germany's continental supremacy into a parallel oceanic supremacy. This neither Britain nor France could view with other than the liveliest fears. Their aim was necessarily the antithesis of Germany's – to call in the favourable balance of power in the oceanic world to restore in Europe a balance less favourable to Germany. When, after 1907, the British Empire cast its lot with France and Russia, this aim became attainable. French and Russian military expansion offset German and Austrian, British naval expansion offset German; and the feverish competition between the two camps achieved a remarkable equalization of power and potential in Europe. By 1914 the balance of power was so even that only a long war of endurance and exhaustion could determine superiority; and the longer the struggle, the more foregone was its conclusion, for the favourable balance of power in the outside world could be imposed more decisively on Europe. The entry of the United States in 1917 made the outcome certain.

The frightening feature of the rival alliances by 1914 was their rigidity and reliability. Each succeeding international crisis, with its latent threat to the security of the great powers, tightened the ties within each group. The tactlessness of the Kaiser's diplomacy contributed to the final débâcle. In October, 1908, he published, in the London *Daily Telegraph*, an article in which he claimed, as proof of his friendship for Britain, the fact that he had worked out a plan of campaign for the Boer War which 'by a matter of curious coincidence' was much the same as that successfully employed by Lord Roberts. It aroused resentful laughs in England, where the Kaiser's telegram to Kruger in 1896 was still remembered; in Germany it raised a storm of angry protest and even led to talk of the

Kaiser's abdication. More dangerous still was his interview with the Austrian Foreign Minister Berchtold in October 1913, at the height of Austrian anger against Serbia for her role in the Balkan Wars. According to Berchtold:

As often as opportunity offered during our hour-and-a-quarter's talk to touch upon our relations as Allies, His Majesty ostentatiously used the occasion to assure me that we could count absolutely and completely on him. This was the red thread that ran through the utterances of the illustrious Sovereign. . . . . His Majesty did me the honour to say that whatever came from the Vienna Foreign Office was a command for him.

The German Emperor had become convinced that war between East and West was now inevitable, and this fatalism – combined with the general tightening of the bonds of the alliances – was itself one factor in the drift towards the abyss.

Whatever the blunders of the Kaiser, it was of decisive importance that Britain and Germany – the greatest world power and the greatest European power – were now competing for supremacy at sea. Nothing more quickly and decisively aroused popular emotions in either country than this naval rivalry. The challenge was first thrown down by the German Naval Laws of 1897 and 1898 which added twelve ships of the line to the existing seven; ten large cruisers to the existing two; and twenty-three small cruisers to the existing seven. This challenge was taken up in earnest by Britain from 1903 onwards, when she began her programme of naval rearmament. Fearing that the greatest military power in Europe would not embark on so large a project of naval construction unless she aimed at the domination of the world, the British Parliament in 1903 approved the formation of a North Sea fleet based on the new naval base of Rosyth. For the first time her disposition of naval power began to face toward Germany rather than France or Russia. Nor could the behaviour of Germany permit of any other interpretation of her intentions. A high seas fleet was needed by Germany only if she intended to use her power outside Europe; and the Navy Law of 1900, which doubled the number of battleships, made the winning of power on the high seas of the world an integral part of German policy. In 1905 Sir John Fisher, engaged in a technical overhaul of British naval strength since becoming First Sea Lord the year before, laid the keel of the first dreadnought. This larger and much more heavily gunned vessel – 'a new type of floating gun-carriage' – made older and smaller ships obsolete. When Germany commenced soon after to build them too, a race began which stirred popular feeling in both countries.

British proposals for agreement to limit naval construction were repeatedly brushed aside by the Kaiser; and after the Triple *Entente* had been completed in 1907, they were doubly suspect by Germany, whose rejections of any suggestion of a 'naval holiday' drove Britain further into the embrace of the *Entente*. Anglo-German rivalry made for Anglo-French cooperation. In the autumn of 1912 it was agreements about dispositions of their naval forces which bound Britain as close to France as any formal pledge of support could have done. It was agreed that French naval strength should be concentrated in the Mediterranean, British in the North Sea. This committed France to defending British interests in the Mediterranean against Austria-Hungary and if need be against Italy, while she left to the British fleet the task of defending her northern coasts and the Channel against Germany. In Britain both Asquith, the Prime Minister, and Sir Edward Grey, his Foreign Secretary, continued to insist that they had made no alliance with France. Notes exchanged between Grey and Paul Cambon explicity stated that the naval agreements were 'not an engagement that commits either government'. This contention may have been formally correct, but in substance both countries now had such vital interests at stake in the faithful fulfilment of these undertakings that no formal alliance could have been morally more binding or materially more reliable.

There was a similar interplay, during the decade, of naval competition and the rising temperature of public opinion in both Germany and France. The *Flottenverein* and the Navy League and other promotional bodies in both countries were especially active in these years; the popular sensational Press in both countries missed no chance to publicize the race; and the notion of a prospective war between the two countries became more and more familiar until it seemed almost inevitable. The need to defend heavy military and naval expenditure in the Reichstag and House of Commons occasioned periodic debates about it and elicited ever more exaggerated claims and assertions.[1] British excitement reached the level of panic in March 1909 when a writer in *The Times* commented, 'The people will be quite sane in a fortnight – they always went like this in March.' The cabinet was divided between those who argued that to build four more dreadnoughts would give the British navy a safe margin of superiority in three years' time, and those who demanded six. Winston Churchill has described how the dispute was settled: 'The Admiralty had demanded six: the economists offered four: and we finally compromised on eight.' The Conservatives and the Navy League took up the slogan 'We want eight and we won't wait'. The hysteria did not, however, die down in a fortnight – it lasted through the summer and was

1. See p. 424.

revived in 1911 by the crisis of Agadir.[1] This was followed by the failure of Lord Haldane's mission to Berlin to explore possible terms of conciliation; it took place in 1912, the year that had, from the outset, been dramatized as 'the critical year' when German naval strength might become great enough to challenge British. The Haldane mission foundered on the German Navy Bill of 1912 (which proposed three new battleships and the creation of a third battle squadron) and on German attempts to insist on political equivalents for any naval limitation. Since political equivalents seemed to demand detachment from France and Russia, or at least a pledge of British neutrality amounting to much the same thing, they could not now be given. Its failure was immediately followed by the Anglo-French redistribution of naval strength. In 1913 a French army law raised the period of compulsory service from two years to three, and the Russian army extended military service from three years to three and a half. It was expected that the German army, now also engaged and with great reserves, would amount to a force of five million men of all arms. Between 1912 and 1914, the rival alliances converted themselves into two great armed camps, preparing feverishly and lavishly for battle. Concessions or limitations seemed out of the question.

By 1914 the balance of power in Europe had been so successfully restored that the nicety of its equilibrium was in itself a menace to peace. It was not that any of the great powers had planned this result. Each power, and each of the rival alliances, had consistently aimed not at an equal balance but at preponderance for itself and its allies. Each wanted, above all, to enjoy a margin of preponderance great enough to give it at least security against aggression, at most a superiority that could ensure success for policies of territorial and colonial expansion. In this purpose each had failed, but all had pursued it with such energy and perseverance that close equality of strength was the outcome. As the English liberal journalist, J. A. Spender, put it:

The stage which Europe had reached was that of a semi-internationalism which organized the nations into two groups but provided no bridge between them. There could scarcely have been worse conditions for either peace or war. The equilibrium was so delicate that a puff of wind might destroy it....

It was out of this strange situation that the First World War erupted.

THE CONDITION OF EUROPE IN 1914

The condition of Europe between 1904 and 1914 has often been called 'international anarchy'. In the sense that there existed no form of inter-

1. See p. 521.

national government, the description is accurate enough. Yet there was nothing new in this absence of international government – that was the normal state of Europe; and the phrase, to mean anything specific, must refer more to the behaviour of the powers in these years than to the nature of their relationships. Did governments, in these years, behave more like anarchists than usually – like those violent, destructive, turbulent anarchists who badgered the First and Second Internationals or assassinated so many monarchs and statesmen? While recreating a balance of power in Europe which had been overthrown in 1871, did they abandon all vestiges of that other idea, of a 'concert of Europe' which, as a legacy of the Napoleonic wars, had prevailed in the earlier part of the nineteenth century?

Concert of Europe. Ideas of a 'concert of Europe' were not entirely abandoned. The Congress of Berlin in 1878 was an impressive general conference of all the powers which attempted to settle general European problems in the East.[1] It left all dissatisfied. But the device of general conferences was repeatedly invoked and it was often successful. The Berlin Conference of 1884–5 settled the future of the Congo.[2] The conference of Algeciras in 1906, attended by representatives of all the powers and of several smaller states as well, laid the basis for a settlement of disputes in Morocco. The Conference of London, summoned to settle the problems of the Balkans in 1912, was attended by ambassadors of all the six powers and sat until August 1913.[3] It proved the most successful of all prewar conferences for relaxing tensions between the powers, and as its initiator, Sir Edward Grey, remarked, 'it was as if we all put out anchors to prevent ourselves from being swept away'. But at that late date its very success was a danger. As Grey adds, 'Then the current seemed to slacken and the anchors were pulled up. The Conference was allowed to dissolve. We seemed to be safe.' But the current, strongly set towards the cataract, was as powerful as ever, and no permanent machinery existed which could again be set in motion to resist it. Yet experiments in international organization were an important feature of the prewar years.

Two conferences were held at the Hague in 1899 and 1907. The first, promoted by the Tsar of Russia, whose Finance Minister could not find the money for modernizing Russian artillery, was proposed in order to bring about general disarmament and make provision for the peaceful settlement of disputes. The proposal was received with the greatest scepticism and suspicion by other governments, who detected in it some hidden trick on the part of Russia and even dangers to the peace of

1. See p. 464.   2. See p. 500.
3. See p. 474.

Europe. They contrived to exclude from its agenda all matters of political importance, but left experts to work out innocuous schemes for arbitration. The conference was saved from complete failure by eventual agreement to set up the first permanent court of international arbitration; but recourse to it was to be entirely optional, and even that innovation seemed dangerous. The second Hague conference of 1907, prompted by President Theodore Roosevelt, was less successful, and from the outset it was clear that no proposals for disarmament were likely to get far. The attendance of representatives of the South American states made it more nearly a world conference, representing forty-four states. Britain and the United States disagreed about the question of immunity for private property at sea ('contraband of war'), and Germany, by backing America, manoeuvred Britain into opposing humane proposals.

These first rehearsals for the 'open diplomacy' (or 'diplomacy by conference') of the postwar years were not auspicious. The powers used the occasion not to promote general agreement but to snatch separate tactical advantages. The net gains for internationalism were slender. It was agreed in 1899 to apply the Red Cross Convention of 1864 to naval warfare. A declaration was drawn up 'prohibiting the use of asphyxiating or deleterious gases'; it was ignored by both sides in 1915. The so-called 'Permanent Court' was at first only an agreed framework of rules, a panel of suitable men who might be chosen to act as arbitrators, and a permanent office and secretariat. By 1914 fourteen cases had been settled by the court, including one of political importance between France and Germany about the Casablanca incident in 1909.[1] At least this international institution, which has grown in usefulness to the present day, was a hopeful product of these years of tension. The Hague Conventions defined and regulated methods of intervention by outside parties in disputes between states; and to recognize the possible value of 'good offices and mediation' in settling disputes was to admit that a war anywhere was a matter of concern to others. They provided for international commissions of inquiry, encouraging their use by states engaged in a dispute; and the method was successfully used by Britain and Russia in their dispute of 1904, when the Russian fleet passing through the North Sea fired on British fishing vessels at the Dogger Bank. But even such rudimentary facilities as did exist were not utilized in 1914; there had grown up no habit of persistently seeking peaceful means of settling disputes, no general propensity to substitute for diplomacy anything other than war.

Other steps toward organizing, or at least recognizing the need for,

1. See p. 521.

some agreed code of behaviour had been taken before 1914. The Red Cross Convention signed at Geneva in 1864 has already been mentioned; its aim was to improve conditions for the wounded in time of war. Ten years later the Postal Union was formed; it was the first universal international union to come into being, and since 1897 every civilized nation has belonged to it. From the start its members were pledged to submit to arbitration all disputes that arose from its working. The interdependence of nations came to be recognized in almost every sphere except the political; during the last three quarters of the nineteenth century over a thousand international congresses were held, all to further some form of social of economic cooperation. The Inter-Parliamentary Union originated in 1889, and was permanently organized in 1892; it reflected the drawing together of political groups in all national Parliaments who were pressing for a more thorough organization of peace. The Universal Peace Congresses, a parallel but non-parliamentary body, represented a wider popular passion to remove the tendencies that were regarded as making for war. International organizations of socialists and trade unionists were well-established.[1] Whatever enthusiastic idealism and piecemeal specialized cooperation could achieve, was achieved. Yet all this activity counted as nothing in preventing war in 1914. What constructive internationalism needed in order to succeed was more time in which to change habits of mind and action, and a basic willingness of governments not to reserve for their separate judgement matters which they regarded as 'vital interests'. Neither prerequisite existed before 1914.

Europe in 1914 was not, therefore, in a condition of unusual 'international anarchy'. The notion of a 'concert of Europe', of efforts to reach a consensus of agreement among the major powers about colonial, territorial, and social matters survived in some strength. In many respects there was even more elaborate, frequent, and systematic collaboration among the nations of Europe than ever before in modern history. But upon certain matters – upon the relative strength and sizes of national forces and armaments, upon the need for reliable allies, upon the determination of what constituted vital national interests – every government was adamantly separatist. The most important characteristic of the whole situation was that European nations were passing through a strange, twilight era of mixed systems: not a stabilized balance of power, but a newly recreated and precarious balance of power; not a concert of Europe, but a residual and imperfect concert, with which was blended a system of divisive alliances; not an international community, but only an embryonic international society in

1. See pp. 390 and 418.

which all political and military decisions remained the jealously guarded preserve of separate sovereign states; not anarchy, but semi-anarchy, liable to make the worst of both worlds. In this conjunction of circumstances, marking a unique phase in the historical development of Europe, lies the most fundamental explanation of why the First World War happened.

The Surface of Friction. Into this peculiar conjunction of circumstances there was thrust a convergence of diplomatic and political disputes. As international contacts had increased, so the surface of friction became larger. Colonial disputes, as has been shown, had for the most part been settled before 1914 – though they had left behind them a sediment of imperialist jealousies and ranking grievances, and in their day had contributed to the alienation of Britain from Germany, and of Italy from France. Two inter-state feuds overshadowed all others by 1914. One was the duel between Britain and Germany for naval power: the other was the violence of hatred between Austria-Hungary and Serbia, bequeathed by the later phase of the Eastern Question. Each of these leading issues was flanked by another. To the Anglo-German was added the older feud between France and Germany. France saw, in Germany's bid for adding supremacy at sea to her existing superiority of military and economic power in Europe, a threat to all prospect of ever recovering the lost provinces of Alsace-Lorraine and even to French national independence on the continent. To the Austro-Serbian was added the older Austro-Russian feud for influence in the Balkan peninsula and in the rapidly disintegrating territories of the Ottoman Empire. This combination of issues, knit inextricably together by the hardening system of rival alliances which was the final outcome of the old diplomacy, yielded a more explosive compound than could be contained within the mixed structure of international relations.

It is probable that the single chance of preventing a general war in 1914 lay in keeping separate the less dynamic and more conciliable disputes of western Europe, and the highly explosive conflicts between dynastic states and erupting nationalism in eastern Europe. Further wars in the Balkans, even involving Austria-Hungary, seemed almost unavoidable. There was occurring one of those great fundamental upheavals of history which have usually entailed considerable violence. That it was not localized was due mainly to the policy of Germany, both in lending unconditional support to Austria and in her habits of brutal diplomacy, which evoked fears and counter-alliances. Germany's crucial central position on the continent and her immense power laid upon her a special responsibility for trying to keep the peace. Far from assuming this responsibility, her government indulged in a restless policy which disturbed the peace. Yet her quarrels with the western powers had none of that quality of historic doom which many have seen in the Eastern Question. Even four years of war brought changes in western Europe which were only marginal and local compared with the drastic transformation of the whole of eastern Europe and the Balkans.[1] It is in linking eastern upheavals with western quarrels, and in preventing the localization of Balkan wars, that German policy and the system of rival alliances which was its nemesis share a special responsibility for the coming of the First World War. By 1914 the sick man of Europe was no longer just Turkey: it was Europe itself, feverish and turbulent, and with strong suicidal tendencies.

How, finally, are these tendencies related to the internal developments of the European nations between 1871 and 1914 (previously described in Part V)? What connexions are there between the growth of democracy and socialism after 1871 and the accumulation of circumstances which led to war? The states that went to war in 1914 had experienced half a century of rapid expansion in population, wealth, and power. The 'age of the masses' had come upon Europe, transforming the foundations, structure, and working of the modern state; and revolutionizing, too, the outlook, expectations, and social loyalties of men and women everywhere. By 1914 this double process was far from complete even in the countries of western and central Europe, and it was only beginning in most of eastern Europe and Asia. The consequence of the incompleteness of industrialization and democracy was a universal surge of social unrest and violence manifest in the great strikes and conflicts of group loyalties. The growth of world trade made nations more economically interdependent than ever before, but the autarchic, protectionist measures of powerful states opposed this tendency. State activity in providing social services and security was at variance with the claims of labour organizations, socialist parties, and churches alike to attract human loyalties that would transcend state frontiers and national allegiances. Huge capitalist organizations had international ramifications in a world where there were no international political institutions. Economics and politics were more closely inter-related than ever before, yet the structure of economic life was nowhere correlated with the structure of political life. These conditions led to a widespread challenge to the cohesion and integrity of national states, which explains the conflict of loyalties and much of the moral and spiritual crisis of the prewar decade.[2] By 1914 the governments of Europe commanded a concentration of economic resources, political authority, adminstrative and mili-

1. See p. 628.
2. See pp. 409–27.

tary power, which none of their predecessors had enjoyed. Yet this power had about it a certain fragility, evidenced by the imminence of a general strike in the United Kingdom in the summer of 1914, the turbulence of political life in most countries, and the prevalence of uncontrolled and unpredictable violence throughout Europe. The established authorities were everywhere subject to a recurrent challenge which struck at the roots of their power – the challenge of mass revulsion against the exacting disciplines of industrial urban civilization. They sat on domestic as well as international volcanoes.

To this precariousness of apparently formidable power a further complication was added by disruptive nationalism. The Irish and the Flemish separatist movements in western Europe were more than matched by the insurgent nationalism of eastern Europe and the Balkans.[1] The dynastic states of the East were immediately and fundamentally threatened by these movements, and by one of them in particular: the Serbian. That is why a collision between Austria-Hungary and Serbia could bring general war. Serbia was the focal point of a triple conflict: that between dynastic imperialism and insurgent nationalism; that between Pan-Germanism and Pan-Slavism; and that between Triple Alliance and Triple *Entente*. This threefold importance explains why assassinations at Sarajevo could precipitate a world war.

Sarajevo, 1914. After the death in 1903 of the pro-Austrian king of Serbia, Alexander Obrenovitch, the Habsburgs faced the third great historic challenge of nationalism to the survival of their multi-national Empire. The political and military leaders of Vienna, led by Berchtold and Conrad, saw in Serbia another Piedmont and another Prussia. In 1859, confronted with the movement for Italian unification, the Habsburgs had been defeated and driven out of Italy by Piedmont. In 1866, faced with the movement for German unification, they had been defeated and driven out of Germany by Prussia.[2] Now, by 1914, there had emerged a comparable movement for national unification of all Slav peoples south of the Danube – that is, within Austria, Hungary, and Bosnia, and within Serbia, Montenegro, and Turkey. The natural leader of this movement was Serbia, a small country of only five million people, but with the independence, energy, and drive to make itself the nucleus of a future Yugoslavia. In 1908 Austria's annexation of Bosnia and Herzegovina had caused a six months' crisis, and had started a continuous drift towards war, because it made clear Austria's intention to check the movement even by annexations.[3] In Vienna Serbian inde-

1. See pp. 476–88. 2. See pp. 300–320.
3. See p. 472.

pendence seemed the latest and greatest historic threat to Habsburg power, and Austrian policy was obsessed by the urge to crush Serbia at all costs.

Serbia also occupied a key position in the clash between Pan-Germanism and Pan-Slavism. Germanic influence was already great in Turkey. Rumania was Austria's ally, and Bulgaria wanted to be. With Serbia, too, under German-Austrian control, Pan-German influence could prevail continuously from Berlin to Baghdad and the *Drang nach Osten* could proceed in favourable conditions. But an independent and restless Serbia, arousing and attracting Pan-Slav sentiments and winning Russian support against Austria, disrupted this whole picture.

Moreover, Serbia was not only the sorest thorn in Habsburg flesh, and an impediment to Pan-German designs; she was also the spearhead of western *Entente* influence in the Balkans. So long as she could be maintained as an independent state, Constantinople could be kept open to pressure from the *Entente* powers, and the extensive French and British interests in the Middle East would be more securely protected. She was a most useful wedge in the German-Austrian-Turkish combination. The crisis caused by Sarajevo was, therefore, a trial of strength between the two grand alliances, not merely between Belgrade and Vienna.

Incongruously enough, the incident that brought war was the murder of the heir to the Habsburg throne by a fanatic whose connexion with the Serbian government could not be proven. There was no reason intrinsically why such an incident should necessitate war between Austria and Serbia. That it did so was due to the policy followed by Vienna. The Archduke Franz Ferdinand had liberal-minded plans for a federal reorganization of the Dual Monarchy, which involved appealing for the support of the southern Slavs against the ruling Magyar minority. Since the aim of fervent Serbian patriots was a southern Slav state completely outside the Dual Monarchy, they regarded with great animosity any plan for prolonging German rule over Slavs. After the Balkan Wars of 1912–13 the Austrian government was confronted with even more positive nationalist agitation for a 'greater Serbia', to include all Slavs south of the Danube and so involving disruption of the Habsburg Empire. That Russian Pan-Slav ambitions lay behind this agitation they had no doubts. They resolved to tolerate no further Serbian gains. When the Archduke and his wife, visiting the Bosnian capital of Sarajevo on 28 June, on a mission intended to win its good will, were fired at and killed by the Austrian Serb, Gavrilo Princip, Vienna regarded the murders as Serbian provocation of war.

The Austrian ministerial council sent to Belgrade on 23 July an ultimatum drafted in terms that were calculated to make its rejection certain. They demanded a reply within forty-eight hours. The demands meant the end of Serbian independence. No restraining hand was extended from Berlin. The Kaiser, on the contrary, assured the Austrian Emperor that he understood the need 'of freeing your Serbian frontiers from their heavy pressure'. The Serbian reply was unexpectedly conciliatory, and went so far towards meeting Austria's demands that even the Kaiser, suddenly filled with misgivings, hailed it with relief because 'with it every ground for war disappears'. In Vienna it was none the less rejected, and war was declared on 28 July. The Russians had advised Serbia to comply; Grey had offered to mediate. But Berchtold was bent upon war, and he lit the fuse when no one had time to extinguish it. From that decisive act everything else followed. Russia ordered general mobilization on 30 July, Germany on 31 July; and Germany declared war against Russia on 1 August, against France on 3 August. Germany's ultimatum to Belgium on 3 August, and its rejection as being a violation of Belgian neutrality, ensured Britain's entry into the war the following day. The bonds of the alliances held firm, and the two armed camps clashed in open battle at last. The British Foreign Secretary, Sir Edward Grey, was a patient devotee of fishing and of wild-bird life, and the gentle amenities of a stable and civilized society. That evening, as he looked out from the windows of the Foreign Office in London, this English country gentleman spoke words that have echoed plaintively down the years. 'The lamps,' he said, 'are going out all over Europe; we shall not see them lit again in our lifetime.'

PART SEVEN

WAR AND PEACE
1914–23

THE war which began in 1914, and which was to last for four years and three months, was in many ways entirely novel in human history. Previous wars, such as the French revolutionary and Napoleonic wars, had involved as many states and had lasted longer. In every decade since 1815 there had been a war somewhere, and thirteen separate wars had been waged in Europe itself, not counting wars fought by European states outside Europe. But if there had not been general peace, there had been no general war. This was the first general conflict between the highly organized states of the twentieth century, able to command the energies of all their citizens, to mobilize the productive capacity of modern industries, and to call upon the resources of modern technology to find new methods of destruction and of defence. It was the first war on a scale large enough to dislocate that international economy which had grown up during the nineteenth century, the first between European nations which collectively controlled most of the rest of the world. It was fought with determination and desperation, because belligerents believed at first that they fought for survival, and later that they fought for high ideals; it was fought in Europe to a point of exhaustion or collapse, and with unprecedented destruction, because the two sides were so evenly matched and had for so long prepared for battle; it was fought on land and above land, on sea and under the sea, for the coming of tank and aeroplane, dreadnought and submarine, made warfare three-dimensional. New resources of economic and even psychological warfare were tapped; for since it was the first war of the masses, a war between whole peoples and not merely between armies and navies, industrial production and civilian morale became of great importance. Generalship on both sides found itself constantly outmoded by the novelties of this kind of warfare, and victories were won as much by the miscalculations of the enemy as by superior insight or strategy. There were times when leaders, civilian and military alike, were literally at their wits' end to keep any control over the course of events.

Those who had expected a general war to be anything like the selective and localized wars of Bismarck could not have been more completely wrong. This war between the grand alliances had many of the qualities of a Frankenstein monster. The accumulation and release of so much concentrated power proved to be not only more destructive of human life and material than any previous wars, but also to be more uncontrollable in its consequences, and completely incalculable in its aftermath. Once begun, war ran its remorseless course of insatiable demands for human sacrifice, discipline, organization, and ingenuity, until it became almost an end in itself. Bismarck's wars had been instruments of precision for attaining diplomatic and political ends, and rested on policies of limited liability and specific objectives. The 'Great War', as it quickly came to be called, got so utterly out of hand as an instrument of policy that it demanded unlimited liability. Its original objectives were soon overlaid with many others which had scarcely been considered when it began. Even the avowed aims of belligerents changed as its course was prolonged, and its outcome was quite different from either the original or the subsequent aims of either side. For this reason it is especially important to keep sharply distinct the war aims originally involved, the peace aims that came to be involved before it ended, and the consequences that are now known to have flowed from it. Its greatest novelty, historically, was a remarkable disparity between the ends sought, the price paid, and the results obtained.

CHAPTER 22

ISSUES AND STAKES, 1914-18

THE WAR AIMS OF 1914

WHEN the Empire of Austria-Hungary went to war with Serbia and when Russia mobilized on Serbia's side, the nineteenth-century Eastern Question reached its culmination. In the views of the men in power at Vienna, it was a war to end Serbian threats to the integrity of the Habsburg Empire and to resist Russian Pan-Slav ambitions in the Balkans and eastern Europe. It was, in this sense, regarded as a war of defence, an ordeal necessary for the survival of a dynastic state. For Serbia, too, since her decision to accept so readily the devastating terms of Austria's ultimatum had been countered nevertheless by a declaration of war, it was also primarily a war of national defence. Behind it, however, lay the sort of demand which the nineteenth century had made popular and respectable: for the national unification and self-determination of all southern Slavs. The initial struggle for Serbia was yet another of the many nineteenth-century struggles between dynasticism and nationalism, and as such it attracted the traditional liberal sympathies of western European nations. The paradox was that the cause of Serbian nationalism was supported by the illiberal dynastic government of Russia, whose aim was to preserve independent Slav states as an obstruction to Austro-German influence in the Balkans. This paradox prevented, from the start, any clear ideological alignment of the powers. The condition of alliances in 1914 placed the western parliamentary democracies of France and Great Britain in the same camp as autocratic Russia; just as it made ill-assorted allies of the German national Reich with its ultramodern economy and efficient military organization, and ramshackle, multi-national, antiquated Austria-Hungary; and before long Turkey of the Young Turks. None of the powers in 1914 was more than a semi-democratic state, in that none rested on truly universal suffrage. But since the presence or absence of democratic institutions was not one of the differentials between the belligerents, democratic ideals were not a war aim in 1914. The only war aims were self-defence and victory.

When war began in 1914, it was essentially a war between great powers (see Map 13). Of the smaller states, only Serbia and Belgium were implicated, in both cases because they were attacked by great powers. Italy kept out for nearly a year, and Portugal had to be discouraged by Britain from entering the war on her side. Rumania, despite her treaty of 1883 with the Triple Alliance, had territorial claims against both Russia (in Bessarabia) and Hungary (in Transylvania), and Russia encouraged her in a policy of 'benevolent neutrality' by promising Bessarabia as a reward. Turkey, afraid that the *Entente* powers would partition her, tempted by a German alliance that would keep her territory intact, and under powerful German and pro-German influences, joined the German side. On 1 November the three *Entente* powers declared war on Turkey, whose closing of the Straits – the Bosporus and the Dardanelles – cut off the main flow of western supplies to Russia. Henceforth Russia was the weakest partner in the Triple *Entente*, for the alternative supply routes of Archangel and later Murmansk were no real substitute. Russia was forced on to the defensive for lack of supplies to equip her armies. The war in its first phase took the shape of a war between the central European powers of Germany and Austria-Hungary, flanked by Turkey, and the western maritime powers of France, the British Empire, and Belgium, supported defensively in the east by Russia and Serbia. Of the overseas self-governing dominions, Canada, Australia, and New Zealand assured Britain of their support before war was declared. The South African government of General Botha promised only that the Union would defend itself, but it alone had Germans on its frontier in German South-west Africa, which South African troops promptly invaded and conquered. Thereafter they also fought in German East Africa and in France. In Ireland the Ulster Volunteers and some of the Irish Volunteers dropped plans for fighting each other and joined the British armies that were setting out to fight Germany.[1] The colonies of Britain, France, and Belgium were automatically at war, and since collectively these included India and nearly all of Africa, they served as a rich reservoir of resources and manpower. Because it was a war of great powers, it was from the start much more than a European war: the spread of Europeans over the globe during the previous century meant that war between them now embraced nearly every continent. In August 1914 Japan also declared war on Germany and overran the German Pacific islands and territorial concessions in China. The war brought her great opportunities for aggrandizement and trade, with the result that Japan emerged in 1919 as a powerful industrial and commercial Empire, hungry for expansion in the Far East and formidable in her naval strength.

Original Issues. The sequence of events with which the war began helped to determine its original issues. The German ultimatum to Belgium, followed by its very proper rejection and the invasion of Belgium

1. See p. 416.

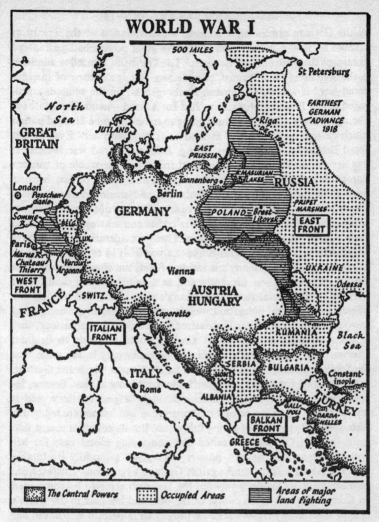

MAP 13. THE FIRST WORLD WAR

The map shows the strategic central position of the powers of the Triple Alliance, but also their disadvantage, in a war against the Triple Entente, of having to fight a land war on two fronts. Except for the Balkans, the main battlefields lay in the three heavily shaded areas of the West, Italian, and East fronts. The small area of the West front was for four years the scene of land battles which cost all participants immense casualties; on the East front, though the Germans penetrated Russia as far as the dotted lines, they did not compel the Russians to make peace until March 1918 (at Brest-Litovsk). By then United States forces and supplies were pouring into the West front.

by the German armies on 4 August, was a violation of the Treaty of London of 1839 in which each of the five great powers had guaranteed to respect the neutrality of Belgium.[1] The German Chancellor admitted in the Reichstag on 4 August, 'Gentlemen, this is a breach of international law.' It was he (Bethmann Hollweg) who on the same day protested to the British ambassador, 'Just for a word – neutrality – just for a scrap of paper, Great Britain is going to make war on a kindred nation which desired nothing better than to be friends with her.' Even in this detail Bethmann Hollweg was wrong. Britain declared war because it was her traditional policy and interest to prevent the whole of western Europe from falling under the domination of a single power; because since 1900 she had abandoned isolation, and made an *entente* with France and Russia in order to preserve some balance of power in Europe; because since 1912 the defence of her coasts and seaways depended on close naval cooperation with France. These considerations would have brought Britain into a general European war in 1914 even had Belgium not been invaded. Germany's invasion of Belgium simply ensured that Britain entered the war promptly and as a united country, and for an obviously good moral reason. Germany's cynical decision to violate a solemn international obligation was defended on diverse grounds: that it would have been militarily disastrous to await a French attack, that it was a strategic necessity, that amends would be made to Belgium afterwards. It was, in truth, a strategic necessity only in the sense that the Schlieffen Plan, officially adopted in 1912, upon which the German generals relied for achieving a swift knockout blow against France, involved swinging the German armies through Belgian territory; and it was a necessity because no other German plan had been prepared which seemed equally capable of giving this result. But its adoption meant that from the first Germany forfeited any convincing moral case for her policy, whereas the western powers were given a morally irrefutable case for taking a firm stand against German aggression. This sacrifice of morality to expediency was not the last such error to be committed by German leaders in the course of the war, and her lack in the world's eyes of an ethically righteous cause proved an important element in her downfall. The most enthusiastic champions of Germany could never claim that Belgium invaded Germany in 1914.

For Belgium, France, and Britain, as for Serbia and Russia, it was therefore a war of self-defence. The Russians fought to keep Austria out of the Balkans and to preserve free passage of the Straits upon which Russia's economic life was felt to depend. France regarded her alliance with Russia as the lifeline of her national independence and of her sur-

1. See p. 170.

vival as a European power. Britain regarded the independence of Belgium and France as providing so vital a safeguard for the security of her own shores that she must fight to preserve it. For Austria-Hungary and Turkey, as already shown, it was also looked upon as a war necessary for their own defence. Germany, likewise, pleaded that she could not afford to risk encirclement by France and Russia, and that solidarity with Austria-Hungary was the cornerstone of her whole position in Europe. This plea lost something of its plausibility in the light of her prewar policy and of her cynical behaviour in 1914. Yet it is probable that most people in most belligerent countries in 1914 genuinely felt that they were fighting for vital national interests which could not be sacrificed without incurring a fatal loss of independence or defensive security. It was the climax to a decade of fear that the greater the power, the more acutely afraid it was of losing friends and allies or of seeing its enemies gain weight in the scales of power. 'Militarism run stark mad' was the comment of the American Colonel House in May 1914. A better word might be panic. Fear, rather than greed or idealism, dominated the decisions of all the powers in 1914.

The First Campaigns, 1914. Because the outbreak of general war marked, in itself, the breakdown of the old diplomacy and of the concert of Europe, and represented the bankruptcy of statemanship, its immediate result was the surrender of control to the professional soldiers and sailors. The German Reichstag, having voted war credits, dispersed and abdicated power to the soldiers. Policy was replaced for a time by technique, and the transition from peace to war meant the submission of governments and nations alike to the technical necessities of mobilization, transport, supplies, and strategic dispositions. The hasty Russian decree of general mobilization on 30 July was prompted not by considerations of diplomacy but by the need to start promptly what was known to be a slow process; German violation of Belgian neutrality was dictated not by policy but by the strategic requirements of the Schlieffen Plan; so, too, French policy became immediately governed by the need to mobilize all her reserves and concentrate them on her vulnerable eastern frontier. Only Britain, given time by her island position and her reliance upon the front-line defence of sea power, relied upon voluntary enlistment and indulged in more leisurely preparation for war. Few foretold that the war would last for years. The pattern of Bismarck's brief, incisive campaigns still dominated military thinking. Six months was a favourite guess. This sort of war seemed too much like an explosion or a volcanic eruption to last longer. A war of attrition was the last thing most governments prepared for, so that after the first six months improvisation became the keynote of strategy.

The object of the Schlieffen Plan, which the German High Command put into operation as soon as war began, was the rapid and total defeat of France by the seizure of Paris and the northern industrial provinces. Its mechanical design was the advance of German armies in a hammer-swing down through Belgium into northern France, hinging on the fortress of Metz in the east. Its success depended upon the surprise overrunning of Belgium and upon having sufficient weight in the hammer head to sweep all before it in the descent upon Paris. Its success was crucial to the whole of German strategy to meet war on two fronts. It would forestall British military action in Europe; and meanwhile, in the East, a small German force and the Austro-Hungarian armies could, it was hoped, keep the Russians at bay for at least six weeks. Evolved with immense care, the plan was admirably suited to the terrain. The eastern Franco-German frontier was unsuitable for the deployment of large forces and for rapid advance, since it was mostly woods and hills and had been well fortified by the French. Further westward the plains of Belgium and northern France offered good facilities for massive advance and rapid movement, and there French fortifications were less formidable. The hammer head was to pass to the west of Paris, and encircle it from the south. The French armies, trapped between Paris and the Vosges in the east, would be enveloped or driven across to Alsace, where fresh German forces lay in wait for them. The whole operation would be completed in six weeks, and Germany left free to deal with a Russia weakened financially and morally by French collapse. There her internal lines of communication and her excellent network of railways would be a decisive advantage. It was a brilliant plan, and the German government pinned all its hopes on its complete success. Yet six weeks later it had decisively failed, and the war became one of attrition.

The explanation for this failure of Germany's first war aim, the collapse of France, was complex. The younger von Moltke, German chief of staff, possibly foredoomed it to failure when he decided to weaken the hammer head in order to strengthen the hinge. He was anxious to prevent a French invasion of Lorraine. The initial resistance of the Belgian army probably delayed the German timetable by two or three days, which had some importance. The attack, launched on 4 August, led to the fall of Brussels, the Belgian capital, on 20 August, and of Namur, a key point on French defence, five days later. The British Expeditionary Force, rushed across the Channel, reached Mons on 22 August. But after rear-guard actions it was driven back, along with the French, until they were nearly cut off from the Channel ports. The force behind von Moltke's hammer was now further weakened, for he detached two corps to hold back the Belgian army at Antwerp, and another two were sent to the Russian front. But by 28 August he concluded that the plan could be completed. He ordered his most westerly first army (under von Kluck) to advance and encircle Paris to the west, the second (under Bülow) to advance directly against Paris, and the third to advance in step with them. In the course of the advance the whole purpose of the plan was wrecked by Bülow. Without consulting headquarters, he persuaded the first and third armies to close in to his support. This caused all three armies to pass well to the east of Paris, for the hammer shaft was shortened in length as it swung. The French generals, Joffre and Gallieni, seized their opportunity to launch a ferocious offensive to the flank of the German armies, and in September, at the Battle of the Marne, they fought the most decisive action of the whole war. The German High Command, still far away in Luxembourg, lost control of the situation. The army commanders on the spot, confused by contradictory orders, withdrew first to the Marne and then still further north to the Aisne. Paris was saved, the plan had failed. Though Antwerp fell, the allies held the Channel ports at the first Battle of Ypres (October-November) and so kept open the flow of British help to France. That autumn both sides dug themselves into trenches, and a deathly stalemate was established which neither side was able to break until 1918.

There was a technical reason, too, for this early conversion of what had been expected to be a war of rapid movement into one of immobility. Warfare had entered upon a phase when defence had caught up with offence. The machine gun and heavy artillery came into use, while motor transport and aviation was still in their infancy and the tank had not yet been invented. Prussia's striking victories of the 1860s had been won by means of artillery and superiority in organization, combined with use of the railways for speedy mobilization and movement.[1] Masses of men entrenched even in open ground behind entanglements of barbed wire, and able to put up the defensive screen of rapid gunfire made possible by the machine gun, could now hold out against cavalry and bayonet charges. They could be driven back only after prolonged pounding by heavy siege howitzers. Troops advancing over ground ploughed up by such pounding were at every disadvantage. Behind the first entrenchments they found others, likewise strongly defended, and the process of heavy pounding had to begin all over again. For this reason the battles of the western front were all fought within a comparatively small area less than two hundred miles long, and the names of the same towns and rivers recur as the battle line swayed to and fro. Slight gains were made at immensely disproportionate costs. The productive capacities of

1. See p. 317.

the two sides were, until 1917, so equal that each could make and transport to the front quantities of guns and supplies large enough to keep the two forces locked in close battle. Mobility became possible again only with the tank and the aeroplane, and only in the final phases of the war was either used in large numbers.

Meanwhile events on the Russian front had contributed to this situation, despite great German victories. Russia began the war with two unexpected advantages. Her mobilization moved faster than anyone had dared hope; and her Commander-in-Chief, the grand duke Nicholas, had learned the war plans of Austria-Hungary from Slav officers in Habsburg service. With these advantages Russian forces invaded Galicia and could spare two strong armies for the invasion of East Prussia. Generals Paul von Hindenburg and Erich von Ludendorff were sent to repulse them. In August and September they won devastating victories against Russia at the battles of Tannenberg and the Masurian Lakes, killing or capturing a quarter of a million Russians. Yet the Russian threat caused the diversion of two German army corps from France at the critical moment of the western campaign, and Russia's victories against Austria-Hungary in Galicia partly offset her reverses in East Prussia. By the end of the year, despite two great attacks by von Hindenburg on Warsaw, and by the Russians on Silesia and Cracow, stalemate was also reached on the eastern front. The dreaded Russian 'steam roller' had been halted, and henceforth its major contribution was to immobilize large numbers of German and Austro-Hungarian troops when they were sorely needed for fresh efforts in the West. In December the grand duke Nicholas had to tell his allies that, since Russia's munitions were exhausted, she must now stand on the defensive.

Elsewhere the war was equally inconclusive at the end of 1914. Serbians repulsed the Austrians in November, retaking Belgrade. But when they then advanced into southern Hungary, they were checked. The German High Seas Fleet stayed in harbour, but powerful forces of the British fleet were immobilized by the need to keep it in harbour. Rumania and Italy clung to a precarious neutrality. The failure of German and Austrian plans for quick victories meant that siege warfare, in various forms, superseded momentous battles. General war in Europe proved to be an exceptionally dreary deadlock. It favoured the western allies in one respect. Since the aims of the Dual Alliance had now been frustrated, and both France and Russia had held the main onslaught, time was likely to work in favour of the Triple *Entente*. Above all, the immense war potential of the British Commonwealth and of the overseas Empires of the western powers now had time to be brought into operation. The grip of the British naval blockade could be tightened. Germany, left by the campaign of 1914 in occupation of Belgium and northern France, was committed to continuing a war of conquest in the West. She was left, also, with the fact of war on two fronts – the old Bismarckian nightmare. But so feeble was concerted action between Russia and her western allies that there was no plan for combined operations or a common war policy. Each side, committed to a long holding action and to a war of unlimited liabilities, had to redouble its efforts to achieve very indecisive results.

For all these reasons, in the first six months of war none of the belligerents had achieved its initial war aims. Germany had not crushed France or even Belgium, but neither of them had kept Germans off their soil; Austria-Hungary had not crushed Serbia, but Russia had not made decisive gains against Austria-Hungary or Germany; neither Britain nor Germany had seriously damaged the other's naval strength. Each fought for victory, but what they had achieved collectively was the one result that none expected or wanted – a prolonged struggle of exhaustion. From this basic situation, at the beginning of 1915, much of the eventual character of the war and its aftermath was to flow. In the quest for circuitous ways to break the deadlock both sides were to spread the field of conflict ever wider, both geographically and politically. As each mobilized more and more of its resources of production and manpower for the struggle, so the acids of hatred bit deeper into national life, and the prospects of rational control over the course of events and of their outcome receded. Each fought desperately, because the only alternative was total defeat. Nobody talked yet of peace aims, because peace seemed too far off. The war became a primordial struggle for survival, of gigantic proportions.

Count von Moltke concentrated nearly two million men for his initial attack in the West. The Belgian army that took the first shock of this attack numbered some 210,000. France could muster about one million semi-professional troops for her first-line defence. The British Expeditionary Force numbered about 160,000, but it was the most highly trained fighting force of any country. Russia, which could mobilize more men than any other state, could put one and a half million into the field, Austria-Hungary could muster two million. Once it became plain that it was to be a war of attrition, what mattered was the war potential of the two sides. In potential manpower Germany rated nine and three quarter million against France's six million, since her population was twenty-five million more than the French. Russia's eventual potential was incalculable but immense, though her chronic deficiencies of equipment greatly diminished this advantage. In 1914 competition in armaments had obliged the powers to spend increasing proportions of their national incomes on preparation for war. Their army estimates for 1914, in millions of pounds sterling, were: Germany 88·4; France 39·4; Great Britain 29·4; Austria-Hungary 28·6; Russia 64·8. Their naval estimates were: Germany 22·4; France 18; Great Britain 47·4; Austria-Hungary 7·6; Russia 23·6. Even in peacetime Austria-Hungary and Russia were each spending more than six per cent of their national incomes on armaments; Germany and France, more than four and a half per cent; Great Britain, nearly three and a half per cent. Prolonged war with heavy casualties forced each belligerent to drain itself of both reserves and resources, and impoverished Europe as a whole in relation to the rest of the world. If it began as a war of self-defence and continued after 1914 as a struggle for survival, salvation could be won only at the price of exhaustion, both human and material. Such were the stakes in the struggles that went on through the years 1915 and 1916.

THE DYNAMICS OF DEADLOCK, 1915-16

At the beginning of 1915, though Germany suffered war on two fronts, she fought in effect two separate enemies. There was little coordination between them, beyond the agreement of Russia and her western allies that neither would make a separate peace. In response to Turkey's entry into the war in November 1914, and to the Russian plea that supplies were exhausted. Britain projected an attack on the Dardanelles which might relieve Turkish pressure on the Caucasus and reopen the supply route to Russia through the Straits. Urged by Winston Churchill as First Lord of the Admiralty, against the opposition of the French, who deplored any diversion of forces away from the western front, a strong Anglo-French naval expedition was sent to the Dardanelles in March 1915. In the same month Britain made a secret treaty with Russia promising her the Straits and Constantinople. The expedition failed in its purpose, and the following month an Allied landing on the Gallipoli peninsula met with such firm Turkish resistance that it had to be given up after great losses of men and materials.

The War at Sea. A more hopeful attempt to open up a new arena was the imposition of the naval blockade on Germany and her allies. Abandoning all distinction between contraband and noncontraband goods (i.e., between munitions and materials of war which could properly be seized, and foodstuffs and other raw materials which should not), France and Britain stopped the shipping of all goods destined for Germany and her allies. Neutral shipping was prevented from making for German ports and was required to stop at Allied ports to have its cargoes examined. Neutral countries were restricted even in their own imports, where these might find their way into Germany by land. The purpose was to starve the enemy and wreck his economy. So great was Anglo-French naval power that it was able to enforce these measures against Dutch, Scandinavian, and even American shipping. This evoked vehement protests, from the United States in particular. She proclaimed the rights of neutrals and 'freedom of the seas', though after she entered the war in 1917 she joined in applying the same measures. American opinion was outraged even more by the consequences of German efforts to counter-blockade Britain by means of mines and submarines. In February 1915 the Germans declared the western approaches to the British Isles to be a zone of war, into which neutral vessels entered at their own risk. Mines were laid, so that passages had to be cleared by mine sweepers. Submarines proved to be a powerful weapon against British maritime strength, and it was a long time before effective protection against them could be devised. In April 1915 a German submarine torpedoed off the Irish coast the British liner *Lusitania*, carrying some munitions of war. Of the 1,200 people drowned, 118 were United States citizens, and President Woodrow Wilson warned Germany that any repetition of such an act would be treated as 'deliberately unfriendly'. This deterred Germany, for the next two years, from unrestricted submarine warfare. It was her return to it in 1917 which provoked the American declaration of war.

Apart from the constant tussle of the blockade and counterblockade, the deadlock of the war at sea was broken only once in 1916, by the Battle of Jutland, and then only temporarily. This strange naval battle, the only major battle of the war between capital ships, seemed to be a minor German success but proved to be a major British victory. The British Grand Fleet, stationed at Scapa Flow and Rosyth, kept guard over the German High Seas Fleet, at anchor behind mine fields in the German North Sea ports. Admirals, unlike generals, refused to give battle unless they were certain of the initial advantage. The naval deadlock arose because the admirals on both sides waited for this initial advantage, which never came. The Germans relied upon mines, torpedoes, and minor naval actions to weaken the British fleet to a point where decisive action might be undertaken with some clear prospect of success. British strategy was guided by the doctrine of 'the fleet in being' – that to maintain supremacy at sea was even more important than defeating the German fleet in battle. Therefore, while no chances were to be lost of inflicting damage, no risks of large-scale defeat could be taken. As Churchill put it, the commander of the Grand Fleet, Admiral Jellicoe was 'the only man on either side who could lose the war in an afternoon'.

The Battle of Jutland was provoked by Admiral Scheer, under pressure of the tightening blockade, in an effort to destroy at least part of the Grand Fleet. Admiral Hipper was sent with a decoy force. The British Admiralty, enjoying the great advantage of knowing the German signal code since August 1914, was able to order the Grand Fleet to sea in good time. On the afternoon of 31 May 1916, a German scouting force of battle and light cruisers under Admiral Hipper made contact with Admiral Beatty's force of comparable strength. Things went badly for the British force, which lost two ships, but the engagement brought the two great fleets under Scheer and Jellicoe rushing to the scene. When after several hours of cautious manoeuvring and occasional contacts night fell, the German ships had inflicted heavier losses than they had suffered. In return for one battleship, one battle cruiser, four light cruisers, and five destroyers sunk by the British, they had destroyed three battle cruisers, three armoured cruisers, and eight destroyers. In officers and men the Germans lost 2,545, the British 6,097. But under cover of darkness the German ships retreated behind mine fields, and at dawn on 1 June the Grand Fleet sailed an empty sea. In August, Scheer made a further bid to lure it into an ambush of submarines, but again he failed. It was all a strange anticlimax to the quarter century of bitter Anglo-German rivalry for naval supremacy which, in itself, had helped to bring about war. Two and a half years later the German Fleet bloodlessly surrendered. Most of it was scuttled by its own crews at Scapa Flow to forestall humiliation.

Deadlock on Land. The deadlock on land, throughout 1915 and 1916, was little affected by the entry of other powers into the war. In April 1915 Italy made with the Allies the secret Treaty of London, which in return for her entry against Austria-Hungary promised her the Trentino and southern Tyrol, Istria and the city of Trieste, and some of the Dalmatian islands in the Adriatic. If Turkey were partitioned, she was to have, in addition, Adalia in Asia Minor; if Britain and France took Germany's African colonies, then Italy would gain colonial territories in Libya and Somaliland. Italy declared war on Austria-Hungary in May 1915; but she did not declare war on Germany until August 1916. She became a belligerent, with great hesitancy on the part of her political leaders and considerable reluctance among her people. Her decision came too late to relieve the pressure of the Austro-German offensive against Russia, and her contribution proved inadequate to turn Germany's flank on the Austro-Italian frontier. In any case the military gains of her accession were offset in October 1915 by the entry of Bulgaria on the other side. In August 1916 Rumania, too, entered the fighting after bargaining with France and Russia to gain Transylvania, the

Bukovina, and the Banat.[1] She proved as much of a liability as an asset, for in November she was overrun by the Germans and Austrians. Her valuable resources of wheat and oil fell into German hands, except for the oil wells hastily destroyed by British agents. A further Allied attempt to open up an important fighting front in the Balkans came to disaster. An Anglo-French expeditionary force was landed in Greece at Salonica in October 1915, and although it stayed there for the rest of the war and tied up nearly a quarter of a million troops, Serbia was overrun, and the Allies made no important headway. By the end of 1916 the war had spread over the whole of the Balkans and Italy. The Central Powers in alliance formed a solid continental *bloc* stretching from Antwerp to Constantinople. The Allies still, however, held the peripheral ring, from the Channel ports eastwards to Salonica, and the stranglehold of the blockade was beginning to reduce the enemy's stamina.

It was on the two great land fronts, in Russia and in France, that the most tense and deadly parts of the struggle were fought. In 1915 General Falkenhayn, successor to von Moltke, decided to concentrate upon Russia. Germany could stand on the defensive in the West, and Allied attacks could be made excessively costly. Russia was the weakest of the Allies, and he wanted to make Austria-Hungary safe from Russia before Italy could attack her from the south. He launched a vigorous offensive against the Russian front near Cracow and in May pierced the line and routed the Russians with immense losses. Warsaw fell in August and the Russians were rolled back out of Poland. Within a month the front was pressed further back to the Bukovina and Carpathians, and all Russian pressure was taken off Austria-Hungary. Serbia, too, was occupied and its army routed. The British and French launched heavy attacks in the West, partly in order to take advantage of Germany's concentration in the East and partly to relieve the pressure on Russia. But they failed to break through the German lines and suffered some 250,000 casualties – double the German number. On the Russian front mobility had been restored, mainly because the Russians lacked heavy artillery and machine guns, and because the front was too long for the close entrenchments of northern France. This new mobility cost the Russians some two million men killed, wounded, or taken prisoner. But since men were more plentiful than munitions, the Russian army remained in being; and although German gains that year were important they could not be decisive. Accordingly, it was to the western front, where alone a clear decision could be reached, that Falkenhayn turned his attention in 1916. There some four million men were entrenched on the two opposing sides.

1. See p. 550.

His new plan for victory in the West was simple, with both the merits and the defects of simplicity. It rested on a tactic of attrition suited to a war of attrition. He looked for a spot in the French defences so crucial that France would be bound to defend it at all cost. Against this he would bring the heaviest possible concentration of attack, and sustain this attack indefinitely. To defend it the French would be compelled to go on drawing upon reserves, who could in this way be systematically slaughtered. France was to be bled to death. For the purpose, he needed not a weak point where he might break through, but a strong point open to attack from several sides at once. The obvious place was Verdun – a fortress situated in a salient of the line so that it exposed a considerable surface to attack. It had been a pivot of the French defence since war began. Against it Falkenhayn massed nineteen divisions with a most formidable array of heavy artillery, all compressed within a few square miles. The plan was ingenious, for it took into account the proven immobility of warfare in the West; the patriotic *élan* of the French army, which was willing to make such great sacrifices; the known inferiority of France to Germany in resources of manpower. Yet it also left two important factors out of account: the proven costliness of the offensive as compared with defence; and the fresh resources of manpower tapped by compulsory military service which the United Kingdom had instituted in January 1916. Even if France alone might have been bled to death, German losses in the attack combined with British reinforcements to France could quickly restore the balance. So it proved to be. The German attack began in February 1916 with nine hours' incessant bombardment of Verdun. For more than five months both sides poured fresh reserves of men, guns, and ammunition into this inferno. The French defenders of Verdun, commanded by General Pétain, created a legend of heroism with their cry, 'They shall not pass.' Germany found herself committed to a stratagem almost as costly to herself as to her enemy. When it ended in July, the lines were much where they had been a year before. Verdun had not fallen, and although the French had lost 350,000 men the Germans had lost 330,000.

On 1 July, partly in the hope of forcing a decision and partly in order to relieve Verdun, the British forces launched on the Somme their first major offensive of the war. Here, too, immense quantities of artillery, as well as a few specimens of that new British invention, the tank, were assembled for the attack on the German lines in Picardy. The Allied purpose was simply to blast a way through the German lines by sheer force, and yet the commanders neglected to use with any effect this new type of armoured gun carrier. Properly developed, it was later to prove capable of surmounting barbed-wire entanglements and trenches; and it was the first effective answer to the machine gun. The Battle of the Somme continued until October and cost more, though it gained no more, than the Battle of Verdun. It cost the Germans 500,000 men, the British 400,000, and the French 20,000, so that once more the offensive proved more extravagant than the defence. In the East, Russia also launched an offensive, at last timed roughly to coincide with the Allied attack on the Somme. Led by General Brusilov the Russians attacked the Austro-Hungarian divisions in the southern sector of the front, and routed them in a fifty-mile advance. By August the impetus of the attack was spent, munitions were again chronically short, and a German counter-attack more or less restored the line to its former position. But Austria-Hungary was gravely weakened by her losses (half a million killed or captured), her attacks on Italy in the Tyrol had failed, and she was saved from Rumanian attack only by German help. In eastern Europe, too, therefore, the essential deadlock remained. Advantages gained were counterbalanced by losses suffered, and advances were followed by retreats. Only against Turkey did the Allies score an undoubted gain. In January 1915 Russia had defeated a large Turkish army on the eastern Turkish frontier, and a year later she captured Armenia. The British, after suffering reverses at Gallipoli in 1916, took Baghdad in March 1917, so restoring both their prestige and their power in the Middle East.

By the end of 1916 the outcome of the war was as uncertain as at the beginning of 1915. The equal balance of power which had existed before the war began [1] had perpetuated itself throughout two and a half years of war. Still neither side had won a decisive victory. Discussions of the possibility of a negotiated peace took place in December 1916, encouraged by President Woodrow Wilson. Even on this question there was insoluble deadlock, since neither side would consider terms tolerable to the other. Meanwhile, at sea, the grim struggle of the blockade and counterblockade went on. The effect on central Europe of the rigorous blockade recalled some of the results obtained against Napoleon.[2] Germany had resources enough of coal and iron, still the sinews of war. But she was short of important raw materials such as cotton, rubber, copper, and lubricating oils, and of such food stuffs as fats and cereals. As the blockade tightened, civilian privations caused anxieties to the government. Food ran very short in the 'turnip' winter of 1916–17. Some goods penetrated the blockade through neutral states, and conquered territories like Rumania brought fresh supplies of oil and wheat; more time was needed before the blockade could prove deadly. The

1. See p. 536.
2. See p. 92.

German counter-blockade, by mine and submarine, was very costly to Britain, despite her naval strength. The number of German U-boats was now much larger, and only fear of provoking the United States into war had restrained their attacks on passenger and merchant ships. After feeling the pinch of the blockade in the winter of 1916 and facing another spring of deadlock on land, the German leaders were tempted to risk everything in a completely unrestricted assault on British imports and supplies by means of their now powerful fleet of U-boats. This decision, which they took in January 1917, was the most fateful since the initial adoption of the Schlieffen Plan. If unrestricted submarine warfare should prove unable to bring Britain to her knees within six months, then it was probable that the United States would go to war with Germany, and ultimate victory for the Central Powers would become impossible. It was with this desperate gambler's throw, to win or lose all, and tacitly admitting that deadlock on land persisted, that Germany began the year 1917.

THE TRANSFORMATION OF 1917-18

Until 1917 the spreading of the war beyond the circle of the original belligerents had not changed its fundamental character. Two major developments of 1917 altered both its course and its outcome. One was the entry of the United States in April, the other was military collapse and revolution in Russia, which by December led to peace negotiations between Russia and Germany. Both events were the direct consequence of German military policy, and in their effects they were closely interlinked.

The Russian Collapse. Germany and Austria-Hungary had shown remarkable capacity to sustain a war on two fronts, and to inflict immense losses on Russia despite the massive forces they had to keep supplied on the western front. One reason for their success was the inefficiency and recklessness of the Russian command and its perpetual dearth of munitions. The real brunt of the eastern fighting was borne by the Russian peasants, drafted in millions into the armed forces, ill-clothed and ill-trained, and always under-equipped. In the course of 1916 Russia had lost another million men, and still the tsarist government had no gains to show for it, nor any ideal to hold before its fighting men other than defence of the régime which most of them hated. Tsarist policy was as bankrupt as its organization, and in March a great epidemic of strikes and mutinies, especially around Petrograd (formerly St Petersburg), brought final paralysis to the régime. On the Ides of March the Tsar abdicated, and the fourth Duma supported a provisional government of liberal nobles and middle-class intellectuals headed by Prince Lvov. Its aim was to pursue the war against Germany with renewed vigour, and to inspire the peasants to fresh efforts by the prospect of establishing democratic constitutional government. In May it was replaced by a new provisional government headed by the socialist lawyer, Aleksandr Kerenski.

This government represented a compromise between the two rival authorities now governing Russia: the executive committee of moderate, liberal, constitutionalists set up by the Duma to exercise power temporarily; and the Petrograd Soviet of Workers' and Soldiers' Deputies, set up at the same time by the insurrectionary workers and mutinous soldiers of the city. One represented the traditional liberal element, the other the proletarian socialist element, in the broad Russian revolutionary tradition.[1] They differed in purpose, for whereas the liberals were resolved to continue the war against Germany and prepared to try to win peasant loyalty by redistributing the land, the socialists were anxious to end the war in order to press on with the social revolution. Neither included the Bolsheviks, whose leaders were mostly in exile until April 1917. In that month the German High Command, hoping to stimulate Russian collapse by encouraging social revolution, gave Lenin and others safe passage in a sealed train from Switzerland to the Russian frontier. Once in Petrograd, Lenin backed the Soviet against Kerenski, seeing in that proletariat body the best means of effecting permanent revolution. The Bolsheviks staged a rising in July, but it was suppressed and Lenin fled to Finland.

In that month the provisional government launched a fresh offensive in Galicia with disastrous results. It became apparent that Russia, after her prolonged ordeal and amid widespread starvation, could not sustain both war and revolution at the same time. This truth was symbolized by the rapid dissolution of the Russian armies. The peasants, hearing that land was about to be redistributed, simply deserted and went home to get it. Lenin waited patiently, planning to effect a Bolshevik revolution as soon as the provisional régime had reached the necessary stage of collapse. His programme was simple: make peace with Germany; distribute land to the peasants; give supreme power to the Soviets. Kerenski planned to summon a constituent assembly, on the traditional model of liberal revolutions in 1848. Lenin countered by demanding an all-Russian congress of soviets. By gaining Bolshevik predominance in the Petrograd Soviet and in many others, by calling upon the mutinous sailors and soldiers, and by skilful use of Bolshevik party agents, he staged a *coup d'état* on the night of 6–7 November. Next morning Petrograd woke up to find the city governed by the Bolsheviks, and the congress of Soviets ruling Russia.[2] In December, Trotsky opened peace negotiations with

1. See p. 336.   2. See p. 582.

Germany, and on 3 March 1918 the Treaty of Brest-Litovsk ended the war between Russia and Germany.

The United States Goes to War. These events had repercussions across the Atlantic. The March revolution removed any repugnance that Americans felt to entering the war as an ally of reactionary, despotic tsardom. The provisional government of liberals and more moderate socialists proclaimed ideals that chimed with the growing belief in the West that the war had become a war for democratic and liberal ideals against militarism and dynasticism. Still more important, Germany had outraged humane feelings as well as American national interests by proclaiming, at the end of January 1917, that she would now resume unrestricted submarine warfare. This meant declaring her intention to sink at sight all merchant ships within a zone of water round the British Isles and around France and Italy in the Mediterranean. President Wilson retaliated by breaking off diplomatic relations and ordering that American ships be armed. Even now he had to move with caution. Isolationist feeling in the United States was still strong. Only three years before, great indignation had been aroused by Great Britain's rigorous enforcement of the naval blockade, which meant irksome interference with neutral shipping. Pro-German or anti-British sentiments were prevalent among sections of America's multi-national population. It was certain the Americans did not want to get embroiled in war. On the other hand, irritation with Germany's methods had been increasing. Her secret agents had been sabotaging munitions plants and stirring up industrial unrest. Her spies had been clumsily busy. Her diplomacy was fanciful. In January 1917 the British intercepted and decoded a telegram from the German Foreign Secretary, Zimmermann, to the German minister in Mexico City. It described how Germany planned, if America should enter the war, to ally with Mexico in order to help her recover her 'lost territories' – that is, Texas, New Mexico, and Arizona, conquered in 1848. The British passed this telegram on to Washington, and it was published in the American Press. The ruthlessness and severity of U-boat sinkings in February and March added to both fears and resentment. They totalled nearly 540,000 tons in February, some 600,000 tons in March. On 2 April the President gained the backing of Congress for a declaration of war on Germany. From the outset he stated peace aims in a way in which none of the European belligerents had so far attempted to state them – in uncompromisingly idealistic terms.

... we shall fight for the things which we have always carried nearest to our hearts – for democracy, for the right of those who submit to authority to have a voice in their own government, for the rights and liberties of small nations, for a universal dominion of right by such a concert of free peoples as shall bring peace and safety to all nations and make the world itself at last free.

Here, in brief, were all the peace aims for which the western allies, in the remaining eighteen months, were to claim to be fighting.

The circumstances in which the United States went to war gave the remaining campaigns their most outstanding characteristic: that of a race against time, since the submarine war was launched on the calculation by the German High Command that it could starve out the British Isles within six months – before American military reinforcements to the Allies could become decisive. It was a calculated risk, in that the Germans regarded American entry as certain before long, but they hoped to make it of little importance; they gambled that a decision in the West would have been reached before the end of the year which they estimated America would need to build up her army. The plan, like other German plans before it, came very close to succeeding. During April the U-boats sank another 870,000 tons of shipping, and Britain was left with stores of food to last only six weeks. At the price of rationing essentials, and real deprivation, it proved to be enough. The German planners had again left important factors out of account. Just as their plan for Verdun underrated French stamina and British reserves, so their plan for the battle of the western approaches underrated British stamina and the extent of immediate naval help which the United States could give. Just as in 1916 they pinned exaggerated hopes on a limited and local operation, so now they overestimated the effectiveness of a single weapon. The British Admiralty invented a series of effective anti-submarine devices – the hydrophone and aeroplane spotting to detect submarines, depth charges and mines to destroy them, and the armed escort to protect whole convoys of merchant ships. The United States navy, already large and powerful, could lend immediate protection. By the end of the year the U-boat menace was beaten, though again at heavy cost of men, ships, and supplies.

The war against the U-boat was complemented by fresh assaults on the western front. General Nivelle, who had succeeded General Joffre as Commander-in-Chief of the French armies, led an attack on a fifty-mile front in Champagne against one of the most heavily fortified German defences. It was repulsed with the loss of more than 100,000 men. In May, Nivelle was replaced by General Pétain, who now had not only to hold German pressure but also to restore the shattered morale of his troops. Muddle and misery combined with heavy losses to breed discontent among the sorely tried French troops, and mutinies broke out. Pétain restored discipline and morale, though not without some severity.

Two further British assaults fared little better than the French. The long dreary battle of Passchendaele brought an advance of five miles at a cost of 400,000 men, many of whom were drowned in the sea of mud which the battlefield had now become. At the end of the year they made a surprise attack near Cambrai, for the first time replacing the usual preliminary of heavy artillery bombardment by a raid of nearly 400 tanks. They crashed through the German lines and penetrated deeply, but with no fresh reserves of infantry to follow them up, or reserves of tanks to replace those that stalled, the ground was soon lost again. In France deadlock still remained, and only in 1918 would United States land forces be available to help break it. The task of France and Britain, all the more now that Russia was deserting them, was to hold on and wait, exhausting Germany to a point where her morale must at last crack. This was no easy task; for Germany – jubilant at her victory over Russia, relieved by the new sources of supplies now available to her in the Ukraine and in the other eastern marchlands stripped from Russia at Brest-Litovsk, aware now that victory or defeat must be determined in 1918 – was preparing yet another tremendous onslaught in the West for the spring of the last fateful year.

The Final Campaigns, 1918. The campaigns of 1918 revealed a new quality of generalship on both sides. For the western allies, supplies of men and munitions and of the shipping to carry them ceased to be a serious problem. With the exuberant productive capacity of the United States open to them, while the stranglehold of the naval blockade tightened on central Europe, they began to be less obsessed by sheer numbers and quantities. The British use of tanks at the end of 1917, timid and half-hearted though it was, was a sign that the crude generalship of mass frontal onslaughts had at last given place to a more intelligent and subtle use of power. To resist the German spring offensive, a unified Allied command was at last set up, with Ferdinand Foch as Commander-in-Chief of all Allied forces in France. By July 1918, when the Germans had made their furthest advance along the Marne, there were nine United States divisions in the line, and American troops were landing in France at the rate of more than 250,000 a month.

Foch waited, as he could afford to wait, until the Germans had stretched their lines to the utmost. Ludendorff's attack had begun on 21 March, on a forty-mile front at the junction between the main British armies (under Douglas Haig) and the French army (under Pétain) entrusted to defend Paris. He hoped that a breakthrough there, to the Marne, would cause Haig to fall back to defend the Channel ports, Pétain to fall back in defence of Paris. Through the gap Ludendorff would pour enough troops to seize the important railway junction of

Arras. Although the British were driven back with heavy losses in killed and captured, they held Arras. Ludendorff next attacked Amiens, but Foch held him. Ludendorff was indulging in what Foch called 'buffalo strategy' – lunging with one horn at one place, with the other at a second place, without real calculation. Foch 'played' his buffalo, by letting him make as many lunges as he chose, until he had exhausted his strength and thrown himself off balance. Then Foch struck with concentrated power at his neck. The buffalo's neck, in this case, turned out to be the central bulge in the German lines produced by their own advances towards the Marne during May and June. The Allied generals had learned the principles of elastic defence – of yielding and holding the front line with a thin screen of troops, parrying each blow as it came but conserving their strength for a final brisk retaliation. In September, with the German lines fully extended and a large indefensible salient in the middle, Foch ordered Mangin – one of Marchand's daring band at Fashoda in 1898 – to strike at the neck of the bulge just below Soissons. Mangin took 30,000 prisoners and the Germans hastily withdrew from the salient. Foch now brought his carefully concerted strategy into operation. It was a skilfully timed sequence of incisive blows at one sector of the front after another, in quick and relentless succession to give the enemy no chance to recover. In August, Haig struck in front of Amiens, taking another 20,000 prisoners, and revealing to Foch that a surprise attack could shake German morale. The following month Haig struck again, at the strongest defences of the Hindenberg Line. As soon as the Germans fell back, the Belgians under King Albert attacked near Ypres. While the main enemy strength was thus held in Flanders, Mangin struck again, and the Americans under General Pershing drove simultaneously towards Verdun and Sedan. A French army, under General Castelnau, attacked in the Ardennes to deliver the *coup de grâce*. This brilliant plan, concerting the separate national thrusts into a grand strategy of offence, took full advantage of Germany's lack of reserves, as well as of her advanced front-line positions. Foch won tactical advantage by the use of tanks. All through September his blows fell according to plan.

Nor was it only in France and Flanders that glimpses of Allied victory appeared. In faraway Salonica, one of the war's forgotten fronts, Serbian, French, and British forces planned in June a daring frontal assault on the mountain frontiers of Bulgaria, designed to knock her out by a surprise attack. It was launched in mid September, and by the end of the month Bulgaria surrendered. Her surrender brought with it the collapse of the whole south-eastern front, for Austria-Hungary was now rapidly disintegrating into its national component parts. Czechs and Poles were deserting the Habsburg cause to assert their own national independence and join the Allies. In Palestine a British army under Allenby captured the whole Turkish army and on 1 October entered Damascus. By the end of the month the Italians had avenged their defeat of Caporetto in 1917 by routing the Austro-Hungarians at Vittorio Veneto – a battle destined to become the basis of the Fascist 'myth' that Allied victory was really due to Italian valour. With her allies deserting her in defeat, and her own armies in the West in rapid retreat, Germany's High Command had no alternative but to sue for peace. With news of unrest at home, even rumours of revolution, it was the nerve of the German generals, especially of Ludendorff, which broke first. By early November the British had broken through into open country, the Americans had reached Sedan, the French were approaching Lorraine. The new liberal German government, formed at the end of September with Prince Max of Baden as Chancellor, wanted to continue the struggle, just as had the government of Prince Lvov in Russia the previous year. With belated enthusiasm for democracy, the Reich was turned into a constitutional monarchy whose Chancellor was responsible to the Reichstag. But Hindenburg and Ludendorff insisted that the fighting must cease. Kaiser William II abdicated on 9 November and escaped to the neutral Netherlands. The armistice was signed in Marshal Foch's railway carriage in the forest of Compiègne. Hostilities ceased at the eleventh hour of the eleventh day of the eleventh month, in the year 1918. But there were no Allied armies on German soil. The timing of the armistice was the most completely successful of all the manoeuvres carried out by the German generals.

Peace Aims. The war ended, as it had begun, as pre-eminently a war between great powers. The lesser powers, Serbia and Belgium from the outset, Bulgaria and Italy subsequently, had never played more than a subordinate role. The victors no less than the vanquished were essentially the great powers, and in 1918 by far the most powerful belligerent – still only realizing her gigantic strength – was the United States. This predominance of the major states in the war was reflected in the conduct of the peace conference of Paris, where all important decisions came to be made by a consortium of the 'Big Three': France, Great Britain, and the United States. Even Japan and Italy, at first included out of courtesy, soon gave up the unequal struggle.[1] But the policies of the decisive powers were very much concerned with the future, with the claims and the rights of the smaller nations. This was because of the shaping of policy in terms of peace aims which took place after the entry of the United States into the war. From the outset, the attacks on

1. See p. 617.

Serbia and Belgium had made the independence of small states an inherent issue of the war. Restoration of their independence was an original war aim. But it was only after the United States went to war and after Russia went out of the war that this cause of independence for all small nations as such came to be an aim of peacemaking. To this result even the policy of Germany and of Bolshevik Russia contributed. The Germans excited nationalist and separatist movements as a tactic of psychological warfare. They promised independence to Poland, exploited Ukrainian hopes, backed the Flemish home-rule movement in Belgium and the Irish home-rule movement in Ireland. Lenin appealed widely to the principle of national self-determination as being a usefully disruptive force in Austria-Hungary. At the Treaty of Brest-Litovsk, Trotsky agreed to the separation from Russia of Poland, the Ukraine, Finland, and the Baltic States. Germany promptly set them up as nominally 'independent' states. President Wilson went further, and in eloquent words that brought fresh hope to all the suppressed national groups of Europe, he proclaimed the doctrine of national self-determination as 'an imperative principle of action which statesmen will henceforth ignore at their peril'. Wilson stood, in general, for the culmination of all the liberal, democratic, nationalist ideals which since 1789 had fermented in Europe. The war became, in his eyes, a war to make the world safe for democracy and for small nations.

In January 1918 Wilson had enunciated peace aims in the famous 'Fourteen Points'. Contrary to popular belief, this programme was concerned less with lofty ideals of humanitarianism than with quite specific proposals to achieve national and international justice by making states more perfect nation-states. The first five points, indeed, outlined general principles of peacemaking. But none of these proved practicable or acceptable after 1918. 'Open covenants of peace openly arrived at' meant abandoning secret diplomacy and negotiation as well as secret treaties, and led to a cult of conferences which achieved small results. 'Absolute freedom of navigation upon the seas outside territorial waters, alike in peace and in war' was a doctrine that neither Great Britain nor the United States had preserved in their blockade of Germany, and it was never accepted by Britain as applicable in war. 'The establishment of an equality of trade conditions among all the nations consenting to the peace' meant in principle free trade, which no postwar state would contemplate. 'Adequate guarantees given and taken that national armaments will be reduced' was an aim that led to several disarmament conferences which rarely achieved important results. 'A free, open-minded, and absolutely impartial adjustment of all colonial claims' was an idealized conception which bore some fruit in the system of colonial mandates, though it was vitiated by conferring no mandates upon the defeated powers. Behind these five general aims lay an implicit theory of what had caused the war: secret treaties, naval jealousies, tariffs, competition in armaments, and colonialism. Remove these causes of war and peace would result. But, as already seen,[1] these were by no means the only or even the main causes of war in 1914. Rather they were the symptoms of the nationalistic fears and rivalries which, in a special set of historical circumstances, produced the system of rival alliances and led to war. Nationalist sentiments were now strengthened, not weakened, by the war.

The remaining nine points covered all the main territorial changes that seemed to be required for a stable settlement in Europe, and they were quite specific. They included the evacuation of all Russian territory occupied at that date; the evacuation and restoration of the invaded Belgian and French provinces and of Alsace-Lorraine; 'a readjustment of the frontiers of Italy . . . along clearly recognizable lines of nationality'; autonomy for 'the peoples of Austria-Hungary'; independence for the Balkan States, including evacuation of Rumania, Serbia, and Montenegro, and access to the sea for Serbia; autonomy for Turkey itself and for 'the nationalities now under Turkish rule'; independence for Poland, with secure access to the sea. Finally, and in Wilson's view of paramount importance, there should be set up 'a general association of nations', with 'mutual guarantees of political independence and territorial integrity to great and small States alike'.

President Wilson elaborated and extended the more general principles of peacemaking in a number of further speeches between February and September 1918, but these specific points were never modified. His most important additions to the general principles were two: that 'each part of the final settlement must be based upon the essential justice of that particular case and upon such adjustments as are most likely to bring a peace that will be permanent'; and that 'the impartial justice meted out must involve no discrimination between those to whom we wish to be just and those to whom we do not wish to be just'. This concept of an absolute justice in the settlement of so tangled a matter as the national frontiers of Europe was to prove a fertile source of profound international grievances. No arrangement conceivable in modern Europe, least of all any arrangement attainable immediately after four years of murderous warfare, could be expected to reach such a standard. The lofty idealism infused into Allied peace aims by Wilson was to be a heavy liability in the years to come.

These formulations of peace aims assumed great significance because

1. See p. 540.

they were broadly endorsed by the Allied governments and were made the basis on which the German government accepted the armistice in November. The Allied governments made it clear, however, that they wished to reserve judgement about the exact meaning of 'freedom of the seas'; and that 'restoration' of invaded territories meant, for them, that 'compensation will be made by Germany for all damage done to the civilian population of the Allies and their property by the aggression of Germany by land, by sea, and from the air'. These principles, aims, and interpretations were all communicated to the Germans before they agreed to end hostilities. The basic principle, clearly enough, was to satisfy as far as humanly possible the desire for national unification and self-determination. There was little attempt to provide that nationalism should be superseded or transcended by larger loyalties, little belief that 'patriotism is not enough'. The reduction of national minorities, combined with liberal national governments, would remove the deeper political causes of unrest. The reduction of tariffs, armaments, and colonialism would remove the deeper economic causes of unrest. A League of Nations to settle disputes between member states would prevent any inflammation of international quarrels. Everything, it seemed, was provided for – except that national frontiers could not be tidily drawn, that nationalist sentiment was unlikely to be pacific or reasonable, that the desire for economic self-sufficiency would resist the abandonment of tariffs and colonies as much as the desire for national security would oppose disarmament, and that to Germans or Hungarians the fact of national defeat could never be made palatable. Peacemaking, in short, was even more formidable a task than warmaking had been, and it was no less liable to produce despondency and deadlock. But this unwelcome truth was little appreciated in 1918. The war was over. The guns were silent. Men could raise their heads again and see the sky. It was grey November, and on every horizon there were heavy clouds.

CHAPTER 23

DOMESTIC CONSEQUENCES,
1914–23

WARTIME COLLECTIVISM

EACH belligerent nation, after more than four years of ordeal by battle, bore lasting scars. The greatest of these was the loss of millions of its fittest men and the permanent disabling of many more. Russia, the heaviest loser, lost more than two million, Germany nearly two million, France and her colonies nearly one and a quarter million, Austria-Hungary one and a quarter million, the British Empire nearly one million. The United States incurred 115,000 deaths, half of them as a result of disease or in the great influenza epidemic that followed the armistice. Some ten million men of all nations lost their lives, and most of them were under forty years old. More than twice that number were wounded, a considerable proportion of them maimed for life. All the wars of the previous century, from the Napoleonic Wars to the Balkan War of 1913, had cost less than four and a half million lives. The French calculated that between August 1914 and February 1917 one Frenchman was killed every minute. Casualties at this rate and on this scale were unprecedented in European warfare. The bearing of the losses upon the recovery of individual nations varied with their ratio to total population. Russia's losses, though numerically the biggest, were less damaging to her whole social fabric than the smaller losses of France, whose population was less than a third of Russia's. But everywhere losses on this scale profoundly affected the structure of population both in sex and in age groups. Among women the loss of life due to the war was relatively slight; among men, it destroyed mainly those born in the last quarter of the nineteenth century. Thus in Great Britain in 1911 there were 1,067 females to every 1,000 males. In 1921 there were 1,093 to every 1,000 males. This abrupt increase in the disequilibrium between the sexes led to much vague postwar discussion of the 'surplus women' problem; it was to a large extent a 'deficit of men' problem. The birth rate, already tending to decline in most European countries before 1914, dipped sharply during the war years and rose sharply again after the war, reflecting the disruption of family life during the war. Even by 1960 this left a deep cut in the groups around middle age, and carried the demographic effects of the war far forward into the post-war years. Thus in 1930 schools that had to deal with unusually few children between the ages of eleven and fifteen had to deal with unusually many children between the ages of nine and ten. An 'age bulge' had to work its way up the educational system after about 1924, which did not cease to cause temporary difficulties until after 1935. When the French began in 1930 to build their heavily fortified Maginot Line along their north-eastern frontier, it was in order to be thrifty with manpower. They planned to complete it by 1935 because they knew that between 1934 and 1939 the annual draft for military service would yield only half the usual number of recruits.

Social and Economic Changes. In every country, too, the war had the effect of accelerating the emancipation of women wherever it had begun to happen before 1914. In Great Britain women over thirty were given the parliamentary vote in 1918 with hardly any opposition. Because modern warfare had demanded a total national effort, civilian morale and industrial production had become hardly less important than the armed forces themselves. Women flocked into factories and shops, offices and voluntary services, hospitals and schools. They took the place of men alongside men, and their claim to equality of status and rights won spontaneous recognition. After so many had acquired and experienced independence, both social and economic, it was impossible that they should be denied it. It became everywhere easier for women to find employment in industry and business, for old conventional barriers against them were down. Barriers of class and wealth, too, were weakened if not entirely demolished by the 'fellowship of the trenches' and by the social solidarity induced by a common national danger and effort. Social ethics significantly changed. Competitive enterprise had given way before national controls and regulations. Private profit-making seemed less obviously good in itself when 'war profiteers' were a special object of scorn and hatred. Danger makes socialists of us all.

Just as the prospect of abundance had, before 1914, made men more impatient of poverty and more intolerant of ignorance and squalor, so the prodigious national effort and the remarkable feats of organization for war left men less daunted by even the forbidding tasks of postwar reconstruction. If necessity could call forth such prodigies of ingenuity, such lavish expenditure, such concerted efforts, then peace, too, could surely bring prosperity and plenty. It became a favourite comment on the failure of governments to deal efficiently with the reabsorption of men into employment after demobilization or their apathy in face of mass unemployment, to contrast such lethargy with the vigour and ingenuity that had been devoted to destruction. It was natural now to look to governments for direction and guidance. They had, in war, commandeered lives and services, property and resources. They had regimented civilians hardly less than soldiers, restricting what food they ate and even how they found entertainment. Nothing had been too great or too menial a matter for the state, if military requirements demanded it.

In Germany, Walter Rathenau, of the great electrical trust, had fought the effects of the British blockade by requisitioning raw materials, organizing special War Companies to run industry and replace wasteful competition by efficient coordination, and encouraging chemists to find substitutes in the laboratory for the natural resources of which the blockade deprived Germany. This scion of capitalist enterprise and big business created what came to be called, quite correctly, 'war social-ism' (*Kriegssozialismus*). A special agency controlled prices and rationed food. It decreed two meatless days a week, and fed Germans on war bread in which turnips and potatoes were mixed with flour. Labour was allocated under a National Service Law of December 1916, which put every male between the ages of seventeen and sixty under the authority of the Minister of War. Trade unions allied with the mili-tary leaders to militarize the country's economic life. Rathenau's achievement in thus creating a novel type of pure 'war economy' (*Kriegswirtschaft*) was well enough described in his own words: 'In its methods it is closely akin to communism, and yet it departs essentially from the prophecies and demands resulting from radical theories.' Rathenau was in the authentic tradition of Bismarck [1] in his subor-dinating of everything to state needs. It was entirely an emergency measure. But not only did it leave Germany with a rich experience of state socialism and economic planning, later exploited by National Socialism, but Germany's 'war economy' became an exemplar of eco-nomic planning for the whole of the postwar world.

The ideal of national economic self-sufficiency, so directly at variance with the prewar growth of economic interdependence through inter-national trade, was born directly of the needs of war. Such *autarky* came to be a favourite notion of the interwar world, and the means to make it possible were discovered during the war. To make explosives the German-Jewish scientist, Fritz Haber, perfected the process of ex-tracting nitrogen from the air, because nitrates could no longer be im-ported from Chile. As a substitute for cotton, cellulose was invented in the laboratory. The exploration of substitute (*Ersatz*) materials, begun during the war in Germany, gave rise to a series of vast new industries making rayons and plastics and an array of synthetic materials some-times found to be superior to the natural products for which they were originally intended as inferior substitutes.

1. See p. 358.

Few other countries embarked upon so thoroughly nationalized an economy as did wartime Germany. But every country moved in that direction. In France special boards of industrialists were set up to plan production to meet government orders and to allocate raw materials that were in short supply. In the United States the War Industries Board, headed by Bernard Baruch, did the same. In the United Kingdom a great political battle was fought about the supply of munitions. At the outbreak of war Lord Kitchener had been appointed Secretary of State for War. He enjoyed great popularity and prestige, but his experience lay in colonial campaigns where mobility mattered more than munitions. By the end of November 1914 the call from the front for munitions of all kinds far exceeded the supply. In all the weapons needed for the new 'war of position' in France – in shells, trench mortars, machine guns, hand grenades – British supplies were both insufficient and in-efficient. Kitchener was widely criticized. In May 1915 when Asquith had to reconstruct his government, he created a new Ministry of Muni-tions and put Lloyd George in charge of it. By means of special legisla-tion he secured almost dictatorial control over British industry, in order to direct its energies to the urgent manufacture of munitions. His task was to equip an army of seventy divisions for a long war in the trenches. A year later he succeeded Kitchener at the War Office and threw his redoubtable energies and genius into the more general conduct of the war. In France the munitions problem was even more acute. By mid September 1914 hardly a month's reserve of shells was left, and German occupation of the industrial provinces robbed France of most of her iron ores and much of her coal. Mobilization halved the number of workers at the great armaments plant of Le Creusot. In May 1915 Albert Thomas, a socialist engineer who had wide experience of labour organizations, was given special charge of artillery and munitions. He had to plan industrial production in the same way as did Lloyd George in Britain. Trade unions, usually reluctantly, had to accept some degree of direction and dilution of labour. National needs took precedence over all else.

Every government, too, had to control foreign trade and credit, and take possession of national assets abroad. Here the United Kingdom's financial strength and long accumulation of capital investment overseas stood her in good stead. Stock held in the United States by British or French investors was sold off to Americans, and the resulting dollars were used to pay for imports. The original stockholders were repaid in domestic currency or bonds. Gold reserves were drawn upon, and large war loans were raised both at home and abroad. The whole process permanently depleted Europe's overseas investments and converted the

United States from a debtor country into the world's greatest creditor. Of Europe's two most advanced industrial nations, Germany was almost entirely excluded from the world's markets by the blockade, and the United Kingdom devoted all its industrial resources to meeting the immediate needs of feeding the population and supplying the troops. Most of the world's shipping was engaged in carrying the cargoes of war, and even neutrals suffered heavily from losses of shipping. The internal balance of the economy of nearly every country in the world was affected, and the prewar pattern of international trade was completely changed.[1] European neutrals were more harshly affected than non-European countries, because the blockade checked their own flow of imports and their continental trade with Germany. The Dutch set up a Netherlands Overseas Trust to handle the rigidly limited quota of imports which they were allowed by the Allies. Other European neutrals – especially Scandinavia and Switzerland – found neutrality difficult to preserve amid the storm that raged around their frontiers. Danish opinion was strongly anti-German, as was Norwegian. Norway lost nearly half her merchant marine. Swedish opinion, on the other hand, was divided between anti-Russian and anti-German movements. The Swiss shared both French and German sympathies but could unite in keeping Swiss neutrality intact. Spain, less encircled by the war, enjoyed a new prosperity in her industrial regions, especially in Catalonia; this strengthened the desire for Catalonian autonomy. All suffered some economic dislocation.

The occupied territories of Europe suffered much more. Belgian territory was subjected to great devastation as a battlefield, to German requisitions of supplies and of labour, and to an increasingly rigorous military control and censorship. Belgian religious and local leaders kept up a brave resistance while King Albert and the remnants of the Belgian army fought on behind Ypres. The country's economy was wrecked, its cities ruined, many of its people refugees or deportees or prisoners of war. In 1915, when the Russians were driven out of Polish territory, the Germans behaved as liberators. Many Poles (including Pilsudski himself) preferred German rule to Russian. Germany's acute labour shortage of 1916 tempted her to try raising a Polish Legion, and in November both Germany and Austria wooed Poland by setting up an 'independent' Polish government to which Pilsudski was admitted as Minister of War. But the new Legion was almost as hostile to Germany and Austria as to Russia, since all three were historically Poland's partitioners and oppressors. Pilsudski was soon in prison, though the Central Powers continued to hold out the lure of national independence in an effort to enlist Polish support.

1. See p. 391.

National Morale. Germany's past record, whether distant or recent, disqualified her as a champion of the rights of small nations, and she could never compete with her enemies in the new weapons of psychological warfare which assumed increasing importance toward the end of the war. As an invading and occupying power, she suffered from the stories of atrocities alleged against her troops. The stories were often true, but even when exaggerated or false, they were accepted as true by a world that remembered the Kaiser's sabre-rattling and the cynical invasion of neutral Belgium. Even on the home front German handling of public opinion was inept. Officialdom issued glowing reports of advances and victories but left calculation of losses and reverses to rumour and Allied estimates. Whispers of the terrible losses in France demoralized civilian families, while rumours of the great privations endured at home undermined the morale of the soldiers. One element in the collapse of German morale in 1918 was the discovery by the advancing Germans, when they found Allied trenches generously stocked with food and supplies, that official German reports had persistently misled them about Allied privations. No government handled public opinion well in the early stages of the war. Both French and British suffered from a tendency to suppress news and so breed rumour, which was usually more demoralizing than even bad news.

Not without reason were governments anxious about public morale and national disunity. The insatiable need for men and munitions made the home front supremely important. Only the imminence of danger held together the disruptive forces that had been so apparent before 1914.[1] Trade-union susceptibilities were handled very delicately, if only because workers and their unions now found themselves in a strong bargaining position. Even so, in July 1915 there was a strike of 200,000 coal miners in South Wales. Ireland, the traditional Achilles' heel of the United Kingdom, flared up in the Easter rebellion of 1916. It was the work of only an extremist minority. Most of the nation, led by John Redmond, backed Britain in the war, and some 250,000 Irish volunteers fought in the British forces. The rebellion was supported by the Germans, who agreed to send a ship with munitions for the rebels and to land the renegade, Sir Roger Casement, from a U-boat. Sinn Feiners, Irish Volunteers, and the Citizen Army of southern Ireland were ready to seize key points. The German ship was intercepted by British destroyers and scuttled by her crew. Casement was put ashore but lost his way and was arrested. The rebels went ahead none the less, and within a week were defeated. Fifteen of their leaders were executed. Casement was tried for treason and hanged. The total effect was to embitter Anglo-

1. See p. 426.

Irish relations and give extremists an advantage over moderates when the future of Ireland came to be settled after the war.

In nearly every belligerent country the winter of 1916-17 brought a national crisis and important political changes. The deadlock of the previous two years reduced every country to a point of exhaustion where it had to tap fresh reserves of energy in order to continue the struggle at all. In December, 1916, Lloyd George succeeded Asquith as Prime Minister of the United Kingdom. He headed a coalition government and a war cabinet of four, including in addition to himself Lord Curzon and Lord Milner (both Conservatives) and Arthur Henderson (Labour party). His leadership, marked by impatience with conventional objections to such devices as the armed convoy and the armoured tank, brought new vigour to the war effort. At the same time in France, Aristide Briand, whose government had survived the ordeal of Verdun amid stormy secret sessions of the Chamber, reorganized his ministry and made General Lyautey, hero of Morocco, Minister of War. In March 1917, Lyautey resigned, and Briand's government fell, to be succeeded in the following six months by weak governments, headed by Ribot and Painlevé, which were distracted by political scandals. In mid November 1917 Georges Clemenceau assumed power and restored something of the original spirit of *union sacrée* – a concerted and indomitable national effort to achieve victory. The despondency and muddle which had bred mutiny earlier in the year were ended, and France recovered her morale through a spirit of dedication to total victory.

Italy was even more rent by dissensions than France. From the outset extreme conservatives were opposed to war; many clericalists were pro-Austrian; and many socialists, pacifist. She was burdened with larger antiwar parties than any other belligerent. Her failure to gain any clear advantages or victories by 1917 was correspondingly more serious for her national unity. The harvest of 1916 had been poor, food was rationed, coal shortage was proving serious, and labour supply was not enough to keep her industries and farming in full production. In the summer of 1917 there were strikes at Turin and rumours of desertions and fraternization at the front. The disaster of Caporetto in October cost her 600,000 men, and happened to coincide with a political crisis in which the government of Boselli fell and made way for Orlando's coalition. The shock of defeat induced a new spirit of unity which carried the nation through to the end without collapse.

In the United States, although national leadership did not change significantly in 1916, President Wilson was re-elected for a second term as 'the man who kept us out of war'. The self-confidence inspired by re-election and by the reaffirmation of his policy enabled Wilson to give a stronger lead against Germany's submarine warfare of 1917 and he led the United States into the war by April.

In Germany national solidarity in war showed signs of breaking by 1917. The Social Democrats began to vote against war credits and went into more continuous opposition. News of the March revolution in Russia and of America's entry into the war in April strengthened their opposition and forced the issue between parties in a way that led to the 'July Crisis' of 1917. But in it the Social Democrats won only a paper victory. They remained hamstrung by the constitutional weakness of the Reichstag itself, in face of the Emperor and his Chancellor. The Kaiser in an 'Easter Message' promised after the war an 'extension of our political, economic, and social life'; by July he had to pledge himself to new electoral laws in Prussia 'before the next elections'. These gestures were intended to placate the old demands of the Social Democrats for greater democratization of both the states and the Reich. They did not prevent the resignation of Bethmann Hollweg as Chancellor, nor stop the Reichstag from passing, by 212 votes to 126, a 'Peace Resolution' drafted by the left. The resolution asserted that 'we are not impelled by the lust of conquest' and that the Reichstag wanted 'a peace of understanding and a lasting reconciliation among peoples' with which 'violations of territory and political, economic, and financial persecution are incompatible'. It led to no change in German policy nor even to a clearer official formulation of German peace aims: Brest-Litovsk seven months later flagrantly contradicted it. After unrest and desertions in the immobilized German navy in the summer of 1917, the unhappy stop-gap Chancellor, Georg Michaelis, was replaced in November by the elderly Count Hertling. Unlike Britain and France, Germany failed to find new and inspiring political leadership. She found no Lloyd George, no Clemenceau, in her time of need.

Austria-Hungary experienced a much more serious political crisis than Germany. Her governments changed with greater frequency as the war dragged on. The population endured the privations and losses of the first two years with remarkable resignation, but the Brussilov offensive of 1916 ended this phase. Economic rivalries were hardening between Austria and Hungary, the one partly industrial the other mainly agricultural. Count Tisza of Hungary even set up a customs barrier between them. In November 1916 the Emperor Francis Joseph died, having reigned since 1848. His successor Charles I attempted reforms and changed ministers and officials. He declared a political amnesty. He summoned the Reichstag, which had been suspended since 1914. The deputies of the various national groups immediately began to claim national autonomy, reinforced in their demands by desertions of Czech and other regiments at the front. In Hungary the Diet at Budapest was beset with similar troubles. The non-Magyar parties clamoured for electoral reforms, and Count Tisza resigned. Czechs and Yugoslavs in exile formed national councils in Paris, seeking recognition from the Allies, and Polish and Czech regiments were formed in France to fight on the western front. Long before November 1918, when Charles gave up all claim to share in the government of Austria and Hungary, the Habsburg dominions had disintegrated into the largest national *blocs* which had underlain the old dynastic state. Yugoslavs, Czechs, and Poles, recognized as belligerent allies by the western powers, appeared equipped with provisional governments ready to assert national independence.

The Eastern Marchlands. Throughout western and central Europe society was already predominantly a national society, and the nation-state was sufficiently stable and cohesive to survive. It was very different in eastern Europe. In the multi-national Empires of Austria-Hungary, Turkey, and Russia, the forces of nationalism worked against the government instead of for it. The result, when collapse finally came, was a dissolution of old frontiers. Dynasticism abruptly went out of fashion. Austria and Hungary were each proclaimed a separate republic. In only two of the defeated states did monarchy survive. When at the end of September Bulgaria signed an armistice, her Tsar Ferdinand abdicated in favour of his son Boris. A month later Turkey, left alone in the midst of advancing Allied armies, and with her Arab territories in revolt, signed an armistice and the Sultan, for a time, kept his throne.

The heirs of the dynasts were the nationalists. Into the emptiness left by the collapse of the old imperial powers flowed the eager eddies of nationalism. From the eastern Baltic shores down through the Polish plains, through the Danube valley and the Balkan peninsula to the deserts of Arabia, the whole of eastern Europe seethed with the great upheaval. Here, where had lain the real storm zone of 1914, the aftermath of war brought its greatest transformation. It took another five years of scuffling and jostling, of diplomatic bargaining and local warfare, to settle the final pattern of the new Europe. Even then the political structure of these lands – the forms of government and the balance of international forces to be established in the long Eurasian frontier – was to remain in doubt. Over the whole of their destiny hung the shadow cast by the most unpredictable of all the war's consequences – the fact that in Russia ruled the first communist government in the world.

The Bolshevik Revolution, 1918–24. The Bolshevik Revolution must be seen as the most extreme manifestation of all the tendencies which general war had released upon Europe.[1] The losses and defeats of

1. See p. 565.

Russia's armies had been more catastrophic, the breakdown of her government more complete, the collapse of her social and economic structure more disastrous, than that of any other state. In such conditions the revolutionary movements, already in 1914 more violently uncompromising in Russia than in any other country, won a complete triumph. Here, in consequence, the nationalizing of society, which was everywhere promoted by the war, was carried to a new intensity. Just as the German Reich, the last of the great Empires to acknowledge defeat, preserved her social and economic order most intact, so Russia, the first to suffer defeat, underwent the most revolutionary change of all.

In November 1917 the Bolsheviks had seized power, not from the tsardom, but from the provisional liberal government which, six months earlier, had overthrown the tsardom. Lenin, who had created the Bolshevik party as the agency of revolution, was the architect of the new state. In the pamphlet *State and Revolution*, which Lenin wrote during the late summer of 1917, he defined his purpose: to set up forthwith 'the dictatorship of the proletariat'. In Marxist theory, of which Lenin now became the interpreter, the proletarian state was an essential prelude to the coming of the 'classless society' of Communism.[1] In Leninist theory it became of indefinite duration and would duly 'wither away' only after it had accomplished tremendous tasks of social and economic reconstruction. At first power would be monopolized by the party, acting as the organized leadership of the proletariat. The capitalist system would be at once abolished, and exploitation of man by man would cease. The new state would be, however, 'the bourgeois state without the bourgeoisie', still coercive in character since the old order had to be transformed and the economy remade under strong central direction. In Marxist doctrine opposing political parties derive only from class conflicts. To eliminate class war means that political parties naturally reduce themselves to only one. All opposition is *ex hypothesi* factious and intolerable. Such was the theory of the first of the single-party totalitarian dictatorships of the twentieth century.

The Council of Commisars, headed by Lenin, with Trotsky in charge of defence and foreign affairs, ruled Russia for the last year of the war in Europe. It relied mainly upon the Red Guard, or Communist militia, and the party's secret police organization to silence rival groups. The Constituent Assembly that met in January 1918 was dispersed, and Russia was given over to Bolshevik party rule. The Bolsheviks repudiated all the foreign debts of the old régime and in March 1918 made peace with Germany in the Treaty of Brest-Litovsk. Russia disentangled herself as quickly and as completely as possible from Europe,

1. See p. 203.

in order to consolidate the revolution and to press on with the drastic programme of collectivizing land and industry which Lenin held to be the immediate task. He took over a country in chaos: the government bankrupt, transport collapsed, industry paralysed, the countryside torn by civil war and hunger, the towns seething with revolution. Adherents of the old régime, formed into 'White' armies, held out against the Communists in certain provinces, and were helped by the western governments that still hoped to bring Russia back into the war against Germany. Lenin's drastic confiscations of land, railways, industries, mines, and banks – without compensation to the former owners – threw increasing numbers into the counter-revolutionary camp. To aid the 'White' armies, Allied expeditionary forces were sent to the fringes of Russia, to Archangel and Murmansk, Sebastopol and Vladivostok. Revolution brought civil war, and civil war brought foreign intervention: intervention of the Japanese to help Admiral Kolchak in Siberia, of the French to help General Denikin in the Caucasus, of the British to help General Yudenitch in the Gulf of Finland, who in the spring of 1919 prepared an advance against Petrograd. The end of the war in Europe freed allied forces for the war of intervention, which continued for another two years.

For three years altogether, civil war raged, countered internally by ruthless terrorism and by prodigies of improvisation on the part of Trotsky to keep the Red Armies fed and supplied in the field. For these years Trotsky lived in a train, keeping in personal touch with his sixteen armies in the field and by telephone with Lenin in Moscow. The unity of command and the dynamic energy of the defence brought the Bolsheviks victory against all their opponents, whom they were able to defeat separately. By the summer of 1920 the only serious threat came from the armies in Poland, strongly supported by the French, who were anxious to keep communism out of eastern Europe. In that year the Poles, under General Pilsudski, tried to capture the rich grainlands of the Ukraine and advanced as far as Kiev. General Maxime Weygand, special aide to Foch, was sent by the French to assist them. But freed from engagements on other fronts, the Red Army was now able to concentrate all its efforts against the Poles, and in its counterattacks almost reached Warsaw. This unhappy prolongation of the war ended in the Treaty of Riga in 1921 (see Map 14). It fixed the Russo-Polish frontiers on a line that left some three million Russians under Polish rule and a legacy of bitterness between the new Poland and the new Russia.

At home Lenin created a system of thoroughgoing collectivization called, significantly, 'War Communism'. It was the Leninist counterpart to Walter Rathenau's 'War Socialism' in Germany before 1918. It in-

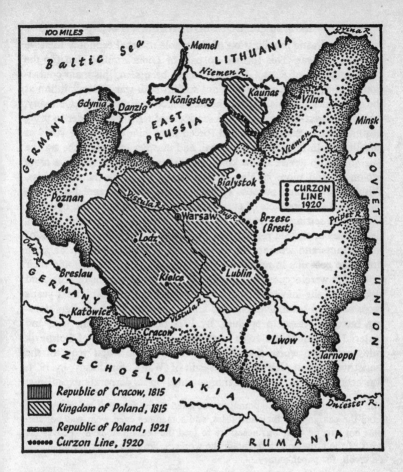

MAP 14. FRONTIERS OF POLAND, 1815–1921

The old Kingdom of Poland, which had disappeared from the map at the end of the eighteenth century when it was partitioned among Austria, Prussia, and Russia, has reappeared in various forms ever since. Napoleon set up a Grand Duchy of Warsaw (see Map 2). In 1815 a Kingdom of Poland was created under Russian domination. Polish revolts in 1830, 1846, and 1863 kept the Polish Question and national spirit alive. As a result of the simultaneous defeat of Russia, Austria-Hungary, and Germany in the First World War, a new Republic of Poland was created with its eastern frontier on the 'Curzon Line'. Under Pilsudski the Poles renewed the war against Russia and advanced the frontier more than a hundred miles eastward, where it was fixed by the Treaty of Riga in 1921. (See also Map 26.)

volved the drastic mobilization of the whole national economy to serve
the needs of war. This formed no part of Lenin's initial plan for the
communization of Russia. In 1917, as has been seen,[1] his main contention had been that Russia could not sustain both war and revolution at
the same time. On this doctrine he had concluded peace with Germany,
making at Brest-Litovsk immense sacrifices of territory in order to bring
hostilities to an end. Events had forced upon him three more years of
hostilities both internal and external, and in order to sustain the war he
was obliged to devise a new kind of social revolution. It meant a more
prolonged and more ruthless requisitioning of goods than was wise.
With the overriding purpose of keeping the armies manned and supplied, food and products of every kind had to be requisitioned by force.
This meant seizing not merely the wealth of the relatively small propertied classes of the old régime, but attacking the interests of the mass of
the peasants and workers. In some provinces the confiscation of grain
drove the peasants in rebellion. They hid their stores of corn and their
cattle, and were accused of sabotage. Annual confiscations of crops and
stock led to the inevitable and traditional peasant reprisal – next year's
crops were not sown, livestock was killed and eaten. With workers starving, factories ceased to produce. By 1920 famine stalked the land and
material conditions, far from improving after three years of Bolshevik
rule, were even worse than they had been in the worst years of the
tsarist war against Germany. The result of 'War Communism', by 1921,
was economic ruin. In 1921 Lenin summed up its desperate expedients:

The peculiarity of war communism consisted in the fact that we really took
from the peasants all their surpluses, and sometimes even what was not surplus but part of what was necessary to feed the peasant, took it to cover the
costs of the army and to maintain the workers. We took it for the most part
on credit, for paper money.

His abrupt abandonment of such a policy in 1921 was dictated by
the attitude of the peasant masses, as well as by Lenin's own sense of
realism. They had reluctantly endured war communism for fear of a
'White' restoration and the loss of their lands. As soon as the war of
intervention was at an end, their resentments flared up unchecked. In
March 1921 Lenin had to admit that 'tens and hundreds of thousands of
disbanded soldiers' were turning to banditry, creating violent peasant
uprisings. His new improvisation, the New Economic Policy (NEP), was
a reversal of the policies of war communism. It was presented as a
temporary halt in the revolutionary policy of collectivization, a step
back in order to move two steps forward later. In effect it reverted to

1. See p. 565.

the inducements of private profit as a stimulus to greater production. Peasants would no longer have their surplus produce requisitioned, but they would pay a tax in kind, calculated as a percentage of the crops harvested. What remained could be sold freely on the market. The new policy came too late to affect the sowing programme of the peasants, and for a second year in succession drought ruined the harvests of the Volga basin. In 1921–2 a terrible famine devastated that area and affected the food supplies of the towns. Only the good harvest of 1922 brought the beginning of real recovery. Meanwhile commercial incentives were also restored in industry and trade. Small industries were permitted and even encouraged, and trading for private profit revived.

When Lenin died in 1924 the new régime had survived. It had weathered famine as well as civil and foreign war, and had tightened its control upon the whole country. Already too – so dynamic was the revolutionary situation in Russia – the basis of large-scale economic planning had been laid. Here again Lenin learned from wartime Germany. Early in 1918 Lenin claimed that socialism had already been realized – the material, economic half of it in Germany in the form of state monopoly capitalism; the other political half in Russia, in the form of the dictatorship of the proletariat. The urgent economic needs of Russia dictated the earliest form this should take: central planning to expand and develop industry by means of extensive electrification. Lenin defined communism as 'Soviet power plus electrification'. In April 1921 a newly created 'state general planning commission' (Gosplan) began its work, which was to bear fruit later in the great Five-Year plans.[1] Their construction of 'socialism in one country' was the climax of that process of 'nationalizing society' which was so greatly forwarded by the war.

The Turkish Revolution. In one other belligerent country similar trends produced a very different pattern of régime. Turkey, when peace was concluded in 1918, was cut back to an Empire of 300,000 square miles. It remained larger in area than any European state apart from Russia, but its population numbered only some thirteen million and its economy was primitive. The Treaty of Sèvres of 1920, which the victorious powers offered to Turkey, was rejected by the Sultan Mohammed VI until British troops occupied Constantinople. When he signed it, the Nationalist Assembly at Ankara repudiated both the treaty and the Sultan and organized national resistance. When a Greek army landed at Smyrna in 1921, there ensued a war between Greece and Turkey (1921–2) which ended in the rout of the Greeks. Eventually, in the Treaty of Lausanne of 1923, the Turks won better terms than those offered three years earlier. In return for Turkey's giving up all her claims to North

1. See p. 692.

African territories and to the Arabian kingdoms, the Allies recognized full Turkish sovereignty over the remaining provinces, cancelled claims for reparations, and gave up their former territorial concessions in Turkey. Internally, in 1922 the sultanate was abolished, and Mustapha Kemal (Kemal Atatürk) was elected president of the Turkish Republic. Kemal set about westernizing the nation in all its aspects. His policy was no less radical than Lenin's revolution in Russia. All former religious, military, and civil titles and privileges were abolished. An elected national assembly and local councils, based on universal suffrage, were instituted, but government remained in the hands of a single party. Islam ceased to be the official religion of the state, and Moslem practices and customs were attacked, as were popular illiteracy and the subjection of women. Although it was 1934 before Turkey, also, introduced a five-year plan for expanding agriculture and industry, by 1923 she was already undergoing a great social revolution, conducted from the centre by a dictatorial government which planned to convert her into a modern western nation-state. Her successfully military defiance of the victorious European powers, closely parallel to Russia's, served to fortify national enthusiasm for the new régime.

In all these diverse ways the main short-term consequence of the First World War, by 1923, was a universal strengthening of nationalist ideals and national institutions. Older nations, like Britain and France, emerged from the ordeal victorious only because they sacrificed so much in the cause of national defence and survival. Germany even more forcibly pointed the way toward a form of state capitalism, the regimentation of national resources, capital and labour alike, in the cause of state power. The new states of the Baltic and the eastern marchlands, whether revivals like Poland, augmentations like Yugoslavia, or new creations like Czechoslovakia, enjoyed separate existence as nation-states.[1] Russia and Turkey, in different ways, embarked upon great new experiments in the social and economic reorganization of the whole community by single-party dictatorships. Everywhere war gave fresh impetus to the growth of the nation-state which was also a monolithic state, claiming an allegiance and competence superior to every other human group.

VOGUE FOR DEMOCRACY

If the first consequence of the war was to carry nationalist enthusiasm and the nation-state to the highest point of fulfilment so far reached in European history, the second was to bring democratic ideals and institutions to peoples who had not known them before. The war

1. See p. 597.

which, at least since 1917, had been announced as a war 'to make the world safe for democracy' seemed in 1919 to have achieved its aim. It was natural enough that the nations who had just attained independence should adopt, as their form of government, the democratic institutions which had brought victory and emancipation. In instinctive hostility to autocracy, which had symbolized their old subjection, nationalists turned to the more enlightened ways of the West. It was perhaps more surprising that defeated powers such as Germany, Austria, Hungary, and Turkey should adopt the forms of government favoured by their enemies. But all had meanwhile undergone political revolution, and the most impressive fact in the world of 1919 was that whereas the dynastic states (including Russia) had gone down into defeat and collapse, the democratic states had withstood all the strains of war and emerged from it victorious. It was the western, maritime, democratic nations that triumphed – Great Britain and France, Belgium and Italy, the United States and Canada, and the other great overseas Dominions nurtured in democratic ways of life. That these also happened to include the most industrialized states and those which collectively dominated the oceans of the world was a fact more often overlooked, since it was obscured by the prewar industrial and naval power of Germany. The power of Germany had indeed been immense – great enough to prolong the war and to exact heavy toll from her enemies in every campaign – but Germany was alone among her allies in being a great industrial and naval power, and tested against the industrial capacity and the manpower of the western allies, her might proved insufficient. These underlying factors of power were less obvious in 1919 than the belief, and the hope, that it was democracy which had won the war. In democracy, it seemed, lay the secret of success in the modern world. Democracy came into vogue, and nationalism appeared to be its natural ally. The optimistic beliefs of the liberal nationalists of 1848 seemed at last to be proved right.[1]

The New Democracies. Accordingly, in one defeated country after another, new democratic constitutions were set up. Germany herself set the pace with her Weimar Republic, one of the most completely democratic paper constitutions ever written. But its prelude was civil war. The political revolution of November 1918, which accompanied the armistice and the abdication of the Emperor, was made by none and wanted by none. It was adopted by the Social Democrats after it had happened, but it rested on no genuinely revolutionary sentiment or movement in the country. It corresponded to 1871 in France – not to 1789 or even 1848 – for it was the outcome of national defeat and the

1. See p. 233.

disappearance of a dynasty. The three focal points of revolutionary action were Kiel, Munich, and Berlin. The sailors and workers of Kiel, on 4 November, set up a Workers' and Soldiers' Council to defy the central authorities, and their example was quickly followed by several other ports and cities. In Bavaria trade unionists and socialists of Munich set up a republic under Kurt Eisner, a Jewish socialist journalist recently released from prison. In Berlin the socialists Ebert and Scheidemann pressed for the abdication of Wilhelm II, and on 9 November Prince Max handed over the office of 'Reich Chancellor' (*Reichskanzler*) to Ebert, who formed a provisional government. Between this government composed of socialists, and the various Workers' and Soldiers' Councils which sprang up all over Germany, there existed a division of authority very like that which had arisen in Russia in November 1917.

The division was ended only by the meeting of the new National Assembly, elected in January 1919. It met at Weimar on 6 February. Most of the Social Democrats, wedded to the idea of a democratic republic based on representative institutions, supported the new assembly. Only the independent Socialists and the Marxian Spartacists, led by Karl Liebknecht and Rosa Luxemburg, echoed Lenin's cry of 'All power to the soviets'. The High Command, under Hindenburg, also backed the Weimar Assembly. The conservative and liberal parties all adjusted themselves to the new situation. Industrialists came to terms with trade unions, and national habits of respect for order and traditions of discipline rallied all save the extremists to the prospect of constitutional government, and so to the provisional government of Ebert. But in conditions of distress and bewilderment the extremists were strong. During December there were frequent clashes between Spartacists and soldiers. At the end of the month the Spartacists formed the new German Communist party and denounced the forthcoming National Assembly as the organ of counter-revolution. In January 1919 came a general strike and an attempted communist revolution in Berlin. Social Democrats cooperated with the army to crush it, and both Liebknecht and Rosa Luxemburg were killed. The meeting of the Weimar Assembly in February was accompanied by a period of civil war in Bavaria, in which Kurt Eisner was assassinated, and by strikes and disorders in most of the industrial areas. The Social Democrats, heirs of a political revolution which they had not made, were forced by events into reluctant alliance with the military and conservative leaders to prevent a social revolution. It was not an auspicious beginning for the new democratic republic which the Weimar Assembly now proceeded to set up.

The abdication of the Kaiser had been the signal for abdication on the part of most German princes. The various forms of republic proclaimed in the different German states were all democratic in spirit. The Weimar Assembly was itself elected on universal suffrage of all men and women over twenty years old, on a system of proportional representation. The decks had been cleared, with the crushing of communism, for the erection of a thoroughly democratic constitution. Even the initial choice of provincial Weimar, home of the humanist tradition of Goethe and Schiller, rather than of Prussian Berlin with its metropolitan mob and its communist threat, symbolized the new outlook. The 423 deputies, unlike their predecessors of 1848, included only one poet. They were mostly party leaders and trade-union officials with considerable political experience. The Social Democrats were now divided into two opposing parties known as the Majority Socialists and the more extreme Independent Socialists. The Majority Socialists won only 165 of the seats, so that although they were the largest party they had no independent majority and were once more forced to find allies. Divided from the Catholic Centre party by faith and from the liberal German Democratic party by social policy, any such alliance would be uneasy. But the Majority Socialist, Philipp Scheidemann, succeeded in forming a coalition government with these Centre and Democratic parties; and this combination, which had framed the 'July Resolution' of 1917 for 'peace without annexation', became the most familiar and characteristic alignment within the Weimar Republic. Ebert was appointed Reich president. In May 1919 the Assembly moved to Berlin. The following month the new government, bitterly reluctant but powerless to resume the war, had to accept the terms of peace dictated by the Allies at Versailles.[1] 'In ten years,' said Max Weber, 'we shall all be nationalists.' The new draft constitution was finally approved on 31 July and came into effect on 14 August 1919. It was mainly the work of Hugo Preuss, a liberal academic lawyer, but it was amended and added to during the Assembly's debates. It borrowed elements from American, British, French, and Swiss versions of democracy.

The constitution establishing the new Republic, unlike all previous German constitutions, provided for both a central and unified state, and it was based on the doctrines of sovereignty of the people organized as a single national entity. The German states kept considerable control over local government but all were bound by the constitution to have a republican form of government based on universal suffrage and proportional representation. The central government enjoyed a more complete national power than that of the old Reich, for it controlled the army, communications, and its own independent finance. A federal

1. See p. 622.

council (Reichsrat) rested on separate representation of the states; but the Reichsrat had little power beyond a suspensory veto on legislation comparable with that of the British House of Lords, so that the power of this upper chamber in no way compared to the power of the United States Senate. The Reichstag, elected on secret, universal suffrage with proportional representation, was the sovereign legislative power. A president, elected by popular vote for a term of seven years, held powers more like those of the French than of the American president. Government was to lie in the hands of the Chancellor who, in the role of Prime Minister, would be chosen by the President but would be responsible along with his colleagues to the Reichstag. A supreme court for the Reich, on the model of the United States Supreme Court, was also set up. The device of referendum was borrowed from Switzerland. The constitution guaranteed the fundamental rights of the citizen – equality before the law, civic freedoms, separation of church and state, and economic freedoms such as the exercise of trade-union rights. Much of the old social and economic order survived almost intact in the judiciary, the bureaucracy, and above all the military authorities. The big landowners and industrial combinations remained, and attempts at nationalization came to nothing. The new political democracy was thus superimposed upon a social order that had changed surprisingly little. An overriding and universal national resentment against defeat, against the terms of peace, and against the Allies, who were responsible for both, was the only common sentiment. The new régime commanded little emotional loyalty, and was soon to be unjustly condemned as having been delivered in the baggage trains of the Allies.

All the elements that were later to amalgamate to destroy the new democracy were there in 1920. Militarism and aggressive nationalism in all their forms were aggravated by the terms of peace and encouraged by the reliance which the new government was forced to place upon them. Even in 1919 the Nationalist party and the conservative People's party, representing the Prussian militarist and nationalist interests, returned sixty-three deputies. The election of Hindenburg in 1925 as president in succession to Ebert marked their revival. Anti-Semitism, not new in Germany, took new and inflamed forms from 1918 onward, stimulated by the immigration of eastern Jews into Germany during the war and by the desire of nationalists to find scapegoats for Germany's ills. Even the technique of the armed patriotic rising to overthrow the legitimate government by force was tried out in the Kapp *Putsch* of 1920. Wolfgang Kapp and a group of professional army officers hatched a plot to seize power. On 11 March 1920 Captain Ehrhardt, commander of two crack brigades of marine troops who were to be disbanded under orders of the Inter-Allied Control Commission, marched 5,000 of his men into Berlin. Overawing the capital, they proclaimed the National Assembly dissolved, the Weimar constitution void, and the government deposed in favour of one headed by Kapp and General von Lüttwitz. Military leaders in Berlin, Silesia, and Pomerania supported them. Ebert and the government of Noske moved to Dresden, and even loyal military officers remained passive. The *putsch* was defeated by the Berlin workers, who declared a general strike and paralysed the city. After five days the insurgents, divided among themselves, gave up the attempt and fled. Despite the weakness of the legitimate government, the republic was saved by the workers, who were united in a resolve to defeat counter-revolution. Those responsible for the rising escaped or were amnestied. The military class were confirmed in their power by the appointment of General von Seeckt to replace General von Lüttwitz as chief of the German Army (Reichswehr); von Seeckt had refused during the crisis to fire upon his fellow officers. In Bavaria the *putsch* led to a right-wing coalition government which paved the way for a further attempt in 1923.

In Munich in January 1919 there was created the German Workers' party (*Deutsche Arbeiter Partei*), one of many little political malcontent movements of the time. It attracted demobilized soldiers, romantic adventurers, and political intriguers. In September an unknown Austrian ex-corporal, Adolf Hitler, joined its political committee, and in March 1920 the party was rechristened the National Socialist German Workers' party (*Nationalsozialistische Deutsche Arbeiter Partei*, or N.S.D.A.P.). In spirit it was anti-Semitic, anti-communist, and antiparliamentary, and it was backed by remnants of the former Pan-German League and other patriotic societies. More important, it was backed by General Ludendorff and his wife. In November 1923 this party attempted a *putsch* in Munich, much on the lines of the Kapp *Putsch*. By then the parliamentary government was more confident and the Reichswehr remained loyal to it. A volley dispersed the insurgents, and Hitler was sentenced to five years in Landsberg prison. There he dictated to his fellow prisoner, Rudolf Hess, the first volume of his autobiography, *My Struggle (Mein Kampf)*. Here were all the bases of the party which, ten years later, was to overthrow the Weimar Republic and undo the work of the peace settlement of 1919.

The Fascist Revolution, 1922. In Italy, where the constitutional monarchy of King Victor Emmanuel III survived the world war, political and social conditions were no more conducive to the working of democratic institutions than in Germany. Although Italy was one of the victorious powers, she had played a minor role in the war and in 1919 failed to exact from the peacemakers of Paris all the benefits of the bargains she had made with the Allies in her secret treaties.[1] She gained the Tyrol, Trieste, part of the Dalmatian coast, and certain islands of the Aegean and Adriatic seas. She did not gain Fiume, and she was not given under mandate any of the former German colonies. Being weaker in natural resources and industrial development, Italy felt the burden of war more acutely than Britain or France. Her parliamentary governments were indecisive and unstable, and in 1919 while brigandage broke out in the south, strikes and industrial revolt broke out in the north. Of all the older parliamentary states in Europe, she was perhaps the most vulnerable to extremist attacks from left or right. The Italian counterpart of the Kapp *Putsch* was the raid on Fiume, carried out in September 1919 by the poet-aviator D'Annunzio in order to claim it for the Italian kingdom. The dashing romanticism of the escapade – D'Annunzio garbed his men in cloaks, crested them with eagle's feathers, armed them with daggers, and flew them to Fiume in aeroplanes – stirred memories of the hectic days of Garibaldi and the *Risorgimento*. The Italian government of Giolitti had the unhappy and unpopular task of driving him out on Christmas Eve, after three months of wild heroics, and of restoring Fiume to the inter-Allied authorities, who later made it a 'free city'.

By the summer of 1920 workers' soviets were being set up in the factories, and the anti-communist war veterans were forming armed bands. Most important of these were the *Fascio di combattimento*, a group of strong-arm fighters founded in Milan the year before by the former socialist journalist, Benito Mussolini. The fasces, symbol of authority carried by the lictors of ancient Rome, consisted of an axe surrounded by a bundle of rods, denoting power of life and death and also of strength, for the bundle was bound tightly together. So the *Fascio* presented itself as the new symbol of authority and strength, necessary if Italy were ever to regain her pride of place in Europe. The movement spread during the next two years of economic distress amid periodic scares of a communist revolution, and attracted to itself discontented youths, frightened *bourgeoisie*, and industrialists who resented the new strength of their workers. In the elections of 1921 the Fascists gained thirty-five seats, and such was the disarray of parties that in October 1922, when Giolitti's ministry resigned, Mussolini was emboldened to stage a 'march on Rome'. Mobilizing 30,000 of his black-shirted followers in disciplined formation, he sent them from Milan to Rome. He himself travelled by train, wearing a bowler hat. But the show of force was enough to win him the backing of 400 non-Fascist deputies, and

1. See p. 633.

the King invited Mussolini to form a government. The chamber voted him dictatorial powers for one year – long enough for the Fascists to take permanent control of the machinery of the state, and to force through a law that entitled whichever party won the biggest vote in elections to claim two thirds of the seats in the chamber. On this semi-constitutional basis Mussolini established the dictatorship that was to last twenty-one years. Democracy in Italy, on the defensive after 1918, was overthrown by 1924.

Hungary and Austria. In Hungary the flirtation with democracy was even briefer. In the moment of defeat the conservative Magyar leaders turned to the liberal aristocrat Mihály Károlyi, who on 31 October 1918, only four days before signing the armistice with the Italians, was asked by the Emperor Charles I to form a provisional government. Károlyi, hoping for better terms, negotiated a separate armistice with the French on 13 November. But the Rumanians continued to pour into Transylvania, and by March 1919 the Hungarians were forced to retreat from even the agreed frontiers. This led to the collapse of Károlyi's government before he had time to do more than distribute his own family estates to the peasants. Power fell to the communist Béla Kun, friend of Lenin recently returned from Russia. Kun proclaimed a Soviet republic and launched a fresh offensive against first Slovakia and then Rumania. The menace of Bolshevism so far west as Budapest alarmed the western powers. They blockaded Hungary and threatened military action. The Rumanians advanced and took Budapest, and on 1 August Béla Kun fled. By November 1919 Admiral Nicholas Horthy, representative of the conservative and military class in command of the army, assumed power. He conducted a 'white terror' against communism, which also liquidated liberalism. Hungary's experience of liberal-democratic rule had lasted for only five months, and she preceded Italy in establishing a semi-fascist dictatorship vowing vengeance for the loss of territories suffered in the peace settlement. The peasants were effectively disfranchised, although Social Democrats and even trade unions survived in the towns. Hungary remained until 1944 a kingdom without a king ruled by an admiral without a fleet.

In Austria a democratic republic was eventually set up by agreement between the two main parties of Christian Socialists (Catholic conservatives) of the provinces and the Social Democrats of Vienna. Both hoped for a union between Austria and the new Germany. When the Allies forbade it, they combined to devise a parliamentary régime for their small population of seven million living in a little landlocked territory. Austrian nationalism hardly existed as yet, for unlike the Magyars the Germans of the Austrian empire had never formed a united national group. Their loyalty had been to the Habsburgs, and now that there was no Habsburg ruler, the strongest loyalty they felt was towards the eight provinces (*Ländern*). The new constitution had therefore to be federal. For some eighteen months the parties negotiated about different drafts, and the constitution was finally passed by the Constituent Assembly in October 1920. Federal legislative power was invested in the National Council, which was elected on universal, secret, direct suffrage of all citizens over twenty years old, by proportional representation. A federal council, elected by the provincial diets, was created but given little power. A federal President, elected by both chambers sitting together as in France, was head of the state; a federal Chancellor and ministers, chosen by the National Council, were to govern. There was provision for popular referendum. The government was kept weak; the National Council which controlled it could not be dissolved and so came to behave irresponsibly towards the government, and the emphasis on proportional representation discouraged political compromise and coherent government. The system was too elaborate and too subtle to be worked well by a people with little experience of self-government, and the constant tension between the two major parties resulted in parliamentary deadlock. These defects, combined with the economic distress of postwar Austria, and with the political manoeuvres of the *Heimwehr*, built by Prince Starhemberg into a private right-wing army, were to prove the ruin of the republic by 1934.

Eastern Europe. Nowhere in central Europe, then, was democracy firmly established within the five years after the war. Eastern Europe had further difficulties of its own. The new Poland, reconstituted as a result of the simultaneous collapse of the three powers which for more than a century had kept her partitioned, fared little better. With their homeland turned by the eastern campaigns into a battlefield, with national leadership divided between the anti-Russian Pilsudski with his Polish Legion, and the anti-German Dmowski who headed the Polish National Committee set up in Paris, the Poles were united sufficiently by the famous Polish pianist, Paderewski, to agree that Pilsudski should become chief of state of the new Republic. A constituent diet assembled in February 1919, and took some three years to produce a new democratic constitution. The strongly nationalistic conservative and peasant forces which predominated in the diet combined to check socialism and the influence of Pilsudski, and to prepare a régime in which parliament closely controlled the government. Modelled closely on the Third French Republic, the Polish constitution also produced unstable government and a weak executive power. The first elections of 1922 yielded a deadlock between conservatives and socialists, from which minority groups profited. The first President to be elected was assassinated within a few days. By 1926 the constitution was forcibly changed by Pilsudski himself, backed by a section of the army and by the communists.

The fragility of democratic institutions in most of the new states of south-eastern Europe was similarly increased by their patchwork structure. The first task of the new régimes in Yugoslavia, Czechoslovakia, and Rumania, as in Poland, was to create nations out of collections of diverse territories. Yugoslavia comprised not only Serbia but westernized areas like Croatia and easternized ex-Turkish areas like Macedonia. Czechoslovakia included industrialized Bohemia, which had been under Austrian rule along with the backward peasant territories of Slovakia, and Ruthenia, which had been under Magyar rule. Rumania had to amalgamate Transylvania, which had been taken from Hungary with Bessarabia, claimed from Russia. Into all three countries were introduced the most advanced political institutions of representative parliamentary government, and such favourite devices as proportional representation, the referendum, and elaborate bills of rights. The Czechs overcame more successfully than did the Poles the problem of amalgamating the National Council of exiles formed in Paris, the Czech Legion which fought against Austria, and the National Committee which set itself up in Prague. Eduard Beneš from Paris collaborated smoothly with the veteran nationalist leader in Prague, Karel Kramář; and when the Czech legionaries duly returned from heroic escapades in Russia, having retreated through Siberia to Japan and the United States, their leader Professor Tomáš Masaryk was acclaimed president of the new Czechoslovak Republic. Beneš and Masaryk led the new multi-national democracy along the civilized road to toleration and free government, despite strong divisive forces of religion, race, and tradition. The combination of more advanced and industrial areas with more backward and agricultural areas was an economic advantage in Czechoslovakia. Bohemia, with three quarters of the industrial plant of old Austria, was balanced by the agricultural additions of Slovakia and Ruthenia. German minorities did not, at first, act as an obstructive force to national unity. It is no accident that Czech democracy proved able to survive longer and attained its ideals more successfully than other Danubian democracies. Liberal democracy and social democracy allied with nationalism more completely there than elsewhere. For staffing the administrative services of the new states it was inevitable that the government should rely heavily upon the large number of experienced officials inherited from the overgrown bureaucracy of the Habsburgs. In Czechoslovakia this gave predominance to the Czechs and led to resentment among the Slovaks.

But liberal policies and concessions held such resentments within bounds.

The politics of Yugoslavia, Greece, and Bulgaria were complicated by the Macedonian question, as well as by communism. Macedonia was divided between Greece and Yugoslavia, and the exchange of minorities between Greece and Bulgaria put many Macedonians under Bulgarian rule. These Macedonians formed an Internal Macedonian Revolutionary Organization (IMRO). Violent and terrorist in its methods, it agitated against the new Bulgarian government of Agrarians, led by Alexander Stambolisky, which after October 1919 ruled in the interests of the eighty per cent of the Bulgarian population who were peasants. Though agitating ostensibly for an independent Macedonia, and therefore hostile to both Greece and Yugoslavia, IMRO mostly favoured the annexation of Macedonia to Bulgaria. In June 1923 it helped to overthrow Stambolisky by a *coup d'état*, and a few days later he was assassinated. A communist rising in September was then crushed with great brutality, and raids on Greek and Yugoslav territory continued into 1924 and 1925. Yugoslavia, rent by internal disputes between Serbs and Croats and Slovenes, reverted to a royal dictatorship by 1929. Just as Slovaks accused Czechs of monopolizing administrative posts, so Croats accused Serbs of the same propensity. Greece, whose political life was disturbed both by the decline of the monarchy under Alexander (1917-20) and George II (1922-3), and by the great influx of some 1,400,000 refugees from Turkey, Russia, and Bulgaria, became a republic in 1924. In 1923, following a frontier dispute between Greece and Albania, Italy as protector of Albania sent warships to bombard and occupy the Greek island of Corfu. It was Mussolini's first defiance of the League of Nations. Although the League made him withdraw troops from Corfu, Greece had to pay Italy an indemnity. The incident was characteristic of the troubled relations between all the Balkan states in these years. Bitter nationalist jealousies prevented the firm rooting of democracy in the turbulent peninsula.

The fate of Albania was a miniature parody of Balkan politics.[1] Set up in 1912 as an 'independent' state by Austria-Hungary and Italy in order to block Serbian expansion in the Adriatic, it was divided between Greece and Italy in 1914, reverted to Austrian occupation in 1915, and was liberated by Serbians, French, and Italians in 1918. In December 1918, a National Assembly met and set up a regency government. When in August 1920 Italy withdrew from Albania, the great powers restored its frontiers to roughly those of 1913 and admitted it to the League of Nations. The leader of one of its most important Moslem clans,

1. See p. 473.

Ahmed Bey Zogu, became its strong-arm Prime Minister. He was driven out by revolt in 1924 but restored with Yugoslav help to proclaim a republic. In January 1925 he became President of Albania. Its economic condition as the most backward state in Europe was not greatly improved by the discovery of an oil field at Petrolia, nor its role as a puppet state by the need to rely upon Italian protection and aid. Nationalist sentiment was strong, but democracy could strike no roots in so uncongenial a soil. Yet it remained within the League of Nations as an independent sovereign state and evolved its panoply of self-government. All the usual lip service was paid to democratic forms until in 1928 a Constituent Assembly was induced to change the constitution and proclaim Zogu as King Zog I of Albania.

In the Baltic borderlands, ceded by Russia in 1918 and recognized as the independent states of Finland, Estonia, Latvia, and Lithuania, extreme democratic institutions were implanted with somewhat more durability and success. Finland preserved neutrality in the war and enjoyed a burst of economic prosperity, both agricultural and industrial. In 1918 a very brutal civil war broke out between two rival Finnish armies – the White Guard led by General Mannerheim and backed by Germany, and the Red Guard supported by the socialist workers and by Russians. With the collapse of Germany, Mannerheim headed a government which was recognized by the Allies, and throughout Finland it conducted a 'white terror' comparable with Horthy's activities in Hungary. Yet in 1919 a new democratic constitution on the standard pattern was introduced, and all parties cooperated in making it work with considerable success. The other three Baltic countries – as in the case of Poland – did not escape from being battlefields until 1920, because of the prolonged war of intervention against Soviet Russia. But in 1920 Estonia, in 1922 Latvia and Lithuania, set up democratic republican constitutions although Lithuania's did not last. These northern peoples of hardy peasants and fisherfolk had a spirit of sturdy independence and of political realism which overcame the immense difficulties of postwar recovery and settlement. The three smaller countries lost their independence after Soviet occupation in 1940; and in 1939–40 the Finns fought the Soviet Union in an effort to preserve their independence.[1]

When the five postwar years are thus reviewed as a whole, they offer little warrant for the view that democratic government was in any sense made safer by the war. For a brief time after the end of hostilities democracy came into vogue throughout Europe. It was adopted for a while by all the new states of Europe, and by all the defeated states, with the exception of Russia. It usually included the most complete and

1. See p. 766.

advanced forms of universal suffrage, proportional representation, referendum. The western political institutions of parliamentary government and elected presidencies were implanted in countries that had little or no experience in any kind of self-government, whose nationalistic passions had been aroused to fever pitch by the war and by prolonged hostilities in eastern Europe after 1918, and whose economic and social life was still very much less advanced than that of the West. The tide of communism lapped their eastern frontiers; formidable tasks of national assimilation and cohesion confronted them internally; and adverse economic conditions beset their efforts to raise their standards of living. It would be difficult to conceive a set of conditions less favourable to experiments in political self-government; and the speedy abandonment of so novel a mode of government is hardly to be wondered at. The wonder is perhaps that in the Baltic states and Czechoslovakia it succeeded so well and survived for so long. It would be wrong to blame democratic government for the turbulence or the ills of eastern Europe after the war. Countries which hardly embarked upon the experiment at all – such as Greece and Bulgaria and Hungary – and which kept or quickly reverted to more familiar autocratic government, fared no better than those which persevered with democratic forms. The failures of democracy are not an explanation of Europe's misfortunes; rather were both the failures of democracy, and the misfortunes of Europe, alike results of the aftermath of war itself, and especially of the economic exhaustion of Europe which undermined the whole postwar settlement, whether national or international, whether made by the separate efforts of nationalities or by the deliberations of the statesmen who gathered in Paris. Any postwar political settlement was necessarily built upon shifting sand, so long as the economic dislocations of war continued to sap its foundations by denying the plenty which peace needed for its fulfilment. There was indeed a correlation between democracy and prosperity, but which was the prerequisite of the other? By 1939 democratic governments survived in most of the dozen countries of the world which had the highest income per head of the population – and hardly anywhere else.

THE ECONOMICS OF EXHAUSTION

The financial cost of the war, though astronomical as compared with the cost of previous wars, was among the least important of the economic burdens that it placed upon all the belligerents. During the twenty years of war against the French Revolution and Napoleon, Great Britain's national debt increased roughly eightfold. During the four years between 1914 and 1918, it increased nearly twelvefold. The total direct expenditure for all the belligerents has been estimated at 186 billion dollars (£45,000,000,000). Even so the amount of property destroyed, of ships and cargoes sunk, of wealth which might otherwise have been produced was incalculable. Immeasurable amounts of materials, labour, energy had been expended for unproductive or destructive purposes. Policies of human welfare, whether in education and health or in social improvement, had been checked or dropped. The barest necessities of life – food and housing, clothing and fuel – were lacking for millions of Europeans in an age when science and technology had promised abundance. The livelihood of most of the peoples of Europe had come to depend upon a stabilized social order and an economic system delicately geared to the flow of world trade, and now this fabric of prewar civilization was violently disrupted and destroyed. What had taken generations to create, including conditions of commercial confidence between nations, could not suddenly be restored at the command of even the most powerful governments.

Economic Dislocation. It was this dislocation of economic life and this disruption of world trade which proved to be the most intractable economic results of the war. The war had undermined the foundations of Europe's industrial supremacy in the world, and industrialized Europe could not thus contract out of the world's economy for four years without finding, when it wished to return, that other continents had found ways of doing without it. Not only had the productive capacity of the United States expanded so that her exports trebled in value, but in South America and India, and in most of the British Dominions, new home industries had developed. In the Far East, Japan, belligerent more in name than in sacrifices, fed with her textiles and other manufactures the markets of China, India, and South America, which had previously been supplied from Europe. The prewar pattern of international trade had been completely changed. Economic reconstruction involved much more than a mere 'return to normalcy', but this was little appreciated when the armistice was signed. To many businessmen and politicians, and to some who were both, 'normalcy' meant the world of 1913. They failed to appreciate that modern war is also a revolution, and that the economic world of 1913 had already passed into history as much as had the Habsburg and Romanoff Empires. It has been pointed out that surprisingly many of the economic slogans of the postwar years began with the prefix *re*: reconstruction, recovery, reparations, retrenchment, repayment of war debts, revaluation of currencies, restoration of the gold standard. The physical exhaustion of the war years was succeeded by mental exhaustion in the postwar years. There was a lack of capacity and of will to think things out afresh. The doctrines that prevailed in 1919, and not only among the peacemakers in Paris, were those implied in the Fourteen Points of 1918: that the trouble had come from secret diplomacy, naval rivalry, tariffs, competition in armaments, and colonialism; and that so long as these evils were now avoided and the doctrine of national self-determination and self-government respected, all that was good and pleasant in the prewar world might still be retrieved.

The satisfactions given to the demands for national self-determination in the postwar settlement even militated against the other policies deemed to be necessary for a peaceful world. Triumphant nationalism, especially in the Balkans, proved to be violently intolerant and quarrelsome, and to prefer the aim of a balanced national economy, achieved if need be by tariffs, to the Cobdenite ideal of world free trade. Nations with infant industries wanted to nurse and protect them, and old industrial powers like Britain and Belgium found it necessary to safeguard their wrecked or disjointed economies against new competitors. In such conditions colonies, and the naval power that went with them, seemed more desirable than ever. The hydra-headed fear of bolshevism added to the sense of insecurity which checked disarmament. The difficulties of collaboration became apparent by 1921 in attempts to organize the economic reconstruction of central Europe. A conference held at Portorose in Istria was attended by representatives of all the new states including Austria and Hungary, as well as the United States, Great Britain, France, and Italy. Its major aim, a general tariff union of the Danubian basin, failed; but several other matters of transport and trade were settled. In 1919 a new International Commission for the Danube was set up, and in conjunction with the reinstated European Commission of the Danube of 1856 it arranged uniform civil, commercial, sanitary, and veterinary regulations for the navigation of the Danube and its delta. In 1922 navigation on the river was made 'unrestricted and open to all flags, on a footing of complete equality'. During the 1920s every Balkan state except Bulgaria made commercial treaties with its neighbours. But no new authority appeared to replace the over-all administrative framework which the vanished Habsburg monarchy, for all its defects and weaknesses, had in some measure supplied. Only visionaries continued to dream of a functional 'Danube Valley Authority', grappling as a whole with the great common economic problems of that important region. Separatism triumphed with nationalism.

French economic recovery was helped by the restoration of the industrial provinces of Alsace and Lorraine, and by the direct reparations in kind gained by the cession of the Saar coal mines for a period of fifteen years. But for France, as for Belgium and Britain, other forms of reparation from Germany could do little to restore prosperity. The vital railway system of Belgium, for example, had 2,400 miles of its track demolished, and only eighty locomotives remained in the country at the time of the armistice. Of her fifty-one steel mills, half were destroyed and most of the rest seriously damaged. Yet by the spring of 1919 traffic on the railroads was almost normal, and this recovery was mainly due to the efforts of Belgians themselves, with the aid of foreign capital. The same story was repeated elsewhere. The initial stages of recovery were difficult and painful: the finding of work for demobilized soldiers, the housing shortage, the reconversion of industry to peacetime production, and the overcoming of financial problems. But within two years most countries had managed to put their internal economies into a condition where immediate consumer goods were being produced in more ample supply. Farming prospered with the demand for foodstuffs; building trades boomed with the need for houses and factories; demobilization made labour more available. In 1919 and 1920 western Europe enjoyed a great industrial boom. Unemployment was slight and there was feverish activity on stock exchanges. Prices rose sharply until, during 1921 and 1922, they began to fall, bringing greater unemployment and a general but temporary depression. The initial boom was less, and recovery was slower, in eastern than in western Europe. The intractable problems of resettlement of migrant populations as well as demobilized soldiers, and of basic reorganization of national economies, retarded recovery. But despite the unevenness of recovery, it seems probable that by 1921 the productive capacity of the world in general was as great as might have been predicted in 1913, even had there been no war. What mattered most was the higher proportion of this productive capacity which now lay outside Europe, and the great impediments to a restoration of international trade, which alone could make this flow of wealth more readily available within Europe. These two factors made the postwar world a less happy place for Europe than was the world of 1914.

International Debts and Reparations. Broadly speaking, standards of living in Europe had risen before 1914 because Europeans as a whole were able to import more than they exported, paying the difference with the interest in overseas investments and with charges for shipping and similar services. The conversion of the largest European creditor nations into debtor nations, by the sale of many of their overseas investments and the raising of foreign loans, now made it necessary for Europeans to export more than they imported. This novel necessity required a restriction of consumption, an austerity in western Europe's standard of living which few were willing to accept in the immediate postwar world, and which at first was hardly seen to be necessary.

Riotous spending was indulged in when great restraint should have been exercised. It was not easy for mass electorates to understand why the lavish expenditure on war could not simply be diverted to an equally extravagant expenditure on the amenities of peace. The great economic difficulties of the apparently simple and attractive process of beating swords back into ploughshares were not easy to explain or to grasp. The wartime projects of 'homes fit for heroes' and a new era of plenty tied the hands of politicians, even when they themselves understood the problems. All European countries were in a position of a family which for more than four years had taken to living on its capital: not only on the great reserves of capital invested abroad, but on stocks of raw materials, on plundering forests and mines and impoverishing even the soil. When it again tried to return to its normal ways of making a living, it had to borrow. Even countries, like Germany and Austria, which had not already incurred large foreign debts as war loans, now incurred big peacetime debts for reconstruction; and it was mainly from American lenders that such loans had to be raised. Only by a combination of massive national effort and foreign financial help could shattered Europe be restored, but the new indebtedness hindered the revival of the normal international exchange of goods which had been the very basis of prewar prosperity. The burning political problem of reparations which caused so much international controversy during the 1920s was important not so much for its own sake as for the way in which it aggravated this inherent difficulty of recreating a healthy world trade. The payment of monetary reparations by Germany to Britain, Belgium, and France had the same effects as the repayment of war debts, for it was a one-way transaction in a world decaying for lack of enough two-way transactions.

The payment of reparations by Germany had been stipulated by the Allied observations on the Fourteen Points, which had themselves spoken of the need to 'restore' Belgium and the invaded portions of France.[1] There could therefore be no doubt that Germany, in accepting the armistice on the basis of the Fourteen Points and of the Allied note about them, had undertaken to pay some form of indemnity. The Allied note of 5 November 1918 had specified that 'compensation will be made by Germany for all damage done to the civilian population of the Allies and their property'. This condition was accordingly included as Article 232 of the Treaty of Versailles which the German representatives signed in June, 1919. But two circumstances made the issue of reparations highly controversial and a great source of international dispute. In the first place, Part VIII of the Treaty, which dealt with reparations, was pre-

1. See p. 573.

faced by Article 231, the famous 'War-Guilt Clause', in which 'The Allied and Associated Governments affirm and Germany accepts the responsibility of Germany and her allies for causing all the loss and damage to which the Allied and Associated Governments and their nationals have been subjected *as a consequence of the war imposed upon them by the aggression of Germany and her allies*'. It was the last seventeen words (in italics) which aroused so much resentment, and they were unnecessary. This enforced acceptance of a very general 'responsibility' was bitterly resented in Germany because it meant admitting under duress that all Germans who had died in the war had died for an unjust cause. It also diverted attention from the obligations Germany accepted by signing the armistice. Secondly, since no sum could be agreed upon by the Allies before the Treaty was signed, a Reparation Commission was set up to determine the amount that Germany should be required to pay and to supervise its collection on behalf of the Allied governments. This meant requiring Germany in 1919 to sign a blank cheque, and projected the wrangles about reparations far into the postwar years.

The issue was beset with both political and economic dilemmas. Belgium and France, which had suffered great devastation, were persistent in claiming the maximum, since reconstruction had to be undertaken as quickly and as completely as possible. Britain, with little devastation on land to repair, soon began to look upon Germany as a potential customer in international trade, which the prolonged burden of reparations merely impoverished. France, apart from the payments in kind received as coal from the Saar, tended to see in reparations not only the barest justice in compensation for her losses, but also a possible means of keeping Germany weak and delaying her economic recovery. These differences of outlook and interest between Britain and France became a wedge driving them apart at the very time when their harmonious cooperation was needed to stabilize western Europe and operate the new security arrangements provided by the Covenant of the League of Nations.

After prolonged haggling the Reparations Commission in April 1921 eventually fixed Germany's liability at 132,000 million gold marks ($33,000 million or £6,600 million), of which 1,000 million marks were to be paid by the end of May. This first payment was not received until August, after a threat to occupy the Ruhr and by means of a loan from London bankers. During the next three years Germany made payments in kind but no further payments in cash, and at the beginning of 1923 her government announced that it could not continue payments. Thereupon the Belgians and the French, led by the intransigent French premier, Raymond Poincaré, occupied the Ruhr, despite the disapproval of Britain and the United States. Germany's creditors 'put the bailiffs in'. The industrialists and workers of the Ruhr, encouraged by the German government, resisted passively and brought most of the mines and plant to a standstill. The government printed paper money recklessly until by November the mark completely collapsed in value. This currency crash, which hit the whole of Germany during the year 1923, effected the social revolution which Germany had hitherto avoided. In 1924 a committee of financial experts, headed by the American General Dawes, was set up to tackle reparations as a purely economic problem – the problem of how, in fact, Germany could pay reparations to the Allies without producing chaos. The Dawes Plan, which both Germany and the Allies accepted in 1924, proposed a two-year moratorium on payments, return of the Ruhr to Germany, and a foreign loan to Germany of 800 million marks ($200 million or £40 million). Germany undertook to resume payment in increasing annuities, and for a time the scheme worked well and even helped to bring prosperity to Germany after the catastrophic collapse of 1923. With new confidence German state and local authorities, as well as business concerns of all kinds, borrowed lavishly abroad for schemes of public works and the expansion of industrial plant. In the following five years, defeated Germany was endowed with a fine new equipment of factories and houses, schools and hospitals, on borrowed foreign capital.

In 1929 a further committee under the American, Owen D. Young, produced a revised scheme of reparations, involving a new international loan to Germany of 1,200 million gold marks ($300 million or £60 million) and payment of reparations over a period of fifty-nine years through a new Bank for International Settlements. Although unwelcome in Germany, where it was condemned as visiting the burden of reparations upon unborn generations, the Young Plan was accepted both by the Reichstag and by popular referendum. Finally, with face-saving assertions at the Lausanne Conference in 1932, reparations ceased. At the same time the growth of German governmental control over foreign trade and exchange, greatly extended after 1933 by the National Socialists, virtually blocked repayment of foreign loans, while the economic crisis in Germany wiped out much other foreign investment. How much, on balance, Germany ever did pay in reparations remains a matter of refined calculation on inadequate data. It seems likely that on balance she paid no reparations at all, save those paid directly in kind after the war, for her creditors (and others) sank and lost as much in investments in Germany as was ever paid out in reparations. The whole dreary issue turned out to be a huge bubble of little substance. Germany had discovered that a debtor nation could force her creditors to keep her afloat and prosperous in the hope of recovering their wealth, and could still cheat them in the end. The indelible mark left on modern Europe was the social revolution inside Germany in 1923.

The experience of a total collapse of currency, in which the German mark depreciated from 20,000 to the dollar in January 1923 to 100,000 in June and five million in August, was bad enough: when it fell from fifty million in early September to 630,000 million in early November, it brought complete economic breakdown. Wages and salaries, revised at first monthly and latterly daily, could not keep pace with prices. There was a perpetual stampede to turn worthless 'hot' paper money into real goods of any kind. All internal debts, whether of individuals or public authorities, were wiped out overnight. Savings and bank balances, mortgages and paper investments, annuities and pensions, became worthless. The whole middle class of *rentier* and pensioner, small businessman and minor official, was ruined. Any owner of real property, whether land or plant or goods, survived and prospered. Everyone who could profit from so fantastic a rise in prices joined the class of new rich which came into existence alongside the new poor: the financial speculator, the big magnate, and the foreign visitor who for a few dollars or shillings could live like a prince. It was no purely economic collapse. It was a psychological collapse as well. It was a failure of public and personal confidence on a gigantic scale, and brought with it the decline of the new democratic régime, whose governments bore the burden of official responsibility for it. When, in 1924, the mark had fallen to utter worthlessness, the government, with an ease that bred considerable suspicion abroad, restored the currency and stabilized economic conditions in time for a new era of great prosperity. The collapse had, perhaps, served its purpose of demonstrating the difficulties and dangers of 'making Germany pay', and it attracted considerable sympathy abroad. The unknown and incalculable result was the mood of black fear and hysteria fostered among the dispossessed middle classes, who alone might have given the new régime stability and permanence. Hitler's failure in 1923 would turn into success ten years later.

Other countries, naturally enough, experienced inflation during the boom period of 1920, and international uncertainties helped to cause depreciation of currencies. In 1919 the French franc stood at only half its prewar value. Because the French treasury believed that economic reconstruction and recovery mattered more than financial stability, it did not, like Britain, impose heavy fresh burdens of taxation. It lived on loans and accepted large deficits in the budget. The result was that when depression set in during 1921 France, being less burdened with taxation than Britain, suffered less. Her industry remained active and her trade brisk. But the damage done by the international crisis of the occupation of the Ruhr in 1923 was all the greater in France. When the German mark collapsed and Britain and the United States reacted unfavourably to French policy, the franc dropped sharply in value. Parliament hastily accepted an addition of twenty per cent on existing taxation in order to redress the budgetary balance and reinspire confidence in France's financial stability. But reliance on loans and deficits instead of on a more severe fiscal system and higher taxation kept French governments at the mercy of millions of subscribers and of foreign investors, and paralysed their efforts to stabilize the franc. By July 1926 the franc had dropped from a prewar value of nineteen cents to only two cents, and Poincaré had to take stern emergency measures to stabilize it at nearly one quarter of its prewar value. A year previously the United Kingdom, which had tried to meet the immense burden of her national debt by heavy taxation, economies in expenditure, and expansion of her export trade, returned to the gold standard and established sterling at its prewar parity. She did not, as did France and Germany, rid herself of debt by means of currency inflation. Like France, she was burdened by immense war debts to the United States, and in 1923 funded this debt of $4,600 million to be repaid over the next sixty-two years. It was only partially offset by repayment of loans by her allies and by receipt of reparations from Germany. Most of the interest on it and the repayment of capital had to come from the depleted pockets of the taxpayer.

The whole question of repayment of war loans had consequences both for international relations and for world trade that were closely parallel to the results of reparations. Both entailed one-way transfers of wealth or of credit between nations at a time when capital was urgently needed internally for economic reconstruction and when the restoration of international trade needed a growing volume of two-way exchanges of wealth and services. In general, France had lent some £355 million to Belgium, Russia, and her other eastern allies, but she had also borrowed £1,058 million from the United Kingdom and the United States. The United Kingdom had lent £1,740 million to Russia, France, and all her other European allies, but she had also borrowed £842 million from the United States. The United States had lent altogether £1,890 million to all her allies. All the Russian debts (£166 million) were irrecoverable, because the Bolshevik government repudiated all the debts of the old régime. But if these Russian debts were omitted, this tangle of international indebtedness could have been eased by linking reparations to war debts, and in effect paying German reparations direct to the United States on behalf of those countries owing the United States. This was frequently proposed by Europeans, but American opinion consistently opposed any such linkage, which was so tempting to the debtor countries, on the grounds immortalized by President Coolidge's remark: 'They hired the money, didn't they?' These debts differed from prewar investments of capital in that all were debts owed by one government to another, not by governments to individuals or by individuals to other individuals. They arose not from profits of industry or payments for services rendered, and could be paid only out of taxation or neutralized by receipt of reparations. It is doubtful indeed whether any monetary reparations went effectively toward the purpose intended, of compensating individuals for damage or loss caused by the Germans. They mostly just neutralized governmental debts to other governments, and after the earliest payments in kind, they became an embarrassment to recipients as well as to Germany. In an age of rising tariffs to keep out industrial imports it was as impossible for Britain to admit Germany's imports free as it was for the United States to admit British goods free. Such one-way payments in goods meant 'dumping' – a charge then levied against Russian trading practices. To insist upon payment without being willing to accept the only possible form of payment marked a low ebb of statecraft.

The total effect of both reparations and war debts on political and diplomatic relations was one of recurrent irritation and exasperation, at a moment when it was important, for the future of the world, to escape from the vindictiveness of wartime and to rebuild confidence between the major nations of the world. The promises of politicians to 'make Germany pay' or, in the words of a British conservative, 'to squeeze Germany until the pips squeak', made better wartime rhetoric than postwar economics. The businessman's attitude that debts must be repaid in full and with agreed interest, at no matter what cost to the peace and prosperity of the world, was inappropriate to a convalescent world in which interdependence had become unavoidable and in which the sacrifices in a common cause had been so unequal. It is difficult to acquit most of the leaders of the nations in the early 1920s of a dearth of farsighted statesmanship, and bursts of genuine but vague idealism consorted strangely with moods of hard-faced and shortsighted bargaining. Not all were blind, and John Maynard Keynes, sent to Paris as a leader of the British financial experts, resigned from his post in protest against what he regarded as the unrealistic and excessive demands for German reparations. He wrote the book that was to play a momentous part in shaping world opinion about the peace settlement. Keynes's polemic on *The Economic Consequences of the Peace* appeared at the end of 1919 and for twenty years to come set the pattern of opinion that the peace-

609

makers had treated Germany harshly and unreasonably. This was much less true than came to be generally believed, and the unexpected effect of this brilliant book was to pave the way for Hitlerite propaganda and assault upon even those terms of the Treaty of Versailles which Keynes would have regarded as quite just. But at least he was correct in predicting that such reparations would not continue to be paid for more than a few years. Attempts to pay them led to a steady draining of most of the world's supply of gold into American vaults, wherein it had to be kept for fear of producing uncontrollable inflation in America. This was not a sensible result when so many of the world's currencies, led by Great Britain, were being put back on to the gold standard. There is a direct line of continuity between the economic problems of the early 1920s and the world economic depression which, beginning in Wall Street in 1929, within a couple of years engulfed the world.[1]

Farming in Eastern Europe. While western and central Europe were concerned primarily with questions of financial stability and currency, with reparations and war debts, with industry and trade, the supreme economic troubles of eastern Europe were agricultural. The political reshaping of eastern Europe from the Baltic to the Balkans had done nothing to change the basic fact that in Rumania, in Bulgaria, and in Yugoslavia more than three quarters of the inhabitants still lived by farming; and that nearly two thirds of the Poles, more than half of the Hungarians, over a third of the Czechoslovaks were peasants. What mattered to them all was who owned the land, on what conditions it was cultivated, and how fertile was the soil in relation to the growing numbers of the population. During and after the war, in Rumania, Poland, and all the former territories of Austria-Hungary land reforms were carried out that were designed to make them what Serbia, Bulgaria, and Greece had already become before 1914 – lands of small peasant proprietors. Big landed estates were broken up and distributed among small holders and landless peasant labourers. This reform went furthest in Rumania, Yugoslavia, and Czechoslovakia, and much less far in Poland and Hungary, which remained predominantly lands of big estates, with smaller holdings prevailing in certain areas. This difference sprang from several sources. In the countries where land reform went furthest, liberal national governments hastened it in order to win the loyalties of peasants as against the counter-attraction of communism. In Hungary and Poland, where the native aristocracies had assumed a leadership in nineteenth-century nationalist movements and where the threat of communist revolution had taken an immediate form and had been crushed, resistance to land reform could take coherent shape in

1. See p. 682.

time to prevent it. In every country it was political or social considerations, rather than economic, which determined the nature and extent of reform. There was no expectation or likelihood that small-scale farming would be more efficient or productive than large-scale, and the immediate effect of subdividing large estates was usually to diminish production. The new owners lacked technical knowledge and equipment, and were given little help by their governments until after 1930. The fall in agricultural prices, brought about first by the competition of imported cereals from America and later by the world economic depression, debased the standard of living of the peasants, which had never been high. Lack of capital, of technical skill, and of honest politics and administration retarded the recovery of most of south-eastern Europe even during the years of comparative progress and prosperity. High infant mortality rates and the spread of tuberculosis and of diseases due to malnutrition continued to make south-eastern Europe a different world from the healthier and wealthier lands of the north-west or even the north-east. In such circumstances the efforts of the agrarian radicals – of men like Alexander Stambolisky in Bulgaria, of Ion Mihalache in Rumania, of Antonin Švehla in Czechoslovakia, and Stephen Radić in Yugoslavia – bore little result in greater economic prosperity. The peasant parties they formed and led tended to voice mainly the interests of the large and medium holders of land, not the dwarf proprietors or the landless farm labourers. They stood for high agricultural prices, protective tariffs, and cooperative marketing, contrary to the welfare of the rural proletariat which (outside Czechoslovakia) constituted half the peasant population. This depressed section of the population, often as much as one third of the whole, was 'surplus' to the amount of land available. Its future lay only in a more thorough industrialization, to which peasant parties were opposed, or in emigration, which was becoming more difficult. Here was no firm social foundation on which to build a lasting settlement in the countries of south-eastern Europe. Disposed by their inherent conditions to desperate remedies as well as economic weakness, they invited the attentions of powerful neighbours – whether German or Russian – who could offer them brighter hopes for the future.[1]

It is desirable to recall these basic economic difficulties of postwar Europe, as well as its short-lived honeymoon with the forms of democratic government, before rather than after examining the nature of the international settlement. This settlement was reached at the Conference of Paris in 1919 and completed in a subsequent series of international treaties. If the peacemakers of 1919 have too often been harshly judged,

1. See pp. 831–7.

it is partly, no doubt, because in a mood of perfectionism and optimism they tried to arrange too much in too short a time. But it is also because the tasks of peacemaking, even while the conference deliberated, were being predetermined and partially settled by men of action on the spot, and by the hardening of a whole set of irreversible circumstances beyond the control of anyone. The men in Paris never had a free hand. Constricted not only by their wartime agreements with one another and by pledges to their peoples at home, but also by the accumulated debris of war itself, they could do no more than try to produce some order from chaos, determine details of frontiers and plan projects of compensations, and leave the achievement of greater precision and perfection to subsequent negotiation and good sense. They were not, as they have sometimes been depicted, men behaving like gods and reshaping a new heaven upon earth. They were tired, harassed, busy but well-meaning men, groping a way as best they could through the appalling aftermath of war, buoyed up by a hope that if only they could set the train on to the track again it might run to some useful destination. The settlement they made at Paris was not so much a basis on which separate nations and statesmen now built: it was the confirmation and acceptance of a new order that was already taking shape around them. The new order was the product of temporary enthusiasms for democratic self-government, of a largely unperceived economic upheaval, and of other results of the war itself. The peacemakers could only trim the edges and try to consolidate. Perhaps the biggest mistake they made was to mention at all ideals of absolute justice or perpetual peace; for these, surely, were a most improbable outcome of the conditions in which Europe found itself when the guns no longer thundered and the men came marching home.

CHAPTER 24

INTERNATIONAL CONSEQUENCES, 1918–23

THE CONFERENCE OF PARIS, 1919

THE conference of spokesmen of the powers of the world which assembled in Paris in January 1919 was a more widely representative body than even the Congress of Vienna in 1814. Crowned heads were now conspicuous by their absence – only King Albert of the Belgians appeared for a short time. Except for President Woodrow Wilson and King Albert, the great powers were represented not by their heads of state but by their Premiers and Foreign Ministers. In all, thirty-two states were represented. The time, place, composition, organization, and procedure of the conference all had some bearing upon what it was able to achieve.

Time. The time – nine weeks after the conclusion of the armistice with Germany – was determined mainly by internal political considerations in the United States and Great Britain. Once President Wilson decided, against all precedent and advice, to attend in person, the conference had to be delayed until after he had delivered his 'State of the Union' message to Congress in December. In Britain, where no election had been held for eight years, Lloyd George was anxious to have a renewal of parliamentary approval before he went to Paris. A general election took place in Britain in mid December. Held at the height of victory-fever, it elicited an unusually rich crop of slogans, ranging from 'Hang the Kaiser' and 'Make Germany Pay' to 'Homes fit for Heroes'. It produced a House of Commons variously described as composed of 'hard-faced men who looked as if they had done well out of the war' and 'the most unintelligent body of public-school boys which even the Mother of Parliaments has known'. That a general election held at such a moment should produce such results was in no way surprising; but the alternative seemed, at the time, even more dangerous, since it could have been maintained that the British representatives at Paris did not represent British opinion. Nor had the Germans, even at the eleventh hour, behaved in a way likely to diminish hatred of them. Not only did they wantonly destroy mines and buildings in France and Belgium during their retreat, but on 16 October 1918 – eleven days after Prince Max of Baden had first approached Wilson to mediate – they torpedoed the

Irish mail steamer *Leinster* and drowned 450 men, women, and children. Such brutal behaviour in defeat left intense feelings of resentment.

The first plenary session of the Conference took place on 18 January 1919. The Treaty of Versailles with Germany was signed on 28 June 1919, the fifth anniversary of Sarajevo. The final session was held on 21 January 1920, and even then peace treaties with Hungary and Turkey remained to be concluded, and the United States did not complete its separate peace treaty with Germany until 25 August 1921. General peace with Turkey was not completed until the Treaty of Lausanne in July 1923, which came into force in August 1924. Thus the process of settlement – even the formal conclusion of peace treaties – lasted very much longer than the Paris Conference. Just as some parts of the settlement were predetermined before the Conference met, so much more of it was made after it dispersed. Considering the size of the Conference (seventy delegates) and the complexity of the issues confronting it, there was small justification for the charges of delay and slowness which were brought against it.

What made any lapse of time seem intolerable was the anxiety of governments and peoples everywhere to press on with urgent labours of reconstruction, and the Allied decision to maintain the naval blockade of Germany until the final conclusion of peace. This decision, subjected to much adverse criticism as being inhumane and vindictive, was not indefensible. With the conditions of peace unsettled, the Allies had to consider the possibility of a renewal of hostilities. The armistice of November 1918 deprived Germany of her navy and most of her military equipment. It did not take away her million tons of merchant shipping or provide for control of her supplies of gold and foreign exchange. Ludendorff and the German High Command still cherished the hope that even the threat to re-engage in battle might force the Allies to grant more favourable terms of peace. Allied and neutral shipping was very scarce, and the first-aid needs of Allied and liberated nations for food and relief were greater than those of Germany. Even so, during the spring and summer of 1919, 100 million gold marks ($20 million or £5 million) were spent on the free delivery of food and other necessities to Germany. The German government refused to permit more than a twentieth part of German gold and foreign reserves to be used for the purchase of foodstuffs, or to release their ships for the transport of them. It was mid March 1919 before it finally gave way, and then the flow of food into starving Germany began at once. During the ten months following the armistice, of all the supplies sent by the Allies to their friends and enemies in Europe more than a third went to Germany and Austria.

Responsibility for civilian hunger in Germany during the Conference lay much more with the German military authorities who had caused the shortage of world shipping and who obstructed and delayed plans to relieve it, than with the so-called 'hunger blockade' of the Allies.

Place. The place of the Conference also had some significance. Geneva in neutral Switzerland had first been suggested, but President Wilson preferred Paris, where American forces were in plentiful supply. The choice of the French capital marked, almost symbolically, the centre of gravity of the *bloc* of western liberal-democratic powers. It made possible such symbolic acts as the signature of the Treaty of Versailles in the Hall of Mirrors at Versailles, where the German Empire had first been proclaimed in January 1871. It also ensured that the aged French Premier, Georges Clemenceau, should by courtesy become President of the Conference, and that French influences in general should bear strongly upon its whole atmosphere and spirit. Being seventy-eight years old, Clemenceau remembered Sedan and 1871 very well. Since neither Lloyd George nor Wilson knew French, and only Clemenceau spoke both French and English, the 'Tiger of France' had certain natural advantages on his home ground.

Composition. The composition of the Conference was even more important. To it came representatives not only of 'the Allies' but also of the 'Associated Powers'. During the final stages of the war many countries had become belligerents largely in order to gain a voice in the final settlement, so the group of 'Allied and Associated Powers' was a large one. Several Central and South American states – Cuba, Brazil, Panama, Guatemala, Nicaragua, Honduras – had entered the war in the wake of the United States. Siam had declared war in July 1917; Liberia and China, in August 1917. Others – notably Bolivia, Peru, Uruguay, and Ecuador – had broken off relations with some of the Central Powers and so were due to sign some of the peace treaties. New states, recognized by the Allies and therefore represented, included Czechoslovakia and Poland. A host of other small nationalities and pressure groups sent unofficial and unrecognized representatives to lobby the powers for consideration; these included Armenians and Zionists, Lebanese and Egyptians, Kurds and Koreans, Irish Sinn Feiners and White Russians. The three major omissions were: the neutral powers, who had no place at what was technically a peace conference to end the Great War; the Russians, still engaged in civil war and the war of intervention; and the ex-enemy powers, Germany, Austria, Hungary, Bulgaria, and Turkey. These absences were supremely important for the future. Whether the absence of neutrals weakened, as has been claimed, the forces of moderation and balance which might have made for more intelligent settlement is doubtful: neutral governments are not notably less self-interested than others. But neutral nations had certainly been profoundly affected by the course of the war and had an undoubted interest in the resettlement of the world. The absence of Russia made easier a territorial settlement of eastern Europe which assumed, in many respects, the shape of a *cordon sanitaire* against the spread of Bolshevism in Europe. The absence of former enemy states, especially Germany, gave peace in Europe the form of a *Diktat*, an imposed arrangement for the shaping of which Germans felt no kind of responsibility since they had not been consulted, and which they were forced to accept in circumstances humiliating to their new republican government. All these consequences, however reasonable the exclusion of such powers seemed at the time, were to prove basic weaknesses in the settlement.

Organization. The organization of the Conference recognized a clear distinction between 'belligerent powers with general interests', which were only the 'Big Five' – the United States, the British Empire, France, Italy, and Japan – and 'belligerent powers with special interests', which comprised all other belligerent states, including separately the British Dominions and India, Poland, Serbia, and the Czechoslovak Republic. The 'Big Five' sent five delegates each, Belgium, Brazil, and Serbia three each, and all the rest one or two each. The Dominions of Canada, Australia, South Africa, and India sent two delegates each, and New Zealand one. Each delegation was accompanied by a number of technical advisers and assistants, which in the case of the United States and Britain numbered as many as two hundred. The Conference could thus claim, despite its important omissions, to be the first great world peace conference. Some three quarters of the population of the world was represented, and the tasks before it surpassed in scale and importance those of any previous international gathering. There were twenty-seven official delegations – thirty-two if the Dominions and India are counted separately. It included many world figures in addition to the leaders of the 'Big Five' themselves – men such as General Smuts of South Africa, Robert Borden of Canada, Wellington Koo of China, and Paderewski the great Polish pianist. Because it was so large and its agenda so varied, and also because the war had been pre-eminently a war of the great powers, control was from the first exercised by a Council of Ten which was a modified version of the Supreme War Council. This select body, comprising two representatives of each of the 'Big Five', made all the preliminary and initial arrangements for the conduct of the Conference. It soon, however, broke down into two bodies, the Council of Five (the five Foreign Ministers) and the Council of Four, consisting of President

Wilson, Clemenceau, Lloyd George, and Orlando, the Premier of Italy. Japan soon lost interest and stayed away, and by the end of April 1919 Orlando also departed. Most important decisions were henceforth taken avowedly, as they had previously been taken substantially, by the famous 'Big Three', upon whose personal attitudes much of the outcome of the Conference ultimately depended.

Many picturesque details have been given of the peculiarities and personal relationships of the American, the Frenchman, and the Welshman. Sir Harold Nicolson has described 'the tired and contemptuous eyelids of Clemenceau, the black button-boots of Woodrow Wilson, the rotund and jovial gestures of Mr Lloyd George's hands'. Lord Keynes wrote of Clemenceau's short decisive sentences and his displays of obstinacy, 'throned, in his grey gloves, on the brocade chair, dry in soul and empty of hope, very old and tired, but surveying the scene with a cynical and almost impish air'; of Wilson's appearance as 'a Nonconformist minister, perhaps a Presbyterian', whose thought and temperament were not intellectual but theological, with all the strength and weakness that implied; of Lloyd George, 'watching the company, with six or seven senses not available to ordinary men . . . compounding with telepathic instinct the argument or appeal best suited to the vanity, weakness, or self-interest of his immediate auditor'. They were indeed a vividly contrasted trio, but perhaps the most important things they had in common were that all were the men who had led their countries in war and victory, all were leaders of democratic countries and therefore sensitive to national feelings at home. In two respects Wilson's status differed from that of his colleagues: he was head of the most powerful single state at the Conference, upon which most of Europe depended for loans and supplies; but whereas in December 1918 Lloyd George had just won resounding victory in the 'Khaki Election' and Clemenceau had been granted an overwhelming vote of confidence (398 votes to ninety-three) by the French Chamber, Wilson's political power at home had just suffered a sharp decline. In the Congressional elections of November 1918 the rival Republican party gained majorities in both Senate and House of Representatives. His paradoxical position was that he, the great democrat preaching and bestowing democracy in Europe, had no majority at home. In Paris the vicious lampooning of the French Press undermined his position and his morale. He became increasingly a lonely and forlorn figure, hugging the Covenant of the League of Nations to veil his political weaknesses and failures, prepared to sacrifice other principles in order to get it accepted by the British and the French.

The organization of the work of the Conference was inevitably elaborate. Delegates suffered from no lack of expert information or advice, which flowed in abundance but was not well digested or coordinated. Although peace had taken most belligerents unawares, and the Allies had been preparing for campaigns instead of conferences in 1919, a great deal of preparatory work had been done in Britain and the United States. It had been envisaged that there would be two separate conferences : one of the great powers to arrange a war settlement and reach a preliminary peace settlement between the belligerents; followed by a plenary conference, in which even ex-enemy and neutral powers might be represented, to settle the broader issues of a final peace settlement. But because the great powers failed to agree upon the first set of problems, both had to be settled simultaneously. In effect, therefore, two conferences met side by side, the more important caucus of the big powers constantly dominating the general conference and casting about to find ways of enlisting the smaller powers in minor parts of the general settlement. There was no clear priority of purpose, no early decision about whether the terms of peace were eventually to be negotiated or dictated. The Conference became what the British delegate, Arthur Balfour, called 'a rough and tumble affair'. 'The great fault of the political leaders,' wrote Colonel House, 'was their failure to draft a plan of procedure.' Fifty-eight committees and commissions were set up to deal with different aspects of the settlement, but all important decisions were finally made by the 'Big Three'.

The muddle that resulted could have been prevented only by a clear distinction, from the start, between matters essential to a preliminary peace (such as the military, political, and reparations questions), which could have been agreed upon by the victorious Allies and dictated to the vanquished; and such long-term problems as disarmament, economic reconstruction, and the League of Nations, which could have been worked out in a calmer, less hurried, and less impassioned manner in general conference. If the urgent issues that underlay popular clamour against the 'dawdlers of Paris' had been speedily disposed of and others left until passions had cooled, it seems likely that a wiser and more durable settlement might have been reached. But any such functional distinction was blurred partly by the general anxiety to get as much as possible settled at once, partly by Wilson's insistence that the League of Nations must be made the first cornerstone of every treaty. Presidents, Prime Ministers, and Foreign Ministers found long absence from home awkward and irksome, and were inclined to press on with the work in whatever order seemed best at the moment. Perhaps the most important consequence – since time and greater order alone might not have brought greater wisdom or justice – was that all the smaller powers were relegated to playing consistently minor roles in the decisions. Even the final draft of the Treaty of Versailles with Germany was presented to the general conference in a brief summary and at short notice. Eight plenary sessions were held during the first five months of the conference, but they were mostly formal and gave no scope for full discussion. The war had been a war of the great powers; it had been won by an alliance of the great powers; and in the event the peace was dictated by the three greatest powers in the world in 1919.

Procedure. The procedure, as distinct from the organization of the Conference, was also determined by these facts. It was decided that all the minor nationalities who hoped to benefit from the settlement should present their claims in writing and should then, by invitation, appear before the Supreme Council to argue their case orally. This not only absorbed a great deal of time, but almost unwittingly gave priority to the claims of the smaller nations as against the basic problem of Germany. It tipped the scales against very much attention being paid to Wilson's dictum of September 1918 that 'the impartial justice meted out must involve no discrimination between those to whom we wish to be just and those to whom we do not wish to be just'. Germany, Austria, Hungary, Bulgaria, and Turkey had no delegates at the Conference to plead their cause. Their most bitter enemies were given repeated facilities to state their case, and every inducement to exaggerate their claims. In such conditions it was improbable that even the most fair-minded attitude on the part of the 'Big Three' who made the final decisions would result in impartial justice to the vanquished. Clauses of the treaty were often hastily approved, despite uneasiness of mind, because of the great pressure for finality and with the reservation that they could always be revised at some future time. Article 19 of the Covenant expressly provided for the reconsideration of 'treaties which have become inapplicable' and of 'international conditions whose continuance might endanger the peace of the world'. It was with this refuge in mind that Wilson was induced to agree to many arrangements that he greatly disliked.

The Big Three. All these circumstances and details of the Paris Conference had importance in helping to shape the settlement. Much has been written about how far the substance of the settlement – especially as regards Germany and Hungary – was a compromise between the two opposing attitudes of Wilson and Clemenceau. Wilson, it is alleged, was the idealist, his eyes fixed above all on absolute justice and on the sacred principles of democracy, of national self-determination, and the Covenant of the League of Nations. Clemenceau was the old-fashioned realist, the narrow nationalist filled with hatred of Germany, to whom nothing mattered as compared with the future security of France and the lasting destruction of German power. In the result the idealist was outwitted at nearly every turn by the realist, aided by the nimble agility of Lloyd George, who used his intermediate position as conciliator to safeguard British interests. This vivid dramatic picture, attractive in its clarity and with just enough footing in fact to be plausible, can be used as evidence that the fair hopes of 1919 were dashed by the intrusion of old-world power politics and national egoism. But it is an interpretation not borne out by the facts. It is true that Wilson left Europe a bitter and disillusioned man, and that he found the stubborn conditions of postwar Europe less conducive than he had expected to remaking a democratic world in which one great war had ended all wars. But this disillusionment was not due only to the wiliness of Clemenceau or Lloyd George: it was due to the quite unrealistic image of European affairs which Wilson had brought with him in December 1918. This image had at first been encouraged by the wildly enthusiastic welcome he was given in Paris and London and Rome as the prophet of the new world. Wilson's collapse was due, also, to the hard facts of postwar trends in Europe, especially in eastern Europe, in which honest efforts to fulfil the specifications of the Fourteen Points only revealed the inconsistencies of the remedies they prescribed. Access to the sea for Poland could be achieved only at the expense of Germany, which would then remain acutely aggrieved; the rival claims of Italy and Yugoslavia in the Adriatic could be solved neither by applying principles of self-determination nor by doctrines of absolute justice, but only by some agreed give-and-take compromise which would certainly satisfy neither. Justice, on the tangled map of the old continent of Europe, might be relative, but it could hardly be absolute. Moreover, as Clemenceau foresaw and as events in Germany were soon to prove, the most democratic constitution was no guarantee against the resurgence of aggressive militarism and inflamed nationalism. Even the first of the Fourteen Points – 'open covenants openly arrived at' – had perforce to be violated with Wilson's connivance in the very conduct of the Paris Conference itself; and attempts to respect it would have led to a slower conference and probably a less desirable outcome. Nor is it fair to judge the treaties by the Fourteen Points alone. They had been formulated in January 1918 before the Treaty of Brest-Litovsk had shown Germany's conception of treaty making, and before the meaning of the Bolshevik Revolution had become apparent.

If Wilson failed in his great mission to set the old world in order, it is to much more than the intransigence of Clemenceau or to personalities in conflict that we must look for an explanation. The settlement, as already suggested, was hardening into shape before the Conference met, and the best that any conference could have achieved would still have fallen far short of Wilson's dream. Moreover, Wilson himself was by no means lacking in the shrewdness and toughness of the politician. There were moments during the Conference when he got his own way by guile and violent measures: as when he threatened to leave Paris rather than give way to Clemenceau over the future of the Rhineland, or when he appealed to the Italian people over the head of their delegate Orlando. To depict Wilson as the gentle humanitarian and Clemenceau as the vicious tiger is a melodramatic distortion. The precise role of Lloyd George also remains controversial. It is certain that his own views and desires about the settlement with Germany were much less vindictive than was at first supposed. The hysterical outcry in Britain for a retributive peace came from Lloyd George's personal enemies, led by Lord Northcliffe and the organs of the Press (especially the *Daily Mail*) which Northcliffe controlled. Headlines like 'Make Germany Pay' and the slogan, repeated daily, that 'The Junkers Will Cheat You Yet' were part of a whole campaign of hate designed to embarrass Lloyd George in Paris. It seems that wherever Lloyd George was not already committed to a line of policy by his own election pledges, or by the inherent demands of British public opinion and his parliamentary majority, he used his influence to moderate the treaty in a liberal manner. His dilemma, indeed, was that of all three statesmen: they were accountable to parliamentary and public opinion at home in a moment of extremely violent anti-German sentiment. For the violence of the sentiment the Germans were themselves mainly responsible, because of their use of unrestricted submarine warfare and their behaviour in defeat. The question of apportioning responsibility for what might later be deemed the mistakes of the settlement is a complex question, ranging far beyond the clashes of personalities within the conference room or the state of mind of the sorely tried victorious nations, to the postwar conditions of physical and moral exhaustion, even to the events of war themselves, still so fresh in the minds of men everywhere.

If there was a conflict throughout the Conference between impulses of idealism and of realism, it was a conflict not between nations or personalities but rather within the hearts of all nations and of most statesmen. The confusion that haunted the Conference haunted also the minds of men in 1919 – a tension between hopes and ideals of a more orderly world as a prize to be snatched from the opportunities of victory, and the human emotions of vindictiveness and vengeance, the natural reactions of peoples who had suffered oppression or aggression and whose recent experiences nourished hatred and fear. That these rival impulses swayed men's minds and coloured their judgements was in no way surprising. This background of the Conference was important in that it helped to produce a settlement of Europe, and especially a treatment of the vanquished, which was harsh where it might better have been lenient and weak where it might better have been strong. It was easy to end by making the worst of both worlds, and to frame a settlement that alienated the vanquished from any heartfelt acceptance of the new order while leaving them free and powerful enough to lay immediate plans to destroy it. To the extent that this was the outcome, the Paris Conference must stand in history as a conspicuous failure; but it was an over-all failure of human intelligence and wisdom, and in part a failure of organization and method. This was not due to either an excess of realism or a lack of idealism, but rather to a misapplication of both.

THE NEW BALANCE OF POWER

The international situation that confronted the peacemakers in Paris was, in the brutal realities of history, the result of a temporary redistribution of the balance of power in the world. The simultaneous military and political collapse of the old Russian, Turkish, Austro-Hungarian, and German Empires and the armed victory of the alliance of western powers brought about a catastrophic change in the power relationships of states within Europe. The prewar hegemony of the central European powers of Germany and Austria-Hungary was, for a time, utterly destroyed; but it had been destroyed only by bringing to bear upon European relations the mobilized strength, not only of Russia and of western Europe – Belgium, France, and Great Britain – but also of the overseas Empires of these powers, of the United States, and, in minor ways, of Japan and South America. The peacemakers were confronted by two supreme tasks. They had to make a settlement with Germany which, so far as they could contrive, would perpetuate a distribution of power in Europe which was unfavourable to German resurgence as an aggressive military state. They also had to redraw the map of central and eastern Europe in a way which replaced the old dynastic frontiers by new frontiers based on realities of national grouping, of economic viability, and of military security. These two tasks were in many ways distinct, but in certain important respects they were interconnected. Thus they could attempt to weaken Germany permanently by depriving her of important territories in the East in the name of granting the right of self-determination to Poles, and of possible allies in the East by a system of alliances between the western powers and the new so-called 'succession' states of eastern Europe. But in general the peacemakers were inclined to avoid such interlocking of methods and to deal with western and eastern issues as relatively distinct problems, to be solved by different methods. The settlement can best be considered, therefore, as falling into two sectors: the treatment of Germany *vis-à-vis* the western powers, and the reshaping of eastern Europe according to principles of national self-determination and security.

The German Problem. The settlement in the West hinged only in minor ways upon readjustments of frontiers and temporary territorial transfers, and predominantly upon joint endeavours to disarm and control Germany. There was no difficulty in ensuring the evacuation of all occupied parts of Belgium and France, or in the restoration to France of the provinces of Alsace and Lorraine; these changes had been stipulated in the Fourteen Points and had been substantially accomplished by the final military operations and the armistice. The Treaty of Versailles stipulated that Germany should surrender to Belgium the small frontier areas around Eupen and Malmédy, and that plebiscites should be held in Schleswig to determine her frontier with Denmark. Germany undertook not to fortify the left bank of the Rhine or a zone fifty kilometres wide along the right bank. Her army was reduced to 100,000 men, recruited by voluntary enlistment for a twelve-year period of service, and her General Staff was dissolved. She was forbidden to make tanks or military aircraft or heavy artillery. An Allied Commission of Control was set up to supervise the carrying out of these military clauses. She ceded the coal mines of the Saar to France for fifteen years, during which the territory would be administered by the League of Nations and after which a plebiscite of the inhabitants would determine its future status. Allied forces of occupation would remain in the Rhineland for fifteen years to ensure fulfilment of these obligations and the payment of reparations, to be determined subsequently by the Reparations Commission.[1] The Allies set up a Conference of Ambassadors to receive reports of the Control Commission and to act as executors of the treaty. The plebiscites held in Schleswig resulted in the northern parts going to Denmark, and the central and southern parts to Germany. The Saar plebiscite was duly held in 1935, and the territory was then restored to Germany.

In naval and colonial matters, which were of especial interest to the western powers, the deprivations imposed by the treaty were more severe. The German navy was not to exceed six battleships of 10,000 tons, six light cruisers, twelve destroyers, and twelve torpedo boats. It was to have no submarines. The naval base of Heligoland in the North Sea was to be demolished. Germany renounced 'all her rights and titles' over colonies, and thus lost her colonial Empire of some million square

1. See p. 605.

miles. The colonies were distributed under mandate to the powers which already occupied them. The Union of South Africa administered German South-west Africa; Britain, France, and Belgium divided among themselves the rest of her African possessions; Japan held under mandate the northern Pacific islands; Australia, German New Guinea; and New Zealand, German Samoa. A Permanent Mandates Commission of the League of Nations was created to receive reports on the administration of these mandated territories.

This western settlement with Germany was not reached, however, without causing profound disagreement among the western powers, especially in relation to the Rhineland. Clemenceau, urged by Foch, at first demanded indefinite control over the Rhine bridgeheads as a military guarantee of French security. Wilson and Lloyd George refused to agree to the indefinite separation of the Rhineland from Germany, for fear of creating a new Alsace-Lorraine in reverse. Instead, they offered the French a joint Anglo-American guarantee to support France immediately if she were attacked by Germany. Reluctantly, Clemenceau accepted this diplomatic guarantee as a bad second-best substitute for the material security of actual occupation. That he was right in his reluctance soon became apparent. The guarantee lapsed on the American side with the Senate's refusal to ratify the treaty, and Britain claimed that this also invalidated her part of the bargain. France henceforth felt that she had been tricked into surrendering a vital element in her material security, and embarked on a feverish quest for more firm safeguards of security. Thus it was she who linked the western settlement with the eastern by making a network of alliances with Poland and of agreements with the 'Little Entente' powers of Yugoslavia, Czechoslovakia, and Rumania. So began the central feature of European relations for the next two decades – the diplomatic and military overburdening of France as the chief mainstay of the treaty settlement.[1]

1. See p. 628.

MAP 15. DANUBIAN PEACE SETTLEMENT
As a result of World War I the Habsburg Empire disintegrated, and from its territories several new states were carved. Austria and Hungary were separated and reduced to two small land-locked states. Italy, Poland, Rumania, and Greece gained additional lands. Serbia became the core of a new composite state of Yugoslavia, while the northern Slav peoples combined to form Czechoslovakia. Bulgaria, as a defeated power, lost lands to Greece and Yugoslavia. Rumania got Bessarabia from Russia, and in all doubled her former size. Special treaties attempted to protect the rights of those alien national minorities which were, inevitably, left on the wrong sides of frontiers.

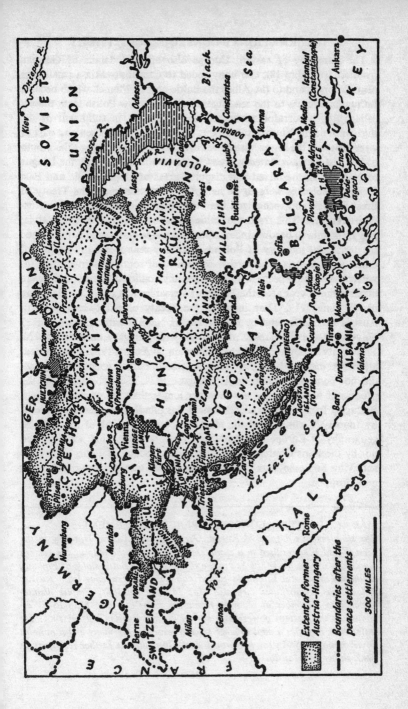

The remaking of eastern Europe also affected details of German frontiers (see Map 18). Germany ceded to Czechoslovakia a small area near Troppau, and to the Allies the Baltic port of Memel, which became Lithuania's access to the sea. She ceded to the new Polish state the so-called 'Polish corridor' giving access to the sea, in fulfilment of the thirteenth of the Fourteen Points. It included most of Posen and part of west Prussia – the lower Vistula valley. The port of Danzig at the mouth of the Vistula was created a Free City to be administered by the League of Nations. In the mixed and disputed areas of Upper Silesia and East Prussia plebiscites were to be held. Germany abrogated the Treaty of Brest-Litovsk and recognized the independence of all the former Russian territories. This freed the Baltic states of Finland, Estonia, Latvia, and Lithuania to become independent sovereign states, and consolidated the territorial integrity of Poland. Germany renounced any project of union with Austria. The further settlement of south-eastern Europe involved treaties of peace with all Germany's allies. Most of these were made within a year after the Treaty of Versailles was signed by Germany on 28 June 1919. They included the Treaty of Saint-Germain with Austria on 10 September, the Treaty of Neuilly with Bulgaria on 27 November and the Treaty of Trianon with Hungary on 4 June 1920. The Treaty of Sèvres, signed by Turkey on 20 August 1920, was rejected; and since the Treaty of Lausanne, to which Turkey eventually agreed, did not come into force until 6 August 1924, it can be said that the process of making peace lasted rather longer than the world war itself. But apart from the Turkish settlement this bundle of treaties, completed by June 1920, constituted the most complete reshaping of the political geography of Europe ever undertaken at one time. They were framed not by the Paris Conference or even by its Council of Four, but by the surviving Supreme War Council from whose title the word 'War' was now dropped.

MAP 16. EASTERN EUROPEAN PEACE SETTLEMENT

The simultaneous defeats of Russia, Germany, and Austria–Hungary in the First World War resulted in a complete redrawing of the map of the eastern marchlands, from the White Sea to the Black Sea. The Baltic states of Finland, Estonia, Latvia, and Lithuania gained complete independence from Russia; Poland was reconstituted (see also Map 14); the Habsburg Empire disintegrated into a number of separate Danubian states (see also Map 15). Welcomed by the western powers as a barrier against Russian bolshevism, these states were to suffer a dual squeeze from a resurgent Germany and a militant Soviet Union between the two world wars. Compare the further reshaping in 1945, shown on Map 26.

INTERNATIONAL CONSEQUENCES, 1918-23

The Reshaping of Eastern Europe. Renner, the Chancellor of 'German Austria' as it was now called, claimed to represent a new nation, as new as any other of the 'succession states'. This claim the Allies rejected, and truncated Austria was treated simply as a defeated enemy power. Accordingly, the Treaty of Saint-Germain was modelled closely on the Treaty of Versailles. Austria was made to cede to Italy Trieste, Istria, and the Tyrol up to the strategic frontier of the Brenner Pass; to Czechoslovakia, Bohemia, Moravia, Austrian Silesia, and parts of Lower Austria; to Rumania, Bukovina; to Yugoslavia, Bosnia, Herzegovina, and Dalmatia. Her union (*Anschluss*) with Germany was forbidden. Her army was limited to only 30,000 men, recruited for long-term voluntary service, and her navy to three police boats on the Danube. She undertook to pay reparations. The new Austria was but a fragment of the old – a quarter of the area containing a fifth of the population. Hungary, the other half of the old Habsburg Empire, received similar but even harsher treatment. She ceded to Rumania alone more territory than the total that she kept, and three million Magyars were placed under foreign rule. The new Hungary was a constricted landlocked relic of the old, and all her former subject nationalities rejoiced in this humiliation of their old oppressors. Bulgaria, claiming like Austria to be a new regenerated democracy but claiming equally in vain, was cut back to roughly her frontiers of 1914. Since she had lost heavily in 1913,[1] Neuilly now confirmed those losses. But otherwise she fared relatively better than Austria or Hungary, and her main new loss in 1919 was of western Thrace to Greece. (See Map 15.)

The chief beneficiaries of the settlement in south-eastern Europe were thus Serbia which, transformed into the new southern-Slav kingdom of Yugoslavia, now rivalled Italy in the Adriatic; Czechoslovakia, the multi-national lizard-shaped democracy comprising Bohemia, Moravia, Slovakia, and Ruthenia; and Rumania, doubled in size by accretions of territory from all her neighbours, including Russia. Greece gained from the settlement, and even more from the collapse of Turkey. Poland, like the three little Baltic states, owed its very existence as a sovereign state to the events of the war (see Map 16). Like the other succession states, she saw in the rigid preservation of the settlement her best security. Among these states France found natural allies in her quest for diplomatic precautions against German resurgence. In 1921 she made a treaty of alliance with Poland. She entered into military understandings with the 'Little *Entente*' of Czechoslovakia, Yugoslavia, and Rumania which, by treaties of alliance concluded among themselves in 1920–21, formed a group of states with common interests in preserving

1. See p. 540.

the settlement. France thus committed herself not only to the maintenance of the Versailles Treaty in which she and Poland had immediate
and direct interests, but also to the preservation of the whole European
settlement. She found herself committed to backing Poland against
Lithuania, Czechoslovakia against Hungary, Yugoslavia and Rumania
against Bulgaria. She assumed, like the Austria of Metternich after 1815,
the position of prime defender of the *status quo*, the implacable enemy
of any proposals for revision of the settlement. France, once the champion of revolution in Europe, now became the mainstay of the conservative forces of Europe. Even so, her inferiority in population and industrialism, and the memory of her tremendous losses and sacrifices in the
war, made her seek eternally for yet further guarantees of security. In-
satiably, she sought for new ways to check German resurgence.

The settlement with Turkey was more complex as well as more belated
than other treaties concerning south-eastern Europe, and it involved new
problems for the great powers. Like the European settlement, it involved
a tangle of wartime promises and secret understandings, as well as a great
insurgence of separatist national ambitions. There was first the question
of Palestine. On 2 November 1917 A. J. Balfour, then British Foreign
Secretary, issued a declaration to Lord Rothschild which he asked to
have made known to the Jewish Zionist Federation. It contained the
famous statement:

His Majesty's Government view with favour the establishment in Palestine
of a national home for the Jewish people, and will use their best endeavours
to facilitate the achievement of this object, it being clearly understood that
nothing shall be done which may prejudice the civil and religious rights of
existing non-Jewish communities in Palestine, or the rights and political status
enjoyed by Jews in any other country.

On 7 November 1918, after the campaigns of Allenby led to the conquest of Palestine and Syria, a joint Anglo-French declaration was issued
simultaneously in Palestine, Syria, and Iraq. It stated:

The goal envisaged by France and Great Britain . . . is the complete and final
liberation of the peoples who have for so long been oppressed by the Turks,
and the setting up of national governments and administrations that shall
derive their authority from the free exercise of the initiative and choice of
the indigenous populations.

This was taken by the Arab peoples of the Near East to involve support
for Arab predominance in Palestine. Thus were misleading and apparently contradictory pledges given, in wartime, to the populations
formerly subject to Turkish rule.

MAP 17. ASIATIC TURKEY – PEACE SETTLEMENT

Like the Habsburg Empire, the Ottoman Turkish Empire in Asia collapsed as a result of the First World War. Iraq and Turkey's eastern Mediterranean territories were mostly placed under mandate to Britain and France. Britain supported a ring of smaller independent Arab sheikdoms in the Persian Gulf, Red Sea, and Indian Ocean. Ibn Saud, ruler of the central Arabian province of Najd, tried to conquer the whole Arab peninsula and succeeded in making a large kingdom of Saudi Arabia. The tangled frontiers of Turkey, Syria, Iraq, Iran, and the Soviet Union remained a source of frequent international dispute.

The basis of Arab nationalism, which in its demand for independence dates from the 1870s, was the westernization that had come from French and American cultural influences and British commercial activities. The centralizing tendencies of the Young Turks before 1914, followed by the British military campaigns in Egypt and Mesopotamia (Iraq) during the war, stimulated and released these Arab demands. In return for guarded promises of independence the Arab leaders agreed to support the British campaigns by organized revolt against the Turks. In 1917 and 1918 T. E. Lawrence won fame as their ingenious organizer. In 1916 the British and French had made the Sykes-Picot Agreement, partitioning Syria and Iraq into a French sphere of influence in the north and a British in the south, but setting aside Palestine for international administration. It was alarm caused among the Arabs by the Balfour Declaration of November 1917 and the publication (in December 1917 by the Bolsheviks) of the Sykes-Picot Agreement that provoked the joint Anglo-French reassurance already quoted. At the San Remo Conference of April 1920 the allied Supreme Council agreed that while the states of the Arabian peninsula should become independent, the Mediterranean areas should become mandated territories. So it was that Palestine, Iraq, and Transjordania were entrusted to Britain under mandate, Syria and Lebanon to France under mandate. But, since conditions in the Near East were clearly so different from those in Germany's former African colonies or Pacific islands, a special form of mandate was devised. 'A' mandates – those in the Near East – defined the task of the mandatory power as 'the rendering of administrative advice and assistance ... until such time as they [the territories] are able to stand alone', and laid down that 'the wishes of these communities must be a principal consideration in the selection of the Mandatory'. In 'B' and 'C' mandates, no such expectation of autonomy was prescribed. The other Arab provinces of the Turkish Empire were given complete independence (see Map 17). Among them was the coastal strip of Arabia bordering the Red Sea and including the Moslem holy places of Mecca and Medina, which became the independent kingdom of the Hejaz (or Hijaz). Its representative attended the Paris Conference. Among them, too, was the central Arabian province of Najd, where the powerful Arab leader, Ibn Saud, now began a policy of conquering the whole Arabian peninsula. He constructed the extensive kingdom of Saudi Arabia, and only the peripheral Arab states, backed by Britain, managed to maintain their precarious independence.

Turkey itself underwent an internal political revolution as a result of defeats in the war.[1] The Sultan Mohammed VI and his conservative

1. See p. 587.

supporters tried to salvage what was left of the Ottoman Empire by accepting the Treaty of Sèvres offered them by the Allies in August 1920. It, too, was on the model of Versailles and was bitterly opposed by Mustapha Kemal and his nationalist followers. They accepted the loss of the Arabian provinces but rejected the Allied plans to partition the old province of Anatolia. In the post of inspector of the army in Anatolia, representing officially the government of the Sultan in Constantinople, Kemal devoted most of the year 1919 to arousing nationalist feeling in the province. When the new Parliament met in January 1920 his supporters were strong enough in it to win adoption of the 'National Pact' asserting the national independence of Turkey within its own frontiers, but in March the Allies sent troops into Constantinople and dissolved the Parliament. The following month Kemal summoned a meeting of the nationalist deputies in Ankara, in Anatolia, and defied both the Sultan and the great powers. He spent the next three years effecting the Turkish nationalist revolution.

He was greatly aided by external events. In 1919 Venizelos, the Prime Minister of Greece who represented Greece at the Paris Conference, had sent Greek forces to occupy Smyrna in Asia Minor. In October 1920 King Alexander of Greece died from the bite of a pet monkey, and was succeeded by the pro-German ex-king Constantine, who was much less acceptable to the Allied powers. The fall of the liberal Venizelos and royalist gains in the elections of 1920 alienated the powers. The Greek adventure in Smyrna, deprived of Allied support, was doomed to disaster. Kemal's troops drove back the Greeks and in September 1922 expelled the last of them. In face of this new, insurgent, efficient Turkey the Allies withdrew from Constantinople and prepared to make peace with Kemal at Lausanne in 1923. In the new treaty, clauses about reparations and penalties disappeared. Since Kemal rejected the old Islamic basis of the state and renounced any claim to territories with Arab majorities, the only frontier in dispute was that toward Greece. There the Turkish frontier was pushed westward beyond Adrianople at the expense of Greece, and Smyrna was included in Turkey. Kemal became president of the new Turkish Republic, and in 1924 the office of Ottoman Caliph, religious head of Islam, was abolished. Relieved of internal problems of Arab nationalism, and reduced to a hard territorial core, the compact new nationalist state of Turkey was free to carry out drastic internal reorganization. For the great powers, however, the growth of Arab nationalism and Zionist hopes of a Jewish national home in Palestine have ever since remained thorny problems.

Even apart from the novel and unpredictable consequences, for the balance of power in Europe, of the new Turkey and the new forces of Arab and Jewish nationalism, the resettlement of eastern Europe created nearly as many difficulties as it removed. It greatly increased the number of middle-sized powers such as Poland, Rumania, and Yugoslavia. It lengthened the frontiers of Europe by some four thousand miles, and in an age of protective tariffs this was important. It diminished the number of people who lived under what they regarded as an alien government, but it created a host of new national minorities. So great was the ethnic and national intermixture in Europe that no tidy national boundaries could be drawn. In an attempt to alleviate this unavoidable grievance, the powers induced all the succession states to enter into treaty obligations to respect the rights of national minorities within their frontiers. Poland, Rumania, Yugoslavia, Czechoslovakia, and Greece all signed such treaties, though under protest that none of the great powers, who also had internal national minorities, showed any willingness to undertake corresponding obligations. Many other states entered into similar undertakings, usually under pressure: former enemy states such as Austria and Hungary, Bulgaria and Turkey, in their treaties of peace; the Baltic states, Albania, and Iraq, when they became members of the League of Nations; Germany and Poland, in a special convention signed at Geneva in 1922. There thus grew up the new international phenomenon of a whole network of special agreements in which sovereign states promised to respect a variety of minority rights – religious and juridical, linguistic and cultural, political and economic. The main question was how these rights were to be guaranteed, and how the obligations were to be enforced. A Minorities Commission of the League of Nations was set up to receive petitions from aggrieved minorities, and the Council of the League was empowered to set up committees to investigate and work out a basis of settlement. Any member of the Council could also ask that a particular minority problem be investigated. The underlying doctrine, like that of mandates, was that sufficient publicity and international attention drawn to such problems would in themselves tend to solve them; but there was no coercive sanction against a government that persisted in dishonouring its promises. The system of encouraging minorities to appeal against their governments to a powerless international body, or alternatively of one government pressing charges against another, did not prove very helpful or effective. The obligations tended to irk national pride, and even to encourage militant minorities in their intransigence without ensuring victimized minorities any certain protection.

This part of the settlement was important because the minorities were so large and were mainly minorities of former enemy nations. Thus three million Germans remained in the Sudetenland within the borders of Czechoslovakia; about a million lived in Poland; over half a million in Yugoslavia. Some 700,000 Magyars were left in Czechoslovakia, one and a half million in Rumania, nearly half a million in Yugoslavia. Rumania's inhabitants included, in various areas, more than half a million Bulgars. Smaller but considerable numbers remained on the other sides of the frontiers: Germany included small Polish minorities, Austria some thousands of Czechs and Slovaks, and Hungary large numbers of Germans, Slovaks, Croats, and Rumanians. In all, Jews formed an important community. Attempts to exchange minorities or transfer them voluntarily were not encouraging. In 1923 limited exchanges were carried out between Greece and Bulgaria, but while most of the Greeks of Bulgaria emigrated, only half the Bulgars in Greece moved in the other direction. A compulsory exchange between Greece and Turkey attempted in the same year was so confused with the existing problem of Greeks who had fled from Turkey as refugees and with policies of indiscriminate expulsions that it caused immense hardship and suffering. It is doubtful whether transfers of population can ever be genuinely voluntary or devoid of hardship. It is even doubtful whether they lead to that radical solution of international disputes which they purport to achieve. As Hitler was later to show, it is as easy to generate agitation for irredentist lands as for irredentist minorities. For a great and aggressive power large minorities abroad may become a military advantage, usable to disrupt a neighbouring state and prepare it for attack; while the uprooting of such minorities leaves ample excuse to demand a return of their lost homeland. There are some international 'problems' to which there is no 'solution', if generosity and civilized behaviour are ruled out of national policies.

The many infringements of Wilson's doctrine of national self-determination and the failure to rearrange Europe into tidy nation-states were mostly due to the sheer mixture of populations. But they were in part due to considerations of economics and defence. A new state like Poland or Czechoslovakia should, it was felt, be shaped not only in accord with national community but also to meet certain desirable conditions of economic welfare and strategic defence. These two criteria – embodied in the conception of 'viability' – had led to the stipulation, even in the Fourteen Points, that Poland and Serbia should be given access to the sea. To give the new Poland access to the Baltic at the mouth of the Vistula meant depriving Germany of some part of her former territory, even if that territory were inhabited, as it was, by a certain number of Germans. It also meant separating East Prussia from the rest of Germany. Geography left no other possibility. Similarly, it seemed wise to respect existing lines of communication by rail and road, and to aim wherever possible at a combination of industrial with agricultural areas so as to achieve some balance within the national economy. On this principle Czechoslovakia was given its long lizardlike shape, including along with industrial Bohemia agricultural Slovakia and Ruthenia. The Sudetenland was also included, despite its predominantly German-speaking population, because the Bohemian mountains were the only militarily defensible frontier for Bohemia and Moravia. It was the hard facts of geography and of economics which often demanded modification of the principle of national self-determination and so led to the acceptance of large national minorities. The certainty that such modifications would be needed made it all the more regrettable that President Wilson and others had announced nationality to be an inviolable basis of the settlement.

The whole settlement of eastern Europe and in some measure the settlement with Germany were coloured by a further very important consideration: fear of the spread of Bolshevism into Europe. Events in Russia were ever-present in the minds of the 'Big Three' when they shaped the peace, for during 1919 western opinion was already shifting away from fear of German militarism towards fear of Russian Communism. The lurking idea that Germany might be used as a bulwark against Bolshevism was already present. There was a strong inclination to make the eastern states, from Finland down to Poland and Rumania, as large and strong as possible in order to serve as a *cordon sanitaire*, a quarantine zone to keep back the tide of Communism. The sporadic communist uprisings in Europe – such as that of the Spartacists in Germany and the Béla Kun régime in Hungary[1] – made this fear real and immediate. It might be argued that no such straggling barrier could be a very effective protection against so great a power as Russia; but what men feared in 1919 was not an armed invasion of eastern Europe by the new Soviet Union – conditions internally forbade that – but rather the infiltration of Communist ideas and local movements which might reproduce elsewhere the events that had taken place in Berlin or Budapest. The peacemakers found some consolation in regarding the new democratic nationalist régimes of the eastern states as what Clemenceau called '*un fil de fer barbelé*' – a length of barbed wire. The French financiers and *bourgeoisie* whose loans to tsarist Russia had been repudiated by the new Soviet government were especially hostile to Bolshevism. Henceforth all French parties except the extreme Left felt that they had two enemies in Europe – the traditional national enemy, Germany, and the new social enemy, the Third International, or Comintern, founded in Moscow in 1919 and dominated by Lenin and the Bolshevik party. Just as

1. See pp. 590 and 595.

the spectre of Jacobinism haunted the peace settlement of 1815, so that of Bolshevism scared the governments of 1919.

The Soviet government disclaimed nationalist ambitions and denounced all imperialist aims. It recognized the newly formed states that had won independence from Russia, and set about establishing official diplomatic relations with them. In 1920 it made peace treaties with Finland, Estonia, Latvia, and Lithuania. In 1921 it made the peace treaty of Riga with Poland, and signed treaties of friendship with Turkey, Persia, and Afghanistan. In the same year it made a commercial agreement with Great Britain and received a British 'trade mission' in Moscow. The British example was soon followed by Italy. In 1922 the Soviet Union and Germany were invited to send representatives to an economic conference of the powers held at Genoa. Lloyd George had hoped to bring about closer relations between the Soviet Union and the western powers. But his intention was frustrated by the insistence of the French and Belgians that Russia's prewar debts should first be recognized, and it was only Germany which, at the nearby seaside resort of Rapallo, signed a treaty of friendship with the Soviet Union. The other powers of Europe were at first indignant and then frightened. The Soviet Union was now officially and fully recognized by a great European power. The ring-fence that had been built round Germany in the East was the same 'line of barbed wire' erected against Bolshevism. Germany and Russia had that much, at least, in common. The two outcast powers of Europe drew together. The fall of Lloyd George soon after the Genoa Conference was in part due to the charge that he had flirted with the Bolsheviks. Rapallo established good relations between Russia and Germany which continued for the next ten years. It aroused all the deepest fears of western Europe, and seemed ample justification for France's efforts to forge close links of alliance with the succession states. Here, in embryo, was the future Nazi-Soviet Pact of 1939 which heralded the Second World War.[1]

Europe in the World. Events such as these emphasized that the balance of power in Europe must henceforth be considered not within the narrow compass of the continent itself, but in relation to the whole balance of power in the world. The preponderance of power in the West suffered a shattering blow when the Senate of the United States refused to ratify the Treaty of Versailles or to support United States membership of the new League of Nations for which the President had fought so hard in Paris. It suffered a further blow when first the United States, and then the United Kingdom, refused to stand by the promise of military aid to France against a German attack. The vast reserves of power

1. See p. 756.

which America could command and which had given the Allies so decisive a preponderance against Germany in 1918 were now withdrawn from their operation in the European arena, and their availability against aggression became quite uncertain. Even the massive resources of the British Empire seemed to be drifting away from Europe, leaving France and Belgium alone to bear the burden of a now more probable German resurgence. The drawing together of Germany and the Soviet Union at Rapallo seemed all the more ominous. The unbalance of power in Europe, on which the Treaty of Versailles depended for its fulfilment, was rapidly being redressed in Germany's favour. The United States and Great Britain were turning their attention overseas – as became evident in 1921 when they made with Japan the Treaty of Washington designed to restrict competition in naval armaments in the Pacific.

By the Treaty of Versailles, Japan acquired from Germany the 'leased territory' of Kiaochow in Shantung as well as a mandate to administer Germany's North Pacific islands. With the eclipse of Russia she was now the only great power on the borders of China. China refused to sign the treaty in protest against the Japanese acquisition of Kiaochow. She already nursed other grievances against Japan. In 1915, while the other interested powers were engaged in Europe, Japan presented to the Chinese government her 'Twenty-One Demands', a secret ultimatum which the Chinese were mostly obliged to accept and which created a virtual Japanese protectorate over China. This was checked two years later by the United States' insistence on the principle of the 'Open Door' in China. The Lansing-Ishii Agreement of November 1917 reached an uneasy compromise. America recognized Japan's 'special' interests; Japan reaffirmed the doctrine of the 'Open Door' in China. Japan's rapid loss of interest in the Paris Conference was followed by feverishly competitive naval construction on the part of the United States, Britain, and Japan. It continued until 1921. At the Washington Conference, however, these three powers, together with six others (France, Belgium, Italy, the Netherlands, Portugal, and China), met to consider how to end this new menace to peace in the Pacific. The five major powers, which had also been the 'Big Five' of the Paris Conference, agreed in 1922 to a ratio at which their naval strengths should be maintained. Then all nine powers reaffirmed the 'Open Door' in China. A further four-power treaty, binding signatories to respect one another's rights in the Pacific and to consult about any future differences, was signed by the United States, Britain, Japan, and France. This was understood to supersede the Anglo-Japanese Treaty of 1902 to which Canada had taken almost as much exception as the United States on the grounds that it had encouraged Japanese aggressions. All these agreements, reached quite outside the framework of the League of Nations, were regarded by Japan as a check and a rebuff. Within a few months civil war broke out in northern and central China, and by 1923 Sun Yat-sen, leader of the nationalist Kuomintang, became head of the government at Canton. He took as his chief adviser Borodin, a Russian who worked for close alliance between Chinese nationalism and Russian Communism. Here too, it seemed, the victimized and outcast nations were beginning to draw together; and here lay the embryo of the future Communist revolution in China. In the East, as in the West, Russia was returning to the stage of international politics.

The full import of all these events in Asia and the Pacific for the fate of the new settlement in Europe could not yet, of course, be foreseen. But Britain, at least, was made aware of what was happening by events in India. There the Hindu Congress party and the rival Moslem League emerged after the war as large active parties openly and violently agitating for national independence. By the Government of India Act, passed in 1919, Britain tried to introduce elements of parliamentary democracy and to make some initial transfers of power to Indian hands. To implant even a limited basis of parliamentary democracy was difficult in face of the widespread illiteracy and poverty and the complex conflicts of religious, racial, and community groups. The attempt only offered fresh facilities for agitation, and in 1920 Mohandas Gandhi launched a campaign of civil disobedience and boycott directed against the British government. Moslems and Hindus constantly engaged in communal riots, and the problem of maintaining order in India – let alone democracy – became acute. Given this new movement to end British power in India, the restless ambitions of Japan, the seething of new forces in China, the isolationist policy of the United States, and the imponderable factor of Soviet power and politics, it was plain enough that European affairs would in future be increasingly affected by what happened in Asia. The problems of Europe still remained crucial to the whole world, and the problem of Germany was still crucial to Europe; but all these matters had now to be viewed in a much wider framework. The settlement resulting from victory of the Allies in 1918 was liable to be changed by countless other factors far beyond the confines of Europe itself. This novel feature of European history became very much more apparent by 1950 than it was in 1920.

So far as this was perceived, however, the League of Nations seemed to be all the more appropriate a framework for building peace and stability in Europe. Here was a world organization contrived to replace the old system of 'power politics'. The methods of secret diplomacy and separate alliances, of rivalries in armed might and quest for a balance of power, were to be replaced by machinery for the peaceful settlement of disputes and arbitration, by constructive cooperation for common ends, and above all by the provision of 'collective security' by mobilizing the will for peace of the peoples of the world. In such terms was the new League and its adjuncts presented to the world, and had these terms been correct and soundly based in realities, it might indeed have been appropriate to the new situation of Europe in the world. How far these were unrealistic descriptions of the new international machinery, and why they proved to be so, may fittingly conclude this examination of 'war and peace' in the decade between 1914 and 1923.

NEW INTERNATIONAL MACHINERY

The peculiarities of the international situation in Europe in 1914 have already been mentioned.[1] They could not accurately be described as 'international anarchy', but were rather 'a twilight era of mixed systems'. A newly recreated and precarious balance of power coexisted with a residual and imperfect concert of Europe disrupted by rival alliances; beneath both there was a rudimentary form of international society in which states cooperated successfully about certain matters of common interest but jealously preserved all political and military matters for separate decision. It was not anarchy but an equally dangerous situation of semi-anarchy, in which the occurrence of colonial and dynastic and national disputes proved liable to send the whole of Europe save for a few fortunate neutrals into the abyss of general war.

The League of Nations. The scheme for a league of nations, sponsored with special enthusiasm and fervour by President Woodrow Wilson but eventually modified in accordance with British and French proposals, could be viewed in two different lights. In one aspect it was the revival and elaboration of the idea of a concert of Europe into a concert of most of the world; that is, it provided regular occasions when the representatives of all member states could meet and discuss not only common problems but any matter that seemed liable to endanger world peace. In providing standing machinery for such gatherings and permanent means of joint discussion, the League was an improved and wider version of the series of congresses which the great powers of Europe had held from time to time throughout the century before 1914. In another light it was something new and very different; it was a multilateral treaty, by which each participant bound itself not only to seek peaceful means of settling any dispute in which it became involved, but also to shoulder

1. See p. 539.

some share of responsibility for defending every other signatory against aggression. This notion, known loosely as a system of 'collective security', was the teeth within the concert – the supposed sanction which, by deterring an aggressor, would keep the peace. In this second aspect only was it based on a new concept; and in this aspect it failed.

The League of Nations was in no sense a superstate or a federation or a world government. It was not a government of any kind, but only a facility to be used by state governments in order to keep the peace – an apparatus of standing machinery created by a covenant among states to eliminate frictions among them and make possible timely common action against any threat to the peace of the world. It made sense and offered prospects of peace only if certain assumptions about the postwar world could be proved correct or be made to be correct. The most basic of these assumptions were that most governments would want peace, would shun war as a means of advancing national interests, and would have the will to use the new machinery. These assumptions seemed reasonable in the immediately postwar mood of revulsion against slaughter and destruction, and amid general anxiety to evolve new habits of interstate relations. They also seemed reasonable on the further assumption that most states would now be democratic states and that democracy would be more peace-loving than the dynastic Empires and autocracies which, it was believed, had been the main source of warlike policies before 1914. The extent to which these beliefs dominated the thought of Wilson is evident from the speech with which he opened the discussion of the League of Nations at the Paris Conference on 25 January 1919. He said:

Gentlemen, the select classes of mankind are no longer the governors of mankind. The fortunes of mankind are now in the hands of the plain people of the whole world. . . . . We are here to see, in short, that the very foundations of this war are swept away. Those foundations were the private choice of small coteries of civil rulers and military staffs. Those foundations were the aggression of great powers upon small. Those foundations were the folding together of Empires of unwilling subjects by the duress of arms. Those foundations were the power of small bodies of men to work their will and use mankind as pawns in a game.

The belief that the autocrats of Europe had caused the war found its fullest expression in the demand to 'Hang the Kaiser' and in Article 227 of the Treaty of Versailles wherein the Allied and Associated Powers 'publicly arraign William II of Hohenzollern, formerly German Emperor, for a supreme offence against international morality and the sanctity of treaties'. They declared their intention to try him before a special tribunal 'with a view to vindicating the solemn obligations of international undertakings and the validity of international morality'. Since William II had found refuge in the neutral Netherlands and the Dutch government refused to surrender him, this Article of the treaty was a dead letter from the beginning. But on the assumption that the new democracies would not only survive but would be more likely than their autocratic predecessors to pursue peaceful policies, the mere provision of facilities for a regular concert of the world's states seemed in itself constructive and hopeful.

It has already been seen how fragile were the new democratic constitutions of Europe, and how speedily the vogue for democracy dispersed. If it is unreasonable to blame the makers of the Covenant for not foreseeing these developments, it is more reasonable to blame them for underrating the militancy of nationalism. The expectation that the territorial resettlement of Europe would contribute to pacification rested on the beliefs that it was imperfect or unfulfilled nationalism that had caused unrest and war and that national self-determination would remove the militancy from nationalism. There was little warrant in nineteenth- or early twentieth-century history for this second notion. Oppressed nationalities had rarely shown a spirit of toleration, generosity, or compromise when they gained political power. The most ingenious redrawing of the frontiers of Europe inevitably raised a new crop of dissatisfied and aggrieved nationalisms. Hungarian minorities were unlikely to be any less restive under Rumanian or Serbian rule than Polish minorities had been under German or Russian rule. The minority treaties already described [1] were attempts to obviate this difficulty, but lack of any sanction to protect minority rights made them of relatively little value. For these reasons, just as the expectation of universal democracy proved unfounded, so the expectation that contented nationalism would make for pacification was also soon dispelled. Once both these expectations were disappointed, there remained no cohesive force which might give the League of Nations the vitality and vigour of action that it needed, other than a mere resolve to preserve the *status quo* and resist every attempt to revise the settlement of 1919. Wilsonian hopes that imperfections in the treaties would be put right by later revisions under Article 19 of the Covenant receded.

Several other circumstances combined to convert this basically conservative role of the League into its major function. On Wilson's insistence the Covenant (a term chosen, he told Lord Cecil, 'because I am an old Presbyterian') was included as the first part of all the treaties made with former enemy states. From its very inception the League of Nations was linked as closely as possible with the whole treaty settle-

1. See p. 633.

ment, including all its imperfections and such vindictive clauses as the arraignment of the Kaiser and the 'war-guilt' clause. This identification of the future world machinery for peace with the settlement of immediate postwar problems was unwise. From the start it made the League suspect to Germany and Russia, who had no share in making the settlement, and even to neutral states, who had no wish to be so closely associated with the war aims of the Allies. Even more important, it helped to ensure the weakening of the treaty settlement itself, for the United States could reject the Covenant only by rejecting the whole Treaty of Versailles. When, in the famous vote of March 1920, the Senate refused to ratify the treaty by the necessary two-thirds majority, it was chiefly because of a recoil from commitments in Europe which fastened upon Article 10 of the Covenant as the main obstacle. Article 10 was the crux of the whole conception of the League as a multilateral treaty for collective security. It stated:

The Members of the League undertake to respect and preserve as against external aggression the territorial integrity and existing political independence of all Members of the League. In case of any such aggression or in case of any threat or danger of such aggression the Council shall advise upon the means by which this obligation shall be fulfilled.

Without this clause, as Wilson correctly protested, the League 'would be hardly more than an influential debating society'. On Article 10 hinged the main provision of the Covenant for 'sanctions' laid down in Articles 16 and 17, whereby member states undertook to take joint action against any member resorting to war in disregard of its obligations under the Covenant.

The failure of the United States to become a member of the League, combined with the exclusion from it of Germany and Russia, was decisive in making the League a mere buttress of the existing settlement. The absence of three major powers and the lukewarmness of Japan toward the new institutions left the British Commonwealth, France, and Italy as the only major powers to be members. These three powers, divided among themselves both by national interests and by differing attitudes towards Germany and towards the very purposes of the League, had to make the League work if it were to work effectively. Italy, under her new Fascist dictator, Mussolini, was prepared to defy the League by the bombardment of Corfu in 1923, and was too dissatisfied by the treaty settlement to have any enthusiasm for the League as a defender of the peace. By 1923 everything hinged upon close collaboration between the United Kingdom and France; and in that year the Belgian and French occupation of the Ruhr, to compel German fulfilment of her reparations payments, alienated British opinion from

France. Thus it was the narrow French conception of the League, as a bulwark against any revision of the settlement, which came to prevail in the formative phase of the League's activities. This conception was not one that France alone, even with the aid of her allies among the eastern succession states and with occasional backing from Britain, could enforce.

Nor, in such changed conditions, was the machinery of the League itself suited for enforcement of obligations. In its Assembly every member state had equal representation and an equal vote. Except for decisions about procedure and the admission of new members, complete unanimity of all members was required. The Council consisted partly of permanent members representing the four major powers (Britain, France, Italy, Japan) and partly of four temporary members (increased to six in 1922 and to nine in 1926) chosen by the Assembly from time to time, but each member had equally one vote. The chief functions of the Council were to hear and consider disputes referred to it, and to report and give advice about what the Assembly should do. It had no power of independent action. These arrangements, admirably suited for the free discussion of matters of general interest and for ventilating the opinions of governments about international affairs, were clearly ill-suited to taking action. The rules of equality and unanimity gave even the smallest state a power of veto over any collective action of the whole League. The League paid full respect to the doctrine of absolute national sovereignty. Not only could no sacrifice of the principle have been secured in 1919, but even the general obligation undertaken in Article 10 proved repugnant to the Republican majority of the United States Senate.

The number of states which adhered to the Covenant and became members of the League by 1924 gave good prospects that, as a forum and vehicle of governmental opinion at least, the League machinery might prove valuable. The number rose from forty-one in 1920 to fifty in 1924. It included all the Latin American states, and the former European neutrals of Scandinavia, Switzerland, and Spain. Germany was not admitted until 1926, nor the Soviet Union until 1934, after Japan and Germany had withdrawn from the League. As an agency for 'collective security' the League was weakened by the fact that there was no moment in its history when more than five of the great powers belonged to it, or when at least two of the great powers did not belong to it. The only two powers who remained members continuously throughout the 'twenty years' truce' between 1919 and 1939 were France and Britain. Any pretension that it was a truly world organization thus collapsed, despite the large number of small and medium-sized states which remained members. For making the League so entirely voluntarist in character – for so tenderly preserving national sovereignty intact and leaving each member in effect free to act or not as it chose, for rejecting the French proposal of 1919 to set up an international force and so leaving all force at the separate disposal of the members – the main justification was that it must be made and kept as world-wide as possible. There was no test of qualification for membership other than a country's political independence. The first Article of the Covenant laid down that 'any fully self-governing State, Dominion, or Colony ... may become a Member of the League if its admission is agreed to by two thirds of the Assembly. ...'. The word 'self-governing' was not taken to require internal democratic government, but only that the applicant must not be governed by any other state. On this footing the new Irish Free State was admitted in 1923. There was, therefore, no attempt to restrict membership to democratic states or even to like-minded nations or trustworthy governments. By completely sacrificing selectivity and solidarity to the aim of being universal, it lost cohesion and decisiveness in action but still fell far short of universality. Provision was made in Article 1 for voluntary withdrawal and in Article 16 for expulsion of members by the Council. There were several voluntary withdrawals, but the first and only state ever to be expelled was the Soviet Union in 1939, when the League was already in collapse.

The Machinery of International Society. In its supreme purpose of keeping peace, the League failed. In both structure and membership, as well as in the circumstances of its birth, it was ill-adapted to this purpose. But it proved useful for promoting peaceful settlement of minor disputes. Wherever states were willing to submit disputes to the procedures of conciliation which it provided, it worked tolerably well. This function was exercised in 1921 in relation to a dispute between Finland and Sweden about the Aland Islands; to frontier disputes between Albania and Yugoslavia, between Poland and Germany, and between Hungary and Czechoslovakia. Frontier quarrels between minor powers were as yet, however, no menace to general peace. Under a secretary-general appointed by the Council and Assembly, the League had a permanent secretariat recruited internationally. This body, which became the pattern for staffing many later bodies including the United Nations, constituted a minor influence for peace in that it was a loyal corps of experienced and internationally minded men and women with professional pride in promoting good international relations. Various special commissions were set up under the auspices of the League; some for specific localities – such as the High Commissariat for the Free City of Danzig and the Governing Commission of the Saar Territory; some for specific purposes – such as the Permanent Mandates Commission and the Minorities Committee of the Council. A number of technical organizations dealt with world problems of health, narcotics, white-slave traffic, communications and transport, and finance. The League sponsored or backed half a dozen special institutes for dealing with such problems as refugees (the Nansen International Office), research on leprosy (at Rio de Janeiro), and intellectual cooperation (in Paris). In all such constructive work on social and economic problems the League helped to widen and deepen that embryonic international society which had already been coming into existence before 1914.

Nor were the League and its subordinate bodies the only pieces of international machinery set up in these years. The Covenant (Article 14) arranged for setting up a Permanent Court of International Justice competent 'to hear and determine any dispute of an international character which the parties thereto submit to it'. The Court was duly set up at The Hague in 1922 after prolonged and careful consideration. It did not replace the Court of Arbitration which had existed since 1900.[1] The new Court was permanent and dealt only with specifically legal disputes between states, such as arose concerning alleged breaches of treaties or different interpretations of international law. It could neither compel a state to appear before it, nor enforce its verdict. Like the League in all its aspects, it depended upon the will of adherents to use it and on their good faith to implement its findings. It began with thirty-four states signing its Statute. Even when the number rose to fifty it still did not include the United States.

Equally dependent on voluntary cooperation among members was the International Labour Organization (ILO), whose constitution was appended to each of the peace treaties just as each was prefaced by the Covenant of the League. It rested on the sound beliefs that economic privation and social injustice were themselves a threat to peace, and that if one nation permitted bad conditions of labour, it placed an obstacle in the way of other nations seeking to improve their own conditions. Its ancestors were the unofficial International Association for Labour Legislation of 1900 and the labour office of Basel set up before 1914. It had its separate annual General Conference to which each member sent four delegates – two representing the government, a third the employers' organizations and a fourth the workers' organizations. The tripartite structure was a unique attempt to introduce functional as well as purely governmental representation, and national delegations did not vote as units. The ILO also had its own Governing Body composed of eight delegates representing the governments of the eight states of great-

1. See p. 538.

est industrial importance; four representatives elected by the group of governmental delegates; and six representatives elected by each of the other two groups of delegates. It had its own Secretariat in Geneva, and national offices in the major countries. Its budget was part of the League budget. One purpose was to collect and disseminate information, but its chief purpose was to frame, and as far as possible apply, international rules governing conditions of labour. It worked by getting states to ratify agreed codes of labour conditions and relations, and to legislate about them. Its own decisions were never binding except in so far as governments legislated or acted upon them. Within these restricted limits it gained a large number of ratifications for rules governing such matters as nightwork of women and children, the rights of combination of agricultural workers, and conditions of employment of seamen. Germany and Austria were members from the outset, and both the United States and the Soviet Union joined in 1934. It survived even the Second World War.

Perhaps the major importance of all these new institutions in 1923 was that they existed at all. They reflected a faith and an ideology which, if not new, had never before been so widely agreed or acted upon by so many governments in the world. That ideology came to be known as 'internationalism' – a creed distinct both from cosmopolitanism, which denied the importance of national communities, and from federalism, which sought to pool authority and power in the hands of some form of world government. Internationalism rested on the fundamental belief that most of the nations of the world – especially if their governments rested on some organized form of popular consent – were capable of cooperating voluntarily and successfully for common purposes to which they had pledged themselves. Without a positive will to cooperate, and without abundant good will and good faith, there was never any hope that internationalism could work at all. The League of Nations and all its concomitant organizations were extensions, into the international relationships of the twentieth century, of the liberal democratic idealism of mid nineteenth-century Europe and early twentieth-century America. Were it not that the war had also been a revolution, that democratic ideals and institutions were too feebly rooted in most of Europe, and that disruptive nationalism proved able to feed upon the imperfections of the settlement of 1919, the future before the new international machinery might indeed have been as glowing as its supporters believed. It attracted the devoted services of gifted men of many nations – of Englishmen like Sir Eric Drummond, first secretary-general of the League, and Harold Butler, first director of the ILO; of the Frenchman, Albert Thomas; the Spaniard, Madariaga; the Norwegian,

Nansen. But the roots of war lay not merely in secret diplomacy, or colonial rivalry, or insurgent national minorities, or in any of the other prewar ills which it became popular to diagnose. War had its roots in the policies of the powers, and especially of the great powers; and states did not have to be dynastic or autocratic to follow policies that led to war. Upon the actual policies followed by the major powers of the world – several of which either never joined or quickly left the League – all this machinery could exert very little influence.

Perhaps the strongest impression left upon any student of the decade of war and peace between 1914 and 1923 is the constant disparity between purpose and achievement, and the power of events to shape subsequent events regardless of the wills of men. The Allies did not go to war in 1914 in order to destroy the Habsburg Empire or the Ottoman Empire, to bring about a communist revolution in Russia or to restore Poland, to create a series of new states in the Baltic or the Balkans, to establish new Arab kingdoms or a Jewish national home in Palestine, or even to begin the new experiment of a League of Nations and an International Labour Organization. The one agreed aim of the Allies in 1914 was to destroy German militarism and to diminish the hegemony of Germany in Europe. Yet all the unintended consequences came to pass, and the one agreed purpose was not achieved. The richest fruits of victory were harvested by the semibelligerents and the nonbelligerents: the United States became the greatest economic power in the world, Japan won a new political ascendancy in China and new economic and naval power in the Pacific, the Irish Free State won complete independence, India made a big stride towards self-government, the Bolsheviks captured control over Russia, the Zionists established strong claims to Palestine. The victorious Allies, even when they achieved particular aims – as France did in recovering Alsace and Lorraine – were bequeathed a most burdensome legacy of devastation, debt, taxation, poverty, refugees, minority problems, frontier disputes, and inter-Allied frictions. It was inevitable that there should spread, throughout western Europe, a revulsion against war backed by the conviction that war could never pay. A mood of outright pacifism pervaded western thought at the very moment when renewed efforts, even a willingness to use force, were most needed to restrain the militant forces of aggrieved national pride which were simultaneously engendered in Italy and Germany and Japan. The central sad theme of European history during the fifteen years between 1924 and 1939 was demolition: the progressive demolition of the settlement, the hopes, the institutions, the distribution of power, which seemed for a brief spell to have been established by 1924.

THE most tantalizing question about the two decades that have come to be known, so pathetically, as the interwar years, is how far they were years of lost opportunities – years that the locusts ate – or how far opportunities that seemed to exist never really existed at all. There was so much optimism in the 1920s that was harshly dispelled by the crashes and crises of the 1930s, so many fair hopes of peace and prosperity were dashed by the collapse of the new world hastily fabricated after 1918, that events suggested a sort of political Manicheeism – a battle between forces of good and of evil which culminated in yet another orgy of slaughter and destruction. It is natural in the conditions of wartime to feel like this. But the historian, as these tragic events recede into history, must question this view. He must probe not merely into the sequence of happenings which preceded the outbreak of the Second World War but also into the whole situation that was created by the First World War and its aftermath; and he must inquire what circumstances and what policies made stability and peaceful progress likely or unlikely. He must try to grade in some order of relative importance the various elements in the situation which made for disruption rather than cohesion. It may be that some opportunities for strengthening tendencies to cohesion and weakening tendencies to disruption were not taken because of the follies and frailties of men. But it may also be that the decisive opportunities – the chance for men in power to give the course of history a new direction – never presented themselves at all. It may be that policies indispensable for mastering the tendencies toward economic collapse and the drift toward war were policies that existing governments were, by their very nature and basis, inhibited from pursuing; and that the really crucial changes could be effected only by events themselves – by new experiences, more knowledge, and a reorientation of mind and of world forces. But if this is true, and if further conflicts and even particular wars were inherently likely in the situation existing after 1919, it does not follow that a further general

MAP 18.   EUROPE, 1923.   See following pages.
This map shows the boundaries of European states as they were eventually fixed by the peace settlement of 1918–23 (see also Maps 15, 16, 17). Although shorn of certain border territories, Germany of the Weimar Republic held a compact, central, and dominant position. Fifteen years later Nazi Germany expanded south-eastward by incorporating Austria and the Sudetenland of Czechoslovakia. She thereby began the sequence of events which led to the Second World War and the redrawing of boundaries shown in Map 27.

EUROPE
1923

- Area lost by Germany
- Area lost by Russia
- Area lost by the Ottoman Empire

Reykjavik ICELAND (DEN.)

FAEROE IS. (DEN.)

NORWAY

Oslo

SCAPA FLOW

Edinburgh

ULSTER
IRISH FREE STATE
Dublin
Liverpool

DENMARK

GREAT BRITAIN

GERM
WEIMAR

Atlantic

Ocean

London Amsterdam
NETH.

English Channel Brussels
BELG.

Hamburg
Bremen
Berlin

Cologne
Frankfurt
Dresden

Paris
Versailles

Metz
Strasburg

Weimar
Prague

Stuttgart
Munich

C Z

FRANCE

SWITZ.

Geneva
Locarno

AUSTRIA

Vienna

Trent

Trieste
Fiume

Bordeaux

Bilbao

Marseilles

Florence

PORTUGAL

Lisbon

SPAIN

Madrid

Barcelona

CORSICA
(FR.)

ITALY

Rome

Naples

Seville

Cadiz

Tangier GIBRALTAR (BR.)
SP. MOROCCO

BALEARIC IS.
(SP.)

SARDINIA
(IT.)

Mediterran

Algiers

MOROCCO
(FR.)

ALGERIA
(FR.)

TUNISIA
(FR.)

SICILY

MALTA
(BR.)

500 MILES

war was inevitable; so the further circumstances that shaped separate conflicts between states into the Second World War must also be examined. The actual consequences of events cannot be taken for granted, any more than their actual sequence was preordained.

It has already been shown, in Part VII, how the processes of warmaking and of peacemaking in the decade before 1924 transformed the map of eastern Europe, Russia, and Turkey (see Map 18). In that transformation ancient states and frontiers were dissolved, new forces of nationalism and democratic fervour released; the whole distribution of wealth, advantages, and power in the world was changed, and new machinery for international cooperation created. All this occurred swiftly and violently, and so much of it was effected by the course of events rather than by any concerted effort or plan, that it was natural enough that it should be followed by a period of unrest and further upheaval. The uncertainty and instability caused by these changes took many forms: first in time, the triumphs of Bolshevism in Russia and of Fascism in Italy; then the upheaval of economic crisis throughout the world between 1929 and 1934; followed by the resurgence of Japan and of Germany as aggressive military powers – all resulting in recurrent challenges to democratic institutions and ideals so recently adopted in many countries. Civil war, in the latent form of a clash between communism and fascism inside many countries, or in the open form of international-plus-civil war as in Spain, preceded international war itself. The new international machinery proved virtually powerless to prevent or even alleviate these conflicts. This was chiefly because it had been granted no power other than that which its supporters chose to put at its disposal. The disturbance and the eventual reversal of the balances of power which had resulted from the victory of the western powers in 1918 were brought about by the deliberate policy of states – pre-eminently Italy, Germany, and Japan – which stood to gain by such changes. Though it might be maintained that prosperity collapsed and that democracy was gradually eclipsed, it is certain that peace was deliberately demolished in the interests of the single-party dictatorships and by conscious policies remorsely pursued.

These events will now be examined in turn. But they, too, had their prelude: the strange, rose-tinted years of the Locarno and Briand-Kellogg pacts, when economic conditions seemed set for stability and progress, dictators had not yet embarked upon programmes of conquest, and good relations prevailed even between Germany and France, between the Soviet Union and the West. With five years of undoubted peace and hopeful cooperation, the drama of contemporary Europe begins.

CHAPTER 25

LOCARNO HONEYMOON, 1924-9

ECONOMIC RECOVERY

BY 1924 a certain basis for economic recovery, and even for economic prosperity, had been laid in each country. But the character of that basis differed from one country to another. British prosperity, which was measured by the decline in figures of unemployment and the rise in figures of exports, rested on a policy of financial solvency and orthodoxy, and on strenuous efforts to balance the budget and so prevent any weakening of the pound. In 1925 Winston Churchill as Chancellor of the Exchequer established the pound at its prewar parity in relation to the dollar and put Britain back on the gold standard. She had not yet been overtaken by either the United States or Germany as the world's most prolific exporter of manufactured goods. Prices were kept low, and the new industries of automobiles and radio, the postwar boom in building, the revival of old industries such as shipbuilding and engineering on which her prewar greatness had in part depended, all helped to promote both material recovery and a sense of prosperity. Yet even this degree of recovery had black spots, and was not securely based. Figures of unemployment never fell below one million; the British share of world exports never returned to prewar levels; in the new industries she was from the start outpaced by the United States; and in her old industries, such as coal mining and textiles, she suffered severe handicaps. With her overseas investments depleted by the war, and her former easy supremacy in world markets challenged no longer by the German Empire but certainly by the United States and Japan, her growing need for larger imports could be met only by heavier exports, which in such conditions were very difficult to attain. The British economy had suffered acutely, as the former workshop and shipper of the world was bound to suffer, from the dislocation of world trade which war had caused. Tending under Conservative governments to retreat behind protective tariffs and abandon those doctrines of free trade which the Liberals and most of the growing Labour party still held sacred, British industries were less robust than they seemed.

The new-found prosperity of Weimer Germany, on the other hand, rested upon quite different foundations.[1] Having ruined almost the entire

1. See p. 606.

German middle class by the currency collapse of 1923, at the same time liquidating all public and many private debts, German policy now relied upon extravagant foreign loans in order to rebuild and modernize German industry. These years were a time of boom in building, in social reconstruction of all kinds, in public and municipal undertakings. But the whole German economy rested not on financial solvency but on the opposite – lavish and mostly short-term borrowing; and for this reason it now stood on a precarious footing, which the first shock to international confidence would rock and probably shatter. The Dawes Plan came into operation in September 1924 and by the end of the year the German government was able to balance its budget and return to the gold standard. The recovery, at about the same time, of Austria and Hungary, which had experienced the same kind of inflation as Germany, was achieved by a combination of international loans and financial control by the League of Nations. The year 1924 brought a general improvement in currency conditions all over Europe, including Scandinavia where Sweden led a return to the gold standard. This general stabilization underlay the new sense of economic recovery which prevailed in 1925. As usual in modern European economic life, once tendencies to revival became apparent in a few major countries, they spread quickly to most of the rest. Economic prosperity, no less than economic depression, tended always to be generalized. European nations were more clearly than ever members one of another, interdependent in their wealth and well-being.

Germany's industry underwent a phase of 'rationalization', which carried even further its prewar tendencies towards the formation of giant trusts and combinations. The number of cartels, both national and international, increased. In 1925 Carl Duisberg created the huge *I. G. Farben* concentration of the chemical and dyestuff industries, whose interest ramified over the whole range of nitrates and fertilizers, drugs and photographic chemicals, motor spirits and perfumes, lubricating oils and varnishes, artificial silks and plastics. By controlling patents in the scientific processes of modern industries, it developed wide international connexions with oil and chemical industries in the United States, Britain, and the Netherlands. It established connexions with various political parties, and the German General Staff showed a discreet but lively interest in its capacity to make substitutes for critical raw materials and strategic necessities. In 1926 Albert Vögler formed the giant steel trust (*Vereinigte Stahlwerke A.G.*) that linked together the large enterprises of Thyssen, Stinnes, Phoenix A.G., and Otto Wolff. Both these trusts played a considerable, though not yet fully assessed, part in the rearmament of Germany and the rise to power of the National Socialist dictatorship. HAPAG regained its old power over shipping;[1] and the *Wiking Konzern* in cement and the *Siemens Konzern* in electrical trades established virtual monopolies. Some of the new industrial magnates, whose power even before the war had been great, enhanced it during the currency crash in 1923 by accumulating fabulous fortunes. The model of such millionaires was Hugo Stinnes, who contrived to erect a giant vertical trust comprising iron and steel, shipping and transport, timber, paper, newspapers, and even hotels. Such men inevitably acquired great political influence and power; a feudal oligarchy was built into the democratic Weimar Republic.

The economic recovery of France and Belgium reflected yet a third pattern, different from that both of Britain and of Germany. They received more in actual reparations payments; and their most urgent problems were those of financial and currency stability and industrial reconstruction, but much less those of world trade. In 1923 foreign trade still played a relatively small role in French economic life; the bulk of her exports and imports was only a little larger than in 1913. But during the war she had experienced an industrial revolution more intensive than hitherto, and this continued after the war. The loss of her richest industrial and mining areas had forced her to develop all other resources to the utmost, and the insatiable demand for munitions boosted the metallurgical and chemical industries. Hydro-electric power was developed to make up for the shortage of coal, and new areas of the country became industrialized. Encouraged by wartime controls and necessities, industrial units became larger. During the postwar years the re-equipment and modernization of her northern industries and the recovery of Alsace and Lorraine carried this revolution very much further. The new plant was more efficient and productive than the old, and by 1927 all the devastated areas had been restored. This combination of innovation and renovation brought an impressive expansion in her whole productive capacity between 1923 and 1929. The emergence of France as a much more industrial state was the most striking feature of western European economy in the postwar years. It meant, too, that she became an exporting nation on a scale larger than before. By 1925 the indexes of her industrial production and railroad transportation were more than double those of 1919. Her balance of trade and payments remained favourable after 1924. The basis of French prosperity seemed firmer and more durable than that of Germany. But even this comforting development called for adjustments and led to fresh problems, both internal and external, which France proved unable or unwilling to face.

1. See p. 376.

Internally, industrialization caused a labour shortage that had to be met by foreign immigrants; it caused new tensions between industrial and agricultural interests, because the deeply rooted traditions of a highly protective agricultural policy kept the price of food and cost of living high, and so made for high wages. Externally, therefore, France entered the export trade handicapped by being unable to cut costs and prices below a certain level, at a time when selling on world markets was becoming increasingly competitive. Home consumption was restricted because the purchasing power of the workers left little surplus for other than necessities. Moreover, international trade itself was about to enter into a phase of rapid contraction after 1929. It was the fate of France to reach a point of economic development just when the kind of activity most necessary for her continued prosperity became especially sensitive to depression. Belgium, whose standard of industrial productivity had exceeded that of France, recovered equally rapidly and for the same reasons; and the Flemish areas particularly prospered both in agriculture and industry. Until 1926 in Belgium, as in France, the depreciation and instability of the franc disturbed the whole economic life of the country. Its stabilization in 1926 brought an expansion of investment and greater economic stability.

Whether economic recovery in Europe followed the British, German or French pattern, it remained fragile and precarious. Yet at the time, after prolonged uncertainties and impoverishment, it was most welcome and it seemed very real. Unemployment, which persisted in Britain and Germany and was liable to occur in Belgium, was alleviated by various means. In Britain the system of unemployment insurance was developed, and in 1920 it already covered roughly two thirds of the employed population. But those who had not enjoyed regular employment for a long enough period remained ineligible for benefits, and even those eligible often needed additional help. Such additional help was given in a somewhat unsystematic and unsatisfactory way by transitional benefits paid out of taxation and poor relief administered by local poor-law authorities. In Germany unemployment insurance was introduced in 1926, as an extension of the existing well-developed system of social security.[1] An efficient programme for housing gave German workers, as well as Austrian, a higher standard of home amenities than was normal in Europe. France in 1928 overhauled her old arrangements for social security and reduced them to a more unified system of national insurance covering sickness, disability, maternity, old age, and death. Unemployment remained sufficiently unimportant in France until after 1930 to call for no special provision.

1. See p. 358.

The Corporative State. Italy under Mussolini's dictatorial régime devised between 1925 and 1929 its so-called 'corporative state', and a Labour Charter of 1927 defined the rights of workers. The labour unions set up by the Fascist party as rivals to the existing socialist and Catholic unions were given a highly privileged position. Employers were induced to recognize them as the sole representatives of the workers for purposes of collective bargaining and wage negotiations. In return the party assured employers that strikes would be forbidden and all disputes settled by arbitration. The legalized unions, having completely ousted the older free unions, were grouped into federations on a national scale, and in 1926 there were formed six National Confederations for unions of employers and another six for unions of workers. A Ministry of Corporations supervised the whole structure. The corporate system was used, in effect, to bring all important sectors of Italian economic life under the disciplined control of the Fascist party and of the state; loyal members were inserted into the corporations as secretaries and organizers. Mussolini was for many years minister of corporations. This whole complicated mechanism was made into a unified system only in 1934, and its structure and operation were never as tidy or as comprehensive as the claims of the party implied. But it enabled the dictatorship to regulate, and in certain ways to improve, the national economy. It facilitated the programme of public works, which was Fascism's chief solution for unemployment and economic recovery. Its most publicized achievement was the draining of the Pontine marshes, and its policy of subsidies for agriculture was dramatized as the 'battle for grain'. In 1927 the lira was stabilized, though at a high rate, which handicapped Italian exports *vis-à-vis* French. Despite all efforts, the standard of living in southern Italy remained low, and the condition of the workers elsewhere remained little better. An auxiliary organization of the party – the National After-Work Organization (*Opera Nazionale Dopolavoro*) – provided all sorts of social, recreational, leisure-time activities for the workers. Despite its propagandist political aspects and exaggerated claims, it did something to improve working-class conditions. In Italy economic recovery depended more directly upon the action of the state than did that of any other country outside the Soviet Union. Even so, Italy, too, suffered from the effects of the economic blizzard which hit Europe in 1930.

Recovery in Eastern Europe. Throughout eastern Europe economic conditions also generally improved in these same years. There, recovery inevitably hinged mainly upon the revival of agriculture and of trade. As already shown,[1] the land reforms extensively carried out in the

1. See p. 610.

Danube valley resulted in a wider diffusion of landed property and thereby increased the independence of individuals and families. But this rarely led to either greater productivity or an amelioration of labour conditions. Peasant families worked hard on their little plots to attain even a low level of subsistence. Only in the more industrialized and commercialized areas, such as western Czechoslovakia and parts of Poland, could the standard of life be considerably raised. The Danubian states, in these years, traded a lot with one another. Austria bought her wheat from Hungary or Rumania. Well over a third of the exports of Austria, Hungary, Czechoslovakia, Rumania, and Yugoslavia went to their Danubian neighbours during the 1920s. But Germany regained much of her prewar trading position in the area, and this was to prove a source of weakness in its economic recovery. When the world economic depression forced Germany, Austria, and Czechoslovakia to cut down their agricultural imports, the effects were immediately transmitted to eastern Europe. The continuing rapid growth of population, in the more constricted conditions of these years, intensified the menace of overpopulation in these still backward economies; and to that menace no effective answer had yet been found. People remained undernourished in countries that were exporting food.

Most dramatic of all, and most far-reaching in its eventual consequences, was the economic recovery of the Soviet Union as a result of Lenin's New Economic Policy.[1] Industrial production, indeed, recovered slowly, and did not reach until 1927 its level of 1913. The major industries all remained in the hands of the state even during the NEP period, and foreign trade was still rigidly controlled. The major industries and foreign trade were, in Lenin's phrase, the 'commanding heights' of the Russian economy. The major concession of the New Economic Policy was to the peasants and to internal traders, both of whom were allowed to sell freely for private gain. Of Russia's whole farming acreage in 1927, only two per cent was held by state or collective farms, all the rest by individual peasant farms run by some twenty-four million households. Although the toleration of individual enterprise and profits in farming made it possible to escape the chaotic famine conditions of 1923, it did little to bring about a positive increase in normal agricultural production or productivity. That could be achieved only by extensive mechanization and more efficient organization.

In 1929 it was decreed that all agriculture should be collectivized within three years. The rigorous and brutal execution of this decree, under the direction of Stalin, reduced the country temporarily to con-

1. See p. 586.

ditions of famine and devastation again. The wealthier peasants (*kulaks*) were driven from their farms. Many thousands were killed or deported to forced-labour camps in Siberia. In the confusion, amounting locally to civil war, the livestock of the country was reduced by half, and production slumped. But in 1928 had been launched the First Five-Year Plan, designed to reorganize and expand Soviet industry as quickly as possible, with special attention to the production of capital plant and agricultural machinery. The early success of the Plan, despite the great shortage of technicians and skilled workers, opened a new vista of prosperity which helped to offset the temporary decline in food supplies.[1]

International Trade. These years also saw some resumption of trade between the Soviet Union and Europe. Russia's urgent need for machinery and technical help provided the spur, and the needs of European nations provided the response. The first British Labour government of 1924 opened negotiations, which were prefaced by formal *de jure* recognition of the U.S.S.R., and were intended to settle outstanding difficulties and arrange a loan to the Soviet government. Though the treaties were not accepted and Ramsay MacDonald's government fell, Italy, France, and a dozen other countries agreed to formal diplomatic recognition of the Soviet régime. Although British relations with the Soviet Union deteriorated, its commercial and diplomatic relations with Italy, France, and especially Germany improved. In 1925 Germany and Russia signed a trade treaty, and the following year made a neutrality treaty in which each undertook to remain neutral should either be attacked by a third power. These treaties proved of value to both countries, and were an extension of the policy foreshadowed four years earlier at Rapallo. The Russians ensured long-term credits at Berlin and prevented a united front against Bolshevism in Europe; the Germans recovered something of their old Russian market, and supplied Russia not only with machinery, but also with engineers. In return, too, the German General Staff gained access to facilities, beyond Allied control, for experiments in aeronautics and in military techniques. During 1927 the Soviet government began to cooperate in the economic and humanitarian activities of the League of Nations, and sent representatives to Geneva both for the general economic conference and for the meetings of the Preparatory Commission for the Disarmament Conference set up by the Council of the League.

In general, the years between 1924 and 1929 were years of economic convalescence but hardly of sound health. There were still signs of debility and fever, and the torn tissue of international trade had not been fully restored. In 1925 European output as a whole was for the first

1. See p. 692.

time as great as it had been in 1913, and by 1929 Europe's share in total world production was as great as before the war. Between these two dates the volume of international trade rose by twenty per cent, though because of falling prices its value increased by only five and a half per cent. The general return to the gold standard by 1925 and the restoration of prewar parity between sterling and the dollar betrayed the general nostalgic assumption that the prewar financial structure for international relations had been good and should now be restored. But it was not obvious that the conditions essential to its prewar success still existed or could now be recreated. The gold standard was not what it had been. It worked differently in a world where gold coins no longer circulated, where paper currency was not in practice convertible into gold, and where the 'gold exchange standard' (whereby some countries held no actual gold reserves but only claims on other gold-standard countries) by no means gave the same security in time of crisis. Italy and most of the eastern European countries adopted a 'gold exchange standard', which meant that any strain in the countries on full gold standard was immediately transmitted to them as well. This more delicate financial nexus between one country and another was one main reason why depression, when it came, affected the whole of Europe.

The prosperity of the 1920s was real: production, trade, and personal incomes were undoubtedly growing. There was more real wealth in the world, per head of population in 1925, than there had been in 1913; and still more in 1929 than in 1925. But this wealth was more unevenly distributed, and there were now more people than before unable to share in the prosperity. There was a larger number of workers unemployed in most European countries – seldom below an average annual rate of ten per cent in the United Kingdom in these years. There were the primary producers of the world, able to supply more of some things than the manufacting areas wanted or than others could afford, with the result that unsold stocks of wheat, sugar, and coffee accumulated. Various devices to increase or forestall purchasing power came into general use; chief among them the device of hire-purchase or deferred payments, which enabled purchasers to mortgage their incomes far ahead of receiving them, and to enjoy the use of goods long before they were paid for. But no such devices could remove the basic maladjustments between the flow of primary and of manufactured goods, nor between the world production of goods which many wanted and the limited power of those who needed them to buy them. The so-called problem of overproduction sprang not from an absence of needs, but from a lack of effective demand. These maladjustments were the basic reason for the economic crash which began in the autumn of 1929, dispelling the growing mood of confidence and prosperity which the previous decade had induced, and toppling over the precarious democratic régimes of central and eastern Europe.

CIVILIAN GOVERNMENT

By 1924 the revulsion against war and military preparedness had gone so far as to become a widespread revulsion against soldiers and armed might of any kind. Pacifist sentiments and doctrines became merged into that creed of 'internationalism' which had been embodied in the Covenant of the League, regardless of their inherent conflict with the notion of 'collective security' which underlay the Covenant.[1] Disillusionment with peacetime neglect of wartime promises bred a spirit of cynicism, when talk of 'Homes fit for Heroes' gave way to the realities of housing shortages and jerry-building, unemployment and niggardly poor relief. Until 1926 postwar democracy entailed the rule, above all, of civilian governments unheroic and unromantic, concerned with intractably obscure matters of currency stabilization and international balance of payments, astronomical war debts and gold standards. Throughout western Europe conservatively minded men held power, though socialist and even communist movements were rapidly gaining in appeal and strength, and in the United Kingdom and France socialists even wielded power on restricted terms and for short periods. The characteristic conservative figures of the time were Harding and Coolidge in the United States, Bonar Law and Stanley Baldwin in Great Britain, Raymond Poincaré and Paul Painlevé in France. The wartime leaders were repudiated, and Lloyd George and Clemenceau fell into the background of public life. (President Wilson and Lenin died in 1924; Clemenceau and Foch in 1929.)

The parliamentary governments destined to grapple with the profound economic and social problems of postwar Europe proved, in general, to be uninspiring and disappointing. It is never easy for parliamentary governments to make unpopular decisions, and in few countries was public opinion in a mood receptive to policies that stressed economy and maintained high taxation, or that demanded further sacrifices and austerity after the hardships of wartime. The flagrant survival of war profiteers, and of others whose wealth and position had obviously been enhanced while so many were ruined or out of work, fostered deep social resentments. The growth of socialist parties and – even more significantly – the new communist parties affiliated with the

1. See p. 642.

Third International of Moscow, made such resentments political, vocal, and effective. The conflicts of social loyalties, which in 1914 had been so abruptly submerged by the outbreak of war, were now remembered and renewed in a still more explosive situation. Moreover, the changes in party alignments which resulted from the war made governments more unstable and short-lived, and made it still more difficult for democratic governments to undertake long-term plans of recovery. Events conspired to implant the belief that democracy was a feeble, hesitant, ineffectual form of government for dealing with postwar problems of great urgency. In all the major countries there appeared, in new form, that conflict between nationalism and socialism which had existed before 1914.[1]

In the United Kingdom the short-lived Labour government of 1924 was followed by five years of Conservative government and, in 1929, by a second Labour government. The biggest political change was the rapid decline of the Liberal party and its replacement, as the second major party in the state, by Labour. Liberalism suffered from its immediate prewar record and from the split between Asquith and Lloyd George; but even more it suffered from its inability to attract the support of trade unions and workers generally. It failed to sponsor the kind of social reforms and modifications in capitalism which organized labour regarded as essential. Its nineteenth-century legacy of *laissez-faire* and free-trade doctrines outweighed its record of social reforms in the decade before 1914. In the coalitions between Labour and Liberals in 1924 and 1929, Labour was inevitably the predominant partner. In France the Chamber elected in 1920 was called the 'Blue Horizon Chamber', because it included so many uniformed officers. With half its members practising Roman Catholics, and its great majority ultranationalistic in outlook, it was the counterpart to the contemporary House of Commons. But the elections of May 1924 brought defeat not only to the conservative 'Blue Horizon Chamber' and to the right-wing government of Raymond Poincaré, but even to the nationalistic President of the Republic, Millerand. They gave victory to the left-wing coalition (*Cartel des Gauches*) which first put the Radical-Socialist, Edouard Herriot, in power, and the independent socialist, Aristide Briand. Their governments were, like the contemporary Labour governments in Britain, essentially coalitions of liberals and socialists, and they too failed to provide the financial stability that France needed. In 1926 a National Union (*Bloc national*) government brought Poincaré back into power to stabilize the franc, and in the general elections two years later his success helped to produce another predominantly conservative

1. See p. 425.

Chamber. Apart from several short-lived ministries, the scene was dominated by Briand, who held power precariously from November 1925 until July 1926, and by Poincaré, who was premier from July 1926 until July 1929.

In Germany the Social Democrats remained strong but never strong enough to enjoy an independent majority in the Reichstag. Every government, therefore, had to be a coalition; and in these years the country was governed by coalitions of the Catholic Centre party (which became an almost indispensable component of any government) and the wealthier middle-class parties, especially the liberal People's party. In the elections of 1924, coincident with the settlement of reparations by the Dawes Plan, the Social Democrats lost heavily and the conservative parties gained. Hitler's National Socialist party even scored its first electoral success by gaining thirty-three seats. But until his death in 1929 the most important leader in German politics, throughout several chancellorships, was Gustav Stresemann of the People's Party. He became Chancellor and Foreign Minister in August 1923, and remained Foreign Minister continuously until 1929. Since foreign relations played so predominant a part in German politics in these years, they justly became know as 'the era of Stresemann'. With never more than fifty supporters of his own party in the Reichstag, he had to maintain himself by subtle coalitions and bargains among the parties. His efforts to consolidate a central *bloc* comprising Centre and Social Democrats came to nothing. But he contrived to steer a remarkably consistent course, directed toward the liberation of Germany from the legacy of Versailles, and a policy of 'fulfulment'. He called off the campaign of passive resistance in the Ruhr in 1923, took strong action against both Hitler and the communists, got the Dawes Plan ratified by the narrowest of margins, and gained Germany's admission to the League of Nations in 1926. He was even awarded the Nobel Peace Prize in 1927. Yet in the war he had supported a policy of annexations and unrestricted submarine warfare, and he had voted against acceptance of the Treaty of Versailles. The confidant of Ludendorff, he belonged to the party of big business and armaments makers, and none could doubt his patriotism and nationalism. He was, in short, the perfect bridge between the nationalist, militarist, and capitalist interests of the Right, who planned only for the resurgence of Germany as a great power; and the more moderate, liberal, democratic, and socialist forces of the Left, who wanted to preserve the Weimar Republic and find a basis of reconciliation and peace in Europe.

In all three major countries of the West, therefore, the elections of 1924 inaugurated a strange interlude of balance and compromise between conservative nationalism and liberal socialism. This mixed phase of politics matched both the stage of domestic recovery and of international reconciliation. From 1926 onwards nationalism began to triumph over socialism. This trend was marked in France by the ascendancy of Poincaré, in Britain by the collapse of the general strike, in Germany by the election, in April 1925, of Field Marshal von Hindenburg, aged seventy-seven, as President of the Weimar Republic to succeed Friedrich Ebert. But in the interval, during 1924 and 1925, left-wing or internationally-minded men controlled the policies of all three countries. This made possible first the negotiations for a Draft Treaty of Mutual Assistance and the Geneva Protocol, conducted by Herriot and Ramsay MacDonald, and then the honeymoon of Locarno, when Briand and Stresemann in company with the British Conservative Foreign Secretary, Sir Austen Chamberlain, explored new paths of pacification in western Europe.[1] The first two sets of negotiations, for reasons which will be explained later, led to no concrete results, and even the Locarno Pacts signed in 1925 had, as seen in retrospect, an ambiguous result. The revival of nationalistic forces from 1926 onwards soon dissolved whatever consolidation of western policies was attained at Locarno, and after the withdrawal of the Allied Control Commission from Germany in 1927 secret rearmament proceeded apace. Political reconstruction, like the apparent economic recovery of these years, proved fragile and short-lived.

Social Unrest. A constant source of friction between conservative nationalism and liberal socialism (or social democracy) was the behaviour of the new communist parties of Europe and of the Third International (Comintern) to which they were affiliated. In 1920-22 communist parties broke away from social democratic parties in most European countries. This had a double effect upon the older social democratic parties themselves. On one hand it freed them from the necessity of the embarrassing prewar compromises between reformist liberal social ism and orthodox Marxism,[2] and made possible that closer alliance with liberal and left-centre parties already noted. Postwar socialism could now ally more whole-heartedly with organized labour to seek immediate social reforms through parliamentary action, and could dissociate itself from violent revolutionary activity or any necessary allegiance to Soviet policy. On the other hand, it gave socialists the novel experience of a distinct and organized party on their left, competing with them for votes and outbidding them for the support of working-class discontent. In Germany the Communist party gained sixty-two seats in the Reichstag in May 1924, and fifty-four in May 1928, and its candidate for the

1. See p. 675.
2. See p. 392.

presidency in 1925 mustered nearly two million votes against Hindenburg's fourteen and a half million. In France the trade union movement was split and a distinct communist section (the *Confédération générale du travail unitaire*, or C.G.T.U.) existed after 1922, seriously weakening the socialist and the working-class forces in the country.

In Britain the clash reached a climax in 1926 in the general strike. This critical event in the interwar history of Great Britain, leaving behind it a legacy of bitterness between capitalism and labour, conservatives and trade unionists, was occasioned by serious discontent in the oldest but most troubled of British industries, coal mining. Since 1920 miners' strikes and disputes of all kinds had been frequent. The report of a royal commission headed by Sir John Sankey had condemned the existing system of ownership of the mines and recommended some form of public management, but conservative governments had shelved the issue. In 1921 a general strike, in support of a mining stoppage involving nearly a million miners, had been only narrowly averted. In May 1926 the miners struck again, after a long deadlock in negotiations over proposed reductions in wages. This time it assumed the proportions of a general strike, as railway and other transport workers, iron and steel workers, builders, printers, and several other trades struck in sympathy. The fate of the miners became a test case for relations between employers, workers, and state. The Trades Union Congress and the Labour party shared something of the political bitterness of the miners. In particular, the Labour party smarted under the successful pre-election stunt of the 'Zinoviev letter', which it alleged had caused the electoral landslide in favour of the Conservatives in October 1924. This document, purporting to be addressed by the Comintern to the British Communist party urging violent revolution, was conveniently published on the eve of the elections. It was almost certainly a forgery, although Zinoviev had undoubtedly sent similar letters to communist parties in other countries. In any case, it was not addressed to the Labour party. But it was used by the Conservative Press and even Conservative candidates as a pre-election scarecrow, and the Conservatives won the elections by a majority of 228 seats over both Labour and Liberals. This unscrupulous sensationalism was treated as a reversion to the hysteria of the Khaki Election of 1918, and made Labour party leaders distrust Baldwin's government to a degree unusual in British politics.

In such an atmosphere the general strike seemed capable of precipitating civil war. The government proclaimed almost a state of siege, sending troops to occupy docks and power stations, and bringing into operation a suspiciously well-prepared system of emergency transport and delivery services. The printers' strike left the nation without newspapers, but Churchill edited the official government sheet, the *British Gazette*. The Trades Union General Council called off the general strike after nine days, so preventing useless chaos and probably bloodshed. The miners' strike dragged on for a further six months and eventually they accepted hard terms. Despite widespread popular sympathy with the miners, the Conservative government scored a positive victory over organized labour. In 1927 it sought to consolidate this victory in a new Trades Disputes Act which declared illegal all 'sympathetic strikes' and strikes calculated to coerce the government and endanger the nation. It stipulated that in future members of trade unions must 'contract in' to paying the union levy for political purposes, instead of as hitherto merely 'contracting out' if they chose. This was felt by Labour to be a particularly petty attempt to undermine the old alliance between trade unions and the parliamentary Labour party. The repeal of the Act became a cardinal item in Labour party policy, and was duly carried out in 1946.

With the forces of capitalism and labour clashing so dramatically even in Britain, the paragon of law-abiding parliamentary government, it is not surprising that these years saw comparable clashes in other lands. In France the financial policies of the *Cartel des Gauches* were resisted by the Right and by the capitalist interests entrenched in the Bank of France. The socialists demanded a capital levy as the only way to restore balance to France's national finances. Although Herriot himself did not support the idea, the mere proposal was enough to split the ranks of the *Cartel* on which his power rested, and to mobilize against it the wrath of the Right. The Bank, it was alleged, engineered the rapid fall of the franc in order to discredit the Left. Poincaré returned to save the franc from further disaster, and by increasing taxes, effecting economies, and balancing the budget, he did so by the end of 1926. These events, like the general strike in Britain, left a new mood of party bitterness and class war which boded ill for the smooth working of parliamentary and democratic institutions. There was some justification for the charges of the Left that French economic life was increasingly dominated by a financial oligarchy. The concentration of industry, even in France, had made great advances since the war. The head of the *Comité des Forges*, the organization of the great ironmasters of France, was de Wendel, and he was also a regent of the Bank of France. Mining, metallurgical, and shipping interests had combined into three great national organizations; and these and other employers' bodies had in 1919 set up a still wider coordinating body, the *Confédération générale de la production française*, which established the closest links with the banks and especially with the Bank of France. The Bank was ruled by fifteen regents elected by the largest shareholders, and by a general council of the 200 largest shareholders. These constituted the famous '200 Families', the central core of the oligarchy of big business and finance which became the favourite butt of left-wing hatred and ridicule until the nationalization of banking in 1945. There were moments when it dictated to the short-lived parliamentary governments. It acted as a powerful brake on any unorthodox financial measures, as well as resisting any policy contrary to the interests of the great concerns heavily represented among its regents.

The European democracies in these years were, therefore, confronted in general with a challenge somewhat different in character from that of the years before 1914. The challenge of militarism, which had haunted France in the time of the Dreyfus case and Germany under Kaiser Wilhelm II, seemed to have receded. But the challenge of economic oligarchy and overpowerful capitalism had become greater, as had the demands of organized labour for social rights and security. In addition, clericalism, from time to time, still raised its head; particularly in France, when Herriot introduced into Alsace and Lorraine the provision for secular education in the schools which had existed in France since the 1880s. The old enemies seemed more real, because more familiar, than the new. Party politics were still conducted in prewar terms to an extent that made them out-of-date in a world of giant capitalist organizations, massive confederations of labour, and communist parties. Clericalism even revived as a bulwark against Marxism. It was only after experience of the world economic crisis that economic and class conflicts appeared in fuller form and the scarecrow of clericalism fell into proper proportions. But after 1926 the issues of nationalism versus socialism appeared more stark and inescapable, and the mid 1920s assumed, in retrospect, an appearance of being a preparation for battle rather than, as they seemed at the time, the dawn of a new era of social harmony and progress in peace.

Stalin versus *Trotsky*. Events in Soviet Russia during these years conform significantly to this same pattern. They marked the height of the quarrel between Stalin and Trotsky, one representing the goal of 'socialism in a single country', the other the aim of 'permanent' world revolution. In April 1922 Josef Stalin, the Georgian of peasant stock who had hardly been outside the borders of Russia, became general secretary of the central committee of the party. In that key post he was well placed to make himself the heir of Lenin, backed by Zinoviev, president of the Communist International and by Kamenev, third member of the triumvirate within the central management of the party. When Lenin died in January 1924, Trotsky was feared as a possible dictatorial successor. A Jew who had been President of the Petrograd Soviet, he had been commissar for war and foreign affairs and had taken a central part in organizing the victorious Red Army during the civil war and the war of foreign intervention. Like Lenin, Zinoviev, Kamenev, and indeed most of the Bolshevik leaders, he had sprung from the gentry, middle classes, and intelligentsia, for his father was an upstart Jewish landowner, and like them he had spent much of his life in exile. Stalin's parents had been born serfs, and he knew from personal experience the poverty and degradation of the masses. His education derived from an ecclesiastical school and the Theological Seminary at Tiflis. He contrasted with the impetuous Trotsky both in temperament and in political doctrine.

By 1925 he persuaded the fourteenth Party Conference to adopt the policy of 'socialism in one country'. This policy involved accepting the fact that the tide of revolution in Europe had ebbed, and that capitalism had temporarily stabilized itself; that the first task of the party was to consolidate and complete the proletarian revolution in the Soviet Union; and that the Marxist goal of world revolution must be subordinated to completing the socialist revolution in Russia. Trotsky regarded both these aims as desirable, but insisted that revolution in Europe was still possible and must precede, or at least accompany, the achievement of socialism in Russia. The Russian Revolution, for Trotsky, was only the prelude to world revolution. To Stalin's concentration upon 'socialism in one country' he opposed the policy of 'permanent revolution', by which he meant seizing every opportunity and sparing no efforts to organize and precipitate revolution in Europe. These differences of emphasis and priority quickly became, in the feverish atmosphere of communist ideological disputes after Lenin's death, a source of ferocious personal and group enmities. Behind them lay both a fundamental difference of personal outlook and an old historical contrast. For Stalin, Russia was not on the periphery of western civilization, dependent upon events in Europe; it was the very heart of a new world civilization. For Trotsky, more familiar with Europe than with Russia, what happened in Europe was decisive, what happened in Russia could not in itself determine events in Europe. It was the twentieth-century version of a nineteenth-century feud; the feud between Slavophils whose faith lay in the special creative genius of the Slav race and of Russia in particular, and the 'westerners' who held that Russia's future lay in her absorption of all that Europe had to offer in science, technology, culture, and ideas.

In January 1925 Trotsky ceased to be commissar for war, a position that had given him great influence with the Red Army, and in December at the Party Congress, Stalin won the day against Zinoviev and Kamenev.

By 1926 the feud between Stalinists and Trotskyites was reaching the point of explosion; and it was taking the shape of a clash between a doctrine and policy which were basically nationalist, and a doctrine and policy which were exclusively antinationalist and revolutionary. For Trotsky, the progress of mankind was hampered not only by capitalism but also by the existence of nation-states. To attempt to build 'socialism in one country' and at the same time to enter into normal international relations with the capitalist nation-states of Europe was to accept as normal the existence of the nation-state. He held that if revolution did not spread to Europe, the revolution in Russia would either succumb to capitalist attacks from Europe or would be corroded in the backward economic and cultural environment of Russia. Even for complete success in Russia, therefore, incessant revolutionary activity in Europe was indispensable. The revolution would either be permanent or it would be betrayed. To a people weary of turmoil and eager for better economic conditions, Stalinism had an incomparably deeper appeal than Trotskyism. Besides, national pride was hurt by the suggestion that Russia could not 'go it alone', but must await events in Europe which – on experience so far – seemed increasingly unlikely to happen. It was not difficult for Stalin to mobilize against his rivals all the sentiments of national pride and hope, as well as the ordinary desire for peace and prosperity.

It was in these circumstances that the outcome of the general strike in Britain assumed crucial importance for Trotsky and Zinoviev as the first clear sign that proletarian revolution, as they had always held, was about to occur in the most industrially advanced country of western Europe. It was the touchstone of their fate. The absence of any revolutionary movement in the strike, the rejection by the Trades Union Congress of money sent to them from Russia, even such characteristic incidents as a football match between strikers and police (which the strikers won by two goals to one), demolished any credit left to the prophets of imminent world revolution. The activities of the Comintern during these years when the Kremlin was seeking to establish commercial and diplomatic relations with the West had anyhow embarrassed all concerned, and the only beneficiaries had been the Fascists and the ultraconservatives. Stalin undertook the elimination of Trotsky and his followers. First Zinoviev and then Trotsky were expelled from the politbureau, the key committee of the party. Zinoviev was deposed from the presidency of the Comintern. During 1927 both were expelled from the central committee and then from the party. In December the Party Congress also expelled seventy-five leading members of the opposition, and Trotsky was sent into exile. Kamenev and Zinoviev recanted but were not reinstated in positions of power. From abroad, from Turkey,

Sweden, and finally Mexico, Trotsky carried on the fight with courage, energy, and ferocious invective. Stalin the nationalist, the ruthless 'man of steel', triumphed completely over his opponents within the party by the same means that the party had used against the Mensheviks: denunciation, skilled manoeuvre, and force. The single-party dictatorship had found its own dictator, and in 1928 the First Five-Year Plan was launched to lay the industrial foundations for 'socialism in one country'. The disasters caused by the decree collectivizing agriculture in 1929 were the first indication of how perilous could be the new concentration of supreme power in the hands of Stalin.[1]

National Consolidation. There was thus a certain political consolidation, on a national basis, in both western and eastern Europe by 1928. Social revolution receded as rightist governments were reaffirmed in power in Britain, France, Germany, and the Soviet Union. In Italy Mussolini's régime seemed to be more than ever firmly based at home, as was Horthy's in Hungary. In the smaller countries, too, conservative nationalism tended to triumph. In Spain, General Primo de Rivera, in September 1923, had proclaimed himself dictator, backed by King Alphonso XIII, the army, and the capitalists of Catalonia, and opposed only by the socialists. The inefficient parliamentary system was overthrown, and for the next six years Spain was governed by a tough military dictatorship, improving material conditions in a heavy-handed way without moving towards the full-dress totalitarian fascism of Mussolini. In January 1930 Primo de Rivera resigned, having lost the support of the army. The following year the King fled and a parliamentary republic was set up.[2] In Portugal, too, General Carmona carried out a military *coup* in 1926, and by 1929 was giving way to his Minister of Finance, Oliveira Salazar, professor of economics and a devout Catholic, whose power was to survive even the Second World War. In Poland, Marshal Pilsudski carried out a similar *coup* in 1926, making himself Premier and Minister of War. He gave the country stronger government and under his rule more rapid economic development took place. But Polish politics remained unstable and turbulent, and his governments of 'colonels' of the old Polish Legion produced few men of political talent and no Salazar. Lithuania, nursing nationalist grievances against Poland about the disputed areas of Vilna and Memel, followed the same road. In 1926 her Nationalist party, exploiting discontent against the moderates and the socialists, set up a strong government under President Smetona, who governed with strong-arm methods until 1939. In south-eastern Europe, as well as in south-western, these same years brought a recession

1. See p. 660.
2. See p. 707.

in democracy that was little related to economic recession. In Austria a Catholic priest, Ignaz Seipel, became Chancellor in 1922. Under his influence until 1929, the country was increasingly diverted away from social democracy toward a clericalist authoritarianism. In Yugoslavia, King Alexander was obliged, by 1928, to assume dictatorial power because parliamentary government broke down, and the Croats set up a separatist parliament at Zagreb.

So widespread, indeed, was this drift towards military or royal or clericalist dictatorships between 1926 and 1929 – in the years of relative economic prosperity – that the eclipse of democracy in Europe clearly cannot be attributed to the world economic depression that only began at the end of 1929. A tendency that appeared simultaneously in Spain and Portugal, in Poland and Lithuania, in Austria and Yugoslavia, was not merely regional in character. It was, like the earlier reversions to dictatorships in Italy and Hungary, due mainly to the unsettled economic and social conditions after the war, to the shallow roots of the new democratic constitutions and the ineptitudes of parliamentary politicians. All these countries were, moreover, strongly Roman Catholic in religion. In each of them conservative clericalism was one of the taproots of reaction against democracy and socialism. The Concordat of 1929 between the Vatican and Mussolini sealed this alliance. The tide of authoritarianism in Europe before 1929 had a nineteenth-century flavour, royalist and militarist and clericalist. The effect of the Great Depression was to intensify this trend and to carry it very much further in the extremist direction of fascism and totalitarian government.[1]

PACIFICATION BY PACT

The League of Nations, as already seen,[2] rested upon a general and potentially universal treaty wherein signatories mutually guaranteed their 'collective security'. Had it been considered effective for this end, separate pacts and treaties and further specific guarantees would have been superfluous. But from the outset France, feeling robbed of the material guarantees for which she had striven at the Conference of Paris, sought special guarantees in treaties of alliance in eastern Europe. Between 1924 and 1929 several attempts were made either to reinforce the existing guarantees of the Covenant or to find additional ways of creating security in Europe. France, the chief 'consumer of security' in Europe, countered every proposal for agreed disarmament with the thesis that far from disarmament being, as the British maintained, a

1. See p. 702.
2. See p. 642.

source and prerequisite of security, greater security was the essential prerequisite of disarmament. Britain, like the United States, tended to think of security as meaning security against war. The French, more pessimistically, thought of it as including also security against defeat in war. Therefore, to maintain national defence in a state of adequate preparedness, to surround oneself with treaties of alliance and mutual guarantee made with reliable and strategically placed allies, and to ensure the continued disarmament and isolation of Germany seemed to the French the plainest common sense. Their obsession with security frequently irritated and alienated Great Britain and other friends of France. French policy seemed too often merely obstructive of proposals for a general scaling down of armaments and all the relief to national burdens which that would have brought. Moreover, the thesis that competition in armaments and the rivalries of alliances had in themselves been an important cause of war in 1914 had sunk deeper into the consciousness of the British and Americans than of the French. The French never forgot that they might easily have been defeated in 1914, as in 1871, had they again been without friends and allies when the German invader came.

Draft Treaty of Mutual Assistance, 1923. The first attempt at disarmament took the form of the draft Treaty of Mutual Assistance. The draft was presented to the Assembly of the League in 1923 by the Temporary Mixed Commission charged with investigating the question of disarmament. It combined vague provisions for future disarmament with specific guarantees for present security. It proposed that within four days of an outbreak of hostilities the Council of the League should decide which party was the aggressor, and that members of the League should then automatically be obliged to give military assistance against the aggressor. Under Article 16 of the Covenant, providing for sanctions against aggression, military sanctions would thus become automatic instead of optional. The draft incorporated, in short, the French thesis that absolute security should precede disarmament. It was rejected by Great Britain and the British Dominions, as well as by the Netherlands and the Scandinavian states, though it was warmly welcomed by France and most of her allies. But in the autumn of 1924, when Herriot and MacDonald coincided at Geneva, a compromise was sought in the form of the 'Geneva Protocol'.

Geneva Protocol. This further attempt to reach agreement, the 'Protocol for the pacific settlement of international disputes', sought to close the existing gaps in the Covenant which still left open the possibility of war. These were mainly two: if the Council should not be unanimous in its judgement on a dispute; and if the subject of the dispute were ruled to be a matter within the domestic jurisdiction of the parties. Under the Protocol all disputes of a legal character were to be submitted to the Permanent Court of International Justice. On other disputes, if the Council (apart from the interested parties) should fail to reach unanimity, it would refer the matter to a committee of arbitrators, by whose decision members previously undertook to abide. Disputes about matters of domestic jurisdiction, though still beyond the jurisdiction of the Council, were to be submitted to the procedure of conciliation under Article 11. This Article entitled the League to take 'any action that may be deemed wise and effectual to safeguard the peace of nations'. No state was to be deemed an aggressor if it had brought the dispute before the League under Article 11. These ingenious arrangements fell short of the automatic military sanctions envisaged by the draft treaty, but would have strengthened the Covenant in the direction that the French desired; and the settlement of 1919 was left intact, as any demand for the revision of a treaty was ruled to be not a 'dispute' to which the procedure of the Protocol would apply. In the conciliatory mood of 1924, France was ready to feel satisfied with this weaker instrument. But again Great Britain and the British Dominions began to have grave doubts. Japan wanted to use the procedure to protest at Geneva against the restrictions on Japanese immigration introduced by Canada, Australia, and New Zealand. Compulsory arbitration and even the application of military sanctions were uncongenial to British opinion. The replacement of the Labour government in November 1924 by the Conservatives under Stanley Baldwin killed the Protocol. In March 1925 Austen Chamberlain, the new Foreign Secretary, informed the Council of the League that Britain refused to ratify it.

Locarno, 1925. Confronted with this further disappointment, France reverted to her quest for specific British guarantees of her Rhineland frontier. From this policy the treaties of Locarno were born. Three years before, the German government had proposed that France and Germany should make a mutual pledge, with which Britain and Belgium would also be associated, not to resort to war against one another for a generation. Poincaré had rejected the proposal. Now, in the more conciliatory mood of 1925, Britain was prepared to guarantee the Franco-German frontier against aggression by either Germany or France. In the course of negotiations in the summer of 1925, the Belgian-German frontier was put on the same footing; the guarantee was extended to include, besides the frontiers, the demilitarized zones in which Germany was forbidden by the Treaty of Versailles to station troops or build fortifications. Italy joined in. Germany, it was agreed, should join the League of Nations. In October 1925 the ministers of all the states concerned met at Locarno in Switzerland and initialled three sets of treaties: the Locarno Treaty guaranteeing the Franco-German and Belgian-German frontiers; treaties of arbitration between Germany, and the group including France, Belgium, Czechoslovakia, and Poland; and treaties of mutual guarantee between France on one hand, Czechoslovakia and Poland on the other. The treaties were all formally signed in London in December.

The principles underlying the additional treaties were that, since Britain would not enter into a guarantee of Germany's eastern frontiers but only of her western, France should guarantee the Czechoslovak and Polish frontiers while Germany undertook to submit to arbitration any disputes arising over these frontiers. It was the best that France could secure in the circumstances. In the favourable atmosphere of 1925 the treaties undoubtedly contributed to the general pacification of Europe. They were the first successful attempt to recognize impartially the needs of both France and Germany. Germany was brought back into the magic circle of great powers, and seemed likely to take her place in international relations as a conciliatory and unaggressive power. Yet the implications of Locarno were sinister as well as reassuring. The implicit grading of frontiers, which recognized Germany's western frontiers as somehow more sacrosanct and permanent than her eastern, implied that the general settlement of 1919 was valid only in so far as it had later been voluntarily endorsed by Germany. Britain's distinction between frontiers that she would guarantee and frontiers that she would not guarantee undermined the general obligations of the Covenant. If the Versailles settlement lacked fully binding force unless it were voluntarily reinforced in this way, it was now more precarious as a whole. France had further overburdened herself by special obligations in eastern Europe without partnership with Britain. If members of the League were to distinguish between parts of the settlement in which they were intimately interested and which they were prepared to guarantee, and other parts in which they were less interested and which they were less likely to uphold by military action, general security suffered from Locarno. There were technical absurdities, too, in the notion of planning any effective military cooperation between the general staffs of Britain and France against possible German attack, if the British staff were at the same moment supposed to be concerting similar action with the Germans against a possible French attack. But such realistic problems were scarcely considered. All these implications were to appear later; at the time they were smothered by the prevailing mood of optimism and good will.

In 1926 Germany duly became a member of the League, and it was understood that she would become a permanent member of its Council alongside Great Britain, France, Italy, and Japan. Provision had been made for an increase in the number of permanent members to six, and now three other powers – Poland, Spain, and Brazil – claimed permanent seats as well. This unforeseen hitch, which could have the effect of cancelling Germany's vote on most important issues if, for example, Poland were given the same status at the same time, was overcome by creating a new category of semi-permanent members. To this category Poland was admitted. But Spain and Brazil, already non-permanent members of the Council, refused to accept the arrangement and withdrew from membership in the League. At the height of this controversy, in April 1926, Germany made a separate treaty with the Soviet Union in which both reaffirmed the Treaty of Rapallo and each undertook to remain neutral should the other be attacked. Again, the process of pacification seemed complete so far as Germany was concerned. But again unpleasant consequences had followed. The three biggest American countries, the United States, Argentina, and Brazil, were now outside the League. (Spain returned in 1928.) Nationalist opinion in Germany was left with strong resentment against Geneva, and with the suspicion that her return to a status of equality with other powers was more apparent than real. The shadow of a German-Soviet alliance had darkened.

Pact of Paris, 1928. The process of pacification by pacts was carried still one stage further in 1928; though by then the mood of optimism was already dispersing. In April 1927 Briand proposed to the United States a pact whereby the two countries would renounce war as an instrument of national policy between them. The American Secretary of State, Frank B. Kellogg, proposed in turn that the pact should be widened to be universal in scope, and Briand agreed. In August 1928, a few days before the Assembly of the League met, representatives of the six great powers, the other three Locarno powers, and the British Dominions and India all met in Paris and signed what came to be known as the Briand-Kellogg Pact or the 'Pact of Paris'. An invitation was extended to every other state to accede to it. The pact declared, simply enough, that every signatory condemned 'recourse to war for the solution of international controversies and renounce[d] it as an instrument of national policy in relations with one another', and that every signatory agreed 'that the settlement or solution of all disputes or conflicts, of whatever nature or of whatever origin they may be, which may arise among them, shall never be sought except by pacific means'. This agreement among fifteen states, including all the great powers except the Soviet Union, to renounce war (or as the phrase went to 'outlaw war') was the high-water mark of interwar pacifism. Almost every other state in the world, including the Soviet Union, but excluding Argentina and Brazil, hastened to adhere to it. In all, sixty-five states signed it.

The Covenant had not banned war as an instrument of national policy. It prohibited only certain kinds of war, but it planned to punish members who indulged in such kinds of war. The Pact condemned all wars, but it made no provision for punishing any. Yet, in the course of framing and endorsing the Pact, signatories had in fact made certain exceptions. A war of self-defence was not condemned or banned, so the Pact was not in this sense completely pacifist. The United States made it clear that the right of self-defence included, in her eyes, any action needed to preserve the Monroe Doctrine. Sir Austen Chamberlain, in a letter to the United States ambassador, made it clear that for Britain it also included the right to preserve the British Empire. 'There are certain regions of the world', he wrote, 'the welfare and integrity of which constitute a special and vital interest for our peace and safety.... Their protection against attack is to the British Empire a measure of self-defence.' This reassertion, by the two major western powers, of special regional reservations chimed oddly with the high moral absolutism of the Pact. They had the effect of making the Pact a declaration of moral principle and intent rather than a contractual obligation or a normal treaty. Each signatory remained the sole judge of its actions, and no machinery for enforcement was even contemplated. National sovereignty was in no way impaired. The Pact, which appeared to go so much further than the Covenant, did not in reality go nearly so far toward creating international security.

In 1929 the British and French governments made a valiant attempt to combine Pact and Covenant, by making the sanctions envisaged by Article 16 applicable to all wars prohibited by the Pact of Paris, and so amending the Covenant accordingly. But discussion of the amendments by the League Assembly was delayed, opposed by Japan and the Scandinavian countries, and eventually abandoned. A parallel attempt to comprise, within a General Act for the Pacific Settlement of International Disputes, all the alternative means of settling disputes – by conciliation, judicial decision by the International Court, and arbitration – and enabling signatories to subscribe to whichever methods they chose, came to little. The Low Countries and Scandinavia subscribed to it, but France and Britain did not ratify it until 1931, and then both the mood and the international scene had greatly changed.

The plethora of pacts in these years was made possible, as was the genuine spirit of reconciliation, by the coexistence and the frequent meetings of Briand, Stresemann, and Austen Chamberlain. These three men, whose personal temperaments and relations were so harmonious, established a remarkable degree of mutual confidence and friendship which in itself helped to stabilize European affairs. Meeting in Swiss hotels, smoking one another's cigars, learning how to reach agreement, they fused their national policies into a general policy of pacification. To this result the very existence of the League contributed. Meetings of the Council and the Assembly brought them regularly together, and after Herriot and MacDonald set the example in 1924, most European states sent their Foreign Ministers to sessions of the Council and Assembly. Geneva in September became the regular meeting place of European statesmen, and consultations were no longer limited to emergency occasions. This much credit, at least, for the pacification of Europe must be given to the League. But in some ways it was almost too easy. The conditions that mattered most, the will to peace among the leading European nations, were temporary because they derived from personalities, from a popular desire for peace, and from the simple inability of either Italy or Germany or the Soviet Union to challenge the still entrenched defenders of the settlement of 1919. These conditions disappeared abruptly when Chamberlain lost office in May 1929, Stresemann died in October, and André Tardieu replaced Briand in November. The economic crisis, which broke at this very moment, diverted the energies of statesmanship toward domestic problems. Franco-German distrust, suspended so blissfully for five years, revived in full force in 1930, when in the German elections of that autumn the National Socialists won more than a hundred seats in the Reichstag.

With Stresemann dead and a more aggressive mood in Germany, all the concessions that France had made immediately became sources of danger. Allied military control of Germany had ended in January 1927. The Young Plan of 1929 for ending the problem of reparations removed the financial controls imposed on Germany by the Dawes Plan. The British Labour government of 1929 pressed for the ending of Allied occupation of the Rhineland, and at the end of June 1930 the last Allied troops left German soil. All material securities against German resurgence had gone; Germany sat on the Council of the League; only her good will and good faith now lay between the continued pacification of Europe and a relapse to preparations for war. And Hitler had a hundred deputies in the Reichstag. Paper pacts seemed a flimsy defence. In December 1929 the French chamber voted the first special credits for building the Maginot line of fortifications along her northern frontier. Was it foolish to do this? Or did French folly lie only in building too little of it, and too late?

CHAPTER 26

THE COLLAPSE OF PROSPERITY,
1929–34

CONTRACTION OF WORLD TRADE

IN economics, no less than in politics and diplomacy, nationalism was in conflict with internationalism by 1929. The legacies of wartime collectivism, the needs of postwar recovery and stabilization, the demand for national protection of important industries, all conspired to make states pursue, immediately and narrowly, national economic policies at the expense of the more long-term expansion of international trade. Yet it was on the prosperity of international trade that the well-being and standards of living of the increasingly industrialized nations of Europe ultimately depended. Just as the Locarno period suspended the former tensions between France and Germany, so it held in check the disruptive forces that since 1918 had threatened a healthy economic life in Europe. It produced half a decade of apparent prosperity and stability.[1] 'Normalcy', it was felt, had practically returned along with 'security'. The basis of this prosperity was the revival of world trade, resting mainly on loans from the United States to the countries of central Europe, which enabled them to invest capital in public works and business enterprises, and so to export goods in exchange for the imports they needed. The wheels of business and industry turned with the wheels of international trade, for they were geared into them. Novel means were found to step up productivity and send cheap goods flowing round the channels of world trade. Standardization and mass production of manufactured goods, livelier methods of salesmanship and high-pressure advertising, big programmes of commercial building and housing, the growth of new industries making automobiles and aeroplanes, radio and gramophones, combined to make a boom in trade.

The centre of this boom was the United States, where it was indeed 'the roaring 'twenties' and the age of material abundance seemed to have arrived. The Federal Reserve Bank encouraged credit inflation and a policy of 'easy money'. This produced a period of speculative investment and feverish activity on the stock markets. The average price of stocks on Wall Street rose by twenty-five per cent in 1928 and by another thirty-five per cent in 1929. Hordes of amateur speculators joined the professional operators in search of quick gains. But these prices and

1. See p. 655.

their rise corresponded in no sense to increases in the supply of real goods or in world trade; industrial employment and production expanded little between 1926 and 1929. They were mere manipulations of the stock market and the system of credit, likely in their irresponsibility to bring disaster if once the bubble should be pricked. When it collapsed with catastrophic suddenness in October 1929 it touched off the Great Depression throughout Europe and the rest of the world. To show the connexions between this speculative boom on Wall Street and the shrinkage of world trade which destroyed the prosperity of the Locarno period, it is necessary to recall the conditions of world trade in 1929.

World Trade. The United States, the supreme creditor nation of the postwar world, neither needed nor wanted the goods exported by other lands. Rich in her own diversified natural resources and her immense industrial and agricultural productive capacity, she erected high tariff walls against imports from other lands. Imports of nearly every kind were regarded as unwelcome competitors with American goods at home. Yet the United States lent lavishly abroad, demanded the repayment of war debts, and wished to sell her own surplus products abroad. There were only two ways in which other nations could pay interest on loans, or repay war debts, or pay for goods imported from America – unless, indeed, Americans should prove amenable to the Christian injunction to 'lend freely hoping for nothing in return'. One was to pay in gold or promises of gold; the other was to pay in goods or services. The second was virtually ruled out by American tariff policy and the expansion of her own shipping and insurance facilities. Debtors to the United States paid in gold until their own reserves of gold ran dry, and the great bulk of the world's gold lay safely buried in American vaults. And even then the only alternative way for the debtor nations to secure dollars for payment to the United States – by exporting goods and so increasing the volume of world trade – was still impeded.

The only way America could ensure the export of her own goods was to lend others the dollars with which to buy them. In a world where war debts were still a controversial issue and where large foreign debts, such as that of Russia, had been repudiated, investors were reluctant to grant the long-term loans that had been normal before 1914. Most borrowing, therefore, was on short-term loans liable to sudden recall, and this gave capital investment a new fickle, flighty character which produced the maximum of instability. Money lent by other nations – such as the former European neutrals, Sweden, Switzerland, the Netherlands – tended to be equally concentrated in short-term loans. Banks and investment corporations in these countries as well as in the United States, finding themselves glutted with money at a time when other nations were hungry for it, readily offered their idle funds to foreign governments and municipalities. They were accepted and welcomed in vast amounts. But such capital was always liable to take flight at every rumour of a devaluation of exchange rates or of political instability, and there were plenty of both in this decade. Large floating balances were deposited on London, Amsterdam, New York, or wherever stability seemed more certain, ready to alight where new opportunities arose. The basis of the economic expansion of the Locarno era was exceptionally fluid and prone to panic.

These conditions, linked with the controversy about reparations, set up a ridiculous cycle of indebtedness which, by its very nature, tended toward a crash. American money flowed into Germany to help her to reconstruct her social amenities and to enable her to pay her reparations. The recipients of these reparations, mainly France and Great Britain, paid their war debts to the United States partly out of such reparations. The flow of such money enabled America to grant more foreign loans. And so on ad infinitum. But the whole cycle did nothing whatever to add to the real flow of international trade; on the contrary, it made it more difficult for European exporters to find markets for their goods. Trade even between European countries was hampered by the need to pay interest on loans or to repay the loans themselves. It was a vicious circle, constantly undermining the only foundations on which a healthy and reliable exchange of goods between countries in need of them could take place.

The Crash of 1929. The first sector of the world's economy to feel the effects of the coming blizzard was, significantly, American and Canadian agriculture. Throughout the North American continent agricultural prices began to fall sharply after 1926. The recovery of agriculture in Europe, and in many places a positive increase in agricultural production, made the vast output of North America largely superfluous to Europe's needs. Grain was a commodity in which Europe as a continent could almost be self-sufficing, and for which its demand was inelastic. The American farmer, faring badly, cut down his own expenditures, and American industry also began to feel the pinch. But it was the bubble of speculation which brought the real crash, and it burst on Wall Street in October 1929. Late on 23 and 24 October – 'Black Thursday' – there was a panic rush of stockholders to unload. On the twenty-fourth alone nearly thirteen million shares were sold, and on Tuesday the twenty-ninth another sixteen and a half million changed hands. By the end of the month American investors had lost 40,000 million dollars. This collapse of the New York stock market brought with it the final collapse of agricultural prices in America and sent a shudder of apprehension round the world. After a temporary recovery in early November prices began to fall again, and continued to fall thereafter, undeterred by the belated efforts of bankers and government to check them.

The repercussions of the collapse on governmental finances and on industry ran parallel to the devastating blow given to producers of food and raw materials. The previous decade had been a time of chronic depression in agriculture all over the world, but especially in those large areas of the world which specialized in primary products for export. North American farmers, Australian fruit and meat growers, Brazilian coffee growers, sugar planters in Java, found world prices for their produce depressingly low. Scientific methods enabled them to grow an abundance of goods which the consumers of the would could not at that time afford to buy. The demand for their products in the more industrialized countries was inelastic, and the underfed masses of Asia and Africa who needed them most could not afford to pay even very low prices. Any further contraction of trade had, therefore, disastrous effects. After the crash of 1929 falling prices spelled ruin for the growers of wheat and cotton, coffee and cocoa, sugar and meat. The ruin of so large a part of so many communities meant a drop in the demand for all the goods which these people could now no longer afford to buy. So general prices dropped further, and the crisis spread from one sector of the world's economy to another. Trade between nations shrank rapidly and steadily from the end of 1929 until 1934, in an ever-contracting spiral. The efforts of most countries to shelter their farmers or manufacturers from this process by protective tariffs or price fixing only tended to check still further the flow of international trade. As bankruptcies occurred, and factories slowed down production or went out of business, millions of workers were thrown out of work. The decline in their purchasing power lowered still more the effective demand for goods. Thus arose, throughout the world, the haunting paradox of 'poverty amidst plenty' – the strange grievance of 'overproduction' when millions went hungry and homeless – the destruction of stocks of food because too many were too poor to eat it.

In its shattering effect upon European prosperity and stability, the Great Depression was comparable with the Great War itself. It had for its victims the same quality of cataclysm or volcanic eruption, as the very earth beneath seemed to open and salvation was beyond hope. The greatest financial powers in the world were humbled. In three years five thousand American banks closed their doors. Americans not only stopped lending money abroad, but withdrew their short-term loans. They pulled away the very foundations of European recovery, especially in Germany and Austria, where the sequence of bankruptcies spread in 1931. First to collapse was the *Kreditanstalt* of Vienna, the largest and most reputable bank holding two thirds of Austria's assets and liabilities. In May 1931 it found itself insolvent. Despite governmental support and a loan from the Bank of England, its failure rocked the finances of central Europe. Foreign investors withdrew much of their capital from Germany, and by the end of the month the German government faced similar difficulties. President Hindenburg issued emergency decrees cutting expenditure and imposing new taxes. The Chancellor, Brüning, sought help from Britain. On 20 June President Hoover of the United States issued his famous 'moratorium', postponing for a year all payments on debts owed to the United States by other governments. He had first consulted Britain but not France. This indicated fresh sources of friction between the two major western countries; for whereas Britain welcomed the moratorium, France, so far only mildly affected by the depression, resented it as an initial step towards cancelling all reparations from Germany.

But by July even British credit began to suffer. It was expected that the next budget would show a deficit. Whereas French budgetary deficits were normal, to orthodox finance in Britain an unbalanced budget was a heresy. With the Bank of England losing gold by withdrawals at the rate of £2½ million a day, some check had to be imposed. The Labour government resigned and a handful of its leaders, led by Ramsay MacDonald, joined in a National Government including the Conservatives and some Liberals. A special supplementary budget imposed further stringent economies, including pay cuts in the armed forces, but these led to mutinous rumblings in the Navy at Invergordon, and this in turn shook foreign confidence and led to further drains on gold. On 2 September the National Government, formed to preserve the gold standard and save the pound, took Britain off gold and allowed the value of the pound to settle about thirty per cent below par. Almost all European stock exchanges closed, and within a short time most other European governments and the Dominions also abandoned the gold standard. A year later the only powers remaining on it were France, Italy, the Low Countries, Switzerland, Poland, Rumania, and the United States. The gold standard, indeed, made little sense in a continent almost devoid of gold.

Governments reacted to the new world economic situation in three different ways. First, they tended to assume more drastic powers to control currency and exchange rates; they raised tariffs; they imposed stiffer quotas on imports; they took, in short, sterner separate measures to shield their countries against the depression. Secondly, they sought regional or sectional arrangements, as did the Scandinavian countries of the 'Oslo Group', or the agricultural lands of eastern Europe, or the British Commonwealth in the Ottawa agreements of 1932. Thirdly, they attempted more comprehensive collective action, as in the ending of reparations by the Lausanne Convention of July 1932, and as in the World Economic Conference which representatives of sixty-six states attended in London in June 1933. In the United States the situation was transformed by the election of Franklin D. Roosevelt as president in the autumn of 1932, and by even America's abandonment of the gold standard in March 1933. The new President brought to American politics a new spirit of courage, vigour, and determination. Not for nothing had he discovered, a cripple thrown on his back for eight years by paralysis, how to overcome the cruellest physical disabilities by force of will and spirit. Believing that American and even world paralysis, too, might be defeated if men were resolved to beat it, he inspired the nation with fresh heart and hope. Just as the collapse had begun in the United States, so too must recovery begin there. 'The only thing we have to fear,' as he put it, 'is fear itself.'

The dislocation caused by the collapse was, indeed, as great as that of a war. In the United States the steel industry was working at only one tenth its capacity. World prices of raw materials were half what they had been five years earlier. Yet the World Economic Conference found that it could achieve little, and neither separate nor group action by governments achieved much. What the world needed, as a tonic, was recovery of faith in itself – in the ability of men to extricate themselves from the absurdities of a world in which thirty million people were known to be unemployed and in which huge stocks of goods were accumulating unsold, when everywhere mankind wanted employment and needed goods. Peoples and governments found themselves in a nightmare world where civilization was choked with its own power to produce abundance, where plenty had actually produced poverty, and where men starved because there was too much wealth. To a commercial crisis, the shrinkage of international trade, had been added a financial crisis – the loss of confidence in all the existing mechanism for getting goods made and distributed, sold and bought, throughout the world. The slump was more than what financiers and economists had at first believed it to be – a particularly severe example of cyclical trade depressions. It was the breakdown of capitalism itself, a crisis in the whole of the economic structure which had developed during the previous two centuries.

CRISIS OF CONFIDENCE

Once international efforts to arrest the crisis had failed, governments reverted to separate internal national action. Each nation adopted ways most suited to its own circumstances. Gradually, by 1934, the conditions of crisis receded and the wheels began to turn again. Because, as was seen above,[1] the foundations of recovery in 1924 had varied in character from one country to another, this national approach proved more hopeful in 1934. In the United States, President Roosevelt launched his 'New Deal', based at first on stringent federal control of credit. One of his earliest and less sensational measures was the Glass-Steagall Act of June 1933, designed to restore confidence in American banking. Combined with the presidential power to control the fortunes of the dollar, the Act began a great extension of the directing and regulating powers of the Treasury Department. The rest of the New Deal involved extensions of federal authority and especially of presidential power to counter the effects of the crisis on industry and mass unemployment.

Emergency Powers. In Great Britain the National Government used emergency powers granted by Parliament as a so-called 'Doctor's mandate' – a general commission to extricate the country from the throes of the economic crisis as best it could. Acting partly through orders in council and partly through the Import Duties Act, it reorganized tariffs in a way which led the free-trade Liberals to resign in September 1932. As only a few members of the Labour party supported it, the National Government was in essence an orthodox Conservative government. Neville Chamberlain as Chancellor of the Exchequer presented a series of balanced budgets. This he achieved mainly by cutting expenditures by one tenth and by additional revenue from the new tariffs. The gradual recovery of trade was strengthened by agreements with Denmark, Germany, Argentina, and even the Soviet Union. After making 'token payments' toward the instalments of war still outstanding, Britain stopped payments in June 1934. All other debtor states, except Finland, did the same. By the end of 1934 the numbers of unemployed had fallen to two million, and relief paid to them was subjected to a quite rigorous 'means test', which caused widespread discontent. Apart from spending more on the armed forces, the government did not embark upon schemes of public works or development plans. Despite the continuing tragedy of mass unemployment, Britain, like the United States, had by the end of 1934 started on slow convalescence. Public confidence returned under the stimulus of firmer government action and with signs of a revival in trade, and confidence was the very lifeblood of financial stability.

1. See p. 655.

France was affected more gently and later by the upheavals of 1931. Her remarkable resilience came from the balance of her economy between agriculture and industry which made her domestic markets relatively more important than her foreign markets, and from the substantial gold reserves which the Bank of France had been able to accumulate. But by the beginning of 1932 she, too, began to suffer, governments collapsed with great frequency, and figures of unemployment began to grow. Governments resorted to the normal course in a crisis – they sought emergency powers and governed by decree-laws controlling wages, prices, and rents. This admission that parliamentary government was fair-weather government, to be put into cold storage in difficult times, was a constant weakness of democracy in France, and her crisis took the characteristic form of a political crisis accompanied by Paris riots. Other countries had known great financial scandals; they had always shaken public confidence both in capitalism and in the government of the day. Clarence Hatry's bogus companies had sent a ripple of uneasiness through Britain in 1929. The collapse and suicide of Ivar Krueger the match-king shook Sweden and other countries in 1932. The association between the Bank of France and the fraudulent activities of Oustric, revealed in 1930, gave fresh ammunition to the critics of the '200 Families'. But when the scandal of Serge Alexandre Stavisky burst upon France in the conditions of January 1934 it caused more violent reactions.

Stavisky, of Russian-Jewish descent, had for eight years indulged in a wide variety of swindles, gaining in impudence and enterprise when he found that he could enjoy immunity from punishment. He was found dead with a bullet in his head, and it was envisaged that the police had shot him to forestall inconvenient revelations. When the Prime Minister, Camille Chautemps, refused to appoint a parliamentary committee of inquiry into the reasons for Stavisky's long immunity from arrest, and it was recalled that Chautemp's brother-in-law was head of the Paris authority which initiated public prosecutions, he drew great suspicion upon himself. In the mood of January 1934 France boiled over. Chautemps resigned. Daladier, another Radical, took over and dismissed Chiappe, prefect of police in Paris. Daladier's new government faced the Chamber of Deputies on 6 February to the accompaniment of tumult in the chamber and ominous demonstrations in the streets of Paris. Who, it was asked, had protected the squalid crookery of Stavisky to the extent that his trial had been postponed since 1927 and his bail renewed nineteen times? The protectors and beneficiaries of Stavisky seemed to include men in high positions in parliament and local government, judiciary and police, the administration and the business world. The extremists of both Left and Right – but especially the agitators of the semi-fascist bands and para-military leagues now so active in France – had no doubts about the explanation. On 6 February rabble-rousing leagues organized demonstrations at strategic points of Paris, and the government feared the march of a mob on the chambers. Amid clashes between demonstrators and police, and under growing 'blackmail of the streets', Daladier resigned. Old Gaston Doumergue, a former President, was brought out of retirement to form an emergency national government that included all save the Socialists and Communists. Marshal Pétain took office as Minister of War. On 12 February the trade unions and the Left organized a general strike to protest against fascist activities which thus threatened the Republic. But the new government weathered the storm, and after some weeks of arrests, suicides, Press hysteria, and the wildest accusations, some degree of public confidence returned. When it resigned in November 1934 there was no recurrence of street riots. Pierre-Etienne Flandin, leading a cabinet that included Pierre Laval as Foreign Minister, succeeded to a more orderly capital.

The Rise of Hitler. One consideration that helped to sober French opinion was the startling political outcome of the comparable crisis in Germany. There, too, a succession of unstable ministries, ruling with the help of emergency powers after 1929, had tried to overcome the drift to economic collapse. Hermann Müller, Chancellor when Stresemann died in 1929, was obliged in March 1930 to ask President Hindenburg for emergency powers under Article 48 of the Weimar Constitution. This provision, inserted as a safety valve, gave the President virtually dictatorial powers in an emergency.

Should public order and safety be seriously disturbed or threatened, the President may take measures necessary to restore public order and safety; in case of need he may use armed force; ... he may, for the time being, declare the fundamental rights of the citizen wholly or partially in abeyance.

This powerful engine, built into the constitution as a safeguard against threats to the Republic, became the chief means of its overthrow. Hindenburg refused the powers to the Socialist Müller and to his successor of the Catholic Centre party, Heinrich Brüning. In September 1930 Brüning asked for general elections, hoping for a popular revulsion against the activities of the extremists. The elections gave a sixth of the votes and 107 seats to the National Socialist party led by Hitler, and seventy-seven seats to the Communists. Without a majority at his command in the Reichstag, Brüning now governed by presidential decrees issued under Article 48, and tried to outbid the National Socialists in his nationalism and authoritarian behaviour. In April 1932 Paul von Hindenburg, aged eighty-four and now very senile, was re-elected President for a second term. But Hitler polled nearly thirteen and a half million votes as against Hindenburg's nineteen and a quarter million. Brüning lasted only another month, decreeing belatedly the dissolution of the Nazi armed bands and grappling ineffectually with the economic crisis at its height. Industrial production in Germany had halved since 1929 while unemployment had trebled from two to six million. Between January 1931 and January 1933 the membership of the Nazi party more than doubled – to 900,000. It won victories in elections to state diets, notably in Prussia. The Social Democrats, the largest party in the Reichstag wih 143 seats, tolerated Brüning's drastic powers but took no effective action against the Nazis. Amid a mood of nationalistic fervour, combined with rising fear lest the currency collapse of 1923 should be repeated, they were too much associated with national humiliation and disaster to serve as a bulwark.

Brüning was succeeded, in June 1932, by a right-wing Chancellor, Franz von Papen, backed by General Kurt von Schleicher and a group of nationalists and conservatives which had for some time intrigued with Hindenburg behind Brüning's back. This group of East Elbian landowners, west German industrialists, politically minded army officers, and adventurer politicians was able to gain power despite lack of popular support only by a tacit bargain with the Nazis. They tolerated the revival of all the Nazi party's activities, and in the July elections the party won thirteen and three quarter million votes and 230 seats. The parties directly supporting von Papen and his government won only a small percentage of the vote; but supported by the Nazis, as the largest single party in the Reichstag, they retained power. Fresh elections in November registered a sharp drop in Nazi support. The Nazis lost two million votes and thirty-four seats, and their funds were depleted. The Communist party, on the other hand, gained eleven seats between July and November. The next month von Schleicher succeeded von Papen as Chancellor, only to be confronted with feverish intrigues on the part of von Papen to regain power. This short-sighted Catholic Rhinelander, misjudging the whole nature of the dynamic revolutionary force he was dealing with, persuaded President Hindenburg that a new right-wing coalition without von Schleicher but including himself and headed by Hitler, could save the situation. On 30 January Hitler became Chancellor, with three members of his party – out of twelve – in the cabinet. The rest were representatives of the nationalist parties, including von Papen as Vice-Chancellor. The men of the German Right – representatives of army and Prussian landowners, big industrialists and financiers – thought they would give Hitler enough rope to hang himself. The clever von Papen, they felt, could be relied upon to outwit the hysterical ex-corporal who lacked experience of high office and government. They thus made themselves the gravediggers of the Republic.

Fresh elections were fixed for 5 March 1933. On 27 February the Reichstag building conveniently caught fire, and an imbecile Dutchman found in it was arrested. Hermann Göring, Nazi Minister without Portfolio in the new government, proclaimed that this was evidence of a Communist plot and proceeded to arrest leaders of the Communist party. The elections took place in a mood of anticommunist frenzy and terror, whipped to fever pitch by the Nazis' propaganda and accompanied by the use of extreme violence against all their opponents. Even so the Nazis gained only forty-four per cent of the votes. But it was enough. One of the first actions of the new Reichstag was to pass an Enabling Act granting Hitler and his government dictatorial power for four years. The Nazis were in the saddle. They could complete their seizure of power by easy instalments, abolishing all opposition parties and taking over all the machinery of state power. In October, Germany left the League of Nations and the already doomed Disarmament Conference. In November, Hitler asked the German nation, by plebiscite, if it approved of his actions, and 96·3 per cent of the votes were for him. In August 1934 President Hindenburg died. Hitler refused to succeed him but as 'Führer and Reich-Chancellor' inherited his presidential powers, including supreme command of all the armed forces. In a further plebiscite ninety per cent of the voters (some thirty-eight million) registered approval. Public confidence under a totalitarian régime was, it appeared, almost boundless.[1]

Meanwhile in Austria, the other main central-European victim of the economic crisis, comparable events took place. It is the simul-taneity of the emergence of authoritarian dictatorships in Europe which is of special significance. There, too, a rapid succession of short-lived chancellorships, after the resignation of Seipel in 1929, dug the grave of the Republic. After the collapse of the *Kreditanstalt* in 1931 the country felt the full impact of the economic blizzard. Already it was rent by the rival forces of the authoritarian *Heimwehr*, virtually the private army of the dashing Prince von Starhemberg, and the less effective *Schützbund* of the Social Democrats. To these were added a new Austrian Nazi party, numbering 100,000 in 1930, working in the closest collaboration with the German Nazis. The Austrian Nazis were affectionately regarded by Hitler as compatriots of his own native land, destined to lead it back into union with the German Reich in defiance of the Treaty of Versailles. In the municipal elections of May 1932 they made alarming gains amid

1. See p. 729.

scenes of riot, terrorism, and virtual civil war. In such circumstances Engelbert Dollfuss, a 'Christian Socialist', formed a ministry in which representatives of von Starhemberg's *Heimwehr* predominated.

This diminutive figure – known to lampooners as 'Millemetternich' or merely Mickey Mouse – played the part von Papen played in Germany. In 1933 the German Nazis, now in power, loudly condemned his 'oppression' of their party friends in Austria. Dollfuss, governing by emergency decrees, sought backing in a new 'Fatherland Front' a patriotic conservative association largely based on the *Heimwehr*. He attacked the socialists and set up a virtual conservative and clericalist dictatorship. The Social Democrats' *Schützbund* was made illegal and in June the Nazi party, too, was dissolved. Dollfuss proclaimed his intention to replace the democratic republic by a 'German Christian Austria', based on a corporative state and authoritarian government, with strong Italian affinities. The new constitution was promulgated in April 1934. But in July, Dollfuss was murdered by the Nazis, who then seized the Vienna radio station and tried to carry out a *coup*. They failed when martial law was proclaimed in Vienna and provincial Nazi risings were broken. Kurt von Schuschnigg, colleague and friend of Dollfuss, became Chancellor. Again a Nazi *putsch* had failed, and Mussolini took the cause of Austrian independence under his wing. He mobilized Italian troops on the Brenner Pass, ready to counter any German attempt to invade Austria. For the moment there could be no *Anschluss*. But democracy in Austria was dead, and only four years later the second Nazi *putsch* would succeed.

Czechoslovakia experienced repercussions of the economic crisis similar to those in Austria. Her industrialized areas were most seriously affected, and they happened to include the Sudetenland where lived some three and a half million of her German-speaking citizens. Although after 1929 the government resorted increasingly to legislation by decree, parliamentary rights were respected and Czechoslovakia produced no von Papen and no Dollfuss. But there arose a Nazi party led by Konrad Henlein, in full sympathy with German Nazism. When it was dissolved, Henlein re-formed it as ostensibly a loyal organization demanding more decentralization and greater freedom for the German minority. The economic slump greatly aided his efforts to arouse resentment against Prague. In the elections of 1935 his party polled more votes than any other. But this warning forced the other parties into closer alliance, and the disruption of Czechoslovak democracy and independence was postponed for a few years.[1]

The First Five-Year Plan. Because of her relative economic isolation

1. See p. 743.

and her controlled domestic economy, the Soviet Union suffered less from the economic crisis than did her western neighbours. But she suffered none the less. The first Five-Year Plan, launched in 1928, was declared to have fulfilled its aims in four years – by 1932. It reorganized large sectors of Russian industry, as well as more than doubling general industrial production. Agriculture suffered severely by the savage drive for collectivization, but by 1932 it was recovering, and some sixty per cent of peasant farms had been collectivized. More than 2,400 machine tractor stations had been set up to supply farms with machinery and power, and to train technicians. The Plan included, in effect, a vast public investment programme devoted especially to production goods rather than consumer goods. But in so far as it relied upon exports for the purchase of such machinery and technical equipment as Russia needed from the outside world, it was impeded by the world slump in prices. In other words, Russia had to export maybe twice as much food stuffs and raw materials as she had bargained for, in order to buy the goods she needed. On the other hand, preoccupation of the rest of Europe with the economic crisis diverted outside hostility away from the Soviet Union, and left it free to proceed without fear with its long-term economic planning. The Five-Year Plan was carried out in a period of freedom from any fear of external attack. Other peoples looked wistfully at the achievements of scientific economic planning with which their own sufferings and confusion compared so unfavourably. These were the years when state planning came to seem a panacea for the undoubted sicknesses of free enterprise and competitive capitalism.

The crisis of the years 1929–34 was thus, in different forms, a general crisis of confidence. The prosperity of the five postwar years was erected on credit; and the foundation of credit is psychological, since it depends upon a prevailing mood of confidence in the established institutions of economics and politics. That confidence was first shaken by the crash on Wall Street in 1929, then by the series of financial crises in Britain and Europe, then by the evident weaknesses of democratic governments in face of growing unemployment and depression. With appreciation of the final paradox of 'poverty amid plenty', faith in the system of capitalism itself began to waver. There was no dearth of rival remedies, ranging from communist collectivization and socialist regulation to the corporative state and the autarchic regimentation of national economy by the state. At the same time, confidence in democratic institutions waned, too. The current in favour of nationalist authoritarian and even militarist dictatorship, already evident in 1926, became a powerful tide by 1934. The wider and deeper consequences of this crisis of confidence in the existing order must next be briefly examined, before assessing the more detailed reasons for the eclipse of democracy in Europe between the wars.

CONSEQUENCES OF CRISIS

By 1934 the word 'crisis' had become the most used and abused of words, applied alike to economic life, parliamentary government, international relations, and even European civilization. Yet it was applicable enough, and expressed the mood of the time which, in itself, was a significant factor in the shaping of Europe's destiny. It had been thought that normalcy was returning, when prosperity had suddenly collapsed; that democratic government had been established, when everywhere it began to creak and decline; that some measure of security and pacification had been achieved, when rabid nationalism again raised its head. The abruptness of the change bred a mood of disillusionment and bewilderment, a moral and psychological crisis that was the most serious of all crises, because, even more than the experience of war or of the immediate aftermath of war, it shattered the ideals and codes of behaviour on which the old order had rested. In 1919 the world had still been buoyed up by a certain faith in the liberal values of personal freedom and equality of rights, by a revival of confidence in capitalism and a generous spirit of social improvement, by a fervent belief that civilization could progress in peace. After 1934 all these faiths were shaken or broken, and Europe lay exposed to the disruptive forces of brutal and inhuman ideologies, as well as to the eruption of violent and destructive tyrannies. Not since the barbarian invasions of the ancient Roman Empire fifteen centuries before had Europe known so complete a challenge to its historic civilization; but now, even more than then, the barbarians came from within the frontiers of civilization itself.

Perhaps the foundation of this moral crisis was an almost universal sense of helplessness, of loss of direction and subjection to blind, impersonal forces beyond the control of men or nations. This feeling first took deepest roots in Germany during the great currency collapse of 1923. Then, as has already been seen,[1] the German government, hard-pressed by Allied demands for reparations, abdicated all attempts to control the depreciation of the mark and let its collapse run the full course before even trying to check the devastating process of inflation. The disaster thus caused to the bulk of the German middle classes, and the revolution in property rights which it brought about, left indelible scars on popular psychology. Mass emotions of panic and hysteria, given full rein in this way, remained liable to return in even more violent and de-

1. See p. 607.

693

structive forms. The panic on Wall Street in 1929, and the chain of bankruptcies and collapses which spread over Europe by 1934, continued this process for the property-owning classes of other countries. In most countries after 1929 the relentless growth of unemployment, matching the equally uncontrolled shrinkage of international trade, implanted similar feelings among the working classes. To the chronic uncertainty and instability of economic life, mass unemployment added a new instability in family life. A society in which thousands of skilled men of the older generation were compelled to spend years in idleness, rejected by the economic system, while their younger sons or daughters could sometimes find employment, effected a moral upheaval in the normal relationships between parents and children. This theme, popular in novels and plays of the time, such as *Love on the Dole* by Walter Greenwood, became one of the most poignant features of twentieth-century industrial society. In America, President Roosevelt spoke of 'the forgotten man'. The tragedy of enforced idleness and poverty sank deep into folklore in such popular songs as *Buddy, can you spare a Dime*. Men kept out of work for years inevitably degenerated in both skill and morale, and the sense of being forgotten or unwanted – thrown on to the scrap heap of an overproductive society – had no fitting place in the mentality of a citizen of democracy. A younger generation, forced into idleness from the start, tended to turn to more violent and revolutionary remedies. From it were recruited many fervent communists and fascists, looking to revolutionary leadership for the hopes which established capitalist democracy denied them.

Behind this social and economic crisis of European civilization lay the more ultimate moral crisis, which was also an intellectual crisis. As a modern British philosopher, T. E. Hulme, has put it:

There are certain doctrines which for a particular period seem not doctrines, but inevitable categories of the human mind. Men do not look on them merely as correct opinions, for they have become so much part of the mind, and lie so far back, that they are never really conscious of them at all.... It is these abstract ideas at the centre, the things which they take for granted, that characterize a period.

The century between 1830 and 1930 had, as these 'abstract ideas at the centre', a set of beliefs about the nature of man in society which may broadly and loosely be described as liberal, capitalist, and internationalist. They had evolved and found embodiment in the liberal and nationalist movements before 1848, in the growth of parliamentary democracy between 1870 and 1919, in the astonishing industrial and commercial expansion of Europe throughout the whole century, and in the experiments establishing a concert of Europe and workable international organizations. Preached and formulated by men like Mill and Gladstone, Mazzini and Cobden, Lincoln and Wilson, they had taken root in men's minds everywhere as self-evident truths, axioms of moral conduct for the good citizen and the successful businessman or statesman. It was assumed that the highest value in social and political life was liberty of the individual, in economic life the greatest production of wealth, in international relations the self-determination of nations. It was also assumed that the best way to reach these ends was to establish in government free representative institutions and civic liberties; in the world of business, *laissez-faire* competitive enterprise and free trade; in international affairs, organizations that governments and peoples could use to promote peace and security. All the most progressive and prosperous parts of Europe had, for a century or more, shared in these ideas, experienced the benefits to be derived from practising them, and enjoyed the rapid expansion of civilized amenities, wealth, and security which appeared to flow from them. Everything good sprang from the vigorous initiative and enterprise of free individuals whether in seeking their own freedom, their own profits, or their own national greatness and strength. There was, it seemed, a certain natural and automatic harmony of interests between men and between nations, whereby each in pursuing freely and intelligently their separate good promoted also the good of all. A whole liberal outlook upon life (or what the Germans call a *Weltanschauung*, a specific texture of thinking interwoven with implicit judgements of value) had grown up and become part of the mental and moral make-up of western man. Thus the British Labour Party, while urging nationalization and planning, clung fervently to the doctrines of free trade.

Now, between 1914 and 1934, that whole outlook had been increasingly broken and destroyed. The First World War, with its voluntary sacrifices of liberty and prosperity in the cause of national survival and security, had in the short run strengthened it. But once the immediate efforts to return to normalcy (which meant reverting to the uninhibited effort to produce the maximum wealth) had passed, war's aftermath produced the first real heart-searchings of doubt. Was not equality of at least as much importance as liberty? Was not the distribution of wealth and the consumption of it more important than production? Was not national security as important as the abstract claim to national self-determination? Europeans began consciously to question and reject the central ideas that had become an almost unconscious part of their thinking. This fundamental revolution in thought and outlook had implications that run far beyond events between the two wars into the shaping of present-day Europe. But its importance for the 1930s lay, first, in the reasons why the old ways of thought had ceased to be appropriate or valid, and, secondly, in the sequence of events by which it led Europe to the brink of the Second World War. The former will be briefly discussed here; the latter will be considered in Chapters 27 and 28 below.

The End of Expansion. One important reason why the old ways of thought were no longer valid was that their presupposition of indefinite expansion, which had once been true, was true no longer. The whole period that had known the expansion of territories of Europeans overseas coupled with a phenomenal increase in their own numbers, had, temporarily at least, come to an end. On these twin foundations, of an ever-expanding population overflowing into ever-expanding frontiers, the optimistic beliefs of the nineteenth century had found their real justification and validity. The greatest historic reception area for European emigrants, the United States, had reached its western limits by the end of the century; and the available colonial areas, too, had nearly all been apportioned among the powers before 1914.[1] The age of wide open spaces and boundless opportunities, of limitless expansion and dynamic productivity, had come to an end. In the century before 1914 a great tide of thirty-five million Europeans had crossed the Atlantic, and the economic growth of America was founded on the labour of the Irish navvy, the Polish farm labourer, the Austrian or German miner, and their counterparts from all other nations. This tide had reached its high-water mark in 1907, when some 1·2 million Europeans entered a land whose existing population was still only eighty-seven million. By then a much higher proportion came from eastern and southern Europe than from western Europe. They were mostly Slavs and Magyars, Latins and Jews.

After 1918 many Americans feared the continuance of this influx from the most troubled areas of Europe. The short depression of 1920 stirred anxieties among the ranks of American labour. Greater mechanization, and the new assembly-line mass-production methods introduced by Henry Ford, ended the old insatiable demand for cheap and unskilled labour. The symbol of the whole change was the decision of the United States to restrict severely all further immigration. In 1921 an Emergency Quota Act imposed maximum figures for immigrants that might be admitted of each nationality. In 1924 the flow from each country was still more severely restricted to an annual maximum of only two per cent of its nationals resident in the United States in 1890. At that date the proportion of British or so-called 'Anglo-Saxon' population had been high, and the proportion of inhabitants from southern and south-eastern

1. See p. 508.

Europe had been low. Aliens ineligible for citizenship – mainly Orientals such as Japanese and Chinese – were completely excluded. Further limitations were imposed in 1929. Under this legislation the entry was limited to a mere trickle of at most 150,000 immigrants, with a heavy preference for those from nations least in need of such an outlet. One American writer has described these measures as doing 'more than the Treaty of Versailles to seal the doom of democracy and capitalism in Europe'. The effect on Europe was accentuated by similar tendencies in the British Dominions and South America. Canada, Australia, New Zealand, having attained virtually complete autonomy in relation to Britain, followed America's example, despite their obvious underpopulation. Before 1914 they had excluded Chinese and Japanese, and followed a policy of white supremacy. For reasons akin to those that operated in the United States, and to preserve their own social homogeneity, they tended to favour not only white immigrants but British immigrants, and they used literacy tests to keep out non-English-speaking people. The cost of travel to the antipodes provided a further automatic deterrent to the emigration of the poorer Europeans. In the 1930s the states of South America, led by Argentina and Brazil, similarly began to restrict immigration both in bulk and by nationality.

The world economic crisis destroyed a second foundation of the older ways of thought – the assumption that what mattered most in economic activity was maximum production and the abolition of scarcity. Twentieth-century Europe, highly capitalistic and industrialized, was freed as never before from the haunting fear of scarcity. It ceased to be predominantly conscious of the evil of scarcity; and in all the most advanced countries, at least, it was believed that there was (or soon could be) plenty for all. The world economic crisis – alleged to be due to 'overproduction' – taught unforgettably the paradox that poverty could exist amid plenty, and might indeed be caused by superabundance. The great new enemy of which men became conscious was not scarcity but poverty, the maladjustment of wealth rather than its insufficiency. This enemy took concrete form in the twin evils of unemployment (or 'social insecurity') and extreme economic inequality. For these evils the old ways of thought, and their correlated institutions of liberal democracy and competitive capitalism, could in themselves offer no remedy. The ground was well prepared, by experience, for germinating and nourishing the socialistic arguments that these institutions were, indeed, the very causes of unemployment, insecurity, and inequality.

Liberal democracy and competitive capitalism had alike been justified by all their most influential defenders on the very grounds that they provided self-regulating mechanisms. They rested upon the fortu-

nate dispensation that the greatest freedom of speech and criticism
would elicit truth; that universal suffrage and free representative institutions would ensure and guarantee the liberty of the individual; that by
the rational pursuit of self-interest the general good would be most
effectively attained; that the laws of supply and demand in a free-market
world would ensure the maximum production of wealth. But by 1914
all the self-regulating mechanisms had only too evidently broken down.
Free investment and speculation had led to the collapse of 1929; free
competitive enterprise had led to the chaos of 1931; the laws of supply
and demand had failed to prevent overproduction; the free interplay of
political parties and deference to popular plebiscites had led to the dictatorship of Mussolini in Italy, and, more recently, to the dictatorship of
Hitler in Germany. Wherever such outcomes had been prevented, it had
been only by assertions of conscious policy and human will; by strong
governments using drastic forms of political power and control, or by
economic planning. Trust could no longer be placed in the capacity of
any providential mechanism to regulate itself. Deliberate acts of policy
and assertions of moral purpose seemed the only alternatives to anarchy
in politics and chaos in economic life.

Such action, conscious and predetermined, purposeful and effective,
could be taken only within the most cohesive and unified forms of social
life, which in twentieth-century conditions meant chiefly the nation-
state. Just as in war national systems of economic production, involving
the planned allocation of sources of raw materials, capital, and labour,
had been inevitable, so now the same devices offered the only hope of
salvation. In every country the economic crisis had been surmounted and
checked only when governments took the initiative, regulating currency
and credit and trade, stimulating recovery by the whole repertoire of
measures urged by modern economists, easing the lot of the unemployed
and effecting some redistribution of wealth by the mechanisms of taxation and social services. The characteristic nineteenth-century divorce
between political and economic activity, enshrined in the doctrines of
laissez-faire and free trade, was abandoned in face of the economic blizzard and the urge of powerful authoritarian governments to dominate
all aspects of national life. Just as modern governments restricted immigration in the name of preserving social cohesion, and regulated trade in
order to safeguard domestic industries, so they went on also to control
credit in the cause of economic stability and the whole of production for
the sake of securing full employment. It is impossible to tell whether
autarchy and economic planning were the root or the fruit of totalitarian
government; for both autarchy and totalitarian alike were the outcome of a generation of economic and political crises engendered by

war and the dislocations of war. The undeniable if unpalatable fact about them was that they involved uprooting those 'abstract ideas at the centre' of all thinking about modern industrial society, and adopting new ideas appropriate to the realities of Europe in the mid twentieth century.

The acceptance of at least some degree of national autarchy and totalitarianism in a continent of nation-states made less and not more soluble the further problems of internationalism. The beliefs and the institutions of internationalism, as they had culminated in the 1920s, presupposed a world of at least predominantly democratic nation-states, anxious to avoid war and willing to seek peaceful means of settling disputes between states.[1] But in a world of democratic, semidemocratic, communist, fascist, and racial states, no natural harmony of interests between states could be assumed. Patriotism alone could not create a cohesive international society, any more than 'collective security', resting on the voluntary cooperation of governments in applying sanctions against aggression, was capable of ensuring peace. Before the successful aggressions of the dictatorships, liberal internationalism went down in humiliating defeat. The single-party states had ready-made remedies of their own design for a new international order. Communism offered, through world proletarian revolution, the prospect of a community of people's democracies united in the common purpose of creating the classless society. National Socialism offered a 'New Order' in Europe, resting on domination by the Master-Race of pure Aryan blood and purged of the poisons of Judaism and Communism. Japan offered, in Asia, her 'co-prosperity sphere' of Japanese imperialism and the expulsion of European intruders.

The capitalist democracies had two alternative forms of international cohesion to offer, but neither of them included Europe. Pan-Americanism, developing through the Havana Conference of 1928 and President Roosevelt's 'Good Neighbour' policy, proclaimed in 1933, acquired new vigour. By 1936 the states of the American continent held, at Buenos Aires, an Inter-American Conference for the Maintenance of Peace. They took steps to ensure collective action in the event of any threat to the peace of the continent from within or without. The British Commonwealth at the same time developed in the direction of greater Dominion autonomy. In 1926 the freedom and equality of all Dominions within the Commonwealth were formally recognized. The Statute of Westminster in 1931 marked the culmination of the century-long movement towards self-government and self-determination for Canada, Australia, New Zealand, the Union of South Africa, and Eire. But both these partial organizations involved a certain drawing apart from Europe, and

1. See p. 640.

even certain conflicts with the cause of stronger international organization in Europe. The Ottawa Conference of 1932, which showed that
economic planning on a Commonwealth scale was ruled out because the
commercial relations of the Dominions cut across their imperial connexions, also encouraged high tariffs against imports from countries outside the Commonwealth. It was bitterly criticized for this by European
countries. The one form of international organization which vitally affected Europe – the League of Nations and its affiliated bodies – proved
to be more ineffective for promoting either prosperity or peace than the
partial organizations of Pan-Americanism and the British Commonwealth. (Even so, Bolivia and Paraguay were at war between 1933 and
1935.) In the realm of international relations the world crisis reached
its climax and its most devastating effects, for here it led directly to the
Second World War.

The keynote of the general world crisis was exclusiveness; its most
important consequence, separatism. The overseas world, pre-eminently
the United States, raised barriers to keep out both European immigrants
and European goods. The British Dominions attained their formal independence and autonomy. The New World was closing itself to the
Old. European nations huddled behind rising barriers of protective tariffs
and defensive armaments, and demonstrated their reluctance to take
effective collective action against powerful aggressors. While Stalin expelled Trotskyites and liquidated *kulaks* in Russia, Hitler expelled Jews
and liquidated all his political opponents in Germany. National minorities in Czechoslovakia and Poland demanded separation from the communities into which it had been hoped, in 1919, they might be integrated.
The expanding world economy of 1914 had broken down into a contracting system of separate autarchic national economies; the universal structure of the League of Nations was abandoned by Japan and Germany,
and only late in 1934 was it joined by the Soviet Union. Everywhere
were forces of disintegration and tightening, exclusive national systems,
intolerant of all that was felt to be alien or nonconformist.

The most significant work produced in these years was Oswald
Spengler's *The Decline of the West* (*Der Untergang des Abendlandes*),
first published in Germany in 1918 and in English translation in 1926–8.
It was widely read throughout Europe and America mainly because it
set out to analyse the contemporary 'decline of that West-European culture which is now spread over the entire globe'. This sombre version of
the doom of European civilization rested on a parallel between twentieth-
century Europe and the later centuries of the ancient world. Spengler
expounded a cyclical theory of human development, in which every
civilization experienced its spring, summer, autumn, and winter. The

twentieth century, far from being an era of democracy, progress, and peace, would prove to be one of tyranny, imperialism, and war. European culture and civilization were on their way down and out. 'We no longer believe in the power of reason over life. We feel that life rules over reason.' There are no reconciliations in history – only the triumph of one side over another. In his emphasis on race and racial domination as a central theme of history, in his identification of Prussianism with socialism so that every citizen and worker is a servant of the state, Spengler paved the way for the triumphs of national socialism. He appealed enormously to German intellectuals, already full of Schopenhauer, Nietzsche, and Wagner; to German youth, in revolt against reason as was the early nineteenth-century romantic movement, but rebelling now against the reason of mechanization, technology, and science; and to Europeans everywhere who sensed, in Spengler's intoxicating, mystical, pessimistic ideas, some hint of explanation of a world in decay and a millennial moment of revolution. If Spengler was right, then the coming of Hitler was predestined, and all efforts to rescue democracy, salvage capitalism, or preserve peace were doomed to failure. He was both the apostle and the prophet of crisis.

CHAPTER 27

THE ECLIPSE OF DEMOCRACY, 1929-39

EMERGENCY POLITICS

By 1928, as already shown,[1] democratic systems of parliamentary government had broken down or had been replaced by more authoritarian governments in Italy, Spain, and Portugal, in Hungary, Austria, and Yugoslavia, in Poland and Lithuania. This recession in democracy in southern and eastern Europe preceded the great economic recession, and is explicable in terms of the unsettled economic and social conditions after the war; the shallow roots of the new democratic constitutions, and the ineptitudes of parliamentary politicians. But it was important that democratic ideas had been to this extent smirched or abandoned, and that parliamentary institutions in all these countries had been discredited or overthrown, before the stronger democratic systems surviving elsewhere were hit by the economic blizzard of 1929. Already a certain pattern of authoritarian government, a technique of undermining and dislocating democratic government, had been demonstrated. Militarist, clericalist, even nineteenth-century in flavour it might be, but it succeeded enough to destroy the optimism of 1919 and to shatter confidence in the appropriateness of free institutions for an age of mass electorates and industrial crisis. Most original and impressive, as well as most highly publicized, was the fascist system set up by Mussolini and his Blackshirts in Italy. That the nation which had aroused so much liberal enthusiasm in the nineteenth century and which ranked among the great victorious Allied powers should have adopted a régime in vivid contrast to the normal parliamentary systems of western and central Europe was startling and significant. That until 1929 it induced greater administrative efficiency and effectively promoted Italian national interests was undeniable. The concordat between Mussolini and the Papacy in 1929 sealed its respectability and lent the régime a new air of permanence and stability. Its recently devised corporate institutions were supposed to bridge the gulf between capital and organized labour, and to afford a defence against industrial unrest and communism. There was little wonder that people in other countries, even when not imitating the ideas and methods of Fascism, tended to treat it with respect.

Emergency Government. Respect for authoritarianism, even in Britain

1. See p. 672.

702

and France, was strengthened in these years by their own experience of the need to abandon normal parliamentary procedures in an effort to meet the Great Depression. As already shown,[1] it became common to entrust drastic emergency powers to 'national governments', broad coalitions usually conservative in character. The considerable extension of presidential authority by President Roosevelt in his New Deal was the American counterpart, just as the use by President Hindenburg of his special powers under Article 48 was the German counterpart. In most democratic systems, indeed, some form of constitutional dictatorship had to be instituted. But much depended on how this was done, and there were important differences between French and British practice. Neither resorted, between the wars, to the extreme measures of declaring a state of siege, which would have been both excessive and inappropriate.

In France the main device was the emergency delegation of law-making power by parliament to the cabinet. The government was empowered, for a limited period and for specific purposes, to issue decree-laws which became immediately operative but could later be annulled by parliament. This power was given to Poincaré in 1926 to enable him to stabilize the franc; to the Doumergue-Tardieu ministry of 1934, again to meet the economic crisis; to Pierre Laval's ministry of 1935 'to prevent speculation and to defend the franc'; and to the Chautemps government of 1937 for the same purpose. In all these instances the control of parliament over government was retained. The abuse of the power by Laval, who issued under its aegis 500 decree-laws, exposed the dangers of the device. It was Edouard Daladier's ministry, which held power from April 1938 until March 1940, which made fullest use of it. During these two years of acute crisis and war, four Enabling Acts were passed which in aggregate meant a surrender of all lawmaking power to the executive authority. They were couched in more sweeping terms, and the chambers virtually abdicated power to the government two years before their more formal abdication to Marshal Pétain in July 1940.[2]

In Britain the prerogative powers of the Crown had always provided a reserve of emergency authority. These were enhanced by the Emergency Powers Act of 1920, which broke with precedent and permanently delegated to any government the right 'to make exceptional provision for the protection of the community in cases of emergency'. The type of emergency visualized was a strike or series of strikes likely to deprive the nation of such essentials of life as food, water, fuel, light, or transport. But a limit of one month was fixed for the validity of any proclamation issued under the act, and parliament had to be immediately

1. See p. 686.
2. See p. 772.

convened. It was thus very far from being an abdication of parliamentary authority. The power so given was used in the coal strike of 1921 and in the general strike of 1926. The economic crisis of 1931 called for different measures, and the National Government of Ramsay MacDonald was given emergency powers by five separate enabling acts. They constituted so radical a break with normal procedure that general elections were held in which the government asked for a 'doctor's mandate'. When it gained 554 seats as against only fifty-two Labour seats and a total opposition of only sixty-one, it could claim to have such a mandate. With so large a majority any legislation that the government wanted could be passed intact, and emergency powers were not again evoked until the outbreak of war in 1939. Then the Emergency Powers (Defence) Act, while preserving parliament's right to annul regulations, gave the government very wide powers to conduct the war with efficiency.

The experience neither of France nor of Britain matched that of Italy and Germany. In both western countries dictatorship was carefully restricted to a constitutional dictatorship. In both a regular opposition survived, parliament could always assert its control over ministers, and it could at any time destroy the government's power by forcing it to resign. The resilience and capacity of adaptation shown by parliamentary democracies in these difficult years has been greatly underrated. France and Britain found effective ways of combining speedy executive action with constitutional safeguards and parliamentary control. They proved remarkably ingenious in showing, in practical terms, that it was perfectly possible to reconcile government with democracy and in refuting the charge of authoritarians that democracy must be weak and ineffectual in a crisis. The French method differed from the British – and the differences were most important – mainly in that in France parliamentary delegations of power sprang as much from the irresponsibility and lack of political courage of parliamentarians as from any resolve to ensure efficient government; and that ministers entrusted with such powers were apt to abuse and discredit them. But in both countries parliament showed a firm resolve not to cut its own throat, as the Italian parliament had done in 1923 and the German Reichstag in 1933.

Outside Germany the aftermath of the Great Depression was more disturbing in its effects on government than were the actual measures needed to deal with the depression itself. The years between 1934 and 1939 saw the rise in almost every European country of stronger extremist movements of both Right and Left. With fascist parties in power in the two great countries of central Europe, fascist movements became active everywhere. It was the activities of the militant Right-wing groups and leagues which precipitated the crisis of February 1934 in France. To such ancient reactionary organizations as the *Action française* of Charles Maurras, dating from the days of the Dreyfus case, were added the Fiery Cross movement (*Croix de feu*) of Colonel de la Rocque, an ex-servicemen's organization founded in 1927 which by 1934 had become a rallying point for the conservative youth of France. With it were linked the *Volontaires Nationaux* and the *Camelots du Roi*. Another relic of the Dreyfus upheaval, the *Ligue des Patriotes*, had in 1924 produced the *Jeunesses Patriotes* of Pierre Taittinger, whose avowed aim was 'to defend the national territory against the dangers of internal revolution, to increase public prosperity, and to improve our public institutions'. In 1933 the perfumer Coty founded a more openly Bonapartist body, *Solidarité française*. Its paper, the *Ami du Peuple*, with its denunciations of republicans, Jews, and communists, attracted the rowdy younger members of the lower middle classes. Taken together, especially the *Action française* and the *Croix de feu*, these bodies provided all the elements of propagandist agitation, private army, and mystique of leadership which in Germany produced Hitlerism. Backed by certain industrialists and ultra-nationalist opinion, they pursued a common purpose of bringing parliamentary government into total disrepute and preparing France for fascism. In the United Kingdom the former conservative and former socialist, Sir Oswald Mosley, formed a British Union of Fascists, blackshirted and violent, modelled closely on Mussolini's. It achieved no electoral victories but contrived to bring much rowdyism into political life. In conjunction with the communists it caused enough disorder in the streets and at public meetings, especially in London, to cause the government to pass in 1936 a new Public Order Act, aimed at prohibiting political uniforms and provocative demonstrations.

In Belgium, whose dependence upon foreign trade made her economy peculiarly sensitive to the depression, an all-party national government was formed in 1937 under Paul van Zeeland. His Belgian New Deal, based on devaluation and structural reforms of the fiscal and banking systems, met with violent opposition from a combination of Flemish nationalists and the Rexists, founded in 1934 by Léon Degrelle. Degrelle showed a remarkable Hitlerian flair for appealing at the same time to sentiments of violent nationalism, to conservative Catholicism, to the prejudices of the army-officer class and big industrialists, to the middle classes who suffered from devaluation, and to the grievances of the unemployed. The Rexists won twenty-one seats in the Belgian Chamber in 1936, but lost ground in the following years. Even Sweden produced a couple of fascist parties, the National party and the National Socialist party, weakened by quarrels with one another and by the prompt prohibition of political uniforms. Balkan states gave birth to their own versions of strong-arm fascist or semi-fascist movements under Cornelius Codreanu in Rumania, General Metaxas in Greece, and Kimon Georgiev in Bulgaria. In Spain the Falangists arose in violent opposition to the Republic, which was proclaimed in 1931. In 1932 the *Falange Española* was founded by José Antonio Primo de Rivera, son of the former military dictator, and it drew support mainly from the army officers and university students. It exploited the difficulties and mistakes of the weak republican governments, until the left-wing gains in the elections of 1936 enabled it to precipitate civil war.[1]

This almost universal and almost simultaneous appearance of fascist movements throughout Europe in the early 1930s was the most ominous political consequence of the Great Depression. Like their prototypes in Italy and Germany, they won support in varying proportions from officers in the armed services and high officials in the bureaucracy, from the church hierarchy and frightened conservatives, from wealthy landowners and big industrialists. In these respects the post-depression fascist movements resembled the pre-depression authoritarian movements that had arisen in reaction against parliamentary government. But the new movements now appealed and won support also from disgruntled ex-servicemen; from disillusioned middle-class people who had suffered from the economic depression; from the ranks of unemployed workers; and from the younger generation of Europe, hungry for leadership and in revolt against national weakness and humiliation. In this respect they also resembled their prototypes in Italy and Germany. It was this support that gave them a more novel, dynamic, and proletarian impulse. Nor were such movements mere imitations, or still less by-products, of the rise of fascism in Italy or national socialism in Germany. They were native and indigenous movements, with roots in the soil of their own countries. A few, such as the national socialist movements formed among Germans in Austria, Switzerland, and Czechoslovakia, were directly German creations. But most were not. They were born of the social tensions, economic dislocations, and political instabilities of postwar Europe. For that reason they were strong, and temptations to ignore or dismiss them as temporary aberrations of a lunatic fringe proved in most countries to be a profound error of judgement.

Popular Fronts. The more immediate consequence of the rise of fascism was an era of 'popular fronts', or combinations of left-wing and moderate forces to resist the advance of fascism and preserve democratic institutions by means of social reforms. In 1936 a Popular Front was formed as an electoral alliance in France, and it resulted in the Popu-

1. See p. 713.

lar Front government headed by Léon Blum. It was supported, for electoral purposes, by the Radicals, Socialists, and Communists, as well as by the main trade-union organizations and other radical groups such as the League of the Rights of Man. This combination won the elections with a large majority, but the Communists refused to participate in the government and reserved the right to coerce it from outside by means of industrial strikes. The programme of the *Rassemblement Populaire* included measures against the fascist leagues, reform of the Press, and the extension of trade-union rights and public education. It also included a programme of nationalization of war industries and credit, fiscal reforms, and measures to diminish unemployment. Blum succeeded in asserting greater state control over the armaments industries and the Bank of France, disbanded the fascist leagues, and set up a national grain board (*Office du Blé*) for marketing wheat. But his more basic reforms were frustrated, and even this relatively mild programme of reforms aroused most bitter opposition. The Popular Front in France failed, in the sense that it lasted barely two years, achieved only part of its aims, and gave way, by uneasy stages, to the Radical government of Daladier in 1938. The fascist leagues tended to form again under other names, and the Press reforms did not eliminate, though they diminished, corruption and violent scurrility in the French Press. The Popular Front did not fail in the sense that every social reform it carried out, except the institution of the forty-hour week which was pressed upon it by the trade unions, survived throughout the Vichy régime after 1940 and into the Fourth Republic. It neither failed nor was overthrown. It was smothered by the looming clouds of international crisis. Hitler had reoccupied the Rhineland two months before it took office, and the aggressions of Italy and Germany transcended and distracted attention from domestic reform.[1]

In the Spanish Republic, too, a Popular Front coalition of the Republican Left, Socialists, and Communists, representing all the major working-class parties, fought and won the elections of February 1936. It was opposed by a corresponding Right-wing combination of monarchists, and conservatives, representing the demand for replacement of the parliamentary republic by a more authoritarian régime. The Popular Front won the elections and returned 267 deputies against the Right's 132, but it did so mainly at the expense of the Centre. This result proved to be the prelude to civil war, because the basic issue was about the future of the régime and the Right forthwith resorted to acts of violence. The Republican leader, Manuel Azaña, was in May elected President of the Republic. The Socialist leader, Largo Caballero, preferred an

1. See p. 734.

alliance with the anarchists and syndicalists rather than with the more moderate socialists or republicans. The Communists were few in number and had a solid backing only in Asturias and Seville, with some support in Cadiz and Malaga. (Seville and Cadiz were also, along with Madrid, the birthplaces of the Falange.) The moderate republican government of the consumptive Casares Quiroga was weak and harassed from both sides. The tactics of the Falangists and extreme Left alike were those of terrorism and violence. The Falangists, especially, attacked the Right with rotten eggs, insults, and broken windows, and attacked the Left with personal terrorism and murder. Judges who condemned Falangists to prison, or journalists who attacked them in the Press, were assassinated. In Madrid cars of *escuadristas* went round the streets, armed with machine guns, shooting down their political enemies. The anarchists and Communists resorted to lightning strikes and shooting affrays. Economic depression and poor harvests wove a backcloth of unemployment and hunger, completing all the conditions favourable to civil war.

The group that took advantage of this opportunity were the army officers, traditionalists, and monarchists, led by Calvo Sotelo, who had been Minister of Finance under the former military dictatorship. When he was murdered on 13 July 1936, the military junta, headed by General Sanjurjo, led an army revolt in the Spanish zone of Morocco and on 16 July occupied Ceuta and Melilla. The next day the officers of the garrisons rose in almost every city in Spain. Sanjurjo was killed in a plane accident and his place taken by General Francisco Franco. It was, in essence, a revolt of the army and the Falangists against the programme of the Popular Front. That it led not, as the rebels hoped, to their speedy seizure of power throughout the whole of Spain, but to a bitter civil war, was due to two developments: the unexpected resistance of the mass of the people, whose courage and energy proved unbeatable for three years; and the intervention of foreign powers, which prolonged the war until the point of exhaustion was reached.[1]

The notion of a 'Popular Front', so much canvassed at this time in every country where fascism made its appearance, was in part the reflection of a new phase in the policy of communism. Fascism, according to the dialectical analysis of Marxism, was the expression of capitalism in its death throes. Faced with the growth of labour organizations and the increasing pressure of working-class demands for social reform, capitalism was preparing to abandon even the forms of liberal democracy which had served it well enough hitherto, and was falling back upon open reaction and violence to oppress the proletariat. It sought to divert popular attention toward national aggrandizement rather than

1. See p. 716.

improvement of social conditions. The strong-arm bands of fascism were the hirelings of the capitalist class, the latest instrument of that class war which was inherent in bourgeois society. The correct response, therefore, according to the communists, was a common front of all democrats, liberals, socialists, and communists to preserve democracy and defeat reaction. This doctrine matched well Stalin's domestic policy of building 'socialism in a single country', for it required peaceful commercial and diplomatic relations with European powers. Moreover, the rise of national socialism in Germany constituted a new menace to Russia, and it was plainly to her interest to prevent fascism from spreading and to support friendly governments in the western powers. The entry of the Soviet Union into the League of Nations in September 1934 marked the positive beginnings of this policy of cooperation with the West, and the demand for Popular Fronts was officially approved at the Congress of the Third International in 1935. Russia's Foreign Commissar, Maxim Litvinov, represented this policy.

The major difficulty in the way of its success was the universal distrust of communism which had meanwhile been instilled into socialist and democratic parties everywhere by the Comintern's tactics of world revolution. For nearly twenty years socialists and communists had been in conflict in trade unions, at elections, and over basic issues of politics and ideology. When communists suddenly became ingratiating and cooperative, and sought the closest affiliation in tones of sweet reasonableness, labour leaders and parliamentary socialists were not unnaturally suspicious that this betokened an insidious tactic of peaceful infiltration and stealth rather than any new-found amity or change of heart. In Great Britain the Communist party sought formal affiliation with the Labour party, and since Labour had split in 1931 the prospect of unity on the Left was attractive. Even Fabian socialists like Professor G. D. H. Cole wrote persuasively in favour of a British People's Front against fascism. But the Labour party, strong in its trade-union support, resisted all such inducements and formally rejected the idea in 1934. Nor was subsequent experience of the Popular Fronts in France or Spain encouraging for socialists, for in each case the communists contrived to evade responsibilities while criticizing their nominal allies. This dilemma of democratic socialism was characteristic of the dilemma of all democrats in these years. Confronted with the triangular enmities of fascism, communism, and democracy, no firm alliance of democrats with either extreme was possible. Communism and fascism tended, indeed, to be twin barometers rising and falling together. Wherever either appeared, the main peril to democracy was that the other would grow too, and that between them they would render parliamentary government unworkable. It was because both throve on economic distress and social tensions that the years after the Great Depression were a time of peculiar difficulty for the working of democracy everywhere.

In their purely domestic setting the victories of the Left in 1936 in France and Spain marked the swing away from the corresponding victories of the Right and the governments of National Union of the preceding five or six years. The continuance of unemployment and economic distress, despite the efforts of the Right to check it, had led naturally enough to a swing of electoral opinion. Internally, Popular Fronts were but another form of 'emergency politics'. But because this swing coincided with the growth of extremist movements at home and with growing international tension between the Soviet Union and the fascist dictatorships of Italy and Germany, it exacerbated both domestic and international tensions. France did not, like Spain, relapse into civil war; but the French Right began to mutter the ominous slogan, 'Better Hitler than Blum', and a 'cold' civil war remained endemic. In Britain, where the National Government of 1931 was succeeded not by a Labour government or by a Popular Front but by the mild conservative government of Stanley Baldwin, the whole political temperature was lowered. A series of events deeply affecting the royal family happened at this time, and had the general effect of rousing a spirit of national unity which fortuitously helped Baldwin in his task. King George V, who had reigned since 1910, held the silver jubilee of his accession in 1935. In January 1936 he died and was genuinely mourned by the whole nation as a monarch whose stalwart devotion to duty, to the British way of life, and to the interests of the Commonwealth had won him and his Queen immense popular affection. He was succeeded by the very popular bachelor Prince of Wales, who became King Edward VIII. By the end of the year rumours began to circulate, despite the great silence of the British Press, of the new King's relations with Mrs Simpson, an American who was about to obtain a divorce from her second husband. Baldwin, backed by powerful influences in the Church, the state, and the Dominions, made the matter of the King's proposed marriage with Mrs Simpson a constitutional issue. The crisis in the monarchy which ensued ousted from public attention all the burning issues of German rearmament, the Spanish Civil War, and the Italo-Abyssinian War. In December 1936 Edward VIII formally abdicated, personally broadcasting his decision to the world. He was succeeded by his brother, the Duke of York, as George VI. The new King perpetuated perfectly the image of the harmonious and dutiful royal family which his father and mother had so deeply implanted in the British mind. His coronation took place in May 1937. Thus for nearly two years – the two most critical years in Europe between the wars – the attention of the island kingdom was repeatedly absorbed by royal events that had no bearing whatever upon European affairs. The Labour party as official opposition refused to oppose the government on the issue of the abdication. The British 'Popular Front' was concerned with saving the monarchy, and it was the only one in Europe which triumphantly fulfilled its purpose.

CIVIL WAR

Just as the First World War had been preceded by a decade of intensifying social and international tensions,[1] so the Second World War, too, had its prelude of civil and international wars. The connexion, first apparent after 1789, between revolution and war persisted into our own times. It was a connexion that both communists and fascists utilized to their own advantage. It in large part explains how Germany could rearm and violate her treaty obligations with impunity, and could commit so many aggressions before uniting the European powers against her. In the 1930s civil war is associated especially with Spain. The war which broke out in July 1936 raged until March 1939, and so greatly implicated other powers that it was a significant prelude to the world war. But the 'hot' civil war in Spain had its counterpart in a 'cold' civil war in other countries in these years. Fundamental to the history of all Europe in the three years before 1939 was an acute social tension created by the aftermath of the Great Depression and the subsequent growth of communist and fascist movements.

If Spain became the classical case of open civil war, it was France which offered the most striking example of the wider tendency to incipient civil war. Her disunity was great; her governments were weak and short-lived, her public institutions in low repute; her national life was lacking in great men. The relapse into violence, so apparent in 1934 and again in 1936, became a recurrent feature of French politics before 1939. The chamber experienced moments of extreme disorder, with deputies assaulting one another and debates reduced to brawls. The Press indulged in violent scurrility and in personal attacks upon national leaders. The country resembled Italy before Mussolini. It became increasingly plain that the real rulers of France were not her revolving-door governments but the power *blocs* of finance and business; or, as the finance committee of the Chamber of Deputies reported in July 1936, 'the Bank is in the hands of an oligarchy which has succeeded in ruling the country over the heads of its chosen representatives.' The *Comité*

1. See p. 540.

des Forges had considerable control over such influential organs of opinion as *Le Temps* and *Le Journal des Débats*. It was partly responsible for setting up the notorious *Comité France-Allemagne* under Fernand de Brinon, to safeguard its close economic links with the German industrialists. At the other extreme the industrial workers whose interests were so slenderly protected by the mild and often ineffective social reforms of the Third Republic, were increasingly drawn towards communism. The improvements effected by Blum in the Matignon Agreement of 1936 were a pale version of a New Deal, but they aroused remarkably ferocious hostility on the Right. That Léon Blum was a Jew and an intellectual made him especially hated both by the traditionally anti-Semitic Right and the new activist leagues. The Senate twice refused to grant him the plenary powers it had given to Doumergue, and the irresistible decline of the franc was attributed to the efforts of the financiers to discredit him. The most sensational discovery of 1937 was the plot of the Hooded Men (*Cagoulards*) a sort of French Ku-Klux-Klan of fascists, driven into secret conspiracy by the dissolution of the fascist leagues. The police unearthed several large private arsenals in Paris and other towns, and most of the arms came from Italy, Germany, and rebel Spain. This organization proved to be the link between several recent incidents, including the murder of the Rosselli brothers, Italian anti-fascist journalists, and mysterious explosions in the Paris offices of the Employers' Federation. Its purpose was to create bewilderment and heighten tension – the trick Göring had played after the Reichstag fire. Strikes were frequent. As late as December 1938 there was an attempt at a general strike, against decrees issued by the government of Daladier under its grant of plenary powers. It collapsed when the government took drastic action. Much of the resilience seemed to have gone out of French public life, and a bitterness between classes dissolved the national unity which had brought victory in 1918, and which was again needed if she were to withstand the even greater menace of Hitlerism.

Several other countries reflected, in varying ways, similar tendencies. In Belgium of the mid 1930s fascist groups, including the Rexists of Léon Degrelle, tended to ally with the more extreme Flemish nationalists. These differed in their avowed aims. Some advocated the disruption of Belgium and the erection of a great Netherlandish state combining the Flemish part of Belgium with the Netherlands; others, such as the Dinasco group (*Dietsch-Nationaal Solidaristisch Verbond*) of Joris van Severen in west Flanders, demanded that this new state be dictatorial and corporative; others, again, such as the V.N.V. (*Vlaamsch Nationaal Verbond*) of Gustaaf de Clerq, which was active in Brussels and Antwerp, were indistinguishable from German Nazism in their programme. Until 1940 all these groups did their best to disrupt the working of parliamentary government. They introduced unwonted violence and vulgarity into Belgian public life before war began, and thereafter gained temporary power as collaborators of Germany after the invasion of 1940.

In Rumania parliamentary institutions, never strong, failed to withstand the corresponding tensions created there by the Great Depression. Chief exploiters of popular disillusionment were the Iron Guard of Corneliu Codreanu, true to the type of Italian Blackshirts and Nazi stormtroopers in their terrorist attacks on parliamentary politicians, Jews, and workers. They were lent every encouragement by King Carol II who was bent on enhancing his own power. In 1937, after turbulent elections in which each party used its armed thugs, the King established his personal dictatorship and guardist leaders were 'shot while trying to escape'. At the end of 1938 Carol established the rule of his own single-party, the 'Front of National Rebirth', resting on police, army, and bureaucracy. In Rumania incipient civil war was crushed by royal despotism. In Poland in 1937 there was open conflict between the reactionary government, newly formed into a 'Camp of National Unity' on the fascist model, and the peasants and some of the industrial workers who organized strikes. The government evaded civil war only by concessions and the promise of electoral reforms. The last four years of the republic in Czechoslovakia were dominated by the rise and activities of Konrad Henlein's Sudeten German party, dedicated to the task of disrupting the republic and seeking union with Germany. As in Austria, Nazi Germany gave direct help to a German minority in order to overthrow the régime.

The Spanish Civil War, 1936–9. But it was in Spain that these general trends were revealed most vividly and to their fullest extent. There civil war ran its full course and entailed foreign intervention on both sides; there the internal crisis and the international crisis most completely coalesced, and the Spanish people were in a real sense the first victims of the Second World War. What prolonged the struggle and frustrated the rebels' plans for a military *coup* was the remarkably even balance of resources between the two sides. On paper all the initial advantages lay with the rebels – the advantages of surprise, of superior armed might, and of greater experience in fighting. On the rebel side, many of the regular officers, the Moorish troops, and the Foreign Legion had seen active service in Morocco. The Civil Guard and such party forces as the monarchist Carlists and the Falangists were already well organized. But the navy was divided, and lack of naval supremacy told against the rebel forces, which initially operated from Morocco. Of the navy's two battleships, one was seized by each side, and other vessels were almost equally shared. If the officers were nationalist, the sailors were republican. On the republican side were a few army officers, particularly General Miaja and General Rojo, a mass of workers and peasants trained in military service, large sections of the urban workers and miners, and most of the Basques and Catalans. They held important economic resources in the industrial areas of Madrid, Barcelona, and Asturias, as well as some of the richest farming areas. By the end of 1936 the nationalists held rather more than half of Spain, mostly in the south, west, and north-west, and the Balearic Islands; General Franco had installed himself at Burgos in northern Castile as 'Chief of the Spanish State' at the head of a 'nationalist government'; and thirty Junker transport planes, helpfully provided by Germany, were ferrying troops to Spain from Morocco. The republican government, eventually transferred to Valencia, was led by the socialist Largo Caballero. It held all eastern and south-eastern Spain, the capital, and most of the northern coastline belt. (See Map 19.)

The war assumed this shape by the end of the first six months, and thereafter it was likely to be a lengthy and exhausting struggle. The republican forces, having recovered from the first shock, were able to organize resistance. The war was also likely to be ferocious, because from the earliest stages extremists on both sides had indulged in great barbarities. In November 1936 Germany and Italy officially recognized Franco's Government and clearly expected a speedy victory. But in the new year General Miaja organized the defence of Madrid, and among the strong reinforcements sent to him was the first International Brigade. It was recruited from among left-wing opponents of fascism in several European countries, including France and Britain. The Soviet Union, too, observing the help given to Franco by Italy and Germany, sent fighter planes to the republican side. Already the civil war was fast becoming international in character, attracting to each side the sympathies and the active support of men in other countries. In March 1937 came the first trial of strength between the major international contingents. Italian troops – ostensibly 'volunteers' but in fact regular Italian troops – launched an attack on Guadalajara as the opening phase of Franco's fresh attempt to capture Madrid. The attack was met – and very decisively repulsed – by the International Brigade. Checked at Madrid, Franco attacked the northern zone of the Basque provinces and Asturias, and by midsummer captured the key port of Bilbao. The republican forces launched diversionary attacks from Madrid and Aragon. In May, Caballero was replaced by another, more moderate socialist, Don Juan Negrin, and by the end of the year, thanks to general conscription, he commanded an army of some eight hundred thousand men.

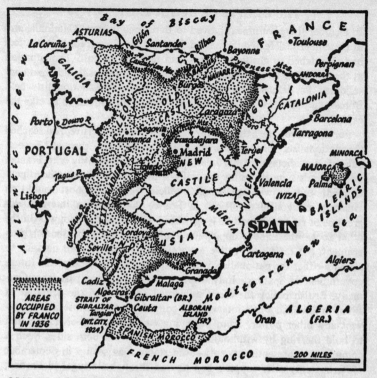

MAP 19.   SPANISH CIVIL WAR

Civil war broke out in Spain in July 1936. By the end of 1936 the rebels under General Franco held most of northern and western Spain; the republican government forces held Madrid and eastern Spain. Rebel strategy was to encircle Madrid and to cut republican Spain in half by advancing eastward from Teruel toward Valencia. By the end of 1937 the government, now at Barcelona, had lost the northern part of Bilbao but had retaken Teruel. During 1938, however, aid from Italy and Germany proved decisive. In February, Franco took Teruel and advanced to the sea. The war ended in March 1939 when he captured Madrid.

715

In October the government moved to Barcelona in loyal Catalonia, and in December it defeated the nationalists at Teruel, where rebel advances had threatened to cut government-held territory in half. The situation at the end of 1937 was stalemate, to the extent that each side had consolidated its defensive positions, and although the nationalists held Bilbao, they had lost the key point of Teruel and had failed to take the capital.

For this reason the extent of foreign help became decisive. Aid reached the nationalists through Portugal, the republicans through France. Salazar, now dictator of Portugal, showed every sympathy with Franco. Léon Blum's sympathies lay naturally with the Spanish republican government, but he was anxious lest official French support should so violently antagonize the Right in France that his own internal programme of reforms would be jeopardized. In Britain the boot was on the other foot – the Labour opposition sympathized with the Spanish government, but the Conservative government of Baldwin had no wish to alienate either the nationalists who it expected would become the future government of Spain, or Italy whom it hoped to keep apart from Germany. British policy therefore welcomed and backed the proposal of Blum to establish a non-intervention committee. Its purpose was to prevent any other powers from becoming engaged in the civil war, and to hold the ring by withholding military aid from both sides. Such a committee, representing twenty-seven states, was set up in September 1936, but only after supplies had poured through Portugal to Franco, and some through France to the government forces.

The Spanish government was induced not to appeal to the League of Nations, and in December 1936 the Council of the League resolved that all other states were under an obligation not to intervene. President Roosevelt had the neutrality laws amended to prevent the sale of American supplies to either side. But these measures did not prevent genuine volunteer brigades from joining the government side, or the fascist dictators from sending troops and equipment to Franco in violation of every agreement. The fact that the policy of non-intervention meant preventing the legitimate government of Spain from purchasing supplies from friendly nations, while the rebels drew considerable illegal help from their fellow fascists abroad, led to bitter recriminations in other countries. It was, indeed, a policy of fear and appeasement, robbing Britain and France of all initiative and striking another blow at democracy as an ideal. It was defensible only if it prevented a widening of the war to the whole of Europe. Attempts by the non-intervention committee to check the flow of supplies to either side by naval blockade and frontier supervision broke down. Britain and France scored only one joint victory at the conference of Nyon, held in September 1937. Ships carrying goods to the Spanish government were attacked by mysterious 'pirate' submarines, known to be mostly Italian. Germany and Italy boycotted the conference called at Nyon to prevent such 'piracy'. Britain and France thereupon organized a joint naval patrol, authorized to attack any submarine, ship, or aircraft illegally attacking a non-Spanish vessel in the Mediterranean. The piracy immediately stopped, and it became evident that a resolute stand could have effect.

But it was too late. In the spring of 1938 Franco, backed by as many as 100,000 Italian troops and efficient German equipment, was strong enough to renew his advance. The government forces, deficient in equipment despite some help from Russian aviation and from the International Brigade which was estimated to number at most 40,000, were torn by internal dissensions. In February the rebels retook Teruel. Driving eastward to the sea, they cut government territory in half. Thereafter it was a long, stubborn fight to occupy more and more territory. Franco resorted to a regular policy of bombing civilians, and defied all foreign protests against it. Barcelona and Madrid, despite heavy and repeated bombing, held out until early in 1939. At last Barcelona fell at the end of January, Madrid at the end of March. Many thousands of Spaniards fled to France to escape the savage reprisals that Franco proceeded to take against his opponents. The non-intervention committee was dissolved, Italian and German legions were withdrawn, and Spain relapsed into the peace of exhaustion. The civil war probably cost her a million in dead or exiles, as well as the destruction of many of her cities and the laying waste of much of her countryside. General Franco had established himself in power where he survived even his sponsors, Mussolini and Hitler. He proceeded to set up a fascist corporative state faithfully modelled after Italy, within which the old groups of army, church, landowners, and grandees continued to rule. The Catalans and Basques lost the regional autonomy they had formerly enjoyed. Communism, anarchism, socialism, and liberalism were driven underground or destroyed. The chief beneficiary of the war was not Mussolini, who had helped most, but Hitler. He had succeeded not only in inflicting another defeat on Britain and France and on the prestige of democracy in Europe, and in securing a potential ally on France's southern frontier; he had also contrived to keep Mussolini preoccupied in Spain while Germany extended her own influence into the Balkans at Italy's expense. Italy, not for the first or last time, had been used as Germany's cat's-paw.

The tragedy of Spain, involving immense human suffering and a degree of blatant brutality unrivalled even in the First World War, was also a tragedy for Europe. It was not that in General Franco the Rome-Berlin Axis (as the alliance of the fascist dictators now came to be called) had found a reliable new ally; he was, in the event, to remain neutral throughout the Second World War, and apart from causing perennial anxiety to France and her allies, he contributed nothing to Axis victories. It was that national opinion in the democracies had been rent asunder by the events in Spain. There, in concentrated drama, was fought the ultimate battle between civilian government and totalitarian dictatorship, between socialism and nationalism, which had for so long underlain the development of European society. The war was not, as the bitter polemics of the time asserted, a war between communism and fascism. Neither the Soviet Union nor Germany was as heavily committed as Italy, and the Spanish government, though supported in the war by communists, was never itself communist in composition. The war remained in essence what it has been in origin – a clash between all the forces in Spain which believed in republican government and a policy of social reforms, and all the other forces which clung to the old order in principle and sought in the institutions of military and fascist dictatorship a more effective means of perpetuating their power.

For the immediate future of Europe the war's chief significance was that it revealed that the aggressive nationalistic dictatorships of Italy and Germany could and would ally together in order to defeat democratic governments, and that they might in face of democratic weakness and disarray succeed in their purposes. In October 1936 Count Ciano, Mussolini's son-in-law who was Italy's Foreign Minister, had met Hitler and signed protocols that embodied an agreement of cooperation between the two dictatorships. It was Mussolini, announcing the agreement on 1 November, who christened it:

This vertical line between Rome and Berlin is not a partition but rather an axis around which can revolve all those European states with a will to collaboration and peace.

The agreement involved other ambitions of the dictators, above all Mussolini's in Abyssinia and Hitler's in Austria.[1] But the date when the Axis was formed is significant. Mussolini had attacked Abyssinia in October 1935; Hitler had invaded and begun to remilitarize the Rhineland in March 1936; the Spanish civil war broke out in July 1936; the Rome-Berlin Axis was formed in October 1936. The success of their concerted action in Spain sealed the alliance of fascism which was to operate in 1940 when Italy attacked a reeling France. In a continent seething with political unrest, the stage was set for a whole programme of action designed to subject Europe to universal dictatorship.

1. See pp. 731 and 741.

SINGLE-PARTY DICTATORSHIPS

It was not only the democratic states which passed through internal crisis in the mid 1930s. The single-party dictatorships of Russia, Germany, and Italy did not escape the consequences of the Great Depression and the acute social tensions to which it gave rise. But in these countries, since formal opposition was impossible, discontent found expression inside the so-called 'monolithic' parties themselves. In each dictatorship it had to be countered by party purges, more intense propaganda, and a general tightening of the grip of the leaders over party and country alike.

The Russian Purge. In 1935 the world was startled by news of a series of very sensational trials in Moscow. Between 1928 and 1933, during the implementation of the First Five-Year Plan, there had been trials, but they had been trials of men accused of wrecking and sabotage. They were explained in many ways, and were regarded as mainly a dramatic manner of accounting for shortcomings and failures, and of diverting blame for them on to alleged enemies of the régime. The party itself must be kept blameless and good, but capitalist enemies at home and abroad and Trotskyite heretics could be made scapegoats. It was quite possible, and indeed probable, that some sabotage had taken place. Certainly there had been muddle and failures. The most puzzling features of the trials of engineers and other technicians in 1928, 1930, and 1933 was the eagerness with which the accused usually confessed their guilt. They even confessed to crimes of which they had not been accused. The sentences were mostly, for Soviet citizens, imprisonment, and for foreigners, deportation; and several accused were acquitted. But the trials of 1935–8 were treason trials, and the accused were not technicians. They included most of the veteran leaders of the Bolshevik party and some of the highest-ranking generals in the Red Army. Here was something symptomatic of a much more profound upheaval within the party itself.

In January 1935 Zinoviev and Kamenev were arrested, charged with plotting to murder Stalin with the aid of the German secret police. These old associates of Lenin and Stalin, who had made their peace with the régime when Trotsky was driven out in 1927, were allegedly implicated in a further plot to separate the Ukraine from the Soviet Union, so they were national as well as personal traitors. Zinoviev was sentenced to ten years in prison, Kamenev to five. In August 1936 they were retried before the Supreme Military Tribunal. They now confessed freely to the most dramatic crimes, gave testimony against each other, and were sentenced to be shot. In January 1937 charges of conspiracy to

719

assist foreign aggressors in an attack on the Soviet Union were brought against Radek, a former leader of the Third International; Sokolnikov, former Soviet ambassador in London; and Piatakov, vice-commissar for heavy industry. The president of the trade-union council and the vice-commissar for war both committed suicide. In June, Marshal Tukhachevsky and seven other Red Army generals were convicted and sentenced to death for military conspiracy 'with an unfriendly state' (presumed to be Germany). The purge reached its height in 1937 with the arrest of tens of thousands of people in all walks of life, ranging from Catholic and Orthodox priests and Soviet commissars to Ukrainian nationalists and humble party members. Many famous Bolsheviks, heroes of the Revolution like Borodin and Béla Kun, were imprisoned or deported, or at least deposed. Even the military judges themselves were eventually liquidated, and of the eight who tried the Red Army generals in 1937, six were degraded by the end of 1938. In March 1938 came a final purge of most of the remaining 'old Bolsheviks' – Rykov who had succeeded Lenin as president of the council of commissars, Bukharin who edited *Pravda*, Rakovsky who had been Soviet ambassador in London and Paris, even Yagoda who was chief of the secret police (N.K.V.D.), and several others. Apart from Stalin and Molotov themselves, the only remaining Bolshevik of the old guard who had been prominent in the days of Lenin was now Trotsky, in exile in Mexico.

Against the arch-enemy Trotsky, relentlessly continuing his vendetta against the betrayal of the revolution and feverishly trying to organize a Fourth International, Stalin had to wait for final vengeance until 1940. In his hide-out in Mexico, Trotsky was busy writing the life story of Stalin. On 20 August 1940, he was visited by a Russian, posing as his supporter, who smashed his head with an axe. The sheets of paper on his desk were spattered with his blood. It was a symbolic ending to the most bloodstained feud of modern history, passing almost unnoticed at a time when the pact between Stalin and Hitler had made possible the German conquest of most of Europe, and when Britain stood alone expecting a German invasion.

Abroad there was boundless speculation about what these trials meant. Their meaning is plainer now. That some party members had remained faithful to the ideas of Trotsky and resented the harsh dictatorship of Stalin seems certain. That some generals, antagonized by the domination of party over army and willing to seek ways of unseating Stalin's ever-heavier power over them, engaged in some sort of conspiracy seems probable. Events after the death of Stalin in 1953, and the further purge of Beria and others in the postwar years, have made it appear more than ever likely that the sensational upheavals of party, state, and army in the 1930s were – above all – incidents in the overweening determination of Stalin and his closest associates to concentrate all power in their own hands at all costs. If this is true, the purges take their place in the physiological history of single-party totalitarian dictatorships, as further evidence that the nemesis of monolithic parties is self-destruction, and the price of absolute power absolute corruption. Only when the entire old guard of Bolshevism had been destroyed could Stalin feel secure. These events have often enough, and aptly enough, been compared with the last stages of the Jacobin reign of terror in 1794 – which they resemble save that Robespierre himself was guillotined in the end, and they took place in Russia not in the early years of the revolution but nearly two decades later.

The effects on the international prestige of the Soviet Union were devastating. The condemned men included former heads of almost every important section of the Soviet system, and they were accused of having worked, from the earliest days of the revolution, for the spy services of Britain, France, Germany, or Japan. Had all these charges been true, the actual survival of the Soviet state would have been inexplicable. This vast conspiracy, reaching to the highest levels, had yielded oddly negligible results. Kirov, governor of Leningrad, had been assassinated by a young opposition communist in December 1934 – an incident which had first touched off the purge. No other important official had been killed – except by Stalin himself in the purge. It was a remarkably disproportionate outcome for so high-powered a plot among men who, on countless occasions, could have killed Stalin himself. No piece of evidence verifiable by ordinary legal procedure was ever produced, and the confessions often included statements of detail known to be untrue. The whole hysterical, unreal procedure could not be explained by any rational desire to find scapegoats for economic failures. Economic conditions actually improved in the years when the purge was being prolonged, and even Stalin did not need so many thousands of scapegoats. Stalin's central motive, in the words of his most authoritative biographer, Isaac Deutscher, was 'to destroy the men who represented the potentiality of alternative government, perhaps not of one but of several alternative governments'. And the destruction of all political centres from which an alternative government might come was 'the direct and undeniable consequences of the trials'.

That Stalin chose 1936 to begin the great purge was due above all to the emergence of Hitlerite Germany as a new European threat to the Soviet régime. The purges, in short, were the Stalinist version of civil war, timed to forestall any combination of internal opposition with external enemy such as produced the civil war in Spain. The first major trials – of Zinoviev, Kamenev, and other former Trotskyites – took place in August 1936, five months after Germany reoccupied the Rhineland and one month after civil war began in Spain. With the long story of Trotskyite opposition in mind, Stalin took no chances. His enemies had to die as traitors, not martyrs; hence the grossly exaggerated charges and the insatiable thirst for confessions. The charges against the generals may, however, have had more substance. By 1937 few men of importance felt safe, and the army was the only organized power strong enough to take measures of self-preservation. There is no evidence that they did so with German help – the Nazi documents produced in 1947 at the Nuremberg trials revealed no hint of a Nazi fifth column in the Soviet government or army. But they had ample motive for planning a *coup d'état* to save themselves from the expected purge. The only general who could play the Bonaparte to Stalin's Robespierre was Tukhachevsky, a man of military genius who was the favourite of the army. He and his colleagues were tried in secret and made no confessions. It is likely that some 20,000 officers, a quarter of the entire officers' corps, were arrested, and several thousand of them were shot. As under Nazism, the one form of opposition which the leader took as seriously as rival leadership within the party was rivalry from the army. In March 1939 Stalin announced that the period of mass purges was at an end. That month Hitler added the whole of Czechoslovakia to his existing conquests of the Rhineland, Austria, and the Sudetenland.

The German Purge. The history of the National Socialist dictatorship in Germany reveals remarkably close parallels to the Stalinist purges. The party in its rise attracted members and votes by a programme that appealed to the twin ideals of nationalism and socialism. Nationalism, in Nazi context, meant the union of all Germans within a greater Germany and the expulsion from the integrated Reich of all alien elements, especially Jews; socialism meant 'abolition of incomes unearned by work' and 'abolition of the thraldom of interest', a corporative state, and organization by that state of all economic and social life in the cause of state power. In its rise to power the party contrived to attract, with this programme, on one hand the support of landowners, army, and big business, on the other the support of the classes dispossessed of savings or employment by the economic crisis. After attaining power, it found it increasingly difficult to satisfy the expectations of both at once. The Jews could be denounced simultaneously as communists and as capitalists. But what then? As in Russia, the first threat to Hitler and his closest colleagues came from within the party itself. Among the many elements drawn into it were men like Ernst Röhm, a swashbuckling soldier of fortune who led the party's earliest storm troopers (*Sturmabteilung*), known as S.A. men or Brownshirts; Catholics associated with von Papen; conservative militarists connected with von Schleicher; socialists grouped round Gregor Strasser. Into the S.A. particularly were incorporated a motley crew of the older generation – ex-servicemen who had been effective enough for street fighting and bashing policemen on the head, but who now hoped only for comfortable jobs under Hitler's auspices, original party comrades whose ill-disciplined civilian outlook went badly with any uniform, and simply workers or lower-middle-class tradesmen attracted to the party by anti-Semitism, economic misfortune, and a taste for shady politics. In power, Hitler and Göring found the demands and even the existence of this body embarrassing. Even more ominous: the Brownshirts included many who took seriously the 'socialist' half of national socialism; and with the persistence of economic distress and the difficulties of finding employment, they began to clamour that the nationalist revolution, now completed, must be followed at once by a second, socialist, revolution, ensuring jobs and prosperity if not for the whole nation then at least for the faithful members of the party. These counterparts to the 'second revolutionaries' or Trotskyites of Russia, the German dictator, too, decided must be purged. He struck on 30 June 1934, a date that became known as 'The Night of the Long Knives'.

Hitler's weapons in the purge were the chief rivals of the Brownshirts, the S.S. men (*Schutzstaffel* or Black Guards) and the secret state police or Gestapo (*Geheime Staatspolizei*) formed by Göring in 1933. Both these organizations were highly disciplined bodies of younger men, mainly bourgeois in origin, vowed to unquestioning obedience to Hitler as their Leader (*Führer*) and acting as a law unto themselves. The events of June 1934 marked the final shift of power from the unreliable, semicivilian Brownshirts of the old movement to the highly efficient and ruthless organizations of S.S. and Gestapo, with whose aid Hitler could dominate the whole nation. As early as July 1933 Hitler had issued a warning to the restless S.A. men. 'I will suppress every attempt to disturb the existing order,' he screamed, 'as ruthlessly as I will deal with the so-called Second Revolution, which would lead only to fresh chaos.' He waged campaigns against grumblers, but in 1934, when economic conditions did not improve, the discontent grew. Röhm, leader of the Brownshirts, was a known rival of Göring; and more and more was heard of the need for a 'second revolution'. At two o'clock on the morning of Saturday, 30 June Hitler and Goebbels with two of their faithful adjutants left in a plane from Bonn. Two hours later they landed at Munich. Picking up five carloads of men from the S.S. headquarters there, they drove out to Wiessee where Röhm, Heines, and a few other drunken Brownshirt leaders were arrested or killed. Hitler then returned to the Brown House in Munich, issued decrees reorganizing the S.A., and flew on to Berlin. Meanwhile, under Göring in Berlin and elsewhere, detachments of S.S. men and sections of the army were also taking action. In Berlin, Klausener, chief of the Rhenish Catholic party, was shot working at his desk. In von Papen's office two of his secretaries were killed at their work. Gregor Strasser was shot. General von Schleicher and his wife were shot at their home. Many of the S.A. chiefs were arrested and shot. Heinrich Himmler took charge of hasty trials and summary executions. Everywhere individual Nazis took the chance to pay off old scores or remove possible rivals. The official version was that seventy-six conspirators, who for months had backed a plot, hatched by von Schleicher and Röhm with the aid of 'a foreign power', to overthrow the régime, had now been killed. It is certain that at least double that number were killed, and possible that several hundred died in what became a general settlement of old accounts. Of some, such as the notorious blackmailer, pervert, and murderer Edmund Heines, commander of the Silesian S.A., the world was well rid; though the blame for his tyranny in Baden lay with Hitler who appointed him to power.

With the S.A. reduced to political impotence, all idea or hope of a 'second revolution' came to an end. The lower-middle classes of the older generation, who had been Hitler's main strength in the past, had become a handicap to his plans now that he was firmly in power. They had wanted to hold him to the socialistic features of his early programme – to an overhaul of the German economic system which would give social security and more butter. But Hitler had chosen the alternative path of militarism and foreign aggression, and opted for guns not butter. His power lay now in the S.S. and the army, and his next move was to reintroduce military conscription in defiance of the Treaty of Versailles. Like Stalin, he had crushed incipient civil war in the cause of national power. But, as in Russia, this left open the question of the relations between party and army. The partnership of Hitler, Göring, Goebbels, and Himmler now held the key positions. Göring controlled the police, Goebbels all the instruments of propaganda, and Himmler since April, 1934, had combined control of the S.S. Black Guards with control of the Gestapo. In the blood bath of June, Hitler disposed of his predecessor as Chancellor, General von Schleicher, and of General von Bredow. When Hindenburg died in August, Hitler took care to inherit his power as Commander-in-Chief of all the armed forces in his new post of *Führer und Reichskanzler*.

Even so the proud Reichswehr with its traditionalist officer corps might be expected to show some resistance to the upstart corporal and his highly unaristocratic followers. But he won the support of the younger Reichswehr officers by his measures for rearmament and military conscription, and the senior officers showed no sign of effective resistance. As General von Blomberg declared later, at the Nuremberg trials in 1946, 'Before 1938–9 the German generals were not opposed to Hitler. There was no ground for opposition since he brought them the successes they desired.' In 1938 two incidents gave him a tighter grip over them, by discrediting the two senior army leaders. General von Blomberg – in the presence of Hitler and Göring – married a lady whom the police dossiers, duly publicized by the Nazis, proved to be a former prostitute. Blomberg was forced to retire. His natural successor, General von Fritsch, was charged by the Gestapo with homosexual practices, and he also was forced to resign the following month. It later transpired that the Gestapo evidence related to a junior officer called Frisch and the General was exonerated by a military court. But Hitler meanwhile assumed personal command of all the armed forces of the Reich, and exacted from the Reichswehr a personal oath of allegiance. With less friction than in Russia, the army was subjected to the absolute will of the dictator.

The Italian Purge. The third of the trio of single-party dictatorships, Mussolini's Italy, fared no better in face of the economic blizzard than did the Soviet Union or Germany. Between the winters of 1926 and 1930 the number of unemployed admitted in official statistics trebled. The figure continued to rise (despite various discreet omissions from the official statistics, such as women dayworkers formerly included) from 765,000 in 1931 to 1,147,000 in the winter of 1932, and to 1,229,000 in February 1933. How much it actually rose above that remains obscure, since Mussolini was more concerned to attack statistics of unemployment than to attack unemployment itself, and repeatedly ordered that fresh categories of unemployed be omitted from the official figures. Even so, official figures registered well over one million throughout the first three months of 1934, and the figures of Italian imports and exports show that the depression continued in Italy throughout that year. The much-vaunted programmes of public works launched by the régime never employed as many as 200,000, at a time when well over one million were unemployed. (In the United States in January 1934 the federal government was giving employment to more than four million workers.) To meet the more severe economic distress of the winter months, the Italians introduced a scheme of public relief described as 'national solidarity', corresponding to the German *Winterhilfe*. As in Germany, it was administered by the party posing as a benevolent institution, though the money was extracted from the pockets of employers and ordinary citizens. By comparison with the relief given to unemployed people in Great Britain or the United States at the height of the economic crisis, relief afforded by Fascism in Italy was extremely small. In the worst winter of 1934 each person received an average amount of fifty centesimi (five cents) a day, while his counterparts in Britain received roughly five times as much, and in New York ten times as much. Yet so inflated was the Fascist effort by propaganda and dramatization that many English and American citizens were persuaded that Mussolini was working miracles.

It was less easy to persuade Italians, who felt the pinch. The régime declined in prestige internally during these years, as it became more and more apparent that the Fascist dictatorship knew no better than the despised democracies how to overcome economic depression. As in other single-party dictatorships, such discontent found voice only within the ranks of the party itself. Mussolini, like Hitler, had attracted to his movement in its rise to power a mixture of elements hoping for diverse things. As in Bolshevism and Nazism, so in Fascism, there was a particularly sharp contrast between those who accepted Mussolini's avowed socialism, and the alleged purpose of the corporative state, as offering genuine hopes of social reform; and those who above all were nationalists and militarists, preferring guns to butter. At the end of 1934 and early in 1935 this 'left wing' of the party was becoming restive and began to press for the 'second revolution'. From this impasse, created by the joint pressure of economic slump and political discontent within and without the party, Mussolini sought escape in the war against Abyssinia.

It began in October 1935. Some 300,000 men were called up for military service, which lowered the figures of unemployment; expenditure on the war served as another form of public work; and the more recalcitrant party members were shipped off to East Africa. The Fascists spoke of the Abyssinian war as a 'revolution'. It was indeed a nationalist revolution, comparable with the 'Night of the Long Knives' in Germany or with the Stalinist purge of Trotskyites in Russia. At one stroke it quelled discontent at home, or at least drowned it in patriotic propaganda and shouts of military glory; it eased the burden of economic stagnation and created a timely diversion; and it opened a new phase in Mussolini's policy of seeking imperial power in the Mediterranean and Africa. This policy was to lead him into engagement in the Spanish Civil War and eventually into war against a stricken France and a threatened Britain in 1940.

The Economy of Dictatorships. If the economic systems of the single-party states were not particularly successful in resisting the results of economic depression, they were admirably geared to preparation for foreign war. In the Soviet Union the Second Five-Year Plan, launched in 1933 and completed by 1937, and the Third, started in 1938, effected the most far-reaching transformation of the country's economy. The greater emphasis still, as in the First, lay on expanding the output of production goods, but more resources could now be devoted to consumption goods. This led to an easing of the burden on the population as a whole, whose standard of living was much improved. Rationing was abandoned in 1935, though control of prices and trade remained. Moreover the Plans could be, and were, modified from year to year to take account of changing needs and conditions. This made it possible to devote more effort to strengthening the armed forces as the clouds of war gathered. The strength of Russia for war could be measured partly in terms of the number of trained men, and this was estimated to be twelve and a half million by 1939. It could be measured, too, in terms of the great industrial revolution carried out by the five-year plans. The output of coal, oil, iron, steel, electrical power, and all other essentials of war production increased many times over production during the years before 1928. Even so, when the Third Plan was fulfilled in 1942, Soviet production of pig iron and steel was still less than that of Germany and less than half that of the United States. In agriculture the revolution consisted mainly of collectivization and mechanization, each making the other possible. By 1940 more than nineteen million peasant households – or more than ninety per cent of the whole peasant population – were established in collective farms, though now less than half the whole population was engaged in agriculture. Nearly 7,000 machine tractor stations provided the machinery and technical labour needed to ensure methods of mass-production farming. But the largest employer of labour was the N.K.V.D. or Commisariat for Internal Affairs, whose forced-labour camps employed millions in building highways, railroads, canals, and in mining.

In the Nazi régime the strong tendencies towards an integrated national economy geared to total war, already existing in Germany, continued in more ruthless form. Hitler said, on one occasion,

I had only to develop logically what social democracy repeatedly failed in because of its attempts to realize its revolution within the framework of democracy. National socialism is what Marxism might have been if it could have broken its absurd ties with a democratic order.... Why need we trouble to socialize banks and factories? We socialize human beings.

National socialism purported to be, and in a large measure it actually was, an extreme form of state capitalism and state socialism combined: a system in which owners of property and workers alike were subjected

to the dictates of the totalitarian state. The huge trusts, the great indus-
rial magnates like Krupp and Thyssen, remained; but they were obliged
to serve the needs of Germany as determined by the Nazi party. Trade
unions of the old type were abolished, and new 'corporative' labour
unions were put in their place; their purpose, too, was to place at the
disposal of the dictatorship all the manpower resources of the Reich,
mobilized through the Labour Front of Robert Ley. At the same time
Nazi leaders, pre-eminently Göring, went into business and industry
themselves, and the Hermann Göring Works set up in 1937 became the
largest industrial combination in Europe. The two German Four-Year
Plans, begun in 1936, transferred control of all economic life to the
state with the twin aims stated by Hitler in that year: to make the armed
forces ready for battle within four years, and to mobilize the economy
for war within four years. By strict control of foreign exchange, allocation of raw materials, controlled investment, and disciplined regulation
of labour, farming, wages, prices, and profits, Germany was made ready
for a complete war economy. Synthetics and substitutes were developed
and the national income was positively increased. Unemployment was
almost eliminated, partly by schemes of public works and rearmament,
partly by the bogus means of creating jobs by removing Jews and all
political opponents, and by overstaffing the vast bureaucracy of state
and party. Helped by Hitler's 'financial wizard', Hjalmar Schacht, the
régime showed great efficiency in attaining its economic objectives. In so
far as it did not attain them, grumbling was simply suppressed by sheer
terror. Italian Fascism, as already seen, was less ruthless and less successful in implementing its economic aims; though in Italy, too, much
of the nation's economic development was state-controlled in the interests of the war machine.

The most important fact about all three single-party states was not
economic but political: the fact that they were governed by men who
wielded, more completely than any other rulers in history, absolute
power of life and death over all their subjects. The unique feature of
modern dictatorship is that it tends to be totalitarian; that is, it con-
trives to concentrate in the hands of the ruling group a degree of power
which enables them to control all aspects of the national life. This
power, in its organized form, rested on two main pillars: on the ability
to control public opinion by every modern resource of public education,
youth organization, censorship, publicity, propaganda by Press, radio,
cinema, theatre, poster, and public meeting; and on the ability to crush
and to keep crushed every form of open criticism or opposition by the
use of secret police, concentration camps, and terror. Ballyhoo and
brutality were made the foundations of the state. Behind the party,

engaged in monopolizing and running all the important organizations of society and state, stood in each country the terrible power of the secret police, striking sometimes openly and in mass, as in the great purges or in the drives against the Jews in Germany, sometimes silently as in the countless isolated arrests of suspects who disappeared to a fate unknown. Any state in which a large and efficient secret police is at the disposal of the single party in power is at the mercy of that party. Each dictator found that he could muster, from modern society, a large enough number of utterly unscrupulous, devoted, and brutal henchmen to gain him this power of terror. It was enough. Given its existence, even the democratic institutions of elections and plebiscites, of parliamentary assemblies and procedures, could be tolerated, because the secret police operated outside the law. The story of tortures and cruelties, of total degradation of the human personality and of vicious sadism, was by the mid-twentieth century familiar enough. There is little mystery left about how a single-party dictatorship works. The more difficult question is how such absolute power could be generated and accumulated in apparently civilized cultured European communities of modern times.

One explanation is the appeal made to fanaticism – the astounding force of ideologies whether Marxist, nationalist, or racialist. Certainly the Stalinist régime based itself on the ideology of Marxism, as interpreted and adapted first by Lenin and then by Stalin; Mussolini claimed for Fascism a new ideology which combined streaks of Hegelian idealist philosophy with an ultranationalism that made all else subordinate to the state; and Hitlerism evolved a complete doctrine of racialism which presented Germans as the 'master race' (*Herrenvolk*) with a historic destiny to rule the world once it had purged itself of contamination by Jews, Christians, liberals, socialists, and communists. Younger generations, indoctrinated in these creeds from early youth, and believing in each case that historic destiny was on their side, produced considerable numbers of devoted young fanatics who abandoned every moral scruple in blind obedience to *Vozhd, Duce*, or *Führer*, as the case might be. Many others, no doubt for diverse reasons, climbed on to the band waggons of successful parties, came to terms with necessity or expediency, and found in the disciplined bossing of others personal satisfaction, lucrative gains, and an exciting career. But what gave these ideologies, propagated at high pressure by all the apparatus of modern publicity, their cutting edge was that propensity of modern civilization to succumb to mass hysteria and herd instincts which was apparent even before the First World War.[1] Stalin, Mussolini, and Hitler would not have been possible a century sooner. They were the products of

1. See p. 372.

modern urban civilization, of postwar upheavals, and of the profound social and economic dislocations of the postwar years.

No less significant than the appeal of fanaticism and ideology, for the rise of the single-party dictatorships, was modern organization. It became possible, as never before in history, for a government that could dispose of all the organizational methods of the modern state to impose its will upon millions of people at one time. The growth of capitalist combinations, labour organizations, and political parties, even before 1914, had revealed the new capacities and opportunities for mass organization and mass action. The First World War had shown, in turn, how such organization could be perfected, brought under central state control, and brought into movement and action for a single end. The trends towards still more large-scale organization had continued after 1918, and had been projected on to an international screen. They included the techniques of economic control, of taxation, of military discipline, of political manipulation of the mass electorates of universal suffrage, of mass education and persuasion. Radio offered new opportunities and electrical amplification made possible the vast mass meetings of Nazism. In this respect, too, the twentieth-century dictators were the heirs of later nineteenth-century developments in technique and social structure.[1] The web of history was untorn, even by the most violent upheavals of war and revolution.

The ascendancy in Europe of three such states, combined with the conditions of 'cold' civil war in so many other countries, made the outbreak of a general war in Europe increasingly likely. All were highly dynamic movements, seeking action and triumphs, missionizing and militant, scorning the notion of an indefinite prospect of peaceful co-existence. There was a drive to war as well as a drift to war, and peace in Europe was deliberately demolished in a way that differed from the pattern of events which preceded 1914.

1. See p. 427.

CHAPTER 28

THE DEMOLITION OF PEACE, 1935–9

THE FAILURE OF COLLECTIVE SECURITY

THE provisions made in the Covenant of the League of Nations for joint action against aggression, even when supplemented by such agreements as the Locarno and the Briand-Kellogg pacts, all presupposed that governments and peoples interested in preserving the peace and in maintaining the settlement of 1919 would be able and willing to act together. That such action might well involve states in war was seldom appreciated by even the warmest supporters of the League. In 1934 the League of Nations Union in Great Britain organized what was called, somewhat misleadingly, a 'National Peace Ballot'. People were asked, among other questions, whether they thought that if one nation attacked another the other nations should combine to stop it by (a) economic sanctions, (b) if necessary, military measures. More than eleven million people answered the first of these questions affirmatively, and the result was taken to show overwhelming support for the principle of collective security. But only two thirds of this number also answered the second question affirmatively. This result accurately reflected the confusion of thought which existed – and not only in Britain. A policy of collective security which shirked military action could never give security against men like Mussolini or Hitler. Too many well-meaning folk thought of 'the League' and even of 'collective security' as things already existing in themselves, and operating apart from the policies of the major League powers whose policies and armed might could alone determine whether or not aggression would be checked.

Japanese Aggression. For wider reasons, too, the League as an agency of collective action was by 1936 already a badly battered instrument. First to attack its principles, and to expose its probable ineffectiveness, was Japan. In September 1931 Japan, still a member of the League, attacked China, which was also a member of the League. The chosen incident was a minor bomb explosion on the south Manchurian railroad a few miles from the Japanese garrison town of Mukden. Forthwith her Kwantung army occupied the main strategic points in south Manchuria, and it became evident that imperialist Japan had resumed her old policy of expansion into Manchuria. The Chinese Nationalist government at Nanking appealed to the League under Article 11, which in the event of war or threat of war empowered the League to take 'any action that may be deemed wise and effectual to safeguard the peace of nations'. It also appealed to the United States under the Briand-Kellogg Pact. The Council of the League asked both parties to withdraw their armed forces to their original positions as preliminary to peaceful settlement. Henry L. Stimson, the American Secretary of State, reminded the parties of their duty to settle differences peacefully under the Briand-Kellogg Pact, and authorized the United States consul in Geneva to sit in on the Council's meetings; but he did nothing more until in January 1932 he refused to recognize any situation – by clear implication, any change in Japanese-Chinese relations – brought about by means contrary to the Pact. Meanwhile the Japanese, undeterred by such gestures, completed the conquest of the whole of Manchuria and in March 1932 renamed it Manchukuo, allegedly an independent state. The League sent to Manchuria a commission of inquiry headed by Lord Lytton. Its report of October condemned Japanese action and dubbed Manchukuo a puppet creation. The League adopted the report in February 1933. In March, Japan gave notice of her withdrawal from membership of the League, and proceeded to invade the Chinese province of Jehol, south-west of Manchukuo. Her speedy conquest of Jehol installed Japanese power at the Great Wall of China. By the end of 1935 she also took control of the provinces of Hopeh and Chahar, and penetrated far into northern China. Neither the League nor the United States took action. Their inactivity and ineffectualness in the Far East lent every encouragement to European aggressors who planned similar acts of defiance.

Italian Aggression. The first to do so was Mussolini, whose plans to attack a fellow member of the League, Abyssinia, reached maturity in October 1935. Here, it seemed, he had found the perfect victim for Italian aggression. Abyssinia (or Ethiopia), under its native Emperor Haile Selassie, was the only remaining independent state in East Africa. It lay between Eritrea and Italian Somaliland, so could be attacked simultaneously from north and south. Once conquered, it could be used to round off the whole Italian East African Empire. Its resources, according to Fascist propaganda, included great riches ranging from pineapples to platinum. Italy already enjoyed certain rights there, though her earlier attempt to make it a protectorate had been decisively defeated at the Battle of Adowa in 1896;[1] and in 1928 she made with Abyssinia a pact of friendship, conciliation, and arbitration. In December 1934 there occurred a clash between Italian troops and Abyssinian escort at the oasis of Walwal, near the border between British and Italian Somaliland, and dispute arose whether the oasis lay in Abyssinian or Italian territory. Although Italy took possession of it, some thirty Italian

1. See p. 502.

colonial troops were killed in the skirmish. When Italy demanded apologies and compensation, Abyssinia appealed to the League under Article 11. The Council succeeded in persuading both sides to seek a settlement under their own treaty of 1928, but in May, 1935, Abyssinia again appealed against continued Italian troop movements. Italian transports, indeed, were moving into East Africa in a steady stream, while at the conference of Stresa in April, Italy joined with Britain and France in protesting against German rearmament. On 3 October without declaring war, Mussolini launched his attack, and the forces from Eritrea soon captured Adowa. This time the Council of the League acted speedily. On 7 October it declared Italy to be the aggressor, and four days later the Assembly agreed to impose economic sanctions against her, excluding coal and oil from its list of goods to be withheld from Italy. A few states – Austria, Hungary, Albania, Switzerland – refused to apply sanctions. President Roosevelt operated the American neutrality laws, restricting trade in arms and ammunition.

All these encouraging signs of a revival in collective action had certain ill effects on British-French relations. France had been more persistent in pressing for resistance to Germany, and was anxious to placate Italy so as to rob Hitler of an ally. Britain, which had been less hostile to Germany and had even, as recently as June 1935, made a naval treaty with her, now set the pace in imposing sanctions against Italy. A British fleet moved to the Mediterranean. In November the National Government was again triumphant in the general elections. Its Foreign Secretary, Sir Samuel Hoare, who had previously had conversations with the French Premier, Pierre Laval, about the Italo-Abyssinian dispute, now resumed these discussions and with him devised a scheme whereby Abyssinia would surrender to Italy a large area of some 60,000 square miles and get in exchange a much smaller area as a corridor to the Eritrean port of Assab. Britain and France were also to secure for Italy a still further concession of 160,000 square miles in southern Abyssina, as an area for exclusive economic development. When it became known, and realized, that nearly two thirds of Ethiopia would thereby be given to Italy, a storm of public indignation in Britain forced Hoare to resign. He was replaced by Anthony Eden, a staunch upholder of the principles of collective security. But export of oil to Italy was not stopped, and other forms of economic sanctions were not enough. In May 1936 the Italians captured the capital of Addis Ababa, proclaiming King Victor Emmanuel III of Italy as Emperor of Ethiopia. Mussolini forthwith organized Ethiopia, Eritrea, and Somaliland into Italian East Africa and made Marshal Badoglio its viceroy. The Council of the League abandoned sanctions in July, and the whole idea of sanctions was discredited by their partial application and their failure to save Abyssinia. That very month the civil war in Spain began. Yet only economic sanctions had been used by the League and these not fully. With the United States, Germany, Japan, and Brazil outside the League, perhaps they could not have been fully effective. The moral generally drawn was that sanctions were unwise or ineffective; perhaps the true moral was that economic sanctions could be effective against a major power only if backed by military sanctions. In any event, the League had suffered a further grave rebuff.

German Aggression. Meanwhile, as a contributory cause of Mussolini's success, it had suffered a further blow from the direction of Germany. On 7 March 1936 Hitler sent his troops dramatically into the demilitarized zone of the Rhineland. It was Hitler's first major territorial aggression, and perhaps the most crucial of all. The move, a frontal challenge to the settlement of Versailles even more serious than his open rearmament of Germany, was opposed by many of his military advisers. It was also a violation of the Locarno agreements which Germany had made not under a *Diktat* but voluntarily. Had France and Britain, or even France alone, marched against him at that time, he was still too unprepared to hope for victory. It was perhaps the biggest gamble of his career. The officers in the operation, it is now known, carried sealed orders to withdraw at once if they met with French resistance. But none came because the government of Sarraut was weak and tottering to its fall, and because it delayed while it consulted Britain and lodged protests with the League of Nations. There is little doubt that vigorous military reprisals taken by a strong French government would, at that moment, have checked Hitler for a time and maybe forever. British opinion, befogged by memories of resentment against French intransigence towards Germany in 1919 and 1923, and confused by talk of Germany's right to go into 'her own back-garden', would hardly have supported French reprisals.

The point so oddly unappreciated was that Hitler could now proceed to build his 'Siegfried Line' of strong fortifications on Germany's western frontier, and so raise the shield behind which his next steps of aggression in south-eastern Europe could be prepared. In one move he had transformed the whole military and diplomatic situation in western Europe. France was exposed to attack, Germany was more defensible against attack; France's allies in eastern Europe were now more cut off from French help and more at Germany's mercy; and a further violent repudiation of the peace settlement had gone unpunished. At home Hitler's political intuition was vindicated, his expert military critics silenced. It was more possible for him to proceed with his programme of aggression, and more certain than ever that he would do so unimpeded at home or abroad. March 1936, was perhaps the last moment when a second world war might have been avoided.

Belgium asked to be released from her Locarno commitments, and huddled back behind her policy of neutrality. France shivered with indignation and apprehension but did nothing. Britain consoled herself with Hitler's assurance, given in January 1937, that 'the so-called period of surprises has now come to an end'. The aggressive powers of the world were more active. In November 1936 Germany and Japan signed an Anti-Comintern Pact, a month after the formation of the Rome-Berlin Axis; and a year later Italy also adhered to it. These were not formal alliances and did not involve military commitments. But they were signs that the dissatisfied powers of the world were drawing together, were prepared to pool their nuisance values, and to concert their separate actions so as to cause the greatest embarrassment to the democracies. Already the Italo-Abyssinian War and the resulting controversy about sanctions had given Hitler the magic moment to reoccupy the Rhineland with impunity. Now the further aggression of Japan was to pave the way for Germany's next moves in Europe. Mussolini's estrangement from the western powers enabled Hitler to secure his approval for that union between Germany and Austria which in 1934 Mussolini had prevented. The Fascist International was proving infinitely more efficient and effectual than the Comintern.

In July 1937, when the situation in northern China had apparently calmed down, the Marco Polo Bridge incident occurred which the Japanese used as an excuse to renew the advance into China. Some Japanese forces on night patrol near Peking had, they alleged, been fired on by the Chinese. By the end of the month they had taken Peking and Tientsin as reprisals. This 'Chinese Incident' became, in fact, an undeclared war between Japan and China which dragged on until Japan was defeated in 1945. China appealed to the League as before, but all the great powers now took strenuous evasive action to avoid being committed to measures against Japan while their hands were so full in Europe. In 1938 and again in 1939 the Council of the League advised individual member states to apply separate sanctions against Japan, but they took no action. Britain was disinclined to act unless the United States, a greater Far Eastern power, acted first. The Soviet Union, however, lent direct technical and material help to the Chinese in their resistance to Japan. The tendency of the policies of all the great powers was to concentrate on the rapidly deteriorating position in Europe, and to leave Far Eastern imbroglios in abeyance until they should either have settled themselves or be forced upon the attention of the world.

Rearmament and Appeasement. By the end of 1937, apart from the continuing civil war in Spain, a certain temporary equilibrium had been reached in Europe. Italy and Germany had made their first positive conquests in Abyssinia and the Rhineland. Both needed a little time to digest these acquisitions. On the other hand France and Britain, at last compelled to take the threat to their security seriously, began large if belated programmes of rearmament. The defence programme outlined in the Conservative party's election campaign at the end of 1935 envisaged increasing the Royal Air Force to a level of parity with the newly created German *Luftwaffe*, upon which Göring was lavishing care and money. Rivalry in air power henceforth almost took the place that naval rivalry had taken in British-German relations before 1914. Even in 1935 it was realized, as it was to be proved five years later, that in any modern battle between Germany and Britain air superiority would be one of the most decisive factors. The British navy, too, was overhauled and reconditioned. In May 1937 Baldwin was replaced as Conservative Premier by Neville Chamberlain, who speeded up the process of rearmament. But Winston Churchill, the leading advocate of strenuous resistance to Nazi Germany, who strove with eloquent voice and pen to sound the alarm against Hitler's plans and measures of rearmament, was still excluded from the Conservative government. His own view later was that he had been fortunate in escaping all responsibility for the errors and inadequacies of these years.

France too, under Daladier, began to strengthen her defences. But her military leaders, with the notable exception of the junior officer Charles de Gaulle, and most of her political leaders, with the exceptions of Paul Reynaud and Georges Mandel, were obsessed with the doctrine that in the Maginot Line – the deep belt of heavily armed fortifications now completed along most of the Franco-German frontier – France had impregnable defences. Chief among the exponents of this doctrine of defence was the venerated Marshal Pétain. De Gaulle and Reynaud contended, against this view, that tanks and warplanes, armoured divisions and fleets of bombers, had revolutionized warfare; and that advantage would in future lie with the state that could command the heaviest concentration of highly mechanized and fast-moving striking power. To counter such power France needed not concrete fortifications, however great in depth and novel in design, but more and better tanks and warplanes, as well as anti-tank guns and anti-aircraft guns. French rearmament, however, neglected these weapons. Her defensive strategy had diplomatic repercussions: France neglected her alliances in eastern Europe with Poland, the Soviet Union, and the Little *Entente*,[1] and they in turn knew that a France that could not

1. See p. 624.

effectively attack Germany was of little use to them as an ally. A disastrously mistaken defensive doctrine of modern warfare contributed to the demolition of peace in Europe.

During the three years before war broke out in 1939, attention focused less upon this doctrine than upon the policy shaped by Neville Chamberlain and soon to be known as 'appeasement'. This policy, too, rested upon a theory that proved to be utterly erroneous. It was that the objectives of Hitler and Mussolini were essentially limited in scope; and that they were limited to reversing the wrongs which, Hitler held, had been done to Germany in 1919, and to the achievement of the colonial aims which Italy had for so long cherished in North and East Africa. Chamberlain accepted the view that the dictators had legitimate grievances and that their countries had had a raw deal. He deduced from this that if Britain and France, instead of intransigently resisting their claims, granted them reasonable and timely concessions, they would settle down peacefully. Their strength at home lay in their capacity to exploit genuine nationalist grievances; remove those grievances and their appeal would be blunted, their propaganda would lose its sting. At the same time, since western military and air power had fallen into neglect, he favoured a vigorous programme of rearmament so as to remove any temptation for the dictators to inflate their demands. Such, at least, is the rationalization usually given of Chamberlain's policy of 'appeasement'. Its basic fallacy was, of course, the assumption that the fascist dictators, and in particular a movement as fanatical and dynamic as German national socialism, had limited objectives. Since that was not true, no policy of appeasement of their demands could do more than postpone war, strengthen them for making further aggressions, and gain time in which the western world could gird itself for the inevitable battle. An alternative explanation of Chamberlain's policy has been that he realized this (or came to realize it), but was determined to avoid war for as long as possible in the hope that circumstances might turn in Britain's favour, and in order to build up the necessary armaments before the probable attack should come. He played for peace and for time, for time he believed was on the side of the western powers. If this is a truer assessment of his policy, it has the merits of greater realism and of sounder logic; though it is certain that some time, at least, was on the side of the dictators, since they too needed time to digest their existing conquests, to build the German Siegfried Line or West Wall, and to complete their preparations for general war.

Perhaps nearer to the truth than either of these explanations is the view that Chamberlain, an intelligent but stubborn man wholly inexperienced in diplomacy and almost wholly ignorant of international affairs, approached the desperate situation in Europe with the common sense of the lay businessman. So far as he could do business with the dictators whose realism he appreciated, and secure British interests and security against them by negotiation and peaceful bargaining, he was resolved to preserve the peace at almost all costs. But he hoped that, should this procedure fail, he would at least have gained enough time for French power to reach a scale big enough to deter the dictators by force or for these countries to face war without risking defeat. If so, his policy succeeded only in part, since France was quickly defeated; it incurred a severe cost for Britain in loss of international prestige and repute, since it involved sacrificing other countries in the cause of appeasement; the Britain herself was saved from military disaster in 1940 by only the narrowest of margins. Its only possible defence was one of sheer necessity – that a war earlier would have been even more perilous and more certain to end in defeat; and that involves complex calculations and speculations which still leave the answer in doubt.

The immediately important feature of the policy, which took shape soon after Chamberlain succeeded Baldwin in May 1937, was that it marked the final collapse and abandonment of the doctrine of collective security. Appeasement as pursued by Chamberlain, whatever the theories behind it, was quite incompatible with the notion of collective security as prescribed in the Covenant of the League of Nations. With the open discarding of it went, too, any further attempt to preserve the settlement of 1919. Hitler knew that he could denounce with impunity any other restrictions imposed in the Treaty of Versailles, and first on his list was its prohibition of the *Anschluss* with his native Austria. The conflict between Chamberlain's policy of appeasement and the policy of collective security was for a time obscured because he retained as Foreign Secretary Anthony Eden who was especially closely identified with support for the League of Nations. Eden held that the best way to check the dictators was to rally together all other nations, including the Soviet Union, within the League, and present the dictators with a common front of resistance to any further aggression. It was the policy that Churchill called the making of a 'Grand Alliance'. This matched more closely Britain's traditional policy of preventing any great power from dominating the continent, of preserving a balance of power in Europe. Eden was strongly backed in this policy, from outside the government, by Winston Churchill. His arguments were already weakened by the plain reluctance of other countries – even France – to support Britain in so defiant a policy. The failures of the League had already been too many, the collapse of collective security measures had gone too far, for Eden's policy to appear very hopeful in the winter of 1937.

The failure of economic sanctions against Italy and the refusal of the powers to take any action against Japan had been fatal blows to it. The breach within the government widened until, in February 1938, Eden resigned and was replaced by Lord Halifax, known to have views very similar to Chamberlain's. Henceforth, until March 1939, Chamberlain had a free hand to pursue fully his chosen policy.[1]

The League of Nations, as an organization intended to keep the peace in the world, ceased from this time to have any importance. It lingered on, in a shadowy existence, until in December 1939 it suddenly sprang into action when Finland appealed to it against Russian attack. It pronounced the Soviet Union an aggressor and expelled it from membership. But with general war in Europe even this unprecedented step had small significance. Its functional agencies and its related institutions, especially the International Labour Organization and the Permanent Court, survived the Second World War. In 1945 many of them were either absorbed into or replaced by the various sections of the United Nations. But the League as a general institution for ensuring peace, upon which so many hopes had centred in 1919 and which had attracted the devoted services and support of many noble men and women, died in humiliation and failure. Its last dramatic action, expulsion of the Soviet Union for aggression, paradoxically sealed its fate. In 1945 its resurrection was impossible because the United States and the Soviet Union had then to be comprehended in any general international organization and both, for contrary reasons, bore grudges against the League. Perhaps its decease mattered little, so long as its successor proved fitted to serve the same ends. Its failures, like its achievements, had derived, as they were bound to derive, from the policies of its leading member states. It existed to facilitate and to encourage cooperation among states. It could not make them cooperate if they did not want to. Its epitaph can be as simple as that.

THE SHIFTING BALANCE OF POWER

European affairs between March 1938 and March 1939 were dominated by the full-scale implementation of Neville Chamberlain's policy of appeasement. If it failed, it could never be said that it had not been tried. If it did not satisfy the ambitions of the dictators, that was because they were in fact insatiable. Perhaps its hidden asset was that it left no shadow of doubt in the world about the peaceful intentions of Britain and France, and their extreme reluctance to contemplate war. When war did begin, every moral advantage lay on the side of the

1. See p. 748.

democracies. Even the patience of the most patient statesmen of modern times had been exhausted, and any future question of war guilt was firmly settled from the outset. This was important even at the time, since in Britain and France it did much to heal the bitter internal disagreements about foreign policy which marked the prewar years. In 1939 both countries entered upon war with remarkable unanimity on the home front. In Britain the major opposition party, the Labour party, had hamstrung its opposition to Chamberlain's policy of appeasement by its previous resistance to rearmament and by the activities of its strong pacifist wing led by George Lansbury. It was strong in its unwavering advocacy of supporting the League of Nations and collective security, but in some confusion of mind it regarded this support as making possible extensive disarmament in Britain. Its leaders, still nursing grievances for the events of 1926 and 1931, claimed that if a Conservative government wanted more arms, it was because it was imperialistic, or war-mongering, or influenced by armaments makers. It was unanimously hostile to both the fascist dictators, yet it condemned equally the appeasement measures, and, at first, the rearmament measures, of the Chamberlain government. It went on pressing for support of the League long after the League had ceased to hold out any real hope of checking aggression. With the opposition thus at sixes and sevens, and anyhow too weak in parliament to overthrow the government, Chamberlain had a free hand to implement his own chosen policy in the knowledge that there was at that moment no clear alternative.

The roots of his policy lay not in the mere inertia with which Baldwin had greeted Hitler's reoccupation of the Rhineland in March 1936, but rather in the idea underlying the Hoare-Laval proposals of October 1935 for the appeasement of Mussolini in Abyssinia. Like those proposals, it involved ignoring the fact that flagrant aggression had been committed against a member of the League of Nations; it meant totally discarding any doctrine of collective security as it was understood in the Covenant; it meant trying to break the Rome-Berlin Axis by detaching Italy from Germany and winning her over to the former 'Stresa Front' of 1935, when Britain, France, and Italy had jointly protested against Hitler's first open denunciation of the Versailles settlement as regards German disarmament. Chamberlain's policy in 1938 was, in short, to go back to 1935 – to the days when Mussolini was still not bound to Hitler, when he had been prepared even to help resist Hitler by sending troops to the Brenner Pass to prevent the *Anschluss* with Austria, and when a certain balance of power had still existed in Europe. If it had indeed been possible to restore the conditions of 1935, this policy might have been wise. But with Hitler secure in the Rhineland

and heavily rearming, with Mussolini secure in Abyssinia, with both dictators cooperating so successfully in Spain, it was unlikely that the Axis could easily be broken. It was proving too useful for both, and the interlude of sanctions had permanently soured Mussolini against the western powers.

Yet Chamberlain resolved to try, and already in January 1937 Britain had signed with Italy a so-called 'gentleman's agreement' in which each recognized that the other had vital national interests in the Mediterranean. Chamberlain now extended this agreement into a more comprehensive and definite settlement of the whole field of Anglo-Italian affairs in the Mediterranean. It was over these negotiations that Eden resigned, but the agreement was finally signed in April 1938. Both governments undertook not to indulge in hostile propaganda, and reaffirmed the existing status of the Suez Canal. Italy disclaimed any territorial aims in relation to Spain or Spanish territories overseas and accepted the British formula for the proportional evacuation of foreign volunteers from Spain. Britain undertook to promote the recognition by others of Italian sovereignty over Abyssinia. The agreement, it was hoped, would bring about a more lasting reconciliation of the two powers, and a corresponding alienation of Italy from Germany. It presupposed, of course, that Mussolini was now satisfied.

The Anschluss. Unfortunately, a month before this agreement was signed in Rome, Hitler had already made his next decisive move. On 12 and 13 March he invaded Austria and annexed it to the German Reich, having this time taken care to catch Mussolini by surprise. Economic cooperation between Italy and Austria had greatly increased during the few preceding years, and the absorption of Austria into Germany was a real loss to Italy economically. It also brought German troops on to the Brenner Pass. News of the *Anschluss* caused considerable popular alarm in Italy, and brought no popularity to the Fascist régime. Yet Mussolini was by now so bound to the Hitlerite chariot that he could get no redress; neither could he risk alienating so powerful a neighbour. Here was warning enough that the policy of seeking to split the Axis, favoured by Laval in 1935 and by Chamberlain in 1938, had little likelihood of success.

The events of the *Anschluss* itself conformed to the now familiar pattern of dictatorial aggressions. It was an aim that Hitler had put on the first page of *Mein Kampf*. His whole conception of German living-space (*Lebensraum*), of a Greater German Reich comprising all Germans in Europe, and personal inclination to regain his native land, all combined to make it the next item on his agenda of conquests. The Austrian Chancellor, Kurt von Schuschnigg, had in July 1936 made an agreement with Hitler in which he undertook to follow a policy friendly to Germany, while Hitler promised to respect the independence of Austria. Schuschnigg personally wanted to continue the pro-Italian policy of Dollfuss, but as Mussolini became engaged in Abyssinia and Spain, the likelihood of his backing Austrian independence against Germany obviously diminished. Schuschnigg therefore began to make closer ties with his other neighbours, the states of the Little *Entente* (Czechoslovakia, Yugoslavia, Rumania), and to this Hitler took violent exception. In January 1938 there was an abortive Nazi *putsch*. Summoning the Austrian Chancellor to Berchtesgaden in February, Hitler forced him to admit Arthur Seyss-Inquart, leader of the Austrian National Socialist party, to the Austrian government as Minister of Public Security. With an avowed Nazi and pro-German in charge of the police, the Trojan horse was inside the gates. Schuschnigg tried to checkmate the scheme by arranging a snap plebiscite for 13 March on the issue of Austrian independence. Hitler stirred the Austrian Nazis to create disorder and demanded that the plebiscite be cancelled. Thereupon Schuschnigg capitulated by handing over the office of Chancellor to Seyss-Inquart. The new Chancellor immediately appealed for German troops to restore order, and on 12 March 1938 German troops marched in. They occupied Vienna and moved on to the Brenner, where they exchanged formal greetings with Italian troops. Hitler drove to Braunau, his birthplace, and visited his parents' graves, through streets bedecked with swastikas and crowded with yelling enthusiasts. By 13 March the *coup* was complete, the union of Austria with Germany announced, and Seyss-Inquart became governor of the new *Ostmark*.

The timing of the *coup* could not have been better. In France the ministry of Chautemps had collapsed on 10 March, and Blum was still busy forming a new, more precarious, reconstruction of the Popular Front. Britain, just shaken by Eden's resignation, was content to repeat the escape formula of 1936, that Germany could hardly be stopped from absorbing Germans who wanted to join the Reich. The abdication of Schuschnigg and the installation of Seyss-Inquart by apparently constitutional procedures obscured the real issues. And just to confirm that everyone wanted what had happened, plebiscites were held in April in both Austria and Germany, wherein the usual overwhelming majorities accepted the *Anschluss*.

In one bloodless victory, Hitler had added seven million Austrians to the sixty-six million Germans of the Reich. He immediately absorbed Austria economically and administratively into Germany. The great *Hermann Göring Werke* took over most of the mines and metallurgical works. The *Reichsbank* took over the Austrian National Bank, together with its gold reserves. The Austrian army was incorporated into the Reichswehr. Nazi S.S. men purged the country of Jews, freemasons, liberals, socialists, and communists, sweeping all who did not flee or commit suicide into concentration camps, or merely murdering them on the spot. Cardinal Innitzer of Vienna and most of the Catholic hierarchy welcomed Hitler, though they soon regretted it when Nazi regimentation (*Gleichschaltung*) extended to Catholic youth movements, monasteries, and church properties. Schuschnigg was imprisoned and subjected to gross ill-treatment. Strategically, Hiter's gains were even more significant (see Map 18). Possession of Austria gave him strategic control over the road, rail, and river communications of the middle Danube valley. It gave him contact with Italy, Hungary, and Yugoslavia, and opened up three sides of the 'Bohemian fortress' of Czechoslovakia, his next objective of aggression. His prestige as well as his material strength and resources, both at home and abroad, were immensely enhanced. Most important of all, the lack of resistance to his *coup* and its total success emboldened him to press on fast with the next items on the agenda.

Toward Munich. It had been said in the time of Bismarck that 'he who controls Bohemia controls Europe'. Czechoslovakia, leading member of the Little *Entente* and keystone of France's alliance system in eastern Europe, had by 1938 become a state of considerable military importance. Its population of fifteen million was large enough to maintain an effective army, and its great Skoda armaments works had a large output of munitions. The strong natural defences of the Bohemian mountains had been reinforced by a smaller version of the Maginot Line, manned by thirty-five well-equipped divisions. It was the strongest and richest of the smaller states of eastern Europe because it was also the most highly industrialized and skilled country in that region. The Great Depression had caused difficulties, both economic and social, in Czechoslovakia as in other countries. The moderate coalitions of parliamentary parties which governed it in these years were beset by a host of minority problems and factious feuds. Most threatening of all was the National Socialist party of Konrad Henlein, which attracted strong support among the three million Germans living along the German borders in the Sudetenland.[1] Here, as in Austria, Hitler had ready to hand a fanatical movement that could be used to disrupt the parliamentary system. Tomáš Masaryk, the revered president of the Republic who had done so much to create it in 1919, retired in December 1935, and was succeeded by his loyal lieutenant and Foreign Minister, Eduard Beneš. (Masaryk died in 1937 at the age of eighty-seven.) With Beneš as presi-

1. See p. 691.

dent and a Slovak, Milan Hodza, as Premier at the head of a coalition government of moderates the country faced the growing threat of Germany with anxiety but courage. In May 1936, the government, like its contemporaries elsewhere, claimed emergency powers under an enabling act to suppress extremist parties and take measures for the defence of the state. This roused agitation not only from the followers of Henlein, against whom the measures were principally aimed, but also from the various other parties – Magyar, Slovak, and Ruthenian – which represented the main minority groups of this multinational state. Henlein was thus able to demand great provincial and local rights for the Germans with some approval from other minority nationalities in the country.

Despite these advantages, the strength of Czechoslovakia was such that Hitler had to move with care and circumspection. Under treaties of mutual assistance with France in 1925 and with the Soviet Union in 1935, the Czechs were assured of immediate aid from both should they be attacked, though the Soviet guarantee was timed to operate only after the French had implemented their guarantee. To preclude Soviet intervention, therefore, it was wise first to preclude French. In March 1938 both France and the Soviet Union reaffirmed that they would honour their obligations to Czechoslovakia. But a week later Chamberlain, in the House of Commons, refused to give assurance that Britain would support France should she be called upon to help Czechoslovakia against German aggression. Britain had no separate commitment to defend the Czechs, apart from that involved in the collective security provisions of the Covenant. Chamberlain, consistently enough, was opposed to any collective efforts to coerce or check the dictators, whether they were made through the League or through the system of mutual assistance organized by France, the Soviet Union, and Czechoslovakia. Such action, he believed, would provoke Hitler to war, whereas he was committed to direct piecemeal negotiation. It was Chamberlain's persistence in this policy, even after the seizure of Austria, which gave Hitler his opening. France would be unlikely to act without Britain, Russia without France. If Britain could be induced to initiate separate negotiations to settle the problems of Czechoslovakia, Hitler was likely to avoid all collective resistance and repeat his former success in demolishing his victims one by one. It was his adept exploitation of this opportunity that led to the Munich settlement.

In April 1938 Henlein, duly briefed during a visit to Berlin, demanded the setting up of a virtually autonomous German province within the Czech state. Beneš and Hodza rejected the proposal but offered wider minority rights that fell short of autonomy. During municipal elections the following month Henlein's Nazi Party behaved with a violence that seemed calculated to invoke German intervention. But the Czech government ordered partial mobilization, Chamberlain warned Hitler that Britain might become involved if war broke out, and the first crisis passed. Like the temporary easing of tension in 1913, it made the next crisis worse. Hitler, who had probably hoped to get what he wanted in May, ordered the plans for a military attack on Czechoslovakia ('Case Green') to be ready by 1 October. He suffered, reported the British ambassador, 'the worst brain-storm of the year'. Chamberlain, alarmed at how near war had been in May, arranged that Lord Runciman – a businessman like himself and equally ignorant of central European affairs – should be sent to Prague in the hope of mediating between Czechs and Germans. The French Foreign Minister, George Bonnet, shared in Chamberlain's views more completely than his Premier, Daladier, and he supported the proposal. Early in August, Lord Runciman arrived in Prague. Within a month the Czech government was persuaded to grant practically all the concessions, amounting to virtual German autonomy, for which Henlein had asked in April. Henlein now rejected all these offers and broke off negotiations, while at the Nuremberg rally Hitler fulminated anew against the 'Bolsheviks of Prague'. After consultations with Daladier, Chamberlain undertook to make a personal appeal to Hitler. On 15 September he flew to Berchtesgaden.

The meeting between the two men in the *Führer's* mountain-nest at Berchtesgaden is one of the most dramatic, and also the most pathetic, scenes in contemporary history. On one side was the anxious, harassed Birmingham businessman, the civilian figure with the umbrella, resolved to avoid the outbreak of war if it were humanly possible, and stubbornly unconvinced that even now there was any international dispute that could not be settled reasonably and finally without war if only each side fully understood the issues involved; on the other, the crazed, paranoiac dictator, the fanatic of the Swastika, equally stubbornly bent on war for the domination of the 'master race' in Europe, but anxious to win all his preliminary victories as cheaply and cunningly as he could. For three hours the interview lasted. Hitler confronted Chamberlain with a blunt insistence that no concession of autonomy would now suffice, and that the territories inhabited by Sudeten Germans must be ceded outright to Germany on the principle of 'self-determination'. This abrupt shift in demand made nonsense of the whole visit, as well as of Lord Runciman's mission to Prague. Hitherto all British intervention had been conducted on the presupposition that there was a real dispute between the Czech government and its internal German minority which could, by adequate concession, be resolved. Runciman, as he himself insisted, had no commission to mediate between Czechoslovakia and the German Reich. By confronting Chamberlain at Berchtesgaden with a demand for the outright cession of the Sudetenland to Germany, Hitler avowed the real objective of his whole policy and shattered the only reasonable basis on which any further British mediation could take place. But he also convinced Chamberlain that he meant to go to war if the demand were not granted, and induced him to make a joint effort with France to extract even this new concession from the Czechs.

It was at this point that Chamberlain's behaviour became most controversial. To mediate, as a sort of arbitrator, in the internal affairs of a foreign state was in itself a doubtful procedure. It was shouldering a responsibility that was unusual and immense, though even that might be justified in the wholehearted search for peace. To undertake the positive coercion of a friendly government into ceding territory to a hostile neighbour was an unwonted role for any British Prime Minister. So intricately had national and international issues become intertwined that Chamberlain, unfamiliar as he was with world affairs, seems scarcely to have appreciated the new role into which Hitler tricked him at Berchtesgaden. 'In spite of the hardness and ruthlessness I thought I saw in his face,' wrote Chamberlain at the time, 'I got the impression that here was a man who could be relied upon when he had given his word.' Daladier and Bonnet visited London, and the two governments drew up a joint plan.

So bent were they upon avoiding a general war at all costs, that on 19 September the British and French governments confronted President Beneš with their joint decision that he must cede to Germany all territories where more than half the inhabitants were Sudeten Germans. They added that they thought the proposal reasonable, and would not consider themselves responsible for the consequences of its rejection. It meant, of course, making Germany a present not only of extensive Czechoslovak territory, but also of some 800,000 Czech citizens and the whole of the Czech Maginot Line, and leaving the rest of the country exposed to any subsequent attack. Faced with no alternative, feeling deserted by their friends, and yielding, as they said, to unheard-of pressure, Beneš and Hodza agreed even to this devastating concession. On 22 September, with this surrender in his pocket, Chamberlain flew to meet Hitler again at Godesberg on the Rhine. Meanwhile Poland and Hungary, eager for any pickings that might be going, put in claims of their own against Czechoslovakia. The Poles coveted Teschen, the Hungarians Ruthenia.

The visit to Godesberg did something to disillusion Chamberlain. Making play with the Polish and Hungarian claims, Hitler now demanded immediate occupation of German-speaking areas by German troops. He swept aside Chamberlain's proposals for a gradual transfer, and a stormy interview followed. Next day Hitler embodied his demands in a memorandum. Military occupation must begin in two days' time, and not a cow must be moved out of the Sudetenland. Chamberlain reported that 'the language and the manner of the document ... would profoundly shock public opinion in neutral countries, and I bitterly reproached the Chancellor for his failure to respond in any way to the efforts which I had made to secure peace'. Hitler, muttering 'You are the only man to whom I have ever made a concession', agreed to move forward the date to 1 October. He declared, with great earnestness, that this was the last of his ambitions in Europe. Plebiscites, he agreed, might be held in marginal areas during November. Even while they were meeting, opinion hardened in Britain, France, and Czechoslovakia.

On 24 September the new Czech government of 'national concentration', under General Syrovy, ordered general mobilization and declared the Godesberg Memorandum 'absolutely and unconditionally unacceptable'. On the same day the French mobilized some 600,000 reservists, and held military consultations with the British general staff. Hitler in Berlin made still more violent speeches against the Czechs, but added, 'This is the last territorial claim I shall make in Europe'. On 28 September the British navy was mobilized, and Chamberlain broadcast: 'How horrible, fantastic, incredible, it is that we should be digging trenches and trying on gas-masks here because of a quarrel in a faraway country between people of whom we know nothing.' He wrote to both Hitler and Mussolini, proposing a four-power meeting of Britain, France, Germany, and Italy to settle the crisis. The French did the same. While he was nearing the end of his speech in the House of Commons, describing his recent efforts to avert war in Europe, Chamberlain was handed an invitation from Hitler to attend a four-power conference at Munich the next morning. He broke off his speech. 'Mr Speaker, I cannot say any more. I am sure that the House will be ready to release me now, to go and see what I can make of this last effort.' It was a quarter past four in the afternoon, and the House broke into an outburst of cheering such as it had seldom known. Next morning Chamberlain flew to Munich, believing that the House of Commons wanted peace at almost any price.

The Munich conference was short and produced an arrangement little different from the Godesberg memorandum, save that the four powers agreed to act as an international commission to supervise the transfer of territories, and agreed to guarantee the new frontiers of Czechoslovakia (see Map 20). The Czech representatives were not admitted to the conversations. On 30 September they were confronted by Chamberlain and Daladier with the agreed terms, which they now had no option but to accept. Collective security for the Czechs had been replaced by collective blackmail to preserve the peace. Late the next afternoon, when Chamberlain alighted at Heston airport in England, he waved above his head a piece of paper. On it he and Hitler had jointly declared that they renounced war in the settlement of any other national difficulties. 'This,' he exclaimed, 'means peace in our time.' There was universal relief that war had been averted. But peace in our time? Only if Chamberlain were right in his belief that 'here was a man who could be relied upon when he had given his word'. It seemed astonishingly late in the day to go on believing that Hitler was such a man. Duff Cooper, First Lord of the Admiralty, did not believe it and resigned his office next day. Chamberlain went on believing it until March 1939.

Chamberlain, nevertheless, now embarked upon a programme of rearmament such as Britain had never before undertaken in time of peace. All her efforts were redoubled. The French also renewed their efforts. The public mood changed in both countries when it came to be realized how much Hitler had gained, and how far the execution of the Munich agreement exceeded even the concessions agreed to. Germany gained the whole defences, most of the industrial areas and vital communications in Bohemia and Moravia, half the Czech coal mines, glass and textile industries, half their largest towns. The western powers had lost an ally, in the strategic centre of the continent, which had possessed 2,000 planes and an army of one and a half million efficient and well-equipped fighting men. Churchill summed up the painful realization in Britain and elsewhere: 'The German dictator, instead of snatching his victuals from the table, has been content to have them served to him course by course.' How true this was became apparant by 15 March 1939. The usual disorders occurred earlier in the month, the German armies in Bavaria and Austria moved toward the frontiers of the truncated Czech state on 13 March, and on the fourteenth the Czech President, Hacha, was summoned to Berlin. From ten o'clock at night until nearly four in the morning he was subjected to third-degree methods until he was induced to agree to surrender his country to Germany, under Göring's threat that Prague would be bombed to rubble if he did not. This, of course, he had no constitutional right to do. But it gave the cloak of pseudo-legality so beloved by Hitler, and at six in the morning the German armies occupied Bohemia and Moravia; Hungary seized Ruthenia. The Republic was extinguished. Germany thereby gained the Skoda armaments works, large stocks of munitions and planes, reserves of gold, and rich economic resources in timber, agriculture, and manpower. Though British opinion

MAP 20. PARTITIONS OF CZECHOSLOVAKIA AND POLAND, 1938–9
The prelude to the Second World War was Germany's demolition of the two main eastern allies of France and Britain. At Munich in September 1938 Czechoslovakia was compelled to give up the Sudetenland, which included nearly three million Germans but also her great western industries and fortifications. Poland and Hungary demanded border territories, Teschen and southern Slovakia. In March 1939 Germany occupied all the rest of Czechoslovakia. In August she made with Russia the Nazi–Soviet Pact which bore fruit, a month later, in their joint invasion and partition of Poland (see also Maps 14, 15, and 26).

was stunned, Chamberlain explained that his guarantee could scarcely apply to a state that had ceased to exist. But at last the policy of appeasement was at an end. Hitler, by violating his most solemn promises of less than six months before, by making abundantly plain that his territorial ambitions were not limited to acquiring Germans for the Reich but extended to indefinite horizons of conquest, by exhausting even the patience of the most ardent apostles of appeasement, ensured that war would come.

Lost Equilibrium. The story of the shift in the balance of power in Europe between 1935 and March 1939 is, in material terms, one of accumulative gains of power by the Axis states. The rearmament and reintroduction of conscription in Germany, the occupation of the Rhineland, of Austria, of Czechoslovakia, were all net gains to the Axis and severe losses to the western democratic powers. In aggregate they demolished all the forms of security against German resurgence which had been devised after 1918 – whether territorial in the Rhineland, diplomatic in the existence of the Little *Éntente*, international in the system of collective security. International relations deteriorated, during the years of appeasement, into a naked conflict of power between rival camps in which more and more of the assets were appropriated by the dictators. They concerted action while Britain and France fell out of step. They pursued dynamic, aggressive policies while the powers most closely interested in preserving the settlement and a balance of power were inert as if paralysed, and were finally tricked even into conniving at the destruction of their own ally. This fact will long remain one of the most puzzling features of contemporary history. But at least a partial explanation is already possible.

First, at least in time, must rank the widespread belief in all democratic countries, but strongest perhaps in Britain and the United States, that the settlement of 1919 had been harsh to Germany and less than just to Italy; that impossible demands had been made on postwar Germany in matters of recognizing war guilt, paying reparations, and enforcing disarmament; and that peace could not be solidly founded until such wrongs had been righted and such grievances removed. Thus every aggressive move that could be presented as a mere redressing of a grievance deriving from the peace settlement of 1919 aroused little protest or hostility. Similarly, minority problems in eastern Europe were treated as imperfections in that settlement, as themselves problems soluble by reasonable arrangements of frontiers. Fascist propaganda was so successful in perpetuating this belief that few realized that the Sudeten Germans had never been within the frontiers of Germany at all. They had been, like the Czechs and Poles, citizens of Austria-Hungary. Minority problems were in every instance the excuse, not the cause, of German action. The worst-treated German minority in Europe lived under Italian rule, which Axis diplomacy found it convenient to overlook; the Sudeten Germans were among the best-treated German minorities in Europe. The tactics of the dictators may be well enough illustrated from the papers of Count Ciano, Italian Foreign Minister. Recording a conversation with the Hungarian minister at the height of the Munich crisis, he records:

M. Villani further informed me, in strict secrecy, that, during the recent conversations in Berchtesgaden, Imrédy and Kánya again expressed to Hitler their firm determination to reach a solution of the Hungarian question. With this in view, it is proposed to *cause incidents to occur* in the areas inhabited by Hungarians and in Slovakia itself. The *Führer* encouraged them....

Minorities were used, as foreign Nazi parties were used, as levers with which to loosen a victim for attack and prepare its destruction. All talk of justice for minorities came ill from a state which, in November 1938, launched a violent pogrom against its whole Jewish minority, and mulcted it of nearly £83 million as a collective fine for the murder of one German official. Yet western statesmen, backed by opinion at home, approached the Munich crisis as if it really were a dispute about minority rights, instead of a major onslaught upon their whole defensive strategy and diplomatic system in eastern Europe.

A further explanation lies in the overburdening of France as the main bulwark of the existing European settlement in Europe. That overburdening dated back to 1919, when France was deprived of the material territorial guarantees against Germany which Foch and Clemenceau wanted, and also of the British and United States guarantees of support in return for which she agreed to forgo the territorial securities.[1] France added to her own burdens by her feverish quest for alliances in eastern Europe – one of which she had to renounce at Munich. Neither in spirit nor in military power was France equal to the task of keeping Europe at peace without the firm support of Britain and the United States. Her faith in the Maginot Line was a fatal form of escapism. Once Britain (and the Dominions) lost faith in any attempt to check German resurgence and sought instead a policy of appeasement, France could do nothing but follow in the wake of Britain. She dared not risk being left alone to resist the might of Germany.

To this situation two further facts contributed. One was the isolationism and separatism of the United States; the other the ostracism of Soviet Russia. Germany and her allies had been defeated in 1918 not by an alliance between France and several small powers, but only by an alliance between France, Britain, Russia, and eventually the United

1. See p. 628.

States. Only some comparable union of power could prevent German resurgence. The contribution of the United States was withdrawn when she refused to ratify the Treaty of Versailles or to join the League of Nations. It was further nullified by her continued policy of isolationism, though events after 1935 modified even this. The new Neutrality Act, passed in May 1937 and derived from experience of the Italo-Abyssinian and Spanish civil wars, gave the President authority to allow the export of goods, other than arms and ammunition, to a belligerent who could ship and pay for such goods on delivery. This 'cash-and-carry' clause was calculated to favour the western powers, who, unlike the Axis, controlled the seas and had large investments and credits in the United States. It was the first big step away from a neutrality that was also isolationism. Cordell Hull, American Secretary of State, began to appeal for 'a cooperative effort' among nations to preserve peace, and to condemn 'aloofness' as an invitation to aggression. President Roosevelt's exhortations and notes during the Munich crisis bore no fruit, and its outcome bred in the United States both fear and a new 'isolationism of disgust'. But the government began to make huge appropriations for the armed services and to stock-pile raw materials needed in war. American power was beginning to make itself felt again in the world, though still at long range and without any decisive influence on the trend of events in Europe.

If the United States was a reluctant dragon, the Soviet Union was a dragon whom her allies feared almost as much as their enemies. In the balance of power in Europe her possible contribution was alternately besought and rejected by French and British diplomacy. Until the Soviet Union joined the League of Nations, there was little expectation that her weight would be felt in Europe as a regular counterpoise to Germany's. But why, thereafter, was it not more systematically felt? It was involved, but without success, in Spain. In 1935 France signed the Franco-Soviet treaty of mutual assistance, and it was ratified in February 1936 – in time for Germany to denounce it as a violation of Locarno, introducing a new balance of power which she must at once redress by occupying the Rhineland. It was accompanied by a Czech-Soviet mutual assistance pact, to operate only if France had already helped Czechoslovakia against an attack. Before and after Munich, Maxim Litvinov, the Soviet foreign commissar, repeated assurances that the Soviet Union would stand by its treaty obligations to the Czechs. Litvinov's slogan that 'peace is indivisible' meant creating an international 'popular front' of peace-loving powers. Yet the Czechs never invoked this proffered help; the Soviet Union was not invited to send representatives to Munich; and the whole crisis was settled with deliberate ostracism of the Soviet Union. It is clear enough why. Chamberlain was anxious to hold a four-power meeting as the only preventative of war, Hitler would not have agreed to any such meeting that included the Soviet Union, and the Czechs neither expected nor wanted Soviet help without French help, which was plainly not forthcoming. But the whole incident convinced Stalin that Britain and France were now concerned to direct Germany's expansion eastward, away from themselves and against Russia. He therefore denounced the pact with the Czechs and prepared to carry out his 'Munich in reverse' when the next opportunity arose. Appeasement, he argued, was a game at which two could play. The result was the German-Soviet Pact of August 1939, and the subsequent partition of Poland.[1]

The fundamental fact behind the whole Munich crisis was that the power immediately available in Europe to check German aggression in September 1938 was insufficient, and the power potentially available for the same purpose – in the British Dominions, the United States, and the Soviet Union – was, for various reasons, uncertain in its application. The rearmament programme of Britain had only half begun, and her air defences in particular were unprepared; the same was true of France. The German air force was numerically superior to the air power of Britain, France, and Czechoslovakia combined. The terror of mass bombing of civilian cities, which proved serious enough in the event, in 1938 filled everyone with an even greater horror in prospect. The Dominions, though loyal to Britain and likely to remain loyal in the event of war, were inclined to feel no less strongly than Chamberlain that Czechoslovakia was 'a far-away country' of which they knew nothing; and Hitler's propaganda against the 'Bolsheviks of Prague' as against the 'Bolsheviks of Madrid', was not without some effect. French opinion, still profoundly divided and paralysed by defeatists and appeasers on the Right, by pacifists on the Left, was only too aware of France's proximity to German bomber fields. United States opinion was still too strongly isolationist, Soviet military power too unreliable after the great army purges and also too incalculable in its motives, to lend much assurance. The arguments in favour of an empirical approach to international disputes – of tackling each dispute on its merits as it arose, in a persistent endeavour to escape from the heartbreak horror of a second world war – still carried widespread conviction. Churchill passed the final verdict on Munich at the time.

We have passed an awful milestone in our history, when the whole equilibrium of Europe has been deranged, and the terrible words have, for the time being, been pronounced against the western democracies: 'Thou art weighed in the balance and found wanting!'

1. See p. 756.

DRIFT TOWARD WAR

The last year of peace was dominated by an atmosphere of fatalism reminiscent of 1914. Both camps were busy gathering strength – the dictators digesting their gains, the democracies making feverish efforts to build up their armaments to a point of better preparedness. Munich taught a bitter lesson: that inferiority of power immediately available in Europe would bring humiliation and might bring general defeat. No time must now be lost. Hitler's cynical occupation of the remainder of Czechoslovakia in March 1939 dispelled all lingering illusions and re-inforced the sense of urgency in rearmament. In April, Britain, for the first time in her history, introduced compulsory military service in peace-time. For good measure, Hitler seized from Lithuania the port of Memel, given to her in the settlement of 1919; on Good Friday, Mussolini, anxious no doubt to claim some compensatory glory when his partner was gaining so much, invaded Albania, which under King Zog had already become virtually an Italian puppet state. This action violated several treaties, ranging from the Treaty of Tirana of 1927 which had made a defensive alliance between the two countries, to the recent British-Italian 'gentleman's agreement' about the Mediterranean. The crown of Albania was transferred to King Victor Emmanuel III of Italy.

Britain retaliated to these fresh aggressions by extending guarantees to the countries most clearly next on the list; to Poland, Greece, Ru-mania, and Turkey. France followed, as was now customary, in Britain's wake. The British guarantee to Poland, given on 31 March 1939, was destined to become the formal reason for Britain's declaration of war on Germany five months later. It was an abrupt departure from traditional British diplomacy, in that it committed Britain to act in eastern Europe and it left the Poles themselves free to determine the occasion when British aid should be invoked. Britain and France committed themselves, in Chamberlain's words, 'in the event of any action which clearly threatened Polish independence, and which the Polish government ac-cordingly considered it vital to resist with their national forces ... to lend the Polish government all the support in their power'. The Soviet proposal, for a six-power conference including Poland, Rumania, and Turkey, was rejected because Poland feared Russia as much as Germany. The next month Britain and France gave guarantees in similar terms to Greece and Rumania, and in May, Britain signed with Turkey a mutual assistance pact, to operate immediately 'in the event of aggression lead-ing to war in the Mediterranean area'. France again followed suit. In April, too, negotiations were resumed with the Soviet Union which now, clearly, controlled the balance of power in Europe. Neither the Axis nor the democracies could henceforth engage in war without reaching some prior understanding with Russia. Litvinov stipulated that any mutual assistance pact or military convention between the Soviet Union and the two western powers should include a guarantee of all the states between the Baltic and the Black Sea. Most of these states were, like Poland, opposed to receiving Russian assistance, which they feared would entail subservience, and the western powers rejected the proposal. It was the final rebuff. On 3 May Litvinov was dismissed and replaced by Molotov. The Russian minister who was most identified with Soviet participation at Geneva, with the era of 'Popular Fronts' and western orientation of policy went, and the man who was a narrower Russian nationalist took his place. It was the crucial turning point in Soviet policy in Europe.

The German-Soviet Pact, 1939. After 31 May 1939 Hitler knew that any attack on Poland (for which his plan of campaign, 'Case White', was ready in April) would involve Germany in war with both Britain and France, and also therefore with the British Commonwealth and the French Empire. Stalin knew this too, and since by mere geography Hitler must invade Poland or Rumania before attacking the Soviet Union, he knew that the Soviet Union now enjoyed an automatic immunity from finding itself attacked without allies. There could not now be war in the East without there also being war in the West. But in the light of the rebuffs at Munich and the more recent rejections of Soviet proposals, he did not draw from this the inference that he could safely ally with the western powers. He drew the contrary inference, that since he now controlled the balance of power in Europe, he could afford to make terms with Germany which would ensure, in any partition of Poland, a large share of Polish territory for himself. This would preserve a buffer of foreign soil between the Soviet Union and Germany, and encourage Hitler to direct his first main onslaught against the West. Stalin used his new-found immunity to buy both space and time, and to gamble on a long, mutually destructive war between central and western Europe from which the Soviet Union could derive both security and profit. The idea of the Nazi-Soviet pact was born of the Franco-British guarantee to Poland. At the same time, it made the German attack on Poland absolutely certain, for the imponderable contribution of Soviet power as a deterrent to Axis aggression was entirely nullified.

The counterweight of United States power began to make itself felt a little more directly in the European arena. In mid April, President Roosevelt addressed to the two dictators a request for assurances that for ten years to come they would not attack or invade a list of thirty countries which he named. It produced outbursts of abuse in Italy and Germany, and Hitler's answer took the form of a long speech to the Reichstag in which he reviewed the whole story of the Nazi rise to power and its battle against Versailles, the League, the Jews, and the other stock targets of Nazi rhetoric. He also took the opportunity to renounce the Anglo-German naval agreement of 1935 and the German-Polish pact of 1934. But when the United States in 1938-9 was appropriating $1,156 million for the navy alone, her power could not be indefinitely ignored. Hitler doubtless relied upon Japan, and American fears of Russia, to re-inforce American devotion to neutrality. When Hitler duly attacked Po-land on 1 September, President Roosevelt broadcast the warning: 'When peace has been broken anywhere, peace of all countries everywhere is in danger.' It had strange echoes of Litvinov's doctrine that 'peace is in-divisible'; but as yet the United States contented itself with 'hemisphere defence', the latest version of the Monroe Doctrine.

With the power of the two greatest non-European states thus kept out of the European arena, Hitler proceeded with his plans to attack Po-land. He and Mussolini, on 22 May, converted the Axis into a formal military alliance, the so-called 'Pact of Steel'. It was signed by Ciano and the Nazi Foreign Minister, Joachim von Ribbentrop, with much ceremony in the presence of Hitler and Göring. It was one of the most frankly offensive alliances in diplomatic history, for Article 3 provided for automatic mutual help 'if it should happen ... that one of them becomes involved in warlike complications with another Power or Powers', regardless of who was responsible for such 'complications'. In effect Mussolini gave Hitler a free hand to attack Poland. On 23 May Hitler held a meeting of his chiefs of staff at which he warned them not to expect a Polish Munich, but to be ready for war with Britain and France, and perhaps also with Russia. A week later he made non-aggres-sion pacts with Estonia and Latvia. The usual flow of propaganda and accusations against the chosen victim was switched on. Polish treatment of its German minority was scandalous and must be improved; the Free City of Danzig, created in 1919 under the League, must fall to Ger-many. Nazi ingenuity was evidently wearing thin. But the master stroke of his preparations, in his own view, was the achievement of the pact with the Soviet Union. It grew out of negotiations of a trade agreement which began as early as May, but only during July and early August did Russian readiness become clear and Hitler's own plans take shape.

On 23 August Molotov and Ribbentrop signed a simple non-aggres-sion pact for ten years' duration, like many others which European states had already signed. Its publication took the world by surprise. But its real purpose was embodied in a 'secret additional protocol', signed at the same time. Therein spheres of influence were agreed for eastern Europe. Germany, in short, was to have Lithuania and western Poland;

the Soviet Union was to have Finland, Estonia, Latvia, the eastern part of Poland and the Rumanian province of Bessarabia. Hitler had no such scruples as Chamberlain or Daladier about sacrificing the independence of the smaller eastern states. It was like Brest-Litovsk in reverse, for Hitler calculated on recovering territories within the Russian sphere eventually by the defeat of that power. He even hoped that the dramatic publication of the pact might stun Britain and France into repudiating their pledges to Poland, and experimented with conciliatory gestures. This hope was dispelled when Chamberlain wrote to him affirming categorically Britain's determination to stand by her pledge, and on 25 August made a formal mutual assistance pact with Poland. That evening Mussolini telephoned a message to Hitler, declaring that 'if Germany attacks Poland and Poland's allies attack Germany, I propose not myself to take any military initiative, given the actual state of Italian preparation. . . .' So much for the 'Pact of Steel'. Hitler cared little, though he would have liked a show of Axis solidarity. He had squared Russia, and could easily defeat Poland.

The Outbreak of War. At dawn on 1 September, in full knowledge that he was starting a general European war but without declaring war at all, he sent his armoured (*panzer*) divisions and planes into Poland. Even now he may have hoped for another Munich. Mussolini and Ciano certainly worked hard for one, knowing Italy's weakness. But on 3 September Britain, and within a few hours France, declared war on Germany. Hitler's interpreter, Paul Schmidt, later described how the *Führer* received the news of Britain's ultimatum.

When I had completed my translation there was silence at first. . . . For a while Hitler sat in his chair deep in thought, and stared rather worriedly into space. Then he broke his silence with . . . 'What are we going to do now?'

That same Sunday morning Neville Chamberlain broadcast the news that Britain was now at war with Germany.

We have a clear conscience, we have done all that any country could do to establish peace, but a situation in which no word given by Germany's ruler could be trusted, and no people or country could feel themselves safe, had become intolerable. . . . For it is evil things we shall be fighting against, brute force, bad faith, injustice, oppression, and persecution. But against them I am certain that the right will prevail.

The major issue of the war, when it began in September 1939, was as simple as that. The policy of appeasement had failed because it was based upon a fundamental misconception of the nature of National

Socialism in Germany and of Hitler himself. Had Nazism been a normal nationalist movement, guided by utilitarian considerations and realistic views of national interests – had the Nazi leaders been even averagely normal men of reason and sense – Chamberlain's policy might have succeeded. It was impossible to set limits to the expansion and tyranny of Nazism other than by destroying it; it was impossible to make any terms with Hitler because he would never be bound by them. Nazism and Hitler were caricatures of the depths of cynicism and mistrust to which lack of respect for treaty obligations or promises had reduced international relations. The movement and its leader were nihilistic – bent upon total destruction of the liberal matrix of civilization which they detested, and if in this they failed, they were bent upon self-destruction. Statesmen acclimatized to the more rational, humane ways of democracy found – with a few notable exceptions – such a movement virtually incomprehensible. They shut their eyes to it as long as they could, submitting to its seductive propaganda and its incessant self-pity; and even when they were forced to look at it straight, they were still so sickened by the thought of general war that they went on deluding themselves with the hope that its dynamism might be spent, its limits found. But the lust for power and further conquest fed on success, the hoped-for limits constantly receded, until the thing had to be confronted in its full horror. The invasion of Prague in March 1939 and the total dismemberment of Czechoslovakia made clear to Britain and France 'the great issues' at stake. They were nothing less than the very existence of all free states of Europe, and possibly of the world. The bestial pogrom against the Jews in November 1938, though only the most spectacular of many previous Nazi onslaughts on the Jews, suddenly illuminated, especially in the United States, the inner nature of Nazism. 'I could scarcely believe,' said President Roosevelt, 'that such things could occur in a twentieth-century civilization.' Nazism was incredible – that was part of its strength.

Yet never had an aggressor made his ambitions known more plainly beforehand, never had a party more repeatedly and consistently given warning of what it proposed to attempt. It was all set out in *Mein Kampf* in 1924, in the party programme, in the speeches and writing of the leaders and above all of Hitler himself. The party could hardly even be charged with deception, for its purposes had been from the first avowed and unashamed. They were so preposterous that no one would believe them. Just as the Nazis grew in strength and captured power in Germany because few took them seriously and some hoped to outwit them, so Nazi Germany came to dominate Europe because civilized men could not believe that so monstrous a régime could exist or succeed. It was overlooked that the resources of power at the disposal of any government of a great modern industrial state are imponderable, and that power, made almost absolute, becomes absolutely corrupting. The Second World War began as the first brave concerted effort of western Europe's two oldest nations to defy and destroy this power.

PART NINE

WAR AND PEACE
1939–63

THE six years' war which Hitler began on 1 September 1939 bore so many resemblances to the Great War of 1914 that from the first it was regarded, accurately enough, as the Second World War. So much had the problem of German resurgence preoccupied the attention of European governments between 1919 and 1939 that the interwar years soon came to be known as the 'Twenty Years' Truce', and the whole era between 1914 and 1945 as another 'Thirty Years' War'. There were, indeed, a thousand subtle affinities and links between the two wars that engulfed Europe within a single generation. Both began in eastern Europe; both arose from treaty obligations towards smaller powers; both involved an initial alliance between Britain and France arrayed against a German-dominated central Europe; both implicated Germany, before their end, in a war on two fronts, and were won by a grand alliance of Britain, France, Russia, and the United States; both changed their character and dimensions as they proceeded, until they engaged most powers in the world; both left behind them tangled problems of reconstruction and resettlement which taxed to the utmost the ingenuity and resources of mankind.

Yet the obvious similarities should not obscure the equally significant differences. The second was much more truly than the first a world war, for it saw prolonged fighting in the Pacific as well as in the Atlantic, in Asia and Africa as well as in Europe, the defeat of Japan as well as of Germany and Italy. It brought the collapse not of Russia but of France, revolution not in Russia but in China, the partition not of Turkey and Austria-Hungary but of Germany itself. The greatest similarity between the two wars was that the eventual outcome of each was quite unforeseen and largely unintended when it began: their main historical significance lies in what the course of events itself led to, rather than in the planned objectives of any belligerent.

Again, it is especially important for the aftermath of war to be considered in the closest possible relation to the course of the war itself. If the period of settlement after 1918 must properly be regarded as lasting at least five years after the end of hostilities,[1] the period of settlement after 1945 – as befits the aftermath of a war which lasted half as long

1. See p. 614.

again and extended over a much larger area of the world – must be regarded as lasting for at least a decade after the end of hostilities. The aftermath included a sequence of secondary wars – wars in Palestine, in Indo China, in Korea, in Algeria – all of which were part of the same great story. It included, too, a series of revolutions, in the internal structure of western European states, in the connexions between these states and their colonial territories, and in the whole fabric of international relations and organizations. These revolutions had taken clearer if not final shape by 1960. For all these reasons, the second great era of 'War and Peace' in twentieth-century Europe must be regarded as extending from 1939 to 1960.

CHAPTER 29

THE SECOND WORLD WAR, 1939–45

FROM EUROPEAN TO GLOBAL WAR, 1939–41

UNTIL the Japanese attacked Pearl Harbour, the United States naval base in Hawaii, on 7 December 1941, the war remained essentially a European war. It remained so despite the immediate entry of the overseas Dominions in September 1939, despite the great material aid then given to Britain by the United States under the arrangements first of 'cash and carry' and then (after March 1941) of 'Lend-Lease', and despite Germany's attack on the Soviet Union in June 1941. Until December 1941 the battlefield was exclusively European and Atlantic; thereafter it became also Asiatic and Pacific. Until that major turning-point was reached, the war in Europe passed through three main phases: the first, of unbroken German victories against Poland, Scandinavia, the Low Countries, and France, ended in the Battle of Britain in the summer of 1940; the second, of Balkan warfare, of desert warfare in North Africa, and of naval warfare, ended with the German onslaught on the Soviet Union in June 1941; the third, the first fierce battles of the eastern front, culminated at the end of 1941 in the advance of Germany 600 miles into Soviet territory.

The first phase began with the swift conquest and partition of Poland, within a month of war beginning. Hitler sent fifty-six divisions against the thirty which Poland could muster to oppose him, and they included nine highly mechanized heavy armoured divisions. They were supported by overwhelming air superiority, which enabled the Germans during the first few days to destroy the 500 planes of the Polish air force. They advanced in two great pincer-movements, one enveloping all the Polish forces and industrial areas west of Warsaw, the other closing its jaws east of Warsaw, leaving the capital to hold out in a siege of remarkable heroism until 27 September. So swift was the German advance, and so decisive its victory, that the Soviet Union had to speed up its own plans. On 17 September it began to occupy the eastern areas of Poland assigned to it in the pact of 23 August. The German and Russian armies met, appropriately enough, at Brest Litovsk. This brought Russian troops to the frontiers of Hungary, which spread alarm throughout the Balkans and Italy. In Moscow Ribbentrop and Stalin met to rearrange the previous agreements so as to allocate Lithuania to the Soviet Union and additional areas of central Poland (including Lublin and Warsaw) to Germany (see Map 20). From a mainly German victory Stalin gained all three Baltic states and half of Poland; Hitler acquiesced, since he wanted to free his hands immediately for action in the West.

This action first took the form of a 'peace offensive' directed at inducing France and Britain, even now, to abandon their pledge to Poland. On 6 October Hitler held out an olive branch to the west. It was promptly rejected, but he held it out again in November. It was mainly for purposes of propaganda inside Germany – to lay the blame for all further hardships on France and Britain, to furnish the régime with an alibi in advance. As he reminded his commanders in chief: 'This does not alter the war aim. This is and remains the destruction of our western enemies.' The German military leaders were in general against attacking in the West, and within the army was formed a core of opposition, contemplating a *putsch* against Hitler. The resistance of the generals achieved nothing, beyond prolonging delays on technical grounds until the spring of 1940. An alleged attempt on Hitler's life on 8 November 1939, when a bomb explosion wrecked the Munich beer-cellar a short time after Hitler had left it, was staged by the Gestapo in order to enhance Hitler's popularity in Germany. It had no connexion with the aims of the army.

But even the delays, at which Hitler chafed, served his purpose well enough. The winter of 1939 was the time of the 'phoney war'. Apart from occasional skirmishes in the Maginot Line and considerable action at sea, the war in the West reached an uncanny anticlimax. After so much feverish preparation, mobilization, bracing for battle, nothing much happened for six months. It created in Britain a false sense of security, in France a mood of relaxed effort which corroded morale and contributed to her eventual collapse. It gave time for German propaganda to soak in, for families in France, a country where five million men were mobilized, to question the need for the war to go on. By May 1940 kindly ladies in that country were appealing for funds to plant rose trees along the concrete desert of the Maginot Line. For both countries, thankful in many ways for the respite in which to get better prepared, a diversion appeared in the form of the Soviet attack on Finland at the end of November 1939. Not only did the suddenly revived League of Nations find Russia the aggressor and expel her from the League, but the heroic resistance of the Finns and the evident inferiority of Russian weapons and planning emboldened Britain and France to send help to Finland. Fortunately for them the Finns made peace on 12 March, before such aid could arrive. Chamberlain called these months the 'twilight war', the Germans called them the *Sitzkrieg*, or sitting war, as opposed to the Polish *Blitzkrieg*, or lightning war. But in April Hitler's new *Blitzkrieg* began, and twilight became night.

On 9 April, without warning, he occupied Denmark and all the main strategic ports in Norway, from Oslo in the south to Narvik in the north. He did this in a single day, though the Norwegians and British and French expeditionary forces continued to fight in Norway for another month. He gained useful air bases against Britain and secured the supply of iron ore from Sweden. The swift success of the blow enhanced the German army's prestige. One result in Britain was a revolt against Neville Chamberlain's conduct of the war. On 10 May he resigned to make way for Winston Churchill, who had hitherto served him as First Lord of the Admiralty. 'As I went to bed at about 3.0 a.m.,' wrote Churchill, 'I was conscious of a profound sense of relief ... I felt as if I were walking with destiny and that all my past life had been a preparation for this hour and this trial ... I was sure I should not fail. Therefore, though impatient for the morning, I slept soundly.'

The man who, at this dramatic moment, took charge of Britain's destinies – and of the destinies of more than Britain – had in the course of a long and colourful life held many high offices, though never until now that of Prime Minister. Before he joined Chamberlain's government in 1939 he had spent eleven years in the political wilderness, thundering in Parliament, Press, and public meeting against the failure to form a grand alliance to meet the ever-growing menace of Nazism. Despite his brilliant achievements in the First World War, when he was in charge of the Admiralty, people in the civilian interwar years did not trust his political judgement. The flamboyance of his character and the vehemence of his utterances did not win wide support. That he was a man of many talents none doubted. 'Churchill might be the right man in time of war,' people said, 'but not in peace.' Now it was war, and the insight he had shown dispelled any remaining doubt about the accuracy of his political judgement. No other elder statesman in the Britain of 1940 could have inspired as much confidence as Winston Churchill. His hour, indeed, had come.

The Defeat of France. On the very day when he became Prime Minister, and proceeded to gather about him the coalition government which, for the next five years with but few changes, was to conduct Britain's war effort, Hitler struck again. He invaded the Netherlands and Belgium at dawn on 10 May. While German tanks, followed by infantry, quickly broke through the thin defences along the frontiers, bombers and parachutists immobilized airfields, bridges, and railroads. Refugees, crowding along the roads, were machine-gunned from the air. Everything was done to create panic and cause total dislocation. Rotterdam was bombed and left in flames. On 14 May the Netherlands Commander-in-Chief surrendered, while Queen Wilhelmina and the government fled to Britain. By 28 May King Leopold of the Belgians capitulated and surrendered himself to the enemy. Breaking through the French armies at Sedan, the Germans drove westward to Abbeville, cutting off the entire British and Belgian forces, as well as many French divisions, from the main French army further south. Hitler had not attacked the Maginot Line. He had come round the end of it, leaving it useless.

After a few allied counter-attacks had failed, no alternative remained but to evacuate by sea as many as possible of the British and French troops cut off in the north-west. Between 27 May and 4 June took place the remarkable evacuation of nearly 340,000 men from the channel port of Dunkirk, under shell-fire and aerial attack. Many French troops were taken prisoner, and all equipment and material had to be destroyed or abandoned. But the bulk of the British forces was rescued, thanks to the combined power of navy and air force, the brave rearguard action of the French, and the hundreds of little boats, summoned from all round the coasts of Britain to go and take part in the evacuation. It was a tremendous disaster: yet so impudently and so successfully was the rescue-work carried out that British morale stood remarkably high. The 'Dunkirk spirit', of bold improvisation and of attempting the impossible, became an asset, not a handicap, in the months that lay ahead.

The battle for France began at once. On 5 June the German attack was resumed, against Paris itself and east of the Maginot Line, heading south toward Lyon. Paul Reynaud, who in March had succeeded Daladier, was resolved to continue the fight even against such odds. General Weygand, whom he had summoned to stem the German advance, soon reported that it was impossible. He advised seeking an armistice, and refused to carry out the Prime Minister's suggestion that he, as Commander-in-Chief, might surrender like the Dutch, whilst the President and government went to North Africa or London to continue the war. General Weygand's demand that an armistice be sought was powerfully reinforced by Marshal Pétain within the government, and by many others who regarded the war as lost and held that the only future for France lay in making the speediest possible terms with Germany. On 10 June Mussolini, anxious to preserve the 'Pact of Steel' when gains were easy and the price low, declared war on France. He sent thirty-two divisions against the six which the French had left on the Franco-Italian frontier; after three weeks of stiff fighting and with the aid of German troops advancing from the rear, they succeeded in moving a few miles into France. After many consultations with Britain and agonizing days of doubt, Reynaud on 16 June resigned. Marshal Pétain formed a new government bent on securing an armistice. On 22 June his representatives signed an armistice agreement, dictated by Hitler, in Foch's railway carriage of 1918 which was specially brought from a museum to its old site in the forest of Compiègne, north-east of Paris. France, as a state, was knocked out of the war. Britain and her faithful Commonwealth stood alone against the tide of Nazism in the West. It was, said Churchill, her finest hour.

The terms of the armistice were such as Hitler considered suitable for an interim settlement with France, until he had completed the conquest of Britain. He put troops of occupation into all northern France, including Paris, and into a zone stretching along the whole western coast. The southern zone, including the Mediterranean coastline and the Pyrenees, was to remain unoccupied (see Map 21). The French government, which now moved to Vichy, would continue to administer both zones, subject in the northern zone to the demands and regulations of the occupying power. France was to pay the costs of the occupation. French prisoners of war, numbering close on two millions, remained as hostages in German hands until the conclusion of peace. The navy was to be disarmed and held in French ports. Weygand, in a phrase which Churchill was to make famous, advised that anyhow Britain would 'have her neck wrung like a chicken's in three weeks'.

The French armistice, so soon after Dunkirk, was a further blow to Britain. But the English Channel, in another phrase of Weygand's, was 'a good tank-ditch', and Britain's immediate anxiety was about the fate of the French fleet. Should the powerful and efficient units of the French navy fall intact into German hands, the balance of naval power would be seriously tipped in Germany's favour. Feeling that in so crucial a matter neither Hitler's assurances in the armistice nor the promises of the men of Vichy that their fleet would not be handed over to Germany were reliable enough, Churchill sent ships and planes to invite French

---

MAP 21.   EUROPE, 1942. See following pages.

The map shows the Empire of Hitler at its height (compare Map 2, showing Napoleon's Empire at its greatest). Germany was in military occupation of Norway, Denmark, the Low Countries, the northern half of France, and vast areas of Russia extending to the gates of Stalingrad. Her allies included Italy (which in turn occupied Albania, and much of Serbia and Greece), Finland, and the group of Balkan satellite states. The only remaining neutrals in Europe were Sweden, Eire, Switzerland, Portugal, Spain, and Turkey. The Vichy Government of France controlled French North and West Africa. But in November 1942 American and British forces invaded North Africa. Hitler was obliged to occupy the whole of France, and he failed to take Stalingrad. Thereafter the tide of war turned against Germany (see Maps 22 and 23).

EUROPE
1942

NORTH CAPE

Ocean

Murmansk

White
Sea

Archangel

LAND

Lake
Onega

Lake
Ladoga

sinki

Leningrad

SOVIET

ESTONIA

Riga

Volga R.

LATVIA

Moscow

Kuibyshev

THUANIA

Smolensk

Tula

SUWALKI

BYELO-
RUSSIA

●●●●● DEC., 1941
FARTHEST AXIS
PENETRATION
●●●● NOV., 1942

UNION

LAND

Kiev

Kharkov

Stalingrad

Volga R.

POLAND

UKRAINE

Donetz R.

Rostov

Don

Astrakhan

Dniester

Maikop

Grozny

*Caspian
Sea*

RUMANIA

Sevastopol

Yalta

TRANSCAUCASIA

Baku

Bucharest

Black Sea

Batum

Sofia

BULGARIA

Istanbul
(TURK.)

Ankara

Tabriz

REECE

TURKEY

IRAN

Athens

SYRIA

Bagdad

IRAQ

CYPRUS
(BR.)

LEBANON

CRETE

500 MILES

HITLER'S 'EMPIRE'

ALLIED WITH GERMANY

OCCUPIED BY THE AXIS

AT WAR AGAINST
THE AXIS

*Relations between the Axis
and Vichy France were governed by the Armistice of
June, 1940, but Germany
occupied the whole of France
in November, 1942*

vessels at Oran, in North Africa, to sail to an allied or neutral port. When they refused they were attacked and wrecked – a tragic incident which left lasting ill-feeling between the two navies. On 18 June, before the armistice was signed, General Charles de Gaulle, the tank-expert who had recently become Reynaud's Under-Secretary of State for War, flew to London and broadcast an appeal to Frenchmen wanting to carry on the fight to get in touch with him. This famous appeal was the origin of the Free French Movement, a movement of volunteers to which in August 1940 Britain gave official recognition and aid, acknowledging de Gaulle as 'Leader of the Free French' (*le Chef des Français Libres*).

In July the French National Assembly, summoned to meet at Vichy to ratify the armistice, was induced to vote plenary powers to Marshal Pétain, surrounded now by Pierre Laval, men of the *Action Française*, anti-republican service chiefs, and a host of defeatists and appeasers. The powers were granted until a 'new constitution' should be promulgated. Pétain was then aged eighty-four. His Vichy governments, destined to survive until 1944 into conditions which none had imagined in 1940, kept for France a unique position among the conquered countries of Europe. Left in control of France so far as German pressure could be resisted, in possession of the remainder of the French fleet and the French overseas territories, and with an 'armistice army' of 100,000 men, Vichy contrived in the course of time to win a precarious semi-independence by taking advantage of Germany's necessities and increasing difficulties. Its characteristic figure was not the senile Pétain, who lent the régime prestige in France, but the agile opportunist Pierre Laval, convinced at first of a German victory but shrewd in bargaining and alert in trickery. His mobile, incalculable tactics did little to help the allies, but also gave little help to the Germans. Vichy never became a mere puppet régime, as did that of Major Quisling in Norway or of the pro-Nazi Mussert in the Netherlands. The French 'quislings', like Marcel Déat and Jacques Doriot, concentrated in occupied Paris and kept up attacks against Vichy almost as vicious as their attacks upon Britain.

The Battle of Britain. After literally dancing with joy at news of the French surrender, Hitler planned his next move: the attack on Britain. Again, his first impulse was to play for a bloodless victory. He had always looked east for German expansion. The war originated in British refusal to give him a free hand in the East. Now, with Poland smashed, with her only remaining western ally defeated, with her own army driven into the sea, Britain surely had no reason to continue. Hitler thought that his victories had cleared the way for a compromise peace, for it was plainly impossible for Britain to prevent German hegemony in Europe. It is strange that Hitler should have expected a policy of appeasement to continue now that Churchill had replaced Chamberlain. But he did, and his care in the armistice with France not to drive the French fleet into joining Britain, or the French government into moving to North Africa, are indications of his hopes. He also very firmly restrained the bellicose Mussolini, thirsting now for great concessions from France. Mussolini's record of achievement left him no grounds for argument. Hitler sent tentative soundings to London through neutral channels. He was waiting, hoping for a sign that Britain would consider peace negotiations. None came. On 19 July he made a long-postponed speech in the Reichstag, appealing 'once more to reason and common sense in Great Britain as much as elsewhere ... I can see no reason why this war must go on.' Count Ciano noted that there was ill-concealed disappointment in Germany at Britain's unaccountable intransigence.

The invasion of Britain in 'Operation Sea-lion', which Admiral Raeder was so reluctant to undertake, required first the establishment of air superiority over the Channel and Channel coast. This was the task entrusted to Göring's *Luftwaffe*. It seems likely that from as early as July onward, Hitler became more and more distracted by thoughts of an attack on Russia, leaving the British unconquered; but that he allowed the air attacks on Britain to continue, at first as preparation for a possible invasion, and latterly to see if Britain could be bombed into considering a compromise peace. On 10 July the first heavy raid was made on southern England, and for a month bombing was concentrated on Channel shipping and ports, then for another month on airfields and London. Thereafter, throughout the late autumn and winter, he continued bombing London and the big industrial cities. But plans for invasion were abandoned after 15 September, when the Battle of Britain reached its climax. By the use of superior fighter-planes directed to their points of interception by radar, and by sacrifice of many of her bravest and most skilled pilots, Britain contrived to inflict upon the *Luftwaffe* losses on a scale which it could not afford. German air superiority proved unattainable. During August and September, Germany lost 1,244 planes and crews. By the spring of 1941 Britain was retaliating with very heavy bombing raids on Germany. The war in the West had to be allowed to fall into stalemate, while Hitler planned his next *Blitzkrieg*, the war against Russia. On 17 September he ordered that 'Operation Sea-lion' be postponed indefinitely; only two days before he had lost fifty-six planes on one day. The principal defenders of Britain were a few hundred young fighter-pilots, British and Dominion, Czech and Polish, Belgian and French. It was the classical revenge of all the countries Hitler had tried to destroy. 'Never,' in Churchill's famous phrase, 'in the field of human conflict, was so much owed by so many to so few.'

Mediterranean and Atlantic. Meanwhile, in the deserts of North Africa, another strange battle was being fought. Under General Wavell small British forces were stationed in the Near East, over an area stretching from Palestine and Egypt to Kenya. In September 1940 a strong Italian force, led by Marshal Graziani, invaded Egypt from Libya. In December Wavell counter-attacked and routed it, pushing 500 miles westward to Benghazi and capturing 130,000 Italians with very small losses. He then withdrew to Egypt, leaving a small Australian garrison to hold Tobruk. These startling victories on land helped to sustain British morale and shake still further Mussolini's tottering fame. In October 1940 he had attacked Greece from Albania only to be driven back deep into Albania. It was only when Germany directed her attentions to the Balkans that Axis victories were won. In March 1941 Bulgaria half willingly was occupied by German troops. In April they also invaded Yugoslavia and overran most of it in a fortnight. At the same time German and Bulgarian troops struck at northern Greece, driving the remnants of the Greek and British forces to the island fortress of Crete. By the end of May, using paratroopers with great effect, they forced the British to retire to Egypt. By the first anniversary of the armistice with France, Germany had occupied the whole of the Balkan peninsula and concluded with Turkey a treaty guaranteeing Turkish neutrality. In the North African desert, however, the British made fresh gains against the Italians. In January 1941 two British columns advanced against Italian East Africa from the Sudan and Kenya. It was a daring attack which took the strong Italian forces by surprise. One column conquered Eritrea and advanced into Abyssinia, the other took Italian Somaliland and also entered Abyssinia. In May the two columns joined forces to defeat the Italian commander, the Duke of Aosta, at Amba Alagi. In five months Mussolini lost his hard-won East African Empire.

At sea the battle raged intermittently, both in the Mediterranean and the Atlantic. In November 1940 a dashing British air-raid from the aircraft carrier *Illustrious* on the naval base at Taranto knocked out three Italian battleships; and the following March the Royal Navy without loss to itself inflicted further heavy damage on the Italian fleet off Cape Matapan in southern Greece. But against British naval strength in the eastern Mediterranean Axis air-power kept up a steady and severe pressure, at Gibraltar, Malta, Alexandria, and Suez. The withdrawal from Crete was costly, and conveying supplies to Malta became a necessary but burdensome task. In the Atlantic German submarines and mines remained a constant menace. But there American aid took various forms. In 1940 President Roosevelt was re-elected President for a third term, and the United States became in his phrase 'the arsenal of the democracies'. In September 1940 she traded fifty over-age destroyers to Britain in exchange for long leases of bases in the Caribbean and western Atlantic. America and Canada set up a Permanent Joint Board of Defence. In March 1941 Congress passed the ingenious Lend-Lease Act, authorizing the President to put American resources at the disposal of any state whose defence he regarded as necessary for the security of the United States. This kept up the steady flow of supplies to Britain and her allies regardless of their ability to pay for them in dollars. The main burden of keeping the Atlantic open for allied supplies rested, however, on the Royal Navy and on the Royal Air Force operating over the western approaches. German U-boats had much greater speed, operational range, and destructive power than their predecessors of 1917, and German pocket-battleships were designed as commerce-raiders. Against this menace, reinforced by new devices such as magnetic mines, Britain mustered a variety of counter-measures, ranging from the conventional armed convoys and escorts, and depth-charges, to bomber-raids on U-boat pens and factories, air-spotting, radar, and devices to protect ships against magnetic mines. By the end of 1940 more than four and a half million tons of allied and neutral merchant shipping had been lost, and another four million tons and more were lost in 1941. The Battle of the Atlantic was the most constant and unremitting of the war (see Map 24).

The Attack on Russia. By the middle of 1941 Germany, now strongly based in the Balkans and the eastern Mediterranean, and (though coming under aerial attack) freed from any immediate threat of invasion from the West, was ready to embark upon her greatest venture of all: the attack upon the Soviet Union. Despite the obvious diplomatic and military preparations for it, it took the world by surprise when, on 22 June 1941, without declaration of war, Hitler threw 160 divisions against his nominal ally in the East. 'Operation Barbarossa' had been prepared, as a strategic plan, since the beginning of the year. In the middle of February Hitler had ordained that any large-scale operations in the Mediterranean must wait until the autumn of 1941, after Russia had been defeated. In his mind everything dictated the conquest of Russia: his long-term ideological battle against Communism, his pan-German quest for expansion in the East, his immediate needs for supplies greater than Russia could give him voluntarily. In Göring's economic directives of May 1941 it was laid down that the overriding need was to use the food-producing areas of the East to supplement Europe's supplies during and after the war. Here was to be the economic foundation of the Nazi New Order in Europe, and it was fully recognized that it would entail ruthless economic exploitation and the death of millions. 'Many tens of millions in the industrial areas will become redundant and will either die or have to emigrate to Siberia.' 'The war can be continued only if all the armed forces are fed by Russia in the third year of the war. There is no doubt that as a result many millions of people will be starved to death if we take out of the country the things we need.' Slavs, in Hitler's view of the world, counted as expendable when the needs of the Master Race were at stake.

There had been one strange prelude to the attack. On 10 May Hitler's deputy, Rudolf Hess, to whom he had dictated in prison the first volume of *Mein Kampf*, took off from Germany in a Messerschmitt fighter and flew alone to Scotland to try to negotiate a peace between Germany and Britain. He did so without Hitler's knowledge, and to his mystification and rage. Landing by parachute near Glasgow, Hess was taken prisoner for the rest of the war. It was a sensational episode, symptomatic of the strange personal relations existing inside the Nazi party. It was damaging to Hitler's prestige, yet also aroused suspicions in Moscow and embarrassment in Britain. It had, it transpired later, no connexion with the attack on Russia and had little real importance.

The choice of the first anniversary of the French armistice for launching the attack was typical of Hitler's superstitious regard for anniversaries: astrology was one of his hobbies. The attack was highly concerted. From Finland a Finnish contingent under Marshal von Mannerheim 'resumed the Soviet-Finnish War'. A northern army group, led by Leeb, attacked Leningrad: a central group, under Bock, struck toward Smolensk and Moscow: a southern group, commanded by Rundstedt, drove into the Ukraine towards Kiev. Against them the Soviet government also opposed 160 divisions, divided into three main groups: under Voroshilov in the north, Timoshenko in the centre, and Budënny in the south. Along a thousand-mile land front, some nine million men were engaged on the two sides. The German forces included units of Rumanians and Slovaks.

The battles moved swiftly and confusingly, centring upon railroad junctions and aiming at large towns, but swaying to and fro at different points as pincer-movements by armed units bit off large 'pockets' containing many prisoners. The Russian strategy was to buy life and time with space, as in the days of Napoleon's war. They retreated readily and scorched the land behind them. They lengthened the German supply-lines and harassed them by air-attack. When they decided to stand and fight, as in the large towns like Smolensk, Leningrad, and Stalingrad, they contrived to exact heavy tolls in German lives and prisoners. Their strategy was that of Foch in 1918 – elastic defence, preparing for a decisive and deadly counter-offensive at the moment of the enemy's greatest extension and weakness (see Map 23). On 3 October, Hitler announced that 'the enemy is already broken, and will never rise again'. On 8 December he declared German operations for the year to be officially ended. At that moment his troops had advanced 600 miles along the front and had taken Tikhvin to the south-east of Leningrad, Kalinin to the north-west of Moscow, Kharkov and Rostov to the west of Stalingrad. But the Russians still held the key cities of Leningrad, Moscow, Sebastopol, and Stalingrad, when the worst winter in living memory descended upon Russia. 'General Winter' proved to be Hitler's worst enemy, as he had been Napoleon's.

Immediately the Red Army's counter-offensive began, proving to the world that far from being annihilated as Hitler had claimed, it was capable of major offensives. It found the German troops short of winter clothing, its guerrillas harried German lines of communication and supply, it regained land west of Moscow, and it retook Rostov. Germany still held nearly the whole of western Russia and the Ukraine : but most of it was scorched earth, devastated by battle and of little economic value that winter. At this moment, too, the whole war was transformed by an event in the far-away Pacific islands of Hawaii. On the morning of 7 December 1941, 189 Japanese bombers swept in low out of the morning haze and bombed United States warships in Pearl Harbour (see Map 24). Eight battleships, three cruisers, three destroyers, and many grounded aircraft were destroyed or seriously damaged. Next day the United States and Great Britain declared war on Japan, followed soon by the Dominions, China, and the Netherlands government in exile. Three days later Germany and Italy, honouring their Tripartite Pact with Japan, declared themselves also at war with the United States. European war, which within Europe left only Eire, Sweden, Switzerland, Spain, Portugal, and Turkey neutral, had suddenly become global war, soon involving the Central American and many of the South American states as well.

From the end of 1941 until the end of the war in 1945 the main theatres of operations were three : the Atlantic and Mediterranean war, which continued until the Atlantic powers landed their combined armies in western Europe and advanced to the conquest of Germany on land; the eastern front, where momentous battles between Germany and the Soviet Union culminated in the advance of Soviet armies into the Balkans, Poland, and eastern Germany; and the Pacific War, reaching its climax in the surrender of Japan in September 1945. Although the three major fronts had constant repercussions one upon the other, and latterly involved careful synchronization of efforts between the three leading partners in the 'Grand Alliance' (Britain, the United States, and the

Soviet Union), they can be most clearly described separately. This will
be done in the three following sections.

THE ATLANTIC ALLIANCE, 1941-5

In August 1941 President Roosevelt and Winston Churchill met on
a battleship in mid Atlantic and drew up what came to be known as 'the
Atlantic Charter'. It was the first serious attempt to formulate peace
aims, as distinct from the simpler war aim of the western powers: resistance to Axis aggressions. It was, in intention, a joint ideological
offensive, agreed upon while America was still technically at peace, and
designed to impress enemy opinion with the justice of the western cause.
Its somewhat hastily drafted eight points included assurances of unaggressive intentions, affirmation of the principles of national self-
determination and of the need for 'the fullest collaboration between all
nations in the economic field', and projects for a peace settlement which
would 'afford assurance that all the men in all the lands may live out
their lives in freedom from fear and want'. Echoing President Roosevelt's enunciation, seven months earlier, of his 'Four Freedoms' – freedom of speech and expression and of worship, freedom from want and
from fear – it struck the first note of a crusading spirit.

By the end of 1941, although the formidable power of Japan was
thrown on to the Axis side, the full entry of the United States into the
war betokened a very much greater addition to the allied side. It meant
that, even should Germany defeat the Soviet Union as Hitler planned
in 1942, the potential forces and resources now arrayed against the Axis
were incomparably greater: so immense, indeed, as to ensure the ultimate defeat of the Axis powers. The Atlantic Alliance, now forged
between the United States and the whole British Commonwealth, was
to endure beyond victory in Europe, into the postwar organization of
economic cooperation and the regional security arrangements of the
North Atlantic Treaty Organization of 1949.[1]

Churchill and the British chiefs of staff spent the Christmas week
of 1941 in Washington, conferring with President Roosevelt and his
advisers. Lend-Lease arrangements had already sent a flow of supplies
to Britain. Roosevelt and Churchill now planned a total unification of
military effort. Combined chiefs of staff were created to direct the
general strategy. It was agreed to regard Germany as the prior enemy
for attack. Many different joint boards were set up, economic as well
as military. On the first day of 1942 representatives of twenty-six 'United
Nations' signed a joint declaration, endorsing the Atlantic Charter and

1. See p. 893.

pooling their war efforts. They included most of the exiled governments of Europe and the Free French, as well as the major belligerent allied governments. Churchill had his 'Grand Alliance' at last – the only weapon great enough to defeat swiftly the Axis powers. This general framework of cooperation was to grow and proliferate during the remaining years of war until it culminated in the United Nations organizations of 1944 and 1945.

North Africa. But on the actual fighting fronts the scene was still gloomy for the western powers. In North Africa the brilliant new Nazi commander, Erwin Rommel, swept back the British Eighth Army and pressed right on to within forty miles of Tobruk. Then, reinforced from Germany, he planned to capture Egypt. In June he captured Tobruk and advanced to El Alamein, only fifty miles west of Alexandria. To mount an effective counterattack meant concerted Anglo-American effort, and in June and July Roosevelt and Churchill, meeting again in Washington, decided to postpone any frontal attack in western Europe and to concentrate instead on a North African campaign. Within three months of the fall of Tobruk the Allies had accumulated materials enough to re-equip the Eighth Army – though most of it had to be sent to Egypt round the Cape and up the Red Sea.

The decisive battle of El Alamein was fought in October 1942. One thousand massed guns opened with an intense barrage, reminiscent in its intensity of the great shell bombardments of the First World War. Then British armoured tanks advanced, and in twelve days the *Afrika Korps* of Rommel and the Italian armies were completely routed. Harassed by bombing and naval bombardment as they streamed back along the coast road to Libya and Mersa-Matruh, they lost some 60,000 men as well as 500 tanks and 1,000 guns. 'Up to Alamein,' said Churchill later, 'we survived. After Alamein we conquered.' The hero of the day was General Montgomery, commander of the Eighth Army which Hitler claimed he had broken in 1940. This skilled and imaginative general, who became henceforth one of the outstanding British military leaders, showed an uncanny flair for predicting what his enemy would do next, as well as a remarkable talent for inspiring confidence and high morale among his troops.

In November 1942, in fast follow-up of this victory, Anglo-American forces landed in Morocco and Algeria, forcing the Vichy authorities there to abandon their carefully cherished attitude of neutrality (see Map 22). Preparations for the coming of the great armada to Casablanca, Oran, and Algiers, involved a tangle of intrigues with anti-Vichy groups and personalities. The chief diplomatic problem had been to find a French leader who might rally the French authorities in North Africa without revealing Allied plans and without prolonged fighting. For this latter purpose de Gaulle and the Free French were useless, since a former move at Dakar had shown that the French colonial administrators remained mostly loyal to Vichy. The Allied choice lay, at first, with General Henri Giraud, a distinguished veteran soldier who had escaped from internment in Germany but had not joined the Free French. He landed secretly in Algeria on 5 November. The Allied armada arrived two days later. It met with serious resistance only at Casablanca. But both German and French reactions were immediate. Hitler at once occupied the whole of France. The remaining units of the French fleet, stationed in Toulon harbour, were scuttled by their officers, on sealed orders of Admiral Darlan, to save them from falling into German hands. To complicate matters still more, Admiral Darlan, Commander-in-Chief of all Vichy forces, appeared on the scene (ostensibly and perhaps actually visiting his sick son in Algiers). He undertook to rally French North Africa to the Allies. Darlan had held high power at Vichy, where earlier in the year he had been Premier under Pétain, and his record had little to commend him to the western allies. But he was accepted as useful by General Eisenhower who was in command of the Allied landings, and General Giraud bowed to Darlan's authority. Darlan ordered the French to cease resistance, and no doubt saved considerable bloodshed. He was, however assassinated on Christmas Eve 1942, and Giraud succeeded him. Darlan's assassination saved the Allies from some of the embarrassments of making so expedient a bargain with a dubious political turncoat, but it did not save Giraud from meeting with intense hostility from General de Gaulle and the Free French, to whom Giraud was scarcely more acceptable than Darlan. Eventually, after prolonged and cumbersome joint arrangements between Giraud and de Gaulle, Giraud too was ousted from power, and North Africa fell to the French Committee of National Liberation, set up in June 1943. This Committee, dominated by de Gaulle, henceforth gained in prestige and strength, until it was able to preside over the initial stages of the liberation of France in 1944.

The Axis reacted in yet other ways to the North African invasion. German forces were sent to Tunisia, Italians to Corsica and Nice. The

MAP 22. WESTERN FRONTS, 1942-5

The Anglo-American landings at Casablanca, Oran, and Algiers in November 1942 led, after hard fighting, to the attack in 1943 upon what Churchill called 'the soft under-belly of the Axis' in Italy. These attacks prepared the way for the opening of a 'Second Front' in France in June 1944, and for the convergence of Allied armies from every point of the compass upon Germany.

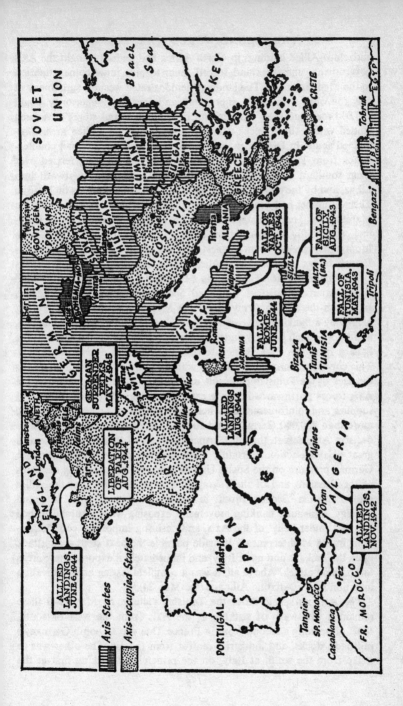

ALLIED LANDINGS, JUNE 6, 1944

GERMAN SURRENDER, RHEIMS, MAY 7, 1945

LIBERATION OF PARIS, AUG., 1944

ALLIED LANDINGS, AUG., 1944

FALL OF ROME, JUNE, 1944

FALL OF NAPLES, OCT., 1943

FALL OF SICILY, AUG., 1943

FALL OF TUNISIA, MAY, 1943

ALLIED LANDINGS, NOV., 1942

Axis States

Axis-occupied States

SOVIET UNION

Black Sea

TURKEY

EGYPT

CRETE

LIBYA

Tobruk

Bengazi

Tripoli

GREECE

Athens

ALBANIA

Tirana

MALTA (BR.)

TUNISIA

Bizerta

Tunis

Algiers

Oran

ALGERIA

FR. MOROCCO

SP. MOROCCO

Tangier

Fez

Casablanca

SPAIN

Madrid

PORTUGAL

ITALY

Rome

Naples

SARDINIA

CORSICA

Nice

Marseilles

SWITZ.

FRANCE

Paris

Rheims

BELG.

NETH.

Amsterdam

Brussels

ENGLAND

London

GERMANY

Berlin

BOHEMIA-MORAVIA

Vienna

SLOVAKIA

HUNGARY

YUGOSLAVIA

Belgrade

RUMANIA

Bucharest

BULGARIA

Sofia

POLAND

Warsaw

GOVT. GEN. OF POLAND

audacious Allied landings in North Africa had, indeed, caught the Axis governments unawares and forced them to give unwelcome attention to the Mediterranean. The landings demonstrated western supremacy at sea, for only with naval supremacy and local air superiority could 185,000 men and their vast amount of equipment and stores have been landed within three weeks. But the problems of the Allied armies remained acute. In December they had to meet a strong German counter-attack from Tunisia, where Hitler now had 150,000 men, ferried over from southern Italy. But the Eighth Army still drove westward into Libya, and by the end of January 1943 it stood at the borders of Tunisia. There Rommel had prepared a strong defensive position, known as the Mareth Line. Here the stage was set for the dramatic final clash. Rommel, powerfully entrenched in Tunisia, faced a double attack from Montgomery in Libya on the east, and the combined Anglo-American-French forces under General Alexander in Algeria on the west.

The final battle for Tunisia was a further triumph not only of Allied coordination but also of combined operations on land, sea, and air. In March the Eighth Army broke the Mareth Line by frontal attack, helped by a flanking movement from the south by the New Zealanders, and by a French column under General Leclerc which had crossed the Sahara from the Free French territory of Chad in equatorial Africa. This combined force joined hands with the armies from Algeria across the neck of the Tunisian peninsula on 7 April, and thenceforth drove the Axis forces northwards into a great battle. There they were robbed of supplies and reinforcements by heavy air and naval bombardment, and more than 250,000 Germans and Italians were taken prisoner. It was a decisive Axis defeat, though Germany calculated that it had value as a great delaying-action. Certainly it did little to relieve the tremendous German pressure on the Soviet Union, or to meet the growing demands of the Russians and of their sympathizers in the West that the Allies should open a 'Second Front' in western Europe. It was, in grand strategy, a gigantic flanking movement, exposing what Churchill called 'the soft under-belly' of the Axis, and ensuring important communications in the Mediterranean It made possible the next steps – an attack upon the Balkans and upon Italy, and immediately it exposed these areas to bombing attack. Above all, it was a complete testing and vindication in action of the Atlantic Alliance (see Map 24).

The Axis Attacked. After the Tunisian victory, by May 1943 there remained two ways of striking at the Axis from the west or south, short of opening a second front in France. One was to bomb Germany's railroads, docks, and industrial centres from the air. The other was to strike from the south at Italy, on the principle of striking first at the weakest point. The Germans claimed that they now sat invincibly within 'Fortress Europe' (*Festung Europa*). The central keep was Germany itself. The outer screen of defences was the occupied or satellite states of Norway, Denmark, the Low Countries, the 'West Wall' in France, the Pyrenees, Italy, the Balkans, Crete, and the Crimea (see Map 21). All these were strongly held. But nothing could prevent the rapidly mounting air strength of the West from reaching the heart of German industry. On 30 May the Royal Air Force made its first thousand-bomber raid on Cologne, followed during the summer by others on Essen and the Ruhr. The autumn of 1943 saw the bomber offensive against Germany stepped up to a scale of still more ferocious intensity. The Royal Air Force concentrated on the Ruhr, and probably reduced German steel production by thirty per cent. Other vulnerable targets were docks and shipping at Hamburg, submarine bases at Lorient and Sainte-Nazaire in France, airfields and rail junctions in France and Belgium, and eventually even Berlin itself, where ten square miles of the city were laid waste. The Americans went at high altitudes by day, the British by night. Many cities were left half in ruins. The *Luftwaffe* concentrated on producing fighter planes and pilots, which gave both Britain and Russia some relief from bombing. The Allied air attacks were to be stepped up more yet, both in numbers of planes and in the weight of bombs carried in each plane. 'Fortress Europe' had no effective defence.

The attack on Italy began on 9 July 1943. The American Seventh and British Eighth armies, numbering thirteen divisions, landed on the coast of Sicily. They swept northwards, and many Italian garrisons surrendered after only token resistance. Then the Eighth Army encountered the German units, which put up much stronger resistance. These were defeated only by mid August, after heavy fighting, and then they mostly escaped to the mainland. The first effect of the invasion was a palace revolution in Rome, which on 25 July brought about the deposition and imprisonment of Mussolini on the orders of the Fascist Grand Council. The King commissioned Marshal Badoglio to form a new government, but Italy remained in the war as an ally of Germany. Hitler took the precaution of sending more German troops into Italy, and she became more obviously than ever a German-occupied country. After heavy air bombardment of southern Italy, the Eighth Army crossed the Straits of Messina into the toe of Italy on 3 September. Continued raids had induced Badoglio to sue for peace on 2 September. Both the negotiations and the terms – unconditional surrender, including surrender of the fleet and demobilization of the army – were kept secret from Germany until 8 September. The next day General Mark Clark landed joint Anglo-American forces on the beaches of Salerno, south of Naples, and engaged in heavy fighting with the entrenched German forces. He was given air cover from captured airfields in Sicily, and constant support from warships which sailed close to shore. Within ten days he was joined by the Eighth Army, driving up from the south, and the united armies forced the Germans to retreat to Naples. On 16 September Badoglio virtually declared war on the Germans, who, after wrecking the fine city of Naples, withdrew by the end of the month toward Rome, and established strong points south of it. There, especially at Cassino, they held out until the end of the year. The Italian campaign settled into a phase of stalemate, pinning down considerable German forces yet also keeping Allied forces and supplies engaged when they would have been useful in the great Allied invasion of France that was planned for 1944. Germany, however, could less afford this dispersal of her strength. She suffered more from the losses inflicted, and from the avowed desertion of her chief European ally. Rome fell on June 1944, Florence in mid August (see Map 22).

Second Front in France. During the first half of 1944 Anglo-American cooperation concentrated on preparations for the frontal assault on France to open the long-pondered 'Second Front'. The U-boat menace was fast being conquered; shipping losses had reached their peak during 1942, but were more than halved during 1943, and shrank to little more than a million tons in 1944. When Roosevelt and Churchill met Stalin at Teheran in November 1943, they told him of their plans, and soon after appointed General Dwight D. Eisenhower Supreme Commander of the Allied Expeditionary Force, to conduct Operation Overlord 'aimed at the heart of Germany and at the destruction of her armed forces'. The United Kingdom was turned into a vast airfield, port, and base, in which men and equipment were accumulated for the great invasion. Some one and a half million Americans had to be trained, transported to Britain, and held ready for 'D-Day'. Countless technical problems had to be overcome – of transport, of landing craft, of security to ensure the tactical advantage of surprise. Against the invasion Germany mustered sixty divisions in France, a quarter of her total army: though by now the losses on other fronts, especially in the east, had been so great that the quality of her troops had considerably deteriorated. The defence was entrusted to Field Marshal von Rundstedt, with Rommel as his subordinate in charge of defending the Channel and Low Countries. But they were kept guessing as to the point and moment of the first attack.

When at last, on 6 June 1944, a mighty armada of 4,000 ships converged upon the beaches of Normandy, it met with no serious enemy resistance from either sea or air (see Map 22). The Anglo-American Alliance had secured absolute air and naval supremacy in the Channel.

For some time before, German coastal defences, radar installations, interior roads, railroads, and airfields had been smashed from the air or by local sabotage. The convoys of landing craft were preceded by minesweepers and followed by complete prefabricated 'Mulberry' harbours towed across the Channel. British assault divisions landed between Caen and Bayeux, American ones west of Bayeux. They were the very beaches from which, in the year 1066, William Duke of Normandy had sailed for his invasion of Britain. Never since then had Britain been invaded: now the Conqueror, in reverse, was General Eisenhower. On the first day he landed 130,000 men. By the sixth day he had landed 326,000 on a bridgehead some fifty miles wide. The initial surprise – so vital for minimizing the costliness of the operation – was complete. Rundstedt and Rommel had expected the attack to come on the Pas-de-Calais, though Hitler, relying as usual on his uncanny intuition, had expected Normandy. A deliberate feint attack in Flanders diverted their attention. Air attacks, in any case, hamstrung their arrangements for focusing troops against the attack. By 2 July, less than a month after D-Day, nearly a million men had landed in Europe, and only 9,000 had been killed, though there were some 61,000 casualties. The main German armour, centred around Caen, kept up fierce counter-attacks. But there they were held, while the mobile American forces broke through into Brittany and Maine and swung eastwards to the Seine. They enveloped 100,000 Germans in the 'Falaise pocket', and the Germans retreated to the Seine. On 15 August a completely new American army under General Patch, with strong reinforcements of French, landed in southern France and advanced northwards up the Rhone valley. Rundstedt was removed from his command, Rommel was wounded and died. By the end of August the Allies had two million men in France, including Canadians and French; Paris was liberated in the latter days of August; and apart from pockets of fanatical Germans holding out stubbornly in some of the French ports, the main German armies were in rapid retreat towards their own frontiers. But they were neither beaten nor destroyed yet, and in the old Siegfried Line of the remilitarized Rhineland they made a last great stand. The war had to continue into 1945.

Germany's Collapse. Even confronted with imminent defeat and collapse, the Nazi régime hit back with great energy and some effect. The attempt to circumvent the Siegfried Line at its northern end, in Holland, by landing large air-borne contingents of British, American, and Polish troops by plane and glider at Arnhem, met with disaster. The Allied forces, which had advanced through France at such high speed, needed time to rest and refit. Soon after D-Day Hitler produced the first of his boasted 'secret weapons' – small, unpiloted aircraft-bombs, which fell after flying a fixed distance, and which were sent over the London area from launching sites in the Pas-de-Calais. Nick-named 'doodlebugs' or 'buzzbombs', they landed at random but in the large built-up area of London did considerable damage, and had very great nuisance-value to the civilian population. Then in August these V-1 weapons gave place to V-2, larger rocket-bombs of greater velocity and destructive power, against which no effective defence could be found in time. The use of this weapon against Britain ended only when its launching-sites were captured. Both gave some hint of how the war might have developed had the Allied invasion of 1944 not succeeded.

On land German resistance remained stubborn and the fighting hard. By the end of 1944 Belgium and France were almost entirely liberated, but the Allied armies were on German soil at only a few points. In mid December the Germans launched a considerable counter-offensive in the Ardennes which almost reached the river Meuse at Dinart, but this 'battle of the bulge' was the last major effort in the West. By the end of January the Germans were again driven out of France, having lost another 120,000 men killed, wounded, or taken prisoner. In March first an American division and then British units crossed the Rhine, and by the end of the month Germany was back within her western frontiers of 1919.

With an equally rapid advance of the Russians into eastern Germany [1] the defeat of Germany was now assured. This necessitated a conference between Roosevelt, Churchill, and Stalin which was held at Yalta in the Crimea early in February 1945. There it was agreed that each should occupy a distinct zone of Germany, and that a fourth zone should be entrusted to France: but that a joint Control Commission should be set up with its headquarters in Berlin. It was also agreed that a conference should meet at San Francisco in April to draft a charter for the United Nations as a permanent international organization. President Roosevelt, who had been elected for yet a fourth term in November, died suddenly on 12 April and was succeeded by the Vice-President, Harry S. Truman. On 25 April American and Soviet forces met on the Elbe and the San Francisco conference opened. Despite desperate resistance here and there, the German *Wehrmacht* was now in rapid dissolution. Thousands of prisoners were taken every day. In Italy, where by the end of 1944 the Allied advance northwards had still only reached Ravenna, the spring offensive launched in April also brought a rapid dissolution of resistance. On 28 April Mussolini was captured and killed ignominiously by Italian partisan fighters. On 2 May hostilities in Italy ceased. On 28 April, too, Hitler gave orders for the last desperate defence of the chancellery of

1. See p. 791.

786

Berlin. There the scene was indescribable. A week before he had celebrated his fifty-sixth birthday by holding conferences with his generals and party leaders. Since the chancellery building itself was badly damaged by Russian shells and bombs, these meetings took place in a concrete air-raid bunker in the garden. Göring and Himmler each began to intrigue for the honour of making peace parleys, and prepared to desert Hitler at the end. Resistance could not be long, for the advancing Russian troops were only a few streets away in east Berlin. On 30 April, having married his mistress Eva Braun, expelled Göring and Himmler from the Nazi party, made his will, and appointed Admiral Doenitz Reich President and Commander-in-Chief of the *Wehrmacht*, Hitler and his wife committed suicide. Their bodies were burned in petrol so that no traces could be found. Only two days after his Axis partner met a squalid death at the hands of Italians Hitler died by his own hand, contriving even at the end to disappear in flames in a veritable Wagnerian climax.

Next day Doenitz broadcast his assumption of authority under Hitler's will and called for continuation of the struggle. He sent proposals to General Montgomery wherein he offered to capitulate in the West but to continue fighting against the Soviet Union in the East. Montgomery demanded unconditional surrender on all fronts, Doenitz agreed on 7 May, and the act of surrender was signed by General Jodl at General Eisenhower's headquarters at Rheims. War in Europe was at an end: so was the nightmare world of Hitler's New Order in Europe. In July the Berlin Conference (held in fact at Potsdam) framed the terms on which Germany was to be governed until a final peace settlement could be made. In the Pacific the war continued, and the immediate problem was to end it as quickly as possible. The Soviet Union, not yet at war with Japan, had at Yalta secretly agreed to enter the war against Japan 'two or three months after the German surrender', on condition that she should recover former Russian territories taken by Japan in Sakhalin, Manchuria, Port Arthur, and the Kurile islands. From Potsdam the three major Allies, and Chiang Kai-shek for Nationalist China, demanded the immediate and unconditional surrender of Japan. But that was not forthcoming until 2 September and much happened meanwhile.[1]

The place of the Soviet Union in the final settlement was conditioned, inevitably, by the large part it had taken in the defeat of Germany and by the positions which Soviet forces occupied at this time in Eastern Europe. Before examining that situation it is necessary to describe the course of the war on the eastern front since 1941, and its consequences for Germany and for German-occupied Europe.

1. See p. 800.

THE EASTERN EUROPEAN WAR, 1941–5

Except on the southern sector of the eastern front, between Orel and the Black Sea, the Germans reached their point of deepest penetration into Russia by the end of December 1941 (see Map 23). Never again, save in the south, were they to get so far east. From the end of 1941 until the end of 1944 the battleline wavered backwards and forwards over the vast borderland between that high tidemark of German advance and the prewar western frontiers of Russia. The scale of land operations on this eastern battlefront dwarfed any in the West, and were rivalled in distances and dimensions only by the scale of naval operations in the Pacific. It was a war of periods of rapid movement and catastrophic retreats, interspersed with grim winter phases of entrenchment and holding-actions. In character, no less than in scale, it was utterly different from warfare in the West until the final land-battles in France after D-Day.

Against Russia Hitler concentrated the major part of his forces and resources, and in tune with his traditional anti-Bolshevism he continued to regard Russia and Communism as his greatest enemies. At first the most that the western powers could do to help Russia was to send her supplies, though both the difficulties of delivery and the shortage of supplies restricted even this form of help. In July 1941 Britain and the Soviet Union signed a mutual aid agreement, and at the end of 1941 America undertook to send aid. Eventually America sent eleven billion dollars' worth of Lend-Lease supplies to Russia. The almost insuperable problem was transportation (see Map 24). British ships ran the gauntlet of German planes and submarines and battled their way through the Arctic Ocean to take supplies by the northern route to Murmansk and Archangel. Other supplies, from both Britain and the United States, had to take the southern route, round the Cape and through Iran. Iran, which Britain and the Soviet Union jointly occupied in August 1941, to save it from falling under Axis control, became one of the main routes. The

---

MAP 23. EASTERN FRONT, 1941–5

Germany's attack on Russia in June 1941 carried her, by the end of that year, to the furthest limits she ever reached save in the southern sector between Orel and Rostov. During 1942 she pushed this southern front eastward to the Volga but was checked at Stalingrad. Thereafter her armies were driven back along the whole front, with immense losses. By the spring of 1944 Soviet armies were fighting on the approaches to Warsaw and the Balkans. Then they, like the allied armies which landed in France in June 1944, converged upon Berlin.

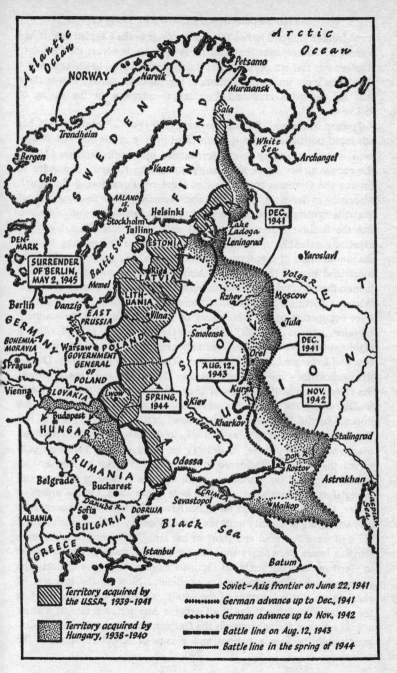

Territory acquired by the U.S.S.R., 1939-1941

Territory acquired by Hungary, 1938-1940

Soviet–Axis frontier on June 22, 1941

German advance up to Dec., 1941

German advance up to Nov., 1942

Battle line on Aug. 12, 1943

Battle line in the spring of 1944

E.S.N. – 42

trans-Iranian railroad linked the Persian Gulf to the Caspian Sea. It had a great advantage, over the other more open route across the Pacific to Russia's Far Eastern ports, in that it delivered supplies to the area where they were most immediately needed, the southern sector. It was there that the Germans launched their major offensive in the spring of 1942.

Toward Stalingrad. During the winter of 1941–2 Germany held her advanced positions on the Russian front mainly in the form of 'hedgehogs' – strategic strong points, surrounded by fortified villages keeping the enemy at bay like a hedgehog's quills. The Russians succeeded in driving the Germans from a few of these positions during the winter, especially in front of Leningrad and Moscow. They also carried out guerrilla fighting behind the front lines against German communications. But the decisive battles had to wait until the spring. This delay was especially valuable to the Russians, who were able to bring up new mammoth tanks of fifty tons, manufactured in their great new industrial hinterland beyond the Urals. By May 1942 the Germans were able to launch their second major offensive on the southern sector of the front. Within a fortnight they advanced another 150 miles. Their objectives were occupation of the whole area of the Caucasus and the southern Ukraine, rich in corn, oil, and hydro-electric power, and affording a highly advantageous southern springboard for further attacks on Moscow and Leningrad. In July they took Sebastopol in the Crimea. During the summer they spread over the lower Don valley and took Rostov at the river's mouth. By September they converged upon the key city of Stalingrad on the Volga. Stalingrad lacked natural defences, and the impetus of the German advance seemed certain to overwhelm it. But the Russian aim was still, as in 1941, to deplete and exhaust German manpower and resources, to destroy her armies. They therefore converted the battle of Stalingrad into a sort of Verdun in reverse – an objective so vital for Germany to win that she poured in her men and material extravagantly, only to lose both to no avail. On the orders of Hitler, General Paulus and his Sixth Army of some 300,000 men went on hammering at the city until the end of January 1943. By then he and his staff were captured and most of his army killed or taken prisoner. Russian losses were heavy too, but by now the shortage of manpower in Germany and the strain on German morale were alike critical. The failure to take Stalingrad was a prodigious blow to the invaders. It checked the whole invasion of the south: with Russian forces holding the west bank of the Volga the Germans dare not, for fear of a flank attack, advance further towards the Caspian Sea. The defence of Stalingrad rightly became a symbol and a saga of Soviet resistance – the counterpart to the Battle of Britain in 1940 or the Battle of Verdun in 1916.

During the second terrible winter in Russia, Germany lost more than men and material. She lost the strategic initiative. She had made her maximum effort, and it had fallen short of its target. This reverse co-incided, moreover, with the Anglo-American landings in North Africa and southern Italy, and with the retreat of Rommel into Tunisia. The Russian spring offensive in 1943 forced Germany on to the defensive in the East, as the Anglo-American Alliance was forcing her in the West. The Soviet armies were now reinforced by drafts from the further Asiatic provinces, and from beyond the Urals flowed the products of a vast recently developed industrial area. The Russians were better equipped, too, with tanks and planes from the West, fed into the crucial southern front, and supplied behind the lines with the help of 200,000 American trucks and jeeps. They proceeded, in 1943, to recapture the cities of Orel, Kharkov, and Kiev, and to drive the invaders back to the Dnieper. The Germans retreated, however, only with tenacious resistance and in good order. By October the Russians were able to cross the Dnieper at several points, and so secure new defensive positions for the third winter of the war. In the four months of fighting between July and October, the Russians could claim to have liberated 140,000 square miles of their country and to have inflicted 900,000 casualties. During the third winter they made further gains in the north, freeing the pressure on Leningrad. In the spring of 1944 they cleared the Crimea of Germans, retaking Odessa and Sebastopol and so recovering command of the Black Sea. The Germans lost another 100,000 men in the process. These great gains in the south exposed to Russian advance, at the critical moment of German collapse, the whole of the Danube valley where Germany's Balkan allies lay especially vulnerable (see Map 23).

War on Two Fronts. The opening of the 'Second Front' in June 1944 brought fresh advantages to the Russians, because it confronted Germany at the moment of her greatest weakness with the traditional night-mare of holding two great land fronts at the same time: indeed three, since by then the only serious resistance in Italy was put up by hard-pressed German units. Seizing full advantage of this opportunity, the Soviet armies smashed ahead to recover all the territories which Germany had occupied, to liberate all Russian territory. Their superiority in numbers was now nearly three to one. In the north they forced back the Finns to Viborg and in September made an armistice with Finland. They reconquered the little Baltic states. By the end of July they stood on the borders of East Prussia, the outskirts of Warsaw, and the Carpathians. They established in Lublin a provisional Polish govern-

WORLD WAR II
PACIFIC THEATRE

Japanese Empire 1940
Occupied Areas June, 1942
At war against Japan, Aug 7, 194[?]

NORTH POLE

Arctic Ocean

CANADA

SOVIET UNION

ALASKA

SINKIANG

SOVIET UNION ENTERS WAR AUG. 8, 1945 ⑤

MONGOLIA

Seattle

Bering Sea

UNITED STATES

TIBET

SAKHALIN

KARAFUTO

Dutch Harbor

San Francisco

INDIA

CHINA

Chungking

MANCHUKUO

Vladivostok

ATTU
F. ALEUTIAN
KISKA

BURMA

KOREA
Hiroshima

JAPAN

ATOMIC BOMBS DROPPED ON HIROSHIMA AND NAGASAKI, AUG.1945
JAPAN SURRENDERS SEPT. 2, 1945 ⑥

Nagasaki

Tokyo

JAPAN ATTACKS PEARL HARBOR DEC. 7, 1941 ①

THAILAND

FORMOSA

IWO JIMA

P a c i f i c   O c e a n

MIDWAY

Pearl Harbor

HONG KONG

INDO CHINA

Manila

U.S. FORCES RE-OCCUPY THE PHILIPPINES OCT. 1944 ④

PHILIPPINE IS.

LEYTE

GREATEST JAPANESE EXPANSION JUNE,1942 ②

HAWAIIAN IS. (U.S.A.)

Singapore

MARIANA IS.

SAIPAN
TINIAN

WAKE

BORNEO

CELEBES

GUAM

YAP
PALAU

ENIWETOK

JAVA

KWAJALEIN

MARSHALL IS.

CAROLINE TRUK
ISLANDS

HOWLAND I. (USA)

Hollandia

NEW GUINEA

GILBERT IS.

Port Moresby

SOLOMON IS.
GUADALCANAL

U.S. FORCES LAND ON GUADALCANAL AUG.7, 1942 ③

TUTUILA (USA)

AUSTRALIA

Coral Sea

NEW HEBRIDES
(BR. & FR.)

FIJI IS. (BR)

Sydney

NEW ZEALAND

⬅ Supply Lines
⬅ Allied Land or Naval Attacks
⬅--- Allied Air Thrusts
⬅····· Soviet Thrusts into Manchuria & Korea

MAP 24. THE SECOND WORLD WAR—PACIFIC AND
ATLANTIC THEATRES
*The war at sea was waged by both sides in close relation to the war on land
(see Maps 22 and 23). These maps emphasize how it was, from 1941 onward,
a 'global war'. Men, equipment, and supplies had to be shipped or flown many*

792

WORLD WAR II
ATLANTIC THEATRE

Hitler's 'Empire'
Allied with Germany
Occupied by the Axis
At war against the Axis

NORTH POLE

GREENLAND (DEN.)

CANADA

UNITED STATES

SOVIET UNION

Murmansk

Kuibyshev
Moscow
Stalingrad

① HITLER INVADES POLAND SEPT. 1, 1939

④ GREATEST AXIS EXPANSION DEC. 1941-NOV. 1942

⑥ GERMANY SURRENDERS MAY 8, 1945

ICELAND

NORWAY

IRAN

TURKEY

UNITED KINGDOM

FRANCE

② FRANCE SURRENDERS JUNE 22, 1940

⑤ ALLIES INVADE NORTH AFRICA NOV. 8, 1942 NORMANDY COAST JUNE 6, 1944

SPAIN

PORT.

SUEZ CANAL

El Alamein

EGYPT

③ UNITED STATES BASES-DESTROYER DEAL SEPT. 2, 1940 ENACTS LEND LEASE MAR. 11, 1941 ENTERS THE WAR DEC. 8, 1941

Casablanca

TUNISIA

ALGERIA (FR.)

LIBYA

CUBA

FR. MOROCCO

PANAMA CANAL

AZORES (PORT.)

CANARY IS. (SP.)

A t l a n t i c
O c e a n

FRENCH WEST AFRICA

FRENCH EQUATORIAL AFRICA

VENEZUELA

CAPE VERDE IS. (PORT.)

Dakar

BRAZIL

Lend Lease Supply Lines

Allied Thrusts

thousands of miles. The United States became, in President Roosevelt's words, 'the arsenal of the democracies'. The Battles of the Pacific and the Atlantic, the Mediterranean and the Arctic, were fought to keep supply routes open as well as to seize strategic advantages. They were no less vital than the great battles fought on land.

ment, based on the Communist-controlled Union of Polish Patriots, and refused to recognize the exiled Polish government. The strong organization of underground resistance in Poland, which was mostly loyal to the exiled government, was destroyed by the Germans – the Russians delaying their taking of Warsaw until this should have been accomplished. In Yugoslavia they likewise supported the Communist-controlled partisans under Tito against the forces, under Mihailovich, which were loyal to the exiled King Peter. In Albania, too, the Communists under Hoxha gained the upper hand. Thus was the ground prepared for establishment of Communist régimes in the border states which the Soviet Union hoped to make a screen against Europe. It was the policy of the *cordon sanitaire* of 1919 in reverse.

In the late summer of 1944 the two Ukrainian armies advanced into the Balkans, and everywhere governments collapsed. On 23 August Rumania surrendered and two days later declared war on Germany. On 5 September the Soviet Union declared war on Bulgaria, which was still not at war with her, and within four days Bulgaria surrendered. Passing through Yugoslavia with Tito's help, the Russians in January 1945 forced Hungary to surrender, and in April they occupied Vienna. Thus, before the final surrender of Germany in May, Russian troops were in occupation of the whole of the eastern marchlands from the Baltic down through Poland and eastern Germany to Hungary, Rumania, Bulgaria, Yugoslavia, and Austria. Only Greece, where British forces occupied Athens in October 1944, remained free of Russian occupation; and there civil war broke out. The powerful Communist guerrilla movement, comparable with Tito's in Yugoslavia, was the National Liberation Front (EAM). When the Greek exiled government returned in October the EAM refused to give up its arms, and turned them against the government. The ensuing civil war, in which the British backed the government, was ended formally at Christmas 1944, but it took another year and more for the government to establish effective control throughout the country. Even then EAM formations, operating from Greece's Communist-controlled neighbours, continued to carry out border raids and provoke risings. Throughout the subsequent negotiations for the settlement of Europe, Greece remained one focus of tension between East and West.

Poland was another. There the disputes were both political and territorial. It was to defend Polish independence and integrity against the demands of Hitler that Britain and France had gone to war in September 1939. Yet by September 1945, it had been agreed that Poland should cede to the Soviet Union her eastern provinces and should take in exchange former German territory to the east of the Oder and Neisse rivers and a southern portion of East Prussia, as well as the former Free City of Danzig (see Map 26). At the Yalta conference of February this rearrangement was broadly agreed, though the final location of Poland's western frontiers was not approved by the Western powers even at the Potsdam conference in August. Once again, as in 1919, one of the initial war aims of the victorious western powers was not attained, and a quite unintentional and unforeseen outcome – a Communist Poland with new frontiers both eastern and western – was determined by the course of events.

By the middle of April 1945, Marshal Zhukov, commanding the central army groups, reached the suburbs of Berlin. At the same moment in western Germany prisoners were being taken by the Western allies at the rate of 50,000 a day and the Reich was in obvious collapse. The situation in mid July, when the leaders of the victorious United Nations met as agreed at Potsdam after Germany's surrender, was that the Red Army was already in occupation of eastern Germany, the western powers in control of western Germany. Whatever might be the general pattern of the new Europe likely to emerge from the war just ending and from the peace settlement already projected, its immediate fate was already in large part determined by two facts. One was the exhausted condition to which Germany and all German-occupied territories had been reduced by the war-effort and the death throes of Hitler's 'New Order'. The other was the nature of the relationship, which Hitler more than anyone else had forged, between the Atlantic Alliance and the Soviet Union. The outcome of the war, on both western and eastern fronts, was on one hand a chaotic and paralysed Europe, on the other a quite new balance of forces and tensions between West and East. It is only if these two overriding facts are set side by side and interrelated, that the consequences of the war can be gauged.

Liberated Europe. The Nazi party had, in effect, governed all Europe save the few neutral states since the middle of 1940. After nearly five years of such rule the national economies of Europe had been in countless ways geared into the wartime needs of the German Reich – needs becoming ever more urgent and exacting as the war progressed. Like the first Napoleon's organization of his continental Empire, Hitler's New Order was no clear-cut scheme, despite its ideological blueprints. It was, like Napoleon's, a complex mixture of ideological schemes, immediate necessities, and temporary expedients. In bursts of tidiness Danes were accepted as Aryans of almost Germanic purity and quality, Dutchmen were transplanted as deputy members of the Master Race to rule over servile Slavs in Poland, and national minorities were moved about to straighten frontiers. The principle was accepted, without question, that the interests of any conquered or satellite country should be sacrificed to the needs of Germany. Jews were systematically persecuted and annihilated. But within this general framework of aims, Europe under German control had remained diversified in the forms of its administration, in the treatment meted out to different nationalities, and in the degree of economic exploitation to which its peoples were subjected.

In a manner which again recalls Napoleon's Grand Empire, Hitler's fell into concentric rings. Its heartland of Greater Germany included the annexed or incorporated territories of the Polish Corridor, Austria, the Sudetenland, Alsace and Lorraine, Luxemburg, and such small areas as Memel, Danzig, Teschen, Eupen, Malmédy, and part of Slovenia. Two further areas, the Protectorate of Bohemia and Moravia and the Government General of Poland (western Poland), were treated as peripheral parts of Greater Germany. Beyond these, other territories were brought under direct military administration and occupation – Belgium and the coastal belt of France including Brittany, Serbia, Macedonia, the Aegean Islands and Crete, the Crimea. Beyond these again were other countries under nominally separate civilian administration but largely German-controlled – Denmark, Norway, the Netherlands, Vichy France, the Ostland (Baltic states), and the Ukraine. As an outer screen lay the satellite states of Slovakia, Hungary, Rumania, Bulgaria, Finland, and for many purposes Italy itself. Italy, however, held occupied or controlled areas of her own – Albania, Dalmatia, Croatia, Montenegro, Greece, the French Alpine frontiers, and Corsica. In general the thoroughness of exploitation varied in proportion to the degree of subservience and control. Poland and the occupied Russian territories fared worst: Denmark, Vichy France, the Netherlands, and the satellite states were better able to resist the more ferocious forms of exploitation. But all were looted, as systematically as possible, of manpower, food, raw materials, and transport for the benefit of the Reich.

German exactions from occupied countries were always heavy, but they mounted to a crescendo of exploitation in 1943 as the strains and drains on Germany's own resources were intensified by heavy losses at the front and by allied bombing of German industrial cities. The first crisis came in 1942, when the losses of the *Wehrmacht* for the first time became very large. In March Hitler appointed Fritz Sauckel, a staunch party member, as plenipotentiary for labour allocation, with almost unlimited powers over the recruitment, utilization, and distribution of labour. Germany's allies could at best provide only small contingents of troops in proportion to her needs. His main concern was to utilize the manpower of the occupied and satellite countries for agricultural and industrial purposes, freeing Germans for military service. Prisoners of war, voluntary workers from occupied countries, and increasing numbers of deported workers, were used in German farms and factories. Industrial plant in other countries was harnessed to Germany's industrial needs by means of controls on credit, labour, and supplies of raw materials. The greatest shortage was always skilled labour. Workers deported from western countries were primarily technicians and mechanics. The strain on transport led to the combing of all Europe for rolling stock and locomotives, oil and automobiles. By May 1943 Sauckel had organized some six and a quarter million foreign workers in German production. In the later stages of the war, as the extent of territory Germany controlled shrank while her needs increased, labour supply was probably her most serious deficiency. The *Organisation Todt*, under Fritz Todt of the SA, had the special task of building fortifications and defence works, harbours and armaments factories. It employed foreign labour extensively in its construction of the 'Atlantic Wall' from Norway to the Spanish frontier, and the 'Ligurian Wall' between Toulon and Spezia. In every way possible all the population and the economic resources of Europe were mobilized for the benefit of the war effort.

So persistent and so exacting a burden did much to excite organized resistance. In every occupied country resistance movements of some kind came into being in the early days of the war. At first they were often just small and local, groups of friends contriving to evade German regulations, or intellectuals printing little clandestine papers for secret circulation. As time went on, and especially after the Battle of Britain and the early German reverses, more and more patriotic men and women recovered sufficiently from the stunning effects of defeat to organize effective sabotage and resistance. The conscription of labour for work in Germany brought them fresh support. Thousands of younger men fled to the hills or took to the open country to evade deportation and, as in France, formed militant groups of the *maquis*, guerrilla bands attacking German guards and trains. The spirit of heroic resistance was encouraged by broadcasts of exiled leaders from London, by the underground Press which flourished all over Europe, and by the parachuting of weapons and supplies to partisan units. These activities provoked the Germans and their henchmen to the most brutal reprisals. Hostages were taken and shot, collective punishments were imposed on villages and towns, resisters were tortured in the cells of the Gestapo. In return collaborators were killed, sabotage increased, occasionally open warfare broke out. Endemic civil war was one of the most unhappy by-products of German occupation – a revival and exacerbation of that tendency to civil strife which had been apparent even before the war in so many European countries.[1]

The activities and organization of the resistance movements changed and widened as the war progressed. After the attack on the Soviet Union in June 1941, Communists in every country, hitherto inhibited by the Nazi-Soviet Pact and the official theory that the war was a war of rival imperialisms, threw themselves wholeheartedly into militant resistance. Although their tactics were often directed more to capturing and controlling organized resistance than to simple cooperation with other groups, they undoubtedly gave a fresh impulse of energy and ingenuity to resistance. Elaborate organizations grew up to assist the escape of Allied airmen and prisoners of war, to concert action with movements in other parts of the country, to supply the Allies with valuable information, to defeat German attempts at preventing sabotage in factories. In the weeks before D-Day sabotage of transport, power stations, telegraph, and bridges was conducted as a regular military operation. In France, under General Koenig, the French Forces of the Interior (FFI) behaved like an army already landed on French soil.

But the unity and harmony of the national movements varied greatly. Most resistance organizations were strongly political and religious in character. In Denmark, Norway, or Bohemia, they managed to sink such differences in a fairly unified movement. In the Balkans, especially in Yugoslavia and Greece where national, racial, and political differences were aggravated during the occupation, partisans were as liable to fight one another as to fight Germans. Nearly everywhere such movements by origin and temper were revolutionary and intransigent, often much more revolutionary than the exiled governments which claimed their support, or than the mass of the civilian population in the country. After four years of such activities no liberated nation was likely to find reconstruction or resettlement easy. It so happened that in the area most exposed to Soviet advance in 1945 – in Poland and the Balkans – the tensions between rival resistance movements and the divorce between internal and exiled authorities were at their greatest. This had the most far-reaching consequences in the postwar years.[2]

The Uneasy Alliance. It was, however, less these tensions than the uneasy alliance between the major allies themselves which boded ill for the prospects of a settled and unified Europe after the war. The alliance between the Soviet Union and the Western powers was in origin a marriage of necessity and convenience. Each side had evaded it as long as it could. The Soviet Union, for the first nine months of the war in the

1. See p. 711.
2. See p. 813.

West, had been formally the ally of Germany, and she had sent her ally a steady flow of economic assistance in the form of food and oil. It was not easy for the Western powers to forgive the action of the Soviet Union in 1939, which had precipitated the war and ensured that Poland would be totally defeated. Their own resistance to Germany and Italy had been regularly denounced in all Communist propaganda as an unworthy war of imperialism – until Hitler turned his forces against the Soviet Union. Then they were denounced for opposing him so feebly. On the other side, it was equally difficult for the Soviet leaders to forget or forgive the period of Munich, when it had seemed that the aim of the Western powers was to divert German attentions eastward at all costs; and still less to forget their precipitate action in 1939 in expelling the Soviet Union from the League of Nations because of its attack upon Finland.

The military alliances which were forged in 1941 and 1942, in the face of the triumphant common enemy, were therefore clouded from the start by memories of recent 'treacheries' on both sides. The unhesitating support offered to Stalin by Churchill in June 1941 did something to dispel these deep-seated animosities. The brave and massive resistance shown by the Red Army to the German invader in the winter of 1941 and throughout 1942 won genuine admiration and respect in the West. But one bone of contention continually recurred. In 1942 the Soviet leaders began to urge that the Western powers should relieve the pressure on Russia by opening a second front in western Europe. It was hoped at first that this might be possible; but in the summer of 1942 it was decided to defer the second front in Europe and to mount a major campaign in North Africa. This decision was unwelcome in Russia, where it was assumed that the Western powers were more concerned with forestalling Russian influence in south-eastern Europe than with aiding the Soviet Union by a frontal attack in the West. The Allied decision was influenced by appreciation of the weakness of Italy, anxiety for supply routes and bases in the Mediterranean and the Near East, and the belief that Rommel's threat to Egypt and the Near East was but one arm of a gigantic pincer-movement, the other arm of which was the German offensive in the Ukraine. Should the two arms of the pincer meet in Iran, all would be lost. To break one of these arms was, therefore, a most effective contribution to Russian security. The Western decision was influenced, too, by the conviction that sufficient transport and forces were not yet available for the perils of a frontal assault. Churchill's view was that Russia could have given Germany a war on two fronts at any time in 1940; that since she had waited until after Dunkirk its absence was as much the responsibility of Russia as of the

West; and that a major assault which failed for lack of accumulated power and momentum would be as much a disaster for Russia as for the Western nations. A diversionary attack on Dieppe by the Canadians in August 1942 proved far from successful. Cross-Channel invasions were not repeated, apart from occasional commando raids for reconnaissance, until D-Day.

But because D-Day was postponed until June 1944, that is, until Soviet forces were well advanced in their great counter-offensives on the eastern front, the eventual invasion of Germany assumed the form of a race between the Eastern and Western Allies to get to Berlin first, and to take possession of the Balkans. This appearance of rivalry was unfortunate, and neither side was free from a desire to forestall the other. This course of events, though determined more by strategic decisions and military timing than by fundamental political policy, created a somewhat uncongenial atmosphere for the crucial meeting of the Allied leaders in the summer of 1945. Other fortuitous events also conspired to change unexpectedly the character of these meetings. President Roosevelt having died in April, the United States was represented by her new President, Harry S. Truman. Churchill, having been defeated heavily in the general elections of 1945, was succeeded halfway through the Berlin Conference by the Labour party leader, Clement Attlee. Of the three great war leaders, Stalin alone survived at Berlin. It is doubtful whether the changes greatly affected the actual decisions taken; these were determined more by the concrete situation and the existing balance of power than by personalities. But the temporary predominance of Stalin was thereby emphasized, and it is possible that his ambitions were all the more stimulated.

On 2 August the Big Three meeting at Potsdam announced the formation of a council of Foreign Ministers of the five Allies (including France and China) to prepare peace treaties for Italy, Bulgaria, Finland, Hungary, and Rumania. As regards the settlement of Germany they enunciated only general principles of political and economic administration to govern the period of Allied occupation, and assigned to the newly formed Polish Provisional Government of National Unity an area of 'administration' extending to the Oder and Neisse rivers in the West, and including Danzig. The frontier was to be finally determined in the future peace settlement. Overshadowing the discussions at Potsdam was the still unsettled issue of Soviet participation in the war against Japan. On this Stalin still temporized. Both Churchill and Roosevelt had kept secret the fast progress made in the manufacture of atomic weapons, and at Yalta they had still been uncertain of the outcome of the experiments. At Potsdam Truman told Stalin of a 'new secret weapon' in

American hands. But since it was still uncertain whether Japan could be beaten without Soviet help, the Western powers conceded to Stalin advantages which they would otherwise hardly have conceded. To assess the relevance of the war in the Far East to the settlement of Europe, it is necessary to take account of the main features of that third sector of the world's battlefronts.

WAR IN THE PACIFIC, 1941-5

Not the whole story of the war in the Pacific is relevant to the story of contemporary Europe. In December 1941 the United States and the British Commonwealth agreed to give priority to the war in Europe. Until the collapse of Germany the major British war effort and a large proportion of United States effort were concentrated upon hostilities in Europe. But Japan's early victories, the overwhelming impetus of her advances in Asia and the Pacific, created for both the Atlantic powers a constant distraction and anxiety. She repeated in the Far East the sequence of early conquests which Hitler, using the same devices of surprise attack and *Blitzkrieg*, had achieved in Europe. Just before her attack on Pearl Harbour, it was believed by United States Army and Naval Intelligence that Japan was more likely to strike first at the Dutch East Indies or Singapore. Already she had exerted pressure on the Vichy French administration of Indochina, under Admiral Decoux, to grant her air bases. German conquest of the Netherlands and France, and the perilous position of Britain, left the Pacific territories of all these states exposed to Japanese pressure and possible conquest. It seemed unlikely that she would forgo this easier prey in order to attack the United States.

But her vainglorious militarist leaders were prepared to tackle all at once. The day before Pearl Harbour was attacked a Japanese fleet arrived in the Gulf of Siam, and poured Japanese troops into French Indochina. Pearl Harbour was the signal for immediate attacks not only on Manila, Luzon, Midway, Wake, and Guam, but also on Singapore, north-east Malaya, Burma, and Hong Kong. On 10 December the British battleship *Prince of Wales* and the battle cruiser *Repulse* were sunk in the Gulf of Siam; this was Britain's counterpart to Pearl Harbour, and a grievous blow to her naval power. By the end of January 1942, Japanese troops had struck through the Malay peninsula and threatened Singapore, while air bombardment paved the way for an attack on the port. On 15 February the Singapore garrison was forced to surrender. At the same time, pressing into Burma, other Japanese forces advanced to take Rangoon, and by the middle of May nearly all Burma, including the important 'Burma Road' or supply route to China, was in Japanese hands. The Philippines fell in the same months. So did the Dutch East Indies – Sumatra, Borneo, the Celebes, Java, Bali, Timor. The tide of Japanese conquest seemed irresistible. The British occupied the island of Madagascar, held by Vichy France, to forestall the tide's lapping even the western shores of the Indian Ocean. An attack on India or Australia seemed by no means impossible.

The Turning of the Tide. But the tide turned in the Pacific in May 1942, with United States victories in the Coral Sea and off Midway which cost Japan the loss of five aircraft carriers (see Map 24). American forces were convoyed to strong positions in Australia, New Zealand, and Samoa. By June they numbered 150,000 and were joined by Australian units recalled from the Near East. In August American troops gained beachheads at Guadalcanal and elsewhere in the Solomons, and Australian and American troops made advances in New Guinea.

The perimeter of Japanese power was being fixed and circumscribed, though vast and rich areas still lay within it. Guadalcanal was entirely retaken by February 1943. Perhaps the first momentous consequence of the Pacific War for the conduct of war in Europe was that it made it impossible to mount a 'Second Front' in Europe even in 1943. American and Allied commitments in the Pacific were so extensive, the task of containing and forcing back Japanese power promised to be so exacting and so protracted, that adequate resources could not be accumulated until 1944 for the major undertaking of an attack in France. This decision, reached, as had been shown,[1] in the summer of 1942, was forced upon the Western powers mainly by the war in the Pacific.

By the end of 1943 New Guinea had been recaptured, and the security of Australia ensured. This also gave the Allies naval and air bases for a counter-offensive northwards. Since the Royal Navy and Royal Air Force were now able to take over more and more of the Battle of the Atlantic, the United States Navy under Admiral Nimitz was freed to concentrate most of its strength and all its aircraft carriers in the western Pacific. Since the Pacific extends over more than half the surface of the globe, the strategy of the war was governed by the enormous distances involved. Its pivots were airfields, or bases where airfields could be built: its chief weapons aircraft and aircraft carriers, as well as warships. Japan's 'Co-prosperity Sphere' in Asia, like Hitler's 'New Order' in Europe, assumed a pattern of concentric arcs. From the islands of Japan, and her older conquests on the mainland in Manchuria and eastern China, spread in a southern arc the inner ring of territories initially seized from the Western powers in 1941—Burma,

1. See p. 799.

Indochina, Malaya, and the Dutch East Indies. In front of these lay the crescent of the Philippines and New Guinea; and east of these yet a further outer screen of little scattered Pacific islands, the Ryukyus, Bonins, Marianas, Carolines, Marshalls, and Gilberts. United States strategy was to strike along this last outer screen of islands, ill-defended and inviting, and so to by-pass or outflank the inner arcs of Japanese-held territories, and strike direct at the heart of Japan itself. Having secured Australia by the recapture of New Guinea, and with firm bases on the Solomons at the southern tip of this outer arc, American forces began the long process of 'island hopping' northwards. They struck at the coral atoll of Tarawa in the Gilberts in November 1943, and took it after some days of very heavy fighting. They moved on to the Marshalls in February 1944, on to the Marianas in June, and raided Japanese bases in the Carolines. From the Marianas Japan was only 1,500 miles away and so within range of the new long-range super-fortress bombers. In September the Americans reached the Palau islands, 550 miles from the southern tip of the Philippines, and so moved into the inner screen of enemy-held territories.

On 19 October a great armada, resembling in scale that other Anglo-American Armada which had sailed towards the Normandy beaches only four months before, carried 250,000 men towards Leyte, in the centre of the Philippine archipelago. It was met by the main Japanese navy, and there took place the greatest naval battle of the whole war. The Japanese lost three battleships, six aircraft carriers, and ten cruisers, and suffered severe damage to several more. The Americans lost one light carrier, two escort carriers, two destroyers, and a destroyer escort. It was a decisive American victory, and made possible the conquest by General Douglas MacArthur first of Leyte and even-tually of the whole of the Philippines. This operation was completed by July 1945, before the Potsdam conference began.

Meanwhile, in February, other units forced their way on to Iwo Jima, a volcanic island 750 miles south of Japan, at a cost of 20,000 casualties. In April divisions of the United States Tenth Army landed on Okinawa in the Ryukyus, only 350 miles from Japan, and after killing more than 100,000 Japanese occupied it by the end of June. Since the previous November Japan, like Germany, had been under continuous and heavy air bombardment, mainly by superfortresses. After the taking of Iwo Jima and Okinawa, this bombardment was intensified to 50,000 tons of bombs a month, paralysing Japanese trans-port and pounding her industrial cities. The surrender of Germany in May relieved Allied forces for yet further concentration of attack by air and sea. Japanese defeat was imminent and certain even before the end of the war in Europe. But that it would almost certainly involve strenuous effort and heavy loss of life seemed evident from the fanatical and tenacious resistance put up by Japanese troops in all the fighting hitherto. One of the American navy's most formidable enemies was the Japanese 'suicide planes', each charged in the nose with a large quantity of explosive and guided to its target by a pilot who had no hope of saving his own life.

In sharp contrast with the steady progress of island-hopping were the more sporadic and often unrewarding progress of jungle warfare in Burma and Malaya, and the land fighting in China. The two were connected, in that the cutting of the Burma supply road robbed the Chinese of most of their urgently needed supplies from the West. In August 1943 a South-east Asia Command (SEAC) was set up under Admiral Lord Louis Mountbatten, and an offensive in northern Burma was planned for the winter of 1943-4. There the British Fourteenth Army under General Slim, guerrilla bands of British and Indian jungle fighters under Brigadier Wingate, General Stilwell's Chinese troops, and General Merrill's American 'Galahad' fighters fought some of the strangest battles of the war. With almost impossible supply lines, they were supplied mainly by air. In an intolerable climate and amid impassable mountains or almost impenetrable jungle, these forces eventually drove the Japanese from northern Burma and saved India from invasion. In southern China the main battle was for the 'rice bowl' of Changsha and the airfields from which American superfortresses flew to raid Japan. By 1944 Burma, like Italy, had become a minor theatre of war, outdistanced by greater operations in the Pacific and in Europe. But the Japanese in Burma were increasingly cut off and isolated. British planes could raid Rangoon or Singapore with impunity, and could supply freely the Allied forces in the jungle and forests. By 22 January 1945, the Burma Road was declared reopened, and in May Rangoon was retaken. The plans to free Malaya and Singapore were never needed: Japan surrendered before they could be carried out. The circumstances of her surrender had the most momentous consequences of all for the future of Europe.

Japanese Defeat. On 6 August 1945 an atomic bomb was dropped on the city of Hiroshima in Japan. It destroyed more than half the city and caused some 80,000 deaths. Two days later the Soviet Union declared war on Japan and invaded Manchuria. On 9 August a second atomic bomb of different type was dropped on the naval base of Nagasaki. On 14 August the Japanese cabinet, on the intervention of Emperor Hirohito, accepted the Allied terms of 'unconditional surrender'. On 2 September Japanese representatives signed the instrument of unconditional surrender on board the battleship *Missouri* in Tokyo Bay. Local Japanese forces everywhere in the Pacific surrendered in the course of next month. The war in the Pacific was over, having lasted only four months longer than the war in Europe.

The circumstances of this happy consummation for the Western powers were, however, of unhappy significance for their future relations with the Soviet Union, both in the Far East and in Europe. Stalin and his advisers had been taken by surprise by the effectiveness of the two atomic bombs and the suddenness of Japan's collapse. Whereas their tactics had been to play for time and to delay the entry of Russia into the war in the Pacific, after 6 August they had to enter that war precipitately in order not to be left out of the Far Eastern settlement. At the same time, the uncomfortable discovery that the United States possessed so devastating a weapon reawakened all their deepest distrusts and fears of American power. They became more exacting in their quest for a defensive screen of satellite countries in eastern Europe.

On the other hand the Western powers, too, were taken somewhat unawares by the catastrophic effect of the new weapon. Had its effects been reliably foreseen at Yalta in February, it seems unlikely that Churchill or Roosevelt would have paid so high a price for the promise of Soviet entry into the war against Japan. Their governments were left with the suspicion that they had paid an exorbitant price for an unnecessary service. If in Europe they had reaped some of the gains of Russia's long and exhausting struggle against Germany, in the Far East the tables were turned. Russia, with a minimum of effort and loss, harvested all the territories formerly taken from her by Japan after the Russo-Japanese War of 1904-5. While Stalin posed as taking 'revenge for 1904' and in Europe played the part formerly played by Tsar Alexander I at Vienna in 1815, it fell to Franklin Roosevelt to undo the Treaty of Portsmouth of 1905 which had been arranged by Theodore Roosevelt.[1] History performed strange tricks on both sides.

The whole sequence of events, which inaugurated so inauspiciously the new atomic age in Europe, was a particularly revealing example of the extent to which history, and especially peacemaking, can be shaped by apparently reasonable calculations which prove in the event to be miscalculations. Because the Soviet Union was not at war with Japan, the Western allies had to consider a contingency in which they would remain for a long time heavily engaged in the Far East while the fate of eastern Europe was being shaped by an unencumbered Russia. They were therefore prepared to pay a high price in Pacific currency to ensure against prolonged Soviet neutrality, and to shorten the duration

1. See p. 508.

of the war against Japan. Stalin raised his price for a promissory note as high as the price that he expected to be able to exact. Both calculations were shattered by the effects of the atomic bomb. The promissory note, already overdue, had to be hastily honoured: the price, no longer justified by military necessities, had still to be paid. The pangs of having to pay it were partly softened by keeping the occupation and control of Japan in exclusively American, not Soviet, hands. But in eastern Europe, for quite different reasons and by an unforeseen process, Stalin contrived to extend Soviet influence far into the Balkans and central Europe.[1]

The most far-reaching consequence of the Pacific war for the western European nations was the colonial revolution which was precipitated though not created by Japanese conquests. The coloured peoples of the overseas colonial territories of Britain, France, and the Netherlands were stirred as never before to revolt against the domination of the white man. This was not only a result of Japanese propaganda and of the blows to European prestige inflicted by Japanese victories. It was also a political outcome of the great social upheaval caused in these lands by experience of invasion, conquest, and liberation. In this sense forces were at work in Burma, Malaya, Indochina, and Indonesia similar to those which operated in the liberated nations of Europe. Nothing strengthens the desire for national self-determination more than to have been for several years completely deprived of it by foreign conquest and occupation: nothing gives more stimulus to social revolution than the revolution of war. Even more important still, for the future of the world, were the repercussions on the largest Asiatic peoples of all, the Indians and the Chinese. The war brought India her supreme opportunity to demand immediate political independence. It also discredited the never strong government of General Chiang Kai-shek and the Kuomintang, and paved the way for the Communist revolution of 1949.

As in 1919, the most momentous indirect results of the Second World War were entirely unintended and unforeseen when it began. The Second World War was begun to preserve the independence and integrity of Poland and to check Nazi domination in Europe. It was not fought to create an independent Burma, republics of Indonesia or Vietnam, two new republics of India and Pakistan, a communist state in China, or a new state of Israel. Yet these were in fact its outcome, and much else besides; whereas the independence and integrity of Poland were not preserved, and postwar Europe was overshadowed almost as much by the threat of Soviet power as it had been darkened

1. See p. 835.

in 1938 by the menace of German power. Pre-eminent among the reasons for these paradoxical results was the extension of the war into the Pacific and Asia which began with the attack on Pearl Harbour. It was evidence enough, if more were needed as late as 1945, that the world had indeed become one world, where events anywhere soon mattered everywhere. The overall revolution brought about in both European and world affairs by the war will be examined in the next section.

THE REVOLUTION OF WAR

The Second World War, like the First, brought in its wake both economic and social transformations and political upheavals, but they were very different in their geographical incidence. In 1919 the main changes in western and central Europe were economic and social, and even in Germany the political revolution of 1919 somewhat missed fire; the main political revolutions came in eastern Europe, where old dynastic Empires gave place to new nation states.[1] In 1945 the most drastic economic and social changes came in central and eastern Europe, where all groups and classes which had supported fascism were discredited, and where many countries underwent a complete economic reorganization under Communist control; the greatest political upheaval came further east still, in the Asiatic countries of China, India, Burma, Malaya, Indo-China, and Indonesia. It was as if the eastwards extension of the forces of nationalism and democracy, again accelerated by war, had now thrust itself far into Asia. Between western and eastern Europe there was still no assimilation, no unity born of westernization. Meanwhile the western nations, suffering as before severe dislocation of their economic life, disruption of trade, and liquidation of overseas investments and assets, were further impoverished in relation to the United States and the overseas Dominions. The consequences of this impoverishment were at first much alleviated by the readiness of the United States and the Dominions to take part in schemes to prevent a repetition of the economic evils of the 1920s.[2] The western nations themselves developed new arrangements for promoting social security and full employment which gave rise to new forms of 'welfare state'. If the western powers made mistakes after 1945, at least they were quite different mistakes from those they had made after 1918.

In the First World War the ideological alignment of the powers had

1. See p. 628.
2. See p. 823.

clarified and simplified as the war proceeded: so that by 1918 it was the western, maritime, democratic states which triumphed, the older dynastic Empires and monarchies which collapsed.[1] In the Second World War the outcome was a duality even in ideology, for although it was the aggressive and authoritarian fascist states which went down into defeat, the victors included both the western democracies and the single-party state of the USSR. This duality was reflected, in the liberated countries, partly by the tension between exiled governments and new parliamentary constitutions, partly by the influence of communism within the resistance movements. It was, however, concealed as between the major allies by the formulas used for purposes of psychological warfare. Allied propaganda hinged upon the Atlantic Charter, with its question-begging reference to 'peace-loving peoples' and its implied distinction between the German people and their rulers. This was a distinction elaborated in subsequent pronouncements and in the trials of enemy leaders at Nuremberg, though it was considerably blurred in demands for reparations and in Allied insistence upon 'unconditional surrender'. Throughout the war the ultimate aim of the propaganda put out by either side was to stimulate revolution against existing governments. This bore singularly little fruit in either camp. No state was beaten because its people rebelled: its people rebelled only when it was beaten, and then under alternative national leadership usually of the military or naval leaders. The political structure of the nation-state proved to be remarkably resilient and tough, even in the greatest adversity. Except among the movements of underground resistance in occupied lands, considerations of ideology and the results of propaganda played relatively little part in shaping the course of events.

Modern Warfare. The broad pattern of events was shaped much more by the nature of modern warfare. The whole war lasted from 1 September 1939 until 2 September 1945 – six years and a day. It fell into two almost equal parts. Until November 1942 most of the advantages and the victories lay with Germany and Japan. After that month, which saw the battles of El Alamein and Stalingrad, the disembarkation of Allied forces in French North Africa, and the establishment of United States forces on Guadalcanal, the tide turned. There began a long series of Allied advances and victories which ended in the liberation of western Europe and south-east Asia, and the surrender of Germany and Japan.

The basic reason for this clear-cut pattern is that more than any previous war it was a war of machines: of tanks and aircraft, motorized columns and heavy artillery, ships and submarines. These

1. See p. 589.

weapons of war, in their nature, are products of great scientific inventiveness and technical skill, and depend for their manufacture in large quantities upon methods of mass production. Such resources are normally available only in the larger and most highly industrialized countries, and demand the disciplined productive efforts of large, skilled, urban, civilian populations. Because civilian production became so essential an element in military power, it also became an essential objective of military attack. Upon the capacity of states to equip themselves with a supply of enough up-to-date weapons of this kind, the methods of mass production impose a severe limitation. Before the plant needed to produce a steady flow of tanks or aircraft can operate, a time-lag of between one and two years must elapse while the machines to make the machines – the machine-tools or jigs – are themselves being designed and manufactured. Moreover, once such plant has been set up, the type of weapons it makes cannot be changed in important respects without causing further delays and a sharp decline in output. Therefore the problem of building up armaments to maximum strength can be solved only in relation to the exact time when operations of war begin. If a government begins mass production too early, it may find its stores of equipment out-of-date; if it begins too late, its output will be too small. This gives immense initial advantages to an aggressor, who can fix the date when war will begin to coincide with his own maximum and optimum output of the weapons of war.

This advantage was fully appreciated and utilized by both Germany and Japan, and it very largely explained their sweeping successes in the first three years of the war. But the same factor brought a great advantage to those states like Britain, the Soviet Union, and the United States which, possessing both superior resources of manpower and greater industrial potential, moved into maximum and optimum production later. Provided these superior resources were properly used, it was inevitable that by the end of 1942 the overall technical advantage in war should swing in favour of the Allies. At the peak of its output in 1943-4, the United States was producing one ship a day and one aircraft every five minutes. In the six years of war this great 'arsenal of the democracies' produced 87,000 tanks, 296,000 aircraft, and 53,000,000 tons of shipping. The first economic burden for the main belligerents was the complete reorganization of their industrial production to mass-produce the equipment of war. This was achieved in Germany by 1940, in her enemies by 1943.

In all countries save the United States and the overseas Dominions this reorganization of the economy was accompanied by immense material destruction: in the United Kingdom, France, Germany, and Japan, by concentrated aerial bombing; in all the occupied countries, the Soviet Union, and Germany, by armed invasion. At sea, despite improvements in anti-submarine devices, total Allied losses of shipping exceeded 20,000,000 tons: a level not reached in the First World War. But this could be more than replaced by the shipping resources of the United States, which was an active belligerent for nearly four years instead of for little more than one year, as in the First World War. The first major crisis of production in Germany, when output lagged behind consumption, came in 1942. Japan reached her comparable crisis for the same reasons in the winter of 1944. In each country the crisis came three years after the beginning of war. The chief reason for this was that strategy for the most effective use of such equipment hinged on the systematic accumulation of it to the point when overwhelming weight and superiority made possible a concentrated and irresistible attack. This was the classical method used by Germany and Japan in preparing their initial surprise attack or *Blitzkrieg*. It was equally the method adopted by the Allies in their counter-offensives at El Alamein, at Stalingrad, and on D-Day.

Because it was so much a war of machines, losses of life on the scale of the great battles of the First World War occurred only on the Russian front. The mobility and speed of most major operations meant that usually more men were taken prisoner than were killed. France, which was twice a major battlefield and was throughout subject to air attack, lost some 500,000 lives, including those killed in the resistance movements: only a third of her losses in the previous war. The forces of the British Commonwealth suffered losses of some 445,000, of which well over half came from the United Kingdom alone. In addition, 60,000 civilians were killed by bombs and rockets. The United States, which had over twelve million troops engaged, lost some 325,000. But the defeated powers, and the Soviet Union which suffered heavy initial reverses on land, lost lives on a scale even exceeding that of the previous war, partly because the Second World War lasted half again as long. Germany lost two and a quarter million killed in battle. Japan, which had been at war continuously from 1937 until 1945, lost 1,174,000 combatants and in addition 330,000 civilians killed in air-raids. Russian losses have been officially given as seven million, but no complete figures are available. Certainly her losses exceeded those of any other belligerent. It was, as never before, a war between whole nations, and women and children figured very high among the death-rolls.

One of its unique characteristics was the enormous uprooting and displacement of people. From the start the Germans in Poland, Belgium, and France used the hordes of civilian refugees as a means of confusing and handicapping the enemy. Bombing made millions homeless. The favourite precaution, evacuation, still meant displacement, and was used by Americans against Japan when they gave precise warnings of the time at which particular cities would be bombed. German conscription of labour in the occupied countries uprooted millions of Europeans from their homes. Each side took millions of prisoners. On the Russian front the ebb and flow of battle wiped out thousands of towns and villages. Displaced persons – the refugee, exile, prisoner-of-war, deported worker, evacuee – were victims of modern war on a scale never before known. They bequeathed to the postwar world a vast problem of resettlement and rehousing, which the division of Germany and the reshaping of the map in Poland and the Middle East made still more intractable. A period of convalescence was inevitable, and it was necessarily protracted and beset with difficulties. If aggregate loss of life was less than before, the amount of human suffering and distress was much greater. Roosevelt's ideals of 'freedom from want and from fear' struck a responsive chord in the hearts of uprooted and homeless people everywhere.

The revolutionary effects of the war were enhanced by the extent to which it was much more truly a world war. This can be measured by the very small number of states which contrived to remain neutral. In Europe Spain and Portugal, Sweden and Switzerland, Eire and Turkey, alone stayed neutral. But all were affected: Spain and Turkey were induced to curtail their exports of rare metals to Germany, Portugal agreed to lease bases in the Azores to Britain, Eire permitted individual volunteers to join the British forces. Switzerland and Sweden clung to their traditional roles as the servants of humanitarian causes, and became intermediaries for Red Cross and postal services. Egypt, though in name neutral, became in fact a battlefield. No South American state remained neutral throughout, though Argentina did not become a belligerent until March 1945. Although the United Nations at first excluded former enemy powers, it was from the outset a more universal body than either the Allied and Associated Powers of 1919, or the original League of Nations. The Charter, which was unanimously adopted at San Francisco in June 1945, was signed by the delegates of fifty nations.[1]

Collaboration and Resistance. In every liberated country two factors making for social revolution, in the sense of a changed balance between social classes, were the purge of collaborators or alleged

1. See p. 876.

collaborators, and the pressure of armed resistance movements. The bitterest legacy of German occupation was the civil strife it engendered between those who had supported Axis puppet régimes or profited from helping the enemy, and those who had engaged in active resistance. Such divisions did not coincide with old class divisions, though anyone of wealth was suspect. In most countries the bulk of the population belonged to neither of these extremes, but included infinite shades of semi-collaboration, acquiescence, surrender to necessity, neutralism, and mild piecemeal resistance. But in the excitement of liberation and amid the chaotic conditions which war left behind, such subtleties were liable to be swept impatiently aside.

Even resistance forces themselves had many nuances, ranging from the few intransigent patriots who had fought on from the beginning, to the 'resisters of the last hour', who had prudently waited to see the direction of events before committing themselves to open defiance of the Germans. Many of the latter were apt to demand purges of collaborators with added vehemence, if only to demonstrate their own implacable purity. In every occupied country trials were held of leading collaborators: industrialists who had made profits from German contracts, militiamen who had fought resisters, politicians and administrators who had served governments subservient to Germany. Such trials might be less than fair to the accused in their procedure and the atmosphere of prejudice in which they were held. A few – most notoriously the trials of Pétain and Laval in France – were so mishandled as to besmirch the provisional governments under whose auspices they took place. But even rougher justice had usually been already meted out, by bands of partisans and city mobs, to alleged collaborators or local traitors seized during the first days of liberation. Local 'liberation committees' or groups of resisters, sometimes Communist in inspiration, tended to seize authority for a time and made lynch law prevail. The formal trials of collaborators were, in part, an attempt by the new provisional governments to regularize and satisfy the general clamour for revenge.

Another of the critical problems confronting such governments was to disarm the resistance organizations, and restore habits of law-abidingness in societies where 'taking the law into one's own hands' had become a habit hallowed by patriotism. So, too, the systematic collection of national taxes, attacks on the prevalent black market, and the implementation of schemes of rationing and price controls, all tasks basic to economic reconstruction, were among the most unpopular and difficult undertakings of the new and often inexperienced administrations. It had been for years a patriotic duty to evade taxes, frustrate German requisitioning of supplies, and defy German regulations. It was not easy suddenly to make people think differently about authority, however nationalistic and beneficent its purposes.

Because of these difficulties, and in order to attract the maximum amount of public credit and support, most provisional governments were combinations of moderates, socialists, and Communists, as in France under the leadership of General de Gaulle in 1945. For a time western Europe was ruled, in effect, by a series of 'Popular Front' governments, brought into being by the very animosities and emergencies which had produced their predecessors of 1936.[1] The same was true at first of the eastern European states which fell under Soviet control – Poland, Hungary, Rumania, Bulgaria, Yugoslavia, Czechoslovakia – but in most of these, where the first coalitions normally included even clericalists and peasant radical parties as well as socialists and Communists, it was the Communists who steadily gained ground. In Belgium, France, and Italy, the Communists were kept inferior in power to their rivals and eventually, in 1947, were ousted from a share in power.

The Iron Curtain. In the eastern countries there were several reasons for Communist ascendancy, apart from the steady inducement of the Red Army itself. In each of them Communists gained initial control of two key departments: the army and the police. The governments were under a double obligation, stipulated by the Allies, to purge their administrations and public life of those who had supported the Axis or had worked against Russia, and to ensure the security of Soviet lines of communication with eastern Germany. Using these formal powers as a weapon and these obligations as an excuse, Stalin directed the liquidation of the old ruling classes of eastern Europe. So many of them had been in outlook anti-democratic and anti-Communist, in record collaborationist, that they were left with little defence. They were, in effect, pulverized and eliminated and the intermediate parties which favoured parliamentary government were too lacking in tradition or experience to be effectual. Thus was the field cleared for complete Communist ascendancy without too obvious Soviet intervention. Where intervention was needed, as in Rumania in the spring of 1945, it was forthcoming. When King Michael refused to dismiss General Radescu as Prime Minister, he was compelled to do so by direct Soviet interference, and the Communist Grozea replaced Radescu. These new Communist revolutions were like the Bolshevik Revolution of 1917 in reverse: they began not with a social revolutionary movement which then built up a police force so powerful that it turned the state into a police state; they began with an all-powerful police force which then, controlled and

1. See p. 706.

manipulated by the Communist party, carried out a social and economic revolution.

This new pattern of Communist revolution emerged only gradually from the chaos of war. It was a pattern broken here and there – in Yugoslavia by the independence of Tito, in Czechoslovakia by the need to effect a formal Communist *coup* as late as 1948. But nowhere did it degenerate into open civil war as in Greece, and it was for the most part a silent sequence of manoeuvres and tricks which left half a dozen nations under solid Communist control.[1]

Meanwhile the first phases of an economic revolution were added to the social and the political revolutions. Industries and transport were nationalized, schemes for more extensive industrialization were prepared. Extensive land reforms distributed land to the peasants. In Poland and Czechoslovakia a whole new peasantry was created by settling families on land expropriated from the Germans. In Hungary, where distribution was most extensive and especially popular, Land Acts of 1945 gave holdings to some 640,000 families. In these three countries, along with Rumania and Bulgaria, more than two million families received land. The Communist revolutions carried out more redistribution of land in a couple of years than had taken place in two decades between the wars. In 1949 the governments began, like their Russian predecessors of 1929, the reverse process of collectivizing the land – much less popular and more hazardous undertaking. The final effect was partly to subordinate the economies of eastern Europe to Soviet needs, and partly to assimilate them to the Soviet pattern of nationalized industry and collectivized agriculture. Thenceforth some ninety million eastern Europeans were brought under direct or indirect Communist government, and the new contrasts between eastern and western Europe were even more definite and more consistent than the old.

The new line of regional contrasts lay not between Russia and Europe, but between eastern and western Europe. The country which in every sense straddled this new dividing-line was defeated and partitioned Germany. From the outset the notion of a joint Four-Power condominium over Germany lost any reality, despite the setting up of the Allied Control Council in Berlin. The one policy all were agreed upon was keeping Germany under military occupation for many years. But the longer each administered its zone for this purpose, the more likely it became that each would try to mould that zone after its own image, thus sharpening the contrasts and increasing the tensions between east and west. Two particular issues furthered this tendency. First, the transfer of the whole area of prewar Germany east of the Oder and

1. See p. 830.

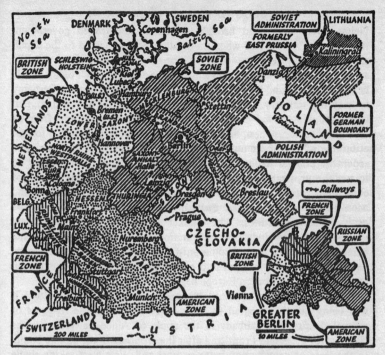

MAP 25. GERMANY AFTER THE SECOND WORLD WAR

The division of Germany in 1945, for purposes of allied military occupation, created four distinct zones, as shown. Berlin, though inside the Soviet Zone, was itself divided into four zones, each of which was separately occupied (see inset). The western frontiers of reconstituted Poland were pushed westward, at Germany's expense, to the Oder-Neisse line, in compensation for the eastern territories of the old Poland now taken by the Soviet Union; and East Prussia was partitioned between Poland and the Soviet Union. The three western zones were increasingly amalgamated, and in May 1949, were made into a new German Federal Republic at Bonn. Five months later the Soviet Zone was converted into the (East) German Democratic Republic.

815

Neisse rivers to Poland brought Communist-controlled government further into Europe; and when the western powers agreed to the expulsion from that territory of its German population they virtually acquiesced in this westward extension of Soviet power. Poland would henceforth be bound to Russia by need for her support against Germany to keep this territory. Secondly the agreement reached at Potsdam, that each occupying power could satisfy its claims for reparations from its own zone of occupation, left each power separately responsible for the economic affairs of its own zone. Concerted policy broke down, and separatist policies led to sharper contrasts. Germany, soon to be no longer the prostrate country of 1945, remained the central ground of contention between East and West, aggravating all other conflicts and accentuating all differences. Eastern Germany was handled like the other eastern satellites. The Junker landlords of Prussia were expropriated, some industries were nationalized, the Social Democratic party was absorbed into a Communist-controlled Socialist Unity party, native Communists were put into office. Eastern Europe now extended to the Elbe, where western Europe began (see Map 25).

If the 'Iron Curtain' was not dropped in Europe until after 1947, it was being quietly prepared as early as 1945. Just as the maggots of mutual distrust were already in the apple of Allied unity during the clamour for a 'Second Front' and after the dropping of the atomic bomb, so the lines of demarcation between East and West were taking shape even while the San Francisco Conference sat. There was never a period after the Second World War when it could be said that world harmony and unity prevailed. Old conflicts subsided into new discords, war gave place to revolution, and at the same moment it became possible that revolution might, in turn, lead to further war. War and peace, as befitted a world seen in terms of the theory of relativity, had ceased to be two distinct processes, cut apart by formal declarations of war and momentous conferences of peace. One merged into the other, imperceptibly and fatalistically, as one single continuum of space and time. The result was not peace but 'cold war' – that peculiarly nihilistic conception, born of the war against nazi nihilism and the impact of the atomic bomb. The consequences of that conception will be examined below.[1] But its first important characteristic has already been described: the 'cold war' was born of the 'cold revolution' in eastern Europe.

1. See p. 837.

CHAPTER 30

EUROPE IN CONVALESCENCE

FIRST AID AND RECONSTRUCTION, 1944-50

IT was recognized as early as 1941 that the economic rehabilitation of Europe after years of German occupation and exploitation would be both difficult and urgent. It was one of the triumphs of western states-manship in the Second World War that even before the tide of war began to turn steps were taken to prepare for this task. The most elaborate organization designed to deal with the problem was the United Nations Relief and Rehabilitation Administration (UNRRA) set up in November 1943. It was a collective international agency, financed by member-states, a provider of first aid for the liberated countries, to follow in the wake of the armed forces and to administer relief of all kinds until the new national administrations could take over respon-sibility. It was to be disbanded as soon as each country had its own system of government, if only on a provisional basis, once more in working order. Its staff was recruited internationally, and it became a pattern and a source of experience for the many other international functional agencies set up under United Nations auspices.[1]

Born of Churchill's pledge of 21 August 1940, to bring relief with victory to the occupied and defeated countries of Europe, and sponsored particularly by Sir Frederick Leith-Ross in Britain and by Dean Acheson in the United States, UNRRA began its work in the field in the spring of 1944. By the end of 1947 it had arranged for the collection, transport, and distribution of more than twenty-two million tons of supplies. It completed its work in that year and formally came to an end in September 1948. The main burden of its work was borne by the United States. It gave help without political discrimination, and was actively supported by Communists and non-Communists. Its main operations were in Greece, Poland, Yugoslavia, Czechoslovakia, Austria, and Italy, and without it the material distress of postwar Europe would have been very much worse than it was. It gave immediately food, clothing, and medical supplies where they were most needed in war-ravaged lands; it helped nations to rehabilitate their agriculture and industry and to get transport working again; it saved millions of Europeans from famine and disease. It was the biggest piece of first-aid work in history, and it

1. See p. 885.

817

was a triumph of international cooperation. Nor was its legacy only temporary. When it was disbanded its work was taken over by the International Refugee Organization (IRO), the World Health Organization (WHO), the Food and Agriculture Organization (FAO), and the United Nations International Children's Emergency Fund (UNICEF).

Of the seventeen receiving countries scattered all over the world, China received most relief. In Europe, Poland, Italy, Yugoslavia, Greece, and Czechoslovakia all benefited very substantially. Even after the end of 1945, when it began to be apparent that a rift was appearing between Communist and non-Communist states, the western nations (especially the United States, Canada, and Great Britain) continued to lavish supplies on potential enemies. Poland and the two Soviet Republics of White Russia and the Ukraine received millions of dollars of supplies, as a free gift, though these areas were clearly the main springboard of Communist power in eastern Europe. The western powers could have given no clearer assurance of their eagerness to build friendly relations between East and West and there was little criticism of this unusual practice of 'feeding the mouth that bites you'. If one motive of Western policy was to kill Communism by kindness it failed. But history records no finer gesture for peace.

Equally unprecedented magnanimity was shown towards former enemy countries. UNRRA played a crucial part in the reconstruction of Italy. Having in Churchill's phrase 'worked her passage home' by contributing to the defeat of Germany, she met with a ready and sympathetic response from the Allies. When the provisional Italian government eventually took over in 1947, UNRRA had poured into Italy more than 418 million dollars' worth of supplies and services. Then the Italian government financed additional programmes of relief and rehabilitation including a large rehousing programme. Austria, too, recognized as more a victim than an accomplice of German aggressions, was saved from collapse by the ready flow of UNRRA supplies. In Germany, while UNRRA was mainly concerned with the care of the millions of displaced persons of other nationalities, immediate relief for Germans themselves was provided by the military authorities of occupation. Allied policy in Germany lacked consistency, in that the dismantling of certain industrial plants went beyond those solely concerned with making armaments, and so clashed with the aim of making 'Bizonia' self-supporting. But the aid it provided enabled the new German Federal Republic, created in 1949, to build economic prosperity on solid foundations. In Japan the United States authorities, who shouldered the responsibility for postwar administration, had to spend several hundred million dollars a year to prevent starvation and to buttress the disorganized industry and trade of the country. Everywhere repairs completely overshadowed reparations as the guiding principle of Western policy towards defeated enemy countries. This was least true of the Soviet Union, where the vast extent of devastation induced the government to show less concern for the rehabilitation of other countries but intense interest in their capacity to pay reparations.[1]

National Reconstruction. Throughout Europe much relief and immediate rehabilitation were provided, quite apart from the work of UNRRA, by the national administrations of the liberated countries. In France, Belgium, the Netherlands, Norway, and Denmark the restored or provisional postwar governments devoted their energies to getting national economies into working order again; to rebuilding railroads and roads, bridges and ports, houses and factories. Even where liberation was a mercifully quick and relatively painless process, as in Norway or Denmark, the dispersal of populations and German exploitation left intricate problems of resettlement and reconstruction. Where, as in France, the land had again become a battlefield during liberation, these tasks were formidable.

The situation in France was an extreme example of the difficulties which existed elsewhere. By the beginning of 1945, although France was freed from German occupation, her whole economy was in a desperate condition. In March her Minister of Production declared: 'We are still in the stage of emergency repairs.' Her two greatest deficiencies were transport and coal. Factories could not begin working again mainly because lack of transport deprived them of coal. Trucks produced by the Renault works remained unusable for lack of tyres. Yet by the summer of 1945, when war ended, French 'emergency repairs' had been carried out with remarkable success. Coal production was back to three quarters of its 1939 level, agriculture output was back to two thirds of prewar output, though factories were yielding only two fifths of their former production. French ports were handling half their prewar traffic, and with a much diminished rolling stock the railways were carrying as many passengers as in 1938.

In Belgium recovery was equally rapid and impressive. Brussels was liberated with unexpected speed on 3 September 1944. When a few days later the prewar government, headed by Hubert Pierlot, returned from London, 60,000 prisoners of war and some 500,000 deported workers were still held captive in Germany. As in France transport, fuel, and food were chronically scarce, and the currency was heavily inflated. The Belgian government was unable to handle the first of these difficulties, scarcity, as swiftly and successfully as the French; but it dealt with the

1. See p. 840.

second, inflation, much more successfully. In October 1944 the Minister of Finance, Camille Gutt, issued a series of carefully drafted decrees replacing the old currency by a new issue of notes. The entire issue of old notes, except for the smallest denominations, was withdrawn, but citizens who surrendered their notes did not at once get in exchange an equivalent amount of the new. All sums over a certain amount were frozen for a fixed period; bank accounts were blocked; and roughly forty per cent of the note issue and bank accounts were converted into part of the national debt, bearing three and a half per cent interest. This ingenious plan not only stabilized the currency and checked inflation, but struck a deadly blow at the operations of the black market, which were almost entirely conducted in notes of large denomination. In France General de Gaulle's Minister of National Economy, Pierre Mendès France, wanted to carry out a similar operation at the beginning of 1945. He failed to get the support of his colleagues, with the result that postwar France continued to suffer from mounting inflation and budgetary instability, and from a black market in nearly all essential goods so extensive that it hamstrung the government's labours of reconstruction.

Comparable difficulties prevailed elsewhere. The Netherlands suffered particularly from savage German reprisals after the Allied reverse at Arnhem in the autumn of 1944, and from flooding of large tracts of fertile land as part of the defence measures taken by the retreating German forces. Even when these difficulties had been overcome, there remained for the Dutch the problem of a rapidly growing population whose standard of living depended on trade with nearby markets in Germany and Britain, and on wealth derived from Indonesia, neither of which was as available after the war as it had been before. Denmark, though not liberated until Germany's surrender in May 1945, enjoyed better material conditions than any other liberated country. Her national larder was fully stocked, her productive capacity was almost intact, and she had no black market. Her economic problems were not inherent, as in France or the Netherlands. They arose from the general European shortage of raw materials, especially of coal and coke which she needed to import, and from Allied control of shipping and trade which prevented her getting high prices for butter and bacon. Norway, on the other hand, suffered severely from currency inflation and the breakdown of transport and communications, especially the loss of half the merchant navy upon which her prosperity had rested. In September 1945 her government carried out a currency reform on the lines of the Gutt plan in Belgium, and prices were kept down by subsidies. By 1947 her whole economy was well on the road to recovery.

Wartime socialization carried in its train peacetime nationalization. This inherent tendency was greatly strengthened by the strongly socialist and Communist political forces which permeated resistance movements everywhere, and by the general swing to the left of public opinion in most countries at the end of the war.[1] As in 1919, years of habituation to stringent governmental controls, the existence of large-scale state undertakings, and the practical need for powerful authority to tidy up war's aftermath, all combined to strengthen the hand of government. This happened just when the principles of socialism were coming into favour. Many were disillusioned with prewar capitalism, and saw in principles of free competition and *laissez-faire* no possible remedy for the ills of postwar Europe. Nor, until 1947, had Communism the scarifying power which it had in 1919 and which it was to have again after 1947. At first, in the era of postwar 'popular front' coalitions, while the appeal of resistance movements survived and there was still a residue of regard for Soviet friendship and some hope of its continuance, socialism seemed only slightly distinguished from new-style Communism. The German habit of damning all resisters as Communists had helped to make Communism as respectable as resistance, and to cast oblivion over the days when, before June 1941, Communism had allied itself with Nazism.

By 1945 there existed, therefore, two main urges toward accepting socialist principles of nationalization and state regulation as the basis of national reconstruction: the collectivization of wartime expediency and postwar necessity, and the collectivism of principle and ideology. It was on this twofold basis that coalitions of moderate liberals and radicals with socialists and Communists became possible in France, Italy, and Belgium. For the first phase of reconstruction, at least, nearly all major parties could move along the same road of economic planning and social control. The austerities and discipline of war were projected far into the postwar years. This was as true of Great Britain as of the liberated countries of Europe. The policy of Sir Stafford Cripps, Chancellor of the Exchequer in the Labour government of 1945-50, became the exemplar of sustained austerity and self-denial in the cause of long-term economic reconstruction. Rationing and price controls, food subsidies and currency regulations, continued long after the end of hostilities, and in the critical year of 1947 they became even more severe than they had been during the war itself.

Between 1945 and 1950 major national resources and industries throughout Europe were increasingly taken under public ownership or management, as a basis for planned economic reconstruction. The Bank

1. See p. 825.

of England and the Bank of France became in name, as well as in fact, governmental agencies. In Britain and France a favourite device was the 'public corporation', entrusted with the management of a particular sector of industry but designed to emphasize business methods rather than bureaucratic regimentation. British coal mines were nationalized and their management given to the National Coal Board; the British Transport Commission supervised all forms of public transport; and corresponding authorities were set up for aviation, gas, and electricity. In France, too, coal mines, gas and electricity, civil aviation, some of the larger insurance companies, and the Renault motor works were placed under the control of corporations representing employees, consumers, and government. Industry as a whole was re-invigorated by the Monnet Plan for the Modernization and Equipment of French Economy, launched in 1946. It concentrated on the six basic sectors of coal, steel, power, transport, building materials, and agriculture. By 1950 its main objectives had been mostly, but unevenly, reached. Whereas in 1950 the private sector of British economy still included four fifths of British industry, between a fourth and a third of France's productive capacity became state-owned. But in both countries private enterprise operated within a complex framework of state regulation and subsidy, and governmental control of credit and trade. Liberal capitalism and faith in the social value of private profit-making declined sharply. It remained stronger in Belgium where no radical policy of nationalization was undertaken. It was weaker in the Netherlands where there emerged a new Labour party, born of the wartime Netherlands People's Movement, canalizing most of the reformist but non-Communist currents in the resistance movements. The new party, founded in February 1946, included Catholics and Protestants, liberals and socialists, and was perforce mildly reformist and socialist in policy. But the extent of eventual nationalization in the Netherlands was little greater than in Belgium.

By the middle of the century the contrast within Europe lay not between free enterprise and collectivism, but between western nations in which state control and certain public enterprises were organized for the benefit of the community as determined by democratically elected governments,[1] and the new 'people's democracies' of eastern Europe in which almost the whole national economy was controlled by single-party states operating within the orbit of Soviet power. The new Communist governments of the East nationalized their main industries and set up planned economies on the Soviet model, until more than ninety per cent of industrial production in eastern Europe, apart from Rumania,

1. See p. 826.

was state-owned. Even anti-Communist Turkey nationalized her railways, shipping, banking, and many other industries. Collectivization of the land also proceeded fast, though by the circuitous route of breaking up the large estates and establishing first peasant cooperatives, and (after 1949) collective farms.[1]

Marshall Aid. In June 1947 a quite novel factor was introduced into the tasks of postwar reconstruction by the dramatic proposals of the United States Secretary of State, George Marshall. Speaking at Harvard, he pointed out that for the next few years at least the requirements of Europe far exceeded her ability to pay for them. He added: 'It is logical that the United States should do whatever it is able to do to assist in the return of normal economic health in the world, without which there can be no political stability and no assured peace.' The Marshall offer was, in short, to finance the recovery and reconstruction of Europe as UNRRA had already financed the relief of Europe. The British and French governments immediately took the initiative in proposing to the Soviet Union a meeting between their three Foreign Ministers in Paris that month, to draft a statement of Europe's needs. The Russians, believing that the scheme would break down because the capitalist world was on the brink of financial collapse, were lukewarm from the start. In July the British and French governments invited twenty-two other European states to a conference on the Marshall offer. The Soviet Union not only held aloof but forbade the attendance of the states under her influence–Finland, Poland, Hungary, Yugoslavia, Rumania, Bulgaria, Albania, and Czechoslovakia. It was in 1947 that the 'Iron Curtain' was first lowered, betokening the new era of 'cold war', dispelling the hopes which for two years had encouraged the United States and Great Britain to disarm, and so perpetuating the division of Germany.[2]

From the organization required to state European needs and distribute Marshall Aid there developed a remarkable series of agencies for European cooperation in the common task of reconstruction. These included, pre-eminently, the Organization for European Economic Cooperation (OEEC) with the immediate task of administering the dollars granted by Congress, but with the final aim of erecting 'a sound European economy through the cooperation of its members'. Its original participants included Austria, Belgium, Denmark, Eire, France, Greece, Iceland, Italy, Luxembourg, the Netherlands, Norway, Portugal, Sweden, Switzerland, Turkey, and the United Kingdom. It thus included both former enemy states and former neutrals, as well as Allied powers. By the end of September these nations submitted to President Truman a

1. See p. 814.
2. See p. 836.

scheme of self-help and mutual aid, as the counterpart to receiving financial aid from the United States. The European Recovery Programme (ERP), commonly known as the Marshall Plan, was approved by President and Congress. Congress appropriated $6.8 billion for the first fifteen months, and undertook to follow this with three further annual grants. Paul G. Hoffman was put in charge of the new Economic Cooperation Administration (ECA) to administer the programme on behalf of the United States. It ensured self-help by stipulating that each recipient should put into a 'counterpart fund' a sum of money equivalent to grants received. Counterpart funds could be spent only with the approval of the American authorities, who took care that they were spent only to develop the nation's economy and promote European recovery in general. By the end of 1948 a total of more than $4 billion had been allocated, Britain receiving about a quarter and France about a fifth of the total. In April 1949 President Truman approved the allocation of a further $5.43 billion for the next fifteen months. By then the three western zones of Germany were also participating.

Three months before, the President had also promulgated a further form of aid to undeveloped countries which gave rise to the Technical Cooperation Administration (TCA). He said: 'We must embark on a new bold policy for making the benefits of our scientific advances and industrial progress available for the improvement and growth of underdeveloped areas. ...' The scheme was not to provide money so much as technical advice and assistance, to enable more backward peoples outside Europe to increase their productivity. In this way, too, the United States made powerful contributions to the economic recovery of the war-shattered world. It made possible more than mere recovery. It helped countries like India to advance towards a standard of productivity and of living higher than they had ever known before.

By 1950 economic recovery throughout Europe was well advanced. Countless problems of recovery remained: exporting countries like the United Kingdom and the Netherlands faced acute difficulties in their balance of payments with dollar areas; shortages of essential materials continued; inflation and financial instability remained recurrent bugbears of many governments. The greatest outstanding world problem was not, as many had feared, economic collapse. It was political tension. Even while Europe passed through the stage of convalescence, old fevers of political antagonism recurred in an even more virulent form. How this came about, and what were the immediate consequences, will be examined in the following two sections.

WELFARE STATES AND PEOPLE'S DEMOCRACIES

The reconstruction of government and administration was no less urgent than the reconstruction of economic life. Experience of Hitlerism revitalized democratic ideals everywhere in Europe. In the new or revised constitutions which came into operation throughout the continent within a year or two after the end of hostilities, it was generally assumed that complete universal suffrage was now inevitable and that the voice of the people as a whole should decide the new régimes. In the eastern states controlled or influenced by the Soviet Union electorates excluded all who had collaborated with fascism, and in the western states, too, a large number of former collaborators who had not fled or been killed were in prison or otherwise deprived of civic rights. By the end of 1946 the great majority of the adult population of Europe had been given an opportunity to register its choice of constitution or of government or of both. In the Soviet Union, Yugoslavia, and Bulgaria ninety per cent or more voted for Communism; in Czechoslovakia, less than forty per cent supported Communism; in France and Finland about twenty-five per cent; in Italy, Belgium, and Hungary, less than twenty per cent; in Austria and Greece, Norway and Sweden, the Netherlands and western Germany, less than ten per cent; in Great Britain, less than one per cent. A rough spectrum appeared, ranging from deep red in the east to the palest pink in the west and north; though the surprise was that in France, Italy, and Belgium such deep hues of red were revealed. This could be explained partly by the conditions of working-class distress in these war-ravaged lands, partly by the success of Communist parties and organizations in exploiting the rebound against fascism, partly by the still strong appeal of the resistance movements in which Communists had contrived to win influence and credit.

The appeal of Communism in the West was part of a larger swing towards the Left in public opinion–a tide of sentiment and political ideas which carried with it a resurgence of social democratic and Christian socialist movements. In Britain the general elections of 1945 (the first to be held since 1935) returned a large Labour party representation of 393 against 213 Conservatives, and a strong Labour government. In France, where the new constitution of the Fourth Republic was eventually approved and came into force in December 1946, the new National Assembly of 618 deputies included 183 Communists, 105 Socialists, and 164 Catholic Democrats (*Mouvement républicaine populaire*, or MRP). In both Belgium and the Netherlands, where strong 'Christian-Social' movements had developed during occupation, the new Catholic parties were widened to include non-

Catholics who were in sympathy with mildly reformist policies. This widening gave the Catholic parties great electoral advantages over the more divided Protestant parties and the Socialists. They won nearly half the seats in the Belgian Parliament and a third of the seats in each chamber of the Dutch States-General. The Socialists held only a third of the seats in the Belgian chambers, and less than a third in the Dutch. In Italy the first free elections since 1921 were held in June 1946. The Constituent Assembly then elected, after rejection of the old monarchy in favour of a republic, had as its largest single party the Christian Democrats with 207 seats out of 556. The Socialists won 115 seats, the Communists 104. As in France the 'big three' parties, controlling between them three quarters of the seats, were Christian Democrats, Socialists, and Communists; and, as in France, the earliest governments were perforce coalitions of these three parties. In the elections of 1948 electoral strength was still further concentrated in these three parties, who then won ninety per cent of the seats in the chamber of deputies.

In Western Germany, where the constitution of a new Federal Republic was born of the labours of the Bonn Parliamentary Council set up in 1948, a somewhat different pattern of parties emerged. It was complicated by recrudescence of the old party system of the Weimar Republic. But in the elections to the new Bundestag of 1949 Konrad Adenauer's Christian Democratic Union polled nearly a third of the votes, Kurt Schumacher's Social Democrats polled only two per cent less. These two large rival parties overshadowed all others, among whom the Communists polled less than six per cent of the votes. In Norway as in Britain the Labour party, for the first time in its history, won a clear majority over all others in 1945. In Denmark the four major political parties of Social Democrats, Liberals, Conservatives, and Radicals were little changed by the war, though postwar elections showed a decline in the strength of the Conservatives and Radicals and gains for the Social Democrats and Liberals.

Throughout the whole of western Europe postwar politics shared, therefore, several common features. In general the old Right, whether outright fascist or merely conservative, suffered eclipse; the old Left, whether social democrat or Communist, showed a new strength; wherever, as in the Low Countries, France, Italy, and Western Germany, Catholic parties had developed strong reformist wings seeking to carry out a Christian socialist programme of reforms, they made dramatic gains at the expense of Social Democrats and Liberals. Everywhere old-fashioned liberalism, devoted to principles of free competitive enterprise and free trade, declined even more than conservatism. Much of the strength of the reinvigorated Christian Democratic movements derived, indeed, from the support of liberals and moderate conservatives to whom neither social democracy nor Communism was acceptable. The mood of the years 1945–50 was for vigorous state action to restore national prosperity, renovate the structure of economic and political life, and ensure enough social reforms to guarantee a measure of social security and 'freedom from want'.

The Welfare State. The great majority of Europeans, with a passion deeper even than in 1919, now wanted democracy. But liberal democracy of the 1919 vintage seemed inadequate. Constitutional liberties, universal suffrage, freedom of association and public meeting, there must be; but these alone no longer aroused the enthusiasm of the masses. Democracy must now be social in character as well as political, and the new state must hold itself responsible for securing the well-being and full employment of its citizens. The emotional drive which lay behind this almost universal demand had three main sources. It came from experience of economic crisis and mass unemployment before the war, from experience of acute personal insecurity during the war, and from the resolve, strong especially in the movements of organized resistance, to build after the war a society within which human dignity and personal fulfilment might be more amply ensured. The tendency after 1919 had been to return to 'normalcy' as quickly as possible. After 1945 the urge to innovate was stronger than the desire to restore.

Characteristic of the ideals nourished by resistance movements was the French 'Resistance Charter' drawn up in March 1944 by the National Council of Resistance. This programme for 'a more just social order' included, in its list of economic reforms, such demands as 'the rational organisation of an economy which will assure the subordination of private interest to the general interest', 'return to the nation of the great monopolies in the means of production, the sources of energy, mineral wealth, insurance companies, and the large banks', and 'participation by the workers in the direction of economic life'. Its social reforms envisaged 'the right to work and leisure', 'measures ensuring security for every worker and his family', 'a guaranteed national purchasing power', 'independent trade unionism endowed with extensive powers in the organization of economic and social life', 'a complete plan of social security,' and a policy extending security to agricultural workers no less than industrial. The main economic reforms, as already seen, were largely achieved in France during the period of convalescence by measures of nationalization, though the participation of workers in the management and direction of business and industry did not proceed very far. The other reforms envisaged by the French resistance movements were partially attained by the introduction of improved systems of social insurance, generous family allowances, and the restoration of full rights to trade unions.

In most other former occupied countries the experience of resistance and the predominance of left-wing opinion after liberation encouraged very similar ideas and led to comparable legislation. But more potent, as an example, than the idealism of resistance was the policy followed by the United Kingdom in elaborating and completing its existing system of social security. In 1942 Sir William (later Lord) Beveridge published his famous *Report on Social Insurance and Allied Services*. It attracted wide international interest as a statement of practical methods of social reorganization in the postwar world. The notion of comprehensive public protection for the individual and the family 'from the cradle to the grave' against sickness, poverty, unemployment, squalor, and ignorance, by provision of minimal social services of public health and medical aid, pensions and family allowances, insurance against unemployment, improved housing, and public education, struck responsive chords all over Europe. That Britain, only two years after Dunkirk, should be debating such a plan caught the imagination of the world. The Labour government of 1945, with little opposition in principle from the Conservative party, passed a series of acts which ended the old poor law system, extended universally the provision of free medical and dental services, and unified into a national scheme of social security the previous systems of insurance against sickness, disability, unemployment, and old age. It was run mainly by the state but with the cooperation of voluntary associations. It left room for provision of additional security by voluntary insurance and schemes of superannuation. The educational system had already been reorganized by the Conservative Minister of Education, R. A. Butler, in the Butler Act of 1944; and a system of family allowances, also advocated in the Beveridge Report, was instituted in 1945. Other countries which trod a similar path were France, Belgium, Norway, and Spain. By 1950 it was widely accepted throughout Europe that extremes of poverty and wealth should be avoided, and that they could best be avoided on one hand by taxation graded according to capacity to pay, and on the other by provision of social services according to need and designed to maintain a minimum standard of living for all.

Nations which accepted these ideas quickly found themselves committed to a further policy: that of raising the average standard of living by deliberate policies of expanding productivity, promoting foreign trade, and maintaining full employment. Without full employment, and without the most efficient use of all national resources, it was unlikely that social services could be maintained, and impossible that they could be extended. Every party in the modern democratic state of universal suffrage had to support such principles or perish. Except where old conflicts of dogma and outlook revived, as between clericalists and anti-clericalists in France and Italy, and except where new extraneous issues arose, such as the conflict in Belgium about the abdication of King Leopold, differences between parties were now for the most part differences of emphasis and priority, procedure and method, rather than conflicts of basic principle. The major exception to this generalization, in spite of agreement about certain measures of nationalization and social security, was in every instance the Communists.

Communist Strategy. For roughly two years after the end of the war, Communists shared in ministerial power in France, Belgium, and Italy, in a succession of what were virtually left-wing coalitions of the 'popular front' pattern. In this respect the governments of these years corresponded to the earlier postwar governments of the eastern European countries.[1] But the record of these two years discouraged the continuation of the experiment on the home front as much as international events of these years destroyed the hopes of smooth cooperation between East and West. In May 1947 the governments of the Socialist Paul Ramadier in France and of the Christian Democrat Alcide de Gasperi in Italy expelled their Communist members, and two months earlier the Belgian socialist Paul-Henri Spaak formed a ministry which excluded the Communists. Thereafter western Communism was everywhere a party of opposition, not of government.

The strategy of Communism in the West after 1945 was to insinuate itself into positions of power, both in the machinery of the state and in trade union organizations. There entrenched, Communists proceeded to use their power to undermine the working of democratic institutions, to exploit the postwar difficulties of new and often inexperienced governments, and to provoke industrial unrest in order to disrupt national recovery. In France, while the large number of Communist deputies acted as a monolithic *bloc* in Parliament and did everything possible to discredit parliamentary government, the grip of the party over the reconstituted unions of the CGT was used to launch waves of strikes in the winters of 1946–7 and 1947–8. In 1947, coinciding with the exclusion of Communists from the ministry, the non-Communist unions of the CGT led by the veteran leader Léon Jouhaux seceded to form the separate *Force ouvrière*. Italian trade unions revived in 1944 and for a time achieved considerable unity, but the Italian General Confederation of Labour (CGIL) came, like the French, to be dominated by

1. See pp. 813 and 831.

Communists and by the Marxist socialists who followed Pietro Nenni. In 1949 the non-Communist unions split away to form the Italian Federation of Labour (FIL), which the following year combined with the Christian democratic unions to form a new non-Communist body, the Italian Confederation of Labour Unions (CISL).

The emancipation of large sections of organized labour from Communist control, and the simultaneous exclusion of Communists from governmental power, marked the failure of western Communism to seize power; but behind this political failure lay the deeper economic reverse, the economic recovery of western Europe and the improvement in standards of living which cut away the basis of Communist hopes – the expected collapse of capitalist economy. Further American aid, foreshadowed by the Marshall Plan of 1947, stirred Communists everywhere to final frantic efforts to undermine recovery before such aid could have its effect. The great strikes which swept over western Europe, most notably France, Belgium, and Italy, in the winter of 1947–8, were in part due to the hardships of inflation. But they were to a large extent stimulated and manipulated by western Communism in order to retard economic recovery and inflict fatal blows on the basic industries and transport services upon which revival must depend. They were the domestic front in the first major campaign of the cold war.

In eastern as in western Europe the first two years after the war were years of 'popular fronts'. At the Yalta Conference of February 1945 the Western powers recognized the predcminant influence of the Soviet Union throughout most of eastern Europe, specifically in Poland, and elsewhere in relation to the armistices which she had concluded with Finland, Rumania, Bulgaria, and Hungary between September 1944 and January 1945. The Soviet Union gained almost unlimited political and economic rights in these countries pending the conclusion of peace treaties. The Western powers established similar rights for themselves in Italy and Greece. In Czechoslovakia Soviet rights were defined by an agreement signed with the exiled Czech government in May 1944; in Yugoslavia Tito's Communist government was recognized by the West on condition that it included representatives of the non-Communist parties. Soviet predominance thus rested on the acquiescence and agreement of the Western powers as well as on the physical presence of the Red Army. But it was intended to be temporary only, and to be limited by the 'Declaration on Liberated Europe' formally agreed at Yalta. This bound all three great powers to help the nations of eastern Europe 'to form interim governmental authorities broadly representative of all democratic elements in the population and pledged to the earliest possible establishment through free elections of governments responsive to the will of the people'. On paper, then, the whole of liberated Europe, east and west, was in 1945 envisaged as passing through a phase of provisional government representing national unity, and resting upon the free electoral expression of national will. At first, since the aim of the Soviet Union was to dispel apprehensions among the Western powers and make its power in eastern Europe as respectable and legitimate as possible, it encouraged the establishment of governments of national unity. But since, from the outset, its aim was also to perpetuate and consolidate its control over eastern Europe, these governments were then used as merely temporary vehicles for Communist dictatorship.

The technique of the 'popular front', thoroughly debated and refined by the Communist International at its seventh congress in 1935, was now used again. It included not only a united front between all the workers' parties (especially Communists and social democrats), but also between these and other parties representing peasants, lower middle classes, and intellectuals. On this principle Tito, in March 1945, set up a National Liberation Front which included, along with Communists, representatives of the exiled government headed by Šubašić of the Croatian Peasant party. In Albania the National Liberation Front, proclaimed by the Communists in November 1944 when the Germans withdrew, was renamed the Democratic Front and included a few non-Communists. In Bulgaria Kimon Georgiev, leader of the Zveno National Union, headed a Fatherland Front including Agrarians led by Petkov and groups of Socialists and Liberals; but Communists held the key posts of justice and the interior. In June 1945 a Provisional Government of National Unity was set up in Poland, with Communists in a majority and in all the key positions, but including Mikolajczyk and other leaders of the Peasant party. The Rumanian Government of National Unity of August 1944 included a predominance of Peasant and Liberal party leaders and a few Communists, as did the Hungarian National Independence Front of December 1944. But each was succeeded by nominal coalitions in which Communists predominated. In Finland and in Czechoslovakia circumstances favoured the non-Communists even more, and in the latter the *coup* of 1948 was necessary to give Communism power.[1]

This initial stage of simulated national coalitions was made susceptible to manipulation by importing native Communists in the train of the Red Army – Gomulka in Poland, Dimitrov in Bulgaria, Anna Pauker in Rumania, Rákosi in Hungary, Gottwald in Czechoslovakia. Manipulation took the form of discrediting and eventually eliminating

1. See p. 833.

one by one the non-Communist members of the governments – Mikolajczyk in Poland, Maniu in Rumania, Petkov in Bulgaria, Bela Kovács in Hungary. Elimination of the peasant and liberal leaders was accomplished by the autumn of 1947, and the moment was chosen in October to set up the new Communist Information Bureau (Cominform) to 'exchange experiences' and coordinate the activities of its member parties. It included representatives of the Communist parties in the Soviet Union, Poland, Yugoslavia, Rumania, Hungary, Bulgaria, Czechoslovakia, Italy, and France. The old Third International (Comintern) had been dissolved in 1943 as a Stalinist gesture towards the West. It was now revived, in this looser form, as a counterblast to the Marshall Plan and as an indication that Communism was consolidating its grip permanently throughout eastern Europe.

This grip, almost complete by the end of 1947, was achieved by the systematic suppression of opposition, which came mainly from the agrarian parties representing the peasant masses. Agrarian leaders were usually untainted with collaboration and had large followings. They stood for small private landownership, as encouraged by the initial redistributions of the land in these states, and they were therefore the main opponents of communist collectivization. They had to be ousted by fraud and force. Petkov was tried for treason and executed, Maniu was imprisoned, Kovács was arrested by the Soviet police, Mikolajczyk was forced to flee, others were sent into exile. Only when all such leaders of serious opposition had been got rid of were elections held and new constitutions drafted. At this stage the decisive factor was Communist control of army, police, and civil administration. Such elections, in every case confirming Communist control by large majorities, were held at the end of 1945 in Albania and Yugoslavia, at the end of 1946 in Bulgaria and Rumania, and during 1947 in Poland and Hungary.

The only exceptions to this consistent pattern were Finland and Czechoslovakia. Communists won about a quarter of the seats in the Finnish Diet in March 1945 and for three years took part in a coalition government along with social democrats and agrarians. In the elections of July 1948 they won only nineteen per cent of the popular vote and were excluded from ministerial power. The main reason for Finland's apparent immunity to Soviet domination, apart from the astute and stubborn resistance put up by her people as a whole, was the decline in Soviet apprehensions about her security in the Baltic. Further pressure or domination seemed unnecessary, and not worth the difficulties it would arouse. Moreover the Soviet Union derived considerable economic advantages from the terms she imposed on the Finns in the peace treaty. In Czechoslovakia, where President Beneš attracted a more solid national support than most exiled leaders, Communists also lost ground between the elections of May 1946 (when they gained nearly thirty-eight per cent of the votes) and the end of 1947. To forestall a reverse in the elections scheduled for the spring of 1948 they therefore staged a *coup*, using their control of the police and their militant 'action committees' which were strong in government offices and labour organizations. In February 1948 a dozen liberal ministers resigned. Beneš was faced with armed demonstrations in Prague and Communist-run strikes in the key industries of the country. He was forced to accept a ministry in which the Communists predominated. A fortnight later his chief lieutenant, Jan Masaryk, son of Tomáš Masaryk who created the state in 1919, died; and in September Beneš himself died. In the elections of May the Communists won the expected large majority and proceeded to set up a new constitution on the regular pattern.

The People's Democracies. The consequence of all these events by the summer of 1948 was that liberal democracy had fallen throughout the whole eastern marchlands with the exception of Finland, and had been replaced by the so-called 'people's democracies' of Communism. On her western borders the Soviet Union had secured an unbroken belt of territories whose governments were likely to prove docile to Soviet demands and hostile to western interests. At that moment only one country managed to assert its independence from Soviet domination. Tito of Yugoslavia had been an orthodox Stalinist Communist, and had joined the Cominform in October 1947. But since the liberation of Yugoslavia owed nothing to the Red Army but much to the efforts of Tito's partisans, and the end of the war found him undisputed master of Yugoslavia, he saw no reason to be either grateful or subservient to the Soviet Union. He refused to accept any orders from Moscow which did not match his country's national interests, and when Stalin called him to order he defied the Kremlin. Even the blast of the Cominform resolution of June 1948, accusing Tito of unfriendliness towards the Soviet Union and of various doctrinal heresies, failed to shake his position or his attitude, and led to his departure from the Cominform. Sympathies with Titoism in other eastern European Communist parties began to be manifest whenever conflict arose between their national interests and the demands of Soviet policy. Already the enforced withdrawal of several eastern states from the European Recovery Programme, from which they had hoped to derive great economic advantages, strained their loyalty to their Soviet masters. The Kremlin's prohibition of the projected economic collaboration of Yugoslavia, Albania, and Bulgaria at the beginning of 1948 strained it further. But outside Yugoslavia obedience could be enforced; and the result was the replacement of native Communist leaders by Russians or minor and more obedient native Communists. In September Gomulka, secretary of the Polish Communist party, was removed from office and publicly denounced. Six months later Kostov, his Bulgarian counterpart, was likewise dismissed, tried, and eventually executed at the end of 1949. In Albania and Hungary former Communist ministers were tried and executed. The purge of native Communists continued as circumstances demanded. Anna Pauker of Rumania was removed in 1952, Slansky and Clementis of Czechoslovakia were executed in the same year.

For this reduction of the 'people's democracies' to the role of Soviet satellites ruled by puppet governments, good theoretical Marxist justification could be found in the doctrine that the victory of Communism everywhere is inevitable, and for any nation to move forward into the historical phase of proletarian dictatorship is therefore essential progress. But the economic, political, and strategic advantages for the Soviet Union of thus consolidating a vast sphere of influence and control in the eastern marchlands were so apparent that some concessions had to be made to wounded national pride. Fluctuations in Soviet policy and behaviour revealed how varied such concessions had to be and, by implication, exposed the strength of national opposition in these countries.

The year 1952 brought considerable economic hardship and intensified police terror. The purges of 1951 and 1952 betrayed strong anti-Semitic trends, and even within the Soviet Union Jews were depicted as public enemies. In January 1953 Jewish doctors of the Kremlin were charged with plotting to poison several party and military leaders. Stalin died on 5 March and was succeeded by Georgi Malenkov. Then the post of Secretary of the Party was transferred to Nikita Khrushchev, L. P. Beria resumed control of the security forces, and Marshall G. K. Zhukov became First Deputy Minister of Defence. There was much talk of the principle of 'collective leadership', and vehement denunciation of the 'cult of personality' which had developed under Stalin. The open jostlings for power in the Kremlin, culminating in the execution of Beria in 1953, the resignation of Malenkov from the premiership in February 1955, and the emergence of Khrushchev as the true heir of Stalin as dictator of the Soviet Union, had important repercussions throughout the European satellites.

Discontent became sufficiently vocal and strong to exact concessions. In Czechoslovakia, where currency reform robbed workers of their accumulated savings, the workers of the industrial centre of Pilsen held a mass demonstration which had to be crushed by troops. In East Berlin strikes broke out, precipitating an East German national rising on 17 June 1953; the régime was saved only by the Soviet army, whose tanks occupied the main cities. Malenkov promised a 'New Course', involving changes in economic planning to permit production of more food and consumer goods. In Poland and Hungary agriculture was decollectivized. There were riots in Poznan.

At the twentieth party congress in February 1956 Khrushchev proclaimed the new doctrine of 'different roads to socialism', and in April he dissolved the Cominform. The policy of strict regimentation of all communist states was now denounced as Stalinist. Titoism seemed to be vindicated, and relations between Yugoslavia and the Soviet Union began to improve. In Poland Gomulka, released from prison in 1955, regained the leadership of the Polish Communist party. In October he became Prime Minister, in spite of Khrushchev's personal visit to Warsaw to try to browbeat the party. In January 1957 relatively free elections were held; they returned Gomulka to power with a large majority.

Events in Hungary followed a more tragic course. In July 1953 Mátyás Rákosi, who had wielded autocratic power for six years, gave up the premiership to Imre Nagy but remained First Secretary of the party. Nagy followed the policy, then in line with Soviet wishes, of limited decollectivization and greater production of consumer goods. Nagy fell after Malenkov had fallen, and Rákosi resumed complete power. By June 1956 there was open criticism of the régime, as Hungarians took literally Khrushchev's doctrine of 'different roads to socialism'. Demands for the removal of Rákosi resulted in his removal on 18 July, but the demand for the return of Nagy was not met. In October, encouraged by events in Poland, students demonstrated in favour of social and political liberties. Soon they were joined by armed workers from the Budapest factories and by groups from the Hungarian army. The security forces and the Soviet troops available were too small to crush the revolt, and the Soviet command signed an armistice. Nagy was immediately restored to power, at the head of a government which included the real leaders of the old socialist and peasant parties.

Nagy's proposal that Hungary be given the same neutral status as Austria might have succeeded had it been energetically backed by the Western powers. But the United States was preoccupied with a presidential election, and Britain and France had engaged in their expedition to Suez, hotly condemned by the United States. Masked by a rival Hungarian government under the pliable János Kádár, which appealed for Soviet help, the Soviet army entered the country and on 4 November attacked Budapest. Despite bitter resistance from the Hungarian workers, the revolution was ruthlessly crushed by Soviet troops. Some 200,000 workers, students, and their families escaped across the Austrian frontier, and for more than a month a general strike continued in Budapest. The Kádár régime was established by Soviet tanks and machine-guns. The spectacle of the Red Army destroy-a genuine workers' government showed Khrushchev's more 'liberal' policy to be a sham, but the fate of Hungary served as a grim warning against similar revolts in the other lands of eastern Europe. One by-product of the Hungarian disaster was renewed tension between the Soviet Union and Yugoslavia, for Marshal Tito had criticized Moscow's policy and Nagy found refuge in the Yugoslav embassy in Budapest, until treacherously arrested after being granted a safe conduct by Kádár.

In November 1957 Marshal Zhukov, while on a visit to Yugoslavia and Albania, was deposed from his public posts in Moscow. Disembarrassed of this last of his possible rivals in 'collective leadership', Khrushchev became more openly the personal dictator of the Soviet Union and chief warder of Moscow's satellite states – a role emphasized still more by his personal tours of Asiatic and even Western countries, including France, Britain, and the United States, during the next three years, and by his spectacular appearances in New York during the meet-ings of the United Nations Assemby in 1960.

THE COMING OF THE COLD WAR

Cold war was no inept description of the series of mounting tensions between East and West which dominated the international scene during these postwar years. Relations between the Western powers and the Communist states of the East were relations of constant manoeuvre for advantage and almost incessant hostility. They were governed by positive aims and strategies like military campaigns, and they involved tactical skirmishes, careful deployment of forces, surprise attacks and improvised counter-attacks, in which each side incurred serious losses or made considerable gains. The persistence of such tensions throughout the 1950s meant that internal and international affairs became more inseparably and intricately inter-related than ever before. The ubiquity of the two demands for social security and for national security con-fronted every European government with the old dilemma of the 1930s – 'guns or butter' – for at a time of world shortages of essential materials and of economic and political convalescence, expenditure on armaments competed with expenditure on social services. The Western effort to 'contain Communism' in Europe, Asia, and Africa encountered the same dilemma. Since, it was held, Communism bred in poverty and harsh social conditions, then relief, aid, loans to non-Communist governments, and timely emancipation of colonial peoples, might be more effective ways of checking the spread of Communism than heavy outlay on armaments. Yet the standing military might of the Soviet Union and the extent of its conquests made apparent the need to 'negotiate from strength'. Both guns and butter seemed to be needed.

The preliminary internal skirmishes took place, as already described, within the Western powers in the spring of 1947, and within the Eastern European powers in the early evolution of the 'people's democracies'. The first international skirmishes took place during the negotiation of peace treaties with the lesser enemy countries of Italy, Rumania, Bulgaria, Hungary, and Finland at the Peace Conference of Paris in the late summer of 1946. The delegates of twenty-one nations there assembled stumbled into the first clear signs of intransigent enmity between the Soviet Union and the Western powers. East-West tension was written into the peace treaties of 1946 even more than it had been into the peace settlement of 1919.

The first pitched battle between the two camps was the Greek Civil War which broke out again in 1947; the height of the battle in Europe was reached, inevitably, in Germany itself in 1948; and the struggle first assumed global proportions in the war in Korea, in 1950. Thereafter the decade of the 1950s was one of repeated tussles, overshadowed increasingly by the competition of East and West for the support of the 'uncommitted peoples' of Asia and the new insurgent nationalities of Africa.

The Peace Treaties, 1946. As in 1919, the eventual settlement made by the five treaties of 1946 was determined by the 'Big Three', who were now J. F. Byrnes of the United States, Ernest Bevin of the United Kingdom, and V. M. Molotov of the Soviet Union. These three men dominated the Council of Foreign Ministers which was entrusted with the drafting of the treaties, and their characters were important. The patient, shrewd, and skilful negotiator Byrnes was usually backed by the more truculent, hard-hitting labour organizer Bevin, against the inscrutable and unpredictable Molotov. All three were men of long experience and training, senior statesmen of their countries. At the first session, held in London in September 1945, they spent three weeks in wrangling and ended in deadlock. The larger conference, meeting in Paris in July 1946, was prefaced by a meeting of the 'Big Three' to which Georges Bidault, Foreign Minister of France, was also admitted. This preliminary meeting, after prolonged negotiations, produced draft treaties for settlements with Italy, Finland, Hungary, Rumania, and Bulgaria. These were presented to the delegates of the seventeen other countries which comprised five British Dominions (Australia, Canada,

1. See p. 830.

India, New Zealand, and the Union of South Africa) four Soviet supporters (Poland, Ukraine, White Russia, and Yugoslavia) and a mixed group consisting of the Low Countries, Brazil, Czechoslovakia, China, Ethiopia, Greece, and Norway. Representatives of the five ex-enemy states affected were permitted to appear and lodge protests, but were given no share in the discussions or the decisions. As in 1919 the settlement was not negotiated but 'dictated'. On many of the votes the five pro-Soviet states lined up against the others, and the whole conference emphasized still further the rift between the rival *blocs*. The United States and Britain rewarded amenable states with generous loans, and punished recalcitrant states by withholding loans. The area of discord was widened, the surface of friction enlarged. The drafts were finally agreed to at a further meeting of the Council of Foreign Ministers held in New York at the end of 1946. They were all eventually accepted by the former enemy countries. The terms of the treaties may be roughly grouped into three categories: territorial changes; economic and military exactions; international arrangements.

Under the first head of territorial changes Italy lost most. The Franco-Italian frontier near Nice was altered to give Briga and Tenda to France; Venezia Giulia went to Yugoslavia, the Dodecanese Islands went to Greece; Trieste was to become a free territory under the protection of the Security Council of the United Nations. The whole Italian African Empire, of more than 1,200,000 square miles in Libya, Eritrea, Italian Somaliland, and Abyssinia, was forfeited. Rumania had to cede to the Soviet Union all Bessarabia and northern Bukovina, and to Bulgaria southern Dobruja, but gained Transylvania from Hungary. Finland, as provided in the armistice terms of September 1944, now lost her Karelian province to Russia and her outlet to the Arctic Ocean at Petsamo (see Map 26).

MAP 26. EASTERN EUROPE—TERRITORIAL CHANGES, 1939–47
The Second World War, like its predecessor, brought a complete redrawing of the map of the eastern marchlands of Europe (compare Map 16). Finland kept her independence but lost some territories to the Soviet Union. Estonia, Latvia, Lithuania, parts of East Prussia and eastern Poland, and Bessarabia were all incorporated into the Soviet Union. Poland was compensated at Germany's expense (see Map 25). With a few minor frontier changes the Balkan states were restored to their shape of 1919. With Communist governments in East Germany, Poland, and the Balkans, Soviet power now extended far into central Europe. After 1947 the 'Iron Curtain' from Stettin to Trieste divided Europe. In the Adriatic, Italy and Yugoslavia disputed various small areas, especially Trieste.

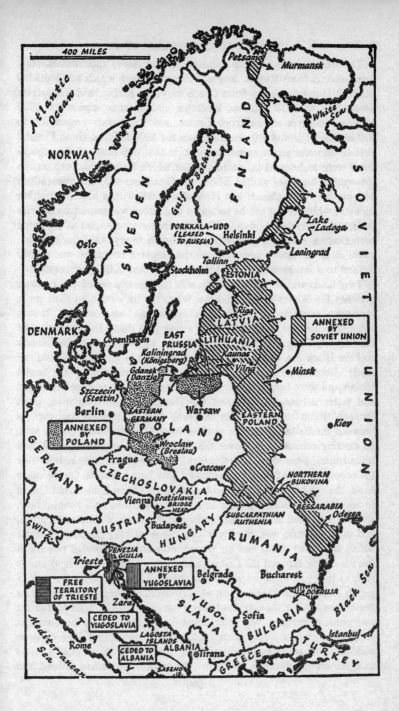

The defeated states were required to pay heavy indemnities. Italy faced claims from Russia, Yugoslavia, and Greece which totalled $330 million; Hungary claims from Czechoslovakia, Russia, and Yugoslavia amounting to $250 million; Rumania claims from Russia for $300 million; Bulgaria claims from Greece and Yugoslavia amounting to $70 million; Finland Russian demands for $300 million. Upon Finland Russia imposed an ingenious stipulation that one third of the reparations were to be paid in machinery for which Finland had neither the materials, plant, nor skilled labour. In September 1952 her reparations account was duly closed; but Finland was left with a new engineering industry which could not be scrapped and which was geared up entirely to Soviet needs and demands. Thus reparations were used as a way of perpetuating economic dependence. In each treaty, too, the military, naval, and air power permitted to the defeated countries was strictly limited to a level which robbed them of any real military strength.

Two international requirements still further sharpened the rivalries between the Soviet Union and the West, for they exposed their more long-term conflicts in the Balkans about trade and security. It was eventually decided to make Trieste a free port under the protection of the Security Council of the United Nations, and to proclaim the Danube and the Black Sea open waterways where ships of all nations could sail freely. Both these decisions were passionately resisted by the Soviet Union and were forced through by the Western powers after prolonged and bitter debates. Trieste and the Danube are the two main gates through which pass the main seaborne flow of imports and exports between the Balkan countries and the West. Had the Soviet Union, with its existing economic grip over the Balkan countries and its good land trade-routes, been also able to control these gates, her domination over the economic life of the Balkans would have been absolute. On the other hand, the internationalizing of these gateways exposed the Soviet Union to security risks. Much greater as a land power than as a naval power, she had witnessed in the Anglo-American invasions of Italy and France, and in the Pacific war, the great long-range striking capacity of states which combined naval and air power. Free entry of foreign powers to the Black Sea exposed the Crimea and southern Russian ports to attack such as they had experienced a century before, and constituted a serious gap in Russia's otherwise strong western defences. Western insistence on these measures, although doubtless prompted mainly by commercial and political motives, was interpreted by the Kremlin as most sinister strategic moves implying hostile intentions in the future. The decision about Trieste was never implemented, for the Security Council failed to agree on appointing a governor. The territory remained divided into two zones until in 1954 the northern half was given to Italy, the southern half to Yugoslavia.

Austria and Germany. The making of peace with the remaining Danubian state, Austria, should have proved exceptionally simple. Austria ranked not as a defeated enemy but as a 'liberated state'. When the Soviet forces entered her in April 1945 they set up a provisional government under the Socialist Dr Karl Renner, which had the broad support of the people and was recognized by the Western powers. This government held general elections in which half the popular vote went to the Catholic People's party, forty-four per cent to the Socialists, and only six per cent to the Communists. The Catholics and Socialists, traditionally enemies, formed successful coalition governments. Renner was elected President of the Second Austrian Republic. Soviet representatives sat amicably with representatives of the three Western powers on the joint Allied Council, but they firmly resisted any attempt to end the four-power occupation of Austria and make a peace treaty. The chief explanation, no doubt, was that the Soviet Union meanwhile enjoyed the rich flow of oil from the wells of Zistersdorf, extracted machinery and supplies as reparations through the 'Soviet Administration of German Assets in Austria', and covered the southern Czech frontier with her troops of occupation. She was in no hurry to depart from so profitable a situation, and it was 1955 before a peace treaty was eventually made. Even then Austria had to agree to deliver to Russia goods to the value of $140 million, and one million tons of crude oil per year for the next ten years. Russia's interest in Austria was throughout economic, revealing her desperate need for oil and machinery no less than her desire for security.

The problems of making peace with Germany, thorniest of all, were deliberately left until last and were then bedevilled by the coming of the cold war. The fate of postwar Germany and the outbreak of the cold war between East and West are inseparable, for each was intensified by the other. Germany in defeat, as agreed at Potsdam, was divided into four zones of military occupation, and it was left to each occupying power to satisfy its demand for reparations from its own zone. From the first the Russians treated their zone in this way, and busily removed from it crops, industrial plant, and labour. After a year of such partition the three Western powers proposed to combine their zones into one, and at the end of 1946 the Russians agreed to discuss plans for reuniting all four zones economically. But no progress was made. The economic benefits of the amalgamation of the three western zones were largely frustrated so long as there was no common reform of currency. In June 1948, freed from any former inhibitions by the *coup* in Prague of

February, the Western powers instituted their reforms of the German currency. Simultaneously controls on prices and rationing were removed, except on food and certain other essential goods. The effects were immediate and stimulating. The Russians, still bent on sucking the utmost from their own zone, were alarmed at the effects which western prosperity would have on the impoverished east Germans. Their reprisal was to attempt to shatter confidence in the Western powers by forcing them to evacuate Berlin. Berlin, like Germany as a whole, was divided into four sectors, each administered by one of the four powers. It lay in the midst of the Russian zone of Germany, so that Russians controlled all means of access to the city by road, canal, or rail. On 24 June 1948, they began their land blockade of the city, cutting off all food and fuel supplies from the West. It could have been interpreted as an act of war. But the answer of the Americans and British was not war. It was an airlift on a scale massive enough to keep the western sectors supplied with food, fuel, clothing, and even raw materials. 'Operation Vittles', involving immense expense and effort, was stepped up in scale throughout the winter of 1948, until, by the spring, an average amount of 8,000 tons a day was being flown into Berlin. On 11 May the Russians admitted defeat by lifting the blockade. Not only had it increased, instead of destroying, German confidence in the Western powers; it had promoted the making of airfields in Germany all pointing eastwards. In devising novel techniques for fighting a cold war, the West had shown itself superior.

Europe Divided. The strategy of the West now crystallized as a 'policy of containment'. The Truman Doctrine and the proof of Western determination to remain in Berlin symbolized the resolve to fix precise limits beyond which further extensions of Communist influence or power would be resisted by all means available. This commitment of total force to specific ends carried with it implicitly the threat of war should these limits be crossed. The strategy of containment operated at two levels, the economic and the military. Hitherto, in granting loans to friendly governments and in the Marshall Plan and technical aid programme, it had operated mainly at the economic level. After the blockade of Berlin it began to operate at the diplomatic and military levels as well. Every inducement was given by the United States to greater unity and closer cooperation on the part of the western European powers. In March 1948 Britain, France, and the 'Benelux' group (Belgium, the Netherlands, and Luxembourg) signed the Brussels Treaty which set up permanent organizations for joint military action in the event of an armed attack 'in Europe'. This impressive form of alliance was not limited to defence against Germany, and was the first specific

Western alliance against Russian attack. A year later it was extended to include the more formidable backing of the North American continent, when the five Brussels Treaty powers entered into the North Atlantic Treaty along with the United States, Canada, Italy, Iceland, Norway, Denmark, and Portugal. Even this substantial power-*bloc* could muster in 1949 less than three million men under arms, as against the Soviet Union's army of more than four millions and its wartime air force of 20,000 planes. But the United States had the atomic bomb, and the Western powers all began programmes of extensive rearmament in the most modern types of weapon. Only a short-sighted foreign policy in the Kremlin could have created, four years after victory, so large and so hostile an alliance.[1]

Meanwhile the Eastern *bloc*, too, was bound more closely together by both economic and diplomatic alliances. Mutual assistance treaties, dating from the later years of the war, existed between the Soviet Union and Czechoslovakia (December 1943), Yugoslavia (April 1945), and Poland (April 1945). In 1948 further similar treaties were made with the other Eastern states, which also made bilateral agreements among themselves. The main political cement of the *bloc*, however, lay more in the all-pervasive control of the Communist parties than in any formal diplomatic arrangements. In January 1949 the existing economic predominance of Russia throughout the whole area was reinforced by setting up a Council of Economic Mutual Assistance, including the Soviet Union, Poland, Bulgaria, Czechoslovakia, Hungary, and Rumania. The quarrel with Yugoslavia led not only to her exclusion from this Council, but also to economic pressures and boycotts against her. In general the aim of the economic plans and economic co-ordination imposed on eastern Europe was to encourage heavy industry and engineering in order to produce machinery. The ill-concealed subordination of the national interests of these countries to Russia's overriding need for machinery later produced much restiveness among workers and peasants alike, which only naked force and successive purges kept in check. Soviet security in Europe was won at the price of considerable instability and oppression, both political and economic, throughout the eastern marchlands.

China and Korea. The new balance of power between the Communist and non-Communist halves of Europe was profoundly affected by events at the end of 1949. These may come to rank as the most momentous of all events in the postwar decade. They happened in China, inhabited by nearly a quarter of the whole of mankind, and they were a direct consequence of the Second World War in that they were

1. See p. 523.

843

precipitated by the defeat of Japan. Tension between the nationalist Kuomintang led by General Chiang Kai-shek and the Chinese Communist party was of long standing.[1] During the prolonged war with Japan, between 1937 and 1945, the two parties sank their differences enough to make common cause against the Japanese, but not enough to make a united front or a common strategy. Both the United States and the Soviet Union recognized and backed the government of Chiang Kai-shek, the latter making a treaty with him as late as 1945. But civil strife between the two parties, always latent, burst into full fury as soon as Japan had been defeated. By now the Kuomintang, after nearly twenty years of power, had become desperately corrupt and inefficient. It had lost both its revolutionary enthusiasm and its popular backing. The Communists, on the other hand, had gained enormously in discipline, coherent policy, and mass support. For four years war raged, the advantage usually falling to the Communists led by a small group of intellectuals including Mao Tse-tung and Chou En-lai. By the end of 1949 Chiang was forced to retreat to the island of Formosa with the remnants of his party and army, and in September the Communists proclaimed the People's Republic of China. Throughout the following year the new government campaigned against corruption, waste, tax-evasion, and bureaucratic incompetence. It won undoubted popularity by comparison with its predecessor. It was Marxist, dictatorial, and often high-handed and heavy-handed, but it reaped all the benefits of ending civil war. The United States, heavily committed to financial support of Chiang and by now engaged in the cold war with the Soviet Union, refused to recognize the new government. The Soviet Union and Great Britain recognized it as the operative and effective government of China. In February 1950 the Soviet Union undertook to give it financial aid, and supplied such technicians and machinery as she could spare. By 1953 China embarked upon a Five-Year Plan on the Soviet model.

The spark which fused the Chinese revolution into the cold war was the outbreak of war in Korea in June 1950, because it raised for the West the problem of 'containing' Communism in Asia as well as in Europe. Korea, after the expulsion of the Japanese, had been divided into two zones of occupation along the thirty-eighth parallel of latitude. The northern zone was occupied by the Soviet Union, the southern by the United States. The ostensible aim, as in the occupation of Germany, was joint occupation in order to restore to the Korean people unity and independence. But in Korea, as in Germany, this purpose was blocked by disagreement between the occupying powers about the future political

1. See p. 638.

colour of the state. In September 1947 the issue was referred to the Assembly of the United Nations, which sent a temporary commission to Korea, but the commission was boycotted by the Russians and the North Koreans. Elections were held, however, in southern Korea in May 1948 and resulted in a national assembly which elected as President Syngman Rhee. The Russians retaliated by setting up a Communist-controlled People's Democratic Republic in their northern zone. The cold-war partition of Germany was thus repeated in miniature in Korea, though by the middle of 1949 each power had withdrawn its troops of occupation.

On 25 June the Communist government of North Korea launched a full-scale invasion of the south. It was universally assumed that the aggression had the approval of the Soviet Union, which stood to gain much and lose nothing by the war. But the United Nations took immediate action. The Security Council called for the immediate withdrawal of North Korean forces behind the thirty-eighth parallel, and when this demand was ignored United States forces were sent to help Syngman Rhee. By October they had driven out the aggressors and approached the Chinese borders in Manchuria. Then Communist China joined in on the North Korean side, and other forces of the United Nations backed the Americans. The cold war had suddenly, in Asiatic territory, became a fighting war in which the major powers were all implicated in varying degrees.

The only hope of preventing the Korean War from turning into a third world war was to keep it strictly localized. It became a remarkable example of a war in which major powers were involved without their regarding it as a war of unlimited commitment. This was possible only because no great power was in a position to engage in total war so soon after 1945, and because none regarded the future of Korea as a matter of vital national interest. The Soviet Union sent no troops, the United States did not use the atomic bomb. It was kept as an 'incident', a more inflamed sequel to such 'incidents' as the Berlin blockade, although there were moments when both China and the United States showed signs of treating it as sufficiently vital to justify full-scale commitment. After the middle of 1951 the fighting relapsed into stalemate, and protracted negotiations for a cease-fire eventually culminated in the armistice of July 1953. The result, too, was deadlock. The line of partition between northern and southern Korea remained roughly where it had been before the war began. Meanwhile most of the country had been laid waste and maybe ten per cent (three millions) of the Korean people had been killed. The Western powers had, indeed, 'contained' Communism in Korea and had vindicated the authority of the United Nations. The

Chinese had secured in North Korea a Communist buffer-state between Manchuria and Western influences, though at the expense of seeing Chiang still more strongly entrenched in Formosa behind the screen of United States naval protection. The Soviet Union, without any cost to herself, had strengthened the Moscow-Peking Axis and obliged Communist China to look to her for arms and supplies.

Elsewhere in Asia it proved less easy to contain Chinese Communism. A Chinese expedition to Tibet succeeded, within a year, in subduing that remote land to Chinese control. In the former colonial lands of south-east Asia – in French Indochina, Siam, Malaya, Indonesia – Communism tended to make common cause with the forces of Asiatic nationalism and anti-colonialism, as it had so successfully done in China. Once independence had been achieved, the tensions commonly apparent in Europe between a native patriotism and the demands of international Communism usually appeared. In Africa, more remote from the centres of world Communism, Arab nationalism and African (black) nationalism generated similar tensions, though Communism made less headway. The colonial revolution as a whole, perhaps the most momentous of all changes during the postwar years, will be examined more fully in the next chapter. It remains, first, to survey briefly some significant trends within the Western European states themselves during the years 1950–63.

WESTERN EUROPE, 1950-63

Western Europe, in the grip of the cold war, clung tenaciously to its traditional democratic institutions, though at times these worked far from smoothly. Endemic instability showed itself in splits within political parties, in the acrimony of parliamentary and electoral contests between parties, and in the emergence of new (often short-lived) political groupings. The issues raised by the cold war, by the colonial revolution, and by dramatic new developments in science, all tended to cut across old party alignments or to demand drastic rethinking of politics.

In Britain the postwar era of Labour Party rule ended in the elections of 1951. Though Winston Churchill's new government had a majority over Labour of only twenty-six, the Conservatives made larger gains in the elections of 1955 and 1959. Labour, in opposition, tended to split over issues of defence, and was weakened in 1963 by the death of its leader, Hugh Gaitskell. The Conservatives, too, suffered repeated splintering over financial policy and survived violent storms over the Suez crisis in 1956 (when Sir Anthony Eden was bitterly opposed by a sector of the party) and the Profumo affair of 1963 (when

Harold Macmillan's Minister for War, John Profumo, was shown to have lied to Parliament and colleagues alike about his relationships with an unsavoury clique). In 1963, when Macmillan made way, after a prolonged internal struggle for leadership, for Sir Alec Douglas-Home, it became apparent that the era of Conservative rule, in turn, was nearing its end.

In France the Fourth Republic failed to solve the riddle of creating a stable government and a coherent policy out of the large number of fluid parties in the National Assembly. Until May 1958 the country experienced a sequence of a score of precarious coalitions, mostly combinations of the centre parties, which neither general elections (in 1951 and 1956) nor agile leaders (like Pierre Mendès France in 1954) could transform into cohesive *blocs*. The political system declined in esteem and was exposed to the attacks of the permanent Communist opposition (numbering some 150 deputies in 1956); of the right-wing Gaullist movement, the *Rassemblement Populaire Français* (RPF) and the tax-resisting activists led by Pierre Poujade; and eventually of a combination of discontented army leaders, Algerian *colons* and ultra-right extremists who conspired to overthrow it in May 1958. The threat of civil war was evaded only by the return to national power of General de Gaulle as, once more, the saviour of France. He came back on his own terms: emergency powers for six months, so extensive as to amount to temporary dictatorship, and authority to remodel the constitution to suit himself. By January 1959 the Fifth Republic came into being. As its President, de Gaulle enjoyed executive authority less restricted by parliamentary controls than any government of the Fourth. In Parliament he was backed, even after fresh elections in 1962, by a solid majority of the new *Union pour la Nouvelle République* (UNR). The new régime tackled with fresh vigour the many social problems of education, housing, taxation, and alcoholism, though with varying degrees of success. Its major achievement was the ending of the long war in Algeria (March 1962) and the grant of full independence to most of France's former colonies in Africa, including Algeria – a strange outcome of a régime first founded on the hopes of the ultra-nationalist right-wing. Charles de Gaulle was to play a dominant role in European and, indeed, in world politics of the 1960s.

The Low Countries, collaborating closely within the union of 'Benelux', reflected in their political developments trends also apparent in Britain and France. Constitutional monarchy survived crises affecting the royal family in Belgium (in 1950 and 1961) and the Netherlands (in 1956). The parliamentary systems encountered difficulties caused by electoral shifts from Labour Party preponderance in 1950 to Liberal or

Christian Democratic party preponderance in the later 1950s, and back again towards Labour in the early 1960s, as well as by dissensions within the parties. All governments wrestled with problems of inflation and consequent demands for wage increases, though all three countries enjoyed a time of great prosperity. Belgium, like France, experienced a revival of old clericalist feuds about education, as well as resurgence of the apparently insoluble Flemish problem.

In Italy, governments between 1948 and the beginning of 1962 were predominantly four-party coalitions of Christian Democrats with the smaller secular centre parties, the Social Democrats, the Republicans, and the Liberals. Then the Socialists, who had joined the Communists in opposition during this time, swung over to supporting the Christian Democrats on a programme of economic planning and social reforms. The Socialists' return to the main stream of Italian political life and the so-called 'opening toward the Left' was accompanied by continuing economic prosperity but by outbreaks of strikes for a larger share in the new wealth. In Germany there existed a comparable polarity between Dr Konrad Adenauer's Christian Democratic Union and the Social Democrats, with Chancellor Adenauer's prestige declining somewhat as the date of his retirement approached in October 1963. German politics were naturally dominated ultimately by the Berlin question and the desire for reunification, issues forced to the forefront of both national and international politics after August 1961 by the erection of the Berlin Wall between east and west Berlin, and the even more significant sealing-off of the German Democratic Republic all the way from the Baltic to the Czech frontier. West Germany's post-war economic boom began to slacken at the same time, causing anxieties about the effects of the Common Market.

The Scandinavian countries showed a slow trend towards the Right and encountered greater difficulties in forming stable coalition governments. Uneasy party coalitions ran into difficulties, as in France, in countering strong inflationary tendencies and persistent economic dislocations. The winter of 1960–1 brought severe strikes in Denmark, as in Belgium. Like the Low Countries in their 'Benelux' organization, the Scandinavian states also evolved machinery for closer regional cooperation, especially in economic matters, in the Nordic Council formed in 1951.

Spain and Portugal survived both economic crises and social unrest with their prewar régimes virtually unchanged. General Franco played off monarchists against Falangists, though both continued to press for concessions. In May 1961 Dr Salazar could celebrate the thirty-fifth anniversary of his 'new state': the cabinet he led had first come into being in 1932. These two régimes, dating continuously in their personal leadership from the 1930s, remained a curious enclave of traditionalism in a rapidly changing Europe. Events in Africa and India in 1961-2 drew them closer together than ever, for Spain backed Portugal in resistance to the revolt in Angola and to India's taking over of Goa, Daman, and Diu.

In general, relations between the states of Western Europe in these years were overshadowed by the cold war and the continued partition of Germany, culminating in the erection of the Berlin Wall as the very symbol of antipathy between East and West; by the necessity for regional military and economic cooperation, and the implicit issues of potential political federation; and by the need to redefine relations between Western European peoples and the underdeveloped countries, most of which had been colonies of the Western powers. Relations between Britain and her European neighbours reached an historic moment in October 1961, when Macmillan began negotiations for Britain's entry into membership of the European Economic Community ('Common Market'); and another in January 1963, when President de Gaulle abruptly ended the negotiations and so excluded Britain from close economic union with the six Common Market countries (France, Western Germany, Italy, and Benelux). The negotiations had revealed both the divisions of opinion within Britain and the contrary pulls of continental and commonwealth loyalties: the rebuff, inflicted so harshly by the President of France, left Franco-British relationships cool and was accompanied by the Franco-Germany Treaty of friendship of January 1963. This treaty, however, bore little fruit in the face of Gaullist lack of consideration for even self-chosen allies. The most significant changes of the years 1950-63 were less in politics than in demographic and economic growth. France, which in the thirties had known little natural increase of population, became one of the most fast-growing populations in Europe. Metropolitan France, in the census of March 1962, had a population of more than forty-six and a half millions. In 1957 the population of the Netherlands for the first time exceeded eleven millions, giving it the greatest density of population of any European country. Infant death-rates – that telling index of a people's real prosperity – fell as low as 15.8 per 1,000 in Sweden in 1958, though Spain's at that date remained as high as 41.1 per 1,000; the United Kingdom's rate was 24 per 1,000, but continued to decrease. Rapid advances in technology resulted in great economic growth, a generally rising standard of living, and an expansion of international trade. Productivity increased as fresh resources of power, new inventiveness, automation, more scientific methods and organization, were

evolved and adopted by industry. The fiscal policies and social services
of the Welfare States spread the benefits of the new wealth more widely
among the population. Even so, disparities of wealth remained very
great, not only between the Western countries but also between classes
within them. Nibbling inflation afflicted different economic groups
differentially, leaving many old people poverty-stricken. Nor did larger
affluence diminish social evils as much as had been expected. Crimes of
violence, juvenile delinquency, prostitution, trade in narcotics, venereal
diseases, and decline in public morals occurred on a scale large enough
to provoke legislation against them in most countries.

Above all, the Western European peoples, as the leading colonial
powers of the later nineteenth century, were now intimately affected
by the colonial revolution. The 1950s and early 1960s brought the
climax of this vast transfiguration of relationships between European
peoples and the peoples of Asia and Africa. It was a decisive element
in the future, perhaps even in the survival, of European civilization:
not least because it was conflicts in underdeveloped areas of the world
– in Korea, Indo-China, the Congo, Cuba, Indonesia – which seemed
most prone to engage the rivalries and fears of the greatest world powers.

CHAPTER 31

THE COLONIAL REVOLUTION

GOVERNMENT OF UNDERDEVELOPED TERRITORIES

COLONIAL ambitions and rivalries played little or no part in the policy of Nazi aggressions which led up to the outbreak of war in 1939. Hitler, pre-eminently continental and racialist in outlook, riveted his gaze upon power in Europe. He thought of the Balkans and south-western Russia as a richer field of colonial gains than overseas territories. Though he never renounced German claims to overseas colonies, he was prepared to subordinate them to conquest in Europe. Colonial issues became prominent only with the entry of Italy into the war, and with the conquests of Japan. Thereafter they remained one of its major issues, and the early reverses of the Western powers – particularly the defeats of the Netherlands, Belgium, and France, and British and American reverses in the Far East – exposed to revolutionary forces the overseas possessions of these powers in Africa and Asia, the Near and the Far East. A few years of Japanese invasion and occupation of parts of Indochina, Malaya, Burma, and Indonesia transformed these countries into more self-conscious, nationalistic, and psychologically detached peoples. The two most powerful states in the postwar world, the Soviet Union and the United States, were both in sentiment and in policy hostile to colonialism. The predominance of left-wing sentiment throughout postwar Europe, whether socialist or Catholic democrat, militated against the more old-fashioned spirit of imperialism. Western opinion in general was now more responsive to the principle that colonial peoples should be encouraged to seek independence and helped to win rights of self-determination. Before the Korean war of 1950 raised the issue of 'containing Communism' in Asia as well as in Europe, any attempt to check the colonial revolution was liable to be denounced as reactionary. Thereafter opinion, especially in the United States and western Europe, swung strongly in the opposite direction, and colonial nationalism was apt to be too closely identified with communism.

Colonial Relationships Before 1939. The colonial revolution was not however, the sudden by-product of the war. Its roots lay deep in the previous century, and by 1939 it had already made considerable advance. Nineteenth-century imperialism had established a certain pattern of relationships between colonies and colony-owners which, until 1914, few in Europe save Marxists and socialists challenged. These were relationships of political dependence, racial inequality, and economic subservience. Politically the colonies were governed by decisions taken in London or Paris, Brussels or Berlin, Lisbon or Amsterdam. Socially the members of the imperial power resident in the colonies established for themselves a position of racial superiority and influence. They were mostly concerned in administering, developing, and generally running the country. They acquired much of the best land, the best houses, and the social amenities of a ruling group. Economically the chief functions of the colonies were to supply raw materials for use in the manufactures of the governing country, to provide markets for its manufactured goods, and to be secure places of investment for its commercial enterprise and its surplus capital. This relationship varied from one Empire to another, and even by 1914 it was modified here and there by limited participation of the native inhabitants in running their own affairs or by the development of certain native industries and enterprises. The British practice of preserving the native princes in India or of indirect rule in Nigeria, the Belgian policy of preserving tribal communities in the Congo, or the French method of making treaties with tribal leaders in North Africa, were all important modifications. But they were exceptional expedients, not the rule. Wherever native police forces were recruited to keep public order, or native levies of troops were used for the defence of colonial territories, they invariably operated under the orders and officers of the governing authority.

The colonial revolution of the twentieth century was much more than a colonial revolt. One of its roots was the growth of population, wealth, literacy, and national awareness among the peoples of the colonial territories: a demand for the ending of that political dependence, racial inequality, and economic subservience which were the substance of later nineteenth-century imperialism. This demand grew with the spread of westernization itself, and it was nourished by the liberal ideals of freedom, equality, and self-determination as well as by the spread of education and industrialism within the colonies. It was a demand greatly accelerated and intensified by two world wars. But the other root of the colonial revolution was no less important. It was the change which took place in the policies, attitudes, circumstances, and needs of the colonial powers, weakening their will to preserve colonial relationships of the old pattern and compelling them to discover new relationship as tutors, trustees, partners, or allies, rather than conquerors, rulers, administrators, or exploiters. This important change happened mainly after 1919, and interacted at many points with the growing pressure of colonial peoples themselves for self-government and independence. Just as nineteenth-century imperialism involved both a push at home and a pull overseas,[1] so the liquidation of it in the twentieth century involved both a push from overseas and a pulling back at home. After 1945 the two trends coincided with dramatic effect. The result was a veritable revolution in colonial relationships, in the course of which the backward peoples, formerly only passive objects of European policy, became driving forces in world affairs with an initiative and motive power of their own.

It was the First World War which produced the first major changes in the standard nineteenth-century pattern. The extent of colonial Empires was in no way diminished. The British, French, Belgian, Dutch, and Portuguese Empires lost none of their territories. Italy gained by additions to Libya and Somaliland, though she gained less than she bargained for. Japan gained even more than did Italy. Germany alone, among the leading powers, lost all her overseas possessions. These were in every instance administered after 1918 by the powers which had seized possession of them during the war. But they were administered under the new principle of mandates, whereby the administering powers undertook specific obligations towards the inhabitants of these territories.[2] For fulfilment of these obligations they became accountable to the Permanent Mandates Commission and had to report annually to the Council of the League of Nations, although neither the Commission nor the League itself possessed power to coerce a recalcitrant state. This solemn acceptance by colonial powers of a code of behaviour and agreed principles of government was important.

Yet even the terms of the mandates contained the significant distinction between 'A' mandates applicable to the former Turkish countries of the Near East, and 'B' and 'C' mandates applying to former German colonies in Africa and the Pacific. 'A' mandates, which governed the British administration of Palestine and Iraq and the French administration of Syria and Lebanon, prescribed the aim of eventual independence, and the need meanwhile to consider 'the wishes of these communities'. Other mandates, which applied to the Cameroons, Togoland, Tanganyika, Ruanda-Urundi, South-West Africa, and the former German Pacific territories, were completely silent on the aim of independence or self-government, and emphasized only the need to respect the interests (though not the wishes) of the inhabitants.

The Covenant of the League spoke in terms of entrusting the government of 'peoples not yet able to stand by themselves under the strenuous

1. See p. 496.
2. See p. 631.

conditions of the modern world' to the 'tutelage' of 'advanced nations who, by reason of their resources, their experience of their geographical position can best undertake this responsibility'. The Covenant thus, in one sense, embodied and perpetuated the doctrine of inferiority and tutelage at the expense of ideas of colonial self-government and independence. Its silence on the principles according to which all the other colonial possessions of the imperial powers should be governed was equally significant. Its chief advance was to stress, for the mandated territories alone, the duty of a colonial power to respect the principle 'that the well-being and development of such peoples form a sacred trust of civilization'. It was no less concerned with securing 'equal opportunities for the trade and commerce of other Members of the League'. Of the territories under 'A' mandates Iraq duly became in 1937 an independent sovereign state. The fate of Palestine, Syria, and Lebanon was not finally decided until the Second World War.

Significant advances in colonial government took place, however, within the British Empire and Commonwealth. These set a new standard of principles and aims in colonial administration. The interwar years brought to the settled Dominions of the Commonwealth the culmination of their autonomy and independence, formally recognized in the Statute of Westminster in 1931. The separate representation of Canada, Australia, New Zealand, the Union of South Africa, and even of India at the Paris Conference in 1919 had already demonstrated the changing status of these five major parts of the Commonwealth.[1] Ideas of equal partnership, rather than of tutelage, were implicit in these new relationships.

The first step toward the participation of Indians in the governing of the country were taken by the India Act of 1919. It introduced elements of representative parliamentary democracy by substituting for the old Legislative Council a two-chamber assembly elected on restricted suffrage, and it increased the Indian membership of the Viceroy's Executive Council. In the provinces such matters as local government, vernacular education, medical relief, sanitation, and agriculture were transferred to Indian hands; but matters of finance, famine relief, labour, and police were reserved for British control. This dividing of responsibility, known as dyarchy, was intended to facilitate the subsequent transfer of reserved matters to Indian control as circumstances allowed, so gradually extending the sphere of self-government. The arrangement was complex. Any attempt to handle the complicated administration of India was bound to be complex. It was also in many ways cumbersome. The experiment was denounced by extreme

1. See p. 616.

nationalists, mostly Western-educated intellectuals who demanded complete self-government at once, and it was at first boycotted by the Congress party under the leadership of Gandhi. After the elections of 1923, when the Congress party won nearly half the seats in the central legislature, it used its power to stultify the new constitutional arrangements. The next twelve years were occupied with a succession of commissions, reports, and conferences, while British governments wrestled with the intractability of communal problems and the intransigence of Gandhi, whose campaign of civil disobedience made any form of government difficult. Yet the process of Indianization went on in the civil service, in the army, and in control over fiscal policy; and in 1935 a new Government of India Act was passed by the British Parliament. It reshaped the constitution of India along federalist lines. The federal legislature was partly elected by constituencies in British India, partly chosen by the provincial legislatures, and partly appointed by the rulers of the Native States. The 1935 Act also separated Burma from India, and gave Burma a distinct constitution of its own. Only thereafter did a political movement of Burmese nationalism take coherent shape, hostile to British and Indians alike and with some pro-Japanese ingredients.

The British had constantly before them not only the memory of American independence and the growing nationalism of India and Burma, but also the recent violent culmination of the movement for Irish Home Rule. As a result of the Anglo-Irish Treaty of 1921 the Irish Free State, under Arthur Griffith and Michael Collins, was set up in 1922 with the status of a British Dominion; but the six northern provinces of Ulster elected to remain separate as Northern Ireland, sending representatives to Westminster and electing also a Parliament of its own under the British Crown. In August Griffith died and Collins was shot, leaving government in the hands of William Cosgrave. Strong hostility to the whole arrangement came from Eamon de Valera and the Sinn Fein party. In 1932, after a decade in the political wilderness, de Valera came to power at the head of a new party, the Fianna Fail ('Soldiers of Destiny'). He proceeded to demolish, bit by bit, the provisions of the Anglo-Irish Treaty and in 1937 promulgated a new constitution. This severed all formal links with the United Kingdom and made the Irish Free State of southern Ireland (Eire as it was now called) an independent sovereign state. Between 1939 and 1945 Eire asserted this independence by remaining neutral.

The tendency to concede increasing measures of independence and responsibility for self-government to parts of the British Empire was therefore strongly present by 1939. The colonial service itself, whose

250,000 officials administered the sixty different territories of the Empire, by then included fewer than 66,000 from the United Kingdom. Everywhere members of the colonial peoples, often educated in British schools and universities, were taking a growing share in the actual administration of their countries. At the same time there took place in Britain and other colonial powers a sceptical reappraisal of the economic advantages of colonialism. In 1937 a League of Nations Committee pointed out that of the world's most important raw materials such as coal, iron, petroleum, cotton, and wool, the total production in all colonial areas was only about three per cent of the world's production. Certain materials, however, came mainly from one or two colonial areas. More than four fifths of the world's rubber and nearly half its tin came from British Malaya and the Netherlands East Indies alone. But in 1938 only eight and a half per cent of Britain's imports came from her colonial territories, which took in exchange only a twelve and a quarter per cent of her exports. The modern colonial Empires, being mainly tropical or semi-tropical, attracted few settlers and provided little outlet for the pressure of population at home. They had, as shown above,[1] considerable economic importance as areas for safe and profitable capital investment before 1914; but between the two wars Britain and France had less capital available for overseas investment. They became in part creditor nations and were faced with economic depression at home. By 1939 much British opinion, especially, had become doubtful whether the material advantages of colonies outweighed the expense, trouble, and opprobrium of governing them.

The mood, however, changed less conspicuously in France, Belgium, the Netherlands, or Portugal, the other colonial powers. In France the theory of colonial rule shifted officially from that predominant before 1914, of 'assimilation', of spreading French culture and civilization throughout her territories and so making Africans not better Africans but better Frenchmen. It changed officially to the theory of 'association', of greater respect for native traditions and ways of life, but a strengthening of their economic and political links with metropolitan France. Such fundamental shifts of colonial policy are easier to formulate in parliamentary speeches and official pronouncements than to implement in detail by changing the routine behaviour of hard-worked colonial administrators on the spot. The change in French colonial policy by 1939 was more apparent than real, more theoretical than substantial. Strong economic interests linked France with her overseas territories, both in finance and in trade. By 1939 France was drawing nearly one third of her imports from her own colonies and sending nearly one third

1. See p. 490.

of her exports to them. These economic links strengthened tendencies to assimilation. At the same time the general distinction was preserved between French 'citizens' (a small minority in most oversea territories other than the older possessions of Martinique, Guadeloupe, and Réunion, and the four communes of Sénégal) and French 'subjects' who had no important political rights. Economic assimilation with lack of political assimilation left most French colonies in effect economically subservient. It goes far to explain the outburst of colonial resistance to French rule after 1945. Thus, when India was gaining and exercising the right to protect her own textile industries by imposing tariffs against the import of Lancashire cottons, Madagascar was obliged to have the same high tariff walls as France, although the free import of cheap textiles would have greatly benefited the inhabitants.

The special characteristic of the Belgian, Dutch, and Portuguese Empires was that in each a small European nation governed a large colonial territory, rich in natural resources. Each could – unlike the British or the French – concentrate upon one territory which constituted the bulk of its Empire. The Belgian Congo, together with the mandated territory of Ruanda-Urundi, was more than seventy-eight times larger than Belgium, with a sparse population of some ten millions; the Netherlands East Indies were fifty-five times bigger in area than the Netherlands, with a large population of more than sixty millions; Portuguese West Africa was twenty-three times larger than Portugal, with some ten million population. Each power could work out a consistent policy of colonial government applicable to its own Empire and adhere to it with considerable persistence. Thus the Belgian administration adopted a paternalist policy of progressive social and economic development, devoid of any notions of partnership in responsibility or of eventual self-government. The economic growth of the Congo was shaped in relation to Belgium's needs. By 1939 the Congo was shipping more than eighty per cent of its exports to Belgium, and deriving from Belgium nearly half its imports. The administration concentrated on improving conditions in agriculture, transport, education, and public health. It treated its colonial dependents as indeed primitive and backward, likely to benefit most from firm guidance and steady rule. Since it regarded the governing of colonies as a matter not of politics but of administration, technical efficiency and improved material conditions for the inhabitants were its main tests of goodness. The Congo was quite unprepared for independence when it was granted in 1960.

Dutch colonial policy was also traditionally firm and paternalist. On the one hand an 'ethical policy' was formulated in 1901, recognizing that Holland owed a moral obligation to the native peoples she governed; on the other, there was a corresponding growth of Indonesian nationalist movements beginning in 1908 with Boedi Octomo ('Beautiful Strife'). As a result various concessions were made to demands for elected local and provincial councils, and for native participation in public life and politics. But trends towards assimilation prevailed, and principles of devolution made little headway. In 1922 the Netherlands' constitution was amended to make Indonesia part of the Dutch Kingdom. The chief internal source of colonial grievances was the contrast between the low level of subsistence at which the mass of the population lived, and the relatively few big Western enterprises in farming, transport, and above all, oil, which made very large profits. Racial discrimination and gross economic inequality rankled. There was virtually no Indonesian middle class. This explosive situation explained the violence of Indonesian nationalism as soon as Japanese invasion loosened Dutch control over the territory.

Portugal, as a neutral in the war, suffered less shock to its colonial status. The Colonial Act of 1933 centralized colonial government in Lisbon, and aimed at strengthening the economic and political interdependence of Portugal and her colonial Empire, unifying its administration and protecting native interests. Trade was mostly with Portugal. The tendency to integration continued uninterrupted by the war, and in 1951 the colonies were made 'oversea provinces'. But dispute arose with India about Goa, the remaining European colony in India.

Colonies in the Second World War. The years of the Second World War brought two strange experiences both to the imperial powers and to their colonial territories. Some, such as French Indochina, Dutch Indonesia, British Malaya, and Italian East Africa experienced a phase of enemy conquest and occupation, during which they were virtually cut off from contact with their normal governors. Others, such as all the African possessions of Belgium and Britain and most of the French colonies, found themselves among their rulers' most valuable assets in the war against the Axis. The French colonial Empire was, in effect, divided between those areas, like French Equatorial Africa, which became the mainstay of the Gaullist Free French Movement; those like French North Africa and West Africa or Madagascar that remained under the rule of Vichy until they were invaded by Anglo-American forces; and those like Indochina that endured Japanese invasion. In all, acute political tensions were introduced, discrediting French government, offering opportunities for every sort of separatist agitation and intrigue, and stimulating internal dissensions between rival groups. Every power was obliged, by war's necessities, to encourage economic development and industrialization in its colonies. This combination of political upheaval with a burst of economic expansion strengthened both the demand for national independence and the concession of greater self-government in colonial relationships.

Moreover, during the last years of the war, ideals inimical to any mere restoration of the old subservience of colonial peoples, inimical even to the very classification into 'advanced' and 'backward' nations implied in the old mandates system, had been spreading throughout the world. Such ideals found both special and general endorsement, of which the two most striking examples were the declaration made by the Brazzaville conference of January 1944 and the 'Philadelphia Charter' of May 1944. At Brazzaville was held the first imperial conference of Free France, presided over by General de Gaulle. It recommended the development of local assemblies to voice colonial opinion, employment of natives in the public services, and direct representation of all France's colonial peoples in the French Parliament. The result was to be one great 'French Union', based on full citizen rights. In May 1946 the French Constituent Assembly proclaimed unanimously that 'From 1 June 1946 all subjects of overseas territories, including Algeria, possess the quality of citizens with the same rights as French citizens in the home country and in the overseas territories'. The distinction between 'citizens' and 'subjects' was ended.

The International Labour Organization met at Philadelphia in April and May 1944. Attended by delegations from forty-one member countries, but not from the Soviet Union, the meeting adopted a declaration of its purposes and principles which included universal equality of rights and status.

All human beings, irrespective of race, creed, or sex, have the right to pursue both their material well-being and their spiritual development in conditions of freedom and dignity, of economic security and equal opportunity; the attainment of the conditions in which this shall be possible must constitute the central aim of national and international policy ...

French representatives fully endorsed the Philadelphia Charter. Both ideas were ultimately egalitarian: both implied ending old legal and political distinctions between 'citizens' and 'subjects', old social and economic privileges of imperial peoples as against colonial peoples. But given the realities of material differences in standards of living and culture, and of violent aspirations for colonial self-determination and political independence, neither of which could be exorcized by general declarations, it was unlikely that the problems of the colonial revolution could be solved by any such simple and universal formulae. The hard compulsion of history was that each imperial power must grope its way toward its own appropriate solution. Relations between peoples that had been woven on so many different looms could not be reshaped into one simple new pattern. Such was the British attitude, and such was the implication of the articles in the United Nations Charter, agreed to in June 1945, creating the system of colonial trusteeship which now replaced the system of mandates.

Colonial Trusteeship. Except for those territories which had been held under 'A' mandates and now became independent states, and except for mandated territories previously held by Japan, former mandated territories were now held under the trusteeship agreements by the same powers as before. The United States held under trusteeship the Pacific islands formerly mandated to Japan. Italy held Italian Somaliland under trusteeship for ten years as from 1950. The Union of South Africa refused to make new arrangements and continued to administer South-West Africa under the terms of the old 'C' mandate. Provision was made for states voluntarily to place any of their own colonial territories under new trusteeship agreements, but none showed itself willing to do this. The basic objectives of the system were stated to be: 'to promote the political, economic, social, and educational advancement of their inhabitants towards self-government or independence as may be appropriate to the particular circumstances of each territory and its peoples and the freely expressed wishes of the people concerned'; 'to encourage respect for human rights and for fundamental freedoms for all without distinction as to race, sex, language, or religion, and to encourage recognition of the interdependence of the peoples of the world'; and 'to ensure equal treatment in social, economic and commercial matters for all Members of the United Nations and their nationals'.

In one respect the new system went beyond the old. Under Chapter XI of the United Nations Charter members with 'responsibilities for the administration of territories whose peoples have not yet attained a full measure of self-government recognize the principle that the interests of the inhabitants of these territories are paramount, and accept as a sacred trust the obligation to promote to the utmost ... the well-being of the inhabitants of these territories'. To this end, they also undertook 'to develop self-government, to take due account of the political aspirations of the peoples, and to assist them in the progressive development of their free political institutions, according to the particular circumstances of each territory and its peoples and their varying stages of advancement'. Acceptance of such aims as applicable to all colonial lands, whether held under specific trusteeship agreements or not, contained some promise of reshaping all colonial relationships.

Against this background of an apparently universal necessity and willingness to rethink and reshape colonial relations there took place, between 1945 and 1963, a series of events so momentous for the future of Europe that they demand closer examination. If the century between 1815 and 1914 had been characterized by the expansion of Europe into Africa, Asia, and the Far East, the years 1945–63 were especially notable for the opposite – for the contraction of Europe, the retreat from empire. This precipitate liquidation of the most characteristic of nineteenth-century achievements was on all counts the most far-reaching historical outcome of the Second World War.

THE CONTRACTION OF EUROPE

When the San Francisco Conference to shape the United Nations was held in 1945, some 600 million people in the world were not fully self-governing, though many had limited self-government and were already moving towards independence. By the end of 1963 the peoples who had not attained full national equality and sovereignty had shrunk to a mere handful.

British Commonwealth. The first and most momentous event in this transformation was the independence of India and Pakistan achieved in 1947. In 1942 Sir Stafford Cripps, on behalf of the British government, had promised India after the war an Indian-made constitution and government by Indians in everything except defence. The offer was then rejected by the Congress party. But Britain was now resolved to leave, and after 1945 the only important question was how she could leave India without precipitating civil war between Hindus and Moslems. The Moslem League, led by Jinnah, demanded a separate sovereign state of Pakistan to include the Moslem areas. On 20 February 1947 the British Prime Minister, Clement Attlee, announced that power would be transferred to Indian hands not later than June 1948; it was for Indians, meanwhile, to agree among themselves how to receive it, and what the future form of their constitution should be. In June Britain put forward a proposal of partition, to reconcile the rival claims of Hindus and Moslems; and although unwelcome to Congress leaders who dreamed of a united India under their party's control, it was accepted because no better alternative could be agreed to. On 15 August 1947 the two Dominions of India and Pakistan were formally instituted. The price of independence was partition, as it had been in Ireland. The riots and disturbances which continued had now to be tackled by Indian governments. Independence was inaugurated with considerable violence and with civil war over Kashmir. Gandhi was assassinated in January and Jinnah died in September 1948. But after a year of independence both new states settled down to constructive work under able statesmen, and the century-old process of achieving national statehood was completed with much less violence than might have been expected. The Conference of Commonwealth Prime Ministers held in London in April 1949 even devised a formula which kept the two new states within the Commonwealth as 'sovereign independent Republics' recognizing the British monarch as 'the symbol of the free association of its independent member nations and, as such, the head of the Commonwealth'.

Independence for India and Pakistan was accompanied by independence also for Burma and Ceylon. In 1945 it was hoped to combine Burmese independence with her continued membership of the Commonwealth. But when a constituent assembly was elected in April 1947 it framed a constitution which involved leaving the Commonwealth, on the Irish rather than the Indian pattern. In January 1948 the Union of Burma came into existence as a sovereign independent republic, and thereafter endured considerable internal turbulence. The following month Ceylon attained full Dominion status within the Commonwealth, having acquired independence by the Ceylon Independence Act of 1947. The entry of India, Pakistan, and Ceylon into Dominion status raised new and fundamental issues for the whole future of the Commonwealth. Hitherto that status had been confined to nations of white settlers, mainly of United Kingdom stocks and tradition. The new Dominions were nations whose cultural heritage was Asiatic and whose political tradition was one of hostility to British rule. Would the subtle bonds of the Commonwealth, which had shown themselves to be so strong under the strains of two world wars, prove capable of holding together these more diverse elements?

The bonds of the old Commonwealth were snapping, meanwhile, in both Eire and the Union of South Africa. In December 1948 the Dail passed the Republic of Ireland Act which severed the last tenuous link with the British Crown and the Commonwealth. In the Union of South Africa General Smuts was defeated in the elections of May 1948. The new Nationalist government of Dr Malan pursued a racialist policy and showed itself resolved upon secession. The presence in the Union of some 350,000 Indians made Malan's policy of racial discrimination particularly disruptive for the Commonwealth. The peculiarity of the new nationalism was that it was not a white nationalism, uniting British and Boer, but an Afrikaner nationalism, exclusive and militant, hostile not only to coloured men but also to other Europeans. When Malan resigned at the end of 1954 he was succeeded, as head of the Nationalist party, by J. G. Strijdom. Strijdom, and after 1958 Dr H. F. Verwoerd, pursued the policy of *apartheid* (racial segregation) with renewed vigour and ruthlessness. A referendum held in 1960 resulted in a small majority for declaring South Africa a republic. But such a republic could remain within the Commonwealth only by agreement of its members, which included several Asiatic peoples. It left in May 1961.

By 1950 every British colonial territory except British Somaliland had a local legislative assembly. In some, such as Tanganyika, Uganda, Nyasaland, Sierre Leone, North Borneo, and Hong Kong, the official (unelected) members were still in a majority; in others, such as the Gold Coast, Nigeria, Kenya, Northern Rhodesia, and Malaya the unofficial (elected) members predominated; in others again, such as most of the British West Indies and Malta, the legislative assembly was entirely elected. To such assemblies, and to the governments which were increasingly made responsible to them, more and more powers were delegated. New universities of the Gold Coast (1948) and Ibadan in Nigeria (1947) offered Africans greater facilities for higher education; in Jamaica, too, a new university college was set up between 1948 and 1950.

The decade of the 1950s brought faster moves toward complete autonomy and fresh experiments in federalism. Within the Commonwealth the colonial revolution gained momentum. Among the African colonies the pioneers in independence were the Gold Coast and Nigeria, each of which gained a new constitution in 1951. In March 1957 the Gold Coast, together with the trustee territory of Togoland, joined to establish the independent state of Ghana with Dominion status within the Commonwealth. Its Prime Minister, Dr K. Nkrumah, had ambitions for making Ghana the nucleus of a future Africa federation, and to this end combined with the former French colony of Guinea in 1958. The Federation of Nigeria developed regional self-government and in 1960 attained complete independence as a Dominion. With its much larger population (more than thirty million) and richer resources, it rivalled Ghana as the model for successful African nationhood.

In central Africa Southern and Northern Rhodesia and Nyasaland were federated in 1953, and the federal government was made responsible for all policy save industrial, mining, and local affairs. But by 1960 the federal Prime Minister, Sir Roy Welensky, was faced with not only strong white separatist forces in Northern Rhodesia but also a powerful separatist African movement in Nyasaland. Yet federalism remained a favourite pattern – adopted in Malaya in 1948 and in the British West Indies in 1958. The task of holding together and administering multiracial societies in an age of militant nationalism called for many experiments with constitutional arrangements calculated to reconcile diversities. When Cyprus became an independent sovereign state in August 1960, its constitution provided for a delicate balance between Greek and Turkish Cypriots. The constitution of Malta, set up in 1947, proved unable to reconcile United Kingdom interests in the island as a defence base, with the interests of the Maltese population. During 1958 attempts to improve the arrangements failed, and self-government had to be temporarily replaced by the 'interim' constitution of April 1959.

Amid so vast a shift in world relationships it is hardly surprising that interludes of considerable violence occurred. In Malaya, with its plural society of Chinese, Malays, Indians, and Europeans, there appeared terrorist organizations led by Malayan Communist groups. Their guerrilla fighting and acts of terrorism continued after federation in 1948 until full independence in 1957. In Cyprus independence was preceded by a decade of civil strife between Greeks and Turks, in which Britain inevitably became implicated. In Kenya, where European settlers numbered some 40,000, and the largest and most politically conscious of Kenya tribes, the Kikuyu, competed with them for land, a secret terrorist organization, Mau Mau, was formed. It murdered Europeans and thousands of its Kikuyu fellow-tribesmen, and from 1952 until 1956 the British had to wage constant war against it. A new constitution of November 1957 was condemned by the Kenya African Congress, led by Tom Mboya, for its efforts to give built-in protection to the rights of the minority groups of Europeans and Asians. Violence most attended the path of self-government when there were internal feuds between rival nationalities or tribal groups.

Indonesia and Indochina. The Dutch in Indonesia, like the British in Malaya and the French in Indochina, reaped the sorry harvest of Japanese occupation. Even after Japan surrendered in September 1945, Indonesia remained under Japanese occupation and the Netherlands had no forces available or adequate to evict them. The task fell to the South-East Asia Command under Admiral Lord Mountbatten, who perforce had to deal with the Indonesian nationalist government of the Republic of Indonesia which had been proclaimed on 17 August 1945. The younger generation of Java and Sumatra, led by Dutch-educated Indonesian nationalists, was resolved to seize these opportunities of independence. They had been armed by the Japanese. Negotiations between the Netherlands government and the nationalists were conducted in 1946 by Dr Van Mook, a Dutchman born in Java, who aimed at replacing the old colonial relationship by freer links of association. When the negotiations broke down and the Dutch reverted to force, war began which continued intermittently until in 1949 Indonesia became completely independent as the Republic of the United States of

Indonesia. Even the polite fiction of a common crown was eventually dropped, and of the former Dutch Empire in Indonesia only Netherlands New Guinea (West Irian) remained. An Empire older than most of the British Empire was liquidated at one blow, and a new Pacific state with some eighty million inhabitants was in 1950 admitted to membership of the United Nations.

The French in Indochina fought longer and more stubbornly to preserve their power, but they too were in the end driven out. In 1939 a small nationalist organization, Veit Minh, or the League for the Independence of Vietnam, had first appeared. One of its leaders was an experienced Communist, Ho Chi Minh, who had lived in Paris, Moscow, and China. As in Indonesia, Japanese occupation of large areas of Tonkin, Annam, and Cochin-China, and delay in evicting the invaders after Japan's surrender, permitted the proclamation of 1945 of Ho Chi Minh as president of the Republic of Vietnam, supported by Chinese nationalist forces. By the end of 1946 French negotiations with Vietnam broke down and open warfare began. It lasted, with increasing strain upon postwar France, until the summer of 1954. French hopes were doomed by the Communist revolution in China, for thereafter Ho Chi Minh could rely upon Chinese support. The coming of the cold war and the Western policy of 'containment' turned the war, in the eyes of the outside world, into a wider issue than French imperialism. The main concern of the powers, as of France's new Premier Pierre Mendès France, was to seek an end to the war which would prevent the whole of Indochina (including the provinces of Laos and Cambodia which had hitherto lain mainly outside the struggle) from falling under Communist control. In July 1954 the Foreign Ministers of the United States, Britain, the Soviet Union, China, France, Vietnam, Laos, Cambodia, and Viet Minh met at Geneva and reached a cease-fire agreement. The dramatic fall of the French garrison at Dien Bien Phu, which occurred before the meeting, settled the matter. The French withdrew from Vietnam north of the seventeenth parallel of latitude, leaving to the Viet Minh the areas of Tonkin and Annam. In the southern areas the non-Communist régime of Bao Dai, ex-Emperor of Annam, was preserved by French power until he was deposed by referendum in October 1955. By the beginning of 1956 French relations with the south had paradoxically deteriorated, and French influence there had been increasingly replaced by American: but French relations with the Viet Minh had greatly improved, both economically and diplomatically, despite the growth of Chinese and Soviet Communist influences in the north. Like the settlement in Korea which was reached a year before the Vietnamese, the basis of truce was deadlock and its price partition. Only when both sides had incurred heavy losses was compromise found. The contraction of Europe left vacuums which tended to be filled by Chinese or Russian Communism, or by anti-Communist American influences, not less than by the pushful forces of colonial nationalism. The colonial revolution merged into the cold war.

Arab Nationalism. While embryonic Asiatic and African nationalisms were dissolving the more outlying colonial Empires of Europe, an even more explosive force than either erupted nearer home. It was the force of Arab nationalism, emerging since the beginning of the century and now impinging upon the Mediterranean territories of the French and British Empires. Although stirred by events of the First World War[1] and especially by the collapse of the Ottoman Empire in 1918, the Arab world had by 1939 made little progress towards political independence. Saudi Arabia, Yemen, and a handful of little sheikhdoms in the Persian Gulf had become independent after 1919. Iraq, old Mesopotamia, had become an independent state in 1937. But all the rest of the Arab world, the 'fertile crescent' extending from Iraq to Morocco, was still divided among European powers. France held Syria and Lebanon under mandate, as well as controlling Algeria, Tunisia, and Morocco. Britain held Palestine and Transjordan under mandate, and kept troops in part of Egypt, with whom she shared a condominium over the Sudan. Italy held Libya. The Mediterranean was in every way a European lake.

The Second World War revolutionized this situation. Not only had important military compaigns been fought along the whole North African coast and in the Mediterranean itself, but the oil resources of the Near East assumed a new global importance in the postwar world. Italy lost Libya, which in 1951 became an independent kingdom under the Amir of Cyrenaica. France implemented the promise of her 'A' mandates over Syria and Lebanon and her proclamations of 1941, when in 1944 those countries became independent republics. Their new parliamentary constitutions were destined to be short-lived preludes to dictatorships. All foreign troops were evacuated by the end of 1946. Britain in 1946 recognized Transjordan as an independent sovereign state which became 'the Hashamite Kingdom of Jordan' with a parliamentary system. None of these Arab kingdoms found their independence easy to maintain. Each of them remained substantially dependent on foreign support of various kinds.

In March 1945 Egypt, Iraq, Syria, Lebanon, Transjordan, Saudi Arabia, and Yemen, representing in all thirty-six million Arab-speaking peoples, formed a League of Arab States. The purposes of the Arab League were wide, ranging from cooperation to expel foreign control

1. See p. 631.

and achieve political federation, to plans for economic and social cooperation. Arab nationalism, being religious and linguistic rather than racial or political, found itself deeply divided by dynastic rivalries. The rulers of Saudi Arabia and Egypt had not interests in common with either the aims of the ruler of Transjordan to dominate Palestine and lead the Great Syria movement, or the more sophisticated republican traditions and tendencies of Syria and Lebanon themselves. The bonds of the League were negative, not positive; and common hostility to Jews, French, and British was not strong enough cement to overcome dynastic rivalries and separatist ambitions. The Arab world lacked unity, whether geographical or cultural, and the pressure of Europe on Islam was its creator. Even so, the very existence of the Arab League was a straw in the wind.

There were three spearheads of Arab revolt: in Palestine, where the enemy was the Jews; in Egypt, where the enemy was Britain; in French North Africa, where the enemy was France. During the postwar decade, although Arab nationalism was still too weak to merge these three revolts into one concerted revolution, it was strong enough in these separate areas to exact heavy concessions from its diverse foes. British attempts from 1936 onward to find a way out of the dilemma in Palestine came to little. Caught between Zionist demands that Jews persecuted in Europe should be free to immigrate into Palestine, and Moslem Arab insistence upon protecting the economic rights of Arabs in Palestine, Britain tried in vain to devise a scheme of self-government for the land she held under an 'A' mandate. Her proposal in 1937 that it be partitioned into an Arab and a Jewish state was flatly rejected by the Arabs. Another British proposal in 1939, that an independent state be set up at the end of a ten-year period, during which Jewish immigration would be limited at first by numbers and then by Arab consent, was rejected by both sides. The issue hung in suspense until 1944. Then the sympathies aroused by the Nazi attempt to exterminate European Jewry, and the pressure of Zionism on United States opinion, combined to produce a United Nations scheme for partition in November 1947. This was again resisted by the Arabs, and the following month fighting broke out between the Jews and forces of the Arab League. It continued into the summer of 1948. Britain surrendered her mandate to the United Nations and withdrew her troops by May. That month the United Nations appointed Count Bernadotte of Sweden as mediator, but in September he was assassinated by a Zionist terrorist. The handling of the whole war reflected little credit upon the United Nations. Armistices were eventually signed between February and July 1949. During the fighting a new state of Israel had come into being with a democratic parliamentary constitution and with Dr Chaim Weizmann as its president. In May 1949 Israel was admitted as a member of the United Nations. The defeat of the Arab states, both in battle and in their general policy, caused internal unrest against governments who had thus failed to satisfy the acrid nationalist feelings which they aroused.

Emboldened by signs of a new ferment in the Arab world, Egyptian nationalists tried to assert leadership over it by wresting power in Egypt from the corrupt hands of King Farouk and pushing aside the Wafd party. In July 1952 a group of young military officers, led by General Neguib and Colonel Nasser, seized power, got rid of Farouk, and dissolved the political parties. They set about purifying government and administration and putting through a moderate but valuable redistribution of the land. Since the big landowners were indemnified for the land they lost at the valuation they had themselves given it in their tax returns, it was their own fault if that valuation tended to be low. The alliance of revolutionary nationalism with state socialism, as in Turkey, became a frequent characteristic of the Arab world, where the younger generation of officials and soldiers had to find support among the discontented masses. The new government agreed with Britain to replace the Anglo-Egyptian condominium by a statute establishing self-government for the Sudan. The Sudan elections of November 1953 brought victory to the pro-Egyptian National Unionist party, but two years later the Sudanese parliament set up a fully independent sovereign state. In July 1954 Colonel Nasser, having ousted Neguib, reached an agreement with Britain whereby the British forces stationed in the Suez Canal Zone would be withdrawn within twenty months. Both parties recognized that the Suez Canal was of international importance, and endorsed the Convention of 1888 which guaranteed freedom of navigation. British troops were duly withdrawn by the end of 1955. The following year Colonel Nasser precipitated conflict with Britain and France by abruptly declaring the nationalization of the Suez Canal Company, in violation of the agreement which he had signed only two years before.

The 'Suez crisis' of 1956 was an outstanding example of how, in the conditions of cold war, the growth of non-European nationalism could precipitate a world crisis: a warning of the inextricable interdependence of world problems. Until 1955 Colonel Nasser had sought and gained aid from the West. The United States made him a substantial loan in 1953 and agreed to support his favourite scheme for economic development in Egypt, construction of the Aswân High Dam. But in September 1955, when he failed to buy arms from the West, he made an agreement to buy Soviet military equipment through Czechoslovakia. In July 1956

John Foster Dulles, American Secretary of State, made a public statement that no American aid for the Dam would be forthcoming; similar statements followed from the British government and the World Bank. Nasser retaliated by nationalizing the Suez Canal Company. Israel was increasingly alarmed by the growth of militant Arab nationalism in Syria and Jordan as well as in Egypt, and France was hostile to Egypt because of the support given by her to the Algerian rebellion. On 29 October 1956 the Israeli army attacked Egypt and won immediate successes. Not only was the threat of a world waterway a matter of international importance, but now the fact of war in the Near East constituted, in the circumstances of the cold war, an immediate threat to world peace.

At this juncture Britain and France joined forces to issue an ultimatum to both belligerents, declaring they would occupy key positions in the Suez Canal zone unless they stopped 'all warlike action by land, sea, and air forthwith'. Nasser rejected the ultimatum and appealed to the Security Council. The first bombs fell on Cairo on 31 October. The Security Council summoned a special meeting at the General Assembly, which carried, by a large majority, an American resolution urging on all participants an immediate cease-fire. In Britain Sir Anthony Eden was confronted with the resignation of two of his ministers and opposition from inside the Conservative Party, as well as with censure motions from the opposition in Parliament and vigorous protests in the country. The escapade produced in Britain a moral crisis more acute than any since Munich. It was noted that, although Australia and New Zealand had voted with Britain in the General Assembly, Canada and South Africa had abstained, and the Asiatic and African members of the Commonwealth were inevitably opposed to an action which savoured so much of old-fashioned colonial wars. The exploit not only alienated the United States but also threatened to split the Commonwealth and public opinion at home, at a moment when the Soviet Union was engaged in suppressing revolt in Hungary: it called for more powerful justification than Eden could produce. The Anglo-French forces obeyed the cease-fire resolution on 6 November, and an international force entered Egypt to take over areas as the Israeli, British and French forces withdrew.

The campaign, called off before its objectives were reached, left Nasser triumphant despite his crushing defeats by Israel. Even more, it left the Soviet Union stronger; for, by crushing Hungary, it tightened its grip on all its European satellites, while by denouncing Britain and France as imperialist aggressors, it won sympathy from the Asiatic and African peoples. Khrushchev's threats of rocket retaliation had much

869

less to do with Anglo-French acceptance of the United Nations resolution than democratic pressures inside Britain, but the Soviet leader was able to pose as a protector of the Arabs. Whatever considerations weighed with the British and French governments when they undertook the campaign, their decision was, beyond doubt, unwise in the larger context of world relations. The chief gains went to Arab nationalism. In February 1958 Egypt united with Syria in a United Arab Republic. In July 1958 pro-Nasser officers overthrew the Hashamite dynasty in Iraq, and a republic was set up with General Abdul Karim el-Kassem as Prime Minister. To prevent further repercussions, American forces landed in Lebanon and British troops were flown to Jordan. This time there was little denunciation of 'colonialism', and in the autumn the Western forces were withdrawn. By 1959 Kassem was beginning to rival Nasser for leadership of the Arab world, receiving Soviet support.

Throughout her three North African territories (known to the Arabs as the Maghreb) France experienced many repercussions of the Arab awakening. In Morocco, Tunisia, and, above all, the older French provinces of Algeria appeared a ferment of anti-European movements for independence, complicated by feuds between Arabs and Jews, between European settlers (*colons*) and the Arabs, and between rival Arab tribal and political leaders themselves. The affairs of Tunisia and Morocco were settled with comparative ease by 1955. France entered into agreements which foreshadowed the gradual transfer to Tunisians of control over police, justice, and their own system of education; and they accepted a settlement in Moroco which loosened France's grip over a territory where, since 1940, her capital investment had been particularly large. The problem of Algeria proved much more intractable, for a revolt which began in 1954 occupied some 500,000 French troops for the next eight years. Economic conditions were bad, and many Algerians migrated to France, where they lived in slum conditions. Since the Algerian *départements* were administered not as colonies, but as part of metropolitan France, there were no native organizations, such as existed in Morocco, which could take over responsibilities from the French. Arab nationalism in Algeria had intimate domestic consequences for France. Moreover, the European population of Algeria numbered over one million in a population of some nine million, and discovery of rich oil and other mineral resources in the Sahara made control of Algeria even more important than ever. The settlers built up a powerful 'Algerian lobby' in French politics, adept in preventing the unstable governments of the Fourth Republic from making any decisive moves to ensure self-government for Algeria.

In 1952 the Algerian nationalist leader Ahmed ben-Bella formed a revolutionary committee in Cairo with Egyptian help. From 1954 onwards this committee organized terrorism against French settlers and their families, and against Moslems accused of helping the French in any way. Under the name of the *Front de libération nationale* (FLN), it fought relentlessly and savagely a war of ambushes and isolated terrorism. In 1955 the French-educated politician Ferhat Abbas became its main spokesman who by September 1958 headed a 'Provisional Government of the Republic of Algeria', based in Cairo and receiving recognition from several Afro-Asian states as well as from Communist China.

These developments, and the continued failure of French governments either to reach a settlement in Algeria or to end the war, precipitated a revolt of the settlers and right-wing movements, backed by dissident French army leaders, in May 1958.[1] General de Gaulle came to power in June, with emergency powers to revise the French constitution and to tackle the problems of Algeria. The solution he sought was acceptable neither to the Algerian nationalists, who wanted independence, nor to the European settlers, who demanded that Algeria should remain French. It provided a large measure of internal self-government and autonomy, suited to preserving Algeria as one multi-racial community, but in conjunction with France within a new commonwealth of African states. During 1960 a dozen former French African colonial territories were given full independence, and all save Guinea remained within the new French Community set up by the constitution of the Fifth Republic. Peoples from Madagascar to Mauretania, from the Congo to the Ivory Coast, thus dramatically entered history as independent states, and soon they also entered the United Nations as independent members, bringing the total membership of that organization to ninety-nine. De Gaulle arranged for a referendum on the future of Algeria to be held in January 1961. It gave a majority of three to one for his policy of self-determination for Algeria. Agreement with the 'Provisional Government' was reached only in March 1962. The Algerian Republic under the leadership of ben-Bella became fully independent. Both in France, where extremists tried to sustain a reign of terror, and in Algeria, where political factions brought the country again to the brink of civil war, the struggle left an aftermath of bitterness and deep distress.

African Nationalism. In these ways the struggles of Arab nationalism stimulated and accelerated the growth of African nationalism. France, like Britain, conceded independence to African states most readily and peacefully where there was no large and influential population of

1. See p. 847.

European settlers. In Kenya and in Algeria, where European minorities were large enough to be important and where racial feelings were also most inflamed, the road to independence was much more thorny. Within colonial territories, as within the world at large, peaceful coexistence proved an aim peculiarly difficult to achieve. Yet the extent of the peaceful revolution of the 1950s in most of the British and French African territories should not be underrated; and the French Community, like the British Commonwealth, kept strong bonds of cohesion which, because they were of evident mutual advantage and rested on reciprocal respect, might be expected to prove durable.

The so-called wind of change which swept through the whole continent of Africa during 1960 was the omen of yet vaster changes still to come. It was the whirlwind reaped by the sowing of the 1950s. The African National Congress, dating from as early as 1912, began during this decade to evolve a mass political organization. In 1952, along with the South African Indian Congress, it launched in South Africa a mass civil disobedience campaign, using the tactics of Gandhi in India a generation before. As the former African colonies of Britain and France progressively won independence, black African nationalism became a dynamic force in its own right. Such men as Dr Nkrumah of Ghana, Tom Mboya of Kenya, Houphouet-Boigny of the Ivory Coast and Diori of Niger became political figures of importance not only within their own states, but as leaders (often in some rivalry) of a wider African nationalism.

The most dramatic explosion of African tribal nationalism occurred in the former Belgian Congo, which was abruptly given independence and a new constitution on 30 June 1960. A round table conference of Belgian and Congolese representatives had been held in Brussels at the beginning of 1960. It accelerated the process of granting independence, although the traditionally paternalist policy of Belgian colonial administration had done little to prepare the Congolese for receiving it. After elections held in some disorder, Joseph Kasavubu was made President of the Republic of the Congo, and Patrice Lumumba became Prime Minister. Provincial and tribal allegiances, however, were considerably stronger than any overriding spirit of nationalism, and the Belgian civil authorities withdrew overhastily. A mutiny in the Congolese *Force Publique* led to a flight of Belgians and to intervention by Belgian troops. The Congolese government appealed to the United Nations, which in mid July sent an international force to maintain order. But utter confusion reigned. Katanga province, under its Premier Tshombe, declared its independence and welcomed Belgian troops; tribal warfare broke out in Leopoldville; Lumumba was arrested by Colonel Mobutu of the Congolese army, while in Stanleyville Lumumba's supporters arrested some opposition deputies; the Soviet Union lent support to Lumumba, while the western powers supported President Kasavubu as the legitimate head of state. Massacres and outrages continued, and at the United Nations the Secretary-General, Dag Hammarskjöld, was variously accused of taking sides in the Congo's internal affairs and of incompetence in handling the United Nations forces. At the end of 1960 the Belgian Congo had become a turbulent centre of tribal, nationalist, and global conflicts. Patrice Lumumba was murdered in February 1961. In Africa only the Portuguese colonies (Angola, Guinea, and Mozambique) remained intact, and even the ancient land of Ethiopia was rent by the upheaval of a palace revolution against the Emperor Haile Selassie, in December 1960. In February 1961 terrorist outbreaks in Angola ended the quiet there. They were savagely crushed by Dr Salazar's reorganized government.

Wider Horizons. The powerful impulses of separatism, so apparent in all the underdeveloped areas of the world, were moderated by two other factors. One was a greater concentration of colonial policy on economic development and social welfare, based on large-scale investment and technical assistance. Under the Colonial Development and Welfare Act of 1945, itself a successor to earlier acts of 1929 and 1940, Britain made available the sum of £120 million (increased in 1950 by another 20 million) to be spent in and on the colonies; during the following decade this sum was spent mainly on developing agriculture and transport systems, and on extending medical and educational services. In 1948 the Colonial Development Corporation was set up, with powers to borrow up to £40 million from the British Treasury, 'to develop the resources and trade of, and to expand the production of, foodstuffs and raw materials in colonial territories'. These years saw the first phase of a real industrial revolution in the colonies. Foundations were laid for a more balanced economy, and therefore for a greater degree of economic independence, no less important than political emancipation.

The second tendency which was transforming colonialism was the growth of new forms of relationship between all states which cut right across, and made irrelevant, the old political relationships. Nations and states increasingly came together not in terms of colonialism or dependency, but of functional cooperation within specialized agencies for promoting mutual interests. The Colombo Plan of 1950 was one such development. Within it the United Kingdom, Australia, Canada, Ceylon, India, New Zealand, and Pakistan, came together with Indochina, Thailand, and the colonial territories of south and south-east Asia, to plan a six-year economic development scheme for India, Pakistan,

Ceylon, Malaya, Singapore, British North Borneo, Brunei, and Sarawak. Its aims were similar to those of the Colonial Development and Welfare Acts of Great Britain. All the functional agencies connected with the United Nations – the Food and Agriculture Organization, the World Health Organization, UNESCO, and the rest [1] – had a similar influence, and were especially concerned with improving conditions of life and work in the more undeveloped parts of the globe. Indonesians, who would not accept directly the technical services of a Dutchman for reasons of national pride and prejudice, would accept them through UNESCO as an international service. In such ways could nationalist barriers and animosities be dissolved within a new context of human relationships.

The shrinkage in area of the Empires of particular European powers did not mean a contraction of the ambit of European civilization in general. On the contrary, Asia sought to use its new independence to adopt more fully the techniques of industrialism and modern science, and even the education and technical advice of Europeans. The two greatest non-European powers in the world, the United States and the Soviet Union, were in reality semi-European powers, each with immediate interests in Europe and each deriving much of its tradition and the basis of its civilization from Europe. Communist China borrowed from Russia what Russia had borrowed from Europe. Never had the impact of European civilization been more truly worldwide than when the range of Europe's political power was being most rapidly contracted. Economic westernization advanced even while political westernization was in retreat.

Significant, too, was the decline of 'continental insularity' in the European outlook. During the 1930s much had been said and written about the cleavage of the world between the 'have nations' and the 'have-not nations'. The former included the colonial powers of Britain, France, and the Low Countries; the latter were especially Germany and Italy which felt underprivileged for lack of large overseas possessions. It was on an assumption that there were two categories of European powers, those with grievances and demands and those whose function it was to satisfy such demands from their own superabundant possessions, that the whole doctrine of appeasement had been founded. In the 1940s and still more the 1950s, the 'have-not' nations were the undeveloped and the dependent peoples of the world; the 'haves' were all the advanced industrial countries upon whose financial aid, technical assistance, and political help the 'have-nots' relied for their own future prosperity and progress. Everywhere horizons had widened, every major

1. See p. 885.

issue became a global issue, and the interdependence of all alike, whether advanced or undeveloped, was more conspicuous than ever before in the history of mankind. Just as events in North Africa could overthrow the Fourth French Republic in 1958, so turmoil in the Congo in 1960 could cause a domestic crisis in Belgium. The globe, men realized, had no edges. Of this change the colonial revolution, in all its aspects, was one great manifestation and one major cause. Another was the rapid multiplication of international organizations of all kinds and purposes, some world-wide and comprehensive, some functional, some regional, but all alike knittting the nations of Europe more closely together with non-European nations. In this way, too, the place of Europe in the world was transformed after 1945: this will be considered in the next chapter.

CHAPTER 32

INTERNATIONAL FABRIC

THE UNITED NATIONS

HISTORICALLY the United Nations began as a grand alliance for fighting the Axis and Japan. The principles of the Atlantic Charter[1] were reaffirmed by the twenty-six allied states on 1 January 1942 in the 'Declaration by United Nations'. Draft proposals for the new organization were prepared under the auspices of the four 'sponsoring powers' (the United Kingdom, United States, Soviet Union, and China) at conferences held at Dumbarton Oaks, near Washington, in the autumn of 1944. They reached agreement on all important matters except voting procedure, and that was settled by the 'Big Three' at Yalta in February 1945. The draft Charter was then discussed, modified, improved, and finally signed by representatives of fifty states at the San Francisco Conference in April-June 1945. They turned the United Nations from a wartime alliance into a permanent peacetime organization for general international cooperation. It formally came into force on 24 October 1945.

United Nations Charter, 1945. The circumstances in which the San Francisco Conference met were in every way transitional and fluid. President Roosevelt, one of the chief sponsors of the project, died a fortnight before it met. The formal surrender of Germany came in the midst of the conference on 7 May. The atomic bomb was still a secret, and war in the Far East was still going on, when the conference dispersed. Turkey, Egypt, Saudi Arabia, and several other states declared war on collapsing Germany chiefly to qualify for attendance at San Francisco as 'peace-loving nations'. The Soviet Union insisted on the separate representation of the Byelorussian and Ukranian Republics of the U.S.S.R., while the United States secured the admission of the neutral Argentine Republic. Other neutrals – Spain, Portugal, Eire, Sweden, Switzerland – were not present, though all but the last later became members of the United Nations. The Charter was thus, in general, the work of the victorious powers and especially of the four great powers. Most of the new states (such as Pakistan, Burma, Israel, Jordan, Indonesia) as well as some ex-enemy states (Italy, Austria, and the Balkan States) were in due course admitted to full membership.

1. See p. 778.

The new organization differed fundamentally from the League of Nations in that both the United States and the Soviet Union were in it from the start, and therefore the real balance of power in the world was reflected in its structure. Yet as it took shape it inevitably came to seem more and more like a resurrection of the League. It, too, had to have a General Assembly in which all member states enjoyed equal representation and equal voting power. The functions of this assembly were, again, to debate matters of common concern, and all important decisions had to be taken by a majority of at least two thirds of the members present and voting. This was a notable advance on the Assembly of the League, where all important decisions required unanimity.

The new body, too, had a Council – now called the Security Council – composed partly of all the great powers as permanent members and partly of six other member states elected to it in two-year rotations by the Assembly. It was granted wider authority than the Council of the League, for under Article 24 members 'confer on the Security Council primary responsibility for the maintenance of international peace and security, and agree that in carrying out its duties under this responsibility the Security Council acts on their behalf'. It was the issue of voting procedure on this body which aroused so much controversy, but the scheme eventually agreed to at Yalta was laid down in Article 27. Each of the eleven members of the Security Council has one vote. On procedural matters an affirmative vote of any seven members is enough. On all other matters decisions require 'an affirmative vote of seven members including the concurring votes of the five permanent members'. This gives each of the great powers a virtual veto over all major decisions. It also makes it necessary, even when all five great powers are in agreement, for them to gain the support of at least two out of the six non-permanent members; but that proviso causes little anxiety. The power of veto, highly valued by each of the great powers, can be condemned as giving large powers an undue importance *vis-à-vis* smaller nations, and as rendering the Security Council ineffective for taking any action against aggression by a major power. But it recognizes the special responsibilities for enforcement action which would lie with the great powers. It certainly gives each great power an absolute veto against the admission of new members, since recommendations for admission lie with the Security Council. The powers repeatedly used this veto and thereby delayed the growth of the United Nations towards universality. The fate of the United Nations, like the fate of Germany and of the colonial revolution, became closely bound up with the cold war. Since non-member states can and do associate themselves with the specialized agencies of the United Nations,[1] this restriction has perhaps mattered little.

Frequent use of the veto has also tended to enhance the role of the General Assembly as against the Security Council. The Assembly has wide terms of reference. It 'may discuss any questions or any matters within the scope of the present Charter', and 'may make recommendations to the members of the United Nations or to the Security Council or to both on any such questions or matters' (Article 10). In November 1950, after the outbreak of the Korean war, the General Assembly passed a resolution.

that if the Security Council, because of lack of unanimity of the permanent members, fails to exercise its primary responsibility for the maintenance of international peace and security ... the General Assembly shall consider the matter immediately with a view to making appropriate recommendations to Members for collective measures, including in the case of a breach of the peace or act of aggression the use of armed force when necessary, to maintain or restore international peace and security.

This Resolution means that a two thirds majority of all members can for certain purposes bypass the veto on the Security Council; and though such a power was probably inherent in Article 10, the Resolution marks the enhanced moral authority of the Assembly as against the Council.

The structure and voting procedure of the Security Council have made it impossible for any great power, or the protégé of any great power, to be condemned as an aggressor by the United Nations. It is, therefore, normally impossible to take punitive action against such a state through the machinery of the United Nations. Since, it may be argued, serious aggression of a kind likely to endanger the peace of the world can come only from the actions of a great power, this fact makes the whole organization ineffectual for its primary purpose, defined in Article 1 as being 'to maintain international peace and security, and to that end to take effective collective measures for the prevention and removal of threats to the peace and for the suppression of acts of aggression or other breaches of the peace....'. It was growing awareness of this which led to the creation of the series of regional security organizations described below.[2] Such organizations have been reconciled with the obligations of the Charter through Articles 52 and 53. These lay down that 'Nothing in the present Charter precludes the existence of regional arrangements or agencies for dealing with such matters relating to the maintenance of peace and security as are appropriate for

1. See p. 885.
2. See pp. 890–96.

regional action'; and even that 'the Security Council shall encourage the development of pacific settlement of local disputes through such regional arrangements or by such regional agencies...'. The Security Council must, however, be kept 'fully informed' of such activities, and they must be 'consistent with the Purposes and Principles of the United Nations'. The 'inherent right' of individual self-defence against an attack is recognized in Article 51.

The picture presented by the United Nations is one of a widely representative general organization resting ultimately upon the voluntary cooperation of all its member states, and most crucially upon the cooperation of the great powers. It represents governments, not necessarily peoples. It rests on the axiom that without the continued concert of the great powers peace cannot be ensured, and that punitive action against aggression by a major power (or by a state supported by a major power) must take place outside the Security Council and not through it. No more than the League is it any form of world government. It is a standing apparatus for the voluntary cooperation of state governments, and works successfully only to the extent to which its most powerful members can reach agreement among themselves. Article 47 of the Charter set up a Military Staffs Committee consisting of the chiefs of staff of the permanent members of the Security Council. It was made 'responsible under the Security Council for the strategic direction of any armed forces placed at the disposal of the Security Council' but had no permanent forces of its own. Lacking any physical coercive power or 'police force', the organization relies for enforcement action (or 'sanctions') upon the will of great powers to put their own forces at its disposal. There is no pooling of force within it, except by *ad hoc* decisions of its members, who are expected under Article 45 to hold air-force contingents 'immediately available' for enforcement action.

This voluntarist character runs throughout all its other organs and the many specialized agencies connected with it. The Charter provided for a new body, the Economic and Social Council, consisting of eighteen members elected by the General Assembly. This Council was charged with the care of 'international economic, social, cultural, educational, health, and related matters', and with coordinating the work of the various specialized agencies concerned with such matters. Since its functions are advisory and auxiliary, not governmental, its decisions are taken by a simple majority of those present and voting. The Charter also provided for a Trusteeship Council, successor to the old Permanent Mandates Commission of the League,[1] which consists of those members administering trust territories, other members of the Security Council

1. See p. 853.

not administering trust territories, and 'as many other members elected for a three-year term by the General Assembly as may be necessary to ensure that the total number of members of the Trusteeship Council is equally divided between those Members of the United Nations which administer trust territories and those which do not' (Article 86). It receives reports from the administering authorities and petitions from the trust territory itself, and provides for periodic visits to the trust territories. Its decisions, too, being advisory and without power of coercive enforcement, are taken by a simple majority of members present and voting. The Permanent Court of International Justice set up in the Covenant of the League was continued by the Charter as the International Court of Justice, and each member of the United Nations undertook (Article 94) 'to comply with the decision of the International Court of Justice in any case to which it is a party'. If it should not so comply 'the other party may have recourse to the Security Council which may, if it deems necessary, make recommendations or decide upon measures to be taken to give effect to the judgement'. The former 'optional clause' was retained.[1] A secretariat, to be 'recruited on as wide a geographical basis as possible', was again set up under a secretary-general, appointed by the General Assembly on the recommendation of the Security Council. The Norwegian Foreign Minister, Trygve Lie, was elected first secretary-general.

By comparison with the League of Nations, the United Nations therefore differs little in pattern or functions. In several respects – in the substitution of a two thirds majority for unanimity in decisions of the General Assembly, in the augmented powers given to the Security Council and to the individual great powers within it, in the authority of the Trusteeship Council to receive petitions and visit trust territories – it is a somewhat tighter organization than the League. Its organs, when they can function at all, can do more. But how far they can function at all depends, as before, on the will of its leading members to make them function. Still greater emphasis is now placed on the role of more elaborate specialized agencies in promoting economic, social, cultural, and technical cooperation. The fabric of international society has been strengthened, even if the political structure for preserving peace and providing international security should prove little more effective than that of the League.

The organization, as stated in its second Article, 'is based on the principle of the sovereign equality of all its members'. This principle, it can be argued, applies more to internal than to external national sovereignty. A subsection of the same Article states that 'Nothing

1. See p. 645.

contained in the present Charter shall authorize the United Nations to intervene in matters which are essentially within the domestic jurisdiction of any State or shall require the Members to submit such matters to settlement under the present Charter'. On these grounds France refused to countenance discussion of Algeria by the United Nations. Member states may be expelled, and new members admitted, by the General Assembly on the recommendation of the Security Council. But the privileges given to the permanent members of the Security Council by the power of veto violate the principle of equality, if not of sovereignty: and the great powers have taken care in other ways to safeguard their separate sovereignty even at the expense of equality. The United States insisted upon the Pacific islands, for which she made trusteeship agreements (Mariana, Caroline, and Marshall Islands) being classed as a 'strategic area', and thus brought under the supervision not of the General Assembly but of the Security Council, where her veto could over-rule any unwelcome decisions about them. From the outset the United Nations became the arena for conflicts between the rival power-*blocs* of the postwar world, none of which was willing to surrender to the untried authority of a novel international organization any of the sovereign rights which it thought necessary for its own security. The Charter, even more clearly than the Covenant, bore the marks not only of wartime alliances but also of postwar jealousies.

Local Wars. By 1960 the United Nations had to take four major decisions: concerning Israel, Korea, Suez, and the Congo. Over the first,[1] it showed neither firmness nor consistency in face of a dynamic new nationalism. It supervised a truce signed on 11 June 1948, and another signed on 18 July. Each truce was broken, but the United Nations took no action. When the mediator whom it sent to Palestine, Count Bernadotte of Sweden, was murdered in broad daylight it made no attempt at reprisals. Instead it welcomed the state of Israel into membership of the United Nations. The question of Palestine was settled not by the United Nations but by a successful war fought by the Jews against the Arabs.

In the Korean dispute, ostensibly a civil war between rival Korean governments but in fact a war of aggression by the North Korean Communist government encouraged by the Soviet Union and China, the Security Council took immediate and decisive action. Since the Soviet Union had withdrawn its representatives from the Security Council in January 1950 and China was represented on it by the government of Chiang Kai-shek, there was no power on the Security Council to veto action. The Council, on United States' initiative, called

1. See p. 867.

for the immediate withdrawal of North Korean forces from all areas south of the thirty-eighth parallel. When this had no effect the United States, followed soon by some other members of the United Nations, sent troops in sufficient strength to drive them back. The subsequent stages of the Korean war – the advance of United Nations forces to the Manchurian border and the consequent intervention of Chinese Communist forces led, as already shown,[1] to a prolonged struggle which ended in restabilizing the frontier along the thirty-eighth parallel. In the end the United Nations decisions had thus been enforced, and the authority of the Security Council upheld. But its legacy was the continued exclusion of Communist China from membership of the United Nations, and a widening of the rift between East and West which bedevilled the whole working of the organization. Decisive action had been made possible, moreover, only by the accidental absence of two major powers which, if present, would have vetoed any action.

The third war in which the United Nations took direct action, the Suez campaign of 1956, began as a renewal of the Israeli-Arab war of 1948 but now involved two major powers, Britain and France.[2] The alacrity with which the General Assembly took action, the amenability of Britain and France in accepting United Nations intervention and agreeing to a cease-fire, and the success with which an international force took over areas as the participating armies withdrew can all be registered as major triumphs for the United Nations as an agency for restoring peace. On the other hand, its intervention meant supporting, in effect, Colonel Nasser's violation of his promise not to nationalize the Suez Canal Company; and its failure to take any measures against the brutal crushing of Hungary by the Soviet Union in these same months was a disastrous submission to one of the world's largest powers. It permitted, by implication, the establishment of a 'double standard' of international ethics, by which aggression is aggression only when committed by Western powers, and Communist conquest of neighbouring lands is not 'imperialism'.

The fourth experiment in United Nations intervention, in the former Belgian Congo after its emancipation,[3] was the most inconclusive of all. The military aspect of the operation, mainly because of the tangle of tribal, racial, and personal conflicts in which it became involved, was only partially successful. Extensive disorders, massacres, and outrages occurred which no one could prevent. Much more successful was the civil administration, whose basic task was to keep

1. See p. 845.   2. See p. 868.
3. See p. 872.

essential services running in conditions of growing collapse and chaos. Politically, the great-power rivalries of the cold war proved the most severe obstacle, for the Soviet Union again seized the opportunity of posing as the saviour of African freedom against aggression of the capitalist powers. The session of the General Assembly in the autumn of 1960 was in many respects a landmark in its history: by reason of the attendance of Khrushchev, Macmillan, and President Eisenhower at some of its meetings; by reason of the attack on the Secretary-General launched by Khrushchev in September, and the subsequent broadening of this attack into a Soviet demand for the reconstruction on a tripartite basis of the secretariat, the Security Council, and some of the specialized agencies; and by reason of the sudden increase in its membership by the admission of the new African states.

Unlike the old League of Nations the United Nations became increasingly universal. Beginning in 1945 with a membership of fifty states, by the end of 1963 it had one hundred and thirteen members. Thirty-five of these were African states, and fifty-eight of them belonged to the Afro-Asian group. The main additions had come in a few clusters. In 1955 sixteen states, whose applications for membership had been previously vetoed by one or other of the big powers, were at last admitted *en bloc* in a 'package deal'. They included three former neutrals (Ireland, Portugal, Spain), three former enemies (Finland, Austria, Italy), four communist countries (Albania, Bulgaria, Hungary, Rumania), and six former colonial countries (Ceylon, Jordan, Nepal, Libya, Cambodia, Laos). Japan was admitted in December 1956. In 1960 seventeen former colonies were admitted as independent member states. The United Nations thus came near to being universal: but four important states were still outside it: both the Germanies, Switzerland, and Communist China. China was represented only by the Formosa government of Chiang Kai-shek, for the United States remained strongly opposed to the admission of the People's Republic. So large an exclusion meant that the United Nations was the voice of only three quarters of mankind. So many small inclusions made the General Assembly now the voice, above all, of the little peoples of the world and of the Afro-Asian group. The exclusion of Communist China was a recurrent bone of contention, not only between the United States and the Soviet Union, but between the western allies themselves. This became apparent in January 1964 when President de Gaulle established diplomatic relations with Peking amid protests from Washington, and Chiang broke off relations with France.

The preponderance of Afro-Asian members raised the question of enlarging the size of the Security Council, and so reasonable a change was supported by many members, including the Latin American *bloc*. But revision of the Charter, which could be vetoed by the Soviet Union or by the United States, was inevitably linked with the issue of Chinese membership. In this characteristic manner world issues became closely intertwined, and the United Nations moved further toward being a forum of discussion, but further away from being an effective guarantor of security. Yet few could doubt that the world would be worse off if the United Nations did not exist. In disputes from Korea to the Congo, from Suez to Cyprus, its services were constantly invoked as mediator, negotiator, holder of the ring or keeper of the peace.

The postwar years brought a series of local wars, none of which the United Nations was able to prevent. In addition to the major wars between the Arab League and Israel in 1948, and in Korea in 1950, there were hostilities between India and Pakistan over Kashmir; between Communist and Nationalist Chinese about Formosa; between Italy and Yugoslavia about Trieste; between Israel and all her Arab neighbours, Syria, Jordan, and Egypt; as well as a Chinese invasion of Tibet and long guerrilla campaigns in colonial territories conducted by the Dutch in Indonesia, the British in Malaya and Kenya, the French in Indochina and North Africa. In India, Korea, Indochina, Palestine, Trieste, prolonged conflicts tended to be concluded by partition of the disputed territories, just as tensions within Europe perpetuated the partition of Germany. Indeed the division of Europe itself by the Iron Curtain from Stettin to Trieste was but another example of this propensity to solve conflicts by partition. With such trends in world affairs, a would-be universal structure such as the United Nations is out of harmony. Only were these trends to be reversed by a larger consensus of agreement and toleration between the rival camps could the hopes of its makers be more amply fulfilled.

The Failure to Disarm. The most signal failure of the United Nations, caused by mutual distrusts among the great powers, was the failure to fulfil Article 26 of the Charter, 'the establishment of a system for the regulation of armaments', and especially the failure to agree upon any scheme for controlling the formidable new power of atomic energy. In January 1946 the General Assembly set up an Atomic Energy Commission to make proposals for the international control of atomic energy. Since the United States insisted on a system of international inspection and control, to ensure that agreements would be carried out, while the Soviet Union rejected all such interference in its internal affairs, the Commission achieved nothing. Voluntary controls in so vital a matter were felt to be inadequate. The Baruch Plan prepared by America would have involved setting up an International Atomic Development

Authority with absolute control over the dangerous uses of atomic energy, and with powers of supervision over its peaceful scientific and economic uses by means of licensing and inspection. Such actions were to be free from the power of veto on the Security Council. The Soviet Union objected to the system of inspection, and insisted upon keeping the power of veto. Without these two provisions the Western powers felt that there could be no security against the secret manufacture of atomic bombs, and therefore no value in the plan. The Baruch Plan was accepted in the General Assembly by forty votes to six, with four members abstaining. But it was vetoed on the Security Council by the Soviet Union. In 1949 it was known that Russia, too, had the secret of the atomic bomb, hitherto kept by the United States and the British Commonwealth. In November 1952 the United States exploded its first hydrogen bomb, much more destructive than the atomic bomb. Within a year the Soviet Union, too, possessed the hydrogen bomb, and in 1957 produced the first earth satellite, the 'sputnik'. In 1958 the United States achieved the same result. By 1960 both had developed ballistic missiles, capable of carrying atomic warheads between continents, and France had joined the 'nuclear club' by exploding atomic devices of her own manufacture in the Sahara.

These rapid advances in destructive capacity, and this spread of such capacity to European nations, made disarmament by agreement more urgently essential, yet also more difficult to achieve. Although no agreement on restriction of armaments was reached, during 1958 agreements were made to suspend nuclear tests for one year, in order to eliminate the danger to public health from 'fall-out'. Except for France's Saharan tests, these arrangements continued tacitly throughout 1960. Competition in nuclear armaments was to some extent replaced by the race to conquer outer space; and, although space rockets and the like had military applications, there was some gain from the shift of emphasis toward rivalry in the exploration of space. The equality of destructive power now reached between the two giant powers led to the strategic doctrine of relying on the 'nuclear deterrent', an admission of deadlock upon which yet further efforts to reach disarmament agreements might proceed.

FUNCTIONAL AGENCIES

Article 55 of its Charter committed the United Nations to promote 'higher standards of living, full employment, and conditions of economic and social progress and development; solutions of international economic, social, health, and related problems; and international cultural and educational cooperation; and universal respect for, and observance of, human rights and fundamental freedoms for all without distinction as to race, sex, language or religion'. Acknowledging that this formidable series of tasks would call for a variety of suitable organizations, it was added in Article 57 that 'the various specialized agencies, established by inter-governmental agreement and having wide international responsibilities ... shall be brought into relationship with the United Nations'. The Economic and Social Council was especially entrusted with the task of making agreements with such agencies, and through consultation, recommendation, and report trying to co-ordinate their activities within the framework of the United Nations.

Several such 'specialized agencies' already existed before the Charter was signed. Some of them had a continuous existence since the late nineteenth century, some dated from 1919, and others were of very recent creation. The International Telecommunication Union of 1865 and the Universal Postal Union of 1875 both become duly linked, in this way, with the United Nations. The old International Meteorological Organization of 1878 was transformed into the new World Meteorological Organization. Such bodies were but modern continuations of those most uncontroversial of all international bodies which originated in the basic needs of modern society.[1] They served their purposes as well as ever. From 1919 dated the International Labour Organization which, like the International Court of Justice, now continued in substantially its old form.[2] An agreement defining its relationship to the Economic and Social Council was made at the end of 1946, and it concerned itself particularly with problems of full employment, migration, and manpower. Some of the work previously done by the technical committees of the League of Nations was now taken over by special commissions of the Economic and Social Council. These included the Commissions on Narcotic Drugs, on the Status of Women, on Transport and Communications, on Population, and on Human Rights. Other tasks formerly performed by the League's technical committees, relating to public health and epidemics, scientific and technical education, or intellectual cooperation, were felt to be sufficiently large and complex to call for new specialized agencies, described below.

In addition to these bodies, there existed in 1945 the Food and Agriculture Organization (FAO) agreed upon by the conference at Hot Springs in 1943, and set up at the conference of Quebec in October 1945; and the two financial organizations created in 1944 by the Bretton Woods Conference, the International Monetary Fund and the Inter-

1. See p. 539.
2. See p. 645.

national Bank for Reconstruction and Development (the 'World Bank'). Each was equipped with a distinct constitution of its own, providing for an annual conference of members and a council to direct operations. Since the functions of the FAO were only advisory and consultative and involved furnishing technical knowledge and assistance when requested by member states, its constitution gave each member state equal representation and accepted a simple majority vote as sufficient for all ordinary decisions. The central bodies of the Fund and the Bank, being executive in character and having power to decide whether or not to permit loans, were constituted not in terms of 'sovereign equality' but according to a highly complex system of weighted voting-power. This gave the 'Big Five', and pre-eminently the United States, control over all operations. The main difference between the two institutions was that the Fund was designed to provide short-term credit facilities to overcome temporary difficulties in the balance of payments and so to discourage such restrictive or competitive monetary measures as sudden devaluations; the Bank was devised to provide long-term loans to facilitate rehabilitation and industrialization. Nevertheless both France (in 1948) and Britain (in 1949) devalued their currencies. The European Recovery Programme after 1948 supplemented the work of the World Bank. In 1957 an International Finance Corporation (IFC), investing in private enterprises to encourage production, was added to this group of agencies.

During the postwar years several further functional agencies were set up, often on the initiative of the United Nations and usually under its general auspices. Most characteristic were three concerned with important matters of world-wide concern, all of which had some precedents in prewar internationalism. The World Health Organization was created in July 1946 and by 1960 101 states adhered to it. It comprised a world health assembly, an executive board, and a director general and secretariat, on the patterns of UNRRA and the FAO. It came formally into being in April 1948 and soon established itself as a counterpart to the FAO. It proved equally effective. Its purpose was to help combat epidemic diseases, to improve nutrition, sanitation, housing, and labour conditions, to promote maternal and child welfare, and even mental health 'as affecting the harmony of human relations'. Secondly, an International Civil Aviation Conference, held at Chicago at the end of 1944, prepared a convention governing the development of civil aviation and air transport. This superseded the Paris Convention of 1919 and the Pan American Convention of 1928. The new organization came into existence in 1947. Thirdly, the Intergovernmental Maritime Consultative Organizations (IMCO) of 1958 performed similar functions for shipping.

Less well-omened efforts were made to set up an International Trade Organization. A proposed charter for it was never ratified by enough states, but it gave rise to a smaller and more limited arrangement in 1947, the General Agreement on Tariffs and Trade, made at first among twenty-three and eventually among thirty-five states (GATT). Tariffs and preferences provided problems much more intractable, largely because they more closely affected basic national interests, than public health and transport. But in such matters as these latter, common interests were strong enough and issues of national sovereignty irrelevant enough to ensure vigorous and valuable organizations. Even so, the Soviet Union and the Ukranian and Byelorussian Soviet Republics withdrew from the WHO in 1949, though they belonged to the Universal Postal Union and the International Telecommunication Union. The International Atomic Energy Agency, set up in 1957, to secure the use of atomic energy for peaceful purposes, attracted seventy member states. Its chief value lay in its future potentialities. Such functional agencies were unable in general to bridge the gulf between East and West. Their achievements lay in strengthening and stiffening the fabric of international society, not in diminishing to any degree the absolute claims of national sovereignty.

Two remaining functional agencies deserve mention. One is the special United Nations International Children's Emergency Fund (UNICEF) raising funds from governments and public appeals to feed some five million hungry or starving children in a dozen European countries and in Asia. Like the International Refugee Organization (IRO), which came into existence in 1948 to deal with the intricate and urgent problems of refugees and displaced persons in succession to UNRRA, UNICEF was intended to be an emergency and, it might be hoped, a temporary organization. But the problems of hunger proved so perennial that it was still very active in 1960. The other is the United Nations Educational, Scientific, and Cultural Organization (UNESCO) which came into being in 1946 on the initiative of Britain and France. It became responsible for promoting those broadest of all objectives listed in the United Nations Charter – 'respect for human rights and for fundamental freedoms for all without distinction as to race, sex, language, or religion'. It works to diffuse knowledge, culture, and international understanding among all peoples of the earth. Its manifold activities, sometimes pretentious and sometimes of realistic value, are a diversified form of the work done before the war by the League's Committee on Intellectual Cooperation. Like most other functional agencies it is an advisory and consultative body, unable to operate in any country without the approval of that country's government. The most important feature of postwar internationalism was that it was always easier to make agreements than to enforce agreements; and the functional agencies, like the security organization, depended for success on good faith, good will, and good sense: on persuasion and appeal to self interest, not on coercion.

Unofficial Agencies. Internationalism was still, as before 1914, much wider than intergovernmental collaboration. A large and increasing number of other less official international organizations existed to serve the common interests of churches, trade unions, professional bodies, and technical interests. The World Council of Churches was set up in 1948 at Amsterdam, representing 147 churches in forty-four countries. Comprising various departments concerned with such matters as aid to refugees, the welfare of youth, overseas missions, and the study of doctrinal differences, it served as a central advisory body. Churches participating included most of the Anglican, Nonconformist, Orthodox, and certain national Catholic churches, but not the Roman Catholic church as a whole or the non-Christian religions. In 1949, on the initiative of the British Trades Union Congress, an International Confederation of Free Trade Unions was set up. It comprised the non-Communist unions which had withdrawn from the Communist-dominated World Federation of Trade Unions, successor to the IFTU of 1913.[1] The cold war split trade unionism just as it divided states and dislocated the United Nations. Many other organizations of even less official kinds, such as the Inter-Parliamentary Union of 1889, the International Chamber of Commerce, the International Council of Scientific Unions, and cultural or professional bodies, constituted a whole further stratum in the pyramid of internationalism quite outside the agencies connected with the United Nations. In all of them European nations took a prominent part.

Principles of Functional Cooperation. The principles underlying this proliferation of functional agencies were that while governments and political leaders might fail to agree, more substantial if limited agreement might be reached among experts; that an accumulation of such agreements about technical affairs of common interest would in itself be valuable, and might make a basis for eventually closer agreement about even higher-level issues of sovereignty and security; and that a habit of international cooperation, acquired and shown to be profitable at such levels of economic and social activity, might strengthen the forces making for peace rather than war. Since the effects of functional cooperation on inter-state relations must avowedly be long-term, it is difficult to assess its contribution to world peace after barely twenty years'

1. See p. 390.

experience. But three facts militate against its contribution to world peace being very substantial. One is that the representative assemblies and governing councils of nearly all such official agencies are composed of governmental representatives, and political considerations have therefore tended to intrude into the conduct of the general policy, if not the day-to-day operations, of these agencies. The experts and technicians do not often get the chance to reach entirely non-political agreements. The second is that most such agencies are essentially advisory, consultative, and persuasive, and it is only when governments decide to act upon their advice or to ratify conventions prepared by them that their work culminates in effective action. At the stage of implementation politics again intervene. Thirdly, they proved less able than it was hoped before 1948, when most of them were created, to heal the rift between East and West. The Soviet Union and its satellites tended either to stay out of them, withdraw from them, or cooperate with them in a suspicious and somewhat obstructive way; though during 1954 these countries rejoined both the ILO and UNESCO.

They have, however, served other ends well. Particularly have they helped to create new and better relationships between the imperial and former colonial powers, between the West and such Asiatic states as India, Pakistan, and Indonesia, and among the nations of the Atlantic seaboard. The functional agencies have provided a wide and expanding surface of agreement, collaboration, and mutual help. Yet the 'growing points' of a world society remain relatively few and scattered, and the most important point of all, the organization of security against aggression, had by 1960 benefited little from the triumphs of functionalism. For this reason mutual security was sought, in a more short-term and restricted form, through regional organizations. Restricted regional groupings were the strongest attainable in the cold war.

REGIONAL ORGANIZATIONS

The development of regionalism was prompted partly by the example of successful regional organization before 1939 (notably the Pan American Union), but even more by the shape imposed upon European affairs by the outcome of the war and the onset of the cold war. France and the United Kingdom took the initiative in March 1947 when they signed the treaty of Dunkirk, providing for mutual defence against any renewal of German aggression and for mutual consultation on economic matters. Three months later General Marshall made his historic offer of United States aid for Europe's economic recovery. This gave great stimulus to wider economic cooperation in western Europe. Meanwhile the Low Countries, in 1944, had agreed to establish a closer economic union among themselves, and in 1948 a common customs union was adopted for Belgium, the Netherlands, and Luxembourg. This became the framework for 'Benelux', not so much an organization as a policy, making for the closest possible economic unification of the three countries. In 1954 the three Scandinavian countries of Denmark, Norway, and Sweden explored possibilities of setting up a common market in certain commodities, having in 1951 set up a Nordic Council for consultation. The same three countries joined with the United Kingdom in 1950 for group cooperation nick-named 'Uniscan'. The Marshall Plan led to the much wider Organization for European Economic Cooperation (OEEC) of 1948. It included Austria, Belgium, Denmark, France, Greece, Iceland, Ireland, Italy, Luxembourg, the Netherlands, Norway, Portugal, Sweden, Switzerland, Turkey and the United Kingdom, and in October 1949 was joined by the German Federal Republic. In 1950 the United States and Canada became associate members.

By 1950 economic cooperation in Europe, extending as widely as from Iceland and Ireland in the West to Greece and Turkey in the East, had developed fast and far. The Council of OEEC consisted of representatives of all member states, meeting at either ministerial or official levels. It had power to make 'decisions' binding on all members, 'agreements' with members, non-members, or international bodies, 'recommendations' to be considered by governments or international bodies, and 'resolutions' concerning the work of the Organization or requesting information from member states. Although 'decisions', to be binding on all, required unanimity, a member's abstention did not prevent others from agreeing and implementing decisions. The prime task of OEEC was to carry out the European Recovery Programme (ERP) by allocating United States aid, but it was designed to continue as a medium of economic cooperation after the end of ERP. It helped to facilitate trade and payments between members, and to create an atmosphere of mutual confidence and common interest. Within six of the countries concerned a still more sensational step towards real integration was taken in 1952, with the formation of the European Coal and Steel Community. The idea, hatched by Jean Monnet who had promoted the Monnet Plan for French economic reorganization, was put forward first by the French foreign minister Robert Schuman, and so became known as the Schuman Plan. France, Italy, the German Federal Republic, and the three Benelux countries combined to set up a single 'High Authority' to plan the production and organize a common market for the coal and steel produced by the six countries. It was the first

European supra-national – as against international – organization, and it was open to any other European country prepared to accept the rules of the treaty. The United Kingdom, though not joining it, became associated with it through a standing Council of Association, set up at the end of 1954.

The six states within the European Coal and Steel Community extended their economic collaboration in 1958, when they set up the European Economic Community (Common Market) and the European Atomic Energy Community (Euratom). The aim of all three bodies was to harmonize policies and achieve a real measure of economic integration, and eventually to reach political federation. Other states within OEEC, preferring looser economic agreements and noncommitment to eventual federation, formed in November 1959 a European Free Trade Association (EFTA); it consisted of Great Britain, Sweden, Norway, Denmark, Switzerland, Austria, and Portugal and, in contrast with the 'inner six', was known as the 'outer seven'. Its aggregate population (eighty-eight million) was little more than half that of the inner six: but the gross national product of the seven was nearly two thirds that of the six, and their trade was large enough, in bulk and value, to constitute a formidable rival *bloc* in any commercial competition. The division within Western European nations, with their economic policies now literally 'at sixes and sevens', led to anxious efforts to repair the breaches. The United States took part in a reconstituted OEEC, initiated in 1961, rechristened the Organization for Economic Cooperation and Development (OECD), and by 1963 even Japan adhered to it. In October 1961 Britain opened negotiations for her own entry to the European Common Market, followed by such members of EFTA as Denmark and Norway. When these were abruptly ended late in 1962 by French opposition, the breach between EEC and EFTA seemed irreparable. But solid material bases for continued economic collaboration remained, as did equally strong sources of economic rivalry within EEC between French and German agriculture. It appeared that certain inherent limits existed, beyond which neither legitimate national interests could be defied nor the urge to collaborate extend. A clumsy yet flexible pattern of overlapping organizations seemed to be the best attainable.

Regional Security. Parallel with this development of both wider and closer economic cooperation there developed comparable arrangements about security. In March 1948 France, the United Kingdom, and Benelux signed the Brussels Treaty, creating a joint organization for military defence. Unlike the Treaty of Dunkirk a year before, which was aimed against a recurrence of German aggression, the Brussels Treaty aimed at preparing defence against Soviet aggression. A Western Union Command, with a commanders-in-chief committee, drew up an integrated plan of air defence, mutual aid in producing arms and ammunition, and combined military, naval, and air exercises. But so small a power-*bloc* was unlikely to be effective alone, and the coming of the cold war brought with it the extension of the organization into the North Atlantic Treaty Organization (NATO), which largely absorbed its functions. This Treaty was signed in April 1949 by twelve states – the five Brussels Treaty states, Denmark, Iceland, Italy, Norway, Portugal, Canada, and the United States; in 1952 by Greece and Turkey, and eventually by the German Federal Republic in 1955. The vital participation of the United States was made possible by the Senate's adoption in June 1948 of the 'Vandenberg Resolution' urging United States association 'with such regional and other collective arrangements as are based on continuous and effective self-help and mutual aid and as affect its national security'. NATO was born against the background of growing tension in the world, the Soviet blockade and the Berlin airlift,[1] and the commitment of the Western powers to a policy of 'containment'. That it so speedily took concrete shape, and established itself as the major security organization of western and central Europe, was a direct outcome of Soviet policy. Only so immediate and persistent a threat could overcome isolationism, neutralism, and separatism to the extent needed for this drastic pooling of military resources.

Continued Soviet pressure was equally responsible for the shape taken by NATO after its first year of existence. The Treaty provided only for the setting up of a North Atlantic Council, which first met in September 1949, and for a year prepared plans. But in September 1950, in the midst of the Korean war, the Council hastened the creation of an integrated defence force under a single command. In January 1951, General Eisenhower assumed command in Paris as Supreme Allied Commander Europe (SACEUR). To make possible West German participation, proposals for a European Defence Community (EDC) with a supra-national authority on the analogy of the Coal and Steel Community, were put forward. But the draft treaty was shunned by Britain and was not ratified by France or Italy. As a result of conferences in London and Paris in the autumn of 1954 it was dropped in favour of less rigid arrangements. The occupation of Germany by the Western powers was brought to an end, the Brussels Treaty was revised and extended so as to bring Italy and the German Federal Republic into a wider group now called Western European Union (WEU), and it was then that Germany acceded to the North Atlantic Treaty. The United

1. See p. 842.

Kingdom undertook to maintain on the continent of Europe four divisions and a tactical air force, or their agreed equivalent, and not to withdraw them against the wishes of the majority of the Brussels Treaty powers. It was the largest and most specific military commitment to continental Europe that Great Britain had ever made in time of peace. Meanwhile three other localized pacts reinforced the system: the Balkan Pact of 1954 between Greece, Turkey, and Yugoslavia; the Baghdad Pact of 1954–5 between Turkey, Iraq, and Pakistan; and the wider organization of the Central Treaty Organization (CENTO) which comprised Britain along with Turkey, Iran, and Pakistan, and was given United States support and cooperation.

By 1960 the security of all Europe west of the iron curtain was defended by an interlaced network of bilateral, regional, and transatlantic alliances, a system of interconnected military organizations, and a unified military command. Under Anglo-American agreements of July 1958 United States ballistic and guided missiles were made available to British forces, and stocks of nuclear warheads were established in Europe. As in economic matters, so in defence, the trend after 1945 was toward regional cooperation, functional integration, and the tightening of links between western Europe and the North American continent.

The Council of Europe. The Council of Europe was a product of those articles of the Brussels Treaty which provided for social and cultural cooperation. It was signed by the five Brussels Treaty powers and by Iceland, the German Federal Republic, Italy, Denmark, Ireland, Greece, Norway, Turkey, and Sweden. Austria was admitted in April 1956. Except that Switzerland, Portugal, and Spain were not members, the membership of the Council of Europe was identical with that of OEEC. Its statute of May 1949 expressly excluded defence from its province, and defined its aim as 'greater unity between its members for the purpose of safeguarding and realizing the ideals and principles which are their common heritage and facilitating their economic and social progress'. Its unique feature was that its consultative assembly was composed of representatives varying in number according to an agreed proportion and chosen not by the governments but by the parliaments of its member states. Its committee consisted of the minister of foreign affairs of each member state, or his deputy. Both assembly and committee met at Strasbourg, and their main activities were drafting conventions about social security, medical services, patents, educational facilities, travel, migrant workers, and codes of human rights, aimed at achieving greater uniformity and reciprocity among member nations. With its wide terms of reference and interparliamentary character, it served as a useful link between OEEC and the 'inner Six' organizations, the functional agencies of the United Nations, non-governmental organizations, and even non-member states.

Interlocking Regions. Through the Commonwealth the United Kingdom became linked with yet further regional groupings of powers throughout the world. The interdependence of all nations, economically and in' defence, made such links of European importance. Under the Colombo Plan inaugurated in July 1951 the sum of £1,868 millions (approximately $5.2 billion) was to be spent over six years in capital investment in India, Pakistan, Ceylon, and the countries of south-east Asia. Of this nearly three quarters was to be invested in India, the largest participant. More than half the capital came from the United States, United Kingdom, Australia, and New Zealand. The programmes concentrated on agriculture, transport, and electric power, the bases for increasing food production which was the supreme need of these countries. It was, on a much bigger scale, the counterpart in the new Dominions to the Colonial Development and Welfare Acts[1] and a supplement to the United Nations Economic Commission for Asia and the Far East (ECAFE) set up in 1947. New security organizations also implicated the Commonwealth. In September 1951 Australia and New Zealand signed with the United States a Pacific Security Pact, pledging mutual aid in the event of an attack on any one of them in the Pacific. It was the Far Eastern counterpart to the Brussels Treaty, and as such led to the 'Anzus' organization for collective defence on the part of these three powers. The Pacific counterpart to NATO was set up in 1945, as the South-East Asia Treaty Organization (SEATO), and the following year it assumed permanent form backed by the United States, Britain, France, Australia, New Zealand, Pakistan, Siam, and the Philippines. The pattern of interlocking regional bodies spread all over the globe.

Regional Communism. Meanwhile the Soviet Union countered these economic and security organizations by comparable systems of its own within the Communist *bloc.* Eastern Europe formed in 1949 its Council for Mutual Economic Aid (COMECON), and in 1955 its Warsaw Treaty Organization designed, in the manner of NATO, to integrate the armed forces of Albania, Bulgaria, Czechoslovakia, Eastern Germany, Hungary, Poland, Rumania, and the Soviet Union. The Soviet Union had made a series of treaties with its satellites in Europe during the early postwar years,[2] and had entered into a network of bilateral trade and aid engagements with them. In February 1950 the Soviet Union made with the new People's Republic of China a Treaty of Friendship, Alliance, and Mutual Assistance. Economic assistance took the form of a

1. See p. 873.
2. See p. 843.

Russian credit of $300 million over a period of five years for industrial development in China, and the sending of technical help. Military aid took the form of mutual pledges of assistance in the event of an attack, against either, by Japan or any state allied with her. The treaty was to last for thirty years. In March joint Sino-Soviet companies were set up to exploit the oil and non-ferrous metal resources of Sinkiang province, and to run civil aviation. Three years later a further trade and aid agreement was signed, supplying China with Russian machinery and other equipment in exchange for raw materials: and on October 1954 the two governments concerted policy and mutual aid programmes still more closely and extensively. China was economically so backward that her alliance brought little immediate addition to Soviet economic strength. In many respects, since the greatest need of all the Communist *bloc* was machinery, Chinese needs competed with Russia's. But the eventual benefits to be got from a modernized, mechanized economy in China were so immense that Sino-Soviet cooperation offered prospects of vast future expansion and power.

BALANCE OF POWER IN MID-CENTURY

If the world were again to relapse into general war, it would not be for lack of facilities for cooperation. These existed in such super-abundance as to arouse suspicion that multiplication of apparatus was becoming a substitute for strength of will and sincerity of purpose – almost an admission that the heart of the matter was lacking. The mania for machinery, the vogue for constitutions, conferences, consultations, and committees, and the plethora of pacts and promises betrayed not confidence but feverish anxiety. Even in economic matters, the coexistence of the 'inner six' and the 'outer seven' betrayed anxieties among allies. The layers of security organizations were multiplied because the veto of the big powers in the Security Council made it more likely that the Security Council could do nothing than that it would do something. Nations retreated into more limited regional alliances, within which common action against aggression would be more reliable, because members were more 'like-minded' and shared common interests and a common outlook. Yet the very splitting of Europe into two rival groups of states, such as was now happening, with each tending to become more highly integrated into OECD, WEU, and NATO on one side, COMECON and the Warsaw Treaty Organization on the other, had traditionally tended to breed war.

The kind of security that can be got from regional arrangements is different in kind, not merely in extent, from the kind of security that could be provided by an effective world organization. It gives reassurance against isolated defeat in war, not against war itself. The fears of nuclear warfare were fears of war itself – fears which could not, therefore, be dispelled by the erection of rival regional organizations. These merely made it more likely that any war would be a general war in which nuclear weapons would be available to both sides. The elaborate new international fabric therefore entirely failed to allay the deepest fears of mankind. The only hope left was that mutual deterrence, the ability of each group to 'negotiate from strength', would in itself prevent war. This meant, in essence, reversion to the time honoured principle of a balance of power.

The balance of power in the mid twentieth century was no different in character, though it was very different in proportions, from the system of balance of power which had operated in Europe a century before. Now, however, that balance was not manipulated within Europe by a Palmerston or a Bismarck according to well-tried methods of diplomatic procedure and technique. The end-product of a century and a half of improvement in methods of organization, both political and economic, and of scientific and technical progress, was the accumulation of power in a few great world centres. Large geographical areas and large populations governed from Washington or Moscow, London or Peking, constituted masses of power in the world which exerted strong gravitational pulls upon less well-organized neighbouring areas and populations. Regional arrangements of security became in effect nuclear alliances, drawing smaller particles within their ambits. The new balance was a sprawling self-operating mechanism, beyond the control of any one individual or nation, and relying mainly upon mutual fears to preserve it.

By 1963, however, there were three important forces at work which could change the whole postwar balance. One was the emergence of many new nations determined to keep apart, as far as they could, from the hardening rival camps of the 'cold war'. In April 1955 the Premiers of India, Pakistan, Ceylon, Burma, and Indonesia sponsored a conference of Asian and African countries at Bandung. It was attended by two dozen other non-European states. These included a Communist power (China) and a NATO power (Turkey), former enemies (China and Japan, Northern and Southern Vietnam), and recently emancipated colonial nations (such as Libya and the Philippines) along with nations soon to become independent (such as Ghana and the Sudan). The common anxiety was to stand together as 'unaligned' in the cold war, though this varied in form from Nehru's austere Indian neutralism to Arab readiness to collect advantages from either side. In the course of the next few years, however, the 'unaligned' states were to divide among themselves. The cement of the potential 'third force' proved brittle. The African states split into two groups. Neither the Accra conference (1958) nor the Addis Ababa conference (1963) produced real solidarity among the thirty or so independent African governments, despite their common hostility to the policies of the South African government. In Asia, nationalist separatism was even more disruptive, as open conflicts broke out between India and China (1962–3) and between Indonesia and Malaysia (1963). Overshadowed by the quarrel between the two great Communist states of China and the Soviet Union, no less than by the older 'cold war', the embryonic 'third force' was a less potent agency for peace in the world by 1963 than its champions had expected five years before.

The second component in the changing international scene was important shifts of personality and policy which took place within and between the Communist powers themselves. Communism ceased even to appear to be the monolithic structure it had seemed before 1950. After Stalin's death in March 1953 intense personal rivalries within the party became evident in the rise and fall of Georgi Malenkov, the overthrow of L. P. Beria, chief of the secret police, and the attack on the cult of Stalin launched by Nikita Khrushchev in February 1956.[1] For a time tension was relaxed both at home and abroad. Khrushchev's doctrine of 'different roads to socialism', his dissolution of the Cominform, and his tours abroad during 1956 were a dramatic switch of policy. By the end of the year it had, indeed, switched back again. The crushing of Hungary showed the narrow limits of freedom allowed to Soviet satellites. The sixth Five-Year Plan for 1956–60, which renewed emphasis on heavy industries as against the production of consumer goods, was combined with a programme of economic aid to Asia, and Russia became more fully than ever a Eurasian power. Khrushchev emerged as the true heir of Stalin. But the new element of Communist China led to further fluctuations of policy. Peking was able openly to challenge Moscow as the exponent of Communist orthodoxy, and henceforth world Communism was a monster which had both the advantages and disadvantages of possessing two heads. At the Kremlin conference of November 1960, attended by representatives of eighty-one Communist parties, Khrushchev ostensibly won the ideological victory against the Chinese thesis that war between capitalism and communism is ultimately inevitable. But the basic Soviet-Chinese quarrel continued underground, and burst into an open clash of both doctrines and interests (as well as of personalities) in 1963. Indeed, the emergence of Red China as a great power was a revolution in the balance of power

1. See p. 835.

in Asiatic, as in world politics, and the policies of India, Pakistan, Southern Vietnam, and Malaysia had to be adjusted to the new balance, no less than had the policies of the Soviet Union and the Western powers. In this respect, too, the blurring of the formerly clear-cut confrontation of East and West, which seemed a happier omen for world peace, brought also a complex of new stresses and tensions which were equally capable, in turn, of endangering world peace.

Thirdly, great overriding world issues were coming to be superimposed on the deadlocks of the cold war, compelling attention and diverting energies from mere preparation for war. One such issue was the prospect, within a decade, of conquering space. The race began in October 1957 with the first *sputnik* in orbit. The Soviet rocket Lunik II struck the moon on 13 September 1959. Lunik III, on 4 October, passed round the moon and transmitted by television a picture of the back of the moon. These achievements, more spectacular than any accomplished by United States Pioneer rockets launched during 1958 or 1959, were partly countered on 11 March 1960, when Pioneer V satellite was put into orbit round the sun between the paths of the earth and Venus. During 1960 each competitor brought animals safely back from journeys into space. The following year was a true landmark in world history, for man himself made journeys into space. The Soviet airman, Major Yuri Gagarin, orbited the earth in April; the American, Commander Alan Shepard, in May travelled 115 miles into space and returned safely. Other manned space flights continued into 1963, as did experiments with inter-planetary rockets. Hope that rivalry in space might prove to be healthier, or at least more harmless, than competition in atomic warfare was encouraged by two events of the summer of 1963. In July the United States, the Soviet Union, and Britain reached a nuclear test ban agreement; and in August were signed Soviet American and Anglo-American agreements to programmes of cooperative experiments with weather and communications satellites in space. 'Telstar' successes in 1963 showed how vast might be the common gains from such scientific cooperation.

Another issue, more earthly and of even more vital concern for all mankind, was the disparity between the rapid growth of world population and that of available food. With an annual increase exceeding fifty millions, and half mankind already undernourished or malnourished, starvation on a vast scale was imminent unless strenuous efforts were made internationally to limit births, expand food production, and improve the distribution of available supplies. In this context allocation of large percentages of national wealth and scientific effort to space research was at times condemned as a diversion from more urgent tasks confronting mankind. Periodic campaigns for famine relief or 'war on want' did something to alleviate local distress: their benefits could only be marginal and temporary. Here was the profoundest problem of all affecting the relations between European peoples and those overseas. Although the Food and Agriculture Organization and other international agencies wrestled with the problem, it was plain that much more systematic efforts would be called for. This tremendous challenge to twentieth-century man, of fundamental importance for the world's future, rivalled the prospect of space travel and of nuclear destruction in its dramatic quality and made national disputes, racial conflicts, and even ideological cold war seem relatively petty issues.

In all these ways Europe of the nineteen-sixties was obliged to assume a more subdued and subordinate role in making the world's greatest decisions than it had played the previous thousand years. Within the political structure of world affairs, the peoples of Europe were not only overshadowed by the two super-powers but were now also outnumbered by the Afro-Asian States. In relation to the balance of power in the world, decisions affecting mankind were now more likely to be made in Washington or Moscow, Peking or even Addis Ababa, than in London or Paris. Both in nuclear weapons and in the space race, Britain and France had fallen into the role of lieutenants of the United States. This very fact lent significance to the efforts of President Charles de Gaulle to make France's 'presence' felt throughout the world, if only by personal intransigence and an eagerness to exploit American or British embarrassments. In the over-all world balance such tensions and frictions among the Western powers were, however, fully compensated by even greater schisms within Communism.

Mundane and traditional problems of the balance of power and of peaceful coexistence therefore continued to dominate policy. The most substantial basis for hope was that experience of the actual wars fought in Korea, Indochina, Egypt[1] and elsewhere showed that even when great powers became themselves implicated in wars, they could connive at keeping them localized engagements of limited commitment. The wars ended when both sides fought them to a standstill, but without using the atomic bomb, or, as in the Suez crisis, when major powers bowed to the force of opinion at home and abroad.

This basis for hope was immensely reinforced by the outcome of the Cuban crisis of October 1962. Having come closer than ever before to the brink of war over installation of Soviet missiles in Cuba, the United States and the Soviet Union then withdrew further toward firm agreement than at any time since 1950. President John Kennedy's skilled

1. See pp. 845, 864, and 868.

900

handling of the crisis matched Khrushchev's realistic appreciation of the danger, and produced a *détente* which yielded agreements in the summer of 1963 about both space research and nuclear tests. One moral drawn in European capitals was that in supreme crisis decisions were likely to be taken without their own close participation. Equally, it could be deduced that ideological conflicts were rapidly becoming less relevant in world affairs, since the Soviet Union was in conflict with Red China despite alleged affinities of ideology, but could make agreements with the United States and Britain despite ideological differences. Most significant of all was the proof given that the inherent threat of mutual nuclear destruction could deter both the world's greatest powers from the final step into the abyss. Peace, in fact, was not quite as 'indivisible' as it had often been proclaimed. The peace of deadlock, exhaustion, partition and even mutual deterrence might be the peace neither of justice nor of heart's desire. It had its heavy price. But a certain balance of power was preserving itself and was finding some stability, however precarious. There was that much margin left between the survival and the obliteration of Europe. It might be just enough.

PART TEN

EPILOGUE: CONTEMPORARY EUROPE

TWENTIETH-CENTURY science, in all its aspects, was a superstructure built upon mathematics and upon the great expansion of scientific knowledge and new methods of investigation which took place in the century before 1914.[1] Within the framework of thought provided by the 'big ideas' of Darwin and Einstein, the basic sciences of physics, chemistry, biology, and mathematics developed rapidly. Through the subsidiary sciences, such as engineering and medicine, these advances exerted a powerful effect upon the life of the individual in society. The intensive quest for new knowledge through experiment and observation called for a degree of precision, a mastery of technique, a dedication to specialization which led to a further fragmentation of science. The frontiers of knowledge were pushed forward so fast and so far that it became increasingly difficult for a single mind, however capacious and flexible, to encompass more than a corner of the new fields brought under cultivation by the insatiable curiosity and enterprise of the human intellect. By mid century it was still not possible to see the wood for the trees, to assess the meaning of modern scientific thought in general philosophical terms.

Yet the whole impact of scientific ideas, experimental methods, and new technologies upon European civilization and culture was never more momentous. This civilization which had become so imbued with science and so dependent on technology was, for other reasons too, a civilization in crisis. The mobile, plastic age of speed, power, and incessant change was also an age of violence, war, revolution, and destruction of old values. There was a constant interplay between the new forces which derived power from mineral energy and technology, and the new forces which derived power from economic and social organization, the manipulation of political controls and administrative machinery, and the surges of mass desires and passions. The totalitarian state was formidable precisely because it harnessed and monopolized both kinds of power, and its threat to science, culture, and civilization alike symbolized the crisis of contemporary Europe.

Since there was a crisis of civilization there was also a crisis of culture: and it was the variations in the attitude of the creative artist to science,

1. See Chapters 13 and 18.

to social needs, and to himself which most clearly revealed the nature of this cultural crisis. Finally, social thought and action themselves – the achievements of the generation after 1914 in discovering more about the operations of man within society – put at the disposal of mankind fresh means for overcoming the dislocations of crisis. It became possible to contrive more effective safeguards for the freedom and welfare of the individual in a scientific but turbulent order. Accordingly this final Part will describe first the more significant of the changes in scientific knowledge, methods, and ideas since 1914; next the main features of change in culture and the arts; then the new lineaments of social thought and action in contemporary Europe. Finally, since these developments were all a culmination of events since 1789, and it is essential to see contemporary Europe against wide horizons and in long perspectives, an attempt will be made to unravel some of the long-term trends which link the present day to the last century and a half of history.

CHAPTER 33

CIVILIZATION AND CULTURE SINCE 1914

SCIENCE AND CIVILIZATION

DURING the half century before 1960 scientific knowledge accumulated more rapidly than ever before, and had a more direct and persistent influence upon European civilization. For this there were three main reasons. First, the basic sciences of physics, chemistry, and biology were able to enjoy the fruits of the brilliant syntheses advanced in the later nineteenth and early twentieth centuries by giants like Darwin and Einstein. Although experimental verification of their theories later brought certain modifications of them, the general effect was to confirm the profundity of the 'big ideas' they conceived. Secondly, these basic sciences entered upon a phase of intensive experimentation, in the course of which whole new sectors of knowledge were explored and charted. So fertile were the new frontiers thus exposed that new hybrid sciences could be cultivated and novel instruments of investigation devised. In this sense scientific discovery acquired fresh momentum. Finally, much of the new knowledge was capable of direct technological application, and the rate at which it was applied technologically in the service of man and society was accelerated.

By mid-century European civilization had become so permeated by scientific ideas, methods, outlook, and material benefits, that the whole relationship between science and civilization shifted in emphasis. Instead of the scientist being one of many different practitioners of intellectual activity he came to dominate the whole sphere of creative endeavour. To a novel degree civilization became the slave of science, the means by which progress in scientific knowledge was sustained and through which its benefits were brought, technologically, into the service of mankind. European civilization, both in Europe and the North American continent and wherever else in the world it had struck root, emerged as the most completely scientific civilization that had ever existed.

Physics. It was in physics that the most far-reaching advances were made after 1914. Research into the structure of the atom conducted by Ernest Rutherford, James Chadwick, and many others, continued after 1919 the basic work which had been done at the beginning of the century. It led to two important discoveries. In 1932 Chadwick discovered the neutron – a particle of small mass and no electrical charge. In 1939 it was found that by using this particle to bombard uranium – the heaviest element known – it was possible to split the atom of uranium. By splitting the heart of the atom, as scientists had long expected, it was possible to release some of the vast amount of energy locked up inside it. During the war it was discovered how to control and collect the energy thus released in atomic piles, or more correctly nuclear reactors. It was also discovered, by 1945, how to make a form of bomb in which energy so released was concentrated in one great explosion which could be timed. After the war physicists and engineers set about solving the technological problem of how to build the most productive and economical nuclear reactors for producing energy which, in the form of electricity, could be used for industrial purposes. By 1960 Britain was well on the way to making atomic energy a usable source of electrical power, likely to relegate coal to the function of a raw material from which various commodities could be extracted, rather than a fuel to be burned. With the construction of large atom-smashing machines, like the 'Bevatron' at the University of California, Berkeley, scientists began to prove the long suspected existence of a sort of mirror universe. Anti-electrons or positrons were discovered by C. D. Anderson in 1932. Now the discovery of anti-protons by E. G. Segrè in October 1955 and of anti-neutrons (announced by Edward Lofgren in September 1956), further confirmed the thesis, first demonstrated mathematically by Einstein, that energy and mass are inter-convertible. Just as nuclear fission enables the scientist to create energy from mass, so the proton, given enormous energy, can form a 'proton pair' when it hits another particle, thus forming mass from energy.

Radioactivity in many different forms came to serve as an indispensable tool for further research, including the investigation of the still little known qualities of cosmic rays. Astrophysics throve alongside nuclear physics. Photography, radioactivity, and electronic devices were all invaluable in this new field of study. It revealed the existence of yet another new kind of particle, called a meson, which proved to exist in different varieties. The exploration of the universe, it seemed, was only beginning. Even such investigations had their concrete and utilitarian values, as evidenced by radar, which played a vital part in the air defence of Britain in 1940, and was widely used by shipping after the war.

The special characteristic of the new science was acceleration: the speed with which discoveries in one field were used to elicit new knowledge in other fields. Scientific progress, so to speak, fed upon itself and thereby acquired new momentum; and the speed with which new scientific knowledge was applied technologically in the service of man correspondingly increased. Only fifteen years elapsed between the laboratory discovery of how to split the atom and the actual production and use of the atomic bomb. It was the devotion of lavish governmental resources to the problem, combined with the great technological skills and facilities of the United States, which made this interval so short. The interval between even the invention of Watt's steam engine and its application to locomotion was more than four times as long. The breakneck tempo of scientific and technological progress was itself a factor preventing a higher synthesis of theory and philosophy.

Biology. While the physicist explored the heart of the atom the biologist explored the inner recesses of the living cell – its nucleus and within that again its chromosomes and genes. He too was aided in his work by adopting new tools borrowed from physics. The use of radioactivity in research and diagnosis, as well as in radiotherapy, put sensitive new instruments into the hands of the medical researcher; the electronic microscope made it possible to magnify objects one hundred times more than by any previous means, and so to identify and observe viruses which had previously been beyond observation; by using radio-isotopes the biochemist learned more about the metabolism of the body; radiation was found to bring about mutation in seeds and to accelerate the rate of mutation in living beings. The first major achievement of biology between the two wars was to fill out Darwinian theory where it was, as Darwin knew, most defective – in its treatment of biological heredity. Darwin had supposed that evolution took place because certain organisms had qualities which enabled them to leave more offspring than their contemporaries, so that an ever-increasing proportion of the population of a species inherited those qualities most valuable for survival. But if it were true, as he also supposed, that heredity involved always the blending of the characteristics of the two parents, then it might be expected that the valuable heredity qualities would be gradually but constantly blurred out of existence by mingling with less valuable ones. Advances in modern genetics removed this difficulty. It was found that there takes place in reproduction not a mingling but a perpetuation, often in latent form, of large numbers of genes both dominant and recessive in character. These can be passed on to future generations, and a particular gene may reappear only when it comes together with a similar gene. There thus exists, so to speak, a large reserve of hereditary variation, which can come into play when a species has to make some adjustment to an important change in environment. It is at that point, mainly, that the selective effect of environment comes into operation.

This and kindred advances in biology came about largely through a certain synthesis which took place during the 1930s between the sciences of biological heredity (genetics) and of cell structure (cytology). C. D. Darlington, J. B. S. Haldane, T. Dobzhansky, and other biologists in Britain and the United States brought together these hitherto specialized sciences, and evolved a mathematical theory of how the frequency of particular genes could increase or decrease within a population under the influence of natural selection. They showed that 'during the history of life there must have been an evolution of evolutionary mechanisms', making for a certain balance between preservation and flexibility. During and after the Second World War biology, like physics, evolved along new lines. On one hand more attention was given to the evolutionary changes produced by environment; on the other research was concentrated on how mutation takes place. Before the war H. J. Muller had discovered how to stimulate mutations by the use of X-rays, and since then many other 'mutagenic' substances, such as mustard gas and other forms of radioactivity, were found to have similar effects. The result was not to produce specific steps in mutation, but rather a random increasing of the frequency of mutations in general. The emphasis thus shifted away from genetics toward the effects of external stimulus, whether environment in general or radiation in particular, upon mutations. This new emphasis had obvious practical applications for the selective stock-breeder and plant-breeder, as well as for the medical researcher. It carried with it, too, an appalling warning against the long-term effects of exposing human beings to intense radiation such as is produced by the atom bomb, for it meant that successive generations might suffer as much as the immediate victims.

The greatest missing link in scientific knowledge was still the relation between the 'nucleus' of the physicist's theories and the 'nucleus' of the biologist's, between energy and life. It was clear that the energy of radioactivity, penetrating through the cell to the nucleus and its chromosomes, could produce considerable effects. How and why those effects were so produced could be discovered only when more was known about the chemistry of genes and of their essential components, protein and nucleic acid. Biochemistry seemed likely to become the crucial field of scientific investigation in the second half of the century, and one possible basis for a new and higher synthesis of scientific knowledge.

Engineering and Medicine. It was a natural outcome of this rapid advance in the physical and biological sciences that the two greatest of the applied sciences, engineering and medicine, should advance equally fast. The adoption of new forms of power for transportation, for example, led to internal combustion engines constructed of lighter metals and capable of generating more concentrated energy and higher speeds: then the development of jet propulsion and even rocket propulsion brought still higher speeds, the need for tougher alloys in metallurgy, fresh constructional problems in aerodynamics. In an age of electricity, electrical engineering likewise made rapid strides, not only for transportation and in the generation of power, but for the thousand amenities of modern society, domestic and industrial. Again, as in the advance of biology, new precision instruments played a large role in the engineer's calculation of stresses and fatigue. The extension of automation, the invention of wonder-working computing machines and 'electronic brains', bore testimony of the constant impact of the physical and mathematical sciences upon technology and industry, and therefore upon the whole of economic life.

Medicine utilized the new knowledge of biology and chemistry as readily and as beneficially as engineering used the new knowledge of physics and mathematics. The discovery of vitamins by Sir F. Gowland Hopkins in 1912, of insulin by F. G. Banting and C. H. Best in 1922, of effective vaccines against most of the great killing diseases of childhood and eventually even against poliomyelitis, of the whole range of sulphonamide drugs and powerful antibiotics such as penicillin and streptomycin, were among the great landmarks in modern preventive and curative medicine. Cancer research, using not only the methods of radical surgery and radiotherapy, but also new treatments suggested by contemporary research in nuclear physics and atomic energy, made some headway after 1945. The new surgery, made possible earlier in the century by the improvement of anaesthetics and the use of radioactivity for diagnosis, became still more delicate. Improved methods of blood transfusion enabled the surgeon to operate on heart, lungs, brain, and the central nervous system in a way previously impossible. Physiotherapy and occupational therapy made recovery after injuries or operations quicker and more complete.

Increasingly, too, the emphasis shifted from curative treatment to preventive measures: which meant that every major advance had to move hand in hand with social organization. Preventive medicine required not only more hygienic conditions in towns, houses, factories, and schools, and an army of medical officers, nurses, inspectors, and instructors to ensure public hygiene, but also constant action by state and local authorities and international cooperation through the World Health Organization and kindred bodies. Curative medicine, too, called for ampler hospital facilities, clinics, costly research facilities such as only public authorities could maintain, and assumption by the community as a whole, and by the state, of heavier responsibilities in training, education, and organization. Public health became an indispensable preoccupation of the welfare state. A 'national health service' was implicit in the whole development of modern medicine no less than in the collectivist trends of modern politics. There was continual interplay between the demands of science upon society, and of society upon science.

Psychology. The advances of the physical, chemical, and biological sciences, as of their derivative sciences engineering and medicine, were thus made along a broad and connected front. This advance was in part due, as has been suggested, to the seminal ideas of Darwin and Einstein, and the broad theoretical basis which their insights afforded. If advance in contemporary psychology was less solid and impressive, if results of investigation were less positive, this was due in some degree to the lack of equally firm theoretical foundations. The basic work of Freud and Jung, fruitful as it was, lacked the comprehensive profundity of a Darwin or an Einstein. Thus, although the influence of Freud on the arts and on non-technical thought was far-reaching, much of the contemporary progress in psychology derived from abandoning introspective analysis for laboratory experiment and observation, replacing behaviourist theories by mathematical analysis. Psychology made fastest progress where it was able to link up with the neighbouring sciences of physiology and medicine, and where its emphasis shifted away from the notion of mind and mental conflicts as separate phenomena to be investigated as such, towards a study biological in character of the behaviour of organisms in relation to environment. Indeed all science, as A. N. Whitehead pointed out, was becoming 'the study of organisms', and he evolved a whole philosophy of organism.

The result of this shift of focus was a great increase in knowledge of neurology and of the role of the nervous system in human behaviour; a better understanding, through laboratory experiments, of the working of memory and of skill; and various psychometric techniques, mathematical in character, which yielded useful if limited results. Even these specialized developments had such obvious practical applications that they were quickly – indeed hastily – adopted in education, criminology, and industry. The effect was to widen knowledge and deepen understanding of human personality, and to alleviate some of the maladjustments which occur, increasingly it seems, in the strains and stresses of modern urban civilization. But more subtle techniques, more reliable generalizations, were necessary before psychology and its associated studies could rest upon a comprehensive and adequate theory of the nature of the human mind and its activities. Exploration of the still more remote and mysterious working of psychic energy, in such fields of extrasensory perception as telepathy, remained sensational in their appeal but inconclusive in their findings. Psychic research, like space travel, had still not advanced much beyond the fringe of magic which always lies along the frontiers of science.

Mid-twentieth-century Europe had thus evolved a civilization which rested ultimately upon mathematics. Its whole organization relied increasingly upon calculation, measurement, precision; and its most useful sciences owed their rapid progress to higher mathematics. Computations of apparently the most abstract kind, of astronomers or of an Einstein, proved to have fundamental meaning for all science. The use of statistics, which brought rewarding results in the fields of quantum physics, medicine, and psychology, spread also to the social sciences, above all to economics and sociology.[1] The widespread application of statistical methods carried with it a certain bias of thought and certain concepts that in turn affected profoundly the way man thought about himself and about society. Statistical methods involved thinking less of individuals than of groups and categories, less of absolutes than of probabilities. Relativity thus came to permeate all thought in subtle and often unperceived ways.

Philosophy. Mathematical concepts and methods spread above all into philosophy. The most influential school of philosophy in Britain and America began at the opening of the century with the efforts of G. E. Moore, Bertrand Russell, A. N. Whitehead, and later the Austrian Ludwig Wittgenstein, to reveal the close affinities between mathematics and all logic, and to overthrow the empire of metaphysical thought. Logical positivism, as developed by Wittgenstein and by philosophers like A. J. Ayer, whose *Language, Truth, and Logic* of 1936 avowedly started from Moore and Russell, came to dominate the field by 1950. The school of neo-Hegelian idealist thinkers, highly influential throughout Europe before 1914,[2] declined sharply in importance after 1918, though eminent individuals such as Benedetto Croce and R. G. Collingwood retained great personal appeal. Throughout the English-speaking world the more empirical and positivist outlook prevailed, in harmony with contemporary progress in the physical and mathematical sciences. Methods of logical and positivist analysis were applied to ethics, aesthetics, and above all to language, until semantics seemed to be the bog in which this river of thought would find its end.

If metaphysical thought of the Hegelian kind fell into discredit, other non-positivist modes of thinking gained in strength, especially in continental Europe. Bergsonian philosophy, emphasizing intuitive know-

1. See p. 930.
2. See p. 436.

ledge, culminated in the highly subjective philosophies of Martin Heidegger and Karl Jaspers, born of the intellectual and spiritual anguish induced by the crises of modern civilization. Wrestling with the problems of 'knowing reality', these philosophies represent some of the repercussions upon moral philosophy of the idea of relativity. The sciences of observation, classification, and generalization deal with a world in which the object known is relative to the knower, and the knower himself essentially relative to the known. The task of finding our way about this world of known objects is the task of the natural sciences. But a scientific and objective psychology cannot, as experience shows, tell us the whole truth about man. Man is aware of himself not only as an object, comparable with other objects in the world, but as the active subjective source of all that he is and does: he is himself 'existence', a dynamism for ever reaching beyond what has already been attained. Knowledge of this kind of 'being' comes from intuition, mystical experience, faith. The Russian thinker, Nicholas Berdyaev, moved to such a standpoint as a reaction against Communism. Similar ideas, transmuted into the French existentialist movement by Jean-Paul Sartre and others, acquired a wide appeal in the conscience-searching, tortured years after 1945. They marked a revulsion against positivism and pragmatism which was not, however, a reversion to Hegelianism or to metaphysics. They revealed an inner crisis in philosophy such as existed in the whole of culture, an overpowering sense of man's having been in Heidegger's phrase 'thrown into a world' which is alien and hostile to him and which ends with an 'absurdity' – death. Yet this effort to repudiate positivism, or at least to escape from its dehumanizing implications, could lead back to a basic materialism and, as with Sartre, to atheism. Finding himself destitute of all values, man can rely only on what his own will controls. This circular nature of philosophical trends throws light on the most striking paradox of the century, the prevalence and widespread acceptance of Marxian materialist determinism: a creed which won power by reason of the very human qualities it denied – the strange capacity of men to live by faith and to die for an abstraction, and by so doing to shape the destiny of mankind.

Against the advance of dialectical materialism, as of other powerful secular creeds such as nationalism and racialism, established religions proved able to offer only partial resistance. Impulses which, in earlier ages, had found expression and satisfaction in religious faith and worship now flowed increasingly into secular moulds. The impulses of man to transcend individuality and to identify himself with a greater whole, to worship a personal deity, found in twentieth-century conditions substitute religions in a faith in science, in national or racial destiny, in the worship of secular leaders. The fanaticism of politics, like the sectarianism of culture, derived from a diversion of religious impulses into secular channels. The revival of Anglo-Catholicism and the revitalization of the Roman Catholic Church in Europe after 1945 came from their capacity to offer, more clearly than the Protestant and Orthodox Churches, a rival 'appeal of the absolute' to those left dissatisfied by economic or political totalitarianism. In the non-European world it remained to be seen whether Hinduism and Islam would offer more effective resistance than Buddhism to the advance of secular faiths.

The Dynamism of Science. Turn where he would for philosophical consolation or explanation, modern man could evade neither the demands nor the consequences of science. It offered the lure of life itself. If a child born in western Europe in 1955 had an expectation of life twenty years greater than one born in 1900, it was mainly because of the dual advances in medicine and in environmental hygiene. If infants in Great Britain were in 1950 dying at the rate of only thirty-one per thousand, instead of at the rate of 142 per thousand as in 1900, this was the reason. As a result of death rates falling faster than birth rates, Europeans continued, though with diminished momentum, their nineteenth-century propensity to multiply; so that the 310 millions of 1900 became the 434 millions of 1962. If such tenacity of life varied greatly still between one European country and another, that variation matched closely the differences in standards of living and hygiene, which in turn had close correlation with the degree of industrialization. Thus Rumania in 1940 had still an infant mortality rate similar to that of France a century before.

More mouths to feed called for a more intensive production of food. Again it was science and technology which provided the remedy in improved stock-breeding, chemical fertilizers, better pest control, mechanization of methods. Nations might find their whole economic status in the world abruptly transformed by the quest of technology for indispensable new resources. Because of the bigger demand for petroleum, oil, rubber, and the lighter metals for the new industries of automobiles and aviation, hitherto poor and backward countries – Malaya and Indonesia with their rubber, Venezuela, Rumania, and the Arab countries with their oil, China, Mexico, and Bolivia with their mineral resources of antimony and tin – assumed a new position in the world's economy. The very roots of that economy were being constantly changed by science and technology: as when France and Italy found unsuspected sources of wealth in their deposits of bauxite and their natural sources of hydroelectric power; or even more dramatically when Canada and the Congo leapt into importance because their uranium was urgently needed for the production of atomic energy. The scientific revolution was also an economic revolution, inescapable and profound in its human consequences throughout the world.

This dynamism of discovery permeated not only material life within the new scientific civilization of Europe, but also its culture and its art. The painter and poet, the architect and sculptor, sensitive to the ever-changing society around him and to the deepening dilemmas of man in such a civilization, showed all the symptoms of a culture in process of equally rapid change. Europe's spiritual and moral crisis was best revealed in its men of art and letters.

THE CULTURE OF CRISIS

Unlike the scientist and the technologist, for whom the challenge of war and the support of war-intent societies brings almost unmitigated benefits in terms of stimulus, encouragement, and facilities, the creative artist finds experience of war, revolutionary violence, or social upheaval intolerably disturbing. There is one basic reason for this contrast. For the scientist the starting-point of his quest for truth is the given object of investigation, the phenomenon of nature to be observed, explored, and if possible explained by means of the proven methods of experiment and verification of hypothesis. For the artist the starting-point of his quest for truth and beauty is his own sensitivity to experience. The mode of his expressing in aesthetic form the truth that he finds is therefore a matter of taste and technique. The more perplexed he is by experience and the more his sensitivity is wounded or shocked by it, the more experimental, esoteric, and introspective is his style likely to become. Such was the fate of much European culture after 1914, betraying all the symptoms of nervous shock. The shattering of traditional values and established beliefs which occurred in war and revolution was accompanied by a wholesale abandonment of traditional taste and technique.

Modernism. From this flowed three different consequences. Some, finding the more conventional forms of expression no longer adequate to express the truth as they saw it, engaged in feverish experiments with free verse, abstract painting, unmelodic music. Others sought escape from the prevailing discord between man and his environment in introspection, the exploration of their own inner consciousness as the only trustworthy register of what experience means if it means anything. Others again, who found in awareness of the anguish and dilemmas of man in a troubled world fresh springs of inspiration, fulfilled one eternal function of the artist in holding up a mirror to his age, revealing with an artist's perceptiveness its tragedies and follies. It was the first two tendencies which at first prevailed, and constituted the 'modernist revolt' of the 1920s. They helped to divorce the artist from society by making art even more esoteric than it already was by 1914, and treating it on one hand as a form of aesthetic gymnastics in which comprehensibility was sacrified to experimental technique, on the other as a form of spiritual hygiene, whereby the artist sought merely relief from his inner torments. Modernism was the culture of coteries.

This self-conscious modernism of the 1920s, so ardently cultivated by *avant-garde* painters, writers, sculptors, and musicians, took several forms: an eager iconoclasm, deserting traditional values along with traditional styles and ridiculing established culture; a readiness for bold experiments in fresh modes of expression, and emancipation from the restrictions of prevalent taste; captivation by the psychological teachings of Freud, Adler, and Jung, which focused attention upon the inner self and especially upon man's unconscious and non-rational impulses. Modernism was therefore not in essence one unified movement but several, variegated in results and mixed in influence; at times creative and refreshing, at others merely destructive and frivolous. Such unity and coherence as it possessed came from its being a revolt, and although it remained in mood a revolt rather than a revolution it had certain effects which proved both revolutionary and beneficial. Twentieth-century culture revealed trends closely equivalent to those already noted in contemporary philosophy: a similar impact of scientific methods and ideas, a like concern with the alienation of man from his environment, and the same tendency, at the extreme, to treat art and philosophy as spiritual exercises. It is no accident that the leading mid-century exponent of existentialism, Sartre, found his most effective medium of expression in drama. The philosopher and the artist responded to the same urges.

Painting led the way to modernism. Whereas the Impressionists had exploited the play of light and shadow captured by the instantaneous photograph, their successors, the Cubists and the Surrealists, broke clean away from any notion or intention of naturalistic representation in which painting could never now hope to rival the camera. The Surrealism of Salvador Dali and his disciples, which flourished during the later 1920s and 1930s, delved ever deeper into the unconscious, exploiting the fantasies of free association used by Freud in his methods of psychoanalysis. Incongruous imagery, the cult of the irrational amounting at times to mere tricks and affectations, were the result. The Cubists experimented with abstract and often geometrical designs, seeking with deliberate distortion and stylization to depict the grotesque and the fantastic. They found congenial inspiration in primitive art, with its strong flat colours and firm but exaggerated outlines. Both movements, in the climate of opinion and the mood of the inter-war years, exerted a far-reaching influence. They served as a strong stimulus to more imaginative modes in art, whether painting, music, or literature. By carrying the possibilities of abstract art to their utmost extreme they revealed both its values and its limits. Experimentalism, even experimentalism run riot, established some aesthetic truths and yielded some creative work. The dominant figures of Pablo Picasso, Henri Matisse, and in sculpture Jacob Epstein, derived inspiration from it. The art of Paul Klee and of Paul Nash demonstrated its higher potentialities. The residual value of the whole movement was found in an art which was modern without being modernist, a culture which was not merely one of cults.

In literature the impulse to escape from the real to an imagined or remembered world was already apparent in the work of Marcel Proust, a chronic invalid whose eleven-novel sequence *Remembrance of Things Past* (*À la Recherche du Temps perdu*) used the sensitive evocations of memory and echo to delineate exquisitely, and often satirically, a world that he had known in his youth. A similar flight inward marked the work of the Irishman James Joyce in his masterpiece *Ulysses* of 1922, and he made similar use of youthful experiences in his *Portrait of the Artist as a Young Man*. Joyce devised, moreover, a new style and even a new vocabulary to express the uninhibited flow of the 'stream of consciousness' through the mind of his central character and of himself. On both Proust and Joyce the impact of Bergson and Freud is obvious enough; equally obvious is their readiness and even resolve to discard conventional prose and seek new, vital, and experimental modes of self-expression. Similar trends can be traced through the novels of Virginia Woolf, the poems of Ezra Pound, the psychoanalytical writings of D. H. Lawrence and Aldous Huxley, and the novels of Franz Kafka.

The figure in literature who spanned the generations and dominated the scene as much as Picasso in painting was André Gide. Established before 1914 as the guiding spirit of the *Nouvelle Revue Française* and of *avant-garde* writing in France, he acquired a world-wide stature between the two wars. The inner contradictions of his own nature and his painful self-questionings reflected the spiritual pilgrimage of the inter-war generation. The characters of his novel *The Counterfeiters* (*Les Faux Monnayeurs*) of 1925 are dupes or shams because each cherishes as 'possible' an aspiration which for him, given his character, is impossible. Men are dupes of their own desires. Gide's influence on thought, and on later existentialist movements, was as great as his stature in literature. He was seen by some as a twentieth-century Goethe, whose self-revelations in his *Journals* are the story of an epoch.

The sharp decline in traditionalism, orthodoxy, and the accepted code of values was equally apparent in music. Aware, like the existentialist philosophers, of a lack of harmony and even an alienation between themselves and their social environment, the younger generation of composers sought expression in revolutionary techniques, in a restless experimentation with atonality and dissonance. Igor Stravinsky's ballet music, beginning with the *Fire Bird* of 1910 which he wrote for Diaghilev, had a style which could be described as 'telegraphic', just as some of Arnold Schoenberg's piano music has been called 'seismographic'. Like the Expressionist and Surrealist painters (and Stravinsky's *Rite of Spring* [*Le Sacre du Printemps*, 1913] shows how great was the influence of Picasso) the modernist composers borrowed rhythms and sounds from primitive cultures. The cultural counterpart to the expansion of Europe was the strong influence of African, Asian, Central American, and Polynesian arts upon European styles in painting, sculpture, and music. The 'primitive' found therein further possibilities of experiment and unorthodoxy. Through the use of primitive contortions of rhythm and sound, colour and shape, they strove to suggest the violence and disintegration of their contemporary world.

Moderations of Modernism. The culture of the 1920s was marked, then, by a spirit of revolt and emancipation, as well as by psychoanalytical introspection. Free verse, free expressionism, was its keynote, and this lent it undoubted vigour, vitality, and originality. Its vices were obvious enough – morbidity, eccentricity, extravagance, frivolity. The *reductio ad absurdum* of modernism was Dadaism, the movement launched from Switzerland in 1919 by Tristan Tzara, which maintained 'the absurdity of art, the identity of contraries' and sponsored irreverence and incoherence as valuable in themselves. But after the initial excesses and the more fantastic features of modernism had passed away, there appeared a marked tendency to seek some reconciliation with more traditional values and forms. By common consent one of the finest and most significant poems of the half century was T. S. Eliot's *The Waste Land* of 1922. It won him esteem as a master of modernist techniques, original yet intelligible. A generation later Eliot was reinvigorating the modern theatre with his poetic dramas *Murder in the Cathedral* and *The Cocktail Party*. Moreover the composite and collaborative public arts such as the opera, ballet, cinema, and radio attracted to their service many of the otherwise esoteric artists. In these years ballet, first popularized by the Russians, became a favourite European art rivalling even the opera. Much modern music was composed for use in ballet, film, or radio. To the painter, designer, and writer these collaborative arts offered new opportunities for a functional development more closely related to other arts and capable of public appreciation. The Welsh poet Dylan Thomas wrote *Under Milk Wood* primarily for radio, and only later was it adapted for presentation on the stage. At the same time classical literature – most successfully Shakespeare – was adapted to films and television with altogether admirable results. The new arts served old and new culture alike.

Such moderations of modernism came, too, from a certain revival of more traditional sources of inspiration. With the Hungarian composer, Béla Bartók, a devotion to European folk-music preserved a basic melody, order, and unifying stability which moderated his use of dissonance and preserved some continuity with the classical tradition. In the novel there persisted one form, established by nineteenth-century novelists like Balzac and Zola and perpetuated by Proust: the vast canvas of a sequence of connected novels in which the writer portrays, in terms of persons and families, the tragedy and grandeur of an age. In Britain John Galsworthy's six volumes of *The Forsyte Saga* (1906–28) gave in the gradual disintegration and growing uncertainties of a middle-class family an epitome of English middle-class life. In Germany, and later in the United States, Thomas Mann portrayed the decline of capitalist society and the corrosion of European civilization in terms of the merchant family of *Buddenbrooks* (1901) or in terms of a universal contagion in *The Magic Mountain* (*Der Zauberberg*, 1924). In France Jules Romains pursued through the twenty-seven interconnected novels of *Men of Good Will* (*Les Hommes de bonne volonté*) the deepening crises of western European society in the quarter century before Hitler. Georges Duhamel depicted petty bourgeois family life in the *Pasquier Chronicles* (*La Chronique des Pasquier*). In contemporary England C. P. Snow, himself a physicist, with his projected eleven-volume sequence *Strangers and Brothers*, stands in the same tradition. The leading novelists of the half-century usually remained in close relation with the moral predicaments of man in modern society and were therefore responsive to the artist's social functions.

The same was broadly true of the dramatists. George Bernard Shaw, by reason of his immense vitality and longevity, continued to be a dominating figure in the European drama. Perhaps the best of his plays, *Saint Joan*, was written in 1923. Shaw was the leading figure in the remarkable Irish literary renaissance which included the dramatists J. M. Synge and Sean O'Casey and one of the century's finest poets, W. B. Yeats, as well as James Joyce. The National Literary Society founded by Yeats in 1891 and the Irish National Theatre of Dublin became the focus of a Celtic culture of great brilliance.

The German expressionists like Georg Kaiser and Ernst Toller held sway in the early years of the Weimar Republic, and after 1917 drama in the Soviet Union passed through a phase of experimentalism and propaganda. But since the theatre, unlike poetry and painting, must find a large and receptive public or cease to function, serious drama, like the novel, was impelled into social criticism and comment as in the plays of W. H. Auden and Christopher Isherwood, into dramatization for film and radio which reached a wide public, and latterly into poetic drama with T. S. Eliot and Christopher Fry. In both novel and drama after 1930 the darkening clouds of world crisis, rampant tyranny, and war's destructiveness brought a more sombre, bitter tone. Arthur Koestler's *Darkness at Noon*, George Orwell's *1984* and *Animal Farm*, Albert Camus's *La Peste*, were characteristic products of the period. Apprehension and fear of annihilation encouraged the grim realism and the hard-boiled brutality found in writers like Ernest Hemingway, Graham Greene, and Sartre, by contrast with which the gentler notes of a Virginia Woolf or a W. B. Yeats seem to belong to a different world. In an age torn by anxieties and moral dilemmas, yet in a world fuller than ever before of resources and potentialities, it was inevitable that literature and indeed the whole of culture should reflect the consequences of this paradox for the human spirit. The culture of crisis suffered, naturally enough, a crisis of culture.

Biography and History. In that branch of literature most completely concerned with understanding and interpreting one personality, the art of biography, the new psychology had great repercussions. A hasty grasp of the ideas of Freud and a smattering of jargon sufficed to produce a host of attempts to write psychological biographies of historical characters, usually misguided in intention and unfortunate in result. But the taste of the 1920s for iconoclasm and satire ('debunking' was the word) induced a series of witty studies serious enough in scholarship to attract and merit attention. The fashion was set by Lytton Strachey, and elaborated by Philip Guedalla, André Maurois, and a sequence of imitators of less brilliant literary craftsmanship. Their favourite subjects, or victims, were the eminent Victorians and their European contemporaries like Napoleon III. By the 1940s the vogue had almost completely given way to more balanced and scholarly biographies, still made attractive and popular by excellence of structure and literary presentation, but lacking the satirical undertones and self-conscious irreverence of their predecessors. Especially was this true in France and Britain. The change can be measured by contrasting Lytton Strachey's studies of Florence Nightingale and General Gordon with their later biographies by Mrs Cecil Woodham-Smith and Lord Elton; or by comparing Strachey's *Elizabeth and Essex* with the work of J. E. Neale or A. L. Rowse, and his *Queen Victoria* with Sir Harold Nicolson's *King George V*. Like the Surrealists in painting and the modernists in poetry, the biographers of the 1920s, by their fresh vivacity, vitality, and literary elegance, compelled biographers to be less portentous and to cultivate a more humanly sympathetic approach to their subjects. In Germany and the United States, less touched by their influence than Britain or France, the older fashion for the three or more volumes of 'steamroller' biography remained on the whole intact, presupposing a stamina on the part of writer and reader alike which seemed hardly justified in contemporary conditions. Even so, it produced such notable works as Erich Eyck's *Bismarck* and Carl Sandburg's *Abraham Lincoln*, and Emil Ludwig's somewhat heavily psychological biographies won an international popularity.

The changing attitude to history was yet another example of similar trends. History flourished as never before in prolific production, standards of scholarship, and literary presentation. In the English-speaking nations history had been once and for all reclaimed for the world of literature largely by the influence of G. M. Trevelyan. (In France it had always been closely linked with literature.) Throughout the whole half-century Trevelyan brought to the writing of histories and biographies an unusual amalgam of the highest scholarship and the highest literary skill. He found effective support from younger writers like Miss C. V. Wedgwood as well as from his most eminent contemporary Sir Winston Churchill. Understanding of the early eighteenth century in English history was enriched as never before by the combination of Trevelyan's *England under Queen Anne* and Churchill's *Marlborough*. The study of early civilizations was entirely rejuvenated by the work of archaeologists and egyptologists, geologists and anthropologists, all of whom enlisted the aid of science in devising new tools. Aerial photography, submarine exploration, pollen analysis, even such by-products of atomic research as the radio-carbon test devised at Chicago in 1949, or the fluorine test which in 1953 exposed the fraud of the Piltdown bones, were all used by archaeologists with great effect. The accumulation of more precise knowledge of remote civilizations added a further dimension to man's understanding of himself, reinforcing and completing the revolution in thought first brought about by Darwin. It was inevitable that this new dimension should arouse the desire for some systematic comparison of all known civilizations, and this Arnold J. Toynbee attempted in his ten-volume *Study of History*, completed over a period of a quarter-century. That Toynbee felt impelled, in Spenglerian fashion, to reflect at length on the reasons for the rise and fall of civilizations was in keeping with the temper of his times; he was rewarded by immense sales of abridgements of his work in the United States and in Britain, and by a world renown.

Technology and the Arts. It was, indeed, to a large extent the influence of technology upon culture which brought the arts back into closer relationship with society. The half-century brought into existence the powerful new media of mass communication, the gramophone, cinema, radio, television; it brought to fruition the earlier trends toward a more literate and intellectually curious public, and the ampler provision of public libraries, museums, art galleries, popular concerts and exhibitions; and through a spate of inexpensive yet high-quality publications, adult education, and more efficient popularization of knowledge, it achieved a wide diffusion of culture never before attainable. Such rich opportunities attracted creative artists, as much by reason of the challenge they offered as the rewards to be won. Machinery which so abundantly brought first-rate drama, acting, and music within the easy and inexpensive reach of all, could not be other than a boon to civilization.

The new technological opportunities were, of course, the mixed blessing that they always are. The earlier silent films and radio stimulated, at their best, new *genres* of art which imposed upon writer, actor, and producer the challenging restrictions which the nature of stone imposes upon the sculptor. These fell partly into decline with the coming of the sound film (after 1925) and of television (mainly after 1945), the techniques of which were inevitably very much alike. By offering almost unbounded technical possibilities and financial rewards at a time when standards of aesthetic value and taste were unstable they proved almost as big a bane as a blessing to creative art. Yet the development of mechanical reproduction of sound and of electronics opened up quite new experimental possibilities for the musician. Composers in the United States and in France experimented in *musique concrète*, sound-strips recording various combinations of sounds at different levels and pitch; electronic instruments challenged the ingenuity of composers; the cartoon-film opened fresh fields for the imaginative artists. The artistic challenge of the century was how to achieve the popularization of the arts without their vulgarization; the diffusion of culture without its dilution and debasement; the utilization of new technical resources with discrimination and good taste. In the arts, as in international organizations, the development of a stricter functionalism seemed to be one possible answer to the problem, provided it too was not carried to excess. Just as the invention of photography had forced the painter to re-think in fresh terms the function of painting in non-photographic and non-representational terms, so other technical changes in the reproduction of sight, sound, and the written word tended to force other artists to formulate anew the essential functions of their arts; and functionalism creates a strong bias towards relating art to society.

The art most directly and completely revolutionized by technology was architecture. The nineteenth century in Britain and most of Europe was almost entirely innocent of any creative developments in architecture. Cities grew up in a chaos of different styles, imitative and ugly, lacking any clear purpose, plan, or inspiration. Large public buildings, railway stations or city halls, churches or factories, might be made of the new materials of steel, concrete, and glass: but they were usually constructed without regard to the fresh possibilities of these new materials for structure and design. The Crystal Palace, a gigantic yet graceful glass-house, was the almost solitary triumph of mid-Victorian architecture. At the end of the century a strong functional reaction set in, heralded by a French architect August Perret and a Swiss engineer Robert Maillart, but led mainly by Louis Sullivan and Frank Lloyd Wright in America, and by Otto Wagner and later Walter Gropius in Germany. It was significant that the two countries most advanced in technology should thus lead the way toward a functional style, austere and efficient, using the new materials as basis for a highly streamlined style of building devoid of ornament yet often very beautiful in its economy and simplicity of line. The impetus came from engineering: ocean liners, suspension bridges, and hydro-electric dams demanded a whole functional philosophy of construction which shunned superfluities. New factories and office buildings, railway terminals and airports were built to serve as efficiently as possible the needs of an age of power.

This approach soon exerted over domestic and public buildings an influence which was almost wholly beneficial. Such austerity could at times become grim and bare, and it struck a blow at sculpture which was at first ignored as a superfluity. But it produced fitting and often beautiful constructions admirably adapted, whether as schools and skyscrapers or as aircraft and battleships, to the public needs of modern society. The development of town planning before and after the Second World War offered to the functional architect still wider opportunities which in most countries he used to the full. Just as buildings can be designed as live structures, in which each component contributes to the stability of the whole and is itself stressed to the utmost, so towns can be planned as living units devised on functional principles. The whole face of European cities was transformed under the influence of men like Le Corbusier in France and Gropius in Germany, and on the whole it was a change for the better.

The final picture of cultural change during the half-century is, therefore, one of phases of experimentalism and introspection, sometimes extravagant and fantastic, sometimes emancipating and creative; and of trends, emerging during the interwar years and strengthening after 1945, toward a great stabilization of values and taste, an absorption of the good effects of experimentalism and a discarding of excesses, and toward more exoteric forms of art. Modernism had too easily forgotten that art has a social function to perform and that for a civilization to be divorced from its culture means a weakening and impoverishment of both. The continued advances of science and technology and the rapidity of social change ensured that there should be no lack of experimentation, no danger of fossilization. It was one of the more hopeful signs of the vitality of European civilization at mid century that even a society so devoted to football pools and national lotteries, to sport and to the lower forms of mass entertainment, had achieved so wide a dissemination of culture and taste. Artists, critics, and public alike were finding it less and not more difficult than a generation before to discriminate firmly between the experimental and the eccentric, the sensitive and the neurotic, the significant and the merely silly.

SOCIAL THOUGHT AND ACTION

Social thinking of the mid-nineteenth century had, as has been suggested,[1] a striking homogeneity with contemporary scientific thought. A science of society resting on a dynamics of competition and conflict, whether between individuals or classes, had affinities with a science of nature resting on a dynamics of energy and a struggle for survival. Bentham and Marx belonged to the same world of thought and the same mode of belief as Victorian thermodynamics and Darwinism. The material achievements of that age were so impressive and so lasting, the intellectual synthesis and coherence it attained were so powerful, that it was a whole lifetime later before the assumptions and basic principles of its system of thought were seriously questioned. In its political forms (liberalism, Marxism, and the various blends of the two within creeds of social democracy) the system of thought assumed the existence of the rational individual seeking his personal fulfilment and happiness. In economics it presupposed that this rational individual, whether as producer or consumer, seller or buyer, entrepreneur or labourer, sought consistently his own self-interest.

The whole system of mid-nineteenth-century social thought was atomistic, in that personal will, interests, actions served as its foundations. It thus matched an atomistic view of the universe, of 'solid atoms'

1. See p. 435.

measurable by weight, of immutable elements in chemistry, and a cellular conception of living matter; and above all it presupposed self-regulating mechanisms, working according to inevitable and discoverable laws, in a providential system within which cohesion was sustained by diversities balancing and interacting. Such laws were the conservation of matter and of energy in physics; the survival of the fittest in biology; supply and demand, the price mechanism, and the 'iron law of wages' in economics; *laissez-faire* in politics. Democratic liberalism believed that the pursuit of the greatest happiness of the greatest number involved only a very marginal intervention by the state, Marxism that proletarian revolution was historically 'inevitable' according to the 'laws' of dialectical materialism. By 1914 grave doubts were being cast upon the validity of one after another of these 'laws', as well as upon the basic concept of the self-evident rational individual, necessarily seeking his self interest. This progressive demolition of the old synthesis, in the natural and social sciences alike, went on throughout the interwar years. It left confusion and destroyed self-confidence. Even by the mid twentieth century signs of a possible new synthesis were still only beginning to appear.

Shifts of Emphasis. Both the atom and the living cell were found to be not simple but highly complex structures, each a further tiny world of its own, reducible to terms in which matter and energy seemed inseparable. Max Planck's Quantum Theory of 1900 revealed that within the atom the accepted laws of physics did not apply. The laws of conservation of matter and of energy were shown to be untrue in their old form, and new laws determining the amount of energy released when matter was destroyed had to be discovered. It was Einstein's famous equation $E = mc^2$, where E represents energy, m the mass of matter, and c the velocity of light, which made him the father of twentieth-century scientific thought. Nor could chemical elements be any longer thought of as immutable.

At the same time, in the social sciences, the old assumptions, concepts, and laws were being likewise demolished. The psychologists and social psychologists, drawing upon the experience of mass behaviour in modern society as well as upon Freudian research, showed that the individual person was also a more complex and mysterious creature, less rationally motivated and less separable from his whole social upbringing and conditioning than liberal thinking had supposed. The sociologists and political theorists analysed society into its component elements, and examined how differently the individual behaves in different groups and how groups interact. They emphasized a pluralistic conception of society and of the state in opposition to the older simpler notions of one community and unitary sovereignty, and these ideas, through French jurists like Léon Duguit, affected legal theory. The economists questioned the rigidity of old economic laws, even of the price mechanism, shifting the emphasis from production to distribution and consumption, from an assumption of scarcity to a postulate of plenty. In every aspect of social thinking the emphasis shifted, sometimes initially as a mere refinement of older principles, sometimes as a frontal attack upon them. Even Marxist thought, more rigidly dogmatic and integrated than most social and political theory, underwent major revision at the hands of Lenin and further modifications in the hands of Stalin, who emphasized the role even in historical dialectic of purposive action by a political elite.

These changes took place not, as a rule, in conscious concord with the changes in scientific thought, though in an age when the ideas of science held universal esteem they had some repercussions upon all intellectual endeavour. Nor did the changes usually take place by a process of borrowing or imitation between one social study and another, although at certain points psychology and sociology impinged directly upon political and legal theory, and the concept of 'economic growth' adopted by economists after 1945 presupposed inner organic principles of social change. They took place, on the whole, as separate adjustments of existing theories to new experience and fresh evidence, as a result of pressing methods of analysis still further and deeper into the recesses of the reliable knowledge available, and fast accumulating, about the behaviour of men in modern society. It was all the more impressive that the final result was an over-all shift of focus and emphasis away from concern with order, law, the principles of political obligation, and modes of economic production, towards concern with change, power, political rights, and the consumption of wealth. The main reason was that thought about twentieth-century society had, of necessity, to be thought about a dynamic society. The era of wars, revolutions, violent upheaval, and economic crisis was an age of eruption in a sense which made even the relatively dynamic mid nineteenth century appear relatively static. If the discoveries of the natural scientist came from experiment, those of the social scientist came from experience.

The crisis of culture, already described above, sprang mainly from this same process of casting off from familiar moorings, a growing sense that the old laws of navigation which had been taken as trustworthy no longer held good in the new uncharted seas of the postwar world, and a consequent nervous insecurity and anxiety, a loss of confidence in canons of taste and form, a quest for new bearings and soundings, to match new experience. In the social sciences, too, the phase of intuitive impressionism and speculation gave way to one of increasing functionalism, improved technical skills, and collaborative productions. The trends of scientific, cultural, and social development in the twentieth century, for all its turbulence and confusion, were more 'of one piece' than anyone noticed or than even seemed conceivable at the time; but that was equally true of nineteenth-century trends.

In the reshaping of social thought two influences were particularly strong: historical method and scientific method, and since historiography had itself previously undergone a phase of 'scientific history',[1] the two influences in part converged. Both the writing of history and studies of society benefited from their fruitful cross-fertilization. On one hand, economic and social history gained from closer understanding of price revolutions and trade cycles; on the other, economics and sociology gained a wider grasp of human motivation and behaviour in society, of industrial trends and 'power *élites*'. Both gained in a sense of realities which destroyed the old abstractions, the 'political man' of old-fashioned history along with the 'economic man' of classical economics. It was important that modern economics and sociology grew up in close relationship of this kind with modern historical study, which explained institutions and social systems in terms of developmental growth in time. The new historiography encouraged a relativist cast of thought, a rejection of absolutes and abstractions, a distrust of static concepts and ideal behaviour, which made economics and sociology better adapted to understanding a dynamic society, as well as more able to absorb scientific notions of evolutionary change and relativity. If the economist must formulate his laws on the proviso 'other things being equal', the historian was there to remind him that other things never are equal. At the same time the influence of scientific method enabled, and indeed demanded, that economists and sociologists would be ever seeking verification of data, precision of measurement and calculation, refinement of hypotheses. Historical and scientific method, combined in a humanizing amalgam, purged social study of abstraction and dogmatism. This was of incalculable importance in an age when economists and sociologists were assuming an increasingly official and responsible status in the conduct of public affairs and government.

Where unhistorical and unscientific dogmatism prevailed, as in the single-party states, the consequences were usually destructive of all humane values. The distortions of biology to justify the racial theories and eugenic measures of Nazi Germany, or to conform with the dogmatic requirements of Marxist materialism in the Soviet Union, were accompanied by parallel distortions of social, economic, and legal

1. See p. 445.

theory to meet the demands of an official political theory. Totalitarianism was the denial of all scientific quality to social studies, a repudiation of all historical experience as well as of all humanity. It was the biological and historical falsehood about 'The Master Race' which made it possible for Dr Goebbels to burn the books of Einstein, Freud, Proust, and Gide.

It was important, too, that the study of contemporary history was acquiring a new and more respectable status at this time. Since social studies are concerned in particular with existing society, it is recent and contemporary history which has special relevance for them; indeed, the writing of contemporary history itself may claim to be one sector of social studies. In an age of speed and cascading events even the historian must work fast if he is to fulfil his social functions. Yet the British and European, if not the American, traditions of historiography frowned upon contemporary history as an unscholarly and journalistic pursuit until, between the two world wars, new possibilities and a new demand for definitive work undermined these traditions. Each of the world wars was followed by massive publication of diplomatic documents in many countries, partly as a result of revolutions (as in Russia and Germany), partly in vindication of prewar policies (as in France, Britain, and the Commonwealth), partly as a result of capturing enemy documents (as in Italy, Germany, and Japan after 1945). These were accompanied by lengthy memoirs written by many of the national and military leaders concerned, and by compilations of extensive 'official histories' published under governmental auspices. New bodies such as the Royal Institute of International Affairs and the Carnegie Endowment for International Peace actively promoted the serious and scholarly study of recent history. As regards both source materials and a receptive public, the contemporary historian had never been more amply provided.

Even so, his failure during the interwar years to dispel the myths about the First World War disseminated by journalism and propaganda showed a need for more strenuous and speedy action. It remained possible, especially in Britain, Germany, and America, for many to believe on one hand that the will for war and drive to aggression of certain prewar national governments bore no share of responsibility for causing the war which broke out in 1914, and on the other that the peace settlement of 1919 was one of undiluted injustice and betrayal perpetrated by vindictive national leaders who enjoyed complete freedom of choice to behave differently. A major reason for this incongruous historical legend was that no balanced analysis of the war and the settlement, comparable in literary brilliance with J. M. Keynes's sparkling *Economic Consequences of the Peace*, circulated widely throughout the world during the 1920s. What many thought about 1919 was conditioned to a remarkable degree by Keynes's passionate and polemical denunciation. From the 1930s onward, however, definitive historical studies of recent events appeared somewhat more promptly, and the tempo of historiography caught up more closely on the tempo of events. J. W. Wheeler-Bennett's study of *Munich* and Sir Lewis Namier's *Diplomatic Prelude, 1938–39* appeared only a decade after the Munich crisis, and Sir Winston Churchill's authoritative account of *The Second World War* became a best-seller between 1948 and 1954. To the firm ascertainment of truth the lawyers and jurists also contributed, and the evidence accumulated and attested at the trials of war criminals at Nuremberg and elsewhere after 1945 threw valuable light upon the history of the war from the defeated side. Explicit and intelligent understanding of contemporary history is the very bedrock of adequate social thought.

Keynesian Economics. The significant shifts of focus and emphasis in social thought can be traced, as has been said, through modern sociology, political theory, even jurisprudence. But they are revealed most sharply in the transformation of economic theory. It was economics, of all the social sciences, which in these years made the firmest and fastest advance, and had the most direct impact on policy. So much did economics become the very hub of policy that by 1960 every national government in the world, and many international agencies too, were engaged in framing fiscal, commercial, monetary, and social policies in accordance with the advice and the principles of economic experts. In Britain after 1941 the annual estimate of 'National Income and Expenditure', even more than the government's budget itself, became the basis for a policy of national investment and full employment. It records what the whole community produces and consumes, not merely what the government collects and spends. It was the totalitarian nature of modern war which made the survey and control of a nation's whole economy a task of national policy. It produced the achievements of Walter Rathenau in Germany of the First World War,[1] the financial wizardry of Hjalmar Schacht in Hitlerite Germany, and the immense formative influence of J. M. Keynes upon British economic policy in the Second World War. Economic theorists, given a new status of authority in policy making, had to adapt their theories all the more closely to realities.

Such developments occurred, it must be noted, for purely nationalistic purposes, just as the elaboration of theories of economic planning took place in Russia after 1917 not as inevitable extensions of Marxist theory but as economic necessities. They were quite distinct in origin and purpose, though not entirely unrelated in consequences, from either the

1. See p. 576.

demands of socialists for greater state regulation of economic life in the cause of diffusing social welfare, or from the Marxist demands of public ownership of the main means of production. These developments in Germany and Britain, and their counterparts in other countries after the world economic crisis and the Second World War, were in origin and purport a revival of 'political economy', a renovation of liberalism dictated by events and imposed upon politicians and economists alike by national needs. The underlying assumption of liberalism, either as *laissez-faire* domestic theories or as free trade principles, included the belief that economics could be to a large extent divorced from politics: that business was business, conducted between individuals or groups, yielding socially valuable results independent of any official interference. Even Marx, whilst insisting on the primacy of economics over politics, regarded them as distinct spheres and believed that the state could wither away to the advantage of society. The task of public authority was to preserve public order, property rights, and freedom of contract, leaving the bargaining, decisions, choices – and their consequences – to the individuals engaged in them.

The liberal system of economic thought rested particularly on the allegedly self-regulating mechanisms of prices and interest. Over-production could occur in particular sectors, but would be automatically ended by the laws of supply and demand: general over-production was impossible, according to what was known as 'Say's Law'. Just as the higgling of the market and the price mechanism tended to equate supply with demand for real goods, so the rate of interest (that is, the price of borrowing funds) would likewise tend to equate the demand for invest-ment with the supply of savings available for investment. If savings became excessive the rate of interest would fall, encouraging capital outlay, and it would continue to fall until capital outlay absorbed all the savings. Thus there might be temporary over-saving or under-investment, and the frictions of a time-lag, but in the end the system would be self-adjusting and must tend towards full employment. State action was unnecessary and likely to be harmful. If the government were to try to alleviate unemployment by a programme of public works it would be merely diverting funds to create employment in some sectors of national life, away from the total amount that the business world would other-wise have used in other sectors. No new employment, in aggregate, could result.

This general classical theory, embodied in magisterial and very refined form in the works of a man like Alfred Marshall at the end of the nineteenth century, held the field in western Europe until after 1914. Marshall's *Principles of Economics* of 1890 remained a standard text for half a century and is still widely read. Systems of economic thought akin to Marshall's were developed by his European counterparts, by the Swedish school of Knut Wicksell and the mathematical Lausanne School of Léon Walras, and by J. B. Clark in the United States. An Austrian school of economists led by Eugen von Böhm-Bawerk and its English exponent W. S. Jevons propounded theories of 'marginal utility' which demonstrated the need for some radical modifications in classical theory. But their arguments could be absorbed without too much damage to the old structure of thinking. Others explored the working of classical laws in conditions of 'imperfect competition', which raised still more basically the question whether conditions, assumed to be abnormal, had not by now become normal; and whether in a world where monopolies or near monopolies, big trusts, powerful labour unions, were the usual units of economic activity, it was still realistic to assume the rational individual producer or bargainer as the unit, or competition as fully operative. Classical theory was not unchallenged, even before 1914, and it had many critics. But in general, apart from the Marxists, they were friendly and moderate critics, questioning particular parts of the older system of thought rather than its fundamental premises. Its laws and mechanisms, it was felt, would operate effectively again once 'normalcy' had returned.

But in the face of wartime experience of state socialism, of postwar inflation and deflation, of world economic crisis and persistent mass unemployment, more radical revision began to seem essential. When liberal capitalism patently went on failing to produce the sort of results that national interests required, and when conditions dismissed as temporary exceptions and abnormalities settled down into being permanent dislocations and sicknesses, then some form of state action was unavoidable. It was in this setting that the bold intellect and persuasive eloquence of J. M. Keynes began to bring about what became known, with reason, as the 'Keynesian revolution'. His radical re-thinking was forced upon him by events, and his thought was hammered out against formidable opposition, for he was a man of affairs as well as an intellectual thinker of great distinction. By the time he came to the major work of 1936 which symbolizes his theory – *The General Theory of Employment, Interest and Money* – he realized whither his thinking was leading him. In a letter to George Bernard Shaw of 1935 he wrote, 'I believe myself to be writing a book on economic theory which will largely revolutionise – not, I suppose, at once but in the course of the next ten years – the way the world thinks about economic problems'. History proved him to be right.

His early pamphlets of 1925–6, *The End of Laissez Faire* and *The Economic Consequences of Mr. Churchill,* marked the beginning of his attack upon the notion of self-regulating mechanisms in economics. The inflations and currency crashes of the postwar years forced economists to scrutinize monetary theory. The gold standard was held, in classical economic theory, to provide the self-regulating mechanism for international trade, and was part and parcel of a *laissez-faire* free-trade economy. It linked the money rates and price levels of each nation with those of every other nation which was 'on gold', and return to the gold standard was a symbol of the return to normalcy. Britain's return to the gold standard in 1925, at prewar parity between the pound sterling and the dollar, had the effect of substantially increasing the prices on world markets of British goods. As a result, major British exports such as coal could not compete in world markets with the expanding exports of the United States. The consequent shrinkage of the markets of those British industries brought unemployment at home. But Keynes opposed Britain's return to the gold standard, and argued instead for a 'managed currency' to be stabilized roughly in terms of real commodities. Irving Fisher in America, Gustav Cassel in Sweden, argued along similar lines for a currency managed in terms of prices; but still prices themselves were assumed to be 'naturally' or 'automatically' determined.

Under the impact of the economic slump and persistent mass unemployment Keynes moved yet further toward urging deliberate management, by governments, of other crucial points of the economy, including even the price of money. His proposals were still guided by a desire to leave most economic decisions to be made privately; but he wanted to determine the trend of those decisions by ingenious political manipulation of the climate of opinion. If the investor or manufacturer were too active and enthusiastic and was producing inflation, he must be curbed and discouraged; if he were tending to sluggishness then he should be deliberately stimulated. Keynes held that there was no thermostat built into the economy which regulated the psychological temperature automatically, and therefore this must be manipulated by governmental policy. There were several means by which it could be done. The rate of interest could be lowered if capital investment were sluggish, raised if it were too active. The amount of money collected in taxes and paid out in public expenditure by the state, being a part of the monetary circulation, could be regulated in a similar way. By budgeting for a deficit in time of stagnation and unemployment, and for a surplus in time of rising prices and excessive activity, the state could powerfully influence the general trend of the economy. It could go even further, and directly create demand for goods and services by a programme of public works, building roads or post offices, dams and power stations.

He overcame the objection of orthodox economics, that such a policy could not result in greater aggregate employment, by a frontal attack on Say's Law. He argued that the very working of the economic system might tend, in certain circumstances, to an equilibrium in which mass unemployment existed. He explained this by introducing the subtle refinement of 'liquidity preference', the psychological factor which may prompt a property owner to keep a proportion of his wealth in the liquid form of cash rather than to invest it in bonds. It is this intrusive consideration which upset Say's Law by relating the rate of interest not to total savings but only to total liquid savings. The rate of interest was the necessary reward for forgoing the advantages of liquidity. What ailed capitalist economy as a whole, on Keynes's analysis, was that the rich, having naturally a greater 'propensity to save' than the poor, and periodically finding no potential investments which seem to promise a profit, tried to commit the sin of the buried talent. They hoarded some as liquid cash, thus sterilizing a lot of savings and leading the community into cumulative economic disequilibrium and depression. One further remedy, therefore, would be to redistribute more income from the rich to the poor who had a greater 'propensity to spend'.

By such a train of thought, argued with immense refinement of mathematics and logic and with rich persuasive eloquence, Keynes arrived at conclusions which in effect overthrew the whole series of allegedly self-regulating mechanisms on which older economic theory was based. His purpose throughout was to preserve, not to attack, liberal capitalism; to plead for restraint and moderation which, with the help of judicious political measures, would remove from the economy its diseases of slump and unemployment. But the inherent logic and eventual drift of his argument were so completely at variance with all the presuppositions of the old system of thought that, the more his conclusions were accepted, in theory and in practice, the more surely did they prove to be revolutionary. Because they invoked at every stage action by the government they also implied a remarriage of economics and politics. They indicated the need for a more completely integrated approach to social studies capable of comprising, in interrelationship, the findings of economists, sociologists, psychologists, and political theorists. Especially striking is the way in which modern economic theory draws upon mathematics and upon concepts, psychological in character, of how and why men behave as they do. The most significant feature of the Keynesian revolution in economics is that it corresponds to the trend already noted in physics and biology; a trend away from a mechanistic (Newtonian) view towards a more organic and relativist (Einsteinian) view of social life. The individual comes to be regarded as an organism in relation to a total environment, and society itself is viewed as an organic economic complex, in which human preferences and propensities must constantly be taken into account.

Planning and Power. Just as the Keynesian revolution in economic thought was itself a series of responses to events and circumstances, so its impact upon the whole of social thought was consolidated by two major events: the adoption of full-scale economic planning in the Soviet Union after 1928, and the Second World War. Economic planning was the central theme of all social thought in the generation after 1928. It had two distinct roots in European history, and two main facets in its modern development. One was planning for national efficiency, which in Germany of 1914, Russia of 1918, Germany and Britain in 1940, meant national efficiency in war. War gave one clear, unifying social purpose in terms of which all planning could be designed: planning for efficiency, efficiency for power, power for victory. It created, automatically, a condition of scarcity in which the most precise allocation of resources and manpower, the systematic and certain fulfilment of quotas and targets of production according to a carefully drawn up time-table, were all vitally necessary. If the peoples of contemporary Europe know so much national economic planning, the chief historical reason is that there have been two world wars in one generation to get them used to it. The other root of planning is the demand for social justice, for a more equitable distribution of wealth and the elimination of destitution and unemployment: and the second main reason for the prevalence of planning is the growth of social democracy, and experience of the world economic depression. The two demands – for national efficiency in production and for social justice in distribution – flowed together after about 1928. Even in wartime some devices – such as rationing of food – served both purposes at once: and during the Second World War price controls, subsidies, war-damage insurance, and a host of other measures were added to rationing as means both of securing efficiency and of satisfying the demand for equalizing the burdens and sacrifices of wartime. The two aims became fused and confused. Both involved scrapping all reliance upon automatic mechanisms. The nineteenth-century image of a self-regulating economy was utterly demolished by events before it was overthrown in theory.

The comparable development in the other two major branches of social study, sociology and political science, was a new concentration upon the role of power in society and the state. Sociologists from the Italians Gaetano Mosca and Vilfredo Pareto to the modern Americans James Burnham and C. Wright Mills explored the working of *élites* in society and politics, and applied to social theory a method of analysis resting on the distribution and transference of power. The Frenchman Bertrand de Jouvenel and the Englishman Bertrand Russell analysed the whole conception of power as, in Russell's words 'the fundamental concept in social sciences .... in the same sense in which Energy is the fundamental concept in physics'. E. H. Carr, in *The Twenty Years' Crisis 1919–1939* (1939), applied this analysis to the study of international relations between the two wars in an avowed attempt to make the study of international politics more scientific. Other economic and social theorists followed similar lines of analysis, stressing always power rather than order.

The trend of such theories was broadly twofold. As adopted and adapted by Italian Fascism and German Nazism, and their imitators elsewhere, the notion of power *élites* was elaborated into a defence of single-party dictatorship and an attack upon democratic institutions. As evolved by democratic thinkers the analysis of power was used to undercut Marxism, to argue that economic power, far from being fundamental to society, is but one important form assumed by power, just as electricity is but one form of energy. It followed, Russell claimed, that 'the laws of social dynamics are laws which can be stated in terms of power, not in terms of this or that form of power'. Economic power might be derived from military power or might be transmuted into political power, but it had none of the supremely deterministic quality accredited to it by Marxism. Another consequence was the close attention given by political scientists to political parties as agencies of power. The inner, more organic, workings of parliamentary and single-party states alike was revealed much more clearly in such studies as Maurice Duverger's *Political Parties* (*Les Partis Politiques*, 1951), R. T. McKenzie's *British Political Parties* (1955), and many close studies of electioneering, voting systems, and party structures. In devices of mass observation, systematic surveys of opinion, and Gallup polls, students of social behaviour followed the economist in attempts to amass reliable data and devise statistical measurement, though more advance was made in description than in significant analysis. In these studies, too, most of the trends already noted were equally evident: abandonment of the isolated rational individual as the basic concept, and insistence upon his relations to groups, parties, and total environment as the significant facts explaining his behaviour. The patent instability and fragility of states, constitutions, political systems, even of economic systems, compelled the focus of attention to shift from legal institutions to social conventions and political movements, from machinery to motivation, from automatism to conscious purpose. The political scientist, like the economist, was induced by his increasing reliance upon concepts of relativity and probability to think more in terms of social context, group, and category, than of personality or individuality.

Despite, therefore, the apparent fragmentation, specialization, and confusion which marked social thinking, the various branches of social study were in fact – like rivers which flow steadily on under the surface of the ocean – moving together in one ultimate direction. There appeared, on the surface, a mere demolition of the older system of thought and a denial of accepted cultural standards, economic assumptions, and social or moral values. At a deeper level there was the making of a new synthesis, the acceptance of a new system of standards, values, and outlooks. In that new system the individual and his whole social environment were organically interrelated, and in the new dynamic amalgam it was necessary for both security and welfare of the whole community and the personal rights and obligations of the individual to be consciously defined, pursued, and reconciled. The co-existence in the world of imminent scarcity and poverty with prospects of potential plenty had begun to produce a whole new pattern of thought and action: commandeering the concentrated power of the centralized nation state, the resources of science, the productive capacities of technology and industry, and new knowledge of how society works, and the whole repertoire of means, administrative and persuasive, by which it was now possible to direct the energies of men towards this new pattern. It was still, in many of its parts, ill-defined and controversial. It was infused with differing and often conflicting purposes in different countries. Its varying labels – the 'age of the common man', 'the social-service state', 'the welfare state', 'the affluent society', 'social democarcy', 'people's democracies' – were all inadequate descriptions, yet they served collectively to stress the many facets of the change. Judging from previous experience, when kindred trends can be detected simultaneously in science, culture, and social thought, it becomes probable that these are historically the most significant trends, and that the future is on their side. When they became embodied, moreover, in a definable pattern of policy and action which prevails over most of Europe, they may properly be treated as the contemporary culmination of a long-range process of change. Can this pattern be more precisely defined?

CHAPTER 34

THE PATTERN OF MODERN EUROPEAN DEVELOPMENT

In 1815, as was described above (Part II), Europe presented a picture of diversity combined with unity, a balance between a common inheritance from the past and divergent developments within different regions and between different national communities. In 1960, after nearly five generations of unusually rapid change affecting every aspect of life, Europe still presented a basically similar picture of cohesion and diversity; but now the lines of both uniformity and cleavage were much more sharply defined. In those respects in which life everywhere in Europe was similar, there tended to be greater uniformity; in those respects in which conditions differed, they differed more sharply.

The prolonged ferment of political and social ideals deriving mainly from the American and French Revolutions – the ideals especially of individual rights to greater freedom and equality and of a nation's rights to self-determination and independence – had made universal suffrage and the nation-state the almost universal bases of government. A peculiarly intimate reciprocal relationship had been created between national communities and states as a result of the triumphs of democracy and of nationalism in 1848, 1871, 1919, and 1945. Even Communism had been captivated by this tendency, from the time when Lenin joined Woodrow Wilson in proclaiming as sacred the rights of national self-determination until the Yugoslavia of Marshal Tito defied (and defeated) Stalin on this very issue, and Stalin's successors devised the doctrine of 'socialist internationalism' to replace the nationally objectionable notion of 'international centralism'. The great countries of Asia and the colonial peoples of Africa were fast asserting precisely the same doctrine, until it dominated the whole world. This was the first and most striking of the new uniformities.

The second was the universal spread of industrialism, and of the mechanization, mass production, specialization of labour, and increased productivity through fresh resources of power, which always accompany industrialization. In 1815 Great Britain was the only highly industrialized country in Europe, though by later standards she stood only on the brink of her first of several 'industrial revolutions'. In 1960 not only had every European country diverted a large proportion of its labour force and its resources into industrial production and transport, but Soviet Russia, Turkey, China, India, had embarked upon vast plans for speedy industrialization, and within the large colonial empires formerly connected with European states industrialism was also striking deeper roots. The whole basis of Europe's economy had shifted, and it had moved toward greater uniformity.

The third of the new uniformities was historically the outcome of the first two: the evolution of that composite structure which may loosely be called 'the welfare state'. Everywhere the state did much more than any state had attempted to do in 1815. It collected more taxes, controlled more effectively more spheres of economic life, wielded greater power over the mass of its citizens, and commanded greater resources of power in time of war, than any state in 1815. But it also undertook more responsibilities towards its citizens than any state of 1815: in providing national systems of education, safeguarding public health, legislating about conditions of labour and housing, organizing a multitude of social services and amenities. And in varying degrees, but always to a large degree by comparison with 1815, such states existed everywhere in Europe.

Yet a fourth uniformity, of a somewhat different kind, must be added. The nation states of Europe were interdependent to an extent and in a sense that they had not been interdependent in 1815. It had then been possible for many European states to pursue policies which, unless they involved direct territorial aggression, caused little concern or interest even among neighbouring states. But by the mid-twentieth century not only had isolation and neutrality become impracticable for all save a few fortunately situated nations, but neglect of generally accepted codes of behaviour, slumps or currency crashes, booms or bankruptcies, within any one community immediately became of direct interest to others. It was the crash of the *Kreditanstalt,* in the otherwise unimportant little state of Austria, which brought the world economic crisis crashing upon the whole of Europe; and the larger and more important the state, the more disastrous were its misfortunes liable to be for the rest of the continent. Europeans had become members one of another in a sense unknown in 1815; and the paradox that proud claims to absolute national sovereignty and independence coincided with this unprecedented degree of interdependence was recognized by the rapid multiplication of articulated international organizations, functional, regional, and worldwide, which Europeans entered into after 1945. The surrender of national autonomy involved in the erection of the Coal and Steel Community would have been unattainable at any date between 1789 and 1950; and Britain's peacetime military commitments to Western European Union in 1954 inconceivable at any date before 1940.

DIAGRAM 6. EUROPE'S USE OF ITS LABOR FORCE, 1950

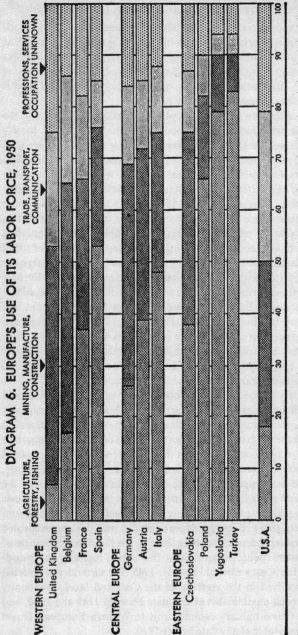

AGRICULTURE, FORESTRY, FISHING ▸ MINING, MANUFACTURE, CONSTRUCTION ▸ TRADE, TRANSPORT, COMMUNICATION ▸ PROFESSIONS, SERVICES OCCUPATION UNKNOWN ▸

WESTERN EUROPE
United Kingdom
Belgium
France
Spain

CENTRAL EUROPE
Germany
Austria
Italy

EASTERN EUROPE
Czechoslovakia
Poland
Yugoslavia
Turkey

U.S.A.

0 10 20 30 40 50 60 70 80 90 100

This Diagram shows three main things. It shows, first, how some of the nations of Europe deployed their labor force in the middle of the twentieth century. The marked segments show approximately the percentages of the total labor force employed in the four main activities of economic life. Proportions in the United States are added for comparison. Secondly, it shows the heavier proportions of people employed in agriculture in Central Europe than in Western Europe, and in Eastern Europe than in either. In all eastern countries except Czechoslovakia, most people made a living by farming. Thirdly, it shows the heavier industrialization of Western and Central Europe than of Eastern Europe. A large proportion of a nation employed in agriculture does not, in twentieth century conditions, reflect high productivity but the opposite—wastage of manpower through neglect of mechanization: but a high proportion employed in industry and transport usually denotes high productivity.

This broad common pattern of development, which led to so solid a substratum of uniformity in European civilization, must be put in the foreground of any assessment of European history since 1789. But the nations of Europe have never been in danger of drab uniformity or excessive standardization. The substantial similarities need prime emphasis if only because it is so easy for them to be eclipsed by the more troublesome contrasts and conflicts between European states. Can these dissimilarities be likewise defined?

Basically, there remained very real differences of nationality, mostly derived from differences of historical experience and fortune. These still took the conspicuous form of different languages and cultural traditions, differing habits of social life and sentiment, different grievances and enmities. National consciousness was strengthened, not weakened, by the Second World War. Even more important, the spread of industrialism was still so uneven in Europe that standards of living, the balance of occupations and interests, and modes of social life still ranged between very wide extremes. When in 1948 the United Nations Department of Economic Affairs tried to assess national differences in standards of living (in terms of the real national income per head of the population in 1938 computed in United States dollars) it was found that European countries ranged from 481 for the United Kingdom to seventy-nine for Greece: a ratio of more than six to one. It was also found that European countries fell into categories which broadly corresponded with the older regional groupings and degrees of industrialization. Thus the bracket $300-500 included the United Kingdom, the Netherlands, Germany, Switzerland, and Scandinavia. Ireland, France, Belgium, and Luxembourg fell within the range $200-300. Spain, Italy, and most of the central and eastern European states fell within the range $100-200. Below that level came Portugal, Greece, Poland, Rumania, Turkey, and Egypt. The report added that 'international disparities have been further intensified during and immediately after the war'. By 1950 (see Diagram 6) north-western and central Europe devoted considerably more of its labour force to mining, manufacture, and transport than did south-western and eastern Europe, and a correspondingly lower porportion to farming. But the postwar Communist governments of eastern Europe were striving to bring their countries in this respect closer into line with the pattern of economy already existing in western Europe. Although economic disparities were still very large, they were being perceptibly diminished.

Moreover the prevalence of the 'welfare state' throughout Europe concealed a great variety of different kinds of purpose and development. In Britain and Germany the growth of social services had a very long history, and the existence of a strong, central government had tended, even before 1914, to induce increasing state intervention in economic and social life to safeguard public welfare. The economic planning introduced by the interwar totalitarian governments usually went hand in hand with still more provision of social services, even though the connexions between such provision and planning for efficiency in war were emphasized by the military terms used – there were agrarian and industrial 'fronts', 'shock brigades' of workers, 'battles' for grain, 'campaigns' for higher productivity, 'targets' of production, and so on. By 1960 there were at least three main types of social-service state in Europe. All were prompted by the double urge for national efficiency and power which had been stimulated by war and its aftermath, and social-democratic demands for greater social justice. The latter came ultimately from that trend which Jakob Burckhardt had noted, even in 1870, as 'the dominating feelings of our age' – 'the desire of the masses for a higher standard of living'.

There was, firstly, the liberal-social-democratic type of Britain, the Low Countries, and Scandinavia, of whom the apostles were Lord Keynes and Lord Beveridge. This mixed system rested upon preservation of as much as possible of competitive capitalism but the superimposing upon it of a system of social security, nationalization, and political control designed to ensure minimum standards of welfare for all. Secondly, there was the type deriving more directly from traditions of a strong, bureaucratic, paternalist national government, to be found in France, Italy, Germany, Spain, and Turkey, tending to place more emphasis than the British on nationalization, less on voluntary associations and self-help to supplement the services that the state provided for all. In the Latin countries and western Germany it owed a special debt to the influence of social Catholicism, for much of the social reorganization had been supported or even performed by powerful Catholic Democratic parties after 1945. Thirdly, there was the more doctrinaire Marxist type of welfare state to be found in the Soviet Union, Yugoslavia, and the eastern European Communist states. There nationalization was more extensive still, liberal capitalism was as far as possible uprooted, economic planning was more rigorous and complete, political freedom more curtailed.

These important differences of motivation and spirit resulted in widely different modes of procedure, administration, and emphasis in the running of national economies and social services. Nor were the three types distinct – Marxism played its part in France and Italy along with both social democracy and Catholic democracy, whereas it played little or no part in Britain, Spain, or Turkey. But the historically significant fact was the convergence and intermingling of these different trends, the broad similarity of answers which they produced to the questions posed for governments in mid-century Europe. There took place a 'nationalizing of socialism' in the East, a 'socializing of nationalism' in the West; and the outcomes of the two processes had both striking resemblances and important differences. To some extent the very impoverishment and stringencies of postwar Europe help to explain the urge to plan national resources more carefully, to redistribute labour force more productively, and to ensure a subsistence level for all citizens.

The greatest line of cleavage within Europe by 1960 was, however, the 'iron curtain', so-called 'polarization' of Europe between the rival pulls of the Soviet Union and the West, a cleavage marked indelibly on the map by the continued partition of Germany (see Map 27). This rift, based mainly on military tensions and security considerations, could be perhaps too easily magnified into a clash of irreconcilable ideologies, totally opposed philosophies and ways of life. The contrasts between the new social democracies of the West and the new 'people's democracies' of the East rested ultimately on long historical conflicts between parliamentary social democracy and Communist 'proletarian dictatorship'. Yet the contrasts, viewed in terms of actual ways of organizing the national economy and of avowed ends of social justice, could be seen as differences of emphasis rather than as two worlds in total conflict. Differences no less significant, no less firmly founded on different philosophical outlooks, divided the Spain of General Franco from France of the Fifth Republic, modern Turkey from contemporary Greece, or Communist China from Soviet Russia. The lines of division within Europe did not, perhaps fortunately, all run deepest or exclusively along the line of the iron curtain.

Nor did the previous century and a half of European history lend

---

MAP 27. EUROPE, 1965. See following pages.

By 1960 Communist governments ruled all eastern Europe except Finland, Greece, and Turkey. All, save Austria and Yugoslavia, were members of the Warsaw Treaty Organization of 1955. The western states, except for Eire, Sweden, Switzerland, and Spain (but including Greece and Turkey), were likewise organized for collective defence within the North Atlantic Treaty Organization of 1949, which included the United States and Canada. Although this alignment of powers seemed capable of tearing Europe apart, various crosscurrents prevented complete 'polarization'. Common membership in the United Nations, and in many world-wide functional agencies, offered a basis for peaceful coexistence'. (See Chapter 32.)

EUROPE
1965

///// Communist Countries

500 MILES

ICELAND
Reykjavik

ARCTIC CIRCLE

FAEROE IS.
(DEN.)

SHETLAND IS.

NORWAY
Trondheim
Bergen
Oslo

ORKNEY IS.

North Sea

SCOTLAND

NORTHERN IRELAND
Edinburgh

DENMARK

EIRE
Dublin

Liverpool
Hull

WALES
ENGLAND
London

UNITED KINGDOM

Amsterdam

Hamburg

Berlin

GERMANY (WEST)
Cologne
Bonn
LUX.
BELG.
Brussels
Rouen

EAST GERMANY
Dresden

CZE.

Atlantic Ocean

English Channel

Paris

Strasbourg

Danube R.

Munich

Vienna

AUST.

Loire R.

Tours

FRANCE

Berne
SWITZ.

Geneva

Milan

Po R.

Trieste

Bay of Biscay

Coruña

Bordeaux

Lyons

Genoa

Florence

Rhone R.

Oporto

PORTUGAL
Lisbon

Bilbao

Saragossa

Pyrenees

Madrid

Tagus R.

Cordoba
Seville
Malaga

SPAIN
Valencia

Barcelona

Marseilles
Toulon

CORSICA
(FR.)

Rome

ITALY

Naples

BALEARIC IS.
(SP.)

SARDINIA
(IT.)

Tangier
GIBRALTAR
(BR.)

Rabat
Casablanca Fez
Marrakech

Oran

Algiers

Mediterranean

Tunis

Palermo

SICILY

MALTA

MOROCCO

ALGERIA

TUNISIA

A F R I C A

Tripoli

LIBYA

support to the view that any alignment of powers, any ideological division, was immovable or even durable. The supreme characteristics of European development have been its flux and mobility, its vitality and resilience. On three occasions during that time Britain and Russia had discarded traditional enmities and ideological conflicts to unite in a successful alliance against great tyrannies in Europe. On all three occasions they had fallen apart shortly after the moment of victory, and yet had continued to find some footing for 'peaceful co-existence'. Although the relative position and power of Europe in the world had shrunk, the continued growth, enterprise, and vitality of European nations in part offset this decline. Even in economic and material terms it was peoples of the old continent who still led the world in the three vital spheres of public hygiene, transport, and the harnessing of atomic power, for in 1960 Sweden enjoyed the lowest infant death rate in the world, France the fastest and most efficient railway system, Britain the most advanced development of atomic energy for peaceful purposes.

The supreme question confronting Europeans at mid century was whether this traditional resilience and these material advantages could be so combined, using intelligence and wisdom, to relegate Europe's internal contrasts and divisions to the function of cultural diversification and enrichment of life, rather than to an intensifying of war-like jealousies and hatreds. Forces both of cohesion and of disunity still coexisted in a precarious balance and dreams of complete integration seemed as far as ever from fulfilment. The result of a century and a half of change was like the situation described by Robert Browning in *Bishop Blougram's Apology:*

> *All we have gained then by our unbelief*
> *Is a life of doubt diversified by faith,*
> *For one of faith diversified by doubt:*
> *We called the chess-board white – we call it black.*

History offered no warrant for either complacent optimism or black despondency. It offered no simple answer: only a challenge to reasonable hope and strenuous, unremitting endeavour.

SELECT BIBLIOGRAPHY

This reading list has been designed to help both the general student and the more specialized student. Its divisions follow the sequence of the parts, rather than the chapters, of this book. But its first section (A) lists books which either survey all or most of the period since Napoleon as a whole, or which cover the history of particular countries during the period. It is Section A, therefore, that the general reader may find most useful.

Section B suggests books which the reader more specially interested in certain aspects, topics, periods, or personalities of the history of modern Europe may find useful. It does not set out to be exhaustive, and makes no attempt to include lists of original sources or – except for special reasons – biographies. It indicates general studies or particular monographs which, in turn, will provide the more specialized worker with appropriate bibliographies of original sources. Its character is determined by the main themes dealt with in the ten parts of this book.

Most of the books mentioned, in both sections, have been published in Britain or the United States, and are in English or in English translation; but certain works in French have been included where no comparable or equally valuable book is known to exist in English. Books in languages other than English or French have been excluded.

A. GENERAL WORKS

General bibliographies may be found in the American publication by Lowell J. Ragatz, *A Bibliography for the Study of European History, 1815–1939* (1942 and subsequent supplements) or in the British publication, A. Bullock and A. J. P. Taylor, *Select List of Books on European History, 1815–1914* (1949, 2nd ed., 1957).

Pre-eminent among works that handle European history in the same manner as it has been handled here are the volumes in the series *The Rise of Modern Europe*, edited by William L. Langer; the volumes appropriate to this period are mentioned in the relevant parts of Section B. The venerable *Cambridge Modern History* is still of value, but it has the double shortcoming that it ends around 1900 and gives much less attention than is now fashionable to economic, social, and cultural history. Volumes 8–12 deal with the years 1789–1900. A completely new version is appearing. In the excellent French series, *Peuples et Civilisations, Histoire Générale*, edited by A. Halphen and

947

P. Sagnac, vols. xv–xix cover the period 1815–1918. For diplomatic history see the efficient survey by R. Albrecht-Carrié, *A Diplomatic History of Europe since the Congress of Vienna* (1958).

There is no completely satisfactory economic history of Europe during this whole period, but standard surveys include W. Bowden, M. Karpovich, and A. P. Usher, *The Economic History of Europe since 1750* (1937); S. B. Clough and C. W. Cole, *An Economic History of Europe* (1941); C. Day, *Economic Development in Europe* (1942); A. Birnie, *An Economic History of Europe 1760–1939* (1930; rev. ed., 1951); L. C. A. Knowles, *Economic Development in the Nineteenth Century – France, Germany, Russia, and the United States* (1932). The modern European economy in a world setting is discussed in W. Ashworth, *A Short History of the International Economy, 1850–1950* (1952). On demography, see A. M. Carr-Saunders, *World Population* (1936).

Economic histories of separate countries include Rondo E. Cameron, *France and the Economic Development of Europe, 1800–1914* (1961), J. H. Clapham, *The Economic Development of France and Germany, 1815–1914* (1921; 4th ed., 1936) and *An Economic History of Modern Britain* (3 vols., 1926–8), which covers the years 1820–1914 in great detail, with an epilogue to 1929. A useful briefer survey which runs to 1939 is W. H. B. Court, *A Concise Economic History of Britain from 1750 to Recent Times* (1954). S. B. Clough, *France: A History of National Economics, 1789–1939* (1939) deals well with French economic policies and development; and W. F. Bruck, *Social and Economic History of Germany from William II to Hitler, 1888–1938* (1938) or G. Stolper, *German Economy, 1870–1940* (1940) does the same for Germany. The economic growth of nineteenth-century Russia is described in J. Mavor, *An Economic History of Russia* (2 vols., 1925) and Sir J. Maynard, *Russia in Flux: Before October* (1941); of Communist Russia in S. and B. Webb, *Soviet Communism: A New Civilization?* (2 vols., 1936) or in E. H. Carr *A History of Soviet Russia*, Vol. 2 (1952) and Vol. 4 (1954), and subsequent volumes yet to appear. The economic growth of other countries is best studied either in the general economic histories listed above, or in relevant sections of the general national histories listed below. Regional studies that throw light on eastern European economic growth are H. G. Wanklyn, *The Eastern Marchlands of Europe* (1941) and H. Seton-Watson, *Eastern Europe between the Wars, 1918–1941* (1945).

The general national and political development of each country can be traced in many excellent books, among which the following have become standard works. For Britain, two volumes of the *Oxford History of England*, ed. G. N. Clark; E. L. Woodward, *The Age of Reform 1815–1870* (1938) and R. C. K. Ensor, *England 1870–1914* (1936); and the great unfinished French masterpiece by É. Halévy, *A History of the English People in the Nineteenth Century* (Eng. trans. by E. I. Watkin in 6 vols., 1927; 2nd rev. ed, 1950). For British relations with Europe, see R. W. Seton-Watson, *Britain in Europe, 1789–1914: A Summary of Foreign Policy* (1937) and its sequel *Britain and the Dictators: A Survey of Post-War British Policy* (1938). For France, J. P. T.

Bury, *France 1814–1940* (1949); J. B. Wolf, *A History of France since 1814* (1940); and D. W. Brogan, *The Development of Modern France 1870–1939* (1940). D. Pickles, *French Politics: The First Years of the Fourth Republic* (1953) carries the story beyond 1940. For Germany, K. S. Pinson, *Modern Germany: Its History and Civilization* (1954) and R. Flenley, *Modern German History* (1953) are excellent modern interpretations of the subject. A. J. P. Taylor, *The Habsburg Monarchy 1809–1918* (1941; new ed. with important changes 1948), despite its concentration on political and dynastic issues, is the best general survey. Austria between the two world wars is described in immense detail by C A. Gulick, *Austria from Habsburg to Hitler* (2 vols., 1948). Russian history is narrated generally in R. D. Charques, *A Short History of Russia* (1956) and in the older work of Sir B. Pares, *A History of Russia* (1926; rev. ed., 1953). Outlines of Italian history are given in A. J. Whyte, *The Evolution of Modern Italy* (1944) covering the years 1720–1920, and since 1861 in D. Mack Smith, *Italy: A Modern History* (1959). Comparable histories of other European countries include: W. C. Atkinson, *A History of Spain and Portugal* (1960); H. V. Livermore, *A History of Portugal* (1947); R. W. Seton-Watson, *A History of the Roumanians* (1936); H. W. V. Temperley, *History of Serbia* (1917); E. S. Forster, *A Short History of Modern Greece 1821–1956* (1957); R. Dyboski, *Outline of Polish History* (1925); B. H. M. Vlekke, *Evolution of the Dutch Nation* (1945); H. van der Linden, *Belgium, the Making of a Nation* (1920); E. Bonjour, H. S. Offler, and G. R. Potter, *A Short History of Switzerland* (1952); J. H. S. Birch, *History of Denmark* (1938); K. Larsen, *A History of Norway* (1948); R. Svanström and C. F. Palmstierna, *A Short History of Sweden* (1934); H. C. J. Luke, *The Making of Modern Turkey* (1936); J. H. Jackson, *Finland* (1938) and *Estonia* (1941).

On the history of political ideas, see Crane Brinton, *English Political Thought in the Nineteenth Century* (1933; rev. ed., 1950); R. H. Soltau, *French Political Thought in the Nineteenth Century* (1931); A. Rosenberg, *Democracy and Socialism* (Eng. trans., 1939, of *Demokratie und Sozialismus,* 1938); R. N. Carew Hunt, *The Theory and Practice of Communism* (1950); M. Oakeshott, *Social and Political Doctrines of Contemporary Europe* (1939); C. J. H. Hayes, *The Historical Evolution of Modern Nationalism* (1931; new ed., 1938); A. Cobban, *National Self-Determination* (1948); E. Kedourie, *Nationalism* (1960). See also the lists for Parts V and VIII below.

Twentieth-century Europe, in the world setting that is so necessary for understanding it, has been discussed briefly by D. Thomson, *World History from 1914 to 1961* (1963), and much more fully by C. E. Black and E. C. Helmreich, *Twentieth Century Europe: A History* (1950; rev. ed., 1959).

B. SPECIAL STUDIES

Part I. Europe in the Melting Pot, 1789–1814

The crisis of the *ancien régime* and the clash between existing institutions and new ideas can be studied in R. R. Palmer, *The Age of the Democratic Revolution: A Political History of Europe and America, 1760–1800* (vol I,

1959); Georges Lefebvre, *Quatre-vingt-neuf* (1939; Eng. trans. by R. R. Palmer as *The Coming of the French Revolution*, 1947); K. Martin, *French Liberal Thought in the Eighteenth Century* (1929; new rev. ed., 1954); P. Sagnac, *La Formation de la société française moderne*, Vol. II, 1715–89 (1946); D. Mornet, *Les Origines intellectuelles de la Révolution française, 1715–1787* (1933).

The ferment of ideas aroused by the Revolution is illustrated in Alfred Cobban (ed.), *The Debate on the French Revolution, 1789–1799* (1945); and is considered in the same author's works on *Edmund Burke and the Revolt against the Eighteenth Century* (1929), *Rousseau and the Modern State* (1934) and *The Social Interpretation of the French Revolution* (1964).

The most convenient general accounts of the Revolution and Napoleon are: Louis Gottschalk, *The Era of the French Revolution, 1715–1815* (1929); Leo Gershoy, *The French Revolution and Napoleon* (1933); J. M. Thompson, *The French Revolution* (1943); and *Napoleon Bonaparte, His Rise and Fall* (1952); G. Salvemini, *The French Revolution 1788–1792* (Eng. trans. by I. M. Rawson, 1954); and a brief critical account by A. Goodwin, *The French Revolution* (1953). Of the many French classics on the subject, F. V. A. Aulard, *Histoire Politique de la Révolution Française* (1901; Eng. trans. by B. Miall as *The French Revolution, a Political History, 1789–1804*, 4 vols., 1910); Louis Madelin, *La Révolution* (1911; Eng. trans. as *The French Revolution*, 1928); and G. Lefebvre, *La Révolution Française* (1951; Eng. trans. as *The French Revolution*, 2 vols., 1962–4) can be specially commended. The best systematic and up-to-date examination of the changes in the government of France during the whole period is J. Godechot, *Les Institutions de la France sous la Révolution et l'Empire* (1951). The magisterial *Lectures on the French Revolution*, by Lord Acton (1910), are still of value.

Among recent studies of special aspects of the Revolution, those most relevant to the discussion in Part I include Norman Hampson, *A Social History of the French Revolution* (1963), C. E. Labrousse, *La Crise de l'économie Française à la fin de l'Ancien Régime et au début de la Révolution* (1944); E. Thompson, *Popular Sovereignty and the French Constituent Assembly 1789–1791* (1952); D. Greer, *The Incidence of the Terror* (1935) and *The Incidence of the Emigration during the French Revolution* (1951); R. R. Palmer, *Twelve Who Ruled* (1941) – on the Committee of Public Safety; D. Thomson, *The Babeuf Plot: The Making of a Republican Legend* (1947); and the Marxist interpretation of working-class struggles by D. Guérin, *La Lutte des Classes sous la Première République* (2 vols., 1946).

Comparable special studies of the Napoleonic period and the effects of the wars on Europe are: F. M. H. Markham, *Napoleon and the Awakening of Europe* (1954); G. Bruun, *Europe and the French Imperium 1799–1814* (1938); H. Butterfield, *The Peace Tactics of Napoleon, 1806–1808* (1929); E. F. Hecksher, *The Continental System: an Economic Interpretation* (1922); G. P. Gooch, *Germany and the French Revolution* (1920) and *Studies in German History* (1948).

Biographical works on the leading personalities abound, but especially relevant are: J M. Thompson, *Leaders of the French Revolution* (1932) and *Robespierre* (2 vols., 1935); J. H. Clapham, *The Abbé Sieyès: an Essay in the Politics of the French Revolution* (1912); J. J. Chevallier, *Mirabeau, un grand destin manqué* (1947); S. J. Watson, *Carnot* (1954); A. Duff Cooper, *Talleyrand* (1932; new ed., 1958). For long the standard English biography of Napoleon was J. Holland Rose, *Life of Napoleon I* (2 vols., 1902), though a more popular study is the same author's *The Personality of Napoleon* (1912). Two works which collate differing interpretations by French historians of this controversial epoch are P. Farmer, *France Reviews Its Revolutionary Origins* (1944) and P. Geyl, *Napoleon – for and against* (1949).

On the peacemakers and the settlement of 1814–15, see C. K. Webster, *The Foreign Policy of Castlereagh, 1812–1815: Britain and the Reconstruction of Europe* (1931) and *The Congress of Vienna, 1814–1815* (1919); G. Ferrero, *The Reconstruction of Europe: Talleyrand and the Congress of Vienna 1814–15* (Eng. trans., 1941); L. I. Strakhovsky, *Alexander I of Russia: the Man Who Defeated Napoleon* (1947); R. Aldington, *Wellington* (1946).

Part II. Europe in 1815

The best general survey of the aftermath of the French Revolutionary and Napoleonic wars is F. B. Artz, *Reaction and Revolution, 1814–1832* (1934), which treats of Europe as a whole as it is handled here. L. S. Woolf, *After the Deluge: a Study of Communal Psychology* (2 vols., 1931–40) considers especially the changes of outlook. The conflicts between the restored monarchy and Church, and the forces of revolutionary change, can be followed in N. E. Hudson, *Ultraroyalism and the French Restoration* (1936); E. L. Woodward, *Three Studies in European Conservatism* (1929 – Metternich, Guizot, and the Catholic Church in the nineteenth century); C. Brinton, *The Political Ideas of the English Romanticists* (1926); A. Debidour, *Histoire des rapports de l'Église et de l'État en France 1789–1870* (2nd ed., 1911) strongly anticlerical in tone, with which may be compared the moderate Anglo-Catholic views of C. S. Phillips, *The Church in France, 1789–1848: A Study in Revival* (1929). And see D. Johnson, *Guizot* (1963).

The basic economic changes in western Europe, especially in Britain, can be studied in P. Mantoux, *The Industrial Revolution in the Eighteenth Century* (1937); three books by T. S. Ashton, *Iron and Steel in the Industrial Revolution* (1924), *The Industrial Revolution, 1760–1830* (1948), and *An Economic History of England: The Eighteenth Century* (1955); W. H. B. Court, *The Rise of the Midland Industries, 1600–1838* (1938); M. C. Buer, *Health, Wealth, and Population in the Early Days of the Industrial Revolution* (1926); and the works by J. L. and B. Hammond, which tend to exaggerate the ill effects of industrialism on working-class life – especially *The Village Labourer, 1760–1832* (1911; new ed., 1948); *The Town Labourer, 1760–1832* (1919). The economic continuity in French life is emphasized in F. B. Artz, *France under the Bourbon Restoration 1814–1830* (1931). The main agrarian changes in Europe are best covered by H. Sée, *Esquisse d'une Histoire du Régime Agraire en Europe au XVIIIe et XIXe Siècles* (1921). A. Goodwin has edited an admirable collection of studies of *The European Nobility in the Eighteenth Century* (1955).

The legacy of the Revolutionary ideals, for France and for modern Europe, is traced in such books as E. L. Woodward, *French Revolutions* (1934); G. Lowes Dickinson, *Revolution and Reaction in Modern France* (1892; new ed., 1927); G. Elton, *The Revolutionary Idea in France, 1789–1871* (1923); J. Plamenatz, *The Revolutionary Movement in France, 1815–1871* (1952). The growth of nationalist feeling in Europe is traced in R. W. Seton-Watson, *The Rise of Nationality in the Balkans* (1917); O. J. Falnes, *National Romanticism in Norway* (1933); R. E. Ergang, *Herder and the Foundations of German Nationalism* (1931); and in the general survey *Nationalism: A Report by a Study Group of Members of the Royal Institute of International Affairs* (1939). Changes made before 1815 which encouraged movements for national unification are discussed in R. M. Johnston, *The Napoleonic Empire in Southern Italy and the Rise of the Secret Societies* (1904); H. A. L. Fisher, *Napoleonic Statesmanship in Germany* (1903); G. S. Ford, *Stein and the Era of Reform in Prussia, 1807–1815* (1922); W. O. Shanahan, *Prussian Military Reforms, 1786–1813* (1945); W. C. Langsam, *The Napoleonic Wars and German Nationalism in Austria* (1930); A. A. Lobanov-Rostovsky, *Russia and Europe, 1789–1825* (1947); E. Tarlé, *Napoleon's Invasion of Russia, 1812* (1942); A. Fugier, *Napoléon et l'Espagne* (1930) and *Napoléon et l'Italie* (1947); M. Handelsman, *Napoléon et la Pologne 1806-7* (1909).

Part III. The Age of Revolutions, 1815–50

In addition to several of the books already mentioned, the following deal with the international politics of the Vienna settlement and the Congress System: W. Alison Phillips, *The Confederation of Europe: A Study of the European Alliance, 1813–1823* (1914, 1920) – an old-fashioned book which still has value; H. G. Schenk, *The Aftermath of the Napoleonic Wars: the Concert of Europe–an Experiment* (1947) is more modern and deals especially with the ideological issues, though not very satisfactorily; H. W. V. Temperley, *The Foreign Policy of Canning, 1822–1827* (1925) is a sequel to C. K. Webster's study of Castlereagh already mentioned, and is equally authoritative.

The special issue of Greece is covered in C. W. Crawley, *The Question of Greek Independence* (1930), and that of Serbia in G. Yakschitch, *L'Europe et la résurrection de la Serbie, 1804–1831* (2nd ed., 1917). The broader issue of the collapse of Turkish power is discussed in W. Miller, *The Ottoman Empire and Its Successors, 1801–1934* (1934). The best study of the Decembrist revolt is A. G. Mazour, *The First Russian Revolution, 1825: the Decembrist Movement, Its Origins, Development, and Significance* (1937).

The prevailing political systems between 1815 and 1848 are described in É. Halévy, *History of the English People in the Nineteenth Century*, Vols. I-IV of English edition (1927–47); J. Lucas-Dubreton, *La Restauration et Monarchie de Juillet* (1926; Eng. trans. as *The Restoration and the July*

SELECT BIBLIOGRAPHY

Monarchy, 1919); H. B. Clarke, *Modern Spain, 1815–1898* (1906); Bolton King, *History of Italian Unity* (2 vols.; 2nd ed., 1912); V. O. Klyuchevsky, *History of Russia* (Vol. V; 1931); B. Winiarski, *Les Institutions politiques en Pologne au XIXe siècle* (1928).

The economic developments of the period are described in the general works cited above (Section A) and also in H. Sée, *La Vie économique de la France sous la monarchie censitaire 1815–1848* (1927); P. Banaerts, *Les Origines de la grande industrie allemande* (1933). J. Kuczynski, *A Short History of Labour Conditions under Industrial Capitalism* (1944–6) deals statistically with labour conditions in Briain and the Empire (Vol. I), Germany (Vol. III), and France (Vol. IV). On the growth of British cities, see A. Redford, *Labour Migration in England, 1800-1850* (1929).

The movements for parliamentary and social reform in Britain have been exceptionally well written up by historians; see especially G. S. Veitch, *The Genesis of Parliamentary Reform* (1913); H. W. C. Davis, *The Age of Grey and Peel* (1929); G. M. Trevelyan, *Lord Grey of the Reform Bill* (1920; 2nd ed., 1929); N. Gash, *Politics in the Age of Peel: A Study in the Technique of Parliamentary Representation, 1830–1850* (1953); M. Hovell, *The Chartist Movement* (2nd ed., 1925); J. L. and B. Hammond, *The Bleak Age* (1934; new ed., 1947); R. J. Cruikshank, *Charles Dickens and Early Victorian England* (1949); R. L. Hill, *Toryism and the People, 1832–1846* (1929). Biographies of particular reformers include J. L. and B. Hammond, *Lord Shaftesbury* (1923; new ed., 1930) Graham Wallas, *The Life of Francis Place, 1771–1854* (1898; new ed., 1925); G. D. H. Cole, *The Life of William Cobbett* (1924) and *The Life of Robert Owen* (1930); S. E. Finer, *The Life and Times of Sir Edwin Chadwick* (1952). The doctrines of radical reform springing from Jeremy Bentham are splendidly analysed in É. Halévy, *The Growth of Philosophic Radicalism* (1901–4; new one-vol. ed., 1949); and the important issues of legal and penal reform have received equally authoritative treatment in L. Radzinowicz, *A History of English Criminal Law,* Vol. I: *The Movement for Reform, 1750–1833* (1948).

The liberal and republican movements in Europe are described in general in G. de Ruggiero, *The History of European Liberalism* (1927), which compares English, French, German, and Italian varieties. That in France is covered by G. Weill, *Histoire du Parti Républicain en France 1814–1870* (new ed., 1928); in Germany (for 1807–1933) by R. Olden, *The History of Liberty in Germany* (1946); in Spain by A. R. Oliveira, *Politics, Economics and Men of Modern Spain, 1808–1946* (1946); in Italy by E. E. Y. Hales, *Mazzini and the Secret Societies* (1956). See also the separate national histories listed in Section A above. For the social consequences of the romantic movement, see D. O. Evans, *Social Romanticism in France, 1830–48* (1951) and L. A. Willoughby, *The Romantic Movement in Germany* (1930).

There are two collections of essays about the revolutions of 1830 and 1848 which remain useful for their many-sidedness, though uneven in quality: *1830: Études sur les mouvements libéraux et nationaux de 1830* (1932) and *The Opening of an Era: 1848* (ed. F. Fejtö; 1948). There is an entertaining study of the year of revolutions as seen from England by R. Postgate, *Story of a Year: 1848* (1955), and a stimulating comparative study by P. Robertson, *Revolutions of 1848* (1952).

Sir L. B. Namier's famous study, *1848: The Revolution of the Intellectuals* (1946) includes a penetrating criticism of the German nationalists; V. Valentin, *1848: Chapters in German History* (1940) gives an account of their activities.

Two classics on the Italian revolution are G. M. Trevelyan's *Garibaldi's Defence of the Roman Republic, 1848–9* (1907, many later edns.) and his *Manin and the Venetian Revolution of 1848* (1923); on its international repercussions, see A. J. P. Taylor, *The Italian Problem in European Diplomacy, 1847–1849* (1934). The best brief history of the revolution in France is in French – J. Dautry, *Histoire de la Révolution de 1848 en France* (1948). On the economic conditions and ferment of ideas see Sir J. Marriott, *The French Revolution of 1848 in its Economic Aspect* (2 vols., 1913; including reprints of Louis Blanc's *Organization of Labour* and Émile Thomas's *The Right to Work*); and D. C. McKay, *The National Workshops*; a *Study in the French Revolution of 1848* (1933).

The ideas and work of the early socialist thinkers is surveyed in Sir A. Gray, *The Socialist Tradition: Moses to Lenin* (1946) and in E. Wilson, *To the Finland Station: a Study in the Writing and Acting of History* (1940; new ed., 1953). There are good biographies of *Karl Marx* by F. Mehring (1920; Eng. trans., 1936; new ed., 1948), by E. H. Carr (1938) and by I. Berlin (1939; new ed., 1948); and of *Friedrich Engels* by G. Mayer (1920; Eng. trans., 1935). On the theories of Marxism, see R. N. Carew Hunt, *The Theory and Practice of Communism* (1950) and G. D. H. Cole, *The Meaning of Marxism* (1948). The chief writings of Marx and Engels relating to this period are *The Communist Manifesto* (1848), of which editions have been edited by C. Adler (1901) and H. J. Laski (1948); and *The Class Struggles in France, 1848 to 1850* (1850), included in the convenient *Karl Marx and Frederick Engels: Selected Works* (2 vols., 1951).

Part IV. The Emergence of New Powers, 1851–71

The most illuminating general survey of these two decades is the volume in the 'Langer Series' by R. C. Binkley, *Realism and Nationalism, 1852–1871* (1935). Though it makes somewhat too much of 'federative polity' as a 'polity that emphasizes the political relations of adjustment among equals rather than political relationships of inferiority and superiority', it offers great insight into the intellectual and economic trends of this very important period. There is a stimulating and even more provocative interpretation by J. S. Schapiro, *Liberalism and the Challenge of Fascism: Social Forces in England and France, 1815–1870* (1949), which dubiously depicts Napoleon III as the 'herald of fascism'.

On the basic question of English and French economic expansion, many of the books listed for Part III extend into this period; and see also L. C. A. Knowles, *The Industrial and Commercial Revolutions in Great Britain during the Nineteenth Century* (1921); L. H. Jenks, *The Migration of British Capital to 1875* (1927); and on French social developments E. Dolléans, *Histoire du Mouvement Ouvrier* (3 vols., 1947–53), the first volume covering the years 1830–71; and G. Duveau, *La Vie ouvrière en France sous le Second Empire* 1946). E. C. Corti, *The Rise of the House of Rothschild, 1848–1870* (1928) and *The Reign of the House of Rothschild* (1928) throw light on international finance.

Comparable developments in Britain, France, Italy, and Germany can be studied in part by means of biographies of the national leaders; such as H. C. F. Bell, *Lord Palmerston* (2 vols., 1936), P. Guedalla, *Palmerston 1784–1865* (1925; new ed., 1942); F. A. Simpson, *The Rise of Louis Napoleon* (1909, 1950) and *Louis Napoleon and the Recovery of France, 1848–1856* (1923), A. Guérard, *Napoleon III* (1943), J. M. Thompson, *Louis Napoleon and the Second Empire* (1954); A. J. Whyte, *The Political Life and Letters of Cavour, 1848–1861* (1930); D. Mack Smith, *Garibaldi* (1956); Bolton King, *The Life of Mazzini* (1902, 1938); C. G. Robertson, *Bismarck* (1919); F. Darmstaedter, *Bismarck and the Creation of the Second Reich* (1948).

As a corrective, however, to an excessively personal interpretation of the Second Empire and the events of the *Risorgimento* in Italy and the *Reichsgründung* in Germany, it is important to study them more broadly. Useful books for this purpose are R. Arnaud, *The Second Republic and Napoleon III* (1930) and O. Aubry, *The Second Empire* (1940); D. Mack Smith, *Cavour and Garibaldi, 1860: A Study in Political Conflict* (1954); W. O. Henderson, *The Zollverein* (1939); H. Friedjung, *The Struggle for Supremacy in Germany, 1859–1866* (1897, 1955); C. W. Clark, *Franz Joseph and Bismarck: The Diplomacy of Austria before the War of 1866* (1934). Classical accounts of internal events in Italy are G. M. Trevelyan, *Garibaldi and the Thousand, May 1860* (1911) and *Garibaldi and the Making of Italy, June–November 1860* (1911).

Such study inevitably leads into the complex diplomacy of the period. This is examined by A. J. P. Taylor in *The Struggle for Mastery in Europe, 1848–1918* (1954), which contains a valuable bibliography. Among the many more specialized examinations of relations between the great powers the most useful are H. W. V. Temperley, *England and the Near East: The Crimea* (1936); G. B. Henderson, *Crimean War Diplomacy, and other historical essays* (1947); L. M. Case, *Franco-Italian Relations, 1860–1865: The Roman Question and the Convention of September* (1932); L. D. Steefel, *The Schleswig-Holstein Question* (1932); R. H. Lord, *The Origins of the War of 1870: New Documents from the German Archives* (1924); H. Oncken, *Napoleon III and the Rhine: The Origin of the War of 1870–71* (1928); G. E. Mosse, *The European Powers and the German Question, 1848–1871* (1958); G. Bonnin, *Bismarck and the Hohenzollern Candidature for the Spanish Throne* (1957).

Special studies of the Eastern Question include V. J. Puryear, *England, Russia and the Straits Question, 1844–1856* (1931); W. G. East, *The Union of Moldavia and Wallachia* (1927). The biography of *Florence Nightingale* by C. Woodham-Smith (1951) gives a vivid account of how the Crimean War affected England, and B. K. Martin, *The Triumph of Lord Palmerston* (1924) is mainly a study of British opinion before the Crimean War. On the general place of warfare in this period, see E. L. Woodward, *War and Peace in Europe, 1815–1870* (1931).

The important agrarian changes in Russia are best studied in G. T. Robinson, *Rural Russia under the Old Régime* (1932), in G. Pasvolsky, *Agricultural Russia on the Eve of the Revolution* (1930; new ed. 1949), and in the early chapters of H. Seton-Watson, *The Decline of Imperial Russia, 1855–1914* (1952). The activities of Russian revolutionaries abroad are described in three works by E. H. Carr, *The Romantic Exiles* (1933; new ed. 1949), *Michael Bakunin* (1937), and *Studies in Revolution* (1950).

The intellectual and cultural currents of the period can be explored in S. Hook, *From Hegel to Marx* (1936); J. Barzun, *Darwin, Marx, Wagner: Critique of a Heritage* (1942); G. Himmelfarb, *Darwin and the Darwinian Revolution* (1959); E. Newman, *Life of Wagner* (4 vols., 1933–47); F. P. Chambers, *The History of Taste* (1932); H. V. Routh, *Towards the Twentieth Century: Essays in the Spiritual History of the Nineteenth* (1937); G. Brandes, *Main Currents in Nineteenth Century Literature* (6 vols., 1901–6); Sir W. C. D. Dampier, *History of Science* (1929; 4th ed., 1948); A. Findlay, *A Hundred Years of Chemistry* (1937); and I. Galdston (ed.), *Social Medicine: Its Derivations and Objectives* (1949).

Part V. Democracy and Socialism, 1871–1914

General histories of this period tend to concentrate on international and imperial relations (see list below for Part VI), rather than upon the pattern of domestic developments. The relevant volume in the 'Langer Series', C. J. H. Hayes, *A Generation of Materialism, 1871–1900* (1941), hinges upon the theme that nationalism and materialism together prepared for the destructive totalitarianism of the twentieth century, and has a strong Catholic bias.

The developments within separate countries are, however, well covered in several works such as R. C. K. Ensor, *England 1870–1914* (1936); D. W. Brogan, *The Development of Modern France, 1870–1939* (1940); B. Croce, *A History of Italy, 1871–1914* (1929); W. H. Dawson, *The German Empire, 1867–1914, and the Unity Movement* (2 vols., 1919); J. B. Trend, *The Origins of Modern Spain* (1934); H. Seton-Watson, *The Decline of Imperial Russia, 1855–1914* (1952).

On the growing pattern of parliamentary democracy in Europe, see R. H. Gretton, *A Modern History of the English People, 1880–1922* (1930); D. Thomson, *Democracy in France since 1870* (1946; new ed., 1964); R. H. Soltau, *French Parties and Politics, 1871–1921* (1930); A. Rosenberg, *The Birth of the German Republic, 1871–1918* (1931); O. Jászi, *The Dissolution of the Hapsburg Monarchy* (1929); Sir B. Pares, *Russia and Reform* (1905); D. Verney, *Parliamentary Reform in Sweden, 1866–1921* (1957); and A. Rosenberg, *Democracy and Socialism* (1939).

On the far-reaching economic developments, see the general economic surveys listed in Section A, and also A. L. Bowley, *Wages and Income in the United Kingdom since 1860* (1938); D. L. Burn, *The Economic History of Steelmaking, 1867–1939* (1940); H. Levy, *Industrial Germany: A Study of Its Monopoly Organizations and Their Control by the State* (1935); A. Gerschenkron, *Bread and Democracy in Germany* (1943); R. Pitrowski, *Cartels and Trusts: Their Origins and Historical Development from the Economic and Legal Aspects* (1933); H. Feis, *Europe, the World's Banker, 1870–1914* (1930); I. Lippincott, *The Development of Modern World Trade* (1936).

On the growth of labour organization, trade unionism, and the co-operative movements, see G. D. H. Cole, *British Working Class Politics, 1832–1914* (1941); S. and B. Webb, *History of Trade Unionism* (1894; new ed., 1920); W. S. Sanders, *Trade Unionism in Germany* (1916); L. Levine, *Syndicalism in France* (1914); W. Milne-Bailey, *Trade Unions and the State* (1934); F. Hall and W. P. Watkins, *Co-operation: a Survey of the History, Principles and Organization of the Co-operative Movement in Great Britain and Ireland* (1934).

On the national movements of socialism and communism, see M. Beer, *A History of British Socialism* (1919; 1-vol. ed., 1940); E. R. Pease, *The History of the Fabian Society* (1916; new ed., 1925); H. Pelling, *The Origins of the Labour Party* (1954); S. Bernstein, *The Beginnings of Marxian Socialism in France* (1933); J. H. Jackson, *Jean Jaurès: His Life and Work* (1943); P. Gay, *The Dilemma of Democratic Socialism* (1952); E. Anderson, *Hammer or Anvil: the Story of the German Working-class Movement* (1945); A. Rosenberg, *A History of Bolshevism* (1934; Eng. trans. of *Geschichte des Bolschevismus,* 1932); G. Brenan, *The Spanish Labyrinth* (1943; 2nd ed., 1950). J. T. Joughin, *The Paris Commune in French Politics, 1871–1880* (2 vols., 1956) examines the significance of the events about which Marx wrote in *The Civil War in France* (1871, 1921). For a general survey see G. D. H. Cole, *A History of Socialist Thought* (4 vols., 1953–60).

On international socialism, communism, and anarchism, see J. Joll, *The Second International, 1889–1914* (1955); F. Borkenau, *Socialism, National or International* (1942); B. Russell, *Proposed Roads to Freedom: Socialism, Anarchism, and Syndicalism* (1919); G. Woodcock, *Pierre-Joseph Proudhon* (1956); J. Joll, *The Anarchists* (1964).

On the growth of social services and welfare legislation before 1914, see the separate national histories listed in Section A and also K. de Schweinitz, *England's Road to Social Security* (1943); W. F. Bruck, *Social and Economic History of Germany, from William II to Hitler 1888–1938* (1938); W. H. Dawson, *Social Insurance in Germany, 1883–1911* (1912), and Chapters X and XI of J. H. Clapham, *The Economic Development of France and Germany, 1815–1914* (1921). H. M. Wodehouse, *A Survey of the History of Education* (1924) relates English to European developments; I. L. Kandel, *Comparative Education* (1933) emphasizes the problems and purposes common to most national systems of education.

The fortunes of the Roman Catholic Church and its conflicts with the state in these years are described in A. Dansette, *Histoire religieuse de la France contemporaine sous la Troisième République* (1951); G. Hoog, *Histoire du Catholicisme Social en France, 1871–1931* (1946); S. W. Halperin, *Italy and the Vatican at War* (1939); L. P. Wallace, *The Papacy and European Diplomacy 1869–1878* (1949).

The developments of science are described partly in the works listed above for Part IV, and also in C. T. Chase, *The Evolution of Modern Physics* (1947); E. Zimmer, *The Revolution in Physics* (1936); F. Wittels, *Freud and His Time* (1931; new ed., 1948); L. R. and H. Lieber, *The Einstein Theory of Relativity* (1945). The relations between scientific ideas and social thought are considered in W. M. McGovern, *From Luther to Hitler* (1946), and in W. Y. Elliott, *The Pragmatic Revolt in Politics* (1928), the former including useful bibliographies. On the arts, see B. Croce, *European Literature in the Nineteenth Century* (1924); J. H. Randall, *The Making of the Modern Mind* (1940); E. P. Richardson, *The Way of Western Art, 1776–1914* (1939); N. Pevsner, *Pioneers of the Modern Movement from William Morris to Walter Gropius* (1936); A. Einstein, *A Short History of Music* (1938). See also the list below, for Part X, and G. L. Mosse, *The Culture of Western Europe* (1963).

The underlying theme of the many-sided challenge to liberal democracy, to the nation-state, and even to traditional western civilization before 1914 is not treated fully in any book. But aspects of it are examined in such books as G. Dangerfield, *The Strange Death of Liberal England* (1936); W. S. Adams, *Edwardian Heritage: A Study in British History, 1901–1906* (1949); G. Chapman, *The Dreyfus Case: A Reassessment* (1955); W. C. Buthman, *The Rise of Integral Nationalism in France* (1939); P. W. Massing, *Rehearsal for Destruction: A Study of Political Anti-semitism in Imperial Germany* (1949); J. N. Figgis, *Churches in the Modern State* (1914); L. Stoddard, *The Revolt against Civilization* (1922). Some of the ideas which were later to assist the rise of racialism and totalitarianism are examined in H. A. Reyburn, *Nietzsche: The Story of a Human Philosopher* (1948); H. W. C. Davis, *Political Thought of Heinrich von Treitschke* (1915), and the work by H. S. Chamberlain, which influenced both Pan-Germanism and Hitlerism, *The Foundations of the Nineteenth Century* (2 vols.; 1911; Eng. trans. of the German *Grundzüge des Neunzehnten Jahrhunderts*, 1899).

Part VI. Imperial Rivalries and International Alliances, 1871-1914

The eastern question in these years has attracted many writers. The most generally useful works are R. W. Seton-Watson, *Disraeli, Gladstone, and the Eastern Question: a Study in Diplomacy and Party Politics* (1935); W. N. Medlicott, *The Congress of Berlin and After, 1878–1880* (1938); E. M. Earle, *Turkey, the Great Powers, and the Bagdad Railway* (1923); E. C. Helmreich, *The Diplomacy of the Balkan Wars, 1912–1913* (1938). On the Balkan states, see C. E. Black, *The Establishment of Constitutional Government in Bulgaria* (1943); W. Miller, *The Ottoman Empire and Its Successors, 1801–1927* (1913; new ed., 1936); H. Baerlein, *The Birth of Yugoslavia* (2 vols., 1922); P. F. Martin, *Greece of the Twentieth Century* (1913).

The expansion of the European powers overseas and their consequent imperial rivalries are topics that have also produced a large literature. See especially P. T. Moon, *Imperialism and World Politics* (1926); R. Muir, *The Expansion of Europe* (1917; 6th ed., 1939); C. P. Lucas, *The Partition and Colonization of Africa* (1922); N. D. Harris, *Europe and the East* (1926); Sir J. T. Pratt, *The Expansion of Europe into the Far East* (1947); and the two most famous polemics against it, J. A. Hobson, *Imperialism: A Study* (1902; new ed., 1938), and V. I. Lenin, *Imperialism, the Highest Stage of Capitalism* (1916 new ed., 1937). On particular areas or forms of colonial expansion, see R. Coupland, *The Exploitation of East Africa, 1856–1890* (1939); L. de Lichtervelde, *Leopold of the Belgians* (1929); H. R. Rudin, *Germans in the Cameroons, 1884–1914: A Case Study in Modern Imperialism* (1938); S. E. Crowe, *The Berlin West-African Conference, 1884–1885* (1942); M. M. Knight, *Morocco as a French Economic Venture* (1937); C. Robequain, *The Economic Development of French Indo-China* (1944, Eng. trans. of *L'Évolution Économique de l'Indo-Chine Française,* 1939); B. H. Sumner, *Tsardom and Imperialism in the Far East and the Middle East, 1880–1914* (1942); B. H. M. Vlekke, *The Story of the Dutch East Indies* (1945).

The policies of the powers which resulted in the system of alliances and the prewar balance of power are well described in N. Mansergh, *The Coming of the First World War, 1878–1914* (1949) or in the older book by J. A. Spender, *Fifty Years of Europe: A Study in Pre-War Documents* (1933; new ed., 1936). Fuller accounts of the same theme are contained in S. B. Fay, *The Origins of the World War* (2 vols., 1929; 2 vols. in 1 and new ed., 1931); W. L. Langer, *European Alliances and Alignments, 1871–1890* (1931) and *The Diplomacy of Imperialism, 1890–1902* (2 vols., 1935); and the work by A. J. P. Taylor already mentioned, *The Struggle for Mastery in Europe, 1848–1918* (1954). A good general account is R. J. Sontag, *European Diplomatic History, 1871–1932* (1933).

The characteristics and interactions of separate national policies are analysed in A. F. Pribram, *England and the International Policy of the European Great Powers, 1871–1914* (1931); R. J. Sontag, *Germany and England: Background of Conflict, 1848–1894* (1938); E. L. Woodward, *Great Britain and the German Navy* (1935); E. Brandenberg, *From Bismarck to the World War: A History of German Foreign Policy, 1870–1914* (1927); G. Michon, *The Franco-Russian Alliance, 1891–1917* (1929); P. Renouvin, *The Immediate Origins of the War* (1928).

Relations between foreign policy and national opinion as influenced by the new popular Press are explored in E. M. Carroll, *French Public Opinion and Foreign Affairs, 1870–1914* (1930); and *Germany and the Great Powers, 1866–1914: A Study in Public Opinion and Foreign Policy* (1939); O. J. Hale, *Publicity and Diplomacy, with Special Reference to England and Germany, 1890–1914* (1940) and *Germany and the Diplomatic Revolution: A Study in the Diplomacy of the Press, 1904–1906* (1931).

The general character of prewar diplomacy is explained by H. Nicolson, *Diplomacy* (1939) and *Sir Arthur Nicolson, Bart., First Lord Carnock: A Study in the Old Diplomacy* (1930); J. Cambon, *The Diplomatist* (1931); G. P.

Gooch, *Before the War: Studies in Diplomacy* (2 vols., 1936–8). Two English works which exercised considerable influence upon Anglo-American thinking about prewar diplomacy are G. L. Dickinson, *The International Anarchy, 1904–1914* (1926) and Sir Norman Angell, *The Great Illusion* (1909; new ed., 1933).

Part VII. War and Peace, 1914–23

The best general military history of the war, in brief form, is C. R. M. F. Cruttwell, *A History of the Great War, 1914–1918* (1934), but see also the more controversial B. H. Liddell Hart, *A History of the World War, 1914–1918* (1934; revised version of *The Real War*, 1930), and the more specialized study of the home fronts by F. P. Chambers, *The War behind the War: A History of the Political and Civilian Fronts* (1939). There is the vast series of volumes, edited by J. T. Shotwell, on the *Economic and Social History of the War* (1921–37), including such works as J. A. Salter, *Allied Shipping Control: an Experiment in International Administration* (1921); A. Fontaine, *French Industry during the War* (1927); Ahmed Amin, *Turkey in the World War* (1930); E. Heckscher and others, *Sweden, Norway, Denmark, and Iceland in the World War* (1930); J. Redlich, *Australian War Government* (1929); and D. Mitrany, *The Effect of the War in South-Eastern Europe* (1936). On the armistices, see Sir F. Maurice, *The Armistices of 1918* (1943).

The large standard history of the Conference of Paris is H. W. V. Temperley (ed.), *History of the Peace Conference* (6 vols., 1920–4), but there is an excellent concise account of it in F. S. Marston, *The Peace Conference of 1919: Organization and Procedure* (1944). Almost all the leading participants left some account of the events, but there are also lively (and often more revealing) personal diaries or accounts by others who were present; such as A. Tardieu, *La Paix* (1921; Eng. trans. as *The Truth about the Treaty*, 1921) and H. Nicolson, *Peacemaking 1919* (1933); and, from the American standpoint, R. Lansing, *The Peace Negotiations: A Personal Narrative* (1921) and S. Bonsal, *Unfinished Business* (1944). Among later reflections upon the conference and its consequences are: P. Birdsall, *Versailles Twenty Years After* (1941); R. B. McCallum, *Public Opinion and the Last Peace* (1944); and T. E. Jessop, *The Treaty of Versailles – Was It Just?* (1942). The classical contemporary indictment was J. M. Keynes, *The Economic Consequences of the Peace* (1920), with which may be contrasted E. Mantoux, *The Carthaginian Peace, or The Economic Consequences of Mr. Keynes* (1946), a French attack upon Keynes's strictures.

The territorial, economic, and political provisions of the treaties which compose the whole settlement of 1918–23 are dealt with in a variety of monographs, including J. W. Wheeler-Bennett, *Brest-Litovsk: The Forgotten Peace* (1939); M. Almond and R. H. Lutz, *The Treaty of St. Germain* (1939); R. Donald, *The Tragedy of Trianon* (1928); R. Albrecht-Carrié, *Italy at the Paris Peace Conference* (1938); F. Deák, *Hungary at the Paris Peace Conference* (1942); I. Morrow, *The Peace Settlement in the German-Polish Borderlands* (1936); C. A. Macartney, *National States and National Minori-*

ties (1934); A. Cobban, *National Self-Determination* (1944). The special issues of reparations, disarmament, and military security bequeathed to the western powers by the terms of the settlement are traced in their subsequent development by W. M. Jordan, *Great Britain, France, and the German Problem, 1918–1939: A Study of Anglo-French Relations in the Making and Maintenance of the Versailles Settlement* (1943); and A. Wolfers, *Britain and France Between Two Wars: Conflicting Strategies of Peace since Versailles* (1940).

The economic aftermath of the war, which would have been far-reaching whatever the peacemakers of 1919 might have done better, is admirably examined in very brief form by A. L. Bowley, *Some Economic Consequences of the Great War* (1930). The controversy about 'war guilt', occasioned by later German propagandist uses of Article 231 of the Treaty of Versailles, is surveyed devastatingly by L. Fraser, *Germany Between Two Wars: A Study of Propaganda and War-Guilt* (1944).

On the League of Nations and the other international institutions set up in 1919, see D. H. Miller, *The Drafting of the Covenant* (2 vols., 1928); Sir A. Zimmern, *The League of Nations and the Rule of Law, 1918–1935* (1936); Viscount Cecil, *A Great Experiment: An Autobiography* (1941); E. J. Phelan, *Yes and Albert Thomas* (1936 – about the I.L.O.); Sir H. Butler, *The Lost Peace: A Personal Impression* (1941); M. O. Hudson, *The Permanent Court of International Justice* (1934; rev. ed., 1943); Q. Wright, *Mandates under the League of Nations* (1930); P. de Azcárate, *League of Nations and National Minorities: An Experiment* (1945); M. Hill, *The Economic and Financial Organization of the League of Nations: A Survey of Twenty-Five Years Experience* (1945); E. F. Ranshoffen-Wertheimer, *The International Secretariat: A Great Experiment in International Administration* (1945); F. P. Walters, *A History of the League of Nations* (2 vols., 1952).

Part VIII. The Age of Demolition, 1924–39

The best concise history of international relations between the two world wars is G. M. Gathorne-Hardy, *A Short History of International Affairs, 1920–1939* (1934; 2nd rev. ed., 1942), though an excellent briefer account is E. H. Carr, *International Relations between the Two World Wars, 1919–1939* (1947). E. H. Carr has also written a penetrating analysis of international policies in these years, *The Twenty Years' Crisis, 1919–1939: An Introduction to the Study of International Relations* (1939; 2nd ed., 1946).

On the working of the new machinery of international organization, see the books listed above for Part VII, and also W. E. Rappard, *The Quest for Peace since the World War* (1940); P. J. Noel-Baker, *The Geneva Protocol for the Pacific Settlement of International Disputes* (1925) and *Disarmament* (1926); D. H. Miller, *The Peace Pact of Paris* (1928); R. Dell, *The Geneva Racket, 1920–1939* (1941). The relevant documents are conveniently collected in A. B. Keith, *Speeches and Documents on International Affairs, 1918–1937* (2 vols., 1938).

On the world economic crisis of 1929–34, see L. C. Robbins, *The Great*

Depression (1934); H. V. Hodson, *Slump and Recovery, 1929–1937: A Survey of World Economic Affairs* (1938); V. P. Timoshenko, *World Agriculture and the Depression* (1933). The crisis is considered in its long-range perspective in G. D. H. Cole, *Introduction to Economic History, 1750–1950* (1952) and in J. P. Day, *An Introduction to World Economic History since the Great War* (1939).

The economic difficulties of the democracies in the interwar years are best studied through separate national histories. In addition to those listed in Section A, see A. C. Pigou, *Aspects of British Economic History, 1918–1925* (1947); George Peel, *The Financial Crisis of France* (1925); R. T. Clark, *The Fall of the German Republic: A Political History* (1935); H. Finer, *Mussolini's Italy* (1935); P. L. Yates and D. Warriner, *Food and Farming in Post-War Europe* (1943); A. F. Sturmthal, *The Tragedy of European Labor, 1918–1939* (1943).

On the rise of the single-party dictatorships, see the standard history of Soviet Russia by E. H. Carr, *The Bolshevik Revolution, 1917–1923* (3 vols., 1951–3); M. Dobb, *Soviet Economic Development since 1917* (1948); I. Deutscher, *Stalin: A Political Biography* (1949); G. Salvemini, *Under the Axe of Fascism* (1936); D. A. Binchy, *Church and State in Fascist Italy* (1942); S. W. Halperin, *Germany Tried Democracy: A Political History of the Reich from 1918 to 1933* (1946); J. W. Wheeler-Bennett, *Wooden Titan: Hindenburg in Twenty Years of German History, 1914–1934* (1936); A. Bullock, *Hitler: A Study in Tyranny* (1952); F. Neumann, *Behemoth: The Structure and Practice of National Socialism* (1942; new ed., 1944); E. Allison Peers, *The Spanish Tragedy, 1930–1936* (1936) and *Spain in Eclipse, 1937–1943* (1943).

The use of emergency powers and exceptional devices in Germany, France, Britain, and the United States are examined by C. L. Rossiter, *Constitutional Dictatorship: Crisis Government in the Modern Democracies* (1948). On particular countries, see C. L. Mowat, *Britain between the Wars, 1918–40* (1955), W. K. Hancock, *Survey of British Commonwealth Affairs* (2 vols., 1942); Sir G. Campion and others, *British Government since 1918* (1950); A. Werth, *The Twilight of France, 1933–1940* (1942); M. MacDonald, *The Republic of Austria, 1918–1934: A Study in the Failure of Democratic Government* (1946); H. Seton-Watson, *Eastern Europe between the Wars, 1918–1941* (1945); G. E. R. Gedye, *Fallen Bastions: The Central European Tragedy* (1939); R. Machray, *The Poland of Pilsudski* (1937); B. A. Arneson, *The Democratic Monarchies of Scandinavia* (1939); M. Derrick, *The Portugal of Salazar* (1939); D. E. Webster, *The Turkey of Ataturk* (1939); B. Ward, *Turkey* (1942).

The ideological conflicts of the interwar years can be examined with the help of the anthologies of writings collected by M. Oakeshott, *Social and Political Doctrines of Contemporary Europe* (1939) and by Sir A. Zimmern, *Modern Political Doctrines* (1939); A. Cobban, *Dictatorship: Its History and Theory* (1939) and D. Spearman, *Modern Dictatorship* (1939); and explored in more detail in R. d'O. Butler, *The Roots of National Socialism* (1941); P. F. Drucker, *The End of Economic Man: A Study of the New Totalitar-*

ianism (1939); E. H. Carr, *The Soviet Impact on the Western World* (1946); J. Plamenatz, *German Marxism and Russian Communism* (1954).

The conflicts and interactions of policies which led to the Spanish Civil War and eventually to the Second World War can be studied partly through examinations of separate national foreign policies, and partly through investigation of their consequences. On the former, see especially E. Wiskemann, *The Rome-Berlin Axis: A History of the Relations Between Hitler and Mussolini* (1949); E. Monroe, *The Mediterranean in Politics* (1937; 2nd ed., 1939); M. Beloff, *The Foreign Policy of Soviet Russia, 1929–1941* (2 vols., 1947–9); R. W. Seton-Watson, *Britain and the Dictators: A Survey of Post-War British Policy* (1938); D. Perkins, *The Evolution of American Foreign Policy* (1948); M. H. H. Macartney and P. Cremona, *Italy's Foreign and Colonial Policy, 1914–1937* (1938); W. d'Ormesson, *France* (1939); C. A. Micaud, *The French Right and Nazi Germany, 1933–1939* (1943); F. J. Vondracek, *The Foreign Policy of Czechoslovakia, 1918–1935* (1937). On the consequences, see N. J. Padelford, *International Law and Diplomacy in the Spanish Civil War* (1939); J. W. Wheeler-Bennett, *Munich: Prologue to Tragedy* (1948); F. L. Schuman, *Europe on the Eve: The Crises of Diplomacy, 1933–1939* (1939) and *Night over Europe: The Diplomacy of Nemesis, 1939–1940* (1941); L. B. Namier, *Europe in Decay: A Study in Disintegration, 1936–1940* (1950) and *Diplomatic Prelude, 1938–1939* (1948).

For all international affairs since 1920, a useful source of both information and documentation is the annual *Survey of International Affairs* edited by A. J. Toynbee, and its occasional supplementary volumes on particular events (e.g., in 1936 on the Abyssinian War, and in 1937 on the Spanish Civil War). The prewar series ran to 1938.

Part IX. War and Peace, 1939–55

The handiest short history of the Second World War is C. Falls, *The Second World War: A Short History* (1948); but see also F. J. C. Fuller, *The Second World War, 1939–1945: A Strategical and Tactical History* (1949); and R. W. Shugg and H. A. de Weerd, *World War II: A Concise History* (1946). A work that is as indispensable as it is colourful is Sir Winston S. Churchill's *tour de force, The Second World War* (6 vols., 1948–54). Chester Wilmot, *The Struggle for Europe* (1952), is a brilliant account of the decisive European campaign by an Australian war correspondent.

Among many studies of special phases or aspects of the war the most relevant are: T. Draper, *The Six Weeks War: France, May 10–June 25, 1940* (1944); E. R. Stettinius, Jr., *Lend-Lease: Weapon for Victory* (1944); A. Werth, *The Year of Stalingrad* (1947); G. C. Marshall, *The Winning of the War in Europe and the Pacific* (Biennial Report of the U.S. Chief of Staff, 1945); H. R. Trevor-Roper, *The Last Days of Hitler* (1947); M. H. H. Macartney, *The Rebuilding of Italy* (1946). A convenient and comprehensive account of Hitler's 'New Order' in Europe and of the underground resistance movements is A. and V. M. Toynbee (eds.) *Hitler's Europe* (1954), one of the War-Time Series of *Surveys of International Affairs* prepared by the Royal

Institute of International Affairs. The outcome in the liberated countries can be pursued in its sequel *The Realignment of Europe* (1955), which includes a full description of the work of UNRRA.

The postwar governments and their work of reconstruction are well surveyed in T. Cole (ed.), *European Political Systems* (1953; 2nd ed., 1959), which deals with the Soviet Union and Eastern Europe, Germany, Italy, Britain, France. The problems of peace-making in 1945, in relation to earlier experience, are discussed in D. Thomson, E. Meyer, and A. Briggs, *Patterns of Peacemaking* (1945), and in E. H. Carr, *Conditions of Peace* (1942). The arrangements made in the peace treaties of 1946 are best studied in the collection of texts published by the U.S. Department of State, *Treaties of Peace with Italy, Bulgaria, Hungary, Roumania, and Finland* (1947). The growth of the 'cold war' is traced briefly in J. H. Jackson, *The Post-War Decade: A Short History of the World, 1945–1955* (1955). The momentum and consequences of communist revolutions are examined admirably in H. Seton-Watson, *The Pattern of Communist Revolution: A Historical Analysis* (1953); M. Einaudi, J.-M. Domenach, and A. Garosci, *Communism in Western Europe* (1951), deals especially with France and Italy; and see F. Borkenau, *European Communism* (1953).

The social and political forces at work in postwar Europe are further described in G. Wright, *The Reshaping of French Democracy* (1950); D. Pickles, *French Politics* (1953); P. M. Williams and M. Harrison, *De Gaulle's Republic* (1960); M. Einaudi and F. Goguel, *Christian Democracy in Italy and France* (1952); M. Grindrod, *The New Italy, 1943–1947* (1947); and *The Rebuilding of Italy: Politics and Economics, 1945–1955* (1955); S. Neumann, *Germany: Promise and Perils* (1950); J. P. Nettl, *The Eastern Zone and Soviet Policy in Germany, 1945–1950* (1951); E. Wiskemann, *Germany's Eastern Neighbours* (1955); B. Sweet-Escott, *Greece: A Political and Economic Survey, 1939–1953* (1955); D. E. Butler (ed.), *Elections Abroad (France, Poland, Ireland, South Africa)* (1959). On labour organizations and social problems, see H. W. Ehrmann, *French Labor from Popular Front to Liberation* (1947); the remarkable study by H. Lüthy, *The State of France: A Study of Contemporary France* (1955); and H. C. Wallich, *Mainsprings of the German Revival* (1955).

The story of the immense transformation in colonial relationships after 1945 has not yet been systematically told, but some of its aspects can be studied in such books as H. V. Hodson, *Twentieth Century Empire* (1948); F. Benham, *The Colombo Plan and Other Essays* (1956); J. H. Boeke, *The Evolution of the Netherlands Indies Economy* (1946); K. Stahl, *British and Soviet Colonial Systems* (1951); and for Britain in two Reference Pamphlets published by the British Central Office of Information, *Constitutional Development in the Commonwealth*, Part I *Member Countries*, Part II *United Kingdom Dependencies* (1955). On the semi-colonial problems of the Near East, see G. de Gaury, *The New State of Israel* (1952); A. H. Hourani, *Syria and Lebanon: A Political Essay* (1946); G. Antonius, *The Arab Awakening* (1946); and of the Far East, Guy Wint, *Spotlight on Asia* (1955); K. S.

Latourette, *A History of Modern China* (1954); and V. Purcell, *China* (1962).

The United Nations organization is described in H. G. Nicholas, *The United Nations as a Political Institution* (1959) and in S. S. Goodspeed, *The Nature and Function of International Organization* (1959); and some of its affiliated functional agencies in J. Huxley, *UNESCO: Its Purposes and Philosophy* (1947); O. Lissitzyn, *The International Court of Justice* (1951); H. D. Hall, *Mandates, Dependencies and Trusteeship* (1948); C .E. Toussaint, *The Trusteeship System of the United Nations* (1956); C. H. Alexandrowicz, *International Economic Organizations* (1952).

Regional organizations are described in Lord Ismay, *NATO: The First Five Years, 1949–1954* (1955); H. L. Mason, *The European Coal and Steel Community: Experiment in Supranationalism* (1955); *Britain in Western Europe: WEU and the Atlantic Alliance* (A Report of a Chatham House Study Group, 1956); and the official publications and reports of the various bodies. See also the British Central Office of Information Reference Pamphlet, No. 11, *Western Co-operation: A Reference Handbook* (1956), and C. A. Colliard, *Institutions Internationales* (1956).

Of the balance of power in the postwar world, little has been written that is not essentially journalistic, but the Communist case for 'peaceful coexistence' is stated in A. Rothstein, *Peaceful Coexistence* (1955) and the world tension between the United States and the Soviet Union is examined in H. L. Roberts, *Russia and America: Dangers and Prospects* (1955). For the views of an English scientist see P. M. S. Blackett, *Atomic Weapons and East-West Relations* (1956). The situation after the death of Stalin in 1953 is covered in P. Calvocoressi, *Survey of International Affairs, 1953* (1956), and the general world scene of 1959 is surveyed in H. Seton-Watson, *Neither War nor Peace: The Struggle For Power in the Postwar World* (1960).

Part X. Contemporary Europe

Many of the works on science, art, and thought listed above for Parts IV and V also include information about the years after 1914. There is a usefully up-to-date review of developments in the arts and sciences in *The New Outline of Modern Knowledge*, ed. A. Pryce-Jones (1956), containing contributions by eminent authorities. Modern evolutionary theories are explained in J. Huxley, *Evolution: The Modern Synthesis* (1942).

On the impact of science and technology on society, see the left-wing work of J. D. Bernal, *The Social Function of Science* (1939; 2nd ed., 1940); J. Huxley, *Science and Social Needs* (1935); W. Esslinger, *Politics and Science* (1955). C. H. Waddington, *The Scientific Attitude* (1941) and F. A. Hayek, *The Counter-Revolution of Science: Studies in the Abuse of Reason* (1952) deal more directly with the effects on modes of thought. B. Russell, *History of Western Philosophy and its Connections with Political and Social Circumstances from the Earliest Times to the Present Day* (1946) deals in its final chapters with currents of modern thought, and the same writer's *Power: A New Social Analysis* (1940) is a good example of one modern mode of political thinking.

SELECT BIBLIOGRAPHY

On literature of the twentieth century, relevant works, out of many, are M. Colum, *From These Roots: The Ideas That Have Made Modern Literature* (1944); H. S. Hughes, *Consciousness and Society, The Reorientation of European Social Thought, 1890–1930* (1958); V. S. Pritchett, *The Living Novel* (1947); H. T. Muller, *Modern Fiction: A Study in Values* (1937); and H. Smith (ed.), *Columbia Dictionary of Modern European Literature* (1947). On the arts, see K. London, *The Seven Soviet Arts* (1937); T. M. Finney, *A History of Music* (1947); W. R. Valentiner, *Origins of Modern Sculpture* (1946); J. M. Richards, *An Introduction to Modern Architecture* (1951); H. Read, *Art and Society* (1937); S. Cheney, *The Story of Modern Art* (1941).

The Welfare State as it has taken shape since 1945 awaits its definitive historians. But useful works for exploring its principles and operation are: R. S. Mendelsohn, *Social Security in the British Commonwealth: Great Britain, Canada, Australia, New Zealand* (1954) – an admirable comparative study; M. P. Hall, *The Social Services of Modern England* (4th rev. ed., 1959); the British Central Office of Information Reference Pamphlet *Social Services in Britain* (1955); *Freedom and Welfare* (a joint publication of the Scandinavian Governments, 1955). See also *International Survey of Social Security* (1950) and *Objectives and Advanced Standards of Social Security* (1952), both issued by the International Labour Office in Geneva; D. Thomson, *Equality* (1949) and *England in the Twentieth Century* (1965); S. L. Benn and R. S. Peters, *Social Principles and the Democratic State* (1959); G. Myrdal, *Beyond the Welfare State* (1960).

INDEX

INDEX

Bavaria *contd.*
trade in, 163; liberal movements in, 171, 209; first German railway in, 181; revolt in, 225; supports Austria in war with Prussia, 313; Prussian treaties with, 314; Bismarck's attitude toward, 319; independent military contingents in, 327; suffrage in, 352; republic of, 590, 593
Baylen, battle of, 121
Bayreuth, 284
Bazaine, Achille, marshal (1811–88), 317
Beatty, Admiral David (1871–1936), 560
Bebel, August (1840–1913), 392, 397, 399, 420, 421
Bechuanaland, 502
Becquerel, Antoine Henri (1852–1908), 430
Beethoven, Ludwig van (1770–1827), 77, 120
Belgian Congo, 259, 852, 857, 872–5, 882–3, 915
Belgium: relations with France during French Revolution and Napoleonic era, 43, 47, 49, 51, 52 (*map*), 64, 66, 67; in 1815, 84, 85, (*map*); and treaties of Paris (1814 and 1815), 92; in Treaty of Vienna, 94; nationalism in, 95, 119; land-ownership in, 109; increase in population, 114; coal production in, 161, 179–80; banking and finance in, 164–5; independence of, 168–70, 244; liberalism in, 175, 189–91; industrialization in, 179–80, 256, 258–60, 384, 658; railroads in, 179–80, 252, 378 (*diagram*), 383, 603; economic crises in, 185–6; social reforms in, 190–1, 358; democracy in, 204, 228–9, 238; French tariff treaty with, 256; education in, 272, 365, 366; government in, 1850–70, 272–5; and Franco-Prussian connivance, 314; suffrage in, 352, 410; and social legislation, 358; local government in, 360; freedom of speech and of the press in, 370–2; total values of imports and exports, 1875–1913, 381 (*diagram*); social and cultural associations in, 387; social democratic party in, 398–402; strikes in, 410; and the First and Second International, 419–22; colonialism and, 498, 501, 851, 852, 857, 872–4, 882; and World War I, 549, 550, 552–5, 570–1; in Wilson's 'Fourteen Points', 572; domestic consequences of World War I in, 578; and German reparations, 604–10; World War I war debt, 608–10; at Paris Conference (1919), 616; and refusal of United States to ratify Treaty of Versailles, 637; economic recovery of, 657–8; in Locarno Pacts, 675–7; emergency government in, 705; incipient civil war in, 712–13; and failure of collective security, 735; German occupation of, 767–8, 786; displacement of people in, 811; national programme of relief and rehabilitation, 819–23; capitalism in, 822; member of OEEC, 823; post-war politics in, 825–9, 848; Communism in, 829–30; at Paris Peace Conference (1946), 838; in NATO, 843; paternalist government of, 872; standard of living in (1948), 941; type of welfare state in, 942
Belgrade, 556
Bellamy, Edward (1850–98), 450

'Belleville Manifesto', 269
Benedetti, Vincente (1817–1900), 314, 316
'Benelux' group, 842, 847, 891. *See also* Belgium; Netherlands; Luxembourg
Beneš, Eduard (1884–1948), 597, 743–4, 746, 832–3
Bentham, Jeremy (1748–1832), 50, 77, 84, 187, 283, 925
Berchtold, Leopold von (1863–1942), 534, 542, 544
Berdyaev, Nicholas (1874–1948), 914
Beresford, William Carr (1768–1854), 136
Bergson, Henri (1859–1941), 438, 918
Beria, Lavrente Pavlovich (1899–1953), 898
Berlin: occupation by Napoleon, 64; revolutionary movements in, 230, 590; Russian influence in, 249; air-lift to, 842, 893
Berlin-Baghdad Railroad, 470, 518
Berlin Conference (1884–85), 500–1, 537
Berlin Conference (1945), 800
Berlin, Congress of (1878), 362, 464–7, 472, 525, 537
Berlin, University of, 120
Berlioz, Louis Hector (1803–69), 284
Bernadotte, Folke (1895–1948), 867, 881
Bernadotte, Jean Baptiste J. (1763?–1844), 72–3, 175–6, 191
Bernard, Martin, 196
Bernstein, Eduard (1850–1932), 399–400
Berryer, Pierre Antoine (1790–1868), 268
Berthelot, Pierre Eugène Marcelin (1827–1907), 276
Bessarabia, 248; Russia surrenders part of, 248, 344; Russia reclaims, 464; Jews in, 482; and World War I, 550; after World War I, 597, 625 (*map*); and World War II, 757, 838
Bessemer process, 286
Best, Charles Herbert (1899–   ), 911
Bethlehem, 243, 246
Bethmann Hollweg, Theobald von (1856–1921), 552, 581
Beust, Friedrich F. von (1809–86), 300
Beveridge, Sir William H. (1879–1963), 828, 942
Bevin, Ernest (1881–1951), 837
Bidault, Georges (1899–   ), 837
Binet, Alfred (1857–1911), 435
Biochemistry, 909–10
Biography, 921–3
Biology: cult of synthesis and, 275, 276–84, 280 (*chart*); influence of Darwin and Einstein on, 432–3, 905, 907; since 1914, 909–10; distortions of, in Nazi Germany and in the Soviet Union, 928–9
Birmingham, 156, 194, 230, 359, 449
Birth rates, 113, 574. *See also* Population
Bismarck, Otto Eduard L. von (1815–98), 237, 288, 294; and unification of Germany, 295, 300, 308–27; and extension of franchise, 353; and labour organizations, 369; dismissed, 374; and Eastern Question, 462–7; resignation of, 469; diplomacy of, 525–6; attitude toward militarism, 531–2
Bismarck Archipelago, 503
Björnson, Björnstjerne (1832–1910), 450, 451
Black Sea, 242, 243, 248, 321, 791, 840

970

INDEX

INDEX

READ MORE IN PENGUIN

In every corner of the world, on every subject under the sun, Penguin represents quality and variety – the very best in publishing today.

For complete information about books available from Penguin – including Puffins, Penguin Classics and Arkana – and how to order them, write to us at the appropriate address below. Please note that for copyright reasons the selection of books varies from country to country.

In the United Kingdom: Please write to *Dept. EP, Penguin Books Ltd, Bath Road, Harmondsworth, West Drayton, Middlesex UB7 ODA*

In the United States: Please write to *Consumer Sales, Penguin Putnam Inc., P.O. Box 999, Dept. 17109, Bergenfield, New Jersey 07621-0120.* VISA and MasterCard holders call 1-800-253-6476 to order Penguin titles

In Canada: Please write to *Penguin Books Canada Ltd, 10 Alcorn Avenue, Suite 300, Toronto, Ontario M4V 3B2*

In Australia: Please write to *Penguin Books Australia Ltd, P.O. Box 257, Ringwood, Victoria 3134*

In New Zealand: Please write to *Penguin Books (NZ) Ltd, Private Bag 102902, North Shore Mail Centre, Auckland 10*

In India: Please write to *Penguin Books India Pvt Ltd, 210 Chiranjiv Tower, 43 Nehru Place, New Delhi 110 019*

In the Netherlands: Please write to *Penguin Books Netherlands bv, Postbus 3507, NL-1001 AH Amsterdam*

In Germany: Please write to *Penguin Books Deutschland GmbH, Metzlerstrasse 26, 60594 Frankfurt am Main*

In Spain: Please write to *Penguin Books S. A., Bravo Murillo 19, 1° B, 28015 Madrid*

In Italy: Please write to *Penguin Italia s.r.l., Via Benedetto Croce 2, 20094 Corsico, Milano*

In France: Please write to *Penguin France, Le Carré Wilson, 62 rue Benjamin Baillaud, 31500 Toulouse*

In Japan: Please write to *Penguin Books Japan Ltd, Kaneko Building, 2-3-25 Koraku, Bunkyo-Ku, Tokyo 112*

In South Africa: Please write to *Penguin Books South Africa (Pty) Ltd, Private Bag X14, Parkview, 2122 Johannesburg*

READ MORE IN PENGUIN

HISTORY

London: A Social History Roy Porter

'The best and bravest thing he has written. It is important because it makes the whole sweep of London's unique history comprehensible and accessible in a way that no previous writer has ever managed to accomplish. And it is angry because it begins and concludes with a slashing, unanswerable indictment of Thatcherite misrule' – *Independent on Sunday*

Somme Lyn Macdonald

'What the reader will longest remember are the words – heartbroken, blunt, angry – of the men who lived through the bloodbath . . . a worthy addition to the literature of the Great War' – *Daily Mail*

Aspects of Aristocracy David Cannadine

'A hugely enjoyable portrait of the upper classes . . . It is the perfect history book for the non-historian. Ample in scope but full of human detail, accessible and graceful in its scholarship, witty and opinionated in style' – *Financial Times*

The Penguin History of Greece A. R. Burn

Readable, erudite, enthusiastic and balanced, this one-volume history of Hellas sweeps the reader along from the days of Mycenae and the splendours of Athens to the conquests of Alexander and the final dark decades.

The Laurel and the Ivy Robert Kee

'Parnell continues to haunt the Irish historical imagination a century after his death . . . Robert Kee's patient and delicate probing enables him to reconstruct the workings of that elusive mind as persuasively, or at least as plausibly, as seems possible . . . This splendid biography, which is as readable as it is rigorous, greatly enhances our understanding of both Parnell, and of the Ireland of his time' – *The Times Literary Supplement*

READ MORE IN PENGUIN

POLITICS AND SOCIAL SCIENCES

Accountable to None   Simon Jenkins

'An important book, because it brings together, with an insider's authority and anecdotage, both a narrative of domestic Thatcherism and a polemic against its pretensions ... an indispensable guide to the corruptions of power and language which have sustained the illusion that Thatcherism was an attack on "government"' – *Guardian*

The Feminine Mystique   Betty Friedan

'A brilliantly researched, passionately argued book – a time bomb flung into the Mom-and-Apple-Pie image ... Out of the debris of that shattered ideal, the Women's Liberation Movement was born' – Ann Leslie

The New Untouchables   Nigel Harris

Misrepresented in politics and in the media, immigration is seen as a serious problem by the vast majority of people. In this ground-breaking book, Nigel Harris draws on a mass of evidence to challenge existing assumptions and examines migration as a response to changes in the world economy.

Political Ideas   Edited by David Thomson

From Machiavelli to Marx – a stimulating and informative introduction to the last 500 years of European political thinkers and political thought.

Structural Anthropology Volumes 1–2   Claude Lévi-Strauss

'That the complex ensemble of Lévi-Strauss's achievement ... is one of the most original and intellectually exciting of the present age seems undeniable. No one seriously interested in language or literature, in sociology or psychology, can afford to ignore it' – George Steiner

Invitation to Sociology   Peter L. Berger

Without belittling its scientific procedures Professor Berger stresses the humanistic affinity of sociology with history and philosophy. It is a discipline which encourages a fuller awareness of the human world ... with the purpose of bettering it.